BRASSEY'S ENCYCLOPEDIA OF MILITARY HISTORY AND BIOGRAPHY

BRASSEY'S
ENCYCLOPEDIA OF
MILITARY HISTORY
AND BIOGRAPHY

Executive Editor

Col. Franklin D. Margiotta,
USAF (Ret.), Ph.D.

Foreword by

John Keegan

BRASSEY'S
Washington • London

Some articles in this work were previously published in 1993, in slightly different
form, in the *International Military and Defense Encyclopedia*.

Library of Congress Cataloging-in-Publication Data

Brassey's encyclopedia of military history and biography/executive
   editor Franklin D. Margiotta; foreword by John Keegan.
         p.   cm.
   Some articles have been previously published in 1993 in the
International Military and Defense Encyclopedia.
   Includes bibliographical references and index.
   ISBN 0-02-881096-1
   1. Military art and science—Encyclopedias. 2. Military
history—Encyclopedias. 3. Military biography—Encyclopedias.
   I. Margiotta, Franklin D.
   U24.B73 1994
   355'.003—dc20

                                      94-33551
                                      CIP

10 9 8 7 6 5 4 3 2 1

PRINTED IN THE UNITED STATES OF AMERICA

DEDICATION

The *International Military and Defense Encyclopedia* was dedicated to the memory of Morris Janowitz (1919–1988), the Distinguished Service Professor of Sociology, University of Chicago. Morris would have been pleased that the world finally had a comprehensive codification of knowledge about the military and defense, international in scope and authorship. For almost half a century, he focused his intellectual life on organizing the study of the military and issues of defense. Through his scholarship, his Inter-University Seminar on Armed Forces and Society, and his scholarly journal, Morris expanded the study of the military and society to all parts of the globe. He was brilliant at opening windows into defense establishments and let us all understand them better. Our only regret is that Morris Janowitz is no longer here to provide the scorching criticism and generous encouragement we always expected. It is only fitting that we continue to remember him upon the publication of *Brassey's Encyclopedia of Military History and Biography*.

INTERNATIONAL HONORARY ADVISORY BOARD OF THE *INTERNATIONAL MILITARY AND DEFENSE ENCYCLOPEDIA*

Admiral of The Fleet Sir William Stavely, GCB, DL
Former First Sea Lord
United Kingdom

General Wu Xiuquan, CPLA
Member, Standing Committee of the Central Advisory
Commission of the Communist Part of China
People's Republic of China

INTERNATIONAL MILITARY AND DEFENSE ENCYCLOPEDIA EDITORIAL BOARD AND SUBJECT EDITORS

ASSOCIATE EDITORS

CONTENTS

FOREWORD

The *International Military and Defense Encyclopedia* has already been widely hailed as an authoritative and indispensable work of reference in its field. It gives me pleasure to write the foreword to its companion volume, *Brassey's Encyclopedia of Military History and Biography*, which brings together from the larger work the military historical and biographical articles that have already been found so useful by scholars and defence community professionals. It also contains new and original entries.

The quality of the publication is guaranteed by the reputation and achievements of the editorial team which designed, compiled and edited it. The editors and advisory boards set new standards by their comprehensiveness and academic quality and in their deliberate editorial choice to break free from the Eurocentric approach to the subject and to provide articles which took the warfare of all continents, cultures and periods as their material.

I was involved with the conception of the *International Military and Defense Encyclopedia* at the outset, and I regret that other commitments prevented me from joining the editorial team in the realisation of the project. Those who did devoted six years to the creation of a work which has no equivalent in any language. The writing of military history or defence studies cannot be undertaken in the future without recourse to this unique source of reference.

The particular quality that informs the *Brassey's Encyclopedia of Military History and Biography* derives from the world view that the editorial team brings to its organisation. Warfare is a universal activity, both in time and place. Because of cultural and technical inequalities, however, it takes widely varying forms. Over time, the Western world has come to excel at the practice of warfare, and Western historiography has therefore neglected the study of warfare in other parts of the world. That neglect has directly affected the course of world events, for Western misunderstanding of Asian forms of war making, in particular, underlay the reverses suffered both by the French and the Americans in Indo-China in the period 1946–1972 and by the Russians in Afghanistan in the 1980s. Faced by enemies who practised strategies of evasion and delay, and who used the dimensions of time and space as weapons, Western commanders experienced deep frustration at the failure of dynamic reaction and of advanced technologies to bring them victory, as such measures consistently had in wars between Western states or alliances.

This encyclopedia's approach to military historiography does much to ensure that the misconceptions stemming from the traditional Eurocentric methodology will not be repeated. This volume, by its emphasis on the importance of Islamic, Ottoman and Chinese military styles and by its coverage of the leading military figures of non-Western cultural zones, strikes a new and creative balance in the recording of military events.

It is also, of course, a valuable and comprehensive guide to the military history and biography of the Western world. I look forward to using it often as a reference source, and I warmly commend it to scholars, military professionals and general readers

JOHN KEEGAN
JULY 1994

PREFACE

Brassey's Encyclopedia of Military History and Biography has a rich and unique history. It is the only English-language encyclopedia of both military history and biography that was supported, advised, organized, and designed by distinguished international boards of military leaders and scholars and was written multiculturally by subject area experts from throughout the world. It is the only such encyclopedia organized alphabetically in separate articles. It is a richer encyclopedia because its articles have been carefully selected out of the much larger six-volume work, the *International Military and Defense Encyclopedia* (*IMADE*).

Brassey's and the Macmillan Publishing Company invested six years of effort and well over a million dollars in *IMADE*, which all seemed worthwhile when the extraordinarily positive reviews and commentaries appeared. It rapidly became clear that the normally very critical reference reviewers had reinforced our notion that in *IMADE* our authors and editors had created something very significant. With the cooperation of Macmillan, it didn't take long for me to decide that it was incumbent upon Brassey's to make readily available to the general public some of the more "popular" parts of the *International Military and Defense Encyclopedia*. While almost 80 percent of the articles in *Brassey's Encyclopedia of Military History and Biography* come directly from *IMADE*'s history and biography section, the depth and breadth of our six-year effort permitted me to include thirty-one carefully selected general historical articles from other areas by experts on such subjects as "The Cold War," "The Cuban Missile Crisis," "Land Warfare," "The Military," "Aerospace Forces and Warfare," and many more.

Because this encyclopedia owes its existence to *IMADE*, it is appropriate to follow the normal tradition in encyclopedic works in which the editor shares with the reader the logic of the encyclopedia's background and development. We will thus explain how we determined there was a need for the parent encyclopedia, how *IMADE* was defined and developed, and what aids we have built in to help the reader find information. We were confident enough to explore the daunting task of compiling this encyclopedia for three reasons: first, we are the oldest book publisher in these fields; second, we have published the largest collection of books and authors in these fields; and third, we are one of the few commercial publishing houses managed by former military officers with operational and combat experience, advanced academic and research experience, and worldwide contacts.

The Need for *IMADE*

To test further our initial research about the need for *IMADE*, Brassey's convened a two-day international conference of distinguished librarians, journalists, scholars, and active and former government and military officials. Strong expressions of support emerged from Mr. John Barry (senior national security correspondent, *Newsweek*); Col. John Collins, USA (Ret.), Ph.D. (senior defense analyst, U.S. Library of Congress); Col. Trevor N. Dupuy, USA (Ret.) (author and eventually editor-in-chief of *IMADE*); Jacques Gansler, Ph.D. (vice president, The Analytic Sciences Corp.); Gen. Paul Gorman, USA (Ret.) (former commander, U.S. Southern Command); Prof. William Kaufmann, Ph.D. (author; former DoD official; faculty member, MIT and Harvard University); Mr. John Keegan (author; defense editor, *Daily Telegraph*, London; faculty member, Oxford University); Col. Fred Kiley, USAF (Ret.) (director of research and press, National Defense University); Prof. Charles C. Moskos (faculty member, Northwestern University; chairman, Inter-University Seminar on Armed Forces and Society); Mr. Thomas Russell (director, National Defense University Library); and Mr. Steven Shaker (author; former Navy program analyst). Based upon this group's preliminary suggestions about content, we then began to define more precisely the purpose and scope of *IMADE*. The first step was to assess more carefully the potential audiences.

Defining and Developing *IMADE*

A wide range of potential users was identified. They included faculty and students in civilian high schools, universities, and educational institutions; private and government academies and military colleges, universities, and training organizations; active, reserve, and retired officers and enlisted personnel of armed forces; and all levels of defense and military personnel in government agencies concerned with security and foreign policy issues. Researchers and staff of research institutes and organizations devoted to the study of security, foreign policy, defense, and the military would also find *IMADE* invaluable, as would all those involved in defense industries or areas affected by defense spending and procurement, including journalists. Finally, the encyclopedia would serve as a ready reference guide for the knowledgeable, informed citizen wanting or needing information about the military and defense.

Brassey's then formed two distinguished boards. The Honorary Advisory Board included British and Indian field marshals, a former chairman of the U.S. Joint Chiefs of Staff, a senior general from the People's Republic of China, and three leading civilian scholars from Germany, Japan, and the United States. Later, we added the former chairman of the Republic of Korea Joint Chiefs of Staff, the former commandant of the United States Marine Corps, the admiral of the fleet from the United Kingdom, and an internationally known scholar in the study of the military and society.

Next, we named an impressive editorial board of seventeen subject editors, each responsible for a subject area. They were experienced, prominent experts from three continents and seven countries. Selecting people of reputation and experience from around the world was a start toward making *IMADE* international in scope and approach. We brought the editorial board to Virginia for a week of debate, discussion, and decision. This was a stimulating experience because of the quality of the individuals involved, their broad range of backgrounds, and the level at which most of them had actively participated in or studied the military and defense. The multicultural basis of *IMADE* was enhanced further by the selection of authors from seventeen countries and the richness of examples used in their articles. Depending on the subject, we sometimes found it essential to select board members and authors who were active duty or retired senior military officers, particularly those who had both operational and academic experiences.

We had a lively debate, but then ruled out including discrete articles on major world figures such as Prime Minister Winston Churchill, President Franklin D. Roosevelt, and others who made their mark as political leaders and were not directly engaged in the military and defense.

Many articles were written by people who have both lived and studied the military and defense subjects of which they wrote. Many of the authors have participated in combat operations. Their unique insights are not normally available to those outside military and defense establishments. Most authors have advanced degrees and academic and/or operational credentials. Collectively, they represent a distinguished international group of practitioners, warriors, scientists and engineers, former high-level commanders, researchers, and scholars.

We recognized the bias that could emerge from *IMADE*'s publication in American English, management by Americans, and the weight of the United States in military and defense matters. The possibility of an unbalanced focus on things American was resisted in many ways. *IMADE* has almost sixty articles from authors from the United Kingdom; more than sixty by German authors; and thirty from Egyptian flag ranks. The advisory board, editorial board, and author list contain experts from seventeen countries and four continents. Our non-American subject editors also insisted on an international approach in articles. During editorial review, articles were returned to authors for examples beyond American or British experience.

This struggle to keep *IMADE* multicultural created significant editorial issues. Articles were written by authors whose English was their second language. At times, we contracted for translations into English. Some articles were revised or rewritten by English-capable associate editors, resulting in team authorship. Sometimes new authors replaced non-Americans if quality and agreement could not be reached. We generally respected the author's spelling of non-English words, especially those in Chinese and Russian. Fortunately, I was able to get assistance from colleagues met during my more than three decades of experience and education in air combat and operations, advanced academic study and teaching at the Air Force Academy and Air Command and

Staff College (ACSC), research and publication, and management of large academic research organizations at ACSC and National Defense University.

Using *Brassey's Encyclopedia of Military History and Biography*

This encyclopedia is presented alphabetically for the convenience of the reader, and a detailed index is presented at the end of the volume. The users of this encyclopedia will find it a rich source of information but will be most successful if they take time at the beginning to understand the many aids we have put in for their benefit. Readers looking for information on a particular area should begin by looking up key words in the index and then scanning the entries to which they are referred. They can also use the significant cross-indexing, which details specialized areas that might be covered in other articles. Another aid is the detailed cross-referencing system to be found at the end of nearly every article, the "See Also" section. This refers the reader to related articles recommended by the author and editors. Almost all articles conclude with a bibliography containing primary source material or longer, sometimes "classic" treatments of the subject.

The front matter of the volume is another valuable source of information: It lists the names and affiliations of the advisory board, subject editors/editorial board, associate editors, and authors. The alphabetical list of entries lists all articles in this encyclopedia and their authors.

These aids should help the reader find solid, objective information on virtually any major subject of military history or biography.

We wish you good and fruitful reading and research.

FRANKLIN D. MARGIOTTA, PH.D.
COLONEL, USAF (RET.)
EXECUTIVE EDITOR AND PUBLISHER
WASHINGTON, D.C.

ACKNOWLEDGMENTS

Hundreds of people are responsible for the development, quality, and publication of Brassey's *International Military and Defense Encyclopedia (IMADE)*, from which *Brassey's Encyclopedia of Military History and Biography* is drawn.

The first general recognition must go to the distinguished international group of military leaders, scholars, research and library experts (identified in the Preface) who strongly suggested in an exploratory meeting that *IMADE* would be a significant contribution to public information and education about the military and defense. They also emphasized that the mere collection of this material into one major work would be of great benefit. Their encouragement, preliminary advice on content, and suggestions on potential contributors sustained us through the next long six years.

We also must thank the International Honorary Advisory Board, which includes seven of the most senior military leaders in the world and four of the most prominent scholars of military and defense matters. Their faith in and support of Brassey's and this project from the earliest days permitted us to attract experts from seventeen countries, whose work is displayed in the articles. Their advice on the selection of the editorial board and authors was especially helpful in broadening the international basis of the work.

The subject editors who formed the editorial board must be acknowledged for their diligence, their positive approach to *IMADE*, and their significant contributions to a better understanding of the military and defense. After helping to define the encyclopedia's scope, weight of effort, responsibilities, and topics, these subject editors signed up author-experts from around the world. They then reviewed and edited the articles, sometimes translating them into English. Without their efforts, this reference work would not exist. We must also recognize those brought on board late as associate editors who pitched in when deadlines neared and we needed to reevaluate and rewrite dozens of articles because of translation problems, late or incomplete work, or monumental changes in the world. Of great importance to this particular encyclopedia of military history and biography was the development work by the *IMADE* subject editor for this area, Curt Johnson.

Most important, of course, are the more than four hundred authors who generously wrote the expert articles, sometimes receiving a modest honorarium, sometimes prohibited by their governments from accepting any compensation. We hope that they will feel that this final product is worthy of their efforts.

The Brassey's and Macmillan staffs, too, deserve special mention. As associate director of publishing for reference works, Deirdre Murphy spent more than three years of her life working with authors and with senior subject editors while managing an impossibly large and complex encyclopedia project. Toward the middle stages, she was joined in these tasks by a first-class contract editor, Jack Hopper. Martha E. Rothenberg completed the contract editorial team and added her substantial skills in computers and database management to our effort. At different times during the six-year gestation period, we were helped by Christine E. Williams and Anne Stockdell. Carrie Burkett helped me start it all, and Elizabeth Ashley helped us finish. At Macmillan in New York, book production was managed with great professionalism by John Ball, Terry Dieli, and Benjamin Barros. I could not have spent the time I did on *IMADE* without our fine book publishing staff who stepped up their efforts and kept the book program alive and well: Don McKeon, associate director of publishing for books; Vicki Chamlee, production editor; and Kim Borchard, director of marketing and public relations.

Special recognition goes to Colonel James B. Motley, USA (Ret.) who particularly assisted *IMADE* during the last six months of manuscript completion. Jim helped us smooth articles, chased authors and editors, rewrote certain articles, and assisted us all with his management and organizational skills. He applied the skills and knowledge he learned in his combat, leadership, and academic assignments. We could not have finished on schedule without him.

LIST OF ARTICLES

xxi

CONTRIBUTORS

Col. John I. Alger, USA (Ret.), Ph.D.
Former Faculty, National War College
United States

Prof. Graham T. Allison, Jr., Ph.D.
JFK School of Government, Harvard U.
United States

Mr. Dwayne Anderson
Author
United States

Mr. Brian R. Bader
Director of Research, Historical
  Evaluation and Research Organization
United States

Lt. Col. Dieter Bangert (Ret.), Ph.D.
Germany

Brig. Gen. Kenneth H. Bell, USAF
  (Ret.)
Author
United States

Mr. James J. Bloom
JB Historical Research Consultants Ltd
United States

Col. James D. Blundell, USA (Ret.)
Institute of Land Warfare, Association of
  the U.S. Army
United States

Mr. Zeev Bonen, Ph.D.
Senior Research Fellow, The Neaman
  Institute
Israel

Mr. David L. Bongard
Military Historian
United States

Prof. Carl Boyd, Ph.D.
Director, Graduate Program of History,
  Old Dominion U.
United States

Col. John R. Brinkerhoff, USA (Ret.)
Former Deputy Assistant Secretary of
  Defense for Reserve Affairs
United States

Mr. Robert Calvert, Jr.
Publisher, Garrett Park Press
United States

Prof. Jack Child, Ph.D.
American U.
United States

Mr. Anthony H. Cordesman, Ph.D.
U.S. Senate Staff; ABC News Military
  Analyst; Prof. of National Security
  Studies, Georgetown U.
United States

Maj. Szabolcs M. de Gyürky, USA (Ret.)
United States

Mr. James F. Dunnigan
Author
United States

Mr. Arnold C. Dupuy
United States

Mr. Fielding Dupuy
United States

Col. Trevor N. Dupuy, USA (Ret.)
Author and Media Military Analyst
United States

Brig. Gen. Uzal W. Ent, USA (Ret.)
United States

Prof. Jiang Feng-bo
Military Science Academy
China

Prof. Arther Ferrill, Ph.D.
Dept. of History, U. of Washington
United States

Maj. David John Fitzpatrick, USA
Faculty, U.S. Military Academy
United States

Mr. Gregory F. Forster
United States

Prof. Suen Fu-tian
Military Science Academy
China

Prof. Janice J. Gabbert, Ph.D.
Chair, Dept. of Classics, Wright
  State U.
United States

Air Vice Marshal Timothy Garden, RAF
Assistant Chief of the Air Staff
United Kingdom

Col. John F. Geraci, USA (Ret.)
United States

Mr. Gwyn Harries-Jenkins, Ph.D.
Dean, U. of Hull
United Kingdom

Mr. Vincent B. Hawkins
Military Historian
United States

Ms. Grace Person Hayes
Author
United States

Mr. Lawrence D. Higgins
Author
United States

Prof. I. B. Holley, Jr., Ph.D.
Dept. of History, Duke U.
United States

Mr. Curt Johnson
Military Historian
United States

Mr. Max George Kellner
Military Historian
Germany

Prof. E. C. Kiesling, Ph.D.
Dept. of History, U. of Alabama
United States

Mr. James K. Kieswetter, Ph.D.
Dept. of History, Eastern
  Washington U.
United States

Mr. Jacob W. Kipp, Ph.D.
Soviet Army Studies Office, Fort
  Leavenworth, Kansas
United States

Mr. Robert E. Knotts
Faculty, U.S. Military Academy
United States

Prof. Phillip E. Koerper, Ph.D.
Dept. of History, Jacksonville State U.
United States

Mr. Robert H. Kupperman, Ph.D.
Center for Strategic and International
  Studies
United States

Lt. Col. Timothy T. Lupfer, USA
United States

Mr. Michael A. Mabe
Major Works, Pergamon Press
United Kingdom

Col. Franklin D. Margiotta, USAF
  (Ret.), Ph.D.
President and Publisher, Brassey's, Inc.
United States

Mr. Edward J. Marolda, Ph.D.
U.S. Naval Historical Center
United States

Col. Donald S. Marshall, USA (Ret.),
  Ph.D.
Peabody Museum
United States

Lt. Col. Albert D. McJoynt, USA (Ret.)
United States

Mr. Mark G. McLaughlin
Journalist
United States

Col. Ralph M. Mitchell, USA (Ret.)
Former Faculty, National War College
United States

Prof. Charles C. Moskos, Ph.D.
Dept. of Sociology, Northwestern U.
United States

Col. James B. Motley, USA (Ret.),
  Ph.D.
Author and Defense Analyst
United States

Prof. Malcolm Muir, Jr., Ph.D.
Chairman, Dept. of History and
  Philosophy, Austin Peay State U.
United States

Capt. David A. Niedringhaus, USA
Faculty, U.S. Military Academy
United States

Lt. Col. Edward C. O'Dowd, USA
Mesa Community College
United States

Mr. John Kennedy Ohl, Ph.D.
United States

Mr. Raymond Oliver
United States

Ms. Rose-Marie Oster, Ph.D.
United States

Mrs. Eloise Paananen
Author
United States

Maj. Harold E. Raugh, Jr., USA
Faculty, U.S. Military Academy
United States

Mr. George A. Reed
U.S. Mission to NATO
United States

Mr. John C. Reilly, Jr.
United States

Prof. R. Dan Richardson, Ph.D.
Roanoke College
United States

Cdr. Hideo Sekino, IJN (Ret.)
Director, Institute for Historical
  Research
Japan

Cdr. Sadao Seno, JMSDF (Ret.)
Japan

Mr. Zhou Shi-chang
Military Science Academy
China

Brig. J. H. Skinner, U.K. (Ret.)
United Kingdom

Lt. Col. John F. Sloan, USA (Ret.)
Faculty, Defense Intelligence College
United States

Maj. Dianne L. Smith, USA, Ph.D.
United States

Maj. Gen. Perry M. Smith, USAF
  (Ret.), Ph.D.
Former Commandant, National War
  College; Author; Military Analyst,
  Cable Network News
United States

Mr. William J. Spahr, Ph.D.
United States

Mr. Paul Stewart, Ph.D.
Southern Connecticut State U.
United States

Prof. Jon Tetsuro Sumida, Ph.D.
U. of Maryland
United States

Mr. Lee A. Sweetapple
Military Analyst
United States

Mr. John E. Tashjean, Ph.D.
President, Conflict Morphology, Inc.
United States

Maj. Gen. A. J. Trythall, CB (Ret.)
Managing Director, Brassey's (UK)
United Kingdom

Prof. Spencer C. Tucker, Ph.D.
Texas Christian U.
United States

Lt. Gen. Franz Uhle-Wettler (Ret.),
  Ph.D.
Former Commandant, NATO Defense
  College
Germany

Ms. Debra van Opstal
Center for Strategic and International
  Studies
United States

Mr. J. E. Wade
Jacksonville State U.
United States

Cdr. Bruce W. Watson, USN (Ret.),
  Ph.D.
Adjunct Faculty, Defense Intelligence
  College
United States

Capt. Kevin J. Weddle, USA
United States

Mr. Gary E. Weir, Ph.D.
U.S. Naval Historical Center
United States

Prof. Everett L. Wheeler, Ph.D.
Dept. of Classical Studies, Duke U.
United States

Mr. Charles E. White, Ph.D.
United States

Mr. Walter P. White
United States

Prof. Max R. Williams, Ph.D.
Western Carolina U.
United States

Mr. Robert S. Wood, Ph.D.
Dean, Center for Naval Warfare Studies,
  Naval War College
United States

BRASSEY'S ENCYCLOPEDIA of MILITARY HISTORY and BIOGRAPHY

A

AFGHANISTAN, SOVIET INVASION OF

The December 1979 Soviet invasion of Afghanistan marked a development unparalleled in Soviet international behavior outside the Warsaw Pact since the end of World War II. The invasion signaled a dramatic and dangerous change in the Soviet approach to resolving international problems. Many countries viewed the invasion as inherent proof of an expansionist tendency in Soviet foreign policy. It shocked the West, especially the United States, which felt a sense of betrayal in light of the sustained efforts of the Carter administration to maintain a policy of detente with the USSR.

The invasion alarmed China, which perceived the Soviet action as part of an elaborate plan to encircle it, especially in light of the Soviet-backed Vietnamese 1978 invasion of Kampuchea (Cambodia). Many developing nations viewed the Soviet use of military force as an atheist assault on their wider religious interests. For the main regional actors (Pakistan, Iran, and India), the Soviet invasion seriously changed the regional balance of power, placing them in the position of having to respond to this action and to cope with its consequences. Pakistan chose to pursue active opposition to the invasion; Iran, although condemning Soviet actions, took a much lower profile. India made no public condemnation of the invasion.

This article provides a historical summary of Soviet-Afghan relations, examines some of the events leading up to the Soviet invasion of Afghanistan, presents some of the most important features of the invasion, and discusses Soviet military strategy. It concludes with comments regarding the significance of the Soviets' withdrawal from Afghanistan.

Historical Summary: Soviet-Afghan Relations

Soviet-Afghan relations followed fairly closely the phases of Soviet policy toward developing nations. Stalin avoided direct involvement and was satisfied with Afghan neutrality. Khrushchev took advantage of mutual hostility toward Pakistan to foster cooperation with the Afghan government during Mohammad Daoud's premiership and in 1955 began providing military aid to Afghanistan.

1

It was not until Brezhnev's phase of activism in developing countries in the early-to-mid-1970s that substantial Soviet involvement in Afghanistan's internal affairs began. The seizure of power by the Marxist-Leninist People's Democratic Party of Afghanistan in April 1978 was the culmination of the increasing Soviet influence in Afghan political and military life.

Prelude to Invasion

April 1978 marks the start of a series of events that led the Soviets, in fewer than twenty months, from providing assistance to Afghanistan to mounting an invasion. Three of these events stand out: the assassination of Mir Akbar Khyber, the kidnapping and death of the U.S. ambassador Adolph ("Spike") Dubs, and the Herat Massacre.

On 17 April 1978, Mir Akbar Khyber, a former police official and a Parcham ideologue, was assassinated by unknown assailants. (Afghanistan has one political party—the People's Democratic Party of Afghanistan, or PDPA. The PDPA has two factions: the Parchami faction, which has been in power since December 1979; and members of the deposed Khalqi faction, which continues to hold some important posts in the military and the ministry of interior.) Shortly thereafter, a massive demonstration by approximately 15,000 people occurred in Kabul. On 26 April the Afghan government began to arrest Khalq and Parcham leaders. Early the next morning Afghan armed forces, some supporting the PDPA and others loyal to Prime Minister Daoud, began fighting. Approximately 1,000 people died including Daoud, his brother Naim, most of their families, and about half of the 2,000-man Republican Guard who defended the presidential palace. By 28 April, PDPA forces had captured the palace, the Kabul airport, Radio Kabul, and the central jail. Two days later, Nur Mohammed Taraki was named head of the Military Revolutionary Command (MRC) and prime minister. His two deputy prime ministers, who would assume prominence in the following months, were Hafizullah Amin and Babrak Karmal. That same day the Soviet Union recognized the new People's Democratic Republic of Afghanistan (PDRA).

The New Government

In Taraki's initial cabinet, the Khalqi faction had eleven seats, the Parchami faction ten. The new government repeatedly denied that the PDRA was a communist party. Between April and August 1978 the government issued a series of decrees that abolished the MRC, abrogated the 1977 constitution, declared racial and ethnic equality, eliminated all pre-1973 debts and diminished payments on subsequent loans (which disrupted the rural economy of the country), and declared a land reform that met with widespread resistance from both landowners and peasants.

On 5 December 1978 the Soviet Union and Afghanistan signed a Treaty of Friendship, Good-Neighborliness, and Cooperation, which was to run for a term of twenty years. Although there were few specifics in the treaty, Article

4 contained an implicit security commitment that would be used in December 1979 to justify the Soviet invasion.

The United States was hesitant to classify the Taraki regime as communist. Thus, it followed a constructive-engagement policy toward the Taraki government until 6 May 1978, at which time the United States recognized the Democratic Republic of Afghanistan (DRA). Beginning in midsummer, other more pressing foreign policy problems confronted the United States: On 29 July 1978, riots in thirteen Iranian cities drew U.S. attention to the problems of the Pahlavi dynasty. The following month, the Camp David meetings began. During the first six months of the Taraki regime, the NATO long-term defense program, the final outline of the Strategic Arms Limitation Talks (SALT) II agreement, and the normalization of relations with the People's Republic of China were all negotiated or finalized. Up until February 1979, the United States continued to watch the situation in Kabul closely while continuing to provide Afghanistan with economic assistance.

Ambassador Dubs' Death

On 14 February 1979, the same day the U.S. embassy was temporarily seized in Teheran and a few days before the Sino-Vietnamese war began, U.S. Ambassador Dubs was kidnapped off the streets of Kabul and taken to a hotel. He and the kidnappers were subsequently killed when the Afghan police, in the presence of several Soviet advisers, stormed the hotel room where Dubs was being held.

As a result of this incident, the United States announced on 22 February that it was terminating further aid to Afghanistan and that, henceforth, U.S. interests in Kabul would be handled by a chargé d'affaires. In addition, the Peace Corps ended its twenty-year program in Afghanistan, and U.S. dependents and most of the embassy staff left the country.

The Herat Massacre

In March, the Afghan Islam resistance forces (the mujaheddin) who opposed the PDPA attacked the city of Herat. The attack, coupled with a local army mutiny, resulted in the capture of Herat and the massacre of the local Soviet advisory group, which included approximately fifty Soviet soldiers and their dependents. In reprisal, an Afghan army unit with Soviet advisers sacked the town of Kerala and killed 640 of its male inhabitants. In April 1979 the United States began a modest program to aid the mujaheddin. During that summer the Soviets provided an increase in military aid and advisers to the Afghan government.

Shortly after the Herat massacre, Amin engineered his own appointment as prime minister. Although the media continued to pay homage to Taraki, increasing power came to rest with Amin. In the following months, however, personal relations between Amin and the Soviet staff in Kabul became increasingly strained.

From September to December 1979 the military situation in Afghanistan continued to deteriorate, prompting the Soviets to decide to: (1) unseat Amin; (2) install Karmal as the leader of a new Khalq-Parcham coalition; and (3) use Soviet troops to gain time for the new regime to restore order and rebuild the Afghan army.

Invasion

The Soviets' invasion of Afghanistan was modeled after their 1968 invasion of Czechoslovakia. Both operations featured elaborate deception, subversion of an "unreliable" communist government, the introduction of airborne troops to seize key objectives in the capital, the movement of motorized rifle troops to link up with air-landed elements, and the replacement of a government with more "reliable" comrades.

On Christmas Eve 1979 the Soviets began landing elements of an airborne division and a *spetsnaz* (commando unit) at the Kabul airport. On 27 December a few hundred spetsnaz troops deployed to the Darulaman Palace outside Kabul and killed President Amin and his bodyguards. Also on the 27th, Soviet troops blew up the main telephone exchange, seized Radio Kabul, and captured most of the central government facilities in Kabul. Serious fighting in the city ended by dawn of 28 December. Karmal was proclaimed president of the Revolutionary Council, general secretary of the PDPA, and prime minister. In the following months the Karmal regime was beset with internal conflict; rather than becoming a puppet, it became a virtual Soviet prisoner with nearly every ministry openly under Soviet control. In May 1986, Karmal—a despised and ineffectual figure—was removed from office and replaced by Mohammad Najibullah, former head of the Afghan secret police, who had better relations with Moscow.

By the end of the first week of January 1980, Soviet troops in Afghanistan totaled 50,000. This number increased to approximately 85,000 by the end of March, equivalent to six Soviet divisions.

International Reaction to the Invasion

In January 1980 the United Nations General Assembly voted 104 to 18 (with 30 absences or abstentions) to "deplore the recent armed intervention in Afghanistan." And in May, although not mentioning the Soviet Union by name, the General Assembly called for "the immediate, unconditional and total withdrawal of foreign troops from Afghanistan."

The significance of the General Assembly vote was that more than two-thirds of the nonaligned nations voted against the USSR. Even some socialist states or fraternal parties either voted against (Yugoslavia) or criticized (Romania) the Soviet Union. China added the removal of Soviet troops from Afghanistan to its demands required prior to a renormalization of Sino-Soviet relations.

The U.S. reaction to the invasion was one of the strongest actions ever taken by the United States in response to a specific Soviet act. Claiming that the implications of the Soviet invasion "could pose the most serious threat to peace since the Second World War," President Carter announced six measures that affected the Soviet Union: (1) blocking the U.S. export of 17 million metric tons of grain; (2) stopping the sale of U.S. computers and high-technology equipment; (3) reducing the allowable catch of the Soviet fishing fleet in U.S. waters from 350,000 tons to 75,000 tons; (4) delaying the opening of the new Soviet consulate in New York; (5) postponing a renegotiation of the U.S.–Soviet Union cultural agreement that was under consideration; and (6) boycotting U.S. participation in the Moscow Olympics, an action later joined by 55 other countries.

The Soviets were surprised by the severity of the international reaction. They attempted through diplomatic measures to shift blame for the conflict to the United States and China and to reassure nations in the area that the USSR had no designs on their territory, resources, or interests. Soviet efforts to develop a favorable peace agreement began in February 1980, but the USSR was unsuccessful in its search for regional allies and its initial efforts to gain a favorable peace were unsuccessful.

Military Occupation and Withdrawal

Over the next nine years, Soviet troops became increasingly bogged down in a bloody occupation of Afghanistan. Soviet strategy was to hold the major centers of communication, limit infiltration, and destroy local strongholds with the minimum risk to its own forces. The use of helicopters, chemical weapons, and terror tactics, key instruments in the Soviet strategy, resulted in hundreds of thousands of Afghan casualties and forced one-third of the population into exile. According to conservative estimates, approximately 1 million of Afghanistan's 12.5 million people had been killed by the time the last Soviet troops left Afghanistan (15 February 1989) and about 5 million had fled as refugees to neighboring Pakistan or Iran. Another million had been displaced from their homes within the country. Most of the deaths were civilians; however, close to 100,000 resistance fighters were also among the dead. The Soviet emphasis on attacking the civilian population from which the mujaheddin drew support eventually led to the deployment of expensive Soviet weapon systems such as the Mi-24 (Hind) helicopter gunship to Afghanistan.

In April 1986, President Reagan ordered the U.S. Central Intelligence Agency to provide the Afghan resistance forces with Stinger antiaircraft missiles—a decision that would dramatically affect the course of the war. With these weapons, the mujaheddin were able to destroy Hind gunships, disrupt Soviet air resupply operations, and reduce the close air support provided by Soviet and Afghan air forces to Soviet ground forces. The Soviet leadership, faced with either increasing its military forces or seeing their effectiveness decline further, decided to withdraw Soviet forces from Afghanistan.

On 8 February 1988, President Gorbachev announced that Soviet troops would begin withdrawing from Afghanistan on 15 May; the withdrawal was completed on 15 February 1989.

The Geneva Accords on Afghanistan of 14 April 1988, concluded under the auspices of the United Nations between the PDPA and the government of

Pakistan and jointly guaranteed by the Soviet Union and the United States, provided the overall framework for the Soviet withdrawal. Although the accords met with widespread international approval and were a diplomatic triumph for the United Nations, they did not provide for the transition to a legitimate government in Afghanistan based on the claims of Afghans to determine their own future free of outside interference. They did, however, prompt Soviet leadership to commence direct talks with the mujaheddin.

Conclusion

The war in Afghanistan was never popular with the post-Brezhnev Soviet leadership, and the growing number of Soviet dead played a significant role in shaping the Soviet public's attitude toward the war. The official Soviet Defense Ministry figure for Soviet military deaths was 13,831, justifying Gorbachev's description of Afghanistan as a "bleeding wound." This figure includes only those killed in action; a more comprehensive estimate of Soviet war deaths from all causes is 36,000.

The decision to withdraw from Afghanistan was one of the most important of the Gorbachev era. It was consistent with the overall thrust of Gorbachev's leadership as embodied in the proceedings of the 27th Congress of the Soviet Communist Party—specifically, reducing East-West tensions and eliminating unsuccessful Soviet commitments in the developing world. Indications are that the Soviets' withdrawal was a turning point in Moscow's foreign policy. These indications have been reinforced by the priority that the Soviet leadership later placed on domestic reform under the rubric of *perestroika* and *glasnost.*

JAMES B. MOTLEY

Bibliography

Collins, J. J. 1986. *The Soviet invasion of Afghanistan: A study in the use of force in Soviet foreign policy.* Lexington, Mass.: D.C. Heath.

Hammond, T. T. 1984. *Red flag over Afghanistan: The communist coup, the Soviet invasion, and the consequences.* Boulder, Colo.: Westview Press.

Oberdorfer, D. 1991. *The turn: From the cold war to a new era.* New York: Poseidon Press.

Saikal, A., and W. Maley, eds. 1989. *The Soviet withdrawal from Afghanistan.* New York: Cambridge Univ. Press.

AIRCRAFT, MILITARY

The twentieth century has been the century of the airplane, as the development of military aircraft led the way to a technological and social revolution. Even more than the automobile, the airplane has dramatically changed the lifestyles of individuals and businesses and the relationships among nations in war and peace. Airplanes have literally shrunk the planet Earth.

The first practical applications of aircraft were military. First there was observation, then reconnaissance, then air-to-ground bombardment, then air-to-air combat. Other combat missions such as air transport and electronic warfare developed rapidly. In fact, most military uses of aircraft had been conceived, developed, and utilized by the time World War I ended, just fifteen years after the first flight of a fixed-wing aircraft.

The principles of physics and aerodynamics that permit an airplane to fly are the same in civilian and military aircraft, but military aircraft differ in several ways from those used by civilians for commercial passengers, freight transportation, pleasure, and rescue. Military aircraft are used for these same purposes, but the most distinct uses are in the defense of a government and country against its enemies, or the posturing of military aircraft to prevent attack by an enemy. In almost all cases, military aircraft are owned and operated by a national government and used for national purposes.

Military aircraft, therefore, may be armored and are designed with more sophisticated technology to permit the effective delivery of a wide range of weapons. The research and development of military aircraft components is often more elaborate than that devoted to civilian aircraft. Military aircraft may be designed to stretch performance envelopes to develop longer range, greater lift capacity, shorter takeoffs and landings, higher air speeds, the ability to refuel in the air, and so forth. These developments enhance the capabilities of the air force's aircraft, but eventually may also be used to improve the capabilities of aircraft used in civilian pursuits.

When considering the enormous variety of military aircraft that are available to the nations of the world at the end of the twentieth century, it is useful to establish categories or mission areas. It should be kept in mind, however, that any categorization is arbitrary and many military aircraft perform two or more types of missions. It is also useful to remember that many civil aircraft can support military missions, especially in military transportation and observation.

Observation

Although almost all military aircraft can accomplish the observation mission, it is secondary for all but a few types of light aircraft. There are a few aircraft, notably light observation helicopters, whose principal mission is observation. The mission is not only to observe and report back the disposition of enemy forces but also to observe and report on terrain, refugees, and other relevant military information. Many modern military forces possess observation helicopters controlled and flown by army officers and noncommissioned officers. In addition to observation helicopters, light, fixed-winged aircraft are dedicated to observation. These observation aircraft provide army commanders with up-to-date, almost minute-by-minute, analysis of the battlefield as well as the area immediately to the rear of the battlefield.

The most serious deficiencies of observation aircraft are their short range, their vulnerability to enemy ground fire, and their general inability to accomplish effective observation in very bad weather and at night. In fact, it is generally accepted doctrine throughout the world that observation aircraft should not fly over heavily defended enemy territory if they are to avoid unacceptable attrition. A good example of a modern observation aircraft is the British Optica Scout. To maximize observation, pilot and observers have marvelous visibility downward, to each side, upward, and to the rear. This 2,000-pound aircraft, very inexpensive to fly and to maintain, takes off and lands in less than 300 meters (1,000 ft.), and has an eight-hour endurance capability.

Reconnaissance

When aircraft are equipped with sensors such as cameras, radar, and infrared detectors, they usually are designated reconnaissance aircraft. Dedicated reconnaissance aircraft that use speed and low-altitude penetration to avoid being shot down are normally called tactical reconnaissance aircraft. The best example of a dedicated tactical reconnaissance aircraft in the Western world in the 1970s, 80s, and 90s is the RF-4 Phantom. First used in combat during the Vietnam War by the United States, it has been modified many times to incorporate more and more sophisticated sensors, a number of which can downlink information directly to analysis centers on the ground.

There is a strong trend in the 1980s and 1990s away from dedicated reconnaissance aircraft and toward the use of reconnaissance pods that are hung on fighter aircraft whenever the reconnaissance mission is of vital importance. Another strong trend in the area of tactical reconnaissance in the 1980s and 1990s is the development and deployment of reconnaissance drones or remotely piloted vehicles. Israel has led the way, having developed sophisticated remotely piloted vehicles and having used them in combat, but a number of other nations have such programs. Their great advantage is that no aircrew is lost if one is shot down or lost over enemy territory. Also, unmanned vehicles can be sent into areas and at altitudes that would be extremely daunting to a pilot flying a reconnaissance aircraft.

Another important trend in recent years in the area of tactical reconnaissance is the rapid analysis of raw reconnaissance information into intelligence that can be useful to the commanders in the field. This is a real challenge since reconnaissance aircraft with many sensors can collect an enormous amount of information on a single sortie.

Military aircraft that fly at very high altitudes and that have sensors that can reach out many hundreds of miles to collect information are normally labeled strategic reconnaissance aircraft. Only the more powerful nations of the world have aircraft dedicated to strategic reconnaissance. Examples of strategic reconnaissance aircraft are the U.S. SR-71 and RC-135, both of which have served with the Strategic Air Command. The SR-71 (now retired) is a Mach-three aircraft, while the RC-135 is a large four-engine subsonic aircraft.

Close Air Support

In the years since World War II, few nations have developed aircraft like the wartime German Stuka, which was dedicated to the specific role of close air support of ground forces in combat. However, the American A-10 aircraft and various armed helicopters (the American Cobra and Apache and the Soviet Hind) have provided fire support and close air support to ground forces as their primary mission. Close air support is an especially challenging mission for manned aircraft since they are vulnerable when they maneuver over the combat area. In addition, they must be careful not to attack friendly forces. Hence, precise target identification is quite important, yet attempts to be absolutely sure that the target is an enemy target often mean even more vulnerability to enemy ground fire. Aircraft that are especially effective for this mission are the A-10, the Alpha jet, the A-4, the Forger, the Harrier, and the A-7, as well as helicopters such as the Hind and the Apache.

Air Interdiction

Interdiction is a natural and appropriate mission for fighter and attack aircraft. Unlike close air support, interdiction is conducted far enough behind enemy territory that all military targets may be considered enemy. The key to interdiction is the selection of targets that will make a real difference in the overall campaign plan. If the intensity of combat is high and the enemy needs a resupply, if lines of communication are fragile, and if there are no major sanctuaries that interdicting aircraft are not authorized to attack (e.g., Cambodia during the Vietnam War) then interdiction can be highly effective and at times decisive to the battle. Military aircraft engaged in the interdiction mission must have the ability to hit targets with precision and persistence; these include bridges, command and control centers, roads and railroads that pass through mountain passes, and major supply areas. These attacks can seriously disrupt the ability of the enemy to support and resupply frontline troops. Precision-guided weapons, long range, and heavy ordnance loads are helpful in ensuring that each interdiction sortie is of high value. It is also very helpful if a significant number of interdiction aircraft can find and destroy targets in inclement weather and at night.

There are two subelements of the interdiction mission: battlefield air interdiction and deep interdiction. Battlefield air interdiction is conducted close enough to the front lines that fairly close coordination is needed with ground forces, although the degree of close control is not as strict as that required for close air support because in battlefield air interdiction friendly troops are not normally endangered by friendly aircraft. Deep interdiction is conducted hundreds of miles deep into enemy territory. It is designed to impede the movement of follow-on forces that might be moving forward to support the immediate battle area. Aircraft that are especially adept at the interdiction mission include the West European Tornado; the Italian Alpha jet; the Soviet MiG-27 Fencer; the U.S. F-117A, F-16, A-7, and F-18; and the new Indian light combat aircraft.

Offensive Counterair

One of the most important roles for military aircraft is the establishment and maintenance of air superiority. One way to ensure this is the destruction of enemy air bases so the ability of the enemy to produce combat sorties is seriously degraded. The classic success story was the Israeli attack on Arab airfields during the 1967 Arab-Israeli war. Within a few hours, the Israeli air force destroyed so many aircraft on the ground that for the rest of the war Israel had not only air superiority, but air supremacy.

Aircraft engaged in the offensive counterair mission must have the range, the payload, the types of ordnance, and the persistence to knock out the key enemy airfields and keep them largely unserviceable throughout the duration of the war. This is a difficult mission if the enemy has a large number of airfields, the airfields are heavily defended by air defense systems, and they have large numbers of hardened shelters to protect aircraft, maintenance, supply, and command and control facilities. This is clearly the case in both Western and Eastern Europe since the mid-1970s. The development in air-to-ground munitions, which will allow an attacking aircraft to do significant long-term damage to runways, taxiways, and shelters, has made the attacking of airfields a feasible mission. Aircraft that are especially useful in this mission are the Fencer, the F-111, the F-15E, and the Tornado since all can carry a large ordnance load and have very long combat radii at low altitude.

Defensive Counterair

Shooting enemy aircraft down in air-to-air combat has been an important and exciting mission ever since World War I. Very high performance aircraft with superb maneuverability, a good mix of air-to-air munitions, and highly trained and aggressive pilots are all required if this mission is to be accomplished successfully. Aircraft that are particularly well designed for the air-to-air mission include the Spitfire and P-51 of World War II, the MiG-15 and the F-86 of the Korean War in the early 1950s, the F-4 and the MiG-21 of the Vietnam War, and the MiG-23, Mirage, Kfir, F-16, and F-15 of the Middle East wars of the 1960s, 70s, 80s, and 90s.

The F-15 aircraft, which was specifically designed for the air-to-air mission, is worth examining in some detail since it has been the best defensive counterair aircraft of the 1970s, 80s, and the early 90s (see Fig. 1). With two powerful afterburning engines, it is the first fighter capable of accelerating while climbing straight up, since the thrust of its engines is greater than its weight. It has superb cockpit visibility and the best long-range radar of any fighter aircraft. The head-up display in the cockpit allows the pilot to spend the majority of his time looking outside the aircraft rather than having to look into the cockpit many times each minute. Critical information is displayed on the windscreen in such a way that the pilot can quickly gain radar, attitude, weapons systems firing parameters, and other information without looking into the cockpit.

Soviet developments in defensive counterair aircraft were quite impressive in the 1970s and 1980s. These decades saw the deployment of large numbers of MiG-23 Floggers, MiG-25 Foxbats, MiG-29 Fulcrums, Su-27 Flankers, and MiG-31 Foxhounds. Some of the most modern Soviet fighters are equipped with infrared search and track systems. The French Mirage 2000 is also an impressive air-to-air fighter as are the Swedish Viggen and Grippen and the new Taiwanese Indigenous Fighter.

Figure 1. Air-to-air front view of two F-15 Eagle aircraft, one directly behind the other. (SOURCE: Courtesy of the U.S. Air Force)

One of the disappointments in fighter developments in the 1980s was the cancellation of the Israeli Lavi. There is a useful lesson here. The design, development, and procurement of the best in air-to-air fighters is very expensive and difficult. Even an advanced nation, Israel, was not able to design, build, and market overseas a fighter appreciably better than the F-16.

Missile development has also been very impressive, and the better defensive counterair aircraft have heat-seeking and radar-homing missiles as well as cannon. Developments to be expected in the 1990s are antiradiation missiles that will allow air-to-air missiles to home in on the radar energy of enemy fighters, attack aircraft, and bombers.

Strategic Bombardment

This is the classic mission for military aircraft. It was the Italian Giulio Douhet, a prophet of airpower, who saw strategic bombardment as the means by which airpower would be decisive in warfare. The idea of air forces, separate and distinct from armies and navies, came about because of the belief in the independent and potentially decisive role of the strategic bomber in warfare. In modern times, a strategic bomber has a combat radius of at least 4,800 kilometers (3,000 mi.) and is normally able to fly much farther as a result of a capability to be refueled while airborne.

The B-17, B-24, B-29, and Lancaster of World War II and the Bear, Bison, Blackjack, Vulcan, B-52, and B-1 in the postwar period have been classic long-range strategic bombardment aircraft. Strategic bombers carry nuclear weapons (in many cases up to 20) or conventional bombs. These bombers can penetrate enemy territory at low altitudes to avoid detection and interception. They often are equipped with terrain-following radar which allows them to fly at altitudes of 60 meters (200 ft.) or less even in bad weather and at night. Most modern bombers can deliver a mix of weapons including freefall bombs, glide bombs, short-range attack missiles, and long-range cruise missiles. Older bombers normally are relegated to the standoff role in nuclear war since they are so likely to be shot down if they try to penetrate. In the standoff role, they launch long-range cruise missiles that have the capability to reach their targets on their own. The latest bombers use stealth technology. The American B-2 is radical in design; it maximizes the uses of airframe and engine geometries, radar absorptive materials, and other techniques and devices to make it very difficult to observe by sensors such as radars and infrared detectors. Large stealthy bombers are extremely expensive and it remains to be seen if they will be built in large numbers, even by the major world powers.

Airlift

Aircraft designed to carry troops or military cargo are called airlift aircraft. The short-range aircraft that can get in and out of small airfields near the battlefield are called tactical airlifters; those that fly long distances and deliver their cargo at airfields to the rear of the combat zone are called strategic airlift aircraft. Examples of strategic airlift aircraft are the American C-141 and C-5 and the Soviet Il-76 Candid, the An-22 Cock, the An-124, and the new six-engine An-225. Examples of tactical airlift aircraft are the U.S. C-130 Hercules, the Casa 235, the Transall C-160, the Kawasaki C-1, and the An-12 Cub. A new airplane slated for operational use in the mid-1990s should span both of these missions quite nicely. The C-17, manufactured by McDonnell Douglas, is designed to fly intercontinental distances, carry oversize and outsize cargo, yet land on short runways near the combat zone. Nations that possess this type of aircraft will have a great advantage over those that do not for there will be no need to offload cargo and troops at a major base and transport them to the battlefield.

Warning and Surveillance

One of the most fascinating developments in military aircraft has been the placement of radar on an aircraft that can look out in all directions. The United States was first to produce an operational system and there are two American aircraft now operational. The E-3 airborne warning and control system (AWACS) aircraft is a Boeing 707 with a large rotating antenna anchored to its top. Aboard the aircraft are a dozen or so radar controllers who have access to all the radar information that the AWACS collects and are in radio communications with friendly fighters. Using air-to-air radios, these controllers direct interceptors toward enemy aircraft. Hence, they control the air battle and make the air-to-air environment over friendly territory much more favorable to the defense. The United States has more than 30 of these aircraft. The North Atlantic Treaty Organization (NATO) alliance has purchased eighteen of the large American AWACS and Britain, France, and Saudi Arabia a few.

There is a fascinating organizational aspect to AWACS aircraft operated by NATO. For the first time in history, an alliance owns a weapon. These aircraft, which have their main operating base in Geilenkirchen, Germany, are manned by airmen from eleven NATO nations. Since the aircraft support air defense throughout the alliance, they serve a useful purpose in helping to standardize air defense procedures from one NATO tactical air force to another. The U.S. Navy also has an aircraft that serves the same purpose—the E-2C. These aircraft are based on aircraft carriers and although they have smaller radars and fewer on-board controllers than the larger AWACS, they play a vital role in controlling the air war at sea. Israel also uses a few E-2Cs. The Soviets developed an AWACS capability with their Tupolev 126 Moss and Ilyushin 76 Mainstay.

Aerial Refueling

Although the capability to transfer aviation fuel from one aircraft to another was demonstrated as early as the 1920s, it was not until the 1950s that dedicated air-refueling aircraft began to appear in large numbers. The U.S. Air Force, immediately after World War II, realized that if it was to carry out its global responsibilities it would need large numbers of air-refueling aircraft deployed around the world to support bomber and fighter aircraft. KB-50s and KC-97s in large numbers supported the Strategic Air Command during the 1950s. These were large, propeller-driven aircraft that offloaded fuel while maintaining a speed of about 200 knots at an altitude of 6,100 meters (20,000 ft.). With the deployment of the B-47, B-52, F-100, and F-105 in the mid-1950s, a high-speed, jet-powered air-refueling aircraft was needed. The KC-135 was the answer, and in the late 1950s and early 1960s more than 800 KC-135s were manufactured by Boeing and deployed throughout the world. In the 1980s and the 1990s these aircraft have been reskinned and reengined and given an additional 30,000 hours of airframe time. As a result the KC-135 could become the first 100-year-old aircraft, since some may still be in service past the middle of the twenty-first century. In the 1980s, the U.S. Air Force purchased 60 KC-10s from McDonnell Douglas. These large tankers not only provide a great deal of jet fuel to various receivers but also have a huge cargo capacity. The KC-10 is a favorite for fighter deployments because it can carry much of a maintenance support team and the team's equipment for its fighter aircraft.

Another innovation of the 1970s and 80s in air refueling is the ability to transfer fuel to other aircraft besides fighters and bombers. For instance, every strategic airlift aircraft in the U.S. Air Force (C-5 and C-141) can receive fuel through air-to-air refueling. Hence, en-route stops of the past are no longer necessary because American airlift aircraft can be topped off with fuel half-way across the Atlantic or Pacific. With the growing uncertainty about overseas bases, every major power can benefit from a significant air-refueling capability. Russia, the United Kingdom, and Israel also have an air-refueling capability. The United States, however, is so dominant in this area of military airpower that it possesses more air-refueling capability than all other nations combined.

Electronic Combat Aircraft

Those aircraft whose primary role is electronic combat are jamming aircraft and hunter-killer aircraft. During the Vietnam War the Americans used "wild weasel" aircraft, which were able to detect enemy radars, lock on to those radars, and launch antiradiation missiles to attack and destroy these radars. The main targets were the radars of North Vietnamese surface-to-air missile sites. A deadly cat-and-mouse game would often take place. The North Vietnamese radars would come on the air in order to locate, lock on, and engage the American attack aircraft. The American wild weasel aircraft would detect the radar signal, lock on to it, and launch antiradiation missiles. The sites would often turn off their radars in order to avoid being destroyed by the American missiles. If the sites turned off their radars, they were unable to guide missiles proceeding toward the American attack aircraft.

Also used extensively during the Vietnam War were jamming aircraft. Aircraft such as the EB-66 flew off the coast of North Vietnam and sent out strong electronic jamming signals aimed at the North Vietnamese radars in order to reduce their effectiveness against attacking American fighters and fighter bombers.

Airborne Command Posts

Starting in the 1950s, there has been development of a new type of military aircraft, the airborne command post. In the era of the nuclear weapon it is terribly important that essential command and control nodes be able to survive the initial nuclear attack so that appropriate retaliation can take place. Airborne command posts serve a deterrent and warfighting purpose in this regard. If nation A knows that nation B can orchestrate nuclear retaliation even after nation A launches a first strike, nation A will be much less likely to launch an attack in the first place. The United States had a command post airborne twenty-four hours a day, 365 days per year, for many decades. The aircraft was a modified KC-135 (code word "Looking Glass") with a general officer on board and sophisticated communications and command-and-control equipment. In addition, the Americans have a larger and more sophisticated command post, the E-4 (a modified Boeing 747) designed to carry the president. There are carefully developed procedures for getting the president into the command post in the case of a nuclear crisis. This aircraft, using air refueling, can remain airborne for a number of days.

There are also tactical airborne command posts, which were used extensively during the Vietnam War. They were C-130 Hercules, which carried a large, self-contained pod. Inside the pod were controllers who gave mission direction to the attack aircraft going to their targets. They also received bomb damage assessment reports. These airborne command posts flew over friendly territory and helped senior commanders manage the air campaign on a minute-by-minute basis.

Special Operations Aircraft

The special operations mission is a fascinating one and has received great interest in recent years. The ability to insert troops deep into the territory of another nation, to keep them supplied, and to extract them on short notice is a particularly demanding mission. This mission is accomplished by three distinct types of military aircraft: specialized helicopters, fixed-wing aircraft such as the C-130, and tiltrotor aircraft such as the V-22 Osprey. Since special operations will become a more important mission in the future, trends in this mission area will be important. This mission area is particularly important to the Soviet Union, the United States, Israel, and Britain, and most of the technological and doctrinal developments come from these nations.

Training Aircraft

There are a large number of aircraft used throughout the world to train military aviators. In fact, the greatest amount of sales competition occurs in this area because so many nations have designed and built training aircraft that they hope to sell to others. With the U.S. Air Force and Navy looking for new trainers in the 1990s, the competition for these big markets is very high, indeed. The Argentine Pampa, the Spanish CASA C-101, the Belgian Squalus, and the British Hawk are all jet powered; the Swiss PC-9 Pilatus and the Brazilian Tucano are powered by turboprop engines. These are just a few of the excellent two-seat military training aircraft that came to the fore in the 1980s.

Trends for the Future

The early part of the next century will be a time of radical change for military aircraft. There will be a strong move toward remotely piloted vehicles, drones, and autonomous vehicles. These will be military aircraft performing military missions; however, the introduction of these aircraft into the inventories of the air forces, armies, and navies of the world will be traumatic for leaders who have been pilots and navigators of manned aircraft. The trend toward autonomous vehicles will result from a number of important factors. First, explosive changes in technology will permit the marriage of very small, efficient engines, light and inexpensive composite materials, and very sophisticated sensors. Second, political factors will encourage national decisionmakers to build vehicles that are stealthy and unmanned, so that if one is lost, there is not the embarrassment of having a downed aviator captured. Third, cost factors will be at play and it will be cheaper to build and maintain autonomous systems. Not having to fly these vehicles on a regular basis to keep the aircrews trained will reduce costs. Autonomous vehicles will be able to take over a major portion of the tactical reconnaissance, close air support, interdiction, and offensive counterair missions. Autonomous vehicles will have less of an impact on the defensive counterair, airlift, strategic reconnaissance, and observation missions. In other words, those missions that require flying over enemy territory will be most significantly affected by autonomous vehicles. Unmanned autonomous military aircraft will also be quite useful in "softening up" the enemy before manned aircraft penetrate enemy airspace. By attacking radar sites, command, control, and communications nodes, surface-to-air missile sites, and gun positions, they can reduce losses of manned penetrating aircraft.

Another significant trend for the future will be the impact of low-observable technology on military aircraft, both manned and unmanned. Stealthy military aircraft, particularly those that are stealthy in many dimensions (hard to detect on radar screens, on infrared detection devices, to the human eye, to photonic systems), will be able to operate over enemy territory for extended periods of time (hours and, in some cases, days) with relative impunity. Most stealthy aircraft will have the capability to make themselves nonstealthy, so they can be picked up on radar in peacetime for air traffic control purposes. This ability to quickly move from visible to invisible (and vice versa) will also have some tactical applications. For instance, a penetrating aircraft may wish to be nonstealthy in order to flush out the interceptors and then become stealthy before being intercepted. This would be an especially useful technique if the stealthy penetrating aircraft were followed by nonstealthy vehicles. If the enemy interceptor force was out of fuel and having to recover for refueling purposes, penetration by nonstealthy aircraft could then be more effective.

Summary

The evolution of military aircraft in the past century has gone through a number of phases. There have been times when developments have been evolutionary and other times of radical change in a short period. Those who wish to plan for the future must study the past while remaining extremely open minded to new ideas, technical developments, and doctrinal innovation. The best military aircraft of the future will be developed by those who can combine doctrinal flexibility, a keen awareness of technological possibilities, and the ability to cut through bureaucratic barriers to creative innovation. In addition, reliability and maintainability must be weighed carefully in the design bureaus of the world. Since airpower may soon become the dominant force in military operations, the nations that stay in the forefront of the development of military aircraft will have disproportionate influence in world affairs in the twenty-first century.

PERRY M. SMITH

Bibliography

Jane's all the world's aircraft, 1987–1988. 1987. London: Jane's.
Jane's all the world's aircraft, 1988–1989. 1988. London: Jane's.
Mason, R. A. 1987. *Air power: An overview of roles.* London: Brassey's.
Singh, J. 1985. *Air power in modern warfare.* New Delhi: Lancer International.
Shaker, S. M., and A. R. Wolf. 1988. *War without men: Robots on the future battlefield.*
    Washington, D.C.: Pergamon-Brassey's.

AIRPOWER, HISTORY OF

Airpower is the use of the air to further defensive or aggressive national objectives. The means by which they are pursued will be an air force, of whatever composition is appropriate to achieve the objectives. But airpower also implies the use of less direct resources such as industry, logistics (including, for example, communications and the supply of fuel), and many other facets of the potential of a nation as a whole for warlike operations. Airpower has developed since the earliest days of aviation and has had failures and successes.

Earliest Steps

The use of the air in war swiftly followed the inventions which enabled man to fly. Unmanned balloons were used in an attempt to bombard Venice with shrapnel as early as 1849 during the Austrian siege of that city; the United States used balloons for surveillance during its Civil War in the 1860s, and the British army used observation balloons in the Boer War. The Wright brothers, while still perfecting their flying machine in 1903, twice offered their invention to the U.S. Army. Military employment has never been far from the minds of aerial inventors. In fact, throughout the history of airpower, the military potential of the use of the air has been a principal stimulus to progress in the field of aviation technology.

The activities of the Wright brothers stirred U.S. military interest in the possibilities of aviation, and on 1 August 1907 the first U.S. military aviation unit was formed, the aeronautics section of the U.S. Army Signal Corps. One year later a nonrigid airship built by Thomas Scott Baldwin, and carrying Glenn Curtiss as flight engineer, was purchased by the corps after a demonstration at Fort Myer, near Washington, D.C.

In 1909, also at Fort Myer, Orville Wright completed the trials of his *Flyer* for the U.S. Army and demonstrated an endurance of 72 minutes and an average speed of 68 kilometers (42 mi.) per hour (Fig. 1). The U.S. Army thus became the owner of the first and only military aircraft in the world at that time.

In the years that followed, small aircraft construction companies sprang up in most industrial countries. During the last three years of peace (1911–14) before World War I, all the major powers were purchasing the new machines for military purposes and training their pilots. Meanwhile in a modest foretaste of

Figure 1. Orville Wright preparing for a flight at Fort Myer, Virginia, 1909. (SOURCE: U.S. Library of Congress)

what was to follow, the Italian army used aircraft to drop 2-kilogram grenades on enemy targets during its Libyan Campaign of 1911.

First World War

But it was during the First World War that use of the air developed from a popular curiosity into an effective means of prosecuting war. When the war began in August 1914 military aviation was limited to a few hundred elementary machines integrated into existing military structures. These aircraft were expected to perform reconnaissance over land and sea, artillery spotting, and courier work. Aircraft were viewed as a supplement to fleets and armies during what was expected to be a short war. Initially, there were no bombs, bombsights, integral weapons, or other equipment for combat in these early machines.

Military aircraft, however, soon took on more robust characteristics as technology was harnessed to the demands of intensive warfare. Three developments were particularly noteworthy. First, more powerful engines and sturdier machines were produced. Second, the introduction of lightweight machine-guns, synchronized to fire through the propeller arc of single-engine aircraft, transformed the early fighters into effective weapon platforms. Third, long production runs meant standardized machines, which in turn made possible formation tactics.

AIR-TO-AIR COMBAT

The demands of air-to-air fighting that emerged began to use resources that might otherwise have been used to meet the growing requirements of land and naval forces for air support. The result was an even more urgent demand for more aircraft, men, and supporting services. Operational pressures for higher performance, so that aircraft could outmaneuver their opponents, led by 1916 to speeds of up to 150 kilometers (93 mi.) per hour in the British DH2 and to ceilings up to 4,600 meters (15,000 ft.) for the French Nieuport II. Endurances of two hours also became common, and although these improvements over the machines of 1914 were not dramatic, they were accompanied by new levels of reliability and maneuverability.

BOMBERS

Long-range bombing, that is, bombing beyond the immediate battle areas, was also introduced. Lighter-than-air airships first undertook this role. Antwerp and Warsaw were attacked in this way by German zeppelins in the early months of the war in raids intended to undermine the morale of the inhabitants rather than to cause any serious physical destruction. These attacks were followed in January 1915 by zeppelin raids on British east coast towns, and by others on London during the spring of 1915, the first strategic bombing offensive in history.

Airships continued to make these sorties, particularly against London and Paris, sporadically throughout 1915 and 1916. Although the raids caused only modest damage and casualties in Britain (556 killed and 1,357 injured; small numbers compared to the slaughter at the war fronts), they alarmed the urban populations and caused grave concern at government level. Defensive measures were put into place in the form of antiaircraft artillery and interceptor aircraft, eventually equipped with deadly tracer and incendiary ammunition.

Rather more serious were the raids made against Britain by Gotha bombers starting in May 1917. On 13 June the first such raid against London killed 162 and injured 432. This and following raids led to a reorganization of the defenses created to counter the zeppelin attacks. Extra searchlights were deployed, as well as barrage balloons that supported curtains of steel cables in the air up to altitudes of 2,400 meters (8,000 ft.). Above that height, intercepters flew patrols.

At the same time as the Gothas were being developed, the British and the French were producing similar machines so that by 1917 all the principal powers had long-range bombers in their inventories. One significant organizational consequence of the Gotha raids was that partly in response to the public outcry about the bombings, the decision was made to amalgamate the air elements of the British army and the Royal Navy—the Royal Flying Corps (RFC) and the Royal Navy Air Service (RNAS)—to form the first independent air arm, the Royal Air Force. This took place in April 1918.

Throughout the war aircraft were also used extensively for support of ground and naval forces. Efforts at coordinated air support for ground forces were made from March 1915 onward, so that at the Battle of the Somme in July 1916, 360 French and British aircraft were engaged. By 1918 air operations had become so extensive that, for example in July of that year, the Allied air forces lost over 500 aircraft in a single month during a counteroffensive that was launched between Soissons and Château-Thierry. Air warfare on other fronts tended to follow the tactics developed in the west, although far fewer numbers were engaged. In Italy, Macedonia, Palestine, East Africa, Gallipoli, and Mesopotamia, aircraft played some part in the operations on land.

NAVAL AND OTHER MISSIONS

Once convoys were instituted in 1917, naval aircraft and airships had an important role in escorting merchant ships. As to main fleet activities, seaplane carriers were able to launch fighters designed to operate from airfields, but the ships were not fast enough to keep up with the fleet. After unsuccessful experiments with a cruiser modified to take an aircraft hangar and a flying-off deck, the Royal Navy in October 1918 introduced the first real aircraft carrier, HMS *Argus,* armed with torpedo bombers, but it joined the fleet too late to enter combat.

By the end of the First World War, aviation had made enormous progress. Some aircraft produced during the conflict, such as the Avro 504N, were still in use as trainers as late as the mid-1930s. At the technical level, the war had produced far more powerful, maneuverable, and reliable aircraft. Special air weapons such as synchronized fixed machine guns, as well as innovations like bombsights, airborne radios, survey cameras, and a host of lesser technologies had all been developed and produced during the war. The war had brought an awareness of the potential of military aviation, and because of the huge numbers of people involved in flying, in support of flying, or in the aviation industry during the conflict, this awareness was widespread throughout the fighting nations. The war had seen the birth of effective airpower.

Interwar Years

During the First World War, the air forces of all the major powers had grown to enormous fleets of machines. Britain, for example, began the war with 110 aircraft. During the war it produced 55,093 machines, and by the 11 November 1918 Armistice over 20,000 were in the inventory, including trainers. After the war, however, the great air fleets of the belligerents were dismantled almost to the point of abolition. As one example, the wartime U.S. Army Air Service grew to about 200,000 men, but by July 1920 only 10,000 remained.

In terms of organization, the air arms of the army and navy in the United States remained apart during and after the war, and bitter bureaucratic argument marked the efforts of Maj. Gen. William L. ("Billy") Mitchell and others in the interwar years to create an independent air force and to gain recognition of Mitchell's claim that the airplane was "the arbiter of our nation's destiny." The two services thus went their own ways, but they did so with some success. In the early 1920s, the U.S. Navy converted a collier into its first aircraft carrier, and two battle cruiser hulls were modified to produce the carriers USS *Saratoga* and USS *Lexington* in 1928. The new carrier USS *Ranger* was launched in 1934, followed by the USS *Enterprise* and the USS *Yorktown* in 1936.

In the case of the U.S. Army Air Corps, the role of coastal defense was stressed. Meanwhile the Air Corps Tactical School at Maxwell Field, Alabama, was exerting a formative influence on the development of airpower thinking, including the importance of the offensive role. On the technical side, aircraft such as the Boeing 299 and the XB-15 of 1935, which contributed to the design of the B-17 and the B-29, were emerging from the advancing technologies of aeronautics.

In Britain, modest resources were spread over the various roles of the Royal Air Force, including that of policing overseas possessions, such as Iraq and the northwest frontier of India, where relatively inexpensive air elements substituted for costly field forces.

INTERWAR DOCTRINE

In terms of doctrine during the interwar years, Douhet's theories of 1921 offered a sweeping vision of how the decisive impact of strategic airpower could replace the attrition of the First World War. His assumptions about the destructive power of the heavy bomber, its ability to prevail in spite of modern air defenses, and the likely effect of bombing on industrialized societies were based on slender evidence, but he offered a very persuasive argument for independent air forces. At the same time, most of the same major powers to whom strategic airpower might have been expected to appeal, had a more immediate preoccupation with security on their frontiers. This concern emphasized the priority of tactical air and of short-range aviation, rather than the expenditure of scarce resources on the long-range heavy bomber. The paradoxical consequences of all this was the emergence of independent air forces in Italy (1923), Sweden (1926), and France and Germany (both in 1933), but very little progress toward a strategic bomber force in any nation.

SPANISH CIVIL WAR

The emphasis on tactical air seemed to be endorsed by the events of the Spanish Civil War of 1936–39. Certainly the experience of the German Condor Legion in that war had a formative influence on the German concept of war fought by a combination of infantry and armor, with airpower acting in direct support and in the interdiction role. Largely because no accurate bombsight was available, bombing from medium levels was found by the Luftwaffe to be less effective than dive bombing, and the use of Panzer divisions, first formed in 1936, together with dive-bombing Stukas was thus to become familiar in the opening stages of the German campaigns in the Second World War.

PREPARATIONS FOR WAR

Meanwhile, in Britain different conclusions were being drawn, this time from the experience of German bombing attacks during the First World War. In analyzing the air threat that Germany was expected to pose to Britain, the Air Ministry fell back on the evidence of the second German air offensive against Britain in 1917. This purported to show that each ton of high explosive would cause 50 casualties. Later revised upward, then extrapolated to the size of the Luftwaffe, this estimate was used to project the casualties that would be produced by the knock-out blow the Germans were expected to deliver at the very start of the war. The official forecast of air casualties for the first day of the war became 1,700 killed and 3,300 injured, with 850 killed and 1,650 injured in each subsequent 24-hour period.

In fact, air-raid casualties in Britain during the whole first year of the war were only 257 killed and 441 hospitalized. But the widely inaccurate forecast led to two developments. One was a massive investment in passive defense measures such as air-raid shelters, fire-fighting equipment, and so on that were to prove invaluable during the later and prolonged German air attacks. The other was a sharp and, as it turned out, decisive acceleration in the air defense program of the Royal Air Force leading to a state of high preparedness by the time of the Battle of Britain.

The Second World War: Early Campaigns

The disparity between expectations and reality was one of the most striking features of the early days of World War II. In fact, the first stages of the war were dominated by tactical, rather than strategic airpower. This was most strikingly the case with German air efforts. Although before the war many Luftwaffe leaders had seen strategic bombardment as the principal mission of the air arm, German rearmament had by 1939 been able to produce only twin-engined bombers. In any case, at the strategic level the German intention was not merely to wage blitzkrieg campaigns, but to wage a blitzkrieg war, in other words, a war that would be swift in execution and short in duration. Strategic bombing might not be necessary.

This certainly proved to be the case in Poland, Norway, France, and the Low Countries. In Poland during the single month of September 1939, both the army and the air force of that country were destroyed. In Norway, the Luftwaffe made a decisive contribution to successful operations by the German army and navy. Against France and the Low Countries, the German offensive began with priority given to air superiority, and although the Allied air forces fought well, those on the Continent were virtually eliminated in the first few days. Thereafter, German aircraft were able to contribute to the assault on the Allied ground forces, which were defeated within a very short time. Notably, however, the evacuation from Dunkirk would not have been possible without air cover provided by the RAF fighter command from bases in Britain.

Battle of Britain

Despite considerable losses during the campaign in France, by July the Luftwaffe was able to launch a major air offensive against the British Isles as the precursor to a full invasion. The initial air objective was defeat of the RAF and its supporting echelons and the destruction of the British aircraft industry. The limited size of the German fighter escort force and the restricted range of the bomber and fighter aircraft, however, confined almost all the attacks to the south of Britain, thus providing immunity to the considerable aircraft industry located in the north and affording sanctuary areas for the training and recuperation of the defending fighter forces.

During August 1940 the air battles of the Battle of Britain developed into costly confrontations as the Luftwaffe pressed home its campaign. For example, between "Eagle Day," 13 August, the day originally planned for the invasion, and 19 August, the Germans lost 284 aircraft, approximately 10 percent of their available force in the west. But just when a collapse of the defenses was within reach, the Luftwaffe switched its efforts to London in a massive daylight attack on 9 September against the docks. The results were highly destructive, and huge fires raged out of control. The damage was then compounded by day and night attacks over the following week. Another massive and destructive daylight attack was made on 15 September, but this raid proved to be the climax of the campaign, and the Luftwaffe scaled down its later efforts. The offensive had been defeated by a skillful defense, greatly assisted by radar and ground control, against German aircraft that were well matched by the defending fighters. But it is doubtful if the defeat would have occurred had the Luftwaffe single-mindedly pursued its attacks against the Royal Air Force's fighter command.

The serious losses suffered by the Luftwaffe in the daylight raids of this period had three consequences. The German invasion plan was canceled; the Luftwaffe switched to night bombing raids; and the RAF was afforded a respite in which to rebuild some of its badly depleted strength.

Meanwhile, the German High Command turned its attention to the east. This left the British (and later the Americans and their allies) free to build up massive airpower resources in the United Kingdom, although German bombing of the United Kingdom continued sporadically throughout the rest of the war, reinforced by V-1 pilotless aircraft attacks and bombardment by V-2 ballistic missiles in 1944.

In the East

In the campaign against Russia, the Luftwaffe again concentrated its initial efforts against the opposing air force, this time in a devastating blow starting in the early hours of the day of the invasion, 22 June 1941. No fewer than 3,275 German aircraft—1,945 of them frontline combat aircraft—had been deployed for the campaign, and the initial air assault was made on 31 Soviet airfields. By the next day 1,811 Soviet aircraft had been destroyed, 1,489 of them on the ground, with a loss of only 35 Luftwaffe aircraft. By the end of June, 4,614 Soviet aircraft had been destroyed, with a loss of only 330 German aircraft. This was an overwhelming air victory, and one that gave German forces the virtual total air superiority. In the months that followed, the Luftwaffe was able not only to give valuable direct support to land operations but also to operate almost unhindered over the Soviet rear areas.

As the war progressed, and particularly as the Allied air offensive over Germany from late 1943 onward drew in more and more of the resources of the Luftwaffe, the Russian air force gradually recovered until it was able in its turn to wrest air superiority from the Luftwaffe in the east.

The Luftwaffe had no answer to this steady and massive buildup. Its aircraft production program was inadequate, and the aircrew training program could not replace the losses of valuable men. But the main failure was a long-term one; the early and easy Luftwaffe victories had caused a misappreciation of the attrition rates likely to be experienced in the prolonged war that became inevitable once the German offensive failed at the gates of Moscow. The result was that by the time the Red Army launched its greatest offensive against the German Army Group Center on 22 June 1944, the Luftwaffe was outnumbered in the East by about 6 to 1.

STRATEGIC BOMBING OFFENSIVES: EUROPE

The early RAF daylight raids on the Continent proved to be expensive failures, and most of the available effort was switched to night bombing. But this, too, was largely ineffective, as well as wildly inaccurate, so in November 1941, bombing by the Royal Air Force was virtually suspended altogether to allow for the re-equipment and expansion of the Bomber Command. It was not until mid-February 1942 that the long strategic bombing campaign could begin in earnest. The first major raid was made by 1,000 aircraft on Cologne on 30 May 1942, and heavy raids against Essen and Bremen followed. On 17 August of the same year, the U.S. Army Air Forces (USAAF) flew their first strategic bombing mission, and from then on a pattern of complementary daylight raids by the USAAF and night attacks by the RAF developed.

The U.S. Army's Eighth Air Force of the USAAF, based in Britain, applied its efforts to specific targets such as oil refineries, shipyards, factories, and other objectives that directly supported the German war effort. Large formations of B-17s and B-24s, escorted from July 1943 onward by early models of long-range fighters, battled their way to the targets and back, sometimes with heavy losses. One of the worst setbacks was the raid on Schweinfurt in October 1943, a target beyond the range of escorting P-47s. Of 291 bombers engaged in the raid, 28 were lost en route to Schweinfurt, and 32 on the return flight. Only 92 suffered no damage at all.

Partly because of the technical difficulties of accurate night bombing, and partly because of a conviction that the will and ability of the enemy to continue the war could be broken by area bombing, the Royal Air Force generally attacked large area targets. Pathfinder techniques were developed by specialist squadrons that made possible concentrated and devastating attacks on major German cities. The bombers flew under the cover of night, relying on the modest protection afforded by on-board machineguns, and on the concentration of the bomber force in time and space to overwhelm the German night-fighter defenses. On many raids the loss rate to the bombers was very low, while on others it was intolerably high. The worst RAF losses were sustained during an unsuccessful raid on Nuremberg on 30–31 March 1944 when 95 out of 795 aircraft were lost, a loss rate of 11.9 percent.

The results of this long campaign of strategic bombing by day and by night were manifold. First, although it did not prevent an overall increase in German arms production, it did set a ceiling on that production at a time when the Germans were desperately short of weapons and equipment on the eastern front. Second, German defensive efforts against the air campaign and the need to repair the vast damage absorbed a huge proportion of the total German war potential. Massive resources in manpower, materiel, guns, and aircraft were all drawn into the battle. German fighter losses during these raids were particularly serious and led to virtual Allied air superiority over Germany from March 1944. In effect, and as Albert Speer admitted, a second front had been opened above Germany long before the Allied invasion of Normandy, and this led to a diversion and attrition of Luftwaffe forces that might otherwise have been available to the German High Command, for example, over the Normandy beachhead. Third, the inability of the Luftwaffe to defeat the attacks led to a loss of confidence in the German air force and encouraged Hitler to devote more of the available limited air resources to tactical support in the East.

Japan

Strategic bombing against Japan during the war in the Pacific took a different form. After initial successes in the early months of the war, the fortunes of the Japanese were swiftly reversed. From February 1943, the Japanese were on the defensive, and by the time Saipan and other island bases in the Pacific were recaptured or seized from the Japanese, some 500 B-29 bombers were available for the strategic bombardment of the Japanese home islands. The main air offensive against the Japanese home islands was launched in November 1944, at a stage of the war when Japanese industry was already in decline and the economy hard pressed, due to shortages in raw materials caused by the destruction of Japanese shipping.

Faced with operational conditions that raised questions about the efficacy of precision bombing relative to area attacks, a policy of area targets that would lead to victory through blockade and bombing alone was decided upon. Attacks using firebombing techniques against the densely built and highly vulnerable Japanese cities were begun in March 1945. Although Japanese industry was very concentrated geographically, and the ground-based defenses could thus be densely deployed, the attacking USAAF XXI Bomber Command suffered only modest losses in these raids. For the Japanese, however, the result was the virtual destruction of 58 cities between May and August 1945. This so undermined morale and the effective functioning of civil and military machinery that surrender became inevitable.

The surrender was hastened by the use of atomic bombs on Hiroshima and Nagasaki in August 1945. These two attacks were a fulfillment of the kind of prophecy that Douhet had made two decades before, yet were on a scale that even he had not envisaged.

The strategic air bombardment of Japan was more effective than that against Germany for several reasons. First, the lessons learned in Europe were incorporated into the plans for the offensive against Japan. Second, the Japanese air defenses were no match for the American air effort. Third, the Japanese economy was already in decline as the result of the American sea blockade. And last, the construction of Japanese cities, which made extensive use of flammable materials, made them far more vulnerable to air attack than those of Europe. Together these factors produced an air campaign of overwhelming success.

HIGHPOINT OF TACTICAL AIR

As Germany was gradually forced onto the defensive, Allied tactical airpower was increasingly brought to bear in North Africa, Italy, and finally in western Europe. It took two main forms. One was the direct support of land forces, and starting in North Africa, techniques of close control of tactical air in the battle area were perfected. Those techniques were then used with great effect in northwest Europe by the new Allied tactical air forces. On D-Day no fewer than 12,837 aircraft including 5,400 fighters were engaged, many of the latter in the close support of armies.

The second form of air support for land operations was that of interdiction. This entailed the destruction in rear areas of enemy resources such as reinforcements before they could reach the battle area and severing and disrupting the routes along which those resources were to travel. Again, the techniques were perfected in the Mediterranean during the campaign in Italy, and applied with devastating effect in preparation for the Allied invasion of Normandy, as well as in operations such as that at the Falaise Gap in 1944 during that same campaign. Interdiction was a highly effective application of airpower; its successes in these instances were enhanced by the massive air superiority that had meanwhile been achieved by the Allied air forces.

AT SEA

At sea, airpower played a key role throughout the Second World War. In the Atlantic and the Mediterranean, both land-based and carrier-borne aircraft helped sustain the vital lines of communication by defeating the German submarine threat. Nearly 60 percent of all U-boats lost in the war were sunk by aircraft. Airpower was also significantly engaged in attacks on German and Italian main fleet units, notably at Taranto in November 1940 and in the sinking of the German battleship *Tirpitz* in 1944.

In the Pacific, it was airpower that opened Japan's war against the United States with the surprise attack on Pearl Harbor by Japanese carrier-borne aircraft on 7 December 1941. In an attack lasting less than two hours, 167 Japanese torpedo and dive bombers sank four U.S. battleships, damaged another four, and destroyed or damaged many smaller vessels and shore facilities. At the same time, 105 other bombers together with 78 fighters destroyed or put out of action 310 of the 400 U.S. Army, Navy, and Marine aircraft, mostly on the ground, on Oahu Island. Meanwhile, other Japanese formations attacked U.S. bases in the Philippines and British forces in Malaya. The Japanese lost only 29 aircraft at Pearl Harbor, but in one critical aspect the raid failed; both of the U.S. aircraft carriers based at Pearl Harbor were at sea, and thus survived to fight in later, decisive battles.

During the next twelve months, the Japanese advance in the Far East was gradually halted, and in the Pacific a series of maritime engagements (including carrier battles at the Coral Sea, Midway, and the Eastern Solomons) took place. During these and other engagements, all fifteen of the Japanese aircraft carriers that had joined the fleet after 1941 were sunk or put out of action, while of the 27 carriers added to the U.S. fleet, only one was lost.

This huge imbalance was decisive in a campaign that was essentially maritime in all its characteristics.

In the entire Far East campaign, because of the vast distances involved, air supply was a crucial feature of Allied operations. Fleets of transport aircraft increasingly supported land and maritime operations, whether in the India-China air link, in Burma, or across the vast reaches of the Pacific Ocean.

WORLD WAR II IN RETROSPECT

By the end of the Second World War, airpower was widely acknowledged as the dominant arm in warfare. In quantity and quality, the development of the air weapon over a period of six years had been phenomenal. Over 300 different types of aircraft saw service during the war, and the principal belligerents produced some three-quarters of a million airframes. The United States alone produced 272,000, and supplied over 45,000 to allies.

In terms of quality, the conflict saw the development not only of the decisive airborne weapon, the atomic bomb, but also of electronic warfare, particularly radar, but including many other devices. It also saw the emergence of the first effective guided weapons in the form of remotely controlled bombs, and finally it greatly accelerated developments in aircraft engines, including jet engines, leading to entirely new levels of aerodynamic performance. If the First World War had seen the birth of airpower, then the Second World War had seen it grow to full maturity.

POSTWAR AIRPOWER: THE STRATEGIC ROLE

By the end of the Second World War, the United States was overwhelmingly the leading proponent of airpower, and within the United States, military aviation had become the largest industry. Meanwhile, and well before the end of the conflict, the leaders of the U.S. Army Air Forces were planning a continuation of this national emphasis on the air arm. They had two objectives: (1) to form an independent U.S. Air Force to give airpower both the voice and the share of national resources that they believed it deserved, and (2) to equip that air force with a minimum of 70 active combat groups.

Within that figure of 70 groups, the emphasis was to be on strategic bombardment. But continuing demobilization, budgetary cuts, and the many problems inherent in separating the new U.S. Air Force (USAF) from the U.S. Army Air Forces meant that the new service was hard-pressed to maintain any strategic force at all after its formation in 1947. Some impetus to the emergence of a separate air force was given by growing Soviet hostility in 1946, and in particular by the U.S.-British Berlin Airlift from June 1948 to September 1949, during a blockade of the city which also served to demonstrate the unique qualities of a logistic air bridge.

Although the Strategic Air Command (SAC) and the strategic mission were given first priority by the USAF in 1948, it was not until the outbreak of the Korean War in June 1950 that the resources to turn intentions into capabilities began to be available. Progress in rebuilding U.S. airpower was then rapid. For example, at the end of 1949, SAC had fourteen bomb groups with 610 strategic bombers, two fighter groups, and six air-to-air refueling squadrons. By 1953, this force had expanded to 37 bomb groups with more than 1,000 aircraft (mainly B-36s and B-47s), as well as six fighter wings and 28 air-to-air refueling squadrons. Between 1951 and 1963, almost 3,000 strategic bombers entered service with the USAF.

This was a high point in postwar U.S. airpower, but two events were to change the strategic situation again toward the end of the Korean conflict. First, Dwight D. Eisenhower became president with a mandate not only to end that war, but to reduce U.S. defense spending. And second, the U.S. exploded the first thermonuclear device in October 1952, followed by the Soviet Union ten months later. The qualitative change that the thermonuclear bomb represented is sometimes overlooked, yet it meant a weapon that was over 500 times more powerful than the atomic bombs that had destroyed Hiroshima and Nagasaki. It also soon became clear that the new weapons could be made smaller in size and in weight than had at first been supposed.

This fact led to profound changes in USAF procurement policies. At the end of the Second World War, air force planners had believed that the manned bomber would remain the principal strategic weapon for many years, and that it would eventually be replaced by cruise missiles. But the development of the lightweight thermonuclear weapon now led the USAF in March 1954 to accelerate the modest Atlas Intercontinental Ballistic Missile (ICBM) program and later to add Titan, Minuteman, and Thor to the USAF missile procurement list. By 1957 it had become clear that Atlas would overtake the most promising cruise missile that had been under development, the Navajo, and the belief that there would be a steady progression from manned aircraft through cruise missiles to ICBMs was abandoned. Progress toward ICBMs became very rapid as technology solved many of the problems that had seemed to argue against ballistic missiles, and by 1963 ICBMs had become the principal U.S. strategic weapon.

This marked the end of an era. Total dependence on conventional aircraft for strategic bombardment was now replaced by a combination of: (1) ICBMs with instantaneous reaction, short flight time, high accuracy, and ability to penetrate all defenses; and (2) an aging, but operationally flexible, force of B-52s supported by tankers.

In the only other Western nuclear power at that time, the United Kingdom, the development of atomic weapons owed much to the wartime cooperation with the United States, and the Royal Air Force was able to deploy a sizable force of nuclear-armed medium bombers from the early 1950s until 1969, when Polaris submarines took over the deterrent role. In the United Kingdom the air-atomic strategy had lasted a little longer than it did in the United States.

Korean Conflict

The invasion of South Korea by the forces of North Korea on 25 June 1950 was thought to be only the first move in a wider Soviet plan of communist expansion. The attack therefore stimulated a rapid and comprehensive Western rearmament program including expanded air forces, but the campaign itself was limited both geographically and in terms of the forces engaged.

From the start, the United Nations (UN) air forces (composed overwhelmingly of U.S. Air Force and U.S. Navy and Marine Corps aviation) held air superiority over all but the northern extremities of the Korean peninsula. The early stages of the campaign were marked by an emphasis on close air support as UN land forces were driven back to the Pusan perimeter. One interesting circumstance was that Second World War piston-engined P-51 Mustangs (redesignated F-51 in 1947) were found to be more effective than the available F-80 Shooting Stars because the jets could not be forward-based from Japan onto the poor airfields of South Korea.

As UN reinforcements arrived in preparation for their counteroffensive, the application of airpower was widened to include attacks by B-29 bombers, not without loss, against strategic targets in North Korea, and growing air efforts against the communists' lines of communications. These and later bombing attacks were indecisive because the real sources of enemy military power lay not in North Korea, but in China and in the Soviet Union. In some respects the attacks were counterproductive, since the Communists were able to make propaganda play out of what they claimed were indiscriminate attacks.

The early interdiction attacks were only the first in a series of eight interdiction campaigns during the three-year war. None was decisive, and all disappointed the air planners. Whether aimed at road, rail, or both networks, these interdiction efforts all failed for the same reasons. First, the logistic needs of Asian-style armies was consistently overestimated. For example, a North Korean division could fight on as little as 50 tons of resupply per day; Western logisticians were more accustomed to thinking in terms of 650 tons per division per day. Second, the staff skills, the ingenuity, and the field engineering capabilities of coolie-style armies had been seriously underestimated. Cuts in roads and railways were quickly repaired, and damaged bridges were rebuilt or replaced with remarkable speed. Third, the Communists learned to disperse their supply columns by day and to move forward under cover of darkness. Fourth, and most telling, the Communists learned to adjust the intensity of their military effort to match the logistic effort that was escaping the interdiction.

In air combat over the extreme north of Korea, the UN forces were more successful. Because Soviet-supplied MiG-15 jet fighters based in Manchuria were unable to dominate airspace over North Korea, the airfields sited there could be kept out of action by UN air bombardment. Thus, the Communists were never able to extend their air effort over the ground battles farther south.

In spite of the application of airpower, the war turned into a stalemate. As a result, it led to considerable rethinking about the future role of airpower. Before Korea, airpower, with its ability to strike the sources of enemy warmaking potential, had come to be the apotheosis of total war. In Korea, not only was it important to prevent the conflict from becoming a total, global war, but the sources of enemy power were in what amounted to sanctuaries. Korea was the first demonstration of limited conventional war in the nuclear era, but it was not to be the last.

Suez Campaign, 1956

Two years after Korea, airpower was again engaged in conventional operations, this time in a struggle for control of the Suez Canal. This brief Anglo-French campaign against the Egyptians was conducted on a considerable scale. Five division equivalents were assigned to the Anglo-French commander, as well as a combined fleet that included five aircraft carriers. Available combat air strength was 125 bombers, 118 fighter/ground attack and reconnaissance aircraft, 159 carrier-borne aircraft, and 24 helicopters, a total of 426 machines, not including the Israeli Defense Force/Air Force or three squadrons of French aircraft based in Israel. The Egyptian air force was composed of about 200 combat aircraft, including 80 MiG-15s.

The air plan for the brief campaign comprised three stages: the destruction of the Egyptian air force; interdiction against military and other installations in what was called an aero-psychological campaign; and direct air support for the amphibious and parachute landings. Although the offensive counter-air effort destroyed about 60 Egyptian aircraft on the ground, the Egyptians succeeded in dispersing the rest of their air force. The limited success of the British and French air forces against airfields was due largely to the fact that the modest force available could not cover all targets adequately. Additionally, the attacks that were made were often too inaccurate to put the airfields out of action. The remaining Egyptian air force was too weak to offer serious opposition to the Anglo-French offensive, however.

With only weak opposition from the Egyptians, the direct air support portion of the campaign was more successful. However, the results of the aero-psychological attacks totally failed to meet expectations. In the first phase of these particular attacks, raids were made against a Cairo radio station, two barracks, and a large railway marshaling yard. The attacks produced an international outcry that caused further attacks to be canceled. The Suez campaign itself was brought to an end by political pressure on the governments of France and Britain after only six days.

Thus at Suez as in Korea, the exercise of airpower was shown to be no longer a question of the uninhibited selection and destruction of targets. Airpower, which in 1943–45 had been able successfully to extend warfare beyond the boundaries of conventional land and sea operations, now found itself restricted by other considerations, including those of international opinion.

Vietnam

A decade later, the United States became involved in another war, this time in Vietnam. Air activity during the Vietnam war from 1965 to 1973 is best viewed in components: strategic and tactical air transport, support to ground forces, air superiority, interdiction, and the use of airpower against strategic targets.

Strategic air transport made an indispensable contribution to logistics, while within Vietnam itself a network of airstrips able to take twin-engine transports had been built across the country as early as 1965 in one of the first U.S. contributions to the defense of South Vietnam. As the conflict developed, some highly adaptive uses of basic transport aircraft were seen, notably when they were employed as flare-ships, as gunships, and in operations to defoliate the forests that covered Vietcong logistic routes.

Considerable air effort was applied in direct support of U.S. and South Vietnamese ground forces throughout the war. On a typical day, between 750 and 800 sorties were flown, either in preplanned missions or in unscheduled support missions. These latter could normally be executed within 35 or 40 minutes by forces in a ground-alert posture. In crisis operations such as that during the Tet offensive of 1968, surge operations could be flown that raised the direct air support effort by about 50 percent. Against an elusive enemy able to concentrate and scatter with ease, this ability to bring mobile and responsive firepower to bear, particularly since artillery was often not available, was a vital element in the U.S. campaign. A further important ground support contribution was made by B-52 bombers used in the tactical role. Their ability to carry the equivalent warload of about five fighter-bombers each meant that they could lay down massive carpets of firepower on areas known to harbor Vietcong concentrations.

A different kind of support was provided in Vietnam by a very considerable force of U.S. helicopters. But all efforts to employ helicopters and tactical transport aircraft in major air-landing operations demanded massive logistic support and served to confirm again the essential prerequisite of air superiority, the need to suppress all ground antiaircraft fire. In smaller operations, however, and particularly in a locally benign air environment, the use of helicopters became an essential and ubiquitous feature of U.S. activity throughout the war.

Air superiority was essential to virtually all other operations in the U.S. air effort, and the Vietcong and North Vietnamese devoted considerable efforts to challenge U.S. domination of the airspace. At the lowest level of effectiveness this included Vietcong small-arms fire in South Vietnam. More telling were the scattered antiaircraft guns used before 1967 along the Ho Chi Minh trail, which was actually a comprehensive system of well-developed roads and tracks. After 1967 the deployment of surface-to-air missiles (SAMs) and more effective AA weapons along the trail made it necessary to cover attacking aircraft with defense suppression missions. North Vietnam deployed highly effective ground-based antiaircraft systems. Those around Hanoi were particularly well sited and efficiently served. Most of the communist surface-to-air missiles in the North were deployed in a 65-kilometer (40-mi.) circle around the capital in some 20–30 battalions that operated a total of perhaps 2,000 launchers.

The effectiveness of the Soviet-supplied SAMs required a considerable U.S. effort to counter them, and by the end of the war the ratio of support to attack aircraft in U.S. attack packages had risen to 4 to 1. These packages were, however, very successful. In 1967 there had been one aircraft lost to each 55 missiles fired; this later fell to one per 100, and by 1972 had fallen to one per 150. Later, during the Linebacker II offensive of December 1972, the Hanoi SAM system was overwhelmed by the density and persistence of U.S. air attacks.

Comprehensive U.S. use of electronic countermeasures (ECM) from 1967 onward made it possible to penetrate North Vietnamese airspace at medium altitude with some assurance of invulnerability from SAMs, and yet be above the range of most of the antiaircraft gunfire. As to enemy fighter defenses, by 1967 there were some 100 MiG-17s and MiG-21s deployed on airfields in North Vietnam. The air-to-air engagements provoked by these fighters were never on the scale of those seen over the Yalu River fifteen years before, and although the communist fighter threat could not be ignored, the MiGs were never a serious inhibition to U.S. air activities.

Efforts to cut the supply routes from the Chinese border and from the port of Haiphong absorbed a great deal of the U.S. air effort in Vietnam. Many of the difficulties encountered during the interdiction campaign in Korea now reappeared. The U.S. air effort still had to deal with a coolie-maintained logistic system and with the proven ingenuity and skill of communist engineers. This made very difficult all attempts to interdict the diffuse and highly resilient network of roads and paths that formed the Ho Chi Minh Trail. Farther north, where limited road and rail communications were being used by the Communists to move their supplies to the combat areas, the American effort was hampered by serious political restrictions that were applied to the air campaign in deference to world opinion and to keep from provoking North Vietnam's Chinese and Soviet allies. In neither the interdiction campaign of 1965 to 1968 nor in that of 1972 could Hanoi or the key harbor of Haiphong be attacked. Furthermore, a 200-kilometer (125-mi.) buffer zone along the Chinese border prevented attacks in that region, while key bridges along the route such as the 1,686-meter (5,532 ft.) long Paul Doumer bridge were off limits until August 1967. The predictable result of these restrictions was that the North Vietnamese instituted a shuttle system between the numerous sanctuary areas, storing military supplies in them by day and moving them forward at night. Thus was interdiction prevented from exercising its full potential, and, as in Korea, the Communists learned to adjust the intensity of their activities to match the supplies evading the U.S. interdiction efforts.

Finally in the Vietnam War, strategic air bombardment was employed by the U.S. air forces. In retrospect, however, one of the principal flaws in the U.S. conduct of the war was the use of air bombardment to send political signals to the North and its supporters, instead of applying the massive military-economic pressure of which U.S. airpower was undoubtedly capable.

Only in the last stages of the war was airpower able to have a decisive impact. There had been various bombing pauses before early 1972 in the hope of persuading the North to come to terms, and pressure was increased again by the mining of Haiphong harbor and by reducing the sanctuary zones around that city and around the capital, Hanoi. This appeared to produce a softening of the communist line at the Paris peace talks and from October all bombing above the 20th parallel was halted. But when it became clear that the Communists were once again procrastinating, the decision was at last made to attack targets in Hanoi and Haiphong with maximum effort.

This was the Linebacker II campaign. It lasted for eleven days beginning on

18 December 1972, and consisted of heavy, coordinated, and escorted B-52 raids. After three nights of bombardment, the efforts by the SAM defenses decreased, and on 26 December a climax was reached when 120 attack and 100 escort aircraft in seven waves struck their targets. All told, 389 sorties were flown by B-52s in these raids, and sixteen of the aircraft were lost. A total of 13,395 tons of bombs was dropped during Linebacker II, and a wide range of targets was hit including railway yards, airfields, petroleum installations, munition depots, docks, and power plants.

It was an expensive war for the United States, and for the U.S. air forces involved. In flying 1,248,105 fixed-wing combat sorties, 1,324 aircraft had been lost to enemy action; and for well over 37 million helicopter sorties, 2,112 machines had been lost in combat and 2,475 to other causes. One reason for the length of the war and for these and other losses was that the slow escalation of the air effort during the whole conflict not only gave the enemy the opportunity to mobilize his population militarily and psychologically against future attacks, but also allowed him to invoke worldwide protest at the same time. The war had seen a serious misuse of airpower, and only when airpower was properly applied during Linebacker II were the desired results forthcoming. The North Vietnamese signed the peace agreement on 15 January 1972, within weeks of Linebacker II.

Falklands/Malvinas Conflict

In another brief campaign in the Falkland Islands/Islas Malvinas in 1982, airpower—both potential and applied—had a considerable impact on both protagonists, although the number of aircraft engaged was small.

On the Argentinian side, the most powerful weapons were five Exocet-armed Super Etendard aircraft, of which only four were serviceable. Yet they not only sank two major British warships, they also obliged the Royal Naval carrier group to operate at the extreme range of its Harrier aircraft. This determined much of the character of the campaign. The British conducted very long-range attacks by bombers that had to be refueled in flight so they could operate from their base on Ascension Island some 6,400 kilometers (4,000 mi.) to the north. These attacks compelled the Argentinians to deploy their most important squadrons of fighters away to the north in defense of Buenos Aires, thus almost certainly tipping the overall balance of power in favor of the British.

Middle East Wars

Three short but intense conflicts took place in the Middle East in 1967, 1973, and 1982, each with its own characteristics from the standpoint of airpower.

SIX-DAY WAR

In the first of these wars, the Israeli Defense Force/Air Force (IDF/AF) on 5 June 1967 launched a pre-emptive attack against nineteen Egyptian airfields in the Sinai and in Egypt proper. These carefully planned attacks achieved complete tactical surprise, and within a few hours, some 75 percent of Egyptian combat air strength had been destroyed. Equally destructive attacks followed on the small Jordanian air force and on that of the Syrians. By the end of the day more than 500 Arab aircraft had been destroyed with a loss of only 20 Israeli machines.

This overwhelming blow enabled the Israeli army to inflict defeats on the Arab land forces, while the Israeli air force followed up its initial success by inflicting heavy losses on large enemy ground forces, particularly in the Mitla Pass in the Sinai Desert. One important and wider consequence of the Israeli destruction of so much enemy airpower on the ground was the construction by the Warsaw Pact of hardened aircraft shelters, starting in 1968, while the North Atlantic Treaty Organization (NATO) followed with a long overdue program in 1974.

WAR OF ATTRITION

The 1967 defeat of the Arabs was followed in the succeeding years by a long Egyptian-inspired campaign of attrition, consisting of constant minor harassing attacks against Israeli positions. The Israeli response took the form of a progressive destruction of most of the Egyptian SA-2 missile batteries. The Egyptians gradually replaced these batteries so that by the end of 1969 a Soviet-supplied, comprehensive air defense system of missiles and guns was in place along Egypt's entire eastern frontier.

OCTOBER 1973 WAR

With their air defenses now secure, the Egyptians planned a surprise assault across the Suez Canal. The Israelis meanwhile had calculated that since they had a superiority in tanks and in operational aircraft, it was extremely unlikely that the Egyptians would risk an attack. In fact the Egyptians had drawn quite different conclusions from the same assessment of comparative strengths. Instead of pitting armor against armor, they employed infantry-fired missiles against tanks and used surface-to-air missiles to dominate the airspace above their army formation when they attacked across the Suez Canal on 6 October 1973. Simultaneously the Syrians attacked the Golan Heights, and both in the north and in the south, the forward Israeli positions were overrun.

The Israeli ground forces were soon so hard pressed that there was no opportunity for the IDF/AF to achieve air superiority. In contrast to the 1967 war, no Arab airfield could be closed by air attack for more than a few hours, and only 22 Arab aircraft were claimed to have been destroyed on the ground. Instead, the IDF/AF, with its 340 or so combat aircraft, was obliged to devote virtually all its efforts to the direct or indirect support of the ground forces.

This meant flying in airspace dominated by SAMs, particularly the SA-6, and by ZSU-23 guns. The Israelis lost about 40 aircraft in the first 48 hours of the conflict. This represented 14 percent of the combat strength of the IDF/AF, and a loss rate of some 3 percent of combat sorties flown. Although the Egyptians contented themselves with a limited advance into the Sinai (and thus retained the dense nature of their ground-based antiaircraft defenses), on the Golan front the pressure became critical, and only the remorseless efforts of the

IDF/AF prevented a Syrian breakthrough into the open plains of Israel. Overall, the intensity of the conflict led to a critical shortage of war materiel on both sides; on 9 October the United States, and on 10 October the Soviet Union, began flying in replacement stocks of arms. The resulting airlifts were a convincing demonstration of the ability of airpower to transfer massive military resources very rapidly over intercontinental distances.

On 15 October, the Israelis were able to launch a counterattack across the Suez Canal, which succeeded in overrunning four of the Egyptian SAM sites. This opened a gap in the air defenses which the IDF/AF was then able to exploit by giving air support to the Israeli ground forces. Ground forces thus contributed to the air superiority necessary to their own continuing operations.

A cease-fire came on 22 October after the Soviets had made preparations to fly in airborne forces and the United States had declared a state of alert. There was much to be learned from the war, particularly about intelligence failures. But as far as airpower was concerned, the Israeli ability to switch effort between the north and the south to meet crises on the Syrian and on the Egyptian fronts had been crucial. The mobility of air at the operational level was paramount. At the tactical level, the protection afforded to ground forces by a careful combination of SAMs and antiaircraft guns was highly effective, although the static nature of the complex deployment carried clear limitations; in highly mobile operations the density of cover would have been less lethal. In any case the lethality was diluted when the United States supplied early warning equipment to counter the new Soviet antiaircraft systems.

Technical surprise had again played an important part in the air facet of a war, this time in the deployment of the Soviet SA-6 and the ZSU-23 and their high effectiveness. This had been crucial when the Egyptians attacked across the canal. On the other hand, their reliance on this ground-based air defense system, together with the fact that most of their air strength was also used in forward areas, meant that Israeli mobilization and reinforcement efforts could proceed virtually unhindered behind the battle zone. The Egyptian offensive lacked the depth that effective airpower might have given it.

The third Middle East conflict took place in June 1982 over the Bekaa Valley in Syria. Employing careful intelligence, excellent training, and superb timing, the Israeli Defense Force/Air Force drew the Syrian air force into an air-to-air battle in which some 86 Syrian aircraft were destroyed and only one Israeli machine was lost. It was a remarkable illustration of the effectiveness of a carefully coordinated air campaign, taking advantage of all the enemy's known weaknesses in the air and in the deployment of SAMs, to achieve a devastating victory.

The Bekaa engagement was also a striking example of an emerging trend in the application of airpower—the rapid execution of independent and accurate air strikes that are carried out with or without a declaration of war. Recent years have seen three other operations of this kind. First was the Israeli air raid on the Iraqi nuclear plant at Tuwaitta near Baghdad in June 1981, carried out with devastating precision by fourteen attack aircraft flying a 2,260-kilometer (1,400 mi.) round-trip mission. Second was the Israeli raid on the Palestine Liberation Organization (PLO) headquarters in Tunis, probably carried out by only six or eight combat aircraft making a round-trip flight of almost 4,840 kilometers (3,000 mi.). Third was the U.S. attack on Libya in April 1986, when aircraft attacked carefully selected targets in Tripoli and Benghazi. For the U.S. Air Force F-111 aircraft, the raid involved a round-trip flight from the United Kingdom of some 8,870 kilometers (5,500 mi.).

1991 Gulf War

The unprecedented air campaign in the 1991 Persian Gulf War was perhaps the most dramatic use of airpower in history. Analysts will study and seek lessons from the following major departures from the past that occurred in the 1991 Gulf War:

- use of large numbers of stealth and other high-technology aircraft.
- extensive use of high-technology and precision-guided munitions including sea- and air-launched cruise missiles and of satellites and airborne systems to provide intelligence; attack warning; control of air defense, strategic and tactical navigation, target selection, and attack.
- development and execution of an integrated air campaign that centralized the targeting and scheduling of aircraft and helicopters of allied air force, army, and navy forces.
- use of army forces at the outset deep within enemy territory against enemy air defenses.
- execution of the campaign as planned with little interference from higher level authorities.
- virtual destruction and demoralization of a large, well-equipped enemy air force and a massive, seasoned, well-equipped army prior to ground combat.
- denial to Iraq of virtually all strategic and tactical intelligence because of the allied airpower threat.
- limitation of allied aircraft losses to far below expectations.
- the demonstration that airpower could achieve all the above if based upon reliable and sophisticated equipment, highly qualified and trained personnel, excellent leadership, and allied cooperation.

Analysts will also study what airpower did not achieve: finding and destroying the leader of Iraq; being able to destroy all mobile Scud missiles; locating and attacking all sites where weapons of mass destruction were made or stored; and successfully enforcing the embargo of materials. Finally, analysts will try to fathom how future wars will be affected by live worldwide television coverage of aerial attacks and suffering in the opposition's homeland.

One thing is certain. The history and the future of airpower were forever altered in this short war.

MICHAEL ARMITAGE

SEE ALSO: Arab-Israeli Wars; Douhet, Giulio; Korean War; Vietnam and Indochina Wars; World War I; World War II.

Bibliography

Armitage, M. J., and A. R. Mason. 1985. *Air power in the nuclear age*. London: Macmillan.

Beaufre, A. 1969. *The Suez expedition*. London: Faber and Faber.

Boog, H. 1983. *Die Luftwaffe. Das Deutsche Reiche und zer Weltkrieg*. Freiburg: Militärgeschichtliches Forschungsamt.

Collier, B. 1957. *The defence of the United Kingdom*. London: Her Majesty's Stationery Office.

Craven, W. H., and J. L. Cate, eds. 1949. *The army air forces in World War II*. Chicago: Univ. of Chicago Press.

Douhet, G. 1942. *Command of the air*. Trans. D. Ferrari. New York: Coward McCann.

Emme, E. M., ed. 1959. *The impact of air power*. New York: Van Nostrand.

Ethel, J., and A. Price. 1983. *Air war South Atlantic*. London: Sidgwick and Jackson.

Futrell, R. F. 1984. *Ideas, concepts, and doctrine*. 2 vols. Salem, N.H.: Ayer.

Futrell, R. E. 1983. *The United States Air Force in Korea*. New York: Duell, Sloan, and Pearce.

Goldberg, A. 1957. *A history of the U.S. Air Force 1907–57*. New York: Van Nostrand.

Momyer, W. W. 1978. *Air power in three wars*. Salem, N.H.: Ayer.

Slessor, J. 1956. *The central blue*. London: Cassell.

Speer, A. 1970. *Inside the Third Reich: Memoirs*. Trans. R. Winston and C. Winston. New York: Macmillan.

Terraine, J. 1985. *The right of the line*. London: Hodder and Stoughton.

ALEXANDER, HAROLD RUPERT LEOFRIC GEORGE [1891–1969]

Field Marshal Earl Alexander of Tunis was one of the outstanding British military commanders of the twentieth century (Fig. 1). Optimistic and self-confident, "Alex" played a significant role in virtually every theater where British troops were involved during World War II.

Early Life and Career

Harold Rupert Leofric George Alexander was born on 10 December 1891, the third son of the fourth Earl of Caledon. He inherited a tradition of public service and a good life marked by dignity, orderliness, and discipline. Alexander attended Harrow, and after graduating from Sandhurst in 1911 he joined the Irish Guards.

When World War I broke out, Alexander's battalion formed a part of the original British Expeditionary Force (BEF), in which he was a 22-year-old lieutenant and platoon commander. Alexander was a chivalric, cheerful, and charismatic leader; during the war he became the youngest lieutenant colonel in the British army, and when the Great War ended he was in temporary command of a brigade. During four years of fighting on the western front he was wounded twice; he won the Military Cross at Loos and the Distinguished Service Order at the Somme. Rudyard Kipling noted, "It is undeniable that

Figure 1. Harold Rupert Leofric George Alexander. (SOURCE: U.S. Library of Congress)

Colonel Alexander had the gift of handling the men on the lines to which they most readily responded . . . his subordinates loved him, even when he fell upon them blisteringly for their shortcomings; and his men were all his own."

Alexander emerged from the crucible of the Great War a solid professional soldier. In 1919–20 he commanded a Landwehr Brigade of German and expatriate soldiers that fought under appalling weather and political conditions to prevent Latvia from succumbing to Bolshevik domination. Successful in this mission, Alexander returned to England with an enhanced reputation for imperturbability, and in time to become a battalion commander in Turkey during the 1922 Chanak crisis. Other interwar assignments included service at Gibraltar and in England, attendance at the Staff College (1926), a short stint in the War Office, then assignment as General Staff Officer 1 (GSO1) in Northern Command at York.

In 1934 Alexander took command of the Nowshera Brigade on the North-West Frontier, an appointment considered exceptional for an officer who had had no connection with the Indian Army. He commanded the brigade for three years in two frontier campaigns: the Loe Agra, as Force Commander, in early 1935; and the Mohmand campaign later that year. Once again Alexander demonstrated his tactical mastery and astute organizational and leadership abilities.

In the wake of Secretary of State for War Hore-Belisha's program to rejuvenate the army, in January 1938 Alexander returned to England as a major general to command the 1st Division, a division designated as part of the British Expeditionary Force in the event British forces were again committed to the continent of Europe.

World War II

At 47 years of age Alexander was indeed fortunate in being at the peak of his intellectual and physical powers when World War II began in 1939. His division, one of the original four of this second BEF, deployed to France and saw little action during the "phony war" of the winter of 1939–40. After the German onslaught in May 1940, the 1st Division was never intensively engaged, but at Dunkirk Alexander was given a task that brought him national renown. He was designated to command the rearguard of the BEF and adroitly conducted the evacuation of the last British soldiers from Dunkirk.

Alexander had earned the trust of Prime Minister Winston Churchill and General (later Field Marshal Viscount) Sir Alan Brooke, the future Chief of the Imperial General Staff (CIGS). Shortly after his return to England, he was promoted to lieutenant general and given command of the I Corps. His mission was to prepare his corps to resist an anticipated German invasion of England.

In December 1940 Alexander was selected to become General Officer Commanding Southern Command, and was later designated to command the first major expeditionary force in a counteroffensive against Europe. The Japanese attack in December 1941 in the Pacific altered these plans, and Alexander was appointed Commander in Chief, Burma, serving under General (later Field Marshal Earl) Sir Archibald P. Wavell, Commander in Chief, India. It was impossible to save Burma and Rangoon, and only by conducting a difficult retreat was Alexander able to save his force.

The defeats of Dunkirk and Burma would have ruined the career of an ordinary general, but shortly after Alexander returned to England in July 1942 he became Commander in Chief, Middle East. He has been criticized for his handling of his difficult subordinate, Lieutenant General (later Field Marshal Viscount) Bernard Montgomery (who later said: "First-class general, Alex—did everything I told him to do"), but North Africa was cleared of Axis forces by May 1943. Alexander reported to Churchill that, "We are masters of the North African shores."

Alexander commanded the 15th Army Group during the invasion of Sicily, then became commander in chief of the polyglot Allied armies in Italy during the difficult advance up the well-defended peninsula. The apex of Alexander's military career was the capture of Rome on 4 June 1944, for which he received his field marshal's baton.

On 12 December 1944 he was appointed Supreme Commander, Mediterranean, and after the success of his Po offensive and the capture of a million German prisoners, Alexander on 29 April 1945 accepted the first unconditional surrender signed by the Germans. Of Alexander's generalship, Harold Macmillan observed: "If Montgomery was the Wellington, Alexander was certainly the Marlborough of this war."

Aftermath

Alexander was selected to succeed Brooke as CIGS, but was requested by Canada to serve as its governor-general. He skillfully and happily served in that position from 1946 to 1952, when he returned to England and served as

Churchill's Minister of Defense from 1952 to 1954. Alexander spent the last fifteen years of his life in semiretirement, serving as director of a number of companies and performing many honorary appointments, including Constable of the Tower of London from 1960 to 1965. He was persuaded to allow his *Memoirs* to be ghost-written in 1960, but they are considered a great disappointment and unworthy of his actual accomplishments. Alexander died of a perforated aorta on 16 June 1969.

Field Marshal Earl Alexander of Tunis, K.G., P.C., O.M., G.C.B., G.C.M.G., C.S.I., D.S.O., M.C., was undoubtedly one of the most skillful, courageous, and charismatic British generals of this century. "Alex's" reputation will rest on his signal achievements as a professional soldier whose life was dedicated to his sovereign and country.

HAROLD E. RAUGH, JR.

SEE ALSO: Civil War, Russian; Montgomery, Bernard Law; Wavell, Archibald Percival; World War I; World War II.

Bibliography

Barnett, C. 1960. *The desert generals.* London: Kimber.
Blaxland, G. 1979. *Alexander's generals.* London: Kimber.
Clark, M. 1950. *Calculated risk.* New York: Harper.
Hillson, N. 1952. *Alexander of Tunis.* London: Allen.
Jackson, W. G. F. 1967. *The battle for Italy.* London: Batsford.
————. 1972. *Alexander of Tunis as military commander.* New York: Dodd, Mead.
Linklater, E. 1977. *The campaign in Italy.* London: Her Majesty's Stationery Office.
Nicolson, N. 1973. *Alex.* London: Weidenfeld and Nicolson.
North, J., ed. 1962. *The Alexander memoirs, 1940–1945.* London: Cassell.
Shepperd, G. A. 1968. *The Italian campaign, 1943–45.* New York: Praeger.

ALEXANDER THE GREAT
(Alexander III) [356–323 B.C.]

Alexander III, King of Macedonia from 336 to 323 B.C., was, quite literally, a legend in his own time. His accomplishments were so unusual and so far removed from those of ordinary men that within his lifetime he achieved a sort of superhuman status, and the process continued after his death. He was a very complex individual, and there is sufficient evidence to see a man who was at one and the same time a visionary, a dreamer, a shrewd politician, and a brilliant military commander. His profound impact on human history is undeniable; he changed the world.

Early Life

Alexander was born in the summer of 356 B.C. to King Philip II of Macedonia and his queen, Olympias. The marriage of Philip and Olympias seems to have been a love match as well as a political arrangement, but the passion died soon after Alexander's birth. Olympias was the second of Philip's seven wives, and a deep hatred developed between them and lasted for as long as they both lived. Nevertheless, Alexander seems to have been genuinely devoted to both of his parents. There are many charming anecdotes told about Alexander's childhood, most of them of questionable validity, but they all seem to indicate an extremely precocious child who learned quickly and was not anxious to remain a child any longer than necessary. When Alexander was about 13, his father decided that he needed nothing less than the famed philosopher Aristotle as his tutor. When he was 16, Alexander was sufficiently skilled and trusted by his father to be given his own army command. Two years later, in 338 B.C., he commanded the victorious right wing of the Macedonian army at the fateful battle of Chaeronea, which confirmed Philip's total mastery of Greece. When Philip was assassinated in 336 B.C. (by one of his bodyguards with a private grudge), Alexander, now 20, was hailed as king without opposition. Nevertheless, as a precaution, he brought about the deaths—by execution or murder—of all possible pretenders.

Preparations for the Invasion of Persia

Philip had been planning the invasion of Persia for several years. Indeed, if he had not been overshadowed historically by his more famous son, his own accomplishments might have entitled him to be called Philip the Great.

Early in his reign, Philip had reformed the Macedonian army into a highly disciplined fighting force equipped with 4.1-meter-long (14-foot-long) pikes (called sarissas [they may have been even longer than this]), which easily overwhelmed the traditional armies of the Greek city-states; yet he was also an able diplomat who rarely had to use his army. After the battle of Chaeronea, Philip forcibly united the Greek city-states into an unequal alliance, called by historians the League of Corinth after the city where the arrangements were made. Philip was the leader of the league with full military command and power to demand troop commitments from each member.

Soon after Philip's assassination, Alexander marched south into Greece with his army and demanded to be installed in his father's place. The demand was not refused. Alexander was tested early in his kingship. Semicivilized Thracian tribes that had been subdued by Philip fought to reassert their independence, believing that with the powerful king of Macedonia dead, they could easily overwhelm a mere boy of 20. Alexander surprised them with the rapidity of his movement and quickly subdued them. Many of the Greek city-states also sought to reassert their independence, and the result was that Alexander destroyed the city of Thebes. These events delayed his carrying out Philip's plan to invade the Persian Empire. He finally crossed into Asia in the spring of 334 B.C. An advance party had been sent over two years earlier and controlled the crossing of the Hellespont (Dardanelles).

REASONS FOR THE INVASION

Alexander, carrying out the plans his father had already formed, made such alterations or adaptations as he thought necessary. The intentions of Philip, and later Alexander, are the subject of much speculation by historians. Philip's invasion of the Persian Empire may have had limited goals—the conquest of Asia Minor, the coast of which was inhabited by Greek-speaking people—or they may have been more extensive. Alexander probably planned much more than the conquest of Asia Minor from the beginning, although whether he planned as much as he actually accomplished is debatable.

An invasion of Persia had been a subject much talked about among Greeks for two generations. Greece was overcrowded and underemployed, and Persia was the traditional enemy since the Persian invasions in the early part of the fifth century. It was also obvious to the Greeks, including Philip, that the Persian Empire was in a state of advanced decay with serious internal problems. Indeed, Darius III, the Persian king at the time of Alexander's crossing, was a usurper who had acquired the throne only three years earlier. The opportunity was simply there.

RESOURCES, ORGANIZATION, AND PLANNING

Alexander's conquest of the Persian Empire was a carefully planned operation. In addition to the fearsome Macedonian phalanx of heavily armed infantry with their sarissas, well drilled and very maneuverable, his cavalry was equally well trained and always deployed to cover the vulnerable flanks of the phalanx. His army included competent engineers for siege warfare, which he used to great effect. His logistics and intelligence operations, although not glamorous, were crucial to his success, and he seems to have appreciated the importance of this kind of support. He had no fleet worthy of the name, but overcame Persian seapower by defeating the Persian fleet on land: he simply overran all of its Mediterranean naval bases. For this early part of the campaign, the presence of the Athenian fleet was useful, but perhaps more as a hostage for the good behavior of Athens than for any operational necessity. Alexander was always outnumbered, yet he never lost a battle because of his combination of good intelligence, astute deployments, skillful maneuvers, and more than a little daring. He was willing to try what was not expected of him.

Conquest of Persia and Egypt

The Battle at the Granicus River in northern Asia Minor was Alexander's first encounter with Persian military forces (see Fig. 1). The Persian plan was apparently to expend all possible effort to kill Alexander himself and thus behead the opposing army. That was not successful, and the Persians were unable to withstand the sudden assault of the Macedonian forces in a bold and skillful river crossing.

For the rest of the year, Alexander continued his march down the coast of Asia Minor, in many cases accepting the submission of the cities along the coast; in some cases it was necessary to lay siege to the cities—always successfully. During the winter months, he campaigned in the interior of Asia Minor and brought under his control some isolated tribes that had not even acknowledged the suzerainty of the Persian king.

The next major encounter with the Persians was the Battle of Issus in Cilicia,

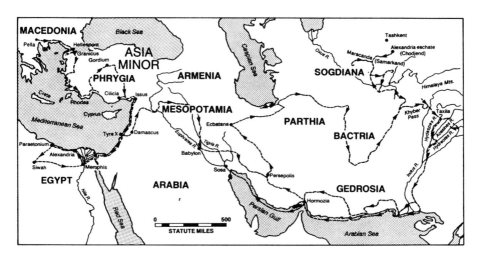

Figure 1. Route of Alexander's army (334–323 B.C.).

where Darius III was himself present. The king's presence did not make his troops fight any better against Alexander, and he fled the scene.

Alexander continued down the coast and was delayed by the siege of Tyre for most of the year 332 B.C. (Tyre was an extremely well-fortified island city and Persia's principal naval base.) The city refused to submit. Alexander's conduct of the siege of Tyre was indicative of his unorthodox character, and it shows his frequent recourse to engineering skills. Alexander determined that the siege of Tyre would be more likely to succeed if Tyre were not an island; therefore, he put his troops and other manpower to work building a causeway from the mainland to the island. It was a time-consuming process, but when he was finished Tyre was connected to the mainland, and it remains so today. It took seven months, but the city finally fell in July of 332 B.C. amid much slaughter by exhausted Macedonian soldiers.

Alexander continued on to begin his conquest of Egypt, where he was happily received by the Egyptians, who were willing to trade a Persian master for a Greek. While in Egypt, he made arrangements for the building of a city, to be called Alexandria, that would be located at the westernmost outlet of the Nile River. This city, begun in 331 B.C., soon became the greatest city of the ancient world.

Pursuit of King Darius

Technically, Persia was still ruled by Darius III. The empire had not fallen and would not until Darius had been captured or killed. Having captured all Persian dominions in the Mediterranean, Alexander left Egypt to pursue Darius into Mesopotamia.

The Battle of Gaugamela took place on 1 October 331 B.C. (the date is secured by a lunar eclipse). This was the largest battle Alexander fought and it proved decisive for the campaign. With only about 47,000 men, Alexander was heavily outnumbered. Darius had assembled an army of more than 200,000 men and had every possible resource at his disposal, including scythed chariots. However, the discipline and training of the Macedonian army, applied in Alexander's brilliant battle plan, prevailed, and Darius fled the field of battle.

Alexander proceeded at leisure to the Persian capitals of Babylon and Persepolis, and whether by accident or design, the royal palace at Persepolis was burned to the ground.

After consolidating control of central Persia, Alexander resumed the pursuit of Darius, who had fled north to Sogdiana and Bactria. As Alexander and his cavalry escort were closing in on Darius, the Persian king was murdered by one of his noblemen, Bessus. Alexander soon caught up with Bessus and had him tortured and executed. There was now no rival claimant for the throne of the Persian Empire. Alexander, king of Macedonia, leader of the Greek league, was now also king of Persia. He would have several other titles before he died.

Campaigns in Afghanistan and Central Asia

Alexander now marched into the Persian provinces of Sogdiana and Bactria (modern Afghanistan, Turkmenistan, and Uzbekistan). The local tribes were more difficult than any people he had encountered on his journey. In one encounter, the inhabitants took refuge at a place called the Sogdian Rock. It was surrounded by sheer cliffs and the leader, Oxyartes, challenged Alexander to reach him at the top of the rock. Alexander called for volunteers to scale the rock, and after that demonstration, Oxyartes and his people surrendered to Alexander. The endeavor had been sufficiently difficult that Alexander thought it prudent to cement the new friendship with the Sogdians by marrying the daughter of the chief, a girl named Roxane, who would bear him a son (born a few months after Alexander's death).

Alexander marched north into Central Asia, crossing both the Oxus and the Jaxartes rivers, decisively defeating and subduing the wild Scythian tribes in that region.

Returning south to Sogdiana, Alexander marched east into what was called India (modern Pakistan, the Punjab area); again he relied on his engineers to defeat the stubborn hill people. A large group had taken refuge in the Rock of Aornos, which was a sheer rock separated from a neighboring hill by a ravine. Alexander simply ordered earth to be moved until the ravine was filled and he could erect a ramp to the top of the rock, at which point the inhabitants surrendered.

War Elephants

Alexander apparently crossed the Khyber Pass and then crossed the Indus River. At the Hydaspes River (a tributary of the Indus) he encountered an Indian force led by their king, Porus, a majestic figure who was reputedly seven feet tall. More impressive than Porus, however, was his use of elephants in warfare. This was the first time the Macedonians had encountered elephants in battle, but by sheer discipline and bravery, as well as excellent tactical moves by Alexander, they won that battle as well. Alexander learned the usefulness of elephants in this encounter, and so did his staff officers, many of whom would later become kings in their own right. Use of the elephant in warfare would become common in the next century.

Mutiny at the Hyphasis River

Alexander then continued his march eastward. But at a small river called the Hyphasis, another Indus tributary, Alexander's troops mutinied. Many of them were veterans who had been with him for fully eight years now, and they had gone as far as they wanted to go. They had conquered the Persian Empire and more, and they saw little need to go on. With great disappointment, Alexander relented and agreed to lead them back home—but he took them home the hard way. They marched and sailed south along the Indus to near modern Karachi. There he built a fleet that he sent westward along the coast of Baluchistan to the Persian Gulf, where it was to rejoin the army near Susa. Meanwhile, Alexander led his army overland through the desert, no doubt planning to secure provisions for the fleet when it reached the shore. The army and the fleet soon lost contact, however, and there was great loss of life on the march through the desert.

Alexander and the remnants of his army finally returned to Susa in 324 B.C. There he took a second wife, Barsine, the daughter of the late King Darius, to cement his position as king of Persia. At the same ceremony, 80 of his officers took Persian wives, and 10,000 of his troops married local women. This was a symbolic attempt to establish the unity of his empire, an empire composed of Macedonians, Greeks, Persians, and many other peoples. The marriages, in general, did not long outlive Alexander.

Death of Alexander

Alexander returned to Babylon early in 323 B.C. and busied himself with administrative details and plans for future expeditions. He became ill in the spring and slowly worsened. He died on 11 June 323 B.C., probably of pernicious malaria. The legend that he died after a roisterous drinking bout is almost certainly inaccurate.

Problems in the Empire

Alexander was not yet 33 years old when he died. It is natural to wonder what more he might have accomplished had he lived, and there were many problems with which he would have had to deal. Many of the governors and other officials he had appointed had become corrupt and disloyal. Although his officers and troops remained fiercely loyal to him to the end, there were grumblings. The occasional conspiracies that arose against Alexander were dealt with rather harshly. On one occasion, not long before his death, he ordered the execution of his boyhood friend on a charge of treason, and also ordered the execution of the man's father, Parmenio—who had been an important staff officer—just to be safe. Many of the Macedonians were displeased with Alexander's growing tendencies to adopt Persian practices and even Persian dress. Yet most of them grudgingly obeyed when instructed to prostrate themselves before their king, something no Macedonian had ever done. The Greek city-states were quite restive because Alexander had insisted that each city take back all of its political exiles, which caused no small amount of political turmoil. He also asked that he be deified and worshiped as a god, something that met with derisive compliance. It remains open to speculation whether a great military commander and an inspired leader could have solved such problems.

Assessment

Alexander changed the world—of that there is no doubt. He changed the political situation, military practices, and the economy. When he was born, the civilized world consisted of the mighty Persian Empire and the independent but very small Greek city-states, with the inconsequential small kingdom of Macedonia on its fringe. Shortly after his death, the political arrangement of the civilized world consisted of three major kingdoms, a few minor independent kingdoms, inconsequential Greek city-states that were under the sovereignty of one of the successor kingdoms, and, significantly, some people called Romans beginning to make their mark in the west. When Alexander was born, strategy was almost unknown and tactics were crude. It was rare for any military encounter to involve more than ten thousand armed men on each side; siege warfare was primitive, and naval activity had not changed for several centuries. After Alexander's death, his successors frequently waged war with 50,000 or more armed soldiers on each side, often mercenaries. Siege warfare under Alexander reached a sophistication not equaled in the West until modern times. He even began a ship design and building program that would result in the large supergalleys of the Hellenistic age. His conquest of the Persian Empire opened up economic opportunities for industrious Greeks, and his dispersal of the hoarded Persian treasure spread wealth unevenly throughout the civilized world and caused considerable inflation. Greek became the common language throughout the civilized world and remained so for over a thousand years in many places. Thus, the Romans learned the Greek language and culture when they eventually conquered most of what had been Alexander's empire.

JANICE J. GABBERT

SEE ALSO: History, Ancient Military; Persian Empire.

Bibliography

Some contemporary accounts are preserved in the *Anabasis of Alexander* by Flavius Arrianus, written in the second century A.D., and Arrian is probably the best source for Alexander. Quintus Curtius Rufus also wrote a useful history of Alexander in the first century A.D. Also useful for personal anecdotes is Plutarch's *Life of Alexander*. Modern literature on Alexander is extensive; a complete overview can be found in the *Cambridge Ancient History*, vol. 6 (Cambridge, 1927).

Adcock, R. E. 1957. *The Greek and Macedonian art of war.* Berkeley, Calif.: Univ. of California Press.

Bosworth, A. B. 1980. *A historical commentary on Arrian's history of Alexander.* London: Oxford Univ. Press.

Engels, D. 1978. *Alexander the great and the logistics of the Macedonian army.* Berkeley, Calif.: Univ. of California Press.

Fox, R. L. 1980. *The search for Alexander.* Boston: Little, Brown.

Fuller, J. F. C. 1960. *The generalship of Alexander the great.* New Brunswick, N.J.: Rutgers Univ. Press.

Hammond, N. G. L. 1981. *Alexander the great: King, commander, and statesman.* Park Ridge, N.J.: Noyes Press.

Holt, F. L. 1988. *Alexander the great and Bactria: The formation of a Greek frontier in central Asia.* Leiden: E. J. Brill.

Tarn, W. W. 1948. *Alexander the great.* Boston: Beacon Press.

Warry, J. 1980. *Warfare in the classical world.* New York: St. Martin's Press.

Wilcken, U. 1967. *Alexander the great.* Trans. G. C. Richards. New York: W. W. Norton.

ALLENBY, EDMUND HENRY HYNMAN
(1861–1936)

At the close of World War I, Gen. Edmund Henry Hynman Allenby (Fig. 1) was the most accomplished and respected British general. His 1918 Palestine campaign is considered one of the most brilliantly conceived and executed successes of the war. The final British offensive in the campaign, initiated by the Battle of Megiddo, was a flawless operation that included the last great horse cavalry battle. It is with justification that Allenby, the architect of the victory, is considered the last great horse cavalry commander. Known for his violent temper and equally violent verbal reprimands, he was respected, if not liked, by those who served under him.

Background and Early Career

Allenby was born 23 April 1861 in East Anglia, of relatively affluent parents. He decided on a military career after failing to pass the Indian Civil Service exam. In February 1881 he entered the Royal Military College at Sandhurst, and upon completing his studies in December 1881 he received a commission in the Sixth Inniskilling Dragoons, stationed in South Africa at the time. He saw considerable service between 1883 and 1888 in South Africa and attended the Staff College at Camberley during 1896–97. At the outset of the Boer War in 1899, Allenby returned to South Africa, where he gained valuable experience in the mobile, hard-hitting style of warfare employed in the conflict. At the end of the war he returned to Britain, where he was promoted to colonel and placed in command of the Fifth Lancers. His competence and proven ability as a cavalry leader were largely responsible for his rise to the rank of major general by the spring of 1910 and his appointment as Inspector-General of Cavalry, a position he held until the outbreak of World War I.

Figure 1. Edmund Henry Hynman Allenby. (SOURCE: U.S. Library of Congress)

Early World War I Service

Allenby took command of the Cavalry Division of the British Expeditionary Force in France during the battles of August and September 1914. Between 29 October and 11 November Allenby's Cavalry Corps (another division had arrived in the meantime from Britain) was heavily engaged south of Ypres by German forces attempting to take the channel ports. Allenby then assumed command of Seventh Corps from Gen. Sir Hubert Plumer in May 1915, at the height of the Second Battle of Ypres. Eight months later he took command of the Third Army from Gen. Sir Charles Monro, who was assigned to the Dardanelles Front. The Third Army was relatively inactive during the Somme offensive of 1916, but in April 1917 it took part in the Arras offensive, making the largest one-day gain on the western front since 1914. But the army quickly lost momentum, and the offensive gradually ground to a halt.

Palestine Campaign of 1917–18

In June 1917 Allenby was sent to Palestine to replace Gen. Sir Archibald Murray as commander of the Egyptian Expeditionary Force (EEF), which to that point had been unsuccessful. Once in command, he used his exceptional leadership and organizational talents to boost morale and prepare the EEF for an offensive against the Turkish Seventh and Eighth Armies in Palestine as soon as cooler temperatures set in. The heavy casualties and poor results on the western front made it vital for morale at home that British troops in Palestine achieve a victory. The British Prime Minister David Lloyd George therefore expected Allenby and his EEF to achieve victory and asked that Jerusalem be taken by Christmas 1917.

The Turks held a heavily fortified position extending from Gaza, on the Mediterranean coast, to Beersheba, approximately 55 kilometers (34 mi.) inland. On 27 October, as a diversion, Allenby opened the offensive with an intense land and sea bombardment of Gaza, while massing the bulk of his force secretly in the vicinity of Beersheba for the main assault. The attack on Beersheba began on 31 October with good results: the city was occupied within 24 hours. The assault on Gaza began on the night of 1–2 November, and Gaza was occupied by the British on the 7th. The retreating Turks occupied a new defensive position at Junction Station, which was taken on 15 November after a two-day fight. The Turks continued their retreat, eventually evacuating Jerusalem, which was occupied by the British on 9 December.

In early 1918 much of Allenby's force was sent to France to help contain the German spring offensives, leaving the EEF depleted of many of its veteran troops. Reinforcements coming from India and Mesopotamia had to be trained and organized throughout the summer. By mid-September Allenby was ready to launch a carefully planned offensive that would drive Turkey from the war.

A series of feints and deception plans carried out by the British caused the Turks to believe the main blow would come on their left flank, north of Jerusalem, and to prepare accordingly. Reversing the procedure of the Gaza battle, the actual attack was launched against the Turkish right on 19 September, achieving complete surprise. A breach in the line was made by the British infantry, and the waiting cavalry pushed through, making deep penetrations, while the Royal Flying Corps harassed the retreating Turkish columns. By 20 September British cavalry spearheads had entered the Plain of Esdraelon, near Megiddo, and shifted east, cutting off retreating elements of the Turkish Seventh and Eighth Armies. Allenby continued the pressure on the Turks as British troops entered Damascus on 1 October. In late October, realizing that any further resistance was impossible, Turkey began to make peace overtures, and on 30 October an armistice was signed.

Postwar Service and Later Life

In March 1919 Allenby was appointed Special High Commissioner for Egypt and was instrumental in Egypt's move from protectorate to sovereignty. Allenby's final days in Egypt were clouded by the murder of the sirdar, Sir Lee

Stack, and a confrontation with Foreign Secretary Austen Chamberlain, over which he ultimately resigned. He left Egypt in June 1925 and returned to England to spend the rest of his life in retirement. He died in London on 14 May 1936, leaving no heirs (his only son, Michael, had been killed in France in 1917). For his accomplishments in the war, he had been promoted to field marshal and raised to the peerage as Viscount Allenby of Megiddo and Felixstowe (the ancient city of Megiddo, the Armageddon of the Bible, was chosen as the name of the climactic battle of the Palestine campaign).

ARNOLD C. DUPUY

SEE ALSO: World War I.

Bibliography

Dupuy, R. E., and T. N. Dupuy. 1970. *Encyclopedia of military history.* New York: Harper and Row.
Gardner, B. 1965. *Allenby of Arabia.* New York: Coward-McCann.
Mansfield, P. 1971. *The British in Egypt.* New York: Holt, Rinehart and Winston.
Savage, R. 1926. *Allenby of Armageddon.* Indianapolis: Bobbs-Merrill.
Wavell, A. P. 1940. *Allenby: A study in greatness.* London: George G. Harrap.

AMERICAN REVOLUTIONARY WAR

After a decade of controversy concerning the place of the colonies of British North America within the empire and in relation to the home country, hostilities erupted near Boston in April 1775. They continued until September 1783 when the Peace of Paris, resulting in an independent United States of America, was signed. During the revolutionary war, the British sought to subdue American insurgents (who composed only a minority of the population) in the thirteen colonies and who were dispersed over several thousand square miles of largely wooded terrain, more than 4,800 kilometers (3,000 mi.) from the British Isles. Because British policy toward the rebels vacillated between conciliation and subjugation, no consistent strategy was pursued. In 1778 France declared war against Great Britain in support of the Americans. Spain, allied with France but not with the United States, entered the war in 1779; and in 1780 Britain declared war on Holland. Thus, the revolutionary war, originally a rebellion, or civil war, became an international conflict.

Balance Sheet

It appeared that Great Britain, a world power by any criterion, had a decisive advantage over the colonists because of its larger population, and material and military superiority. By contrast, the Americans had no proven continental government, no treasury or credit, no regular army or navy, no military tradition beyond the short service of militia and volunteers, and little experience in continental cooperation of any kind.

INTERNAL DIVISIONS

The American people were fragmented into three groups of roughly equal proportions: the indifferent, the Tories, and the patriots. Class and sectional antagonisms, manifest in disagreements as to wartime objectives, also proved divisive. Only after adoption of the Declaration of Independence (4 July 1776) did a determination to persevere characterize the patriot cause. There were also serious disagreements within the British body politic. The Friends of America (men such as Isaac Barré, Edmund Burke, Charles James Fox, and William Pitt) believed that the rebels were merely protecting their historic rights as Englishmen against the tyranny of King George III. Some of Britain's ablest generals and admirals declined service against the Americans.

THE ARMIES

While the British army was composed of professional regulars trained and disciplined on the European model, the Americans had only their militia tradition and the limited experience gained in the colonial wars on which to build. To confront forces, which grew to about 42,000 British regulars and nearly 30,000 German mercenaries, the Americans organized two sets of forces: the Continental, or national, Army and the various state militias. The Continental Army ranged in size from roughly 5,000 to 20,000, depending on its fortunes. The largest single American field army numbered about 17,000 and was composed of Continentals and militia. By 1778 the Continental Army was reliable and, considering its brief history, surprisingly well trained, but the militia was unpredictable throughout the war. There were notable exceptions, such as at Bunker Hill and Cowpens, where militiamen performed well. South Carolina irregulars under Francis Marion, Andrew Pickens, and Thomas Sumter were especially effective in harassing British outposts, field armies in motion, and lines of supply and communications.

The generalship of both British and American commanders was undistinguished. Service in North America tarnished the reputation of every major British general who fought there: Thomas Gage, William Howe, John Burgoyne, Henry Clinton, and Charles Cornwallis. There were no geniuses among the American generals, but Henry Knox, Daniel Morgan, Nathanael Greene, and George Washington were competent. An enigma, Benedict Arnold showed great promise in the Quebec campaign at Valcour Island and in the Saratoga campaign, but his name became synonymous with treason when he defected to the British. Commander in chief George Washington's leadership was crucial to American military success. Although he sometimes took dangerous risks, Washington kept his army intact and demonstrated in all circumstances a determination to endure until independence was achieved (Fig. 1). He became the embodiment of the patriot cause.

THE NAVIES

The greatest disparity between Britain and the United States was in naval forces. The Americans had no navy when hostilities began, while the British had 131 ships of the line and 139 ships of other classes. From the first Wash-

Figure 1. On the night of 25 December 1776, Washington's army crossed the Delaware River and attacked a Hessian garrison at Trenton, New Jersey. Of 1,400 Hessians, more than half were captured by Washington's forces. (SOURCE: U.S. Library of Congress)

ington feared British naval supremacy, and as early as September 1775 he sought to arm New England merchantmen so that they might interrupt the flow of British supplies to Boston. "Washington's Navy," a flotilla of six schooners and a brigantine, took 35 prizes valued at more than US$600,000 before it was disbanded in 1777. Meanwhile, the Continental Congress created an American navy composed initially of eight ships. These ships, mounting only 110 guns among them, were ordered to clear American waters of 78 British ships armed with 2,000 guns. While the Continental and state navies eventually commissioned nearly 100 ships, the British fleet was increased from 270 to 468 ships between 1775 and 1783.

Clearly overmatched, the American navies prudently engaged in actions against isolated warships and unarmed merchantmen. Some 2,000 privateers were authorized to prey on British commerce, but they had little effect in offsetting the supremacy of the Royal Navy in American waters. Capt. John Paul Jones, whose exploits became legend, emerged as America's greatest naval hero, but he did little more than harass British ships around Britain's home islands. Fortunately for the Americans, at the outset of the war the British fleet was in deplorable condition and was poorly directed by Lord Sandwich.

Because of unchallenged British naval predominance before the French entry into the war, British armies were easily transported from one military objective to another. Not until 1780, with the British fleet divided among American, West Indian, and European waters, did the United States and its allies overcome Britain's naval superiority. Reorganized after 1763, and in a high state of morale and efficiency, the French navy was essential to the American victory at Yorktown.

The War

At some time between 1775 and 1781 the British occupied every major American city—Boston, New York, Philadelphia, Charleston, and Savannah—but were never able to destroy Washington's army or the American will to resist.

STRATEGY

The British appear to have envisioned several strategic initiatives, including the following:
1. to occupy major American seaports and to pacify the surrounding countryside;
2. to isolate New England by controlling Lake Champlain, Lake George, and the Hudson River;
3. to divide the southern states along the line of the Santee River from a base at Charleston;
4. to use naval superiority to blockade the American coast, to transport army units as necessary, and to provide logistical support; and
5. to enlist the support of American Loyalists wherever and whenever possible.

None of these strategies was pursued with vigor, imagination, or consistency. After 1778 British priorities shifted to protection of the empire as the long struggle with France resumed.

Washington clearly recognized that the British had naval superiority, Canada as a base of operations, and larger, more professional armies; but he also knew that the British were faced with the problem of controlling a vast geographic area and subduing a widely dispersed populace. He understood that patriot hopes depended on the survival of the Continental Army. It was essential that he avoid decisive defeat and keep the army in the field.

CAMPAIGNS AND BATTLES

Except for the abortive American invasion of Canada (1775–76), the successes of Brig. Gen. George Rogers Clark in the West (1778–79), and George Washington's joint Franco-American action against Cornwallis at Yorktown, the military initiative in the revolutionary war lay with the British. After it became apparent that occupation of American cities would not result in general submission, the British undertook two major campaigns, one prior to European intervention and one after.

THE SARATOGA CAMPAIGN

Perhaps the best prospect for British success lay in the 1777 campaign proposed by Lt. Gen. John Burgoyne for a three-pronged advance on Albany, New York. Burgoyne was to invade New York from Canada via the Richelieu River–Lake Champlain route so as to reach the upper Hudson River Valley; a smaller force of British regulars and Indians, under Brig. Gen. Barry St. Leger, was to reach Lake Ontario via the St. Lawrence, land at Oswego, and advance down the Mohawk to Albany; and Maj. Gen. George Clinton, with a portion of Howe's army, then ensconced in New York City, was to proceed up the Hudson. The combined forces of Burgoyne, St. Leger, and Clinton would isolate New England from the other rebellious colonies, and American resistance would then be broken. Lord George Germain, British secretary of state for the American colonies, and principal architect of British strategy, approved Burgoyne's plan; but he also approved a contradictory plan whereby Howe would occupy Philadelphia. Because of the consequent division of effort, and Washington's recognition of its implications, the Saratoga campaign, a British disaster, ensued. St. Leger was forced to turn back, and Clinton never started up the Hudson. Moving overland from Canada, Burgoyne, burdened by excess baggage and troubled by poor supply, moved slowly through dense New York forests. Near Saratoga he met an American army under Horatio Gates, reinforced by major contingents sent from Washington's army. Isolated there without hope of relief from St. Leger or Clinton, Burgoyne gave battle at Freeman's Farm (19 September) and Bemis Heights (7 October) before surrendering his army of 5,000 to the Americans on 17 October 1777. Burgoyne's defeat was symptomatic of other British failures during the revolutionary war. The campaign plan was too complex, given the poor transportation and communications prospects; poor planning and coordination in Britain and America also contributed to the defeat. News of the American victory at Saratoga was partly responsible for France's decision to enter the war against Britain.

THE SOUTHERN CAMPAIGN

Subsequently, although British strategists considered North America a less important theater of war than the West Indies, Europe, and India, another major campaign to crush the American rebellion was mounted. The British had long believed that, because of the large number of Loyalists in Georgia and the Carolinas, victory in the South was attainable. As early as 1776 a joint army-navy expedition to capitalize on Loyalist sentiment among Southerners was undertaken, but the British arrived in North Carolina waters after Loyalists had been defeated in the Battle of Moore's Creek Bridge (27 February 1776) and were thereafter unable to capture Charleston.

The British concentrated their efforts elsewhere until late 1778. Then the British, at the urging of George III, who still believed that thousands of Loyalists were awaiting an opportunity to serve their king, took Savannah easily. From that base, the Georgia backcountry was pacified and royal government was restored. After a bitter siege, Charleston fell to the British on 12 May 1780, and Maj. Gen. Benjamin Lincoln surrendered 5,500 American defenders, the largest army captured by either side to date. Events in the South had taken an ominous turn for the Americans. Against Washington's advice, the Continental Congress sent Horatio Gates, the victor of Saratoga, to command its Southern Army with instructions to hold the Carolinas. From Charleston the British moved inland, and Cornwallis surprised and routed Gates at Camden, South Carolina, on 16 August 1780. Gates was replaced by Nathanael Greene who found the army battered and demoralized. Moreover, thousands of Tories were entering the king's service. Intensive fighting characterized the conflict between patriots and Tories in the Carolinas. At the Battle of King's Mountain (7 October 1780) about 1,700 patriots from the mountains and beyond attacked about 900 Tories holding high ground in a bloody fight. The Tory commander, Maj. Patrick Ferguson, the only Briton in the fray, was slain and his entire force either killed or captured. Thereafter it was more difficult to recruit Tories.

A series of small engagements in 1780 and 1781 were interspersed with two battles of major importance. Greene split his army, and Brig. Gen. Daniel Morgan moved westward in hopes of menacing the British flank and rear. He was pursued and forced to give battle by Lt. Col. Banastre Tarleton at Cowpens in northwestern South Carolina. There, on 17 January 1781, Tarleton with some 1,100 men (slightly more than Morgan had) attacked the Americans, who had the swollen Broad River at their backs. Mistaking a readjustment of Morgan's lines as a panicky retreat, Tarleton ordered his men to attack. Morgan dealt a stunning defeat to the British, utilizing green militiamen to good advantage. The main armies of Cornwallis and Greene met at Guilford Courthouse on 15 March 1781, where the British gained a Pyrrhic victory in a bloody engagement. Consequently, Cornwallis decided to link up with the British navy, first at Wilmington, North Carolina, and then at Yorktown, Virginia. Hopelessly trapped at Yorktown by the French fleet under Admiral De Grasse and a combined Franco-American army of superior numbers, Cornwallis surrendered his army of about 8,000 men to Washington and French Gen. Jean Baptiste, Comte de Rochambeau on 19 October 1781. The victory at Yorktown virtually ended the war and made possible the final separation of the thirteen colonies from the British Empire.

Assessment of the Revolutionary War

The Whig historians George Otto Trevelyan, Sir Lewis Namier, Richard Pares, and others have contended that the Americans were defending their rights as Englishmen against royal tyranny and that the government of George III was shamefully inept in prosecuting an unpopular war. Eric Robson believed that the scales were weighed against the British from the outset because of distance, difficult terrain, poor communications, and the British commitment to European strategy and tactics. Many scholars have emphasized European intervention as critical; Samuel Flagg Bemis has stated flatly that the outcome was determined by France. More recently Richard B. Morris has postulated that the American patriots would have won the War for Independence in any event.

Perhaps, as Robert Middlekauff has argued, American morale and commitment to the "Glorious Cause" of liberty and self-government were of paramount significance in determining the outcome. Based on the experience of the American Revolutionary War, it would appear that an insurrectionary movement, upheld by a determined, highly motivated minority willing to sacrifice life and fortune for its cause, might well prove impossible to quell. The Napoleonic French in Spain, the British in South Africa, the Americans in Vietnam, and the Russians in Afghanistan might have studied the American Revolution to advantage.

MAX R. WILLIAMS

SEE ALSO: Suffren de St. Tropez, Pierre André; Washington, George.

Bibliography

Alden, J. R. 1962. *The American Revolution, 1775–1783.* New York: Harper.
Bonwick, C. 1977. *English radicals and the American Revolution.* Chapel Hill, N.C.: Univ. of North Carolina Press.
Flexner, J. T. 1968. *George Washington in the American Revolution, 1775–1783.* Boston: Little Brown.
Gruber, I.D. 1972. *The Howe brothers and the American Revolution.* Chapel Hill, N.C.: Univ. of North Carolina Press.
Higginbotham, D. 1971. *The war of American independence: Military attitudes, policies, and practice, 1783–1789.* New York: Macmillan.
Mackesy, P. 1964. *The war for America, 1775–1783.* Oxford: Oxford Univ. Press.
Middlekauff, R. 1982. *The glorious cause: The American Revolution, 1763–1789.* New York: Oxford.
Miller, J. C. 1948. *Triumph of freedom, 1775–1783.* Boston: Little, Brown.
Robson, E. 1966. *The American Revolution in its political and military aspects 1763–1783.* New York: Norton.
Shy, J. W. 1976. *A people numerous and armed: Reflections on the military struggle for American independence.* New York: Oxford.
Ward, C. 1952. *The war of the revolution.* 2 vols. New York: Macmillan.

ARAB CONQUESTS [A.D. 632–732]

The Arab conquests dramatically altered the political and religious status quo in the Mediterranean basin. United into one nation by the Prophet Muhammad and motivated by the tenets of Islam, the Arabs destroyed the Persian Empire and from the Byzantine Empire won Palestine, Syria, Egypt, eastern Anatolia, and the north coast of Africa. In the space of 100 years, the Arabs conquered an empire extending from the Pamirs in the east to the Atlantic coast of Morocco in the west, and northward into southern France.

The Arab Military

An Arab field army consisted of four elements: vanguard, center, wings, and rearguard. The troops in each element were recruited from the same tribe.

The cavalry, drawn from the nomadic Bedouin tribes, were either lancers, armed with swords and lances, or horse archers, armed with swords and bows and arrows. Some cavalrymen also carried javelins. During their early campaigns, the horse archers did not use stirrups, and as a result, their effectiveness was limited. The Arab cavalry, therefore, relied primarily on the lance and the sword.

Initially, the cavalryman was lightly armored, his personal armor consisting, usually, of a helmet and mail shirt. After contact with the Byzantine and Persian heavy cavalry, the Arabs adopted the armor of their opponents.

The infantry, drawn from the town-dwelling Arabs (al-Hadhar), consisted mainly of foot archers who, along with their bows and arrows, carried swords. Occasionally, other weapons—including javelins, slings, and spears—were used. Infantry armor consisted of a helmet and mail shirt. In Arabia and the conquered territories, Arab townsmen formed militias for both garrison duty and field operations.

TACTICS

The cavalry deployed either in extended order (line) or in a compact mass (column). When present, the infantry formed the center and the cavalry the wings. Tactics were centered around the cavalry charge with supporting fire supplied by the horse archers and the infantry, the latter serving as both a tactical pivot and a fire-support base. The objective of the charge was to break the enemy's formation. Once the enemy forces were in disarray, the Arabs attacked and defeated each unit separately.

Arab tactics were based upon the *razzia*, the traditional Bedouin raid. In fact, most campaigns were just a series of raids. The traditions of the *razzia* also explain a major weakness of Arab tactics. After the cavalry had driven home the charge, each warrior engaged in single combat with an enemy soldier—just as if he were on an intertribal raid in Arabia. All unit cohesion disappeared.

REASONS FOR ARAB VICTORIES

Despite the glaring weaknesses of their tactical system, the Arabs won victory after victory over the Byzantines and Persians, the dominant military powers of the day. The superior mobility of the Arabs, their high morale, the weakness of both the Byzantine and Persian empires following the conclusion of their 25-year war, and the support of native populations all contributed to Arab victories. Another contributing factor was Arab generalship. The victories of Khalid ibn al-Walid, Amr ibn al-As, and Saad ibn Abu Waqqas were won against superior enemy forces. The ability of the Arab commanders to exploit the advantages of terrain, especially the desert, and to draw the enemy into fighting on ground favorable to the Arabs, accounts in large part for the string of Arab victories.

The Conquests: First Phase (632–56)

INITIAL OPERATIONS IN IRAQ

Abu Bakr, the successor (caliph) of the Prophet Muhammad, chose Iraq and Palestine as the initial targets for Arab expansionism. In 634, Khalid ibn al-Walid led a force of 4,000 cavalry into southwestern Iraq. He was joined there by Muthanna ibn Haritha, chief of the Beni-Bakr, and his warriors. With his reinforced army, Khalid took al-Hira and transformed it into his operational base. Located 320 kilometers (200 mi.) northwest of Basra (up the Euphrates River), al-Hira was strategically situated. Its strong walls also made it a highly defendable refuge in case of trouble. From al-Hira, Khalid raided the Persians at will, penetrating as far as Ctesiphon, the Persian capital (located approximately 80 kilometers [50 mi.] south of modern Baghdad, on the Tigris River). Advancing northwestward up the Euphrates, Khalid defeated a Persian army at Firad (480 kilometers [300 mi.] upriver from al-Hira). In recognition of his success, Abu Bakr named Khalid governor of Iraq.

Operations in Palestine and Syria. While Khalid was advancing along the Euphrates, Abu Obeida, with a force of 24,000, commenced operations in Palestine. His army was divided into four columns. The first column, commanded by Amr ibn al-As, was to advance from Akaba to Gaza, then to Jerusalem. The second column, commanded by Yazid ibn Abu Sufyad, had Damascus as its objective. The third and fourth columns formed the reserve.

Amr occupied Akaba, then crossed the Negev Desert and captured Gaza. Initial Byzantine resistance was light, but as Amr neared Jerusalem, resistance stiffened. Both the first and second columns were stopped.

His advance stalled, Abu Obeida faced a new threat: rebellion behind his lines. Fearing that Abu Obeida's forces would be cut off and destroyed, Abu Bakr ordered Khalid from Iraq to Palestine. In July 634, Khalid led a force of 9,000 cavalry across the Great Syrian Desert, entered Palestine, and overwhelmed the rebels. Joining forces with Amr, Khalid defeated the Byzantines at Ajnadayo. The advance northward resumed, bypassing Jerusalem. Khalid and Abu Obeida laid siege to Damascus in March 635; the city surrendered, on lenient terms, in September. Homs and Aleppo surrendered shortly thereafter.

Persian counterattack in Iraq. While Khalid was conducting operations in Palestine and Syria, the Persians counterattacked in Iraq. At the Battle of the Bridge, the Persians defeated Muthanna ibn Haritha. Arab losses totaled 4,000. In October 634, Muthanna stopped the Persian offensive at the Battle of Buwaib. During the battle, Muthanna was mortally wounded.

Byzantine counterattack in Syria. In 636, the Byzantine emperor Heraclius led a force of 200,000 men to Antioch. He sent most of these, under his brother Theodorus, toward Damascus. As the Byzantines approached, Khalid abandoned Damascus and withdrew southward. The Byzantines pursued. Khalid continued to fall back until he reached the confluence of the Yarmuk and Jordan rivers (near the modern towns of Baqura and Ashdot Ya'aqov). Under cover of a sandstorm, Khalid launched his army of 40,000 against Theodorus's 150,000. The Battle of Yarmuk lasted three days. Khalid maneuvered his forces so that eventually the Byzantines were caught in a narrow passage between two converging Arab columns. Theodorus was slain and his army annihilated. So decisive was the Battle of Yarmuk that Heraclius withdrew from Antioch and returned to Constantinople. Khalid, at the head of his victorious army, reentered Damascus only to be deprived of his command and recalled by the new caliph, Omar, who had appointed Abu Obeida governor of Syria. In January 637, Amr ibn al-As occupied Jerusalem. With the exception of Caesarea and Antioch, all of Palestine and Syria—two of the richest provinces of the Byzantine Empire—were in Arab hands.

Conquest of Iraq. Omar appointed Saad ibn Abu Waqqas governor of Iraq in 636. Saad, with 30,000 men, defeated a Persian army 100,000 strong at Qadisiya. Advancing up the Tigris River, Saad occupied Ctesiphon. At Jalula (80 kilometers [50 mi.] north of Baghdad), Saad again defeated the Persians. Saad wished to pursue the Persians into Iran, but Omar, the caliph, forbade it. The victories of Saad ibn Abu Waqqas gave the Arabs control of all of Iraq except for the Mosul region.

CONQUEST OF EGYPT

The conquest of Egypt was entrusted to Amr ibn al-As, the conquerer of Jerusalem. With a force of 4,000—later increased to 10,000—Amr crossed the Sinai isthmus into Egypt in December 639. Pelusium and Heliopolis quickly fell to the Arabs. In April 640, Amr besieged Babylon, a mighty Byzantine fortress on the site of modern Cairo. Babylon surrendered in March 641 on condition that the garrison be allowed to withdraw to Alexandria. Three months later, Amr laid siege to Alexandria, capital of the province of Egypt and headquarters of the Byzantine fleet in the Levant. In November 641, Cyrus, the Byzantine viceroy, surrendered the city to Amr. Once again, Amr granted the Byzantines lenient terms and allowed the defenders of Alexandria to withdraw from Egypt. All of Egypt was secured by 643, and Amr was appointed governor of the province. In 645, Alexandria revolted, spurred on by the appearance of the Byzantine fleet offshore. Amr, however, quickly quelled the rebellion, and the Byzantines withdrew.

Abdullah ibn Saad replaced Amr as governor of Egypt in 646. To counter the threat posed by the Byzantine navy, Abdullah created an Arab navy, and in 649, it captured Cyprus. At the Battle of the Masts (Dhat al-sawaib) in 655, the Arabs soundly beat the Byzantine navy, thereby wresting control of the eastern Mediterranean from the Byzantine empire.

CONQUEST OF PERSIA

Saad ibn Abu Waqqas recommenced operations in northern Iraq in 641, securing Mosul. Then, in 642, he crossed into Persia (Iran) and, at Nehawend, decisively defeated the Persian emperor Yazdagird, who fled eastward leaving 60,000 Persian dead on the battlefield. After Nehawend, the Arabs gradually extended their control over all of Persia. In 649, Saad ibn al-As, governor of Kufah, commenced operations along the Hamadan-Ray-Jurjan-Khurasan axis, while Abdullah ibn Amir, governor of Basra, advanced along the Fars-Kerman-Tabas-Nishapur-Marv axis. Although the Arabs encountered sporadic, and sometimes stiff, resistance, their advance was aided by the conversion of many Persian aristocrats to Islam. The once mighty Persian Empire was finally secured by 652.

END OF THE FIRST PHASE

The first phase of the Arab conquests was ended by the outbreak of the First Arab Civil War. Fought between the Alids, followers of Ali—the son-in-law of the Prophet Muhammad—and the followers of the Omayyads, the war revealed deep religious and tribal divisions within the Arab nation.

The Conquests: Second Phase (661–80)

The victory of the Omayyads in 661 restored stability to the Arab Empire—at least temporarily. Unity restored, Arab expansion continued, with Arab forces becoming active in North Africa and Central Asia.

The conquest of North Africa was assigned to Oqbah ibn Nafi, nephew of Amr ibn al-As. By 670, Oqbah had reached Tunisia, where he founded Kairouan (Qairawan).

Ziyad ibn Abihi campaigned in Afghanistan and occupied Kabul in 664, after which he proceeded northward into Transoxiana, reducing Samarkand in 676.

The outbreak of the Second Arab Civil War ended the second phase. Hussein, son of Ali, revolted against the Omayyads in 680. The war ended quickly, Hussein was slain in the Battle of Kerbala, and his followers were ruthlessly suppressed.

The Conquests: Third Phase (680–732)

The defeat of the Alid rebels paved the way for the resumption of operations in North Africa and Central Asia.

Oqbah ibn Nafi resumed his westward march in 683. Tangier fell and all of the Moroccan coast as far as modern Agadir (on the Atlantic coast) came under Arab control. Oqbah's conquests, however, were short-lived. On the journey back to his base at Kairouan, Oqbah divided his army into a number of columns—it was a fatal blunder. At Bishra, Berbers ambushed and annihilated Oqbah's column.

Twenty-two years passed between the death of Oqbah and the resumption of operations in North Africa. The capture of Carthage from the Byzantines was the only Arab success of note. In 704, however, Musa ibn Nosair was named governor of North Africa. Through a combination of military action and diplomacy, Musa persuaded the Berbers to make peace with the Arabs and to accept Islam. With the conquest of Mauritania in 705, all of the Atlantic coast of North Africa was added to the domain of the caliph.

CENTRAL ASIA

While Musa ibn Nosair was pushing the western frontiers of Islam to the Atlantic, Qutaba ibn Muslim began operations to reconquer Transoxiana where, during the Second Arab Civil War, the Turks had reasserted their independence. This proved a formidable task. The Arabs met stiff resistance from the Turkic horse archers, whose skill with horse and bow far surpassed that of their Arab counterparts. Bokhara was taken in 709; Samarkand not until 712. By 714,

Qutaba had pushed the eastern frontiers of Islam as far as Farghana, though tradition claims he reached Kasghar in Chinese Turkestan.

Between 710 and 715, Arab forces commanded by Mohammed ibn Kasim reconquered Afghanistan and extended Arab rule over the Punjab and Sind, thus adding the Indus River valley to the empire of the Omayyads.

IBERIAN PENINSULA

Tariq ibn Ziyad, the governor of Tangier and a subordinate of Musa ibn Nosair, crossed the straits of Gibraltar (Tariq's Rock) with 7,000 men in 711. Taking advantage of Visigothic disunity, Tariq rapidly occupied Algeciras, Cadiz, Málaga, and Córdoba. On 19 July 711, Tariq annihilated the army of the Visigoth king, Roderick, at the Battle of Wadi Bekka (Salado River). With the death of King Roderick, all organized resistance ended. Granada and Toledo, the Visigoth capital, surrendered.

Musa ibn Nosair, upon learning of Tariq's adventure, crossed over to Spain with 10,000 men. By the end of 713, all of Iberia except for the northern provinces of Asturias and Navarre had been secured.

SOUTHERN FRANCE

From their base in Spain, successive Arab governors launched operations against southern France. In 717, al-Hurr ibn Abd al-Rahman al-Thakafi conducted the first of these raids. Al-Samh ibn Malik al-Khaulani occupied Septimania in 720 and established a forward base at Narbonne. In 721, al-Samh laid siege to Toulouse. It was during this siege that al-Samh was slain and the Arabs withdrew to Narbonne. In 732, Abd al-Rahman ibn Abdullah al-Ghafiqi advanced northwestward along the Garonne River with about 50,000 men and occupied Bordeaux. Advancing northward from Bordeaux, the Arabs penetrated central France, reaching the Loire River near Tours. Charles Martel, de facto ruler of the Merovingian Frankish borders, led an army of more than 50,000 to meet the Arabs, who retreated to protect their train of booty. Somewhere between Tours and Poitiers, near the confluence of the Clain and Vienne rivers, the Franks caught up with the Arabs, and decisively defeated them. This Battle of Tours (October 732) marked the farthest Arab penetration of Europe. Although the Battle of Tours blunted Arab expansionism, it did not end Arab military activity in France. In 734, Arab raiders seized Avignon. In 743, they raided Lyon. The Arabs remained a military threat until the loss of their base at Narbonne in 759.

End of the Conquests

The Arab conquests lost momentum after 732 for a number of reasons. After withstanding four Arab attacks on Constantinople, and repeated attempts to occupy Asia Minor, the resurgent Byzantine Empire took the offensive, reoccupied the Syrian coast, and threatened Arab possession of Palestine.

In the east, Arab expansion into Chinese Turkestan was blocked by the Uigher Turks. And behind the Uighers stood the Chinese Empire. In the west, the growing power of the Franks under the son and grandson (Charlemagne) of

Charles Martel, proved a barrier to further Arab expansion into western Europe.

Arab disunity also contributed to the end of the Arab conquests. The simmering hatred between the Omayyads and the Alids, reflected in the continuing Sunni-Shiite split, undermined both the stability and unity of the Arab nation. The overthrow of the Omayyads in 750 by the Abbasids—a Persian family of Arab origin—further undermined Arab unity. The banner of Islam passed from the Arabs to the Seljuk and Ottoman Turks.

LAWRENCE D. HIGGINS

SEE ALSO: Byzantine Empire; Charlemagne; History, Medieval Military; Khalid ibn-al-Walid.

Bibliography

Brice, W. C., ed. 1981. *A historical atlas of Islam.* Leiden: E. J. Brill.
Butler, A. J. 1902. *The Arab conquest of Egypt.* London: Oxford Univ. Press.
Gibb, H. A. R. 1923. *The Arab conquests in central Asia.* London: Royal Asiatic Society.
Glubb, Sir John. 1963. *The great Arab conquests.* London: Hodder and Stoughton.
Hitti, P. K. 1956. *History of the Arabs.* 6th ed. New York: Macmillan.
Levy, R. 1957. *The social structure of Islam.* Cambridge: Cambridge Univ. Press.
Lewis, B. 1958. *The Arabs in history.* 4th ed. London: Hutchinson.
Nutting, A. 1964. *The Arabs: A narrative history from Mohammed to the present.* New York: New American Library/Mentor Books.
Pipes, D. 1981. *Slave soldiers and Islam: The genesis of a military system.* New Haven: Yale Univ. Press.
Spuler, B. 1960. *The age of the caliphs.* Leiden: E. J. Brill.

ARAB-ISRAELI WARS [1947–82]

The long struggle between Israel and various coalitions of surrounding Arab nations began with the Israeli War of Independence (First Arab-Israeli War) in 1948–49 and has since included four more wars, plus almost continual conflict with various levels of violence, ranging from military interventions to terrorism. The last three wars served Western and Soviet military planners as paradigms for a hypothetical clash in Central Europe.

The basic issue concerns territorial rights in the former Ottoman-Turkish administrative district of Palestine, which is located in the heart of what the Arabs of the Middle East regard as an exclusively Islamic domain. Britain and France had, since 1918, administered (under League of Nations mandates) the lands in the Fertile Crescent liberated from Germany's Turkish ally in World War I. This arrangement was intended to midwife the native nationalist movements to independent nationhood. British wartime diplomacy, however, resulted in separate and conflicting promises of self-rule in Palestine to both the native Arab populace and the Jewish Zionist nationalist movement. It was subsequently impossible to satisfy the claims of either the Zionists or the Palestinian Arabs, and spiraling violence from both parties, directed primarily at the British occupation apparatus but also at each other, ultimately brought the matter to the attention of the United Nations (UN) in 1946. That body voted to partition the mandate into separate Jewish and Arab areas, with Jerusalem a neutral international zone. The Zionists accepted this (as half a loaf), but the Arab League nations vowed to nullify the decision by force. Israeli success in 1948 resulted in the flight of most of the original Arab inhabitants ("Palestinians"). Confined to tent cities in countries of refuge, the plight of the stateless Palestinians was the impetus (some say pretext) for their patrons' revanchist efforts to undo the Zionist fait accompli. Since then, brief bursts of intensive all-out warfare punctuated extended truces during which the conflict continued in economic and guerrilla-terroristic modes.

Arab-Israeli War of 1948–49

The first round officially lasted one and a half years. It was a stop-start series of clashes, the longest of which lasted four weeks, with combat operations totaling about ten weeks. Long truces divided the war into distinct phases.

Phase I was the period of "civil war" between the Palestinian irregular armed bands—remnants of a 1936–39 uprising—and the Jewish self-defense force. The waning yet vigilant British presence prevented the Arab League states from invading Palestine, but they could not prevent village-based Arab bands from waging a guerrilla war. There were two irregular "fighting organizations" loyal to the exiled Grand Mufti of Jerusalem, each numbering about 1,500 men, which had on call some 35,000 armed villagers, an informal local militia available for short-term and rather static actions. Car-bombing and random sniping in the towns was expected to wear down Jewish morale while the Battle of the Roads would choke isolated Jewish settlements. The patchwork pattern of Jewish settlement meant that the Arab villages sat astride vital communications links. Thus the Palestinians were able to mount roadblocks and ambushes on an ad hoc basis. Haganah, the underground Jewish army, had to rely upon armed convoys for resupply and reinforcement at this early stage. This method was only sporadically successful and exacted a high toll in lives and vehicles.

A small "Arab Liberation Army" composed of Palestinians and volunteers from other Arab countries was operating against Zionist settlements by January 1948. By the end of March 1948, in anticipation of invasion by neighboring Arab countries on expiration of the British League of Nations mandate, Haganah had mobilized and integrated various contingents: a core of 3,000 idealists in the elite Palmach striking force, with another 1,000 in reserve; a mobile field force, HISH, about 10,000 strong with a pool of 35,000 World War II veterans on tap; and a home guard–style static settlement defense force, HIM, numbering 20,000. There were nine brigade-sized units activated, enough to implement Plan D, an offensive designed to seize and hold the Arab wedges separating Jewish sectors. There were also two politically dissident independent terrorist groups, Irgun and Stern, totaling about 1,500. By 15 May, the Jewish consolidation effort was girded for the all-out Arab invasion on the heels of the departed British.

On 15 May—the day following British abandonment of the League of Nations mandate—Egypt, Transjordan, Syria, Iraq, and Lebanon sent forces into Palestine against the Israelis, thereby initiating Phase II of the war. Of all of these, only the Transjordan contingent—the Arab Legion—was a truly effective fighting force. Forces allocated to the task by each of the mutually suspicious Arab allies were quite small relative to strength left at home to check dissident domestic rivals. Each sent brigade-sized expeditions (Egypt allocated two brigades) reinforced by tanks, ground attack planes, artillery, and armored cars. Much has been made of the imbalance of these assets, but the Arab forces could not coordinate the various arms and had to employ them piecemeal, in rigid field-manual fashion.

Most serious was the lack of a unified war plan, which left the various armies to run independent operations without provision for mutual support. All were stunned by tenacious and aggressive reaction of the Jewish border settlements and considerably altered their initial "Anaconda" program (a plan to cut off incoming resources by closing Israel's borders) to settle for a few threatening bridgeheads on the periphery of the Jewish state. Egyptian columns stalled far short of their objectives—Tel Aviv and Jerusalem—unable to eliminate the chain of Negev settlements from whence wasp stings paralyzed overextended communications. The Arab Legion, however, had secured most of the Old City of Jerusalem. Had the invasion forces made a concerted, coordinated attack instead of accepting an 11 June 1948 truce, it is likely that there would be no Israel today.

Phase III operations were all Israeli initiatives using enlarged and up-gunned mobile brigades. The Israeli Defense Force (IDF) succeeded in blunting the Arab Legion east of Tel Aviv, in containing the Iraqi probe at the narrow "waist," and in decisively thrashing the volunteer army in central Galilee. The Legion still menaced the main corridor between Tel Aviv and West Jerusalem at Latrun, but an improvised bypass rendered Latrun less relevant.

In October 1948, the Israelis began Phase IV with maneuvers that achieved a new sophistication, primarily directed at the Egyptian picket line across the main roads to the Negev. The offensive shattered the Egyptian front, leaving a defiant Egyptian pocket at Faluja and a main threat at Gaza-El Arish, which was dealt with in Phase V (December 1948–January 1949).

This phase began with a wide envelopment presaging the freewheeling maneuvers in Sinai of 1956 and 1967, including the coordinated use of armor, artillery preparations, and air support. A series of armistices (no treaties or recognition was in sight) and a last-minute grab for the Negev's deep "V" corridor to the Gulf of Aqaba left the Jews in control of a considerably larger Israel than the UN had contemplated, but with a crazy-quilt border that was particularly vulnerable opposite the Transjordanian (later Jordanian) salient, now known as the West Bank since it is west of the Jordan River.

Sinai Campaign, 1956 (Operation Kadesh)

Israel had been frustrated by the failure of its reprisal raids to deter border incursions and sabotage by Palestinian exile terrorist/commando groups during the early 1950s. The escalating pattern of reprisals only seemed to intensify these fedayeen attacks, which in 1954 were openly sponsored by Egypt's Gamal Abdel Nasser. In early 1956, Israel decided to stop these terrorist incursions.

In his bid for leadership of the Arab world, Nasser sought to head the confrontation with Israel, stepping up the pressure by sealing Israel's Red Sea outlet with artillery that commanded the narrow Tiran Straits and declaring a military alliance with Syria directed against Israel. Most worrisome for the IDF was Egypt's massive purchase of Czech and Soviet arms in summer 1955, which would provide Egypt with a decisive edge in one to two years. Thus, the Israeli decision to take military action to halt terrorist attacks was probably to some extent influenced by a determination to prevent the Egyptian forces from integrating their new and sophisticated equipment into effective field units. This then was to some extent a "preventive war," but firm evidence of Egyptian war plans is lacking.

Shortly before the planned Israeli attack on Egypt, France "invited" Israel to coordinate its own campaign with an imminent Anglo-French operation, Musketeer, to seize the Suez Canal. Nasser had recently nationalized the canal in retaliation for withdrawal of Western capital from his Aswan High Dam project. Israel's opening gambit would be to pose a credible "threat" to the canal zone, bringing Egyptian units into the area, in turn triggering Musketeer, ostensibly to buffer the two converging forces in order to keep the canal open. The "distraction" of the Anglo-French maneuvers would draw off sufficient Egyptian strength to allow Israel to accomplish its objectives of wiping out the Gaza fedayeen bases and removing the Egyptian forces covering the Tiran Straits, neither of which entailed incursions near the canal.

To avoid alerting Egypt's armored forces held west of the canal as well as its worrisome air strength, the first phase of "Kadesh"—an airborne incursion east of the Mitla Pass—was to appear to be merely a deep-strike counter fedayeen raid. If the Egyptian High Command were deceived by this and thought they were dealing only with another Israeli retaliation, they would hold back their air support and not alert the strong, well-dug-in defenses holding the northeast Sinai "triangle": El Arish–Rafah–Abu Ageila. The second phase would be the opening of an alternate supply corridor to the first phase units deep in Sinai by breaching the formidable Egyptian defense "hedgehog" at Abu Ageila. The final operations would involve the annihilation of the pocketed raider bases in the Gaza Strip while mobile units overran the Egyptian artillery bases at Sharm el Sheikh.

Phase I went according to plan, although some unauthorized probes into the Mitla Pass created a perilous situation for a few hours. The Egyptian air and armored reserves were not drawn off from the canal—largely because of the diversion created in Nasser's rear by the concentration of the Anglo-French task force on Crete. The Israeli airborne brigade near Mitla turned south to Sharm el Sheikh, while an infantry brigade from Eliat began an arduous trek along the converging axis through terrain barely passable for wheeled vehicles; civilian transport borrowed for the job often broke down.

Two Israeli mechanized infantry brigades opposite the Um Katef/Um Shehan hedgehog in the center were held at bay by accurate preranged fire from dug-in Egyptian armor and artillery. Impatient with delay, the IDF's sole all-tank brigade, supposedly in reserve, probed along the southern fringes of the defensive complex and found an unguarded pass through which to circle to the rear of Abu Ageila. Contrary to the plan, and without informing headquarters, one tank battalion filtered through and began pounding the Egyptian self-propelled guns from the rear, while the other battalion raced southwest to assist the mechanized brigade beginning its thrust to Sharm el-Sheikh.

The northern Israeli task force then began its combined-arms reduction of the second major Egyptian fortified zone between Rafah and Gaza, one unit racing westward flanking the sector along "impassable" terrain and disrupting its rearward communications, while the other assaulted from the front, exploiting the rather rigid Egyptian defense plans. Finally, the mopping up of the Gaza Strip's Palestinian and Egyptian raiding forces occurred while the two columns descending toward Sharm el Sheikh besieged the garrison there. By this time, the Egyptian high command had ordered all forces in Sinai to pull back to reinforce the main effort against the Anglo-French landings at Suez; this facilitated Israeli operations under way in the two main fortified belts in northeast Sinai. The IAF had dealt decisively with two Egyptian armored columns that had attempted to relieve the hard-pressed units at Abu Ageila and Rafa, proving the value of air superiority over the battlefield, especially in herding retreating vehicles into killing zones at bottlenecks. The inability of Israeli mechanized infantry to penetrate the Um Katef defenses, combined with the success of the armored spearheads, led the Israelis to decide that the tank was the decisive weapon, and that infantry should be used to exploit *after* the armor had punched through or bypassed the main enemy concentrations.

Although Israel won a clear-cut military victory, the war was a political disaster for her Anglo-French allies, who were compelled by pressure from the UN, and especially from the United States and the Soviet Union, to withdraw from Suez. This in turn compelled the Israelis to withdraw from Sinai, although the Straits of Tiran were opened and the postwar UN force in the Sinai limited terrorist attacks on Israel from Egyptian bases. The war left Nasser in a much stronger political position, as he had successfully weathered a crisis and frustrated Anglo-French goals.

Six-Day War, June 1967

After his 1956 military defeat, and political triumph, Nasser rebuilt his forces with Soviet equipment and deployed much of his revitalized army in the forward positions that had caused the entire Sinai command structure to unravel when these linchpins were cracked in 1956. His claim to military leadership of the confrontation with Israel was questioned by Syria in May 1967 when Nasser failed to honor his military commitment (another alliance was patched together in 1966) after an Israeli retaliatory air patrol shot down six Syrian MiGs. Reacting both to the goad and to a supposed threat of an imminent Israeli invasion of Syria (contrived by Soviet incitement), Nasser reimposed the blockade against shipping from Eilat, demanded the evacuation of the UN buffer force from the border areas in Sinai, stirred up the Egyptian masses with martial rhetoric defying Israel, and signed a pact with Jordan and Iraq, placing the alliance forces under Egyptian command. Thus, all the previously announced Israeli tripwires to war had been broken. Yet apparently Nasser did not really expect Israel to attack.

PRELIMINARY AIR STRIKE, 6 JUNE 1967

Israel adopted a low-key posture while secretly mobilizing reserves, updating war plans, and apparently demonstrating a concentration toward Jordan. The Arab air threat was seen as the most crucial factor, both in terms of equipment and numbers. So the Israelis opened their unambiguously preventive war with a meticulously executed, simultaneous air strike on eighteen Egyptian air bases, exploiting the predictability of the Egyptian morning stand-down pattern, underflying Egyptian radar, and dodging SAM-2 missile shields by flying out to sea and circling back from the west. An incredible turnaround time, one-third that of the United States Air Force standard, effectively trebled the Israeli Defense Force/Air Force (IDF/AF) order of battle and convinced Nasser that the United States was participating in collusion. Later that day, Jordan and then Syria, crediting Egyptian propaganda that the Israeli attackers had been blown from the sky, launched limited, futile fighter-bomber attacks on Israeli bases and depots. This spurred the IDF/AF to mount additional strikes against their air bases, including an Iraqi base in Jordan, catching planes on the ground as they returned from their initial missions. In all, over two-thirds of total Arab airpower was eliminated in eight hours, thereby giving the IDF/AF a free hand to neutralize the Arab superiority on the ground in armor, artillery, and manpower.

SINAI FRONT

Taking advantage of intelligence that Nasser's war "coalition" was a self-deluding myth, the IDF resolved, as it had in 1948, to exploit its central position to deal separately with each threat, trusting the unmolested partners to sit on their hands. The first priority was the most dangerous adversary, Egypt, to be dealt with by three divisional task forces (*ugdahs*), each designed and structured for a unique tactical situation along its designated line of march. Southern front commander Gavish employed his 700 tanks and 50,000 troops to punch through the two northernmost Egyptian blocking positions and race to the passes along the Sinai's western ridge line. There he trapped and destroyed the withdrawing Egyptian forces as they channeled through the gorges, utilizing unopposed air support to suppress dug-in firepower and block counterattacks.

Meanwhile, a deceptive feint, where a brigade masqueraded as a division using dummy tanks and illusory reinforcements, opposed the one offensively oriented Egyptian division (Division Shazli) poised along the southern Negev gateway to Tel Aviv and ensured that it would stay there, safely away from the main thrusts.

Ugdah Israel Tal slashed through Egyptian fortifications along the north coast while isolating and reducing Palestinian infantry units entrenched in Gaza. Ugdah Yoffe exploited a soft, heretofore "impassable," seam between two major hedgehogs to join with Tal's southern detachment in racing to the Khatmia Pass and trapping an Egyptian counterattack force at Bir Gifgafa. Yoffe was also able to send part of his force southwest toward an Egyptian deployment at Jebel Libni. Ugdah Ariel Sharon, farther east, mounted a complex, set piece concentric night attack on the greatly expanded (since 1956) Um Katef–Abu Ageila defensive complex. Then, moving cross-country southwest to Nakhl, Sharon cut off Egyptian forces lining the southern axis. Although dangerously overextended and depleted, Yoffe's force captured garrisons at Bir Hasneh and Bir Thamada before sealing the Mitla and Giddi passes. Sharon's force was able to ambush an Egyptian column near Thamad and hold it for the IDF/AF to finish off.

CENTRAL FRONT

The campaign on the central front was to some extent improvised, since the Israelis had expected Jordan to abstain from the fight. Under pressure from Nasser to show solidarity, King Hussein seems to have hoped that perfunctory long-range shelling of Israeli air bases, Jewish Jerusalem, and Tel Aviv with 155mm "Long Toms" would satisfy Nasser yet at the same time demonstrate enough restraint to stay Israel's hand. However, the long-range artillery threat to the runways at the important Ramot David air base set Gen. Uzi Narkiss's central front forces in motion. This readiness demonstrated that the contingency was not entirely unexpected.

The Israelis immediately attacked in Jerusalem to contain a Jordanian battalion in its defensive position, while other elements of the Jerusalem Brigade advanced south toward Hebron. Reinforcements released from Southern Command reserve allowed Narkiss to send three brigades into the Battle of Jerusalem, the main task falling to Col. Mordechai Gur's paratroop brigade. A reinforced Jordanian brigade commanded by Brig. Ata Ali garrisoned the old walled city, Gur's assigned objective. The night assault stalled in the face of obstinate resistance, but elements of Gur's brigade were more successful in driving out two Jordanian infantry brigades holding commanding positions northwest and east of Jerusalem. This action enabled the main effort force to capture intervening posts along the northern ridge line, making contact with a beleaguered Jewish outpost on Mount Scopus.

Meanwhile, early on 6 June, elements of Ben Ari's armored brigade took up positions astride key terrain north of Jerusalem and worked cross-country through territory considered impassable to tanks to gain control of Ramallah by dawn on the seventh. A reserve infantry brigade, striking toward Ramallah in a wide arc through Jordanian positions at Latrun, consolidated Israeli control of the heights dominating the Jerusalem area while the infantry brigade holding the southern approaches closed the ring.

The Jordanian 60th Armored Brigade, held in reserve around Jericho, mounted an effort to relieve the Jerusalem garrison. The relief column, consisting of a battalion each of tanks and infantry, was caught by the IDF/AF and Israeli ground forces. It was wiped out on the night of 5–6 June. Another relief attempt mounted by the Qadisiyeh infantry brigade on 6–7 June also failed.

Concurrently with operations around Jerusalem, Northern Command and elements of Central Command mounted a series of concentric pincer thrusts into Samaria. Jordanian antitank defenses at Jenin stalled one armored brigade, but a mechanized brigade hooked around from the southeast to surprise the Jenin garrison. A particularly effective Jordanian armored counterattack was halted at Kabbatya junction.

An Israeli feint down the Jordan Valley distracted other Jordanian units, as did the advance from the coastal strip by a Central Command infantry brigade, threatening Jordanian armor at Jenin from the rear. The infantry brigade had to fight its way through determined Jordanian armored counterattacks and move cross-country to encircle Nablus from the southwest, while the mechanized brigade could only extricate itself from desperate fighting in Jenin with the help of air support, allowing it to approach Nablus from the northwest, completing the conquest of that town and, with it, the West Bank.

NORTHERN FRONT

True to expectations, the Syrians, stripped of their air force, largely confined their activities to artillery bombardment of Israeli targets from their formidable fortified complex atop the more than 600-meter (2,000-ft.) Golan escarpment. Shuffling forces from the Jordanian front, the Israeli attack went in on the fourth day of the war. Facing six Syrian brigades on line, with six more in reserve east of Kuneitra, Northern Command concentrated its available forces along the northern anchor of the Syrian line at the Dan-Banyas area, flanking the foothills of Mount Hermon, for an initial advance onto the Golan Plateau. Israeli attack planes concentrated on silencing Syrian gun positions. The key to the Syrian defenses was the fort of Tel Fakhr. There was no scope for maneuver; tank-backed APCs took the hedgehogs straight-on, assisted by armored bulldozers moving ahead to clear boulders littering the steep gradient. Infantry dismounted for the final lunge for the trench lines. Fresh troops passed through depleted units, picking up the remnants. The next day, other Israeli units forced their way up the ridge north of the Sea of Galilee and units fresh from the heavy fighting in the Jenin-Nablus action crossed into Syria along the sea's southern shore. Heliborne troops, leapfrogging with an armored column, menaced Kuneitra from the south.

Meanwhile, the breakthrough units to the north pushed through the crumbling Syrian Golan defenses and pressed on across the plateau to converge on Kuneitra from the north and west, joining the units redeployed from the Jordanian front coming up through the Yarmuk Valley to surround Kuneitra, as an armored unit entered and held the key Syrian assembly point. The imminent Israeli threat to Damascus was warded off by a bluntly worded Soviet ultimatum. The previously announced UN cease-fire took hold on 10 June, with Israeli forces controlling the entire Sinai Peninsula, the West Bank salient, and the Golan Heights—all three declared by Israel as nonnegotiable, essential strategic buffer zones.

War of Attrition

Victory in the Six-Day War netted Israel a strategic warning belt against Egypt in the Sinai. However, the security demands of policing thousands of restive Arabs in the captured territories left Israel with a new internal security problem, tying down troops that were thereby unavailable to guard the distant Suez defense line, which in itself posed logistical and deployment problems in the event of war.

The Egyptians were reequipped massively by the Soviets with modern tanks and field guns. They determined to make life along the canal untenable for the Israeli garrison force and, in September-October 1968, fired intermittent intense artillery barrages from 150 positions along the canal, initially inflicting heavy casualties on the unprepared Israelis. Nasser, anticipating heavy Israeli retaliation, also evacuated civilians from the canal zone. Saboteurs and small raiding parties infiltrated through unguarded sectors, but these were almost always intercepted and this tactic was abandoned. Israeli artillery could not match the Egyptian barrages, and Israel came to rely instead on deep air strikes on industrial sites and arms depots in the Egyptian hinterland as well as spectacular commando forays into ostensibly impenetrable Egyptian military installations.

The air strikes prompted Nasser's Soviet patron to set up an integrated air defense net of antiaircraft guns overlapped by SA-2 ground-to-air missiles. When this system failed to deter the IDF/AF, Soviet pilots began to fly air cover in the Egyptian interior. The United States engineered a cease-fire after several Soviet pilots were shot down in dogfights and the situation threatened to create a superpower showdown. Egypt defied the cease-fire terms by secretly installing an interlocking line of SAM emplacements along the canal's west bank. For their part, the Israelis constructed fortified observation bunkers with a linking command and communications network on their side of the canal. This so-called Bar-Lev line was designed to be a line of observation posts and a delaying tripwire rather than a rigid rampart against an Egyptian attack.

October 1973 Mideast War

Underlying the failure of Israeli intelligence to accurately read the incipient two-front attack of 6 October 1973 was their conviction that the Arabs would not attempt to move forward without absolute air supremacy and their belief that the IDF/AF had developed effective tactics to foil the SAMs in 1970. Nor did the IDF contemplate Arab willingness to settle for a *limited* objective under the protection of a static, tightly integrated, multilayered air defense shield. Nor could the Israelis imagine the precision of the Egyptian attack plan, a well-rehearsed, precisely orchestrated, shallow mass assault. Inconceivable as well, based on the lessons of 1967, was the very idea of Arab initiative and multifront coordination between allies. Egyptian ingenuity and the adaptation of Soviet doctrine and technology combined with a successful deception plan contributed to the successful cross-canal assault. This began with a massive artillery preparation, which covered the opening stages of the assault. Once across, teams of sappers ingeniously cut pathways through the Israeli sand rampart and blew holes for bridging units while 70,000 infantrymen fanned out laterally from the crossing points to set recoilless rifle and antitank missile ambushes. The IDF/AF's scramble to wipe out the widening bridgeheads was foiled by the deadly SAM umbrella underpinned by radar-guided AA batteries and hand-held infrared SAMs. Reserve armor was sent forward as it mobilized—piecemeal—and was badly mauled on D + 2 as it entered the infantry antitank killing grounds.

The Egyptians crossed two corps-sized armies that consolidated shallow bridgeheads along an 80-kilometer (50-mi.) front. On the second day, the bulk of the IDF/AF was redirected to the northern front to try to stem the Syrian advance, also begun on 6 October.

Syria had committed about 75 percent of its total armor (800 tanks) to the attack, which sent four columns westward north of the Sea of Galilee. Preceded by heavy artillery fire, three mechanized infantry divisions (in 2,800 APCs) preceded two armored divisions, ultimately 1,400 tanks, against less than 200 Israeli tanks that redeployed to specially prepared chokepoint ambushes with interlocking fields of fire. By this method, the Israeli armor was able to make the Syrians pay dearly for their initial breakthrough. An assault by heliborne infantry seized the fortified Israeli observation post on the commanding heights of Mount Hermon.

The IDF turned its major attention to this front as posing the most immediate threat to Israeli territory. By the second day, Israeli reserves were arriving in sufficient numbers (an entire division) to put their highly accurate long-range tank gunnery to good use. The IDF/AF at first flew into the missile umbrellas regardless of cost, but soon developed evasive tactics and was able to hit a fresh column of armor along the southernmost axis by coming in at treetop level over Jordanian territory, stopping it after an advance of almost 29 kilometers (18 mi.)—the Syrians' deepest penetration. The Syrians soon outran their lines of communication and then changed their formation to line abreast, whereupon Israeli air chewed them up. In this way, the Israelis bought 36 vital hours. Without a follow-on echelon to extend its incursion, and lacking the improvisational capacity to regroup and explore alternate lines of advance, the Syrians were driven back with hammer blows, making a stubborn fighting withdrawal toward Damascus and Sasa, clear off the Golan Heights to their start line by the 10th. On 11 October, advancing Israeli tanks were able to turn to deal decisively with Iraqi and Jordanian armored attacks on their southwest flank.

On the 14th, the Egyptians responded to desperate Syrian appeals by launching a major assault out of their secure defensive laagers. Backed by unmolested air cover, the Israelis were able to neutralize the infantry antitank teams with artillery fire, while long-range precise tank fire picked off advancing Egyptian T-62s before they could bring their turret guns to bear, disabling over 250 tanks.

The next day, exploiting a seam discovered between the two Egyptian bridgeheads during the early containment probes, the IDF activated a contingency plan to bridge the canal into Egypt proper. Using improvised bridging equipment, the Israelis advanced to the canal through the gap between the two Egyptian army sectors. The Egyptian Second Army, on the northern flank of the crossing, belatedly recognized the threat and mounted a concerted effort to seal the corridor (Battle of the Chinese Farm). This effort was repulsed by Gen. Abraham (Bren) Adan's division, which then crossed the canal into the bridgehead held by General Sharon's division. As Adan passed through to the southwest, Sharon attempted to seize Ismailia but was stopped. Adan's southward push toward Suez City began the Israeli main effort. The Egyptian Third Army—astride the canal—was encircled. By this time international pressure brought about a cease-fire, just as Adan was repulsed from Suez City. Israel had managed to turn near disaster into a muted victory, losing 3,000 men in the effort. The losses were commensurate with the intensity of the fighting but unacceptable by Israeli standards. The grand strategical winner appears to have been Egypt, which secured eventual return of the Sinai and a "cold peace" with Israel.

1982 War in Lebanon

In 1976 civil war flared in Lebanon, partly due to the activities of the Palestine Liberation Organization (PLO), which was able to establish a base for terrorist operations against Israel in southern Lebanon, and partly a result of long-standing hostilities between Lebanese Muslims and Christians. In March 1978, the Israelis made a limited incursion to crush the PLO presence in southern Lebanon. This had led to the establishment of a UN Emergency Force in Lebanon, but this proved to be unable to halt PLO rocket attacks on settlements in northern Galilee. In early 1982, Israel decided that it must eliminate the PLO bases.

The attempted assassination of Israel's ambassador to England by Arab terrorists on 4 June was the starting gun for Israel to initiate the long-planned sequel to the truncated 1978 effort. The problem was that there were actually two war plans. The first, known as Operation Peace for Galilee, had been agreed to by the full Israeli cabinet and known to the Israeli staff and field command. It involved the removal of PLO bases from a security belt running 40 kilometers (25 mi.) north from the Israeli border, designed to place PLO gunners beyond range of Israel. The second, the so-called Big Plan, a secret apparently shared between defense minister Ariel Sharon and the IDF chief of staff, was concealed from the cabinet and IDF commanders. It involved scouring the entire country up to Beirut to eliminate the entire PLO presence in Lebanon and install a Phalangist Christian government in full consonance with Israel's security goals.

Massive air strikes on 5 June on PLO installations throughout Lebanon drew the expected heavy PLO artillery and rocket retaliation along the entire northern frontier. The next day—6 June—the IDF pushed north on three main axes. Believed ultimately to be comprised of seven *ugdahs* (divisional task forces), the easternmost combined three *ugdahs* into a corps-sized task group of 35,000 men and 800 tanks. The westernmost column, proceeding along the coastal plain, was allocated 22,000 men and 220 tanks. The central column, about 20,000 men and 200 tanks, was to link its operations with those of the two main efforts on the flank. Total Israeli manpower mobilized for the operation amounted to 76,000 troops, with 1,250 tanks and 1,500 APCs. The PLO regular fighting forces were organized in brigades of 1,000 to 1,500 men each, totaling about 9,000, with another 12,000 militia in the refugee camps. They had arsenals of heavy weapons, including tanks, APCs, field guns, rocket launchers, and mobile antiaircraft and antitank weapons sufficient to equip two division equivalents, though much of this was either in storage or parceled out haphazardly among the various units.

The Syrians had two tank divisions and other units in Lebanon, totaling about 50,000 men and 600 tanks. In the central Bekaa Valley area, PLO concentrations were shielded by Syrian forward elements.

On the coast, major PLO camps near Tyre were enveloped by a small Israeli amphibious landing and units moving up from Galilee on 6 June. That evening, a larger amphibious force landed at Sidon and began the isolation of trapped PLO formations, sending detachments north to Damour on the coast and inland to push PLO defenders into the mountains, while fresh units coming up the coastal highway bypassed PLO camps that were left to mop-up crews. The latter had to stalk PLO fighters in street fighting in the camps, attempting to avoid hitting civilians interspersed with and often indistinguishable from the PLO militia. The militia generally gave a good account of themselves, though fighters in the uniformed "regular" units often fled after their officers shed their uniforms and melted away.

A central column entered the "pivot" at the bend of the Litani River, heights that commanded roads north and west, a vital crossroads from which the coast could be reinforced through Nabatiye and other units sent north along the key Arsouf-Jezzine axis. A small force took Beaufort Castle, a PLO mountaintop observation post that overlooked northern Galilee. The Syrian outposts in the southern Bekaa Valley were quiet, being under constraint not to engage the Israelis unless directly threatened, the PLO plight notwithstanding. For its part, the IDF sought initially to avoid a fight with the Syrians. On the third day, with the western and central columns advancing toward Beirut and the Beirut-Damascus highway, the Israelis decided to move against the Syrians. The IDF/AF moved decisively to take out seventeen of the nineteen SAM batteries in the northern Bekaa, applying advanced electronic countermeasures devised for the task. Dogfights with Syrian MiG-21s and -23s on that day destroyed 29 of the Soviet-built aircraft with no Israeli losses. Another 60 Syrian planes were shot down over the next few days.

At the same time, the Bekaa Valley Group advanced to engage the Syrian 1st Armored Division, facing T-72s for the first time, defeating it in a major tank battle east of Lake Kairouan. The arrival of Syrian reinforcements slowed the Israeli advance. An Israeli-Syrian cease-fire on 11 June left the Syrians bleeding, the PLO inert, and the Israelis within long artillery range of Damascus and closing on Beirut.

The cease-fire applied only to the Bekaa sector, and IDF units in the west continued the encirclement of Beirut through the Shouf hills on the southeast perimeter in the teeth of tenacious PLO-Syrian resistance. Fierce resistance of the PLO in the Ein Hilweh camp near Sidon was bypassed by Israeli armored columns. Other Israeli forces advanced up through the Beirut airport on the south. After a sharp fight near the southeastern quadrant of Beirut, the Israelis linked with Phalangists and closed the ring around Beirut on 12 June.

In renewed fighting south of the Beirut-Damascus road on 22–26 June, the Israelis succeeded in controlling the highway for ten miles east of Beirut. A second cease-fire, this one on 26 June, ended offensive combat operations. Sharon, however, continued to press for his grand strategic solution through siege operations. While American mediator Phillip Habib negotiated the terms of disengagement in Beirut, the IDF and Phalangists surrounding the city sent artillery shells and bombs into the Muslim western half after dropping leaflets urging all noncombatants to evacuate southward via the Israeli-controlled coastal highway. Periodic barrages, air strikes, and utilities stoppages continued for two months amid growing international condemnation of the Israeli siege, unprecedented protest demonstrations in Jerusalem and Tel Aviv, and dissension among the IDF commanders themselves.

The PLO withdrawal and dispersal among several reluctant Arab states was finally arranged at the end of August and was completed by 2 September, when the siege was lifted and an international truce supervisory force entered. The assassination of the newly elected Christian Phalangist president in mid-September prompted the Israelis to cross into Muslim West Beirut on the pretext of protecting Palestinian civilians from the wrath of rioting Christian mobs. The northern front commander was ordered by General Eitan, the chief of staff, to allow Phalangist militia to enter the Sabra and Shatila Palestinian camps in Beirut to root out any PLO combatant remnants. Predictably, the Phalangists indiscriminately slaughtered hundreds of unarmed residents. A chastened and internationally scorned IDF immediately pulled out and was replaced by the international force. A commission of inquiry several months later placed indirect blame for the massacre upon War Minister Sharon, Chief of Staff Eitan, and Prime Minister Menachem Begin, all of whom either resigned or were relieved of their positions.

The Israeli army left an occupation force in the area of Southern Lebanon controlled by the allied Christian Southern Lebanese Army. Its presence, as well as the overreach of the 1982 invasion, drew the wrath of Muslim and Druze fighting factions that had at first applauded Israeli actions against their unwelcome PLO neighbors. These former friends began their own resistance struggle against the Israelis and their Phalangist surrogates. The financial and human cost of continued occupation forced the Israelis to withdraw from all save a strip of southern Lebanon within the year, leaving a fractious and evermore hostile neighbor to their north and the Syrians in firmer control than before. Though operationally impressive, the deceit that the defense minister and chief of staff exercised toward both the cabinet and their field commanders obscures the "lessons." On balance, the 1982 war marks a low point for vaunted Israeli purity of arms.

JAMES J. BLOOM

SEE ALSO: History, Modern Military.

Bibliography

Adan, A. 1980. *On the banks of the Suez*. Novato, Calif.: Presidio Press.

Barker, A. J. 1980. *Arab-Israeli wars*. New York: Hippocrene Books.

Bloom, J. J. 1982. From the Litani to Beirut: A brief strategic assessment of Israel's operations in Lebanon, 1978–1982. *Middle East Insight*, November/December.

———. 1983. Six days plus ten weeks war. *Middle East Insight*, January/February.

Cordesman, A. H., and A. R. Wagner. 1990. *The lessons of modern war*. Volume I: *The Arab-Israeli conflicts, 1973–1989*. Boulder, Colo.: Westview Press.

Dayan, M. 1966. *Diary of the Sinai campaign*. New York: Harper and Row.

Dupuy, T. N. 1984. *Elusive victory: The Arab-Israeli wars, 1947–1974*. Fairfax, Va.: HERO Books.

Dupuy, T. N., and P. Martell. 1985. *Flawed victory: The Arab-Israeli conflict and the 1982 war in Lebanon*. Vienna, Va.: HERO Books.

Eshel, D. 1989. *Chariots of the desert: The story of the Israeli armored corps*. London: Brassey's.

Gawrych, G. 1990. *Key to the Sinai: The battles for Abu Ageila in the 1956 and 1967 Arab–Israeli wars*. Fort Leavenworth, Kans.: U.S. Army Command and General Staff College.

Herzog, C. 1984. *The Arab-Israeli wars*. Rev. ed. New York: Vintage Books.

Lorch, N. 1961. *The edge of the sword: Israel's war for independence*. New York: Putnam.

———. 1976. *One long war*. Jerusalem: Keter.

Marshall, S. L. A. 1958. *Sinai victory*. New York: William Morrow.

Safran, N. 1969. *From war to war*. New York: Pegasus.

———. 1981. *Israel: The embattled ally*. Cambridge: Harvard Univ. Press.

Schiff, Z. 1985. *A history of the Israeli army: 1874 to the present*. New York: Macmillan.

Young, P. 1968. *The Israeli campaign 1967*. London: Kimber.

ARDANT DU PICQ, CHARLES JEAN JACQUES JOSEPH [1821–70]

Charles J. J. J. Ardant du Picq was a French soldier and military theorist of the mid-nineteenth century whose writings, as they were later interpreted by other theorists, had a great effect on French military theory and doctrine.

Life and Career

Ardant du Picq was born at Périgueux in the Dordogne on 19 October 1821. On 1 October 1844, upon graduation from the Ecole de St. Cyr, he was commissioned a sublieutenant in the 67th Regiment of Line Infantry. As a captain, he saw action in the French expedition to Varna (April–June 1853) during the Crimean War, but he fell ill and was shipped home. Upon recovery, he rejoined his regiment in front of Sevastopol (September). Transferred to the 9th Chasseurs à Pied battalion (December 1854), he was captured during the storming of the central bastion of Sevastopol in September 1855. He was released in December 1855 and returned to active duty. As a major with the 16th Chasseur battalion, Ardant du Picq served in Syria from August 1860 to June 1861 during the French intervention to restore order during Maronite-Druze sectarian violence. Like virtually all his peers, he also saw extensive service in Algeria (1864–66), and in February 1869 was appointed colonel of the 10th Regiment of Line Infantry. He was in France at the outbreak of war with Prussia on 15 July 1870 and took command of his regiment. He was killed leading his troops at the Battle of Borny, near Metz, on 15 August 1870.

Military Theorist and Author

Ardant du Picq's fame rests more with his writings than with his martial exploits. By the time of his death, he had already published *Combat antique* (*Ancient Battle*), which was later expanded from his manuscripts into the classic *Etudes sur les combat: Combat antique et moderne*, often referred to by its common English title as *Battle Studies*. This work was published in part in 1880; the complete text did not appear until 1902.

Although comparatively little is known of his life, his small corpus of writings has earned him a place in the ranks of the great military analysts. His principal interest was in the moral and psychological aspects of battle; as he himself wrote of the battlefields of his day: "The soldier is unknown often to his closest companions. He loses them in the disorienting smoke and confusion of a battle which he is fighting, so to speak, on his own. Cohesion is no longer ensured by mutual observation." Nor did Ardant du Picq neglect the decisive importance of modern firepower, noting that it was necessary for the attacker to "employ fire up till the last possible moment; otherwise, given modern rates of fire, no attack will reach its objective." Despite these words, much of his work was later used to help justify the unfortunate doctrine of the *offensive à l'outrance*, put forward principally by Colonel Grandmaison.

Assessment

In sum, Ardant du Picq was a talented analyst and, had he lived, would have gained a fine reputation as a military historian. His analyses stressed the vital importance, especially in contemporary warfare, of discipline and unit cohesion. With Karl von Clausewitz, he was one of the first military analysts to pay particular attention to psychological and behavioral factors in combat.

DAVID L. BONGARD

SEE ALSO: Clausewitz, Karl von; History, Modern Military.

Bibliography

Ardant du Picq, C. J. J. J. 1942. *Etudes sur les combat: Combat antique et moderne.*
     Paris: N.p.
——. 1921. *Battle studies: Ancient and modern battle.* Trans. J. M. Greely and R. C.
     Cotton. Harrisburg, Pa.: Military Service.
Porch, D. 1981. *The march to the Marne.* Cambridge: Cambridge Univ. Press.
Possony, S. T., and E. Mantoux. 1943. Du Picq and Foch: The French school. In
     Makers of modern strategy, ed. E. M. Earle, et al. Princeton, N.J.: Princeton
     Univ. Press.
Snyder, J. 1984. *The cult of the offensive in European war planning, 1870–1914.* Ithaca,
     N.Y.: Cornell Univ. Press.

ARMED FORCES AND SOCIETY

The term *armed forces and society* summarizes the complex relationship that
exists between military organizations and social systems, while the term *armed
forces* relates to just the organized groups that are involved in the managed
application of violence. Since the former term refers to regular and irregular
military organizations and standing armies as well as voluntary or auxiliary
formations, it is wider in its coverage than the term *armed services*, which
applies specifically and exclusively to those institutions and organizations that
are part of the state. The concept of "society" is also more extensive in scope
than the notion of the "state," for while armed forces are, as a rule, national
instruments, they are also an international type of social institution, the characteristics, structure, and functions of which transcend political boundaries.

General Characteristics

Although the study of armed forces over the centuries has created an extensive
literature of military science and history, specific interest in the analysis of the
relationship between those forces and the parent society is of more recent
origin. Two contributions that were prepared in the 1930s provide a multidis-
ciplinary approach to the study of the field. The first of these major works was
Karl Demeter's pioneer study, *Das Deutsche Heer und Seine Offiziere.* This
constituted the first extensive and major historico-sociological research on a
specific group of military personnel. It drew heavily on both historical and
sociological methodology even though its sociological stance was more implicit
than explicitly formulated. Nevertheless, the sociological theory that is used is
an important contribution to study in this field, for it is a development of Max
Weber's brilliant and penetrating analysis of military institutions. In the same
way that this theory has had a continuing impact on the social scientific community, the work of Demeter is also a valuable commentary on Alfred Vagt's
The History of Militarism, which appeared in 1937 and which offered a clear
and noteworthy distinction between "militarism" and the "military way."

In his classic study of the German officer corps, Demeter meticulously laid down the framework of much subsequent research into the social origins, education, and career development of an elite group. This later research owed a very considerable debt to the earlier work. It is no exaggeration to conclude that Demeter's study was the prototype for a whole generation of more elaborate and more explicitly sociological analysis of military professionals, professionalism, and professionalization. At the same time, Demeter recognized that the military professional is also an armed bureaucrat who works in a highly structured organization. The emphasis that is increasingly placed on the more systematic application of organizational theory to this field reflects the evolution of this analysis of the military profession and the military organization as one of the most developed aspects of the study of armed forces and society.

In the second area—that of civil-military relations—the genesis of much subsequent study was the publication in 1941 of Harold D. Lasswell's classic essay, "The Garrison State." Drawing on his earlier conceptual statements, Lasswell refined the analysis of the dangers of militarism in an advanced industrialized society that was subject to a sustained threat of war. His basic hypothesis completely rejected earlier notions of military dictatorship, for he argued that militarization and militarism in these advanced societies could not be—and would not be—characterized by direct rule by military elites. Rather, it would be identified by expansion of the military into those political roles that are traditionally held by civilian elites. The trend of the time, he argued, was away from the dominance of the specialist on bargaining—the businessman— toward the supremacy of the soldier as the specialist in the application of violence.

This general study of society and social systems expanded rapidly in the 1940s and early 1950s, particularly in the United States. During World War II and immediately afterward, social scientists began a critical examination of the military system. In *The American Soldier*, S. A. Stouffer and his colleagues produced a classic study of combat behavior, morale, and buddy relationships under stress. This complemented other work that looked at the contribution of the primary group to the maintenance of military cohesion. This type of research paralleled the interest shown by social scientists, on the basis of their experience, on the concept of the military as an ideal-type bureaucratic organization. One important study, S. Andreski's *Military Organization and Society*, was a major contribution to the analysis from a general perspective of the relationship between armed forces and society. This introduced the concept of the military participation ratio (MPR)—that is, the ratio of military-utilized individuals to the total population—as an indicator of postulated changes in the structure of the parent society. Even so, specific interest in the further analysis of the relationship between armed forces and that society did not truly develop until the late 1950s.

The most significant development was the publication of two major studies, one by Samuel Huntington and one by Morris Janowitz. These studies share a common overall perspective, for they both stress the concept that the military career-officer is a member of a profession that possesses certain characteristics which contribute to effectiveness and responsibilities. However, it is the difference between these two theorists that highlights the conceptual and problematic questions associated with the study of armed forces and society.

In *The Soldier and the State*, Huntington argues that military officership is a fully developed profession because it manifests, to a significant degree, three principal characteristics of the ideal type of professional model: expertise, corporateness, and responsibility. The military, however, carries out its purpose within a political environment without regard to political, moral, or other nonmilitary considerations, so its professionalism can be summarized as its expertise over lethal violence, a corporate self-identity, and ultimate responsibility to the larger polity.

According to Huntington, only officers involved in and dedicated to the central expertise of the management of violence are members of the military profession. This implies that neither commissioned specialists such as lawyers and doctors nor enlisted personnel can be typed as military professionals. Furthermore, the characteristics of the latter are derived from and are shaped by the content and function of the military task. Thus, the professional officer is, above all, obedient and loyal to the authority of the state, competent in military expertise, dedicated to using his skill to provide for the security of the state, and politically and morally neutral. His sense of professional commitment is shaped by a military ethic that reflects a carefully inculcated set of values and attitudes. These are seen to constitute a unique professional outlook or military mind that may be characterized as pessimistic, collectivist, historically inclined, power-oriented, nationalistic, militaristic, pacifist, and instrumentalist—in short, realistic and conservative. Huntington approaches the analysis of the relationship between armed forces and society from the perspective of interest group politics. Civil-military relations constitute a subsystem of a pluralistic political system; the nub of most problems of civil-military relations, accordingly, is the issue of the relative power of the armed forces and other groups within society. Huntington suggests that the more professionalized the officer corps, the more likely it is to be an efficient and politically neutral instrument of state policy. The dominant political beliefs affect the nature of this relationship. Huntington argues that a conservative ideology (rather than a liberal, fascist, or Marxist one) is most compatible with the military ethic and professionalism.

This widely read and influential text was complemented in 1960 by the publication of Morris Janowitz's seminal work, *The Professional Soldier*. In common with Huntington, Janowitz was concerned with the critical issue of the subordination of the military to the duly elected government. He, however, treated the military as a social system in which the professional characteristics of the officer corps change over time. They are variable in that they encompass norms and skills, including, but also going beyond, the direct management of violence. While he specifies the characteristics that make officership a profession—expertise, lengthy education, group identity, ethics, standards of performance—he identifies the profession not as a static model but as a dynamic bureaucratic organization that changes over time in response to changing conditions. This recognizes the extent to which the form of existing military organizations and professionalized officer corps has been shaped since the turn of the century by the impact of broad social transformations. This implies that armed forces are experiencing a long-term transformation toward convergence with civilian structures and norms. It can be hypothesized that as a result of broad social changes, the basis of authority and discipline in the armed forces has shifted to manipulation and consensus; military skills have become more socially representative; membership of the elite has become more open and the ideology of the profession has become more political. As a result of this, the traditional heroic warrior role has given way to an ascendant managerial-technical role. In short, the military profession as a whole has become similar to large, bureaucratic, nonmilitary institutions. It has, in effect, become "civilianized."

The Military Community

A common feature in this research is the emphasis placed on the significance of the military community. Armed forces are something more than a bureaucratic organization. They are not simply "General Motors in Uniform." Their characteristics as a profession resemble those of other occupational groups claiming this status, but they also uniquely reflect the nature of the military task. Armed forces form a community that unites the work and life of its members much more completely than do most other social organizations. Within this milieu, two distinctive lifestyles can be identified. That of officers is characterized by a ceremonialism that is a heritage of the long historical traditions of officership. Seen by its critics to be anachronistic, this military style of life is expected to enhance group cohesion, encourage professional loyalty, and maintain martial spirit. Political indoctrination is effective in this milieu because of the relatively closed community environment in which military officers continue to work and live.

The community life of enlisted men is very different. The distinction between officers and men is visibly reflected in differences in uniforms and insignia. It is seen in differences in remuneration and types of accommodation. Socially, greater privileges and status are attached to officership. Although gradations in the lifestyle of enlisted personnel can be made between noncommissioned officers (NCOs) and privates, the separation of officers and enlisted personnel is most marked. This is particularly noticeable with reference to recruitment, socialization, rights, and privileges (Moskos and Wood 1988). Although the increased recruitment of women into national armed forces has modified traditional customs and mores, the characteristics of the exclusively male combat unit constitute the archetypal image of this military community. With its distinctive subculture, characterized by a distinctive language and a strongly developed informal organization, socialization and life in this tightly knit occupational community produce a self-image that reflects its self-sufficiency.

The Military Bureaucracy

Armed forces constitute a purposive organization. The formal structure of the military closely resembles the classic model of bureaucracy described by Weber. Since the primary function of armed forces is the effective management and application of violence, an organizational form is required that is designed to do this effectively and the defining characteristics of bureaucracy—hierarchy of command, impersonality, precision, routine, and regulations—are seen to ensure this. This is particularly so when these qualities can be linked to an emphasis on the importance of patterns of traditional authority. The creation of a bureaucratic structure with a formal, highly detailed, and often monolithic body of rules and regulations also recognizes the presence within armed forces of a specialized division of labor. From a very early point in the historical development of armed forces, the training of the military man as a multiskilled generalist was paralleled by the evolution of the military specialist. This encourages the development of armed forces as bureaucracies, many features of which are also to be found in civilian organizations. Theories of military organization are, therefore, closely related to general theories of sociology. For all the romance, ritual, and history associated with the regiment, ship, or air squadron, the military is a rational-legal institution in which the structure of power and authority closely resembles that of other large-scale organizations. As in any other bureaucracy, the principle of hierarchy prevails. The office guarantees that the individual will enjoy all the authority associated with his rank. The military, however, now faces the major problem of bringing this traditional authority into line with technological developments that have materially affected ways of waging war.

In the past, the authority structure widely associated with the military was that of a rigid hierarchy of command. The model was simple. The principle of hierarchy rested on a broad base of basically unskilled enlisted men under the command of an officer who was aided by a few trusted noncommissioned officers who put his orders into practice. At each successive echelon or rank grade, there was an officer of higher rank who directed several more or less functionally similar units. This created the traditional hierarchical pyramid that is a defining characteristic of all bureaucracies.

The introduction of new weaponry and increasingly sophisticated technology materially affected this structure. Many enlisted men—and women—possess vital skills not easily replaced. This can give rise to major questions about their reluctance to accept orders solely on the basis of the authority of rank of the person from whom such orders emanate. This is very noticeable if such orders should be seen to go contrary to their own technical judgment. The diverse components that nowadays come under the direction of even a unit commander often exceed the technical competence of the officer in command. To direct them effectively he is therefore forced to rely on the knowledge of others, either from within his own unit or from a technical expert attached to a higher staff. Dependence on highly technical knowledge at ever lower echelons gives the technical staff officers a set of informal roles in which they enjoy considerable de facto authority, resolving problems outside the regular command channels and frequently without the knowledge of the commanding officer. Such deviation from "correct" procedures may be widely condoned. Thus, many relatively junior officers exercise authority to which they are entitled neither by their rank nor by their formal position in the hierarchy. This implies that too precise an adherence to hierarchical channels will discourage this type of informal communication among officers sharing responsibility for a mission.

The issues that are implicit in this debate can be seen more clearly in the wider discussion of the difficulties of introducing innovation into military organizations. Armed forces are traditionally held to distinguish between *structural* innovation and *operational* innovation. The former may be more readily accepted because it supports the quest for certainty about the internal and external environment. By contrast, dismantlement of one weapon system in favor of a new one always has a destabilizing effect on military organization, and the remote and uncertain advantages promised by their adoption in peacetime must always be balanced against the costs and disruptions of change of any sort. Hence, in the past, armies have almost invariably gone into battle with strategic concepts and weapons whose only improvement over those used in the previous war consisted of the elimination of obvious deficiencies. Such generalized resistance to new weapons is shown by the unwillingness to motorize the cavalry, to switch from battleship to carrier, and to give up the bomber in favor of missiles.

In view of the current emphasis both armed forces and the parent society place on weapons development, the problem of introducing major innovations into the military is of critical importance. There are some indications that despite their comparative willingness to accept structural changes and notwithstanding their innate organizational advantages, armed forces lag behind comparable civilian organizations in their ability to innovate. And it can be argued that, despite a heavy commitment to research and development, change in the military cannot be readily effected other than in peripheral matters. If, therefore, military organizations continue to insist on some outmoded structural forms, there must be some reason.

To begin with, investing structural means with a special sanctity is a feature of military organizations. Individuals everywhere who hold authority and responsibility fear being bypassed by subordinates. In addition, however, there are some specific factors within the military that encourage adherence to some routines, even after their utility has been questioned. Clear channels and routinized procedures are thus thought to help reduce uncertainty. They are considered to create a sense of confidence that during a crisis officers and soldiers at all levels of the organization will respond in accordance with their training. The second factor that inhibits the introduction of innovation is the tendency of every military institution to build its routines on the normal and its expectations on the expected. This being so, there can be no adequate test of the appropriateness of many military practices short of actual war.

The Military Professional

Traditionally, the term *military professional* referred to those soldiers whose lifetime career in the armed forces contrasted markedly with the lesser commitment of the citizen soldier, reservist, or auxiliary volunteer. Today, it also means that a member of the armed forces has characteristics in common with others who identify themselves with the professional self-image: doctors, lawyers, priests, accountants, and so on. It is, however, very evident that the military self-image predates the evolution in the nineteenth century of other occupational groups claiming professional status. Accordingly, while many of the characteristics of that early military self-image were adopted without change by those groups, others remain uniquely military. The degree of collegiality that is implicit, for example, in the notion of officership is not replicated in other occupations. The traditions of the officers' mess, the willing acceptance of a code of ethics, the retention of a sense of honor, and so on, emphasize the uniqueness of this form of professionalism. Not unexpectedly, therefore, the concept of the profession of arms is traditionally associated with officers and not enlisted personnel. This can be readily rationalized. The particular set of values and attitudes that makes up the professional ethos is seen to be most prevalent among commissioned officers, is rarely to be found among noncommissioned officers, and is thought not to exist among enlisted men.

Increasingly, however, this traditional image of the military profession is under critical review. There are two particular developments. First, armed forces are a unique example of the total fusion of profession and organization. Since the military professional can only be employed within the structure of the total institution, many of the characteristics of the ideal type are modified. As the organization becomes increasingly bureaucratized, these characteristics begin to change very markedly. Expertise becomes skill; the commitment of the professional to the client is recast as the subordination of the soldier to the government of the day; professional responsibility is confused with organizational loyalty; collegiality conflicts with the rigid hierarchy of formal rank. For many members of the military, this change to the traditional military image is the source of considerable personal stress and occupational strain. This is particularly marked among those whose perception of the armed forces recognizes that the military is more than just an organization.

A second development encourages a shift away from the traditional professional model of the military toward an occupational model. The concept of the professional soldier has never been static. Over time, a number of significant changes have transformed the officer corps from a group of part-time employed, neo-feudal soldiers to a well-educated, technologically competent, and managerially trained group of experts recruited on the basis of their achievement and skill. As part of this transformation, there has been a shift away from the concept of the soldier as the professional working within an institutional format to one that resembles more and more an occupational ideal type.

In the institutional model, the military profession is legitimized in terms of its values and norms. Self-interest is subservient to a presumed higher good.

Membership in the armed forces is seen to be a vocation in which a paternalistic remuneration system based on rank and seniority may not be comparable with marketplace trends. The high status enjoyed by the military is, however, some compensation for employment conditions and the dangers inherent in combat. In the occupational model, the military career is defined in terms of the marketplace. The cash-work nexus implies a priority of self-interest that contrasts markedly with the traditional preference for community interest. The military professional is now seen to be no different from any other worker in terms of the attitudes and values that are projected.

An alternative approach sheds doubt on the efficacy of this model as an indicator of the dimensions of change within the military organization. This argues that institution and occupation are not opposite poles in a comparable dimension but are really two relatively autonomous positions, the developmental trends of which may well be in the same direction. This does not reflect a zero-sum situation; rather, it draws attention to the utility of the concept of pragmatic professionalism as a measure of institutional and occupational concerns. The central feature of this interpretation of military professionalism is the conclusion that the military is essentially a bureaucratic profession. Here, the fusion of profession and organization is most evident. The introduction of unions into the military is a case in point. Traditionally, the absence of trade unions within armed forces, other than for civilian employees, seemingly confirmed the validity of the institutional model. Linked to the innate conservatism of armed forces and their tendency to promote a traditional self-image that was heavily dependent on established norms and values, this rejection of unionization implied an extreme stance. Yet the gradual introduction of military unions into the organization did not lead to the loss or replacement of the unique features of the military organization. Many military unions resemble professional associations rather than civilian trade unions. Although there has been a change in the basis of authority and discipline in the military establishment by virtue of a shift from authoritarian domination to greater reliance on manipulation, persuasion, and group consensus, it has not gone as far as it has in civilian organizations. The armed services in industrialized and many developing nations remain a highly professionalized and distinctive social organization. In some instances, however, armed forces do not attain this status. Guerrilla units, for example, are noticeably distinctive social organizations with well-developed cohesion and ideology, but they do not fall into the category of highly professionalized organizations.

Originally, the issue of recruitment was of significance solely in terms of the numbers inducted into the military. Subsequently, it was important because of the level of professionalism associated with entry into the armed forces. The types of people who were recruited provide valuable information on changes in social composition and in the motivation of personnel. The issue was also important since, as the officer corps became more socially representative and more heterogeneous, it became difficult to maintain organizational effectiveness. In addition, the recruitment process was of fundamental significance because it provided the means to continue the organization's existence.

For many years, a major issue in industrialized countries was the debate about the legitimacy and potential effectiveness of a system of universal conscription or national service as a means of recruitment, as opposed to a selective service system in which lotteries, appeals to local draft boards, and the like meant that only a fraction of those potentially liable to conscription were actually inducted. Extensive sociological studies were complemented by perceptive analyses of the economic advantages and disadvantages of conscription. In the United States, however, the end of the war in Vietnam and the concomitant cessation of the draft meant that the major issue became that of the problematic nature of recruitment into an all-volunteer force (AVF). This led very naturally to an evaluation of the probable social composition of an all-volunteer force in the United States. Two conflicting schools of thought could be identified. One viewpoint, influential at top American policy-making levels, argued that with proper monetary inducements an all-volunteer force could be recruited that would in general terms be representative of the larger society. The opposite view held that an all-volunteer force, especially in the ground combat arms, would grossly overrepresent less well educated and minority groups.

Outside the United States, much of this debate reflected a specific rather than universal management problem. Few issues could be readily identified as methodological and conceptual questions that were of more than local interest. One of these, however, is the emotional issue of the role of women in armed forces. This has a wider importance than the basic question of the general problems of recruitment into the contemporary military organization. Three questions of critical import can be identified. First, there is the major issue of the identification and evaluation of the role of women in the military organization. Second, there is an increasing awareness of the effect upon organizational issues of enhanced recruitment of female personnel: relative costs, problems of socialization, morale and attrition rates, and fundamental questions of operational effectiveness. The third issue, in common with much research into the complex area of race relations and ethnicity in armed forces, is more concerned with the societal implications of changing established and traditional manpower policies. In this context the issue is not simply the technical competence of women soldiers. Nor is it solely a question of the impact that the recruitment of women has had on the organizational effectiveness of the military. Rather, the critical area of interest is part of a more general concern with the implications for society of contemporary manpower changes within the military organization.

To a very great extent, the crux of these manpower issues is the fundamental problem of recruiting an adequate number of suitably qualified personnel. This is linked not only to immediate questions of cost but also to more fundamental issues of social policy. Maintaining the armed forces is a classic example of choice under uncertainty. It involves politicians in choices about the desirable size and composition of various budgets. This in turn encourages a welfare-warfare controversy in which the competing claims of the military and civil sectors of society have to be judged. For some countries, the choice is between guns and butter. Since the military is a heavy user of material and human resources, the creation of large and expensive armed forces prevents the development of other parts of the social system. This trend may be justified if the military makes a qualitative and quantitative contribution to the creation and perpetuation of innovation. This modernizing role is rationalized on the grounds that the military is the most modern institution in a country, that its leaders are the most effective managers, that military socialization most readily transmits culture, and that it serves as the symbol of nationhood. Such justification is less rational in those industrialized countries where the choice is more dichotomized as welfare or warfare.

The problem is particularly acute when the scarce resource is that of manpower. When faced with this problem, governments have traditionally adopted one of five options. First, some relied heavily on conscription as a means of bringing into the military organization an adequate number of recruits. Alternatively, in adopting an all-volunteer force structure, governments depended on a whole variety of motivating factors, ranging from market forces to appeals to patriotism, as a means of meeting manpower targets. Third, smaller and, it can be argued, less vulnerable states in the West created military structures based on the notion of the "citizen-soldier," which is the assumption that a small cadre of professional soldiers could be readily supplemented in time of emergency by civilian reservists. A fourth option, in contrast, depended for its effectiveness not on the mass availability of manpower but on substitution policies that replaced men with machines. Finally, governments continually used their preferences for compromise solutions to devise mixed strategies that combined one or more of these options.

Military Effectiveness

Initially, the effectiveness of a military organization is linked to the suitability of its organizational structure. The simple system of organization, which is adequate for peacetime operations, is transformed in time of conflict into a complex form capable of responding to the exigencies of wartime. Effective combat performance is thought to result from the effective operation of the formal military organization. This includes positive military leadership, discipline, and the esprit de corps of the military formation. Military effectiveness is also defined in terms of combat effectiveness. Many studies of the latter originated during the course of World War II. These stressed that a key explanation of such effectiveness was the solidarity and social cohesion of military personnel at the small-group level. In the abnormal situation of combat, men from different socioeconomic backgrounds, of different ethnic origins and lifestyles are expected to unify as a single fighting unit. Individual and group performance in terms of courage, discipline, enthusiasm, and willingness to endure is initially very dependent on the solidarity of the small group with whom the individual identifies. Cohesion can be identified with the peer relationships that occur within the primary group. Participant observation in Korea suggested that while the basic unit of cohesion in World War II followed squad or platoon boundaries, this had changed to the two-man or "buddy" relationship. Subsequent operations indicated that the "brick" or four-man patrol was the smallest effective subdivision. In all instances, this horizontal cohesion or peer bonding is associated with a common sense of mission within a specific technical proficiency, a deep appreciation of the importance of team-work, and a reliance on mutual trust, respect, and friendship.

It is complemented by other forms of bonding. Vertical cohesion involves the relationship within the organization of enlisted personnel, noncommissioned officers, and officers. This comprises not only formal military authority but also more subtle features of leadership such as concern, example, trust, and sharing of risks, which transcend the officially laid down bureaucratic hierarchy. Or-ganizational cohesion, in contrast, stresses the importance of normative con-cepts of tradition, patriotism, valor, heroism, nationhood, and ideology; these bond the individual soldier or officer to the subunit within the broader context of the military system. These explanations of combat motivation, originating in the social science studies of World War II, tend to de-emphasize ideological considerations. The attention they give to the role of face-to-face or primary groups in formulating the motivation of the individual stresses that this moti-vation is a function of his solidarity and social intimacy with fellow soldiers at small-group levels. An alternative explanation, however, finds combat motiva-tion resting on the presumed national character of the general populace. The varying effectiveness of different national armies has often been popularly as-cribed to the putative martial spirit of their respective citizenries. The use of national-character explanations of military effectiveness, however, is not unique to popular folklore. In recent American history, certain prominent spokesmen invoked such broad cultural determinants to explain the allegedly poor perfor-mance of American prisoners of war in the Korean War. All of this can be seen, in part, as cultural cohesion—that is, the relationship of the military and the individual to society at large. An increasingly important aspect of this is the willingness of a society to support the military system it has established. Some of this support will be reflected in the size of the national defense budget; some will be linked to the expressed preference for a conscript or all-volunteer military force. All will reflect the extent to which armed forces are recognized by society as a reflection of the norms, values, mores, and cultural ethos of that society.

Civil-Military Relations

The term *civil-military relations* summarizes the complex network of political interests that exists between the various branches of the military and the var-ious sectors of civilian society. Traditionally, the doctrine of civil-military re-lations presumes a series of checks and balances. Armed forces are identified as the managers of violence; civil power on the other hand exercises political control over the military. This democratic model of civil-military relations en-sures that the civilian and military elites are sharply differentiated, for the civilian political elites exercise control over the military through a formal set of rules that ensures the objective control of the armed forces. This model is seen not as a reflection of historical reality but rather as an objective of governmental policy. It contrasts markedly with an aristocratic model where the civilian and military elites are socially and functionally integrated. The narrow base of recruitment for both elites and the presence of a relatively monolithic power structure combine to provide for the comprehensive subjective control of the military. It is also different from a totalitarian model in which political regimes manipulate a whole series of control mechanisms to ensure the politicization of military personnel. It can also be distinguished from the garrison state model, which identifies the rise to power of the military elite under conditions of prolonged international tension.

The contemporary preference for the ideology of the democratic model is most marked. Even so, the dangers inherent in the perception of civil-military relations are not ignored. The danger of praetorianism is very real. Praetorianism characterizes a situation in which the military elite within a society exercises independent political power by virtue of an actual or theoretical use of force. In terms of organization and coherence, armed forces possess many advantages over comparable civilian organizations. Centralization, a hierarchy of authority, discipline, a communications network, and a commonly accepted ethos indicate that the military is more highly organized than civilian bodies. A concern with order, which stems from the function of armed forces as crisis organizations, encourages the development of hyperbureaucratization. This ensures that armed forces are not only the most highly organized association but are also a continuing corporation with an intense sentiment of solidarity.

This power makes it possible for armed forces to intervene in the domain of the civil authority and, under certain conditions, to supplant that authority. Whether the military will have the motive or, indeed, the opportunity to so intervene will depend on a number of complex factors. In some countries, the tendency of armed forces to intervene, the motive to intervene, and the opportunity to intervene are such that the military coup d'état is an almost endemic feature of political life. This is not a new phenomenon. In the nineteenth century, many European and Latin American countries were plagued by coups. In the present day, military intervention frequently occurs in the states that have won their freedom from colonial domination. This is especially noticeable where the civilian government cannot assert its legitimacy, or where such a government is ineffective. In the latter case, the military represents a relatively efficient and stable instrument of power.

Once power has been seized, the ability of the armed forces to continue in office and to govern efficiently invites critical evaluation. Notwithstanding their structural and organizational advantages, armed forces have little technical ability to administer the complex modern state. The demands of a sophisticated economy, the promotion of schemes of social welfare, the need for a highly developed division of labor, and the wish to ensure the effective management of innovation favor the employment of civilian technicians and bureaucrats. Tasks such as resource allocation, the provision of specialized skills, and the need to respond to "civilian" problems create cross-pressures for armed forces. It may be possible for a military organization to respond to these pressures through enhanced internal differentiation. Alternatively, a valid response may result in the creation of specialized units, either on an ad hoc basis or as part of a more regular plan of activity. A third solution, however, is for the military to cooperate more and more with civilian agencies.

A more major and persistent critical issue is the legitimization of the military's claim to remain in power. Following a military coup, the questions that ultimately arise are: How is the intervention in politics to be legitimized? And to whom can the military look in search of legitimacy? In rare instances, the legitimacy of armed forces is unquestioned. The military is uniquely identified with the national interest. Armed forces are seen to be the origin of the independent nation-state and the last bastion of nationhood. Armies are not merely part of the administrative bureaucracy. Their claim to a monopoly of arms gives them a special status that enables them to symbolize, as well as make effective, the distinctive identity of the state. From this point of view, no other national institution so symbolizes independence, sovereignty, or equality with other peoples as a country's armed forces. Armed forces are the synthesis of the nation and the purest image of the state. Their power is legitimate, because it is based on an authority exercised in the establishment and maintenance of goals that are defined in terms of the basic needs of the state.

In most cases, the claim of the military to effective and general legitimacy is less easily established. True legitimacy can only be ensured by the transfer from direct military rule to various types of civilian rule. There are two major modes of transfer: abdication and civilianization. In the former, armed forces willingly or unwillingly hand back the reins of power to the civilian elite; in the latter, the military elite itself becomes civilianized. In both instances the pattern of civil-military relations recognizes that true legitimacy exists only when the respective political roles of the military and civil elite can be sharply differentiated. Even the special relationships between the military and industry that are implicit in the controversial term *military-industrial complex* do not weaken this preference for the distinctiveness of those political roles.

Future Developments

The traditional interpretation of the concept of armed forces and society draws heavily on historical models. These were very well established in Western society. The pattern of relationships that evolved from the seventeenth century onward was not only accepted in Western Europe; it was exported overseas and retained by new nations as they gained independence. The basis of the relationship was the role and function of the military in two distinct but related areas. First, armed forces were seen to have the major objectives of protecting the state from an external aggressor and the promotion of its political interests through the coercion of other states. Second, the legitimate role of the military was identified with the protection of the state from internal threats. This objective included maintaining the duly elected government. Both distinctive external and internal functions represented the formal purpose of the military organization.

Over time, this formal structure has been considerably amended. The domestic function of the military has been extended to include the responsibilities of armed forces as agents of modernization. In many developing countries, the social and political significance of these armed forces as agents of economic development are most marked. A wider analysis of the role of the military in national modernization questions the changes that the intervention of armed forces brings about. Structural and attitudinal changes contrast with the effects of sociodemographic change. The potential for sustained natural growth invites an examination of the quality and quantity of military-sponsored change in terms of economic differentiation, communication, urbanization, and political development. In the latter area, the military's effectiveness invites a particularly critical examination. This reflects the awareness of the major role of armed forces in such areas of political growth and the institutionalization of political organization.

An alternative feature of this future development is the changing role of armed forces in an era of nuclear stalemate and the effect of this change upon traditional interpretations of the relationship between armed forces and society. The use of force as an instrument of foreign policy has been so changed that the future role of the military can be identified with the constabulary concept. While this provides a continuity with the past experience of armed forces, it reflects a radical interpretation of future military purpose. The military establishment is seen to become a constabulary force where it is always prepared to act and committed to the minimum use of force. Its goal is the attainment of satisfactory international relations rather than victory, and it incorporates a protective military position (Janowitz 1960). When the trend toward the internationalization of these constabulary forces is added to this adoption of a pragmatic doctrine, the traditional perception of the relationship between a military organization and the parent society is much altered. Nevertheless, for the moment, the complex relationship between armed forces and the parent society persists. Change in the internal dynamic of the military organization will be inevitable; society will reflect, in its attitudes toward the military, the impact of altered norms and values. Armed forces and society, however, will continue to be an important element of a necessary and realistic public discussion about the control of an all-powerful purposeful organization.

GWYN HARRIES-JENKINS

Bibliography

Andreski, S. 1954. *Military organization and society*. London: Routledge and Kegan Paul.

Demeter, K. 1935. *Das Deutsche Heer und Seine Offiziere*. Berlin: Verlag von Reimar Hobbing.

Edmonds, M. 1988. *Armed services and society*. Leicester: Leicester Univ. Press.

Harries-Jenkins, G. 1977. *The army in Victorian society*. London: Routledge and Kegan Paul.

————, and C. C. Moskos. 1981. Armed forces and society. *Current Sociology* 29:1–170.

Huntington, S. P. 1957. *The soldier and the state: The theory and politics of civil-military relations.* Cambridge, Mass.: Harvard Univ. Press.

Janowitz, M. 1960. *The professional soldier.* New York: Free Press.

————. 1977. *Military institutions and coercion in the developing nations.* Chicago: Univ. of Chicago Press.

Lasswell, H. D. 1941. The garrison state. *American Journal of Sociology* 46:455–68.

Moskos, C. C., Jr., and Frank R. Wood, eds. 1988. *The military—More than just a job?* McLean, Va.: Pergamon-Brassey's.

Stouffer, S. A., et al. 1949. *The American soldier.* Princeton, N.J.: Princeton Univ. Press.

Van Doorn, J. 1975. *The soldier and social change.* Beverly Hills, Calif.: Sage.

ARNOLD, H. H. ("HAP") [1886–1950]

"Hap" Arnold played a vital role in the history of United States military air-power (Fig. 1). As chief of the U.S. Army Air Forces during World War II, he established the doctrinal patterns and organizational structures that influenced the U.S. Air Force for many years subsequently.

The Emergence of Air Power

Arnold was born at Gladwyne, Pennsylvania, on 25 June 1886. He entered West Point in 1903 and in 1907, after graduation, he received an infantry assignment. His first post was in the Philippines, where the Army Signal Corps was forming an Aeronautical Division. The new flying machine's obvious potential for observation suggested its assignment to the Signal Corps. Arnold decided to become an aviator.

In 1911, Arnold was assigned to aeronautical duty with the Signal Corps at the Wright Aircraft flying school, Dayton, Ohio. After flight training, he became the 29th pilot licensed in the United States. With a small cadre of airmen, Arnold brought two Wright planes to the College Park, Maryland, airfield. The group trained pilots and mechanics and established a nomenclature for airplane parts. They also experimented with bomb sights and mounting guns on planes and practiced air-to-ground communications.

In 1911, Arnold became the first pilot to deliver U.S. mail by air. In 1912, he gained national publicity by flying to an unprecedented altitude of 6,540 feet, and an aerial reconnaissance won him the first Mackay Trophy for "the most meritorious flight of the year." A near-fatal accident that same year grounded him for a short time, but he soon tired of desk jobs and reapplied to the infantry. There he participated in the Batanga, Philippines, maneuvers under the command of Lt. George C. Marshall. The two developed a mutual respect that played an important part in their future military careers.

Figure 1. Henry Harley ("Hap") Arnold. (SOURCE: U.S. Library of Congress)

In 1916, Arnold returned to the Aviation Section of the Signal Corps. When the United States entered World War I the next year, he was assigned to Washington with the temporary rank of full colonel—at 31, the youngest in the army at the time. Arnold was appointed executive officer of the Signal Corps Air Division. In May 1918, the Aviation Section separated from the Signal Corps and became the Air Service of the Army of the United States. Arnold became assistant director of military aeronautics, the number-two man in the Air Service.

The Armistice ended World War I before Arnold got to Europe. Disappointed because he had not been in combat, he considered resigning. However, his broad experience in aviation was much respected, and he became an articulate spokesman for a concept of national airpower. Military operations were only a part of Arnold's vision of airpower. He advocated mass production of aircraft by companies dedicated primarily to making planes (rather than automobile manufacturers). He also promoted civilian air transportation and, in 1925, was involved in the beginnings of Pan American Airways.

Arnold was promoted to temporary brigadier general in 1935 and became commander of the First Wing of the newly created General Headquarters Air Force. Now in a position to influence military doctrine and policies directly and officially, he saw distinct objectives and operations in air warfare, and struggled for an independent air arm. He supported the basic tenet of airpower advocates that long-range bombers were the nation's primary defensive need. Seeking to develop a long-range, high-altitude strike force, Arnold promoted the development of the B-17 bomber (the "Flying Fortress") and sought appropriations to develop pressurized cabins in such aircraft.

In 1939, Arnold became chief of the Air Corps. With the support of his old friend General Marshall, Arnold developed an air plan that allowed the Air Corps to sustain Britain's air forces when the United States entered the European War, but did not compromise the buildup of the U.S. Army Air Corps. Arnold faced an enormous and complex task. He obtained funds, directed development of improved aircraft designs, prodded companies to work faster, built air bases, recruited and trained air crews, and selected leaders. A major problem was whether primary emphasis should be placed on developing bomber or fighter planes. Arnold favored bombers and struggled to acquire long-range aircraft capabilities. General Marshall's support of Arnold in initiating development of the B-29 "Superfortress" was taken as an official recognition of the independent, strategic mission of the Air Corps. When Marshall appointed him deputy chief of staff for air, Arnold became the first airman to serve on the General Staff.

World War II: Airpower Comes of Age

After the attack on Pearl Harbor, Arnold's challenge was to train and organize effectively the massive resources of men and materiel being mobilized for the new Air Corps. Fortunately, he knew many outstanding airmen, like Doolittle, Spaatz, Eaker, and others, whom he appointed to critical command and logistical support positions.

Early in the war, the United States established the Joint Chiefs of Staff (JCS) to work with the British Chiefs of Staff Committee. Arnold's participation in the JCS rendered him equal to General Marshall and Admiral King, chiefs of the Army and Navy services, and to Admiral Leahy, chief of staff to the President. He also became a member of the seven-man Combined Chiefs of Staff (CCS), which included three members of the British Chiefs of Staff Committee. The CCS, under the direction of President Roosevelt and Prime Minister Churchill, was responsible for the strategic direction of the Allied global war effort.

In addition to the strategic responsibility he carried as a member of the JCS and CCS, Arnold faced many difficult airpower issues. His major concern was to make strategic bombing work in the fashion he and others had envisioned. Allied air commanders learned many exacting lessons. The daylight raids over Germany were more costly than most had estimated. Long-range escort fighters were needed to protect the bombers, and target selection was often ineffective, as postwar analyses were to point out. But overall, U.S. airpower prevailed with quality air crews, innovative technology, and sheer numbers—

elements of U.S. airpower for which Arnold was fundamentally responsible.

The U.S. air effort was sustained by an exceptional new logistical system. Arnold understood airpower's reliance on emerging aeronautical technology and airmanship skills, much of which depended upon civilian institutions. He gave the fullest attention to training and efficient support activities, and pushed the military airlift to its fullest potential. In operational matters, Arnold also resorted to special civilian support. In 1942, he authorized a Committee of Operations Analysis, mostly civilians, to assess selection of bombing targets and to study penetration tactics.

After the success of the D-Day landings in Normandy (6 June 1944), Arnold knew that the war was won and that the air war in Western Europe had entered its final phase. He turned his attention more fully to the Far East. His hope that airpower could reduce further Allied casualties in ending the Pacific war depended mainly on the use of new long-range bombers in sufficient numbers. In 1944, the 20th Air Force, composed of B-29s, was established. Arnold followed the bomber's progress with keen interest, for he believed strongly in its evolutionary potential. The pace of wartime production presented many difficulties in the aircraft's development. The initial attempts to bomb the Japanese mainland from bases in China were not successful. In November 1944, B-29s flying from Saipan began a devastating campaign against Japan. In 1945, the B-29 was matched with the atomic bomb; the consequences of that match demonstrated once and for all the utility of the long-range bomber.

After Arnold suffered four heart attacks during the last two years of the war, General Spaatz became his deputy and assumed many of his responsibilities. Following the Japanese surrender, Arnold retired with five-star rank—the only U.S. Air Force officer to hold that rank. Marshall and Arnold were the only members of the American-British CCS to serve in the same post from the first day of the war to the last.

Arnold died 15 January 1950 at his home in Sonoma, California. He had lived to see the independent U.S. Air Force he always sought. He left the Air Force with an abiding model for long-range planning. Well aware of the revolutionary impact the atomic bomb and jet propulsion were having an airpower, he knew that military planning would have to deal more effectively with the increasingly rapid development of technology. One of his last acts was to engage Dr. Theodore von Karman to conduct an extensive study of a science-oriented military future. Many findings of the study influenced U.S. Air Force developments, and civilian scientists have continued to contribute to long-range U.S. military planning.

ALBERT D. MCJOYNT

SEE ALSO: Marshall, George Catlett, Jr.; Spaatz, Carl A.; World War II.

Bibliography

Arnold, H. H. 1949. *Global mission*. New York: Harper.
Coffey, T. M. 1982. *"Hap."* New York: Viking Press.
Copp, D. S. 1980. *A few great captains: The men and events that shaped the development of U.S. air power*. New York: Doubleday.

Kuter, L. S. 1973. How Hap Arnold built the AAF. *Air Force Magazine* 56(9):88–93.

Mason, H. M. 1976. *The United States Air Force: A turbulent history, 1907–1975.* New York: Mason/Charter.

Mauer, M. 1987. *Aviation in the U.S. Army, 1919–1939.* Washington, D.C.: Office of Air Force History, U.S. Air Force.

Sherry, M. S. 1987. *The rise of American air power.* New Haven: Yale University Press.

ART OF WAR

The art of war refers to the skill or ability of individuals or groups to wage war. While the term *art* can be applied to either utilitarian or nonutilitarian purposes—that is, aesthetic purposes—the art of war encompasses only the basic utilitarian abilities pertinent to the prosecution of war.

Ancient War

Primitive war refers to war that occurred before written histories were recorded and generally involved fighting between tribes with the object of vindicating offended mores. Battles were nearly always fought on foot, and the common weapons were the club, spear, and knife. Until the advent of herding and agricultural tribes, war was seldom fought for conquest or economic advantage.

The first recorded images of war date to about 4000 B.C. Babylonian carvings from that period depict men wearing helmets, armed with spears, carrying shields, and arranged in close order. One of the significant innovations in warfare in the ancient period was the introduction of the horse as a participant in battle, first as the motive power of a chariot, later as the mount of a horseman. Early horsemen had neither saddles nor stirrups to control their beasts, but their size and strength alone altered the balance in a battle.

In the 500 years before the birth of Christ, the Greek city-states were in frequent conflict. The chief protagonists in these wars were Athens and Sparta, and their chief fighting formation was the phalanx. Battles were generally won by brute force, but notable exceptions occurred at the Battle of Marathon (490 B.C.) and at Leuctra (371 B.C.). At Marathon, the Greeks defeated the invading Persians by presenting a weak center and then, with the strength of both flanks, routing the whole of the Persian force. At Leuctra, a Theban force of 6,000 under Epaminondas defeated a Spartan force of 11,000 by weighting the left flank and thereby defeating the strong right of the Spartans, a maneuver since referred to as the oblique order, using the techniques of the refused flank.

Further significant developments in the art of war of the ancients occurred during the reign of Alexander the Great of Macedonia (336–323 B.C.). Two years after ascending the throne, Alexander began a campaign against Persia that lasted eleven years and ended with his death. Although only 23 years old at the start of the campaign, Alexander combined the skill and discipline of his foot soldiers with the mobility of his cavalry and consistently defeated more numerous forces.

The conquest of the Mediterranean basin by the Romans, and Rome's subsequent decline, marked both the zenith and the end of the ancient period of war. The first major wars for control of the Mediterranean, known as the Punic Wars, occurred between Rome and Carthage. Hannibal commanded the Carthaginian forces in the second Punic War, and although successful in his invasion of the Italian peninsula, particularly at the Battle of Cannae (216 B.C.) where he annihilated a larger Roman army in a classic double envelopment reminiscent of Marathon, Hannibal was ultimately forced to return to Carthage after the Roman senate adopted a successful strategy of sending forces to attack Carthage. The most notable achievement in the rise of Rome was the defeat of Hannibal and Carthage by Publius Correlius Scipio at the Battle of Zama (202 B.C.).

Julius Caesar's contribution to the art of war was initiated by his conquest of semicivilized Gaul, today made up of France, Switzerland, Belgium, the Netherlands, and the Rhineland of Germany. His conquest was marked by significant engineering achievements, notably his bridging of the Rhine, the construction of an extensive system of military roads, and the successful conduct of siege warfare. From this beginning he demonstrated his genius by consistently defeating the best (next to him) Roman generals in the Great Civil War.

Warfare in the ancient period was characterized by close formations, a tradition of citizen-soldiers, and a predominance of thrusting and throwing weapons. The Romans replaced the thrusting spears of the Greeks with throwing spears, such as the pilum or javelin. Some machines of war—such as the catapult, onager, and trebuchet—were widely used, particularly in siege warfare. Toward the end of the empire, the citizen-soldiers were replaced by barbarian mercenaries, an act typical of the social and political decline of Rome.

Navies consisted of oared vessels that sought to defeat their enemies by ramming or by boarding an enemy's ship and gaining control through hand-to-hand combat.

Medieval War

The Middle Ages span the 1,000 years from the fall of Rome (ca. A.D. 500) to the emergence of gunpowder as a significant force in the art of war (ca. 1500). Cavalry was in its prime, and religion increasingly dominated the affairs of citizens and states. Threats to the remnants of the western portion of the Roman Empire came from Scandinavian pirates known as Vikings and from Magyar horsemen. Threats to the Eastern Empire came first from Persian and later from Muslim invaders. Heavy cavalry dominated the fighting forces, and the bow and arrow was the arm of distant engagement.

Technology was largely responsible for the growing importance of both cavalry and archers. The introduction of the saddle and stirrup (ca. A.D. 300–800) gave the rider a stable seat to support the traditional mounted weapons of war:

the sword, the spear, and the lance. The crossbow, a bow set crosswise on a stock, which had dominated warfare in China since the second century B.C., appeared in Europe in the eleventh century. Although it was slow to arm, its arrow, or bolt, could pierce light armor. Bows were commonly used by Eastern horsemen, and in the thirteenth century the longbow, a 2.7-meter (6-ft.) bow made of yew or ash, became a favorite weapon of English foot soldiers. It could shoot farther and much more rapidly than the best crossbow and was equally good at penetrating armor.

In the west, the fragmentation of the Roman Empire meant that local leaders had to organize defensive forces to protect against barbaric invaders, and the resulting social system was known as feudalism. Local autonomy prevailed except when strong leaders were able to impose organization and discipline over vast geographic areas. Charlemagne was such a leader. Although semi-literate, his edicts established a military standard that brought unity and strength to what is today France, the Low Countries, Switzerland, most of Germany, and large parts of Austria, Italy, and Spain. Charlemagne strength-ened the cavalry by forbidding the export of armor; he levied subordinate leaders for troops and equipment. His greatest contribution to the art of war was really the revival of an old Roman practice: the building of fortifications that were permanently manned in order to maintain control of a region after the army had passed through. These sites—at Bremen, Magdeburg, and Pader-born, for example—became important political and economic centers.

Charlemagne's empire passed intact to his son, Louis the Pious, but Louis's three sons fought bitterly and hastened the empire's decline. Feudalism thrived, partly in response to the military necessity resulting from Viking in-vasions. Feudalism achieved its most thorough development in the ninth and tenth centuries.

During this period, the power of the Christian church was expanding. The church restricted the use of the crossbow, calling it a barbaric and highly destructive weapon that allowed the lowly archer to best the chivalrous and noble knight. And the church attempted to excommunicate anyone who fought between Thursday night and Monday morning. The church was also responsi-ble, as a result of an appeal from Pope Urban II in 1095, for the Crusades, military expeditions to the Holy Land that spanned a period of over 150 years.

The purpose of the Crusades was to recover the holy sites of Christendom from Muslim occupiers, to avenge mistreatment of Christian pilgrims, and to protect both the sites and the pilgrims from Seljuk Turks and other Muslim warriors. The logistical effort necessary to support the Crusades was enor-mous, and the dominance of the mounted horseman was challenged by both mounted and dismounted bowmen. But neither the logistics system devised nor the effectiveness of the Eastern bowmen had a profound effect on the prevailing state of the art of war in western Europe. The horseman remained the dominant force on the continent of Europe, but the longbows and the crossbow were increasingly used with good effect. The lasting military impact of the Crusades was the bringing to Europe of new ideas regarding fortifi-cations and the opening of commerce between East and West.

Warships remained oared during the Middle Ages, and ramming and board-ing continued as the principal options available to naval commanders.

Having successfully defended its institutions from the Vikings, from the Moors in Spain and southern France, from pagans of Prussia and Lithuania, and from periodic Muslim threats to the Byzantine Empire, the feudal system began to weaken. The church, a central feature of feudalism, was threatened by greed and corruption. The feudal lords were increasingly in conflict with their neighbors and their vassals. And the dominance of the mounted warrior was threatened by the longbows of England, the discipline and pikes of the Swiss infantry, and the introduction of gunpowder in the middle of the fourteenth century. Primitive hand cannon were used during the Hundred Years' War (1337–1453), but the potential of the destructive power of gunpowder was not fully evident until the walls of Constantinople fell to the artillery of the Turks in 1453. By the dawn of the sixteenth century, significant new conditions influenced the art of war.

Discovery, Renaissance, and Reason

Columbus's discovery of the New World half a millennium ago corresponded with the rebirth of knowledge in European cities. The accumulation of wealth and the consequent growth of banking further spurred the growth and magni-fied the importance of cities. The protection of cities also increased in impor-tance as feudal arrangements were supplanted by the power of hereditary kings. Through war, inheritance, and marriage, new centers of power arose around the Tudors in England and the Valois in France, around Ferdinand of Aragon and Isabella of Castile in Spain, and around the institution of the Holy Roman Empire in German-speaking lands. The feudal arrangement of exchang-ing military service for land gave way to a system of exchanging military service for money or gold, and mercenary armies were hired and rigorously trained to protect and defend the new monarchs.

As sovereigns attempted to protect and extend their temporal powers, they needed larger and better-equipped armies. New methods of recruitment were introduced, and new, highly disciplined formations were created. No longer was the soldier a peasant who took up arms from time to time to fulfill a feudal obligation; he became instead a full-time professional who was trained, equipped, and paid to serve the monarch's wishes.

The first writer to explore the new forces operating in renaissance society was Niccolò Machiavelli (1469–1527). Disgusted with the *condottieri*, mercenary fighters of the Italian city-states, Machiavelli proposed that a trained militia be established. He argued that a militia would be more effective than mercenaries because motivation by identification with institutions would lead to a more effective soldier than would motivation by money only. He also believed that peace was maintained by power, and that war was a natural condition between states. Though marked by wisdom and a timeless quality, Machiavelli's ideas had little general effect on the art of war in the Renaissance era.

The impact of technology and organizations on the art of war, however, was profound. The Swiss had shown that the mounted horseman could be defeated by mass, phalanxlike formations armed with the pike and halberd. The Spanish used similar mass formations but with large numbers of gunpowder weapons in the hands of the infantry. Late in the fifteenth century, Gonzalo de Córdoba combined harquebuses and pikes in a formation that became known as the Spanish *tercio*. The harquebus was the first of the shoulder-fired weapons to come into general use. It consisted of a metal tube mounted on a stock. The tube was loaded with a measure of gunpowder, followed by a metal ball or round stone. A touchhole in the tube allowed a glowing match to ignite the powder and fire the ball or stone in the general direction in which the tube was pointed. Inaccurate and unreliable, particularly in wet or damp weather, the harquebus was nonetheless effective when used in mass. Tercios commonly numbered between 1,500 and 3,000 men.

The tercio was still in use during the Thirty Years' War (1618–48), but the harquebuses had been replaced by muskets, which used a lock, or trigger mechanism, to ignite the powder in the breech of the weapon. The Thirty Years' War had its roots in religious conflict, but as the war grew more general, it directly or indirectly involved all the major powers of Europe.

The destruction and horror of the war were extreme. The town of Magdeburg, for example, was destroyed in 1630, and its 30,000 inhabitants slaughtered. Some historians have claimed that three-quarters of the German-speaking people of the world were killed in that war or died of disease, particularly of plague, which was carried from town to town by the itinerant armies.

The art of war seemed hardly an art form in the midst of such wanton destruction, yet it was greatly advanced during the Thirty Years' War through the efforts and genius of Gustavus Adolphus, King of Sweden. He instituted a national military service obligation to replace the mercenary system that Machiavelli and others had complained of. He instituted a training system that ensured that soldiers were well drilled in battle evolutions. He reduced the weight of weapons by replacing the heavy wooden rest used to support the early muskets with a light iron pole. He further lightened the infantryman's load by discarding armor, which had little protective value against musket fire. He introduced the paper cartridge, which combined ball and powder in a single package and greatly simplified the loading of the musket. He changed the basic fighting formation from one ten ranks deep to one only six ranks deep, and occasionally utilized formations in which the musketeers were formed three ranks deep. The increase in mobility and firepower was significant. He standardized the sizes of artillery pieces and lightened the weight of artillery gun tubes. He established a system of depots to supply his army on campaign. He returned shock action to the cavalry by restoring the charge with sword rather than the standoff that often resulted from the use of fire tactics with ineffective pistols. The Gustavian reforms proved their worth at Brietenfield in 1631, when the unwieldy tercios of the Imperial armies were routed by the Swedish force. Gustavus's genius covered the gamut of the art of war. He established a solid base, had a superb system of supply, moved his army quickly, struck decisively, and employed all the tools of war in a masterful way.

In England during the civil wars (1642–49), the lessons of the Swedish reform were generally adopted, although it is not clear that it was simply a case of emulating success. Oliver Cromwell, like Gustavus, recognized that discipline, training, and a professional force were necessary components of victory. Through discipline and leadership, Cromwell bested the king's forces and became the first to conquer and rule over all the British Isles.

In the late seventeenth century, France became the leading military power in the Western world, and like the Macedonians, the Romans, the Swiss, the Spanish, the Swedes, and every other group that had set the pace regarding the development of the art of war, France took the lead as a result of innovation and reform. The key to French reform was wealth and the desire for greater wealth. Gold from the New World had filled the coffers of the Spanish during the Thirty Years' War, and now France sought to be a leading power in Europe and a major colonial power. The sinews of war are said to be gold, and Louis XIV's finance minister, Jean Baptiste Colbert, put the finances of France on a firm footing through taxation and a mercantile policy. Military reform, led by Louis's secretary of state for war Michel le Tellier and his son, the Marquis de Louvois, who succeeded him, was greatly facilitated by the wealth of the state. Uniforms were adopted for general use throughout the army. Arsenals, hospitals, and retirement centers were built. And an efficient quartermaster department was established to correct the abuses in the supply system that had earlier prevailed. Civil servants ran the army, and the modern system of bureaucracy imposed itself on the art of war.

By the early eighteenth century, all the armies of Europe recognized the value of fixed magazines and depots for the successful prosecution of war. To protect these depots and the frontiers of the modern states, fortifications were built to block the advance of any invading army. Thus, fortifications became the key to a nation's defense, and fortification design and construction became important aspects of the art of war. Chief among the military engineers of this and every other era was Louis XIV's military engineer, Sébastien Le Prestre de Vauban. Vauban developed three systems of complex defensive works, each designed to stop the progress of an invading army by exhausting it in time-consuming sieges. To counter his virtually impregnable defensive works, Vauban devised a system of offense against defensive works that was known as the system of parallels. By digging approach trenches, parallel trenches, and establishing artillery batteries at critical points, Vauban was able to again turn to geometry and mathematics to solve the practical problems facing commanders in the field.

Although the armies of Louis XIV were well trained, well disciplined, well financed, and well supplied, they were sometimes defeated by superior generalship and powerful coalitions. The generals who served France so skillfully in the seventeenth and eighteenth centuries, chief among them Henri Turenne; Louis, Prince de Condé; and Hermann Maurice, Comte de Saxe, were some-

times defeated when faced by forces commanded by such luminaries as Raimondo Montecuccoli; John Churchill, Duke of Marlborough; Eugene, Prince
of Savoy; and finally, Frederick the Great of Prussia. By the time of the Seven
Years' War (1756–63) France's military hegemony was eclipsed by Britain at sea
and Prussia on land.

The limited warfare that generally prevailed in Europe after the Thirty Years'
War continued during Frederick the Great's reign (1740–86), but the limitations did not affect Frederick's willingness to take risks, to commit to battle, or
to the skill and discipline that he demanded of his soldiers and their leaders.
The key to Frederick's success lay in his own energy and determination. His
army was well equipped, particularly with regard to the iron ramrod and
artillery—the former being far superior to the wooden version still used by
other European armies. Frederick's artillery was light in comparison with that
of other European powers, but it was highly mobile. Furthermore, one-third of
Frederick's artillery consisted of very effective howitzers. The discipline in-
stilled in the army paid dividends when Frederick was compelled to fight a
major battle against the French at Rossbach (7 November 1757), then march
270 kilometers (170 mi.) to defeat the Austrians at Leuthen just one month
later.

Much discussion about Frederick as a general concerns his use of the oblique
order, which had been used with success by Epaminondas at Leuctra over
2,000 years earlier. It worked for Frederick on two of four occasions (at Leuthen
and Torgau—it failed at Zorndorf and Kunersdorf), but he gave greater credit
for his success to his use of artillery. Significantly, Frederick won only half his
battles, but he established Prussian military institutions as preeminent in the
Western world. He mastered the use of the army as an instrument of policy and
raised the art of war in the age of limited war to unprecedented heights.

Like war on land, war at sea was greatly affected by the introduction of
gunpowder. The ship was an ideal platform for the heavy siege cannon of the
period, but the weight of the cannon made ships too heavy to be propelled by
oars. The great age of sail began in the sixteenth century and extended well into
the nineteenth. Cannon facing outward along the sides of ships meant that a
line of ships maneuvered to place its broadsides toward its enemy so that
maximum firepower could be brought to bear. A strong navy was essential to
any state that sought to be a colonial power, and the French victory off the
Chesapeake capes, which led to the surrender of Cornwallis at Yorktown (1781),
demonstrated the dominant role that seapower would play in a world joined by
oceans but contested on land.

The Napoleonic Age

No military commander has dominated the events of the age in which he lived
to the extent Napoleon did. Yet he is surrounded by controversy. He was a hero
to some, a villain to others; an innovator and superb strategist who was lucky
when successful and foolish when defeated; a military genius and a brazen
exploiter of the ideas of others.

Without question, the events following the overthrow of the Bourbon regime in 1789 had extraordinary impact on the art of war. Of greatest significance was the institutionalization of the *levée en masse*, the concept that the entire population of the state had obligations in time of war. The *levée* meant large armies—not since the time of Attila the Hun had such large armies been placed under arms. It also meant that the rigorous training that had typified the professional, mercenary armies of Frederick the Great and Louis XIV would be impractical. Instead of the common soldier's being a valued commodity in the system of war, he could be quickly and readily replaced. The generals who commanded the French forces in the early years after the *levée* recognized the difference, but Napoleon saw in the *levée* an opportunity to change the fundamental nature of war. With greater resources, Napoleon expended his resources more readily and sought not just victory but the annihilation of his foes. Thus the *levée* gave Napoleon the opportunity to command a nation in arms, not just an army.

The larger armies also made command, training, and logistics far more complex. But Napoleon was equal to the task. He established a corps system in which his corps commanders were given considerable autonomy. He used his cavalry extensively as a reconnaissance force, and he was demanding in the face of adversity. The strict linear formations employed during the period of Frederick the Great were put aside, and columns were more widely used in the attack. The column required far less training and gave depth and staying power to the attack, and it mattered little if it was inefficient. Manpower in the Napoleonic Age was an expendable resource. A further change in the formations for battle involved the use of skirmishers, men sent in advance of a main formation as a reconnaissance and early reaction force. Their role was simply to find the enemy and disrupt his formations before the arrival of the main body of troops.

To supply his army, Napoleon relied on the system of depots and magazines established by his predecessors, but the larger armies also meant that foraging as a means of supply had to be used extensively. Far more factories were needed to generate the materiel of war, and the beginnings of industrialization helped by meeting the voluminous demands of the army and by making weapons with interchangeable parts. The system worked effectively until 1812 when distances, the Russian army, Russia's deliberate destruction of abandoned crops and supplies, and the Russian winter combined to bring the first major defeat on land to Napoleon's French Empire.

Technologically, there was little innovation in the arsenal of weapons employed by Napoleonic armies. The smoothbore muzzleloading musket was still the dominant firearm of infantry, and even though Gribeauval had standardized French artillery late in the reign of Louis XVI, Napoleon had little or no technological advantage in artillery. He introduced heavier armor for some of his cavalry and experimented with a mechanical telegraph system, but generally he relied on the weapons of war that had been available to his predecessors.

As a planner, Napoleon was unrivaled. He was a man of infinite detail, and his knowledge and constant updating of the disposition of his forces was essential to his ability to concentrate superior force against his enemies at the decisive moment. He constantly looked for opportunities to divide his enemies and defeat them in detail or to maneuver his force in a way that blocked his enemy from their base of supply. His example became the school for leaders and generals in the post-Napoleonic world.

American Civil War to World War I

The wars of Napoleon were characterized by little technological innovation and superb generalship; the American Civil War was characterized by significant technological innovation and generally poor generalship. Both the Industrial Revolution and the benefits of commerce contributed to the significant changes that occurred in the manufacture and design of the weapons of war between the defeat of Napoleon at Waterloo and the close of the American Civil War. The developments that had the greatest impact were the rifling of muskets and the introduction of railroads.

The basic shoulder arm of the infantry had changed little in the 100 years before the introduction of the rifled musket. Effective rifles had been used by hunters and some elite soldiers since the sixteenth century, but, with few exceptions, they were muzzleloaders and very slow to load since the bullet had to be forced down the grooves of the rifling as it was inserted into the barrel. For some models, a mallet was needed to tamp the bullet into the barrel. The key to the development of a militarily effective muzzleloading rifle was the creation of an undersized bullet called a "minié ball." Named after its inventor, Claude Minié, the elongated bullet had a hollow base into which an iron thimble was placed. When the weapon was fired, the thimble was driven into the bullet, the walls at the base of the Minié bullet expanded into the grooves of the rifling, and the bullet was given spin as it traveled down the barrel. The spin gave increased velocity, accuracy, and range to the bullet. The new rifle-muskets of the U.S. Army also employed a percussion cap system. Instead of relying on a flint to provide the spark necessary to ignite the powder in the chamber, a small cap containing fulminate of mercury was placed over a nipple that took the spark to the chamber. This percussion cap gave much greater reliability to the weapon, since the ignition system was now essentially watertight. Some breechloaders and a few repeating rifles were introduced during the Civil War, but the net effect of the rifle-muskets and other rifles was to increase the lethality of the most common of the weapons of the battlefield and to force soldiers to dig trenches for protection even from small arms.

The development of a system of railroads affected the strategy and logistics of war. Troops could now be moved rapidly from one theater of war to another, and the delivery of mass supplies was greatly facilitated.

Communications on the battlefield was aided by experimental telegraph systems, and balloons were again used to facilitate reconnaissance. Improvements in iron allowed cast-iron artillery to be mass produced, and Robert P. Parrott developed a method of reinforcing the breech of rifled cannon by heat-shrinking a heavy wrought-iron band around the breech. Like the rifled musket, the Parrott guns used an elongated projectile, similar in design to the minié ball. Artillery was also improved by the adoption of the friction primer, which consisted of a tube of primer that was placed in the touchhole and a roughened, twisted wire that was perpendicularly inserted in the tube. When the wire was yanked from the tube by the lanyard, a sulfurous substance on the wire ignited the primer, and the tube carried the flame to the main powder charge in the breech.

Innovation came to naval vessels, too. The first ironclads opposed each other in the American Civil War, and the invention of the screw propeller in 1836 meant that steam engines could be used on ocean-going ships armed with cannon and guns. Steam gave predictability to the navy because movement at sea was no longer dependent on the winds.

Despite the many innovations in technology, the Civil War saw few, if any, consistently bold strokes of leadership. Stonewall Jackson was brilliant in the Shenandoah Valley campaign in 1862, but tardy when needed near Richmond. Robert E. Lee was brilliant at Chancellorsville in May 1863, but reverted to bloody, unrewarding frontal assaults at Gettysburg less than two months later. Ulysses S. Grant was effective in the western theater, but ordered repeated, costly assaults in the Virginia campaign of 1864. Ambrose Burnside was ineffective; George McClellan was slow. Positive contributions to the development of the art of war seemed confined to the world of logistics and technology.

The attention savants gave to the Civil War was short-lived, for the wars of German unification quickly turned military interest to the world of the Prussian military machine. Quick victories over Denmark (1864) and Austria (1866) were followed by an equally impressive victory over the French in 1870–71. The Prussians employed the Dreyse needle gun in their victories; it was the first breechloader to be standardized for use on the battlefield. Still, far more than technology influenced the Prussian victories. Perhaps the greatest innovation regarding the art of war to be demonstrated in the Prussian victories was the staff work accomplished by the great general staff. Efficiency was the byword, and success was the result.

The World Wars

Continued improvements in the weapons of war and wholly new dimensions of war marked the most significant changes that occurred in the art of war during the two great wars of this century. Among the notable technological advances was the invention of smokeless gunpowder, which was not literally smokeless but burned white rather than black and caused far less fouling of small arms and artillery. It made rapid-fire weapons effective, and rapid-fire weapons made life between heavily manned, entrenched lines impossible.

New ideas and new weapons were used in attempts to breach the enemy's trenches. Gas warfare was attempted. Mass attacks were attempted. Radios facilitated communications. Tanks were tried. New tactics, among them the Hutier tactics of the Germans, were tried. And airplanes were used, but without any decisive result. Submarines prowled the seas and wrecked havoc on commercial shipping, but the stalemate in the trenches continued. The arrival of Gen. Jack Pershing and the American Expeditionary Force (AEF) had only a minor impact on the outcome of the war; ultimately, the Germans sued for peace because in a bloody war of exhaustion, they were the first to be exhausted.

In the years following World War I, diplomatic initiatives sought to outlaw the use of chemical weapons, to limit the size of navies, and to eliminate war as an instrument of policy among nations. Meanwhile, the tank was further developed as an effective ground fighting vehicle. The airplane became an effective weapons platform, and advocates of airpower argued that an independent air force would be the decisive arm in future conflicts. The French believed that the defensive would dominate future wars and invested in an elaborate series of fortifications, known as the Maginot Line, that extended in depth all along France's border with Germany. While the Western powers focused on hopes of peace, the Germans, Italians, and Japanese focused on plans for retribution and conquest.

In stark contrast to the stalemate of the defensiveness of World War I, World War II was a war of vast and rapid movement. Tanks and airplanes dominated the land and air, and at sea, battleships, aircraft carriers, and submarines engaged in costly battles throughout the oceans of the world. Sophistication marked further weapon developments. Radar provided eyes to see distant attacks developing in and from the air. The Norden bombsight improved the accuracy of high-level bombers. Guidance instruments allowed planes to navigate effectively at night and in marginal weather. Machine guns were improved. Huge railroad guns were developed. Antiaircraft weapons were perfected, and pilotless bombs, the dreaded Vergeltungswaffen rockets, were unleashed. The ultimate weapon of war, the nuclear bomb, was developed and used with devastating effect on Hiroshima and Nagasaki to bring an end to the destruction in the Pacific.

Open formations were used by all ground forces, and the combined arms team of infantry, tanks, and artillery was employed wherever possible. Aircraft were used in close support roles, but the bulk of air resources were used in strategic bombing offensives against the enemy homeland and industrial base.

Examples of good and bad generalship occurred on all sides, and major problems in war leadership involved the resolution of differences between civilian heads of government and the generals in the field. Hitler's megalomania, Mussolini's obsequiousness, Stalin's lack of resources, Churchill's dogged determination, and Roosevelt's poor health all affected the conduct of the war.

Man remained the ultimate determinant of the outcome of war, but as technology made some tasks easier, it made moral choices much harder.

Cold War to the Present

Notable changes have affected the art of war since the conclusion of World War II. Nuclear weapon arsenals have increased dramatically—to the point where it is possible to destroy the world many times over. Attempts to limit the number of nations possessing nuclear arms have been moderately successful, and attempts to reduce the size of the great power arsenals have met with limited success. Improved delivery systems, from sophisticated stealth bombers to midget intercontinental ballistic missiles, continue to demand high production and deployment costs. Nations have agreed to the peaceful uses of space, but spy satellites, communications satellites, and a continually manned Soviet space station ply the heavens.

Closer to the firmament, new weapons of war are still in abundance. Jet aircraft continue to improve in speed, maneuverability, carrying power, and staying power. Their electronic navigation and target acquisition systems are complex, yet reliable—and made possible in large part by computers and electronic miniaturization. Supersonic transports routinely fly from continent to continent, and helicopters perform myriad functions in support of the soldier on the ground. Computers are pervasive, and their role in future wars will be extensive.

Tactics have changed from the preponderance of frontal attacks that marked World Wars I and II and the Korean War to a preference for guerrilla methods where stealth and surprise can overcome the sophisticated and lethal weapons of one's enemies, particularly if a developing nation is in conflict with a major power. A logical extension of guerrilla war is the terrorist war, and Western nations have invested costly resources in special operations commands to deter and counter acts of terrorism. While nations meet to place further bans on the use of chemical, biological, and nuclear weapons, evidence of chemical use is abundant.

This review illustrates some of the dominant factors—among them economic, social, and political institutions—that have affected the art of war. Other factors are generalship, the state of military thought and doctrine, the state of logistics and administration, strategy, and tactics. Clearly, technology has been, and will continue to be, a major factor. The constant in the art of war is man, his avarice and greed, his sacrifice and his courage. The future of war is a great unknown, but the obligation of civilized nations to be prepared for war when it comes is absolute. Skill in the practice of war and study of the art of war are essential features of man's existence.

JOHN I. ALGER

SEE ALSO: Alexander the Great; Charlemagne; Civil War, American; Crusades; Feudalism; Frederick the Great; Gonzalo de Córdoba; Graeco-Persian Wars; Gustavus Adolphus; History, Ancient Military; History, Early Modern Military; History, Medieval Military; History, Military; History, Modern Military; Napoleon I; Punic Wars; Roman Empire; Science of War; Thirty Years' War; Vauban, Sébastien Le Prestre de; Vikings; World War I; World War II.

Bibliography

Adcock, F. 1957. *The Greek and Macedonian art of war.* Berkeley, Calif.: Univ. of Calif. Press.
Amstutz, J. B. 1986. *Afghanistan: The first five years of Soviet occupation.* Washington, D.C.: National Defense Univ. Press.

Chandler, D. G. 1966. *The campaigns of Napoleon.* New York: Macmillan.
Delbruck, H. 1975. *History of the art of war.* Trans. W. J. Renfroe, Jr. Westport, Conn.: Greenwood Press.
Esposito, V. J., ed. 1959. *West Point atlas of American wars.* New York: Praeger.
Griess, T. E., ed. 1985. *The West Point military history series.* Wayne, N.J.: Avery.
Hastings, M., and S. Jenkins. 1983. *The battle for the Falklands.* New York: Norton.
Howard, M. 1979. *The Franco-Prussian war.* London: Granada.
Liddell Hart, B. H. 1931. *The real war, 1914–1918.* Boston: Little, Brown.
Montross, L. 1944. *War through the ages.* New York: Harper.
Oman, C. W. 1885. *The art of war in the Middle Ages.* Oxford: Oxford Univ. Press.
Parker, G., ed. 1988. *The Thirty Years' War.* London: Routledge, Chapman & Hall.
Preston, R. A., and S. F. Wise. 1970. *Men in arms.* New York: Praeger.
Rees, D. 1964. *Korea: The limited war.* New York: St. Martin's Press.
Ritter, G. 1954. *Frederick the Great.* Heidelberg: Quelle and Meyer.
Ropp, T. 1959. *War in the modern world.* Durham, N.C.: Duke Univ. Press.
Spaulding, O. L., H. Nickerson, and J. W. Wright. 1925. *Warfare: A study of military methods from the earliest times.* New York: Harcourt, Brace.
Thucydides. 1954. *The Peloponnesian war.* Trans. R. Warner. Middlesex, Eng.: Penguin.
Williams, T. H. 1952. *Lincoln and his generals.* New York: Knopf.
Wright, G. 1968. *The ordeal of total war, 1939–1945.* New York: Harper.
Wright, Q. 1942. *A study of war.* Chicago: Univ. of Chicago Press.

ASSYRIA, MILITARY HISTORY OF

Assyria began as a small northern Mesopotamian city-state called Assur. Under a succession of aggressive, warlike kings, Assyria created a highly professional army and, with it, an empire that, at its height, included the entire Fertile Crescent as well as much of Asia Minor. Although Assyria's rise to supremacy was a slow process, its fall was swift and complete.

Militarization of Assyria

Located at the junction of important caravan routes in northern Mesopotamia, Assyria was open to attack from all directions. During the second millennium B.C., it suffered greatly from the chariot forces of Indo-European invaders.

THREATS TO ASSYRIAN SECURITY

By 1550 B.C., Assyria was, in effect, encircled and threatened by potential and actual enemies. To the southeast, Babylonia, under the Indo-European Kassites, constituted a perennial threat. To the east, it was prey to frequent raids by various mountain tribes. To the north, the Kingdom of Mitanni, and later the Kingdom of Urartu, seriously threatened both the commerce and survival of Assyria. The most formidable threat, however, lay to the northwest. The Hittites, with their chariots and iron weapons, were an aggressive, expansive power. Under Mursilis I (1550–1530 B.C.), the Hittites not only conquered Syria but also sacked Babylon.

ASSYRIAN ARMY

Assyria answered the threats confronting it by creating a professional, standing army. Assuruballit I (1366–1331 B.C.) reorganized the army according to weapon type: chariots, infantry, and engineers—including sappers and siege artillery. While his opponents emphasized the chariot, Assuruballit made the heavy infantry the core of his army. Following the Hittite example, he armed his soldiers with iron weapons and provided them with light body armor.

Assuruballit marshaled his troops in formations according to branch. The smallest unit consisted of ten men. Building on the basic unit of ten, formations of 100 (company), 1,000 (regiment), and field armies of 120,000 or more were mobilized.

Information on Assyrian military tactics is fragmentary. On the strategic level, the Assyrians proved themselves masters at exploiting terrain to the best advantage. In Mesopotamia, for example, the Assyrians used the rivers and canals not only for logistical purposes but also to screen movements, to provide flank protection, and to channel enemy movements. The Assyrians also developed riverine and amphibious warfare capabilities, as demonstrated by the campaigns of Sennacherib (705–682 B.C.) against the Elamites.

Assyrian Expansion

Assyrian expansion occurred in two distinct phases: the Middle Assyrian Empire and the New Assyrian Empire.

MIDDLE ASSYRIAN EMPIRE, 1356–1209 B.C.

Enlilnirari I (1330–1321 B.C.), son of Assuruballit, established the unalterable, central principle of Assyrian policy in Mesopotamia: control of Babylonia. Although Enlilnirari succeeded in reducing Babylonia to vassalage, his successors were frequently required to remind the Babylonians of their duty to Assyria.

Under Adadnirari I (1308–1276 B.C.) the Assyrians first clashed with the Hittites. The Assyrian conquest of Mitanni, a Hittite vassal, provoked numerous border skirmishes. Although the bulk of the Hittite forces were engaged in the ongoing struggle with Ramses II of Egypt over control of Syria and Palestine, the Hittites were too strong to be challenged directly.

Blocked by the Hittites to the northwest, Shalmaneser I (1275–1246 B.C.) attempted to expand northward at the expense of the Urartu, a tribal confederacy. His operations met with only limited success. Tukultininurita I (1245–1209 B.C.), angered by Babylonian collusion with the Hittites, crushed the Kassites, thereby ending their 450-year rule over southern Mesopotamia. Babylonia was incorporated into Assyria as a province and Tukultininurita took for himself the ancient title of the kings of Babylon, "King of Sumer and Akkad."

The disintegration of the Hittite Empire around 1200 B.C. offered Assyria an opportunity to expand westward to the Mediterranean Sea. Assyria, however, came under attack from Aramean and Chaldean tribesmen moving eastward from Syria. From 1200 to 1117 B.C., Assyria fought to survive against these new invaders as well as a reinvigorated Babylon.

NEW ASSYRIAN EMPIRE, 1115–612 B.C.

The first great king of the New Assyrian Empire was Tiglathpileser I (1115–1077 B.C.), who accomplished what his predecessors had been unable to do: conquer Syria to the Mediterranean coast. He also reimposed Assyrian suzerainty over the troublesome Babylonians.

Tiglathpileser was the ruler to initiate the terror tactics that have become synonymous with the name Assyria: the mass deportation of conquered people, or their mass execution by immurement, flaying alive, or impalement. Faced with barbarian invaders and rebellious vassals, the Assyrians employed barbarous means of coercion.

Tukultininurita II (890–884 B.C.) continued the policies of his ancestors. His great innovation was the introduction of cavalry, which was done in response to the depredations caused by a new wave of invading Indo-European cavalrymen, ancestors of the later Medes and Persians.

Tiglathpileser III (745–728 B.C.) extended Assyrian power over most of Asia Minor and Palestine to the Egyptian border.

Shalmaneser V (726–722 B.C.) suppressed a rebellion by the Arameans of Damascus and their ally, the Kingdom of Israel. Israel was destroyed and its people deported to northern Mesopotamia. Sargon II (722–705 B.C.) defeated the Elamites and brought the Babylonians to heel once again.

Sennacherib (705–682 B.C.) added no new territory to the empire. He did reassert Assyrian suzerainty over the Kingdom of Judah (Judea) and devastated Elam in the 690s B.C. Against Babylon, Sennacherib took drastic measures. In 689 B.C., he ordered the ancient city destroyed and forbade its rebuilding for 80 years.

Esarhaddon (681–670 B.C.) lifted his father's ban on Babylon in 679 B.C. and rebuilt the city on a grand scale. He also imposed Assyrian suzerainty over the Phoenician city of Sidon. Esarhaddon's most significant achievement was the conquest of northern (Lower) Egypt, completed in 671 B.C. with the occupation of Memphis. Esarhaddon, however, never completed his conquest of Egypt. He died in 670 B.C. while leading a new expedition against the Egyptians, and with him died the last period of Assyrian expansion.

Decline and Fall of Assyria

With the exception of Assurbanipal III (668–625 B.C.), under whom Mesopotamian civilization experienced its penultimate flowering, the last Assyrian kings were weak nonentities. In the summer of 612 B.C., Nineveh, the Assyrian capital, fell to the Medes and Babylonians. Although a junior member of the royal family attempted to revive Assyria, by 609 B.C. mighty Assyria was no more.

Cyaxares, king of the Medes, imposed his rule over the former Assyrian provinces of northern Mesopotamia and the vassal states of Asia Minor and Urartu.

Nabopolasser, founder of the Neo-Babylonian Empire, accepted the homage of the states of Syria and Palestine. His son, Nebuchadnezzar II (605–561 B.C.), destroyed the rebellious Kingdom of Judah in 586 B.C. and deported the Judeans to Babylon, where they remained until freed by Cyrus the Great.

LAWRENCE D. HIGGINS

SEE ALSO: History, Ancient Military; Persian Empire.

Bibliography

Olmstead A. T. E. 1908. *Western Asia in the days of Sargon of Assyria.* Ithaca: Cornell Univ. Press.

———. 1923. *History of Assyria.* New York: Scribner's.

Rigg, H. A. 1942. Sargon's "eighth military campaign." *Journal of the American Oriental Society* 62:130–38.

Saggs, H. W. F. 1962. *The greatness that was Babylon.* New York: New American Library (Mentor Books).

Smith, S. 1928. *Early history of Assyria to 1000 B.C.* London: Chatto and Windus.

Tadmor, H. 1958. The campaigns of Sargon II of Assur: A chronological-historical study. *Journal of Cuneiform Studies* 12:22–40; 77–100.

Wright, E. M. 1943. The eighth campaign of Sargon II of Assyria. *Journal of Near Eastern Studies* 2:173–86.

ATTILA THE HUN

The Huns, a people of Turanian stock, began to appear as a political and military power during the second century B.C. They emerged from the pastoral peoples living on the northern steppes of Europe and Asia and reached the height of their power in the West between A.D. 350 and A.D. 470. From their earliest appearance in Europe (fourth century A.D.) they gained a reputation as fierce warriors.

The Eastern Huns (chronicled by the Chinese as *hsiung-nu*) attained their greatest power under King Mao Tun in the early first century A.D. In central Asia, some nineteen tribes, known as the Southern Huns, consolidated their power during the first and second centuries A.D. They gained control of the Altai region and modern Kazakhstan, expanding into northern India, Pakistan, and Afghanistan.

The Huns, or hsiung-nu, became known to the Romans after the defeat of Crassus's legions by the Parthians at the Battle of Carrhae in 54 B.C. The captured legionaries were resettled on the Parthians' eastern frontiers where they became mercenaries in the service of Chih-chih, hsiung-nu shan-yu, the king of the Southern Huns. The term *hsiung-nu* (archaic Chinese) derives from the ancient Iranian word for ruling king and was used by the Huns when referring to themselves.

Recent excavations of early Hun sites have provided evidence that the Huns had both agrarian knowledge and weapons-fashioning skills. Agricultural tools and large storage areas for cereal grains were found along with weapons made from iron and bronze. The Hun ruling class (Logades), as best as can be determined, spoke an ancient Eastern dialect similar to Saka-Iranian.

There is little reason to believe that there was a concerted sociopolitical life within the Hun empire that would have united the Eastern, Southern, and Western Huns. Instead, each evolved separately, modifying their languages and sociopolitical and military organizations as they formed alliances, subjugated other peoples, and developed political, economic, and military spheres of influence.

Also, it is evident, from the brief period of Western Hun supremacy (A.D. 350–470) and its rapid decline after the death of Attila (A.D. 453), that it was Attila's political and military skills, as opposed to consolidated Hun political and military power, that held his part of the empire together. This is further strengthened by the fact that the Western Huns were far outnumbered by the people they ruled, the majority of whom were Germanic.

The Western Huns' peak military power occurred sometime after Attila's birth (ca. A.D. 406) with the unification of the Western Hun tribes under one all-powerful king, Karaton (A.D. 412). Prior to this, Balamer (ca. A.D. 320–390), Karaton's father, appeared to be "first among equals" in his relationship with the loosely federated tribal chieftains.

Organization and Equipment

The Hun military organization was based on the tribe. Each tribe numbered 50,000–60,000 individuals, of whom about 10,000 were military-age males. This 10,000-man unit of mounted archers, which represented the tribe's war-making capability, was called a *tumen.* The basic building block of the tumen was ten light horsemen, who were combined into elements of 100 and then 1,000. The highest title among the Huns, next to that of king, was "commander of the Ten Thousand Horsemen," also known as the khan among many Turanian peoples.

The Hun tumen were the epitome of fast, light cavalry. The horse was essential to their way of life and mode of fighting. The Hun horses were small and hairy with long manes and long, bushy tails. They had large, long heads and short legs with broad hooves. Their eyes were large, and they were apparently faithful companions to their masters. These hardy horses survived quite well on grass and sparse vegetation, could tolerate extreme cold or heat without noticeable fatigue, and were rarely sick.

These horses responded equally well to bridle commands, the rider's verbal commands, and the unit commander's signals, thus leaving the rider's hands free to handle the war bow and other weapons. When the enemy's defensive line was penetrated, the Hun horses would bite and kick the enemy's troops, wreaking great havoc and consternation.

The saddle consisted of a wooden frame covered with leather and stuffed with horse hair or other materials. The stirrups were wood covered with leather. The leaders rode horses whose saddles and bridles were richly decorated with silver and gold.

The Hun's principal weapon was the reflex composite bow, which measured 140–160 centimeters (55–63 in.) in length, and which when unstrung curved outwards. In fact, the entire Hun system of warfare and tactics evolved around this bow, which was still used by the Hungarians as late as the early fifteenth century. The bow was not symmetrical, the bottom extending a shorter distance from the grip than the top. It was made of seven different materials—including wood, bone, and sinew—by expert bow makers. The quiver consisted of a wooden frame covered with leather and highly ornamented. It hung from either the saddle or the rider's belt.

The effective combat range of the Hun bow was 70–100 meters (230–330 ft.). The maximum range for "arrow showers" was 175 meters (575 ft.). The war bow was commonly referred to as the Scythian bow, and its origin and design were most likely Iranian.

The Huns complemented their use of the bow with the lasso, which was used to thin an enemy line by roping enemies out of the ranks and dragging them away. Other weapons included short, curved Iranian-type swords, daggers, maces, and pickaxes. Thrusting and jabbing lances, while known to have been used, were rare. A small shield of wood covered with leather completed the Hun warrior's equipment. Depending on the owner's rank and wealth, the weapons were decorated with silver, gold, and precious stones.

Clothing and combat attire were equally rich and again were used to display rank and wealth. The warrior wore a leather-covered conical helmet (made on a metal frame), with a peak that pointed forward. Chain mail covered the neck and shoulders, and sometimes the upper body, but body armor was usually made of hard leather, which was greased with animal fat for waterproofing. The leather armor was skin tight and bone plaques were sewn to the outer part for additional protection. Up to four layers of this armor were worn over a shirt or blouse. The warriors also wore baggy pants of goat skin, and soft boots. The boots were only good for riding as they were too fragile for dismounted use. Over this clothing, the warrior wore a knee-length split-felt or fur coat, often richly embroidered.

The Hun warrior rarely cut his hair or beard. His hair was combed and parted on top of his head. Sometimes his beard was also parted, and both the beard and hair might be plaited with colorful ribbons. During cold and rainy seasons, animal fat was thickly smeared over the warrior's face and hair for protection against the elements.

Tactics and Strategy

The Hun system of warfare was characterized by rapid movement during tactical marches toward an objective, as well as during combat itself. The Huns had no infantry or siege equipment and, therefore, depended upon rapid movement to catch their enemies off guard with city garrisons ill-prepared for defense. Movement over great distances occurred so quickly that no one, regardless how distant from the great Hungarian plains, felt secure. This mobility was provided by the horse, with each warrior having at least one remount. Some sources indicate that the Huns had as many as seven remounts. When a mount was killed in combat, the warrior changed to another. The mounts were saddled and equipped with a spare quiver and standard rations, which made each horse an individual logistical package, enabling units of 1,000 and more to travel hundreds, even thousands, of miles from home without the need for an operational support base.

In addition to individual horses, the Huns used light, two-wheeled, chariot-like carts drawn by two to three horses.

It must be noted that the armies of Balamer, Mundzuk, and Attila became progressively less Hun-like as they absorbed Gothic elements, which were mainly infantry. The Goths, Gepids, and Quadi fought dismounted, as infantry, preferring hand-to-hand combat. The Huns rarely dismounted and preferred to use their bows from a distance. Close combat was used only for finishing off the enemy in the final assault.

The Huns and other Turanians preferred to avoid hand-to-hand combat for several reasons: first, while their armor was quite effective against arrows, it offered almost no protection against the heavy cut-and-thrust weapons used by the Roman legions or Germanic tribes. Second, the Hun horses were vulnerable to the spear and lance at close combat range. Third, a limited population base and the ever-present need to protect the tribe made the heavy losses sustained in close combat unacceptable.

If the tumen of 10,000 warriors incurred heavy casualties, the tribe was endangered, since it could no longer protect itself and its livestock from marauders. Therefore, the tribal tumen was usually split. Half the warriors would remain behind to protect the tribe, while half would go on military expeditions and raids. Thus, even if the tribe's entire offensive capability was lost in war, it remained formidable defensively.

The Huns placed great value on long-range reconnaissance, deception, and concealment. The full force was never within view of their enemy. Any part of the main body might be hidden in forests, ravines, or riverbeds. In battle, units would be arrayed over wide fronts.

Skirmishes, aimed at thinning the enemy ranks, would always precede an assault. Groups would dash out from the line, fire a few well-placed arrows, wheel right, fire several more arrows, and return to their position in the line. This maneuver was repeated until the enemy ranks had been thinned sufficiently to permit the decisive tactical maneuvers to be initiated.

Units of 1,000 would then approach within bow range (70–100 m, 230–328 ft.). The front ranks would then fire direct, well-aimed shots, while the rear ranks would fire arrow showers overhead. These arrow showers would force the enemy troops to lift their shields to protect their heads and shoulders, thereby exposing their bodies to the direct fire from the Hun front ranks.

The attacking tumens would move forward quickly, then turn back and move forward again. Some elements would ride around to the enemy's rear and flanks and engage his cavalry and rear guard. Through these seemingly random forward and rearward movements the attacking Huns would attempt to lure the enemy's main body into pursuit, which was always attended by some disorganization. Another ruse was the simulation, on signal, of the flight of the entire Hun force. If the enemy pursued into the trap, units that had been kept out of sight attacked from all sides and destroyed him. If the enemy did not fall for the feint and kept his formation, a frontal assault was executed in wedge formation by units of 1,000 or by massed tumen, depending on the total size of the army.

Rivers were never an obstacle to the Hun warriors. They all carried inflatable skins. In addition rafts would be built to carry heavy equipment and carts. Individual warriors normally would ride their horses into the water and swim across. The major river-crossing sites were well guarded.

The Attila Period

Attila was brought to kingship as co-ruler by his brother Bleda (Buda, A.D. 434–445), who was the ruling king. This dual kingship was common among the pastoral peoples of the East. The elder partner was responsible for general administration and political and spiritual leadership, while the younger partner led the military forces.

Attila was by nature cautious and preferred above all to gain his political and military objectives through cunning political maneuvers rather than bloodshed, as the Roman chronicler Ammianus Marcellinus noted. If he had to fight, he used his confederates and allies as much as possible rather than risking Hun forces. Although he was called a savage and a barbarian by his enemies, this assessment may not be entirely fair, particularly when considering his abilities as a military commander. Attila often led armies of 60,000 to 100,000 troops from what is now central Hungary into Gaul, Italy, Illyria, Greece, and Spain. There, he conducted siege operations and fought pitched battles. What is even more impressive is the fact that his armies were multilingual, making command and control difficult.

Attila's main adversaries were the Roman legions, at that time the best trained, disciplined, equipped, and supplied military formations in the world. They were ably led by professional noncommissioned officers and officers. Attila's ability to effectively meet and defeat the Roman legions places his military and intellectual powers on a par with the great commanders of his time.

After the death of Attila's uncle, Ruga, in A.D. 434, good relations with the Roman Empire ceased. Bleda and Attila engaged in almost constant warfare with the Eastern Roman Empire until Bleda's death in A.D. 445. When Attila assumed sole rule, he ruthlessly made war against the Western and Eastern empires, enjoying great success.

It appears from historical accounts that no amount of monetary tribute from the Roman Empire satisfied Attila, who was bent on conquering Rome. At that time Roman military strength was heavily committed to Asia Minor, Africa, and Gaul. This left Rome the option of paying off the Huns to keep peace.

Attila made peace in the East to free his southern flank for an attack on the Western Roman Empire. He used, as justification for this attack, the refusal of Valentinianus III to accede to his demand for the hand of his sister, Honoria, in marriage. Attila appeared, unexpectedly, at the gates of Metz on Easter Sunday, 7 April 451. His army killed and looted as far south as the Loire River. At Orléans, he reached the frontier of the kingdom of the Visigoths, having burned everything in his path. When the Roman army, under Aetius, arrived, Attila and his allies were still besieging Orléans. Attila immediately raised the siege to look for a battlefield where he intended to fight a pitched battle. This decision to stand and fight was uncharacteristic of the Huns, who avoided close combat, especially when conditions were not totally in their favor.

Attila found a suitable field on the plains of Châlons (Catalaunian Plains). Here, near the city of Troyes, close to a small village called Mauriacum, he prepared for battle. Because he was superstitious and believed he would lose, he placed his Huns in the center around himself. The Ostrogoths with Walamir were placed on the left, facing the Visigoths, and Ardaric and the Gepids were on the right facing the Romans. Aetius, who was concerned about the loyalty of his Alans, placed his Romans on the left flank, the Alans in the center, and Theodoric and his Visigoths on the right.

The battle, which began around 3:00 P.M., ended late in the evening. Although Theodoric was killed, Attila clearly lost control toward evening, and the battle then turned in Aetius's favor. At dark, the Huns withdrew into the wagon fort that was their camp. When morning came, the Romans and Visigoths had withdrawn from the field. Aetius, for political expediency, had left Attila free to depart. Attila, however, turned south, invading Venetia and Aquileia (452), devastating northern Italy, and taking Milan and Apuleia. In desperation, Pope Leo I came out of Rome to meet Attila and dissuade him from sacking Rome. It is said that the pope succeeded in persuading Attila to relent and spare Rome, but it is more likely that the invasion of his home territory (modern-day Hungary) by the armies of the East Roman Emperor Marcianus cut short his Italian expedition.

Attila died a year after returning home (453) of a sudden nosebleed on the evening of his marriage to Ildiko. None of his sons was strong enough to keep Attila's allies subjugated and his empire intact. The Hun empire, within twenty years of Attila's death, disintegrated from bloody internal power struggles and fighting with the Romans. The main Hun tribes, under the leadership of Attila's two Hun sons, Irnik and Dengizik, returned to the areas between the Dniester and Don rivers. Some Hun tribes remained in the Carpathian Basin, but these either posed no threat to Rome or they entered Roman military service. Irnik also entered Roman service at some later date. Dengizik tried stubbornly to reestablish his father's empire, but was killed in combat against East Roman forces.

Szabolcs M. de Gyürky
Cheryl de Gyürky

See Also: History, Ancient Military; Roman Empire.

Bibliography

Eckhardt, S., et al. 1986. *Attila es Hunjai* (Attila and his Huns). Ed. G. Nemeth. Budapest: Hungarian Academy Press.

Fuller, J. F. C. 1954. *A military history of the Western world.* Vol. 1. New York: Funk and Wagnalls.

Maenchen, O. J. 1973. *The world of the Huns.* Berkeley, Calif.: Univ. of California Press.

Padanyi, V. 1956. *Dentu Magyaria.* Buenos Aires: Transylvania.

Phillips, E. D. 1969. *The Mongols.* London: Thames and Hudson.

Zajti, F. 1939. *Magyar Evezredek* (Hungarian millennia). Budapest: Arpad Fodor Press.

B

BALKAN WARS

First Balkan War, 1912–13

In 1912 Bulgaria, Serbia, and Greece—each seeking to eliminate Turkish power in its region of the Balkans, and each seeking to increase its own territorial area—entered into a military alliance to take advantage of Turkey's involvement in a war with Italy. Tiny Montenegro was informally associated with the allies. The pretext for war was Turkish misrule in Macedonia.

Turkey had about 140,000 troops in Macedonia, Albania, and Epirus, and another 100,000 in Thrace. The allies were rightly confident that Greek command of the Aegean would prevent rapid and direct transfer of other Turkish forces to the Balkans. Bulgarian active military strength was approximately 180,000, Serb 80,000, and Greek 50,000, and each had about an equal number of trained, readily mobilizable reserves. Montenegrin militia strength, capable only of guerrilla operations, was about 30,000. Courage and stamina of the opposing forces were equal, but the tactical leadership of the allies was superior to that of the Turks, despite recent German assistance in reorganization of the Ottoman army.

ALLIED INVASIONS

Almost simultaneously, the allies moved into Turkey's European provinces on 17 October 1912. Three Bulgarian armies under Gen. Radko Dimitriev invaded Thrace, moving generally on Adrianople. In Macedonia, Gen. Radomir Putnik's three Serbian armies from the north, and Crown Prince Constantine's Greek army from the south, converged on the Vardar Valley with the intention of compressing hastily grouping Turkish elements between them.

Operations in Macedonia. While a small Greek force invaded Epirus in the west, Constantine's main army pressed on to the lower Vardar Valley. He defeated the Turks at Elasson on 23 October. Most of the Turkish force withdrew toward Monastir, but Constantine did not pursue since, contrary to prior agreements, a Bulgarian division (ostensibly aiding the Serbian invasion) was advancing toward Salonika, which was coveted by both Bulgaria and Greece. Constantine headed eastward to try to forestall the Bulgarians. Turkish resistance in unexpected strength at Venije Vardar on 2 November at first held up the Greek advance. At the same time, other Turkish units defeated Constantine's flank detachments at Kastoria and Yiannitsá. Despite these setbacks, on 5 November Constantine finally overwhelmed the Turks at Venije and pressed on to Salonika (Thessaloniki). The isolated Turks to his northwest withdrew to Yannina (Ioánnina).

Meanwhile, the Serbs met and defeated a Turkish covering force at Kumanovo on 24 October. Turkish resistance stiffened in the Babuna Pass, near Prilep, and checked the Serbs until a threatened double envelopment in the hills forced the Turks to evacuate Skopje and retreat to Monastir. There, reinforced to a strength of 40,000, they again gave battle.

At Monastir, on 5 November, a Serb division impetuously stormed commanding ground to threaten an envelopment of the Turkish left. An Ottoman counterattack, with reinforcements drawn from the center of their line, retook the height, almost annihilating the Serb division. But the Turk center was so weakened that a Serbian frontal attack broke through. Faced with a threatened Greek advance from the south, Turkish resistance collapsed. Nearly 20,000 Turks were killed or captured. The remainder, scattering to the west and south, finally reached the fortress of Yannina, where they were besieged by the Greeks.

In the face of Greek preparations for an all-out assault on Monastir, the Turkish garrison of 20,000 surrendered on 9 November. Constantine occupied the city one day before the frustrated Bulgarian division arrived. This incident, and the subsequent dispute over possession of Salonika, worsened relations between the Bulgarians and the Greeks.

By the end of the year, the only Turkish forces still holding out west of the Vardar were the garrisons of Yannina (besieged by the Greeks) and Scutari (Shkoder, besieged by the Montenegrins).

Operations in Thrace. In Thrace, a Turkish army group commanded by Abdalla Pasha met Dimitriev's Bulgarians in a series of fiercely contested engagements (22–25 October) and was driven back to a line between Lüle Burgas and Bunar Hisar, where it regrouped. The Bulgarian Second Army, on the right, invested Adrianople, while the other two Bulgarian armies wheeled to the east against the position of the Turkish field armies. The Battle of Lüle Burgas ensued.

The Bulgarian battle plan envisioned a strong frontal attack against the Turkish position followed by an envelopment of the Turkish left (southern) flank, intended to drive the Turks off their line of communications to the south and Istanbul. The Bulgarian attack, however, when it developed on 28 October, was poorly coordinated. On the first day only the Bulgarian left engaged the Turks. On the second day the fighting became general, but the Bulgarian units again failed to coordinate their efforts, and the attacks were delivered piecemeal. Nonetheless, the Bulgarian right was successful in turning the Turkish left, and the Turks were forced to withdraw in some confusion. The Bulgarians did not pursue. The Turks subsequently reorganized behind the permanent fortifications of the Chatalja Line, between the Black Sea and the Sea of Marmara, protecting Constantinople.

The Bulgarians, launching a premature assault, were driven back with heavy losses (17–18 November). A stalemate continued along the Chatalja Line until, on 3 December, an armistice between Bulgarians and Serbs on one side, and Turks on the other, temporarily ended hostilities. Adrianople remained in Turkish possession. Greece and Montenegro ignored the armistice.

ABORTIVE PEACE NEGOTIATIONS

Beginning on 27 December, representatives of the combatants and of the European Great Powers met in London, where they vainly tried to settle their conflicting aims with respect to the Balkans and the crumbling Turkish Empire. The conference collapsed.

On 23 January 1913 the Turkish government was overthrown by the Young Turk nationalistic group, led by Enver Bey. The Young Turks denounced the armistice and, on 3 February, hostilities resumed.

RESUMPTION OF HOSTILITIES

On 3 March the Turkish garrison of 30,000 surrendered Yannina to Crown Prince Constantine. This was followed on 26 March at Adrianople by a combined Bulgarian-Serb assault against the eastern face of the fortress, breaching the Turk lines despite an allied loss of 9,500 men. Shukri Pasha surrendered Adrianople with his garrison of 60,000.

Meanwhile, in mid-March, a Serb force had come to the assistance of the irregular Montenegrin besiegers at Scutari, but they left on 16 April after a month of continuing disagreements. The Turks then surrendered to the Montenegrins.

TREATY OF LONDON

On 30 May the Great Powers finally imposed an uneasy peace, the Treaty of London, on the combatants. Turkey lost all of her European possessions save the tiny Chatalja and Gallipoli peninsulas. Bitter squabbles broke out between Bulgaria, on the one hand, and the Greeks and Serbs, on the other, over the division of conquered Macedonia. Montenegro was forced to abandon Scutari to the newly established state of Albania.

Second Balkan War, 1913

At the end of the war, Bulgaria's five armies were arranged as follows: the First faced the Serbs between Vidin and Brokovitsa, with the Fifth on its left; the Third lay above Kustendil; the Fourth about Koccani and Radaviste (Radovic); the Second faced the Greeks between Strumitsa (Strumica) and Serres (Serrai).

The Serb Second Army was on the old Serb-Bulgarian frontier; the First, in the center, at Kumanovo and Kriva Palanka; the Third, on the right of the First, was concentrated along the Bregalnica.

The Greeks were assembled between the lower Vardar and the mouth of the Struma.

Bulgarian Offensive

On 30 May the Bulgarians attacked Serbia and Greece without a declaration of war. The Fourth and Third armies, moving to the Vardar, attacked the Serbs. The Second Army drove in Greek advance elements. Both Serbs and Greeks were disposed in depth, however, and the Bulgarian attack soon lost its momentum.

Serbia's General Putnik, responsible for the success of the Serbian defensive, seized the initiative on 2 July. While the Third Serbian Army checked the Bulgarians on the upper Bregalnica, the First Army broke through, driving on Kyustendil and pushing the Bulgarians back in a northeasterly direction. On 3 July the Greeks attacked the Bulgarian Second Army, forcing it back. On 7 July the Greeks outflanked the Bulgarian left and drove them north up the Struma Valley. A counteroffensive by Bulgaria's Third and Fourth armies against the Serbian Third, toward the upper Bregalnica, was checked on 10 July.

Intervention of Romania

Romania declared war on Bulgaria on 15 July, and Romanian troops advanced into Bulgaria toward Sofia practically unopposed. At the same time, the Turks issued from the Chatalja Line and from Bulair (Bolayr) to reoccupy Adrianople. A Bulgarian attempt to regroup and attack the Greeks in the Struma Valley was unsuccessful. On 13 July Bulgaria sued for peace and hostilities were formally ended by the Treaty of Bucharest (10 August).

Bulgaria's brilliant successes in the First Balkan War caused her to underestimate her former allies' military capacity. The end result of the Second Balkan War was to deprive the Bulgarians of all gains made in the previous conflict.

TREVOR N. DUPUY

SEE ALSO: Ottoman Empire.

Bibliography

Ashmead-Bartlett, E. 1913. *With the Turks in Thrace.* London: W. Heinemann.
Barby, H. 1913. *La guerre des Balkans.* Paris: B. Grasset.
Dupuy, R. E., and T. N. Dupuy. 1986. *The encyclopedia of military history.* New York: Harper and Row.
Ford, C. S. 1915. *The Balkan wars.* Fort Leavenworth, Kans.: Press of the Army Service Schools.
Howell, P. 1913. *The campaign in Thrace, 1912.* London: H. Rees.
Kiraly, B. K., and D. Djordjevic, eds. 1987. *East central European society and the Balkan wars.* Boulder, Colo.: Social Science Monographs.
Schurman, J. G. 1914. *The Balkan wars, 1912–1913.* Princeton, N.J.: Princeton Univ. Press.
Wagner, H. 1913. *With the victorious Bulgarians.* Boston: Houghton Mifflin.

BOER WARS

The origins of the Boer Wars—sometimes called the Anglo-Boer or South African wars—can be traced back to the French Revolutionary–Napoleonic

Wars. In 1795 a small British force seized the Dutch Cape Colony, which had been established in 1652, at the southern tip of South Africa. This was returned to Dutch control in 1802 under the Treaty of Amiens.

After the renewal of the war between France and England, the British in early 1805 again occupied Capetown and the Cape Colony. In 1814 the Treaty of Paris granted the colony to Britain.

From the beginning of British rule, there was friction between the British administrators and the Dutch colonists, known as Boers (the Dutch word for farmers). Between 1835 and 1837, in a migration known to history as the "Great Trek," some 12,000 Boers migrated northward from the Cape Colony to establish independent states west of Natal, in the fertile valleys of the Vaal and Orange rivers. In 1852 Great Britain renounced its sovereignty over the Transvaal region, which was soon proclaimed the South African Republic. In 1854 Britain also recognized the independence of the neighboring Orange Free State. Over the next 40 years, despite frequent friction with both Zulus and British in Natal, the Boers firmly established themselves in their two new homelands.

The discovery of diamonds (1868) and gold (1888) in and adjacent to the territory of the two Boer states complicated what had become a three-way—British, Boers, Zulus—rivalry over the region. The British reannexed the Transvaal region in 1877. The Boers protested vigorously and began to plan rebellion. In 1879 in a bloody and hard-fought war, the British defeated the Zulus and established a protectorate over Zululand. Then, in late 1880, the Boers of the Transvaal again proclaimed their independence from Britain.

First Boer War, 1880–81

This action by the Boers of the Transvaal precipitated the First Boer War. Although they were undisciplined militiamen, the Boers were superb marksmen, and they operated as highly mobile mounted infantry. Although they had the best of the fighting in several sharp battles with British troops, the most important of which were Laing's Nek (28 January 1881) and Majuba Hill (27 February), they were unable to prevent British reoccupation. On 5 April 1881, in the Treaty of Pretoria, Britain compromised, granting independence to the South African Republic, but under a British protectorate.

Second Boer War, 1899–1902

Friction between British and Boers continued, as much due to the ambitions and machinations of Cecil Rhodes, the governor of the British Cape Colony, as to the obstreperous stubbornness of the Boers. In October 1899, President Paul Kruger of the South African—or Transvaal—Republic became concerned by the arrival of British troops in Natal for what appeared to the Boers to be a British expeditionary force. Kruger issued an ultimatum, giving the British government 48 hours to disband all military preparations. The ultimatum was refused. The Orange Free State announced its alliance with the South African Republic.

BOER MILITARY ORGANIZATION

The Boer military organization was extremely sketchy, a localized militia system grouped into so-called commandos that varied in strength with the population from which they were recruited. Every individual, however, was a marksman, armed with a modern repeating rifle, and every man was mounted. The riders of the veldt were hunters, trained from childhood to take advantage of cover and terrain. The result was an irregular firepower capability that could pulverize, from concealed positions, the ranks of any close-order formation. These irregulars were also capable of rapidly disappearing from the field when seriously threatened. The Boers also had a small quantity of modern German and French field artillery, on the whole well served. On the other hand, the Boers lacked discipline and control, and few of their leaders had any real concept of tactics or strategy.

BOER OFFENSIVE

Beginning on 11 October 1899, fast-moving Boer columns advanced, both east and west from the Transvaal. Two days later, Transvaal general Piet A. Cronje invested Mafeking, which was valiantly defended by a handful of British troops and militia under Col. Robert S. S. Baden-Powell. On 15 October, Free State forces besieged Kimberley.

Meanwhile, on 12 October, the Boer main effort, 15,000 strong, under Transvaal general Jacobus Joubert, pushed through the Natal Defense Force, equal in number, under Gen. Sir George White, at Laing's Nek. After brushes at Talana Hill (20 October), Elandslaagte (21 October), and Nicholson's Nek (30 October), Joubert, on 2 November, bottled up White's troops in Ladysmith.

British relieving forces were unwisely divided by the British commander in South Africa, Gen. Sir Redvers Buller, who tried to check the Boers everywhere at once. Gen. Lord Paul Methuen's column, nearly 10,000 men with sixteen guns, moved to the relief of Kimberley. Transvaal and Free State Boer commandos, about 7,000 strong, under Transvaal generals Cronje and Jacobus H. De La Rey, contested the advance in a series of delaying actions. On 28 November, Methuen won a hard-fought battle to reach the Modder River, after losing 72 men killed and 396 wounded, but his troops were so exhausted that he paused to await reinforcements. Boer casualties were negligible.

The Boers under Cronje near the Modder River, then about 8,000 strong, occupied an entrenched hill near Magersfontein. At dawn on 10 October, in the rain, Methuen attacked frontally in mass formation. He was repulsed in a two-day battle with the loss of 210 men killed (including one general officer), 675 wounded, and 63 missing. Again, Boer casualties were negligible.

Buller himself led 21,000 men of all arms to relieve Ladysmith. Crossing the Tugela River on 15 December, he attempted to turn the left flank of Free State general Louis Botha, entrenched near Colenso with 6,000 men. The British flank attack, entangled in difficult terrain, was decimated by small-arms fire. British batteries, unlimbering to support the frontal attack, found themselves at the mercy of a concealed force of Boer marksmen. The British were driven back with losses of 143 killed, 756 wounded, and 220 men and 11 guns captured. Boer losses in this, the Battle of Colenso, are believed to be not more than 50 men.

On 20 December, a British force under Gen. Sir William Gatacre got lost in a night move against an invading Boer spearhead from the Orange Free State, 112 kilometers (70 mi.) north of Queenstown. The British were ambushed and suffered heavy losses.

ROBERTS'S REORGANIZATION

At the end of Britain's "Black Week," General Buller was so badly beaten that he advocated the surrender of Ladysmith. He was at once relieved of the supreme command and replaced by Field Marshal Frederick Sleigh Roberts, Viscount of Kandahar, with Gen. Horatio Kitchener as his chief of staff.

Realizing at once that mobility was the keynote for success against the Boers, Roberts and Kitchener began revamping British field forces (Fig. 1). To meet the Boer fluidity of fire and movement, a progressive buildup of mounted infantry began around the existing militia units, a long and arduous task against conservative British military opinion. Meanwhile, along the southwest border of the Orange Free State, Brig. Gen. John D. P. French, with two small brigades of cavalry, kept up a spirited campaign against De La Rey and Free State general Christiaan R. De Wet, who were proving themselves to be natural leaders of light cavalry.

Figure 1. Royal Munster Fusiliers fighting behind the redoubt at Honey Nest Kloof, South Africa (ca. 1900). (SOURCE: U.S. Library of Congress)

BRITISH OFFENSIVE

In late January, General Buller began the first of two successive attempts to cross the Tugela River. He was defeated in his first attempt on 23 January at Spion Kop. He tried again on 5 February and was repulsed at Vaal Kranz. British losses in these battles were 408 killed, 1,390 wounded, and 311 missing. The Boers lost some 40 killed and 50 wounded.

On 15 February, General French reached Kimberley, bringing the Boer siege of that city to an end.

Meanwhile, in late January, Field Marshal Roberts had set out toward Kimberley with 30,000 men. While French was driving directly on Kimberley, the main British force marched past General Cronje's left flank at Magersfontein, threatening his communications. On 6 February, the Boer leader began a slow withdrawal.

On 18 February, near Paardeberg, Cronje's retreat across the Modder River was blocked by French, who had come rushing back from Kimberley. As the main British army approached, Roberts, temporarily sick, turned his command over to Kitchener, who made a tempestuous frontal piecemeal attack on the Boers' fortified laager (wagon train). The British were repulsed with losses of 320 killed and 942 men wounded.

Roberts, recovering, took command again and began a systematic encirclement and bombardment of the Boer laager. Cronje might have broken out with his 4,000 mounted men, but he stubbornly refused to abandon his wounded and his train, and was surrounded and besieged. With his men starving, he finally surrendered on 27 February.

On 17–18 February, General Buller, on the Tugela, made a third attack and finally succeeded. As he advanced toward Ladysmith, the besiegers withdrew and the relieving force made contact with the garrison on 28 February. The tide had turned.

OCCUPATION OF THE ORANGE FREE STATE

The British, now heavily reinforced, advanced on all fronts. On 13 March, Roberts took Bloemfontein, capital of the Orange Free State; pushing on, he reached Kroonstad on 12 May. Buller, in Natal on 15 May, swept Boer resistance away at Glencoe and Dundee. Nine days later the Orange Free State was annexed by Britain.

On 17 May, a flying column of cavalry and mounted infantry under Maj. Gen. Bryan T. Mahon relieved the garrison of Mafeking after a siege of more than seven months.

INVASION OF THE TRANSVAAL

Roberts now pushed into the heart of the Transvaal. Johannesburg fell on 31 May, then Pretoria on 5 June. On 4 July, Roberts and Buller joined forces at Vlakfontein, ending all formal resistance. President Kruger fled to Portuguese Mozambique, and then sought Dutch protection. On 3 September 1900, Britain formally annexed the Transvaal. In December, Roberts went home, leaving Kitchener in command.

Guerrilla Warfare

De Wet, De La Rey, Botha, and some minor leaders rallied the disbanded burgher forces to their respective commandos. For eighteen months they played havoc with British communications and defied all attempts to corner them. Erection of a line of blockhouses to protect the rail and other communication lines was the first remedial action taken by the British. But the raiders seemed to plunge at will through this cordon defense. Kitchener then turned to a war of attrition. The country was swept by flying columns of British mounted infantry; the farms on which the Boer raiders depended for sustenance were burned, and some 120,000 Boer women and children were herded into concentration camps, where an estimated 20,000 of them died of disease and neglect. Under these harsh measures, all resistance collapsed. In the spring of 1902, the guerrilla leaders capitulated.

On 31 May 1902, in the Treaty of Vereeniging, the Boers accepted British sovereignty. As part of the very lenient terms, Britain granted them £3 million compensation for the destroyed farms.

Total British casualties in the war were 5,774 killed and 22,829 wounded. The Boers lost an estimated 4,000 killed; there is no accurate total of the wounded, but they probably exceeded 10,000. About 40,000 Boer soldiers had been captured.

Assessment

It took the British Empire two years and eight months to subdue a foe whose manpower potential was 83,000 men of fighting age and who never had in the field at one time more than approximately 40,000 men. In the beginning, the number of British forces engaged did not total more than 25,000, but before it was over some 500,000 British troops were in South Africa—drawn from empire resources around the world. For the first time since the War of 1812, the British army met hostile mounted riflemen and small-arms fire. The experience of some 85 years of formal and informal wars in Europe and around the world was of little use, and an entirely new system of tactics and techniques had to be evolved on the battlefield.

Trevor N. Dupuy

Bibliography

Bond, B., ed. 1967. *Victorian military campaigns.* New York: Praeger.
De Wet, C. R. 1902. *Three years' war.* New York: Scribner.
Dupuy, R. E., and T. N. Dupuy. 1986. *The encyclopedia of military history.* 2d rev. ed. New York: Harper and Row.
Farwell, B. 1976. *The great Anglo-Boer war.* New York: Harper and Row.
Hillegas, H. C. 1899. *Oom Paul's people.* New York: Appleton.
Pakenham, T. 1979. *The Boer war.* New York: Random House.
Reitz, D. 1929. *Commando.* London: Faber and Faber.

BOLÍVAR, SIMÓN [1783–1830]

A great South American independence leader, Bolívar is hailed as *El Liberta-dor* (the Liberator) (Fig. 1). A soldier-statesman, his victories over the Spanish in the early 1800s won independence for Venezuela, Colombia, Peru, Ecuador, and Bolivia. Bolívar's life struggle was marked by severe vicissitudes—defeat, victory, adulation, and finally, rejection by the newly liberated states.

Early Years

Bolívar was born in 1783 in Caracas, Venezuela, of wealthy Creole parents, who died when he was young. He was sent to Europe in 1799 by his guardian to complete his education. There he married, but his wife died in Caracas of yellow fever in 1803. Bolívar returned to Europe in 1804 and studied Locke, Rousseau, and Voltaire. His idea of independence for Latin America probably originated during that time.

After his return to Venezuela from Europe, the young Bolívar joined a group of Venezuelan patriots who wrested Caracas, the colonial capital, from Spain in 1810. After a third trip to Europe that year—largely to seek aid from England,

Figure 1. Simón Bolívar. (SOURCE: U.S. Library of Congress)

which agreed only to remain neutral—he returned to Venezuela, where independence was declared in July 1811.

The Fight for Independence

In 1811 Bolívar took command of a liberation force occupying the Venezuelan port of Puerto Cabello. When Spain retook Venezuela in 1812, Bolívar fled to Colombia to join liberation forces there, and returned to Venezuela in 1813 at the head of an expeditionary force. After fighting the Spanish to the gates of Caracas, he entered the city and assumed dictatorial powers. However, he was defeated and driven out in mid-1814 by a band of *llaneros* (plains cowboys) organized by the Spanish.

Bolívar then made his way to New Granada (now Colombia) and then to Jamaica. In 1815 he went to Haiti, where he obtained arms and support from that newly independent country's president. In 1816, after two unsuccessful efforts to invade Venezuela, he decided to penetrate into Colombia, and he set up a base at Angostura, now Ciudad Bolívar. After several indecisive actions, he and his army, reinforced by British and Irish mercenaries, moved against the Spanish in 1819. His army marched over the Andes and attacked and defeated the Spanish army at Boyacá. He entered the capital, Bogotá, a few days later and assumed dictatorial powers. Bolívar returned to Venezuela with an army in 1821 to win the Battle of Carabobo (24 June), thus liberating the country. He quickly sent a trusted general, Antonio José de Sucre, into Ecuador at the head of a liberation force, freeing that territory from the Spanish. The territory of *Gran Colombia* (Colombia, Venezuela, and Ecuador) had now been liberated and was recognized by the United States.

There remained only Peru. The next year (1822) Bolívar met with José de San Martín, an Argentinean, the other great liberation figure of Latin America. San Martín had been instrumental in liberating Argentina and Chile, and then went to Peru to help in the nationalist struggle there. No one knows exactly what occurred in the meeting of San Martín and Bolívar, but apparently they disagreed. San Martín, perhaps wishing to avoid dissension in the liberation forces, returned to Argentina. Bolívar then moved into Peru, entered Lima in September 1823, and became that country's new dictator.

Finally, Bolívar's army (led by General Sucre) defeated the Spanish at the Battle of Ayacucho in Peru in 1824, which effectively ended Spanish power in Latin America. Sucre then marched eastward into the Presidency of Charcas, southeast of Peru, where he established a new republic named Bolivia, in Bolívar's honor, in 1825.

The independent *Gran Colombia* of several sovereign states that Bolívar envisioned did not survive. One by one, the newly liberated states withdrew from the union. By 1828, Bolívar governed only what is now Colombia. Sentiment against Bolívar's dictatorial rule grew stronger, there were insurrections and struggles for power by ambitious local leaders, and Bolívar narrowly escaped assassination at one time. In 1830, shortly before his death, Bolívar resigned as president of Colombia and went into exile.

Bolívar as Soldier and Statesman

As a commander, Bolívar was noted for his swift decisions and rapid reactions. His tactics often featured a strong element of surprise. For example, his victory at Boyacá, which liberated Colombia, was possible because he had led his forces through a difficult area of plains and mountains to attack a surprised Spanish army from an unexpected direction. Bolívar's military successes were enhanced by capable and aggressive subordinates, most particularly Sucre.

Bolívar took advantage of the political climate and condition of the time, which favored Latin American independence. A spirit of freedom and revolt against the old order arose in the Old and New Worlds following the French and American revolutions. Spain, which had been colonial overlord of most of Latin America for three centuries, had been weakened by Napoleon's invasion in 1806 and by internal unrest in the 1820s. The times were ripe for Bolívar and Latin American independence.

Bolívar left several important political statements, largely written in exile, which defined and inspired the Latin American struggle. The most important of these was *La Carta de Jamaica,* which outlined a grand scheme for a free Latin America stretching from Chile to Mexico.

His leadership was marked by a strong authoritarian streak. In devising constitutions for the liberated countries, Bolívar followed a vague Western model: a president for life, who would be, in fact, a dictator, and two legislative houses without any real power. This led to his downfall.

WALTER P. WHITE

SEE ALSO: Latin American Wars of Independence; San Martín, José de; Spanish Empire.

Bibliography

Johnson, J. J. 1968. *Simón Bolívar and Latin American independence.* Princeton, N.J.: Van Nostrand.
Lecuna, V. 1950. *Chronica Razonada de las Guerras de Bolívar.* 3 vols. Clinton, Mass.: Colonial Press.
Madariaga, S. de. 1967. *Bolívar.* Coral Gables, Fla.: Univ. of Miami Press.
O'Leary, D. F. 1970. *Bolívar and the war of independence.* Ed. and trans. R. F. McNerney, Jr. Austin, Tex.: Univ. of Texas Press.

BRADLEY, OMAR NELSON
[1893–1981]

General of the Army Omar Nelson Bradley (Fig. 1) was one of the most influential American military men of the twentieth century. His military career began when he entered the U.S. Military Academy at West Point in August 1911 and officially ended with his death at age 88 in 1981. Bradley was commissioned a second lieutenant upon graduation from West Point in 1915. He served in a variety of peacetime positions that ultimately prepared him for

Figure 1. Gen. Omar Bradley (left) with Under Secretary of Defense Stephen Early in 1950. (SOURCE: U.S. Library of Congress)

America's largest field command in history in World War II and subsequently the highest military position in the American defense establishment, the chairman of the Joint Chiefs of Staff.

Early Life and Civilian Career

Bradley was born to a family of limited economic means on 12 February 1893 near Clark, Missouri. As a boy, he excelled in school and became involved in hunting, fishing, trapping, and other outdoor pursuits, including such sports as football and baseball—interests that would remain with him for the rest of his life. When his mother moved the family to Moberly, Missouri, in 1908, Bradley met his future wife, Mary Quayle. It was also in Moberly where he applied for an appointment to West Point. To his great surprise, Bradley passed the entrance exams with excellent scores (surpassing those of the candidate endorsed by his congressman) and received the appointment. He subsequently entered West Point on 1 August 1911.

Bradley graduated with the class of 1915, later called the "class the stars fell on" for its large number of future general officers. Bradley's classmates included his fellow five-star general Dwight D. Eisenhower and the future four-star general James A. Van Fleet. He was actively involved in sports at West Point, where he played varsity baseball and football. He later wrote that his sports activities hurt his overall academic standing, but he never regretted them. Bradley graduated 44th out of 164 in June 1915 and began his active military career as a second lieutenant in the infantry.

Early Military Career

Bradley's military career after graduation was characterized by vain attempts to be assigned to a unit that was deploying to France. He later wrote that the period of American involvement in World War I was "professionally, the most frustrating of my early army career."

Bradley's career in the period between the two world wars was similar to that of many American officers. In the early 1920s he taught mathematics at West Point. That was a time of agonizingly slow promotions; Bradley was promoted to major in 1924 and remained a major for twelve years. It was at West Point that Bradley's only child, a daughter, was born. It was also during his West Point assignment that Bradley became interested in military history.

Following a school assignment at Fort Benning, Georgia, Bradley and his family traveled to their first overseas tour of duty at Schofield Barracks, Hawaii. He served with the 27th Infantry Regiment for three years before returning to the United States to attend the Command and General Staff College at Fort Leavenworth, Kansas. The year at Fort Leavenworth was followed by another assignment to Fort Benning, this time as an instructor. Bradley was later to call his decision to join the faculty at Fort Benning "the most fortunate decision of my life." It was here that Bradley first caught the eye of the future Chief of Staff of the United States Army, George Catlett Marshall. For the next twenty years Bradley was to serve intermittently with Marshall. Bradley spent four years under Marshall at Benning before he was selected to attend the Army War College in 1933. After his year at the War College, Bradley was again assigned to West Point, this time in the Department of Tactics. Bradley spent four years at West Point and profoundly influenced many of the Academy's outstanding graduates, including William C. Westmoreland and Creighton W. Abrams. Upon the completion of his second tour of duty at West Point, Bradley had spent thirteen years of his 23-year career as an instructor of some sort.

Bradley's final peacetime assignments were as assistant secretary to the General Staff and as commandant of the Infantry School at Fort Benning in February 1941. Bradley owed appointment to both of these important positions to Marshall. The commandant's job brought Bradley promotion to brigadier general. Soon after America's entry into World War II, Bradley was promoted to major general and briefly commanded first the 82d Infantry Division and then the 28th Infantry Division; he was the first man in his class to command a division.

World War II

Bradley's first wartime overseas assignment came early in 1943 when, on Marshall's advice, he was cast in the awkward role of Gen. Dwight D. Eisenhower's personal representative at the front in North Africa. It was as Eisenhower's "eyes in North Africa" that Bradley began his often stormy relationship with Gen. George S. Patton, Jr. Bradley was later elevated to assistant II Corps commander under Patton. He later assumed command of the II Corps and led it successfully until the end of the North African campaign. Promoted to lieutenant general, he also commanded the II Corps during the Sicilian campaign (10 July–17 August 1943).

In October 1943, largely as a result of Patton's much-publicized slapping of several soldiers under his command, Bradley was placed in command of the U.S. First Army, the American ground force for the Normandy invasion. (Bradley's command would ultimately consist of more than 1.3 million men.) Shortly after the "Overlord" landings on 6 June 1944 and immediately after the breakout of his First Army at St. Lô on 26 July, Bradley was named commander of the Twelfth Army Group.

As commander of the Twelfth Army Group, Bradley learned the harsh realities of modern coalition warfare when he experienced several disputes with Britain's Gen. (later Field Marshal) Bernard L. Montgomery. Montgomery and Bradley both opposed General Eisenhower's broad-front strategy approach, but Bradley wished to have the narrow thrust performed by his First or Third Army, while Montgomery wanted it for his British First Army. Both were overruled by Eisenhower. These disputes came to a head during the Battle of the Bulge (16 December 1944–mid-January 1945) when Montgomery claimed much of the credit, at the expense of the American troops, for the ultimate Allied victory.

Despite the setback in the Ardennes Forest, and despite Eisenhower's diversion of resources to Montgomery, Bradley's forces beat their British counterparts in crossing the Rhine River. Bradley subsequently was promoted to full general (12 March 1945). He was indeed fortunate to have such outstanding subordinates as Patton and Gen. Courtney H. Hodges as army commanders. With those aggressive, offense-minded generals leading the way, Bradley's forces soon linked up with the Russians at the Elbe River in April 1945. By May the war was over. It was during the European campaigns that Bradley earned the nickname "GI General" for his compassion for the common soldier.

Postwar

Immediately after the war Bradley became veterans affairs administrator. Shortly thereafter, on 7 February 1948, Bradley succeeded Eisenhower as chief of staff of the U.S. Army. Finally, on 16 January 1949, he became the first chairman of the Joint Chiefs of Staff. He was promoted to five-star rank in September 1950. Bradley served in these high positions during some of the most trying days of the early cold war.

Although a five-star general cannot officially "retire," Bradley stepped down from active duty on 15 August 1953. He served in a variety of positions in private industry while still giving military guidance when called upon. Bradley died on 8 April 1981 at age 88. He is buried at Arlington National Cemetery.

KEVIN J. WEDDLE

SEE ALSO: Eisenhower, Dwight D.; Marshall, George Catlett, Jr.; Montgomery, Bernard Law; Patton, George Smith, Jr.; World War I; World War II.

Bibliography

Ambrose, S. 1970. *The supreme commander*. New York: Doubleday.
Bradley, O. 1951. *A soldier's story*. New York: Holt, Rinehart and Winston.
———, and C. Blair. 1983. *A general's life*. New York: Simon and Schuster.

Eisenhower, D. 1948. *Crusade in Europe.* New York: Doubleday.
Pogue, F. 1954. *The supreme command: U.S. Army in World War II.* Washington,
 D.C.: U.S. Dept. of the Army.
Whiting, C. 1971. *Bradley.* New York: Ballantine.

BRAUCHITSCH, WALTHER VON [1881–1948]

German Field Marshal Walther von Brauchitsch, the future commander-in-chief of the German army (ground forces), was born in Berlin on 4 October 1881. Like many of his now-famous contemporaries (Field Marshals Blomberg, Busch, and Goering), Walther von Brauchitsch graduated from the Hauptkadettenanstalt Gross-Lichterfelde in Berlin. Upon receiving his commission as a lieutenant on 22 March 1900, he was posted to the Third Guard Grenadier Regiment at Berlin-Charlottenburg. One year later, he requested a change in his combat arms' designation and was reassigned to the Third Guard Field Artillery Regiment. On 18 October 1909 he was promoted to the rank of first lieutenant, Field Artillery.

His capabilities in the assessment of situations during tactical exercises brought him to the attention of his superiors. This resulted in his appointment to the German Great General Staff on 18 December 1913, about the same time as his promotion to captain.

Assignment to the Great General Staff included attendance at the Imperial War Academy. The three-year curriculum concentrated primarily on tactics and military history, with secondary emphasis on staff procedures for tactical support. The first year's studies centered on regiment- and division-level operations, while the second year covered supply and special problems, again at the regimental and divisional levels. The third year emphasized military history, tactics, and more special problems, with additional concentration on terrain analysis and studies. The last year's studies, however, were approached from the level of army corps operations.

World War I

At the start of World War I, Brauchitsch was a General Staff officer with the XVI Army Corps at Metz. By 1915, he was posted to the 34th Infantry Regiment, then located in the Argonne Forest, as its General Staff officer. He distinguished himself at Verdun in August 1916 and was awarded the Knight's Cross of the Order of the House of Hohenzollern. This was the second highest award for military valor, surpassed only by the Ordre Pour le Mérite, commonly known as the Blue Max.

Brauchitsch's rapid rise in the Great General Staff was no small feat, given that the selection criteria for training and final appointment were high, and competition was keen. Only the best troop unit officers were appointed to the Great General Staff. There were other general staffs and staff schools in the

German Imperial Army, such as the Bavarian, whose members in no way met the selection criteria for the Great General Staff.

At the close of World War I, Brauchitsch was a major on the General Staff of Army Group "German *Kronprinz*."

Interwar Years

In 1921, Brauchitsch returned to troop duty, and commanded the Second Detachment of the Sixth Artillery Regiment in Minden, Westphalia. On 1 July 1923, while at Minden, he was promoted to lieutenant colonel. In November 1927, he was reassigned to the Sixth Infantry Division as its chief of staff. He was selected for promotion to colonel on 1 April 1928, well ahead of his peers. With this promotion, Brauchitsch was posted to the Ministry of Defense as chief of the Army Training Branch. He served in this critical position until his promotion to brigadier general on 1 March 1932. At that time, he became inspector general of Artillery. Thus, he was already a general officer when Adolf Hitler assumed the Chancellorship of Germany.

Drastic changes in the Ministry of Defense, instituted by Hitler, resulted in Blomberg's appointment to the post of Defense Minister. This left vacant the position of commanding general, First Division, located in Koenigsberg, East Prussia. Brauchitsch was given command of the division and was also appointed commanding general of Wehrkreis Kommando I, also located in East Prussia. East Prussia was considered extremely vulnerable because it was separated from Germany proper by the Polish Corridor under the Treaty of Versailles.

Upon Hitler's repudiation of the Treaty of Versailles and the reinstitution of universal military conscription, Major General Brauchitsch was promoted to *general der artillerie* (lieutenant general) and was assigned to command I Army Corps (20 April 1936).

The continuing, rapid expansion of the armed forces did not allow him much time in this command. When the new Fourth Army Group was formed at Leipzig, Brauchitsch was posted there as its commander on 1 April 1937. Almost a year later, 4 March 1938, he was promoted to full general (*general-oberst*).

German troops under Brauchitsch's command entered Austria in March 1938, for the Auschluss. In October 1938, he led his troops in the occupation of the Sudetenland and in March 1939 entered Bohemia and Moravia. He was also responsible for the planning and execution of the army's tactical plan for the occupation of Poland (September 1939). For this, he was awarded the Knight's Cross of the Iron Cross.

World War II

Although Brauchitsch vigorously opposed "Case Yellow," the plan to attack France, he proceeded to build up the divisions required for this plan. Attempts to dissuade Hitler from the attack proved fruitless, and Case Yellow, which began on 10 May 1940, was executed successfully with speed and élan. The outstanding performance of the army earned him promotion to field marshal on 19 July 1940.

In the spring of 1940, German forces under Brauchitsch's operational command, concluded successful operations against Yugoslavia, Greece, and Crete. Upon completion of the Balkan Campaign, he received Directive 21 for Operation "Barbarossa," the German campaign against Russia. The operational planning was carried out under the direction of Gen. Franz Halder, chief of the Army General Staff.

By now, both Brauchitsch and Halder were seriously disillusioned with Hitler's methods. In particular, they were concerned about his approach to command and control as well as his allowing political motives to overshadow sound military considerations in the planning of operations.

The attack on the Soviet Union, which began on 22 June 1941, three months later than originally planned, bogged down by December 1941. Incredibly high casualties were inflicted on the army, which bore the brunt of the campaign. The stresses of the campaign became too much for Brauchitsch, already weakened by severe heart disease, and he requested permission to retire. His request was granted on 19 December 1941.

Shortly after this, the field marshal underwent heart surgery and lived in retirement for the remainder of the war. When World War II ended, he became a British prisoner, confined first in England and later in Munsterlager. He died of a heart attack while still a prisoner of war, on 18 October 1948.

Significance

Walther von Brauchitsch's military significance lies both in his rapid rise in rank and in his competence as a military strategist. By virtue of his talents and abilities, he rose to the rank of brigadier general during the turbulent years of the Weimar Republic before Hitler became chancellor. He later earned his marshal's baton on his own merits, and remained true to the ideals and concepts of the General Staff. Although he disagreed on occasion with Hitler, as was his right, he nevertheless performed his duty to his country and to its highest authority, the Führer. It could be argued that he should have been more forceful in the expression of his disagreements; on the other hand, had he been more forceful, he might have been relieved and thus have lost all influence. Under his leadership, the German army successfully executed all its operations from the prewar annexations of the Sudetenland, Austria, Bohemia, and Moravia, to the invasions of Scandinavia, the Low Countries, France, the Balkans, and Greece. The Russian Campaign, as conceived by Brauchitsch, was a sound tactical plan and could have progressed well had it not been for Hitler's meddling in operational matters. Considerable credit for these accomplishments, particularly the planning, goes to his chief of staff, Franz Halder. Walther von Brauchitsch was one of the last worthy examples of traditional and apolitical general officers produced by the German Great General Staff.

SZABOLCS M. DE GYÜRKY
CHERYL DE GYÜRKY

SEE ALSO: History, Modern Military.

Bibliography

Department of the Army. 1955. *The German campaign in Russia—Planning and operations (1940–1942)*. Department of the Army Pamphlet no. 20–261a. Washington, D.C.

The German general staff corps: A study of the organization of the German general staff. April 1946, produced at GMDS by a combined British, Canadian, and U.S. Staff.

Goerlitz, W. 1953. *History of the German general staff 1657–1945*. Trans. B. Battershaw. New York: Praeger.

Heuer, G. F., 1978. *Die Deutsche General-Feldmarschalle und Grossadmirale*. Rastatt/Baden, Germany: Erich Pabel Publishers K. G.

Kennedy, R. W. 1956. *The German campaign in Poland (1939)*. Department of the Army Pamphlet no. 20–255. Washington D.C.: Department of the Army.

BROOKE, ALAN FRANCIS
(1st Viscount Alanbrooke)
[1883–1963]

As chief of the Imperial General Staff (CIGS) December 1941–46, Lord Alanbrooke was commander in chief of Britain's military forces during much of World War II, and was Prime Minister Winston Churchill's key military adviser. In these positions, he played a vital role in developing Allied strategy. His daily diary, which he maintained during the war, has been an important source of historical information.

Early Years

Brooke was born in Bagueres de Bigorre, France, on 23 July 1883. His father, Sir Victor Brooke, was an Irish landowner who moved to France because of a lung infection. Brooke attended a French school but spent his summers in Ireland, where he developed his lifelong love of fishing and ornithology.

His family had a strong military tradition. An older brother died in service in the First World War, and Churchill had served as assistant adjutant to another brother during the Boer War. Brooke entered the Royal Military Academy at Woolwich and graduated in 1902 with a commission in the Royal Artillery.

World War I and Interwar Years

Brooke began his active service as a subaltern, serving four years in Ireland before being transferred to India, where he remained until the outbreak of World War I. In September 1914 he debarked at Marseilles as captain in an Indian cavalry brigade. By the end of the war, he was chief artillery officer for the British First Army where he adapted the French system of creeping barrages to support and encourage attacking troops.

Between the wars, Brooke attended the Staff College at Camberly and became known as a skilled trainer. Later, he served as director of military training for the War Office, commanded the experimental mobile division, and was in charge of the Anti-Aircraft Command.

In appearance, Brooke was the very model of a British general, with a trim figure, a close-cropped mustache, and a stern military bearing. He was strong willed, highly disciplined, patient, and seemingly without nerves. Some felt his daily diary entries helped him get rid of some of the frustrations of his job. He was criticized by some as remote and aloof, an unsmiling man who expected efficiency and speed from subordinates. Yet, off duty he was relaxed, friendly, and mingled freely with troops of all ranks. His American counterpart, Gen. George C. Marshall, commented that Brooke was "determined in his position, yet amenable to negotiation, generous in his judgments, and delightful in his friendship."

World War II

At the outbreak of the war in 1939, Lieutenant General Brooke was given command of one of the two corps of the British Expeditionary Force (BEF) in France. A stickler for discipline and training, he was upset by the casual attitudes of senior French generals and by the seemingly low morale of their troops.

When the German armies struck through the Low Countries in May 1940, Brooke moved his corps north to reinforce the Belgian army. This began for Brooke what was to be only a nineteen-day campaign, which began to unravel with the sudden surrender of the Belgian army. As the overpowered BEF withdrew toward the English Channel and eventual evacuation, Brooke's corps was called upon to delay the German advance. Communication was difficult, and Brooke relied on daily personal visits to his division commanders to direct overall strategy and to improve morale. His best division commanders were Bernard Montgomery and Harold Alexander, and Brooke became their champion from that time on. To ensure his availability for later assignments, Brooke was ordered back to England on 29 May.

A few days after his return he was ordered to return to France and take command of the 150,000 British troops still with the French army. Once in France, and sensing the growing collapse all around him, Brooke urged that no more British troops be sent to the Continent and, later, received permission to evacuate the remnant of the BEF through Cherbourg. In July 1940, Brooke was given command of the British Home Forces and, with only fourteen weak divisions, he began to rearm, retrain, and reinspire the British army and to prepare defenses against the expected German invasion.

In December 1941, Brooke was appointed chief of the Imperial General Staff, succeeding Sir John Dill, and three months later was also asked to serve as chairman of the Chiefs of Staff Committee.

Once America entered the war, British planners led by Brooke dominated much of the early Anglo-American strategy sessions because of their firsthand experience fighting the Germans, and through superior staff work. The Americans wanted to attack the European mainland in late 1942 or 1943, but Brooke favored first sapping German strength by blockade and aerial bombing. He was very impressed with the high caliber of the German soldier and wanted to make sure that ample resources were available before any campaign was launched. Brooke was in favor of campaigns in North Africa, Sicily, and Italy, but discouraged efforts by Churchill to expand the war into the Balkans.

Key Relationships

After the war, Brooke wrote, "Churchill is the most wonderful man I have ever met." During the war, however, he wrote, "He is quite the most difficult man to work with I have ever seen." On balance, he and Churchill made a good team, the patient and tireless Brooke listening to Churchill's ideas and exercising a moderating influence. Night after night, after a hard day's work, Brooke would be called in by Churchill for a meeting or conversation, which might be followed by the showing of a new film and a sandwich at 2:30 A.M.

Brooke and the Supreme Allied Commander, Gen. Dwight D. Eisenhower, were never close. Churchill had promised Brooke command of the Allied invasion of Europe, but this was withdrawn when the scope of America's participation became clear. In his diary, Brooke often criticized Eisenhower's grasp of strategy but later admitted that Eisenhower was a good team leader and coordinator. Eisenhower wrote later, "Brooke did not hesitate to differ sharply . . . but this never affected the friendliness of his personal contacts or the unqualified character of his support. He must be classed as a brilliant soldier."

Postwar Years

In January 1944 Brooke was promoted to field marshal and after his retirement from military service in 1946 was made Viscount Alanbrooke.

Brooke married twice. His first wife died at his side in an automobile accident in the 1920s, leaving him with two children. One of them was a son who served in the British army in the war. Brooke later remarried and had two more children.

On his retirement, he spent much of his time studying and talking about nature, presenting numerous illustrated lectures on birds. Like Marshall, he did not write memoirs or seek to capitalize on his reputation.

Brooke died of a heart ailment at Wintney, Hampshire, England, on 17 June 1963, a few days before his 80th birthday.

ROBERT CALVERT, JR.

SEE ALSO: Eisenhower, Dwight D.; Marshall, George C.; Montgomery, Bernard L.; World War II.

Bibliography

Alanbrooke, Lord. 1939–46. Diaries.
Bryant, A. 1957. *Turn of the tide.* Garden City, N.Y.: Doubleday.
———. 1959. *Triumph in the West.* Garden City, N.Y.: Doubleday.

Churchill, W. 1949–51. *The Second World War.* 5 vols. Boston: Houghton Mifflin.
Fraser, D. 1982. *Alanbrooke.* New York: Atheneum.
Irving, D. 1981. *The war between the generals.* New York: Congdon and Lettes.

BYZANTINE EMPIRE

The Byzantine, or Eastern Roman, Empire fell heir to the heritage of the Roman Empire in A.D. 476. In that year a Gothic general, Odavacer, dethroned Romulus Augustulus, Emperor of the West, and recognized Zeno, Emperor of the East, as the sole ruler of the Roman world. The Byzantine Empire maintained the traditions of Rome, through alternating periods of greatness and decline, until the fall of Constantinople in 1453. The longevity of the empire depended to a large extent on the professionalism and efficiency of its armed forces.

The Byzantine Armed Forces

The Byzantine armed forces exhibited, throughout the existence of the empire, an ability to adapt to changing strategic and tactical situations. Organization, weapons, and tactics changed to meet the threat. "Threat assessment" was a continual process within the Byzantine high command, as the empire's frontiers were rarely free from foreign intrusion, and the threats were usually multiple.

Although elements within the Byzantine defense structure were subject to periodic change, the professionalism and effectiveness of its combat formations—cavalry, infantry, specialist units, naval forces—and Byzantine generalship remained constant.

COMBAT FORMATIONS

The greatest contrast between the Byzantine army and the Roman army of the Republic and Empire was the former's reliance on cavalry. However, the Byzantine army, the heir to the traditions and genius of the army of the Caesars, had inherited its cavalry from the Roman army of A.D. 378, not the army of 33 B.C. After the Gothic victory over the emperor Valens at Adrianople (A.D. 378), the Romans adopted the cavalry organization, weapons, and tactics of the Goths and relegated the infantry, the principal arm of the old army, to a secondary role. The Byzantine cavalry later adopted the arms and tactics of the Persians, the perennial enemy of the empire for its first 159 years.

The cavalry was divided into heavy cavalry and light cavalry. The heavy cavalryman wore personal armor consisting of a helmet, thigh-length mail shirt, mail gauntlets, greaves, and heavy boots with spurs. Weapons included a lance, sword, axe or mace, dagger, and bows and arrows. Heavy cavalry horses were also armored, and the Byzantine saddle was fitted with stirrups. So equipped, the Byzantine *cataphract* resembled his Persian counterpart and prefigured the knight of the European Middle Ages.

The light cavalryman was lightly armored; his armor consisted of a helmet and a waist-length mail shirt. Weapons were either bows and arrows or javelins, as well as a sword.

Although secondary in importance to the cavalry, the Byzantine infantry was not allowed to atrophy. The infantry, like the cavalry, was divided into heavy and light formations. The heavy infantry (*scutati*) were equipped with helmet, waist-length mail shirt, gauntlets, and greaves. Offensive weapons were the lance, sword, or axe. Heavy infantrymen also carried large shields (*scutum*) from which they derived their name.

The light infantry (*psiloi*), like the light cavalry, wore little personal armor. When worn, armor consisted of a helmet and a waist-length mail shirt. Weapons included bows and arrows or javelins. Often the infantryman carried an axe and a small, round shield.

Specialist support units consisted of engineer, transportation, supply, and medical units. Besides constructing and repairing roads and bridges, the engineers conducted siege operations. In the field, transportation, supply, and medical assets were drawn from the civilian population and were paid on commission. These units were under command of a *tuldophylax*.

The Byzantine navy dominated the Mediterranean and faced little opposition until the rise of the Arabs in the seventh century. The backbone of the navy was the *droman*, a lateen-rigged, two-masted galley with two banks of oars. Depending on the size of the ship, it had from 30 to 40 oars per side. Normally, 300 men crewed a *droman*.

BYZANTINE GENERALSHIP

The Byzantine approach to the study and practice of war was both professional and scientific. The strengths and weaknesses of enemies and potential enemies were researched. Enemy tactics were analyzed and countertactics developed.

Byzantine combat studies and threat assessments produced a number of treatises on the art of war. These treatises were the equivalent of modern military field and technical manuals. Surviving examples include *Strategikon*, attributed to the emperor Maurice (582–602); *Tactica*, attributed to the emperor Leo VI, "the Wise" (886–912); and *Nicephorus Praecepta Militaria*, attributed to the emperor Nicephorus II Phocas (963–69) but likely written by a staff officer.

The Byzantine high command and general staff were part of the imperial household. The imperial bodyguard functioned as the training ground for officers destined for the highest levels of command.

STRATEGY AND TACTICS

Byzantine strategy has often been characterized as defensive. This generalization, however, is contradicted by the aggressive policies of Justinian I, Heraclius, Nicephorus II, John I, and Basil II. Each of these emperors justified his policy on religious and historical grounds. The Byzantine emperor envisioned himself as the anointed protector of Christianity. As the heir of the Caesars, the emperor felt it his duty to reclaim land once part of the Roman Empire, to restore the unity and greatness of the Roman *imperium*. As the *imperium* and

Christendom were considered synonymous, Byzantine expansionism was religiously, politically, economically, and historically justified.

Byzantine conduct of war included not only military operations but also diplomatic maneuvers, as well as such niceties as espionage, sabotage, bribery, psychological warfare, subversion, and so forth. Fifteen hundred years before the term became popular, the Byzantines attempted to destabilize enemy governments, either as a prelude to military action or as its substitute. Belisarius, the great general of the Age of Justinian, echoing the sentiments of the Chinese theoretician Sun Tzu, stated that it is best to force the enemy to abandon his objective without resorting to battle. Any means that accomplished this end were felt to be justified.

The basic tactical formation of the Byzantine army was the *numerus* (*bandon*), equivalent to a modern battalion. The size of the *numerus* varied from province to province, ranging from 300 to 500 men under the command of a count (*comes*) or tribune. From three to eight *numeri* formed a *turma* (*moirach*). The strength of the *turma* ranged from 1,500 to 2,400 men, equivalent to a reinforced regiment or demi-brigade. The *turma* was commanded by a *turmarch*. The largest tactical unit was the *thema* (*meros*) consisting of from two to three *turmae*. Commanded by a *strategos*, the *thema* deployed between 4,500 and 7,200 combat troops. Garrison commands were organized on the basis of a *clissura*, a unit roughly equivalent to a *numerus*, commanded by a *clissurarch*.

The Byzantines deployed for battle according to the nature and size of the enemy forces and the nature and size of the Byzantine forces available. All tactical formations were composed of a center and two wings. The composition of the wings was invariably cavalry; that of the center depended upon the availability of heavy infantry. When present, the heavy infantry formed the center and acted as the tactical pivot of the Byzantine line. After receiving the initial enemy assault, the center would hold the foe while the cavalry counterattacked. When the infantry contingent was small, or none was present, heavy cavalry units formed the center, often dismounting when faced by enemy infantry to receive the enemy assault. The armament of the *cataphract* allowed him to function as infantry when necessary.

Byzantine commanders usually deployed their light cavalry hidden in prepared ambush sites. During the battle, these units would attack the enemy flanks and rear.

Byzantine Expansion during the Age of Justinian

The accession of Justinian I, the Great (527–65), initiated the first phase of Byzantine expansion. Justinian, a native of the Latin-speaking province of Illyria, was conscious of his responsibility, as heir of the heritage of Rome, to restore and strengthen the Roman *imperium*. At the time of Justinian's accession, North Africa was controlled by Vandals, Berbers, and Moors; Spain (Hispania) had been overrun by the Visigoths; Italy had fallen prey to the Ostrogoths. Justinian was determined to win back these lands and restore the Roman Empire.

In 533, Belisarius landed in North Africa with a force of 15,000. Of the troops available to him, Belisarius relied on his 5,000 cavalry, composed of his own bodyguard and Hun mercenaries. At the battles of Ad Decimen and Tricameron, Belisarius was victorious. Gelimer, king of the Vandals, surrendered to Belisarius in 534 and Africa (modern Tunisia, as well as much of Algeria and Morocco), once again became a province of the empire.

Justinian's next target was Italy, then under the control of Ostrogoth King Witiges. The emperor gave Belisarius an army of 10,000 with which he was to reconquer Sicily and Italy from a Gothic army ten times the size of his own. Landing in Sicily, where he was welcomed as a liberator, Belisarius quickly secured the island. Crossing the Straits of Messina, Belisarius rapidly advanced as far as Naples, where he encountered stiff resistance. Naples fell after an intrepid detachment of Byzantines penetrated the city defenses by way of the aqueduct system. Rome was occupied in December 536. After withstanding a year-long siege by the Ostrogoths, Belisarius advanced northward from Rome. Defeated in battle after battle, the Goths surrendered in 537.

In 541, the Byzantine hold on Italy was seriously threatened by Totila, the new Ostrogoth king. Raising the banner of rebellion, Totila advanced as far south as Naples before being stopped. Belisarius was able to reoccupy Rome in 546, but was forced to relinquish control of the Eternal City in 549. Justinian recalled Belisarius in 552 and replaced him with Narses. At the battle of Tagina in A.D. 552, Narses crushed the Ostrogoths. The following year, Narses defeated an army of invading Franks at Casilinum. By 554, all of Italy was secured.

The Byzantine reconquest of Italy proved short-lived. In 568, the Lombards invaded Italy and forced the Byzantines into the southern part of the peninsula. However, southern Italy and Sicily remained Byzantine until the advent of the Normans. The Byzantine reconquest of Spain, completed in 554, was somewhat more successful. The empire held the southern third of the Iberian Peninsula until 616, when the Visigoths reclaimed their lost territories.

The Military Reforms of Maurice (582–602)

The Byzantine army of the Age of Justinian possessed many advantages over its enemies in North Africa and Italy. The tactical skill of Belisarius and Narses, as well as the quality of their troops, enabled the Byzantines to overcome numerically superior enemy forces. The flexibility of the *cataphract*, who could fight on foot as well as on horseback, allowed the Byzantine commanders greater latitude and multiple options in operational planning and execution.

The glaring weakness of the Byzantine army was its reliance on foreign mercenaries. The use of mercenaries, a practice inherited from the later Roman Empire, placed a heavy financial burden on the imperial treasury. More troubling, mercenaries tended to desert when the tide of battle turned against their employer. It was for good reason that Belisarius and Narses took steps to reduce vulnerabilities resulting from doubtful troops. Finally, to the extent they had loyalties, mercenaries were loyal to their generals and not to the *imperium*. The specter of a military coup, another legacy of the Roman Empire, was all too real to Justinian and his successors.

The emperor Maurice, a successful general, ascended the throne in 582. Maurice advocated the reorganization of the Byzantine armed forces. First, he greatly reduced the recruiting of mercenaries. Second, all officers were to be appointed by, and responsible to, the imperial government. Third, all soldiers were required to swear loyalty first and foremost to the government, not to their generals.

Maurice's most important reform was the creation of the *themes*. Each *theme* was, in fact, a territorial defense unit under the command of a *strategos*. Under the *strategos* were a number of *turmae*, each having a strength of 2,000 men or more under the command of a *turmarch*. Each *turma* consisted of from six to eight *numeri* (battalions) or *clissurae* (garrisons). The actual tables of organization varied from *theme* to *theme* and depended on such considerations as population and proximity to the frontier.

The *theme* drew its manpower from the large and small landowners within its borders. Officers were recruited from among the large landowners, while the rank and file were drawn from the small landowners. Both officers and men received pay and tax exemptions for their service. Although used primarily in defense of its own territory, each *theme* provided contingents to the national army in times of crisis.

The *theme* system had much in common with the military system of Persia and the later feudal system of western Europe. All three systems tied military service to landholding. All three supplied a specified type of soldier in exchange for land and other perquisites. The *theme* system differed from the other two in that both large and small landowners formed the fighting force of the *theme*. In many respects the *theme* system married the feudal system of Persia with the ancient military tradition of the Greek city-states and the Roman Republic, the tradition of the citizen-soldier.

The *theme* system, begun under Maurice, was not completed until the reign of Leo III (717–41). In the interim, the Byzantine Empire suffered a series of crises and military defeats that threatened its very existence.

The Slavic War

During the reign of Maurice, the empire faced multiple threats on multiple fronts. To the north the Avars, the Slavs, and the rising power of the Bulgars loomed ominously. To the east, Persian expansionism once again threatened Syria, Palestine, and Asia Minor. The Slavic penetration of the Balkans was countered with a war of annihilation. Maurice entrusted the war to General Priscus. In one year in the late 590s, the Byzantines slaughtered 28,000 Slavs. The next year, Slav casualties amounted to 30,000 slain. Priscus finally crossed the Danube and systematically destroyed Slav settlements and put the inhabitants to the sword. Yet, before the Slav onslaught relented, the provinces of Thrace and Illyria—the two principal Latin-speaking provinces of the empire—lay in ruins.

The Persian War (602–630)

In 602 Maurice was overthrown and slain by one of his generals, Phocas, who assumed the imperial dignity. Chosroes II, king of Persia, used Maurice's murder as an excuse to break his treaty with the empire and invaded Syria. Conquering Syria, the Persians advanced into Asia Minor. By 608, the Persians were within sight of Constantinople. Phocas's misrule led to the rebellion of the province of Africa (northwest Africa). The Byzantine general Heraclius, son of the exarch (military governor) of Carthage, assumed leadership of the rebellion. In 610, Heraclius overthrew Phocas and ascended the throne.

For the first twelve years of his reign, Heraclius fought a defensive war against the Persians. All resources of the empire were concentrated on the defense of Constantinople. Consequently, the Persians succeeded in occupying Damascus and Antioch in 613, Jerusalem in 614, Chalcedon in 615, and Egypt in 619. In the west, the Visigoths recovered southern Spain in 616. The Avars once again besieged Constantinople in 619, but were repulsed.

Heraclius took the offensive in 622. Making a surprise amphibious landing on the coast of Cilicia, Heraclius outflanked the Persians and threatened their lines of communication. The emperor out-maneuvered the Persian forces and cut their lines of communication with Egypt, Palestine, and Syria. He won a decisive victory at the Battle of the Halys. At the end of the campaign season Heraclius withdrew to Byzantine territory, having inflicted severe damage on the enemy.

The following year Heraclius, after a feint toward Syria and Palestine, sailed to Trebizond, then swiftly advanced eastward through Armenia. From Armenia, he penetrated the Persian satrapy of Media. With the Persian homeland in peril, King Chosroes recalled his Persian units from Syria. Hoping to force Heraclius' withdrawal from Media, Chosroes convinced his Avar and Slav allies once again to besiege Constantinople.

Even with Constantinople under siege, however, Heraclius remained in Persia, cutting a destructive path through Media. Chosroes had no option but to return to Persia with all available forces. For four years, Heraclius marched through the western provinces of Persia, winning battle after battle. On 12 December 627, the Byzantines won the decisive battle of the war within sight of the ruins of Nineveh, the ancient Assyrian capital. Forced to seek peace, Chosroes agreed to pay a heavy indemnity and return all territories seized from the Byzantines.

The Byzantine Empire had emerged from its 28-year-long war with Persia victorious. Heraclius was hailed as both hero and savior and, quite deservedly, took his place among the great generals of Roman and Byzantine history. He did not long enjoy the fruits of victory. The war had drained both the Persian and Byzantine empires. To Persia, postwar weakness proved fatal. A new enemy arose on the southern fringes of civilization that swept away the ancient kingdom of Persia and drove the Byzantine Empire to the brink of destruction.

The Arab Conquests

The Arabs burst upon the war-torn Middle East in 634. Damascus fell in September 635 to the combined forces of Abu Obeida and Khalid ibn al-Walid. In 636, Heraclius arrived at Antioch with a strong force. The bulk of this force, commanded by Theodorus, the emperor's brother, reoccupied Damascus without a fight; Khalid ibn al-Walid had withdrawn southward. The Byzantines pursued the retreating Arabs until, at the confluence of the Jordan and Yarmuk rivers, Khalid turned and offered battle. The Battle of Yarmuk (20 August) ended in an Arab victory. Heraclius, upon learning of the defeat of his army and the death of his brother in battle, returned to Constantinople, leaving Syria and Palestine to the Arabs.

The Arabs next invaded Egypt. With the surrender of Alexandria in November 641, Egypt was secured. Three of the richest provinces of the Byzantine Empire—Egypt, Palestine, and Syria—were in Arab hands. Arab armies threatened North Africa, Asia Minor, and Constantinople itself. In 649 the newly created Arab navy took Cyprus, and in 655 it defeated the Byzantine fleet at the battle of the Masts (Dhat al-sawaib, off Phoenix, Lycian coast).

The Fight for Survival (642–842)

In the 200 years between the death of Heraclius and the rise of the Macedonian Dynasty, the Byzantine Empire waged a desperate struggle for survival. Four times during this period the Arabs laid siege to Constantinople. The sieges of 673–78 and 717–18 were conducted by both ground and naval forces. Constantinople survived all four sieges through a combination of good fortune, courage, and "Greek Fire." The first siege cost the Arabs 30,000 killed; the second, 70,000 killed.

The reign of Leo III, "the Iconoclast" (717–41), marked the turning point in the empire's struggle with the Arabs. Besides successfully repelling the last Arab siege, Leo completed the reorganization of the empire into *themes*. Army reform progressed slowly, but by the end of Leo's reign the Byzantines were able to take the offensive against the Arabs in Anatolia (Asia Minor), scoring a major victory at Akroinen in 739.

In 745 Leo's successor, Constantine V (741–75), initiated operations against the Arabs in Syria. The Byzantine navy defeated an Arab fleet and retook Cyprus in 746. Imperial campaigns in Armenia (751–52) also were successful. Only the loss of Ravenna to the Lombards in 751 marred the rebirth of Byzantine military prowess.

A new enemy now arose to challenge the empire. In the northeastern part of the Balkans, the Bulgar czars embarked on a program of territorial expansion. Between 755 and 764 the Byzantines campaigned against the Bulgars, gaining victories in 759 and 760. War with the Bulgars broke out again in 772, and the Byzantines again were victorious.

Leo IV (775–80) renewed the war with the Arabs in Anatolia. By 800 the Byzantines and the Arabs had reached parity in Asia Minor. Skirmishing continued between the Arabs and the Byzantines, with the border between the caliphate and the empire solidifying along the line of the Taurus Mountains.

In the Balkans, the Bulgars continued to threaten the empire. Leo V (813–20) stopped a Bulgar advance southward at Mesembria in 817.

The Age of Conquest (842–1050)

The accession of Basil I (867–86), first emperor of the Macedonian Dynasty, ushered in the second great period of Byzantine military glory. Basil launched a series of campaigns against the Arabs between 871 and 879. Samosata, on the upper Euphrates, was occupied in 873. During the campaign of 878–79, both Cappadocia and Cilicia were liberated. In Italy, Basil I regained control of Bari (875), Tarentum (880), Sicily (878), and Calabria (885).

Leo VI, "the Wise" (886–912), warred with the Bulgars and their aggressive czar, Symeon. Leo allied with the Hungarians in his struggles with the Bulgars.

Constantine VII (912–59) suffered a series of reverses in the ongoing struggle with the Bulgars. Although the Byzantines successfully repelled a Bulgar attempt on Constantinople in 913, Adrianople fell to the Bulgars the next year; the Bulgars, however, were not able to hold on to the city. At the battle of Anchialus in 914, the Bulgars were victorious. They once again attempted to take Constantinople in 924, again in vain. The only major victory won by Byzantine arms during this period was at the Garigliano River in southern Italy, in 915, when an Arab attempt to gain a foothold in Italy was repulsed.

In 920, Romanus Lecapenus (920–44) became Constantine's co-emperor. During this joint reign the Byzantines, under the command of John Kurkuas, retook Erzerum (928) and Melitene (934). In 941 the Byzantine fleet soundly trounced a Russian fleet attempting to enter the Bosporus. This was the first intrusion of Russian arms into the empire.

During the short reign of Romanus II (959–63), the Byzantines reoccupied Crete in 960–61. In 963 Romanus died and Nicephorus Phocas, who had commanded the successful operation in Crete, seized the throne and married Romanus' widow, Theophano.

NICEPHORUS II PHOCAS (963–69)

Nicephorus ascended the throne as co-emperor with his infant stepsons, Basil II and Constantine. Under Nicephorus, the *theme* system reached fruition, tactics were reformed, and the power and might of the empire reached new heights.

Nicephorus introduced a new tactical formation. Regiments were deployed for battle in a wedge. The front line of the wedge had twenty *cataphracts* abreast; the second line, 24 abreast; the third, 28; the fourth, 32; and so forth—each succeeding line was four men wider than the one to its front until the last (12th) line had 64 *cataphracts* abreast. (In the smaller *cataphract* regiment of 300 men, the formation was nine ranks deep.)

The *cataphracts* of the first four ranks were armed with swords or maces; those from the fifth rank on, with lances. Light cavalry archers were deployed within the wedge from the fifth rank back. A *cataphract* regiment of 500 men contained a detachment of 150 horse-archers; a *cataphract* regiment of 300 men had 80 horse-archers. Nicephorus demanded that the regimental commander lead the regiment from a position in front of the first rank.

Nicephorus initiated operations against the Muslims in southeastern Asia Minor in 964, occupying Adana. Tarsus fell in 965. The Byzantines retook Cyprus the same year. The emperor invaded Syria in 968, occupying Antioch and Aleppo. Nicephorus' victories so impressed the Muslims that they nicknamed him "The White Death."

When not fighting the Muslims in the east, Nicephorus was fighting the Bulgars in the Balkans. In 966, he formed an alliance with Sviatoslav, king of the Kievan *Russ*, against the Bulgars. By 969, Bulgaria had been overrun and the surviving Bulgars sued for peace.

In late 969, Nicephorus was overthrown and killed by his nephew, John Tzimisces, who as John I became the second co-emperor of Basil II. John I aggressively prosecuted the war against the Muslims. Operations in the east, however, were halted by a Russian invasion led by the empire's erstwhile ally, Sviatoslav. In 969 John defeated Sviatoslav near Adrianople at Arcadropolis. The Byzantines then pursued the Russians to Silistria, where they fought six engagements. During the sixth engagement, the battle of Dorostalon in July 971, John positioned himself before his regiments and personally led the final charge. The Russians wavered before the advancing Byzantines, then broke and ran. The Russians eventually sued for peace in 972.

With the Russian threat ended, John again turned his attention eastward. Edessa and Nezib were occupied in 974. He led the Byzantines into Damascus and Beirut in 976. Reaching the vicinity of Jerusalem in 976, John died suddenly and the Byzantines withdrew to Antioch.

BASIL II, "THE BULGARSLAYER" (976–1025)

Basil II became sole emperor upon the death of John I. Basil's fame and sobriquet resulted from his long and ultimately successful wars against the Bulgars and their czar, Samuel (976–1014). Basil's Bulgar Wars did not begin auspiciously. In 981, at the Battle of Sophia, the Bulgars defeated the Byzantines. Thereafter, the Bulgars penetrated Greece as far as the Peloponnesus. Fifteen years later, Basil launched a series of campaigns against the Bulgars that spanned a period of eighteen years. The emperor's victory at Spercheios in 996 led to the withdrawal of the Bulgars from Greece. In 1002 Basil reconquered Macedonia, only to lose it to Samuel in 1003. Samuel's counteroffensive reached Adrianople, which he sacked. At Balathista, however, Basil destroyed the Bulgar army. Macedonia was once more Byzantine. Basil ordered the 15,000 Bulgar prisoners blinded. One man in 100 was allowed to keep one eye so that he could lead 99 of his totally blinded comrades home. According to tradition, the sight of his blinded soldiers caused Samuel to die of shock. In 1018, the Bulgars submitted to Byzantine suzerainty.

During Basil's reign, the Byzantines first came into contact with the Normans, whom the Byzantines would later contest for control of southern Italy. Their first encounter, at Cannae in 1018, resulted in a Byzantine victory over the Normans and the Lombards.

During the reigns of Basil's immediate successors, Michael IV (1034–41), Michael V (1041–42), and Constantine IX (1042–55), Byzantine arms continued to dominate despite occasional reverses. Campaigns against the Muslims continued.

A Byzantine fleet commanded by Harald Haardrada (future king of Norway and unsuccessful candidate for the English throne in 1066) crushed the Muslim pirates who infested the Aegean (1034–35). A joint operation of the Byzantine army and navy, commanded by Georgios Maniakes and Haardrada, took the Muslim strongholds of Rametta and Dragina in 1038. In 1042, Maniakes defeated the Normans at the Battle of Monopoli. In their first encounter with the Seljuk Turks, at Stragna (1048), the Byzantines were victorious.

BYZANTINE DECLINE AND THE BATTLE OF MANZIKERT

The reigns of Theodora (1042–56), Michael VI (1056–57), and Isaac I (1057–59) marked the decline of Byzantine power. Under Constantine X (1059–67), the empire lost Calabria to the Normans (1060). In Asia Minor the Seljuks, led by Alp Arslan, raided Armenia and occupied its capital, Ani, in 1064.

Romanus IV Diogenes (1067–71) assumed the imperial dignity upon the death of Constantine. In Italy, the Normans took Otranto (1068) and Bari (1071), ending Byzantine rule in southern Italy. In the east, Seljuk raids increased in both frequency and severity. Convinced that the Seljuks were mounting a full-scale invasion, Romanus in 1068 drove the Turks, under Alp Arslan, from Phrygia and Pontus. He then led an army 60,000 strong into Armenia. In 1069 and 1070, Romanus drove the Turks out of most of the eastern provinces of the empire. Alp Arslan returned to Iraq and raised new forces. Assembling east of Lake Van, the Seljuks in 1071 rapidly advanced westward, skirting the southern shore of the lake. Near Manzikert, the Seljuks surprised the Byzantines and—aided by treachery in Romanus' army—crushed them. Romanus was captured by the Turks. Exploiting their victory, the Seljuks advanced into Anatolia, where Sulaiman Beg established the Sultanate of Rum (Iconium). The loss of Anatolia proved disastrous to the empire. Not only were the rich agricultural lands of the region in enemy hands, but with the loss of Anatolia the empire had lost its prime recruiting ground for the army.

The Comneni, the Crusades, and the Latin Emperors

Following Manzikert, the Byzantine Empire suffered the rule of two incompetent emperors: Michael VII (1071–78) and Nicephorus III (1078–81). Michael neglected the military. His answer to Seljuk aggression was recognition of Seljuk sovereignty over Anatolia. In 1078, Michael was overthrown and murdered by Nicephorus Botaniates. Nichephorus III himself was overthrown in 1081 by General Alexius Comnenus.

Under Alexius I (1081–1118), the Byzantine Empire experienced its penultimate period of greatness. His reign began inauspiciously, however, with a Norman incursion into the Balkans. Robert Guiscard led the Normans to victory at Pharsalus, then occupied Durazzo in Epirus (1082). In 1083, the Normans occupied Macedonia, but a victory of a combined Byzantine-Venetian fleet at Corfu in 1085 turned the tide in the favor of the empire.

The First Crusade provided Alexius the means to retake Nicaea, Dorylaeum, and the Anatolian coast. When Bohemund, son of Robert Guiscard, refused to do homage to Alexius for Antioch, the empire embarked on a new war with the Normans. In 1104, the Byzantines repelled a Norman attempt to retake Durazzo. After four years of inconclusive fighting, Bohemund recognized Byzantine suzerainty.

War resumed between the empire and the Seljuks in 1110. At the Battle of Philomelion, Byzantine arms prevailed. The Peace of Akroinen in 1117 returned western Anatolia to the Byzantines.

John II Comnenus (1118–43) succeeded his father. During his 1120–21 campaign against the Seljuks, John regained southeastern Anatolia. In 1122, he defeated a Patzinak invasion. Between 1122 and 1126, John was at war with Venice over trading rights. He retook Cilicia between 1134 and 1137, and reasserted Byzantine suzerainty over Antioch. John was succeeded by his son, Manuel (Manuel I Comnenus, 1143–80).

War with Roger of Sicily broke out in 1147. The Byzantine fleet, neglected and decayed, was unable to stop the sea-borne Normans. Manuel was forced to hire the Venetian fleet. In 1149 the Venetians took Corfu and, in 1151, Ancona. The war finally ended in 1158, with a return to the *status quo ante*. The bad blood between the Byzantines and the Franks was further exacerbated by the Second Crusade (1147–49).

Between 1152 and 1156, the empire was at war with the Kingdom of Hungary. The first Hungarian war ended in 1156 with Hungarian recognition of Byzantine suzerainty.

Manuel I successfully reimposed Byzantine suzerainty on Antioch in 1159. In 1161, he signed a peace treaty with the sultan of Rum, Kilidj Arslan, who recognized the emperor as his suzerain.

The second Hungarian war ended in 1168. The empire gained control of Dalmatia and part of Croatia. King Bela III of Hungary recognized Manuel I as his suzerain.

Manuel I drifted into war with his erstwhile allies, the Venetians, because of his refusal to renew their trading rights within the empire. In 1171, the Venetians took Ragusa and Chios, but they failed in their attempt to capture Ancona in 1173. The Venetian-Norman alliance of 1175 forced Manuel to seek peace. The empire was forced to renew Venetian trading privileges and pay a heavy indemnity.

The last years of the reign of Manuel I were marked by a new war with the Seljuks of Rum. The stunning Seljuk victory at Myriocephalon in 1176 was partially offset by the Byzantine successes in Bithynia in 1177.

The short reigns of Alexius II Comnenus (1180–83) and Andronicus I Comnenus (1183–85) marked the decline of the Comneni and the empire. In 1185, the Normans captured Durazzo and Thessalonica. Andronicus I was murdered and replaced by Isaac Angelus (1185–95).

With the exception of the victory over the Normans in 1191, the history of the empire continued to be one of decline. In 1185, the Bulgars threw off the Byzantine yoke. The Bulgar war of 1190–94 enlarged the newly independent kingdom at Byzantine expense.

The Fourth Crusade (1202–1204) proved more dangerous to the empire than Bulgar aggression. The crusaders, in alliance with Venice, took Durazzo in 1203. Reaching Constantinople in June 1203, the crusaders forced Alexius III (1195–1203) to flee. The crusaders then installed Alexius IV, son of Isaac Angelus. Alexius was a mere front for the crusaders. On 25 January 1204, the citizens of Constantinople rebelled and deposed Alexius IV. Alexius V Dukas (1204) ascended the throne. On 12 April 1204, the crusaders stormed and sacked the city, while Alexius V fled. (This was the first time Constantinople was ever assaulted successfully.) The crusaders installed one of their own, Baldwin of Flanders, as the first Latin emperor. The Latin emperors ruled a truncated and feudalized empire until 1261.

The Paleologi and the Fall of Constantinople

The rule of the Latin emperors led to the breakup of the empire into feudal domains on the western pattern. Besides his own rowdy, insubordinate vassals, the Latin emperor had to contend with three rival Byzantine successor states: the Despotate of Epirus; the Empire of Trebizond; and the Kingdom of Nicaea. In 1259, Michael Paleologus became king of Nicaea and, upon the recapture of Constantinople in 1261, Emperor Michael VIII (1259–82). Michael reconquered the southeastern Peloponnesus (Morea) in 1261 and the Despotate of Epirus between 1262 and 1265. Victory in a war with the Bulgars (1264–65) returned part of Macedonia to the Byzantine Empire.

The reign of Michael VIII promised a return of the glory days of the empire, but the promise proved illusory. During the reigns of the co-emperors Andronicus II (1282–1328) and Michael IX (1295–1320), Athens was lost to the Catalans, while Brusa and Nicomedia fell to the Ottoman Turks. Although Andronicus III (1328–41) won control of Chios (1329), Thessaly (1334–35), and Lesbos (1336), the victories of Stephen Dushan, king of the Serbs, threatened the empire. The war against the Serbs was complicated by civil war. For six years, Andronicus III and John V Cantacuzene (1341–76) fought for the throne. Each made use of Serbian and Ottoman troops. The triumph of John V did not bring peace to the empire. The internal power struggles continued throughout the reigns of John V, John VI Cantacuzene (1347–54), Andronicus IV (1376–79), and John VII (1390)—father, sons, and grandson.

The accession of Manuel II (1391–1425) ended the 50-year-long struggle over the throne. The empire had been reduced to Constantinople, Thessalonica, and Morea. Catalans, Venetians, Genoese, Normans, Angevins, and Ottoman Turks had picked the bones of the once mighty Byzantine Empire. The greatest danger to the empire was the growing power of the Ottoman Turks. Three times during the reign of Manuel II the Turks laid siege to Constantinople: 1391–95, 1397, and 1422.

During the reign of John VIII (1425–48), Thessalonica (1430) and Corinth (1446) were lost to the Turks. Constantine XI (1448–53) presided over the final destruction of the empire. In 1453, under Sultan Muhammed II, the Turks captured Constantinople. Morea fell in 1460, and the last remnant of Byzantine power, the Empire of Trebizond, was conquered in 1461.

LAWRENCE D. HIGGINS

SEE ALSO: Arab Conquests; Attila the Hun; Crusades (1097–1291); History, Medieval Military; Khalid ibn al-Walid; Ottoman Empire; Roman Empire; Turkic Empire.

Bibliography

Bivar, A. D. H. 1972. Cavalry equipment and tactics on the Euphrates frontier. *Dumbarton Oaks Papers* 26:273.

Brand, C. M. 1968. *Byzantium confronts the West, 1180–1204*. Cambridge: Harvard Univ. Press.

Browning, R. 1987. *Justinian and Theodora: The Byzantine recovery*. London: Thames and Hudson.

Bury, J. B. 1958. *History of the later Roman Empire*. 2d ed. New York: Dover.

Diehl, C. 1957. *Byzantium: Greatness and decline*. New Brunswick, N.J.: Rutgers Univ. Press.

Isaac, B. 1990. *The limits of empire: The Roman army in the East*. London: Oxford Univ. Press.

Procopius. 1914. *History of the wars*. 6 vols. Trans. H. B. Dewing. London: Heinemann.

Obolensky, D. 1971. *The Byzantine commonwealth: Eastern Europe, 500–1453*. New York: Praeger.

Ostrogorsky, G. 1968. *History of the Byzantine state*. 2d ed. Oxford: Basil Blackwell.

Ure, P. N. 1951. *Justinian and his age*. Harmondsworth, UK: Penguin Books.

Vasiliev, A. A. 1958. *History of the Byzantine Empire, 324–1453*. 2d ed. Madison, Wisc.: Univ. of Wisconsin Press.

Whitting, P., ed. 1972. *Byzantium: An introduction*. New York: Harper and Row.

C

CAESAR, JULIUS [100–44 B.C.]

Gaius Julius Caesar (Fig. 1) was born in 100 B.C., the son of C. Julius Caesar and Aurelia. Caesar belonged to the Julians, one of Rome's oldest patrician families, and was the nephew of Marius, one of Rome's greatest generals and seven times a consul. In 87 B.C. Marius appointed Caesar a priest of Jupiter. In 83 B.C. Caesar became allied with the popular, or plebian, party through his marriage to Cornelia, the daughter of Lucias Cinna. Caesar's political position put him in direct opposition to Sulla, dictator of Rome and leader of the patrician, or aristocratic, party and led to his proscription. Although he was later pardoned, he left Rome in 82 B.C. for Asia Minor and the East and summarily joined the army.

After Sulla's death in 78 B.C., Caesar returned to Rome and began his public career. Caesar's intelligence, public appeal, and administrative skill caused him to rise quickly. In 74 B.C. he was elected a military tribune and *pontifex*, a member of the highest priestly order. In 68 B.C. he was elected *quaestor*, or treasurer, and was sent to Spain to settle its finances. The following year he married Pompeia, cousin of the Roman consul Pompey. In 65 B.C. Caesar was elected *curule aedile*, a magisterial post, and earned great acclaim for the splendor of his public games. In 63 B.C. he was elected *praetor*, in charge of administration, and *pontifex maximus*, the head of the Roman religion. In 61 B.C. Caesar was appointed *propraetor*, or governor, of Further Spain. He began a long military career and earned his first laurels with his victories over the Lusitanians.

In 59 B.C. Caesar was elected consul, one of the head magistrates of Rome. With the collusion of the general Pompey the Great and the wealthy senator Marcus Crassus, Caesar formed the First Triumvirate, establishing the three men in the official political alliance that dominated Roman politics. By previous agreement and with the help of his two partners, Caesar created for himself an extraordinary provincial command, including the provinces of Cisalpine Gaul in Northern Italy, Illyricum across the Adriatic, and Transalpine Gaul in the southern part of modern France.

Figure 1. Bust of Julius Caesar. (SOURCE: U.S. Library of Congress)

Campaigns in Gaul

In 58 B.C., after his year-long term as consul in Rome, Caesar moved to his provinces and immediately became embroiled in the fighting that led to the conquest of all Gaul up to the Rhine River. The Helvetii from modern Switzerland, 380,000 strong, tried to migrate into central Gaul. Caesar was afraid that their presence north of the Roman province would be disruptive, so he quickly moved against them. With six legions he met the Helvetii invaders at Bibracte and completely defeated them.

The war for Gaul at first pleased the central tribes that had been allied with Rome in the past. They did not initially realize Caesar's intentions; they thought he was simply making central Gaul safer for them. In the summer of 58 B.C., after he had defeated the Helvetii, Caesar turned against a warlike German tribe led by Ariovistus that had crossed the Rhine River into Gaul. After driving the Germans back from Vesontio, Caesar decisively defeated them in open battle, leaving but a few survivors to recross the Rhine into their own territory.

Caesar's campaign successes were impressive, but they resulted in provoking fear among the northern Celtic tribes, collectively called the Belgae, who subsequently began to prepare for war against Rome. In 57 B.C. Caesar marched his legions far to the north and defeated the Nervii, the most fearsome of the Belgic tribes, in a desperate, close-run battle on the banks of the Sambre River. Caesar, in a critical moment at the height of the struggle, personally exposed himself to great danger in an effort to turn the tide.

The following year Caesar moved against the Veneti of Britanny, a coastal tribe with a fleet of high, flat-bottomed boats. A Roman fleet led by Decimus Brutus, later one of Caesar's assassins (not to be confused with the more famous Marcus Brutus), was constructed at the mouth of the Loire River. The Romans crushed the Veneti by the innovation of using long poles with sickles attached to cut down the enemy rigging, thereby rendering their boats immobile and enabling the Romans to board the enemy vessels and defeat their crews at will.

Campaigns in Germany and Britain

Since Gaul seemed to be safely under Roman control, Caesar decided to deal with threats on the periphery, especially in Germany and Britain. In the summer of 55 B.C., he crossed the Rhine over a trestle bridge built by his military engineers, demonstrated on the opposite bank for nineteen days, and then marched back across the river, destroying the bridge behind him. This "message" had an awesome effect on the Germans. Not only did the Romans have the technical knowledge and skill to build such bridges—a feat far beyond the scope and limited capabilities of the more primitive Germans—but they could build them so easily that they could tear them down and build them again if necessary! This exemplifies a chief characteristic of Caesar's generalship; he took complete advantage of Rome's technological superiority as demonstrated by its military engineers.

Late in August of 55 B.C., Caesar crossed the English Channel and invaded Britain with a small expeditionary force. He quickly returned to Gaul, but the following summer he went back to Britain, this time with a fleet of more than 800 ships, the largest naval force in the Channel until World War II. Caesar won a major victory in England and imposed an annual tribute on the Britons. It would be another century, however, before the area was organized as a Roman province under the Emperor Claudius.

Conquest of Gaul

Following his victory over the Britons, Caesar was occupied with suppressing revolts in northern Gaul. In 52 B.C. a major rebellion broke out in central Gaul under the leadership of the Gallic chieftain Vercingetorix. Caesar broke Gallic resistance by his successful siege of Alesia, one of his greatest achievements. It took another year to completely suppress the insurrection, but by 50 B.C. Caesar had finally gained total mastery over Gaul. By a combination of military skill and force of character, Caesar had subjugated Gaul and ensured Roman dominance over the region for the next 500 years.

Civil War

By this time, Marcus Crassus had been killed in a misguided invasion of Parthia, and the other triumvir—Pompey, who had married Caesar's daughter, Julia, in 58 B.C.—had been illegally appointed sole consul by the Roman Senate. Jealous of Caesar's successes in Gaul, Pompey maneuvered the Senate into demanding that Caesar relinquish his provinces, disband his legions, and return to Rome or face charges of treason. Caesar replied to these orders by marching his troops across the Rubicon River into Italy in January of 49 B.C. By so doing he broke Roman law, which forbade the bringing of armed forces into Italy proper without the consent of the Senate, and thus initiated a civil war against the Senate and Pompey.

In a brilliant 66-day campaign, Caesar stormed down the Italian peninsula, taking Rome and driving Pompey and most of the Senate across the Adriatic. Caesar, however, had no fleet with which to pursue, and while one was being built he decided to go overland to Spain and deal with Pompeian forces there. In another quick campaign, he defeated the Pompeian army of Spain at the Battle of Ilerda (49 B.C.). He then returned to Rome where the remnants of the Senate appointed him dictator. With this appointment Caesar became the sole leader of Rome and a virtual monarch, effectively bringing to an end the Roman Republic. In January, 48 B.C., despite the superiority of the Pompeian fleet, Caesar crossed the Adriatic with part of his army, landing in southern Illyrium. There he was soon joined by Mark Antony and the rest of the army. He besieged Pompey at Dyrrhachium but was forced to give up the siege because of insufficient forces.

Withdrawing into Thessaly, Caesar was pursued by Pompey. The two rivals fought a great battle at Pharsalus (August 48 B.C.). Although outnumbered two to one, Caesar's skillful tactics and bold leadership enabled him to repulse Pompey's cavalry and then counterattack. Defeated, Pompey fled to Egypt where he was killed upon arrival. Caesar pursued and defeated Pompey's adherents. After helping Cleopatra secure power in Egypt, Caesar went to Auataba, where he defeated King Pharnaces of Pontus (47 B.C.) in a five-day campaign. He reported his victory to the Senate with his famous "Veni, vidi, vici" message ("I came, I saw, I conquered"). He then returned to Rome.

In 45 B.C. Caesar sailed to North Africa where surviving Pompeians had regrouped. Another brilliant campaign culminated in his victory at Thapsus after a bloody battle. Some Pompeians escaped to Spain. Caesar followed, and in March of 45 B.C. at Munda he fought the most difficult and bitterly contested battle of his military career. He prevailed, however, and finally brought the civil war to an end.

Dictator and Final Years

Upon his return to Rome in September of that year, Caesar was selected as dictator for life, and consul for the next ten years. Caesar then threw himself into the business of reforming the legal, political, and economic affairs of the state, fully utilizing his organizational skill and administrative talents. Some Romans, fearful of Caesar's growing autocratic despotism and believing that he intended to make himself king, formed a conspiracy against him. Resistance to Caesar grew as he planned a great war against Parthia, Rome's powerful civilized neighbor to the east. It was on the eve of his departure for that campaign, on the Ides (15) of March 44 B.C., that Julius Caesar was assassinated in the Senate by a band of Roman senators led by Cassius and Marcus Brutus, the latter a favored subordinate.

Assessment

Julius Caesar combined myriad talents and abilities with a high degree of intelligence and a keen perception that marked him as one of the great men of history. He is best described by Charles Bennett, an editor of Caesar's *Gallic Wars:*

> He was general, statesman, orator and man of letters; and in each of these fields he displayed consummate genius. His military campaigns have evoked the admiration of masters of the art of war. His statesmanship brought order out of anarchy. As an orator he was magnetic. As a man of letters he has left us accounts of the Gallic and Civil wars, admirable for their directness and luminous simplicity of statement.
>
> His essential qualities were those of a man of action—clearness of vision, promptness of decision, energy in execution and indefatigable perseverance. Needless cruelty and bloodshed at times stained his conduct, but these cannot obscure the greatness of his personality or essentially alter the measure of his achievements.

ARTHER FERRILL

SEE ALSO: History, Ancient Military; Roman Empire.

Bibliography

Brady, S. G. 1968. *Caesar's Gallic campaigns.* Harrisburg, Pa.: Stackpole.

Dodge, T. A. 1892. *Caesar: A history of the art of war among the Romans down to the end of the Roman Empire, with a detailed account of the campaigns of Gaius Julius Caesar.* Boston: Houghton Mifflin.

Fuller, J. F. C. 1965. *Julius Caesar: Man, soldier, and tyrant.* London: Eyre and Spottiswoode.

Grant, M. 1974. *The army of the Caesars.* New York: Scribner's.

Vegetius, F. 1944. T. R. Phillips, ed. *Military institutions of the Romans.* Harrisburg, Pa.: Stackpole.

CHARLEMAGNE [742?–814]

Charlemagne (Charles the Great), king of the Franks and first Holy Roman Emperor, was the eldest son of Pepin III, "Pepin the Short," king of the Franks. He acceded to his father's throne in 771. An accomplished soldier, he was the central figure of the early Middle Ages in Europe.

Life and Achievements

In 770, Charles married the daughter of Desiderius, king of the Lombards, but in 771, he repudiated her. Desiderius, resenting the slight upon his daughter, planned revenge. Later that year, when Charles's brother Carloman died, Charles appropriated his kingdom (southern Gaul), excluding his brother's infant sons. Carloman's widow fled with her children to the court of Desiderius, who supported their claims, which he urged on the pope.

In 772, the new pope, Hadrian, endangered the safety of the Papal States by refusing Desiderius and appealing to Charles for aid. Since Charles was preoccupied with his first Saxon campaign, Desiderius plundered and conquered at will in central Italy. But in autumn 772, Charles demanded satisfaction from the Lombards for himself and for the pope. Desiderius was defiant. Charles took two Frankish armies across the Alps, seized Verona, and besieged Desiderius in Pavia. Charles captured Pavia and Desiderius in the summer of 774, and took the title of king of the Lombards.

From 774 to 799, Charles again waged war against the Saxons east of the Rhine and north of Hesse and Thuringia. The Frankish army was much superior to that of the Saxons, but the terrain favored the Saxons. The Franks could only field their army during the summer and could not garrison areas they conquered. The Saxons would submit during the campaign and revolt later. As a result, the conquest of Saxony required fourteen campaigns; however, once they were completely conquered, the Saxons became a strong component of the Frankish empire. In the midst of these campaigns Charles had returned to Italy (775) to crush a Lombard rebellion and to take control of Benevento (780 and 787).

The Franks also fought against the Moors in Spain. In 778, Charles had commanded the abortive expedition against Saragossa. As the Franks retreated across the Pyrenees, their rear guard was destroyed in the Pass of Roncesvalles—by Christian Basques, not Arabs. This rear guard was commanded by Roland, Charles's nephew and count of the Breton March, who became the subject of a famous medieval epic poem.

In 788, Charles annexed Bavaria after deposing Tassilo, the last Bavarian duke, for conspiring with the Avars. Bavaria became a strong center of the East Frankish kingdom. From Bavaria, Charles came into conflict with the Avars, who had lived on the steppes to the east (later Hungary) since 568. Later, in 805, the Avar khan, finding himself pressed by the Slavs, became a Christian and accepted the emperor's protection.

In 799, a Roman faction accused Pope Leo of various crimes. So in November 800, Charles returned to Rome and spent three weeks reviewing the situation. On 23 December, Leo cleared himself to Charles's satisfaction.

On Christmas Day, as Charles attended mass at St. Peter's Basilica, Leo crowned him emperor, the successor of the emperors of Rome. This was the most important event of the early Middle Ages because it not only created the Holy Roman Empire but also led eventually to a centuries-long struggle between pope and emperor.

In 801, Charles began a war with the Byzantines over Istria and Dalmatia, primarily a naval war in the Adriatic conducted by his son Pepin.

At the end of his reign, Charles's main enemies were the Greeks of Byzantium, the Danes, the Vikings, and the Arab pirates of the Mediterranean. In 809, he built a fort at Itzehoe to protect the Elbe River from Danish pirates. Charles also had fleets at Boulogne to protect the northern coasts and in the Mediterranean to control the coast from Narbonne to the Tiber, guarding against Arab pirates. In the meantime, he had also conquered Corsica, Sardinia, and the Balearic Islands.

Charles encouraged learning and assiduously studied Latin grammar. Many of the oldest manuscripts remaining from the classical writers were copied during his time. He died on 28 January 814 of pleurisy and was buried in the chapel at Aachen (Aix-la-Chapelle).

The Frankish Army

Frankish warriors traditionally used single-handed axes and spears and fought from behind a shield wall. By Charles's time they were in transition from foot soldiers to true knightly cavalry of the medieval type: riding horses and sometimes fighting from horseback. They developed a long, well-made Frankish sword, which was renowned throughout Europe. They were mostly unarmored, but the cavalry wore leather jackets onto which metal pieces were sewn.

The Frankish army was not a regular, standing force but was called up seasonally. All Frankish free men were required to serve without pay on campaign, if summoned, or be fined and punished. Compensation came from the division of booty. The usual muster was in the spring, and the army served for three to six months.

Each soldier brought his own three-months' food supply, arms, armor, tools for entrenching, and other items. Charles had a well-organized supply organization and excellent transport. Advance planning worked out the movements, and supplies, when needed, were requisitioned. Cattle were herded with the baggage trains that accompanied the forces. On the march, the army did not forage or plunder unless in conquered territory, such as Saxony, where it was done more for punishment than for provisioning.

Charles had an extensive and detailed intelligence service that provided terrain analysis and estimates of the enemy population, methods of war, agricultural resources, and lifestyles. He generally divided his army into two major forces, one under his direct command and the other under a trusted noble. This confused the enemy, and when he united the forces they were usually able to overpower the opponent.

In battle, the cavalry charged en masse, and the infantry followed. The close combat was just a mass melee of infantry supported by horsemen. The army was not structured tactically but was divided, administratively, into the groups brought by various nobles and other officials.

JOHN F. SLOAN

SEE ALSO: Arab Conquests; Byzantine Empire; Feudalism; History, Medieval Military; Prussia and Germany, Rise of; Vikings.

Bibliography

Buckler, F. W. [1931] 1978. *Harunul-Rashid and Charles the Great.* New York: AMS Press.
Contamine, P. 1984. *War in the Middle Ages.* Trans. M. Jones. Oxford: Basil Blackwell.
Delbrück, H. 1990. *History of the art of war within the framework of political history.* Vol. 3, *Middle Ages.* Trans. W. Renfroe. Lincoln: Univ. of Nebraska Press.
Einhard. 1972. *Vita Karoli Magni: The life of Charlemagne.* Eds. E. S. Firchow and E. H. Zeydel. Coral Gables, Fla.: Univ. of Miami Press.
Notker Balbulus. 1890. *Gesta Karoli Magni.* Leipzig: Dyksche Buchhandlung.

CHARLES XII, KING OF SWEDEN [1682–1718]

Charles XII was, after Gustavus Adolphus, the greatest warrior-king of Sweden. By the age of 20, he had earned a place as one of the foremost generals in Europe. Although his invasion of Russia ended in disaster, he recovered from that failure and during the last two years of his life did much to restore the military position of Sweden, which had decayed during his long absence.

Early Life

Charles was born in Stockholm on 17 June 1682, the eldest son of King Charles XI and Queen Ulrika Eleonora and their only son to survive childhood. He received an excellent education, largely directed by his father, and following the queen's death in 1693 he became his father's closest companion and principal confidant. He succeeded to the throne when his father died on 5 April 1697, although Charles was not yet 15 and the country was at first governed by a regency. The regency was ended early, in view of Charles's demonstrated ability and maturity, in November of that year.

First Stages of the Great Northern War

In April 1700, Sweden was attacked by a Polish-Russian-Danish alliance, and Charles found himself at war. The allies, hoping to have the advantage over a young and inexperienced monarch, were soon disabused of this notion. Although Charles had not planned the initial Swedish operations, he played his part in the conquest of Zealand in April 1700 with great energy and notable success, and so was able to conclude the favorable Treaty of Travendal with Denmark on 28 August. Determined to carry the war to his enemies, he landed in Livonia at the head of an army on 16 October and marched to Narva, then besieged by a large Russian army under the command of Czar Peter I. Charles launched an attack during a driving snowstorm on 20 November, an unexpected move that caught the Russians off guard and enabled the Swedes, who numbered barely 10,000, to defeat 40,000 Russian regulars and another 30,000 militia.

Capitalizing on this success the following spring, Charles led his army to the relief of Riga, where he defeated a Russian-Polish-Saxon army at Dünamünde on the River Düna (Dvina) on 18 June 1701 and then went on to relieve Riga on 27 June. He then occupied Courland and invaded Lithuania between August and October. He began the campaign of 1702 by marching on Warsaw and capturing it on 18 May, and then headed west into Germany to seek battle with his enemies. He defeated General Steinau's larger Saxon-Polish army at Kliszow on 19 July and then went on to capture Kraków, in the process continuing to undermine the control over Poland exercised by Augustus II, king of Poland and elector of Saxony. He smashed another but much larger army under Steinau at Pultusk on 1 May 1703, and placed Stanislaus Leszczynski on the Polish throne the following year. He defeated new Saxon armies at Punitz and Wszawa in 1705 and so largely pacified Poland, a considerable achievement.

Invasion of Russia

Charles then returned to the Baltic provinces and drove Ogilvie's Russian army out of Lithuania in August and as far into Russia as Pinsk by late September. Capitalizing on these successes, Charles compelled Augustus II to sign the Treaty of Altranstadt on 4 October 1706 and thereby abdicate the Polish throne and break his alliance with Russia. He rejected Czar Peter's overtures and, determined to have vengeance on Russia, planned to invade Russia the following year. Charles spent the next year improving his supply services and raising more troops. Charles invaded Russia on 1 January 1708 and captured Grodno on 5 February. He halted his army near Minsk from March to June to wait out the endless mud of the spring thaw. Charles then led his army across the Berezina River and defeated Prince Repnin's larger army at Holowczyn on 12 July 1708, while forcing a crossing of the Bubitch River. He reached Mogilev on the Dnieper River on 18 July, but by this time his campaign was hampered by Russian scorched-earth measures, and his troops were harassed by skirmishers. He continued his advance on Moscow and mauled Prince Golitsyn's small force at Dobroje on 11 September, but as winter drew near he turned south to seek aid from Hetman Ivan Mazeppa's Ukrainian Cossacks. This strategy was wrecked by the destruction of General Löwenhaupt's vital column of supplies and reinforcements at Lyesna on 9 and 10 October and the ouster of Mazeppa in late October.

Charles kept his weary and dispirited army together throughout the harsh winter from November 1708 to April 1709 and advanced on Voronezh as good weather returned. He stopped to besiege the fortress of Poltava on the Vorskla River, but his efforts, lasting from 2 May to 7 July 1709, were hampered by scarcity of both cannon and supplies. Czar Peter, recognizing the dangerous Swedish position, hurried there with most of his army and had assembled his forces in the area by mid-June. Charles was wounded in the foot in a skirmish on 17 June while maneuvering against Peter's relief attempts. Realizing his desperate situation, Charles determined to attack Peter's army and laid careful plans. The assault, when it began during the early morning hours of 9 July, enjoyed initial success, but the weakness of the Swedes (16,000 men in 18 small infantry battalions and 12 cavalry squadrons, against 40,000 Russian regulars in 30 regiments and 30 cavalry squadrons, plus nearly 40,000 militia) and the inability of Charles's generals to cooperate effectively doomed the Swedish effort. At the end of nearly eighteen hours of battle, the Swedes had been driven from the field, and Charles escaped the destruction of his army accompanied only by Mazeppa and perhaps 1,500 cavalry.

Flight and Return to Sweden

Charles fled to shelter in Turkish Moldavia, where he settled into camp at Bender (Fig. 1). He induced Turkey to enter the war as his ally in October 1710, and he continued a valiant effort to govern Sweden from Bender for most of the next five years (1709–1714). He was briefly besieged in his camp at Bender in January and February 1713 when he quarreled with his Turkish hosts. Charles left Turkey in November 1714 and traveled across Hapsburg lands to reach Swedish Pomerania in just fourteen days. Back on Swedish soil, he waged a vigorous campaign to restore the Swedish position in northern Germany and save the cities of Stralsund and Wismar, but he was finally compelled to abandon them and return to Sweden in December 1715.

Back in his own country for the first time in more than ten years, Charles spent the winter rebuilding the Swedish army, which had been decimated by nearly twenty years of continual warfare. His efforts were successful, and he forestalled an allied invasion of Sweden in the summer of 1716. Emboldened by this success, he raised yet more troops in 1717 and planned campaigns to bring about an advantageous negotiated peace. He invaded southern Norway and was killed by a musket shot (according to some tales a silver bullet) at the siege of Fredrikshald (Halden) on 30 November 1718.

Assessment

Charles was a highly intelligent man, gifted with a vigorous mind and accompanying physical energy. As a commander he was bold and daring, traits that sometimes inclined him to rashness and folly. He was a gifted and innovative tactician and generally showed himself an able strategist. His greatest error was his refusal of Peter I's peace overtures in autumn 1706 and his subsequent

Figure 1. Charles XII, king of Sweden, at Bender. (SOURCE:
U.S. Library of Congress)

decision to invade Russia. His youth and his demonstrated martial abilities
combined within his own lifetime to make him a contemporary Alexander the
Great.

DAVID L. BONGARD

SEE ALSO: Gustavus Adolphus; Peter the Great; Thirty Years' War.

Bibliography

Adlerfelt, G. 1740. *Histoire militaire de Charles XII, roi de Suède.* 4 vols. Amsterdam:
    J. Westein and C. Smith.
Bengtsson, F. G. [1935–36] 1960. *The life of Charles XII.* Trans. N. Walford. 2 vols.
    Stockholm: Norstedt.
Chandler, D. G. 1976. *The art of warfare in the age of Marlborough.* New York:
    Hippocrene.

Gade, J. A. 1916. *Charles the Twelfth, King of Sweden*. Trans. from the ms. of Karl Gustafson Klingspor. Boston: Houghton Mifflin.

Hatton, R. M. 1968. *Charles XII of Sweden*. London: Weidenfeld and Nicolson.

CHIANG KAI-SHEK [1887–1975]

Chiang Kai-shek (31 October 1887–6 April 1975), also known as Chiang Chungcheng and Jiang Jieshi, was the supreme military and political leader of the Chinese Nationalists (Kuomintang) from 1927 to 1975, and president of the Republic of China from 1928 to 1975 (Fig. 1).

Early Life and Career

Chiang Kai-shek was born near Shanghai in the Fenghua District of Ninpo Prefecture in the Province of Chekiang, China. Although Chiang's ancestors were farmers, his grandfather and father left farming and started a small salt-trading business. After the death of Chiang's father in 1896, his mother raised him and five other children on a small income.

Chiang began planning for a military career at a young age and attended local schools in Ningpo and Fenghua. Following the Russo-Japanese War (1905), Chiang went to Japan to study military affairs. He returned to China in 1907 to continue his studies at the Paoting Military College in Hopei, one of China's first modern military schools. Chiang joined Sun Yat-sen's Chinese United League (Chung-kuo T'ung-meng Hui) in 1908 and returned to Japan for two years of study at the Shimbu Gakko, a preparatory school for the Japanese military academy.

In October 1911, the Wuchang Revolution to overthrow the Ch'ing Dynasty swept across China and Chiang participated in several military actions, including a plot to seize an arsenal in Shanghai and thereby break Manchu power in that important city. In recognition of Chiang's efforts the revolutionary government of Shanghai gave him a regimental command.

During the next ten years Chiang divided his time between periods of study in Japan and periods of agitation in China. Time spent as a financial speculator in Shanghai gave Chiang strong connections with the early Nationalist revolutionaries, local militarists, and the important secret societies of Shanghai.

In the fall of 1922 Chiang assumed new military duties in the KMT (Kuomintang or Nationalist Party) forces of Sun Yat-sen. From 16 August to 16 December 1923, he studied military affairs in the Soviet Union. During the First National Congress of the Kuomintang (20–30 January 1924), Chiang was appointed to the party's Military Council, and on 3 May 1924 he was assigned as commandant of the newly established Whampoa Military Academy. This put Chiang in the perfect position to build a power base among the bright and loyal young officers of the Nationalist Party.

In July 1926, Chiang was elected to the Central Executive Committee of the KMT's Second National Congress. At the same time, he was assembling

Figure 1. Generalissimo Chiang Kai-shek. (SOURCE: U.S. Library of Congress)

eight armies for a "Northern Expedition" to destroy the local military strongmen in north and central China and to unite the country. The expedition left Canton on 9 July 1926 and by 24 March 1927 it had captured Nanking and Shanghai.

This first phase of the Northern Expedition was followed by a pause while Chiang dealt with problems of Party unity that had become evident in the drive north from Canton. He believed that the policies of the Chinese Communists (CCP) on labor organization, antiforeign agitation, and dual membership in the KMT and CCP were incompatible with the interests of the KMT. On 12 April 1927, Chiang purged the Communist and leftist elements from the KMT, and on 18 April he organized a new national government in Nanking.

Following a summer of factional strife within the KMT and battles with warlords in the Hsuchow area, Chiang retired to Japan to prepare for his wedding to Soong Mei-ling. The wedding cemented ties with the powerful financier J. V. Soong, brother of the bride, but created animosity with Soong Ch'ing-ling, the widow of Sun Yat-sen and sister of the bride.

In the late winter of 1928, Chiang launched the second phase of the Northern Expedition, with four armies targeted on Manchurian warlord Chang Tso-lin, who then controlled the Peking government. By 6 June 1928, troops allied with Chiang had seized Peking. On 10 October 1928, Chiang became chairman of the National Government.

As chairman, Chiang faced enormous problems. After the anti-Communist purge of April 1927, the Communists had turned their attentions to creating a peasant revolution in south central China. To destroy the Communists, Chiang launched five "encirclement" campaigns that ultimately forced the Communists to begin their "Long March" away from Chiang's forces.

While Chiang engaged in campaigns against the Communists, Japanese actions grew more ominous. Chiang had temporized in the face of Japan's increased belligerence in northwest China and its virtual annexation of Manchuria. This policy created animosity among other Chinese leaders who believed Japan was a greater threat than the Communists. On 12 December 1936 Chiang was kidnapped in the northwest city of Sian by Marshal Chang Hsueh-liang (son of Chang Tso-lin) and the Communists. As a condition of his release Chiang was forced to agree to a United Front with the Communists against the Japanese.

World War II and the Chinese Civil War

Six months later (7 July 1937) war began when the Japanese moved against Peking and Tientsin. By the end of 1938 the KMT had lost all of north central China and much of southeast China. Chiang moved his capital to Chungking. From this base in southwest China, Chiang entered formal military alliances with the United States and Great Britain after 7 December 1941. Chiang's relationship with his allies was stormy because Chiang never diverted his attention from his primary goal of destroying the Communists. As a result, Chiang frequently held views different from his allies and sometimes seemed to be a burden to the allied effort against Japan.

Chiang spent the years immediately after World War II attempting to expand his political control throughout northern China while angling for advantage in U.S.-sponsored negotiations with the Communists. When the civil war escalated from isolated actions to a war of maneuver by large-scale military forces, Chiang lost three critical campaigns (Manchuria, Huai-Hai, and Peking-Tientsin) in the last six months of 1948. On 20 April 1949, Chinese Communist troops met only token resistance when they crossed the Yangtze on their final push into south China. Chiang and his government fled to Taiwan. In April 1950, Chinese Communist armies captured Hainan Island. Only Taiwan, the new base of Chiang's government, remained unconquered.

Chiang and the Republic of China on Taiwan

During the flight from Communist armies, Chiang had retired from the presidency. On 1 March 1950, he reassumed that title. From 1950 until his death on 6 April 1975, Chiang retained ultimate power in the Republic of China government on Taiwan. His rule was authoritarian and oriented toward the economic development needed to achieve his goal of national reunification under KMT leadership.

EDWARD C. O'DOWD

SEE ALSO: Mao Tse-tung; Stilwell, Joseph Warren; World War II.

Bibliography

Boorman, H. L. 1967. Chiang Kai-shek. In *Biographical dictionary of republican China*. Vol. 1. New York: Columbia Univ. Press.
Crozier, B. 1969. *The man who lost China: The first full biography of Chiang Kai-shek*. New York: Weybright and Talley.
Furuya, K. 1981. *Chiang Kai-shek: His life and times*. Abridged by Chang Chun-ming. New York: St. John's Univ. Press.

CHU-TEH [1886–1976]

This article briefly traces the life of Chu-Teh, the revolutionary Chinese general and military strategist.

The Formative Years: 1886–1928

Originally named Zhu Daizhen, Chu-Teh was born into a peasant family on 1 December 1886 in Ma'anchang in Longxian County of Sichuan Province. Having finished his primary education in a private school, in 1909 he enrolled in the Infantry Section of the Yunnan Military Academy. That winter he joined Tong Meng Hui (the Revolutionary League). In 1911, he was made a platoon leader in the Yunnan Newly Organized Army. When the Revolution of 1911 (against the Manchu [Qing, or Ch'ing] Empire) broke out in October, he took part in the armed uprising in Yunnan as a company commander. He then became a military instructor in the Yunnan Military Academy and was made a battalion commander, then assistant regimental commander, and finally regimental commander of the Yunnan troops. He took part in the War to Safeguard the Republic against Yuan Shikai's restoration of the empire (December 1915–March 1916) and the War to Safeguard the Constitution against the dictatorship of Prime Minister Duan Qirui (1–12 July 1917). Because of his distinguished services, Chu-Teh was made a brigade commander in 1917.

Following the October Socialist Revolution in Russia, he left office and in 1922 went to Shanghai and Beijing, in pursuit of Marxism and Leninism, and to seek out the Chinese Communist Party (CCP). He went to study in Germany in September, and in November joined the Communist party with Chou En-lai and others as his sponsors. He was arrested twice for his revolutionary activities and was eventually exiled. In July 1925, he went to the Soviet Union to study military affairs. When he returned to China a year later, he was appointed the Party representative to the Twentieth Army of the National Revolutionary Army in Sichuan. He was one of the leaders in the Huzhou and Shunqing Uprising and led the struggle against the British warships that bombarded Wanxian County. He arrived in Nanchang in early 1927 and was the chief of staff of the Fifth Front Army of the National Revolutionary Army, the commander of the officers' Educational Regiment of the Third Front Army, and later (concurrently) the director of the Nanchang Public Security Bureau.

Chu-Teh was a leader of the Nanchang Uprising of August 1927 and the vice-commandant of the Ninth Front Army. After suffering setbacks when he led his troops southward to Guangdong, he and Chen Yi led the remnant troops to the Fujian-Jiangxi-Guangdong border area. The following January, he mobilized the peasants in dozens of counties in Hunan to launch uprisings before the Lunar New Year, and he set up the workers and peasants' army and government. In April 1928, he led his troops to the Jinggang Mountains and joined forces with the army led by Mao Tse-tung. The new army was named the Fourth Army of the Chinese Workers' and Peasants' Red Army with Chu-Teh as commander.

Military Operations Against the Kuomintang

During this period, the military-political struggle was against the Kuomintang (KMT) forces of Chiang Kai-shek. Chu-Teh and Mao Tse-tung summed up the experience of the fighting and condensed the basic principles of guerrilla warfare into the following: "The enemy advances, we retreat; the enemy camps, we harass; the enemy tires, we attack; the enemy retreats, we pursue."

In early 1929, Chu-Teh and Mao Tse-tung led their troops to southern Jiangxi and western Fujian, where they founded a new revolutionary base area (later, the Central Revolutionary Base Area). From July 1930 to November 1931, Chu-Teh was successively the commander in chief of the First Army Group of the Workers' and Peasants' Red Army, the commandant of the First Front Army, vice-chairman of the Military Commission of the Party Central Committee, and chairman of the Military Commission of the Party Central Committee of the Soviet Republic of China; he also held several other posts. Under the direction of Chu-Teh and Mao Tse-tung, the First Front Army adopted the tactical principles to "lure the enemy in deep" and "concentrate a superior force to destroy the enemy forces one by one." The army smashed three successive campaigns launched by Chiang Kai-shek's troops during January–September 1931. In his article *How to Create an Iron Red Army*, published around that time, Chu-Teh elaborated on the nature of the Red Army, the leadership of the Chinese Communist Party (CCP), and the importance of political training. In the spring of 1933, under the command of Chu-Teh and Chou En-lai, the Central Red Army again smashed the KMT's fourth campaign of "encirclement and suppression" following the strategy of using large units to ambush the enemy. Chu-Teh supported the policy advocated by Mao at the enlarged conference of the Political Bureau of the Central Committee, convened at Zunyi in Guizhou province. After the meeting, he assisted Mao in leading the Red Army across the Chishui River four times, succeeded in breaking through the KMT's encirclement, and eluded enemy interception attempts. It was a decisive victory in the course of the Communist's strategic retreat, which came to be known as the "Long March." After the First Front Red Army linked up with the Fourth Front Red Army, Chu-Teh firmly defended the collective leadership of the Party Central Committee, upheld unity within the Red Army, and waged an unremitting struggle against Zhang Guo-tao's attempt to split the Party and the Red Army.

World War II and the Third Revolutionary Civil War

When the War of Resistance against Japan (World War II) started in 1937, Chu-Teh was the commanding officer of the Eighth Route Army of the National Revolutionary Army (later called the commander in chief of the 18th Division) and concurrently the secretary of the Front Branch of the Central Military Commission (later the North China Army Branch). He led the main force of the Eighth Route Army to the North China front to conduct independent guerrilla warfare in coordination with the military operations of the KMT troops. Meanwhile, he exerted every effort to mobilize the mass of the people and established the anti-Japanese democratic base areas in the enemy's rear in North China. In his article entitled *On Anti-Japanese Guerrilla Warfare*, published in early 1938, Chu-Teh gave an overall exposition of the significance and tactics of anti-Japanese guerrilla warfare. From March 1938, he was successively the chief commanding officer of the East Front Army in the Second War Zone and its adjutant general. He directed the coordination of military operations between the 1st Division of the KMT army and the Eighth Route Army to defeat the Japanese who marched on the Southeast Region of Shanxi Province in nine columns.

Chu-Teh returned to Yan'an in May 1940 to take part in directing the Chinese People's War of Resistance against Japan. He initiated the Nanniwan Policy by which the army reclaimed wasteland to achieve partial self-sufficiency through production. This played an important role in overcoming the extreme hardship in rear-base areas and enabled the people there to continue their protracted struggle.

At the Seventh National People's Congress of the Communist Party of China, held in April 1945, Chu-Teh delivered a military report entitled *The Battle Front of the Liberated Areas*. When the Soviet Union declared war against Japan in August, Gen. Chu-Teh, as the commander in chief of the Yan'an General Headquarters, issued an order to the army and the people in the Liberated Areas to launch a general offensive to recover the vast territories controlled by the Japanese in north and central China.

During the Third Revolutionary Civil War (September 1945–September

1949), Chu-Teh, as vice-chairman of the Military Commission of the Party Central Committee and commander in chief of the Chinese People's Liberation Army (PLA), assisted Mao Tse-tung in directing military operations across the whole country. In May 1947, Chu-Teh and Liu Shaoqi presided over the daily work of the Party Central Committee in north China as members of the Central Work Committee. From October to November, he personally commanded the Field Army of Shanxi-Chahar-Hebei, which won the battles of Shijiazhuang and of Qingdengdian. He also wrote articles to elaborate systematically on the tactics of storming heavily fortified points. After September 1948, Chu-Teh assisted Mao in planning and directing the three major campaigns of Liaoxi-Shenyang, Huai Hai, and Beiping-Tianjin. Following the victorious conclusion of these campaigns, he and Mao jointly issued a command to the PLA, ordering it to cross the Changjiang River to complete its mission: the liberation of the entire country.

Chu-Teh's Significance

After the founding of the People's Republic of China (PRC) in 1949, Chu-Teh served successively as the commander in chief of the PLA, vice-chairman of the Central People's Government, vice-chairman of the Central Revolutionary Military Commission, vice-chairman of the PRC, vice-chairman of the National Defense Committee, and chairman of the Standing Committee of the National People's Congress. He was awarded the rank of field marshal in 1955. He participated in the formulation of the Party's lines, principles, and policies and helped complete the historical change of the PLA from a single-branch army to a combined-arms army. He also made unremitting efforts in the development of a socialist economy and the consolidation and defense of national security. He was also an alternate member of the Third Session of the Sixth National People's Congress, a member of the Political Bureau of the Central Committee and of the Secretariat after the Fifth Session of the Sixth NPC, vice-chairman of the Party Central Committee, a member of the Political Bureau of the Central Committee of the Ninth NPC, and a member of the Standing Committee of the Political Bureau of the Central Committee of the Eighth and Tenth NPC. One of the founders of the Chinese PLA and an important leader of the CCP, Chu-Teh died of an illness in Beijing on 6 July 1976. His major works were included in *The Collected Works of Zhu De* (1983).

SUEN FU-TIAN

SEE ALSO: Mao Tse-tung; World War II.

Bibliography

Collected works of Zhu De. 1983. Beijing: People's Publishing House.
Comrade Zhu De during the war times. 1977. Beijing: People's Publishing House.
Military Museum. 1986. *Marshal Zhu De—An everlasting monument.* Shanghai: People's Publishing House.
National Document Research Institute. 1986. *A chronicle of Zhu De's life.* Beijing: People's Publishing House.

Smedley, A. 1979. *The great road: The life and times of Chu De.* Beijing: PLA Soldiers' Publishing House.

CIVIL WAR

Civil war is a conflict between indigenous factions (including colonial governments) in a single country with the objective being to gain or retain control over the state or to establish a new, independent state. An essential prerequisite of civil war is the ability of both parties to arm their followers. Furthermore, civil wars must be of sufficient extent, intensity, and duration to distinguish them from other forms of violence such as mutinies, riots, banditry, and piracy. It should also be noted that Marxists tend to include an element of class warfare in their view of civil war. For example, one Soviet source defines civil war as "organized, armed struggled for national power between individual classes and social groups within a country; this is the most violent form of class struggle."

Many other varieties of conflict are closely akin to civil war. These include coup d'état, putsch, rebellion, revolt, uprising, insurrection, people's war, revolutionary war, partisan warfare, and guerrilla warfare. In some cases, a clear distinction between such conflict and civil war is all but impossible to make. The effort to distinguish civil wars from these other forms of conflict has been further complicated in recent times by such developments as the expanded use of terrorism by extremist groups and measures of intimidation aimed at a nation's people by the police apparatus of the government.

Major Types of Civil War

One basis for a discussion of civil wars is to divide them into two basic categories. In one type, the issue is division of power; in the other, the focus of the conflict is on control of power. This latter category includes wars of secession and wars of unification.

Armed conflicts of secession are at times colonial wars, in which an area that is controlled by another power seeks to gain independence from the jurisdiction of that foreign power. Wars of this type are relatively few now, since most colonial empires collapsed soon after World War II.

Other wars of secession occur where a foreign colonial power no longer rules the area but where a political or religious minority seeks independence from the central ruling authority of a larger state. Examples are Biafra's effort to secede from Nigeria, the secession of Bangladesh from Pakistan, and the Katangese attempt to secede from the Congo (now Zaire).

Perhaps more common than armed conflicts of secession are struggles within a nation over control of power. This type of civil war begins when social, political, or cultural groups disagree over living conditions and power sharing. In some cases, this involves ethnic rivalries, as in the brief but deadly civil war in Burundi in 1972 and the long-running conflict in South Africa. In other cases, civil wars are sparked by religious tensions, as in the case of Ireland's conflict between Protestant and Catholic Christians and in Lebanon, where the conflict is principally between Muslims and Christians. Elsewhere, ideological conflicts have split societies into warring factions and produced new governments, as in the case of Mao Tse-tung's communist revolution in China and Fidel Castro's overthrow of the Cuban government of Fulgencio Batista.

These different motives seldom occur in pure form. In most cases, several factors are involved in various combinations. Thus, the religious wars in Ireland and in Lebanon are also motivated in part by differences between social classes and by differing views of how these countries should be governed.

As noted earlier, the Marxist view implies that civil war emerges as a consequence of the development of classes within the state. In an antagonistic society, contradictions in the area of socioeconomic conditions normally give rise to armed conflict.

Experience indicates, however, that a major cause of civil wars may be the structural imperfections that emerge in developing countries—there exists a correlation between unresolved economic and ethnic-cultural problems, the absence of political cohesion, and the use of military force.

One condition that occurs frequently in developing nations is that education and urbanization outstrip agricultural and industrial-technical progress. The larger the disparity, the greater are the extent and intensity of violent conflicts in a society. At some point, the disparity becomes so great that the claims of entire groups of society, although they are subjectively considered legitimate, cannot be met. The educated segment of society becomes frustrated and combines with other elements of the society that are already disenchanted. Members of the educated group become the leaders and organizers of a struggle against the government that aims to restore some form of balance and social justice in national developmental processes. Thus, the better-educated urban middle class essentially becomes the avant-garde of revolutionary movements and civil wars. Here, examples are the French Revolution of 1789, the urban guerrilla movements in South America, and the resistance groups in the black townships of South Africa.

From the standpoint of a ruling elite, the revolutionizing of the middle class is the worst conceivable situation. Until this revolutionizing process is complete, the only threat to the elite is that the government will lose legitimacy. As legitimacy is lost, the ruling group will attempt to compensate through reforms and development programs. If the reforms are only perfunctory, they will not prevent civil war. Indeed, bogus efforts to improve the conditions in a country are often found in a period preceding civil wars.

Origins and Nature of Civil War

As noted in the opening section, a wide variety of conflicts are similar to civil war. In at least some cases, these other forms of violence actually contribute to civil wars. An example of this point is the relationship between revolutionary wars and coups d'état or putsches.

The concept of revolutionary war always implies the intention to make changes in one or all of the structures of a nation—social, political, and economic. Such a goal contrasts sharply with the intent of a coup d'état or putsch, which aims to do little more than change the faces in a country's circle of rulers. Yet in changing the leadership, a coup d'état may trigger a wider rebellion that overthrows the entire power structure. Similarly, it is possible to see a relationship between civil war and guerrilla or partisan warfare, when the latter two forms of warfare essentially describe tactics used to achieve the goals of rebels fighting a civil war.

At times, civil war has resulted from the efforts of a minority to overthrow the majority. Examples include the rebellion of the Choung Clan in China around 1050 B.C., the revolt of Soga Clan in Japan in 642 B.C., the slave rebellion in Rome that was led by Spartacus, a peasant uprising in Germany in 1525, the American Revolution of 1776–83, and the Algerian revolt (1958–63). If the rebel minority is successful, its numbers will grow; with this expansion, its military power increases relative to the military power of its opponent. This occurred in the successful revolution in which the Chinese Communists under Mao Tse-tung overthrew the Chinese Nationalists under Chiang Kai-shek. However, the opposite may occur and the strength of the rebels may steadily decline, as in the case of the Polish insurgencies of 1830–31, 1848, and 1862–63. At other times, factions in the revolting forces may begin fighting among themselves, even as they are fighting the established government.

On some occasions, antigovernment forces seek not to overthrow the ruling government, but only to secure concessions. This occurred in France's Huguenot Wars of the sixteenth century and during the Thirty Years' War of the following century. Thus, religious wars and wars of secession may have as their goals anything from complete autonomy for the rebelling group to a simple improvement in legal status for the rebels.

At times, civil war expands beyond the borders of the state where the war occurs. This can happen in one of two ways: a foreign power foments rebellion in a country, or foreign powers intervene in a civil war after it starts. After the Spanish Civil War began in 1936, the Soviet Union intervened on behalf of the Loyalists, and the Italians and Germans supported the forces of Francisco Franco. An example of the first case is India's stimulation of rebellious activities in East Pakistan, which eventually became Bangladesh.

In spite of these numerous variations, it is possible to lay out a model of the general causes and characteristics of civil war, with the following elements.

- A situation develops in which a state cannot peacefully resolve the problems of modernization.
- The inability to solve these problems leads to a decline of legitimacy, which then expands into a government crisis when parts of the population begin to oppose the government openly or covertly. The opposition takes the form of strikes, protests, and demonstrations.
- Economic and social programs are implemented in an effort to restore support for the government, and force is used to suppress those who continue to oppose the government.

• The government's use of force begets resistance by force. After a phase in which limited covert action is confined to one area, the armed conflict may expand into an open civil war.

This model is generally valid for most of the civil wars that have occurred throughout history, from the time of Gracchian Rome (133 B.C.) to the Spanish Civil War (1936–39).

Civil War as a Problem for Governmental and Legal Systems

THE POLITICAL PROBLEM

A war between two independent nations rarely challenges the integrity of either warring state. Indeed, internal cohesion is of prime concern during wartime, and nations tend to unite when faced with an external enemy. On the other hand, a civil war tends to bring about a collapse of the entire social and political fabric of a country. This tendency has increased in modern times because radio and television allow more rapid communication with more people than has been possible in the past.

To be certain, theories of the "social contract" from Thomas Hobbes (1588–1679) to Raymond Aron (1905–83) did not exclude the possibility that the contract could be voided by rebellion of the subjects or by tyranny of the ruling leader. But, according to their views, this would occur only rarely. The twentieth century has proved the theorists wrong. If we look only at the half century since the end of World War II, we cannot help but notice that the number of traditional wars fought between states has been small compared to the number of civil wars. Border disputes sometimes degenerate into armed conflicts, but generally these expressions of violence occur intermittently or over a limited period of time. Moreover, they are not usually threatening because they seldom lead to territorial changes. Important exceptions are the Kashmir conflict between India and Pakistan and the Chinese-Indian conflict.

Military history since World War II also tends to refute the socialist view of warfare. According to socialist thinking, civil war in developing countries is a special case in which the rebellion of the working masses is stimulated by the armed intervention of imperialist powers in support of the reactionary forces of the state. In the context of this paradigm, the United States is blamed for interference in Korea between 1950 and 1953 and in Vietnam during the period from 1964 to 1973, while any such activity by the socialists is seen as assistance in support of the struggle for freedom.

During the height of the cold war, the world's revolutions were seen as a serious threat to the safety of the planet. While the superpowers were always too cautious to become involved in a direct confrontation, it was feared that the United States and USSR might be drawn into a general war with each other as a result of their supporting opposing sides in one of the world's revolutions.

THE MORAL/ETHICAL PROBLEM

Today, the position taken throughout the world with regard to civil war is generally dominated by Western thought. Throughout much of history, violent conflict between the citizens of a country has been seen as evil. Up to the eighteenth century, political philosophers and theologians based their views of civil war on the principle that the ruler was responsible for a legitimate order that the citizen must respect. Indeed, the ruler tended to be seen as drawing his right to rule from God. As a result, rebellion was seen as a sin. Not only did this view support the worldly power of the prince, but it also tended to protect the church from rebellion by its supplicants. In more recent times, violence between citizens of a democracy has tended to be seen as unlawful and unnecessary, since democracy should offer the means for bringing about social and political changes by peaceful processes.

THE PROBLEM OF INTERNATIONAL LAW AND PHILOSOPHY

Civil war is not easily comprehended by international law. Law is a philosophical framework for resolving disputes and is based upon such concepts as rationality and consent—concepts largely missing from civil war, which is a resort to force of arms to resolve disagreements that seem insoluble by other means. In classical international law, Hugo Grotius (1583–1645), Emmeridi DeVattel (1714–67), and Johann Kaspar Bluntschli (1808–1881) concurrently took the position that a domestic conflict was a form of criminal activity rather than a civil war. This meant that the legal aspects of such things as rebellions and uprisings were to be treated under the state's criminal law. Only when the insurgents were recognized as a belligerent party could the conflict be accorded the status of civil war, and this determination was the prerogative of the sovereign. The extent and intensity of the rebellion had little to do with this determination by the king. As a result, those who rebelled were normally treated as criminals rather than as soldiers.

Although civil war had been largely incompatible with international law, it had found a firm place in the political philosophies of the West by the time of the American Revolutionary War. For example, toward the end of the seventeenth century and in the eighteenth century, French philosophers such as J. J. Rousseau and C. A. Helvetius considered civil war the means whereby a people could rid itself of despotism. In the mind of Thomas Jefferson, civil war in the face of tyranny was both legitimate and necessary.

The American Revolution itself was an impetus to change in the classical perception of the nature of civil war. This conflict gave rise to the view that a civil war was a rebellion in which the intensity of the conflict reached a level normally found in war and in which those rebelling developed an organization equivalent to that of the state against which they rebelled. Still, it has remained difficult for rebels to gain recognition for their rebellion as a civil war. Only five times in history—and none of these in the twentieth century—have uprisings been accorded the status of civil war.

In the second half of the nineteenth century, a body of legal principles derived from international law began to be applied as principles of the law of war. Various conventions held in Geneva played a critical role in this process; special significance is usually attached to the first convention in 1864, which established the International Red Cross (the Red Crescent in the Islamic world). Since the first convention, Geneva has become synonymous with efforts to restrain war through conventions, agreements, and treaties. Until after World War II, however, the Geneva conferences devoted little attention to civil wars.

In 1949, the United Nations and the International Committee of the Red Cross achieved a fundamental definition of civil war and gained agreement for the application of the principles of the international law of war. Civil war was defined as "as armed conflict of a noninternational nature." The international standards of the law of war can thus be applied to civil wars independent of any formal recognition of a conflict as a civil war.

Conclusion

Since 1949, the following principles of international law are considered applicable to civil wars:

- The intensity of combat is the only criterion for distinguishing civil war from other forms of violence within a state.
- The armed conflict must have assumed a form that approximates traditional warfare.
- The adherence to the *ius in bello* depends on the individual phases of combat.
- The fact of a revolt is ruled out for any provision based on international law.

In more recent times, efforts to apply these principles to civil wars have been clouded to some extent by the influence of ideology. Increasingly, foreign nations have tended to intervene in civil wars. As a result of this development, in 1971 and 1972 the International Committee of the Red Cross proposed to designate as international wars those civil wars in which a third party intervened. These efforts failed.

Results were quite different where so-called wars of national liberation were concerned. Between 1972 and 1974, a majority of the United Nations decided that the application of all four Geneva Conventions would be extended to wars of liberation against colonial rule and racist regimes. This decision was considered consistent with the United Nations Charter of 1945 and the UN Resolutions of 1973.

Currently, it is not apparent to what extent the tension between national sovereignty and the right of a people to self-determination has been and can be resolved. Furthermore, it seems inconsistent to ban international wars yet accept the legitimacy of civil wars. Categories that are consistent and recognized on a worldwide basis are required to guarantee the control of international law. In addition, a system of sanctions consistent with international law has yet to be developed for use against groups resorting to civil war.

DIETER BANGERT

SEE ALSO: Civil War, American; Civil War, Russian; Korean War; Vietnam and Indochina Wars; War.

Bibliography

Asprey, R. B. 1975. *War in the shadows: The guerrilla in history.* 2 vols. New York: Doubleday.
Bond, J. E. 1974. *The rules of riot: Internal conflict and the law of war.* Princeton, N.J.: Princeton Univ. Press.
Wheatcroft, A. 1983. *The world atlas of revolutions.* New York: Simon and Schuster.

CIVIL WAR, AMERICAN

The American Civil War was fought from 1861 to 1865 between eleven seceding states (known as the Confederacy) and 25 states (known as the Union) that remained loyal to the federal government of the United States. (Two of the latter became states after the war began.) The central and underlying cause of the war was slavery.

Inability of the agrarian South and the largely industrializing North to reach agreement over their socioeconomic and political differences, highlighted by states' rights impasses pertaining to westward expansion, led to secession by the southern states in the following order: South Carolina (20 December 1860); Mississippi (9 January 1861); Florida (10 January 1861); Alabama (11 January 1861); Georgia (19 January 1861); Louisiana (26 January 1861); Texas (1 February 1861); Virginia (17 April 1861); Arkansas (6 May 1861); North Carolina (20 May 1861); and Tennessee (8 June 1861). States remaining with or joining the Union during the conflict were California, Connecticut, Delaware, Illinois, Indiana, Iowa, Kansas, Kentucky, Maine, Maryland, Massachusetts, Michigan, Minnesota, Missouri, Nevada (1864 statehood), New Hampshire, New Jersey, New York, Ohio, Oregon, Pennsylvania, Rhode Island, Vermont, West Virginia (1863 statehood), and Wisconsin. Of these, Delaware, Maryland, Kentucky, and Missouri were slave states that elected not to secede; the latter three had divided loyalties.

From a military standpoint, the Civil War was the mightiest spectacle of the nineteenth century. To win it, the United States had to conquer a rebellious confederation of states that, at the outset of the war, occupied 749,000 square miles of territory—much more than Napoleon's armies had captured during fifteen years of campaigning in Europe earlier in the century.

Resource comparisons in 1860 favored the Union in every category. In the tremendous surge of economic expansion between 1848 and 1860, the North had greatly surpassed the South. It held a three-to-one advantage in miles of railroad track, had control of most inland waterways, and maintained a virtual monopoly on coastal and overseas shipping. Manufacturing, finance, and trade were also monopolized by Northerners. The North had far greater food production than its agrarian neighbors to the south. Population figures in 1860 showed 22 million inhabitants in the North and only 9 million in the South, of whom 3.5 million were slaves. Neither side expected or wanted a long war, but the North was far better able to fight one than the South. Throughout the war, resource ratios between the two steadily increased in favor of the North.

To offset such preponderant Northern advantages, the South relied initially on a more united home front, a sharp sense of grievance, and a stronger motive for survival. Throughout the war, the Confederacy attempted unsuccessfully to get foreign recognition, and therefore allies, to even the balance. U.S. economic ties with Europe were strong, and no foreign nation was willing to undermine its relationship with the Union to recognize a new and rival government that seemed hopelessly outmatched in people and resources.

The Confederacy needed only to survive long enough to convince the Union that restoration of the United States to its antebellum status would never occur. Unable to prevent secession, the federal government had the more difficult task of restoring the United States. This meant subduing the rebellious states by attacking them and forcing them back into the Union.

The Path to War

On 6 November 1860, Abraham Lincoln was elected president of the United States. Southern states saw the election as the culmination of 40 years of frustration over Northern dominance and a threat to their slave-based agrarian economy. They determined to secede in order to preserve that way of life. On 20 December 1860, South Carolina took the first major step toward war by declaring, "The union now subsisting between South Carolina and other States under the name of the United States of America is hereby dissolved." Other states followed suit, and on 4 February 1861 a congress of representatives from all Southern states that had passed ordinances of secession met in Montgomery, Alabama. On 8 February they adopted a provisional constitution; the next day they elected Jefferson Davis of Mississippi the president and Alexander Stephens of Georgia the vice president of the Confederate States of America. Abraham Lincoln was inaugurated president of the United States on 4 March 1861.

The first shots of the war had been fired on 9 January 1861, when Confederates drove off a steamer carrying provisions for the Union garrison at Fort Sumter, South Carolina, in Charleston harbor. On 12 April Confederate forces commanded by Brig. Gen. Pierre Gustave Toutant Beauregard bombarded Fort Sumter. Two days later the garrison commander, Maj. Robert Anderson, surrendered. The United States declared war on 15 April and President Lincoln called for 75,000 state militia volunteers to put down combinations or alliances against the Union. The Confederacy had adopted similar measures with a broader call-up of 100,000 men on 4 March and had passed a general conscription law on 9 April. On 19 April, Lincoln ordered a naval blockade of all Southern ports. On the same day, Confederate forces seized the Federal arsenal at Harpers Ferry, Virginia (now West Virginia), and followed that with the capture of the large U.S. Navy Yard at Norfolk, Virginia. Many abandoned military forts and other installations were subsequently seized by Confederate state militia forces.

On 18 April, Lincoln had offered command of the Union Army to Col. Robert E. Lee. Lee refused, resigning his U.S. Army commission on 20 April so he could offer his services to his native state of Virginia, against which he would not take up arms. A total of 286 out of 1,066 regular U.S. Army officers and 322 out of 1,322 regular U.S. Navy officers chose the same course and became instrumental in the organizing and fighting of the Confederate forces.

1861–62

When the war began, both sides thought the conflict would be brief. Each had a fixation on the other's capital. The Union general in chief, 74-year-old Winfield Scott, was the only officer on either side who had ever commanded as many as 5,000 troops. It was he who suggested a campaign designed to squeeze the life out of the South by naval blockade and land attacks to create north-south and east-west cleavages. Derisively dubbed the "Anaconda" by Northern politicians in 1861, it was essentially this plan that Ulysses S. Grant used to defeat the South in the end.

Forced onto the defensive in 1861, the South soon dispelled any ideas the North had of ending the war quickly. In the East at Manassas Junction on 21 July, combined forces under Beauregard and Brig. Gen. Joseph E. Johnston routed Union forces commanded by Brig. Gen. Irvin McDowell in the First Battle of Bull Run. This led the U.S. Congress to authorize $500,000,000 and a volunteer force of 500,000 men. Maj. Gen. George B. McClellan was hurriedly called from some earlier successes in western Virginia to replace McDowell. He organized and trained the Army of the Potomac, but, to Lincoln's great distress, was slow to take it into battle.

In the West, both sides attempted to control the border states of Missouri and Kentucky. On 10 August a Union force under Brig. Gen. Nathaniel F. Lyon was defeated at Wilson's Creek, Missouri, by stronger Confederate forces under Brig. Gens. Sterling Price and Ben McCullough. Lyon was killed, but his aggressive operations had saved Missouri for the Union. Paducah, Kentucky, was occupied on 6 August by Brig. Gen. Ulysses S. Grant, thus safeguarding Cairo, Illinois, at that time a strategically significant town. Gen. Albert S. Johnston, commander of all Confederate forces in the West, established a defensive line across Kentucky to block movements down the Mississippi and up the Cumberland and Tennessee rivers. On 7 November, Union forces under Grant struck a Confederate camp at Belmont, Missouri, the western point on Johnston's line, to relieve growing Confederate pressure in Missouri. On 18 November, Maj. Gen. Henry W. Halleck replaced Maj. Gen. John C. Fremont as commander of all Union forces west of the Mississippi. Brig. Gen. Don Carlos Buell commanded Union forces in central and eastern Kentucky.

Naval activities in 1861 centered around a Union blockade from the Potomac River to the Gulf of Mexico and scattered actions by a few ill-equipped Confederate privateers prowling the Atlantic Coast. War with England was narrowly averted when, on 8 December, Confederate commissioners James M. Mason and John Slidell representing President Davis were forcibly removed from a British vessel by a Union warship. To defuse the crisis, the United States had to disavow the action and place Mason and Slidell on a British warship to continue their mission.

In the West in 1862 Grant, in cooperation with a naval force commanded by Commodore Andrew H. Foote, captured Fort Henry (February 6) on the Tennessee River and Fort Donelson (February 16) on the Cumberland River. This broke the Confederate defensive line across Kentucky. The Confederates fell back to a new line along the Memphis and Charleston Railroad passing through Memphis, Tennessee, on the left, Corinth, Mississippi, in the center, and Chattanooga, Tennessee, on the right. On 11 March, Lincoln placed Halleck in overall command in the West. Moving through Tennessee against Johnston's new line of defense, Grant was surprised and nearly defeated by a Confederate attack at Shiloh on 6 April. The timely arrival of reinforcements under Buell and Grant's counterattack on 7 April turned defeat into victory and allowed Union forces to control the upper Mississippi River almost as far south as Memphis. A. S. Johnston had been killed at Shiloh, and Confederate command fell to Beauregard, who withdrew to Corinth. That city fell on 30 May, and Memphis on 6 June. Most of the Mississippi River north and south of Vicksburg was now controlled by Union forces. Beginning operations on 18 March in one of the most dramatic naval actions of the war, Adm. David G. Farragut conquered Confederate forts along the southern Mississippi River. By 28 April he had opened the Mississippi all the way north to New Orleans.

On 17 June, Beauregard was replaced by Gen. Braxton Bragg, who was placed in command of the Confederacy's western campaign. With Halleck's July departure for Washington to be general in chief, the Union's western command fell to Grant and Buell commanding the armies of the Tennessee and Ohio, respectively. Grant retained Memphis and Corinth by defeating Confederate Maj. Gens. Sterling Price and Earl Van Dorn in the Battles of Iuka (19–20 September) and Corinth (3–4 October). Meanwhile, in late July, Bragg moved slowly north from Chattanooga. Buell first withdrew, then advanced and fought part of Bragg's force to a draw at Perryville, Kentucky, on 8 October. Bragg withdrew to Tennessee. Buell failed to pursue and was replaced by Maj. Gen. William S. Rosecrans on 30 October. Rosecrans occupied Nashville on 6 November and fought Bragg's forces to a draw in the Battle of Murfreesboro (31 December 1862–2 January 1863).

During the last months of 1862, Union armies under Grant and Maj. Gen. William T. Sherman tried unsuccessfully to capture Vicksburg. The Confederate defenders occupying the "Gibralter of the West" stubbornly held out. At the end of the year, the Mississippi River from Vicksburg to Baton Rouge remained under Confederate control.

The use of naval gunboats to support land forces operating near inland waterways was validated by Union successes on the Mississippi, Cumberland, and Tennessee rivers in 1862. More important was the ushering in of a new age of naval warfare during a battle of the ironclads on 9 March of that year. In four hours of battle at Hampton Roads, Virginia, the Union *Monitor* and the Confederate *Merrimac* (rechristened CSS *Virginia*) fought to a draw, demonstrating the relative invulnerability of armored ships.

As activities in the West continued practically unabated during 1862, the campaigns in the East kept pace. Goaded into action by Lincoln, McClellan determined to attack Richmond, the Confederate capital, by moving his army down the Chesapeake Bay to Fortress Monroe; from there he could advance up a peninsula formed by the York and James rivers. Using this route, he could avoid direct assault against Johnston's Confederate army, which was facing Washington. That army would be forced to turn and meet him in order to protect the Confederate capital. A large force under McDowell was to move overland to join McClellan's forces in their attack on Richmond, but a masterful campaign by Maj. Gen. Thomas J. ("Stonewall") Jackson in the Shenandoah Valley threatened Washington and prevented McDowell's forces from moving south. In six weeks, with less than 18,000 men, Jackson had tied up 70,000 Federal troops and ruined McClellan's campaign plan. McClellan, nevertheless, began his advance on 4 April. On 1 June, Lee was ordered to replace the wounded Joseph E. Johnston as commander of the Confederate forces opposing McClellan. By 25 June, McClellan was four miles from Richmond, and the Seven Days Battles (25 June–1 July) began. In those battles Lee attacked aggressively, preventing McClellan from taking Richmond and causing him to withdraw to Harrison's Landing on the James River.

Lincoln called Maj. Gen. John Pope from the West and on 26 June appointed him to command the newly formed Army of Virginia. Halleck was also brought to Washington and appointed general in chief on 11 July. McClellan retained command of the Army of the Potomac, which was recalled to Washington on 3 August. Lee sent Jackson to observe Pope in central Virginia and slowly followed him north. In the Second Battle of Bull Run (29–30 August), Pope thought he had Jackson trapped but was surprised by Lee and Maj. Gen. James Longstreet, who struck his flank and caused his forces to withdraw toward Washington.

With President Davis's approval, Lee crossed the Potomac into Maryland. They hoped that a successful campaign would gain foreign recognition for the Confederacy, spark revolt in Maryland, and relieve Virginia for a time from the ravages of war. McClellan received a captured copy of Lee's order for the disposition and movement of his forces and moved slowly to engage him. On 17 September 1862, near the town of Sharpsburg, Maryland, the Battle of Antietam was fought. In what became known as the bloodiest day in American history, McClellan's uncoordinated attacks failed to dislodge Lee's army from its defensive positions, but did prevent it from conducting further offensive operations. Lee withdrew across the Potomac, and McClellan did not follow until ordered by Lincoln to do so. On 23 September, Lincoln took advantage of McClellan's strategic success against Lee and issued the Emancipation Proclamation, which ordered the freeing of all slaves in the rebellious states on 1 January 1863.

On 7 November, Lincoln replaced McClellan with Maj. Gen. Ambrose E. Burnside, who moved south and attacked Lee at Fredericksburg, Virginia, on

13 December. Fourteen successive Union assaults were repulsed, at terrible cost to Burnside's army. Lee had won the Battle of Fredericksburg. Still seeking a general who could defeat Lee and the Army of Northern Virginia, Lincoln replaced Burnside with Maj. Gen. Joseph Hooker on 26 January 1863.

1863

On 27 April, Hooker crossed the Rappahannock River to attack Lee. Maj. Gen. John Sedgwick was to demonstrate by forcing a crossing of the river at Fredericksburg, while Hooker would cross the river above, into the Wilderness, and flank Lee's left. Longstreet's corps was away gathering provisions, but screened by Maj. Gen. J. E. B. Stuart's cavalry, Lee was well aware of Hooker's movements. On 1 May, Lee left a small force at Fredericksburg to contain Sedgwick's attack and moved rapidly west to meet Hooker's main thrust. Separating his forces a second time on 2 May, Lee had Jackson envelop Hooker's right wing, completely demoralizing that force. That night, however, Lee suffered a loss he could not overcome. Returning from a reconnaissance of Union lines, Stonewall Jackson was mortally wounded by fire from his own troops. Lee resumed the attack against Hooker on 3 May, then turned to attack Sedgwick the next day. Hooker withdrew across the Rappahannock on 5–6 May. After his greatest tactical victory, Lee prepared for his second invasion of the North.

Lee hoped that, if he invaded the North and defeated Hooker's army decisively, he might yet gain foreign recognition for the Confederacy and force an end to the war as well. At least Virginia would be spared further invasion, and Maryland and Pennsylvania offered ample supplies of food and clothing. Lee moved northward into those two states. Hooker was slow to respond. Bickering with Lincoln and Halleck, Hooker offered to resign and was replaced by Maj. Gen. George G. Meade on 28 June. Learning that the Army of the Potomac was moving north, Lee concentrated his army near Cashtown, Pennsylvania, on 29–30 June.

On 1 July a Confederate infantry brigade and a Union cavalry brigade clashed on a road west of Gettysburg. The greatest battle ever fought on the continent had begun. Both sides rushed forces to the town. By the end of the day, Union forces had been driven back with heavy losses to Cemetery Hill, the high ground south of Gettysburg. On 2 July Lee continued to attack. Delays in getting Southern forces to attack positions and the constant flow of fresh Union troops to the battlefield prevented a Confederate victory. On 3 July, Lee made one more attempt to break the stalemate with an attack concentrated on the Union center. Known as "Pickett's Charge," this attack across almost a mile of open ground was repulsed with heavy Confederate casualties. Between 4 and 14 July, Lee withdrew across the Potomac. Meade followed cautiously and lost an opportunity to exploit his victory. There were no major operations in the East for the remainder of the year.

The South's last chance for a favorable decision in the East was lost at Gettysburg on 3 July. One day later, Vicksburg fell. Grant, with Sherman assisting, concluded a two-month campaign against Lt. Gen. John Pemberton's forces at

Vicksburg and those of Joseph E. Johnston (recovered from his wounds and now overall Confederate commander in the West) at Jackson, Mississippi. Grant had abandoned his supply lines to place himself between the two Confederate forces, inflicting losses on both and finally causing the Vicksburg defenders to surrender after a well-orchestrated siege. The Western Confederacy was split from north to south. The area west of the Mississippi, known as the Trans-Mississippi Confederacy, could no longer be counted upon to provide the remainder of the Confederacy with badly needed food and raw materials. The death knell had sounded, but the war would drag on for almost two years longer.

As the actions around Vicksburg unfolded, Rosecrans outmaneuvered Bragg and forced him to withdraw to Chattanooga in early July. After some delay, and with a brilliant maneuver, Rosecrans forced Bragg to evacuate the city on 7 September and pursued him into northwestern Georgia. Meanwhile, Longstreet, one of "Lee's Lieutenants," had been rushed westward to bolster Bragg's forces. After his arrival, Bragg advanced and attacked Rosecrans's forces near Chickamauga Creek on 19–20 September. The Battle of Chickamauga ended with Rosecrans's defeat and the withdrawal of his Army of the Cumberland to Chattanooga, where it was surrounded by Bragg's forces and cut off from outside help.

On 27 October, Lincoln placed Grant in command of all Union forces between the Mississippi and the Alleghenies. Grant hastened to Chattanooga and ordered Sherman and his Army of the Tennessee there also. Replacing Rosecrans with Brig. Gen. George H. Thomas, who had fought valiantly at Chickamauga, Grant set about breaking Bragg's siege of Chattanooga. On 23–25 November, in bold attacks against Bragg's well-entrenched forces, Grant broke the siege and drove Bragg's army from the city. With this victory, the path lay open for an attack into Georgia to cut the Confederacy once again. By the close of 1863, Union armies had gained control of Arkansas, Kentucky, Tennessee, most of Louisiana, Mississippi, Florida, the Rio Grande Frontier of Texas, and the entire length of the Mississippi River.

Naval operations through 1863 continued apace. The Union naval blockade was taking its toll. Still, blockade running had become big business and was therefore attempted with regularity. The meager Confederate high-seas fleet consisted of only a few vessels and was no match for a constantly expanding Union Navy.

1864–65

On 9 March 1864, Lincoln appointed Grant to be general in chief of all Union armies. Grant wasted no time organizing his huge forces for what would be the final crushing blow to the Confederacy. In giving Grant a free hand to conduct operations, Lincoln had told him: "The particulars of your plan I neither know nor seek to know. . . . I wish not to obtrude any constraints or restraints on you." Grant appointed Sherman commander of all Union armies in the West and South. His plan was to launch simultaneous offensives against Lee's army in the East and Johnston's armies in the West. While Grant operated against Lee, Sherman would split the Confederacy again by attacking eastward until his forces reached the Atlantic Ocean. From there, he would turn north and advance until Confederate resistance ended.

While moving south, Grant determined to keep constant pressure on Lee's army "wherever it may be found" and give him no respite from battle. Lee attempted to keep his army between Grant and Richmond. On 4 May, Grant advanced, seeking to envelop Lee's right flank. The armies clashed in confused fighting in the Battle of the Wilderness (5–7 May) near the old Chancellorsville battlefield. The fight ended in a draw. Rather than break off the engagement as previous Union commanders had done after a difficult battle, Grant slipped around Lee's right flank and headed south. Lee had anticipated this move and rushed to Spotsylvania Court House, where a five-day series of piecemeal engagements ended without victory for either side.

Grant continued his flanking maneuvers, and Lee countered them in a series of brilliant maneuvers that took both forces just north and east of Richmond. The fighting was bloody. On 3 June at Cold Harbor, Grant lost 8,000 men in an unsuccessful one-hour attack against Lee's forces. In the course of the battles leading to the outskirts of Richmond, Lee suffered two irreplaceable losses. Longstreet, his best remaining corps commander, was severely wounded; Stuart, his trusted cavalry commander on whom he relied heavily for information was mortally wounded in a battle with Maj. Gen. Philip H. Sheridan's cavalry near Yellow Tavern.

After Cold Harbor, Grant moved south of the James River, surprising Lee, who had expected an attack in force against Richmond. Lee quickly recovered and moved his forces south to defend Petersburg. Grant attacked him on 18 June, but Lee held, and the siege of Petersburg had begun. Grant planned to take Petersburg and then move upon Richmond from the southeast. That operation was delayed when Confederate major general Jubal A. Early's corps moved north in July and threatened Washington. Union reinforcements were rushed north to counter this threat, but it was not until mid-October that forces under Sheridan finally drove Early's corps from the Shenandoah Valley. This cleared the way for a more complete concentration against Lee at Petersburg. Operations dragged on for the rest of the year with trench warfare and spectacular sorties and maneuvers during which Grant slowly extended his partial encirclement of the Richmond-Petersburg area. During the winter, half-starved Confederate defenders watched their resources shrink as the well-fed, well-supplied Union besiegers steadily became stronger.

In the West, Sherman left Chattanooga on 5 May to begin his advance into Georgia against Johnston's armies. Johnston skillfully opposed Sherman in a series of delaying maneuvers. Sherman countered by outflanking Johnston's forces, but, while forcing them to withdraw steadily, he could not defeat them. After arriving at the outskirts of Atlanta and preparing for a counterattack, Johnston was replaced by the impulsive Confederate Lieutenant General John B. Hood, who repeatedly attacked advancing Union columns and was repulsed. By 31 August, Hood was forced to evacuate Atlanta, which was occupied by

Sherman's forces the next day (Fig. 1). Hood then attempted to move back into Tennessee to cut Sherman's long lines of communication and impede Union army operations eastward from Atlanta. Sherman continued his advance toward Savannah, but dispatched Thomas to counter the threat from Hood. In the battles of Franklin (30 November) and Nashville (15–16 December), Hood was decisively defeated and forced to withdraw from Tennessee. Johnston was recalled to replace Hood, but there was little he could do to stop the march to the sea. By 21 December, Sherman had taken Savannah.

Naval operations helped tighten the Union's grip on the Confederacy. Union warships sank most of the remaining Confederate warships and closed major harbors along the Gulf of Mexico and the East Coast. This all but denied blockade runners access to the Confederacy. Submarine warfare claimed its first victims on 17 February 1865, when the CSS *H. L. Hunley*, a true submarine, torpedoed and sank the steam frigate USS *Housatonic* of the federal squadron blockading the Charleston harbor. The *Hunley* sank with its prey.

On 31 January 1865, President Lincoln met with Confederate peace commissioners, led by Vice President Stephens, on a Union warship in Hampton Roads. Lincoln offered complete amnesty if the South would rejoin the Union and abolish slavery. The Confederate representatives insisted on independence, so the conference failed to accomplish anything. On 3 February, President Davis appointed Lee to supreme command of the Confederate armies. Lee immediately placed Johnston in command of all the scattered Confederate elements in the Carolinas. By 17 February, Sherman had moved north into Columbia, South Carolina. The same day, Charleston fell. Sherman then moved toward Goldsboro to attack Johnston, but was surprised when the latter attacked him at Bentonville on 19 March. After a fierce battle, Johnston was forced to withdraw. Sherman reached Goldsboro on 23 March and decided to

Figure 1. On 31 August 1864, the Confederate army at Jonesboro, Georgia, fifteen miles south of Atlanta, was attacked by Sherman's army. General Hood's communication line was cut and he evacuated Atlanta that night. (SOURCE: U.S. Library of Congress)

rest his exhausted forces for three weeks. He planned to join Grant near Petersburg in mid-April.

In the meantime, Grant continued to press Lee's defenses around Petersburg, causing him to stretch his already overextended and weakened lines. On 25 March, Lee attempted vainly to break Grant's grip with a surprise assault against Fort Stedman. The fort was taken, but Union forces rallied and regained it. Following Sheridan's return from the Shenandoah Valley on 26 March, Grant decided to "end the matter." He sent Sheridan to outflank Lee's right and, that accomplished, ordered a general assault on Lee's positions. Lee attempted to escape and link up with Johnston south of Danville, where Jefferson Davis had set up a temporary capital. That effort was thwarted when Union forces blocked all avenues of escape. The city of Richmond surrendered on 3 April. On 9 April at Appomattox Court House, Lee surrendered the Army of Northern Virginia to Grant. President Lincoln was assassinated by John Wilkes Booth on 14 April. On 26 April, Johnston surrendered to Sherman. Jefferson Davis attempted to escape, but he was captured on 10 May by Union cavalry at Irwinsville, Georgia. All other Confederate forces had surrendered by 26 May. On 29 May, President Andrew Johnson's proclamation of amnesty officially ended the war.

Casualties

The Civil War was the bloodiest war in American history. On both sides, one of every three soldiers who participated in the conflict became a casualty from enemy fire or disease. During the war, 2,261 battles were fought. Of approximately 2,000,000 Union participants, 359,528 died—110,070 died in battle, 224,586 from disease, and 24,872 of other causes. Confederate force estimates are less exact and vary from 600,000 to 1,000,000. Of those, approximately 258,000 died. How many of those died from disease or other causes is not known. Hundreds of thousands more on both sides were wounded or suffered from disease but recovered. Union and Confederate innovations in the treatment and evacuation of the wounded produced military and civilian hospital and ambulance systems that remained valid well into the twentieth century.

To this day, the Civil War remains the most cataclysmic event in the history of the United States.

RALPH M. MITCHELL

SEE ALSO: Civil War; Farragut, David Glasgow; Grant, Ulysses Simpson; Jackson, Thomas Jonathan ("Stonewall"); Lee, Robert Edward; Scott, Winfield; Sherman, William Tecumseh.

Bibliography

Boatner, M. M. 1988. *The Civil War dictionary.* Rev. ed. New York: Times Books.
Catton, B. 1962. *The Army of the Potomac.* 3 vols. Garden City, N.Y.: Doubleday.
Johnson, R. U., and C. C. Buel, eds. 1887. *Battles and leaders of the Civil War.* 4 vols. New York.

Livermore, T. L. 1957. *Numbers and losses in the Civil War.* Millwood, N.Y.: Kraus Reprint.

Long, E. B. 1985. *The Civil War day by day.* New York: Da Capo.

Mitchell, R. M. 1975. *Improvisation, adaptation and innovation: The handling of wounded in the Civil War.* Unpublished master's thesis, Rice Univ., Houston, Tex.

Vandiver, F. E. 1987. *Their tattered flags: The epic of the Confederacy.* College Station: Texas A & M Univ. Press.

CIVIL WAR, RUSSIAN [1918–22]

The Russian Revolution of 7 November 1917 was little more than a coup d'état in St. Petersburg and Moscow. The Bolsheviks seized power in the name of the *soviets* (councils), promising to rule until free elections convened a constituent assembly. After only one session, the Bolsheviks dissolved the assembly. That act, more than any other, sparked the Russian Civil War (1918–22), although it did not fully blossom until after the humiliating peace with Germany in 1918. During the next five years there were concurrent civil wars between revolutionaries, counterrevolutionaries, and ethnic minorities; war with Poland; foreign intervention; and implementation of revolutionary socialism under the banner of world Communism. Finland, Estonia, Latvia, Lithuania, and Poland won their independence, while Poland, Turkey, and Romania acquired pieces of the Soviet borderlands. The civil war was the class struggle that the revolution bypassed. It shaped the institutions and perceptions of the Soviet state and resulted in the adoption of autocratic institutions to stamp out counterrevolution.

Beginning of the Civil War

It is difficult to state exactly when the civil war began. Socialist revolutionary terror, including an assassination attempt on Lenin in August 1918 and an uprising in July 1918, failed to dislodge the Bolsheviks, who retaliated with Red Terror on a scale unmatched by the czars. Because Lenin had promised "peace, land, and bread," he declared an armistice with Germany in December 1917, stating, "No war, no peace." The Russian army dissolved as soldiers "voted with their feet," and the German army moved into the void and seized huge tracts of land. Lenin conceded defeat in order to save the revolution (Treaty of Brest Litovsk, 3 March 1918). Latvia, Lithuania, Estonia, Poland, the Ukraine, and Finland received their freedom as puppet states of the Germans. Only Germany's defeat in the west (November 1918) saved the treaty from full implementation.

The former czarist chief of staff, Gen. M. W. Alekseev (1857–1918), created an anti-Bolshevik "White" army early in 1918, but he died soon afterward of natural causes. His successor, Gen. L. G. Kornilov (1870–1918), the former commander in chief of the provisional government's army, who had led an aborted counterrevolution against Kerensky, was captured in March 1918 during an attack on Ekaterinodar and executed. The subsequent leader of the White movement in the south was Gen. A. I. Denikin (1872–1947), the former commander of the western front, who had been imprisoned for his part in the Kornilov affair against Kerensky, escaped, and joined Alekseev's forces on the Don. In the north, the French and British supported a secessionist government under the socialist Nikolai Chaikovsky. To the west, in Estonia, a force under Gen. Nikolai Iudenich threatened Petrograd. A bizarre twist occurred in May of 1918 when 40,000 Czech prisoners of war, being transported to Vladivostok via the Trans-Siberian Railroad, mutinied and fought to throw off Bolshevik rule in Siberia. Within three months nearly 8,000 kilometers (5,000 mi.) of railroad were under Czech control. On 8 June, a Committee of Members of the Constituent Assembly formed a government in Samara (on the Volga River). A provisional Siberian government (the All-Russian Directory) founded in Omsk in June 1918 was joined by the Ural and Orenburg cossacks. On 16 July a local Bolshevik commander executed the royal family in Ekaterinburg when White forces approached.

National Liberation Movements

The drive for independence by ethnic minorities of the Russian Empire did not rest solely with German initiatives. Finland, the Baltic states, and Belorussia had already declared their independence in 1917. In 1918, the Ukraine, Poland, and the Transcaucasus states of Armenia, Azerbaijan, and Georgia did so as well. The Bolsheviks claimed a doctrine of self-determination but wanted to keep the multinational empire intact. Lenin was interested in the international class struggle and world revolution, not the creation on the borderlands of the Crimean Tatar, Bashkir, Kirghiz, and Kokand republics, the emirates of Bokhara and Khiva, or the Menshevik-dominated Caucasus states. Once the Red Army had expelled the more threatening White armies and it was apparent that world revolution was not going to occur, the Bolsheviks moved in on these smaller states and brought them back under control, except for the Baltic states, Poland, and Finland.

Foreign Intervention

Foreign intervention actually began in February 1918 when German, Austrian, and Turkish troops seized huge chunks of Russian territory. Fourteen allied nations also sent troops and supplies, originally to defend war supplies shipped to the provisional government in Arkhangelsk and Murmansk, but later to contain and overthrow the revolution and keep it from spreading to Western Europe. Allied participation has been exaggerated by historians and Bolshevik propagandists. Japan's intervention was the largest (more than 60,000 troops). It backed Gregory Semenov in eastern Siberia in hopes of expanding onto the Asian continent and regaining the northern half of Sakhalin Island. (The Japanese did not withdraw their troops until 1922 and kept Sakhalin Island until 1925.) The United Kingdom sent about 40,000 troops, but confined most of its operations to Denikin in the southeast around the Black Sea and in the north.

The French and Greeks each sent two divisions but centered their operations in the southwest (Black Sea and Crimea). The United States sent about 10,000 men to the north and Siberia. The most influential intervention force, the Czechs, was not "sent" at all. Most of the aid from the Allies went to train and supply White troops, but the bulk of such efforts occurred in the summer of 1919 after the crucial battles had already been lost. No major battles were fought between the Allies and Bolsheviks. The Allies' blockade of October 1919–January 1920 (too little, too late) was most significant in evacuating troops and civilians once the tide of battle had turned. The Allies' home front was tired of war and wanted their boys to come home. West European states were more interested in redrawing the map in Central Europe and the new League of Nations than in the civil war in Russia.

Denikin's "Volunteer Army"

The greatest threat to Soviet rule was General Denikin's White Volunteer Army, joined in the summer of 1918 by the Kuban and Don cossacks. During the spring of 1919, a circle of enemies threatened the Bolshevik center from all sides. A Red Army was growing, but there were not enough troops to fight in all the border areas. Denikin's army, composed mainly of former czarist officers and Don cossacks, occupied the Ukraine and advanced on Moscow, the new capital. By October 1919, Denikin had victory within his grasp, but then everything fell apart. A Russian nationalist, Denikin wanted to retain the integrity and institutions of the former empire. He refused to institute a land-reform program to win the support of the peasantry, and his civil administration was inefficient. Initial successes were due more to Bolshevik weaknesses than to his generalship. Denikin conquered nearly 910,000 square kilometers (350,000 sq. mi.) of land from the overextended Red Army (which had to fight through the Ukraine to reach him), but he was unable to consolidate his gains or secure local peasant or cossack support. He fought in isolation and was unable—or unwilling—to link up with the Siberian resistance. After defeating Iudenich in Estonia, the Red Army was able to confront him piecemeal and force him back to the sea, where he was replaced by Baron P. N. Wrangel (1878–1928).

Kolchak's Offensive in Siberia

The Siberian provisional government proclaimed the former commander of the Black Sea Fleet, Adm. A. V. Kolchak (1875–1920), Supreme Ruler of Russia—that is, military dictator—following a coup on 17 November 1918. Kolchak received Western military aid and in the spring of 1919 he launched the Ufa offensive, advancing 400 kilometers (250 mi.) in eight weeks and almost reaching the Volga. However, the spring thaw set in and his army, mired in mud, fell victim to a Red counteroffensive. He was also hampered by poor military organization and logistics, a lack of popular support following his coup, an inefficient government, and a conservative economic policy that refused concessions to the peasants. In November 1919, Omsk fell. Kolchak was captured and executed by the Bolsheviks on 7 February 1920.

The Russo-Polish War of 1920–21

The liberation of Poland from the Russian, Austro-Hungarian, and German partitioning powers created a new state, bound together by a fierce national identity and strong historic ambitions, existing in a political vacuum in which borders were determined by the most powerful state. The Allies supported the Curzon line along the Bug River (which matched ethnic lines) for the eastern border. The Poles, under Marshal Joseph Pilsudski (1867–1935), dreamed of re-creating the medieval Polish kingdom that had stretched from the Baltic to the Ukraine. On 25 April 1920, the Poles launched an attack against the newly independent Ukrainian state; by 6–7 May they had conquered Kiev, throwing out both the Ukrainian nationalists and the Red army. The overextended Polish force was vulnerable to a Bolshevik counterattack under Mikhail N. Tukhachevsky (1893–1937) and S. M. Budenny (1888–1973), who fought their way to the Vistula River and the very "gates of Warsaw" (16–25 August). The Soviets, however, were hampered by poor transportation, a shortage of trained troops, and command conflicts between Tukhachevsky and Egorov/Stalin. With the help of French advisers and military aid, the Poles defeated the counterattack. The Treaty of Riga (18 March 1921) secured a Polish state (smaller in real territory than when the war began) and Bolshevik survival.

The Last Gasp of Wrangel

In April 1920, the last White army was commanded by Baron Wrangel, a brilliant czarist officer who had commanded a cavalry brigade at the age of 39 and won fame for his defense of Tsaritsyn against Voroshilov. Wrangel did have a land-reform program and attempted to rule without alienating the peasants with food requisitioning, but his goal was not to overthrow Bolshevism. He simply wanted to withdraw his forces. By 1920, it was too late to change the course of the civil war and the battle-hardened Red army could now concentrate on isolated White remnants. Wrangel successfully evacuated nearly 150,000 soldiers and civilians from five ports on the Black Sea in November 1920. For all practical purposes the war was over.

Why Bolshevik Success?

The Whites were united only in that they were all anti-Bolshevik. They were nationalistic Russians who wanted to oust Bolshevism and re-create the old empire; each general saw himself as the new ruler. This inability to link up and provide a united campaign hurt them because it made it possible for the Soviets to pick them off one at a time.

The war-weary foreign interventionists also lacked common goals; they had no clear support for any one army and no clear objective. Allied success in the West kept the Germans from overthrowing the Bolsheviks.

National revolts were separate and small; none could confront the Soviets alone. Only those with excellent leaders (Mannerheim in Finland) or foreign support (the Baltic states) were able to retain their freedom. The Poles were a threat, but all they wanted was statehood, not the overthrow of Lenin.

White Terror and Leftist Terror (Socialist revolutionaries) were matched atrocity for atrocity by Red Terror. The Red army under Trotsky, reinforced by czarist officers (specialists) such as Vatsetis and Kamenev and converts such as Mikhail Tukhachevsky, was a match for the Whites.

The Bolshevik heartland between Moscow and Petrograd, comprising over 2.5 million square kilometers (nearly 1 million sq. mi.), 60 million people, and an excellent railway system, provided enough land in the center to trade space for time. The Bolsheviks promised "peace, land, and bread," and at great cost provided it. Their claim to rule in the name of the independently elected *soviets* also gained national support.

Conclusion

The Russian Revolution of November 1917 was a political coup in a power vacuum in isolated cities. The civil war, as a social, economic, political, and military force, was the real revolution in Russia.

DIANNE L. SMITH

SEE ALSO: History, Modern Military.

Bibliography

Adams, A. E. [1963] 1973. *Bolsheviks in the Ukraine: The second campaign, 1918–1919.* Reprint. Kennikat.

Erickson, J. 1984. *Soviet high command: A military-political history, 1918–41.* London: Westview Press.

Kenez, P. 1971. *Civil war in south Russia, 1918: The first year of the volunteer army.* Berkeley, Calif.: Univ. of California.

———. 1977. *Civil war in South Russia, 1919–20: The defeat of the Whites.* Berkeley, Calif.: Univ. of California.

Kennan, G. 1967. *The decision to intervene.* New York: Atheneum.

Luckett, R. 1971. *The White generals: An account of the White movement and the Russian civil war.* London: Longman.

Mawdsley, E. 1987. *The Russian civil war.* Boston: Allen & Unwin.

Mayzel, M. 1979. *Generals and revolutionaries: The Russian general staff during the revolution: A study in the transformation of a military elite.* Osnabrück, Germany.

Pipes, R. 1917. [1954.] *The formation of the Soviet Union: Communism and nationalism.* Cambridge, Mass.: Harvard Univ. Press.

Shokolov, M. 1934. *And quiet flows the Don.* New York: Knopf.

CIVIL WAR, SPANISH

Revolt, revolution, and civil war engulfed Spain in July 1936 as a result of long-brewing internal problems. Because of the ideological climate of Europe at the time, the Spanish war immediately assumed major international importance. Unfortunately for the Spaniards, their country became an arena in which the violent political and ideological passions of the time vied for superiority.

In the military sphere, the war was used as a testing ground for new technologies and tactics by the Germans, Italians, and Russians, all of whom intervened militarily. It also became a classic battle of attrition, with each side raising armies of a half million or more. It was ferociously fought with no quarter asked or given, lasted almost three years, and cost perhaps a half million lives.

The War Begins

The war began with a revolt by part of the army against the leftist "popular front" government of the Republic. The revolt was not a complete success, but won sufficient territory and military and civilian support to sustain itself. It undermined the normal forces of order in the state to the extent that the government armed numerous party and union militia forces (Fig. 1). This, in turn, allowed a violent upsurge of leftist revolution.

At the outset neither side had a strong military force. The only combat-ready part of the army, commanded by Gen. Francisco Franco, was blockaded in Morocco by the government-controlled fleet. Franco overcame this by launching the first major airlift in history, flying some 20,000 troops across the Strait of Gibraltar between July and September. With these units as its spearhead, the Nationalist drive to Madrid began in early August. Foreign support was received (mainly aircraft and pilots) during this period by the Nationalists (from Italy and Germany) and by the Republic (from France).

Soviet Intervention and the Battle of Madrid

By the first week in November the Nationalists had fought to the outskirts of Madrid, but had failed to take the city by frontal assault. This failure was due in large part to two factors: first, the Republican forces substantially outnum-

Figure 1. Soldiers in the Spanish Civil War. (SOURCE: U.S. Library of Congress)

bered the 20,000 or so Nationalists, and second, the timely arrival of Soviet materiel, a cadre of advisers and technicians, and the Comintern-sponsored International Brigades, which substantially increased the capability of the Republic's military forces. Stymied in their efforts to take the city by frontal assault, the Nationalists made several attempts to envelop it by wide flanking attacks, none of which proved successful.

The Northern Campaign

By March 1937 the Nationalist command shifted its main effort away from Madrid to concentrate on the destruction of the isolated Republican enclave in northern Spain. This campaign (April to October 1937) was characterized by several factors that favored the Nationalists. Since the area was isolated from other government territory, and the Nationalists had almost complete air and naval superiority in the area, the strongest military forces of the Republic could not provide reinforcements or supplies. In addition, this area of Republican Spain was rent by political disunity and military discord, while the Nationalists enjoyed a unified command.

Successful conclusion of the northern campaign provided the Nationalists with Spain's major coal deposits, most of its steel production, its major arms factories, the important port and industrial city of Bilbao, some 12,000 square miles of territory (much of it good agricultural land), and 1,500,000 people. In addition, some 100,000 prisoners of war were taken, many of whom were conscripted into the Nationalist army, while the rest were put to work in other capacities. This victory also allowed the Nationalist army and air force to concentrate entirely on objectives in the remainder of Republican territory and to concentrate the fleet in the Mediterranean.

Republican Offensives

The Republic attempted several offensive operations designed to force the Nationalists to divert forces from the north. These operations revealed some of the military deficiencies that were to plague the Republic's army throughout the war: lack of adequate training among field-grade officers, lack of initiative in the junior officer and noncommissioned ranks, lack of mobility, and poor coordination. Even with the benefit of local air and ground superiority, no breakthroughs of consequence were achieved, and the Nationalists did not have to disrupt their ongoing campaign in the north.

The Two Armies

The Spanish conflict was one in which each side had to build an army while fighting a war. By the summer of 1937 each had conscripted more than 300,000 men, and by the end of 1937 each army numbered about 500,000.

The new Republican Popular Army came into existence in October 1936 with the organization of its first six brigades, primarily formed from the ranks of the Communist Fifth Regiment militia forces. From the beginning the Communists occupied most of the command positions. Of the 3,000 or so officers of the prewar Spanish army who served the Republic, most were politically suspect, many were unenthusiastic, and few held commands in frontline units. A political commissar system was introduced into the army; the red star was adopted as its symbol; and the clenched fist salute replaced the traditional one. Soviet advisers played a major role, particularly in the elite units (including the International Brigades) that were consistently called upon to do most of the fighting.

The Nationalist army was more traditional and was derived more directly from the prewar Spanish army. Its leading commanders throughout the war were regular officers; discipline and hierarchy never broke down; and the vacuum of authority and leadership so evident in the Republican army never existed. Franco and the Spaniards remained thoroughly in charge, even while benefiting from the aid, advice, materiel, and personnel of their German and Italian allies.

The Air War

When the war broke out, the government retained the vast majority of the planes and at least half of the pilots of the Spanish air force. Because the planes were obsolescent and the pilots, for the most part, were unfit for combat, the government sought foreign aircraft and personnel from virtually the first day of the war. The Nationalists, with few aircraft under their control, did the same. Each side received approximately the same number of planes during the first months of the war: the government mainly from France, the Nationalists mainly from Italy and Germany. The government recruited foreign fliers, and the Nationalists received Italian and German air force pilots. The Nationalists used their airpower more effectively from the beginning, first in airlifting troops from Morocco, second in developing the technique of close support of ground operations, and third, in achieving, by October 1936, almost complete air superiority.

This situation was reversed in early November by substantial Soviet air intervention. From that time through much of 1937, the Republic maintained air superiority, although this was not brought to bear in the northern campaign. Throughout 1937 the air war was fought primarily by foreigners, the Germans and Italians on one side and the Soviet air contingent on the other. Some Spanish fliers fought on both sides from the beginning, and both soon initiated programs to train Spanish pilots. The Republic sent many recruits to the Soviet Union for flight training while the Nationalists relied mainly on Italian training facilities. By 1938 the Nationalists had achieved both numerical and technical superiority.

The Naval War

In the naval sphere the Republic began with an overwhelming superiority in ships. But this potentially critical advantage was never successfully exploited because of ineffective leadership and a lack of trained officers. As early as

September 1936, the much smaller but competently and aggressively handled Nationalist fleet won control of the Strait of Gibraltar, never to relinquish it. Operating from Mallorca, the Nationalist fleet harassed shipping bound for Republican ports, making it a high-risk enterprise to run war materiel to the Republic by sea, and effectively neutralized the Republican fleet. In no sphere of operations did the disparity in technical expertise and aggressiveness between the two sides show more clearly than in naval operations.

The War of Attrition

Following the successful conclusion of the northern campaign in October 1937, Franco decided to turn once more to the conquest of Madrid. The Republic, forewarned by its intelligence services, launched a preemptive attack in Aragón, surprised the Nationalists, and captured the provincial capital of Teruel. Franco, as always unwilling to allow any advance to go unchallenged, shifted his forces and, by the end of February, had retaken Teruel. The Nationalists followed up with a major offensive through Aragón that resulted, by April, in driving a wedge through Republican territory to the Mediterranean.

Franco then turned his forces south against Valencia. While the bulk of the Nationalist army was thus engaged, the Republic, having regrouped its forces in Catalonia, launched an offensive across the Ebro River. Once more, Franco abandoned his own operation and turned to counter the enemy initiative. The Nationalist army spent the fall of 1938 retaking the territory seized by the Republican forces and, in the process, destroying the remnants of the Popular Army in Catalonia.

Defeatism, steadily deepening in the Republic since the reverse at Teruel and the breakthrough to the sea, now became almost universal. The Nationalist offensive into Catalonia met only half-hearted and sporadic resistance, and the city of Barcelona fell without a fight. The remnants of the Popular Army in Catalonia, some 200,000 men, were herded across the French frontier into exile.

Only the Communists in the Republican forces continued to demand resistance to the end. This led to an anti-Communist coup within the Popular Army engineered by professional officers in the Madrid zone, an event that signaled the final collapse of the Republic and Nationalist victory.

Why the Nationalists Won

The Nationalists did not win because of greater resources or more foreign support, but because they used their resources more effectively. Throughout the war the Nationalists held the initiative, conquered territory, and forced the Republic to take the defensive. Even the Republic's offensives were for defensive purposes, and they were never successful in the long run.

Nationalist victory also reflected the political realities of the war. The Republic was a disunited, quarreling, and mutually suspicious organization of autonomous "states within the state," and the ideological contingents often-seemed more interested in waging internecine political struggles than in winning the war.

Nationalist Spain, on the other hand, was organized first and foremost for waging war. Political unity of command was the concomitant of military unity of command. From the early stages of the war, Franco was both generalissimo of the armed forces and head of state. The Republicans used too much time and energy making politics and revolution, while the Nationalists concentrated on making war.

R. DAN RICHARDSON

SEE ALSO: Civil War.

Bibliography

Alcofar Nassaes, J. L. 1971. *Las fuerzas navales en la guerra civil española*. Barcelona: Editorial Euros.
Bolloten, B. 1979. *The Spanish revolution*. Chapel Hill: Univ. of North Carolina Press.
Carr, R., ed. 1971. *The republic and the civil war in Spain*. London: Macmillan.
Cattell, D. T. 1955. *Communism in the Spanish civil war*. Berkeley: Univ. of California.
Payne, S. 1970. *The Spanish revolution*. New York: Norton.
Richardson, R. D. 1982. *Comintern army: The International Brigades in the Spanish civil war*. Lexington: Univ. of Kentucky Press.
Salas Larrazábal, J. 1969. *La guerra de España desde el aire*. Barcelona: Ediciones Ariel.
Salas Larrazábal, R. 1974. *Historia del ejército popular de la republica*. 4 vols. Madrid: Editorita Nacional.
Thomas, H. 1986. *The Spanish civil war*. New York: Harper and Row.

CLAUSEWITZ, KARL VON
[1780–1831]

Karl Philipp Gottlieb von Clausewitz (Fig. 1) was a major-general in the Prussian army who played an important role in the Prussian alliance politics and military reforms that helped to defeat Napoleon. The reforms also laid the foundations for the Prussian and German general staff and concomitant ideals of military leadership and the professional development of officers. His classic work, *On War*, has had global influence.

Clausewitz was born in Burg, Prussia, a small town on an inland canal connecting the Havel and the Elbe northeast of Magdeburg. His father was a lieutenant in the army, but left the service following the Seven Years' War and became a collector of excise taxes. Karl, the youngest of four brothers who had successful military careers, grew up in an atmosphere of devotion to the Prussian army.

Military Career

At the age of 12, Clausewitz took part in the Rhineland campaign during the War of the First Coalition. In 1795, upon conclusion of the Peace of Basel, he was posted to garrison duty at Neuruppin near Berlin. He spent six years there, building the foundation for his subsequent ascent. Clausewitz studied the Seven

Figure 1. Karl von Clausewitz. (SOURCE: U.S. Library of Congress)

Years' War, the deeds of Frederick the Great, and Frederick's general principles of war in the *Instruction* for his generals, edited by Scharnhorst in 1794 (Rothfels 1980). He also played a role in the regimental school for lance corporals and ensigns. In 1801, he was admitted to the Berlin military academy, newly reorganized by Scharnhorst.

The reorganization of the academy was necessarily significant in a state so dependent upon, and dominated by, its army. The formation of the officer corps was, potentially, an activity of high statecraft. Prussia, adjusting slowly and painfully to the passing of enlightened absolutism and of the turbulent 1790s, was attracted to, but disturbed by, the option of "defensive modernization" (Wehler 1987).

Clausewitz was deeply affected by these changes in military theory. He began his education studying the orthodox art of generalship as exemplified by Frederick; in turn he created a genuine theory of war rising above tradecraft, principles of war, and service doctrine.

As a star graduate of the military academy, Clausewitz became a protégé of Scharnhorst, the leader of the military wing of a budding reform movement. In 1804, Clausewitz began his essays on strategy (Clausewitz 1937), in which he adopted Machiavelli's elastic concept of victory (*Discourses* II:22) and elaborated it into a theory of culmination (Tashjean 1988). The theory analyzes the changing relations between offense and defense; on that basis, it highlights the culmination point as a criterion for war termination in a limited war. The essays of 1804 also predicted Napoleon's defeat should he invade Russia.

Clausewitz was briefly held captive in France after the Prussian defeat by Napoleon in 1806. Subsequently, he joined Scharnhorst in Königsberg to perform confidential tasks of Prussian rearmament. Between 1809 and 1812, he produced a first draft of *On War*, lectured at the military academy in Berlin on general staff work and guerrilla war, and worked on a new infantry manual.

In the spring of 1812, his disgust with the Prussian alliance with Napoleon drove Clausewitz into the service of Russia; the flaming patriotism of his "Confession" made him a spokesman for Prussian officers leaving their country's service. Clausewitz helped to bring about the Convention of Tauroggen, which detached the Prussian auxiliary corps from Napoleon's army and ushered in the wars of liberation. Only the year before, when Gneisenau had proposed following the Spanish example of popular liberation war, King Frederick William III had commented only, "Nice poetry" (Niemeyer 1987). Now, in December 1812, following the Russian debacle, the beginning of the end was at hand for Napoleon. Despite some setbacks, the anti-Napoleonic coalition led to the events of Leipzig and Napoleon's defeat. In 1815, Clausewitz rejoined the Prussian army at the rank of colonel. He served as chief of staff of the III Army Corps and authored the plans for his corps' operations at Ligny and at the critical battle of Wavre in the Waterloo campaign.

After 1815 came the forces of restoration. Clausewitz became director of the War Academy in Berlin, where he drafted the massive manuscript for *On War*. In 1831, he served as chief of staff of Gneisenau's army of observation when Poland revolted against the Russians. Cholera took his life in Breslau on 16 November, 1831. His wife Marie, née Countess Brühl, published *On War* as the first three of ten volumes of his writings. On 19 November 1971, his mortal remains, transferred from Breslau to his native town, were interred with military honors in the East Cemetery of Burg (Rehm 1980, p. 363).

Essential Teaching

Clausewitz articulated three complementary concepts of war. The trinity of war—political direction, the armed forces (including generalship), and the popular base—is multivariate. In other words, any of its elements may vary substantially from war to war. Political direction dominates, because war is the continuation of state policy with an admixture of other means. (*On War* presupposes an international system of sovereign nations.)

Clausewitz also posits that friction—a negative "force multiplier"—makes the great difference between any theory of war and actual war. But no theory of war can encompass all that matters in a war, because theory can account for only potential frictions. The scope of this concept is disputed.

For example, each belligerent in a contest may be personified metaphorically as a wrestler. This abstraction is useful for reasons of intellectual economy, but, in fact, the multiplicity of simultaneous combats escapes theoretical grasp. Such an abstraction requires corrective concretion by the concept of friction.

At the international level, war is dialectical: the trinity of war is assumed away, as is most friction. What comes into view here are the military dialectics of attack and defense, as well as material and moral factors from threat perception through outbreak scenarios, escalation, and culmination, to war termination and peace.

The dialectical concept of war is the starting point of most Western military theory since Napoleon. But Clausewitz teaches that any such conception of war is, by itself, grossly truncated and misleading.

JOHN E. TASHJEAN

SEE ALSO: Frederick the Great; Napoleon I; Principles of War; Prussia and Germany, Rise of; Scharnhorst, Gerhard Johann David von; Seven Years' War; War.

Bibliography

Aron, R. 1976. *Penser la guerre, Clausewitz*. 2 vols. Paris: Gallimard.

Clausewitz, C. von. 1977. *The campaign of 1812 in Russia*. Westport, Conn.: Greenwood Press.

———. 1937. *Strategie aus dem Jahr 1804*. Hamburg: Hanseatische Verlagsanstalt.

———. 1984. *On War*. Ed. and trans. M. Howard and P. Paret. Princeton, N.J.: Princeton Univ. Press.

Dill, G., ed. 1980. *Clausewitz in Perspektive*. Frankfurt a.M.: Ullstein.

Doepner, F. 1987. Die Familie des Kriegsphilosophen Carl von Clausewitz. In *Der Herold*, vol. 12, pp. 53–68.

Niemeyer, J. 1987. Einleitung. In *Scharnhorst-Briefe an Friedrich von der Decken 1803–1813*, pp. 7–39. Bonn: Duemmler.

Paret, P. 1976. *Clausewitz and the state*. Oxford: Clarendon Press.

Rehm, W. 1980. Clausewitz in der DDR. In *Freiheit ohne Krieg?* E. Wagemann and J. Niemeyer, eds., pp. 363–77. Bonn: Duemmler.

Rothfels, H. 1980. *Clausewitz, Politik und Krieg*. Bonn: Duemmler.

Tashjean, J. 1988. Zum Kulminationsbegriff bei und nach Clausewitz. In *Clausewitz, Jomini, Erzherzog Carl*, ed. M. Rauchensteiner. Vienna: Oesterreichischer Bundesverlag.

Wehler, H. U. 1987. *Deutsche Gesellschaftsgeschichte*. 2 vols. Munich: Beck.

COLD WAR

The term *cold war* was first used in its present context by American political commentator Walter Lippman in 1948 to describe the political rivalry that developed between the United States and the Soviet Union after World War II. Although the antagonists were not formally at war with one another and had not engaged in armed combat, the rivalry was marked by a hostility characteristic of enemies waging total war. The intensity of the conflict derived from two diametrically opposed conceptions of international order and the shared perception of the rival as the chief obstacle to the attainment of a just world order.

The rivalry endured for the better part of four decades, became global in scope, and was punctuated by shooting wars between proxy states of each and between proxy states and one of the superpowers.

Origin and Development

The meeting of victorious Soviet and American troops at the River Elbe in Germany (25 April 1945) symbolized the beginning of a new era in world politics. The exhaustion of the United Kingdom and France coupled with the defeat of the Axis powers created a power vacuum in central Europe and east Asia. The United States, a maritime power, had assumed the leadership of the Western democracies, waging global war while providing its allies with materiel for their own war efforts. The Soviet Union, a Eurasian power, had survived twenty million war deaths to overwhelm the German army from the East. The Soviet Union thus emerged from World War II as the other dominant world power.

Realist theorists who emphasize the historic and geographic dimension of power rivalries see the conflict as an inevitable power struggle between a continental land power trying to extend its dominions and an insular maritime power trying to prevent the dominant continental power from gaining hegemony over the Eurasian continental land mass. To explain the inevitability of the cold war rivalry, these theorists point to historic analogs such as the clash between Napoleonic France and Great Britain and between Imperial Germany and Great Britain.

This analysis is necessary in understanding the origins of the cold war, but it alone does not suffice as an explanation for the beginnings of the postwar competition between the United States and the Soviet Union. One must also examine the nature of the rival regimes and the motivations and objectives of the major statesmen. Leaders of the Soviet Union had traditionally proclaimed that there could be no lasting peace between socialist states and capitalist imperialism. Woodrow Wilson, U.S. president from 1913 to 1921, abhorred V. I. Lenin's Soviet regime; the half-hearted Allied interventions in the Russian Civil War only served to reinforce the fundamental antipathy between the Soviets and the West. From a Marxist-Leninist perspective, diplomatic recognition and trade agreements with the West were manifestations of inherent capitalist weakness and a favorable shift in the correlation of forces. Failure of the Western democracies to respond to Stalin's diplomatic overtures to form an anti-Nazi alliance in the 1930s only reinforced Soviet hostility.

Based on a draft by British prime minister Winston S. Churchill, the U.S. war aims for World War II as presented in the Atlantic Charter (14 August 1941) were strikingly similar to Wilson's Fourteen Points (January 1918). The Wilsonian principle of self-determination of nations is the seminal theme of the Atlantic Charter. The Molotov–von Ribbentrop Pact (Non-Aggression Pact between the Soviet Union and Nazi Germany, 23 August 1939) was diametrically opposed to the principles embodied in the Atlantic Charter. Whether described as a correct estimate of the correlation of forces or successful attainment of Russian irredentist claims, the Non-Aggression Pact helped initiate hostilities by an act of armed aggression against Poland. Following the German invasion of the Soviet Union, Stalin was chiefly concerned with only one clause of the Atlantic Charter, "the final destruction of the Nazi tyranny." This common bond between the Soviet Union and the Western Allies masked profound differences regarding the nature of just government and the framework of the postwar international order.

The fate of Poland was the emblematic expression of these differences. The Soviet betrayal of the Polish underground resistance forces in Warsaw (29 July–2 October 1944) signaled that Stalin's intentions regarding the governance of Poland were decidedly different from those of the Western leaders. Churchill unsuccessfully attempted to get Stalin to aid the Warsaw uprising with weapons and supplies, or to permit U.S. and British aircraft landing privileges at Soviet airfields in order to supply the Poles. At the Teheran Conference (November 1943) Churchill had suggested the Curzon Line as the postwar Soviet-Polish border, with Poland receiving territorial compensation from Germany. At the Moscow Conference (9–17 October 1944) Churchill attempted to negotiate Polish acceptance of the Teheran proposal in exchange for Stalin's acceptance of the Polish Government in Exile's inclusion in the Polish provisional government. He failed, as the exiled Poles in London refused to accept the Curzon Line.

At Moscow, Churchill also fashioned an ad hoc sphere-of-influence proposal, conceding Soviet dominance in Bulgaria, Romania, and Hungary in exchange for Anglo-American dominance in Greece and an equal share in Yugoslavia. In December 1944 British troops forcibly suppressed an indigenous communist uprising in Greece, while Stalin stood by without offering any assistance to the Greek communists. Churchill was favorably impressed by Stalin's inaction in Greece; both he and American president Franklin D. Roosevelt approached the Yalta Conference (4–12 February 1945) trusting that they, with Stalin, could forge a new international order predicated upon the principles of the Atlantic Charter and strengthened by the newly formed United Nations Organization.

At Yalta the Big Three (Churchill, Roosevelt, and Stalin) reached accords calling for democratically elected governments in Eastern Europe. However, the stipulation calling for election supervision by international observers was conspicuously absent from the final protocol. Failure to include this requirement for elections in Soviet zones of occupation in Europe was the most glaring omission in the Yalta accords.

The Western Allies lost other opportunities to revise the postwar settlement on terms more favorable to the West. Following the Soviet failure to reconstitute the Polish government on a more democratic basis and the establishment of communist regimes in areas under Soviet control, Churchill urged strong diplomatic censure. U.S. State Department officials, speaking for a gravely ill Roosevelt, thought it better to cooperate with the Soviets. U.S. officials were concerned that noncommunist elements would jeopardize land reform programs and would be branded as fascist by the Soviets. Churchill had also argued unsuccessfully for U.S. and British forces to advance beyond previously agreed-upon occupation zones in the final stages of the war in Europe, to pressure the Soviets to adhere to the political provisions of the Yalta accords. The European conflict ended with the forces of the Western Allies further east than antici-pated, but two months after the armistice U.S. and British forces withdrew 240 kilometers (150 mi.) to the west.

Imbued with an abiding faith in rule of law and the legal nature of diplomatic agreements, U.S. policymakers were slow to take the measure of the differ-ences between their perception of the political good and Stalin's. They sin-cerely hoped that, through Western-Soviet cooperation, Stalin would share in the effort to transform world politics through an international organization predicated upon rule of law and self-determination of nations. Moreover, U.S. policymakers were only too aware that the American people wanted to con-clude the war against Japan and that Soviet military assistance would facilitate attainment of this objective.

Roosevelt's successor, Harry S Truman, was intent on carrying out his pre-decessor's foreign policy, but at the same time was determined not to be bullied by the Soviets. At the Potsdam Conference (15 July–1 August 1945) the West-ern Allies clashed with the Soviet Union over adherence to the Yalta agreement on democratic elections in Eastern Europe; they failed to arrive at a final agreement regarding the political future of the divided continent.

The Soviets and Americans again clashed in 1946, this time over the re-moval of Soviet troops from Iran and stoppage of food supplies from Soviet-occupied Germany to the western occupation zones. Both actions violated previous agreements. Under diplomatic pressure from the United States, Sta-lin removed Soviet troops from Iran. In retaliation for Soviet cessation of food supplies for the western occupation zones in Germany, western-zone repa-ration payments to the Soviet Union were suspended and preparations were begun to merge the western zones into a single entity (July 1946). Thus, although the Warsaw Uprising may be considered the opening of hostilities over the constitution of the postwar European order, it was not until 1946 that U.S. policymakers began to fully understand that the armed struggle against the Axis had been supplanted by a new and different type of power struggle.

Policy of Containment

To counter the threat of Soviet expansion the Truman administration adopted a broad policy approach known as containment. Career diplomat George F. Kennan defined containment in an article titled "Sources of Soviet Conduct." Using the byline "X," Kennan explained that, although Soviet leaders were resolute in purpose, Marxist-Leninist ideology afforded strategic and tactical flexibility. He argued that communist ideology fit Russian national character, which was formed by centuries of struggle in which patience, flexibility, and deception had enabled the Russians to survive. Kennan averred, "The main element of any United States policy toward the Soviet Union must be that of a long-term, patient but firm and vigilant containment of Russian expansive tendencies" (Kennan 1984, p. 119). Kennan had been the catalyst in America's adoption of containment. While stationed in Moscow as Minister Councilor he responded to a State Department request for his views on Russia with an 8,000-word memorandum, the "Long Telegram" (22 February 1946), which warned that accommodation with the Soviets was doomed to failure.

Two weeks after the Long Telegram, Churchill delivered his famous "Iron Curtain" speech at Fulton, Missouri, calling on the United States to assume a dominant role in checking Soviet expansion. Kennan's warnings, reinforced by Churchill's speech, spurred the United States to action to halt Soviet expansion by aiding friendly powers who requested it. Negotiations with the Soviets hereafter would be conducted without expectation of achieving meaningful agreements.

CONTAINMENT IN ACTION: THE TRUMAN DOCTRINE

An opportunity to aid friendly countries came on 21 February 1947 when the British Foreign Office informed the United States that it could no longer support the efforts of Greece in its civil war against communist insurgents. The British also declared that they were unable to continue to bolster Turkey, which was being pressured by the Soviets. On 12 March 1947 Truman requested US$400 million in economic and military aid for both Greece and Turkey, proclaiming that it was the United States' duty to assist "free peoples" (Halle 1967, p. 121) in their struggle against totalitarianism. The Truman Doctrine, as it came to be called, was tantamount to a policy of containment. Although neither Greece nor Turkey was a constitutional democracy, the U.S. Congress granted Truman's request for financial and military aid. Truman and his advisers knew that communist victories in Greece and Turkey would strengthen the Soviet presence in the Mediterannean and the Middle East. U.S. assistance helped defeat the communist forces in Greece (1949) and stabilized conditions in Turkey.

CONTAINMENT IN ACTION: THE MARSHALL PLAN AND THE BERLIN BLOCKADE

Devastated by war, the economy and morale of Europe were in shambles. Germany, its industrial base destroyed and its territory occupied and divided, faced a population swollen by immigrants from the east. Domestic conditions in Great Britain were poor, and conditions in France were equally disastrous. Hostile to capitalism and enamored with the role of the French Communist party in the anti-Nazi resistance, one-fourth of the French voted Communist in 1946. In Italy, also beset with postwar anomie, the Communists controlled one-third of the electorate.

Faced with the prospect of the imminent economic collapse of Europe and the political instability sure to follow, Truman and his foreign policy advisers moved with dispatch. On 5 June 1947, U.S. Secretary of State George C. Marshall announced the U.S. foreign policy objective to promote European economic recovery with a massive infusion of economic aid to all of Europe.

The Soviets summarily refused aid for themselves and other Eastern European communist regimes, but representatives of sixteen European nations, including Britain and France, formed the Committee of European Economic Cooperation (12–16 June 1947) and subsequently issued a report stating their economic needs for the next four years. The United States responded with the Economic Cooperation Act (3 April 1948), allocating US$5,300 million to Europe's economic recovery.

When it appeared that the democratically elected coalition government of Czechoslovakia might accept Marshall Plan aid, the Soviets engineered a coup d'état and installed a Czech Stalinist regime (25 February 1948). Four months later Stalin directly challenged Truman's resolve in implementing containment. On 22 June 1948, Soviet forces blockaded West Berlin. The United States and Great Britain countered the blockade by airlifting more than two million tons of supplies to Berlin. Faced with Anglo-American air superiority and the indomitable will of the people of Berlin, the Soviets lifted the blockade on 12 May 1949. The end of the Berlin Blockade was a major cold war victory for the West, but Berlin remained a symbol of the division of Europe and a future battleground for other political tests of will.

NATO: CONTAINMENT'S POLITICO-MILITARY ARM

Britain, France, and the Low Countries moved to action by the Soviet-directed coup in Czechoslovakia, signed the Brussels Treaty (17 March 1948) as the first step toward forming a political-military alliance to counter the threat posed by Soviet troops deployed in Europe. The chairman of the U.S. Senate Foreign Relations Committee, Arthur Vandenberg, sponsored a resolution that called for the United States to associate "by constitutional process, with such regional and other collective arrangements as are based on continuous and effective self-help and mutual aid, and as affect its national security" (Dougherty and Pfaltzgraff 1986, p. 72). The Vandenberg Resolution passed with overwhelming bipartisan support, preparing the way for the United States to sign a long-term defense treaty with Western European nations. The North Atlantic Treaty Organization (NATO) was formed on 4 April 1949, and the United States formally entered NATO on 21 July 1949.

NATO member states pledged to strengthen democratic political institutions and to promote economic cooperation. Invoking Article 51 of the UN Charter, the member states also pledged that an attack against one was an attack against all. Following the Soviet detonation of an atomic bomb (23 September 1949) and the North Korean invasion of South Korea (25 June 1950), the NATO allies instituted a formal military command structure with Gen. Dwight D. Eisenhower as NATO's first Supreme Commander (December 1950). NATO's role as the linchpin of containment in Europe was solidified with the deployment of U.S. troops to NATO in 1951.

CONTAINMENT IN ASIA: THE CHINESE CIVIL WAR AND KOREA

The Roosevelt administration had believed that the Chinese Kuomintang Party headed by Chiang Kai-shek would provide effective government for China and serve as the key to maintenance of international order in East Asia. However, Stalin did not wish to see a strong communist or nationalist China develop; he played a double game, signing a treaty of alliance and friendship with the Kuomintang while delaying movement of Kuomintang forces to Manchuria until the arrival of Chinese Communist Party (CCP) forces. CCP propaganda skillfully exploited the weakness of Chiang's regime, its political corruption, and its insensitivity to poverty. Despite massive amounts of U.S. aid, the Kuomintang suffered complete defeat at the hands of CCP leader Mao Tse-tung and his superior guerrilla strategy.

Following Mao's triumph in China, U.S. Secretary of State Dean Acheson defined American defense perimeters in the Pacific (12 January 1950), stating that the United States would not take unilateral action to maintain Korean security. Korea had been partitioned at the end of World War II, with Soviet troops occupying north of the 38th Parallel (17 August 1945) and U.S. forces deploying south of that line. Prior to their official withdrawal (25 December 1948) the Soviets had helped build up North Korea's military; the United States recognized the South Korean regime of Syngman Rhee before withdrawing its troops on 29 June 1949.

In April 1950 a group of State and Defense Department officials headed by Paul Nitze drafted a classified policy statement, National Security Council Paper No. 68 (NSC-68), which stressed the need to defend the entire periphery of what geopolitical analysts called the Eurasian heartland. When North Korea invaded South Korea in June 1950, Acheson viewed armed response to the invasion as consistent with the NSC-68 concept of containment. Accordingly, the United States took advantage of the Soviet boycott of the UN Security Council (initiated in January 1950 over UN failure to recognize Mao's communist regime) to pass a resolution censuring the North Koreans for the invasion. To bolster crumbling South Korean resistance, the United States moved quickly under the aegis of the United Nations to intervene militarily.

The three-year Korean War had unintended consequences for both superpowers. The United States accomplished its goals of preserving South Korea and containing Soviet expansion in the region, and bolstered its credibility with its allies. The UN drive into North Korea, however, led to Chinese entry into the war, which virtually precluded any chance for U.S. rapprochement with Mao. While the conflict redounded to the immediate advantage of the Soviets through heightened U.S.–Sino rivalry, it may also have contributed inadvertently to the Sino-Soviet rift. Mao apparently was angered by the Soviet-supported North Korean invasion, because it forced him to commit troops in Korea at a time when he was consolidating his power base.

The Korean War also had the unintended effect of strengthening the concept of containment advanced by NSC-68. The Soviets apparently had approved the North Korean invasion in part because they had misinterpreted Acheson's public declaration of U.S. Pacific defense perimeters. The invasion of South Korea by a Soviet client state made it possible for the backers of NSC-68 to win congressional approval and popular support for the increased

U.S. defense budget and dominant U.S. presence in NATO put forth by the security council paper.

CONTAINMENT AND THE FOUNDATIONS OF DETERRENCE

In 1946 Bernard Brodie and other prominent defense intellectuals wrote a highly influential book about the nature of atomic weapons and their significance in the practice of warfare (Brodie 1946). The authors of *The Absolute Weapon* argued that atomic weapons would be employed as had other weapons throughout history—that is, against military forces. They also wrote that cities would be the primary targets of atomic attacks. By virtue of the power of atomic weapons, it followed that once the Soviet Union had developed atomic weapons both superpowers would be able to strike each other at will. The writers averred that the powerfully destructive weapons would be used by each superpower to prevent attacks by its rival, thus setting the foundation for the strategy of deterrence through mutual assured destruction (MAD).

The authors of *The Absolute Weapon* advocated international control as a means of maintaining world order with atomic weapons, but plans to do so failed to win approval. The Soviets summarily dismissed the Baruch Plan, which would have placed atomic weapons under UN supervision.

Truman's decision not to use atomic weapons in Korea, despite pleas from UN Forces Commander Gen. Douglas MacArthur, illustrated further the prescience of *The Absolute Weapon* regarding atomic weapons and pointed to their limitations as an instrument of containment. Truman's successor, Dwight D. Eisenhower, through his Secretary of State John Foster Dulles, announced on 12 January 1954 that the United States would use "massive retaliation" to stop communist aggression, in effect a declaratory policy of containment through deterrence. Eisenhower had previously threatened effectively to use the atomic bomb to induce the Chinese to agree to terms for the cessation of hostilities in Korea. In 1955 he used similar tactics to bring an end to the Chinese shelling of two Kuomintang-controlled islands off the coast of the People's Republic of China (PRC).

From Containment to Accommodation

EISENHOWER, DULLES, AND THE POLICY OF ROLLBACK

Dulles professed a new declaration policy of rollback, or liberation, as an alternative to containment. Dulles declared that to win the cold war it would be necessary to "roll back" the Soviets in Eastern and Central Europe. The ideas of New York University philosophy professor James Burnham (1953), as expressed in *Containment or Liberation?*, were the intellectual mainspring of Dulles' declaration policy of rollback.

While employed by the Office of Strategic Services (OSS), Burnham had written an internal memorandum on the nature and stakes of the developing cold war, which may have influenced the drafting of the Truman Doctrine and served as the basis for *Containment or Liberation?* Like Kennan, Burnham understood that the cold war was not just an ideological conflict but a geopolitical power struggle as well. Burnham, however, like Acheson and the authors of NSC-68, favored a perimeter defense, as opposed to the point defense of Kennan's fully expounded doctrine of containment.

Burnham believed that reliance on containment was necessary but not sufficient to win the cold war. He believed that the offensive was an essential element in achieving victory in the struggle with the Soviet Union, whose legitimacy and international appeal were predicated upon an expansionist ethic. Provocative actions challenging Soviet prestige were imperative and could be achieved through the conduct of "all sided political warfare" (Burnham 1953, p. 223), the use of varied political, psychological, military, and economic means to exert pressure on weaknesses within the Soviet empire. Political warfare as advocated by Burnham came directly from Lenin's emendation of military theorist Karl von Clausewitz: peace is the continuation of warfare by other means.

HUNGARY AND SUEZ: THE FAILURE OF ROLLBACK

Following Stalin's death (5 March 1953) Eisenhower moved quickly to launch a diplomatic counteroffensive in response to the post-Stalinist Soviet peace offensive, by calling for the reunification of Germany on the basis of free elections, an Austrian peace treaty, international control of atomic energy, and an end to the Korean War (16 April 1953). Discontent in Eastern Bloc countries followed the implementation of the declaratory policy of liberation and anti-Soviet broadcasts by Radio Free Europe and the Voice of America. Soviet troops forcibly suppressed anticommunist riots in Berlin (16–17 June 1953); the Soviets subsequently eased domestic controls and recognized East German sovereignty. On 14 May 1955 the Warsaw Pact was created to lend legitimacy to Soviet domination of Eastern Europe and in response to NATO's approval of West German rearmament and integration of its forces in NATO.

A Soviet treaty with Austria ended Soviet occupation in that country (15 May 1955) and led to the first Summit Conference at Geneva, Switzerland, in July 1955. The four-power conference was highlighted by superpower engagement in political warfare. Eisenhower proposed an Open Skies policy to prevent surprise attack and to keep the Soviet Union on the diplomatic defensive. General secretary of the Communist Party of the Soviet Union (CPSU) Nikita Khrushchev denounced the Open Skies proposal as an attempt to practice unlimited espionage against the Soviet Union. Soviet premier Nikolai Bulganin's proposal calling for the dissolution of both NATO and the Warsaw Pact and the removal of all non-European troops from Europe was rejected.

Khrushchev's denunciation of Stalin at the 20th Congress of the CPSU exacerbated tensions within the Eastern Bloc, leading to a workers' revolt in Poland and full-scale revolution in Hungary (23 October–4 November 1956). Soviet troops quelled the Polish workers' revolt. When the Hungarians established an anti-Soviet government, the United States failed to extend formal recognition to the Hungarians despite a Soviet pledge to withdraw troops (28 October) and a temporary halt in the fighting. In response to U.S. inaction the Soviets quickly crushed the revolt and reestablished a pro-Soviet regime.

In the Middle East, Great Britain and France cooperated with Israel in an attempt to reverse Egyptian President Gamal Nasser's nationalization of the Suez Canal and prevent Soviet penetration in the Middle East. Israeli military forces launched a surprise attack on Egyptian forces in the Sinai (29 October 1956). Then, under the guise of enforcing a cease-fire, Anglo-French air forces struck Egyptian bases (31 October), and Anglo-French troops subsequently launched an assault on the canal (5 November 1956). Eisenhower angrily condemned these actions. The United States thus found itself in the awkward position of joining the Soviets in protesting aggression by U.S. allies, while at the same time denouncing Soviet aggression in Hungary. U.S. denunciation of its allies did not lessen Nasser's hostility toward the United States; instead he strengthened his ties with the Soviet Union. U.S. condemnation also planted seeds of discord among the NATO allies that redounded to the advantage of the Soviet Union.

In response to the Suez crisis, Eisenhower pledged that the United States would use force to prevent communist regimes from coming to power. With the promulgation of the Eisenhower Doctrine (1 January 1957), the United States extended its policy of containment to the Middle East.

CRISIS IN BERLIN, THE U-2 INCIDENT, AND REVOLUTION IN CUBA

On 27 March 1958, Khrushchev ousted Bulganin and became head of the Soviet Union and the CPSU. On 10 November 1958, he asserted that the Soviet Union would end NATO rights to Berlin; this violated the postwar agreement on the city that, according to Eisenhower, could be changed only by mutual consent of the city's four occupying powers. The U.S. president pledged to use armed convoys to keep open corridors to Berlin. On a visit to the United States in September 1959, Khrushchev formally renounced any deadline on the Western presence in Berlin in exchange for an agreement for a four-power summit conference. The proposed summit never took place, however, as a U.S. U-2 reconnaissance plane was shot down over Soviet territory on 6 May 1960. Khrushchev denounced the United States and demanded an apology. Eisenhower adamantly refused, claiming such flights were necessary to offset the numerous Soviet espionage agents in the United States and to guard against a Soviet surprise attack.

In January 1959 the Soviets had made an unexpected gain in the Western Hemisphere, when the revolutionary Fidel Castro deposed Cuban dictator Batista. Castro subsequently announced that he was a Marxist-Leninist and that he intended to pursue a foreign policy congenial to that of the Soviet Union. The Cuban Revolution and the U-2 incident were the last two major cold war defeats during Eisenhower's presidency, an era that had begun auspiciously with the conclusion of the Korean War and the declaratory policy of rollback.

THE NEW FRONTIER AND BEYOND

In his successful 1960 presidential campaign, John F. Kennedy chided the Eisenhower administration for its inability to depose Castro, and claimed the existence of a "missile gap" that favored the Soviet Union. According to some

Western intelligence analysts, the Soviets had indeed made the decision in 1959 to achieve nuclear superiority over the United States. Kennedy's inaugural address asked for dedication in "a long twilight struggle" against Soviet communism. Kennedy appealed to developing nations to emulate the American experience rather than the Soviet style of anti-imperialist revolution, and urged Americans to steel themselves "to bear the burden of a long twilight struggle . . . against tyranny, poverty, disease, and war itself. . . ." Accordingly, the Kennedy administration adopted the theme of the New Frontier, in which cold war rivalry and the struggle against other ills were coterminous, each a means of winning the other struggle.

Kennedy suffered an early defeat in a cold war battle that cast a shadow over his subsequent dealings with the Soviet Union. On 15–20 April 1961 a U.S.-sponsored invasion of Cuba by Cuban emigres failed at the Bay of Pigs. Kennedy had doubts about the invasion (planning for which had begun during the Eisenhower Administration) but nevertheless approved its go-ahead. His cancellation of U.S. air support for the invasion added to the embarrassment of the defeat. Kennedy accepted full responsibility for the Bay of Pigs, but it was an enormous blow to the international prestige of the United States and his last attempt to implement a policy of liberation.

Other cold war confrontations preceded and endured beyond the Bay of Pigs debacle. In the first year of Kennedy's presidency, communist Pathet Lao forces extended their control over Laos. At a June 1961 superpower summit conference in Vienna, Kennedy and Khrushchev agreed to a peaceful resolution of that struggle, preparing the way for negotiations that led to the neutralization of Laos in June 1962. At Vienna, Khrushchev again raised the issue of the Western presence in Berlin, threatening to deny Western access to the city. Like his predecessors Kennedy pledged to defend Western access. In August 1961 East Germany began construction of the Berlin Wall, cutting off the flow of refugees from the East.

Following the Kennedy administration's endorsement of tacit understanding in Laos, Khrushchev implemented application of the Leninist concept of "wars of national liberation" to Cuba. Under the so-called tacit understanding in Laos, it had been agreed that communists and anticommunists would exercise control of their respective spheres of influence. Khrushchev had interpreted this understanding as U.S. consent to North Vietnamese use of bases in Laos for their war of liberation. Since Cuba had waged a successful war of national liberation, it was fitting for the Soviets to ensure the preservation of the outcome by installing nuclear intermediate-range ballistic missiles (IRBMs) in Cuba. Aware that the "missile gap" had been illusory and that the Soviets had few effective intercontinental ballistic missiles (ICBMs), the Kennedy administration viewed deployment of the missiles as an offensive threat. In the tensest moments of the cold war, Kennedy demanded their removal. Khrushchev assented to the demand. Kennedy was lauded for having averted nuclear war and for achieving a major political victory. Contemporary critics such as former Acheson aide Charles Burton Marshall looked less favorably upon the resolution of the missile crisis. Writing in *The New Republic*, Marshall claimed that Khrushchev had achieved a strategic-political gain by getting Kennedy to pledge that the United States would not attempt to forcibly remove Castro from power. Marshall argued Kennedy's pledge had assured the Soviets a base of operations in the Western Hemisphere, thereby making the Monroe Doctrine obsolete.

Kennedy himself depicted resolution of the missile crisis as a diplomatic stalemate; it nonetheless dramatically changed his thinking on strategic nuclear deterrence. In the wake of the crisis Kennedy changed U.S. nuclear doctrine from a counterforce damage-limiting strategy to a strategy predicated upon MAD. Kennedy and U.S. secretary of defense Robert S. MacNamara had originally favored deploying an antiballistic missile (ABM) system and using civil defense measures; successful ABM tests had already been conducted by the United States in June 1962. MAD remained the dominant strategic posture of the United States into the 1970s. The Soviets continued to augment their offensive strategic nuclear missile forces, building a second, third, and fourth generation of missiles over the next two decades. Doctrinal adjustments to meet the continued buildup of Warsaw Pact conventional forces and the flexible response doctrine added credibility to the United States' NATO theater force deterrent. These changes were intended to assuage the fears of European allies and to serve notice to the Soviets of U.S. resolve in Europe.

In South Vietnam, Kennedy attempted to suppress communist guerrilla warfare through the use of U.S. Army military advisers to aid and instruct anticommunist forces. The United States also slowly increased the size of its forces in Vietnam as North Vietnamese–Viet Cong forces intensified their efforts. In November 1963 Kennedy assented to a coup d'état in Saigon to revitalize the South Vietnamese regime. South Vietnamese president Ngo Dinh Diem was assassinated, but his successors proved equally inefficient and more corrupt.

On 22 November 1963 Kennedy himself was assassinated. His successor, Lyndon B. Johnson, continued to support the South Vietnamese regime. Following the attack on U.S. Navy patrol boats in the Gulf of Tonkin (August 1965) Johnson won congressional approval for increased U.S. military involvement in Vietnam. As Johnson stepped up the U.S. war effort, the new Soviet leadership of Leonid Brezhnev and Alexei Kosygin continued to supply war materiel to the North Vietnamese. The Soviets also sanctioned use of Laos to infiltrate South Vietnam, in violation of the tacit understanding of Laos.

The continued supply of Soviet weapons and technical assistance to Egypt and Syria—in Soviet eyes an effort to uphold the national liberation of these countries—was viewed by U.S. policymakers as destabilizing and a Soviet attempt to maintain a foothold in the region. Israel's pre-emptive strike against the Arab states (1 June 1967) and its subsequent victory in the Six Day War deepened Arab hostility to the United States. This sentiment combined with increased Arab dependence on Soviet aid to keep the Middle East very much a cold war crisis spot.

As a new decade of cold war struggle approached, U.S. counterinsurgency operations and escalation of the conflict netted tactical victories but failed to break the will of the North Vietnamese and Viet Cong. Ironically, the turning point in the war was the Tet Offensive (30 January–29 February 1968), a military defeat for the communist forces. The communist ability to achieve surprise during Tet belied official U.S. statements about winning the war. U.S. news media coverage of the operation had a chilling effect on American citizens with whom involvement in Southeast Asia was becoming increasingly unpopular. Frustrated by growing domestic opposition to the war and the inability to conclude it on favorable terms, Johnson refused to run for re-election and agreed to negotiate with the North Vietnamese (10 May 1968).

Johnson's efforts to improve relations with the Soviet Union did not lessen Soviet intentions to aid communist forces in North Vietnam. Neither did they deter the Soviets from using armed intervention to depose dissident communist leader Alexander Dubcek and prevent Czechoslovakia's defection from the Warsaw Pact in August 1968. The military intervention in Czechoslovakia was a manifestation of the so-called Brezhnev Doctrine, proclaimed in *Pravda* (26 September 1968): Once a country had adopted a Marxist-Leninist form of government, it was the right and duty of the Soviet Union to employ force if necessary to defeat counterrevolutionary forces.

DETENTE, VIETNAM, AND THE AMERICAN REGIME

One year before he was elected president, Richard M. Nixon predicted that the United States was about to conclude an era of confrontation and begin an era of negotiation with the Soviet Union. Nixon and his national security adviser (later secretary of state), Henry A. Kissinger, attempted to negotiate an end to the Vietnam War by getting North Vietnam to agree to withdraw its troops from South Vietnam. This goal was also intended to induce the Soviet Union to end its cold war rivalry with the United States. Nixon and Kissinger established detente with the PRC and the Soviet Union, playing on their mutual hostility and their shared desire for Western markets and technology to hold the balance between the two nations. Nixon and Kissinger also predicated detente with the Soviet Union upon perceived mutual superpower interests such as the environment, exploration of space, continued economic growth, and strategic arms limitations negotiations. Progress on these separate but related issues were linked. The policy of linkage was designed to ensure Soviet cooperation by rewarding good behavior and by giving the Soviet Union a share in building the new international order.

Progress on limiting the deployment of nuclear weapons was viewed as the key to success in other areas. The Strategic Arms Limitations Talks (SALT) Treaty and subsequent agreements were predicated upon the assumption that the Soviet Union shared belief in the MAD doctrine. U.S. belief was clearly evidenced in the 26 May 1972 ABM Treaty in which the United States forfeited its advantage in ABM technology by agreeing to limit deployment of strategic defensive systems.

The Vietnam War was to be the last exercise of containment. On 26 April 1969 Nixon initiated "Vietnamization" of the war. To facilitate South Vietnam's efforts to assume conduct of the war and to facilitate U.S. withdrawal, Nixon resumed bombing of North Vietnam and authorized U.S. ground forces to carry out limited operations in Cambodia to destroy North Vietnamese strongholds. The last U.S. troops were withdrawn from Vietnam on 29 March 1973.

Despite Nixon's policy of Vietnamization, domestic opposition to the Vietnam War had continued during his first term. Antiwar feelings affected Nixon's and Kissinger's perceptions of American attitudes toward defense issues and foreign affairs. An end to the cold war rivalry was seen as vitally important. Nixon's policies were fashioned out of recognition that the United States should seek accommodation with the Soviet Union because the postwar world and American political culture had changed.

America had indeed been demoralized by its Vietnam experience. In the frustration over the U.S. role in Vietnam, the study of revisionist history of the cold war that placed blame on the United States became fashionable. The late 1960s and early 1970s were characterized by campus unrest and civil disobedience. American consensus was further eroded when the Watergate affair forced Nixon to resign from office.

The North Vietnamese conquest of South Vietnam (April–May 1975) did not spell the end of detente. The North Vietnamese attack was not the first major invasion conducted with Soviet weapons and approval during detente. Less than four months after the signing of the Agreement on the Prevention of Nuclear War (21 June 1973), Egyptian troops had used Soviet-built military equipment to launch a massive invasion across the Suez Canal at the start of the 1973 October War. The Soviets had been aware that the invasion was imminent but did not inform the United States, in contravention of the Agreement of the Prevention of Nuclear War. Cold war tension reached a crisis point on 25 October when U.S. forces were placed on alert to avert unilateral Soviet intervention in the Middle East. Meanwhile U.S. Secretary of State Henry Kissinger brought pressure to bear on Israel and Egypt to end the fighting. A UN Security Council sponsored cease-fire went into effect on 27 October 1973, ending the war and the superpower crisis.

The Helsinki Security Conference (30 July–2 August 1975) was a major step in the transformation to a new world order. Statesmen from 35 nations agreed to respect human rights, including free passage of citizens across international borders and the sanctity of international borders. The latter agreement in effect acknowledged the legitimacy of postwar European borders, a political triumph for the Soviet Union. The Helsinki Accords and the arms control agreements signed on 24 November 1975 by Brezhnev and U.S. president Gerald R. Ford made the Soviet Union an equal partner in the new international order. The cold war was indeed winding down, if not finished.

From Accommodation to Confrontation

Amid growing suspicion that the Soviets were attempting to achieve superiority in strategic nuclear weapons, Ford commissioned a group of independent policy analysts and defense scholars to study data used by regular intelligence analysts. Contesting intelligence estimates and analysis, a team led by Harvard's Richard Pipes concluded that the Soviets were attempting to achieve superiority. Doubts about detente were growing in the Ford administration when Ford lost the 1976 presidential election to Jimmy Carter. Carter desired to get beyond the cold war with a foreign policy that emphasized human rights and accommodation with developing nations and the Soviet Union. Carter's first major foreign policy address (22 May 1977) proclaimed, "We are now free of that inordinate fear of communism which once led us to embrace any dictator who joined us in that fear." He decried America's efforts in Vietnam to contain communism. He further castigated both the United States and the Soviet Union for participating in what he termed "a morally deplorable" arms race.

The Soviets summarily dismissed Carter's initial arms control proposals, which called for deep cuts in strategic arsenals. Under Brezhnev's leadership, the Soviets continued to pursue an activist foreign policy and to modernize their armed forces at all levels, developing a blue-water navy, vastly improved strategic nuclear forces, and enhanced ground-force capabilities. Expansionist Soviet foreign policy of the 1970s, conducted while pursuing arms control negotiations, was the result of Soviet interpretation of U.S. foreign policy changes as a decisive shift in the correlation of forces.

Carter's diplomatic triumph at Camp David (which led to a treaty between Israel and Egypt in 1979) did not mute growing criticism of his foreign policy by policy analysts who were alarmed by the apparent Soviet effort to achieve a nuclear first-strike capability and Soviet adventurism in developing nations in Africa and elsewhere. Carter was also criticized for his decisions not to deploy enhanced radiation warhead (ERW) neutron bombs in Europe and not to modernize aging U.S. strategic bomber fleets by deploying the B-1.

To allay criticism, boost support for SALT II negotiations, and increase the credibility of U.S. strategic forces, Carter adopted a new strategic nuclear force doctrine. Presidential Directive 59 (PD-59) called for increased counterforce targeting without abandoning countervalue options. The new countervailing strategy sought to satisfy advocates of the MAD posture while quieting critics who challenged the credibility of a countercity strategy.

The SALT II Treaty signed by Carter and Brezhnev in Vienna on 18 June 1979 was faulted for its lack of adequate verification provisions and its failure to substantially limit deployment of fourth-generation Soviet counterforce missiles. The SALT II Treaty was not ratified by the U.S. Senate, but Carter said he would abide by the terms of the treaty even without its ratification.

Carter's prestige was severely tarnished by the takeover of the U.S. Embassy in Iran in 1979. The Soviets, seeing the failure of their client Afghan regime and sensing ineffectiveness in U.S. power projection, intervened militarily in Afghanistan in December 1979. In reaction to the Soviet invasion, Carter declared that the United States would use force if necessary to prevent the Soviet Union from becoming the dominant power in the Persian Gulf. The Carter Doctrine, a reassertion of containment, effectively put an end to nearly a decade of accommodation with the Soviet Union. Carter also announced a boycott of the 1980 Moscow Olympics and invoked a grain embargo against the Soviet Union. These actions, and Carter's approved request to Congress for aid to Afghan resistance forces, moved the United States toward the policy of liberation advocated by James Burnham almost 30 years earlier. Unable to solve the Iranian hostage crisis, however, Carter was defeated for re-election in 1980 by Ronald Reagan, who pledged to rebuild U.S. defenses and the U.S. image in world politics.

The Reagan Doctrine and Liberation

During Reagan's presidency NATO forces began deploying high-technology improved conventional weapon systems to increase the credibility of flexible response deterrence. The U.S. Navy began building up to a 600-ship goal. Reagan continued to pursue the two-track policy begun under the Carter administration, adopting the "zero-zero" option to eliminate all medium-range nuclear missiles in Europe while simultaneously testing the Soviet Union's desire for arms control treaties. Reagan promised to abide by the unratified SALT II Treaty but began negotiating a new treaty. The acronym START (Strategic Arms Reduction Talks) signified that his goal was a genuine reduction in strategic arms. At the same time the United States qualitatively improved all three legs of its strategic triad.

Speaking before a joint session of Parliament (8 June 1982), Reagan challenged the Soviets to engage in ideological warfare with the United States, asserting that Western constitutional democracy was a superior, moral form of government that would triumph in the struggle with Marxist-Leninism. The speech attacked totalitarian regimes and advocated the adoption of constitutional democracy on a global scale. This speech and Reagan's denunciation of the Soviet Union as an "evil empire" (8 March 1983) were manifestly in the mold of Burnham's policy of liberation.

Reagan employed other tactics that fit the strategy of liberation. He continued aid to Afghan resistance fighters and provided military and economic aid for El Salvador in its struggle against Marxist-Leninist insurgents. Continued violation of human rights by the El Salvadoran military made it difficult to overcome political opposition to aid for the Contras, anti-Sandinista insurgents operating against Nicaragua from neighboring Honduras.

In Central Europe, Reagan extended his political warfare operations to the heart of the Soviet empire. In July 1980, Polish labor leader Lech Walesa founded the independent trade union, Solidarity, in response to profound economic failure in Poland. With 10 million members Solidarity posed a major threat to the Soviets. On 13 December 1981 Polish Communist leader Wojciech Jaruzelski declared martial law and arrested the Solidarity leadership. Reagan responded by imposing economic sanctions upon Poland. Although U.S. and Western European leaders differed over aspects of the sanctions, the Jaruzelski regime eased and eventually lifted martial law.

In Western Europe the Soviets also actively engaged in political warfare to penetrate European peace movements and galvanize opinion against deployment of U.S. Pershing II and ground-launched cruise missiles (GLCMs). On 21 December 1982 Brezhnev's successor, Yuri Andropov, proposed to reduce the Soviet SS-20 IRBM force from 280 to 162 missiles, at parity with the British and

French missile forces, in exchange for a U.S. promise not to deploy Pershing IIs or GLCMs. The United States, Britain, and France refused to consider the British and French forces in negotiations. When U.S. intermediate nuclear force (INF) missiles were deployed on 23 November 1983, the Soviets withdrew from the INF, START, and Mutual Balanced Force Reductions (MBFR) negotiations.

Postdetente cold war rivalry was not limited to nonviolent acts of political warfare and military aid to U.S. and Soviet surrogates. The Soviet Union continued its armed conflict with the Afghan resistance, and the United States invaded the Caribbean island of Grenada to topple its Marxist-Leninist regime (25–30 October 1983). Reagan considered the successful invasion of Grenada an important cold war victory because—contrary to Marxist-Leninist propaganda—it demonstrated that nations under communist rule could be liberated.

As the Soviets had used their improved ICBM force and blue-water navy to project global power in the 1970s, so the Reagan administration used America's renewed political volition, military buildup, and technological expertise to regain the initiative in the 1980s. Reagan challenged the doctrine of MAD by proclaiming that the United States would conduct research and development of a spacebased ABM defensive system. Dubbed "Star Wars," the Strategic Defense Initiative (SDI) caused a heated debate in the U.S. national security community and exacerbated relations between the superpowers. The Soviets denounced SDI as a violation of the ABM Treaty, while simultaneously conducting their own research and development on the military use of space and building a giant phased-array radar, the latter a violation of the ABM Treaty.

In March 1985, Mikhail Gorbachev came to power in the Soviet Union, intent on revitalization of the Soviet economy and restoration of a sense of civic pride in the Marxist-Leninist regime. At a summit meeting in Iceland (October 1986) the Soviet leader attempted to get Reagan to abandon SDI in exchange for a comprehensive strategic arms control agreement. Reagan refused the offer and continued prosecution of the Reagan Doctrine, which promised U.S. aid to developing countries seeking to overthrow Marxist-Leninist regimes. U.S.–supplied Stinger surface-to-air missiles greatly helped the Afghan resistance in its war against Soviet troops and Soviet-backed government forces. The United States also provided aid to UNITA, the Angolan anticommunist resistance movement that had some success in battling Soviet-advised and Cuban-assisted forces.

In the late 1980s, a remarkable chain of events throughout Eastern Europe and the Warsaw Pact marked the beginning of the end of the cold war. Gorbachev agreed to accept Reagan's zero-zero option; Reagan and Gorbachev agreed to eliminate their INF forces in Europe (8 December 1987). The INF Treaty was ratified by the U.S. Senate on 27 May 1988. Confronting intractable economic problems at home Gorbachev announced unilateral troop withdrawals from Eastern Europe (7 December 1988) and initiated sweeping domestic political changes intended to revitalize the faltering Soviet economy and restore faith in the Soviet political system. *Perestroika* (restructuring) and *glasnost* (opening) were designed to enable Gorbachev to eliminate his domestic political rivals and centralize power under his authority. Reforms in the USSR increased domestic unrest and led to demands for reforms within the Soviet Bloc. Solidarity led the way in Poland, forcing the communist leadership to hold parliamentary elections (4 and 18 June 1989). On 24 August 1989 the Polish parliament selected a member of Solidarity, Tadeusz Mazowiecki, as prime minister. Without Soviet support, local communist leaders were easily ousted throughout Eastern Europe by the end of 1989. Most impressive was the destruction (10 November 1989) of the Berlin Wall, emblematic of the cold war division of Germany and Europe and the site of Reagan's bold challenge to Gorbachev to "tear down this wall" to demonstrate Soviet sincerity about freedom. After free elections in East Germany and agreement to reunite Germany, Gorbachev dropped his objections to East German membership in NATO and agreed to withdraw Soviet troops from East Germany by 1994. Outside of Europe, the Soviets suffered a setback when the Soviet army withdrew from Afghanistan after nearly 10 years of inconclusive warfare (15 February 1989).

Destruction of the Berlin Wall may be seen as the symbolic end of the cold war. The end of nearly 45 years of superpower rivalry was replete with irony, as the Nobel Peace Prize was awarded to Mikhail Gorbachev, while Polish citizens in Gdansk awarded former U.S. President Ronald Reagan a sword for helping them defeat communism and honored him with *stolat*, a praise sung only for heroes.

While the tumultuous events of 1989–90 brought an end to the intense rivalry of the cold war, some observers had lingering doubts as to whether these events signaled not an end to hostilities, but a *bellus interruptus*. They pointed to Soviet repression in Lithuania and Gorbachev's appointment of hardline communists to the Soviet government as evidence that, despite defeat in the cold war, confrontational politics between the United States and the USSR could resume if these communists increased their power. Skeptics also decried Gorbachev's attempt to negotiate an end to the Gulf War on the eve of the U.S.–led coalition's offensive to liberate Kuwait (23 January 1992). These critics called for the Bush administration to end its strong support of Gorbachev's policies and lend greater support to anticommunist reformers within the Soviet Union. They charged that Gorbachev's reluctance to drop communism was a barrier to further reform and would only lead to triumph of the unreconstructed communists. Their fears seemed justified when communist hardliners in Gorbachev's government attempted a coup d'état in August 1991. The coup failed, as Russian Republic President Boris Yeltsin led a popular uprising in defiance of communism, preparing the way for the dissolution of the Soviet Union four months later (25 December 1991), and removing any doubt as to the final demise of the cold war.

CHARLES R. SMITH

SEE ALSO: Cuban Missile Crisis; Korean War; Vietnam and Indochina Wars; War.

Bibliography

Acheson, D. 1969. *Present at the creation: My years in the State Department.* New York: Norton.

Brodie, B., ed. 1946. *The absolute weapon: Atomic power and world order.* New York: Harcourt, Brace.

Brzezinski, Z. 1989. *The grand failure: The birth and death of communism in the twentieth century.* New York: Collier.

Burnham, J. 1947. *The struggle for the world.* New York: John Day.

————. 1949. *The coming defeat of communism.* New York: John Day.

————. 1953. *Containment or liberation? An inquiry into the aims of United States foreign policy.* New York: John Day.

————. 1975. *Suicide of the West: An essay on the meaning and destiny of liberalism.* New Rochelle, N.Y.: Arlington House.

Dougherty, J. E., and R. L. Pfaltzgraff, Jr. 1986. *American foreign policy: FDR to Reagan.* New York: Harper and Row.

Dupuy, R. E., and T. N. Dupuy. 1986. *The encyclopedia of military history from 3500 B.C. to the present.* New York: Harper and Row.

Francis, S. 1984. *Power and history: The political thought of James Burnham.* Lanham, Md.: University Press of America.

Gaddis, J. L. 1982. *Strategies of containment: A critical appraisal of postwar American national security policy.* Oxford: Oxford Univ. Press.

————. 1987. *The long peace: Inquiries into the history of the cold war.* New York: Oxford Univ. Press.

Gilbert, M. 1986. *Winston S. Churchill.* Vol. 7, *Road to victory, 1941–1945.* Boston: Houghton Mifflin.

————. 1988. *Winston Churchill.* Vol. 8, *Never despair, 1945–1965.* Boston: Houghton Mifflin.

Halle, L. J. 1967. *The cold war as history.* New York: Harper and Row.

Hannah, N. B. 1987. *The key to failure: Laos and the Vietnam War.* Lanham, Md.: Madison Books.

Hoffman, S. 1987. *Janus and Minerva: Essays in the theory and practice of international politics.* Boulder, Colo.: Westview Press.

International Institute for Strategic Studies. 1990. *Strategic survey, 1989–1990.* London: Brassey's.

Johnson, P. 1983. *Modern times: The world from the twenties to the eighties.* New York: Harper and Row.

Kennan, G. F. 1984. *American diplomacy.* Chicago: Univ. of Chicago Press.

Kissinger, H. A. 1982. *Years of upheaval.* Boston: Little, Brown.

Lenin, V. I. 1940. *Left-wing communism, an infantile disorder: A popular essay in Marxist strategy and tactics.* New York: International.

Lukacs, J. 1966. *A new history of the cold war.* Garden City, N.Y.: Anchor Books.

Rood, H. W. 1980. *Kingdoms of the blind: How the great democracies have resumed the follies that so nearly cost them their life.* Durham, N.C.: Carolina Academic Press.

Rubinstein, A.Z. 1989. *Soviet foreign policy since World War II: Imperial and global.* Glenview, Ill.: Scott, Foresman.

Sarkesian, S. C., and R. A. Vitas. 1988. *U.S. national security policy and strategy: Documents and policy proposals.* New York: Greenwood Press.

Seabury, P., and A. Codevilla. 1989. *War: Ends and means.* New York: Basic Books.

Soviet military power, 1990. 1990. Washington, D.C.: Government Printing Office.

Spanier, J. 1988. *American foreign policy since World War II.* Washington, D.C.: Congressional Quarterly.

COLONIAL EMPIRES, EUROPEAN

The impulse toward colonial expansion was always present in European civilization. Early expansion during the sixteenth, seventeenth, and eighteenth centuries arose concurrently with the discovery of the Americas and the commercial revolution. England, France, Holland, Portugal, and Spain founded empires in the New World in an early wave of imperialism that relegated the colonies to a subservience to the mother country that reflected the mercantile theories of the age.

Imperial enthusiasm waned with the collapse of the early British, French, and Spanish colonial empires between 1763 and 1820. The years 1815 to 1870 were dominated by imperial apathy as the European world struggled between the forces of reactionism and liberalism.

The decades after 1870 witnessed a revival of overseas expansion that is called the "new imperialism." Under the pretext of Europeanizing "backward" regions as part of the "white man's burden," the imperialist nations competed in a scramble for rich and strategic territories in the Middle East, Africa, Asia, and the Pacific Basin. The industrialization of Europe compelled the nations to seek new markets, more food for the growing populations, new sources of raw materials, new regions for capital investment, and strategic supply bases and coaling stations for commercial and naval vessels.

British Expansion

The British Empire in 1870 included the Dominion of Canada, Australia, New Zealand, and India. Lesser colonies of the empire included crown colonies and protectorates such as Gibraltar and Malta in the Mediterranean; Aden, Ceylon, Lower Burma, and Hong Kong in Asia; British Honduras, the British West Indies, British Guiana, Bermuda, and the Falkland Islands in the Western Hemisphere; and Gambia, Sierra Leone, Cape Colony, and Natal in Africa.

AFRICA

Britain politically entered Egypt by acquiring a considerable share of the Suez Canal in 1875 and increased its military control by suppressing the Ahmed Arabi revolt in 1882. The defeat of fanatic Muslim warriors at the Battle of Omdurman (1898) brought the Upper Nile (Sudan) under British control. The Fashoda crisis in 1898 resulted in an agreement with France that created the Anglo-Egyptian Sudan.

Early explorers in East Africa—Richard Burton, David Livingston, and John Speke—led to an interest and eventual protectorates in Kenya, Somaliland, Uganda, and Zanzibar. In West Africa, Britain took control of Nigeria and Sierra Leone and annexed the Gold Coast region after winning the Third Ashanti War (1893–94).

After wresting South Africa from the Dutch in 1814, the discovery of gold and diamonds ultimately led to the Anglo-Boer War (1899–1902) and British annexation of the Orange Free State, Transvaal, and Natal. The earlier imperialistic endeavor of Cecil Rhodes had led to British control of Bechuanaland, Nyasaland, and Rhodesia. Zululand had been annexed at the end of the Zulu War in 1879.

ASIA AND THE PACIFIC

The British continued to consolidate and expand the Indian Empire in Asia. They occupied the Indus Valley, Baluchistan, and Afghanistan to forestall Russian advances toward the Indian Ocean. Britain established influence over Tibet in 1904 and joined Russia in partitioning Persia in 1907.

In 1886, Britain deposed the Burmese ruler and completed the conquest of Burma. Earlier, Britain had opened China to British commerce by winning the Opium War (1840–42) and the Second Chinese War (1856–60). Then, during the so-called new age of imperialism, it took control of the Straits Settlement, Hong Kong, Singapore, Sarawak, British New Guinea, and the Malay States.

In the Pacific, Britain continued to support the growth of the various Australian colonies in the nineteenth century and in 1900 implemented the Australian Commonwealth Act. New Zealand, which began as a joint stock company in 1838, was annexed in 1840 as a crown colony. The British won the Maori Wars (1860–72) and New Zealand became a dominion in 1907. Smaller Pacific possessions annexed or claimed by Britain included Pitcairn Island, Fiji, the British Solomon Islands, Gilbert and Ellis islands, the Southern Solomons, and (jointly with France) the New Hebrides Islands.

French Expansion

The French Empire had been seriously reduced during the wars of the eighteenth and early nineteenth centuries. In 1870, France held Algeria, Senegal, and portions of the Ivory Coast in Africa; Cochin China and Indian territory in the Bay of Bengal in Asia; and a few small Caribbean possessions.

During the decades after 1870, France added Tunis, French West Africa, Morocco, French Guinea, Tunisia, Dahomey, the French Congo, French Somaliland, and Madagascar in Africa; Indochina and Siam in Asia; and (jointly with Britain) the New Hebrides Islands, New Caledonia, the Loyalty Islands, and the Marquesas in the Pacific Basin.

The acquisition of these possessions involved aggressive conflicts by the French trading companies in Africa and Asia, an armed expedition into Cochin China, and a clever policy of war and diplomacy in Indochina.

German Expansion

Germany, distracted by its own dissension and unification efforts, had no interest or role in overseas exploration and colonization before 1870. But rapid expansion of German industrialization and the growth of commercial interests led to aggressive imperialistic activity.

In 1884, Germany declared a protectorate over Southwest Africa, Togoland,

and the coast of the Gulf of Guinea (Cameroons). German East Africa (Tanganyika) was added as a protectorate in 1885.

The murder of two missionaries in China in 1897 resulted in German intervention and the conquest of Kiaochow. In Pacific Oceania, Germany took a portion of New Guinea and the Bismarck Archipelago, the Marshall Islands, the Mariana Islands, part of the Samoan Islands, Palau, the Caroline Islands, and smaller island groups in the Pacific for bases and coaling stations for the German navy.

Italian Expansion

Italy completed its unification in 1870 and embarked on an imperialistic policy despite political and economic pressures at home. The Italians, settling for the barren leftovers in Africa, took the Somali coast on the Horn of Africa in 1885. In 1912, Italy seized Tripoli and Cyrenaica (Libya) from the declining Ottoman Empire as a result of the Tripolitan War. Italy suffered several embarrassing imperial adventures. France faced Italy down over Tunisia in 1896 and the Italians were humiliated when they were defeated by poorly armed Ethiopian soldiers during the Ethiopian War (1895–96).

Expansion by Other European Nations

Prior to the outbreak of World War I, several other European states were trying to maintain declining empires or were endeavoring to build small ones. Spain was the master of the colonies of Río de Oro, Adrar, and portions of the Moroccan and Guinean coasts of Africa, but lost the Philippine Islands, Puerto Rico, Guam, the Spanish West Indies, and Cuba during the Spanish-American War in 1898.

By 1914, the Dutch controlled the islands of Sumatra, Bali, Java, Celebes Island, and portions of New Guinea and Borneo, but this was also an effort to maintain the remnants of an empire established before 1870.

In 1878, King Leopold II of Belgium established an international company to develop the Congo River basin. Leopold was very unscrupulous and the Bantu natives were mistreated and massacred. In 1908, the Congo Free State became the Belgian Congo.

Portugal had a sizable empire in 1870 that consisted of the Cape Verde Islands, Portuguese Guinea, St. Thomas Island, and Príncipe Island in Africa; Macao in China; Portuguese India; and the island of Timor in the Malay Archipelago. After 1870, Portugal enlarged its holdings with the addition of protectorates over Mozambique and Angola in Africa.

Russian imperialism was almost totally concentrated on the Asian mainland. Blocked in Afghanistan and Persia, Russia expanded to the Pacific Ocean until Japan defeated it in 1905 in a war over Manchuria. Russia was also active during the brief period of the European economic division of China around 1900.

The Versailles Treaty and the European Colonies

The Versailles Treaty, which ended World War I, was the last great change in the empires established by the various European states. Germany was forced to forfeit her overseas possessions: Tanganyika was given to Great Britain; Togoland and the Cameroons were divided between Britain and France; and Southwest Africa was placed under the Union of South Africa. In the Pacific, the Marshall Islands, Mariana Islands, and Caroline Islands were given to Japan; Samoa was handed over to New Zealand; and Northeast New Guinea went to Australia. These mandates were to be held in trusteeship under the League of Nations.

The Versailles Treaty and the Treaty of Sèvres (1920) completed the breakup of the Ottoman Empire. France received Syria as a mandate; Britain acquired Palestine and Mesopotamia as mandates; and the Turkish island possessions were divided between Greece and Italy.

Decline of the European Empires

Nationalism, which had originally stimulated the European expansion known as the new imperialism, began to develop among the various peoples of the great European empires. The twentieth century was witness to the breakup of these empires by various means. Spain's empire was virtually destroyed by the Spanish-American War while Germany's empire was divided among the winners at Versailles in 1919. After World War II, France reluctantly freed its colonies after the embarrassments of Indochina, Algeria, and Morocco. Great Britain provided a better example as an imperial power by the creation of the British Commonwealth, which permitted the independence of most of its colonies by peaceful means. Like the other imperial powers, however, Britain also faced violent colonial clashes over independence in colonies like India, Palestine, and Egypt. The two world wars, the rise of economic powers like the United States and Japan, and the ideological struggles of the twentieth century added to the problems of maintaining empires. The colonial liberation movements helped to spawn the new Third World idea, which has led during the second half of the twentieth century to clashes between the economically developed West and its disadvantaged former colonies.

PHILLIP E. KOERPER

SEE ALSO: Latin American Wars of Independence; Ottoman Empire; Seapower, British; Vietnam and Indochina Wars; World War I.

Bibliography

Hollis, C. 1941. *Italy in Africa.* London: Hamilton.
Knaplund, P. 1970. *The British empire 1815–1939.* New York: Fertig.
Langer, W. L. 1965. *The diplomacy of imperialism, 1890–1902.* New York: Knopf.
Pratt, J. T. 1947. *The expansion of Europe into the Far East.* London: Sylvan.
Prosser, G., and W. R. Lewis. 1967. *Britain and Germany in Africa.* New Haven, Conn.: Yale Univ. Press.
———. 1971. *France and Britain in Africa.* New Haven, Conn.: Yale Univ. Press.

Roberts, S. H. 1963. *History of French colonial policy*. Hamden, Conn.: Archon.

Smith, W. D. 1978. *The German colonial empire*. Chapel Hill, N.C.: Univ. of North Carolina.

Sumner, B. H. 1968. *Tsardom and imperialism in the Far East and Middle East, 1880–1914*. Hamden, Conn.: Shoe String.

Thornton, A. P. 1968. *Theories of imperialism*. London: Dobson.

Winks, R. W. 1969. *The age of imperialism*. Englewood Cliffs, N.J.: Prentice-Hall.

Winslow, E. M. 1948. *The pattern of imperialism*. New York: Columbia Univ.

Wright, H. M. 1961. *The new imperialism: Analysis of late nineteenth century expansion*. Boston: Heath.

CONDÉ, LOUIS II DE BOURBON, PRINCE DE [1621–86]

Louis II de Bourbon, Prince of Condé (Fig. 1), was one of the foremost French military commanders of the seventeenth century, worthy of rank with his great comrade-in-arms (and sometimes adversary) Turenne, and most certainly superior, in martial talent, to his formidable protégé, the Marshal-Duke of Luxembourg.

Youth and Early Career

Condé, who was known as Duke of Enghien until his father's death, was born in Paris on 8 September 1621, the son of Henry II de Bourbon, Prince of Condé, and his wife, Charlotte Marguerite de Montmorency. Since his father was a

Figure 1. Eighteenth-century bust of Louis II of Bourbon.
(SOURCE: U.S. Library of Congress)

cousin of King Henry IV (reigned 1589–1610), Enghien was a "prince of the Blood Royal"—and heritor of tremendous wealth and virtually boundless privilege.

Enghien's advantage of birth was compounded by an excellent education and marriage, in 1641, to Claire Clémence de Maillé, niece of Cardinal Richelieu, France's premier. The young duke made his first campaigns in 1640 and 1641, serving at the Siege of Arras (13 June–9 August 1640) and several subsequent sieges. (France was then engaged in the Thirty Years' War on the side of Sweden against Spain, the Empire, and Bavaria.)

Enghien's palpable dislike for his 13-year-old wife and his equally open, politically tactless affection for a group of attractive, influential *belles amies* (as he styled them) earned Richelieu's displeasure. The cardinal's death (6 December 1642) probably prevented a serious political rupture between the two powerful, headstrong men. Richelieu was succeeded as premier by the capable but malleable Jules, Cardinal Mazarin.

Rocroi, Freiburg, and Allerheim

In 1643, at the age of 21, Enghien was given command of the Army of Picardy and charged with the defense of France's northeastern frontier, which was threatened by the veteran Spanish Netherlands army led by Francisco Melo de Braganza. When Melo invaded and invested the frontier town of Rocroi in the Ardennes, Enghien moved to the town's relief. The Battle of Rocroi that followed (19 May 1643) was a remarkable French victory, due almost entirely to Enghien's tactical genius (although he quite properly lavished praise on his lieutenant, Jean de Gassion). The Spanish were practically annihilated, the redoubtable infantry of the *tercios viejos* bravely resisting to the last, and 150 years of Spanish military predominance on European battlefields was ended. In one stroke, France supplanted Spain as Europe's foremost land power. Enghien followed his triumph by taking Thionville and Sierck.

In late spring 1644, Henri de la Tour d'Auvergne, vicomte de Turenne, commander of the French Army of Germany, appealed to Enghien for assistance against Franz von Mercy's Bavarian army, which was besieging the key fortress of Freiburg im Breisgau. Enghien marched to Turenne's aid and the two French armies joined at Breisach, near Freiburg (2 August). Freiburg, meanwhile, had fallen to Mercy, and the cunning Bavarian commander had prepared a fortified defense in depth based securely upon the mountainous, wooded terrain that restricted the practicable approaches to the city. Since the opposing forces were about equal in strength, the attack of Mercy's position was a forbidding task, but Enghien, in overall command by virtue of his station as Prince of the Blood, determined to undertake it. In two days of severe fighting (3 and 5 August), punctuated by a pause to regroup, the French pushed Mercy back on Freiburg. On 9 August, with his line of communications threatened by envelopment, Mercy quit Freiburg and retreated through the Black Forest to safety. He conceded the Upper Rhine to the French, who capitalized by taking Philippsburg and other places. Enghien, in the meantime, returned to France.

Mercy launched a counteroffensive in spring 1645, surprising Turenne at Mergentheim (Marienthal) on 5 May and driving the French into Hesse. Enghien once again marched to Turenne's assistance, while Turenne reorganized his army and drew in Hessian and Swedish reinforcements. The combined armies then marched against Mercy, who fell back into Bavaria but turned and gave battle at Allerheim, near Nördlingen, on 3 August. The Battle of Allerheim was one of the bitterest and bloodiest on record (in terms of the percent of casualties per day): the French right wing of cavalry was swept from the field, and the French infantry in the center was destroyed in repeated, murderous attacks on the town of Allerheim, which Mercy had turned into a strongpoint. Enghien was wounded several times, and Mercy was killed by a bullet in the head. Turenne, however, saved the day, driving the Bavarian right wing from the field and confronting the Bavarian center and left in an unbroken line of battle at nightfall. Both armies were crippled by casualties, but during the night the Bavarians withdrew, conceding the field of battle.

Like Freiburg, Allerheim was a dismal, Pyrrhic victory. Won by Turenne's genius and Enghien's invincible determination, it was significant mainly because Mercy's death removed the principal obstacle to Franco-Swedish success in Bavaria, finally achieved by Turenne and the Swede Wrangel in 1648.

Flanders

In 1646, Enghien was sent to Flanders, where he served under the nominal command of the king's uncle, Gaston, Duke of Orléans (known as "Monsieur"), against the Spanish. Monsieur was a seedy political malcontent who was less harmful in the field than at court, where he was the focus of numerous plots against ministerial absolutism, but, as the king's uncle, was relatively invulnerable. He and Enghien enjoyed great success in Flanders that year, taking the Spanish fortress-towns of Courtrai (28 June) and Mardyck (23 August) before Monsieur left the army to pursue his plots against Mazarin and the queen mother. Enghien capped the campaign by taking Dunkirk (11 October) after a brief siege. That winter, Enghien's father died (26 December), and the duke succeeded to the title of Prince of Condé.

Catalonia: Graveyard of Reputations

The perpetually discontented Spanish province of Catalonia had rebelled in 1640 and cast its lot with France, electing King Louis XIII Duke of Barcelona. But Catalonia, except as a diplomatic pawn, was as much trouble for the French as for the Spaniards. A succession of French viceroys had been unable to make real progress against the Spanish army there, and particularly against the great fortress of Lérida, scene of French defeats in 1644 and 1646.

In January 1647, Condé was designated to command in Catalonia. He arrived in Barcelona in April and was received favorably by the people, who were always volatile and usually divided by factionalism. He decided to move against Lérida, which was invested on 11 May. However, the remarkable resistance of the garrison, inspired by the governor, Don Gregorio Brito, the alarming reduction of the French army through disease and desertion, and the approach of a strong relief force led Condé to raise the siege in June. Condé kept the field with his diminished force but was too feeble to effect much against the Spanish field army, commanded by the Marquis of Aytona. In late October, however, Aytona was forced to withdraw across the Ebro by the shortage of forage, and the French army was left in control of the Catalonian countryside.

Condé's overall success in Catalonia was wholly erased by his failure before Lérida. He departed Catalonia in November, returning to Paris, where he and Mazarin were mocked by seditious *mazarinades* called "Léridas." Nevertheless, the military situation in Catalonia was of less consequence than that in Flanders, where the Spanish had a new commander and a reinvigorated army.

Lens: A "Second Rocroi"

In the late summer of 1648, as the Thirty Years' War ground inexorably to a close, a Spanish army under Archduke Leopold William, brother of Holy Roman Emperor Ferdinand III, invaded Artois and besieged Lens. The French were initially too weak to oppose the archduke, but Condé was rushed to the scene, and the French army was reinforced by cavalry sent from Turenne's army in Germany. On 20 August, Condé confronted the Spanish on the plain west of Lens. The Spanish were deployed on a ridge and showed no disposition to attack. Condé tempted them from their strong position by feigning a disorderly retreat. When the Spanish entered the plain to pursue, Condé ordered his "retreating" lines to "about face" and march directly at the Spanish. The Spanish were surprised by the maneuver and after some sharp fighting were defeated and annihilated. Lens has been characterized as a "second Rocroi," since it resulted in the destruction of another Spanish field army. Its principal results were to preserve Artois at a time when France was entering the first stages of the civil war known as the Fronde and to force the emperor to negotiate seriously to end the Thirty Years' War.

The Fronde

Condé's conduct during the Fronde (there were actually three frondes during 1648–58) is controversial. The politics were complex, as were the shifting politico-military alignments. Suffice to say that in the First Fronde (1648–49), Condé put down the revolt of the *Parlement* against Mazarin's policies; in the Second (1649–51), Condé was arrayed against Mazarin, arrested, and imprisoned for thirteen months; and in the Third (1651–58), Condé led a rebellion against the queen regent in alliance with the Spanish, who made him general. This rebellion was plainly treason, and Condé was condemned to death in absentia (25 November 1654).

The fighting of the Fronde was nearly coincident with the ongoing Franco-Spanish War (a conflict that had continued even after most of Europe had concluded peace in 1648). Condé and the Spanish had their brief moments of success, but Turenne finally prevailed at the Battle of the Dunes (14 June 1658), where, after a brief combat, they were routed and scattered.

Dutch Wars

In the aftermath of the Dunes, the Spanish signed the Treaty of the Pyrenees (1659), ending hostilities and, incidentally, protecting Condé's life. A much-chastened Condé was pardoned (January 1660), but for nearly a decade after he was denied a field command. His one diversion, which he took seriously, was an abortive pursuit of the elective Polish crown.

Finally, in 1668, Condé was entrusted with the command of a field army. His performance in the French blitz of the virtually defenseless Spanish Franche-Comté impressed the king sufficiently that henceforth he was a major player in French military affairs. In 1672 (Second Dutch War), Condé initially had joint command with Turenne of the main army operating against the Dutch and was wounded in the famous assault passage of the Rhine near Arnhem (12 June 1672). He subsequently served in Alsace, then returned to the Spanish Netherlands to defeat the Prince of Orange's invasion army in a brilliantly conducted battle at Seneffe (11 August 1674).

Final Campaign, Retirement, and Death

Seneffe was Condé's last victory. Aging, increasingly infirm, he was no longer equal to the rigors of campaigning. Yet duty beckoned once again when Turenne was killed by a cannon shot at Sasbach in Baden (27 July 1675) while opposing Montecuccoli's imperial army. Turenne's Army of Alsace, stunned by the loss of its revered leader, fell back across the Rhine in confusion. The threat was such that Condé was ordered to Alsace to assume command. In the campaign that followed, neither Condé nor Montecuccoli displayed much energy, but the imperial army was checked. On 11 November, the Army of Alsace went into winter quarters, and Condé's military career ended.

An interesting fact is that the campaign of 1675 was the last for three of the century's greatest soldiers. Turenne died a soldier's death; Condé retired; and Montecuccoli, reportedly complaining that he no longer had an adversary worthy of his sword, retired also.

Condé spent his last years at his magnificent chateau of Chantilly and busied himself with family matters and the intellectual pursuits that were so dear to him. He converted to Roman Catholicism in April 1685, although in fact he had long been inclined toward the church's doctrines. He died on 11 December 1686, so peacefully that initially his passing went unnoticed by those at prayer in his chamber.

Significance

That Condé was one of the great men of military history is beyond question. Nevertheless, Napoleon omitted him from his brief list of great captains and censured him for Freiburg and Allerheim, where he had faced the wily Mercy, who *never* fought at a disadvantage. Unfortunately, Condé's reputation has suffered by comparison with that of Turenne, who was no doubt the greater soldier and a different person from the point of view of character and personality. But in this case, the comparison is invidious. Condé's brilliance and tenacity won many battles, including two battles of annihilation, and it is worth remembering that Turenne had the greatest regard for Condé's generalship, which helped establish France as Europe's preeminent military power in the mid-seventeenth century. Richelieu, Le Tellier, and Louvois provided the sword, and Condé and his comrades in high command wielded it with consummate skill.

CURT JOHNSON

SEE ALSO: France, Military Hegemony of; Spanish Empire; Thirty Years' War; Turenne, Henri de La Tour d'Auvergne, Vicomte de.

Bibliography

Aumale, Henri Eugene Philippe Louis d'Orléans, duc d'. 1863–96. *Histoire des princes de Condé.* 7 vols. and atlas. Paris: Michel Lévy.
———. 1872. *History of the princes of Condé in the XVIth and XVIIth centuries.* Trans. R. B. Borthwick. 2 vols. London.
Blancpain, M. ca. 1986. *Monsieur le prince: La vie illustre de Louis de Condé, héros et cousin du Grand Roi.* Paris: Hachette Litterature.
Camon, H. 1933. *Deux grands chefs de guerre du XVIIIe siècle: Condé et Turenne.* Paris: Berger-Levrault.
Duhamel, P. G. ca. 1981. *Le grand Condé, ou l'Orgueil.* Paris: Perrin.
Godley, E. C. 1915. *The great Condé.* London: J. Murray.
Stanhope, P. H. 1845. *The life of Louis, prince of Condé, surnamed the great.* London: J. Murray.
Schaufler, H. H. 1980. *Die Schlacht bei Freiburg im Breisgau.* Freiburg im Breisgau: Verlag Rombach.

CRIMEAN WAR [1853–56]

A monkish squabble over jurisdiction within the Holy Places of Turkish-ruled Jerusalem in 1853 brought France (protector of the Catholics) and Russia (protector of the Orthodox clergy) into sharp diplomatic controversy, with Turkey squeezed between. Czar Nicholas I saw the problem in Jerusalem as an opportunity to dominate Turkey and to secure entrance into the Mediterranean through the Turkish Straits. As a result, a Russian army began occupation of Turkey's Romanian principalities (July). France had no intention of letting its rival become more powerful in the Near East, and England opposed any change in the balance of power. Accordingly, British and French fleets, operating independently, arrived at Constantinople to encourage the Turks.

On 4 October 1853 Turkey declared war on Russia. A Turkish army under Omar Pasha (Croatian-born Michael Lattas, a good soldier) crossed the Danube. On 4 November Omar defeated the Russians in southern Romania, near the Danube.

On 30 November a Russian fleet attacked the main Turkish fleet in the harbor at Sinope (Sinop). Russia's Adm. Paul S. Nakhimov, with six ships of the line, three frigates, and several smaller craft, attacked Turkey's Adm. Hussein

Pasha's seven frigates, three corvettes, and two small steamers lying in the harbor. The Turkish flotilla was destroyed in a six-hour engagement, the outnumbered and outgunned Turks fighting to the end. The most significant aspect of the encounter was the enormous damage done by the Russian shell guns—a new type of naval ordnance making its first appearance in warfare.

On 3 January 1854 a Franco-British fleet sailed into the Black Sea. On 12 March both nations, forgetting momentarily their mutual jealousies and suspicions, allied themselves with Turkey to protect the Turkish coast and shipping.

On 20 March a strong Russian army under Marshal Ivan Paskievich invaded Turkish Bulgaria. As a result, Britain and France declared war on Russia on 28 March. On 10 April they concluded a mutual alliance. A Franco-British expeditionary force moved to Varna to assist in repelling the Russian invasion, which had now reached and was besieging Silistria (Silistra). On 16 April the British frigate *Furious* was fired on while trying to enter Odessa under a flag of truce. In retaliation, a Franco-Britain squadron bombarded the shore batteries, inflicting serious damage.

On 20 April, after entering into a defensive alliance with Prussia against Russia, Austria massed an army of 50,000 men in Galicia and Transylvania. With Turkish permission, Austria moved into Turkey's Danube principalities. In the face of this threat, Russia abandoned the siege of Silistria (9 June) and later withdrew its forces from the area (2 August), but Russia rejected the joint peace conditions set by England, France, Prussia, and Austria (Vienna Four Points, 8 August) that specified Russia must keep its hands off the Ottoman Empire.

Invasion of the Crimea

The Russian evacuation of the Balkans achieved the principal objective of the allied expeditionary force at Varna, which was now rotting with cholera. But in September 1854, London and Paris decided to use the force at Varna to break Russian power in the Black Sea by crippling the great naval base at Sevastopol. The expedition was decided upon without any consideration of the magnitude of the task, and without any adequate prior reconnaissance. Britain's Maj. Gen. Fitzroy James Henry Somerset, Lord Raglan, age 66, and France's Marshal Armand J. O. de Saint-Arnaud, age 53 (who was already seriously ill with cholera), commanded jointly.

The allied force sailed from Varna on 7 September. It was transported to the Crimean Peninsula in a great convoy of 150 British and French warships and transports. Typical of the haphazard conduct of the campaign, it was not until the convoy lay offshore that a decision was made as to the point of debarkation. Equally typical was that no attempt was made by Prince Alexander Sergeievich Menshikov, Russia's commander in the Crimea, to oppose the landing.

On 13 September the allies began landing at Old Fort, on an open beach with no harbor, some 48 kilometers (30 mi.) north and west of Sevastopol. Bad weather and the weakened condition of the troops combined to delay the debarkation. Beginning on 29 September the expeditionary force—51,000 British, French, and Turkish infantry; 1,000 British cavalry; and 128 guns—moved south, the British on the landward flank. The fleet kept pace along the seacoast. Menshikov, with 36,400 men, elected to defend on the bank of the Alma River, his left flank out of range of the allied fleet, his right anchored on a ridge. The allies crossed the river without much difficulty, but the British then found themselves facing a steep slope, which was won only after a hard fight. Menshikov then withdrew without molestation. Allied casualties (mostly British) were about 3,000 men; the Russians lost 5,709 men.

By 25 September the allies were in sight of Sevastopol, whose harbor channel had been blocked by sunken ships, rendering naval cooperation in an assault from the north impossible. Without a base, siege was impractical. The only solution was a flank march around the fortress to the south side and the establishment of bases at the ports of Kamiesch and Balaklava. As the allies, abandoning their line of retreat, made the 24-kilometer (15-mi.) circuit with their flank unmolested, Menshikov left a garrison within the works of Sevastopol and wisely marched the remainder of his army north to Bakhehisarai to join Russian reinforcements now moving in. Actually, the opponents marched across one another's front without knowing it. The allied army safely made the circuit and on 26 September regained contact with the fleet. The British based themselves on Balaklava and the French on Kamiesch.

Siege of Sevastopol

The southern defenses of Sevastopol had not yet been completed. An immediate assault might have been successful. Instead, while the British contingent and one French army corps protected the operation from attack by the Russian field army, a siege corps was extemporized and investment began. St. Arnaud died of cholera on 29 September, and Gen. Francois Certain Canrobert took command. By 17 October, when the first bombardment began, Col. Frants E. I. Todleben, the Russian chief engineer, had done an amazing job of fortification. The bombardment and counterbattery fire caused serious losses on both sides but no permanent damage to the works. The port was blockaded by the fleet of Adm. Sir Edmund Lyons.

Battles of Balaklava and Inkerman

On 25 October Menshikov's field army attempted to drive between the besieging lines and the British base at Balaklava. A penetration was made and some Turkish guns taken. Russian cavalry attempting to exploit the breakthrough were repelled by the British Heavy Cavalry Brigade and the stand of the 93d Highlanders ("the thin red line"). The Light Cavalry Brigade, through circumstances never satisfactorily explained, now charged the Russian field batteries to their front, riding up a narrow, 1.6-kilometer-long (1 mi.) valley, exposed at the same time to fire from the captured Turkish guns on their right flank and other Russian guns on their left (Fig. 1). They reached the guns, rode through them, clashed with Russian cavalry beyond, and then the survivors rode back through the cross fire of the "Valley of Death" made famous by

Figure 1. The charge of the Light Brigade at Balaklava, painted by R. Caton Woodville. (SOURCE: U.S. Library of Congress)

Tennyson's poem. The charge will stand forever as a monument to gallant soldiers doomed to death by the arrant stupidity of Brig. Gen. James Thomas Brudenell, Lord Cardigan, commander of the brigade, and Maj. Gen. G. C. Bingham, Lord Lucan, commander of the Cavalry Division. The return of the survivors was assisted by the equally gallant charge of the 4th French Chasseurs d'Afrique, who rode down part of the flanking Russian artillery. Of 673 mounted officers and men entering the 20-minute-long Light Brigade charge, 247 men and 497 horses were lost. A most fitting epitaph was the remark of French general Pierre F. J. Bosquet, witnessing the charge: "It is magnificent, but it is not war." The Russians retained possession of the Vorontosov ridge, commanding the Balaklava-Sevastopol road. The allies retained Balaklava.

On 5 November Menshikov again tried at Inkerman to break through between the besieging troops and their field support. The brunt of the action fell on the British, in an all-day struggle during which all coordinated control was lost on both sides. The arrival of Bosquet's French division finally tipped the balance, and Menshikov withdrew, with a loss of 12,000 men. The allied loss—mostly British—was 3,300 men.

The Siege Continues

Theoretically, the allies, with sea communications unhindered, should have had little difficulty in their siege operations, whereas the Russians, although their northern line of communications was open, had a long, tenuous overland supply problem. Actually, the allies were totally unprepared for a winter campaign, while a heavy storm (14 November), which wrecked some 30 transports lying at Balaklava, destroyed most of the existing stores of rations, forage, and clothing. To make matters worse, the Russian field army still sat astride the only paved road from Balaklava to the siege lines. Wagon haulage over the muddy plain was almost impossible.

The British troops, without shelter or adequate winter clothing, were also actually semistarved. Cholera raged; men died like flies in shockingly inadequate medical facilities. By February, British effectives were down to 12,000. Canrobert, whose administration was much better handled, had 78,000 men on hand and took over part of the British sector. But the cable and telegraph were pouring out the grim story as seen by William Howard Russell, war correspondent for the London *Times*. An outraged British public forced the fall of the government of George H. Gordon, Lord Aberdeen. There were immediate remedial results, one of the most important being the establishment of proper medical and hospital facilities under Florence Nightingale. Meanwhile, despite serious casualties to the working parties from the allied bombardments, Todleben's incessant activity and engineering genius countered the damage done by the allied guns, and the defensive works grew in strength.

On 26 January 1855, a contingent of Sardinians arrived to reinforce the allies. These 10,000 troops were commanded by Gen. Alfonso Ferrero di La Marmora.

A new road and a railroad over the mud plain now linked the Balaklava base to the siege corps. On 17 February the Russian field army, now commanded by Prince Michael Gorchakov (replacing Menshikov), made a halfhearted attempt at Eupatoria to interfere with this construction. This was repulsed by the Turks. The siege lines drew closer.

From 8 to 13 April, in a so-called Easter Bombardment, a major part of the Russian defenses was destroyed by allied artillery. Russian troops drawn up to meet an expected assault lost more than 6,000 men, but the attack never came. Allied field commanders and home governments were wrangling via telegraph over conduct of the operations. Canrobert, enraged by the interferences, resigned his command. His successor, Gen. Aimable Jean Jacques Pelissier, like his predecessor a veteran of the Algerian wars, brought new vigor to the allied operations.

On 24 May a well-handled joint expedition cleared the Sea of Azov (Axovskoe More), captured Kerch, and severed Russian communications with the interior.

Closing in on Sevastopol

On 7 June the allies assaulted the fortress and captured part of the Russian outer defenses; there were 8,500 Russian casualties and about 6,900 allied. On 17–18 June the allies renewed their assault. The objectives were two principal Russian strong points, the Malakoff and the Redan. Lack of coordination brought utter failure. The French attack on the Malakoff dwindled into an indecisive fire fight, while the British assault on the Redan was caught in the cross fire of 100 heavy guns and thrown back with heavy losses. The allies lost 4,000 men in this effort, the Russians 5,400. Raglan, heartbroken, died ten days later; he was succeeded by Gen. Sir James Simpson.

Russian losses through bombardment were draining Sevastopol's strength— some 350 died each day during July. The Russian field army decided to make one final effort to break through the allied curtain between Balaklava and the fortress. This led to the Battle of the Traktir Ridge on 16 August. Two corps of

Gorchakov's army were thrown against some 37,000 French and Sardinian troops on the height above the Chernaya River. A five-hour combat ended in Russian defeat, putting to rest the last hope for relieving Sevastopol, despite the dogged determination of the Russian infantry.

The one perfectly planned and executed operation of the war took place on 8 September. After an intense bombardment (5–8 September) softened the defenses, Bosquet's entire corps launched a long-prepared mass assault on the Malakoff fort. Meticulous attention to detail included a last-minute check by staff officers to ensure that each of the three assaulting columns would have easy egress from the trenches, now only 27 meters (30 yd.) from the Russian strong point. To preserve secrecy, no signal was given for the assault. Synchronization of watches—for the first time, perhaps, in military history—governed the move. On the stroke of noon, the corps surged forward, each column led by its commanding general, while Bosquet established his command post on the parapet of the outermost French trench.

The assault gained the outer wall and swept into the inner defenses, where the Russians disputed every casemate and traverse in hand-to-hand combat. By nightfall, the Malakoff was safely in French hands.

A simultaneous British assault on the Redan was thrown back, but from the Malakoff the French now turned their fire on the Russians in the Redan and drove them out with heavy losses. That night, after blowing up the remainder of the fortifications, Gorchakov evacuated Sevastopol. The next day the allies occupied the city. In all, the allies suffered more than 10,000 casualties in this final assault, the Russians 13,000.

Bombardment of Kinburn, at the mouth of the Bug River, was anticlimactic, but on 16 October, three French steam-powered floating batteries made history as ironclad warships made their first appearance in battle. They demolished heavy masonry works while Russian round shot and shells spent themselves harmlessly on the iron plates at ranges of 900 meters (1,000 yd.) or less.

Caucasus Front, 1854–55

Severe but indecisive fighting between Turks and Russians took place in the Caucasus and Transcaucasus during 1854 and 1855. The principal operation of note was the Siege of Kars by the Russian general Michael Muraviev. On 29 September 1855, the Turkish garrison, commanded by Sir William Fenwich Williams (Williams Pasha), British commissioner and a lieutenant general in the Turkish army, repelled a savage Russian assault. Omar Pasha, after the fall of Sevastopol, took a force of 15,000 men to the relief of Kars, but the fortress succumbed to starvation and disease before his arrival. Williams surrendered on 26 November 1855.

Naval Operations in the Baltic

On 7 August 1854 a French squadron landed 10,000 men under Gen. Achille Baraguay d'Hilliers at Bomarsund, Aland Islands. After an eight-day siege, during which naval gunfire from Sir Charles Napier's allied fleet took joint part, the 2,400-man garrison surrendered and the fortress was destroyed.

A year later, on 7–11 August 1855, a Franco-British fleet, after demonstrating before the fortress of Kronstadt (Kronshtadt), bombarded Sveaborg (fortress in Helsinki harbor) without success.

Peace

On 1 February 1856, preliminary peace conditions were agreed to at Vienna. Final ratification took place at the Congress of Paris (28 February–30 March).

Comment

The outstanding aspect of the war was the abysmal mismanagement on both sides, featuring indifference in governments and senility and incompetence on the part of field commanders. Russia, fighting England, France, Turkey, and Sardinia, lost—from all causes—some 256,000 men. The allies lost about 252,600. Actual Russian battle deaths were an estimated 128,700; those of the allies, 70,000. Disease—mainly cholera—accounted for the rest. The combatants themselves displayed raw courage under great handicaps. Back home, the awakening of national interest in the welfare of the troops was unprecedented, particularly in Great Britain, where accounts by war correspondents spread the news of shocking conditions on the fighting front.

TREVOR N. DUPUY

SEE ALSO: History, Modern Military.

Bibliography

Dupuy, R. E., and T. N. Dupuy. 1986. *Encyclopedia of military history.* New York: Harper and Row.
Gibbs, P. 1960. *Crimean blunder.* New York: Holt, Rinehart and Winston.
———. 1963. *The battle of the Alma.* London: Weidenfeld and Nicolson.
Hamley, E. 1891. *The war in the Crimea.* London: Seely.
Kinglake, A. W. 1863–87. *The invasion of the Crimea.* 8 vols. Edinburgh: William Blackwood.
Slade, A. 1896. *Turkey and the Crimean war.* London: Smith, Elder.
Woodham-Smith, C. 1953. *The reason why.* New York: McGraw-Hill.

CROMWELL, OLIVER [1599–1658]

Although he did not begin his military career until well into middle age, Oliver Cromwell (Fig. 1) proved an exceptionally able general. A deeply religious man, he was also just, capable of great compassion, and a fearless and ruthless warrior. He was largely responsible for England's one brief flirtation with "republican" government during the 1650s.

Early Life

Oliver Cromwell was born in Huntingdon on 25 April 1599, the son of Robert Cromwell, a prosperous landowner, and his wife, Elizabeth. He entered Sidney Sussex College at Cambridge University in April 1616, but left the following

Figure 1. Oliver Cromwell. (SOURCE: U.S. Library of Congress)

June after his father's death. His stay at Cambridge was not graced with academic achievement, for Cromwell apparently had a keener interest in the playing field than in the classroom. Before he married Elizabeth Bourchier in August 1620, Cromwell spent some time at the Inns of Court in London studying law.

He passed most of the next twenty years as a prosperous rural landowner, although he served in the Parliament of 1628–29 as member for Huntingdon. About 1630, he experienced a deeply felt spiritual awakening to full-fledged Puritanism. As England neared political crisis in the late 1630s, he sided with King Charles I's political opponents. He was elected to Parliament as a member for Cambridge in April 1640 and again in November (the so-called *Long Parliament*). An eloquent and often impassioned speaker, he played a role in the momentous political events of 1640–42, and raised a troop of horse in late summer 1642 after the outbreak of civil war.

Military Commander in the First Civil War, 1642–46

Cromwell led his troop at the Battle of Edgehill on 23 October 1642, but probably arrived on the field late and so fought only in the battle's later stages. Over the first winter of war, Cromwell became a member of the Eastern and Midlands Associations, gaining a colonel's commission and with it command of a regiment of horse. He led a charge against Royalist cavalry at Grantham on 13 May 1643 and routed the enemy at the cost of but two of his own men. Following this success, he captured Burleigh House on 24 July, and led the right wing at the relief of Gainsborough four days later.

He was soon appointed governor of Ely, and led the vanguard against the Royalists at Winceby on 11 October. When the Earl of Manchester was appointed General of the Eastern Association's army over the winter of 1643–44, Cromwell became his lieutenant-general of horse. Further, Cromwell's own regiment, now nicknamed the "Ironsides," grew to fourteen troops of horse, twice the size of most regiments. At the great battle of Marston Moor (2 July 1644), Cromwell and his cavalry played a decisive role, and he gained the thanks of Parliament for his part in that battle, which cost the Royalists the north of England.

He enjoyed less success at the Second Battle of Newbury on 26 October, and attacked the Earl of Manchester in Parliament for the Earl's lack of zeal, thereby provoking a major political crisis, which led to the creation of the "New Model Army" during the winter. By spring 1645 Cromwell was lieutenant-general of horse to General Lord Thomas Fairfax, commander of the New Model. He led the right wing at the Battle of Naseby on 14 June 1645, again showing his ability to keep tight control of cavalry on the field. Following that victory, he and Fairfax won a victory at Langport on 10 July, and the next spring found Cromwell besieging Oxford, the Royalist capital. As hostilities died down in summer and autumn 1646, Cromwell settled in London and resumed his political career.

First General of the Republic, 1646–51

Parliament's efforts to reach an accommodation with King Charles, undertaken from early 1647 through February 1648, were undermined by Charles's stubbornness and Presbyterian (especially Scottish) political opposition. Cromwell returned to military service when the Second Civil War broke out in spring 1648 and was ordered to south Wales, where he besieged and captured Pembroke (early June to 11 July). Cromwell then led his army northward to meet the invading Scottish army of James, Duke of Hamilton. Cromwell smashed Hamilton's ragged army at Preston in a free-wheeling three-day battle from 17 to 19 August.

He stayed to pacify the North, and returned to London in early December. Building on his success and the support of the army, he pressed for the trial of the king. He won appointment as one of 135 commissioners for the trial, and employed his full will and eloquence to persuade his fellow commissioners to sign the king's death warrant in late January 1649.

In the wake of the king's execution, Cromwell was chosen first chairman of the new Republic's Council of State, and suppressed a radical "Leveller" mutiny within the army that spring. His most urgent task was to settle the situation in Ireland, which had been in uproar since 1640–41. He assembled an army and sailed for Ireland, landing at Dublin on 13 August 1649. Faced with considerable resistance from Irish Catholics, he besieged the Catholic stronghold at Drogheda, and then stormed it on 10–11 September. His forces (probably not at his direction but certainly with his permission) massacred a large part of the garrison and many civilians. Even in Ireland, where massacres and blood feuds were hardly unknown, the brutality of this event was shocking, and the garrisons of many Catholic strongholds hastened to submit to spare themselves Drogheda's fate.

Despite the moral effect of Drogheda, Cromwell had to storm Wexford on 11 October and Waterford the following month. Next, he led his army inland to subdue Munster and besiege Clonmel in April 1650. After Clonmel fell in May, Cromwell entrusted command to his son-in-law, Henry Ireton, and returned to England. He arrived just as the Third Civil War with Scotland broke out in June. He took command of the entire army after Fairfax resigned command on 23 June, and marched north.

He campaigned around Edinburgh in August without success, and retired to the small port of Dunbar to await badly needed supplies and reinforcements. Trapped there by Alexander Leslie's larger Scots army (Cromwell had perhaps 12,000 men to Leslie's 23,000), Cromwell turned and launched a successful counterattack in a rainstorm on 3 September, after Leslie's army had descended from the hills to deploy for battle. Worn by the stress of campaigning and the labors of trying to pacify Scotland, Cromwell fell ill at Edinburgh in February 1651, and suffered a relapse in May. He was thus unable to resume operations until June.

He moved northward, and allowed Leslie's army to invade England along the west coast. He followed swiftly, gathering reinforcements as he went, and caught the Scots army at Worcester on 3 September 1651, destroying it utterly. All the British Isles lay under the same government, which Cromwell headed.

Statesman and Lord Protector, 1652–58

Barely had peace returned to Britain than war loomed with the Dutch, sparked by long-festering commercial disputes. Cromwell entered the war without enthusiasm, disliking the idea of war with a sister republic. Exasperated with the Rump of the Long Parliament, he dissolved it by force in April 1653, reputedly dismissing it with the words: "You have sat long enough; let us have done with you. In the name of God, go!"

Cromwell was unable to work with the ensuing "Barebones Parliament" either, and he dismissed it in turn late that autumn. Struggling to create an effective government, Cromwell became Protector under John Lambert's *Instrument of Government* on 16 December. Disputes and quarrels with Parliament continued, and he dissolved it again in January 1655, instituting regional government through the major general of the army.

The prospect of war with Spain compelled him to call a new Parliament to raise money in September 1656, but this body proved no more amenable to his wishes than had its forerunners, although most of its members had been appointed by Cromwell's officials. Cromwell refused the offer of the crown on 8 May 1657 after two months of political wrangling, but he accepted the "Humble Petition and Advice" on 25 May. This made him "Lord Protector" (and king in all but name), and created a new upper house of Parliament. Ironically, this last step weakened Cromwell's hand, as many of his supporters in Commons were promoted out of political expediency. Still unable, despite his new rank and powers, to get along with Parliament, he dissolved it again (February 1658) and subsequently ruled without one, thereby echoing the recourse of Charles I, which had turned so many people like Cromwell against him in the 1630s.

Cromwell fell ill in August and died in London on 3 September 1658. He was succeeded as Lord Protector by his son Richard, who had none of his father's talent for leadership. Within sixteen months the monarchy was restored under King Charles II. Cromwell's remains were dug up from their resting place, and together with the corpse of Ireton (dead since 1652) were hung from the Tyburn gallows, and then interred beneath them.

Assessment

Oliver Cromwell has a mixed reputation. Admired for his skills as a general and a statesman, his reputation has suffered (with some justification) for his activities in Ireland, especially Drogheda, and his central role in the trial and execution of Charles I. Cromwell was a man of deep and sincerely held religious faith, and possessed great strength of character. This latter quality, especially, stood him in good stead as a general, and his grasp of military science was remarkably clear and thorough for a man who began soldiering so late in life. His career as a statesman and politician was less successful, in part because he was unable to create a popularly acceptable alternative to the monarchy.

DAVID L. BONGARD

SEE ALSO: France, Military Hegemony of; History, Early Modern Military; Seapower, British.

Bibliography

Abbot, W. C. 1937–47. *Writings and speeches of Oliver Cromwell.* 4 vols. Cambridge: Cambridge Univ. Press.

Ashley, M. P. 1972. *Oliver Cromwell and his world.* New York: Putnam.

Firth, C. H. 1900. *Oliver Cromwell.* New York: Defau.

———. 1962. *Cromwell's army.* New York: Barnes and Noble.

Fraser, A. 1973. *Cromwell: The lord protector.* New York: Knopf.

Hill, C. 1970. *God's Englishman: Oliver Cromwell and the English revolution.* London: Dial Press.

Kenyon, J. 1988. *The civil wars of England.* London: Weidenfeld and Nicolson.

Rogers, H. C. B. 1968. *Battles and generals of the civil wars.* London: Seeley.

Wedgwood, C. V. 1964. *The trial of Charles I.* London: Collins.

CRUSADES [1097–1291]

The Crusades, a series of campaigns by West European Christians from 1096 to 1291, were attempts to regain the Holy Land from the Muslims.

The Crusades were an expression of the revival of religious feeling and missionary zeal that had begun in Europe in the tenth century. Contemporaries stressed this aspect of the Crusades: "holy wars" to defend Christ's sepulchre. However, individual participants and groups also acted from a variety of secular motives including personal, political, and economic expansionism.

The Crusades were also part of the secular policy of the papacy. The popes had a number of reasons for desiring to direct the faithful to a great war of Christianity against the infidel. For the papacy the Crusades provided an opportunity to divert and channel the warlike energies of their most troublesome subjects away from the destructive violence endemic within Christendom.

For many of the faithful, the Crusades were a new avenue to gain salvation by making a pilgrimage. Such pilgrimages had been taking place throughout the previous four centuries, as had continual fighting between Christians and Muslims in those theaters where they shared a common frontier, including Spain, Sicily, Italy, Asia Minor, and at sea.

Immediate Causes of the Crusades

Although Muslims captured Jerusalem in A.D. 637, their policy of religious tolerance allowed continual communication between the Christian churches in the Holy Land and their coreligionists in Europe. In the early eleventh century, however, the situation changed when the caliph Hakim began to interfere; at the same time, relations between the Latin and Byzantine churches were rent by the schism of 1054. The situation became even worse when the Seljuk Turks captured Jerusalem from the Egyptians in 1071, the same year they destroyed a Byzantine army at Manzikert and seized Asia Minor up to the Hellespont.

Naval powers such as Pisa, Genoa, and Venice were gaining vital control of the Mediterranean. The Normans were particularly active, not only in conquering Sicily and southern Italy and in assisting Christians in Spain, but also in efforts to wrest territory from the Byzantines. Thus, when the Byzantines were severely pressed by the Seljuk Turks, the emperor of the Eastern Roman Empire, Michael VII, appealed in 1073 to Pope Gregory VII (whom the Normans nominally supported), hoping to transfer Norman attentions from taking his domains in Greece to helping him recover others in Asia Minor. The appeals for assistance were later repeated by Byzantine emperor Alexius I Comnenus to Pope Urban II and other Western leaders. Thus the stage was set for the pope's initiative of 1095. The confluence of factors can be listed as follows:

• unprecedented difficulty for Christians desiring pilgrimage directly to Jerusalem

- extraordinary weakness of the Byzantine Empire, including losses to the Turks
- increased military power of Western Europeans, especially Normans and French, and restless eagerness on the part of military leaders to put it to their own use
- increased Christian naval strength throughout the Mediterranean, and heightened desire of the naval cities to exploit this power for commercial advantage
- papal interest in an expedition to Asia Minor and Palestine and in asserting more control over the internal affairs of Western Europe
- popular ideological and cultural interest linking religious fervor to concept of crusade
- a period of increased local famine and disease in Europe, which encouraged the masses to undertake dangerous treks in search of a better life

The crusade movement resulted in an almost continuous flow of individuals and groups, armed and unarmed, from Western Europe to the Levant. Hardly a year passed without several nobles arriving with their retainers. Nevertheless, the period between 1096 and 1291 witnessed eight specific campaigns considered sufficiently discrete to be numbered as named Crusades.

First Crusade, 1097–99

Leaders:
Godfrey of Bouillon, duke of Lorraine
Baldwin of Bouillon, of Lorraine
Raymund of Toulouse, leader of Provençals
Bishop Adhemar, from the Provençals
Bohemund of Otranto, Norman of Sicily
Tancred of Otranto, Norman of Sicily
Hugh of Vermandois, brother of King Philip I of France
Robert of Normandy, brother of the king of England
Stephen of Blois
Robert of Flanders

Opponents:
Kilij Arslan, sultan of Iconium
Yagi-sian, ruler of Antioch
Kerbogha, emir of Mosul

In Europe, the immediate outcome of Pope Urban II's appeal in 1095 was the generation of a religious fervor that swept warrior and civil classes alike. The result was something different from what either pope or Byzantine emperor had in mind. The first to turn desire into action were the common people, whose lack of either property to look after or military understanding to counsel preparation enabled them to take up the cross on the spot. Five large bodies of common folk coalesced under various self-appointed leaders and moved from the Rhine across Bavaria, down the Danube to Constantinople. Three of these mobs were destroyed in Hungary due to their own wild excesses. Two reached

Constantinople and crossed into Asia Minor, only to be completely destroyed by the Seljuks.

The real military forces took longer to assemble and organize. Beginning in March 1096 as individual knights and members of medieval hosts, they marched and sailed from throughout France and the Low Countries toward Constantinople, arriving there between December 1096 and May 1097.

In May the crusaders crossed the Bosporus and entered the domain of Kilij Arslan. They first captured Nicaea and then defeated the Seljuk field army at Dorylaeum. They marched unmolested across Asia Minor to Antioch, held by Yagi-sian, and besieged the city (21 October 1097 to 3 June 1098). The great leader of the siege was Bohemund. He repelled two attempts to relieve the city, which was finally taken as a result of treachery within the garrison. After this success the Crusader army moved south along the coast. Bohemund remained in Antioch while Raymund besieged Acre (February to May 1099) and attempted to capture Tripoli. With Raymund and Bohemund feuding, Godfrey of Bouillon took the leadership and pressed on to Jerusalem. The army arrived there in June and after a relatively brief siege took the Holy City on 15 July, bringing the formal crusade to an end. The result was the creation of several crusader states that drew the attention of Europe for the next 200 years.

Second Crusade, 1145–48

Leaders:
Conrad III, king of Germany
Louis VII, king of France
Baldwin II, king of Jerusalem

Opponents:
Muin-eddin-Anar, vizier of Damascus
Nureddin, emir of Aleppo (in background)

The emir of Mosul captured Edessa on Christmas Day 1144. This signaled the beginning of the destruction of the Latin kingdom of Jerusalem. The news reached Pope Eugenius III early in 1145, and he immediately appealed for a new crusade. King Louis VII of France took the vow, followed by the German king, Conrad III, the next year. With the leadership in the hands of two great kings the prospects for success seemed greater than for the First Crusade. However, such was not to be the case. The knights from England and the Low Countries sailed down the Iberian coast; they stopped to help the Portuguese gain control of Lisbon from the Moors, the only success of the campaign. They then continued on to Antioch. Meanwhile, Conrad marched overland on the well-worn road through Hungary to Constantinople, while Louis arrived later by sea. En route, the German army attempted a raid into the Sultanate of Iconium and was defeated at Dorylaeum in October 1147. At this Louis decided to march by the long, roundabout coastal route. The result was that by the time the French and German forces reached the Holy Land in 1148, both had lost most of their troops. Here Conrad and Louis joined the Frankish king Baldwin

III to plan some action. They foolishly decided to besiege Damascus, their one Muslim ally, to block the advance of the more powerful Emir Nureddin from Allepo and Baghdad. The siege failed after four days, but helped reunite the Muslims.

Conrad returned to Constantinople and Louis to France. The effect of this great movement was detrimental to the Frankish position in the Holy Land. In addition, the fiasco so discredited the whole crusading idea that efforts to recruit a new force in 1150 failed.

Third Crusade, 1189–92

Leaders:
Richard I, king of England
Frederick I (Barbarossa), Holy Roman Emperor
Philip Augustus, king of France
Conrad, marquis of Montferrat
Guy de Lusignan, king of Jerusalem

Opponent:
Saladin, sultan of Egypt

The loss of Jerusalem on 2 October 1187 and most of the Holy Land to Saladin after the battle of Hattin in July 1187 generated another papal appeal throughout Europe. This time the state powers took up the call. The great German emperor Frederick I (Barbarossa), who had participated in the Second Crusade, organized a fine army. The kings of England and France temporarily laid aside their conflicts to join together for the expedition. But this crusade was little more successful than the second. The German army marched across the Balkans, crossed the Bosphorus, and passed through Asia Minor practically unscathed, only to fall apart immediately on the accidental drowning of their emperor. Only 1,000 men reached Acre in October 1190 under command of the emperor's son, Frederick of Swabia.

The French and English sailed from southern France, stopped over the winter of 1190–91 in Sicily, then reached Acre in midyear. (Richard had conquered Cyprus en route).

The initial rout of the Franks after the battle of Hattin had been checked at Tyre, their last remaining stronghold in the south, by the last-minute arrival of Conrad of Montferrat. He advanced with the remnant of crusader forces to the siege of Acre, the key seaport for Jerusalem. Here they were in turn besieged by Saladin with the combined Muslim hosts of Egypt and much of Syria. The arrival of the French and English enabled the crusaders finally to take the city and a little more of the seacoast, but they were unable to even consider an attempt on Jerusalem with Saladin's army so near. Philip quickly returned to France. Richard accomplished more through diplomatic negotiations with Saladin than by force of arms.

The crusade failed in its objective, but it did at least buy some time by saving Antioch, Tripoli, and some of the coastal cities. Its main results lay in Europe itself, where it represented the shift in control of crusades from the religious power of the papacy to the secular power of the state.

Fourth Crusade, 1202–04

Leaders:
Theobald III of Champagne (until death in 1201)
Boniface of Montferrat (after 1201)
Baldwin of Flanders
Enrico Dandolo, Doge of Venice
Louis of Blois

Opponents:
Alexius III Angelus, Byzantine emperor (usurper, having deposed and imprisoned his brother, Isaac II)
Alexius V Ducas Mourtzouphlous (leader of second city defense)

In 1199 Pope Innocent III raised a crusade in France with the objective of attacking the center of Muslim power in Egypt. The French chivalry (i.e., mounted men at arms) led by Theobald III responded. However, after he died, the newly elected leader, Boniface, was persuaded by his cousin, Philip of Swabia (the Hohenstaufen Holy Roman Emperor), with the aid of Venice to divert the French crusaders to Constantinople. Philip's aim was to aid his brother-in-law, Alexis, in restoring his father, the dethroned emperor Isaac Angelus. With the Venetians supplying the sea power and transports, the effort succeeded. Isaac was restored, but a subsequent revolt gave the crusaders the excuse to capture the city and place Baldwin on the throne as the first Latin emperor of Constantinople.

The result of this excursion was the further diversion of crusades from spiritual motivation and papal control to secular (political and economic) motivations and secular state control. It was a major setback for the efforts to save the Holy Land: not only was a large portion of Frankish fighting strength diverted from Jerusalem for years to come, but also Byzantine support, never very extensive, was further eroded.

Fifth Crusade, 1218–21

Leaders:
Pelagius, cardinal legate of Pope Innocent III
John of Brienne, king of Jerusalem

Opponents:
Sultan Malik-al-Adil (died 1218)
Sultan Malik-al-Kamil

Undaunted by the disastrous miscarriage of his plans for the Fourth Crusade, Pope Innocent III urged yet another at the Fourth Lateran Council of 1215. The initial reception was auspicious. The great Emperor Frederick II took the cross in Germany. In 1217 the duke of Austria and the king of Hungary went to the Holy Land. In 1218 another army from northwest Europe joined them. By this time it was clear to the crusaders that the real locus of Muslim power was Egypt. Innocent declared that the purpose of the crusade would be to capture the Egyptian stronghold at Damietta and then seek to take Cairo as well. The crusaders took Damietta by the end of 1219, but spent all of 1220 waiting there for the arrival of Emperor Frederick II, the nominal leader. The sultan offered very favorable terms, which were rejected. In 1221 Pelagius, over the protests of King John, ordered an advance on Cairo.

The crusader army reached the new Mameluke fortress at Mansura in July. The sultan again offered terms that were rejected, and the crusaders were driven back to Damietta. At this the cardinal agreed to a treaty (August 1221) to gain the freedom to withdraw. The crusader evacuation of Egypt ended the crusade. The failure was due in part to the failure of Frederick II to arrive, since his presence would have greatly strengthened the crusader cause; and in part to the intransigence of Pelagius in refusing to heed the advice of the experienced King John.

Sixth Crusade, 1228–29

Leader:
Emperor Frederick II (Stupor Mundi), Holy Roman Emperor (1212–50)

Opponent:
Malik-al-Kamil, Sultan of Egypt

The Sixth Crusade succeeded but under circumstances that made its success even more disastrous than the failure of the preceding crusade. This crusade was unique in that instead of receiving a papal blessing its leader was actually excommunicated. It was also the only crusade that included no hostile acts against the Muslims. Frederick undertook the crusade as king of Jerusalem, despite being under excommunication by Pope Gregory IX. Without striking a blow he managed to obtain a treaty of ten years' duration; during that time he regained the city plus other territories connecting it to the coast.

Later, again due to the nobles' stupidity, they lost the city for the last time. In 1244 they decided to ally with the ruler of Damascus against the sultan of Egypt. In the resulting battle of Gaza they were deserted by their erstwhile ally and defeated by the great Mameluke general and future sultan, Bibars.

Seventh Crusade, 1248–54

Leader:
Louis IX (Saint Louis), king of France

Opponent:
Malik-al-Salih Najm al-din Ayyub, sultan of Egypt and Damascus

After the loss of Jerusalem in 1244, a new crusade was urged at the Council of Lyons in 1245. The nature of medieval politics is revealed in the promise of Pope Innocent IV to grant crusader status to all who would take up his cause, not only in the Holy Land, but more especially against Emperor Frederick II himself. Thus the papacy turned the concept of crusade to its own secular objectives.

Meanwhile, King Louis of France took up the cross. He moved to Cyprus in 1248 and in the spring of 1249 landed in Egypt. Again the crusaders succeeded in capturing Damietta and in marching as far as Mansura, where they were again defeated. This time the king was captured as well. After paying ransom and surrendering Damietta, he moved to Acre in 1250, where he remained for four years vainly seeking to enlist aid from Europe and to capture Jerusalem. Finally the death of his mother forced Louis to return to France in 1254.

Eighth Crusade, 1270–72

Leaders:
Louis IX (Saint Louis), king of France
Charles of Anjou, brother of Louis and king of Sicily
Edward, Prince of England

Opponents:
Bey of Tunis
Bibars, sultan of Egypt

The successes of Bibars in capturing Caesarea in 1265 and Antioch in 1268 led King Louis to consider another crusade. His brother, Charles of Anjou, meanwhile had supplanted the Hohenstaufen as king of Sicily and was planning crusades himself, to Constantinople as well as Jerusalem. Louis, however, had got the notion that the bey of Tunis might be converted; he decided to begin his crusade at that location before moving east. Charles did not like this idea, but was forced to forgo his own plans in order to support his brother. Prince Edward of England was also enlisted in the enterprise. No sooner had Louis landed in Africa than he fell sick and died. Charles successfully negotiated a favorable treaty from the bey for his own Sicilian kingdom. By the time Prince Edward arrived the war was over. He proceeded to Acre where he entered into unsuccessful negotiations with the Mongols in Persia in hopes of finding a military force capable of ousting the Mamelukes. He returned home in 1272, the last of the Western crusaders.

JOHN F. SLOAN

SEE ALSO: Byzantine Empire; History, Medieval Military; Saladin.

Bibliography

Brundage, J. A. 1964. *The Crusades: Motives and achievements.* Boston: D. C. Heath.
Contamine, P. 1984. *War in the Middle Ages.* Trans. M. Jones. London: Basil Blackwell.
Finucane, R. C. 1983. *Soldiers of the faith.* New York: St. Martin's Press.
Grousset, R. 1970. *The epic of the Crusades.* Trans. N. Lindsay. New York: Orion Press.
Heath, I. 1978. *Armies and enemies of the Crusades 1096–1291.* Sussex, England: Wargames Research Group.

Lamb, H. 1930. *The Crusades*. New York: Doubleday, Doran.
Runciman, S. 1964. *A history of the Crusades*. 3 vols. New York: Harper Torchbooks.
Wise, T. 1978. *The wars of the Crusades 1096–1291*. London: Osprey.

CUBAN MISSILE CRISIS

The Cuban missile crisis of October 1962 is the classic nuclear crisis. For thirteen days, President John F. Kennedy and Chairman Nikita Khrushchev contemplated choices that could have led to war, even nuclear war. At the time, Kennedy estimated the risks of war as "between one-in-three and even." Khrushchev spoke of "the smell of burning" in the air. Cloudy though it is, the missile crisis remains the best window available for scholars and policymakers who want to pursue questions about nuclear confrontation and superpower crisis management.

The missile crisis ranks among the most studied events of all time. About no analogous event is so much information available. This includes firsthand memoirs by participants, tens of thousands of pages of highly classified documents that have been made public, and even secret audio tapes of the most private deliberations at the top levels of the U.S. government during these events—all accessible during the lifetime of participants who can be cross-examined. While Soviet perceptions, motivations, and decision-making processes remain unclear, *glasnost* has made more information available, including interviews with Soviet participants, than scholars have had about any equivalent decisions of the Soviet government.

Answers to Ranke's question of "what really happened," whether in the missile crisis or elsewhere, do not depend solely on the evidence available. Conceptual frameworks that analysts bring to their inquiry, assumptions historians make, and categories they use in framing questions shape what are accepted as satisfactory answers. The missile crisis has provided fertile ground for competing arguments not only about the crisis itself, but also about larger questions of theories of foreign policy analysis and crisis management. These debates, however, are not likely to improve on President Kennedy's own conclusion about the missile crisis, namely, that the "ultimate decision remains impenetrable to the observer—often, indeed, to the decider himself . . . there will always be the dark and tangled stretches in the decision-making process—mysterious even to those who may be most intimately involved."

The Facts

The thirteen days of crisis began on 14 October 1962 when the United States discovered that the Soviet Union was in the midst of a secret attempt to deploy strategic nuclear missiles to Cuba. A U.S. high-altitude U-2 overflight of Cuba took photographs that provided clear evidence of an ambitious Soviet deployment of 48 medium-range ballistic missiles (MRBMs, range 1,100 nautical miles) and 24 intermediate-range ballistic missiles (IRBMs, range 2,200 nautical miles) at four separate sites in Cuba. The U.S. government's reaction was, in the words of the president's brother, Atty. Gen. Robert Kennedy, one of "shocked incredulity." Never before had the Soviet Union stationed nuclear weapons outside Soviet territory. Khrushchev had given Kennedy the most solemn private pledges that the Soviet Union would not undertake any such action. Relying on these assurances, Kennedy had rebutted charges made by Republican opponents in the midterm congressional elections by drawing a line that declared Soviet installation of significant offensive capabilities in Cuba, specifically including strategic missiles, "unacceptable."

Thus, from the outset, President Kennedy determined that the missiles must be removed. The question, then, was *how* the missiles could be eliminated without war. To assist him in assessing the predicament and fashioning a response, the president assembled his most trusted advisers as the Executive Committee (Excomm) of the National Security Council. Since the Soviet government was unaware that its clandestine initiative had been uncovered, the president and his advisers had the luxury of a week for private deliberation. In the beginning, the president and most of his advisers favored a direct air strike to destroy the missiles. After full analysis of the pros and cons of this and other options, Kennedy chose a naval quarantine of all Soviet arms shipments to Cuba as the initial response.

On Monday, 22 October, the president announced to the Soviet Union, the American public, and the world the U.S. discovery of the Soviet deception (Fig. 1) and the U.S. response with a naval quarantine. U.S. forces worldwide were raised to alert status. President Kennedy's speech warned the Soviet Union that any attack from Cuba would be met with a "full retaliatory re-

Figure 1. Low-altitude reconnaissance photo over Cuba showing 5 medium-range missiles on trailers, a missile-ready tent, and a number of fueling and checkout vehicles (October 1962). (SOURCE: U.S. Dept. of Air Force)

sponse." (In an initial private letter, Khrushchev assured Kennedy that the Soviet Union, not Cuba, had full control of the missiles in Cuba.)

There ensued a week of public and private bargaining. U.S. allies in Europe and Latin America supported the American position that the Soviet initiative was illegal and unacceptable, and that the missiles had to be withdrawn. The U.S. naval quarantine went into effect on Wednesday. Soviet ships tested the blockade. Ships carrying additional Soviet missiles, specifically the *Poltava*, approached the blockade line but then stopped. While U.S. intelligence was not certain of the presence of nuclear warheads on Cuba, the U.S. government had to act as if they were there. (By the late 1980s, Soviet sources had confirmed the presence of twenty nuclear warheads on the island.)

On Thursday, the U.S. government received a letter from the Soviet government proposing to withdraw the missiles in response to an American pledge not to invade Cuba. Before the United States was able to respond, a second letter arrived on Friday, raising the ante: U.S. missiles in Turkey were the price demanded for Soviet missiles in Cuba. The U.S. government responded to the first proposal, without reference to the second. U.S. officials argued both in the Excomm and publicly that the United States could not trade away missiles deployed for the defense of a North Atlantic Treaty Organization (NATO) ally in the context of a crisis. On Saturday, a Soviet surface-to-air missile (SAM) in Cuba shot down a U.S. U-2 flying over Cuba. Reversing a previous decision to retaliate against SAM sites that attacked U.S. forces, President Kennedy paused. Arguments in the Excomm became bitter. The president decided to communicate to Khrushchev a clear warning that unless he announced withdrawal of the missiles immediately, the United States would take unilateral action to eliminate them. Most members of the Excomm expected the president to authorize an air strike against the missiles in Cuba at the meeting scheduled for Sunday morning. Most of the participants anticipated a Soviet response against U.S. missiles in Turkey, or in Berlin, or elsewhere. Thus, as they left "Black Saturday," they wondered whether they would live to see another week. Some of the participants' families left Washington, D.C.

At 9:00 Sunday morning, Washington time, Chairman Khrushchev's announcement that the missiles would be withdrawn was broadcast live from Moscow.

The Context

The larger context in which these thirteen days occurred includes three ongoing competitions between the United States and the Soviet Union. The overriding competition was, of course, the cold war. Regaining the initiative in the cold war had, in effect, been Kennedy's principal theme in the presidential campaign of 1960. Attacking the Republican administration's complacency in meeting Soviet threats, Kennedy pointed to the "missile gap," the "space gap," and Soviet successes in the Caribbean and Southeast Asia. His inaugural speech as president sounded the trumpet, pledging that Americans would "pay any price, bear any burden . . . to assure the success of liberty."

Two weeks before Kennedy's own inauguration, Khrushchev announced that the Soviet Union would vigorously support "wars of national liberation." The Kennedy administration read this as a virtual declaration of war in the developing world. Fidel Castro's Cuba illustrated the subtlety of Soviet tactics. Having come to power in 1958 as a nonaligned revolutionary, Castro had increasingly allied himself with the Soviets, in a violation of the Monroe Doctrine. Like the Eisenhower administration before it, the Kennedy administration declared the Castro government "illegitimate." In April 1961, the Kennedy administration sponsored a halfhearted invasion of Cuba by 1,500 Cuban exiles directed by the CIA (the Bay of Pigs incident). This effort was decisively defeated by Castro. After first attempting to deny U.S. involvement, Kennedy accepted full responsibility for the failure. In the aftermath, U.S. covert actions against Castro increased significantly, including several attempts to assassinate him.

The third strand of the broader context was the competition for nuclear advantage. Through the 1950s, the United States maintained a significant nuclear superiority. This posture offset Soviet conventional advantages in Europe and provided the backdrop for the Eisenhower administration's doctrine of "massive retaliation." After the Soviet launch of Sputnik, Khrushchev touted massive increases in Soviet missile-launched nuclear capabilities. Kennedy targeted this emerging "missile gap" as a major issue in the 1960 presidential campaign: for the first time, the Soviet Union would exercise nuclear advantage over the United States.

After taking office, the administration soon learned that the Soviet Union had failed to exploit its potential to build missiles in the way Khrushchev had threatened. Nonetheless, the U.S. rapidly expanded its own deployment of nuclear weapons. By late 1961, the United States was deliberately communicating to the Soviet Union that the Soviets were on the short end of a missile gap. In fact, by late 1962, U.S. advantages were approaching a capacity for what has been called a "splendid first strike"—namely, an attack after which the Soviet Union could have been incapable of responding with a major attack on the United States. (During the crisis, the United States estimated that the Soviets had 75 operational intercontinental ballistic missiles [ICBMs]; subsequent U.S. estimates reduced this number to 44 operational launchers. More recent Soviet information indicates that the Soviet government may not have been confident of the capacity even of these 44 weapons.)

Central Questions

The central questions about the missile crisis are three: (1) Why did the Soviet Union deploy missiles in Cuba? (2) Why did the United States respond with the blockade? and (3) Why did the Soviet Union withdraw the missiles? Answers to each have been, and remain, a matter of continuing debate.

The issue of why the Soviet government had attempted such an unexpected and dangerous initiative arose at the first meeting of the Excomm. They identified five hypotheses: (1) bargaining barter—Khrushchev deployed the missiles as a chip that could be traded for U.S. missiles in Turkey, or Berlin, or something else; (2) diverting trap—if this lightning rod drew U.S. fire, the Soviet Union could take the occasion to move against Berlin (as it had moved against Hungary in 1956 while the world was diverted by the Franco-British action at Suez); (3) Cuban defense—fearing a follow-up to the abortive Bay of Pigs invasion, Moscow moved to assure the defense of its Cuban ally; (4) cold war politics—the missile crisis posed "the supreme probe of American intentions and resolve"; that is, if the United States failed to respond, U.S. cowardice would be exposed and the Soviet Union could act boldly elsewhere; (5) missile power— facing a real missile gap in terms of intercontinental strategic missiles, Moscow chose the only short-term fix available to redress its strategic nuclear inferiority.

The Excomm considered arguments for and against each of these hypotheses, examining specific evidence about the Soviet deployment. Thus, for example, the hypothesis of Cuban defense was rejected by the Excomm, and has generally been rejected by subsequent analyses, on the grounds that the Soviet Union could have achieved this objective more efficiently and at less risk without deploying strategic nuclear weapons. Soviet troops armed with conventional weapons would have sufficed. Certainly Cuban defense would not require IRBMs that threaten New York and Strategic Air Command (SAC) bases in Nebraska in addition to the MRBM threat against Washington.

Scholarly attempts to answer this question have pointed more broadly to the array of factors that must have influenced Soviet decision making. Yet even these analyses have tended to resolve the competing hypotheses with conclusions about "the objective" or "the primary objective" of the Soviet government—on the assumption that the various objectives of relevant individuals in the Soviet government can appropriately be summarized as if the Soviet government were a unitary rational actor.

Other scholars, employing different assumptions, have argued that individuals in the Soviet government must have been moved by different considerations: Khrushchev perhaps by his preoccupation with possible U.S. military action against Cuba; other members of the Politburo, spurred by the Soviet Strategic Rocket Forces, were more concerned about Soviet strategic inferiority. Evidence from the Soviet Union gives these analyses additional plausibility and color.

In his memoirs, Khrushchev states that his overriding concern was what he believed to be the impending American military invasion of Cuba. Other Soviet sources (including Sergei Mikoyan, on the basis of conversations with his father Anastas Mikoyan, at the time the first deputy premier) emphasize the following: Khrushchev's impulsiveness, which led him to make decisions without an adequate assessment of the risks; the origin of the idea during Khrushchev's visit to the Crimea where he was struck by equivalent U.S. deployments just across the Black Sea in Turkey; a real fear by Khrushchev and other Soviet leaders that a U.S. military invasion of Cuba was imminent; and a general concern about strategic nuclear inferiority. In the spirit of *glasnost*, Soviet participants in these events later offered accounts of the decision-making process from which the deployment emerged.

Why the United States chose to respond to Soviet missiles in Cuba with a blockade has generated less debate. The historical record shows that the Excomm considered options ranging from doing nothing to a major air strike and invasion. The explanation the U.S. government gave at the time for its choice has been widely accepted in subsequent analyses. Essentially, the argument is that the costs and risks of other alternatives simply exceeded those of the blockade. The blockade was a golden mean between inaction and aggression: firm enough to communicate determination but still not so precipitous as a strike. It placed on Khrushchev the burden of choice for the next step. It capitalized on U.S. naval superiority in the region and emphasized the advantages of U.S. conventional arms if further steps were required.

The general acceptance of this official explanation is a reminder of the three perils all historians face. First, it is no accident that the concepts of rationality, rationale, and rationalization have a common root. Had the U.S. government chosen a different option, it would have provided an explanation for that choice, emphasizing the benefits of an air strike or doing nothing versus the costs and risks of the other alternatives. Reasons given to explain and justify an action are not identical with causes. Second, after an episode, there is a powerful temptation for participants to adjust their positions and even their memories about their own views and about the merits of arguments at the time. As a result, the sharper edges of arguments are blunted. Third, after a decision that produces successful results, it becomes harder to visualize real, reasonable alternatives. The certainty of what was chosen and what occurred thus overwhelms the uncertainties the actors faced when making decisions.

Subsequent analyses have noted the number of additional causal factors that shaped the selection of the blockade. The fact that U.S. intelligence discovered the missiles during the process of deployment, rather than two weeks later, after deployment had been completed, provided the opportunity to choose an option like blockade. Had the missiles already been operational, such a choice would have been irrelevant. Similarly, while the costs and risks of any surgical air strike may have outweighed, on balance, the potential benefits, in this specific instance, the U.S. Air Force estimated that it would not be able to assure destruction of all Soviet missiles. That estimate, based upon standard U.S. Air Force estimating procedures, turned out to have mistakenly assumed that the Soviet missiles were "mobile." During the second week of the crisis, after this mistake was corrected, the option of a surgical air strike became live again as part of the deliberations. Similarly, finer-grained analyses give greater weight to the sharp differences among individual members of the Excomm. Robert Kennedy once observed, "The fourteen people involved were very significant. ... If six of them had been president of the U.S., I think that the world might have been blown up." Discounting exaggeration, one should nonetheless note differences among Secretary of Defense Robert McNamara, who judged the Soviet missiles of no military significance and was thus prepared to tolerate them; the presidential assistant for national security affairs McGeorge Bundy, who appears to have favored a private diplomatic approach to Khrushchev rather than risk a public confrontation; Robert Kennedy, who was impressed by the "Tojo analogy," unable to explain to himself or others how a great and good power could initiate a surprise air strike on a small island nation; and the former secretary of state Dean Acheson, who wrote: "As I saw it at the time, and still believe, the decision to resort to the blockade was a decision to postpone the issue at the expense of time within which the nuclear weapons might be made operational." Competing groups in the Excomm were labeled "hawks" and "doves," terms that entered the political vocabulary thereafter.

Explorations of why Khrushchev withdrew the missiles have tended to follow naturally from accounts of the merits of the blockade. The blockade signaled a willingness to use local nonnuclear forces but left open a "staircase of ascending steps in the use of force." In the background was overwhelming U.S. nuclear superiority. Having no real alternative, Khrushchev withdrew.

Competing analyses of the Soviet withdrawal of missiles reject the hypothesis that the blockade worked. They focus instead on the events of the final Saturday of the crisis and specifically on Kennedy's partially public and partially undisclosed decision to present Khrushchev with a combination of stick and carrot. The stick consisted of the threat to bomb the missiles if Khrushchev did not act immediately to remove them. The carrot was an arrangement that had both a public and a private clause. The public clause was a pledge not to invade Cuba or support invasions of Cuba. The private clause promised removal of U.S. missiles from Turkey after the crisis was successfully resolved. The private arrangement was known only to the president, his brother, the assistant for national security affairs, the secretary of defense, and the secretary of state. Denied by the U.S. government publicly, it was not even hinted to other members of the Excomm. Not until the twentieth anniversary of the crisis, after scholars had pointed to the likelihood of such an understanding, did those party to the private pledge acknowledge this arrangement.

Emerging Evidence

Evidence about the missile crisis has emerged in waves. The first was dominated by Kennedy administration officials. Both in press coverage, and then in memoirs that emerged shortly after the assassination of President Kennedy, the missile crisis was featured as his administration's "finest hour." Second, academic analyses of the crisis began appearing shortly thereafter, and have continued to do so at a steady rate. The missile crisis is one of the few historical episodes about which articles continue to appear in major foreign affairs journals. A third wave of evidence about the crisis consists of U.S. documents declassified after the Freedom of Information Act or provided to the presidential libraries. The National Security Archive in Washington has undertaken to index the thousands of pages of such documents. The secret audio tapes of Excomm meetings on three of the thirteen days of the crisis have now been transcribed and made available to the public, and the others are being transcribed by the JFK library. Finally, *glasnost* permitted Soviet participants in the crisis to begin to write and give interviews. Some Soviet historians reviewed relevant Soviet documents.

While statements by such individuals have provided clues to Soviet perceptions and motivations, the documentary evidence released so far is sparse, selective, and partial.

GRAHAM T. ALLISON, JR.

SEE ALSO: Cold War.

Bibliography

Abel, E. 1966. *The missile crisis.* Philadelphia: J. B. Lippincott.

Allison, G. T. 1971. *Essence of decision: Explaining the Cuban missile crisis.* Boston: Little, Brown.

Allison, G. T., and W. L. Ury, eds. 1989. *Windows of opportunity: From cold war to peaceful competition in U.S.-Soviet relations.* Cambridge, Mass.: Ballinger.

Blight, J. G., and D. A. Welch. 1989. *On the brink: Americans and Soviets reexamine the Cuban missile crisis.* New York: Farrar, Straus and Giroux.

Dinerstein, H. S. 1976. *The making of a missile crisis: October 1962.* Baltimore, Md.: Johns Hopkins Univ. Press.

Divine, R. A., ed. 1971. *The Cuban missile crisis* (collected essays). Chicago: Quadrangle.

Hilsman, R. 1967. *To move a nation: The politics of foreign policy in the administration of John F. Kennedy.* New York: Doubleday.

Kennedy, R. F. 1967. *Thirteen days: A memoir of the Cuban missile crisis.* New York: W. W. Norton.

Khrushchev, N. 1970. *Khrushchev remembers.* Boston: Little, Brown.

———. 1974. *Khrushchev remembers: Last testament.* Boston: Little, Brown.

Larson, T. 1978. *Soviet-American rivalry.* New York: W. W. Norton.

National Security Archives. 1988. *Preliminary catalogue of documents on the Cuban missile crisis.* Washington, D.C.: Government Printing Office.

Schlesinger, A. M., Jr. 1965. *A thousand days.* Boston: Houghton Mifflin.

Sorensen, T. 1965. *Kennedy.* New York: Harper and Row.

Tatu, M. 1969. *Power in the Kremlin.* New York: Viking Press.

Wohlstetter, A., and R. Wohlstetter. 1965. Controlling the risks in Cuba. *Adelphi Paper no. 17.* London: International Institute for Strategic Studies.

CUNNINGHAM, SIR ALAN G.
[1887–1983]

Gen. Sir Alan Gordon Cunningham served Great Britain with distinction in World War I and World War II and as the last British high commissioner of Palestine. He is most famous for his lightning campaign in spring 1941 that liberated Ethiopia and for the "Crusader" offensive he led in November of that year as the first commander of the British Eighth Army.

Early Career

Born in Dublin on 1 May 1887 to a prominent Scottish family he was the younger brother of Andrew Browne Cunningham, later admiral and Viscount Cunningham of Hyndhope. Cunningham graduated from the Royal Military

Academy and was commissioned in the Royal Artillery in 1906. His early career included an assignment in India, from which he returned at the outbreak of World War I. Arriving on the western front in 1915, Cunningham served there as a brigade major until the end of the war, having earned the Companion of the Distinguished Service Order (DSO) and the Military Cross (MC).

Although not a graduate of the Staff College, Cunningham held two staff appointments during the interwar period, the first in Singapore, the second at the Small Arms School at Netheravon from 1929 to 1931. After attending the Imperial Defense College in 1937, he served briefly as the commander of Royal Artillery of the 1st Division. Upon his promotion to major general in 1938, Cunningham took command of the 5th Anti-Aircraft Division. After the outbreak of war in 1939, he commanded, in succession, three different divisions stationed in England.

Campaigns in Ethiopia and the Western Desert

Cunningham's opportunity for a combat command came in November 1940 when he took command of all Commonwealth forces in Kenya. Consisting mostly of African troops and roughly equivalent to four brigades of infantry, his force was to be the southern pincer in the efforts by Gen. Archibald Percival Wavell to liberate Ethiopia.

Winston Churchill characterized Cunningham's conduct of the subsequent campaign as "daring and highly successful." Feigning an attack along the direct route from Nairobi to Addis Ababa, Cunningham's main effort drove along the coast into Italian Somaliland. After the capture of Mogadishu on 25 February, Cunningham turned inland and moved 1,130 kilometers (700 mi.) to the Ethiopian town of Jijiga in just seventeen days. Turning west, he next captured Addis Ababa, almost 800 kilometers (500 mi.) away, on 6 April. The Duke of Aosta, commander of Italian forces in Ethiopia, surrendered on 16 May 1941. In this brilliant campaign, Cunningham's soldiers advanced over 1,600 kilometers (1,000 mi.), averaging 56 kilometers (35 mi.) per day, captured 936,000 square kilometers (360,000 sq. mi.) of enemy-controlled territory, and took 50,000 prisoners at a cost of less than 500 casualties. For his efforts in Ethiopia, Cunningham was awarded the Knight Commander of the Bath.

Cunningham's conquest of Ethiopia, combined with simultaneous British disasters in the Western Desert, afforded him the opportunity to command a field army. Wavell's retreat across northern Libya to the Egyptian border in the spring of 1941 had allowed the Germans to besiege Tobruk. After several failures to retake that vital port, Wavell was relieved as commander in chief in the Middle East and replaced by Gen. Sir Claude Auchinleck. Auchinleck quickly reorganized Commonwealth forces in the Western Desert into the Eighth Army and appointed Cunningham its commander.

Taking command in August 1941, Cunningham's immediate concern was to ready his army for battle with Erwin Rommel and his Afrika Korps and then to undertake the relief of Tobruk sometime in November. It was a daunting task. The Eighth Army consisted of two corps (XXX and XIII), which between them had the equivalent of seven divisions. Cunningham had never commanded so large a force, and many of the units that were to take part in the upcoming campaign were not yet in Egypt. Moreover, he estimated that only two of the divisions were properly trained. The sheer vastness of the Western Desert also awed Cunningham, and he had but two months to become intimately familiar with the nature of the terrain and the environment. Finally, although battles in North Africa were typically dominated by tanks, he had never commanded armor, and he understood little about the nature of tank warfare. All of these factors did not bode well for Cunningham.

Opening on 18 November, Cunningham's attack, dubbed Operation Crusader, was initially successful. By dusk the next day the British spearhead had penetrated to within 16 kilometers (10 mi.) of the Italian lines that surrounded Tobruk. There the advance came to a halt. Initially fooled by the location and scope of the offensive, Rommel quickly recovered, and because of the qualitative superiority of his tanks and antitank guns, as well as his tactical genius, he successfully counterattacked and halted the British while raiding Cunningham's rear. At this point, Cunningham appears to have lost his nerve (Correlli Barnett argues that Cunningham was "a spent man" although he does not conclude, as some do, that he had a nervous breakdown [Barnett 1982]) and requested permission from Auchinleck that he be allowed to break off the action. Flying to the front to analyze the situation for himself, Auchinleck determined that Cunningham had become defensive-minded, relieved him of command of the Eighth Army, and sent him to a hospital in Alexandria.

Later Years

After his recovery, Cunningham was assigned first as the commandant of the Staff College, then as commander of troops in Northern Ireland, and finally, in 1944, as the commander of the Eastern Command in England. When Lord Gort, the British high commissioner in Palestine, fell ill in late 1945, Cunningham, now a general, was appointed to take his place. It was a job he held until 1948 and one that he performed well in the face of heightening tensions in that region. For his service there he received the Knight Grand Cross of St. Michael and St. George (KCMG), the last military commander to receive that award.

Having retired from the army in 1946, the end of the British mandate in Palestine effectively ended Cunningham's public career, although he served on the council of Cheltenham College from 1943 until 1961. General Cunningham died on 30 January 1983 at the age of 95.

DAVID JOHN FITZPATRICK

SEE ALSO: Rommel, Erwin; Wavell, Archibald Percival, 1st Earl; World War II.

Bibliography

Barnett, C. 1982. *The desert generals.* 2d ed. Bloomington, Ind.: Indiana Univ. Press.
Dupuy, R. E., and T. N. Dupuy. 1977. *The encyclopedia of military history.* New York: Harper and Row.

Esposito, V. 1959. *The West Point atlas of American wars.* Vol. 2. New York: Praeger.
Young, P. 1974. *Atlas of the Second World War.* New York: Berkley.

CUSTOMS AND ETIQUETTE

Customs and etiquette among members of the military community generally
serve much the same purpose as those followed in civilian life. They are the
"oil" that helps the military society and machine to function smoothly with
minimal friction.

The Salute

Perhaps the oldest and most ubiquitous military custom is that of the salute
(Fig. 1). Although most commonly given by hand, a salute can also be rendered
by guns, swords, banners, or music. Many writers have suggested that the hand

*Figure 1. "After the victory," a painting of Napoleon I, emperor
of the French, by Maurice Orange, 1912.* (SOURCE: U.S. Library
of Congress)

salute dates back to the time when man still lived in caves. When encountering a stranger, one could never be sure whether the approaching individual was friend or foe. A raised right arm, hand empty and extended, was a reliable indication of nonhostile intent.

The raised right arm salute was universally practiced by the Romans. Indeed, the English word *salute* is derived from the Latin word *salutare*, meaning "to greet." Before engaging in mortal combat in the arena, Roman gladiators would form before Caesar, and with upraised arm cry out: "Ave Caesare. Morituri te salutamus" ("We who are about to die greet you"). Other writers believe that the practice of raising the hand to the peak of the headdress originated in the age of chivalry. The theory goes that when armored knights met, they would raise the visors of their helmets both to enable mutual recognition and to convey the message that there was no hostile intent. On the other hand, given the inordinately heavy, uncomfortable, and clumsy full armor of the era, it is unlikely that knights would routinely ride about so attired (much less with the vision-restricting visor in place), unless prepared to engage in immediate battle.

Today, the salute is practiced by virtually all organized military forces. Customarily, the salute is not only rendered among members of the same nation's forces but also between members of friendly foreign nations—that is, countries with which we are not at war. There are, however, historical examples of prisoners of war saluting the officers of the capturing armies, for whom they had great respect (such was the case with Field Marshal Erwin Rommel). In effect, the salute has become a comradely greeting between fighting men who share common values, dangers, and ethics.

A fact sometimes overlooked is that it is not absolutely necessary that the salute be initiated by the junior, although many a junior officer has received a dressing-down for not recognizing that retired officers are still officers and entitled to all the courtesies of rank—including a salute. In the American armed forces, it is not improper for the senior to initiate the greeting. Even the most senior American officers will initiate a salute to a soldier of any rank wearing the Medal of Honor.

When a group of soldiers is engaged in outdoor work, the senior person in charge salutes for the detail while the others continue working. The same procedure is followed at athletic events. The participants continue the sport, the one in charge salutes.

Depending on national custom, a soldier carrying a rifle salutes by bringing either hand to some point of the rifle, depending on how the weapon is being held at the time. Since the rifle will normally be in the right hand, the salute is rendered with the left.

A salute can also be fired. Friendly foreign naval vessels are sometimes saluted with blank cannon fire, and heads of state and other dignitaries of friendly nations are also often greeted in this manner upon arrival. The custom supposedly started when ships and/or shore batteries would harmlessly discharge their cannon to show that they were now unloaded and there was no hostile intention. Usually, the maximum number of rounds is 21, although any number of guns may participate in a salute battery.

A final rifle salute is commonly fired over the grave of a fallen warrior. This appears to be not so much a tribute as the carrying on of the old superstition of frightening evil spirits away from the grave. Customarily, three volleys are fired by an honor guard.

While the wearing of swords has been relegated to ceremonial roles—usually by officers—in modern times, a salute is rendered with swords when they are carried unsheathed. In a parade, unit banners, guidons, and unit flags are customarily "dipped" before reviewing dignitaries and officials. The national colors or standards of the United States, however, are *never* lowered or dropped, although this custom is not universal in all armies. Salutes may also be rendered musically, not only by full bands but also by bugles, drum rolls, bagpipes, or other suitable instruments. All have the effect of calling attention to the importance of the occasion or the personage being honored. Some of these ceremonies can be extremely elaborate and instill great pride.

Banners

Perhaps the second oldest custom is that of unit banners. General Sir John Hackett traces the usage to Roman times. Their purpose was originally for ease of unit identification, but they also became symbols of unit identity, cohesion, and pride. For a unit to lose its colors ranks among the most shameful of events, and captured colors are displayed with great pride by the captors. In bygone years, the "color sergeant" was a position of great honor and responsibility. In battle, he was the one entrusted with safeguarding the unit's colors. When flown with national colors, unit colors are always in a subordinate position—that is, to the left, or below. National colors are normally escorted by an honor guard armed with rifles, pistols, or sabers.

Etiquette

Several present-day customs derive from the days when the primary weapon was the sword. A gentleman always walked on the right of a lady so that his sword arm (presumably his right arm) was free to draw the sword in the event of danger. Even today, the senior officer is always on the right. There is a slightly "tricky" variation of this having to do with entering and exiting automobiles, aircraft, and ships. Here, the junior officer enters first. This is to allow the senior officer the place next to the exit so that he can exit first.

Good manners are quite prevalent in the military. One rises when a senior officer enters the room, as one does when a lady enters. At social functions, it is expected that the junior officers will seek out the seniors and initiate conversation. Ranking persons and ladies are not left alone and unattended. Unless the subject is introduced by the senior officer, the junior is well advised to avoid "shop talk." Nor should one monopolize the senior officer, unless of course he or she should request that the junior remain as part of the conversation.

Guests of whatever rank should receive much the same courtesies as senior officers. Each nation has its own protocol for equating status. In the United

States Army, for example, a bishop receives the same courtesies as does a major general.

Dinners and banquets may hold special significance, requiring strict observances of customs and formalities. Once at table, with colors (if present) having been honored and posted, one or more toasts are often proposed. The origin of this custom is obscure, but it is thought to derive from an ancient ritual of dipping bread (a "toast") into the wine goblet before consuming it. The first toast is always to the head of state or the sovereign. At multinational functions, a number of toasts may be drunk to various national leaders or to senior military personnel. (This in no way implies the consumption of great quantities of alcohol since one need only take a small sip at each toast.) Toasts, with rare exceptions having to do with special occasions, are always made standing. In affairs of purely national character, toasts such as "to the ladies" or "to the regiment" are often proposed, usually by the senior officer present. After introductory remarks, dinner is served.

At dinner one is expected to converse with those on the right, left, and across. To ignore anyone close is a serious breach of courtesy. Even in a multinational setting where languages may differ, one is still expected to make a proper effort at friendly communication. Toward the end of the dinner there may be speakers.

A particularly stylized function, found primarily in the British armed forces, is called a "dining-in." Normally these events include only military personnel. Spouses are rarely, if ever, included; civil dignitaries are infrequently invited unless being honored or speaking.

Rank and Insignia

Several points are perhaps worthy of special attention. There are certain commonalities as to insignia of rank among the forces of most countries, naval rank possibly being the most universally accepted by means of gold braid—half and full bands—on the sleeve of a blue coat. These are often replicated on the shoulder boards worn with coat or shirt. Some navies have adopted miniature versions of the ground forces insignia and they are worn on the shirt collar when appropriate.

Titles of rank differ considerably, though the designation "captain" is widely used. The U.S. Navy, like those of other former British colonies, favors the use of most of the British ranks (this applies in all services with few exceptions). A number of Latin American navies have adopted the rather interesting custom of inserting the title of "captain" into two lesser ranks. Thus the fourth rank "up" is Capitan Corvetta, the fifth Capitan Frigata, and finally Capitan Naval, which corresponds to the Western European and American titles.

The most common land force rank insignia for officers is a single small mark— square, lozenge, or circle—called a "pip" in the British army and those of its Commonwealth affiliates and former colonies. Thus one, two, and three pips refer to officer ranks one, two, and three, respectively. Above that level, pips are still used but are either larger, more impressive, or in other ways more distinctive, or they may have the addition of another device identifying fourth and sixth rank, as is done in the Bundeswehr of the FRG.

Except as noted, the armies of the Western Hemisphere and parts of Asia favor other systems, perhaps of a more symbolic nature. In the Republic of Korea, for example, one, two, and three diamond-shaped metal pins denote officer ranks one (second lieutenant), two (first lieutenant), and three (captain). Field-grade officers wear one, two, or three small insignia in the form of the Korean national flower; generals wear the requisite number of stars. These insignia are symbolic in that the diamond is valuable and found in the ground, the flower is more important because it is found above the ground (over the diamond), and the stars are most important because they are found above both the diamond and the flower.

The U.S. Army uses similar symbolism: gold and silver bars (below ground but of great value), oak leaves (much higher and denoting great wisdom) eagles (soar above the trees and are a symbol of great power), and stars (above the eagle). As a sidenote to the American system, it is interesting to note that silver insignia "outrank" the gold: that is, second lieutenants wear a single gold bar, while first lieutenants wear a silver bar, and captains two silver bars. Majors wear a gold oak leaf, while lieutenant colonels wear a silver one; general's stars are silver. This arrangement came about as a result of officer uniforms during the Civil War era. Second lieutenants wore plain, gold-trimmed shoulder boards on their jackets. First lieutenants had a small silver bar on the board, which provided a nice contrast. Field-grade officers wore gold shoulder boards with tassels. A major simply wore the board. A lieutenant colonel wore a silver oak leaf on his board. Later, when the cumbersome boards were phased out on all but dress uniforms, something was needed to identify the second lieutenant and the major: the gold devices were selected.

In dealing with rank, the question frequently arises as to the apparent inconsistency in titles for general officers. Up to a point, the order seems quite logical: colonel general (in forces that have them; the United States does not), outranks a lieutenant general, yet the lieutenant general outranks a major general. This is a vestige of history. Originally, the title in full was sergeant major general, who of course would be outranked by the lieutenant general.

Another point of interest is the distinction between the titles brigadier and brigadier general. In the American military, the brigadier general is, in fact, a general officer entitled to all honors and privileges due that distinguished company. In the British forces and many that have adopted the British system of titles, however, brigadier is the senior field officer rank; he is not a general officer, nor is he accorded such honors.

Particularly in European armies, one finds the rank of field marshal. Other armies, such as that of the United States, use no such title, at least in peacetime. However, in order to assure consistency, during World War II the United States adopted the rank of general of the army, a five-star rank equal to field marshal.

In the enlisted grades, titles of rank become far more complex. In general, sergeant major would be the senior grade. Below this, however, are a plethora of titles and grades. To complicate matters further, in some armies titles, grades, and insignia of grade change with some frequency. Thus, in the U.S. Army, between the end of World War II and the 1960s, the number of enlisted grades increased from seven to nine, "corporal" was abolished then restored, and "T" (technician) grades were abolished then replaced with distinctive "non-combat" insignia that were replaced with "specialist" insignia. Concurrently, enlisted grades eight and nine were established, which provided greater pay for first sergeants and sergeants-major, respectively, whereas previously these were the same as the grade seven master sergeant. The other U.S. armed forces have also adopted nine pay grades, but with different titles. In a few forces, certain senior grades of noncommissioned officers are saluted.

Distinctive Uniforms and Customs

The uniform is a relatively modern convenience. Gen. Sir John Hackett, in his authoritative *The Profession of Arms* (1983), places the advent of uniforms to the era of Louis XIV. But beyond general commonalities within forces, there is a rich and proud tradition of unit customs, dress, and courtesies. Many units have achieved such distinction of valor in battle that they are entitled to special uniforms or accouterments. One of the oldest of these, practiced only by certain Scottish and Greek units, is the wearing of the kilt, or skirt. Scotsmen so attired won the respect of their German enemy, who nicknamed them "the ladies from Hades," during the First World War. In World War II, American paratroopers were similarly honored by the Germans, who called them "devils in baggy pants." The beret is frequently used as a distinctive head covering in elite units or those that have distinguished themselves in some manner. Other distinctions include unit shoulder patches, regimental crests, and other heraldic emblems.

A number of British units still wear distinctive bearskin hats, although reserved for ceremonial functions, while others, such as the First Life Guards, wear the chromed Roman-styled helmet, sometimes with a high bear-fur plume.

Naval Customs and Traditions

Navies, because of the nature of their environment, have had a long and colorful history of traditions, customs, and etiquette, harkening back to the days of sail. Sailing a fully rigged ship was no easy job. The trim of the sails needed to be changed according to the winds, tide, and course, and this required a sizable number of hands. Voice commands and instructions, some of which would be somewhat lengthy, would be difficult if not impossible to understand under conditions of wind, sea, and/or battle. To alleviate this problem, the boatswain's pipe was developed as a communication device to transmit commands or orders regarding the sails. Its high-pitched sound carried far enough and remained loud enough to be heard under adverse conditions. The fact that it was also musical lent itself to transmitting a great number of possible orders; in a word, it was a highly flexible tool under shipboard conditions.

Later, as navies became more professional and organized, the pipe was used to honor senior dignitaries in and out of uniform, thus the custom of "piping aboard."

In the U.S. Navy at least, if not in many others as well, the tradition remains that individuals of importance are announced when boarding or departing ship. Since the captain and his ship are almost universally considered a single entity among seafaring men, when he boards any ship he is announced as "Nelson boarding" if the name of the ship he commands is the *Nelson*, for example. The custom holds for commanders of groups of ships as well. Thus an admiral commanding, for instance, an entity called the North Atlantic Battle Fleet would be announced as "North Atlantic Battle Fleet boarding." If a ranking officer who is not the commander of a ship boards, he is announced as "Captain so-and-so boarding." A staff flag officer would also be announced as "Admiral so-and-so boarding."

The strong bonds among sailors who share the same rigors and the rather lonely life at sea have brought about many other traditions and courtesies. For example, when ships meet in passing, the junior commander always honors the senior. This is a custom followed not only within a nation's navy but is a courtesy exchanged between ships of friendly foreign powers as well.

A daily "ration" of rum or some other alcoholic drink is also customary in many navies. The British navy still quaffs its daily ration of "Nelson's blood," but the U.S. Navy no longer receives any alcoholic ration. In fact, in the U.S. Navy, alcoholic beverages may not be brought aboard ship.

At sea, the bridge is the ship's command post when under way, while the quarterdeck serves this function at anchor. One enters only with permission of the ship's captain. To enter uninvited would be a gross breach of courtesy, if not discipline. In many navies, officers below the rank of commander (fifth grade up in rank) are addressed informally as "mister." Written and formal verbal communications are, of course, addressed to rank. Chief petty officers are informally addressed as simply "chief," but as with junior officers, formal address is to grade.

When boarding or departing a ship, one is expected to salute the quarterdeck. This is an ancient custom from times when a pagan altar was carried on ships to appease the gods. Later, in the Christian era, ships displayed a crucifix there, and so the custom has survived.

Navies tend to have a language all their own. Under conditions of darkness and low or restricted visibility, approaching craft are sometimes "hailed," something akin to a sentry on land giving a challenge. The cry is "Boat ahoy?" rather than the landlubbers' "Who's there?" Examples of proper responses include: "Aye, aye" (a commissioned officer), "No, no" (a warrant officer), "Hello" (an enlisted grade), name of the ship if it is the commanding officer, or the name of the command if it is the commander. Navies have a tremendous store of customs and terms, with which those not belonging are normally unacquainted. Nonnaval personnel who expect to board or serve aboard should learn basic vocabulary and customs.

Air Force Traditions

Air forces in most nations are ordinarily the junior service, being, in most cases, the last to be formed. Those air services that sprang from the army tend to retain most fundamental army etiquette and customs. However, in the relatively brief existence of air forces, rich traditions have developed. Perhaps adopted from the navy, when an aircraft is to be abandoned the pilot is the last to leave. A highly emotional tribute to a deceased aviator is the flying over of the "missing man" formation—a normal formation but with a wingman missing. Certainly many more service-specific customs will develop with time.

Miscellaneous Customs and Traditions

Customs vary from nation to nation. Some Latin American countries, for example Ecuador, let a senior officer without an assignment stay at home without any particular duties. He bears, then, the title Coronel en Casa, literally "Colonel at Home." Such an individual expects to be given an active assignment as circumstances warrant. In the U.S. Army, five-star generals are never considered retired; they remain on the active list until death. For other ranks, it is not uncommon for retired officers to be recalled for limited purposes, such as serving on various boards or performing specific assignments of relatively brief duration in which they have requisite expertise. Naturally, in an all-out war, retired status holds little meaning.

The British army, while strictly observing tradition, on occasion will end an evening with a variety of "games," which can include rough physical contact as a "manly" pastime. One fortunate enough to be invited to a dining-in of another nation's forces would be well advised to familiarize himself with the proper dress and protocol. A well-run dining-in can be a memorable experience.

In the American as well as many Western European field artillery units, St. Barbara's Day, which falls on 4 December, may be celebrated. St. Barbara is traditionally the patron saint of artillerymen.

A custom that is on the wane, due to the availability of loud-speaker communication, is that of bugle calls. The bugle seems to be almost as old as warfare itself. Before the era of modern communications, the bugle call was often the only communication possible in battle. Its sound could be heard over distances far greater than that of the human voice, and the "tune" itself could carry orders. With the great troop dispersions and deafening noise of modern battle, however, the usefulness of the bugle has long since passed. Still, many military installations continue the custom, broadcasting either "live" or taped bugle calls for day-to-day operations. Few events will evoke greater emotion in "old" soldiers than hearing "taps," "charge," or "to the colors." The armies of the People's Republic of China used bugle calls to considerable effect during the Korean War.

A custom that can cause confusion is the rank referred to as warrant officer. In U.S. forces, warrant officers hold the same status as officers and are entitled to the salute. But in the forces of the United Kingdom, they are senior non-commissioned officers. In Canadian forces, they hold much the same status as in the U.S. military. In general, warrant officers are specialists in technical fields such as administration, supply, maintenance, medicine, aviation, and so on. "Mister" is probably the most common form of address for warrant officers.

An interesting religious custom is adhered to by many navies and air forces, especially in Portugal, Spain, France, Italy, and several other European nations with strong Catholic backgrounds. One of the three chapels in the shrine of Our Lady of Lourdes in southern France is almost a military museum. Crews of fighting ships and aircraft have dedicated themselves to Our Lady of Lourdes and have hung magnificently detailed, and often large, models of their ships and planes in this chapel. The shrine is also the location of an annual three-day pilgrimage by Catholic military, especially those in the army, of nearly every country in Western Europe. American forces have also participated. It is literally an international military encampment.

For many centuries, a French contribution that has enjoyed a measure of popularity in and out of France has been the *nom de guerre,* or "wartime name." The *nom* is an alias, in some cases blatantly so—for example, "Beau-visage" ("handsome"). The custom seems to have been especially prevalent in the Foreign Legion, in which enlistments of criminals and deserters was common; or they may simply wish anonymity for some personal reason. The custom further dictated that one retained the name until he disgraced himself in battle, at which time he lost the name.

Among the odder customs are those that show particular esprit de corps. The Italian Bersaglieri, proud of their traditionally extraordinary physical fitness and stamina, always parade at a trot. The French Foreign Legion is also rich in its own traditions and customs. Certain men in each unit who have been killed in battle are singled out as heroes. At unit roll calls their names are still called and answered "present."

Customs that seem virtually universal include the arch of swords or sabers at military weddings and the wearing of awards and decorations. Both spring from very old heritage. The former is from the time when groom's "men" were pledged to protect the wedded couple from harm, the saber arch symbolizing this protective commitment. The latter originated during the Crusades when knights wore their badges of honor over their hearts, further protected by the shield usually carried by the left arm. Thus the high value placed upon these badges was clearly demonstrated.

Conclusion

All this barely dents the treasure trove of these customs and can only provide a most basic familiarity. There are any number of publications that deal with these subjects in much greater length and detail, both for the arms or services, as well as the nationalities.

JOHN F. GERACI

SEE ALSO: Flags and Symbols; Uniforms and Accouterments.

Bibliography

The air force officer's guide. Annual. Harrisburg, Pa.: Stackpole Books.

Hackett, J. 1983. *The profession of arms*. New York: Macmillan.

Melagari, V. 1972. *The world's great regiments*. London: Hamlyn.

Perret, G. 1989. *A country made by war*. New York: Random House.

Service etiquette. 1988. 4th ed. Annapolis, Md.: U.S. Naval Institute Press.

D

DECORATIONS, HONORARY ORDERS, AND AWARDS

Awards for gallantry or service have been presented for as long as nations have been fighting each other. History does not record when decorations or medals first appeared, but it is known that the ancient Greeks rewarded their heroes with crowns of laurel leaves in addition to arms or armor. Some modern medals and decorations still include laurel wreaths in their designs. The Egyptians and Romans awarded special plaques of gold or silver to soldiers on the battlefield. The Romans were fairly liberal in awarding decorations, which were in the form of necklaces, armbands, and ornamental bosses worn on the soldier's breastplate. Some decorations were attached to the harness of horses in much the same manner as horse brasses are used today. One high honor was for saving a comrade's life, while another—the mural crown—went to the first man to reach the top of the wall of a besieged town. Some honors were limited to certain ranks, such as the silver spearshaft that went only to officers.

The terms *decoration* or *medal* may have different meanings depending on who is using them. A decoration is usually given for a specific act of gallantry or military service, and the decoration itself is often in the form of a cross, star, sunburst, or other distinctive shape. A medal is awarded for a variety of services—for example, participating in designated wars, campaigns, or expeditions or performing services in support of combat activities. A medal is often in the form of a disk, such as the U.S. Army's Good Conduct Medal, and is usually a slightly lower level of honor than a decoration. To make things even more confusing, decorations may have the word *medal* in their titles, such as the United States's Medal of Honor or Distinguished Service Medal, or the French Military Medal (*Medaille militaire*).

Another form of honor is the honorary "order," the badge or insignia of a group in which membership is an honor (Fig. 1). Some orders might trace their histories to knights who fought in the Crusades or to societies founded by kings and emperors hundreds of years ago. Among the more famous orders are the English Order of the Garter, the British Distinguished Service Order, the French Legion of Honor, and the Order of St. John of Jerusalem.

Decorations and Medals

While the Romans and the nations that came after them honored their heroes with various decorations, badges, orders, titles, and distinctions throughout the centuries, the beginnings of medals and decorations as we understand them today came in the mid-nineteenth century when the British started giving decorations in the form of medals of a standard design to all officers and men. Before that, commemorative medals had been struck for specific victories but were usually awarded only to the highest officers. The British Victoria Cross, instituted in 1856, was among the first awards for gallantry open to all ranks of the army. Other European nations and the United States soon developed their own awards. As awards evolved, there came to be four general types: decorations for valor in combat, medals for being in a campaign, medals for services not directly involved with combat, and medals for long service.

The numbers and types of decorations and medals have multiplied many times since the late nineteenth century as the various nations issued metal and enamel crosses, stars, sunbursts, disks, shields, hearts, and other shapes to honor gallantry or service. Many are suspended from a colorful ribbon that is worn by itself when it is not appropriate to wear the entire decoration. Sometimes rosettes are worn instead of the decoration, especially on civilian clothes.

A description of each decoration and medal would require an encyclopedia by itself, so this article is limited to a selection of the better known.

Queen Victoria established the British Victoria Cross (V.C.) in 1856, perhaps on the suggestion of her Prince Consort. She presented the first 62 crosses to veterans of the Crimean War in June 1857. The decoration was a pattée cross made from bronze taken from a cannon captured at Sebastopol. Since then, almost 1,300 British soldiers, officers, and enlisted men have received the honor. The supply of bronze from captured cannons ran out years ago, but the V.C. remains the nation's highest and most prized decoration. The second highest British decoration for gallantry for all services is also considered an "order of chivalry"—the Distinguished Service Order (DSO).

The three British armed services use crosses to honor acts of gallantry by junior officers that do not quite merit the V.C. The navy's Conspicuous Service Cross, started in 1901, became the Distinguished Service Cross in 1914. The army's Military Cross also began in 1914. The Royal Air Force's Distinguished Flying Cross was instituted in 1918 when the RAF became a separate service. The Air Force Cross, also from 1918, honors bravery in the air that does not involve active operations against an enemy.

Gallantry medals for British enlisted men also came about during World War I. The Distinguished Service Medal for petty officers and seamen started in 1914, followed by the Military Medal for the Army in 1916. The Distinguished Flying Medal and Air Force Medal for enlisted men were also instituted in 1918.

King George VI established the George Cross in 1940 as a civilian counterpart to the DSO. It honors acts of bravery for which military awards are not strictly applicable. The George Cross has, for example, been awarded to soldiers doing bomb disposal work where the enemy was not present and to agents behind enemy lines. An entire nation was honored with the George Cross during World War II when it was presented to the people of Malta for defending their island.

France's Military Medal (*Medaille militaire*) was instituted in 1852. It goes to enlisted men for gallantry in action and sometimes to high-ranking officers (generals and admirals who commanded major forces) for distinguished service in wartime. The War Cross (*Croix de Guerre*) was introduced in 1915 and was awarded to officers and enlisted members of the armed forces. Thousands of the War Cross were awarded during the two world wars, making it the most famous of the French decorations. It can be worn with a variety of emblems on its ribbon—ranging from star to laurel branches, depending on the reason for the award. In 1956 the French established the Cross of Military Valor for peacetime operations.

The former Soviet Union's Order of the Red Banner was instituted in 1924 and awarded in large numbers for service during the Revolution, Civil War of 1919–23, and World War II. It was also pinned on the officers who shot down the U.S. U-2 spy plane in 1960.

Perhaps the best known of the Soviet decorations, the gold star of Hero of the Soviet Union, was instituted in 1934 to honor outstanding services to the nation and gallantry in action. It was the star seen often on the suits of Soviet leaders. In World War II, 11,066 stars went to Soviet soldiers for bravery in action. When a Hero of the Soviet Union received a second star, he or she also received the Order of Lenin. In addition, a bust of the recipient was placed in a position of honor in the person's hometown. A third award included a bronze bust of the recipient displayed in the Palace of the Soviets in the Kremlin.

Among the most recognizable decorations in the world is the German Iron Cross. Prussia's King William III instituted the Iron Cross in 1813 and awarded it for gallantry in the last years of the Napoleonic Wars. It had two classes: the first pinned directly on the uniform, the second hanging from a ribbon pinned to the wearer's tunic. The Iron Cross was also awarded during the Franco-Prussian War and World War I. Between 1813 and 1918, some three-quarters of a million German soldiers received Iron Crosses. In 1939, the Iron Cross was again awarded in such vast numbers that just about every German soldier and, subsequently, thousands of souvenir hunters got one or more. Today, the once-proud decoration is a common item at flea markets, gun shows, and collectors' fairs.

The top U.S. decoration, the Medal of Honor, began during the American Civil War. The navy version dates from December 1861 while the army's is from July 1862. It was apparently intended to be awarded only during that war, but it remained in use for minor conflicts afterwards as well as the wars of the twentieth century. The United States Air Force used the army version of the Medal of Honor until its own design became available in 1965.

New decorations came about in 1918 to honor service in World War I. Among them were the Distinguished Service Cross (roughly equivalent to the British DSO), the Navy Cross, and the army and navy Distinguished Service medals. These remain in use as does the Distinguished Flying Cross, which was established in 1926 to recognize heroism in the air, and the Soldier's Medal for bravery not in the face of the enemy.

The Silver Star started in World War I as a tiny star on the ribbon of the Victory Medal for either gallantry in action or for a wound received in action. This caused some confusion but helped bring about the establishment in 1932 of the current Silver Star and Purple Heart decorations.

The Purple Heart was established in 1932 to be awarded only to those wounded in action while serving with the U.S. armed forces. It is the traditional descendant of the nation's first decoration for bravery, the Badge of Military Merit, established in 1782 by Gen. George Washington and apparently awarded only three times (Fig. 1). That badge was a purple heart of cloth worn over the left breast on the uniform coat. General Washington might have chosen the color purple because of the wood used in certain gun carriages. The wood, called purpleheart, is a smooth-grained wood of a rich plum color from South America. Military engineers in Washington's time believed it to be the best wood in the world for gun carriages and mortar beds because it could withstand violent stress better than oak or any other available wood, thus providing sturdy and reliable support for the guns. Perhaps Washington wanted everyone to see the recipients of the new decoration as sturdy and reliable soldiers. The Badge of Military Merit was a high decoration for valor, not for wounds. It might even be considered the forerunner of the Medal of Honor.

Honorary Orders

Honorary orders have the most colorful histories of all the honors since some are connected with the orders of chivalry that originated in the Middle Ages, when knights in armor fought in the Crusades, in the wars among European

Figure 1. Orders from a variety of countries. (SOURCE: Iconographic Encyclopaedia)

princes, or in tournaments. This period also gave us the many stories and legends of such heroes as Roland and his companions, King Arthur and his knights of the round table, Richard the Lionheart, Robin Hood, and the Black Prince. (The "real" King Arthur, of course, lived several hundred years before the Middle Ages, but stories about him are often set in that period.) The medieval orders were select bands of knights pledged to serve their king or a religious ideal. Membership was a great honor open to a select few as a reward for service or as a result of family connections. Although many of the orders disappeared as feudalism declined, their memories remained to appear again in later centuries.

The insignia or badge of the medieval orders was usually very simple—a cross or perhaps an animal. Some orders had no special insignia; membership was what counted. The elaborate systems of insignia now associated with the orders started around the sixteenth century. The orders had only one class until 1802 when Napoleon established the French Legion of Honor in five classes. Most orders now have several classes. Each successive higher class has a more ornate badge and sometimes ribbons, chains, robes, shields, uniforms, and such special clothes as knee breeches, silk stockings, and hats.

Orders can be divided into three general groups: the religious-military orders, such as the Order of St. John of Jerusalem (perhaps better known as the Knights of Malta); dynastic orders of royal houses, such as the Order of the Garter; and national orders of merit, which are the most common and often are actually decorations.

The most famous of the orders is the British Order of the Garter founded in 1348 by King Edward III. The name is said to come from the king's helping a lady who lost her garter during a dance. To save the lady the embarrassment of having to pick up her garter, the king retrieved it and tied it around his leg, commenting "evil to him who evil thinks" (*honi soit qui mal y pense*). This strange incident somehow led to the very exclusive order of knighthood consisting of the king and 26 knights whose main insignia is a garter embroidered with King Edward's comment. Today, the Order of the Garter includes an elaborate uniform and a badge, called the George, that features an enameled figure of St. George and the dragon. For other than special occasions, members wear an eight-pointed star of silver showing the red cross of St. George surrounded by the garter and motto.

Another order, the Most Ancient and Most Noble Order of the Thistle, was founded by the King of the Scots in 787, but it died out only to be revived in 1687 by King James II of England (James VII of Scotland). It consists of the sovereign and sixteen knights. King George III founded the Most Illustrious Order of St. Patrick in 1783 and limited it to the sovereign, the Lord Lieutenant of Ireland, and 22 knights. Both orders have elaborate insignia.

The Most Honourable Order of the Bath dates from 1399. Its name honors the ritual bath candidate knights underwent to ensure purity before getting their insignia. A bath was a rare event in those days. The order became dormant—perhaps because the nobles felt a bath was too great a sacrifice—until revived in 1725 by King George I. Until the Battle of Waterloo, it was given only to high officers for distinguished war service. Afterward, it was expanded to three classes: Knights Grand Cross (GCB), Knights Commander (KCB), and Companions (CB). After 1847, civilians could also receive the Order of the Bath. Recipients, however, are no longer required to take a bath.

King George III founded the Most Distinguished Order of St. Michael and St. George in 1818 to reward citizens of the Ionian Islands that became British possessions during the Napoleonic Wars. In 1859, the islands became part of Greece, but the British kept the order to honor their subjects for service overseas. The order has three classes: Knights Grand Cross (GCMG), Knights Commander (KCMG), and Companions (CMG). The initials brought about the joke that the holders of the order could say they meant "God calls me God," "Kindly call me God," and "Call me God."

As noted above, the DSO, while a decoration for valor, is also a highly honored order of chivalry. The most common of the British orders of chivalry is the Most Excellent Order of the British Empire established in 1917 by King George V. It features both military and civil divisions, with five classes in each division and is open to both men and women.

One of the most famous of the medieval orders was the Golden Fleece, which is still used by Spain. Its emblem is a golden sheepskin suspended from the recipient's neck. The order was founded by the Duke of Burgundy in 1430 to celebrate his marriage. The duke might have been thinking of the Greek myth of Jason and the Argonauts, who went on a perilous journey to find the golden fleece. On a more prosaic level, the duke might have chosen fleece because his fortune came from the wool trade. In 1477, the Golden Fleece became the main order of knighthood in Austria after the marriage of Mary of Burgundy to Maximilian of Austria. When their son, Philip, became King of Castile in 1504, he established the Spanish branch of the order, which still survives. It is given to members of the royal family, heads of state, and other nobles. When Gen. Francisco Franco came to power in Spain, he founded the Imperial Order of the Yoke and Arrows to replace the Golden Fleece as the top Spanish honor. The colorful award is based on an ancient emblem of the arrows that freed Spain from the yoke of the Moors.

An order famous mostly for its unusual shape is Denmark's Order of the Elephant, which dates from 1462. Its badge is a golden elephant enameled in white with gold tusks and blue trappings. On one side is a diamond cross. On its back is a red-bricked enamel tower decorated with diamonds. On its head is a rider armed with a gold spear. The badge is said to be a favorite of its recipients' children. It is presented to kings, princes, and heads of state.

Czarist Russia had several orders whose insignia featured stars and jewels, but these were abolished in 1917 except for the Order of St. George, founded in 1769 for bravery. The Communists turned the Order of St. George into the Soviet Order of Glory, retaining the czarist order's orange and black ribbon.

The Soviet Union awarded several orders, but these were actually decorations for gallantry. The highest was the Order of Victory, established in 1943. Others were named for military and naval heroes of the past: Aleksandr Suvorov, Ushakov, Mikhail Kutuzov, and Paul S. Nakhimov. In 1942, the Soviets resurrected the Czarist Order of Alexander Nevsky but added a hammer and sickle to the badge to make certain nobody got the wrong idea.

Germany's Order of Merit (*Pour le mérite*) started in 1667 as Brandenburg's Order of Generosity. In 1740, Frederick the Great of Prussia renamed it and used it primarily as a decoration for valor—its main use until the end of the German Empire in 1918. In 1951, the Federal Republic of Germany established a new Order for Merit in eight classes for science and literature.

The pre-1918 Order for Merit is perhaps best known by its nickname "The Blue Max" made famous by a popular novel and movie in the mid-1960s. The source of the "blue" part of the name is obvious since the decoration is a blue Maltese cross. The "max" part, however, is subject to various stories. One story has it honoring World War I fighter pilot Max Immelmann because the decoration's blue enamel reflected on his pale, war-weary face making him the real Blue Max. Somehow, according to the story, the nickname attached itself to the award. Another story says Max was a disparaging nickname for Frederick the Great, used only behind his back. Some Prussian officers who resented Frederick's giving a French name to his highest honor also used his nickname for the award. A third and somewhat more logical story is that "max" is short for "maximum," which means the same in German as it does in English. The Blue Max, therefore, was Prussia's maximum or highest decoration.

Napoleon founded the French Legion of Honor (*Légion d'honneur*) in 1802 to recognize bravery in action, twenty years distinguished military service, or civilian service in peacetime. It was the only French award for gallantry until 1852 when the Military Medal came into being. Napoleon began the practice of dividing orders into several classes—the Legion of Honor has five—a practice adopted by many other nations. Previous practice had been to have only one class for each order, since they were usually given only members of royal families, nobles, or the highest ranking military officers who tended to be nobles anyway. Napoleon's innovation created classes for all levels of society and made the honor available to everyone.

The French Legion of Honor inspired the United States's Legion of Merit, which was authorized by Congress in 1942. It has four classes to be comparable to the European orders and is similar to the French award in name and appearance. It can be awarded to foreign heads of state and other foreign military service members, the class depending on their positions and the importance of their services to the United States. Members of the U.S. armed forces usually receive the lowest class. The Legion of Merit is the official successor to the Badge of Military Merit, a cloth badge in the shape of a purple heart, which was awarded three times for services during the Revolutionary War.

Japan adopted the idea of orders as it adopted many other Western ideas during the nineteenth century. Its major orders all came about in the latter part of the century. The Order of the Chrysanthemum and the Order of the Rising Sun both started in 1876. The Order of the Sacred Treasure came about in 1888. Other Asiatic and some African nations also set up orders.

Summary

All nations and all armed forces have used decorations and orders to reward bravery and meritorious service. The complete history and description of this topic is a subject for specialists and enthusiasts. The significance and detailed descriptions of specific decorations and awards may be obtained from the references listed in the bibliography.

RAYMOND OLIVER

SEE ALSO: Feudalism; Flags and Symbols; Uniforms and Accouterments.

Bibliography

Angus, I. 1973. *Medals and decorations.* New York: St. Martin's Press.
Boatner, M. M. 1976. *Military customs and traditions.* Westport, Conn.: Greenwood Press.
Castano, J. B. 1975. *The naval officer's uniform guide.* Annapolis, Md.: U.S. Naval Institute Press.
Crocker, L. P. 1988. *The army officer's guide.* Harrisburg, Pa.: Stackpole Books.
Darling, H. T. 1974. *Ribbons and medals.* Garden City, N.Y.: Doubleday.
Edkins, D. 1981. *The Prussian orden pour le mérite.* Falls Church, Va.: Ajay.
Fitzsimons, B. 1973. *Heraldry & regalia of war.* New York: Beekman House.
Kerrigan, E. E. 1964. *American war medals and decorations.* New York: Viking Press.
———. 1967. *American badges and insignia.* New York: Viking Press.
Lovette, L. P. 1959. *Naval customs, traditions and usage.* Annapolis, Md.: U.S. Naval Institute Press.
Mack, W. P., and R. W. Connell. 1980. *Naval ceremonies, customs, and traditions.* Annapolis, Md.: U.S. Naval Institute Press.
McDowell, C. P. 1984. *Military and naval decorations of the United States.* Springfield, Va.: Quest.
Napier III, J. H. 1986. *The air force officer's guide.* Harrisburg, Pa.: Stackpole.
Riley, D. L. 1980. *Uncommon valor: Decorations, badges and service medals of the U.S. Navy and Marine Corps.* Marcaline, Mo.: Wadsworth.
Robles, P. K. 1971. *United States military medals & ribbons.* Rutland, Vt.: Tuttle.
Rosignoli, G. 1986. *The illustrated encyclopedia of military insignia of the 20th century.* Secaucus, N.J.: Chartwell Books.
Wilkinson, F. 1970. *Battle dress.* Garden City, N.Y.: Doubleday.

DE LATTRE DE TASSIGNY, JEAN [1889–1953]

Few men better exemplify the conflicting elements of French military tradition than Marshal Jean de Lattre de Tassigny. Carrying to extremes the highest military virtues—courage, professional competence, strategic insight, leadership, and the panache that earned him the nickname "Le Roi Jean"—de Lattre also manifested that pernicious sense of political mission that has so often put the French officer corps at odds with the regime.

Early Life and Career

Jean Marie Gabriel de Lattre de Tassigny was born in the village of Mouilleron-en-Pareds in the Vendée on 2 February 1889. Of Catholic and aristocratic background, classically educated, and an enthusiastic horseman, de Lattre prepared for a career as a cavalry officer at the college of Sainte-Geneviève, the French military academy at St. Cyr, and the cavalry school of Saumur.

Lieutenant de Lattre fought with distinction in World War I. Wounded by a shell fragment in August 1914, in September he killed two German cavalrymen with his sword during a mounted skirmish before his chest was impaled by a lance. After his recuperation, de Lattre transferred to the 93d Infantry Regiment, with which he spent sixteen months in the Verdun sector. By the war's end, de Lattre had been mentioned in dispatches eight times and wounded five. One of the youngest chefs de bataillon (major in Anglo-American usage) in the French army, he was already an officer of the Légion d'Honneur.

De Lattre served in Morocco from 1921 to 1925 and was cited for gallantry. The spring of 1927 saw two further triumphs, his entry into the highly competitive Ecole Superièure de Guerre and marriage to Simonne Calary de Lamazière.

In 1933 de Lattre joined the staff of General Weygand, the military head of the French army. As Weygand's foreign affairs expert and liaison with the legislature, he demonstrated considerable political zeal. Fearing a rapprochement between Germany and the Soviet Union, de Lattre set out single-handedly to create a Franco-Soviet alliance and persuaded Weygand to dispatch a military attaché to Moscow. De Lattre's disregard of the ban on political activities by soldiers threatened his career when he participated in discussions about installing a broadly based reform government in response to the riots of 6 February 1934. Only Weygand's refusal to dismiss his aide saved the man now reviled by the Right as the "Red Colonel," capable of negotiating with Moscow, and by the Left as the mastermind of a coup d'état.

World War II

The German attack of 10 May 1940 found de Lattre in command of the 14th Infantry Division, which he led with great skill and daring throughout the campaign. Unable to withdraw his division to North Africa, de Lattre remained in France as a major general in the Armistice Army. Like many officers under the Vichy regime, he believed in the army's special mission to restore French national pride. Concern with French morale led de Lattre to establish a camp for young soldiers in the village at Opme where communal outdoor life, physical training, and lectures on the glories of French history were to dissolve class barriers and inculcate principles of leadership, teamwork, and patriotism.

Alone among divisional commanders in advocating open resistance to the German occupation of Vichy France in November 1942, de Lattre was arrested by French authorities and condemned to ten years' imprisonment. He served eight months before his wife and 15-year-old son Bernard engineered the jailbreak that brought him to London.

Joining Charles de Gaulle's Free French, de Lattre went to North Africa to assume command of the French troops assigned to the liberation of France. Landing in southern France on 15 August 1944, de Lattre led his French First Army in a campaign that confirmed his military reputation. His politics of national unity also bore fruit as he integrated into his army the resistance fighters from the French Forces of the Interior. De Lattre's campaigns culminated in his witnessing on behalf of France the German Act of Capitulation in Berlin on 8 May 1945.

In November 1945 de Lattre was appointed to head the French army as chief of staff and inspector general. Again fascinated by the army's socializing potential, he created the Light Camps, open-air bivouacs based on the Opme model, where the postwar army, poor as it was in military materiel, could learn leadership and patriotism. The experiment proved too expensive, however, and the government saved the budget from de Lattre's enthusiasm by promoting him in May 1947 to the posts of wartime commander in chief and, as of 1948, commander of French land forces in Western Europe.

Later Life

In 1950, de Lattre was called upon to revive the failing fortunes of French forces in Indochina. Although the task boded ill for the aging general's health and reputation, he accepted on the grounds that young French officers in Indochina, his own son among them, deserved better leadership than they had found there. Arriving in Indochina on 19 December 1950, he so restored the morale of the Franco-Vietnamese forces that they won their first major success at Vinh-Yen in January 1951 (Fig. 1).

Ever aware of the political implications of warfare, de Lattre saw Indochina not as a military problem but as a test of French capability to transform its anachronistic empire into a union of states. He hoped to create a state capable of partnership with France and defended by a self-sufficient national army. The French officer commanding one of the new Vietnamese units was his 23-year-old son, Bernard, a soldier since his 16th year, who died at Ninh Binh on 30 May 1951.

Although shattered by Bernard's death, de Lattre traveled to the United States with a plea for financial support that sowed the seeds of American concern about the future of Indochina. His health broken, he died in Paris on 9 January 1953. The president of the Republic placed the baton of a marshal of France on his coffin.

De Lattre's career was an object lesson in military-civil relations in twentieth-century France. Willing to overthrow one government in 1934 and to disobey another in 1943, deeply concerned about the role of the army vis-à-vis the nation and the nation vis-à-vis its colonies, de Lattre represented both the glory of French arms and their wielders' ever-problematic relationship with the state they defended.

EUGENIA C. KIESLING

Figure 1. Jean de Lattre de Tassigny with his son, Bernard, 1951. (SOURCE: U.S. Library of Congress)

SEE ALSO: Vietnam and Indochina Wars; World War II.

Bibliography

Bankwitz, P. C. F. 1967. *Maxime Weygand and civil-military relations in modern France.* Cambridge: Harvard Univ. Press.

De Lattre de Tassigny, J. 1988. *La ferveur et le sacrifice: Indochine 1951.* Paris: Plon.

————. 1984. *Ne pas subir. Ecrits 1914–1952.* Paris: Plon.

————. 1985. *Reconquérir. Ecrits 1944–1945.* Paris: Plon.

De Lattre, S. 1972. *Jean de Lattre, mon marie.* Paris: Presses de la Cité.

Dinfreville, J. 1970. De Lattre à l'état-major de Weygand. *Revue de Deux Mondes,* June, pp. 70–92; July, 558–578.

Salisbury-Jones, G. 1955. *So full a glory: A life of Marshal de Lattre de Tassigny.* New York: Praeger.

DOENITZ, KARL [1891–1980]

Karl Doenitz was born on 16 September 1891 in Grünau near Berlin, the son of Emil Doenitz, a successful engineer, and his wife, Anna. Karl attended the Realgymnasium in Weimar, where he showed a keen interest in and an aptitude for military life. On 1 April 1910 he entered the training school of the Imperial Navy. He was assigned to the light cruiser *Breslau* in 1912 and was commissioned in 1913.

World War I

At the outbreak of World War I the *Breslau* and the battle cruiser *Goeben* eluded the British Mediterranean Fleet and entered the Dardanelles to take advantage of Turkey's benevolent neutrality. Doenitz remained in Near Eastern waters until October 1916, when he was transferred to the U-boat, or submarine, service.

In the spring of 1916 Doenitz had married Ingeborg Weber, the daughter of General Weber. This union produced two sons and a daughter. Both sons eventually joined the navy and were killed in action during World War II.

Doenitz served as watch officer on the *U-39* until 1918, when he was given command of the *U-68*. On the night of 3–4 October 1918, while attacking a British convoy en route to Malta, the *U-68* was sunk; Doenitz, along with most of his crew, was taken prisoner.

While in captivity Doenitz devised new tactical theories to improve the combat effectiveness of the U-boats. His experience as a U-boat captain had shown him that the "lone wolf" tactics of single, unsupported boats attacking enemy shipping were inefficient and dangerous. A single U-boat was hard-pressed to inflict any serious damage and its operations ran the crew to exhaustion, thus rendering it ineffective and more susceptible to destruction. Doenitz reasoned that a number of U-boats operating in support of one another, or in wolf packs, could cause significantly greater damage to enemy shipping and at the same time increase their individual vessels' chances of survival.

Interwar Years

Doenitz was repatriated in July 1919 and, eager to test his new ideas, applied for service at the new naval headquarters in Kiel. Although the Versailles Treaty expressly forbade the building of U-boats and had effectively rendered the German navy impotent, Doenitz, in the hope that Germany would again be allowed to build U-boats, reentered the service. In the meantime, he improved his knowledge and skill in surface warship tactics. Upon his return to active duty he was given command of a torpedo boat and in 1923 was assigned to the torpedo boat inspectorate in Kiel.

Doenitz was then transferred to naval headquarters in Berlin. In 1927 he returned to sea duty as a navigation officer on the flagship of Vice Admiral von Loewenfeld, commanding officer of naval forces in the Baltic. In early 1930 Doenitz was given command of a destroyer flotilla. Later that same year he was appointed head of the Admiralty Staff Division of the High Command of the North Sea. Doenitz held this post until 1934, when he was promoted to captain and given command of the cruiser *Emden*.

On 31 January 1933 Adolf Hitler became chancellor of Germany, and Doenitz's long-standing hopes for naval rearmament and the resurgence of the U-boat service were fulfilled. Hitler initiated the "Z Plan" calling for immediate naval construction; an integral part of the Z Plan was to be the U-boat service. This policy endeared Hitler to Doenitz, and although he never joined the National Socialist Party, Doenitz became an avid supporter of Hitler.

On 27 September 1935, Doenitz's greatest dream came true when Adm. Erich Raeder, commander in chief, Naval Forces, appointed him head of the new U-boat fleet with the specific task of rebuilding and training that service. Doenitz, finally given a chance to put his theories on U-boat tactics into practice, threw himself into the job with relish, overseeing every aspect of the U-boat fleet's development. As there were no training manuals for the crews, Doenitz wrote them himself. Working both from theory and from practical experience, Doenitz devised the two major concepts by which the U-boat fleet was to function: first, that the primary objective of the U-boats was the enemy merchant fleet, not its warships; second, that a U-boat was basically a surface vessel that could submerge when necessary and whose silhouette made it almost invisible at night. The latter characteristic, combined with the vessel's speed, convinced Doenitz that the U-boats should operate in groups and make surface attacks at night.

Doenitz also devised an intensive six-month training program designed to drill his crews to perfection in every aspect of U-boat warfare and to attain the highest possible degree of war readiness. This program was implemented on 1 October 1935, with the newly raised Weddingen Flotilla, the first of the U-boat groups to see service. Along with the training of the crews, Doenitz was also responsible for the design and development of new U-boats. Under his direction, faster and more efficient boats with longer range capabilities were built.

Doenitz was unsuccessful, however, in getting the High Command to build the 300-boat fleet he felt would be necessary to win another war with Great Britain. Under the Z Plan, the surface fleet had construction priority, and Doenitz's arguments to the contrary were ignored.

World War II

As Doenitz had feared, the outbreak of war on 1 September 1939 found the U-boat fleet unprepared. Of the 56 U-boats in service, only 46 were operational; of these only 22 were suitable for duty in the Atlantic Ocean, the rest fit only for North Sea operations. Of the 22 available for Atlantic duty, only seven at a time could be deployed for action, the remainder being either en route to or from duty, or in port undergoing repair and replenishment. With such minor forces at his disposal, Doenitz was reduced to conducting a series of "pinprick" attacks against Britain's merchant fleet instead of an all-out assault against its supply lines.

Doenitz's strategy of unrestricted U-boat warfare was also initially hampered by the rules of the Hague Convention and certain restrictions imposed by Hitler himself. The convention required U-boats to stop and search unescorted ships for military contraband and, if any were found, to see to the safety of the crew before sinking the ship. Hitler, not wishing to broaden the war and increase animosity against Germany, forbade the sinking of any passenger liners even if they were known to be carrying military supplies. Despite these restrictions, by the end of 1939 the U-boats had sunk 114 merchant ships totaling 421,000 tons.

January and February 1940 showed a dramatic increase in U-boat successes, with 85 ships, a total of 281,000 tons, sunk. From March to June the U-boats were assigned to cover the German troop landings in Norway. By July they were back in the Atlantic on blockade duty. On 17 August, Hitler withdrew all previous restrictions and ordered the U-boats to sink any and all enemy ships on sight. With his hands no longer tied, Doenitz unleashed the wolf packs from newly acquired bases along the French coast. From July through October the U-boats ran rampant and by the end of 1940 had sunk 285 ships totaling over 1,111,360 tons. Doenitz was promoted to vice admiral the same year.

There was a decrease in U-boat kills in 1941, as Hitler ordered the transfer of boats from the Atlantic to security duty in the Mediterranean and the Arctic to protect the supply lines for the North African campaign and to attack Allied convoys bound for Russia. Doenitz was incensed by the use of the U-boats as defensive weapons (for which they were totally unsuited), instead of as offensive weapons, where they had just begun to demonstrate their effectiveness as offensive weapons. In an attempt to assist the weakened Atlantic Fleet, Doenitz requested an air support squadron, but even this was not enough to make up for the loss of so many of his boats.

The entry of the United States into the war on 7 December 1941 gave Doenitz a new hunting ground for his U-boats. The United States had virtually no defense against the U-boats and, in the first six months of 1942, lost 585 ships totaling over 3,081,000 tons. As the United States began to establish coastal convoys to protect its shipping, the U-boats returned to the central Atlantic. By June the number of U-boats in service had risen to 140 with more being produced daily. Doenitz realized that he had to keep inflicting heavy losses to counter the Allies' superior production capability. When the Allies began using aircraft-mounted radar to detect the U-boats, Doenitz countered with Metox, a device that bounced back the radar signal, effectively hiding the U-boats.

In November the Allies landed in North Africa, and Doenitz immediately dispatched all available U-boats to the area. Finding the landing areas covered by numerous escort vessels, he moved as many of the U-boats as possible back to the now relatively unguarded Atlantic. By the end of the year the U-boats had sunk a total of 1,160 ships (over 6,226,215 tons) with a loss of only 87 boats of their own. As a result of these successes Doenitz was promoted to admiral.

On 30 January 1943 Doenitz replaced Admiral Raeder as commander in chief of the navy. That same month at the Casablanca Conference the Allies decided on a concentrated campaign against the U-boats for control of the Atlantic. The first three months of 1943 were nevertheless good ones for Doenitz, the U-boats sinking more than 102 ships. But by May the tide had turned, and in April alone 41 U-boats were lost. The British had begun sending small escort carriers, converted from unfinished merchantmen, to accompany their convoys.

This factor, plus the development of a longer range, aircraft-mounted radar and the breaking of the German naval codes, allowed the Allies to track down the U-boats with devastating effect. Faced with staggering losses, Doenitz ordered the U-boats to abandon the convoy lanes on 24 May. After some small successes in the Indian Ocean, Doenitz again sent his U-boats into the Atlantic. The convoys were simply too powerful, however; in November, Doenitz suspended the wolf pack tactics as they were now causing more losses to the U-boats than to the convoys.

The situation continued to worsen in 1944. By 6 June, when the Allies began their Normandy landings, the U-boats were reduced to the secondary role of tying down enemy forces. By the beginning of 1945, the new Type XXIII U-boats were sent into action; however, even they could do little against the convoys. Although Doenitz continued to send out his U-boats, the control of the seas was clearly in the hands of the Allies.

On 30 April 1945 Hitler committed suicide in Berlin and, as stipulated in his will, Doenitz was appointed his successor. Doenitz immediately set about trying to save as many lives as possible. He attempted to negotiate a separate peace with the Western Allies in an effort to keep millions of German soldiers and civilians from falling into the hands of the Russians. His terms were refused, however. With no other choice left, Doenitz authorized Gen. Alfred Jodl to sign the terms of surrender at Rheims on 7 May. Doenitz continued to serve as head of the government, although his authority was not recognized by the Allies. On 22 May his presence was demanded aboard the steamship *Patria*, the headquarters of the Allied Control Commission. Upon his arrival he was placed under arrest and charged with war crimes.

At his trial in Nuremberg, Doenitz was charged with the crimes of waging aggressive war and waging war against noncombatants. To his surprise, Doenitz was aided in his defense by the letters of hundreds of American and British seamen and the written testimony of Adm. Chester W. Nimitz. Nimitz stated that American submarines were ordered to engage in unrestricted submarine warfare as of 7 December 1941, and that it was not the practice of submarine crews to rescue survivors if such an effort constituted an undue hazard to their vessel. Eventually, the court found Doenitz guilty on the ambiguous charge of having committed crimes against peace but not having conspired to commit them. He was thus guilty of war crimes and was sentenced to ten years' imprisonment in Spandau prison in Berlin. On 1 October 1956 Doenitz was released. He retired to Hamburg where he wrote his memoirs, *Ten Years and Twenty Days*, which were published in 1958. He died on 24 December 1980 of a heart attack.

Doenitz was a talented leader and strategist as well as a brilliant U-boat commander. His development and handling of the U-boat fleet demonstrated his abilities as an innovator and naval tactician just as his brief term as head of the German government demonstrated his compassion. As Doenitz was loved and admired by his men, so was he equally respected by his enemies.

VINCENT B. HAWKINS

SEE ALSO: World War I; World War II.

Bibliography

Davidson, E. 1966. *The trial of the Germans*. New York: Collins Books.
Doenitz, K. 1959. *Ten years and twenty days*. New York: World.
Pfannes, C. E., and V. A. Salamone. 1984. *The great admirals of World War II*. Vol. 2, *The Germans*. New York: Kensington.
Wistrich, R. 1982. *Who's who in Nazi Germany*. New York: Bonanza Books.

DOMINICAN REPUBLIC: 1965 CRISIS

In April 1965, Dominican army troops attempted to overthrow the ruling civilian triumvirate in the Dominican Republic. This resulted in an armed struggle for control of the government between dissident troops (rebels), who were joined by civilians, and loyalist military forces seeking to establish a military junta. The ensuing anarchy in the city of Santo Domingo led to intervention by U.S. military forces at approximately the same time that President Lyndon B. Johnson made the decision to commit ground troops to Vietnam. Complexity characterized the Dominican factional dispute, the U.S. military operations in the Dominican Republic that attempted to separate the two opposing forces and stop the fighting, and the activities associated with the search for a cease-fire and a negotiated peace. Although the U.S. intervention was a controversial issue at the time, it proved successful both politically and militarily and brought unprecedented stability to the long-troubled Dominican Republic. The intervention was not a mission of conquest, but rather an effort to safeguard the lives of U.S. and other nationals and to restore order in the country without taking sides in the dispute.

In the initial days of the intervention, U.S. political and military goals were obscure. The goal of evacuation of threatened civilians was obvious to all, but the U.S. military were not sure of additional missions. Contingency plans envisioned a much smaller force than that actually used, which caused military commanders to make last-minute changes. Although varying interpretations exist regarding communist influence in the rebellion, a rapid U.S. intervention in strength was intended to prevent a communist takeover.

In addition to providing security of U.S. property and evacuating American citizens from the Dominican Republic, U.S. military forces conducted urban warfare operations in the city of Santo Domingo, participated in civil affairs and psychological warfare programs, supported diplomatic efforts to achieve a political settlement, and provided troops for the Inter-American Peace Force (IAPF). After the creation of the IAPF, the primary duties of U.S. military forces were to maintain order in Santo Domingo, ensure that rebel forces were contained in their stronghold in Santo Domingo, and restrain the loyalist forces from attacking rebel strongholds. After a political settlement was obtained between opposing Dominican factions, U.S. military forces withdrew from the country and the IAPF disbanded on 20 September 1966.

The establishment of the IAPF was a historical first. It demonstrated the advantage of organizing and committing an inter-American force on a peace-keeping mission within the territory of a member state. Moreover, the IAPF demonstrated that multinational forces can work together effectively.

Although dated, in the sense that more recent U.S. military actions have been conducted in Latin America (Grenada, 1983; Panama, 1989), the Dominican Republic crisis provides invaluable lessons that continue to be pertinent. (Comparison of U.S. intervention in these three countries is beyond the scope of this article. There are, however, striking similarities and several differences that are identified in the Grenada and Panama entries of this encyclopedia.)

Background

The causes of the Dominican crisis of 1965 can be traced to the period of Rafael Trujillo's dictatorship (1930 to 1960). Thirty years under the rule of Trujillo had left the Dominican Republic without qualified political and social leaders. As in other Latin American countries, Dominican military officers played an important role in the political life of the country.

In September 1963, a group of military officers led by General Elías Wessin y Wessin (who would play a major role in the 1965 crisis) ousted Juan Bosch, the first constitutional president of the post-Trujillo era, forcing him into exile. Bosch, an ineffective leader, had not only alienated the upper classes of the country but also quarreled with senior army officers over corruption within the military. Furthermore, he had been labeled pro-communist. Bosch's inability to cope efficiently with the nation's problems led to his overthrow and the establishment of a civilian triumvirate backed by the military. The triumvirate eventually became a two-man regime dominated by the former foreign minister, Donald Reid Cabral, a moderate.

Unrest in the country continued under Reid's regime. He made himself unpopular with military leaders by reducing the military budget and shutting off lucrative smuggling activities by senior officers. Junior officers disapproved of the slow pace of Reid's reforms, especially in retiring high-ranking officers left over from the Trujillo regime. Many of the younger officers and enlisted men favored the progressive policies and social welfare programs that had been advocated by Bosch and disapproved of the return of the military-backed Reid government to the constitution of 1962. They wanted reinstitution of the liberal Bosch constitution of 1963. This split in the military was the immediate cause of the 1965 revolt, but other groups (farmers, laborers, merchants, and small businessmen) also opposed Reid because of his harsh economic measures.

The Dominican Revolt

On 24 April 1965, a group of young officers and leaders of Bosch's revolutionary party initiated a coup d'état that toppled the Reid government and led to an armed uprising. Pro-Bosch forces intended Dr. Molina Ureña, the highest-ranking member of the 1963 Bosch government then on Dominican soil, to be sworn in as provisional constitutional president pending the return of Bosch. However, General Wessin y Wessin, commander of the Armed Forces Training Center, who had led the anti-Bosch coup in 1963, decided to fight the movement to restore Bosch to power.

The following day, in an effort to prevent Molina Ureña from being sworn in, the presidential palace was strafed by the Dominican air force and shelled by naval vessels. Thus, what began as a coup to overthrow the Reid government became a fight between pro- (rebel) and anti- (loyalist) Bosch forces in Santo Domingo, a city of about 300,000 persons.

By Monday morning, 26 April, mobs and agitators ran riot in the city. Trained teams, many led by communists, organized commando and paramilitary groups. Armed civilians outnumbered the rebel soldiers. It was difficult to determine who, if anyone, controlled the revolt. On Tuesday, a sizable loyalist force of tanks, artillery, and infantry under the command of Wessin y Wessin crossed the Duarte Bridge and advanced several blocks into the city against stiff rebel resistance. Hundreds of people, mostly civilians, were killed or wounded in this battle, one of the bloodiest single battles in Dominican history. The battle at the Duarte Bridge and the arrival of about 1,000 additional loyalist forces led the rebels to negotiate.

Faced with an apparently hopeless situation, the Molina Ureña government collapsed. U.S. officials believed that the rebellion would cease and that General Wessin y Wessin would assume control of Santo Domingo. On Tuesday night and early the next morning (27–28 April), however, the rebels regrouped, resupplied their forces, and consolidated their positions in the city. The loyalists formed a three-man military junta led by Col. Pedro Bartolome Benoit of the Dominican air force, to rally anti-Bosch support. This self-proclaimed government represented some semblance of authority and with police support controlled most of the Dominican Republic except for the rebel-held areas in downtown Santo Domingo.

U.S. Military Intervention

On Wednesday, 28 April, President Johnson authorized the landing of 500 U.S. Marines to assist in the security and protection of U.S. citizens and property in Santo Domingo. He limited their actions to defensive operations and ordered that their weapons be fired only in self-defense. Helicopters transported the marines from a U.S. amphibious assault ship, the *Boxer*, stationed off the coast of the Dominican Republic, to the evacuation site without meeting opposition. American citizens were evacuated to the *Boxer*. Later that evening, in a television broadcast, President Johnson informed the American people of the crisis and urged both Dominican factions to agree on a cease-fire. The president did not mention U.S. officials' fear of a communist takeover in the Dominican Republic. This failure to fully inform the American public subsequently cast doubt on the administration's credibility and became a controversial subject concerning U.S. intervention.

On Thursday, 29 April, senior U.S. officials discussed a plan to establish an international security zone that would include the residential area of Santo Domingo and extend from the Embajador Hotel to the U.S. embassy and then to the sea. It was felt that by interposing U.S. military forces between rebel and junta forces and sealing off the rebel stronghold in downtown Santo Domingo, the two factions would agree to a cease-fire; thereafter, the United States would request the Organization of American States (OAS) to negotiate a political settlement. This discussion formed the background for a subsequent meeting that evening during which President Johnson decided on rapid U.S. military intervention to prevent a Castro-type takeover in the Dominican Republic.

On Thursday, additional U.S. personnel were evacuated. Based on reports of rebel movement toward Santo Domingo, President Johnson considered the 500-man marine force already ashore too small for securing the international security zone under consideration. He ordered an additional 1,500 marines ashore at the evacuation area.

Once it became apparent that the United States might become involved in the crisis, the Johnson administration began pressing for the active participation of the OAS in an inter-American peacekeeping force in the Dominican Republic. Given past U.S. actions in the Caribbean, however, OAS member states were reluctant to approve such a plan. They feared it would encourage the United States to return to an interventionist policy and also that it would appear as if one Latin American nation were acting against another at the request of the United States. During the night of 28–29 April, Latin American ambassadors and members of the OAS were informed of the marines' landing. The failure of U.S. officials to inform the OAS sooner became another controversial issue during the crisis.

A series of orders over the next few days implemented the president's decision. In addition to the 2,000 marines already in the Dominican Republic, 2,000 U.S. Army paratroopers were committed on 30 April and another 2,000 troops on 2 May. The president also directed that an additional 4,500 troops be landed as soon as possible. The U.S. military commitment eventually reached a peak strength of more than 23,000 by the middle of May.

Missions assigned to U.S. military forces were:

- To protect the lives of Americans and foreign nationals;
- To evacuate U.S. citizens and foreign nationals who desired to leave the Dominican Republic;
- To perform humanitarian missions as ordered, including distribution of food and medical supplies, without regard to nationality or faction;
- To assist in the establishment of stable conditions conducive to the development of an effective political settlement under the aegis of the OAS; and
- To help prevent, in keeping with the principles of the American system, the establishment of another communist state in the Western Hemisphere.

U.S. Military Operations: An Overview

AIR OPERATIONS

Although the U.S. Air Force furnished fighters, reconnaissance aircraft, and many other services in support of Dominican ground operations, air operations focused on the airlift of troops and supplies from the United States to the

Dominican Republic. Transport aircraft delivered approximately 80 percent of the American ground troops to Santo Domingo. Only two squadrons of air force fighters and elements of another squadron of air force reconnaissance aircraft deployed to the area. This limited deployment was due to the small likelihood of counterair operations by hostile forces, the lack of need for air strikes support by U.S. military ground forces, and the availability of U.S. marine and naval fighter aircraft in the objective area.

Six U.S. RF-101s and three RB-66 aircraft provided reconnaissance support for the Dominican operation. These aircraft furnished visual and photographic reconnaissance, photographic processing, and interpretation, and disseminated intelligence products to requesting organizations.

HELICOPTER OPERATIONS

During the Dominican operation, U.S. Marines, army troops, and naval forces used helicopters extensively for command and control and to increase the mobility of troops. The versatility of the helicopter made it ideal for rapid transport, liaison, observation and reconnaissance, medical evacuation, supply, and communications. This use of helicopters in the Dominican Republic served as a prelude to their employment in South Vietnam.

GROUND OPERATIONS

Urban guerrilla warfare characterized ground operations in the Dominican Republic. The enemy consisted primarily of individual snipers or small groups of individuals using hit-and-run guerrilla tactics. Many of the snipers were *tigres*, young thrill-seeking hoodlums who enjoyed carrying out their own private guerrilla warfare in the city of Santo Domingo. U.S. ground operations varied widely in scope, from security of U.S. property and assisting in the evacuation of Americans to dealing with snipers, conducting house-to-house searches, and fulfilling peacekeeping missions. At the same time, U.S. forces were subject to strict rules of engagement regarding the types of weapons fired, their use, and so on.

Ground troops established a three-mile corridor through the heart of downtown Santo Domingo that sealed off the principal rebel forces in the city from the rest of the country. Once established, the corridor also linked the separate enclaves of American forces, thus improving their communications and making their military positions mutually supportable. More important, once the corridor was established much of the fighting between the rebels and junta troops ended, allowing U.S. forces to adopt a more neutral position in the days that followed.

NAVAL OPERATIONS

The activities of U.S. naval forces in the Dominican operation, like those of the air and ground forces, varied widely. In addition to evacuating personnel, naval ships were prepared to provide off-shore gunfire support to ground forces.

Until early June, U.S. air and surface naval forces blockaded the island of Hispaniola to prevent Cuban or other forces from interfering with U.S. operations. Destroyers, minesweepers, and amphibious vessels conducted surveillance and patrol of the sea approaches to the Dominican Republic to detect any infiltration of arms or personnel. U.S. naval ships also established special patrols to warn of any commando raids or shore bombardments by the Dominican navy directed against the rebel stronghold.

Other U.S. naval tasks involved retrieval of Dominican dead floating out to sea, ship visits to Dominican ports to deliver medical supplies and food, and towing and salvage operations.

HUMANITARIAN OPERATIONS

Humanitarian operations included the evacuation of American and foreign nationals from the Dominican Republic and the provision of food and medical aid to needy Dominicans. Distribution food points often fed as many as 4,000 people daily.

Although most of the humanitarian work was conducted in the city of Santo Domingo, U.S. military doctors and chaplains made many trips to outlying towns and villages. Doctors treated Dominican civilians for everything from head colds to appendicitis. Chaplains, in the absence of Dominican priests, held religious services and baptized children in remote areas. American military engineers established water supply points in outlying towns and trucked water into Santo Domingo to alleviate serious shortages. Daily trash runs were made by U.S. military forces to assist in restoring sanitation to the city.

SPECIAL OPERATIONS

U.S. Army Special Forces (SF) conducted several special operations during the Dominican crisis. They performed intelligence-collection missions and were also used in U.S. psychological warfare operations that played an important role during the crisis. All three forces—U.S. military forces, loyalists, and rebels—used radio broadcasts and printed material to influence the attitudes and behavior of groups opposed to them.

The goal of the U.S. psychological warfare campaign was to explain that the U.S. intervention was not a mission of conquest but rather to safeguard the lives of U.S. and other nationals and to restore order within the country without taking sides in the dispute. The United States used the Voice of America, locally generated radio broadcasts, trucks and ground-emplaced loudspeakers, and air-dropped and truck-distributed leaflets to carry its message to the Dominican people.

The Inter-American Peace Force and Establishment of a Political Settlement

After establishment of the three-mile corridor on 2 May and the subsequent cessation of armed hostilities between the two Dominican forces, the way was opened for peace negotiations.

On 4 May, the pro-Bosch rebels installed Col. Francisco Deno Caamano as constitutional president of a provisional regime. The next day the Caamano and Wessin y Wessin forces signed a formal truce negotiated by OAS and U.S.

officials. During the truce, the loyalists formed a new five-man civilian-military government under Gen. Antonio Barreras Imbert and Colonel Benoit. The new regime, called the Government of National Reconstruction, was sworn in on 7 May but never recognized by the United States.

The day before the creation of this interim government, the OAS foreign ministers approved by a 14-to-5 vote a historic U.S. resolution to establish a peace force. This multinational force, initially called the Inter-American Force but later redesignated the Inter-American Peace Force, would operate under OAS direction to "cooperate in the restoration of peace in the Dominican Republic, maintain the security of its inhabitants . . . and establish an atmosphere of peace and conciliation to permit the functioning of democratic institutions." Peace force contingents would include troops from the United States, Brazil, Honduras, Nicaragua, and Paraguay, and a platoon of police from Costa Rica.

On 22 May, Gen. Hugo Panasco Alvim of Brazil was named commander-in-chief of the IAPF with U.S. Lt. Gen. Bruce Palmer as deputy commander. The next day with the signing of the formal document (The Act Creating the Inter-American Force), a unique experiment in OAS cooperation had produced a new organization and concept for collective action. It was the first time that sovereign states within the Americas had joined together to form a regional multinational force. (At its maximum strength of approximately 14,000 men, the IAPF contained fewer than 2,000 Latin American troops, the majority of whom were Brazilian. The bulk of the force consisted of U.S. troops.) This act also represented a fundamental change in the way the United States would move to influence future events in Latin America.

By 23 May all the Latin American contingents except that of Paraguay had arrived in the Dominican Republic, and the IAPF began operations. Three-man teams of peace force observers, each composed of an American, a Honduran, and a Costa Rican, began patrolling junta territory on 23 May to enforce the terms of the truce agreement.

With the arrival of the Brazilian troops in late May, President Johnson ordered the withdrawal of 600 U.S. Marines. The withdrawal began on 26 May and was completed on 6 June when the final marine units departed. With the buildup of the peace force and the gradual withdrawal of U.S. forces from the Dominican Republic, the final stages of a political settlement began, although incidents between IAPF troops and rebels occurred almost daily through June.

By the end of June, agreement was near on the composition of a provisional Dominican government. An OAS committee proposed Hector García-Godoy Caceres, who had briefly been Bosch's foreign minister, for provisional president. He was accepted by the competing factions and assumed office on 3 September 1965. The United States recognized the provisional government the following day.

The IAPF defended the provisional government against two rightist coups prior to the national elections in June 1966 at which time the Dominicans elected Dr. Joaquin Balaguer as president. In his last act as provisional president, García-Godoy signed on 29 June 1966 a law reintegrating the former constitutionalist rebels into the armed forces, thereby officially recognizing the end of the violence that began in April 1965. Balaguer assumed office on 1 July.

After the election, the OAS passed a resolution calling for the withdrawal of the IAPF from the Dominican Republic within three months. Troops began leaving on 1 July; the last U.S. military forces departed on 19 September 1966. Operations of the IAPF formally ended one day later.

Conclusion

As a military operation, the U.S. intervention in the Dominican Republic was a success. Despite little warning, and with Vietnam absorbing most of the attention of the U.S. leadership, American military forces responded rapidly and effectively to an ambiguous situation. Order was introduced into a chaotic situation by interposing U.S. troops between opposing Dominican factions. The operation demonstrated the capability of U.S. military forces to deploy to a distant area on short notice to stabilize a crisis situation. It also reaffirmed the requirement for joint doctrine and the need to deploy sufficient military force, properly organized, to accomplish its mission. Strategic air and sea mobility were essential in deploying ground forces and in supplying them with heavy tonnage items such as ammunition, fuel, and rations.

As with any military operation, however, the U.S. intervention was not flawless. Several military problems were encountered. During the early stages of the intervention, the lack of adequate strategic communications hampered U.S. command and control. Pertinent intelligence and the availability of maps were lacking. No joint public affairs organization representing the Department of Defense, the State Department, and other U.S. government agencies, able to present a consistent and credible explanation of the U.S. intervention, was ever established in Santo Domingo.

The Dominican crisis was not without its cost in human lives and suffering. U.S. military casualties were 44 dead (of whom 27 were killed in action), 172 wounded in action, and 111 injured. Latin American casualties within the IAPF were 6 Brazilians and 5 Paraguayans wounded in action.

Losses among the regular Dominican military (loyalists) and national police were about 500 killed or missing in action for the armed forces and 325 for the police, plus an undetermined number of wounded. Among the rebel military (constitutionalists), the best estimate was about 600 dead and an undetermined number wounded. A reasonable estimate of total Dominican casualties (both sides, civilian, and military) is about 6,000 people, with the bulk of these occurring during the early phase of fighting in April and May 1965.

In sum, there are costs and limits to military interventions such as the Dominican Republic. Military action can stabilize conditions but cannot solve a country's political, social, and economic inequities.

JAMES B. MOTLEY

Bibliography

Johnson, L. B. 1971. *The vantage point: Perspectives of the presidency 1963–1969.* New York: Holt, Rinehart, and Winston.

LaFeber, W. 1984. *Inevitable revolutions: The United States in Central America.* Expanded ed. New York: W. W. Norton.

Lowenthal, A. F. 1972. *The Dominican intervention.* Cambridge, Mass.: Harvard Univ. Press.

Mansback, R. W. 1971. *Dominican crisis—1965.* New York: Facts on File.

Palmer, B., Jr. 1989. *Intervention in the Caribbean: The Dominican crisis of 1965.* Lexington, Ky.: Univ. Press of Kentucky.

Schoonmaker, H. G. 1977. United States military forces in the Dominican crisis of 1965. Ph.D. diss. University of Georgia, Athens.

DOUHET, GIULIO [1869–1930]

Giulio Douhet was an Italian army officer and airpower theorist. He was most noted for his advocacy of the use of airpower for strategic bombardment, recommending bombardment of the enemy's industrial and population centers to destroy both the enemy's ability to wage war and its morale. He also advocated an independent air force that was separate from the army.

Early Life and Military Career

Son of a military family long associated with the house of Savoy, Douhet was born 30 May 1869 in Caserta. He graduated first in his class at the Italian military academy and was commissioned in the artillery. He later studied at the Polytechnical Institute at Turin and the Command and Staff College. Intensely interested in mechanizing the army, he was given command of an experimental motorcycle battalion of elite *bersaglieri*. Wilbur Wright's visit to Italy in 1909 inspired him to write a visionary article in *Lapreparazione*, a service journal, predicting the appearance of a separate air force coequal with the army and navy. Given command of Italy's first aviation battalion, he published what was probably the first doctrinal manual for airpower, *Rules for the Use of Airplanes in War in 1913.* Denied official funding to construct bombers, he conspired with industrialist Count Caproni to develop a bomber in his battalion workshops. Although relieved of his command for this evasion, Douhet's initiative helped set Caproni on his way toward becoming a major producer of bombers capable of strategic operations, which the Italians used in mass formations against the Austrians in World War I.

While serving as chief of staff of the Milan Division during World War I, Douhet continued to urge the use of strategic bombardment to win the war. Frustrated at the ineffectiveness of the Italian command, he indiscreetly expressed his views to a civilian official; for this breach he was court-martialed and sentenced to a year in confinement, a period he used to draft elaborate schemes for Allied air bombardment of the Central Powers. Exonerated after the Italian collapse at Caporetto in 1917 validated his criticisms, Douhet served as director of technical services in the Italian air arm until his retirement.

Concepts of Airpower

A prolific writer, Douhet in retirement published a stream of articles in *Revista Aeronautica* and other journals, but he is best remembered for his major work, *Il dominio dell'ario* (*Command of the Air*), published in Rome by the War Ministry in 1921, the year he was promoted to major general on the retired list in recognition of his services. The main themes of this book, which he supplemented with articles, can be stated briefly: command of the air is to be won by the strategic use of bombs and gas to destroy the enemy's factories, cities, and especially the will to fight. These, not the enemy's armed forces, should be the principal objectives. The traditional services, the army and navy, should be employed defensively, leaving the main offensive to an independent air force.

Because Douhet was convinced that massive surprise air attacks would quickly render the enemy helpless, he was inclined to minimize or neglect defensive preparations. He envisioned bombers as cheaply converted civilian transport craft that could be flown by commercial pilots who merely changed their uniforms.

World War II was to reveal the overall validity of Douhet's concepts, as well as serious flaws in much of his thinking. The damage inflicted by conventional bombing, prior to the advent of nuclear weapons, was far less than he had predicted; civilian morale turned out to be more resilient, and bombers were more expensive and required far more elaborate defenses than he anticipated.

Attracted by Mussolini's emphasis on youth and modernization, Douhet was an early adherent of the Fascist movement. He was rewarded with a government post as commissioner of aviation but soon resigned to devote his energies to writing. Although in his early writings he was at pains to limit his prescriptions for airpower to the particular situation of Italy, his subsequent essays dropped this qualification. After retirement, when he was no longer constrained by the exigencies of the service, his writings became more speculative and less practical. In 1927, when revising *Command of the Air* for reissue, he proposed doing away entirely with all tactical air devoted to cooperation with the army and navy. Far better, he now argued, to spend the money on bombers to assure an initial knockout blow. This stance embroiled him in his declining years with the advocates of air support for land and sea forces who challenged his neglect of tactical airpower.

Assessment

Although honored by the Fascists in Italy as a great visionary, valuable for propaganda purposes, Douhet actually had little impact on the Italian air force, *Aeronautica Regia*. Mussolini allotted the air arm fewer resources than the army or navy, and the weapons procured did not reflect the emphasis on strategic bombardment espoused by Douhet. In the United States he was scarcely known and then largely indirectly through Air Corps translations of French journal articles. His major work, *Command of the Air*, was not published in English until 1942. Despite a lively discussion of Douhet's doctrine, neither the French nor the Germans adopted it. Ironically, Britain and the United States, where Douhet was least discussed, were the principal adherents of strategic bombardment doctrine.

Douhet died 15 February 1930 in Rome. He was brilliant, intensely emotional, often tactless, and dogmatic. Especially in his later writings, he was more polemicist than scholar. Nonetheless, he merits his place as one of the first systematic thinkers on the significance of airpower.

I. B. HOLLEY, JR.

SEE ALSO: Airpower, History of.

Bibliography

Cappelluti, F. J. 1967. The life and thought of Giulio Douhet. Ph.D. diss., Rutgers Univ., New Brunswick, N.J. (microfilm order no. 67–14. 762).

Douhet, G. [1942] 1983. *Command of the air*. Rev. ed. Trans. D. Ferrari. [New York: Coward McCann] Washington, D.C.: Government Printing Office.

Segre, C. O. 1979. Douhet in Italy: Prophet without honor? *Aerospace History* 26:69–80.

Sigaud, L. A. 1941. *Douhet and aerial warfare*. New York: Putnam.

Tomlinson, W. H. 1966. The father of air power doctrine. *Military Review* 46:27–31.

Warner, E. 1943. Douhet, Mitchell, Seversky: Theories of air warfare. In *Makers of modern strategy*, ed. E. M. Earle. Princeton, N.J.: Princeton Univ. Press.

———, and D. MacIsaac. 1986. Voices from the central blue: The air power theorists. In *Makers of modern strategy*, ed. Peter Paret. Rev. ed. Princeton, N.J.: Princeton Univ. Press.

E

EDWARD I [1239–1307]

Edward I (Fig. 1), the son of King Henry III of England, was the ablest of late medieval English monarchs. He was a resourceful general and a gifted strategist, as well as a ruler and administrator of unusual ability.

Early Life

Edward was born at Westminster on 17 June 1239, the eldest son of Henry III and his wife, Eleanor of Provence. In 1254 he received from his father large grants of land and several titles. These steps were undertaken in preparation for his trip to Castile, where he married Eleanor, the half-sister of King Alfonso X, in late October 1254. On his return to England, Edward was faced with revolt in his lands bordering the still-independent principality of Wales. His efforts to subdue the unrest in the autumn of 1255 were fruitless, for he lacked support from both his father and his border lord vassals. Some of his difficulties may have sprung from his close ties to his mother, which made him unpopular, and in reaction he drew closer to his powerful uncle, Simon de Montfort. When King Henry and Montfort clashed over the Provisions of Westminster in October 1259, Edward supported Montfort against his father, but reconsidered, deserted the baronial party, and was forgiven by Henry in May 1260. Partly to get him out of England, Henry sent his son to Gascony, where Edward stayed for three years. Returning to England in 1263, Edward found the country braced for civil war between his father and Montfort, but the prince's quarrelsome nature damaged the royalist cause. At the Battle of Lewes on 14 May 1264, his headlong charge routed part of the baronial army, but his impetuous pursuit enabled the rest of the barons to defeat and capture King Henry while Edward careered about the countryside. Shortly afterward, Edward surrendered to Montfort, who imprisoned him.

Chafing in captivity, Edward escaped in May 1265 after less than a year's confinement. Once free, he assumed leadership of the scattered but still powerful royalist forces. Hastily raising an army, Edward began the most brilliant military campaign ever fought on British soil by defeating Montfort at Newport

Figure 1. Edward I, king of England. (SOURCE: U.S. Library of Congress)

on 8 July 1265. Capitalizing on his success, Edward drove Montfort's chastened army into Wales, but was threatened by another baronial army under Montfort's son, Simon the Younger. Retracing his steps, Edward met Simon's army at Kenilworth on 1 August and virtually annihilated it. The elder Montfort was not yet subdued, and Edward had to rouse his troops for another forced march and a final battle at Evesham on 4 August, where he at last rescued King Henry. The grateful king rewarded his son with virtual control of the royalist cause, but Edward's harsh retributions probably delayed a final peace by prolonging resistance until the summer of 1266.

Aware of his own unpopularity and still eager for action, Edward made plans to join King Louis IX of France on a crusade, but problems in raising the necessary monies postponed his arrival in the Holy Land until after Louis's death in August 1270. Undeterred, Edward landed at Acre and from that stronghold led a series of raids into the Muslim-held hinterlands between May 1271 and September 1272, achieving little of concrete value but enhancing his own reputation for bravery and energy. He was in Sicily on his way back to

England when word reached him of his father's death on 16 November 1272, but he journeyed home slowly. In spite of his absence and his earlier unpopularity, his accession to the throne was not contested, and he postponed his coronation until 19 August 1274. At first his energies were taken up with legal and administrative matters, and the talent he showed as a lawmaker earned him the title "Lawgiver."

Conquest of Wales

Edward's first military exploits as king grew from continuing border quarrels with Wales, which peaked late in 1276. In spring 1277, Edward, accompanied by woodcutters and laborers to build roads and supported and supplied by a fleet offshore, led an army of 6,000 men along the northern coast. Overawed, the Welsh prince Llywelyn ap Gruffydd hastened to make peace in November. The resulting Treaty of Conway lasted for four years, postponing but not forestalling a final conflict. Llywelyn and his brother David led a revolt and captured Roger Clifford, the justiciar of North Wales, in March 1282 and so provoked a major military response from Edward. He led a large army into Wales, defeated the insurgents, and captured the last major Welsh stronghold at Bere Castle in April 1283. Although the country was in his hands, Edward recognized the likelihood of future revolts and began the construction of the chain of castles that are his most enduring physical monument, encircling the center of Welsh unrest with a line of fortified bases. Designed purely as military strongholds, the castles of Rhuddlan, Conway, Caernarvon, Beaumaris, and Harlech are probably the finest examples of medieval fortification in western Europe. Operating from these fortresses, Edward's troops maintained royal control over Wales despite the revolts of 1287 and 1294–95.

Intervention in Scotland

Edward traveled to Gascony in 1286, staying there for three years and working diligently to restore order and reform the administration. His presence on the continent, however, exacerbated a long-standing quarrel with France. Edward returned to England in 1289. When Margaret of Norway, granddaughter of King Alexander III of Scotland and the last clear heir to the Scottish throne, died in 1290, Scotland was plunged into a succession crisis. Anxious to prevent civil war, the desperate Scottish magnates asked Edward to arbitrate among the various claimants. Edward accepted but in return demanded that the Scots accept his suzerainty, which they did in 1292. After considerable investigation and deliberation, Edward chose John de Baliol as king over his rival Edward Bruce in November 1292. After receiving Baliol's homage, Edward lent him support to gain the throne. In his quest for unity and order in Britain, Edward wanted to bring to Scotland the same settlement he had created in Wales. Unfortunately for his plans, he did not realize the dimensions of his undertaking, for Scotland was both far larger and far wilder than Wales and also much farther from the centers of English authority.

Despite Baliol's gratitude for having gained the throne through Edward's good offices, the new Scots king, supported by most of his people, was determined not to let the country become a mere province of England, and Baliol summoned his own parliament in October 1293. The growing crisis with France, which led to the outbreak of war in 1294, gave the Scots an opportunity to break with England and the Scots browbeat Baliol into a French alliance in October 1295. Infuriated by this betrayal, Edward assembled a large army and invaded Scotland in March 1296, supported by a fleet close inshore, and endeavored to repeat the successful pattern of his first Welsh campaign. Edward smashed the Scots army at Dunbar in April, then swept through the Lowlands and received Baliol's abdication. He then made a rapid circuit of the Highlands before summoning a parliament at Berwick in August, named the Earl of Surrey guardian of the kingdom in his absence, and returned to England.

The following year, Edward was involved in a desultory and unfruitful campaign in France between August and October. While he was away, William Wallace began a revolt in Scotland, and in the spring of 1298 Edward led a second army into Scotland. Although he gained a great victory over Wallace's ragtag army at Falkirk on 22 July 1298, he was unable to capture either Wallace or his chief confederate, Robert the Bruce, the grandson of Baliol's rival. As long as those two leaders and their followers remained at large, Edward's vigorous campaigning, which earned him the title "Hammer of the Scots," could do little to restore peace to Scotland. Edward's capture of Stirling in 1304 seemed to mark a turning point, and he managed to capture Wallace and execute him in 1305. With Scotland in a precarious state of peace, he returned to England that year, but renewed revolt broke out, led by Robert the Bruce, while Edward was away. Determined to maintain English dominance in Scotland, he was on his way north with yet another army when he fell ill and died suddenly at Burgh by Sands near Carlisle on 7 July 1307.

Edward I as a Monarch

Although Edward's efforts to annex Scotland were unsuccessful, this failure should not obscure the real achievements of his reign. Tall, strong, and imposing, he certainly looked the part of a king. He was also both a gifted tactician and a talented strategist, the latter an ability that placed him in the upper reaches of medieval monarchs, among whom warriors were common, but generals rare. He was a bold and inspiring leader and a careful, just ruler who sought the advice of intelligent and independent counselors, partly to curb his fierce temper and his tendency to autocracy. He was possibly England's greatest monarch and certainly its greatest medieval lawmaker.

DAVID L. BONGARD

SEE ALSO: Crusades; History, Medieval Military.

Bibliography

Morris, J. E. 1901. *The Welsh wars of Edward I*. Oxford: Clarendon.
Powicke, F., et al. 1964. *The battle of Lewes, 1264*. Lewes: Friends of Lewes Society.

Prestwick, M. 1972. *War, politics, and finance under Edward I.* New York: St. Martin's Press.

Salzman, L. F. 1968. *Edward I.* New York: Praeger.

EDWARD III [1312–77]

Edward III is well known as the victor of the famous Battle of Crécy in 1346, but this monarch, one of the greatest of late medieval England, was also notable for his campaigns in Scotland and for the justice, liberality, and kindness of his reign.

Early Life

Edward was born at Windsor Castle on 13 November 1312, the eldest son of King Edward II and Queen Isabella. His childhood and youth were unsettled by the great political struggles of the day, for he fled to the continent with his mother to escape the influence of Hugh le Despenser and his family in 1325. While there he was betrothed to Philippa of Hainaut. He returned to England with Isabella and her lover, Roger de Mortimer, in September 1326. Mortimer and Isabella led a revolt against King Edward II, who was first deposed and then brutally murdered in September 1327. Edward III's reign nominally began with his father's deposition (25 January 1327), but real power rested in the hands of Isabella and Mortimer, acting as regents. Edward III took part in an unsuccessful campaign against the Scots during the summer and was thereby compelled to accept the treaty of Northampton in 1328, which recognized Scottish independence.

Coronation and Start of the Hundred Years' War

Edward married Philippa on 24 January 1328; following the birth of his son Edward on 15 June 1330, he captured Mortimer in October, had him executed the following month, and assumed personal rule after respectfully banishing his mother to a royal manor. Determined to reverse England's sagging fortunes, he intervened in Scotland in support of Edward de Baliol; after crushing a Scottish army at Halidon Hill on 19 July 1333, he helped Baliol gain the Scottish throne. Soon afterward he quarreled with King Philip VI over the homage Edward owed the French king for the duchy of Gascony. Edward was also unhappy with Philip's succession to the throne after the death of King Charles IV, and he took the opportunity to revive an old claim to the French throne. These developments led to the outbreak of war in 1337, and Edward began hostilities by establishing bases in Flanders for attacks on France. After he assumed the title "King of France" in January 1340, he destroyed the French fleet in the fierce Battle of Sluys on 24 June. Despite this victory, his campaign in Brittany in 1342 was indecisive, but Edward remained undeterred.

He raised a new army and landed near Cherbourg in Normandy on 12 July 1346. After advancing inland and capturing Caen on 27 July, his army of 12,000 men was nearly trapped by a French army of about 35,000 under King Philip VI. Closely pursued by the French, Edward and his troops escaped across the Seine River. On 26 August, near the village of Crécy, Edward turned to fight, carefully choosing his ground on a gentle rise. The impetuous French knights attacked headlong, trampling their own crossbowmen, but their advance suffered heavily from English longbow fire, and the dense blocks of English men-at-arms repulsed the French attacks with heavy losses. Edward then led his army to besiege Calais for a year and finally captured it in August 1347. While campaigning in France, he instituted the Order of the Garter in 1348 and, despite the near-catastrophic effects of the Black Death, continued to prosecute his war with Philip VI, albeit at a reduced level.

Faced with intervention in Philip's support from Castile, Edward led his fleet to victory over a Castilian fleet off Winchelsea in 1350, although English shipping was sometimes harassed by Castilian privateers even after this English success. Edward spent most of the next ten years in England, although he was often concerned with the war, and sent his eldest son Edward, surnamed "the Black Prince," to France to lead the campaigns. The Black Prince won a great victory over the French at Poitiers on 19 September 1356 and captured the French King Jean II. Despite this great success, Edward did not take the field again until 1360, when he led a triumphal march across France to the walls of Paris and then gained the very favorable terms of the Treaty of Brétigny, at the price of relinquishing his claim to the French throne (24 October).

Later Reign

Despite this apparent success, France remained unsubdued, and following French constable Bertrand du Guesclin's support for Gascon rebels, Edward renewed the war in 1368, entrusting its prosecution to the Black Prince. Following the death of Queen Philippa the next year, Edward fell increasingly under the influence of a succession of mistresses, notably the much-disliked Alice Ferrers (ca. 1371–76). He left the administration of the kingdom largely in the hands of his fourth son, John of Gaunt, and his last years were clouded by the death of the Black Prince on 8 June 1376. Old and ill, he died at Richmond barely a year later, on 21 June 1377, leaving the throne to the Black Prince's 9-year-old son, Richard II.

Edward as King and Commander

Edward III was a ruler of unusual energy and ability, far closer to his grandfather than to his father. As a general he was a fine tactician but lacked Edward I's strategic insight. In the affairs of his own realm, he strove to be just, open-handed, and kind, although he abdicated many of his responsibilities toward the close of his reign, much to the detriment of his kingdom. Personally brave and an eager soldier, he was at heart a knight.

DAVID L. BONGARD

SEE ALSO: History, Medieval Military; Hundred Years' War.

Bibliography

Allmand, C. T. 1973. *Society at war: The experience of England and France during the Hundred Years' War*. Edinburgh: Oliver and Boyd.

Burne, A. H. 1976. *The Crécy war: A military history of the Hundred Years' War from 1337 to the peace of Brétigny, 1360*. London: Eyre and Spottiswoode.

Froissart, J. 1968. *Chronicles*. Trans. and ed. G. Beresford. New York: Viking Press.

Hewitt, H. J. 1966. *The organization of war under Edward III, 1338–1362*. Manchester: Univ. of Manchester Press.

Nicholson, R. 1965. *Edward III and the Scots: The formative years of a military career, 1327–1335*. London: Oxford Univ. Press.

Prestwick, M. 1980. *The three Edwards: War and state in England, 1272–1377*. New York: St. Martin's Press.

Seward, D. 1978. *The Hundred Years' War*. New York: Atheneum.

EISENHOWER, DWIGHT DAVID
[1890–1969]

Dwight David Eisenhower (Fig. 1) was one of the United States' principal Army commanders in World War II and the nation's 34th president. Eisenhower acquired much of his leadership skill, and his ability as a mediator and strategist, during his interwar service in various staff positions in the U.S. Army. As commander of Supreme Headquarters, Allied Expeditionary Force, during 1944–45, he played a major part in the successful conduct of coalition warfare against Italy and Nazi Germany. His two-term presidency in the 1950s lacked the drama of his wartime service, but was characterized by domestic prosperity and cold war tension with the Soviet Union.

Early Life and Army Career to World War II

Eisenhower was born on 14 October 1890 in Denison, Texas, the third son of David and Ida Eisenhower. His original name, David Dwight Eisenhower, was later reversed to Dwight David, and in boyhood he acquired the nickname "Ike," which was to remain with him for life. Growing up in Abilene, Kansas, the young Eisenhower developed a lifelong interest in outdoor recreation and sports. In 1910 he obtained an appointment to the United States Military Academy. He was admitted in 1911 and graduated in 1915, 61st in a class of 164, with a commission of second lieutenant in the infantry. Athletics at West Point greatly interested him, and he both played and coached football. Academically, Eisenhower was an average student, but he successfully met the challenges of the rigorous program of military instruction and from it learned discipline and a sense of duty.

His first assignment after graduation was as a supply officer with the 57th Infantry Regiment at Fort Sam Houston, Texas. In July 1916 he married Mary

Figure 1. Gen. Dwight D. Eisenhower. (SOURCE: U.S. Library
of Congress)

(Mamie) Geneva Doud. Following the United States' entry into World War I
in 1917, Eisenhower was stationed at Fort Oglethorpe, Georgia, to train officer
candidates. This was the first of several training assignments, including one
with the Army's Tank Corps, in which he was to serve for the duration of the
war. Although he later lamented his lack of overseas service in France, Eisenhower gained valuable experience as a leader and organizer while he performed
his training duties.

At Camp Meade, Maryland, in 1919 Eisenhower met Maj. George S. Patton,
Jr., and the two officers studied the art of armored warfare. Together, they
unsuccessfully tried to persuade the U.S. Army to exploit the potential of the
tank to break the deadlock of trench warfare. In 1920 Eisenhower was promoted to major, a rank he was to hold for the next two decades. From 1922 to
1924 he was an executive officer in an infantry brigade at Camp Gaillard,
Panama. In 1926 he graduated first in a class of 275 from the Command and
General Staff College at Fort Leavenworth, Kansas. In the next year he worked
under General John J. Pershing, then head of the American Battles Monu-

ments Commission, and compiled a guidebook to U.S. World War I battlefields in Europe.

Eisenhower graduated from the Army War College in 1928, and, in 1929, as an assistant executive in the Office of the Assistant Secretary of War, he helped write an industrial mobilization plan to convert peacetime industry to a wartime footing. In February 1933 Eisenhower was assigned to the Office of the Chief of Staff, a post held at that time by Gen. Douglas MacArthur. He accompanied MacArthur to the Philippines in 1935 and served under him as military adviser until 1938. As the U.S. Army expanded in the early 1940s, Eisenhower assumed positions of increasing responsibility, first as chief of staff of the 3d Division in November 1940 and then of the IX Army Corps in March 1941, when he was promoted to full colonel. In September 1941 he was promoted to brigadier general in recognition of his performance as Third Army chief of staff during the Louisiana maneuvers in August–September 1941.

World War II Service

Upon the entry of the United States into World War II, Eisenhower's interwar service and the professional reputation he had established with Pershing and MacArthur immediately attracted the attention of Army Chief of Staff General George C. Marshall, who in December 1941 appointed him assistant chief of staff, and head of the Army War Plans Division, which became the nucleus of the new Operations Division in 1942. Eisenhower and Marshall subsequently formulated the overall strategic plan for the conduct of the war by the Allies: a defensive holding strategy against the Japanese in the Pacific theater until Nazi Germany was defeated by an invasion of occupied France and an offensive into Germany. Promoted to major general in March 1942, Eisenhower was posted to Europe two months later and in June took command of the U.S. Army in the European Theater of Operations. He quickly proved himself an adept negotiator and compromiser in managing various high-level tasks of the coordinated Anglo-American war effort. The British did not endorse his and Marshall's plan for an immediate cross-channel invasion of Nazi-occupied Europe, but rather advocated a strategy of first defeating the Axis powers in the Mediterranean.

In July 1942 Eisenhower became a lieutenant general and was chosen to head the first major Allied military effort, Operation "Torch"—the invasion of North Africa. The Allies landed in North Africa in November 1942 and in May 1943 completed the conquest of Tunisia. Throughout the campaign, Eisenhower demonstrated his mastery of coalition warfare, directing and coordinating the efforts of U.S., British, and Free French land, sea, and air forces to drive the Axis powers from North Africa. Promoted to full general in February 1943, he commanded Allied forces in the invasion of Sicily in July–August and the invasion of mainland Italy in September.

In December 1943 Eisenhower was appointed to command Supreme Headquarters, Allied Expeditionary Force (SHAEF), for the planned invasion of northwest Europe—Operation "Overlord." As "Overlord's" supreme commander, Eisenhower directed the complex and comprehensive planning effort, as well as the massive logistical buildup and training program required to assemble the invasion force. It was his decision on 6 June 1944 that launched the successful amphibious assault against Normandy. Once Anglo-American forces had broken out from Normandy in August, Eisenhower directed that the operations across France and into Germany be conducted under a "broad-front" strategy by all Allied ground forces. His decision was political as well as military, for he had to negotiate the conflicting demands of his most vocal subordinates, British Gen. (later Field Marshal) Bernard L. Montgomery and U.S. Lt. Gen. George S. Patton, Jr., who requested that Allied strategy employ a single-thrust advance with the majority of supplies and support provided to their respective armies.

On 1 September 1944 Eisenhower assumed direct command of ground operations in France. His first major command decision was to approve Montgomery's ill-fated ground and airborne offensive, Operation "Market-Garden," despite its seeming violation of the broad-front strategy. Eisenhower was promoted to the newly created rank of general of the army in December 1944, the same month the Germans launched the Ardennes offensive (the Battle of the Bulge). After defeating the German attack, Allied forces resumed their offensive in February 1945, crossed the Rhine River in March, and pushed into Germany until the unconditional German surrender in May.

Postwar Career

From July to November 1945, Eisenhower commanded the American Occupation Zone in Germany. In December 1945 he became army chief of staff. He relinquished that position in February 1948. As chief of staff he oversaw the demobilization of the army and recommended universal military training and unification of the armed forces. After retiring from the army, he became president of Columbia University in June 1948. In December 1950 he was recalled to active duty to serve as the Supreme Allied Commander, Europe, in command of North Atlantic Treaty Organization (NATO) forces in Europe.

Throughout the first seven years of his postwar career, Eisenhower repeatedly turned down offers from both major parties to run for president of the United States. However, in 1952 he resigned his commission and entered politics as the Republican presidential candidate. He won the election in 1952 and ran successfully for a second term in 1956. His presidency was marked by events such as school desegregation and the U.S. intervention in Lebanon in June–August 1958, the latter incident part of the "Eisenhower Doctrine" to protect the Middle East from communist aggression. In July 1953 communist and United Nations negotiators at Panmunjon signed an armistice ending the Korean War, keeping Eisenhower's campaign promise to the war-weary American public to end the conflict in Korea honorably. In domestic politics, an important event of Eisenhower's presidency was the creation of the Department of Health, Education, and Welfare (HEW) in 1953. Eisenhower retired from public life in 1961 and died after a lengthy illness on 28 March 1969.

Assessment

Eisenhower's personal traits of devotion to duty and humility, coupled with his intellectual capabilities as a strategist and organizer as well as his innate political talent, made him the ideal Allied commander for the invasion of northwest Europe. He carefully balanced the conflicting desires of his British and American lieutenants and guided his decision making toward the goal of an expeditious defeat of the European Axis powers. During his presidency he maintained the peace despite cold war tensions, and practiced fiscal responsibility, in large measure due to cuts in the budget of the Defense Department.

SEE ALSO: Korean War; MacArthur, Douglas; Marshall, George Catlett, Jr.; Montgomery, Bernard Law; Patton, George Smith, Jr.; Pershing, John Joseph; World War II.

BRIAN R. BADER

Bibliography

Ambrose, S. E. 1983–84. *Eisenhower.* 2 vols. New York: Simon and Schuster.
Brendon, P. 1986. *Ike: His life and times.* New York: Harper and Row.
Butcher, H. 1946. *My three years with Eisenhower.* New York: Simon and Schuster.
Davis, K. S. 1945. *Soldier of democracy: A biography of Dwight Eisenhower.* Garden City, New York: Doubleday, Doran.
Eisenhower, D. D. 1948. *Crusade in Europe.* Garden City, N.Y.: Doubleday.

EUGENE, PRINCE OF SAVOY-CARIGNAN [1663–1736]

Prince Eugene was one of the greatest soldiers of the late seventeenth and early eighteenth centuries (Fig. 1). He directed the Austrian campaigns that liberated Hungary and Croatia from Turkish rule, and together with the Duke of Marlborough, his famous comrade-in-arms of the War of the Spanish Succession, he won an exceptional series of victories over the French armies of Louis XIV.

Early Life

Eugene was born in Paris on 18 October 1663, the son of Maurice, Prince of Savoy-Carignan, and Olympia Mancini and through his mother the grandnephew of Cardinal Mazarin. As a child he was small, ugly, and weak, and he was early destined for an ecclesiastical career, an idea that appalled him. His repeated entreaties to King Louis XIV to enter the French army were brusquely denied, and in desperation Eugene fled France in July 1683. Ever after he harbored bitter memories of the callous treatment he had received in France.

Traveling to Passau, Eugene met Emperor Leopold I, who accepted him for service in the Austrian army. Soon thereafter he won distinction fighting against

Figure 1. Eugene, prince of Savoy. (SOURCE: U.S. Library of Congress)

the Turks under Charles V of Lorraine at the climactic Battle of Vienna (12 September 1683). In recognition of his services, he was rewarded with command of the Kuefstein Dragoon Regiment in December, and he led his regiment with bravery and skill during the campaigns in Hungary between 1684 and 1688. He modeled his behavior on that of his commanders, Charles V of Lorraine and Louis of Baden. Exploiting his Savoyard connections, the emperor sent Eugene on a diplomatic mission to Savoy, where he won Duke Victor Amadeus to the imperial cause in July 1690. Eugene was appointed to command the cavalry of Antonio Caraffa's imperial army in Italy later that year. Between 1690 and 1692 he relieved Coni, captured Carmagnola, and defeated the forces of French Marshal Catinat, but he was prevented from gaining a decisive success by the conservatism and timidity of Caraffa and the Duke of Savoy. In 1692, during the unsuccessful Austrian invasion of Dauphiné, in eastern France, Eugene's capture of Gap and Embrun won him promotion to *feldmarschall* (field marshal) in 1693. He was appointed to supreme command in Italy the next year, at the age of 30.

Eugene's efforts in Italy were hampered by the poor quality of his troops and by the continued timidity of the Duke of Savoy. Thus he must have been pleased in 1697 when he was appointed commander in chief on the Hungarian frontier. Applying his usual energy, he reorganized and revitalized the Austrian army there, won a great victory over the Turks at Zenta on 11 September, and confirmed his reputation as one of the leading generals of his day. He went on to capture Sarajevo in October 1697.

War of the Spanish Succession and Cooperation with Marlborough

At the outbreak of the War of the Spanish Succession with France in 1701, Eugene led a small army across the mountains from Hungary to Italy. He defeated his old opponent Marshal Catinat at Carpi on 9 July and repulsed Marshal Villeroi's assault at Chiara on 1 September. Eugene captured Villeroi during an otherwise unsuccessful surprise attack on Cremona (1 February 1702). Short of troops and supplies, he was unable to defeat Villeroi's successor, Marshal Vendôme, at Luzzara on 15 August 1702. He returned to Vienna late that year to become president of the *Hofkriegsrat* (war council). In that post Eugene strengthened the imperial cavalry and made supply more flexible. The following year he went to Hungary and reorganized the forces there. In early 1704 he led those troops into southern Germany in concert with Marlborough's descent on Bavaria between May and July.

Eugene joined forces with Marlborough and his army on 12 August. Next day they won a great victory over the armies of Marshals Tallard and Marsin and Elector Maximilian of Bavaria at Blenheim. Their collaboration in this victory led to an enduring friendship between Eugene and Marlborough. Eugene returned to Italy, where he claimed victory over Vendôme at the inconclusive Battle of Cassano on 16 August 1705. In the following year's campaigns, Eugene slipped past Vendôme's army in July and marched on Turin to assist Duke Victor Amadeus. After seizing Parma on 15 August 1706, he joined forces with the duke near Turin on 31 August. Together, Eugene and Victor Amadeus attacked and defeated the French army of the Duke of Orléans and Marshal Marsin at Turin on 7 September 1706. Building on his victory, Eugene drove the French from Italy between September and December. He invaded southern France in July and August 1707, although he received scant support from Victor Amadeus.

In 1708 Eugene led his army north to the Low Countries, again to join forces with Marlborough. He hurried ahead of his troops and arrived in time to join Marlborough on the field of Oudenarde, where they defeated Vendôme's army on 11 July 1708. The two allied generals operated in concert over the next several years. Next Eugene successfully besieged and captured Lille between 14 August and 11 December 1708 while Marlborough led the covering force. Eugene also took part in the siege and capture of both Tournai, between 28 June and 29 July 1709, and Mons, between 4 September and 26 October of that year. The efforts of the French Marshals Villars and Boufflers to relieve Mons resulted on 11 September in the Battle of Malplaquet, where Eugene led the allied right and center in that murderous struggle, while Marlborough led the army's left. In 1710 he captured both Douai, on 10 June, and Bethune, on 30 August, but returned to Vienna after the death of Emperor Joseph I late that year to ensure the orderly election of Charles VI as Holy Roman emperor.

Eugene returned to Flanders just after Villars attacked and routed part of the allied army at Denain on 24 July 1712, and between August and October he waged a defensive campaign of maneuver against Villars's army. He urged Charles VI to make peace, and gained favorable terms from Villars in negotiations at Rastatt, which culminated in a peace treaty there on 6 March 1714.

Campaigns Against the Ottomans and Later Career

The end of the war with France was not the end of campaigning for Eugene, and he assumed command in Hungary when war with Turkey broke out again in spring 1716. He gained a notable victory over the Turkish army of Damad Ali Pasha at Peterwardein on 5 August and then went on to besiege and capture Temesvar between 1 September and 14 December 1716.

The following year Eugene invested Belgrade on 29 June and inflicted a crushing defeat on Shalil Pasha's relief army on 16 August 1717. The Austrian victory induced the Turkish garrison to surrender on 18 August. Within a year the war ended with the Treaty of Passarowitz, signed on 21 July 1718.

Following the Turkish War, Eugene became a trusted adviser to Emperor Charles VI. He was known over the following years for his moderation and pragmatism. Most of his activities during the years from 1718 to 1733 were related to peacetime administration and economic development, but Eugene retained an active interest in military affairs.

During the War of Polish Succession, Eugene exercised command in the Rhine Valley from April to September 1733, but age (he was nearly 70) and an indifferent army hampered his efforts. In his last campaign Eugene prevented an invasion of southern Germany by a French army under the Duke of Berwick. He then returned to Vienna, where he died on the night of 20 April 1736.

Assessment

Eugene was a gifted commander, renowned for the speed of his movements and his skill in maneuver. He was popular with his soldiers, who appreciated his efforts to keep them well supplied. As a military administrator and organizer, he had few equals in his day. He enjoyed considerable success as a diplomat, and his cordial and very fruitful cooperation with Marlborough is almost unique in the history of alliance warfare. In sum, Eugene was probably the foremost soldier of his generation and certainly assembled the most impressive list of victories. He also was known for his patronage of the arts, and his library was famous throughout Europe for its depth and variety.

DAVID L. BONGARD

SEE ALSO: France, Military Hegemony of; Marlborough, John Churchill, Duke of.

Bibliography

Arneth, A. von. 1864. *Prinz Eugen von Savoyen.* 3 vols. Vienna: W. Braunmüller.
Braubach, M. 1963–65. *Prinz Eugen von Savoyen.* 5 vols. Munich: R. Oldenburg.
Chandler, D. G. 1976. *The art of warfare in the age of Marlborough.* London: Batsford.

Eugen, Prinz von Savoyen. 1876–92. *Feldzüge des Prinzen Eugen von Savoyen*. 20 vols.
    Vienna: Abteilung für Kriegsgeschichte des Kaiserlich-Königliche Kriegsarchiv.
Henderson, N. 1965. *Prince Eugen of Savoy*. New York: Praeger.
McKay, D. 1977. *Prince Eugene of Savoy*. London: Thames and Hudson.
Quincy, C. S., Marquis de. 1736–37. *The military history of the late Prince Eugene of
    Savoy*. Ed and trans. J. Campbell. 2 vols. London: C. Du Bosc.

F

FARRAGUT, DAVID GLASGOW
[1801–70]

Admiral David G. Farragut was the most famous U.S. naval officer of the nineteenth century (Fig. 1). His tactical skill, acumen, and decisiveness in battle, qualities that were exhibited most explicitly at the Battle of Mobile Bay, were among the strengths of this remarkable naval leader.

Early Life and Career

Born as James Glasgow Farragut on 5 July 1801 near Knoxville, Tennessee, Farragut was the son of George Farragut (1755–1817), who had served as a young merchant and naval sailor in Spain and Russia before he became a privateer lieutenant for the American forces in 1776. Later, he served as a cavalry officer in the Carolinas and in the frontier militia in Tennessee, and then became a sailing master during the War of 1812. The family was friendly with the family of Capt. David Porter, and when George Farragut's wife died of yellow fever in 1808, young James became the ward of Captain Porter. Out of gratitude and devotion to Porter, James later changed his first name to David.

In 1810, the young Farragut accepted an appointment as a midshipman from Tennessee and served under Porter on the frigate *Essex* during the War of 1812. The *Essex* captured many British merchant and whaling ships and, because Porter had such respect for Farragut, he put the 12-year-old lad in charge of the *Alexander Barclay*, one of the prizes. Already an expert ship's officer by the age of 20, Farragut served under Porter in 1823 during the U.S. naval operations against pirates in the Caribbean. In 1824, he was given his first official command in the U.S. Navy, the *Ferret*.

Civil War

For more than three decades Farragut served on routine assignments in the navy, then he served brilliantly in the Civil War, being promoted to the newly created rank of rear admiral in July 1862, to the newly created rank of vice admiral in December 1864, and to full admiral in July 1866. These accomplishments were particularly notable, given the fact that Farragut was considered a

Figure 1. David Glasgow Farragut. (SOURCE: U.S. Library of Congress)

southerner and therefore was suspect in the eyes of his superiors as the North entered the Civil War.

Farragut spent the initial period of the war on land (September–December 1861) as a member of a naval retirement board in New York City, but his late guardian's son, Cdr. D. D. Porter, interceded on his behalf. This influence overcame the suspicions against Farragut, and in December 1861 he was made commander of a Union squadron engaged in blockading operations in the western region of the Gulf of Mexico. While there, he was ordered to proceed up the Mississippi River and capture the port of New Orleans, which was then an important receiving point for Confederate war supplies. Sailing from the Gulf of Mexico in February 1862, Farragut proceeded to the Mississippi. The War Department recommended that Farragut first attack and neutralize two forts that were situated downstream from New Orleans. On 18 April Farragut's forces began a bombardment of the forts that lasted for six days but was ultimately unsuccessful. On the night of 24 April Farragut led his force past the forts while under fire, and engaged and destroyed a Confederate river squadron that was stationed just upstream from them. Troops were then disembarked from Union transports, and they captured both the forts and New Orleans.

In 1862, as Gen. Ulysses S. Grant advanced on Vicksburg, Mississippi, Farragut led his naval forces past heavy Confederate defenses at Fort Hudson and interdicted Confederate traffic along the Red River. Closing this supply route greatly assisted Grant, and Vicksburg fell to the Union in July 1863. The entire Mississippi River area was under Union control soon thereafter.

In the subsequent weeks, Farragut's forces continued to operate in the Mississippi and the Gulf of Mexico. After a brief return to New York, Farragut, on board the *Hartford*, voyaged to Pensacola Harbor in January 1864. For the next several months, he commanded the Union blockade of his assigned portion of the Gulf of Mexico.

BATTLE OF MOBILE BAY

His next major operation was against the port of Mobile at Mobile Bay, Alabama, which was heavily defended by several forts and by the Confederate ironclad *Tennessee*. The entrance to the bay was protected by Fort Morgan and Fort Gaines, and by mines, called "torpedoes," which were laid in a pattern that forced enemy ships to pass within close range of the guns of Fort Morgan.

On 5 August 1864, Farragut formed his force of armored monitors, frigates, and other ships into two columns, each led by monitors. The *Tecumseh*, the leading monitor, proceeded to engage the Confederate *Tennessee*, but was destroyed when it struck a mine. The *Brooklyn*, the leading wooden ship, stopped and tried to back clear of the mines, and the entire column of ships drifted aimlessly under the guns of Fort Morgan. Farragut shouted his famous words, "Damn the torpedoes, full speed ahead," to the *Brooklyn*, and swung his own ship, the *Hartford*, clear of the other ships and headed her across the mines, which failed to explode. The other Union ships followed Farragut, and the force subsequently anchored safely upstream from the forts. The *Tennessee* sailed forth from the protection of the forts to engage the Union ships. It was rammed several times, and, after intense fighting, surrendered. The forts were thus isolated and their occupants subsequently surrendered.

Mobile Bay was the climax of Farragut's career. Although poor health plagued him, he was placed in command of the European Squadron in 1867, and embarked on the frigate *Franklin* for a triumphal cruise of Europe. He returned home in November 1868. He died less than two years later, on 14 August 1870, on the dispatch boat *Tallapoosa* during its visit to Portsmouth Navy Yard in New Hampshire.

Significance

Farragut had an excellent understanding of the strategic realities of the Civil War and was noted for his excellent planning and brave execution of operations. These traits, combined with his tactical skill and decisiveness in the confusion of battle, accounted for his success. His most critical successes were against land fortifications, shore forts and batteries, which he considered to be vulnerable in wartime. Farragut's accomplishments made him the most famous U.S. admiral of the period between the Revolutionary War and the twentieth century.

BRUCE W. WATSON

SEE ALSO: Civil War, American; Grant, Ulysses Simpson; Naval Warfare.

Bibliography

Hoyt, E. P. 1970. *Damn the torpedoes! The story of America's first admiral: David Glasgow Farragut*. London: Abelard-Shuman.
Lewis, C. L. 1980. *David Glasgow Farragut*. New York: Arno Press.
Mahan, A. T. [1892] 1970. *Admiral Farragut*. St. Clair Shores, Mich.: Scholarly Press.
Reynolds, C. G. 1978. *Famous American admirals*. New York: Van Nostrand Reinhold.
Spiller, R. J. 1989. *American military leaders*. New York: Praeger.

FEUDALISM

Feudalism was a personal contractual relationship in medieval Europe in which a lord bestowed land upon a noble servitor in exchange for military service. Feudalism included a decentralized political system, a system of values, and a military system based on the castle and mounted knight.

Origins

Historians dispute the origins of feudalism, although most agree it was a blend of Roman and German institutions and customs. During the late Roman Empire, a *precarium* was a grant of land held by someone at the will of the donor; tenure could be terminated at any time. The *precarium* continued into the Frankish empire, where it was held for a specific period in return for rent or performance of a stipulated service. It was then often found in ecclesiastical lands that could not be given away.

Under Roman *patrocinium* (patronage), men provided service to a powerful patron in exchange for protection. Tacitus described a German tribal fealty rite (*comitatus*) whose name he coined from the companions (*comites*) of the chief. The men followed him (in peace and war) in exchange for military equipment, other goods, and a share of the booty. The voluntary relationship could be terminated at any time.

Nevertheless, the institutions we identify as feudal did not appear until the eighth century. The term *vassal* dates from the 730s and describes a man who received a *benefice* (usually an agrarian estate, including the serfs, or nonfree tenants) in exchange for military or political service. This coincided with the introduction of the stirrup and armored, heavy cavalry into Western Europe, which laid the groundwork for the development of the mainstay of feudalism, the mounted knight, who needed financial support (land in the precapitalist economy) to pay for his horse and armor. Carolingian vassalage was a personal relationship restricted to fighting men; *benefices* (granted from royal lands or confiscated estates) were held on condition of military service and could not be inherited. This military benefice was called a *fief* (Latin *feudum*).

Basic Principles

Feudalism was a mutual obligation between a lord and his vassal. The vassal promised to faithfully provide advice and military aid when requested; the lord had a reciprocal duty to support and defend his vassals. If either defaulted on the obligation, the contract was void and the guilty party declared a felon. A code of conduct (chivalry) outlined the vassal relationship. This relationship was reflected in two rites: *homage* and *fealty*. During the rite of homage, the vassal knelt before the lord and placed his hands between his lord's as a symbol of his subordination, acknowledging sole service to that lord. An oath of fealty taken after the ceremony of homage provided a religious sanction to the new relationship.

Institutions

The basic institutions were the lord, the vassal, and the fief (normally a landed estate, although monetary fiefs did exist). It was possible for a vassal to parcel out his fief to junior servitors and become a lord in turn for his estate, mirroring the rites and obligations at a lower level. This was known as *subinfeudation*. There was no limit to the number of subdivisions, as long as the grant was sufficient to finance the new vassal's obligations. Since a vassal could receive fiefs from different lords in different locations, discrepancies and conflicts of loyalty could result. Usually, one primary lord was designated the *liege lord*, to whom the vassal owed *liege homage*, which took precedence over ordinary homage owed other lords.

The lord had rights over his vassal's fief known as *feudal incidents*. The fief was held for the period of service; but if there was an heir, the lord was obligated to pass it on to him. The new vassal swore homage and fealty and received an *investiture* (a symbolic object to mark his formal possession of the fief), and he paid the lord a sum of money, called *relief*. If the vassal died without an heir, the lord declared the fief *escheat* and regranted it to another of his choice. Primogeniture demanded that the fief be passed intact to the eldest son. If the eldest son was a minor, he was declared a ward and the lord took the fief (pocketing any revenue), supporting the heir until his majority. If the vassal died with only a daughter as an heir, the lord picked a bridegroom, and the new husband assumed homage. If the vassal was declared a felon for violating feudal law, he forfeited his estate and the lord would regrant it to another vassal.

Feudal Service

The vassal owed the lord military, political, and financial service. The vassal was expected to provide mounted troops from among his own vassals (usually a pre-set quota) at his own expense for a specified term of service. The length of the term of service varied—40 days was common after A.D. 1100. When the time limit expired, the vassal was legally free to pack up and go home, even if a campaign was in progress. A lord might get around this, especially during a siege, by calling up vassals sequentially so that new servitors appeared as the obligation of those on duty expired.

Political service was called suit to court. When summoned to court by the lord, the vassal had to appear at his own expense. He might then advise the lord on affairs of state or serve on a feudal court when an errant vassal was tried by his peers.

The lord could demand financial service on special occasions such as the knighting of his son, the marriage of his daughter, a crusade, or payment of ransom (e.g., Richard the Lionheart). When the lord and his retainers visited a vassal (*hospitality*), the vassal had to foot the bill. Fines levied during judicial proceedings and income derived from the feudal incidents also were forms of financial service.

Feudal Military

The two basic institutions of the feudal military were the mounted knight and the castle. The concept of mounted, mailed warriors evolved following the introduction of the stirrup, which, in Western Europe, occurred probably after A.D. 500 (the approximate date is a matter of controversy). However, the huge expense of providing a warhorse and armor was prohibitive for a lone warrior. In the precapital economy, it was beyond the means of a sovereign to finance a national army. Feudalism provided kings with military manpower, and fiefs funded their equipment. Command and control of feudal armies depended upon feudal and social relationships. There was no military rank structure. Lords called upon their vassals to form an army for a campaign. The commander of the force was not chosen for his military expertise; rather, the noble with the senior title assumed command. Armies formed into three "battles." All three battles attacked simultaneously; there was rarely a reserve, because knights feared missing out on battlefield booty. Terrain was rarely taken into consideration when choosing a field of battle. Indeed, few actual "great" battles took place. A small number of mercenary infantry accompanied the feudal host, but such service was not usually viewed as honorable, as shown by the French knights' massacre of their own mercenary crossbowmen at Crécy. Mercenaries' loyalty lasted as long as their pay (derived from taxes and feudal obligations).

A knight began his training at age 7. The son of a knight would enter the service of his father's lord or another knight as a *page;* at about 15 he would become a *squire* and accompany his master into battle. At about 20 the squire could be knighted, either in peacetime or on the battlefield, by another knight tapping him on the shoulder with a sword (*accolade*).

Medieval castles (from *castellum*, fort) evolved from simple *motte* (natural or man-made hill) and *bailey* (walled court) structures into quite elaborate structures (Fig. 1). Each castle, however, had common features. The fortress was surrounded by a moat, or ditch, which was crossed by a drawbridge. Outer walls (battlements) were high and very thick. Projecting over the battlements were ledges (ramparts) from which the defenders fought. Along the battlements were towers. Defenders fought with arrows, rocks, hot liquids, and, later, crude artillery. A smaller, inner fortress called a *keep*, or *donjon*, housed the lord, his treasury, and bodyguards. It could continue the defense even if the outer fortress fell. Well-situated fortresses with an independent water supply and sufficient foodstuffs could usually outlast a siege manned by a feudal army. The development of cannon made the medieval castle's high wall progressively vulnerable.

Heyday and Decline

Feudalism reached its apogee in the twelfth century. It had developed in response to a decentralized political system with a weak central government and an economy consisting only of lords, knights, and peasants. By the fourteenth century, with the growth of commerce and the rise of cities, a new middle class developed between the knights and the peasants. The merchant class had wealth in capital, not land. Even as early as the thirteenth century, English barons could pay a sum of money, *scutage* (shield money), to avoid field service. The old personal relationship declined into a set of financial obligations. Fiefs became property that could be inherited outright. Strong central governments with salaried officials and mercenary forces (England, France, and the Holy Roman Empire) displaced the feudal knights. New mil-

Figure 1. Military engineering of the Middle Ages. (SOURCE: Iconographic Encyclopaedia).

itary technology and the rise of the bowman and pikeman (infantry) in the fourteenth century eventually rendered the mounted knight obsolete.

Geographical Occurrence

Feudalism spread throughout Europe in various degrees from the Frankish kingdom of the Loire and Rhine valleys, Carolingian lands in southern France, Spain, Palestine, and Germany, and in lands conquered by the Norman French (England, southern Italy, and Crusader states in the Near East). Elements of feudal institutions also appeared in Scandinavia and Russia. Some historians have identified feudalism in samurai Japan and China (Shang and Chou epochs ca. 1500–200 B.C.) because of the characteristic decentralized power, the importance of the warrior, and subinfeudation.

Marxist Interpretation of Feudalism

Karl Marx viewed history as a constant dialectical class struggle based on changing modes of production. All societies would necessarily go through five economic stages: slavery, feudalism, capitalism, socialism, and communism. All five stages had to occur in that order. None could be skipped. All political, religious, and social institutions were derived from the given economic system. This has created problems for Marxist historians (and revolutionaries) who had to identify each stage in their national history and who, arguably, had to wait for each stage to evolve before the expected socialist revolution could occur.

DIANNE L. SMITH

SEE ALSO: Charlemagne; Crusades; History, Medieval Military; Roman Empire.

Bibliography

Beeler, J. H. 1971. *Warfare in feudal Europe, 700–1200.* Ithaca, N.Y.: Cornell Univ. Press.
Bloch, M. 1961. *Feudal society.* Chicago: Univ. of Chicago Press.
Oman, C. W. C. 1953. *The art of war in the Middle Ages.* Rev. and ed. J. Beeler. Ithaca, N.Y.: Cornell Univ. Press.
Painter, S. 1951. *Mediaeval society.* Ithaca, N.Y.: Cornell Univ. Press.
Turnbull, S. 1985. *The book of the medieval knight.* London: Arms and Armour Press.
Wise, T. 1976. *Medieval warfare.* New York: Hastings House.

FISHER, JOHN ARBUTHNOT, 1st BARON FISHER OF KILVERSTONE [1841–1920]

John Arbuthnot Fisher was Britain's most important naval leader during the decade that preceded the outbreak of the First World War. As service chief (First Sea Lord) of the Royal Navy from 1904 to 1910, he implemented a series of administrative reforms that greatly increased the fighting efficiency of the fleet, and was associated with the introduction of the battleship *Dreadnought*, which set new standards for capital ship design that were subsequently emulated by all major naval powers. Driven from office in 1910 by opposition to his policies and methods, Fisher returned to the Admiralty as First Sea Lord in October 1914, serving until May 1915.

Early Life and Career

Fisher was born in January 1841 in Ceylon, the first child of eleven sired by a less than prosperous but well-connected English planter. Fisher was sent to England at the age of 6 for his education, joined the navy in July 1854 as a naval cadet, and served in the Baltic during the Crimean War. He became a midshipman in 1856 and, after seeing action in China, was promoted in 1860 to mate and then acting lieutenant. In 1861, following a brilliant performance in the examinations for the rank of lieutenant, Fisher was promoted to that rank with the date of promotion made retroactive to November of the previous year. He attained the rank of commander in 1869, and captain in 1874 at the age of 33. Fisher was married in 1866.

Early Military Career

As commander of HMS *Excellent*, the gunnery school of the Royal Navy, from 1883 to 1886, and Director of Naval Ordnance from 1886 to 1891, Fisher played a major role in the adoption of breech-loading big guns, quick-firing guns, and naval range finders. Promoted to rear admiral in 1890, Fisher became the Superintendent of the Portsmouth Dockyard in 1891. As Third Sea Lord and controller on the Board of Admiralty from 1892 to 1897, Fisher was in charge of the procurement of naval materiel, which gave him the opportunity to invent the destroyer and expedite the introduction of water-tube boilers. Fisher was promoted to the rank of vice admiral in 1897 and took command of the North America and West Indies station for a brief period during that year. After that he assumed command of the Mediterranean Fleet (then the premier seagoing appointment in the Royal Navy), serving there until 1901, in which year he also became an admiral. Made Second Sea Lord in 1902, Fisher formulated a fundamental reform of naval education that was subsequently implemented, after which in 1903 he became commander in chief at Portsmouth.

Influence on Naval Policy

In October 1904 Fisher became First Sea Lord with instructions to reduce naval expenditures substantially, but also with a mandate to introduce major changes in administration and warship design. In his first two years in office, Fisher made drastic alterations in the management of the dockyards, the manning of the reserve fleet, and training in naval gunnery. He scrapped many obsolete warships, withdrew major units from foreign stations in order to concentrate the main strength of the Royal Navy in home waters, and orchestrated the adoption of turbine propulsion and the all-big-gun system for capital ships. Fisher's administrative reforms and the disruption of foreign building programs by the advent of the all-big-gun battleship *Dreadnought* made it possible for Britain to reduce its naval expenditures significantly from 1905 through 1908 without undue diminution of its naval security. By 1909, however, Fisher's radical administrative and technical changes, certain shortcomings in policy, and heavy-handed style of leadership had bitterly divided the service, creating public controversy that caused him to retire in 1910 as an Admiral of the Fleet, a rank that he had attained in 1905.

Fisher's close friendship with the young Winston Churchill, who became First Lord of the Admiralty in 1911, allowed him to play a significant unofficial role in the formulation of naval policy, including important decisions on naval materiel that resulted in the adoption of heavier caliber main armament guns and the replacement of coal by oil fuel for the battleships of the 1912 program. Shortly after the outbreak of World War I, Churchill recalled Fisher to the Admiralty as First Sea Lord. Fisher's quick action in response to the British defeat at Coronel led to the major British naval success at the Falkland Islands in December 1914, and he formulated the plans that largely determined the course of British warship construction for the rest of the war. His opposition to the diversion of substantial naval resources to the Dardanelles and his demands for the construction of battlecruisers of unprecedented speed and firepower, however, disrupted his relations with Churchill, and in May 1915 he resigned in the hope that he would be recalled with the greater authority that he required to control operations and implement his building program. To his dismay, Fisher found himself politically isolated and never again held a major office, although he served as chairman of the relatively inconsequential Board of Invention and Research from 1915 to 1918. He died in July 1920 at the age of 79.

Summary

Fisher was a man of quick intelligence, strong opinion, vigorous industry, and unbending resolution. He possessed great personal charm, respected talent, and delegated authority easily. He was also devious, unforgiving, and ruthless. Thus, while he won politically influential patronage and the loyalty of capable subordinates, he was distrusted by many of his naval peers. Fisher was also a technological radical. By 1904, he was convinced that the battleship was obsolete as a type and that it should be replaced by the battlecruiser, an opinion that caused him to oppose proposals to build the *Dreadnought* in 1905, and in later years to press for the construction of battlecruisers instead of dreadnought battleships. In more general terms, Fisher believed that what mattered in naval war was not numbers but quality, and that Britain's naval supremacy could therefore only be maintained through a policy of building capital ships that were much more capable than those of rival powers. Neither the bureaucratic development of the Admiralty nor Fisher's brand of personal rule, however, was adequate to the task of managing the kind of research and development effort that was needed to produce the succession of technological breakthroughs in naval materiel required to realize such an advanced strategy.

JON TETSURO SUMIDA

SEE ALSO: British Seapower; Churchill, Sir Winston Leonard Spencer; Naval Warfare; World War I.

Bibliography

Bacon, Sir R. H. S. 1929. *The life of Lord Fisher of Kilverstone.* 2 vols. Garden City, N.Y.: Doubleday, Doran.

Fisher, J. A., Baron. 1920. *Memories and records, by Admiral of the Fleet, Lord Fisher.* . . . 2 vols. New York: George H. Doran.

Kemp, P. K., ed. 1960–64. *The papers of Admiral Sir John Fisher.* 2 vols. London: Navy Records Society.

Mackay, R. F. 1973. *Fisher of Kilverstone.* Oxford: Clarendon Press.

Marder, A. J., ed. 1952–59. *Fear God and dread nought: The correspondence of Admiral of the Fleet Lord Fisher of Kilverstone.* 3 vols. London: Cape.

———. 1961–70. *From the Dreadnought to Scapa Flow: The Royal Navy in the Fisher era, 1904–1919.* 5 vols. New York: Oxford Univ. Press.

Sumida, J. T. 1989. *In defence of naval supremacy: Finance, technology, and British naval policy, 1889–1914.* Boston: Unwin Hyman.

FLAGS AND SYMBOLS

"Great is the value of the standard," British general Sir Charles Napier explained a century and a half ago. "It contains the symbol of the honor of the band, and the brave press round its banner." To Napier, who fought under Wellington in Spain against Napoleon (1808–14) and who gained fame for himself by leading the relief of Hyderabad in the Sind War (1843), few things were more important to a soldier than his regiment's colors. To the common private the flag was the rallying point amidst the disorder of combat. To the generals it was, as Napier put it, "the telegraph in the center of the battle" by which commanders could follow the progress of units and issue orders. Whether as a symbol of honor, a rallying point, or a communications device, the unit standard has led men in war for at least 5,000 years (Fig. 1).

Earliest Times

The first recorded evidence of soldiers being led into battle by flags or standards comes from the tombs of ancient Egypt. On the cosmetics palette of King Narmer, who ruled circa 3000 B.C., are depictions of Egyptian soldiers carrying long poles atop which are perched representations of animals such as jackals and birds. Short streamers are attached to these poles. Similar drawings have been found on temple walls. The account of Pharoah Ramses' battle with the Hittites at Kadesh, along the banks of Lebanon's Orontes River, in 1294 B.C. includes references to the divisions of "Re and Amon" being preceded by charioteers holding aloft the symbols of these gods on totem-style standards.

Other ancient peoples used similar standards as symbols of authority and organization. Wall paintings discovered at Mari, a former trading and military

Figure 1. Raising the American flag over Mt. Suribachi, Iwo Jima, 1945. (SOURCE: U.S. Library of Congress)

post of the Sumerian Empire (ca. 2700 B.C.) on the Euphrates River, show Sumerian troops being led into battle by a standard-bearer. The Old Testament repeatedly mentions invading armies following the "banners" of the kings of Babylon, Assyria, and other empires of the ancient Middle East.

There are references in Chinese history to the use of military flags in the twelfth century B.C., and a book written in the fifth century B.C. mentions flags being used by cavalry units. Despite that reference, even in China, as in most ancient empires, a rigid, carved symbol on a pike was apparently favored over a flag. Chinese forces of the T'ang Dynasty (600 B.C.–A.D. 900), for example, are pictured in drawings being led by men carrying staffs topped with an inverted crescent moon.

The Phoenician navy and the soldiers it hired to fight in its far-flung Mediterranean trading empire did so beneath an identifying standard. The fleets of the Peloponnesian wars (460–404 B.C.) raised standards and may have unfurled simple banners from their ships as a means of identifying friend from foe in the confused actions of the day.

The armies of Europe also followed banners and standards. The earliest evidence of cloth flags in use by land forces in Western Europe is found in the tombs of the Etruscans (ca. 300 B.C.) of northern Italy. Depictions of soldiers carrying a rounded, intricately designed cloth attached to the staff of a spear have been found on Etruscan funeral urns.

Roman Standards

The Roman armies that conquered Italy and the rest of the Mediterranean basin did so beneath the standards of the legion. Initially it was a simple device, such as a triangular piece of beaten metal stamped with a number or the representation of an animal, afixed to a pole. The standards grew larger as medals, medallions, mottos, and other symbols of victories and honors were added to the standard. The standards on a relief in the church of San Marcello in Rome, for example, have at least five such devices, ranging from an outstretched hand to a castle, and include crescent moons, circles, wreaths, and the imperial eagle.

Each legion had a unique symbol that represented the god or goddess who protected the unit or that showed the zodiac symbol under which its founding general or emperor was born. Pliny the Elder wrote that Republican legions often had five standards, each of which carried a different symbol, such as a wolf, boar, minotaur, horse, or eagle. Under the Republic, legionary standards bore the inscription "SPQR" (*Senatus Populusque Romanus*—the Senate and the People of Rome). In the first century B.C., Marius made the eagle the supreme symbol of the legion, a practice that was continued by the emperors. An imperial eagle topped most legionary standards, although many retained the SPQR inscription as a token of allegiance to the senate.

The eagle and other symbols on the standard were made of, or were at least gilded with, gold or silver, and this rather heavy and unwieldy device was entrusted to a standard-bearer, the aquilifer. These standard-bearers ranked just below centurions in the chain of command and were exempt from menial duties. They wore an animal-skin headdress and robe that could either be of the animal symbol of the legion or its station, such as the African lion or a wolf (as a remembrance of the legend of Romulus and Remus, the founders of the Roman state who were allegedly raised by a she-wolf in the hills of central Italy).

Like those of Ramses, the legionary standards had a religious significance. They were blessed with sacred oil, were kept in a special shrine (the *sacellum*) in the legionary headquarters, and were used for both military and religious gatherings. When new recruits joined the legion they swore an oath to protect the standard. The reverence that standards were shown drew early Christian writers to equate them with pagan symbols.

Roman generals used standards as part of their command system. Trumpeters would sound the commands, and the standard-bearers would then face the standards in the direction they were ordered to march, or would wave them about to indicate a change of formation.

Some generals, notably Julius Caesar, made limited use of flags for signal purposes. In his *Commentaries*, for example, Caesar describes how he raised a red flag on a pole as a danger signal that his fort was under attack. The Romans made limited use of unit flags for their navy and cavalry. Instead of a legionary standard, cavalry units carried a device known as the vexillum, a small flag attached to a bar, which is itself attached as a crosspiece to a short spear or staff. The flag was often fringed and usually carried an inscription or other device. Small, specialized units of infantry and cavalry, or of a mixed force, also bore the vexillum, and because of this were known as "vexillatio." Detachments from a legion were also given special vexillia. One of those, which was found in a tomb in Egypt, is in the collection of the Hermitage Museum in St. Petersburg, Russia.

The loss of a standard was considered the greatest dishonor a legion could suffer. Emperor Augustus waged wars in Germany and Persia just to reclaim the lost eagles of the legions of Crassus and Varus that had been wiped out at Carrhae (53 B.C.) and Teutoburger Wald (A.D. 9), respectively. Like the soldiers of Napier's days, Roman legionnaires placed their honor in their standards.

The Dark Ages

The barbarian hordes that swept from the steppe into Europe, and which eventually buried the standards of the Roman Empire, also carried standards. According to the historian Arrian, the Scythians carried fluttering dragonlike pennants made of dyed cloth that "even hiss in the breeze" as the horsemen bearing them sped past. Sarmatian auxiliaries introduced these dragon flags into the Roman army in the mid-fourth century A.D. According to the historian Vegetius, they became so popular that within 50 years each cohort of the legions carried the dragon banner known as the "draconarius."

Each of the barbarian hordes that came west had its own standard, usually symbolizing their gods or a device favored by their ruler. The armies of Islam that swept out of Arabia in the sixth century carried huge colored flags (usually green) that bore inscriptions from the Koran, the Muslim holy book. The Carolingian Franks raised the "draco" over their forces in the eighth, ninth, and tenth centuries. The "draco" was based on the draconarius of the Roman Empire and was a bag made of plaited straw attached to a lance. Some were made in the shape of a dragon spitting flames, while others were made to look like large fish with flapping tails and fins.

The Vikings who raided the coasts and waterways of Europe also had standards and symbols, notably the famous "Raven Flag" that appeared in the later part of the ninth century. When William of Normandy invaded England in 1066, some of his men carried small swallow-tailed flags called *pennons* on their lances. The Bayeux Tapestry shows that only a few men, possibly commanders or their aides, carried the pennons. William himself is seen holding a pennon emblazoned with a cross, while other nobles have simple symbols such as circles or stripes sewn onto their pennons.

English King Harold's Housecarls (regular infantry) also carried pennons, but these had three or more tails instead of the two found on the Norman pennons. Harold himself is depicted in the tapestry as standing next to a man holding a royal standard that appears to be a "draco." The standard is a flying dragon, complete with wings, attached at the mouth to a thick staff.

While pennons would be added to lances later on in the Middle Ages as a means to identify a knight and prevent a couched lance from becoming stuck in the body of its victim, that practice was not in wide use when William and Harold clashed at the Battle of Hastings. Most of the knights and foot soldiers depicted in the tapestry carry only bare spears, which are being thrust overhead rather than couched as a lance. The few pennons displayed, therefore, presumably marked the location of leaders and their commands.

The cross that William bore on his own pennant was awarded to him by the Pope, who sanctioned his invasion of England as a religious crusade. The symbol of the cross soon became the centerpiece of military flags throughout Europe, as Western armies were sent East under the holy cross to spread Christianity and recover the Holy Land from the Muslims.

Crusaders and Heralds

The simple red cross on white cloth was adopted by the Crusaders as their flag as they marched east in 1095. Knights wore it on their surcoats and foot soldiers carried it on huge banners to proclaim their faith. The knightly holy orders of the Hospital and the Temple, along with a host of other militant monastic groups that fought in the Holy Land, northeastern Europe, Spain, and other places, all took variations of the cross as their symbol. White, black, and red crosses on backgrounds of white, red, or yellow were found on the banners of the Knights of Santiago in Spain, the Teutonic Knights in Prussia, and the Orders of the Knights of St. John and the Temple in Jerusalem. Many of the knights who journeyed east set aside their own colors, or at least wore the crusader surplice.

The use of the cross grew as the kings of Europe took for themselves such religious standards as the English cross of St. George, the French Oriflamme of St. Denis, and the Scottish cross of St. Andrew, to name a few. The crusaders who swept into the Baltic also brought the cross with them, and this crusading symbol remains in the national flags of the Scandinavian countries today.

In Europe proper, the basic, almost crude symbols that adorned the pennons of the Normans and Saxons at Hastings proliferated. As the Middle Ages progressed the heraldry that adorned the shields, surcoats, horsebards, and pennons of the nobility was transferred to flags. By the mid-twelfth century, the laws that governed heraldry were applied to flags, and seven different types of flags, ranging from the small lance flags, called the pennoncelle, to the giant banners of sovereigns, were specified. This led to a colorful array of flags with a wide variety of size, color, mounting, and design, with religious symbols, personal badges, and royal coats of arms proliferating.

In the East the armies of Islam retained their sacred banners, and the invading steppe armies of the Mongols raised huge silk flags over their regiments. Each body of 1,000 Mongol cavalry, known as a Minghan, had its own flag, which was used in the same manner as the Roman standard—that is, to signal orders across the battlefield. Mongol armies were famed for their mobility and their ability to carry out complex and almost choreographed maneuvers in response to commands transmitted by flags.

Like the European nobles, the Samurai warrior elite of Japan transferred their family crests and symbols to flags. Large vexillum-like flags were carried by foot soldiers, and cavalry later had tall banners attached to staves as part of their individual equipment.

Early Modern Flags

By the mid-sixteenth century the religious flags and royal banners of the Middle Ages began to be superseded by national and regimental flags. Some units began to wear costumes of uniform color or style, and regular, standing armies began to appear. The Spanish regiments of pike, crossbow, and sword companies carried colors that, unlike the banners of the ad hoc feudal units or mercenary companies of the Middle Ages and early Renaissance, were passed down over the years as the *colunellas* and *tercios* (regiments and brigades) remained in service. Other professional units, such as the Russian *strelsti*, the French *compagnies d'ordonnance*, and the regiments of the Swiss cantons became as devoted to their flags as the Roman legions had been to their standards.

The religious wars of the sixteenth and seventeenth centuries brought the last great rush of holy symbology to flags, as banners expressing faith in one creed and damnation to the followers of another were raised. By the end of the seventeenth century the nations of Europe had accepted a code of flags that set the standard for the next 250 years. Infantry regiments carried a regimental flag that attested to the province or region where they were raised, a royal or king's flag that showed their allegiance to a sovereign, and company flags or *guidons* (so called because the troops could be guided by them) for each company that made up the regiment. Cavalry units carried smaller flags, called *standards* (often square). In many cases the only distinction between the regimental and royal flags was a reversed color scheme, a streamer, or a crest.

The age of the regimental flag reached its peak in Western Europe in the late eighteenth and early nineteenth centuries, the age in which Sir Charles Napier, whose quote opened this article, lived. In this era victory was measured more in terms of flags captured than in men killed or ground taken, as the loss of a flag was an admission by a unit, and an army, that it had lost its fight. As slaves had been marched in processions behind the Caesars to mark their triumphs, so captured flags were carried as trophies on parade by victorious European armies.

As with the standards of Rome, European soldiers risked their lives to save the flags. Regiments were known to stand their ground and die to give their standard-bearer time to escape with the flag. Emperor Napoleon I of France reintroduced the eagle to the growing cult of the flag, and each of his regiments boasted a gilded eagle atop the flagstaff. A unit was punished for cowardice by the loss of its eagle, or rewarded for bravery by the attaching of battle honors to the flag. In the British army a regiment that participated in a victory won the right to have the name of that battle embroidered on its flag.

National flags, many of which grew from the royal or religious banners of the past, became the norm by the time of Napoleon, and throughout the nineteenth century the national flag slowly began to replace the other banners carried by units. By the time of the First World War few units carried their regimental flags into battle. National flags were sometimes raised aloft to lead a charge, but that made the ensign who carried it a target for the long-range and rapid-fire weapons of modern warfare. Moreover, with the introduction of radio and telephone communications, flags were no longer needed as a device to transmit orders.

The flag, however, has not disappeared from the battlefield. Polish and Russian cavalry carried guidons and larger standards up through the early years of World War II. Japanese banzai charges were led by officers carrying a Rising Sun flag, and British tank commanders, at least in the early months of the war in the Western Desert, had guidons attached to their tank antennae—until German gunners began to look for these easily identifiable targets. Chinese infantry in Korea (1950–53) and Iranian human wave attackers in the Gulf War (1980–88) carried flags into battle. Warships still fly their naval ensigns, however, and as late as the Second World War a ship still signified its surrender by striking its colors.

On the whole flags are no longer used on the battlefield but are reserved for parades, ceremonies, and other peacetime displays. As a symbol of a nation, or a regiment, however, the flag today remains as much a "symbol of the honor of the band" as it did for Sir Charles Napier in 1840 or the Roman legionnaires of Julius Caesar 50 years before the birth of Christ.

Mark G. McLaughlin

SEE ALSO: Customs and Etiquette.

Bibiliography

Funcken, L., and F. Funcken. 1966. *Le costume et les armes des soldats de tous les temps*. 2 vols. Paris: Casterman.
———.1975. *L'uniforme et les armes des soldats de la guerre en dentelle*. 2 vols. Paris: Casterman.
———.1977. *Le costume, l'armure et les armes au temps de la chevalerie*. 2 vols. Paris: Casterman.
Lemonofides, D. 1971. *British infantry colours*. London: Almark.
Saxtorph, N. 1972. *Warriors and weapons of early times*. New York: Macmillan.
Smith, W. 1975. *Flags through the ages and across the world*. New York: McGraw-Hill.
Webster, G. 1985. *The Roman imperial army*. Totowa, N.J.: Barnes and Noble Books.
Wise, T. 1977. *Military flags of the world, 1618–1900*. New York: Arco.
———.1981. *Flags of the Napoleonic wars*. 3 vols. London: Osprey.

FOCH, FERDINAND [1851–1929]

Ferdinand Foch, marshal of France, was given command of the Allied armies during the last stages of World War I. He is credited with stopping the German advance at the Marne River in 1914 and halting the Ludendorff Peace Offensives of 1918. He was also the architect of the plan that led to final Allied victory in World War I.

Background

Born 2 October 1851 at Tarbes, France, Foch received a conventional Jesuit education. Although he enlisted in the French infantry in 1870, he saw no action in the Franco-Prussian War. He was commissioned in the field artillery from the Ecole Polytechnique in 1873. His early career was undistinguished, although he had a reputation as a fine horseman. Devout Catholicism may have retarded his early advancement as a result of the French army's anticlericalism in reaction to the Dreyfus affair. In his early career, Foch began to show his inclination toward an academic approach to tactical problems, which would become his trademark. He also gained a reputation as a military thinker and teacher while serving on the faculty of the Ecole de Guerre from 1895 to 1900; in 1907, he became the school's commandant.

Military Doctrine

Foch's major contribution to doctrine, contained in his *Principles de la guerre*, published in 1903, was his unwavering belief in the spirit of the offensive, which became known as *élan*. He was convinced that an indomitable will to win would carry the fight on the battlefield. He believed that the enhanced firepower of early twentieth-century weaponry gave as much advantage to the attacker as it did to the defender. Foch's emphasis on the offensive, however, was often perverted to extremes by some of his disciples and subordinates, such as Col. Louis Loizeau de Grandmaison. Élan became a blind offensive doctrine of *l'offensive à l'outrance*—attack at all costs without consideration of alternatives. This spirit, which permeated the French army in the early phases of World War I, contributed to the frontal assaults and correspondingly high casualties that characterized the war.

Service in World War I

In 1913, Foch was given command of the XX Corps, a crack unit stationed on the frontier with Germany and headquartered at Nancy. In the opening days of World War I, as the Germans withdrew from this sector to execute a turning movement on the French at Morhange, the XX Corps fought with considerable élan and correspondingly high casualties. Foch was rewarded for this action with command of the newly formed Ninth Army, which found itself covering a critical gap between its own right and the left of the Fourth Army southeast of

Paris. Foch responded to the massive German offensive of 8 September 1914 with his own counterattack, remarking, "My left yields, my right is broken through: situation excellent; I am attacking." In spite of over 35,000 casualties, Foch is often credited with the decisive role in the Battle of the Marne. In reality, it was his ability to withstand the attack rather than inflict a decisive defeat on the Germans that was significant.

Based on his performance during the Battle of the Marne, Foch was appointed to coordinate the operations of the Allied armies of the North even though no agreement existed with the British or Belgians for overall French control. In this capacity, Foch was heavily criticized for his perceived reluctance to commit French reserves. Although his decision appears to have been correct in the long run, his hesitancy infuriated Allied field commanders.

With the failure of the Battle of the Somme in late 1916, during which he nominally commanded the French forces, Foch was transferred to an insignificant advisory post where he would remain until early 1918. In March 1918, the Germans launched a final series of massive offensives that threatened to push the British into the sea and destroy the French outside Paris. Foch was appointed generalissimo of the Allied armies on 3 April 1918 with the concurrence of the British and the newly arrived Americans. Foch immediately began reorganizing the front and his efforts gradually exhausted the German drive. With the help of fresh American troops, he was then able to launch the successful offensive of August–September 1918, which resulted in the final Allied victory two months later.

Later Life

In August 1918, Foch was made a marshal of France, and the following year he was gazetted as a British field marshal. In January 1920, he became president of the Allied Military Committee at Versailles, which was responsible for administering the terms of the armistice.

Often criticized for the high casualties associated with élan, his military theories were vindicated by ultimate victory and justifiably he was credited with turning the possible defeat at the hands of Erich Ludendorff in 1918 into victory. Foch died on 20 March 1929 and was interred under the dome of Les Invalides beside Napoleon and Turenne.

ROBERT E. KNOTTS

SEE ALSO: Ludendorff, Erich; World War I.

Bibliography

Atteridge, A. H. 1919. *Marshal Ferdinand Foch: His life and his theory of modern war.* New York: Dodd, Mead.

Falls, C. B. 1939. *Marshal Foch.* London: Blackie & Son.

Foch, F. 1918. *The principles of war.* Trans. H. Belloc. London: Chapman and Hall.

———. 1931. *Memoirs of Marshal Foch.* Garden City, N.Y.: Doubleday.

Liddell Hart, B. H. 1932. *Foch, the man of Orleans.* Boston: Little, Brown.

Windrow, M., and F. K. Mason. 1975. *A concise dictionary of military biography: Two hundred of the most significant names in land warfare, 10th–20th century.* Reading, Pa.: Osprey.

FRANCE, MILITARY HEGEMONY OF

The military hegemony of France in Europe and in many regions overseas began on 19 May 1643 with the destruction of the Spanish Netherlands Army at Rocroi by a French army led by the 21-year-old Duke of Enghien (later Prince of Condé, the "Great Condé"). The young duke's remarkable victory over Spain's hardened veterans signaled the end of Spain's military predominance (which dated from the sixteenth century) and represented the fruition of the military reorganization initiated by King Louis XIII's premier, Armand Jean du Plessis, cardinal-duke of Richelieu.

On the foundation laid by Richelieu, talented military leaders like Condé, Turenne, Luxembourg, Vauban, Catinat, Villars, Vendôme, Boufflers, and Saxe, and a succession of accomplished royal ministers, like Colbert and Louvois, built the edifice of France's military greatness.

France was ruled during its ascendancy by the "Sun King," Louis XIV (reigned 1643–1715), whose ambition and territorial designs caused many of the great wars that wracked Europe during the last decades of the seventeenth century. French hegemony was first checked by coalitions led by England and Holland and finally ended by Great Britain in the Seven Years' War (1756–63), a true world war in which France lost most of its great colonial empire.

Henry IV (*"le Grand"*)

The end of the long period of religious-civil wars in France (Edict of Nantes, 1598) was also the end of the latest French struggle with Hapsburg Spain (Treaty of Vervins), with which France had been at war more or less continually since the beginning of the sixteenth century. The new French king, Henry IV, had triumphed over his enemies, foreign and domestic, but was shrewd enough to recognize that he had gained as much by compromise and cynical accommodation as by military prowess. The conflict with the Spanish Hapsburgs (and their Austrian cousins) was more suspended than resolved. The debilitating domestic religious question was solved temporarily by permitting the Huguenots to erect a kind of independent republic based on their centers of influence, chiefly in the south and southwest of France. But, fundamentally, the religious question had been deferred, not settled. Much depended on the king's political skills and vision, not only for France, but for Europe.

At this time, the kingdom's energies were directed toward re-establishing order and rebuilding the economy, as the *Mémoires* of the Duke of Sully recount. In foreign affairs, the king conceived a fantastic project for a "United States of Europe," a precursor of the present-day European Union. But how serious he was, and what the results of his various schemes might have been, remain subjects for conjecture: Henry IV was assassinated by a fanatic in 1610. He was succeeded by his son, Louis XIII (reigned 1610–43), who was 9 years old.

Louis XIII (*"le Juste"*)

INTERNAL CONFLICTS

Louis's reign was troubled by internal division, conspiracy, and conflict. In part this was due to the king's youth and the constant jockeying for power and influence at court among regents, favorites, advisers, and councilors; in part it was due to the renewed outbreak of religious and civil wars, as the problems left unresolved at the accession of Henry IV resurfaced.

It is remarkable that, at this time, France was virtually bereft of armed forces. The "peace dividend" attendant to the accession of Henry IV was manifest in the purposeful neglect of the army and navy. In particular, Henry had allowed the ancient companies of gendarmes (regular heavy cavalry) to dwindle to nothing, since they had been arrayed against him in the civil wars. Even the royal household troops, the fabled *Maison du Roi*, had been cut back severely, and some units existed only as sinecures for Henry's old comrades in arms.

Louis XIII, his favorites, and his ministers gradually rebuilt the *Maison*, adding new units and reinforcing the old ones, so that the Royal Army always had a well-drilled, professional core. In the dizzying succession of internal wars that beset the country until the final defeat of the Huguenots (1628), the professionalism of the Royal Army made the difference.

Louis's enemies did not want for armed men, nor for enthusiastic amateurs to lead them, but the armies of the nobles (*les grands*) and the Huguenots could not stand up to the Royal Army in the field. The wars were characterized by sieges—in particular, the epic siege of the Huguenot stronghold of La Rochelle (1627–28). At the end of the wars, the king's chief minister, Cardinal Richelieu, stood in triumph over his enemies. Henceforward until his death (1642), he was effectively France's ruler.

RICHELIEU

The conclusion of the internal wars allowed Richelieu to turn his attention to foreign affairs, his true *métier*. In Richelieu's eyes, France's principal enemy was the House of Hapsburg, and particularly the Spanish Hapsburgs, whose domains or dependents confronted France on all its land frontiers. Thus, from 1629 until 1659, France was almost continually at war with Spain, either at first-hand or by proxy.

These wars included the War of the Mantuan Succession (1629–32) and the Franco-Spanish War (1635–59), which just preceded open French involvement in the Thirty Years' War (French phase, 1636–48) and continued long afterward. In this series of conflicts, France was ultimately successful, despite political divisions manifested by the various civil wars of the antiministerial *Fronde* (1648–53) and the treason of Condé, who threw in with the Spanish after his defeat as the leader of the *Frondeurs* (he served as a Spanish *generalissimo* until 1659).

France's success in this period may be attributed almost entirely to the policies of Richelieu. He reformed and reorganized the army, eliminating some of the worst abuses of the oligarchic spoils system by subordinating the entirely aristocratic officer corps to central authority. He achieved some success in enlarging and professionalizing the native French forces and ending the Crown's dependence on the superb but not always reliable mercenary contingents that historically had constituted the fighting core of the French army.

Richelieu also virtually founded the French navy, which had hardly existed as a permanent force before his ministry. For a brief (and remarkable) period the navy won several victories against the Spanish. The greatest French admiral of the period was the cardinal's brilliant nephew, Maillé-Brézé (1619–49).

But Richelieu's achievements did not long outlast him. His successor, Cardinal Mazarin (Giuilo Mazarini, premier 1642–61), allowed the navy to sink into decline, and it was of little military value until its true foundation as a professional service around 1669 by the great navy minister, Jean-Baptiste Colbert (1619–83). The army, however, retained a measure of efficiency, and its greatest moments were ahead of it.

Louis XIV (*"le Roi Soleil"*)

The Sun King's reign had begun in 1643, but in fact Mazarin ruled France until he died in 1661, when Louis proclaimed that henceforth he would be his own chief minister. The next 54 years were a period of splendor and magnificence for France, not only in the arts but also in military affairs. France was at the zenith of its power.

In the military sphere, France was organized for war so thoroughly that no one power could long hope to withstand it. And Louis's ambition for territorial aggrandizement might have startled even his more aggressive ancestors.

LOUVOIS

While Colbert reorganized the financial structure of the nation and launched an ambitious naval building program, his bitter enemy, the equally remarkable war minister François Michel Le Tellier, marquis de Louvois (1641–91), reorganized the army. Louvois was assisted in this work by Turenne, who was made marshal-general in 1660 to give him authority over all his redoubtable contemporaries in the marshalate. Turenne in turn was assisted by three brilliant but largely forgotten subordinates—Martinet, Fourilles, and Du Metz—each responsible for the reorganization of a single combat arm: infantry, cavalry, and artillery, respectively. The result of this immense effort was the first truly modern army: a permanent professional force, well organized, trained to a relatively high degree of efficiency, and subordinated to a powerful minister supported by a large, proficient civilian bureaucracy.

Logistical support of field armies was facilitated by the magazine system created by the great engineer Vauban. The rationalization of logistics, combined with the centralized control and direction of the marshaled human and material resources of the nation-state, made larger armies possible. Whereas, during the Thirty Years' War, the average field army had numbered about 19,000 men, the late-seventeenth-century wars of Louis XIV were fought by field armies two to three times larger. To compound France's advantages in this period, the magnificent armies created by Louvois were led by perhaps the greatest galaxy of military talent ever assembled.

THE WARS OF LOUIS XIV

Louis's wars of aggression, conducted between 1667 and 1714, involved his blatant and barely rationalized attempts to expand France's frontiers, particularly in the northeast (Flanders) and east (along the Rhine), at the expense of the moribund Spanish Empire and the hopelessly divided, invitingly weak Holy Roman Empire. These expansionist wars began in earnest with the War of Devolution (1667–68) and the Dutch War (1672–79), in which France gained Franche-Comté and many strong places along the frontiers. France's principal enemy was Holland, the architect of strong coalitions which alone could hope to oppose France. Indeed, in this period, France was virtually isolated diplomatically. The French armies, led by Turenne and Condé, won brilliant victories in the field, notably at Seneffe (11 August 1674), where Condé defeated a Dutch-Spanish army led by William of Orange, the Dutch *stadtholder*, and at Sinzheim (16 June 1674), Enzheim (4 October 1674), and Turckheim (5 January 1675), in which Turenne gained a trio of remarkable victories against the coalition armies along the Rhine.

The period following the Treaty of Nijmegen (6 February 1679) was marked by French bullying along the Rhine and further French expansion as Louis's "Chambers of Reunion" decreed several territories and towns "French" (since at one time or another they had belonged to any of several recent French territorial acquisitions). French troops promptly moved in to enforce the decisions of these courts, and the German emperor was forced to accede to this latest aggression. Louis followed up by revoking the Edict of Nantes, which had guaranteed freedom of worship to the Huguenots (1685). Europe was appalled, and France was much weakened by the emigration of thousands of her most industrious people.

Further French threats and aggressions along the Rhine led to the formation of the Dutch-inspired anti-French League of Augsburg, which consisted of virtually all the powers of Europe except for England (9 July 1686). But the English Revolution of 1688 led to the exile of the English king James II. When William of Orange and his wife, Mary, James's daughter, took the English throne, England joined the League, which became the Grand Alliance (12 May 1689).

Meanwhile, the War of the League of Augsburg (1688–97) had broken out, and France confronted the coalition on land and sea. A new generation of French military leaders soon proved their mettle. In Flanders, the Marshal-Duke of Luxembourg, Condé's protégé, won great victories over the coalition at Fleurus (1 July 1690), Steenkerke (3 August 1692), and Neerwinden (1

August 1693). In Italy, Marshal Catinat knocked Savoy out of the war after winning the decisive Battle of Marsaglia (4 October 1693). At sea, however, the French were beaten badly at Cap La Hogue (May 1692).

This war was also a true "world war," since it involved the American and Indian-subcontinent colonies of the belligerents. In America, it was known as King William's War and involved fighting between the French and English and each side's Indian allies. The Treaty of Ryswick (1697) that ended the war was unremarkable. In the complex territorial provisions, France gained Alsace and Strasbourg.

The imminent extinction of the Spanish Hapsburg dynasty preoccupied Europe in the years following the Treaty of Ryswick. When Charles II, Spain's feeble-minded, childless king, finally died in 1700, Louis advanced the claim of his grandson, Philip of Anjou, to the Spanish throne. Since the European powers could not countenance a union of Spain and France, this brought on the War of the Spanish Succession (1701–1714), in which France once again squared off against an all-European coalition.

In this war, France for once was decidedly deficient in military talent. Against the genius of the great allied commanders Marlborough and Eugene of Savoy, France had mostly second-rate marshals and generals (Luxembourg had died in 1695). The allies won a succession of striking victories: Blenheim (1704), Ramillies (1706), Turin (1706), and Oudenarde (1708). The French gained some successes in Italy and prevailed in Spain. The allies won the bloody Battle of Malplaquet (11 September 1709) at tremendous cost, and England retreated from the war effort in revulsion at the casualties. The French cause was helped immeasurably by the brilliant Marshal Villars, whose victories improved France's negotiating position as the war wound down.

In 1713 and 1714, the exhausted belligerents negotiated treaties ending the war. Philip of Anjou was recognized as king of Spain, but the crowns of France and Spain were permanently separated. Louis XIV died in 1715 and was succeeded by his great-grandson, Louis XV.

Louis XV ("*le Bien-Aimé*")

The reign of Louis XV (1715–74) was marked by the gradual decline of the military machine created by Louvois and Turenne. The officer corps grew alarmingly, until by mid-century the proportion of officers to enlisted men was 1 to 15. Moreover, the quality of the officer corps deteriorated: many were weak, incompetent, venal, or amateurish. Inevitably, discipline suffered, and the once-proud army became the object of contempt—an "unqualified mediocrity" in the eyes of many.

The reign was marked by the complete reversal of Louis XIV's foreign policy, but France's military commitments did not diminish appreciably, as Europe's coalition wars continued undiminished. France was allied with recent enemies Britain, Holland, and Austria against its former ally Spain in the War of the Quadruple Alliance (1718–20). In the War of the Polish Succession (1733–38), France supported the claim of Stanislas Leszczynski (Louis XV's father-in-law) to the Polish crown against Saxony, Austria, and Russia. France's most distinguished soldier during this period was James Fitzjames, duke of Berwick and marshal of France. Berwick, an illegitimate son of England's King James II, was killed in action at the Siege of Philippsburg (12 June 1734). The Philippsburg campaign was also the last for a long-time antagonist of France, Prince Eugene of Savoy.

THE WAR OF THE AUSTRIAN SUCCESSION (1740–48)

Although a guarantor of the Pragmatic Sanction, in this war France was allied with Prussia, Bavaria, Saxony, Savoy, and Sweden against Austria, Russia, and Britain. France did not officially enter the war until 1744, but French "volunteers" served from 1741—a decidedly modern piece of disingenuousness.

The war marked the emergence of one of France's greatest soldiers, Maurice, comte de Saxe (1696–1750), a German by birth—one of 300-odd illegitimate children of Augustus II "the Strong," elector of Saxony—a military genius and himself a prodigious womanizer. Campaigning in Flanders, the Austrian Netherlands, and Holland, Saxe won victories against the allies at Fontenoy (10 May 1745), Rocourt (11 October 1746), and Lauffeld (2 July 1747).

Saxe's success in the Low Countries was not matched by his contemporaries in other major theaters—Italy and Germany. At sea, the British had the upper hand against the French and Spanish fleets. In North America (King George's War), France fared miserably, incurring serious defeats by the British and British colonials and native American allies. In India, however, Dupleix was successful at Madras and in the Carnatic.

The Treaty of Aix-la-Chapelle (1748), ending the war, restored all colonial conquests to their prewar status. France gained nothing by the European provisions; essentially, the war had been a failure.

THE SEVEN YEARS' WAR (1756–63): THE NADIR

In the Seven Years' War in Europe, France and its principal allies, Austria (the Empire) and Russia, contended against the numerically inferior forces of Prussia and Great Britain. The allied powers, operating on exterior lines, made several poorly coordinated attempts to crush King Frederick the Great of Prussia by convergent invasions of Hanover and Prussia. Initially, the French, under Marshal Louis d'Estrées, were successful against the British-Hanoverian army led by the son of King George II, William Augustus, duke of Cumberland—whom Saxe had beaten at Fontenoy (despite the splendid bravery of the British-Hanoverian infantry).

Defeated at Hastenbeck (26 July 1757), Cumberland was trapped at Kloster-Zeven (Zeven) and forced to concede Hanover to the French. The Convention of Kloster-Zeven was the worst British surrender until Dunkirk (1940), not excepting Yorktown. D'Estrées' replacement, the Marshal-Duke Louis de Richelieu, failed to cooperate with Charles de Rohan, prince de Soubise, and the prince of Saxe-Hildburghausen at the head of the Franco-Reichs army. Despite great numerical superiority, the allies were defeated badly by Frederick at Rossbach (5 November 1757).

The great victory at Rossbach eliminated one of two French armies committed to Germany and effectively allowed Frederick to concentrate his energies on the Austrians and Russians. Henceforth, the French were opposed on the Rhine front by the gifted Prince Ferdinand of Brunswick. Louis, marquis de Contades, was defeated by Ferdinand at Minden (1 August 1759) and the French were driven back to the Rhine. Subsequently, Ferdinand contended successfully against the French (1760–62), finally driving them across the Rhine.

In the New World, the French, led by the brilliant Louis Joseph, marquis de Montcalm-Gozon, were initially successful (French and Indian War), but Montcalm was defeated by James Wolfe at Quebec (13 September 1759), and the British conquest of Canada was completed within a year. Both Montcalm and Wolfe died in the battle that decided the fate of a continent.

In India, weak French forces were led by Count Thomas Arthur Lally, a distinguished veteran of Irish descent, who was beaten as much by the ineptitude and machinations of his officers as by the genius of the British soldier Sir Eyre Coote. Lally lost India and went to the scaffold for it, a miscarriage of justice memorialized by Voltaire in *Fragments of India.*

The French navy was no match for the British at sea. British naval superiority contributed to the relative isolation of French colonial forces and the disparity in strategic mobility, numbers, and resources wherever the two powers confronted one another.

The Treaty of Paris (1763) marked the political and military humiliation of France and the ascendancy of Britain in Europe and overseas. France lost most of its North American and Caribbean empire, including Canada, and French India was practically dismantled. In Europe, France had sunk so low that it was almost eclipsed by a resurgent Spain, led by King Charles III (reigned 1759–88).

Military Reform and Rebirth

France had always been a congenial environment for military thinkers—and not a few eccentrics. Among the great theorists of the eighteenth century were Jean Charles, chevalier de Folard (1669–1752), and Marshal Saxe, whose *Mes rêveries* is still read and admired today. During the Seven Years' War, the innovative Marshal-Duke Victor-François de Broglie, victor over Brunswick at Bergen (13 April 1759), had introduced the all-arms division organization, a necessary precursor of the larger Napoleonic army corps.

Thus, despite the stagnation and enervation so pronounced at midcentury, it is not surprising that the French armed forces were reformed and modernized during the reign of Louis XVI (1774–92). The principal agent of reform was the war minister, Claude Louis, comte de St. Germain (1707–78), who was assisted in his work by Jacques Antoine Hippolyte, comte de Guibert (1743–90; tactics and doctrine), Jean Baptiste Vaquette de Gribeauval (1715–89; artillery materiel and organization), and Jean Baptiste Donatien de Vimeur, comte de Rochambeau (1725–1807; tactics and infantry organization).

Although the old army was swept away in the Revolution (1789), these reformers were directly responsible for creating the professional core of the successful Revolutionary armies. However, the fine quality of the reformed French army was already evident in 1780 in the small but magnificent expeditionary corps that Rochambeau led to America and that played such an important part in the Yorktown campaign.

CURT JOHNSON

SEE ALSO: Colonial Empires, European; Condé, Louis II de Bourbon, Prince de; Saxe, Hermann Maurice, Comte de; Seapower, British; Seven Years' War; Spanish Empire; Suffren de St. Tropez, Pierre Andre de; Thirty Years' War; Turenne, Henri de La Tour d'Auvergne, Vicomte de; Vauban, Sebastien Le Prestre de.

Bibliography

Aumale, H. E. P. L. 1867. *Les institutions militaires de France: Louvois—Carnot—Saint Cyr.* Paris: Lévy.
Dollinger, P. 1966. *Histoire universelle des armées.* Vol. 2. Paris: Laffont.
Kennett, L. 1967. *The French armies in the Seven Years' War.* Durham, N.C.: Duke Univ. Press.
Susane, L. A. V. V. 1974. *Histoire de la cavalerie française.* 3 vols. Paris: Hetzel.
———. 1874. *Histoire de l'artillerie française.* Paris: Hetzel.
———. 1876. *Histoire de l'infanterie française.* 5 vols. Paris: Dumaine.
Weygand, M. 1953. *Histoire de l'armée française.* Paris: Flammarion.

FRANCO-PRUSSIAN WAR

This war, also known as the Franco-German War, ended French military and political pre-eminence in Europe and established Prussia-Germany as the dominant power of continental Europe.

Unexpected by French emperor Napoleon III was the success of the Prussian chancellor Otto von Bismarck in rallying the north German states, in the 1860s, into the anti-French North German Confederation. A Prussian effort to place a Hohenzollern prince on the Spanish throne in mid-1870 threatened France with the possibility of a two-front war. Napoleon was further provoked by Bismarck's misrepresentations of a meeting at Ems between King William I of Prussia and the French ambassador. Believing the French army to be invincible, the French emperor decided to precipitate a war he now believed inevitable.

On 15 July 1870 France declared war. Immediate mobilization followed in both countries. Mobilization and troop concentrations of the North German Confederation followed a well-directed plan, using the rail net to the fullest. French mobilization was haphazard and incomplete. In the next two days, the South German states joined Prussia and the North German Confederation in a coalition against France. Bavaria, Baden, and Württemberg began to mobilize.

German Offensive

By 31 July three well-equipped German armies—totaling 380,000 men—were concentrated on the Franco-German frontier west of the Rhine: the First, with 60,000 men under Gen. Karl F. von Steinmetz, was between Trier and Saarbrücken; the Second, with 175,000 men, under Prince Frederick Karl, assembled between Bingen and Mannheim; the Third, with 145,000 men, under Crown Prince Frederick William, was between Landau and Germersheim. An additional 95,000 troops were held back in central Germany until it was certain that Austria would not intervene on the French side.

Nominally commanded by King William, the actual direction of Prussian-German operations was conducted by Gen. Helmuth von Moltke, chief of the efficient Prussian general staff. Prussian intelligence had determined the complete French order of battle. The Prussian objective was to destroy the French armies in the field, and then to capture Paris.

The French army, some 224,000 men in eight army corps, lay behind the frontier from Thionville to Strasbourg and echeloned back to the fortress line Metz-Nancy-Belfort. In stark contrast to German efficiency, French transport was improvised, munitions scanty, and units below war strength. Napoleon III, at Metz with his incompetent war minister Marshal Edmond Leboeuf, was in command. The only plan was the cry of the French populace: "On to Berlin!" French intelligence was nonexistent. Napoleon ordered a general advance.

A skirmish on 2 August near Saarbrücken, between units of the German First Army and the French II Corps, alerted the French only to the fact that the enemy was near. Napoleon belatedly directed the grouping of his troops in two armies: the Army of Alsace (consisting of the three southernmost corps under Marshal Marie E. P. M. de MacMahon) and the Army of Lorraine (the remaining five corps under Marshal Achille F. Bazaine). No army staffs existed; the two army commanders had to function with their own individual corps staffs assuming the additional planning and administrative burdens.

Early on 4 August the Crown Prince's army, advancing in four columns, surprised the leading division of MacMahon's corps on the Lauter River near Weissenburg. The other two French corps had not yet joined him, although one division came up later that day. After a sharp action in which the badly outnumbered French lost 1,600 men killed and wounded and 700 prisoners—against German casualties of 1,550—MacMahon pulled back and concentrated defensively on a wooded plateau fronting on the Lauter.

This led, on 6 August, to the Battle of Froeschwiller (or Woerth). A German reconnaissance in force was repulsed by MacMahon's right. The Crown Prince built up his strength, overlapping both French flanks, with the main effort against the right supported by the fire of 150 guns. MacMahon sacrificed his cavalry in gallant, suicidal charges but was unable to halt the envelopment. He fell back on Froeschwiller, covered by his reserve artillery. He clung there until nightfall, then retreated without interference to Châlons-sur-Marne (7–14 August). German losses, out of 125,000 men and 312 guns engaged, amounted to 8,200 killed and wounded and 1,373 missing. The French, who had had

46,500 men and 119 guns engaged, lost 10,760 killed and wounded and 6,200 prisoners. The Vosges barrier had been pierced, the road to Paris opened. The Crown Prince's army marched methodically westward toward the Meuse and Paris.

The pattern of tactical operations had been set; the French *chassepot* rifle was superior to the Prussian needle gun in accuracy and volume of fire, but the French artillery, thanks to a mistaken reliance on machine guns (*mitrailleuses*) in place of cannon (about one-fourth of French artillery pieces were *mitrailleuses*), was far inferior to the German.

Metz Campaign

Meanwhile, the German First and Second armies moved into Lorraine, where Bazaine's army was spread in three separate areas, out of mutual supporting distance. Attacked by Steinmetz and a corps of Frederick Karl's army, Gen. Charles August Frossard's II Corps held the heights of Spicheren, southeast of Saarbrücken, for an entire day (6 August) until threatened by envelopment on both flanks as the German piecemeal attack gradually built up. Bazaine made no attempt to reinforce Frossard. In this Battle of Spicheren, the French had 29,980 men engaged and lost 1,982 killed and wounded and 1,096 missing. The Germans, who had put 45,000 men into action, lost 4,491 killed and wounded and 372 missing. As the II Corps withdrew in good order, there was no immediate pursuit by the exhausted Germans.

Moltke now ordered pursuit across the entire front. He sent the Third Army after MacMahon and personally followed hard on Bazaine's trail with the First and Second armies. The rapidity of the advance of the German spearheads and the boldness of their operations gave the French no respite. The Prussian sweep was a strategic penetration between the two French armies. By 15 August the Germans were threatening Bazaine's line of communication.

Shaken by these early defeats, Napoleon surrendered all initiative and betook himself to Verdun. Leboeuf was relieved and replaced by Gen. Charles G. M. Cousin-Montauban, Count of Palikao. Bazaine, put in full command of a reorganized Army of the Rhine, fell back on the fortress of Metz while Mac-Mahon regrouped at Châlons.

In the Battle of Borny, on 15 August, the Prussian First Army forced Bazaine to retire across the Moselle. He hoped to gain Verdun and a juncture with MacMahon, but the German Second Army, crossing at Pont-à-Mousson, cut him off. Still hoping to break out, Bazaine concentrated between the Orne and the Moselle, facing south with his left resting on Metz.

On 16 August, there was a series of battles at Mars-la-Tour, Vionville, and Rezonville. Frederick Karl, moving north at dawn across the Verdun-Metz highway, collided with the French. His leading corps attacked immediately while the remainder of the army hurried to the sound of the guns. A French cavalry charge was repulsed with much loss. The German offensive built up in the usual German pattern of concentration on the battlefield, and a piecemeal engagement developed into a full-blown battle. Successive cavalry charges on both sides ended in a cavalry duel in the afternoon; great masses of horsemen mingled in an almost aimless melee for nearly an hour until both sides broke off in exhaustion. Frederick Karl finally assaulted along his entire front, pushing into Rezonville.

Actually, the combat—or series of combats—was a drawn battle, for both sides bivouacked on the field after the hardest-fought engagement of the entire war. German losses were some 17,000; the French lost more than 16,000. The next day, Bazaine, giving up hope for a breakout, retired unmolested on Metz, pivoting about his left flank; his army of 120,000 men took up a new position, some 9.5 kilometers (6 mi.) long, facing west on a ridge between the Moselle and the Orne. The bulk of the German armies—about 200,000 men, now between Bazaine and Paris—began moving into this area, only a reinforced corps remaining in observation east of Metz.

On 18 August Moltke, who had taken personal charge of operations near Metz, attacked Bazaine, making his main effort on his own left with the Second Army. The walled village of St. Privat le Montaigne became the key point of combat. Frederick Karl squandered the Prussian Guard in a series of charges against the hamlet, which was defended by Marshal Canrobert's VI Corps. From early morning until dusk, Canrobert's 23,000 men held out against 100,000 assailants, while Bazaine ignored his requests for reinforcement. Then a Saxon corps reached Roncourt, to the north, outflanking the French and threatening their rear. After house-to-house combat through the village, Canrobert pulled the remnants of his troops back into Metz. Meanwhile, on the German right, an almost independent battle was fought. Two German corps battered their way east of Gravelotte, then became entangled in a ravine beyond. Attempts at disengagement turned into panic, and hordes of German refugees poured west through Gravelotte. A brilliant French counterattack was checked only by Gen. Prince Kraft zu Hohenlohe-Ingelfingen's artillery and the personal efforts of Moltke, who led reinforcements and averted disaster. Not until midnight, when news of the success of St. Privat reached Moltke, were the Germans sure of victory in this Battle of Gravelotte–St. Privat. Had Bazaine made a general counterattack that night—or even the next morning—with the forces still at his disposal, he might have broken free. Instead, he remained passive, relinquishing all control to his corps commanders. Moltke, after waiting for a counterattack that never came, proceeded to seal Bazaine within his perimeter.

Sedan Campaign

Meanwhile, MacMahon, responding to frantic appeals from the government, on 21 August moved out of Châlons with 120,000 men and 393 guns to the relief of Bazaine, his strength and movements widely advertised in the French press. Napoleon III accompanied him. MacMahon's stupid choice of a northerly route invited a turning movement. Moltke accepted the opportunity. While the German First Army and part of the Second—all under Frederick Karl— invested Metz, the remainder of the Second Army—now called the Army of the

Meuse and under the command of Crown Prince Albert of Saxony—struck west to cooperate with Frederick William, whose Third Army was driving rapidly westward through the Argonne Forest to bar MacMahon's advance.

On 29 August MacMahon sent part of his army across the Meuse at Douzy. The Prussian Army of the Meuse, advancing north on both sides of the river, forced him northward toward Sedan after sharp clashes at Nouart (29 August) and Beaumont (30 August). Another clash at Bazeilles (31 August), where MacMahon was wounded, forced the French into a bend of the river at Sedan itself. Again, the Prussians lay between a French army and Paris.

The Crown Prince's Third Army, arriving from the southeast through Wadlincourt and Conchery on the left bank of the Meuse, crossed the river on pontoon bridges and moved into the plain north of Sedan, completing the envelopment of the French army. Meanwhile, Bazaine's halfhearted attempt to break out of Metz on 31 August was repulsed by Frederick Karl.

Gen. Auguste Ducrot, replacing MacMahon in command at Sedan, found himself, on 1 September, with his back to the Belgian frontier while nearly 200,000 German troops under Moltke pressed in on the south, west, and north. The French cavalry made a desperate attempt to break out to the northwest, but it was shattered by German infantry fire while 426 German guns, ranged in a semicircle on the heights above Sedan, raked the French positions in a day-long bombardment. German cavalry charges were repelled in turn by the French machine guns. Thwarted in his northwesterly drive, Ducrot attempted a southerly assault in the afternoon. This, too, was repulsed.

By 5:00 P.M., the Battle of Sedan was lost; the French army was crowded into the fortress and town, which was pummeled by devastating German artillery fire. Gen. Emmanuel F. de Wimpffen, who had succeeded to command, urged the emperor to place himself at the head of his troops and make one last charge. Napoleon refused to have any more of his men sacrificed; early on 2 September, he drove out under a white flag and surrendered as an individual to the king of Prussia. Wimpffen then surrendered the army: 83,000 men and 449 guns. French losses were 17,000; German 9,000.

French Resurgence

The war, it seemed, was over. Half of France's regular organized field forces had been captured, the other half immured in Metz. All that remained were the other fortresses studded along the eastern frontier—Strasbourg, Verdun, and Belfort being the most important. While German reinforcements methodically went about reducing these, and the First and Second armies tightened their iron ring about Bazaine in Metz, the Third Army and the Army of the Meuse rolled on toward Paris. But as they marched, all France flamed in an amazing demonstration of patriotic resiliency.

In Paris, on 4 September, the empire was toppled in a popular uprising. A provisional government of a new Third Republic rose, with Leon Gambetta its torchbearer and Gen. Louis Jules Trochu its president. Trochu, as military governor of the city, manned its forts with 120,000 hastily recruited soldiers (including many veterans, reservists, and 20,000 regular marine infantry), 80,000 *gardes mobiles* (untrained recruits under the age of 30), and 300,000 highly volatile and anarchistic-minded *gardes nationales* (militia recruits between the ages of 30 and 50).

Siege of Paris

Moltke had no intention of squandering his troops in assaults upon the deep-sited and massive system of fortifications ringing the city in two belts. He invested Paris on 19 September. Elaborate siege works sealed the French capital, King William established his headquarters at Versailles, and Moltke waited for starvation to bring the great metropolis into his hands. Much to his astonishment, he found his line of communications harassed by *franc-tireurs* (guerrillas) and a new French army gathering in the Loire Valley.

Gambetta, escaping from Paris by balloon—Paris's sole link with the outside world—established a provisional government at Tours on 11 October and organized nationwide resistance. Moltke now found himself concurrently engaged in two major sieges, a field campaign, and constant guerrilla warfare along his long line of communications—severely straining the efficient German war machine.

On 27 October Bazaine's army of 173,000 men surrendered after a 54-day siege. It had been defeated more through the vacillation of its commander and by starvation than by force of arms. After the war, Bazaine was court-martialed, unfairly convicted of treason, and imprisoned.

War Across Northern France

Moltke at once utilized the besiegers of Metz to conduct an increasingly large-scale operation in the Loire and Sarthe valleys as the inexperienced French army of the Loire made several gallant but unsuccessful attempts to move to the relief of Paris. With the French holding the initiative, fighting continued through the winter, marked also by harsh treatment of guerrillas that were captured on the German line of communications.

Despite famine, Trochu's forces in Paris harassed the besiegers. The task was complicated by the behavior of the *gardes nationales*, whose mutiny (31 October) seriously compromised the defense. Two major sorties (29–30 November and 21 December) were repulsed after some initial success.

On 9 November, in the Battle of Coulmiers, a French victory over a Bavarian corps caused German withdrawal from Orléans, but the subsequent French advance was then checked by Prussian reinforcements. This led to the Battle of Orléans on 2–4 December. Two days of heavy fighting between Gen. Louis J. B. d'Aurelle de Paladines's French Army of the Loire and the army of Frederick Karl ended with the unwise division of the French forces and reoccupation of Orléans by the Germans. While Gen. Charles D. S. Bourbaki hurried to the east to assist the garrison of Belfort, which was under German investment, Gen. Antoine E. A. Chanzy, with the remainder of the Army of the Loire, kept up a constant struggle against a much superior force.

Bombardment of Paris

After an acrimonious debate with Chancellor Bismarck, who was supported by the king, Moltke, on 5 January, reluctantly ordered the bombardment of Paris. As Moltke had anticipated, the German shelling caused more resentment than damage, while the war in the provinces continued unabated.

Meanwhile, in the north, French general Louis L. C. Faidherbe, on 23 December, opposed with mixed success German efforts to pacify northern France in the Battle of the Hallue. He fought another drawn battle with Gen. August Karl von Goeben at Bapaume on 2–3 January. On 19 January at the Battle of St. Quentin, however, he was severely defeated by Goeben. Faidherbe withdrew in good order and repulsed German pursuit. He immediately prepared to renew his offensive, adding to the alarm of the Germans, now seriously overextended by the unexpectedly effective French resistance in all of the outlying provinces.

On 10–12 January at the Battle of Le Mans in the Loire Valley, the Germans repulsed a desperate offensive effort by Chanzy. The untrustworthiness of his troops forced Chanzy to retreat to the west, but he still threatened the German hold on the Loire.

In the east, Belfort was the only important French frontier fortress still resisting. On 15 January Bourbaki, with a woefully inexperienced army of 150,000 men, initiated the Battle of Belfort by attacking the 60,000 German besiegers under the command of Gen. Karl Wilhelm F. A. L. Werder. Bourbaki's main effort was against Werder's positions on the Lisaine River, within cannon shot of the fortress. Thanks to his own ineptness and that of famed Italian patriot Giuseppe Garibaldi (a volunteer fighting for France), Bourbaki was thrown back after three days of furious fighting. German losses were nearly 1,900, French more than 6,000. Bourbaki attempted suicide but failed and was replaced by Gen. Justin Clinchant. With the arrival of a German reinforcing army under Gen. Edwin von Manteuffel, Clinchant found himself pinned between two German armies with the Swiss frontier at his back. On 1 February, with 83,000 men, he moved into Switzerland and hospitable internment at Pontarlier.

On 18 January 1871, at Versailles, Bismarck achieved the triumph of years of planning. In the Hall of Mirrors, King William I of Prussia was proclaimed emperor of a united Germany. Prussian preeminence in Germany was assured while French influence in western and southern Germany was ended.

Surrender of Paris

A third and final sortie of the Paris garrison on 19 January was decisively thrown back when the *gardes nationales* treacherously fired at their comrades. On 26 January, with all hope lost and the population on the verge of starvation, Trochu obtained an armistice.

On 28 January, in the Convention of Versailles, Paris capitulated and all hostilities ended, except at Belfort. All French regular troops of the garrison and the *gardes mobiles* became prisoners of war; the forts around the city were occupied by the Germans. At French request—unwisely, as it turned out—the terms did not include disarmament of the *gardes nationales,* who were supposed to become a police force to control the restive population of Paris. The victors marched triumphantly into the city on 1 March.

Indomitable Belfort

Col. Pierre M. P. A. Denfert-Rochereau, commanding the fortress of Belfort, had resisted siege since 3 November 1870. An engineer officer who had been in command of the ancient fortress for six years, he utilized the existing works, extended an outer line of resistance, and with a garrison of some 17,600 men, mainly *gardes mobiles* and *gardes nationales,* carried on an elastic defense. Not until late January were the Germans established within cannon range of the inner fortress. Even then, their progress was slow. Only upon an imperative order from the French General Assembly in the temporary capital at Bordeaux (15 February) did Denfert-Rochereau capitulate. The garrison marched out with the honors of war—under arms, colors flying—with all their baggage and mobile equipment. In a siege of 105 days, French losses were some 4,800, while 336 of the townsfolk had been killed by bombardment. German losses had been about 2,000. The defense of Belfort was an epic of the French army.

Paris Commune

While a peace treaty was being negotiated at Frankfurt, the *gardes nationales* seized power in Paris, overthrowing the municipal government. The National Assembly, which had returned to Paris from Bordeaux, fled to Versailles. While Paris suffered a reign of terror, the German government authorized the rearming of the captured armies of Metz and Sedan to permit the French government to re-establish control of the capital. On 2 April the French army, under Marshal MacMahon, began operations against the Communards who had seized all of the fortifications of the city. On 21 May, after capturing all of the outer forts, the government troops entered Paris. The Communards ruthlessly murdered hundreds of hostages, including the archbishop of Paris, as the army fought its way into the city. After the so-called Bloody Week, government control was re-established on 28 May.

All of this activity was passively observed by the German army of occupation from garrisons surrounding Paris.

Treaty of Frankfurt

On 10 May, by the Treaty of Frankfurt, France agreed to cede Alsace and northeastern Lorraine to Germany and to pay an indemnity of 5 billion francs (US$1 billion). A German army of occupation was to remain in France until the indemnity was paid. To the amazement of Germany, this was completed by a patriotic financial effort on 15 July 1872, and the Germans evacuated France over the next year.

TREVOR N. DUPUY

SEE ALSO: Moltke the Elder; Prussia and Germany, Rise of.

Bibliography

Dupuy, R. E., and T. N. Dupuy. 1985. *Encyclopedia of military history.* New York: Harper and Row.

Dupuy, T. N. 1977. *A genius for war: The German army and general staff, 1807–1945.* Englewood Cliffs, N.J.: Prentice-Hall.

Fuller, J. F. C. 1956. *A military history of the western world.* 3 vols. New York: Funk and Wagnalls.

Goerlitz, W. 1953. *History of the German general staff, 1657–1945.* Trans. B. Battershaw. New York: Praeger.

Hohenlohe Ingelfingen, K. zu. 1898. *Letters on artillery.* Trans. N. L. Walford. London: Edward Stanford.

Howard, M. 1961. *The Franco-Prussian war.* New York: Macmillan.

Kitchen, M. 1975. *A military history of Germany: From the eighteenth century to the present.* Bloomington, Ind.: Indiana Univ. Press.

Rousset, Lt. Col. 1911. *Histoire Générale de la guerre Franco-Allemande (1870–1871).* 2 vols. Paris: Librairie Illustrée, Jules Tallandier.

Schlieffen, A von. 1931. *Cannae.* Authorized translation. Ft. Leavenworth, Kans.: The Command and General Staff School Press.

Verdy du Vernois, J. A. F. W. von. [1897] 1971. *With the royal headquarters, 1870–71.* Reprint. New York: AMS Press.

Weygand, M. 1938. *Histoire de l'armée française.* Paris: Flammarion.

FREDERICK THE GREAT
(Frederick II) [1712–86]

Frederick Wilhelm II (Fig. 1) was born on 24 January 1712 in Berlin. He was the third and eldest surviving son of King Frederick Wilhelm I of Prussia and Sophia Dorothea of Hanover, the sister of King George II of England.

Frederick's childhood was an unhappy one. A retiring child, fond of music and literature, Frederick was subjected to constant berating and abuse from his tyrannical and militaristic father. At the age of 14, Frederick was appointed a major in the Potsdam Grenadiers, his father's giant bodyguards. This position, however, only served to increase his father's dominance over his life. Frustrated beyond endurance, Frederick—in the company of two of his friends, Lieutenants Keith and von Katte—attempted to escape to France on 5 August 1730. The plot was discovered, and Frederick and Katte were caught. Frederick's father reacted brutally to this act of rebellion; Katte was executed, and Frederick was imprisoned in the fortress of Küstrin under suspended sentence of death.

Frederick remained under strict supervision for fourteen months until January 1732, when he was formally reconciled with his father and appointed colonel of the Ruppin Infantry Regiment.

On 12 June 1733, Frederick, against his wishes, married Elizabeth Christine of Brunswick-Bevern. Although she was a pleasant and understanding woman, Frederick developed an intense hatred for his new wife and had little to do with her. This unhappy union produced no children.

Figure 1. Frederick the Great. (SOURCE: U.S. Library of Congress)

In 1734 the War of the Polish Succession began. In an attempt to further his military education, Frederick was allowed to serve with the Prussian contingent in the Rhineland under Prince Eugene of Savoy. An eager student, Frederick learned a great deal from Prince Eugene's discourses on the art of war.

In that same year, Frederick began to correspond with Voltaire. The next six years Frederick spent happily in pursuit of his studies, music, and correspondence.

King of Prussia

On 28 May 1740, Frederick's father died; three days later Frederick was crowned King of Prussia. A proponent of the theories of the Enlightenment, Frederick immediately began putting these liberal theories into practice in

Prussia. He outlawed torture of civilians, allowed freedom of religion, abolished censorship, guaranteed the freedom of the press, and became a fanatical devotee of the freedom of expression. Frederick took a much greater personal interest in his subjects than did most rulers of the time, and tried to improve both their standard of living and their allegiance to the state.

The Silesian Wars

The death of Emperor Charles VI of Austria on 20 October 1740 left Austria without a male heir and the right of succession to the throne of the Holy Roman Empire open to question. Charles had intended that his daughter, Maria Theresa, and her husband, Francis of Lorraine, should succeed him, but he had failed to acquire the necessary support for the succession among the electors before his death. Further, he had left his daughter an empty treasury and a deplorable army with which to enforce her claim to the throne.

Frederick's father had left him a large, well-trained army and a substantial treasury, and Frederick determined to use both to enlarge his kingdom. Deciding to take advantage of these circumstances, which offered little risk to himself, Frederick launched an invasion of the Austrian province of Silesia on 16 December 1740.

At the Battle of Mollwitz on 10 April 1741 the Prussians won a narrow victory that saved Silesia from Austrian reconquest. Frederick, advised by General Schwerin to leave the field when the action turned against the Prussians, was informed later of his army's victory. As a result of this embarrassment, Frederick resolved never again to leave the battlefield before a decision was reached. Frederick then set about repairing the shortcomings of his army that had become apparent during Mollwitz, most notably the poor showing of the Prussian cavalry.

Frederick resumed military operations in February 1742 and advanced to within sight of Vienna. He was forced to retire to Bohemia, however, when a Moravian peasant uprising threatened his communications. The Austrians then moved against Frederick and caught him with his army scattered and in need of rest. He quickly reassembled the army and on 17 May won another narrow victory at Chotusitz.

Convinced that his army still needed improvement, Frederick resorted to diplomacy. On 11 June, the Peace of Breslau was signed, ending the First Silesian War. This settlement gave Frederick all of Silesia and the county of Glatz.

Frederick spent the next two years expanding and training his army. During this time, however, the Austrians made significant progress against Prussia's French and Bavarian allies, and on 17 August 1744, Frederick reentered the conflict.

Frederick again advanced into Bohemia and after a short siege took Prague on 16 September. Unable to find the main Austrian force, and with his supply and communications severely harassed by raiding parties, Frederick fled back into Silesia. Rampant desertion and anarchy during the retreat cost the Prussians tremendous losses.

Reforming his army, Frederick advanced against the Austrians and their new Saxon allies. On 4 June 1745, Frederick caught them at Hohenfriedberg, beating first the Saxons and then the Austrians. Now highly trained, Frederick's cavalry performed brilliantly. Charging at the most opportune moment, it rode down twenty Austrian battalions, capturing 2,500 prisoners and 66 colors.

Attempting to surprise Frederick, the Austrians and Saxons attacked his camp at Soor on 30 September, but Frederick reacted quickly and drove off the attack. He followed up his victory with two more, at Katholisch-Hennersdorf and Görlitz on 23 and 24 November. The Austrians tried one more assault near Dresden, but Frederick's lieutenant, General Leopold of Anhalt-Dessau ("the old Dessauer") defeated them at Kesselsdorf on 15 December.

The Treaty of Dresden on 25 December ended the Second Silesian War. Frederick's claim to Silesia was acknowledged, and Prussia was established as a leading European power.

Between the Wars

During the next decade Frederick worked diligently to improve the army and strengthen the country. He enlarged the army, adding horse artillery units to provide quick support for the cavalry, which he also further improved, and he established yearly exercises and reviews designed to drill his men to perfection. He strengthened the economy and enlarged the war chest and he also improved the road systems, built new factories, and saw to the development of the Prussian mercantile system.

Frederick also found time to build himself a new palace, "Sans Souci," as well as to indulge his interests in writing and music. In 1746 he began writing the remarkable *Histoire de mon temps*, and in 1747 he privately published his treatise on the art of war, *The Instruction of Frederick the Great for his Generals*. During this period he also wrote several libretti, 25 flute sonatas, four concerti, and various other pieces.

The Seven Years' War

On 16 January 1756, Frederick formed an alliance with Great Britain, the Convention of Westminster. The French, believing that Frederick had abandoned them, formed an alliance with Austria, the Treaty of Versailles, on 1 May. Frederick, worried that Russia and Saxony would join Austria in an overwhelming coalition against him, decided to strike first. On 29 August 1756 he invaded neutral Saxony.

After occupying Dresden, Frederick pushed on to attack the Saxons in their camp at Pirna. News of Austrian forces massing in Bohemia forced Frederick to abandon his blockade of Pirna and turn to meet the new threat. He encountered the main Austrian army under Field Marshal von Browne at Lobositz on 1 October and, after a bitter fight, the Austrians withdrew. On 17 October the Saxon army capitulated and was forced to "volunteer" in the Prussian army. Frederick then led his army into winter quarters.

During the winter and spring of 1756–57, Russia, Sweden, and the states of southern and western Germany joined the coalition against Prussia and Great Britain. Frederick decided to strike a decisive blow against Austria, and on 18 April 1757 he invaded Bohemia. Frederick caught and defeated the Austrian troops at Prague on 6 May, driving them into the city. Leaving a force to besiege Prague, Frederick then turned to attack the Austrians under Field Marshal Daun in their entrenched camp at Kolin on 18 June. The attack was defeated with heavy losses, and Frederick was forced to raise the siege of Prague and fall back into Silesia.

With French, Austrian, and Russian armies converging on him, Frederick was compelled to fight from a central position. He adapted his strategy to one of attacking from interior lines, concentrating his army against each opponent in turn. In this way he hoped to destroy each army in turn or, at the very least, to prevent them from joining forces.

Frederick turned on the French first. Despite nearly 2-to-1 odds against him, Frederick crushed the French in a brilliantly maneuvered victory at Rossbach on 5 November. He then marched swiftly into Silesia and met the Austrians at Leuthen on 6 December. Although again greatly outnumbered, Frederick attacked and decisively defeated the Austrians in a masterpiece of battlefield maneuver. The Austrians withdrew from Silesia in disorder, leaving 17,000 men stranded in Breslau to surrender on 20 December.

In 1758 Frederick launched another offensive against Austria. He advanced into Moravia and from May to June besieged the fortress of Olmütz. Learning that a strong Russian army was moving to invade East Prussia, Frederick marched swiftly north to prevent the Russians from crossing the Oder River. Frederick attacked the Russians at Zorndorf on 25 August, and after a bitter and costly drawn battle the Russians withdrew. Frederick quickly returned to Saxony to relieve his brother, Prince Henry, who was facing two Austrian armies under General Loudon and Field Marshal Daun. Daun's army surprised Frederick in his camp at Hochkirch on 14 October and came close to destroying the Prussians. Frederick's army was seriously mauled and nearly routed—some of the Prussian regiments turning their backs to the enemy for the first time—but managed to extricate itself and escape.

Frederick spent the winter of 1758–59 reorganizing his army and training new troops. Upon learning that the Russian general Saltikov had beaten a Prussian force at Kay on 23 July 1759, and had joined Daun's Austrian army, Frederick took immediate action. He attacked the Austro-Russian army at Kunersdorf on 12 August but was repulsed with severe losses. A counterattack by the allied cavalry broke the remnants of his army, and for the first time the Prussians were routed off the field. Fortunately for Frederick, the allies fell out amongst themselves and did not pursue, allowing the Prussians to escape.

The Prussians were defeated again on 20 November at Maxen where, due to Frederick's obstinacy as commander, an entire corps was left isolated against superior numbers and subsequently forced to surrender. The remnants of Frederick's army spent a hard winter quartered near Dresden.

Frederick began the campaign of 1760 by allowing another isolated Prussian corps to be defeated at Landeshut on 23 June. After an unsuccessful attempt to retake Dresden by siege, Frederick moved to deal with the allied armies converging on Silesia. Facing a precarious strategic situation, Frederick was forced to shuttle back and forth against three allied armies—each stronger than his own—desperately trying to keep all of them at bay. On 15 August he defeated repeated attacks by Daun's Austrians at Liegnitz. He then diverted General Czernichev's Russian army by a clever piece of disinformation. On 9 October allied troops occupied Berlin. Frederick marched at once on his capital, which he relieved on 12 October. He next attacked Daun's army in its fortified camp at Torgau on 3 November. In a fierce battle, he forced the Austrians to retreat after severe losses to both sides.

In 1761 Frederick, too weak to risk battle, resorted to maneuver in an effort to hold off his more numerous foes. Eventually brought to bay, he retreated into his fortified camp at Bunzelwitz from 20 August to 25 September. Facing a hopeless military situation, Frederick nevertheless mustered 60,000 troops for yet another campaign. Instead, Prussia was saved by the timely death of Czarina Elizabeth on 5 January 1762 and the succession of Peter III to the Russian imperial throne. A great admirer of Frederick and all things Prussian, Peter withdrew from the allied coalition, made peace with Prussia, and joined sides with Frederick through the Treaty of St. Petersburg on 15 May. Although Peter was later deposed by his wife, Catherine II (the Great), his brief reign saved Prussia from disaster and gave Frederick time to consolidate his position.

Going over to the offensive, Frederick attacked and defeated Daun at Burkersdorf on 21 July and regained control of Silesia. An armistice was concluded in November, and the Peace of Hubertusburg on 16 January 1763 ended the Seven Years' War in Europe.

Final Years

Frederick now dedicated all his efforts to rebuilding his war-ravaged country. Within three years most of the major damage had been repaired, and Prussia was well on the road to recovery. In 1772 Frederick joined the empresses Maria Theresa and Catherine II in the first partition of Poland, through which Prussia received the territory of West Prussia.

On 3 July 1778, Frederick took the field against Austria for the last time, leading the Prussian army in the War of the Bavarian Succession, or the "Potato War." There was little fighting and all of it was done by Prince Henry, Frederick by now having lost his taste for war. After some maneuvering and a few minor skirmishes, the war ended with the Treaty of Teschen on 13 May 1779, by which Austria renounced all claims to Bavaria.

Frederick spent the remaining years of his life in relative peace, playing his music, maintaining his correspondence, and reviewing his army. On 17 August 1786, the great king died quietly at Sans Souci.

Frederick the Great was a classic example of an enlightened despot. A skillful commander and tactical genius, he sometimes let his obstinacy, self-confidence, and position as king override his better military judgment. Although sometimes harsh and unforgiving to the point of brutality, he had a great affection for his soldiers and tried to take care of their needs. His liberal government policies worked well for Prussia, producing a strong state with a deep sense of patriotism and national pride. Frederick's civil, military, and national policies influenced Prussia for years to come and laid the foundation of later German nationalism.

VINCENT B. HAWKINS

SEE ALSO: History, Early Modern Military; Prussia and Germany, Rise of; Seven Years' War.

Bibliography

Dorn, G. and J. Englemann. 1986. *Die Schlachten Friedrichs des Grossens.* Hanau, Germany: Podzun-Pallas.
Duffy, C. 1974. *The army of Frederick the Great.* New York: Hippocrene Books.
――――. 1986. *The military life of Frederick the Great.* New York: Atheneum.
Luvaas, J. 1966. *Frederick the Great on the art of war.* New York: Free Press.
Mitford, N. 1970. *Frederick the Great.* London: Hamish Hamilton.
Prussian General Staff. 1901–1914. *Die Kriege Friedrichs des Grossen.* 13 vols. Berlin: Ernst Siegfried Mittler und Sohn.

FRENCH REVOLUTIONARY–NAPOLEONIC WARS

The French Revolutionary–Napoleonic Wars, lasting from 1792 to 1815, generally continued the long-standing Anglo-French rivalry and other continental rivalries, with the addition of the fervor and ideology of revolutionary France. These wars are usually designated by the names of the coalitions that opposed France (see Fig. 1).

War of the First Coalition

When Austria and Prussia formed an alliance to restore the French monarchy, the French Assembly declared war (20 April 1792). The Kingdom of Sardinia (Piedmont) soon joined the alliance. Although neither side was militarily ready for war, major campaigning began in August, when an allied army under Charles William, duke of Brunswick, invaded France (19 August). Capturing Longwy and Verdun, Brunswick was stopped at Valmy (20 September) by a mixed force of revolutionary volunteers and Old Regime regulars under Charles C. Dumouriez and François C. Kellermann. As a result, Brunswick and the Prussians retreated into Germany. Dumouriez pursued the Austrians into the Austrian Netherlands (Belgium), defeating them at Jemappes (6 November) and conquering Belgium, a long-standing French goal. Simultaneously, France attacked Piedmont and Savoy and invaded Germany.

In February 1793, Britain, Holland, and Spain joined the alliance against France, and counteroffensives were begun against the disintegrating French

Figure 1. Battles of the French Revolution and Napoleon.

forces. Austrians under Frederick Josias, duke of Coburg, defeated Dumouriez at Neerwinden (18 March 1793), leading to the defection of Dumouriez and the rise of the Jacobins to power in France. The allies captured Condé and Valenciennes (10 and 29 July), while the British occupied Toulon (23 August). Spain and Sardinia launched offensives, but the allies disagreed on priorities.

France's war minister, Lazare Carnot, inaugurated reforms, which revitalized the French armies. Raw recruits were brigaded with veterans, supplies were provided on a regular basis, the proportion of horse artillery in the armies was increased, and victory returned to France. Jean Houchard defeated an Anglo-Austrian force under Frederick Augustus, duke of York, at Hondschoote (8 September) and Jean-Baptiste Jourdan defeated Coburg at Wattignies (15–16 October). The allies retreated across the Rhine. Meanwhile, Jacques E. Dugommier, aided by Napoleon Bonaparte's artillery, recaptured Toulon (19 December). These victories reflected not only French zeal but also improving French discipline and tactics.

French victories continued with Jean Pichegru's defeat of the Austrians at Tourcoing (18 May 1794). The decisive battle of this period occurred at Fleurus (26 June) where Jourdan soundly defeated Coburg, a victory that helped bring about the fall of Maximilien F. de Robespierre and the end of the Reign of Terror. The French then reoccupied Belgium and invaded Holland. Meanwhile, Dugommier and Adrien Moncey defeated the Spanish and penetrated both flanks of the Pyrenees. France now had achieved her natural frontiers, and both France and its enemies were exhausted. The First Coalition collapsed in 1795, leaving Austria and Britain the only major belligerents.

In 1795, Jourdan and Pichegru crossed the Rhine to attack Austria in Germany, but were driven back. In 1796, Jourdan and Jean Moreau again attacked into Germany while Napoleon campaigned in northern Italy. Archduke Charles of Austria defeated Jourdan at Würzburg (3 September) and drove Moreau back to the Rhine River. Napoleon, however, decisively defeated the Austrians in Italy, conquered Lombardy, and invaded Venetia in 1797 while French successes were renewed in Germany. In an attempt to strike at Britain in 1796, French general Louis Lazare Hoche led an expedition to invade Ireland and exploit Irish unrest. The invasion was unsuccessful, as Hoche decided to return to France after a gale had scattered his ships off the coast of Ireland. But Austria, its homeland invaded by Napoleon and Barthélemy Joubert, made peace at Campo Formio (17 October 1797). Britain now stood alone.

Egyptian Campaign

France then considered an invasion of England but instead sent Napoleon, in May 1798, to attack British interests in Egypt and the Middle East. His expedition captured Malta (12 June) and landed in Egypt (1 July). He defeated the Mameluke cavalry at the Battle of the Pyramids (21 July), although Lord Horatio Nelson destroyed the French fleet at Aboukir Bay (1–2 August), cutting him off from Europe. Threatened by a Turkish army near Damascus and possibly seeking a route back to Europe, Napoleon marched against Syria. Turkish troops and a British squadron under Sydney Smith halted him at Acre (March–May 1799). The French then retreated back to Egypt, crushing a Turkish landing at Aboukir Bay (25 July). Then Napoleon, learning of French defeats in Europe, sailed for France (23 August), leaving his troops under Jean Baptiste Kléber.

War of the Second Coalition

The battles that brought Napoleon back to France were fought by the Second Coalition and were engineered by Czar Paul I of Russia, who was allied (December 1798) with Turkey and Britain. Naples, Austria, Sweden, and Portugal joined them. The allies planned to drive the French from Italy and invade France through Germany. Although the French won initial victories over Austria in Italy, Archduke Charles defeated Jourdan at Stockach I (25 March 1799), and Barthélemy Scherer was beaten by Paul Kray's Austrians at Magnano (5 April). Other defeats by the Austrians and Russians followed in Italy and Switzerland, and an Anglo-Russian force invaded Holland. But the tide turned before Napoleon actually set foot in France. André Masséna defeated Alexander Korsakov at Zurich (25–26 September) and thwarted Archduke Charles's planned invasion of France. Guillaume Brune checked the Anglo-Russians in Holland, and Britain agreed to evacuate. Russia thereupon broke its British alliance (22 October) in disgust and Austria remained France's only major land enemy.

In the spring of 1800, Moreau launched a campaign across the Rhine; Napoleon, now first consul, crossed the St. Bernard Pass to attack the Austrians from the rear. At Marengo, Napoleon and Louis Desaix defeated Michael Melas's Austrians (14 June), virtually ending this Italian campaign. Then Moreau decisively defeated Austria's Archduke John at Hohenlinden (3 December). Invaded by Moreau from Germany, by Jacques Macdonald from Switzerland, and by Brune from Italy, Austria ended hostilities (9 February 1801), and Britain made peace (27 March 1802).

Anglo-French dissension continued, however, and in 1803 Napoleon established an Army of England to prepare for invasion. War was formally renewed (16 May 1803), although little action occurred in Europe until 1805.

War of the Third Coalition

With Europe antagonized by French expansion, Britain easily formed the Third Coalition with Russia, Austria, Naples, and Sweden. To avenge their previous defeats and losses, they hoped to crush the small French force in Italy and then attack France through Germany—a battle plan similar to that of 1798–99. When Austria moved against Bavaria (August 1805), Napoleon secretly marched the Army of England, renamed the Grand Army, into Germany, while Masséna maneuvered against Archduke Charles in Italy. Crossing the Rhine before the Austrians knew he had left Boulogne, Napoleon forced the surrender of the Austrian army of Karl Mack von Leiberich at Ulm (17 October), and Masséna defeated Charles at Caldiers (30 October). The Austrians then joined the Russian armies under Michael Kutusov and Czar Alexander I. Napoleon, preventing other forces from joining them, defeated these combined armies at Austerlitz (2 December). The Russians then retreated into Poland, while Austria made peace (26 December). After Austerlitz, the Third Coalition collapsed.

Meanwhile, an unsuccessful French attempt to distract the British fleet from the Channel, begun in early 1805, had led to the destruction of the French and Spanish fleets by Nelson at Trafalgar (21 October 1805).

After Austerlitz, Russia remained belligerent, and Prussia, resentful of French domination, was inclined to hostilities. Thus, in 1806, Britain formed a Fourth Coalition with Prussia and Russia.

War of the Fourth Coalition

In late September 1806, Prussia demanded that France withdraw west of the Rhine. Napoleon quickly concentrated to the southeast of the Prussian army and rapidly outflanked it. The French crushed the main Prussian forces at Jena and Auerstädt (14 October), defeated their reserves at Halle (17 October), and occupied Berlin (24 October). The French then moved east to the Vistula and seized Warsaw. Simultaneously, they induced Turkey to break its alliance with Russia and England, initiating a war that lasted until 1812.

Meanwhile the remnants of the Prussian army united with the Russians, who continued the war. In January 1807, the Russians under Lévin Bennigsen attacked Michel Ney's winter quarters, driving him westward and leading to Napoleon's marginal success at Eylau (8 February). To meet a Russian spring counteroffensive, Napoleon split the enemy forces and crushed Bennigsen's Russians at Friedland (14 June). The Treaties of Tilsit between France and Russia (7 July) and France and Prussia (9 July) ended the coalition. The major threat of war then shifted to the Iberian Peninsula.

IBERIA

After Tilsit, Portugal remained the only country officially open to British trade. Therefore, a French army under Marshal Andoche Junot invaded Portugal (November 1807). Then, ostensibly to guard the Spanish coasts, Marshal Joachim Murat led an invasion of Spain (March 1808). When Napoleon installed his brother Joseph as king of Spain, a popular uprising and guerrilla war erupted against the French. The British responded with aid. A British landing in Portugal was followed by Junot's defeat at Vimeiro (21 August) by Gen. Arthur Wellesley, later duke of Wellington, and Junot evacuated Portugal.

Simultaneously, French difficulties in Spain increased. Gen. Pierre Dupont capitulated to Spanish levies at Baylen (22 July), the first capitulation of a Napoleonic army in Europe, and Madrid was abandoned. Napoleon himself then led a new army into Spain, winning against Spanish regulars and recapturing Madrid (4 December). Meanwhile, a British contingent under Gen. Sir John Moore had landed at Corunna. Napoleon pursued the British, then turned command over to Marshal Nicholas Soult, who followed Moore to Corunna, where an indecisive battle was fought (16 January 1809). The British then withdrew from Spain. The French capture of Saragossa (21 February) after a long siege appeared to restore their position in Spain, although guerrilla warfare continued. The French invaded Portugal but were driven out, and Wellesley invaded Spain, winning a victory at Talavera (28 July). The French threat to Portugal was now temporarily ended. The French, however, pushed farther into southern Spain, defeating a Spanish army at Ocaña (19 November) and occupying most of Andalusia. Meanwhile, Austria, in a new coalition with Britain, had risen against Napoleon.

War of the Fifth Coalition

Hoping to drive France out of Germany, Archduke Charles invaded Bavaria, while Archduke John attacked in Italy. Napoleon rushed to Bavaria from Paris, and in a week of rapid action drove Charles across the Danube. Napoleon occupied Vienna (13 May) and attempted to cross the Danube but was defeated by Charles at Aspern and Essling (21–22 May). Napoleon then bridged the Danube from Löbau Island and soundly defeated Charles at Wagram (5–6 July). The French also defeated a British landing on Walcheren Island. Austria then made peace with France (14 October) and the Fifth Coalition ended. War, however, continued in the peninsula where Britain, without major allies, was on the defensive.

In 1810 the French attacked Wellington (Wellesley) in Portugal. Masséna captured Ciudad Rodrigo (10 July), but the British stopped him at the Lines of Torres Vedras in October. After skirmishing over Ciudad Rodrigo and Badajoz, which controlled passes from Spain into Portugal, Masséna retreated into Spain. Wellington defeated him at Fuentes de Onoro (5 May 1811), while William Beresford defeated Soult at Albuera (16 May). In 1812 Wellington's renewed offensive captured Ciudad Rodrigo (19 January) and Badajoz (19 April). His crushing defeat of Auguste Marmont at Salamanca (22 July) led to Joseph Bonaparte's evacuation of Madrid in August. Wellington, however, was temporarily driven back in the fall.

War of the Sixth Coalition

After three years of uneasy peace in central Europe, the Sixth Coalition developed over a two-year period. Napoleon invaded Russia (24 June 1812), which was allied with Britain and Sweden, hoping to defeat two main Russian armies separately, but they united under Barclay de Tolly, who retreated, then fought and lost at Smolensk (17 August). Kutusov then replaced Barclay. Napoleon, seeking a complete victory, pursued Kutusov and defeated him at Borodino (7 September). The French occupied Moscow (14 September) but, when Alexander refused to make peace, they abandoned the city (19 October). Failing to defeat the Russians at Maloyaroslavets (24 October), the French retreated, harassed by Russian attacks and devastated by severe winter weather. The heroism of the soldiers of Ney and Nicolas Oudinot and of Jean-Baptiste Eblé's sappers permitted the remnants of the army to fight off three encircling Russian armies and to recross the Beresina (26–28 November). The Grand Army then disintegrated. Hans Yorck von Wartenburg, commander of the Prussian contingent of the Grand Army, joined the Russians (30 December), allowing them to pass freely through the territory under his control.

Wars of Liberation

In early 1813, the Germans began to rise against the French, and once again Prussia allied itself with Russia, Sweden, and Britain (27 February). Napoleon hoped to confront the allies separately and defeated them at Lützen (2 May) and Bautzen (20–21 May), driving them back and capturing Dresden. But with allied strength increasing, he accepted an armistice (2 June–13 August). The war resumed with Austria joining the allies, and three major allied armies moved against the French. Napoleon won his last major victory in Germany at Dresden (26–27 August). The allies renewed their offensive; a combined army defeated Napoleon at Leipzig (16–19 October) and ended French power in Germany. Napoleon retreated to France, followed by the allies, who began to cross the Rhine (21 December).

Meanwhile, the transfer of French troops from Spain led to renewed offensives and advances by Wellington, who crushed Jourdan's army at Vittoria (21

June 1813). Wellington invaded France (7 October), repeatedly defeating Soult and besieging Bayonne in December.

Campaign in France

Three allied armies invaded France through the Low Countries, the Belfort Gap, and Lorraine. Fencing with them, Napoleon defeated Gebhard Blücher's army at Champaubert, Montmirail, Château-Thierry, and Vauchamps (10–14 February 1814) and then turned to defeat the Austrians at Montereau (17–18 February). But a series of allied victories in March led to the capture of Paris (31 March) and Napoleon's unconditional abdication (6 April). Meanwhile, Wellington had taken Bordeaux (12 March) and dealt Soult a final defeat at Toulouse (10 April).

War of the Seventh Coalition

When Napoleon returned from Elba (1 March 1815), the allies renewed their alliance. Hoping to defeat the allied armies before they could unite, Napoleon invaded Belgium and defeated the Prussian advance guard at Charleroi (15 June). He drove Blücher back at Ligny (16 June), but Ney was temporarily checked at Quatre Bras the same day. Napoleon, detaching Marshal Emmanuel de Grouchy to pursue the Prussians, moved north against Wellington. But Blücher eluded Grouchy and united with Wellington in time to defeat Napoleon at Waterloo (18 June). The French army then disintegrated, and the allies entered Paris (7 July). The wars came to an end with Napoleon's final abdication (22 June) and exile and the Second Peace of Paris (20 November.)

The wars of the French Revolution and Napoleon saw the introduction to warfare of mass citizen armies (the nation in arms). France expanded to its natural frontiers and briefly dominated Europe. Political change was stimulated throughout Europe, especially the rise of nationalism in Germany and Italy. And even after Napoleon's defeat, the old order, swept away by the wars, was not restored.

JAMES K. KIESWETTER

SEE ALSO: British Seapower; History, Modern Military; Napoleon I; Nelson, Lord Horatio; Prussia and Germany, Rise of.

Bibliography

Chandler, D. G. 1966. *The campaigns of Napoleon.* New York: Macmillan.
———. 1979. *Dictionary of the Napoleonic Wars.* New York: Macmillan.
Chuquet, A. 1887–96. *Les guerres de la révolution.* 11 vols. Paris: Cerf.
Jomini, A. H. 1820–24. *Histoire critique et militaire des guerres de la révolution.* 15 vols. Paris: Anselin et Pochard.
Lynn, J. A. 1984. *The bayonets of the republic.* Urbana: Univ. of Illinois Press.
Oman, C. 1902–30. *A history of the peninsular war.* 7 vols. London: Oxford Univ. Press.
Phipps, R. W. 1926–39. *The armies of the first French Republic.* 5 vols. London: Oxford Univ. Press.

FULLER, J. F. C. [1878–1966]

Known throughout most of his life as "Boney," because of both his small stature and his military interests, John Frederick Charles Fuller was born on 1 September 1878 in Itchenor in southern England. He was the son of an Anglican clergyman and of a French mother who had been educated and brought up in Germany. He died on 10 February 1966 in Cornwall. During his long life he made a contribution to military thought that has become increasingly recognized as one that places him foremost in rank below Clausewitz.

Early Military Career

Fuller was commissioned from Sandhurst in 1898 into the 1st Battalion of the Oxfordshire Light Infantry, now part of the Royal Green Jackets. He joined his regiment in Ireland where he spent his time reading ancient and nineteenth-century philosophy, an unusual occupation for a Victorian subaltern. In 1899 the regiment moved to Plymouth, and in December embarked at Southampton, bound for Capetown and the Boer War.

Fuller's first experience of hostilities was interrupted by an appendectomy and five months' sick leave in England. In time he was given command of 70 unreliable native scouts and the job of watching a large tract of the Orange Free State, which was only partially pacified. The use of black troops was not to the liking of the Boers, and Fuller was threatened with execution should he be taken prisoner. When the war ended in May 1901, Fuller rejoined his regiment and was stationed in Chatham. In 1903 the regiment went to India. Here Fuller first met the notorious occultist Alastair Crowley and so began his interest in magic. It was to be an association that boded ill for Fuller's personal reputation in British society and among his contemporaries in the army. In 1906 he returned to England and met and married Margarethe Karnatz, of Polish-German extraction, known generally as Sonia. He next became a volunteer or reserve forces adjutant, then rejoined his regiment and studied for the Staff College Examination. At this time he also began to write and publish pamphlets and articles on training, mobilization, and troop entrainment.

In 1914, he entered the Staff College where he fell foul of the commandant because he embraced the concept of tactical penetration rather than envelopment. At the Staff College he also developed an interest in the principles of war.

World War I

The outbreak of the First World War in August 1914 found Fuller employed as an embarkation staff officer at Southampton, involved in the dispatch of the British Expeditionary Force (doubtless the price he paid for his pamphlet on entrainment). Because of this and another posting, he did not go to France until July 1915, soon after which he wrote a seminal article on "The Principles of War with Reference to the Campaign of 1914–1915," which was published anonymously by the Royal United Services Institute (RUSI) in February 1916.

In France he had several staff appointments, and soon concluded that (1) victory would only be achieved by penetration, and (2) the method of penetration did not exist, because the front line could not be outflanked, and machine gun, rifle, and artillery fire made frontal assault suicidal. On 20 August 1916 Fuller saw his first tank and realized that tanks were the means of penetration. In December he was posted as a staff officer to the headquarters of the new Heavy Branch of the Machine Gun Corps (or Tank) organization and began devising tactics for the use of tank forces. In April 1917 he became a lieutenant colonel and was the planner of the victory at Cambrai, which failed to achieve lasting results because the overall plan for battle did not provide for proper exploitation of the initial success of the tanks. In March 1918 he observed the British retreat in the face of the German offensive and concluded that the British were retreating because the command was paralyzed. This gave him the concept of "strategic paralysis" as the means for victory and in due course he produced a plan to win the war in 1919 by inflicting such paralysis on the enemy. This was "Plan 1919," possibly one of the most visionary projects in military history. It called for a massive and swift penetration of the front line at points on a 145-kilometer (90-mi.) front without artillery preparation— which would simply alert the enemy to the forthcoming attack. The penetrating force would consist of 790 new Medium D tanks (as yet unproduced but to have a 320-km [200-mi.] range and a speed of 32 km [20 mi.] per hour). This force would destroy the primary objective, the area between German divisional and army headquarters. The secondary objective, the front line, would be broken by 2,592 heavy tanks and 30 Medium Ds, and exploitation from the primary objective would be undertaken by a pursuing force of 820 Medium Ds and 400 other medium tanks. Bombing by airplanes of supply and road centers would add to the confusion as would the bombing of the German Western GHQ.

Although it received official support, Plan 1919 was never put into effect because the war ended. It was, however, a brilliant conception and the germ of blitzkrieg and "deep battle"—whether it would have worked against a resolute enemy would have depended on the minimization of "friction" and the solution of the technological problems posed by the Medium D.

Post–World War I

In August 1918 Fuller returned to London to head a new branch responsible for tanks in the War Office. In that appointment he succeeded in setting up the Royal Tank Corps as a permanent establishment. He also began his writing career in earnest, turning from persuasion to shock tactics when he found the forces of equine conservatism (i.e., the horsed cavalry and their supporters) opposed to his ever more radical views on armored and mechanized warfare. His basic thesis was that, since horse and human flesh cannot withstand bullets, all movement on the battlefield should be by armored vehicles. He gave a lecture at the RUSI in 1920 on "The Development of Sea Warfare on Land and Its Influence on Future Naval Operations," which was a veritable blueprint of the distant future and contains the splendid, if somewhat hopeful sentence:

"There is nothing too wonderful for science—we of the fighting services must grasp the wand of this magician and compel the future to obey us."

In the same year, he also won the RUSI Gold Medal Military Essay Prize with an essay that called for the total mechanization of the army. The forces of reaction in Whitehall were quick to stigmatize it as "violent military Bolshevism" and Fuller's reputation in official circles as a military menace was born. In June 1920 he met Basil Liddell Hart and there began a most important friendship and partnership for them that, with one notable break caused by Fuller's Fascist sympathies in the late thirties and early forties, lasted until Fuller's death.

At this time, Fuller began to become a prolific writer of military books, his most important publication of the time being *The Reformation of War* (1923).

In January 1923 Fuller became an instructor at the Staff College and thoroughly reorganized its syllabuses, even to the extent of making Xenophon's *Cyropaedia* a required text. In due course, he turned his own lectures into a book, *The Foundations of the Science of War* (1926), which he was not allowed to publish until he left Camberley. This book was Fuller at his most visionary, most philosophical, and worst. It is very hard to read and contains some very strange metaphysics such as The Threefold Order. However, its analysis of the causes, objects, instruments, and conditions of war is stimulating and the final chapter, "The Application of the Science of War," is well worth reading. *The Foundations of the Science of War* did Fuller's reputation no good and met with undeserved ridicule.

In 1926, at the suggestion of Liddell Hart, the Chief of the Imperial General Staff (CIGS), Gen. Sir George Milne, took Fuller on as his military assistant. The *Sunday Express* described him as "probably by far the cleverest man in the Army." Unfortunately, he eventually proved too clever for the CIGS and for his own career. In 1927 Fuller was told that he had been selected to command the Experimental Force, an organization designed to test tank and mechanized structures and tactics. For reasons that are not entirely clear (but were connected with his unwillingness to act as a garrison commander, and probably Sonia's to be a garrison commander's wife), Fuller turned the post down. This was the beginning of the end of his active military career. He held a series of other appointments, including in 1929 that of Commander of the 2d Rhine Brigade in Wiesbaden. This command ended after three months, however, when the Rhine Army was withdrawn. In 1930 he was promoted to major general and was eventually offered the post of GOC of a Second Class District in India. He refused the appointment. He was not offered another and after a period on half pay, was retired from the army in December 1933 at the age of 55.

Nonmilitary Career

As a career soldier, Fuller had only modest success, although as a serving military thinker and planner he was outstanding. There was no doubt that his radical abrasiveness and extreme intellectuality made him unacceptable in the

British military establishment of his time. He devoted the remaining 31 years of his life to military history, military thought, politics, and the occult. At first he sought to reason, but found that few people paid attention to him. In despair he joined Oswald Mosley's British Union of Fascists because he thought that the achievement of power through Mosley would enable him to reform and mechanize the army and so save the British Empire and Western civilization from the forces then stirring in central and eastern Europe. Mosley claimed that he would have made Fuller his generalissimo had he come to power.

Fuller's books included: *On Future Warfare* (1928), *The Generalship of Ulysses S. Grant* (1929), *Lectures on FSR II* (1931), *Lectures on FSR III* (1932), *Generalship: Its Diseases and Their Cure* (1933), *Memoirs of an Unconventional Soldier* (1936), *Towards Armageddon* (1937), and *Decisive Battles* (1939 and 1940).

Many of these books contained Fascist and anti-Semitic undertones, but Fuller withdrew as a Fascist parliamentary candidate in 1938 because he was conscious of how much Leslie Hore-Belisha (a Jew) had done for the army as Secretary of State for War. He did, however, attend Hitler's 50th birthday parade in 1939.

At the outbreak of World War II, he met with the CIGS about the possibility of being brought back to the active list as Deputy CIGS but, not unsurprisingly, this came to nothing. Throughout the war he continued to write, generally critically, both books and as a journalist. In fact he had done a lot of journalism in the thirties and visited the Abyssinian and Spanish wars as a newspaper correspondent. He was particularly critical of Churchill's policy of unconditional surrender.

In 1946 he published *Armament and History*, a penetrating study of the relationship between weapon development and historical events. In this book, he put forward again his law of military development and his constant tactical factor, which he had first developed in the early thirties. The law stated that "civilization is environment, and armies must adapt themselves to its changing phases in order to remain fitted for war"; the factor holds that

> every improvement in weapon power has aimed at lessening the danger on one side by increasing it on the other. Therefore every improvement in weapons has eventually been met by a counter-improvement which has rendered the improvement obsolete: the evolutionary pendulum of weapon-power, slowly or rapidly, swinging from the offensive to the protective and back again in harmony with the pace of civil progress; each swing in a measurable degree eliminating danger.

These truths were significant insights, but just before the book was published, Fuller was forced to rethink his position and write a new chapter because the atom bomb was dropped on Japan. This rewriting, at the age of 64, he did effectively, and he predicted that cities would be "girt about by radar sets, ceaselessly 'listening-in' for the first jazz note of the broadcast of annihilation." Admittedly he also stated that "the whole idea of maintaining peace through the power to destroy is unadulterated madness."

After the war, Fuller continued to write. He became friendly again with Liddell Hart. He produced much quieter and more scholarly books, of which the best are probably *The Decisive Battles of the Western World* (1954, 1955, 1956) and *The Conduct of War: 1789–1961* (1961). In 1963 he and Liddell Hart were presented with Chesney Gold Medals in the RUSI. Gen. Sir John Hackett called Fuller "the gadfly of Socrates, pricking people to awareness of false complacency, not always a popular pursuit in armies." In February 1966, he died while on a visit to Cornwall at the age of 87, the author of 45 books, hundreds of articles, the inventor of tank tactics, and a very considerable military thinker and philosopher, if an aberrant politician.

Contribution

First and foremost Fuller was a most atypical army officer. He was a man of superb intellect and encyclopedic knowledge, and also of high moral courage; he was a fine writer in a lively, pungent, amusing, and highly controversial style. Not all that he wrote was sensible, but much was either profound or full of incisive insight and very effective analysis. He was, above all, a philosopher and scientist of war as well as a military theoretician. He attempted to create a science of war, but failed because war is an art, although science plays a large part in its conduct. He did not have the rigorous academic training of an academic philosopher, but his rational thought brought him to positions many philosophers would have admired. As a politician, his views were distorted and often regrettable; he distrusted democracy as the cause of violence and irrationality but was always a patriot; as a journalist, he was highly successful; as a historian he made a unique contribution and his system for writing military history and drawing lessons from it are useful devices for the military profession. He denied being a prophet, but he gave voice to some remarkable prophecies, which subsequently came true, notably Indian partition, the decline of white global supremacy, the use of military rockets, the weakness of airpower in antiguerrilla warfare, and the limitation of war through weapon development. He was a scholar of the occult and saw a connection between generalship and the art of the white magician in that they both sought control over others.

In short, Fuller was a genius but his genius was flawed; he was a profound tactical and strategic thinker, a philosopher of war, a man whose frustrations led him for a while into strange political waters but who, in the evening of his life, became a wiser man. He had great influence throughout much of the world and was the colleague and mentor of Liddell Hart. He carried the process of rationality too far to be a career success, but this failure led him to devote his enormous intellectual energies to thinking about war—and indeed peace—and in this sphere of activity his life and work will be long remembered and greatly valued.

A. J. TRYTHALL

SEE ALSO: World War I.

Bibliography

Fuller, J. F. C. 1926. *The foundations of the science of war*. London: Hutchinson.

———. 1932. *Lectures on FSR III*. London: Sifton Praed.

———. 1936. *Memoirs of an unconventional soldier*. London: Nicholson and Watson.

———. 1949. *Armament and history*. London: Eyre and Spottiswoode.

———. 1954–56. *The decisive battles of the western world*. Vols. 1–3. London: Eyre and Spottiswoode.

———. 1961. *The conduct of war, 1789–1961*. London: Eyre and Spottiswoode.

Holden Reid, B. 1987. *J. F. C. Fuller, military thinker*. London: Macmillan.

Luvaas, J. 1965. *The education of an army*. London: Cassell.

Trythall, A. J. 1977. *Boney Fuller, The intellectual general: 1878–1966*. London: Cassell.

G

GENGHIS KHAN [ca. 1167–1227]

Genghis Khan, the "Master of Thrones and Crowns," created the largest land empire in world history and passed it on, intact, to his sons and grandsons. Genghis Khan created not only the Mongol Empire but also the Mongol nation itself. Before Genghis Khan's rise to supremacy, the Mongol people were divided into numerous tribes and clans. After Genghis Khan, there was but one Mongol people, one Mongol nation.

Birth and Ancestry

The future Genghis Khan was born circa 1167. His father, Yesugei, was a minor chieftain of the Kiyat clan. Yesugei had gained a small following as a result of his success in battle. When his first son was born, Yesugei, following custom, named the boy Temujin after a captured Tatar chieftain.

Temujin's mother was Houlun, whom Yesugei had abducted from her husband, a member of the Merkit tribe, shortly after her wedding. Yesugei and Houlun had three other children besides Temujin.

Although the son of a chieftain, Temujin's lifestyle differed little from that of the common folk. He had, however, something the common folk lacked, an illustrious ancestry: the royal line of the Mongols, the Borjigin (Blue-Eyed Men).

Temujin's great-great-grandfather, Kaidu Khan, had been the first Mongol king. His grandfather, Kabul Khan, and his great-uncles Ambakhai Khan and Khutula Khan, had also borne the royal title. However, the Mongol kingdom was short-lived. Antagonism between the Mongols and the Tatars and the foreign policy of the Kin dynasty of North China undermined the Mongol kingdom. Both Kabul Khan and Ambakhai Khan died at the hands of the Kin, after their capture by the Tatars. With the death of Khutula Khan, the Mongol kingdom disintegrated.

Early Life

Such was the fragility of tribal unity among the Mongols that, when Yesugei died, the clans that had gathered around him quickly deserted his widows and children and left them alone and destitute. Temujin was only nine years old when his father died, leaving him and his brothers and half-brothers to glean a living from the steppe.

Nature was not their only enemy. Steppe bandits were a constant threat. The greatest danger to Temujin, however, came from his cousins the Taychiuts, once followers of Yesugei. The Taychiuts captured Temujin, kept him prisoner in their camp, and forced him to wear a cangue, a heavy wooden collar. Faced with slavery or, more likely, death at the hands of his cousins, Temujin escaped with the help of Sorkhan-shira and his family.

As they survived the perils of the steppe and grew, Temujin and his brothers were able to stabilize the precarious situation of their family. Temujin also was able to gather a small following of other destitute families. More important, with the improvement in his family's fortunes, Temujin was able to renew the friendship forged between Yesugei and Toghrul Khan, king of the Keraits, a Turkic tribe. With the support of Toghrul, Temujin pressed his claim to the hand of Borte, to whom he had become betrothed shortly before his father's death. In due course, Temujin and Borte were married.

Temujin's fortunes took a turn for the worse when a large Merkit raiding party, greatly outnumbering Temujin's followers, attacked the Mongol camp. Temujin was forced to flee, leaving Borte at the mercy of the Merkits. The Merkit raiders gave Borte to a relative of the man whose brief marriage to Houlun had ended with her abduction by Yesugei.

Temujin sought the aid of Toghrul Khan in rescuing Borte. Toghrul gladly agreed to help in the rescue, as did Jamukha, khan of the Jalairs. Jamukha had been Temujin's *anda* (blood brother) when the two were children. The combined Mongol-Kerait-Jalair forces easily scattered the Merkits and freed Borte. Nine months later she gave birth to Juchi, whom Temujin acknowledged as his first-born son despite questions concerning the boy's paternity.

Supremacy over the Mongols

The successful rescue of Borte and the renewal of the Kerait alliance increased Temujin's stature among the Mongols. In 1190, the princes of the Kiyat clan— including Prince Altan, son of the last Mongol king, Khutula—asked Temujin to accept the title of king. As a member of a junior branch of the clan, Temujin at first refused, suggesting instead either Prince Altan or one of the princes of the Jürkin, the senior line. When the other princes refused, Temujin agreed to become king.

The Mongol princes knew the Kerait alliance was a personal one between Toghrul and Temujin, not between Keraits and Mongols. Without the alliance the newfound importance of the Mongols would evaporate. Therefore, the princes elected Temujin to be their leader in war and in the hunt. Temujin, however, conceived his role differently.

Temujin realized that without a strong leader the Mongol peoples were fated to remain dispersed and disunited, prey not only to each other but to outside forces as well. To create a single, united people—a nation—Temujin had to neutralize the dissident factions within his own kingdom and then defeat and incorporate into the Mongol kingdom the other ethnic Mongol tribes.

WAR AGAINST THE TATARS

The Kin dynasty of North China followed the traditional Chinese policy of setting one group of barbarians against another. When the Mongols became too strong, the Kin allied with the Tatars to neutralize the Mongol menace. With the Tatars now a threat, the Kin reversed themselves and offered an alliance to Temujin.

Temujin realized that the alliance with the Kin would be temporary, and, given the nature of their foreign policy, the Kin might quickly switch their support back to the Tatars. Therefore, the Mongols, in alliance with the Keraits, had to bring the maximum force possible against the Tatars in the shortest possible time. In a series of lightning moves, Temujin defeated the Tatars and crippled their war-making potential by slaying all Tatar males taller than the linchpin of a wagon wheel.

PURGE OF THE JÜRKIN PRINCES

Temujin declared the Tatar War a national war of vengeance. The Tatars had helped bring about the deaths of both Kabul and Ambakhai. Temujin's own father, Yesugei, had died poisoned by a Tatar. Therefore, he considered the war to be just punishment for the crimes of the Tatars.

When Temujin marshaled his forces for the war, the Jürkin princes were absent. After the war, Temujin called his uncles to account for their treason. The Jürkin princes paid with their lives, smothered to death lest their royal blood be spilled.

END OF THE KERAIT ALLIANCE

The defeat of the Tatars and the purge of the Jürkin princes greatly strengthened Temujin. However, his very success caused concern among his allies, the Keraits and Jalairs. Jamukha Khan convinced Toghrul that Temujin had designs on the Kerait kingdom. There followed numerous combinations—of Jalairs, Merkits, Naimans, Tatar remnants, and Keraits under the vacillating Toghrul—against Temujin.

FOUNDING OF THE MONGOL EMPIRE

After years of warfare, including a near-disastrous war with the Keraits, Temujin emerged victorious. In the spring of 1206, a general council (*khuraltai*) was held. The Mongol princes not only reaffirmed Temujin's kingship but also conferred upon him a new title: Genghis Khan (*Chinggis Khahan*), "King of the Sea-Surrounded Land." Genghis Khan decreed that, henceforth, all his subjects—including Merkits, Tatars, Keraits, Naimans, and Oiyats—would be known as Mongols, members of one Mongol nation (*ulus*).

Structure of the Mongol Empire

The Mongol Empire was an absolute monarchy. Genghis Khan held all executive, legislative, and judicial powers. Although ruthless toward his enemies, Genghis Khan valued loyalty and friendship above all else. Men who betrayed their leaders to Genghis Khan were summarily executed. A victim of the all-too-common Mongol tendency to betray and prey upon one another, Genghis Khan gave short shrift to traitors but magnificent rewards to friends and loyal companions.

COMPANIONS OF GENGHIS KHAN

Long before his rise to unchallenged power, Genghis Khan had attracted warriors to his cause. His first companion was Boguechi, who as a youth accompanied an equally youthful Temujin in tracking down stolen horses. Boguechi remained with Temujin to become one of his "Four Heroes." Tribal origin was no obstacle to entry into the emperor's retinue. Besides Boguechi, the other Four Heroes were Mukhali of the Jalair; Chilaan of the Taychiuds, a son of Sorkhan-shira; and Borokul of the Jürkin, one of the emperor's adopted brothers. Khubalai of the Barulas, Jelme of the Uriyangkhadai and his younger brother Subotai, and Jebe the Merkit were feared as the "Four Hounds" of Genghis Khan. To these men, to his brother Kasar, and to his four sons by Borte—Juchi, Chagatai, Ogadai, and Tuli—Genghis Khan delegated responsibility for the administration of the empire and command of the Mongol army.

YASSA

The governance of the empire was regulated by a series of laws decreed by Genghis Khan and enumerated in the *Yassa*. The *Yassa* established the Mongol Army on a permanent footing. In its regulations concerning marriage, theft, and quarrels between his subjects, Genghis Khan sought to end the internal conflicts that had plagued his people for centuries. With the expansion of the Mongol Empire, the *Yassa* became the supreme law for all subject peoples.

Expansion of the Mongol Empire

Political and economic factors explain the expansion of the Mongol Empire in the 21 years between its creation and the death of Genghis Khan. Military campaigns and the resulting booty were necessary to channel the Mongol tendency to raid and plunder—each other if no one else was available—a tendency that, if not controlled, would have destroyed the empire from within.

The campaigns against the Kin of northern China solved another crucial security problem. The Kin posed a direct threat to the very existence of the Mongol Empire through their foreign policy toward the barbarians. The only way to neutralize the threat posed by the Kin was the total destruction of their empire.

Mongolia lay astride the traditional caravan route between China and the Middle East, the famous Silk Road. Control of the Silk Road gave Genghis Khan the power to collect transit taxes from Chinese, Persian, and Arab merchants. The Mongol conquest of the kingdoms of Hsi-Hsia and Kara-Khitai strengthened Mongol control of the Silk Road.

Death of Genghis Khan and His Legacy

Genghis Khan died in August 1227. In obedience to the wishes of Genghis Khan, his third son, Ogadai, was elected emperor by the princes and high-ranking officers of the empire. The Mongol Empire, instead of disintegrating, as had the Mongol kingdom of earlier times, continued to flourish under the sons and grandsons of Genghis Khan. Charged by Genghis Khan with the task of perpetuating and expanding the empire, his successors eventually conquered China, Korea, Iran, present-day Iraq, most of Russia, parts of Poland and Hungary, Indochina, and Burma. The Mongol army, led by veteran generals such as Subotai, annihilated the armies of countries with manpower resources far greater than that of the Mongols.

The most enduring legacy of Genghis Khan was the Mongol nation itself. Although the Mongols were later subjugated by Manchu and Russian, the concept of Mongol nationhood, as conceived by Genghis Khan, survived. In Mongol folk religion, Genghis Khan still holds an exalted position as an incarnation of the Everlasting Blue Sky and the special protector of the nation. So strong is Mongol identification with Genghis Khan that the Mongol people celebrated his 800th birthday despite the official disapproval of the Mongolian Communist Party and the displeasure of the Soviet Union.

LAWRENCE D. HIGGINS

SEE ALSO: Mongol Conquests.

Bibliography

Boyle, J. A. 1958. *The history of the world conqueror by 'Ala-ad-Din 'Ata-Malik Ju-vaini.* 2 vols. Manchester: Manchester Univ. Press.

Grousset, R. 1966. *Conqueror of the world.* Trans. M. McKellarand and D. Sinor. New York: Orion Press.

Haenisch, E. 1941. *Die geheime geschichte der Mongolen* [The secret history of the Mongols]. Leipzig: O. Harrassowitz.

Heissig, W. 1980. *The religions of Mongolia.* Berkeley: Univ. of California Press.

Kuo-yi Pao. 1965. *Studies on the secret history of the Mongols.* Bloomington, Ind.: Indiana Univ. Press.

Lamb, H. 1940. *The march of the barbarians.* New York: Literary Guild of America.

Legg, S. 1970. *The heartland.* New York: Farrar, Straus and Giroux.

Martin, H. D. 1977. *The rise of Chingis Khan and his conquest of North China.* New York: Octagon Books.

GEOGRAPHY, MILITARY

Military geography is that part of military science that deals with the characteristics of the area of operations as they relate to military missions and forces. Military geography is the application of the geographic method of analysis to military problems.

Geography

Geography is the science that deals with the spatial distribution of phenomena at or near the surface of the earth. Geography is used to explain the patterns and relationships of natural and human phenomena: people and the artifacts of their cultures, animals, vegetation, climate, oceans, and landforms. These patterns and relationships are significant only in terms of a problem to be solved. Geography may be broken down into branches according to the type of problem being addressed. Economic geography covers the spatial distribution of factories and ports and the movement of goods and dollars among various locations. Human geography covers the way in which people live and relate to their environment. Urban geography covers the relationships among the different parts of cities. Political geography covers patterns among nation-states or other political entities. Physical geography covers the natural features of the earth's surface, such as rivers, mountains, plains, storms, and soil. Finally, geography is concerned with regions defined by the nature and scope of the problem being addressed. The geographic method of analysis seeks to define appropriate regions and explain the spatial distribution of phenomena in the region in the context of a problem.

Military Geography

Military geography is applied in regions defined by the missions of the military forces. Military geography is subdivided into four major branches: terrain analysis; theater analysis; geopolitics; and topical military geography. The first three of these may be related to the tripartite division of military art as follows:

LEVEL OF WARFARE	SCOPE	BRANCH OF MILITARY GEOGRAPHY
Strategy	Global	Geopolitics
Operational art	Theater of operations	Theater Analysis
Tactics	Battlefield	Terrain Analysis

TERRAIN ANALYSIS

Terrain analysis is used to determine the effect of the natural and man-made features of an area of operations on tactical military operations. It includes consideration of natural phenomena such as landforms, relief, drainage patterns, vegetation, animal and insect life, and surface materials. It includes consideration of works of man such as buildings, roads, railroads, airfields, dams, pipelines, and cultivation, but it does not usually consider humans in the area of interest. Terrain analysis may also include consideration of weather and climate.

Terms other than *terrain analysis* are also used to describe the application of military geography at the tactical level. *Terrain appreciation* is often used interchangeably with terrain analysis, although it implies a narrower and deeper study of the landforms of the area. *Terrain intelligence* implies more emphasis on basic data compilation than on mission-oriented analysis. *Military topography* was used formerly to mean the study of landforms from a military viewpoint, but now it refers primarily to map making and map reading. *Topography* still means the landforms of an area.

Terrain analysis is mission oriented. The area of operations is defined by the mission, and the significance of a terrain feature will vary depending on the nature of the mission. For example, a hill or a river has a different significance if the mission is to defend rather than to attack.

Terrain analysis is dynamic. The evolving military situation constantly changes missions and viewpoints, and thus constantly changes the significance of the terrain for the military commander. Changes in military weapons and technology can also alter the relative significance of terrain features. A river, which was a formidable barrier, can become a trivial problem with the introduction of improved combat bridging equipment. A distant target, which was not worth considering, can become important with the introduction of long-range weapons. The terrain itself also changes. It is modified by natural forces such as erosion and earthquakes, and it is also modified by man's construction of roads, airfields, and bridges. It is modified by military operations from the effects of troop movements, artillery fire, air strikes, and demolition of structures.

The military components of terrain analysis are:
1. Obstacles: terrain features that slow down or stop momentarily the movement of either enemy or friendly forces.
2. Fields of fire: the tendency of an area to facilitate or hinder direct fire by flat-trajectory weapons and missiles.
3. Observation: the tendency of an area to permit or deny visual or sensor detection of the enemy.
4. Concealment: the tendency of an area to facilitate avoiding observation by the enemy.
5. Cover: the tendency of an area to afford protection against being hit by enemy direct-fire weapons and missiles.
6. Routes of communication: roads or paths for movement of troops and vehicles.

An essential element of terrain analysis is the definition and interpretation of the spatial relationships among terrain features. For example, if the military mission is to seize a crossroads, several factors must be noted: the precise location of the crossroads, the distance and direction of the crossroads from the military unit, the characteristics of the intervening ground, and the relative position of terrain features (i.e., whether they will help or hinder the unit in accomplishing its mission). All of these factors must be taken into account along with the capabilities of the unit's weapons, equipment, and troops, to determine not only the time it will take to accomplish the mission, but also whether the mission can be accomplished at all.

Terrain analysis also varies according to the level at which it is carried out. Smaller units use a greater level of detail than larger units. For an individual rifleman or gunner, for example, a single tree or a small hill or hollow offering cover and concealment are of paramount interest. At the rifle company level, however, a clearing or the next ridgeline are the significant terrain features and fields of fire the primary concern. At the infantry or tank battalion level, the commander's interest is in obstacles such as villages, forests, or streams, while at the division level routes of communication may be the most important features.

Terrain is evaluated differently by different commanders, depending on the type and extent of influence the terrain will have on their units. A tank company commander, for example, with great organic tactical mobility, will draw conclusions about an area different from the conclusions drawn by an airborne rifle company commander with few or no vehicles. An air assault division commander with several hundred helicopters will draw different conclusions about the nature of his area of operations than would an armored division commander with several hundred tanks. Each commander must perform terrain analysis that is appropriate for the mission, role, and circumstances of the unit.

THEATER ANALYSIS

Theater analysis, or strategic area analysis, is the application of military geography at the level of operational art. Theater analysis is used to describe the influence on military operations of the characteristics of an actual or potential theater of war.

Theater analysis, unlike terrain analysis, does include humans in its consideration of natural and manmade features in the theater of operations. The occupancy patterns of human activity, consisting of towns, agricultural areas, roads, railroads, and airfields are of interest, as well as landforms, drainage, vegetation, and climate.

There is also a difference in scale between theater analysis and terrain analysis. Theater analysis takes into account the entire area of operations; terrain analysis has a more restricted or localized viewpoint. To the division commander, a river is an obstacle either to be crossed or defended. To the theater commander, the same river is only part of a total pattern of drainage indicating likely defensive positions or avenues of approach for an offensive. The principles are the same, and the influence of the river is likely to be similar, but the scale is different.

Theater area analysis also tends to be less mission-oriented than terrain analysis. At the theater and army group levels, missions are generally stated in broad terms, significant mission changes occur infrequently, and the planning cycle may be several weeks or months. For an army corps, the planning cycle may be several days or a few weeks, for a rifle company it may be measured in minutes.

Theater analysis tends to be more predictive than terrain analysis. Estimates used in the planning process at the theater headquarters must predict the impact of the area of operations on operations several weeks or months in the future. Terrain analysis deals with the immediate impact; theater analysis, with future impact.

The intelligence sections of theater headquarters or major land, air, or naval headquarters in the theater are responsible for theater analysis. In peacetime, the primary activity of theater analysis is compilation of data on the physical and human characteristics of the theater of operations. This includes descriptions of landforms and underlying geology, climatic data, distribution of vegetation and fauna, and demographic data. Special studies are made of trafficability, highway networks, railroads, ports, navigation channels and straits, airfields, airways, pipelines, power and communications networks, urban and built-up areas, and other characteristics of interest.

Theater analyses provide the basis for planning military operations in the theater. If the winter will be severe enough to require special clothing, that will have to be taken into account in planning the campaign. If the cloud cover will restrict air operations, that has to be considered in planning the kind and amount of air force units to be employed. If the terrain in a particular location is unsuitable for tanks, that should be taken into consideration when organizing the forces for combat. The presence of civilians has implications for nuclear and conventional fire support planning. The impact of refugees on the movement of troops and supplies may cause a diversion of resources. All of these factors must be taken into account in theater analysis.

Finally, the spatial perspective is an essential element of theater analysis. Because the distances are greater and the times longer, the interaction of space-time factors with military forces becomes more important at the level of operational art (theater analysis) than at the tactical level (terrain analysis). This is particularly true for selection of targets for battlefield or long-range interdiction, major defensive positions, or offensive axes of advance. Properly conducted, the theater analysis constitutes a complete application of geographic method to the military problem.

GEOPOLITICS

The application of military geography at the strategic or global level is called geopolitics. Geopolitics integrates political, diplomatic, sociological, economic, and military considerations into an overall strategic approach. Geopolitics is concerned with relative power among nations and coalitions. It includes consideration of the foundations of national power: population, industry, commerce, financial status, internal stability, resources, and national will, as well as military forces.

The essence of geopolitics is consideration of the size, shape, location, and characteristics of nations with respect to one another. History offers numerous examples of the importance of location and terrain. Poland, a nation between two great powers, but without natural lines of defense, has suffered repeated invasions. Switzerland has remained neutral and untouched through several major wars in its alpine bastion. The United States, secure from invasion and remote from Europe, needed only a small navy and an even smaller army from 1865 to 1917. Japan, lacking a large land area and raw materials, sought security by expanding into China and Southeast Asia.

Geopolitics recognizes tension between nations that are maritime powers and those that are land-based powers. Alfred Thayer Mahan advanced the concept of maritime power based largely on the experience of the British, who, invulnerable to invasion from the European continent, ruled a global empire for 140 years by virtue of a superior navy and a substantial merchant marine. In 1904 Sir Harold Mackinder identified the plains of Russia as the Heartland of Europe and predicted eventual global supremacy for the ruler of the Heartland. In Germany before World War II, Karl Haushofer bolstered German war aims by asserting that a combination of Germany, Russia, and Japan was unbeatable. Hitler's invasion of the Soviet Union, against Haushofer's advice, forced a coalition between the maritime power of the British Empire and the United States and the land power of the Soviet Union, which led ultimately to the defeat of Germany in 1945. In 1943 Nicholas Spykman advanced the concept of the Rimlands in opposition to the Heartland concept. According to Spykman, a combination of the economic and industrial superiority of the Rimlands—the United States, Western Europe, and the nations of the Pacific basin—would be more powerful than the Soviet Heartland.

Geopolitics is a major element of military strategic thinking in the nuclear age. Geopolitical concepts of relative location and power are important in maintaining a global balance of power by coalitions between the superpower and the medium powers. Geopolitical ideas underlie the current debate in the United States between advocates of a maritime strategy and adherents of a coalition (land-based) strategy. Geopolitics helps to understand how future changes in the relative power of nations will affect potential military operations.

TOPICAL MILITARY GEOGRAPHY

Topical military geography covers a particular, well-defined type of phenomena (a topic) on a worldwide basis. The major military applications of topical geography are:

Environmental studies. Environmental studies of climate, vegetation, and fauna are important in providing the correct equipment and training for military forces to be employed in various parts of the world. Troops employed in arctic regions need to be trained and equipped differently from troops employed in low-latitude deserts. This kind of topical military geography is often employed in the research and development process as new equipment, clothing, and supplies are developed.

Military geology. Geology is a scientific discipline dealing with the nature of the rock formations underlying the surface of the earth. Military geology provides a sound basis for protective construction for cover against conventional or nuclear explosions. It is also used to locate sources of water. Military geology is sometimes considered to be separate from military geography.

Geodesy. Geodesy is the science of global earth measurement that allows the precise location of points on the surface of the earth. Surveying, geodesy on a smaller scale, has been important in military operations since the introduction of field telegraphy allowed the use of indirect fire control with artillery. The advent of nuclear weapons and very long-range missiles has increased the importance of knowing the exact location of potential targets.

Military topography. Military topography originally meant the study of the impact of landforms on military operations, but the term now applies to the making and, particularly, the reading, of maps. Topographic maps are a representation of a portion of the earth's surface, usually of a land area, and include a means to represent altitude or relief. Relief is the difference between the high points and low points of landforms in the area. Relief is shown on a topographic map by contour lines that connect points of equal elevation, by color tinting, by shading, or by hachure marks to depict mountains and other elevated landforms.

Cartography. Cartography is the science of making maps, including topographic maps, aerial charts, and naval charts. Aerial charts provide a representation of the land or sea surface, emphasizing recognizable landmarks and information on navigational aids and airfields. Navigational charts provide a representation of sea or ocean areas, coastal areas, water depth in coastal areas, and hazards and aids to navigation.

Influence of the Area of Operations on Warfare

The characteristics of the area of operations have had enormous influence on the nature of combat and warfare throughout the ages. Generally, the confluence of terrain and technology on the battlefield has determined tactics. The nature of the theater of operations has been the primary basis for campaign planning and execution. Time and distance relationships among various regions of the world along with considerations of resources and statecraft have determined strategy. The nature of the terrain and weather affects all forms of warfare. The most obvious influence is on land warfare, but air and naval warfare are also influenced by the nature of the surface of the earth.

Armies fight on and must conform to the nature of the earth's surface. Therefore, military commanders and planners must appreciate the interaction of men and equipment with the terrain and weather. Streams and forests are both barriers and avenues of advance and supply; mountains are both barriers and bastions; gaps and passes historically have had great military significance; hills are easy to cross and easy to defend; dry plateaus resemble the sea and favor rapid, mobile warfare; wet plateaus are rugged and make it difficult for military forces to move rapidly; and the boundary between land and sea—the coasts—are important for amphibious warfare and for access to the interior. Man-made structures have become increasingly important both as objectives and as defensive positions. Intimate knowledge of landforms and how to take advantage of them is a valuable tool for accomplishing a military mission.

Air and naval forces do not fight on land, but they are both dependent ultimately on land bases, although the nuclear-powered aircraft carrier and its nuclear-powered escorts may operate for extended periods of time without returning to base. So it is important to understand what influence the land will have on military operations by air and naval forces. Air forces fight from and over land, and their concerns in the area of operations are the suitability of the land for airfields and the adequacy of supporting roads and railroads. The nature of the terrain also influences the tactics and munitions that are appropriate to attack ground targets, particularly for low-flying aircraft such as helicopters and close-support attack aircraft. Despite great advances in high-technology navigation systems, aviators may have to rely sometimes on recognition of terrain features to locate themselves and their targets.

Navies also must learn the lay of the land. The nature of coastlines determines the availability of safe harbors and anchorages, for storms remain a dangerous foe for ships at sea. The distance of naval combat from supporting bases is still a major factor in planning and implementing naval warfare, although the time that a fleet can remain at sea without resupply has increased. The configuration of the ocean bottom is a major factor in undersea warfare. Even space warfare would be influenced by the wind patterns of the atmosphere and the shape and nature of the earth below.

WORLD WAR II

World War II was a truly global war, which necessitated an appreciation for military geography by both sides. Although the major land battles early in the war were fought in Europe, ultimately the Allies also conducted major ground campaigns in the Middle East, the Mediterranean area, China, Burma, the southwest Pacific, the central Pacific, and Manchuria. The nature of the war in each of these major theaters was dictated by the relative priority of the theater for resources and by the terrain and climate. Combat occurred in frozen mountains in Italy, on hot deserts in North Africa, across the stormy North Atlantic, on the vast ocean expanses of the Pacific, and in the moist tropical rain forests of Burma. The Allies had to produce uniforms and equipment, tactics, and techniques suitable for operations under these varied conditions. That they did this successfully reflects the best use of military geography until the Persian Gulf War of 1990–91.

On the tactical level, there were pluses and minuses. The Allies planned carefully for the breakout of armed forces from the landing areas secured by the Normandy invasion in June 1944. However, the planners had paid insufficient attention to the implications of the local hedgerows. These were formidable stone walls overgrown with thick vegetation and were characteristic of that part of France. It took a field expedient, attaching blades to tanks to clear out the hedgerows, to free the British and American armies to move to the Rhine.

Earlier, in May 1940 the Germans and the French did take note of a terrain feature—the Ardennes Forest—but drew different conclusions. To the French the Ardennes was an obstacle impassable to vehicles and worthy only of a light defense; to the Germans the Ardennes was an avenue of attack capable of handling the main effort of the German blitzkrieg.

In North Africa the Germans under Rommel and the British under Montgomery each adapted their operations to the realities of the desert, but in different ways. Rommel operated on a shoestring with rapid mobility and improvisation to take advantage of the ease of movement over most of the area. Montgomery adopted a mobile defense backed with air superiority, which could strike the Germans and Italians almost at will. Ultimately, the British prevailed when the Germans could not resupply their fighting forces.

In Russia, the Soviets learned from their earlier war with the Finns and adapted their clothing and tactics to snow and ice while the Germans froze and bogged down in the mire.

In the Pacific, the Japanese underestimated the ability of the U.S. construction troops to carve airfields and ports out of what was thought to be impassable and unusable terrain. This lack of appreciation of the capability of 1940s technology to alter the terrain cost the Japanese heavily as they were repeatedly outflanked during General MacArthur's island-hopping campaigns.

At the Ardennes Forest late in 1945 weather played an important role in the ability of the Allies to hold back the last desperate offensive by the Germans. The U.S. troops holding out in Bastogne were cut off from supplies and air support for several days because of bad weather, but when the clouds cleared, the U.S. and British planes were able to do their job and help defeat the Germans decisively. Terrain and weather were important elements during World War II.

KOREAN WAR

The invasion of South Korea by North Korea brought on some of the fiercest land fighting of the modern era. Korea was an infantryman's war. The navy supported and shelled, and the air forces attacked the North Koreans almost unchallenged. They both played important roles in the war, but the nature of the terrain in Korea was such that the outcome had to be decided on the ground.

Except for the western plain and small areas on the coast, Korea is a mountainous country with high relief. Relief is a measure of the difference in elevation between high points and low points and indicates the ruggedness of the land. Korea is a land of steep slopes, long ridges, and narrow valleys. Initially, the North Koreans took advantage of the roads and railroads to move swiftly southward with their tanks and trucks.

The U.S. forces, thrown unprepared into the breach, at first failed to appreciate the significance of the terrain; they moved in the valleys, which invited ambush and defeat. Adding to their misery was the cold and snowy weather for which the U.S. troops were also unprepared, with respect to both clothing and tactics. The North Koreans and the Chinese, however, took advantage of the terrain and weather. They fought at night in the worst weather, keeping to the ground and moving along the ridgelines to bring plunging fire to bear on the road-bound Americans in the valleys below. Fighting desperately, the U.S. and Republic of Korea (ROK) forces gradually adapted to the terrain and weather. They learned to fight on the ridges and make sure they had the high ground. They used artillery to attack North Korean troops dug into defensive positions high in the mountains. They learned how to live and fight in cold weather. Eventually, they fought their opponents to a military and political draw. The early stages of the Korean War illustrate the consequences of a lack of attention to military geography. Things that should have been known were not, and lives and battles were lost as a consequence.

VIETNAM WAR

The terrain and weather of Southeast Asia had a major impact on the Vietnam War, and the time and distance of the area of operations from the United States influenced the strategy and the outcome of the war. The long distances involved increased the difficulties of establishing and maintaining the logistical pipelines of supplies and replacements. While the materiel problem was solved by the application of massive resources, the distance of Vietnam from the United States made the problem appear remote and may have contributed to the loss of public support that eventually ended the war without the United States having achieved its strategic objectives.

The nature of the theater had a definite influence on campaign planning. The three major regions of Vietnam where U.S. and allied troops fought were the northern coastal plain, the Central Highlands, and the Mekong Delta. At the outset the U.S. campaign plan was to find and defeat decisively the North Vietnamese forces while simultaneously conducting counterinsurgency operations against the Viet Cong. This led the United States to distribute its forces across the nation more or less in proportion to the population rather than to the threat. Key terrain was defined tactically and not for the entire theater, and the option of closing off the border between South and North Vietnam extending into Laos was not pursued aggressively or with overwhelming force. Although the United States consistently won on the battlefield, the campaign turned into a war of attrition, which was won by North Vietnam as the United States lost its will to fight.

At the tactical level, the rugged and mountainous terrain in the Central Highlands and the heavy rainfall in the Mekong Delta slowed the tempo of operations and made it difficult for the United States to bring to bear fully its advantage in modern weapons. The thick vegetation of the triple-canopy rain forest diminished the effects of air attacks and made bomb damage assessment difficult. The vegetation also offered the attacking North Vietnamese and Viet Cong the advantage of concealment, which they used to great effect in ambushes. The United States responded by removing the protective vegetation, cutting down the trees, and killing them with chemical defoliants.

Fighting a new kind of warfare without fronts, the U.S. and South Vietnamese forces tried to overcome the terrain with new technology—primarily helicopters. This worked to a certain extent and made it possible for the U.S. and South Vietnamese forces to win almost all tactical engagements. After losing a few early battles conclusively, however, the North Vietnamese refused to stand and fight in decisive battles. They appreciated the nature of the terrain and took advantage of it to build combat power slowly and steadily under the concealment offered by the terrain until they had sufficient force to defeat the South Vietnamese forces in conventional combat. The U.S. and South Vietnamese forces fought well and won most of the time but in the end were defeated by the terrain and the will of their opponent.

PERSIAN GULF WAR

The Persian Gulf War took place in a region entirely different from Southeast Asia. The terrain in Kuwait, Saudi Arabia, and Iraq is desert with low elevations, little vegetation, and little rainfall.

Kuwait is 7,000 miles from the United States, but the United States had for several years been building a capability to project its armed forces rapidly to just such a remote location. Airlift, sealift, and pre-positioned equipment and supplies were on hand when President Bush decided to commit U.S. forces to defend Saudi Arabia and then to free Kuwait from Iraq. The strategic time and distance factors, however, did cause great anxiety for the U.S. commanders who were forced to wait for several weeks until the U.S. and coalition forces were sufficient to defend Saudi Arabia and another several weeks until enough forces had been assembled in the theater to take the offensive.

From a theater viewpoint, the man-made features of Saudi Arabia were critical to the success of the U.S. and coalition forces. Saudi Arabia had constructed modern airfields, ports, and roads in the northern area near Kuwait and Iraq in anticipation of this contingency. The availability of these facilities was crucial to the success of the U.S. buildup and resupply operations. If these facilities had not been available, it would have been much more difficult—and perhaps impossible—for the United States to have done what it did. The shallow seas of the Persian Gulf and the coastal islands off the coast of Kuwait made naval operations difficult and contributed significantly to the decision to make an amphibious operation a feint rather than a real attack.

Tactically, the lack of cover and concealment for the Iraqi forces was very important. The U.S. and coalition aircraft, having beaten the Iraqi air forces, could attack ground targets that could not hide. Although there were some problems due to unfavorable weather, in general the area was ideal for air operations. The mobility afforded ground vehicles in the desert areas west of Kuwait made possible the gigantic single envelopment that struck deep into Iraq and then turned to cut off the Iraqi Republican Guard from behind. Although the Iraqis sought to create artificial obstacles, they found it a difficult task lacking terrain favorable for the defense. Finally, modern high-technology tank guns and missiles were at their best in the flat terrain and able to fire accurately at long ranges over excellent fields of fire. The success of the United States and the coalition against Iraq is evidence of sound appreciation of the terrain and weather in the area of operations and illustrates the application of military geography at its best.

Overall Characteristics of Military Geography

Military geography is mission oriented. The mere compilation of data on a military theater or area of operations does not constitute an application of military geography. The essential nature of the geographic process comes into play only when the spatial relationships and impacts of the area are interpreted in light of a mission. If the mission changes, the effect of the features of the area of operations changes also.

Military geography is part of the commander's planning process. The planning process begins when a new mission is received from higher headquarters. After the commander has analyzed and elaborated on the mission, the next step is to make an estimate of the situation. The estimate of the situation includes consideration of the mission, friendly forces, enemy forces, and a military geographic analysis of the characteristics of the area of operations. Alternative courses of action to accomplish the mission are drawn up and evaluated. The commander decides upon a course of action and issues orders to that effect. The products of the planning process are missions for subordinate units. The receipt of these new missions at lower levels in turn initiates a new cycle of military planning, including additional estimates of the situation and geographic analyses of new areas of operations.

The area of operations is the geographic region defined by the military mission. It comprises the area directly influenced by the forces and weapons under the control of the commander. It includes the area occupied by the opposing enemy force, terrain features designated as objectives to be seized or held, area held by adjacent friendly units, and the support area of the military organization itself. The commander needs to know everything about the area of operations, and is also interested in major events in a larger area of interest, which includes the area of operations. The commander may assign reconnaissance resources to report on the area of interest or request intelligence on the area of interest from higher headquarters.

Military geography is an element of military intelligence and the responsibility of the staff intelligence officer. The compilation of data on natural and man-made terrain features and on human factors in a theater or area of operations usually is performed by intelligence sections and organizations. In intelligence terms, combat intelligence corresponds to terrain analysis, and strategic intelligence corresponds to theater analysis.

Military geography is three-dimensional. Warfare takes place in the oceans below the earth's surface and in the atmosphere above the earth's surface, as well as on the surface. Time and distance factors and the importance of relative positions take on different meanings when it is possible to deliver munitions by aircraft or missile or observe from a satellite. Submarines, aircraft, and satellites in earth orbit, with the possibility of manned space stations, must be considered in making the estimate of the situation. The area of operations is in reality a three-dimensional volume ranging from below the surface of the earth to the outer boundary of inner space.

Military geography uses the latest in modern technology and methodology. Earth satellites are used in geodesy and cartography. Aerial and space photography is used in cartography, terrain analysis, and theater analysis. Computers are used to calculate time and space factors and target locations, and to compile, manage, and analyze geographic data. Modern methods of mathematical, statistical, and spatial analysis are applied to military geographic problems.

Problems of Military Geography

There is a general lack of knowledge about military geography. All military forces employ the various elements of military geography, but most of them do not realize that they are using military geography. Terrain analysis is always part of tactical doctrine. Theater analysis is an accepted part of the intelligence process. Geopolitics is employed in politico-military strategic studies. These applications of military geography often are used without an appreciation for the spatial viewpoint of geographic analysis.

Military geography is seldom taught as a unified discipline. Terrain analysis and theater analysis are taught in military schools as part of courses on tactics or intelligence, and the elements of geopolitics are taught at war colleges. The essential appreciation of geography as a discipline unified by the process of spatial analysis, however, has been lost.

The inclusion of area analysis in the intelligence staff function has the advantage of providing a sponsor for this activity. It has the disadvantage of reinforcing the tendency of commanders and operations officers to concentrate on enemy and friendly forces and ignore or relegate to secondary importance the characteristics of the area of operations.

Value of Military Geography

Military geography has had substantial impact on military combat in the past. The Russian winter played a part in defeating both Napoleon and Hitler. The defensible landforms (*cuestas*) north of Paris helped France stop the invading Germans in 1914. The hedgerows of Normandy stalled the Allied advance in 1944. The vastness of China thwarted Japanese attempts at military domination in the 1930s. The nature of the Persian Gulf area made it possible for U.S. technology to crush the Iraqi army overwhelmingly in short order. It is logical to believe that military geography will also have a substantial impact on combat in the future.

The value of military geography is that it integrates the effects of the area of operations by a process of spatial analysis. Military geography does not live up to its potential because it is seldom applied by trained geographers or by military personnel who understand geographic method. Even so, the ideas and concepts of geography are now, more than ever, essential to the planning and conduct of military operations.

JOHN R. BRINKERHOFF

SEE ALSO: Mahan, Alfred Thayer; Maps, Charts, and Symbols, Military.

Bibliography

Able, R. F., M. G. Marcus, and J. M. Olson, eds. 1992. *Geography's inner worlds: Pervasive themes in contemporary American geography.* New Brunswick, N.J.: Rutgers Univ. Press.

Faringdon, H. 1986. *Confrontation: The strategic geography of NATO and the Warsaw Pact.* London and New York: Routledge and Kegan Paul.

Gray, C. S. 1988. *The geopolitics of super power*. Lexington, Ky.: Univ. of Kentucky Press.

Hartshorne, R. 1962. *Perspective on the nature of geography*. Association of American Geographers. Chicago: Rand McNally.

James, P. E., and C. F. Jones, eds. 1954. *American geography: Inventory and prospect*. Association of American Geographers. Syracuse, N.Y.: Syracuse Univ. Press.

O'Sullivan P., and J. W. Miller. 1983. *The geography of warfare*. New York: St. Martin's Press.

Rosen, S. J. 1977. *Military geography and the military balance in the Arab-Israeli conflict*. Jerusalem: Hebrew Univ.

Zoppo, C. E., and C. Zorgbibe. 1985. *On geopolitics: Classical and nuclear*. NATO Advanced Science Institutes Studies. Dordrecht: Martinus Nijhoff.

U.S. Department of the Army. 1972. *Field manual 30–10: Military geographic intelligence (terrain)*. Washington, D.C.: Government Printing Office.

GIAP, VO NGUYEN [1912–]

Senior General Giap (Fig. 1), five-star former commander in chief of North Vietnam's army, as well as its defense minister, is the only North Vietnamese general widely known in connection with the Indochina-Vietnam wars. Giap (also known as Anh Van, or Tran Van Lam) won his place in world history by leading the Viet Minh peasant forces that decisively defeated U.S.-supported French Mainland, Foreign Legion, Colonial, and collaborating Vietnamese regular and auxiliary forces in Dien Bien Phu in 1954, thus winning the First Indochina-Vietnam War (the Viet Minh War).

Subsequently, Giap brought sufficient continual military pressure on U.S., Free World (including Asian-Pacific allies), and South Vietnamese armed forces. This pressure, combined with the results of North Vietnamese political-diplomatic maneuvering, forced the governments of the United States and its allies to retire their troops from the field in 1973. Demoralized, unsupported South Vietnamese forces were then overrun by North Vietnamese troops in 1975. Giap's self-taught strategic, logistical, and tactical abilities, combined with North Vietnamese political-diplomatic maneuvering and Sino-Soviet support, enabled Eastern peasants to defeat Western professional military commanders, their citizen-soldiers, and their doctrine, to win the Second Indochina-Vietnam War (the Vietnam War).

Giap's determination and willingness to spill his troops' blood enabled Third World socialist forces to overcome the will of democratic powers' East-West alliances. The Western nations' complex political maneuvering, economic predominance, technological superiority, massive military strength, and immense firepower fell to this one-time history teacher's able organizational talents, his cunning, and his single-minded will power. While Giap is now a larger-than-life legend, American critics are downplaying his strategic abilities and his ideas on "People's War" by focusing on the huge losses suffered by his troops and their tactical defeats. But Senior Gen. Vo Nguyen Giap's military-political

Figure 1. Vo Nguyen Giap. (SOURCE: Presumed to be a North
Vietnamese official photo)

achievements—necessarily coupled with those of a wily and tenacious Ho Chi
Minh—are and will remain monumental.

Giap the Individual

Vo Nguyen Giap was born in 1912 (or 1911 or 1909—many published "facts"
about Giap are questionable) in Quang Binh/Vinh (or Thanh Hoa) in the then-
French protectorate of Annam. Officially from a peasant family, he was reportedly the son of a hardworking, low-ranking mandarin scholar who sacrificed
much to have his son educated.

Giap began working at age 14, immediately becoming involved with the Tan
Viet Nationalist revolutionary party. In 1930 he took part in demonstrations
against the French, earning two or three years in jail on Puolo Condore Island—
where he read extensively. Giap then attended the French-operated Lycée
National (with classmate and future adversary Ngo Dinh Diem), assisted by a
future father-in-law. Later, while studying law at Hanoi University, he was first
a journalist and then a high school history teacher, becoming known for his

interest in Napoleon and for his inflammatory speeches. Awarded a less-than-M.A. degree in three years, Giap failed his fourth-year entrance exam, although some believe he received doctorates in political science and in law.

Giap was persuaded to embrace communism by Truong Chinh, later chief ideologue of the Vietnamese communists. Giap married his first wife, Minh Thai, in 1934, and they joined the Indochina Communist Party. In 1936 he was a founding member of the Democratic Front. Giap and Phan Van Dang then published anti-imperialist newspapers. Giap published his first book in 1938, coauthoring with Truong Chinh *The Peasant Question*. Regarded by the French as a subversive document and a guide to revolution, it was seized and destroyed.

When communism was outlawed in France in 1939, the French repressed the Indochinese Communists; and Giap went to China with Pham Van Dang, later premier of North Vietnam. There he became allied with Ho Chi Minh, leader of exiled Vietnamese Communists. He helped start the Viet Minh "League for the Independence of Vietnam" at the Tsin Tsi Conference in 1941. During World War II Giap worked in the mountains of Vietnam, gathering information to sell to the Republic of China and eliminating local opposition to communism. (Giap did not hesitate to eliminate challengers, including fellow Viet Minh.) In December 1944 he commanded the 34-person armed propaganda "Brigade" for National Liberation, which evolved into the People's Army of Vietnam (PAVN). This group reportedly attacked the French on 19 December 1946 in retaliation for earlier French shelling of Hanoi, thus initiating the Viet Minh War.

For a short time Giap was interior minister of the newly declared independent Democratic Republic of Vietnam but was soon promoted by Ho Chi Minh to general and commander in chief. He became defense minister in 1946, and in that year married his second wife, Dan Thai Ha, daughter of the minister of education, Dang Thai Mai. Giap often appeared in public with her and they had two children.

In Giap's early days of command he was, to Western eyes, a slight and rumpled figure—seeming strangely out of place near the tall French officers of the army he would eventually defeat or striding in review of his peasant soldiers. Later, the stern face that glared from the cover of *Time* magazine better fit Western ideas of a powerful military figure. Throughout Giap's career he has been *Nui Lua*, the "snow-capped volcano," as Ho Chi Minh referred to the calm exterior that barely concealed his seething interior. Occasionally he has exploded violently—once resigning as defense minister.

Forceful and arrogant, imaginative and impatient, energetic and ambitious, Senior General Giap has an analytic mind. Reported to have an "encyclopedic knowledge of military history" (Bowman 1985), he first received military training in 1940 from the Chinese Communists, later supplemented by reading Western and Eastern military works and studying Chinese Communist warfare against Japanese invaders. Giap alleges that he was influenced by the ancient Chinese strategist Sun Tzu, and by the early Vietnamese guerrilla warrior

Trang Hung Dao, who defeated Kublai Khan's Chinese in 1287. The deaths in French jails of his first wife and child, his father, two sisters, and others of his family, plus the guillotining of his sister-in-law, strengthened Giap's hatred of the French and his determination to prevail. Although less well known and perhaps less sophisticated than Ho Chi Minh—even needing someone like Ho to fully succeed—Giap nevertheless approaches him in historical significance.

Giap's Accomplishments

Employing the philosophy of many successful military commanders, Giap urged his forces not to lose sight of the main objective of fighting—destruction of the enemy. He believed more in armed struggle than political struggle (in contrast to his former coauthor and subsequent doctrinal archrival, Truong Chinh), although conceding the need for both. Focusing on frontal attacks rather than the guerrilla tactics he had employed so well, Giap seemed first to follow the direct, "real warfare" philosophy of Germany's Clausewitz rather than the indirect approach offered by Sun Tzu. But his complex thoughts possibly parallel the in-between combat philosophy of Japan's Musashi.

An anonymous U.S. analyst (Giap's Use . . . 1969) noted that the classic principle of war, "economy of force," was used by great offensively minded commanders of history: Napoleon, Jackson, Lee, Rommel, Bradley, and Giap— and that Giap's application fitted his time. He organized only a few main force units and used them to attack isolated posts—first French, then American. But his irregular organizers were protected by guerrillas; they shunned contact, and concentrated on the enemy's rear. The reaction was what Giap expected: Counter–main force units were organized and fielded. The attention of enemy commanders was held rigidly to the relative handful of Giap's main forces— while the enemy's rear crumbled. From late 1946 until 1949, the French thought the lull in military activities meant they had won the war; they were not finding anyone to fight. Lulls while fighting the Americans in 1968 and 1969 were similar, the analyst stated. (At one time during the American phase, 95 percent of the combat elements of the U.S. expeditionary force was dispersed in territory where only 5 percent of the population was located.) Giap's most important force was conquering the real battlefield (the people) while his "economy of force" units (regular battalions) kept U.S. forces occupied elsewhere. Giap did not, however, neglect his assumed need for the final "big push."

Giap's determination to use periodic, unrelenting uniformed force—at first defeated again and again by the French—took him to the heights of conventional military success at Dien Bien Phu. There he brought artillery into terrain considered impossible by the French, establishing so vigorous a siege (with a four-to-one artillery dominance) that faraway U.S. supporters following the situation decided not to interfere by providing the troops, air strikes, or nuclear weapons requested by the French. The French surrendered.

Giap's willingness to learn about his foe, without regard to the number of men he lost, was demonstrated at the 1965 battle of Ia Drang. There he continued to send troops into battle against U.S. forces to see how the Americans fought, in order to develop a strategy and tactics to counter them. If his critics are correct, Giap did not learn. He continued to use frontal attack combat tactics (which had been successful at Dien Bien Phu) at the siege of Khe Sanh, in the Tet Offensive, and in the Eastertide Offensive. This reportedly caused his removal from office (Zabecki and Montpelier 1988; Summers 1985). He was replaced as vice chairman of the National Defense Council in 1971. In 1975, Chief of Staff Van Tien Dung (a proponent of political pressure) succeeded Giap as commander in chief. In 1977–78, when Vietnam initiated the Third Indochina War, Giap attempted to dissuade his colleagues from the proposed Soviet-style over-the-border overt invasion and occupation of Kampuchea, but his advice was ignored. He retired as minister of defense of the Socialist Republic of Vietnam in 1980, and from the Politburo in 1982. His work shifted from military commander and strategist to leader of an effort to improve the Vietnamese economy and future prospects through the use of science and technology. Giap's change of emphasis and offices, following the death of Ho Chi Minh (whom he once was expected to succeed), may be related as much to the loss of his patron as to arguments about strategy (Gurtov 1970).

Senior Gen. Vo Nguyen Giap was highly respected by his opponents as well as his fellow Communists for his policy, strategic (especially logistical), and tactical accomplishments. The West's most knowledgeable scholar of North Vietnam and Indochina reported (Pike 1966, p. 36) that Giap had redefined Mao Tse-tung's "three stages" into the National Liberation Front's (NLF) "third generation," and that "Mao-Giap became to revolutionary warfare what Marxism-Leninism is to Communist theory." Pike has provided two careful evaluations (1966, pp. 49–51; 1987, pp. 339–43), concluding that Giap cannot be regarded as a military genius (except, perhaps, a logistics genius). Despite his achievement of tactical skills and his energy, audacity, and meticulous planning, Giap was a competent but not brilliant commander, a first-rate military organizer (once past the stage of innovative conceptual work), and a meticulous planner. As a strategist, Giap was at best a "gifted amateur." Nevertheless, organization of the "Legion of Porters" and architecture of the logistical miracle of the Ho Chi Minh Trail, with its ubiquitous bicycles that moved tons of supplies, shows that this user of "floating bridges" and the willing backs of his people surely was a consummate logistician.

But more significant than specific incidents of successful strategic or tactical surprise, superb logistic movements, or other strictly military accomplishments in battle (despite costly failures through frontal combat in major engagements) are the global implications of Giap's ultimate victories over Western powers and their Eastern allies. To the nations and peoples of today's developing countries (who first were shown the possibility of victory by the East when turn-of-the-century Japan defeated the West—the Russian fleet at Tsushima), Giap demonstrated clearly the feasibility and the specific means for seemingly weak "resistance movements" to overcome apparently overwhelmingly strong "great powers." Richard Nixon notes (1978, p. 269) that Giap stated in 1965: "The war against South Vietnam was a model for the communist movement around the world; if such a style of aggression could succeed there, it could work elsewhere."

Giap's Future

Vo Nguyen Giap will always provide an example of how to use military thinking to achieve political ends, not just a general who was important in battle for a brief period in history. Although the target of political enemies and of whispering campaigns, Giap remains a "national treasure" of Vietnam. He seems to have overcome a reported deadly illness, and continued to write and be written about (Pike 1987, p. 343; Davidson 1988). With a continuing stream of his own publications, and others writing about him and his philosophy, both Giap's accomplishments and his purported failings will provide clear examples of military thought put into practice.

DONALD S. MARSHALL

SEE ALSO: Ho Chi Minh; Mao Tse-tung; Musashi, Miyamoto; Vietnam and Indochina Wars.

Bibliography

Bowman, J. S., ed. 1985. Vo Nguyen Giap. In *The Vietnam war: An almanac*. New York: World Almanac.
Davidson, P. B. 1988. *Vietnam at war—The history 1946–1975*. Novato, Calif.: Presidio Press.
Dobbs, C. 1988. Vo Nguyen Giap. In *Dictionary of the Vietnam War*, ed. J. S. Olson. New York: Greenwood Press.
Fall, B. B. 1966. *Hell in a very small place: The siege of Dien Bien Phu*. Philadelphia: J. B. Lippincott.
Giap's use of the "economy of force" principle. 1969. LORAPL Papers, Indochina Archive, Univ. of California, Berkeley.
Giap, V. N. 1962. *Dien Bien Phu*. Hanoi: Foreign Language Publishing House.
———. 1967. *Big victory, great task*. New York: Praeger.
———. 1975. *Unforgettable days*. Hanoi: Foreign Language Publishing House.
———. 1976. *How we won the war*. Philadelphia: Recon.
———. 1979. *War for national liberation*. Hanoi: Su That Publishing House.
Gurtov, M. 1970. *Some recent statements by North Vietnamese leaders: General Giap*. Rand Document D-20026-ARPA/AGILE. Santa Monica, Calif.: Rand Corp.
Jenkins, B. 1972. *Giap and the seventh son*. (P4851) Santa Monica, Calif.: Rand Corp.
Nixon, R. 1978. *The memoirs of Richard Nixon*. New York: Grosset and Dunlap.
O'Neill, R. J. 1969. *General Giap: Politician and strategist*. New York: Praeger.
Pike, D. B. 1966. *Viet Cong*. Cambridge, Mass.: M.I.T. Press.
———. 1987. *PAVN: People's Army of Vietnam*. Novato, Calif.: Presidio Press.
Summers, H. 1985. Giap, Vo Nguyen. In *Vietnam war almanac*. New York: Facts on File.
Zabecki, D. T., and R. P. Montpelier. 1988. Unlimited expense account. *Vietnam* 1(2):43–49.

GONZALO DE CÓRDOBA
[1453–1515]

Gonzalo (Gonsalvo) Fernández de Córdoba y Aguilar played a key role in the transition from medieval to modern warfare. He developed the Spanish infantry to the point where it replaced heavy cavalry as the principal combat element. His carefully planned campaigns, which coordinated infantry, cavalry, and artillery, replaced the medieval cavalry duel. He fitted his infantrymen with light armor and steel helmets and armed them with short swords instead of cumbersome Swiss halberds, or with harquebuses instead of crossbows. He divided his men into captaincies, which he combined into larger units, prototypes of regiments or Spanish *tercios*. In Italy his inspiring leadership in wars against France forged his poorly paid soldiers into a disciplined army that outmoded Renaissance condottiere warfare.

Early Life

Born in the family castle of Montilla, 40 miles south of Córdoba, the son of Pedro Fernández de Córdoba, Gonzalo and his brother Alfonso de Aguilar were carried into battle virtually from infancy, against the Muslims of Granada or against their own cousins, the counts of Cabra. As boys they had suits of chain mail. Gonzalo represented his family at the court of Princess Isabella of Castile and her husband Prince Ferdinand of Aragón, but he withdrew in 1473 in accordance with the politics of the marquis of Villena, his brother's father-in-law. Gonzalo returned to Isabella's service in 1479 after she had gained his release from captivity by his Cabra cousin. Commanding a hundred knights of the Order of Santiago and funded by his brother against Alfonso V of Portugal, he helped Isabella gain the Castilian throne.

Gonzalo emerged as an outstanding commander in the campaigns against Granada (1481–92) in which feuding Castilian vassals united and fought under royal leadership to finish the Reconquest, ending the 700-year Muslim presence in Spain. The queen rewarded him by making him a knight commander of Santiago and giving him twelve towns.

Gonzalo's Italian Campaigns (1495–97 and 1500–1504)

Commanding an expedition to protect Naples against the invasion of Charles VIII of France, Gonzalo lost his first battle against the French at Seminara because of poor coordination with his Italian allies. Afterwards he concentrated on training and organizing his men, refusing challenges for a field battle with D'Aubigny, the French commander in Calabria. By July 1496, however, when the allied army assembled at Atella, Gonzalo had gained control in Calabria with the guerrilla-like tactics he had used in the Granada wars. His men hailed him as "The Great Captain." Speed and skill in taking fortresses at Atella and Ostia further enhanced his reputation.

In 1500 Gonzalo returned to Italy and nearby waters as captain-general of a large armada, ostensibly to support a Venetian war against the Turks, but Ferdinand had already agreed with Louis XII of France to conquer and divide the Kingdom of Naples. Again Gonzalo, with Pedro Navarro and Antonello da Trani, demonstrated brilliant siegecraft in taking the Turkish fortress of Saint George on Kephallenia (Cephalonia).

Although the Franco-Spanish conquest of Naples in 1501–1502 presented few difficulties, major warfare soon broke out between the two victors. For nine months Gonzalo, headquartered in Barletta, restricted himself to small operations and raids launched from a line of advanced fortified garrisons. Finally, reinforced and supplied, he assembled his forces for a grueling march to his chosen battlefield near Cerignola on a rising slope among vineyards. Arriving late in the afternoon of 28 April 1503, the Great Captain established a defensive base of operations, ordering his exhausted men to dig a long trench and build a parapet behind it with the dirt they extracted. The French, under the viceroy, the duke of Nemours, arrived at dusk, and attacked at nightfall. The Franco-Swiss infantry stumbled into Gonzalo's trench, and were then hit by harquebus fire from behind the parapet. A French cavalry charge fared no better and Nemours was killed. Gonzalo then led his Italian-Spanish cavalry in a counterattack, turning the battle into a rout.

Fabrizio Colonna, an Italian commander in Gonzalo's army, said disdainfully that a mere ditch had won the battle. In fact, that battle changed warfare forever. Gonzalo's soldiers halted their pursuit of the retreating Frenchmen to mutiny for pay. He placated them with appeals to national pride and allowed them to sack the city of Bari, the Castel Nuovo in Naples, and even his own house. But later he hanged the leaders of the mutiny.

Louis XII sent another army to Italy, and Gonzalo, outnumbered three-to-one, fought another campaign that year, this time in the valley of the Garigliano River. Again, with headquarters in San Germano, he established garrisons to hold a defensive perimeter while avoiding a major confrontation. The Roccasecca garrison diverted the French approach to San Germano, and the two armies faced each other across the river in a war of attrition. The marquis of Mantua, who had replaced the duke of La Trémouille as French commander, retired and the marquis of Saluzzo replaced him. After the French army withdrew from the flooded river banks to winter quarters, Gonzalo assembled his army and attacked during a terrible rainstorm on 27–28 December. He surprised and completely defeated the enemy in this Battle of the Garigliano.

Gonzalo's Loyalty to Ferdinand "the Catholic"

King Ferdinand made Gonzalo viceroy of Naples, duke of Terranova, and rewarded him generously, but he also surrounded him with spies and bureaucrats. In consequence the beleaguered viceroy presented royal officials with the famous "accounts of the Great Captain," including fictitious sums paid to the clergy for prayers. After Isabella's death in 1504, her daughter Juana inherited Castile. The future of the union of Castile and Aragón was in grave jeopardy. Many of the great vassals of Castile, including Gonzalo's kinsmen, turned to support Juana and her husband, Philip of Hapsburg. As a consequence, threatened King Ferdinand was still less trustful of his viceroy in Naples. The Venetians and the pope had already offered him command over their armies, and rumors circulated that he intended to make himself ruler of Naples.

However, Castilian Gonzalo remained loyal to the Aragonese king, illustrating in his own life the emergence of transcending national loyalty. Relieved of his Italian command in 1507, Gonzalo returned peacefully to Spain. Denied his promised reward, the mastership of Santiago, he withdrew to his Castilian estates. When Gonzalo's nephew, the marquis of Priego, revolted and Ferdinand pulled down Montilla Castle as punishment, the uncle counseled submission. In 1512, after Spain's defeat at Ravenna, the king called on the Great Captain to lead a new Italian expedition, but then reneged. Gonzalo accepted this disappointment, too, and remained a loyal Spaniard. He died three years later on 1 December 1515 from malaria, which he had contracted during his long stay in southern Italy.

PAUL STEWART

SEE ALSO: Arab Conquests; Italian Wars.

Bibliography

D'Auton, J. 1889–95. *Chroniques de Louis XII*. Editions de la Société de l'histoire de la France, vols. 245, 250, 264, 278. Paris: Renouard.
De Gaury, G. 1955. *The grand captain*. London: Longmans.
Lojendio, L. M. 1952. *Gonzalo de Córdoba, el gran capitán*. Madrid: Espasa-Calpe.
Pieri, P. 1952. *Il Rinascimiento e la crisi militare italiana*. Torino: Einaudi.
Quatrefages, R. A. 1977. A la naissance de l'armée moderne. *Mélanges de la casa de Vélasquez* (Paris) 13:119–59.
Rodríguez Villa, A., ed. 1908. *Crónicas del Gran Capitán. Nueva biblioteca de autores españoles*. vol. 10. Madrid: Balliére.

GRAECO-PERSIAN WARS

The military encounters between the Persian Empire and the Greek city-states in the early part of the fifth century B.C. were among the most pivotal events of human history. As a result of the eventual Greek victory, the culture of Classical Greece would flourish and have a profound effect on subsequent human history. The major source of information on this time is the Greek historian Herodotus, who, about the middle of the fifth century B.C.—a generation after the wars ended—compiled a lengthy account of the wars. There are other sources that can be used to add to and correct the account of Herodotus, but details remain uncertain.

Causes

The Persian Empire was at its most powerful and most expansionist during the reign of Darius I (521–486 B.C.), who may have had designs on Greek territory. The genesis of the Graeco-Persian wars can be found in the revolt of the Ionian

Greeks in 499. Ionian Greek city-states on the coast of Asia Minor had been absorbed into the Persian Empire a generation earlier, but in 499 they broke into open revolt and sought aid from the older city-states of the Greek mainland. Assistance came from only two cities: Athens and Eretria. The revolt was eventually crushed, and Darius seems to have resolved to punish Athens and Eretria for the aid they offered to the rebels. But even without vengeance as a motive, Darius had incentive to conquer Greece (Fig. 1). His empire contained a large number of different ethnic groups, including the Greeks of Asia Minor, and to rule over some of the Greeks but not all would be a constant source of danger in the future. Thus, the attempted conquest of Greece by the Persian Empire may be viewed as simple expansionism, as a desire to more efficiently incorporate ethnic peoples into the empire, as simple vengeance, or, and more likely, as a combination of these.

It should be noted that throughout this period contact between Greeks and Persians was regular and frequent. Greece was rife with political factionalism, and throughout the campaigns the Persian emperor had the advice of Greek expatriates who resided at his court. It is likely that the preparations by each side were well known to the other.

Campaign of 490 B.C.

In the summer of 490 B.C., Darius sent an invading force under the command of his generals Datis and Artaphernes by ship from Asia Minor across the Aegean Sea. Herodotus suggests that there were approximately 600 ships and

Figure 1. Greece in the fifth century B.C.

25,000 to 30,000 men, including a sizable cavalry contingent. Some modern historians, however, doubt the Persian land troops much exceeded 10,000 in number. After receiving the submission of the small islands along the way, who were in no position to resist, the Persian force landed on the island of Euboea off the coast of Attica and laid siege to the city of Eretria. Although assistance was sought from Athens, and promised, Eretria was eventually betrayed by some of its inhabitants, and the Persians entered the city and destroyed it. The Eretrians were killed or sold into slavery. The Persian fleet then made a landing at Marathon in northeast Attica, about 42 kilometers (26 mi.) from Athens. This particular spot was chosen on the advice of an exiled Athenian tyrant named Hippias, who believed it would be an ideal place for the deployment of cavalry. In the account of the battle, however, little use seems to have been made of the cavalry.

BATTLE OF MARATHON (12 SEPTEMBER 490 B.C.)

A force of about 10,000 heavily armed hoplites (armored spear or pikemen), mostly Athenian, was at Marathon to meet the Persians, but the Persians had no difficulty disembarking their troops and making camp.

The battle plans of either side are difficult to determine. The Persians were apparently in no hurry to engage the Athenian force and may have expected to simply overawe the opposition with their numbers. The Athenian force under Miltiades seemed intent on just blocking the land route to Athens, although it was easily possible for the Persians to re-embark and sail around Attica to Athens (which they eventually did). The Athenians also appeared to be in no hurry to engage, and several days were spent with each side observing the other and repositioning their forces. Finally, apparently as the Persians began to re-embark some of their troops, Miltiades ordered an attack. The Persians were surprised, not only by the unexpected charge, but also by the fact that 10,000 Greeks in heavy armor were bearing down on them in dense array. The shock was effective, as was the Athenian tactic of strengthening the wings at the expense of the center. The Persians seem to have driven back the Athenian center but were in turn enveloped by the wings. A rout ensued, and the casualty figures are striking: 6,400 Persian dead, 192 Athenian dead. The remnant of the Persian force re-embarked and sailed around Cape Sunium to Athens, only to find that Miltiades had marched his victorious army overland and was waiting for them on the beach. The Persians did not attempt a landing; instead, they abandoned the effort and sailed back to Asia.

Marathon marked the end of the first campaign in Greece proper, but there was little doubt that another attempt would be made. The next invasion attempt was delayed ten years, however, by internal problems within the Persian Empire.

Campaign of 480 B.C.

The Persian invasion of 480 B.C. was several years in preparation. Herodotus gives specific information, which modern scholars find difficult to accept. We are told that the Persian force numbered 1.7 million infantry, 80,000 cavalry, and 1,200 warships with crews of approximately 200 each, for a total of about 2 million fighting men. There were in addition more than 3,000 smaller vessels and transports, and numerous support personnel and camp followers, a total of nearly 4.2 million. This force was prepared under the direction of the Persian king Xerxes (486–465 B.C.), who had succeeded his father, Darius. Herodotus describes in detail the method of mustering and counting the troops as well as the considerable logistics involved in transporting and feeding a force this size. Nevertheless, the great German military historian Hans Delbrueck considered Herodotus's figures to be a gross exaggeration, and estimated that Xerxes's army "cannot have numbered more than some 75,000 warriors, including the allied Greeks" (Delbrueck 1975, pp. 35–36). The route of march was through Asia Minor, across the Hellespont (a bridge was built of ships lashed together and covered), and then through what is now northern Greece, reaching the objective, Athens, from the north. The land force was to stay near the coast; the fleet would sail alongside.

The Greeks had undertaken some advance planning as well. For the first time in Greek history, a large number of Greek city-states put aside their quarrels with one another and their insistence on complete independence and formed an alliance, usually referred to as the Hellenic League. Thirty-one states were involved, under the nominal leadership of Sparta, which was generally agreed to be the strongest military power among them. The land forces available to the Greek alliance probably numbered about 70,000, although they were never all mustered in one place, and were commanded by King Leonidas of Sparta. In Athens, the statesman and general Themistocles had convinced the Athenians to build up their navy, which now numbered nearly 300 ships and was by far the strongest naval force among the Greeks. Although the nominal command of the naval forces was conferred on a Spartan, the practical command lay with Themistocles. Like the Persians, the Greeks saw the necessity of coordinated land and sea activity.

After considering all the options, the Greeks decided to post a blocking force at the pass of Thermopylae in central Greece. The easiest passage from northern Greece to southern Greece and the only practical way to move a large army was along the coastal road, which at Thermopylae traversed a defile that, at its narrowest, was only about 13 meters (40–50 ft.) wide between the steep, rugged mountains and the sea. (Changes in the seacoast have substantially widened the pass in subsequent centuries.) It was a place where the superior numbers of the Persians would provide little advantage. Not far offshore, the island of Euboea provided a convenient base for blocking the accompanying Persian fleet, which would either have to go around the island or sail through the Euripos channel; in either case, it could be outflanked and attacked in detail by taking the other route. Therefore, the Greek fleet, which numbered about 400 ships, positioned itself at the northern end of the island of Euboea near a place called Artemisium, a location close enough to Thermopylae to maintain contact with the land army.

BATTLE OF THERMOPYLAE

The Greek forces at Thermopylae numbered about 10,000 heavily armed troops; only 300 were Spartans. Sparta had sent only the king and his body-guard because of religious festivals at home (a similar situation had prevented them from aiding the Athenians at Marathon in 490). It is doubtful that the Greeks ever expected to do more than delay the Persian advance by their stand at Thermopylae. In that, they succeeded. The Persian movement was halted for perhaps as long as two weeks, during which time many of the cities to the south were evacuated in an orderly manner. The Greek stand at Thermopylae not only cost Xerxes valuable time—it was already September and winter would soon be upon the Persians—but it seems he also took heavy casualties both on land and sea.

For several days the Persians assaulted the Greek position, only to be driven back by the Greek soldiers; the 300 Spartans under King Leonidas particularly distinguished themselves. At the same time, the Persian fleet was unable to dislodge the Greek fleet from the narrow waters off Artemisium. There were no victories at sea for the Greeks but no defeats either. Although the naval encounters were indecisive, they were costly for the Persians, who had no intimate knowledge of the waters and weather patterns, and suffered severe losses from shipwrecks during storms. The land battle at Thermopylae was finally won by the Persians when the Greek position was turned by a small Persian force that had been guided along an undefended mountain path by a Greek traitor. This came as no surprise to King Leonidas; it was just a question of when, not if, the Persians would find the path. When he learned from his scouts that the position was no longer tenable, Leonidas ordered most of the Greek force to withdraw and remained with his 300 Spartans and a few other troops to buy a little more time. Leonidas and his Spartans fell to the last man. Once the land battle had been lost, the Greek fleet retreated from its exposed position and regrouped off the island of Salamis near Athens.

NAVAL BATTLE OF SALAMIS

The land army of Xerxes marched south into central Greece while his fleet sailed around the promontory and arrived in the Saronic Gulf, near Athens. Xerxes received the submission of some of the smaller towns that were still inhabited, but most of the cities had been evacuated and were plundered and burned. Athens, whose inhabitants had fled, was sacked and burned.

The Greek land forces took up positions on the narrow Isthmus of Corinth to prevent a Persian advance into the Peloponnesus. The land forces saw no further action, however; the decisive battle of this second and final Persian campaign was a naval battle in the Straits of Salamis, between the island and the mainland. The subsequent Greek success at Salamis was due entirely to the efforts of Themistocles. The Greeks were disunited and fearful, and there was great sentiment for fleeing, either to avoid the Persians or to protect one's own family, city, and territory. Themistocles had detailed knowledge of the local topography, sea conditions, and winds. He managed to convince the Persians by secret messages that their best hope was to trap the Greeks in the narrow straits of Salamis and annihilate them there; while at the same time he persuaded the Greeks that their best chance for a victorious battle was at Salamis. The Greek ships, obscured from Persian view by the irregularities of the coast on the island of Salamis, were lying in ambush for the Persian fleet as it entered the narrow channel on 23 September. Persian superiority in numbers was irrelevant. Just after the battle got under way, the winds and the current changed, causing the Persians to run afoul of one another and making the Greek task of ramming and boarding easier. As at Thermopylae, the Greeks gave battle in a location where superior numbers could not be used to advantage. Half of the Persian ships were sunk or captured; the Greeks lost only 40 ships.

The Sequel

With the defeat at Salamis, Xerxes had little choice but to withdraw most of his army and navy from Greece. A force so large could not be maintained in a hostile land for any length of time, particularly without command of the sea. He left an army in Greece under his general Mardonius and withdrew the remainder into Asia. Mardonius's army suffered many deprivations during the ensuing winter, and what was left of it was annihilated in a battle at Plataea in the spring of the following year. Only a few stragglers made their way back to Persia. That spring (479 B.C.) the Athenian fleet sailed through the islands of the Aegean and to the coast of Asia Minor to liberate the Greek cities remaining under Persian rule.

There was never again a Persian invasion of Greece, and the entire episode may be viewed as the genesis of the Athenian Empire of the fifth century B.C.

JANICE J. GABBERT

SEE ALSO: History, Ancient Military; Persian Empire.

Bibliography

The primary sources are Herodotus, as well as Aeschylus's play *The Persians*, and the biographies by Plutarch of Themistocles and Aristides. A full treatment of modern scholarship on the subject can be found in *Cambridge Ancient History*, Vol. 4 (Cambridge, 1926, rev. 1964).

Adcock, F. E. 1957. *The Greek and Macedonian art of war.* Berkeley: Univ. of California Press.
Delbrueck, H. 1975. *History of the art of war within the framework of political history.* Vol. 1, *Antiquity.* Trans. W. J. Renfroe, Jr. Westport, Conn.: Greenwood Press.
Ferrill, A. 1985. *The origins of war: From the Stone Age to Alexander the Great.* London: Thames and Hudson.
Frost, F. J. 1980. *Plutarch's Themistocles: A historical commentary.* Princeton, N.J.: Princeton Univ. Press.
Hammond, N. G. L. 1967. *A history of Greece to 322 B.C.* Oxford: Clarendon Press.
Pritchett, W. K. 1971–85. *The Greek state at war.* 4 vols. Berkeley: Univ. of California Press.
Rodgers, W. L. [1937] 1964. *Greek and Roman naval warfare.* Reprint. Annapolis, Md.: U.S. Naval Institute Press.
Warry, J. 1980. *Warfare in the classical world.* New York: St. Martin's Press.

GRANT, ULYSSES SIMPSON
(1822–85)

Ulysses Simpson Grant (Fig. 1), the chief architect of the Federal forces' (or Union) victory over the Confederacy in the American Civil War, rose from an inauspicious prewar business career to become one of the most prominent leaders in American military history.

Early Life and Pre–Civil War Activities

Grant was born on 27 April 1822 at Point Pleasant, Ohio, the first of six children of Jesse Root and Hannah Simpson Grant. Christened Hiram Ulysses Grant, when he entered the United States Military Academy at West Point, New York, he altered his name to Ulysses Simpson Grant, the name provided by the

Figure 1. Ulysses S. Grant. (SOURCE: U.S. Library of Congress)

congressman who applied for his appointment. Growing up in Ohio, Grant led a comfortable frontier life, attending school and working on his father's farm. In 1839, his father, unbeknownst to Grant, secured for him an appointment to West Point. Grant accepted it without enthusiasm and went on to become a mediocre cadet with a distaste for military life and no intention of remaining in the army. He achieved distinction at West Point primarily for his accomplished horsemanship, but he also collected a substantial number of demerits and at graduation in 1843 ranked only 21st academically in a class of 39.

In September 1843, Grant joined the 4th Infantry Regiment in St. Louis. One year later, the unit assembled with Gen. Zachary Taylor's Army of Occupation in Corpus Christi, Texas. Taylor moved against the Mexican army in May 1846, and Grant served under him in battles at Palo Alto and Resaca de la Palma (8–9 May 1846) and Monterrey (21–23 September 1846). Grant participated in Gen. Winfield Scott's 1847 Vera Cruz–Mexico City campaign, along with numerous other future Civil War leaders, both Confederate and Federal. He saw action at Vera Cruz (9–29 March 1847), Cerro Gordo (17–18 April 1847), Churubusco (20 August 1847), Molino del Rey (8 September 1847), and the storming of the hilltop fortress of Chapultepec (13 September 1847), where he was breveted captain for bravery. On 16 September 1847, Grant was commissioned a first lieutenant, the rank he held at the end of the Mexican War (1848).

Grant returned to the United States in 1848 and married Julia Dent, whose acquaintance he had made while stationed in St. Louis. In 1854, after duty in New York, Michigan, the Pacific Northwest, and California—enduring separation from his family and suffering from excessive drinking while on the Pacific Coast—Grant resigned with the rank of captain. Until 1860, he lived with his wife and children in Missouri, where he tried his hand at farming, real estate, and other occupations. In 1860, he started work with a family-owned business in Galena, Illinois, and remained there until the outbreak of the Civil War.

Civil War Generalship

Grant trained a company of Galena militia and then worked in the Illinois Adjutant General's Office in Springfield, the state capital. He tendered his services to the army in May 1861 and was ignored. He was, however, soon appointed colonel and made commander of the 21st Illinois Volunteer Infantry Regiment. Promoted to brigadier general in August 1861, Grant took command of the District of Southeast Missouri, with headquarters in Cairo, Illinois. On 7 November 1861, he commanded Federal forces in an inconclusive battle at Belmont, Missouri. In February 1862, he scored major victories in capturing Forts Henry (6 February) and Donelson (16 February), actions that earned him promotion to major general of Volunteers and the nickname "Unconditional Surrender" from a message he sent to the Confederate commander at Fort Donelson. Although temporarily removed from command due to failed communications with his superior, Gen. Henry W. Halleck, Grant regained his position as head of the Army of the Tennessee in March. On 6–7 April 1862, a Confederate army under Gen. Albert Sydney Johnston surprised Grant's troops encamped at Shiloh (Pittsburg Landing), Tennessee, and pushed them back until Grant rallied his troops and then, reinforced, drove the Southerners from the field in severe fighting. After Shiloh, Grant again temporarily lost command of the Army of the Tennessee to Halleck, but resumed it in July 1862 and, following victories by Maj. Gen. William S. Rosecrans at Iuka (19 September) and Corinth (3–4 October), initiated his campaign to open the Mississippi River and divide the Confederacy.

Cooperating with the river gunboats of Rear Adm. David D. Porter, Grant conducted a long campaign, beset by natural obstacles and Confederate resistance. Finally, in April 1863, he moved his forces south of Vicksburg, crossed the river, and marched overland to Jackson, Mississippi. He defeated Confederate general John C. Pemberton's army at Champion's Hill (16 May 1863). Grant then invested Pemberton's army at Vicksburg and forced the surrender of the Confederate garrison on 4 July. With the Federal victory at Port Hudson on 9 July, the Union effectively controlled the entire Mississippi River.

Grant earned his promotion to major general in the regular army with his victory at Vicksburg and received command of the newly created Military Division of the Mississippi on October 1863. His next actions came at Chattanooga, Tennessee, where he took command of the besieged Federal army (October) and won a decisive victory at Lookout Mountain–Missionary Ridge (24–25 November 1863).

President Abraham Lincoln was greatly impressed by Grant's achievements; he brought Grant to Washington, promoted him to lieutenant general, and appointed him general in chief in March 1864. Although Grant exercised command over all Federal armies, he remained in the east with Gen. George G. Meade's Army of the Potomac for the rest of the Civil War. Using the telegraph, he directed the overall Union army war effort, sending Gen. William T. Sherman through Georgia and the Carolinas, while directly overseeing the crucial campaign in Virginia. His drive on Richmond was carried out in accordance with a simple but effective strategy and was characterized by brutal fighting with Gen. Robert E. Lee's Confederate army at the Wilderness, Spotsylvania, Cold Harbor, and the attack on Petersburg (May–June 1864). Grant continued undeterred from his goal to wear down Lee and laid siege to Richmond and Petersburg. The Virginia campaign thus entered a new stage of fighting, foreshadowing the static trench warfare of World War I. After a nine-month siege, the overwhelming Federal strength and dwindling Southern resources forced Lee to evacuate his defensive line around the Confederate capital and march westward (April 1865). Grant pursued, sending part of his army to cut off the Confederate retreat. Lee surrendered at Appomattox Courthouse, in Virginia, on 9 April. Lee's capitulation doomed the Confederacy.

Postwar Activities

In 1866, Grant was promoted to general of the army and, in 1868, following an increasingly turbulent political relationship with Pres. Andrew Johnson, accepted the nomination by the Republican party as candidate for president of the

United States. Grant was elected in 1868 and served two terms. He appointed a number of unscrupulous or incompetent officials to his administration posts, and his presidency suffered for it. Financial scandals such as the Black Friday episode (1869), the Whiskey Ring (1872), and the Credit Mobilier crisis (1873) rocked his terms in office. Grant was politically naive and not personally involved in the corruption. Negative sentiment prevented his renomination for a third term in 1880. Moving to New York City in 1881, he invested his life's savings with a banking firm and lost it when the business went bankrupt due to mismanagement by fraudulent partners. This financial catastrophe coincided with the onset of throat cancer, the disease that eventually killed him.

Grant spent the remainder of his life writing his autobiography, proceeds from which restored his family's finances. He completed the highly acclaimed literary work only four days before his death on 23 July 1885.

Grant achieved his place in history as a "Great Captain" from his accomplishments during the Civil War, both in the western and eastern theaters. In the Vicksburg campaign he proved to be an able tactician and strategist. In Virginia, his determination and persistence were most evident. After the intense battle at Spotsylvania, he demonstrated a strong will in continuing to press Lee by stating that he would "fight it out on this line if it takes all summer" (Dupuy 1969, p. 109). Lincoln held Grant in particularly high esteem. When urged by influential politicians to replace him, Lincoln refused with the response, "I can't spare this man. He fights!" (Heinl 1966, p. 135). Grant's great determination and personal courage remained through his final years.

BRIAN R. BADER

SEE ALSO: Civil War, American; Lee, Robert Edward; Scott, Winfield.

Bibliography

Dupuy, T. N. 1969. *The military life of Abraham Lincoln: Commander-in-chief.* New York: Franklin Watts.
Fuller, J. F. C. 1929. *The generalship of Ulysses S. Grant.* New York: Dodd, Mead.
———1957. *Grant & Lee: A study in personality and generalship.* Bloomington: Indiana Univ. Press.
Heinl, R. D., Jr. 1966. *Dictionary of military and naval quotations.* Annapolis, Md.: U.S. Naval Institute Press.
Lewis, L. 1950. *Captain Sam Grant.* Boston: Little, Brown.
Grant, U. S. 1952. *Personal memiors of U. S. Grant.* Ed. with notes and an introduction by E. B. Long. Cleveland: World (reprint).
Porter, H. 1897. *Campaigning with Grant.* New York: Century.

GRENADA, U.S. INTERVENTION IN

The events that triggered the U.S. intervention in Grenada, code-name Urgent Fury, began long before the 24 October 1983 presidential directive. Beginning in 1974, when Grenada gained its independence from Britain, corruption and political repression were trademarks of successive Grenadian prime ministers. The execution of Prime Minister Maurice Bishop on 19 October 1983, however, set into motion a series of events that would culminate in the largest U.S. military operation since the Vietnam War.

The intervention was overwhelmingly supported by the American public but condemned internationally and likened by some to the Soviets' 1979 invasion of Afghanistan. The decision to launch Urgent Fury, however, proved to be a sound one, both militarily and politically. Documents captured by U.S. forces revealed that almost every communist satellite regime under Soviet influence had representatives and observers, at some stage, in Grenada. These individuals were helping to transform the island into a major military camp, as revealed by U.S. forces' discovery of artillery, antiaircraft weapons, ammunition, armored personnel carriers, and rocket launchers. Moreover, a democratically elected government was subsequently restored to Grenada, an island that for years had suffered under autocratic, corrupt, and ruthless regimes. For Cuba and the Soviet Union, the intervention was a serious blow.

By 15 December 1983, less than two months after they were ordered into action, U.S. combat forces were withdrawn from Grenada. Some maintained that the victory re-established the professional competence of the U.S. military, which had been lost in Vietnam. However, others pointed out that Grenada was not a flawless military operation but had come close to being a military disaster. William S. Lind, a staff aide to former Senator Gary W. Hart, was highly critical of the operation. The press coverage of his allegations was partly responsible for demands for a congressional investigation, but an investigation was forestalled by the Chairman, Joint Chiefs of Staff's written responses to the allegations.

Overall, U.S. military operations in Grenada succeeded beyond expectations against a small and marginally equipped group of defenders. According to former Secretary of Defense Caspar W. Weinberger, it was a "complex operation in which we saved a lot of lives and a lot of misery." The operation showed the ability of the U.S. military to mount a swift, well-executed attack on short notice. More important, it demonstrated U.S. public support for the use of selective military force to accomplish limited political-military goals.

History

The island of Grenada was discovered by Columbus in 1498. Thereafter, it passed through Spanish and French hands and finally came under British ownership during the eighteenth century; England governed the island until the late 1950s. During the early 1960s, Britain sponsored two attempts to form its Caribbean colonies into a single federation. Failing in this, the individual islands were given independence within the British Commonwealth system, starting with Grenada in 1974. Grenada's first prime minister was Sir Eric Gairy, whose administration was known for its corruption and political repression. In March 1979, Gairy was overthrown in a bloodless coup led by Maurice Bishop. Bishop took power as head of Grenada's Provisional Revolutionary

Government (PRG) in the name of his New Jewel Movement Party (NJMP), an acronym that stood for the Joint Endeavor for Welfare, Education, and Liberation.

The New Jewel Movement

Bishop and his NJMP faced both political and economic problems but saw a solution in the example of Cuba. Over the next few years, Bishop invited increasing assistance from both Cuba and other communist states. This, plus Bishop's lack of interest in holding elections, brought PRG into conflict with U.S. foreign policy in the region, a situation aggravated by the PRG's announcement of its most ambitious project—construction of a new international airport at Point Salines. The airport was to be built by Cuban workers and feature a 2,750-meter (9,000-ft.) runway. Its purpose was to improve Grenada's sagging tourist trade, because the existing airport could accept only twin-engine air traffic. U.S. military forces, however, captured documents revealing that the Cubans had planned to use the airport as a staging area to airlift supplies to their troops in Africa and as a refueling stop for Soviet planes en route to Nicaragua.

By late summer 1983, the NJMP had split into two factions. One faction, led by Bishop, wanted closer ties with the West. The other faction, led by Deputy Prime Minister Bernard Coard, wanted to retain Grenada's communist connections and to speed up the country's conversion to a Marxist state. (By the time of the U.S. intervention, Grenada had agreements with the Soviet Union, Vietnam, Czechoslovakia, North Korea, Cuba, and East Germany for supply of modern sophisticated military equipment and technical logistical assistance.) The crisis between the two factions came to a head on 13 October, when Coard, with the PRG military's backing under Gen. Hudson Austin, ordered Bishop to step down from office for failure to carry out the orders of the NJMP's Central Committee. Bishop and a number of his ministers were placed under house arrest and subsequently executed on 19 October. A 24-hour curfew was then imposed and notice given that violators would be shot on sight.

Events in Grenada: 19–28 October 1983

On the night of 19 October, General Austin announced the formation of a 16-man Revolutionary Military Council (RMC) with himself as head. No mention was made of Coard; however, he would serve as an adviser to Austin. Over the next four days, a number of prominent citizens were arrested.

On 21 October, the leaders of six small nations (Dominica, St. Lucia, St. Vincent, Montserrat, St. Kitts-Nevis, and Antigua) composing the Organization of Eastern Caribbean States (OECS) met to consider collective action against Grenada. They voted to intervene militarily to restore order to the region. However, because none of the six possessed the necessary forces, they recognized that an appeal for assistance would have to be made to nonmember states Jamaica and Barbados, regional neighbors, and to the United States.

The following day, the Caribbean Community (CARICOM) met. A majority of the delegates supported the idea of intervention, if the RMC would not peacefully accept a CARICOM fact-finding commission and a Caribbean Peace-keeping Force.

On 23 October, the British deputy commissioner in Barbados and two U.S. diplomats met with Grenadian officials. The diplomats found the officials "obstructionist and uncooperative." (Early that morning, 241 U.S. Marines stationed in Beirut had been killed by the explosion of a bomb-laden truck driven by a suicide driver. After an all-day meeting between President Reagan and his advisers on the situation in Beirut, attention shifted to Grenada. The president expressed concern over the possibility of U.S. hostages because of the 1,000 U.S. citizens on Grenada, most of whom were students and faculty of St. George's University Medical School, an American-run institution.) The next day, two additional U.S. diplomats arrived on Grenada. Grenadian officials demanded six hours' advance notice for any evacuation flights and warned the diplomats they could not guarantee the safety of foreigners. U.S. officials became concerned that the RMC was planning to use the safety issue of American citizens as a bargaining chip.

A formal request for assistance under Article 8 of the OECS charter was presented to Jamaica, Barbados, and the United States on 23 October. President Reagan met with senior U.S. officials the next day and that evening signed the directive committing U.S. military forces into action. Early on the morning of 25 October, a combined force of 7,000 military troops from the United States, Jamaica, Barbados, and the six OECS states landed on Grenada by sea and air. By Friday, 28 October, the force had secured all significant military objectives and had defeated the People's Revolutionary Army and Territorial Militia and captured about 600 Cuban construction workers. Forty-nine Russians, seventeen Libyans, fifteen North Koreans, ten East Germans, and three Bulgarians were found on the island and quickly repatriated.

Justification for U.S. Action

The Grenada operation was the first time since the Dominican intervention of 1965 that U.S. forces had been ordered into combat in the Caribbean. Elaborate justification for the action was given by senior U.S. officials. President Reagan's 25 October announcement of the "rescue mission" outlined the main reasons for the operation: to ensure the "personal safety" of between 800 and 1,000 U.S. citizens on Grenada, to "forestall further chaos," and "to assist in a joint effort to restore order and democracy" there. He also strongly emphasized that the operation had been mounted in response to "an urgent, formal request" from several eastern Caribbean states.

Secretary of State George Shultz, the U.S. representative to the Organization of American States, Ambassador J. William Middendorf, and United Nations Ambassador Jeanne Kirkpatrick also elaborated upon the president's statement and provided further justification for the intervention: the lack of governmental authority on the island, international law requirements, regional security concerns, and the reality of the use of military force in world politics.

U.S. Domestic Reactions to the Intervention

Despite the Reagan administration's efforts to portray the Grenada operation as a humanitarian rescue mission, a response to an urgent request for help by friendly democratic neighbors, and the successful foiling of a Soviet-Cuban colony, the U.S. public supported the intervention because it was swift, conclusive, and relatively free of cost. Several polls affirmed the American public's overwhelming support of the operation. Many Americans believed that the intervention demonstrated that the United States had overcome the "Vietnam syndrome," that is, the reluctance to use military power to defend U.S. interests and values.

Initial congressional reaction, however, was largely negative, due in part to the administration's failure to consult Congress prior to the intervention. But as the medical students began returning from Grenada and as U.S. forces uncovered evidence of Cuban and Soviet weapons, congressional criticism diminished markedly and shifted toward other issues associated with the military operation. Two such issues were the restrictions that had been placed on journalists, prohibiting them from going on the island until several days after the operation had begun, and the accidental U.S. bombing of a mental hospital that claimed several patients' lives.

International Reactions

Although U.S. domestic opinion supported the intervention, international opinion did not. From 25 to 27 October, the United Nations Security Council debated U.S. and OECS actions. Of 63 countries that spoke regarding the intervention, only the United States and the OECS states defended the action. On 28 October, by a vote of eleven "yes," one "no," and three "abstain," a UN resolution was passed that "deeply deplored the armed intervention in Grenada" as "a flagrant violation of international law and of the independence, sovereignty and territorial integrity of that state." An identical resolution was introduced in the General Assembly on 2 November and was passed without debate with over 100 states voting "yes."

The European allies of the United States also expressed initial disapproval of the intervention. But as the Reagan administration continued to produce evidence showing that the U.S. students had been in danger and that Grenada had become a Soviet outpost, European opposition began to soften.

U.S. Military Performance

The United States deployed elite military units to Grenada that included airborne, ranger, and special operations forces, and marines. By the time hostilities were officially declared over, these forces equated to nine infantry battalions. (Grenada was divided roughly in half, with the marines responsible for the northern part of the island and the army for the southern part.) Missions that were accomplished included the seizure of key objectives and the securing of the island with minimum casualties and destruction. American ground units were supported by a naval carrier battle group complete with ground attack aircraft, naval gunfire, air force and helicopter gunships, army artillery, and massive logistical support. The forces opposing U.S. military units consisted of about 750 Grenadian troops and 600 Cuban "construction workers," all of whom were of questionable morale, with no air or naval forces, no tanks, no artillery, and only a few outdated antiaircraft guns.

Although Urgent Fury was a success, U.S. military operations were not without their problems, most of which remain classified. However, based on open source material, the most highly publicized were the bombing of U.S. troops by their own aircraft, intelligence failures, the lack of maps, and problems with special operations.

A report of lessons learned from the U.S. intervention was submitted to the Chairman, Joint Chiefs of Staff on 6 February 1984 by Adm. Wesley L. McDonald, the commander of Task Force 120, the combined headquarters that controlled military operations. The report identified a number of problems: the lack of understanding of interservice close air support procedures, the confusion caused by the lack of maps, the need for senior liaison officers from all commands at the controlling headquarters, the lack of equipment and preplanning to deal with prisoners of war, and the lack of experience with communications systems.

In addition to these problems, Admiral McDonald said that there was confusion with the insertion of the Caribbean Peacekeeping Force; air assets were "not always properly controlled"; "helicopters are highly vulnerable to well-aimed ground fire"; and "medevac operations at night became a great concern because Black Hawk pilots had not been trained to land on seaborne helicopter platforms and were denied permission to land." Although some have maintained that there were "unforgivable blunders" in intelligence, Admiral McDonald's report stated: "Available basic intelligence was generally adequate for overall planning purposes" and that the estimate of enemy strengths "was within an acceptable range of uncertainty."

Costs and Implications

Almost a decade after the end of the Vietnam war, the U.S. intervention in Grenada reintroduced the use of military power into U.S. foreign policy. However, Urgent Fury cost the lives of eighteen U.S. servicemen killed in action. A total of 116 were wounded in action. Nine U.S. helicopters were either destroyed or damaged. American citizens evacuated from the island totaled 599.

Of the approximately 600 Cubans on Grenada, 24 were killed in action and 59 wounded. No official attempt was made to separate Grenadian casualties into military and civilian totals; the combined total was 45 killed and 337 wounded.

The loss of Grenada was a severe blow to Cuban prestige worldwide and, more directly, to its plans in the region. The exposure of Grenada's secret agreements with East Bloc countries revealed the subversion that was underway, which, if left uncontested, would have threatened both regional and U.S. interests.

Militarily, Urgent Fury demonstrated the readiness, capability, and professionalism of the U.S. armed forces. The entire operation was planned and executed in less than a week. While operating under stringent rules of engagement, U.S. forces accomplished their mission. When the operation was over, Americans felt a renewed sense of pride in their military forces.

In the final analysis, the U.S. intervention in Grenada revealed that the use of military power, tempered by effective and determined leadership, remains a valid tenet of international politics.

JAMES B. MOTLEY

SEE ALSO: Dominican Republic: 1965 Crisis; Land Warfare; Panama, U.S. Invasion of.

Bibliography

Adkins, M. 1989. *Urgent Fury: The battle for Grenada*. Lexington, Mass.: D. C. Heath.

Dunn, P. M., and B. W. Watson, ed. 1985. *American intervention in Grenada*. Boulder, Colo.: Westview Press.

Motley, J. B. 1984. Grenada: Low-intensity conflict and the use of U.S. military power. *World Affairs* 146 Winter 1983–84, (3):221–38.

Russell, L. E., and M. A. Mendez. 1985. *Grenada 1983*. London: Osprey.

Seabury, P., and W. A. McDougall, eds. 1984. *The Grenada papers*. San Francisco, Calif.: Institute for Contemporary Studies.

Schoenhals, K. P., and R. A. Melanson. 1985. *Revolution and intervention in Grenada*. Boulder, Colo.: Westview Press.

Weinberger, C. 1990. *Fighting for peace: Seven critical years in the Pentagon*. New York: Warner Books.

JCS replies to criticism of Grenada operation. *Army* (August 1984):28–37.

GUDERIAN, HEINZ [1888–1951]

Heinz Guderian was born on 17 June 1888 in Kulm, East Prussia. His father was an army officer and an aristocrat. In 1900 Heinz entered the cadet school at Karlsruhe in Baden, transferring in 1903 to the Main Cadet School at Gross Lichterfeld outside Berlin.

An eager and highly intelligent student, Heinz easily passed his cadet training and was assigned to the 100th Hannover Jaeger Battalion, then his father's command. On 27 January 1908, he was commissioned a lieutenant in the battalion.

In 1912 Guderian was selected to join a newly formed radio company. During this assignment Guderian learned to appreciate the importance of effective radio communications, and the flexibility they provided in the exercise of command.

In 1913 Guderian was selected to attend the War College. In October of that same year he married Margarete Goerne. The War College was closed upon the outbreak of war in 1914, and Guderian was given command of a wireless station in the headquarters of the 5th Cavalry Division in the Third Army.

World War I

In April 1915 Guderian was transferred to the headquarters of the Fourth Army to serve as assistant signals officer. He was promoted to captain and, in April 1917, was transferred to the General Staff of the 4th Infantry Division in Champagne, France.

Except for one month when he commanded the 2d Battalion, 14th Infantry Regiment, Guderian continued to hold staff positions from division to army level throughout the war. He was assigned in February 1918 to the Army General Staff and in October to the prestigious Operations Branch as general staff officer.

Interwar Years

In May 1919 Guderian was assigned to the staff of the "Iron Division" in Latvia. The "Iron Division" was a Freikorps unit involved in halting Bolshevik expansion from Russia into Latvia and East Prussia. In June, after the withdrawal of German troops from the Baltic states, Guderian returned to Hannover and a staff appointment with his old battalion. At the end of 1919 he was selected as an officer in the newly formed Reichswehr, the small 100,000-man defensive force allowed Germany under the terms of the Versailles Treaty.

In January 1922 Guderian was assigned to Reichswehr headquarters and posted to the new Office of the Inspectorate of Transport Troops. He threw himself into the job with his customary eagerness and intensity. Along with the study of motorized troops, Guderian developed an interest in the tank and read all the available works on tank development and tactics, most notably those by Fuller, Liddell-Hart, and Martel.

Guderian quickly made himself a leading tank expert. He began to supplement his income as well as to disseminate his theories by writing articles for various military periodicals on the uses of tanks and troop transports on the battlefield.

In October 1924 Guderian was assigned to the 2d Division as instructor of tactics and military history. He used his new position to develop further his concepts of mobile warfare. In 1927 he was promoted to major and in October was reassigned to Reichswehr headquarters. Posted back to the Transport Section, he was given the specific tasks of studying motorized troop transport and of instructing members of his section in the operational uses of tanks.

Guderian worked zealously at developing an armored (panzer) force for the army. In February 1930 he was given command of a motor transport battalion and immediately began transforming it into an armored reconnaissance battalion. Despite resistance to his ideas, Guderian persevered in his belief that fast, mobile armored units were the wave of the future. In October 1931 he was promoted to lieutenant colonel and offered the post of chief of staff by his old friend, General Lutz, now inspector of Transport Troops. Lutz had always been a supporter of Guderian's ideas, and the two of them began to work toward not only the development of a panzer force but also its acceptance by the High Command.

Under Lutz, Guderian was given free reign to experiment and to develop his theories of mobile warfare. By the time of Hitler's accession to power in 1933, Guderian had already laid the groundwork for the building of Germany's panzer forces. By 1934 the first panzer division was created and Guderian was promoted to colonel and made chief of staff to the Commander in Chief, Panzer Troops. By 1935 three panzer divisions had been created and Guderian, although still only a colonel, was given command of the 2d Panzer Division at Wuerzburg.

In 1936 Guderian's book, *Achtung! Panzer*, was published. In it he detailed his theories on using massed armored formations, supported by artillery and air attacks, to breach the enemy's lines and then to fan out into their rear areas. Once through, the panzers would use their mobility to exploit the breach further, while accompanying motorized infantry would clear the breach and hold it open for the follow-on forces. Guderian emphasized the importance of panzer mobility. As long as the panzers kept moving, they could keep the enemy off balance and deny it a chance to concentrate.

Later in 1936 Guderian was promoted to *generalmajor* (brigadier general). In 1938, as a result of the Blomberg-Fritsch crisis, Lutz was forced into retirement by Hitler. Guderian was then promoted to *generalleutnant* (major general) and made acting commander of the XIII Corps. In November he was promoted to *general* (lieutenant general) of Panzer Troops and succeeded Lutz as commander in chief of Mobile Troops.

By January 1939 Guderian had five panzer divisions operational and a sixth on the way. He was also preparing the four light divisions for quick conversion into panzer divisions if the need should arise. Shortly afterward, Guderian was finally given the command he desired most: commander in chief, Panzer Troops.

World War II

On 22 August 1939, Guderian was given command of the XIX Corps for the planned invasion of Poland. The XIX Corps was composed of the 3d Panzer and the 2d and 20th Motorized divisions and had the important role of spearheading the German drive across the neck of the Polish Corridor. The German offensive opened on 1 September, and Guderian, leading his corps from the front, proceeded to put his theories to the test. By the evening of 4 September, Guderian's troops had crossed the corridor and by the 16th had taken Brest-Litovsk, inside the allocated Russian zone of influence, effectively ending the campaign.

On touring the battlefield, Hitler was amazed and impressed by the destruction wrought by the panzers. Guderian had proven his case for the effectiveness of massed, highly mobile panzer forces. He was awarded the Knight's Cross in October during the victory celebrations in Berlin.

During the preparation and planning stages of Case Yellow (code name for the planned invasion of France) Guderian helped Gen. Eric von Manstein, Chief of Staff of Army Group A, persuade Field Marshal Gerd von Runstedt, Army Group A commander, of the soundness of a surprise armored thrust through the Ardennes Forest. Guderian also encouraged Manstein to approach Hitler with this strategic concept.

Upon acceptance of Manstein's plan, Guderian's XIX Corps was assigned the difficult operation of spearheading the drive across the Meuse River. The XIX Corps was now composed of the 1st, 2d, and 10th Panzer divisions and the Grossdeutschland Regiment, whose battalions alternately served as Hitler's personal escort. Guderian's corps was one of three that formed Panzer Group Kleist. Kleist's group contained five panzer divisions—half the entire German panzer force.

On 10 May, Guderian's corps drove through the Ardennes in eastern Belgium and smashed into the French lines. By the 13th he had taken Sedan and forced a crossing of the Meuse. On the 20th his panzers reached Abbeville on the French coast and by the 23d had taken Calais and Boulogne before receiving Hitler's order to halt. Guderian was furious at not being able to finish the destruction of the French and British troops, now trapped with their backs to the sea, but Hitler was adamant. When the Germans renewed their offensive southward into France on 5 June, Guderian drove to the Swiss border before halting again. Guderian's success was a direct result of his tactics of mobility, command from the front, and an excellent working relationship with the Luftwaffe unit that supported the panzer group.

The French surrendered unconditionally on 22 June; for his part in the victory Guderian was promoted to *generaloberst* (general) on 19 July. Guderian then returned to the task of raising and training new panzer divisions. Within the year he had increased the number of panzer divisions to twenty but had not increased the strength of the panzer force. Much to Guderian's displeasure Hitler had ordered the creation of the new divisions but had equipped them by taking panzers from the existing divisions. This was to become a standard practice for Hitler. Combined with the inability of the German automotive industry to keep pace with the necessary production requirements, it severely weakened the further development of the panzer forces.

At the beginning of the Russian Campaign (22 June 1941) the Wehrmacht boasted four panzer groups. Guderian was given command of the 2d Panzergroup (later called Panzerarmee Guderian and then 2d Panzer Armee). This, with General Hoth's 4th Panzergroup, formed the spearhead of General von Bock's Army Group Center.

Guderian launched his panzers into Russia with the same skill and tenacity as in Poland and France. Forming a pincer with Hoth's corps, Guderian raced across Russia, slicing deep into enemy territory. Guderian and Hoth met on 27

June outside Minsk, having covered more than 320 kilometers (200 mi.) in five days and encircling nearly 300,000 Russian troops. They repeated this tactic at Smolensk on 27 July, trapping another 100,000 Russians.

In August, Hitler shifted the axis of advance from Army Group Center to Rundstedt's Army Group South. Guderian was incensed that Hitler could not see the ramifications of not pushing on to take Moscow and only against his better judgment moved his army south to support the drive on Kiev. On 15 September, Guderian linked up with Kleist near Lokhvista, completing the encirclement of over 600,000 Russians.

Guderian was then ordered to turn north and resume the advance toward Moscow. Although he succeeded in penetrating south beyond Moscow, the onset of winter and the exhaustion of both men and equipment convinced Guderian that the city could not be taken and that the army's only recourse was to retreat to prepared winter positions. Hitler, however, ordered the army to stand fast regardless of the losses from exposure. Guderian, Rundstedt, and Bock opposed this idea and withdrew their forces in spite of Hitler's orders. On 26 December, Guderian and the others were relieved of their commands and assigned to the reserve officers' pool.

Guderian remained literally unemployed until February 1943 when Hitler, realizing that the military situation demanded all of his experienced officers to stem the tide of German reversal, recalled him to act as inspector general of Panzer Troops. Guderian immediately buried himself in the duties of his new position, which involved the training, organization, and development of the panzer forces.

After the abortive assassination attempt on Hitler's life on 20 July 1944, Guderian was appointed to replace General Zietzler as chief of the General Staff of the Army High Command (OKH) on 21 July. One of his first duties was to act as chairman of the army tribunal that investigated those implicated in the assassination conspiracy. The tribunal had the responsibility of turning over hundreds of the accused to a People's Court for trial and summary execution. Guderian found the entire affair disgusting but was virtually trapped by his position as chief of staff.

He did use his new position to fight for an increase of troop strength on the eastern front. Guderian predicted that the Russians would launch a major offensive that would result in a collapse of the German lines if they were caught unprepared. He spared no pains to challenge Hitler on this issue whenever necessary. When the Russian offensive began in December, Guderian's predictions came true. With the Allies closing in on Germany from east and west, Guderian urged Hitler to make peace with the western powers. Hitler had had many violent disagreements with Guderian in the past but this was too much. He dismissed Guderian for reasons of failing health on 21 March 1945. Guderian retired to the Tyrol to await the end and was taken prisoner by American forces on 10 May. He was held in captivity as a war criminal until June 1947 when the charges against him were dropped and he was released.

In 1951 his memoirs, *Erinnerungen eines Soldaten*, were published. In them he brutally lambasted the dilettante mentality of the High Command that resulted in Germany's defeats on the eastern front. Guderian died on 15 May 1951 in Schwangau bei Fussen.

A brilliant tactician, organizer, and commander, Guderian was the mastermind behind the creation of the panzer forces, the cutting edge of the German blitzkrieg.

VINCENT B. HAWKINS

SEE ALSO: Manstein, Erich von; World War II.

Bibliography

Guderian, H. 1952. *Panzer leader*. London: Michael Joseph.
Keegan, J. 1973. *Guderian*. New York: Ballantine Books.
Pfannes, C. E., and V. A. Salamone. 1980. *The great commanders of World War II*. Vol. 1, *The Germans*. New York: Kensington.
Wistrich, R. 1982. *Who's who in Nazi Germany*. New York: Bonanza Books.

GULF WAR, 1991

Iraq's invasion of Kuwait on 1 August 1990 triggered a series of events that led to one of the largest-scale conflicts of the modern era. Although the actual fighting lasted only 43 days, it involved massive air and armored operations and the widespread use of new military technologies ranging from stealth attack aircraft to modern tank fire-control systems with thermal imaging sights.

The war also marked a major shift in East-West relations and within the developing world itself. It became a contest between a regional superpower, under the leadership of an ambitious dictator, and a broad coalition of United Nations forces, led by the United States and Saudi Arabia and operating in a political context where the United States had the political support of the Soviet Union. As such, it may well have been the first conflict of the post–cold war era.

Iraq's Invasion of Kuwait

Unlike most conflicts, Iraq's invasion of Kuwait was an act of naked aggression with little political justification or sophistication. In the period before the invasion, Iraq claimed that Kuwait was violating its oil quotas and improperly draining oil from the Rumalia oil field—a large reservoir largely in Iraq but whose southern tip is in Kuwait. In fact, Iraq had never agreed to a quota of its own, and most of Kuwait's modest production from the Rumalia field had gone to sales that aided Iraq during its war with Iran (1980–88). Further, Kuwait had provided Iraq with billions of dollars in aid during that war, and had offered both to cut its exports and halt production from the Rumalia field before the Iraqi invasion.

Iraq also undermined any justifications for its actions during the first days of the invasion when it first claimed to be supporting a nonexistent uprising by prodemocratic Kuwaiti forces, stated that it was withdrawing from the country but then moved toward outright annexation, and sent its forces to Kuwait's southern border with Saudi Arabia.

While Iraq then claimed it was simply liberating territory stolen from it by Britain, these claims had equally little historical justification: Iraq had no claim to Kuwait as a successor state because modern Iraq had been created by Britain after the collapse of the Turkish Empire at the end of World War I. Even the Turkish Empire had had an uncertain claim to Kuwait, since it exercised only limited or dual jurisdiction over the area, and Kuwait had normally existed as a small independent Bedouin settlement on the Persian Gulf coast. Kuwait's boundaries as a city-state were set by the British in the 1920s, and only in reaction to the threat of a Saudi invasion.

The true causes of Iraq's invasion were a mixture of economic problems and the ambitions of Saddam Hussein. Under Saddam's leadership, Iraq had continued to expand its military machine after the cease-fire in August 1988. It did so even though it had obtained more than US$60 billion worth of arms during 1980–88, and the war had cost Iraq as much as one-third of its gross domestic product. Further, Iraq was spending additional billions on missiles and biological, chemical, and nuclear weapons. At the same time, Iraq spent billions on ambitious civil development projects like the reconstruction of Basra and Al Fao.

This saddled Iraq with a foreign debt of some US$80–100 billion at a time when oil prices were depressed and there was a significant world surplus of oil exports. As a result, Iraq could not continue to pay for its military machine, could not meet its debt payments, and experienced steadily greater problems in giving its people the kind of economic development and reconstruction they expected at the end of the war with Iran.

The invasion of Kuwait thus offered Saddam Hussein a means of distracting Iraq's population, a potential source of vast wealth, and the strategic asset of a deep-water port on the Persian Gulf. Kuwait's Fund for the Future had investments worth more than US$100 billion. Kuwait was capable of adding at least 2 million barrels a day of oil to Iraq's exports of roughly 3.5 million, and it offered the opportunity to increase Iraq's total oil reserves from 100 billion to 198 billion barrels (a total of nearly 25% of the world's total reserves). At the same time, it placed Iraqi forces on Saudi Arabia's border and within easy striking range. Even if Iraq did not attack Saudi Arabia's nearby oil fields and oil facilities, this strategic position gave it political and military leverage over nations that possessed an additional 28 percent of the world's total reserves.

International Reactions and the Forging of a U.S.-Led Military Coalition

The success of Iraq's invasion depended, however, on the reaction of its neighbors, the United States, and other regional and world powers. Saddam Hussein seems to have calculated that neighboring states like Saudi Arabia would be too frightened to act and that the United States would either not send forces or not be willing to go to war. As it turned out, he fatally miscalculated the reaction of his neighbors, the United States, and the other nations of the world.

Instead of paralysis, Saudi Arabia immediately gave the Kuwaiti government-in-exile its full support and consulted with the United States. Rather than be intimidated when Iraq moved its divisions to the Saudi border, in position to invade Saudi Arabia, Saudi Arabia sought outside military aid. Further, Saudi Arabia immediately obtained the support of other Gulf Cooperation Council states—Bahrain, Oman, Qatar, and the United Arab Emirates.

President George Bush of the United States also acted immediately to check Iraqi aggression. Consulting with France, Britain, and many of the same allies that had supported joint naval action in the Persian Gulf in 1987 and 1988, President Bush sent a delegation to Saudi Arabia that pledged the commitment of massive military forces to defend Saudi Arabia. At the same time, President Bush took immediate action to freeze Iraqi assets and to obtain UN support for a naval blockade of Iraq and an embargo on all Iraqi imports and exports other than medicine and food for humanitarian purposes. If Saddam Hussein counted on what he perceived to be weakness demonstrated by the U.S. withdrawal from Vietnam and Lebanon, he was proved totally mistaken. On 7 August, less than a week after the first Iraqi troops entered Kuwait, the United States announced it would send land, air, and naval forces to Saudi Arabia.

Most of the rest of the world proved equally decisive. Britain, France, the other members of the North Atlantic Treaty Organization (NATO), Japan, most Eastern European nations, and the Soviet Union immediately joined in condemning Iraq's actions. While the Soviet Union jockeyed for political position and made its own efforts to seek Iraqi withdrawal from Kuwait, it consistently supported the United States in the United Nations and never gave Iraq any support for its actions. Most of the remaining Arab world proved equally firm. On 3 August 1990, the Arab League Council voted to condemn Iraq and demand its withdrawal from Kuwait. Egypt and Syria strongly opposed Iraq and sent military forces to defend Saudi Arabia and liberate Kuwait. So did other Arab states including Algeria. Only Jordan, Libya, Mauritania, the PLO, the Sudan, and Yemen gave Iraq significant political support during any point of the crisis.

The shift toward cooperation between East and West had an equally important impact in allowing the United Nations to take unprecedented action against Iraq. On 2 August 1990, the Security Council voted 14 to 0 (Resolution 660) to demand Iraq's immediate and unconditional withdrawal from Kuwait. The Security Council then passed resolutions that ordered a financial and trade embargo against Iraq (6 August), declared Iraq's annexation of Kuwait null and void (9 August), demanded that Iraq free all the foreign hostages it had taken (18 August), established an international naval blockade (25 August), halted all air cargo shipments (25 September), declared Iraq liable for all war damages and economic costs (29 October), and authorized the nations allied with Kuwait "to use all necessary means" if Iraq did not withdraw from Kuwait by 15 January 1991 (29 November).

For the first time since the Korean War, the United Nations was allowed freedom of action in checking an aggressor. As a result, Iraq suffered a complete naval and economic blockade, could not export oil, and lost any access to arms imports. Its economic and military strength was severely undermined, and it was forced to deploy a steadily increasing portion of its best forces to defend the Saudi-Kuwaiti border and its border with Saudi Arabia. By the UN deadline, Iraq had sent 545,000 men and 12 armored (heavy) and 31 mechanized infantry (light) divisions to the Kuwaiti theater of operations.

Force Ratios at the Beginning of the Conflict

Time did not favor Iraq or Saddam Hussein. His military inaction during the months of diplomatic maneuvering—1 August to 15 January—gave the powers who opposed him time to build up a massive international force. The United States built its forces from a few tactical air squadrons, which it deployed to Saudi Arabia shortly after the Iraqi invasion, to a massive land-sea-air force of 527,000 men and women, including over 110 naval vessels, 2,000 tanks, 2,200 armored personnel carriers, 1,800 fixed-wing aircraft, and 1,700 helicopters.

The U.S. forces were the largest element of what became a 38-nation coalition that included major contributions by other nations. Saudi Arabia contributed 118,000 troops, 550 tanks, 179 aircraft, and over 400 sites for artillery bases. Equally important, it made its modern air bases and military infrastructure available to the other nations of the coalition. Britain contributed naval forces, 43,000 troops with 170 tanks, an armored division, and 72 combat aircraft. Egypt contributed 40,000 troops with 2 armored divisions and 250 tanks. France contributed 16,000 troops with tanks, helicopters, a light armored division, and combat aircraft. Syria contributed 20,000 troops and 2 divisions. Other allied nations, such as Canada and Italy, contributed air and naval forces, and Oman, Qatar, and the United Arab Emirates deployed a significant portion of their small forces.

The end result was the largest set of opposing forces since the Korean War, and the largest mix of modern armor and air units since World War II. While experts still argue over the exact numbers involved, U.S. reports after the war indicate that, in toto, the coalition had well in excess of 600,000 land troops to Iraq's 545,000; 3,360 tanks to 4,230; 3,633 artillery weapons to 3,110; 4,050 other armored vehicles to 2,870; 1,959 helicopters to 160; and some 2,700 aircraft to 770. Moreover, the coalition had a massive technological advantage in virtually every category of weaponry, munitions, communications, and command and control. It also had an effective monopoly over photo, signal, and electronic intelligence.

Air Phase of the War

The 1991 Gulf War began on 17 January 1991 when U.S.-led air units launched a devastating series of attacks on targets in Iraq. These targets included command and control facilities, communications systems, air bases, and land-based air defenses. The war began when AH-64 Apache attack helicopters knocked out Iraq's forward radar system. The United States then used F-117 stealth attack fighters, which flew 31 percent of the attacks during the first day and attacked even heavily defended targets such as downtown Baghdad with complete impunity. They also involved the first significant use of sea-launched cruise missiles and a wide range of precision-guided weapons.

As early as the third day of the war, the coalition air forces were able to shift their attacks from Iraq's main air defenses to such strategic targets as key headquarters, civil and army communications, electric power plants, and Iraq's plants and facilities for the production of biological, chemical, and nuclear warfare.

The coalition also took full advantage of its monopoly on long-range reconnaissance, photo and signal intelligence from satellites, electronic intelligence aircraft, refueling capability, air control and warning aircraft (AWACS), and sophisticated targeting aircraft like the JSTARS. This gave it further advantages in both air-to-air and air-to-ground combat.

The advantage in air-to-air combat became clear during the first days of the war. Iraq had 770 combat aircraft, 24 main operating bases, 30 dispersal bases, and a massive network of some 3,000 surface-to-air missiles when the coalition attacked. Coalition air forces, however, were so superior that Iraq was unable to win a single air-to-air engagement and lost a total of 35 aircraft in air-to-air combat. By the end of the first week of the air war, Iraq ceased to attempt active resistance in the air, and Iraqi aircraft began to flee to Iran in hopes that Iran would return the aircraft and pilots after the war. Iraq halted even token efforts to use its aircraft in combat after the fourteenth day of the air war, and Iraq's land-based air defenses then proved vulnerable to electronic warfare, infrared and other countermeasures, and antiradiation missiles throughout the rest of the war.

At the start of the second week of the air war, coalition air forces shifted their focus and began attacking the Iraqi field army in the Kuwaiti theater of operations. This phase of the air conflict lasted for the next 26 days. The coalition was able to use its AWACS and refueling capabilities, maintain extremely high sortie rates, and concentrate up to 600 aircraft in the air over a country as small as Kuwait. It then used a mix of highly sophisticated attack fighters like the F-15E and F-16 with the LANTIRN night targeting system to launch precision-guided weapons against Iraqi armor and artillery. Other lighter aircraft—the AV-8B, F-18A/B, A-10, and AH-64—also played a major role in striking Iraqi army targets in Kuwait.

These strikes were backed by bombers like the B-52 and F-111, using a mix of guided and unguided ordnance, and heavy attack fighters like the Tornado. These aircraft were able to keep Iraq's air bases suppressed and to conduct massive strikes on land targets. Typical bomber targets included Republican Guard concentrations, key supply and communications facilities in the rear and border area, dug-in artillery positions, and Iraq's defensive barriers and positions near the border area.

Almost from the outset of the war, Iraq realized it had no way to retaliate against the coalition's attacks except to launch its long-range modified Scud missile. Iraq began these missile strikes by attacking Israel and Saudi Arabia on the second day of the war and persisted in them until the cease-fire. Iraq launched a total of 40 Scud variants against Israel and 46 against Saudi Arabia, but these missiles never succeeded in doing major military damage. They also failed to provoke Israel into retaliating against Iraq, largely because the United States rushed Patriot defense missiles to both Israel and Saudi Arabia; the Patriot's ability to hit most incoming Scuds provided a vital boost in public confidence. Israeli restraint may have played a key role in ensuring that the Arab members of the coalition continued to support it throughout the war.

In retrospect, the only major impact of the Scuds was to force the coalition's air forces into a massive game of hide and seek in trying to kill Iraqi Scud units. Even here, however, the Scuds also imposed new costs on Iraq. While the attacks on the Iraqi Scuds diverted sorties from other targets, they increased the damage to Iraqi targets outside the Kuwaiti theater of operations. The only strategic damage Iraq was able to inflict on Kuwait and the coalition was to set fire to some 600 Kuwaiti oil wells. These fires, however, did nothing to affect allied air operations or slow the pace of the war.

By the time the ground war began at 0400 hours on 24 February 1991, Iraqi ground forces had been hit by more than 40,000 attack sorties. While the resulting damage estimates are controversial, coalition airpower claimed to have destroyed or severely damaged: all of Iraq's nuclear reactor facilities, eleven chemical and biological weapons storage facilities and three production facilities, 60 percent of Iraq's major command centers, 70 percent of its military communications, 125 ammunition storage revetments, 48 Iraqi naval vessels, and 75 percent of Iraq's electric power–generating capability. Logistic supply to the theater had been cut by up to 90 percent, and the U.S. command estimated that at least 1,300 Iraqi tanks, 800 other armored vehicles, and 1,100 artillery pieces had been destroyed from the air.

These air attacks continued throughout the air-land phase of the war that followed. By the cease-fire of 28 February, coalition air forces had dropped a total of 88,500 tons of ordnance, of which 6,520 tons were precision-guided weapons. A total of 216 Iraqi aircraft had been destroyed, along with nearly 600 aircraft shelters. Coalition air forces had also destroyed 54 bridges or made them inoperable—playing a major role in cutting off Iraqi land forces from their final route of escape along the Tigris north of Basra during the last days of the war.

Air-Land Phase of the Battle

Once the ground phase of the war began, it proved to be extraordinarily quick and decisive. The coalition not only attacked a gravely weakened Iraqi army and had a massive advantage in intelligence and virtually every area of tactical technology, it had vastly superior tactics. The coalition forces used the "air-land battle" concept, which the United States had developed to meet the Warsaw Pact's most modern forces in Europe, against an Iraqi force that was equipped with modern weapons but had trained and organized to fight a relatively static trench war against an Iran that lacked significant airpower.

While coalition land forces did not enjoy a significant superiority in weapons strength and manpower over Iraq, they did consist largely of highly motivated professionals. In contrast, the majority of Iraqi forces were poorly trained conscripts who seemed to have poor morale and little motivation. It is impossible to determine how much of this weakness stemmed from having to invade an Arab "brother," poor leadership and organization, or the coalition's air attacks. All three combined to undermine Iraqi military capabilities.

Iraq's one "success" in the land war occurred long before coalition land forces began to liberate Kuwait. Several Iraqi brigades made a brief incursion into the Saudi border town of Khafji on 29 January. But the town had been evacuated, and the Iraqi forces were driven back the next day by Saudi, Qatari, and U.S. Marine forces. The net result was that Iraq did more to reveal its weaknesses than advance its own cause.

The attack on Khafji also did nothing to keep coalition land forces from making a massive shift from positions along the coast and to the south of Kuwait, to areas near the Iraqi-Saudi border to the west of Kuwait. These shifts later allowed coalition land forces to drive deep into Iraq and Kuwait.

The shifts of land forces began on 17 January, the same day the air phase of the war began. They involved massive logistic and movement difficulties, but they eventually positioned the U.S. Marine Expeditionary Force and Saudi, Syrian, and Egyptian forces where they could drive north from the center of Kuwait's southern border toward Kuwait City. At the same time, French and U.S. forces in VII Corps moved far to the west, where they could launch an attack to cut off southern Iraq from Baghdad and then drive around Kuwait to move against Basra from the west. British and U.S. Army forces in XVIII Corps moved to areas on the Saudi-Iraqi border just west of Kuwait.

In a move he later called his "Hail Mary play," the allied commander, Gen. H. Norman Schwarzkopf, was able to position two full armored corps along the Iraqi border to the west of Kuwait without the Iraqis detecting these movements. He was able to keep them undetected through the use of special forces and extensive frontline patrols, and because coalition airpower denied Iraq any air reconnaissance capability, even near its own border.

This element of surprise played a key role when the air-land battle began on 24 February 1991 (Fig. 1). Two major simultaneous attacks quickly crossed Iraqi defensive positions. The first consisted of Pan-Arab (Saudi, Kuwaiti, Qatari, and Omani) forces and U.S. Marine forces attacking on a broad front from the northern "notch" in the Saudi-Kuwaiti border to the coast and penetrating the Iraqi defenses along the southern Kuwait border. These forces advanced as far as half the distance to Kuwait City within twelve hours. This attack was aided by the fact that many of Iraq's forces were kept pinned down by a U.S. deception operation that convinced Iraqi commanders that U.S. Marine amphibious forces might strike at any point along the coast.

The second attack occurred at the far western edge of coalition positions along the Iraqi-Saudi border. The French 6th Light Armored Division and one brigade of the 82d Airborne Division drove 90 miles north to seize an airfield at Al-Salman. The U.S. 101st Airborne Division then launched the largest air assault operation in military history, and U.S. heliborne forces moved first to a forward logistic base in Iraq and then to positions near Samawah on the Eu-

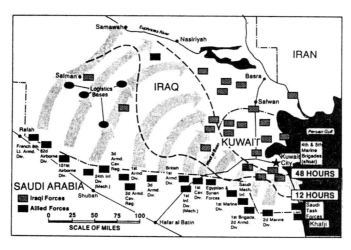

Figure 1. The first two days of the air-land battle, 24–25 February, 1991 Gulf War. (SOURCE: AUSA 1991)

phrates. This attack cut Iraqi forces off from the main routes from Basra to Baghdad that run south of the Euphrates.

The coalition attacked along a third major line that same afternoon. The 3d Armored and 24th divisions of XVIII Corps drove across the Iraqi border and toward the Wadi al-Batin and the western approaches to Kuwait City. Immediately to the east, U.S. and British land forces also advanced into Iraq. The 1st U.S. Division forced a breach in the Iraqi defenses that was rapidly exploited by the 1st British Armored Division and the 2d Cavalry Regiment and 1st and 3d Armored divisions of the U.S. Army. This advance rapidly turned into a deep thrust against the Republican Guard forces west of Kuwait City, north of Kuwait, and west of Basra. Finally, Egyptian and Saudi forces, backed by Syrian fire support, launched a fourth attack on Iraqi positions to the east of the gorge of Al-Batin on the 25th.

These attacks, and the relentless air attacks that had preceded them, quickly shattered the remaining organization, morale, and war-fighting capability of most of the Iraqi army, while the Republican Guards remained pinned down outside Kuwait. As a result, coalition forces were able to drive up through Kuwait to strike positions south and west of Kuwait City, while VII and XVIII corps forces moved deep into Iraq, to positions south of a line drawn from the border to Nasiryah.

On 26 February, forces of VII and XVIII Corps closed on the Iraqi Republican Guard forces and reserves defending Basra in the longest sustained armored advance in history (Fig. 2). They destroyed the key Republican Guard divisions holding the area just north of the Kuwaiti border. Other coalition forces, including the 1st and 2d Marine Divisions, reached positions on the edge of Kuwait City and began fighting for control of the international airport. These advances took place despite extraordinarily bad weather, which created substantial amounts of mud and interfered with air cover.

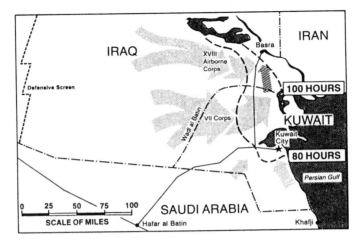

Figure 2. The final push of the 1991 Gulf War, 26–27 February.
(SOURCE: AUSA 1991)

The war ended with a devastating series of engagements where Iraqi forces were able to put up only limited resistance. The thermal sights and superior fire-control systems of coalition tanks allowed them to achieve massive kills against Iraqi armor, backed by lethal systems like the AH-64 attack helicopter and the Multiple Launch Rocket System. The coalition's vastly superior intelligence and night vision devices, combined with the use of new navigation aids that provided precise location data from global positioning satellites, gave its land forces control of both the desert and the night.

From 27 February to President Bush's order to halt operations on 28 February, the remainder of Iraq's 43 divisions in the theater were destroyed or rendered ineffective. The VII Corps shattered the remainder of the armored (heavy) Republican Guard divisions; the XVIII corps moved close to Basra. British and U.S. Army forces liberated northern Kuwait. Saudi and other Arab forces liberated Kuwait City, and U.S. Marine forces secured the southern and western outskirts of Kuwait City.

The scale of the coalition's success in fighting a 1,000-hour air battle and the 100-hour air-land battle that followed is indicated by the fact that coalition land forces succeeded in reaching every major objective ahead of schedule and with far fewer casualties than their commanders dared to hope for. They achieved a rate of advance so fast that many units did not bother to halt at their intermediate objectives.

The scale of the coalition's success is also indicated by U.S. estimates that coalition forces had destroyed nearly 4,000 Iraqi tanks, more than 1,000 other armored vehicles, and nearly 3,000 artillery weapons. In contrast, the coalition suffered combat losses of four tanks, nine other armored vehicles, and one artillery weapon. Although coalition aircraft flew a total of 109,876 sorties by the end of the war, the coalition lost only 38 aircraft—the lowest loss rate of any air combat in history and less than the normal accident rate per sortie in combat training. The difference in manpower losses is even more astounding, although no precise estimates are possible. U.S. intelligence issued rough estimates after the war that 100,000 Iraqi soldiers died in combat. Allied killed—less casualties to friendly fire—totaled less than 200.

Political and Military Consequences of the Conflict

It will be years before all the lessons of the 1991 Gulf War are fully analyzed and its strategic political consequences are clear. It is, however, already apparent that the coalition victory had a number of complex impacts.

The war substantially shattered Iraq's military organization. While substantial Iraqi forces still remain, largely composed of units never deployed to the Kuwaiti theater of operations, these are incapable of offensive action against neighbors like Iran, Turkey, and Syria, or against Kuwait and Saudi Arabia as long as they have American backing. Iraq has little chance of intimidating the conservative southern Gulf states, and a new and far more stable balance of power has been established within the region.

Elsewhere in the Middle East, the war had more ambiguous effects. It critically weakened a military threat to Israel, but it has also demonstrated Israel's vulnerability to missile attacks and its potential vulnerability to weapons of mass destruction. It has further shattered the myth of Arab unity without bringing any new concept of regional order in its place. It created new opportunities for an Arab-Israel peace initiative, but Palestinian and Jordanian alignment with Iraq also made some aspects of such negotiations more difficult.

The war ended with the United States emerging as the leader of a 38-nation coalition and as a pre-eminent military power that took only 43 days to inflict one of the most decisive military defeats in military history. Nearly two decades after the U.S. withdrawal from Vietnam, and almost a decade after U.S. withdrawal from Lebanon, the reputation of U.S. military forces has been decisively restored. The United States demonstrated a combination of strategy, tactics, readiness, training, weaponry, and manpower quality that clearly had no equal. At the same time, it showed that the United States was heavily dependent on time to deploy its powers and access to the ports, air bases, and facilities of nations in the forward area. Further, it showed that American military freedom of action was heavily dependent on an international consensus and allied military support.

The implications for the future of East-West relations were equally complex. The coalition victory came at a time when the Soviet Union was already in a deep political and economic crisis and drifting toward dissolution. The Warsaw Pact ceased to exist a few months after the cease-fire, and the Soviet Union transformed itself into the Union of Sovereign States only a year after Iraq first invaded Kuwait. The bipolar world that existed from 1945 to 1990 had begun to vanish without creating any clear movement toward the "new world order" that President Bush had mentioned in some of his speeches before the war.

Like most victories, the war also produced new issues and uncertainties. There is no doubt that the coalition scored a major victory in grand strategic terms. It liberated Kuwait, it destroyed Iraq's ability to invade or use military pressure against its neighbors, it destroyed most of Iraq's capability to build and use weapons of mass destruction, and it forced Iraq to agree to cease-fire terms that promised to steadily weaken its military capabilities for years to come.

The importance of superior technology was evident. Advanced weapon systems provided the coalition forces with a clear-cut advantage over Iraq, a nation which itself was equipped with some very modern Western systems. The war, which received unprecedented television coverage, marked the dawn of a new technological era. Precision-guided munitions (PGM) proved immensely effective. Cruise missiles, antiballistic missile defenses, advanced reconnaissance systems, F-117 stealth aircraft, and Apache helicopters were all used successfully for the first time in major combat.

Land and naval forces played key roles in the U.S.-led coalition's strategic plan. Airpower, however, provided the decisive element. For 38 days, allied aircraft methodically attacked Iraq's offensive machine, leaving a shattered, demoralized, and disorganized army to be mopped up in 100 hours by coalition ground forces. Factors contributing to the successful application of airpower against Iraq included:

- Highly accurate navigation and weapon delivery systems that could deliver PGMs to within one meter (3 ft.) of their target.
- Stealth technology, which returned the element of surprise to air warfare.
- Night attack systems to maintain pressure around the clock.
- Surveillance and intelligence-gathering systems, space systems, and tactical reconnaissance aircraft that provided coalition commanders with theater-wide situational awareness.

The importance of technology and airpower should not be overstated, however. The extent to which the early collapse of Iraq's air defense system was due to allied technology as opposed to human factors remains unanswered. And it should be noted that the war was conducted in terrain that has historically favored air operations. But the bottom line is that high-technology weapon system dramatically increased the effectiveness of coalition forces.

The war did not, however, destroy Saddam Hussein's control over Iraq. It left the rivalry between Iraq and Iran intact and caused new tensions between the southern Gulf states and Yemen and the Sudan. It did not bring more liberal or democratic regimes to any state in the region. The Arab portions of the coalition that defeated Iraq did not hold together, and no new security structure arose in its place. Enforcing the terms of the cease-fire rapidly became a major challenge, and Iraq constantly attempted to cheat on its terms in every area—from recognition of Kuwait's sovereignty to preventing the destruction of its weapons of mass destruction. Rather than marking the end of history, the legacy of the 1991 Gulf War was one of creating further sources of instability in a radical period of change.

© ANTHONY H. CORDESMAN

Bibliography

Association of the U.S. Army (AUSA). 1991. *Special report: The U.S. Army in Operation Desert Storm: An overview.* Arlington, Va.: AUSA Institute of Land Warfare.
Blackwell, J. 1991. *Thunder in the desert.* New York: Bantam Books.

Friedman, N. 1991. *Desert victory: The war for Kuwait*. Annapolis, Md.: U.S. Naval Institute Press.
U.S. Department of Defense. 1992. *Conduct of the war report*. 15 February.
Woodward, B. 1991. *The commanders*. New York: Simon and Schuster.

GUSTAVUS ADOLPHUS (Gustavus II) [1594–1632]

Gustavus Adolphus (Fig. 1), called the "Father of Modern Warfare" by military historians, was known as the "Lion of the North" during his time. A skilled statesman and conscientious ruler, he is most famous as an innovative early modern military leader.

Early Years: Scandinavian and Baltic Campaigns

Gustavus was born in Stockholm on 9 December 1594. His grandfather, Gustavus I (1496–1560), was the first of the Swedish royal house of Vasa. While still a teenager Gustavus Adolphus successfully led Swedish troops against Danish invaders. In 1611, at the age of 17, he succeeded his father, Charles IX, as Gustavus II Adolphus.

With the crown he inherited three persistent conflicts with Denmark, Poland, and Russia. He quickly took the field, and with skillful tactical command and careful strategic judgments, he was able to obtain reasonable treaties with Denmark (Treaty of Knäred in 1613) and Russia (Treaty of Stolbovo in 1617). He then focused on a more serious challenge—King Sigismund III of Poland. The Polish king, who claimed the Swedish throne, withstood several military defeats and agreed only to a series of truces. Initially, Gustavus needed the truces to begin the reforms in the Swedish army for which he became famous. However, his continued war with Poland was handicapped by his increasing interest in the Thirty Years' War in Germany, and by the very effective command of Polish forces under Stanislaw Koniecpolski.

Satisfied that he had effectively established Sweden as a power among the Scandinavian and Baltic states, and had secured sufficient security for his homeland, Gustavus agreed to a six-year truce with Poland, signed at Altmark on 26 September 1627. He then prepared to go to war against the Emperor Ferdinand of Hapsburg, whose forces had largely defeated the armies of the Protestant states of northern Germany. Gustavus's brilliant achievements in the Swedish phase of the ongoing Thirty Years' War are best appreciated by understanding his reforms of the Swedish army.

Formation of the Modern Army in the Age of Gunpowder

Gustavus Adolphus's legacy to military art was far more significant than his conquests, which were too extensive for Sweden to hold. As a monarch, he inherited his command, but he had to develop his military force. The warrior-

Figure 1. Gustavus Adolphus. (SOURCE: U.S. Library of Congress)

king had a unique advantage; he played the part of both combat commander and logistic administrator. Gustavus's interest and authority spanned the spectrum of military organization and employment. He could introduce innovations with the full knowledge and control of their implementation—rarely the case in military history.

Seventeenth-century military institutions were struggling to adapt to the use of gunpowder. In addition, it was essential for a small nation with limited resources, like Sweden, to be efficient in warfare. Military reform was given high priority by Gustavus, who saw both his country and religion threatened by larger powers. Gustavus was an avid student of military history. He understood the essence of mobility plus force, and he sought to establish these elements in each of the arms on the battlefield.

Gustavus built upon the concepts of the great Dutch general, Maurice of Nassau. What made Gustavus's contribution unique was his vision. He did not just improve muskets and cannon, he also addressed the structure of field formations and logistics. One of his most effective reforms was to emphasize the use of cavalry as a shock weapon.

Gustavus restructured the infantry formations to enhance the firepower of the muskets. He reduced the battle formations to six lines in various postures (standing, stooping, and kneeling) while delivering their fire. He redesigned artillery pieces both to limit the logistics of supporting varied calibers and to enhance the mobility of some of the field pieces. He developed battlefield artillery as far as the manufacturing techniques of his time allowed, and directed the manufacture of light guns (some made of metal-reinforced leather and wood) to allow rapid horse-drawn or manhandled movement. He had shot and powder packaged in cartridges for both artillery and infantry.

He did not focus on weapons alone, but emphasized training, discipline, and professionalism—such as making his artillerymen military personnel, rather than civilian specialists. He trained his army to emphasize coordinated employment of infantry, cavalry, and artillery on the field. His reforms stretched into logistics and troop discipline.

Although Gustavus's reforms sustained the Swedish army for some time following his death, they fell short of a self-perpetuating institution. In the long run, the inheritors of Gustavus's military ideas were other great leaders, in other nations. Bernhard of Saxe-Weimar, who took command of the Swedish army at the battle of Lützen after the king fell, introduced Gustavus's ideas into the French army and, in particular, to the great French general, Turenne. Gustavus's cavalry shock tactics were adopted in France by Turenne, implemented in England by Cromwell, and later fully exploited by the Duke of Marlborough. Gustavus's use of artillery in an effective mobile balance with other arms was never fully achieved until Napoleon, who benefited from newer casting technology and the reforms of Gribeauval.

Campaigns in the Thirty Years' War

In the early phases of the war the military successes of the Imperial (i.e., Holy Roman Empire) forces in Germany posed a threat to Swedish power in the Baltic Sea. Gustavus also saw a threat to the Protestant cause, but religion was not the primary motive behind most of the actions at this time. In fact, the French, under royal minister Cardinal Richelieu, subsidized a considerable part of the Protestant king's campaigns against the Catholic Hapsburgs.

Delegating much of the duties as regent of the Swedish Kingdom to his chancellor, Count Axel Oxenstierna, Gustavus led his army of 16,000 to northern Germany in June 1630. Gustavus was fortunate in that soon after his arrival, one of the ablest commanders of the Imperial forces, Albrecht von Wallenstein, was dismissed. Thus, Gustavus did not have to confront him during the critical early phase of his campaign. In a short time, Gustavus drove the Imperial forces out of Pomerania and marched south.

On 3 April 1631 his army stormed Frankfurt-on-Oder, but was unable to prevent the sack of Magdeburg by the Imperialists on 20 May. Though his army was weakened by a lack of supplies, Gustavus defeated the Imperial army under Count Tilly near Werben in late July. When the Imperialist army started to lay waste to Saxony, Gustavus secured support from Brandenburg and Saxony, and on 17 September 1631, again confronted the Imperial forces under Count Tilly, at Breitenfeld, near Leipzig.

The Battle of Breitenfeld was the first test of Gustavus's new army against the deeper, less maneuverable formations of the Imperialists. Gustavus defeated the initial attack of the Imperial army on his right and then directed his forces to deal with the collapse of his Saxon allies on his left wing. He led a cavalry attack that captured a large portion of the Imperial artillery. The Imperial army's inflexible formations collapsed under the intense Swedish artillery bombardment and massed cavalry charges. Tilly, who had been wounded, withdrew his army, which had suffered heavy losses (approximately 11,000). The Saxons and Swedes lost only about 4,500 men.

Gustavus then undertook a campaign to consolidate his position in northern Germany. He seized the strategically important town of Mainz on 22 December 1631, and in the following year marched south toward Vienna. Tilly had formed another army and attempted to prevent the Swedish army from crossing the Lech River. In the ensuing Battle of the Lech (15–16 April 1632), Gustavus won a decisive victory and Tilly was killed.

The emperor, recognizing the severity of the threat, recalled Wallenstein to succeed Tilly in command of the Imperial forces. While Wallenstein lacked the finely honed army that Gustavus possessed, he was a clever strategist and highly capable tactician. Wallenstein quickly formed an army and moved to prevent Gustavus from joining up with the Saxons. For weeks the two armies maneuvered around Nüremburg.

Finally the two armies met in the Battle of the Alte Veste. Neither commander allowed himself to be lured into an engagement that the other attempted to develop. Gustavus realized that his supply line was too vulnerable to maintain such a southern position and made a series of futile attacks against Wallenstein's well-defended position on 31 August–4 September 1632. Failing in this, Gustavus disengaged and moved north.

Wallenstein followed Gustavus to Saxony. There, on 16 November 1632, the two commanders engaged in the bitterly fought Battle of Lützen. It was here that Gustavus's recklessness led him into the enemy's formation during a cavalry melee and he was killed. The Swedish army rallied to gain this last victory for their fallen leader, and rushed forward in mass to overpower the Imperial army.

Gustavus Adolphus was a popular leader, and imparted a structure and reputation to the Swedish army for some time after his death. His excellent leadership qualities included the selection and training of highly capable subordinate commanders. While these commanders ensured excellent terms for Sweden in the Treaties of Westphalia, which ended the Thirty Years' War, they were not monarchs nor did they have the genius of Gustavus.

Significance

The integrated, combined arms employment of forces was the most advanced of Gustavus Adolphus's concepts. He showed his grasp of the integrated effect of combined arms as it is understood today. Further, he demonstrated fully the traditional concepts of streamlined organizational structure for effective command and control, and appreciated the value of rapid, aggressive action. The significant thrust of many of his innovations was to give firearms more potential in the offense.

His personal leadership qualities were exemplary, both as a monarch and as a field commander. He elicited the highest morale from his troops and love from his subjects.

ALBERT D. McJOYNT

SEE ALSO: History, Early Modern Military; Thirty Years' War.

Bibliography

Ahnlund, N. 1983. *Gustavus Adolphus*. Trans. M. Roberts. Westport, Conn.: Greenwood Press.
Dodge, T. A. 1895. *Gustavus Adolphus*. 2 vols. Boston: Houghton Mifflin.
Dupuy, T. N. 1969. *The military life of Gustavus Adolphus, father of modern war*. New York: Franklin Watts.

H

HALSEY, WILLIAM F. ("Bull")
[1882–1959]

Adm. William Frederick Halsey, Jr., U.S. Navy, nicknamed "Bull" Halsey by the press, was a major U.S. naval leader in the Pacific theater during World War II (Fig. 1). He directed the Guadalcanal, Solomon Islands, and Philippine Islands campaigns, and the controversial battle of Leyte Gulf. A great proponent of sea-based airpower, he had a positive effect on the scope and operational development of carrier airpower in World War II.

Early Life and Career

Halsey was born on 30 October 1882 in Elizabeth, New Jersey. He came from a naval tradition, as his father had graduated from the U.S. Naval Academy in 1873 and retired from the navy as a captain. Graduating from the Naval Academy in 1904, Halsey served on the battleship *Kansas* as that ship steamed around the world as part of President Theodore Roosevelt's Great White Fleet.

As a navy commander during World War I, Halsey commanded first the destroyer *Benham* and then the *Shaw*. He was awarded the Navy Cross for his wartime service. Following the war his various assignments included duty at the Naval War College in Newport, Rhode Island, and the Army War College in Washington, D.C. His attention then turned to naval aviation; he qualified as a naval aviator in 1935 at the age of 53. He subsequently commanded the carrier *Saratoga* and then the Pensacola Naval Air Station. In the spring of 1940, Admiral Halsey was designated Commander Aircraft Battle Force, commanding all the carriers of the Pacific Fleet.

World War II

On 7 December 1941, Halsey's force, consisting of the carrier *Enterprise*, three cruisers, and nine destroyers, was 240 kilometers (150 mi.) west of Oahu when the Japanese attacked Pearl Harbor. Refueling at Pearl Harbor, Halsey's force sortied on 9 December in search of enemy submarines. In January 1942, Admiral Nimitz ordered a carrier force under Halsey's command to attack Japanese bases in the Gilbert and Marshall islands, and on Wake Island and Marcus

Figure 1. Admiral William F. Halsey. (SOURCE: U.S. Library of Congress)

Island. In April Halsey's title was changed to Commander Carriers Pacific, and he delivered Lt. Col. James Doolittle's B-25 bombers to their launch point in the Pacific Ocean, from which they sortied to bomb Tokyo on 18 April.

Halsey fell ill and was unable to participate in the Battle of Midway in June 1942. He returned to duty in October and became commander of the South Pacific Force and Area. He directed his forces in victories off the Santa Cruz Islands and Guadalcanal in October and November.

After the Japanese evacuated Guadalcanal on 9 February 1943, Halsey planned and directed an offensive up the Solomon Islands that lasted throughout 1943 and into 1944. His strategy was to bypass the Japanese strongpoints, including Rabaul, sealing them off with airpower and leaving their garrisons stranded. U.S. forces then constructed new air and naval bases in less strongly defended locations several hundred miles closer to Japan. In November 1943, carrier-based aircraft pounded Rabaul while aircraft from Bougainville continued to destroy enemy air forces. By 25 March 1944, Rabaul was neutralized and the war in the South Pacific had ended.

BATTLE OF LEYTE GULF

Halsey was made Commander Third Fleet in June 1944; in August he directed carrier support for the Philippines campaign, the timetable of which he had moved up after his probing perceived weak enemy defenses. In reaction to the

American landing on Leyte Island on 20 October, the Japanese committed their entire fleet against American forces. This fleet was divided into three forces: the southern, central, and northern. The southern force, consisting of battleships and cruisers, was to pass through Surigao Strait and rendezvous with the powerful central force that was to move through San Bernadino Strait and come around Samar from the north. The northern force, built around four carriers, was to lure Halsey's carrier force northward, away from Leyte Gulf. As combat began, forces under Adm. Thomas Kincaid engaged the southern force, sinking several ships and sending the remainder fleeing. Halsey's aircraft had engaged the central force and he overestimated the damage his planes had incurred. When the northern force was discovered moving southward, Halsey moved his forces northward to engage them, thereby leaving San Bernadino Strait unguarded. While Halsey's forces engaged and sank all four Japanese carriers in the battle off Cape Engano, the powerful Japanese central force left San Bernadino Strait unopposed and approached the northern entrance to Leyte Gulf undetected. It then attacked Kincaid's escort carrier forces off Samar Island and the ensuing action was among the bloodiest and most gallant in U.S. naval history. Since the Japanese lacked airpower, the Americans were able to defeat their fleet, which had more than ten times the U.S. naval firepower. The Japanese fleet was damaged so severely in the battle that it could no longer mount an offensive, but in the battle's aftermath Halsey was strongly criticized for leaving the beachhead undefended and open to enemy attack.

In the final months of the war, Halsey's forces launched strikes on Japanese installations on other Philippine islands, Formosa, Okinawa, and the Chinese coast. Following the bombing of Hiroshima and Nagasaki, Japan surrendered unconditionally on 14 August 1945. The official surrender took place on 2 September on board Halsey's flagship, *Missouri*, anchored in Tokyo Bay.

Halsey was promoted to fleet admiral in December 1945, retired from the Navy in 1947, and died 16 August 1959 on Fishers Island, New York.

Halsey's Significance

Halsey was an aggressive risk-taker who welcomed hazardous situations. He was an early supporter of airpower, and stressed its flexibility, importance, and effectiveness. He had great confidence in his carrier-based forces and the effect that they could have in war. He believed that such airpower could establish command of the air at a required place and time and thereby establish the conditions necessary for successful amphibious operations.

Halsey spent his final years defending his decision at Leyte Gulf, and that battle has been replayed continually in U.S. war games and strategy sessions. The correctness of his decision is still disputed, reflected in the fact that the navy has not named a class of ships after him, while a class of destroyers was named after Admiral Spruance, who participated in the Battle of Midway. His supporters point out that he had a talent for selecting the brightest and most capable officers to be on his staff, for rarely going against his staff's recommendations, and for defending his staff when it was criticized. He was extremely popular with the press and the navy's rank and file, and has gone down in history as one of America's most colorful admirals.

BRUCE W. WATSON

SEE ALSO: Naval Warfare; World War II.

Bibliography

Halsey, W. F., and J. Bryan, III. 1976. *Admiral Halsey's story.* New York: Da Capo Press.
Keating, L. A. 1965. *Fleet admiral: The story of William F. Halsey.* Philadelphia: Westminster Press.
Merrill, J. M. 1976. *A sailor's admiral: A biography of William F. Halsey.* New York: Crowell.
Potter, E. B. 1985. *Bull Halsey.* Annapolis, Md.: U.S. Naval Institute Press.
Reynolds, C. G. 1978. *Famous American admirals.* New York: Van Nostrand Reinhold.
Spiller, R. J. 1989. *American military leaders.* New York: Praeger.

HANNIBAL BARCA [247–183 B.C.]

Hannibal Barca, commonly referred to as Hannibal, was a Carthaginian general renowned for his daring attack on Rome using an indirect approach across the Alps during the Second Punic War (218–202 B.C.). Also known as the "Father of Strategy," Hannibal successfully commanded Carthaginian armies in the Siege of Saguntum (219), at the River Ticinus (Ticino) (218), and at the Trebbia in 218. He won another victory at Lake Trasimene in 217 and destroyed eight Roman legions at Cannae in 216. Hannibal campaigned vigorously against the Romans in southern Italy, but although he won many battles, he was unable to force Rome to sue for peace. Scipio Africanus's invasion of Africa in 204 forced Hannibal's recall to defend Carthage, but he was defeated by Scipio at Zama in 202 and was forced into exile. Greatly feared by his Roman enemies, all that is known about him is derived from Roman accounts.

Early Career

Hannibal was born in 247 B.C., the son of Hamilcar Barca, a member of a distinguished Carthaginian noble family. Hamilcar had, following Carthage's defeat in the First Punic War (264–241 B.C.), directed Carthaginian expansion in Spain. Hamilcar took his son and his son-in-law, Hasdrubal, to Spain with him in 237. Popular legend has it that Hannibal swore an oath before he left for Spain never to be a friend of Rome. Over the next nine years he was almost constantly at his father's side, gaining a thorough education in war. Hamilcar was drowned while on a campaign in 228, and Hannibal returned to Carthage to complete his education while command of the army in Spain fell to Hasdrubal.

Hannibal the General

Hannibal returned to Spain in 224 and took command of the cavalry in Hasdrubal's army. Hasdrubal was assassinated in 221, just after he had concluded a treaty with Rome that set the Ebro River as the boundary between Roman and Carthaginian Spain. Hannibal was chosen to succeed his brother-in-law as commander in Spain, and over the next two years he led two effective campaigns to subdue the northwest part of the country between early 221 and autumn 220. He won the respect and loyalty of his soldiers; Roman chroniclers noted that "he never required others to do what he could not and would not do himself."

In spring 219, Hannibal moved his army against the port of Saguntum. Although this city lay south of the Ebro, Roman envoys warned him that any attack upon it would lead to war. Hannibal prosecuted the siege with his accustomed vigor, and Saguntum fell in late autumn that year after an eight-month siege. The following spring, Rome declared war on Carthage, and Hannibal marched northward. He led about 60,000 troops, including some 80 elephants, across the Ebro and into Gaul in July 218. Continuing toward Italy, Hannibal eluded the army of P. Cornelius Scipio near Massilia and headed up the Rhone Valley, making an epic crossing of the Alps in September and October. Hannibal soon acquired allies among the Gallic tribes of northern Italy and defeated a force of Roman cavalry and light troops at the River Ticinus (Ticino) in November. The following month, he defeated the main Roman army of T. Sempronius Longus at the River Trebbia.

Early the following spring, Hannibal moved his army (now numbering about 40,000) south and evaded the army of G. Flaminius near Pisea in March 217 before turning and destroying Flaminius's army in an ambush at Lake Trasimene in April. Hannibal led his army south, passing west of Rome, hoping to find allies among the Greek subject cities of southern Italy. The Romans, frustrated at their inability to defeat the nimble army of Hannibal, raised a force of sixteen legions (four consular armies totaling about 80,000 men) and placed it under the command of both consuls, G. Terentius Varro and L. Aemilius Paulus. Hannibal met this formidable army at Cannae on 2 August 216 and, employing his superiority in cavalry, encircled the Roman center and nearly annihilated it, inflicting some 55,000 casualties.

Despite this great victory, strategic success eluded Hannibal, as Rome refused to make peace and continued to field new armies. Even the success at Cannae failed to induce Rome's allies to desert it in any numbers. Hannibal continued to campaign vigorously in southern Italy. Although his first attack on Rome was repulsed by M. Claudius Marcellus at Nola (215), he had more success at Capua, the Silarus River, and Herdonia in 212. A second attempt on Rome in 211 also failed, but Hannibal blunted a Roman offensive against his bases, winning battles at Second Herdonia and Numistro in 210. Hannibal's position in Italy was severely damaged by the loss of his valuable base at Tarentum to Q. Fabius Maximus in 208, but he still retained the edge in the field.

Rome Ascendant

The following year (207), Hannibal's younger brother, Hasdrubal, led a reinforcing army from Spain to Italy, following in Hannibal's footsteps. Unfortunately for Hasdrubal, his messengers to Hannibal were captured by the Romans. Thus forewarned, Consul G. Claudius Nero left a force to cover Hannibal's army and hastened north. At the River Metaurus in summer 207, Hasdrubal's army was destroyed and he was killed by the forces of Nero and M. Livius Salinator. Hannibal heard of the disaster only when his brother's head was hurled into his camp.

Although he realized that his cause was nearly hopeless, he withdrew to Bruttium and continued the struggle. In 204, P. Cornelius Scipio (the son of the general mentioned above), capitalizing on a series of successes in Spain, invaded Africa. Although he was forced to lift the siege of Utica soon after, he won notable success in a series of battles with Hasdrubal Gisco and Syphax in early 203. Scipio won a great victory at Bagbrades in early autumn 203 and captured Syphax. The desperate Carthaginian Senate recalled Hannibal and his brother Mago (leading a small army in Liguria) to Africa to defend Carthage. Hannibal led a new army, some 48,000 strong, built around his veterans from Italy, into the field in early 202. He met Scipio's army on the plain of Zama in early March. Despite some initial success, and the stout resistance of his Italian veterans, Hannibal's army was overwhelmed and defeated when the Numidian cavalry of Massanissa, having defeated Hannibal's own cavalry, fell on the Carthaginian rear. For this success, Scipio gained the honorific "Africanus."

After Zama

As the leading Carthaginian general, Hannibal played a major role in convincing his more bellicose countrymen that peace was preferable to the destruction of Carthage. Elected Suffete (a post similar to consul) in 196, his moderate politics had aroused distrust and suspicion in both Carthage and Rome, and he was exiled at Roman insistence. He took shelter at the court of King Antiochus III the Great of Syria and raised a naval squadron for him from the cities of Phoenicia. He attacked Rhodes but was defeated at Eurymedon, off Side, by Eudamus of Rhodes and L. Aemilius Regilus in 190.

Following Antiochus's defeat by Rome in 188, Hannibal fled first to Crete and then took shelter in Bithynia. There, to avoid capture by the Romans, he took poison in 183. As he lay dying, he is alleged to have said, "Let us release the Romans from their long anxiety, since they think it too long to wait for the death of an old man."

Evaluation

Hannibal was certainly the ablest general Carthage ever produced. He was resolute in adversity, eager to seize opportunities when they arose, but cautious when he needed to be. He was a supremely gifted strategist, and as a tactician he was able to coax remarkable performances from his disparate forces.

The information about Hannibal is drawn entirely from the Romans, who in general both feared and hated him.

LEE A. SWEETAPPLE

SEE ALSO: History, Ancient Military; Punic Wars; Roman Empire; Scipio Africanus.

Bibliography

De Beer, G. R. 1969. *Hannibal: Challenging Rome's supremacy.* New York: Viking.
Dodge, T. A. 1891. *Hannibal.* Boston: Houghton Mifflin.
Dupuy, T. N. 1969. *The military life of Hannibal.* New York: Franklin Watts.
Livy (Titus Livius). 1965. *The war with Hannibal.* Trans. A. de Selincourt, ed. B. Radine. Baltimore, Md.: Johns Hopkins Univ. Press.
Polybius. 1922–27. *Histories.* 6 vols. Trans. W. R. Paton. Cambridge, Mass.: Harvard Univ. Press.
Proctor, D. 1971. *Hannibal's march in history.* Oxford: Basil Blackwell.

HINDENBURG, PAUL VON
[1847–1934]

Paul von Hindenburg was a German field marshal during World War I and president of Germany during the Weimar Republic (Fig. 1). Exhibiting strength of character and a strong sense of duty, he was the most popular figure in Germany during the First World War and in the 1920s. Controversy surrounds his dependence upon more brilliant subordinates during the war and his selection of Adolf Hitler as German chancellor in 1933.

Life Prior to the First World War

Born in Posen, Prussia, on 2 October 1847 with the full name of Paul Ludwig Hans Anton von Beneckendorff und von Hindenburg, he was from an old Prussian aristocratic ("Junker") family, whose line went back to the Teutonic Knights of the Middle Ages. Upon achieving fame in the First World War, he used the surname of von Hindenburg, although prior to that he was listed in the army records under the surname of von Beneckendorff und von Hindenburg.

He became a cadet at age eleven, and served with distinction as a junior officer in the Austro-Prussian War (1866) and the Franco-Prussian War (1870–71), and was awarded the Iron Cross. Hindenburg was then selected to attend the school of the German General Staff, the Kriegsakademie. As a member of this elite and powerful general staff, his assignments alternated between staff duties and troop duties. He retired as a general in 1911. There is some suspicion that his retirement was hastened by his performance as a commander during a maneuver exercise in 1908, during which he "defeated" the opposing forces commanded by the kaiser. In later years, however, Hindenburg denied that this incident had affected his decision to retire.

Figure 1. Paul von Hindenburg. (SOURCE: U.S. Library of Congress)

The First World War

The outbreak of war in 1914 provided Hindenburg with the opportunity to return to active service. The German plan to win the war quickly, the Schlieffen Plan, called for German forces to hold the slower-to-mobilize Russians in the east, while the bulk of German forces swept through Belgium to conquer France. As the war began, Gen. Max von Prittwitz, the commander of German forces in the east (the Eighth Army), panicked when the Russians massed two field armies on the border and advanced into East Prussia. The German high command relieved Prittwitz and his chief of staff, and named Hindenburg the new commander. On the train specially assigned to carry him east to his new command, Hindenburg met his newly appointed chief of staff, Maj. Gen. Erich Ludendorff, for the first time. Under the Imperial German system, the chief of staff was more a partner of the commander than a subordinate; the two shared responsibility for the performance of the unit. The meeting of Ludendorff and

Hindenburg was the beginning of a command team that would eventually direct the entire war effort of Germany.

Hindenburg was deliberate, calm, and self-effacing. Ludendorff was brilliant, intense, and subject to extremes of temperament. Working together, the two men complemented each other superbly. They demonstrated their collective abilities immediately by reversing the situation on the eastern front. With two Russian armies entering East Prussia (but not cooperating with each other), the H-L team (to use an abbreviation that Winston Churchill devised) concentrated first against the southern army and annihilated it at Tannenberg, then massed against the other army and drove it out of East Prussia. The victories were the result of cooperative efforts, not only of the H-L team, but also with significant contributions from Lt. Col. Max Hoffmann of the operations staff and from the impetuous I Corps commander, Gen. Hermann K. von François. But the object of public adoration was Hindenburg. He received fan mail and presents from an adoring public and the nation's highest decoration from the kaiser. To his credit, Hindenburg never allowed this adulation to go to his head.

After Tannenberg, Hindenburg assumed command of all German forces on the eastern front and was promoted to field marshal. With Ludendorff at his side, he directed more spectacular victories over the Russians, driving them deeper into Russia. Germany, having failed to conquer France in 1914, now fought a two-front war. The H-L team had bitter disputes with the chief of the General Staff, Gen. Erich von Falkenhayn, who directed the national war effort and believed that the war would be won by concentrating efforts in the west. The H-L team felt that Falkenhayn was both denying adequate resources for their efforts in the east, and interfering with their conduct of operations. When Falkenhayn's plans to win the war proved unsuccessful by August 1916, Hindenburg was named to replace him as chief of the General Staff. Ludendorff, as first quartermaster general, accompanied Hindenburg to the new post.

The H-L team thus assumed control of the entire German war effort. The kaiser was an indecisive figurehead, and no German politician appeared on the scene to lead the nation. By default, the military leaders assumed responsibilities that were well beyond their scope and experience. Hindenburg was so popular that, by threatening to resign, he and Ludendorff could impose their will on national policy, even forcing the resignation of the chancellor. The policies advocated by the H-L team included resumption of unrestricted submarine warfare (which brought the United States into the war) and aggressive territorial demands (which eliminated any hope of a negotiated peace).

The End of the War

In 1917 the German armies fought a masterful defensive campaign on the western front and drove Russia to internal collapse on the eastern front. The year 1918 was the year of decision. Germany had to destroy the Western Allies before the full military power of the United States could be brought to bear. The great German offensives of the spring of 1918 were largely the result of

Ludendorff's efforts. They achieved initial success for which Hindenburg was awarded a national decoration that had not been bestowed since the Napoleonic Wars. But the flaws in Ludendorff's conduct of the operations, the exhaustion of Germany, and the resilience of the Western Allies caused Germany's last gamble to fail. By late 1918 it was clear that Germany could not win the war. In the bitterness of that realization, Ludendorff became the object of widespread German resentment, and resigned. Ludendorff and many others felt that Hindenburg had callously allowed Ludendorff to absorb the blame, while the field marshal remained serenely at his post. Even when the kaiser abdicated, Hindenberg remained as chief of the General Staff, supervising the withdrawal of German forces into Germany, where they crushed uprisings of radicals and restored order. Hindenburg's support for the new and fragile republic was crucial, for he was the symbol of continuity and order for the psychologically distraught German people. The field marshal's influence was also critical in the painful decision to accept the terms of the Treaty of Versailles (although Hindenburg's name was never publicly associated with that acceptance). With his popularity still high, Hindenburg retired in 1919.

Political Career

Despite his lifelong commitment to the German monarchy, Hindenburg agreed to run for president of Germany in 1925, at the age of 77. He entered politics from a genuine sense of patriotic duty, but his lack of political experience and his old age did not serve him well in the treacherous political climate of Germany during the interwar years. By the early 1930s, Hindenburg was the only national figure whose popularity exceeded that of the rising Adolf Hitler. Hindenburg defeated Hitler in the presidential election of 1932. Like many other respectable Germans, Hindenburg mistakenly believed that extremists like Hitler could be tamed or manipulated by the more reasonable elements of German society, never realizing that Hitler was always one step ahead of those elements in his plans to undermine and revolutionize German society. Political pressure forced Hindenburg to name Hitler chancellor in 1933. Hindenburg died on 2 August 1934, not living to see the results of his misjudgment. He was buried as a national hero.

Assessment

Hindenburg was an able military commander. He was not merely a figurehead in the First World War; his was the final decision in several critical situations. He bore himself extremely well under great pressure, persevering under the uncertainties of battle better than Ludendorff. His military career demonstrates the importance of combinations of personalities in modern war, a factor that is often overlooked in societies that emphasize and analyze individual contributions in isolation. Hindenburg also never allowed his enormous popularity to cloud his thinking. However, as he grew older in the murky political climate of the 1920s and early 1930s, he deferred too often to the last opinion he had heard. Like so many of his countrymen, Hindenburg never grasped that a determined megalomaniac could bend Germany to his own will. The tragedy of Field Marshal Paul von Hindenburg is that his outstanding service in the First World War gave him the popularity and respect to stand as the last obstacle to Hitler, a final role in which the aged field marshal failed.

TIMOTHY T. LUPFER

SEE ALSO: Ludendorff, Erich.

Bibliography

Craig, G. A. 1964. *The politics of the Prussian army.* Oxford: Oxford Univ. Press.
Dupuy, T. N. 1970. *The military lives of Hindenburg and Ludendorff of imperial Germany.* New York: Franklin Watts.
————. 1977. *A genius for war.* Fairfax, Va.: Hero Books.
Goerlitz W. 1953. *The German general staff.* New York: Praeger.
Hindenburg, P. von. 1920. *Out of my life.* London: Cassell.
Lupfer, T. T. 1981. *The dynamics of doctrine: The changes in German tactical doctrine during the First World War.* Ft. Leavenworth Kans.: Combat Studies Institute.
Wheeler-Bennett, J. W. 1936. *Wooden titan: Hindenburg in twenty years of German history.* New York: William Morrow.

HISTORY, ANCIENT MILITARY
[Prehistory–A.D. 476]

The military arts underwent an impressive development from prehistoric times to the fall of the Roman Empire. Large, fully integrated armies moved out of Egypt and Mesopotamia in the ancient Near East, and in the Roman Empire armies of Napoleonic proportions defended the frontiers. During the reign of Theodosius the Great (A.D. 379–395) the Roman army numbered about 500,000; this compared with the army of 600,000 that Napoleon I led into Russia. Many of the armies of antiquity were as large as or larger than the armies of the Middle Ages and Early Modern times.

Prehistoric Warfare

The origins of war go back to prehistoric times. Some anthropologists have argued that war is a creation of civilized man and that in prehistoric times there was no armed aggression of man against man. Archaeological discoveries of the twentieth century, however, have produced ample evidence that prehistoric man did wage wars. No one knows when men were first organized into armies, but they appeared at least by Neolithic times and possibly earlier. When Narmer moved down the Nile and united the two kingdoms of Egypt at the beginning of Egyptian history, he did it with an organized army, at least according to the stone relief sculpture that has survived from those early times. When man first learned how to write, he had wars to write about.

The earliest man-made weapons were chipped stone tools and fire-hardened spears. There is very little evidence for the bow and the sling in Paleolithic times. The famous cave paintings of France and Spain (20,000–30,000 years old) contain few scenes of human figures and none that unequivocally depict man killing man. Most of the pictures are peaceful and show beautiful animals, many of which are now extinct.

Although some scholars believe that the bow may be 50,000 years old, there is no definite evidence for it until the Late Paleolithic, around 12,000 B.C. A cemetery site discovered in excavations during the building of the Aswan dam on the Upper Nile has skeletons with what appear to be arrowheads embedded in the bones. The first clear evidence of the use of the bow is from the Neolithic period in the Eastern Mediterranean (8,000–7,000 B.C.). Neolithic cave paintings from Spain depict man fighting man in an organized fashion, deployed in column and line. The sling is illustrated in drawings found at Çatal Hüyük in modern Turkey.

The most impressive evidence for warfare in the Neolithic period is the ruins of the great walls and fortifications of prehistoric settlements, the most famous of which are Jericho and Çatal Hüyük. The massive stone walls of Jericho even had towers. At Çatal Hüyük there were no surrounding walls, but the dwellings were all built with contiguous walls. The only entrance into them was up ladders through holes in the roof, and the ladders could be pulled up if there was an attack. Since the walls of the settlement were contiguous, there was in effect an outside wall, and if an attacker managed to get through it, he would find himself inside a single room. It was an ingenious form of military architecture.

In the Neolithic some villages contained a few thousand inhabitants. Jericho's population is estimated at 2,000; and the number of fighting men at 500 to 600. The wall enclosed an area of about ten acres and was 700 meters (765 yd.) long. It has been suggested that the new developments in warfare are what caused man to settle down in the Neolithic villages and discover agriculture; man had to live in permanent settlements behind strong walls for his own protection against the new missile weapons of the bow and the sling.

Ancient Egypt and Babylonia

Civilization first appeared in the river valleys of Egypt and Mesopotamia in the fourth millennium B.C. In the course of Egyptian history there were many wars, and much is known about the army of the pharaohs from literary and pictorial evidence. Although Egypt was well protected by deserts and relatively isolated from the other centers of civilization in Syria-Palestine, Asia Minor, and Mesopotamia, the pharaohs always had an army. Under warlike pharaohs such as Tuthmosis III and Ramses II, the mobile field army numbered around 20,000. It consisted of infantry armed with spears, swords, and bows, and of fast, light, horse-drawn chariots. At the Battle of Kadesh in 1285 B.C. Ramses II marched several hundred miles out of Egypt into Syria where he fought the king of the Hittites in a major battle. Although the Egyptian army was caught in an ambush as it marched up to Kadesh and was hit hard in the flank, Ramses personally rallied his panic-stricken troops and led them to a tactical victory over the Hittites. They were not able to take the fortified city, however, and the campaign ended in a strategic stalemate.

In Babylonia the war chariot appeared much earlier than in Egypt. There is pictorial evidence that it appeared at least as early as the third millennium although the earliest ones were four-wheeled carts drawn by asses. The so-called Standard of Ur also depicts infantry pikemen in formation. From early times in Lower Mesopotamia, organized armies fought one another as the Sumerian cities competed for precious territory in the rich, fertile valleys of the Tigris and Euphrates rivers. In the last half of the third millennium, Sargon the Great sent armies on raiding expeditions as far away as Asia Minor, and by the time of Hammurabi in Babylon (ca. 1750 B.C.) the military empire of the Amorite kings was extensive. Because Mesopotamia was relatively open to attack in comparison with isolated Egypt, military developments were faster and more effective. The last two great Mesopotamian empires, the Assyrian and Persian, both conquered Egypt.

Assyria and Persia

The army of the Assyrian Empire (900–612 B.C.) was one of the finest in the history of the ancient Near East. Numbering at least 150,000 men, it contained infantry, cavalry, chariots, skirmishers, and special forces (such as sappers, siege troops, mountain troops, infantry, cavalry, and chariot shock forces). Assyrians excelled in siege warfare. Walled and fortified cities were unable to stand against the Assyrian army. Although the Assyrians did develop cavalry, chariotry retained its pride of place in the armed forces. The logistical system of the Assyrian army was advanced enough to permit the army to move vast distances of up to 1,600 kilometers (1,000 mi.) and to fight effectively at the end of the march.

The rise of Assyria corresponds with the beginning of the Iron Age. Although iron had been used earlier as an ornamental metal, it was not until the early first millennium B.C. that it became available on a wide enough scale to have an impact on warfare. Iron is one of the earth's plentiful metals, much more so than the tin that was necessary for making bronze weapons in the earlier period. As a result the Assyrians were able to build a mighty arsenal.

Eventually, however, the Assyrian Empire fell, as much the result of internal rebellion as of external threat. Nineveh was destroyed in 612 B.C. After an interlude of about one-half century, during which the Neo-Chaldeans of Babylonia and the Medes dominated the eastern Mediterranean, Cyrus the Great (559–530 B.C.) wrested control for his Achaemenid dynasty and launched the Persian Empire with extensive conquests.

The Persians introduced two new ingredients into the warfare of the civilized states around the east coast of the Mediterranean. Although the Assyrians had used some cavalry, they relied mainly on chariots. Persia abandoned the chariot for the horse cavalry. Also, although the Persians were not sailors, they organized the first great fleet of triremes to dominate the sea. It was composed of ships provided by their allies, mainly the Phoenicians and also some of the

Greek cities along the coast of Asia Minor. It is uncertain whether the trireme was invented by Phoenicians or Greeks, but it was the Persians who actually organized the first large fleet. With it they were able to dominate the Aegean and the Syria-Palestine coast. Under Cyrus's successors, the Persian Empire expanded to include all the ancient Near East from Egypt to India. It extended across the Bosphorus into European Thrace, and by 500 B.C. the expansion of Persia brought the empire into contact with the Greek cities of Athens and Sparta.

Early Greek Warfare

Despite Homer's epic poems, the *Iliad* and the *Odyssey*, little is known about Greek warfare in the Bronze Age. The Trojan War remains semilegendary after more than a century of excavation in modern Turkey and Greece. The Minoans and Mycenaeans were familiar with the war chariot and also with Bronze Age warships. Homer implies that they fought duels as champions in the fashion of Achilles and Hector, but it is possible, and even likely, that they fought in formation.

In the Greek Dark Ages, when Homer lived, the duel of champions may have been common, but by 700 B.C. the Greek cities had adopted a new style of fighting with heavy infantry called the *hoplite phalanx*. Greek warriors wearing helmet, shield, breastplate, and greaves, carrying a six-foot thrusting spear, fought in a close-order formation eight ranks deep, the phalanx. The warrior was called a *hoplite*, meaning a shield bearer. This new heavy infantry dominated the warfare of classical Greece. Individual champions were powerless against it. The Spartans became the foremost practitioners of this style of fighting, which required considerable discipline because it was essential that the individual warrior hold his place in the line. The most important thing was not to panic and run. As one Spartan mother is supposed to have told her son, "Come home with your shield or on it." In other words, it was better to die in action and to be carried home on the shield than to throw it away and desert in the face of the enemy. Because the Greek hoplites fought with thrusting spears, they engaged in shock, or hand-to-hand combat, which requires courage and discipline.

In the period from 700 to 500 B.C., the Greeks were developing their distinctive type of warfare while the Persians (in the last half of that period) were conquering their empire, including the Greek states of Ionia on the coast of Asia Minor. In 499 those Greek states revolted against Persia, and Athens agreed to come to their aid. The Persians were too strong, however, and by 494 they had reconquered the Ionians and decided to invade the Greek mainland to protect the northwest frontier of their empire.

The Persian Wars

In 490 Darius, king of Persia, sent an expeditionary force across the Aegean against Athens. It landed at Marathon, about 40 kilometers (25 mi.) across the Attic Peninsula from Athens. The Athenians probably surprised the Persians by sending their army out to meet them in the field rather than defending the walls of their city. Considering the Persian superiority in siege warfare this proved a wise decision on the part of the Athenians. The Athenian general Miltiades, after occupying a position in the foothills surrounding the plain of Marathon so that the Greek army could not be attacked by the Persian cavalry, moved out against the enemy after thinning his line in the center so that he would not be outflanked by the larger Persian force. The Athenian army numbered about 10,000 and the Persian about 20,000. When the two armies were about a kilometer apart, Miltiades ordered the Athenians to attack on the run in order to reduce the amount of time they would be under the fire of the Persian archers. The Persians advanced against the weak center of the Greek line, but as they did so, the heavier Greek wings wheeled around and caught the invaders in a double envelopment. The Persians were driven back to the sea, and they withdrew from mainland Greece in their fleet.

In 480 Xerxes, successor to Darius, invaded Greece again. This time the Persian king personally accompanied the army, and it was the full army of Persia, not just an expeditionary force. It was so large, perhaps 150,000 to 250,000 strong, that no Greek army could hope to stand against it. The Athenian leader, Themistocles, realized that the Persian army was too large to live off the land in Greece and that it would have to be supported by the fleet. Therefore, if the Greeks could defeat the Persian fleet, they could force the army to withdraw. And Themistocles believed that it would be much easier to defeat the Persian fleet than to defeat the army. On the sea the Greeks would be outnumbered but not so much as on the land.

The Spartans, who had been given overall command of the Greek forces in the war, wanted to defend a wall they were building across the Isthmus of Corinth. Since Athens and a few other Greek cities were north of that line, however, the Greeks decided to stop the Persians farther north, in narrow constricted areas where the Persians would not be able to take advantage of their superiority in numbers. The main stand came at Thermopylae where the Spartans under their King Leonidas fought to the death in a three-day battle before the Persians finally breached the Greek position by learning of an alternate route that took them behind the Spartans. On the same three days, the Greek fleet fought a losing battle in the nearby waters of Artemisium. After this defeat on land and sea it was necessary to evacuate Athens, and the Greek fleet fell back to Salamis to help with the evacuation. The Persians moved up to offer battle, but in the narrow and constricted waterway that was favorable to the Greeks, they were decisively defeated.

King Xerxes then moved the bulk of his army back into Asia because the Greeks now controlled the western Aegean and were in a position to cut off the Persian line of retreat across the Hellespont. He left an army of about 50,000 in Greece under General Mardonius, but it was defeated in spring of 479 in a battle at Plataea. According to tradition, on the same day the Greek fleet defeated the Persian fleet again, this time in the eastern Aegean at Mycale. This marked the end of the Persian War; the Greeks had repelled a full-scale invasion by the Persian Empire.

The Peloponnesian War

Until the last half of the fifth century B.C., the Greeks relied almost exclusively on heavy infantry, the hoplite phalanx. There were few cavalry, skirmishers, or light infantry. During the Peloponnesian War between Athens and Sparta, skirmishers and light infantry made an appearance, but cavalry was very limited until the fourth century.

When Sparta invaded Athens in 431, the Athenian leader Pericles responded by having the Athenians abandon their fields and fall back behind the safety of their walls. Periclean strategy dictated that under no circumstances should the Athenians meet the well-disciplined and trained Spartan army in a pitched battle on land. Instead, the Athenians used their fleet to feed their city since they controlled the sea-lanes for the grain trade from the Black Sea, and they also circumnavigated and attacked the coast of the Peloponnese. Because the Athenians had greater financial resources, they could outlast Sparta in a war of attrition.

Except for a plague that swept through the city in 429 (among its victims was Pericles), the first few years of the war went well for Athens, culminating in a victory at Pylos (425) where the Athenians forced some Spartan hoplites to surrender. Under the leadership of the demagogue Cleon, however, the Athenians abandoned Periclean strategy and became more aggressive on land. This led ultimately to a major defeat at Amphipolis (422). In the following year, both sides, wearied by the conflict, agreed to end the war by the Peace of Nicias, named after the Athenian who negotiated it. It was supposed to last for 50 years, but only lasted about seven.

During the interval between the first and second phases of the war, the Athenians mounted a Sicilian expedition. A Greek city on Sicily asked Athens for help against a neighbor, closely allied with the large city of Syracuse, which in turn had good relations with Corinth and Sparta. In Athens an ambitious young leader, Alcibiades, nephew and ward of Pericles, saw the invitation to intervene in Sicily as an opportunity to weaken the Peloponnesian League that Sparta dominated. In 415 B.C. Athens sent a fleet of 134 warships, about 5,000 hoplites, 480 archers, 700 Rhodian slingers, 120 light infantry, and 30 cavalry to Sicily. Unfortunately, the Athenians broke the principle of unity of command by naming three equal leaders—Alcibiades, Nicias, and Lamachus. Alcibiades, the one most likely to succeed, was removed from the expedition at the start because of a religious scandal.

In Sicily the Athenians moved against Syracuse and became bogged down in a siege that lasted until the summer of 413. Before it was over, Athens sent an additional 73 triremes and 5,000 troops, but the large armada failed to breach Syracusan defenses and was eventually totally destroyed. The losses numbered nearly 40,000 men, including the crews of the 200 ships that were also lost. The hoplite phalanx was outstanding on a level field of combat, but not particularly good for siege warfare. Syracuse was simply too far away from the center of Athenian vested interests, and Athens overcommitted its forces.

In the following year Sparta decided to renew the Peloponnesian War. The King of Persia, who had lost control of the Aegean to Athens after the Persian wars, saw an opportunity to regain much of Persia's former position, and he promised the Spartans strong financial support for the duration of hostilities. From 412 to 404 the war was fought on the sea, and Athens was often victorious in battle, but the Persians always helped the Spartans to rebuild their fleet, and eventually, at the Battle of Aegospotami in 405, the Spartan commander Lysander destroyed the Athenian fleet and blockaded the Athenian harbor at Piraeus. In March 404 Athens surrendered and the war was over. Sparta became the dominant city of the Greek mainland, and the King of Persia regained control of the Greek cities of Asia Minor.

Heavy infantry, the traditional force of the Greek states, had not been the decisive factor in this war. The need for lighter troops, for effective siege units, and for a navy was becoming widely recognized. What the Greeks lacked, and what the ancient Near Eastern states had long produced, was an integrated army, one composed of heavy and light infantry, skirmishers, heavy and light cavalry, and special forces. Exclusive reliance on the hoplite phalanx was beginning to decline.

Sparta and Thebes

The most important battles of the first half of the fourth century, the Battles of Leuctra and Mantinea between Sparta and Thebes, were fought by phalanxes. In them the Theban commander, Epaminondas, defeated the vaunted Spartan phalanx by stacking his own left wing in a formation 50 shields deep against the best troops on the Spartan right. In previous phalanx battles, the full force of the fighting had been felt all along the line and there had been no attempt at turning the flanks of an army (although it sometimes happened by accident). But Epaminondas deliberately massed his strength on one wing and used it against the best troops of the enemy. In that way Thebes won at Leuctra in 371 and again at Mantinea in 362, using the same tactics. At Mantinea, however, Epaminondas was killed in the fighting, and his death signaled the end of the Theban hegemony in Greece.

Significant changes were beginning to occur in Greek warfare. The simple catapult was invented in Syracuse in 399 B.C., and by the 350s the sophisticated and powerful torsion catapult was in use. At the beginning of the century the famous march of Xenophon and the Ten Thousand into the heart of Persia nearly to Babylon taught the Greek mercenaries a great deal about the art of logistics and the importance of cavalry and skirmishers. The Greeks were beginning to realize that light troops had their uses and that the best army was an integrated one. The first person to create such a force was Philip II of the northern kingdom of Macedon (359–336 B.C.).

Philip and the Macedonian Army

At the very start of his reign Philip reorganized the Macedonian army and fashioned one of the greatest fighting forces in the history of war. The premier arm of the new army was its cavalry. Macedonian aristocrats were horsemen, and the best of them were organized into the King's Companions, heavy cavalry that served as shock troops. They fought in a wedge formation and carried lances made of cornel wood. In weight and size the Macedonian lance was similar to the Napoleonic lance of modern times, but the Macedonian one had an iron point on both ends. For reconnoitering, skirmishing, and light cavalry, Philip used Thracians and Paeonians. His Thessalian allies provided another large contingent of heavy cavalry, and altogether the Macedonian cavalry numbered about 5,000.

In addition, Philip created the Macedonian phalanx which was heavier than the hoplite phalanx. This infantry fought sixteen deep, and the phalangites carried two-handed pikes (*sarissas*) that were probably about 4 meters (13 ft.) long. Front rankers wore very heavy armor. The formation was not very mobile, and it had a specialized tactical function—to meet and pin down the enemy line while the Macedonian cavalry attacked the flanks of the enemy or penetrated gaps in the opposing line. This represented the introduction of so-called hammer-and-anvil tactics in the Greek world. The phalanx was the anvil against which the surrounding cavalry, the hammer, smashed the enemy forces. The king trained these troops intensively to face in any direction by wheeling in an arc, and he could double the length of his line by stepping the last eight men in the files to the right or the left and moving them up. Although the usual battle order was in phalanx, the men were trained to fight in other formations, too, and Alexander (Philip's son) used them in sieges and mountain warfare.

Philip also used light infantry and skirmishers on a wide scale. *Peltasts* could perform as either: they were armed with javelins and could fight in a line or individually. There were units of archers and slingers in the Macedonian army. Philip also revolutionized logistics in the Greek world. He abandoned the use of carts and required his men to carry their own supplies, and he reduced the number of servants the troops were allowed. He was able to move his army an average of 25 kilometers (15 mi.) per day, and for short periods much more than that. Until the advent of the railroad in the nineteenth century, no armies exceeded these speeds. The new mobility increased the strategic range of Macedonian power. Alexander marched all the way to India, an impossibility for earlier Greek armies. Finally, Philip trained his new Macedonian army with the rigor that is today devoted to commandos, sending them often on training marches of nearly 65 kilometers (40 mi.) under full pack. His mobile, integrated army became, under his son Alexander, one of the world's finest armies.

Philip was able to dominate Greece with his army, and at the Battle of Chaeronea in 338 he defeated Athens and Thebes, formed the League of Corinth, and planned to lead the Greeks on a great crusade against Persia to free the Greek cities of Asia Minor. However, he was assassinated in 336 on the eve of his departure, and the young Alexander became king.

Alexander the Great

Alexander became one of the best generals in the history of warfare. He was an inspirational leader of men, a legend in his own lifetime, whose feats even today are remarkable. After devoting two years to securing his position on the throne of Macedon, he was ready in 334 to launch the crusade against Persia. He never turned back until he reached India about ten years later.

Almost immediately after crossing the Hellespont with his army he met the Persians at the Granicus River where he led a charge across a stream into the heart of the Persian defenders and breached their line. The Persians tried, but failed, to kill Alexander, and after his victory he marched triumphantly down the coast of Ionia in Asia Minor freeing the Greek cities as he went. Most opened their gates to him, although he was forced to overcome resistance at Miletus and Halicarnassus.

Then, in 333 B.C., the young king went through central Asia Minor to the city of Gordium where he untied the famous Gordian Knot and announced that he would become, as the legend promised, the Lord of Asia. As he moved down into Tarsus, the Persians tried unsuccessfully to stop him in the narrow mountain pass at the Cilician Gates. Alexander turned the corner from Asia Minor down the Syria-Palestine coast. He had decided to conquer all Persia, and first he needed to neutralize the Persian fleet by capturing its land bases around the eastern Mediterranean because his fleet was no match for the Persians'.

Darius III, King of Persia, marched the full Persian field army (perhaps 200,000 to 500,000 strong) in behind Alexander as the Macedonians advanced down the coast. Alexander immediately turned around and charged back against the Persians at Issus, where they fought a great battle. The Persians lost much of their numerical advantage by using the coastal road since the terrain forced them into a narrow area between mountains and sea. They took a strong defensive position along the Pinarus River, facing south, but since the ground was hilly on their left, Darius massed all his cavalry on his right.

Alexander, with a smaller army of about 45,000, approached in traditional formation with cavalry on both wings. He normally fought with the right cavalry and put the left wing of his army under the command of his senior general, Parmenio. In any event, Alexander advanced against the Persians so rapidly that he had to move from line of column into line of battle in the face of the enemy. As soon as the battle began, he charged with his right-wing cavalry into the left wing of the Persians and breached a gap in their line. Then he wheeled against the Persian center, where Darius personally fought, and threatened the rear of their line. The Persians panicked, including Darius, who fled from the field, abandoning his chariot, armor, and members of his family who had accompanied him on the expedition. In defeating the main army of Persia, under Darius, Alexander had won a major victory (November 333 B.C.).

The Macedonians continued their march down the coast, and the cities of Lebanon surrendered to them—Sidon, Byblos, Beirut—but the city of Tyre offered only neutrality. It was an island city about a kilometer off the coast with splendid defenses including strong walls, in some places about 45 meters (150 ft.) high. Alexander decided to build a mole, or walkway, across the sea to the walls of the city. The siege proved extremely difficult and lasted for almost seven months, from January to July of 332. Alexander was helped when the Phoenician fleets, which had formerly served Persia, defected to him. Eventually he used those warships against the walls of Tyre, and after several disappointments the Macedonians stormed that city, opening the road to Egypt.

After a brief siege at Gaza, Alexander entered Egypt without resistance and spent the winter of 332–331 there. Having gained control of the entire eastern coast of the Mediterranean, the King of Macedon was ready to strike into the heart of Persia against Darius. The Persian king had mobilized a new army and was waiting for Alexander on the plains of Babylon. The Macedonian had followed the Fertile Crescent north, and when he crossed the Euphrates River he decided to continue eastward toward the Tigris River rather than meet Darius on terrain that permitted the Persians to take advantage of their numerical superiority. Darius had no choice but to march up the Tigris, and the two armies met (September–October 331 B.C.) on the field near the village of Gaugamela.

The Battle of Gaugamela (often called the Battle of Arbela, which was the largest city in the vicinity; about 110 kilometers [70 mi.] away) proved decisive in the war for Persia. The Macedonians were outnumbered at least three or four to one. Alexander extended his line in echelon formation on the left wing, where he ordered Parmenio to fight a holding action. On the right he looked for an opportunity to lead a charge. When the Macedonians were on the verge of defeat, after their left wing had been enveloped, Alexander attacked through a gap that developed on the Persian left, wheeled around (as he had done at Issus), and moved against the rear of the Persian center. Again, Darius panicked and fled. Although victorious, Alexander was forced to help the beleaguered Parmenio on the Macedonian left, and Darius escaped. The full Persian army, however, was never reassembled.

Alexander then marched unopposed into Babylon and Susa, the Persian capital. After some opposition he also took the ancestral shrines at Persepolis, which he put to the torch in revenge for what the Persians had done to Athens during the Persian Wars of the fifth century B.C. Darius was killed in 330 by his own nobles, and Alexander spent the years 329–327 fighting a guerrilla war for control of northeastern Iran. Finally he was able to move into India, which had also once been part of the Persian Empire (the area known as the Punjab in modern Pakistan).

The Punjab was so far from the Greek world that Macedonians knew about it only vaguely in myth. When they arrived at the tributaries of the Indus River, Alexander thought he had discovered the source of the Nile because there were crocodiles in the rivers, and the Nile was the only river he knew where they existed. While in India, a shipment of equipment arrived from Macedonia, a tribute to Alexander's logistical system.

The main opponent in the valley of the Indus was a king named Porus, who took a strong position on the east bank of the Hydaspes River (the modern Jhelum River). He defended it with an Indian army of 30,000 infantry, 4,000 cavalry, 300 chariots, and, perhaps most important, some 200 war elephants. The elephants were effective—Alexander's men and horses were not trained to fight them, and horses unaccustomed to elephants are frightened of them (see Fig. 1). Since he could not move directly across the river against Porus, Alex-

Figure 1.Elephants and camels were used in the time of Alexander, who originally saw them in use in the Indian Army.
(SOURCE: Iconographic Encyclopaedia)

ander marched under cover of darkness 27 kilometers (17 mi.) upstream, crossed the river, and marched down against the Indians. Porus wheeled his army around and rushed to meet the invaders. Alexander won the great cavalry battle that developed on the Macedonian right and Indian left, gained control of the Punjab, and became friends with his former foe, Porus.

By this time Alexander had decided that he wanted to march to the end of the earth. Greeks believed that an ocean stream flowed around the world, and Alexander heard that there was only one more river valley to conquer before reaching it, but after he reached the Hyphasis (modern Beas), his army refused to go farther. After weeping in his tent for three days, the king finally agreed to take the men home. By one modern estimate they had marched over 27,000 kilometers (17,000 mi.) since leaving Macedonia. They returned down the Indus, and at the mouth of the river, Alexander took part of the force overland across southern Persia; the rest went under the command of Nearchus by sea in a fleet the army built. Both forces suffered severely, but Alexander and Nearchus made it back to Babylon.

Alexander died there in 323 B.C. at the age of 32. His conquests are among the most extensive in history, and his generalship was superb. Characterized by decisiveness and speed, the quality of his command has rarely, if ever, been exceeded. In strategic thought he made few questionable decisions, and he was tactically successful as well. The most common criticism of his generalship is that he exposed himself to personal injury too often and recklessly, which, although true, is also part of what made him such an inspirational leader. His integrated army was as well trained as any in premodern times. Discipline was firm, and the quality of his senior officers was brilliant.

Alexander had a tremendous impact on warfare. From his time forward, armies were able to strike hundreds or thousands of miles from their home base. Ancient Near Eastern armies had also performed long-distance operations, and they too were integrated and had good logistical support. What the Macedonians added was outstanding heavy infantry and rigorous discipline. As a result of his invasion of India, one of Alexander's legacies was the introduction of elephant warfare into the Mediterranean; a new way of fighting for the Greeks, and through them the Romans.

Early Rome

When Alexander died in Babylon, the Romans in Italy were just starting to become a world power. According to legend, their city had been founded on 21 April 753 B.C., by its first king, Romulus. Late in the period of the monarchy, Rome adopted a phalanx army similar to those used at the same time in Greece. The Roman army successfully defended the fledgling republic during the fifth century B.C. against attacks by the neighboring hill people, and around 400 B.C. they won their first war against a major civilized state, the Etruscan city of Veii. Shortly afterward, however, Gauls from the Po Valley in northern Italy sacked Rome (390 B.C.) and humiliated the army. It was probably at that time that the Roman military hero Camillus, who had defeated Veii, reorganized the phalanx army into legions.

The Roman legion was arranged in maniples, each consisting of 120 men (except for the maniples in the rear ranks which were only 60 strong). Altogether the legion numbered about 4,200. In addition to the legions, Rome's allies provided auxiliary units equal in manpower to the legions. Generally, the Roman army was strong in infantry and weak in cavalry. It normally depended on mercenaries for archers, mounted and unmounted. Discipline in the Roman army was notoriously severe—decimation is the most famous example.

The Roman army usually fought in three lines. Those in the first line were called *hastati* and *velites*. The *velites* were the youngest (1,200 in all), and they served as skirmishers with swords, javelins, and circular shields. The *hastati* and the troops in the second line, the *principes*, carried the short sword (*gladius*), two javelins, and the oval shield (*scutum*). There were 1,200 of each. In the third line stood the veterans, the *triarii*, 600 strong, who carried a pike instead of javelins. Each line wore a distinctive uniform. The cavalry squadrons attached to the legion numbered 300.

Normally, when a consul went into the field he took two legions plus an equal number of allied troops, nearly 20,000 men altogether. Sometimes in a grave crisis consular armies were doubled in size. All Roman legionaries were conscripts, and they were also property owners. The Romans did not want to arm the landless poor.

After conquering most of the Italian peninsula south of the Po Valley, the Romans faced the Greeks of southern Italy. Greeks had been in Sicily and southern Italy for centuries, and they had always fought with the neighboring Italian hill people. In the 280s B.C., one of the Greek towns, Thurii, asked the increasingly powerful Romans to help them against attacks. Rome responded by sending troops and angered the Greek city of Tarentum, which believed that southern Italy was Tarentum's sphere of influence. Tarentum was bold enough to oppose Rome because a king from the Greek world, Pyrrhus of Epirus, offered to help the Tarentines.

Pyrrhus was an ambitious Hellenistic king and general with an army of about 25,000 professional troops trained to fight in the Macedonian style. He crossed to Italy in the spring of 280 B.C. and defeated the Romans at the Battle of Heraclea. The following year he defeated them again, at Asculum, making good use of his elephants in both battles. His losses were heavy in both battles, and after the second he is supposed to have exclaimed, "Another such victory and I am lost." His problem was that he could not besiege Rome as long as Rome's Italian allies remained loyal because they would mobilize a relief army and pin him down around the walls of the city. Thus, although he had won great tactical victories, he was far from winning the war strategically. Despondent, he accepted an invitation to help the Greek cities of Sicily in a war against Carthage and left Italy. Although he was successful against Carthage, his Greek allies eventually turned against him, and he returned to Italy in 275 to resume the war with Rome. He was defeated at the Battle of Beneventum and left Italy to return to Epirus. He became King of Macedon and died a few years later in a street fight in the city of Argos. During this time the Romans organized the Greek cities of Italy into the Roman alliance system.

The Wars with Carthage

The conquest of Greek Italy brought Rome into direct conflict with the Carthaginian Empire of North Africa. Until the early third century B.C. Rome and Carthage had been friendly because they had no conflicts of interest. The traditional enemies of both states were the Etruscans and Greeks. Rome finally defeated both, and brought them into the Roman confederation. Because the Greeks of Italy had close ties with the Greeks of Sicily, Rome soon became involved in Sicilian affairs. However, Carthage occupied the western end of Sicily, and within ten years of the war with Pyrrhus, Rome was at war with Carthage.

The first Carthaginian War (or Punic War; *Punic* was the Latin word for Phoenician, and Carthage had originally been a Phoenician colony) became a war of attrition, lasting an entire generation from 265–241 B.C. Carthage was a major naval power, and Roman strength was in infantry, but because the Romans had to fight overseas, they built a fleet. Knowing they were inferior to the Carthaginians in standard naval battle maneuvers, the Romans added a large gangplank onto a special mast near the prows of their vessels. Attached vertically, it could be released to fall onto the deck of the enemy ship as it approached. The gangplank had a spike in its end to pierce the Carthaginian deck; it was called a crow (in Latin, a *corvus*, because the spike resembled a crow's beak). The Romans then sent their legions across the crow to board the Punic warship. With this new invention the Romans inflicted heavy losses on the Carthaginians.

The Roman forces surprisingly fared better on sea than on land. The Carthaginian army dug in on Sicily, and the Roman army could not dislodge them. In 256 B.C. the Romans used their fleet to carry the war to North Africa against Carthage, but the army, under the Consul Regulus, was defeated outside the city, and Regulus was captured. Although the Romans resumed the war at sea, they suffered heavy losses in storms, either because their ships were made unseaworthy by the heavy extra mast for the crow, or simply because they lacked naval experience. In 242 both states built new fleets, and the Romans won. In the following year Carthage agreed to give up Sicily. and a few years later Rome seized Sardinia and Corsica.

Hannibal and the Second Punic War (218–201 B.C.)

In the First Punic War Carthage had been defeated but not destroyed. Its North African empire was still intact, and Hasdrubal, the best Carthaginian general, decided to pursue Punic designs on Spain. Spain was far from Rome, and the Romans paid little attention to Carthaginian activities there. Rome fought the Gauls of the Po Valley in the 220s and sent troops across the Adriatic to protect the shipping of the Greek cities of southern Italy against piracy. The Carthaginians under Hamilcar, and eventually under his son Hannibal, strengthened their position in Spain and grew strong on the mineral resources of that country. In 219 Hannibal put Saguntum (a Spanish city allied to Rome) under siege, although he knew it would lead to renewed war between the two major powers.

In 218 the Romans prepared for war. Determined to avoid the pitfalls of the earlier conflict with Carthage, they wanted a quick victory; they sent out two armies, one to Sicily and the other, under P. Cornelius Scipio, to Spain. Hannibal, however, achieved strategic surprise with his march across southern France and over the Alps into Italy. Although he suffered heavy losses crossing the Alps, he caught the Romans off guard and defeated them in three major battles in the first three years of the war. The Carthaginians overwhelmed the Roman army at the Trebia in December of 218 and at Lake Trasimene in 217. Following these defeats, the Romans, under the dictator Fabius Maximus, followed a strategy of exhaustion against Hannibal (popularly misnamed "Fabian tactics") and refused to offer conventional battle. Hannibal faced the same dilemma as had Pyrrhus earlier in the century. Carthage could not put Rome under siege as long as the allies in Italy remained loyal. Hannibal needed decisive victories in the field in order to incite Rome's allies to defect. Fabius hoped to deny Hannibal that opportunity, but Fabian tactics were not popular in Rome, and the Senate decided on a bold attempt to defeat Hannibal in Italy.

In 216 a large army (possibly 80,000 strong) met the Carthaginians in southern Italy at Cannae. There Hannibal put out strong cavalry on both wings, placed his weakest infantry in the center in a crescent formation, and stationed his best veterans on both sides of the crescent. The Romans drove back the weak troops in the center, but the Carthaginian wings wheeled around while their cavalry easily defeated Roman cavalry and then hammered the rear of the Roman line, catching the entire Roman army in a classic double envelopment. The defeat at Cannae was the darkest moment of the war for the Romans. Philip V of Macedonia declared war the next year, and the Italian city of Capua defected to Carthage. Even Syracuse on the island of Sicily abandoned a long and loyal Roman alliance.

Hannibal, however, could not offer Capua or Syracuse much protection since he did not want to pin his own army down in a besieged site. The Romans retook these cities in the next few years, and in Spain, where they had sent an army at the outset of the war, a young general named Scipio won a total victory. In 205 Scipio won election to the consulship on a promise to carry the war to North Africa against Carthage. He left in 204 and a year later the Carthaginians recalled Hannibal from Italy—he had won many great battles, but he had not achieved strategic victory.

In North Africa at the Battle of Zama in 202 Scipio (later known as Africanus) defeated Hannibal, and in 201 Carthage accepted the terms Scipio imposed. Carthage lost all of her empire and was reduced to the status of a city; Rome took Spain and the Kingdom of Numidia (roughly modern Algeria), and Carthage became a Roman ally. Carthage was also forbidden to wage war without Roman permission. In geopolitical terms, Rome became dominant in the central and western Mediterranean and emerged as the leading power in the world.

Rome quickly demonstrated that power. First the legions humbled the Macedonian phalanx at the Battle of Cynoscephalae in 197, and then defeated the army of Antiochus the Great, ruler of the Seleucid Empire, at the Battle of Magnesia in 189. The Ptolemies of Egypt quickly adopted a peaceful policy toward Rome, and the legions of the west became the master of the world. Around 100 B.C. the Roman general Marius reorganized the Roman army and left an indelible stamp on Roman history.

Marius, Sulla, Pompey the Great, and Caesar

Marius abandoned the draft and property requirement for service in the army and called for landless volunteers. He promised them booty and land grants as a reward for service, rewards that were guaranteed by the commanding general rather than the state. The result was that the army became more attached to its general than to the government, and it was not long before Roman armies were willing to march on Rome itself if the general ordered it. Marius also streamlined the logistical supply system, following Alexander's father's example, by making Roman troops carry most of their own supplies. The army became known as Marius's Mules. He also made some tactical changes, organizing the legions around cohorts made up of six centuries each, and each century consisted of 80 men. There were ten cohorts in a Roman legion, and on paper each legion numbered slightly more than 5,000 men, although legions, like modern military divisions, were rarely up to paper strength. Some of Caesar's legions later were only about 2,000 strong. But the new legions of Marius, now highly politicized, were also extremely effective on the battlefield. It is at this time that they began to acquire the famous legionary standards and names. Marius is sometimes credited with creating a professional army; although this is not so, he did lay the foundations for it.

The armies of the Late Roman Republic made tremendous conquests and played a major role in Roman politics, often placing their generals in control of the government. Pompey the Great and Julius Caesar are the most famous examples of military dynasts. Pompey defeated Mithridates in Asia Minor and added Syria to the Roman Empire. Caesar conquered all Gaul. Then in a great civil war Caesar defeated Pompey and became dictator. Caesar's generalship was characterized by decisiveness (or Caesarspeed), personal bravery, and firm discipline. He also doubled legionary pay. In war there are many paths to popularity, but generosity and victory are perhaps the best.

Augustus and the Grand Strategy of Preclusive Security

The loyal support of the legions, however, was not enough to prevent Caesar's opponents in the Senate from assassinating him on the Ides of March, 44 B.C. Eventually, after a major military confrontation between his successors, Octavian and Mark Antony, Octavian emerged as the sole ruler of Rome and became known as the Emperor Augustus. It was Augustus who completed the transformation of Roman troops, begun by Marius, into a standing professional army.

After the victory over Antony and Cleopatra at Actium (31 B.C.), Augustus demobilized the great army that had developed during the period of the Second Triumvirate, reducing his forces to 28 legions (and an equal number of auxiliary troops). He pursued extensive conquests, especially along the northern frontier of the Rhine and Danube rivers, and stationed most of the legions along that line. Only a few, particularly in Egypt and Spain, were kept for internal police purposes.

The emperor also regularized the length of service. Legionaries served for 20 years, members of the Praetorian Guard (an elite force of about 7,000 men stationed in Italy) for 16, and auxiliaries for 25. There were also two fleets, one stationed at Ravenna and the other in the Bay of Naples. Pay, bonuses, and retirement benefits also were controlled by the government, and a new military treasury was created for the pension system.

The imperial defense system was characterized by economy of force. The army, after the loss of three legions across the Rhine at the Teutoburg Forest in A.D. 9, was only 25 legions strong, and with auxiliaries numbered around 250,000 to 300,000 men. For an imperial frontier of several thousand miles this force was small and efficient. Training and discipline made the Roman imperial army one of the finest in the history of the world. Under Augustus and the Julio-Claudians, Romans used "client kings" or satellite states to help in the defense of the frontiers, but by the end of the first century A.D. there were about 30 legions, and the client kingdoms had been incorporated as provinces. In the second century the Romans had a fully developed system of preclusive security protecting the imperial frontiers which were rigidly defined. Hadrian's Wall in England is the most famous example. Some analysts have argued that the flaw in Roman grand strategy was that the legions were all deployed on the frontier and there was no central reserve.

The Collapse of the Third Century and the Recovery
Under Diocletian and Constantine

In the third century A.D. military defense of the Roman Empire broke down in a half century of civil war (235–84 A.D.), sometimes referred to as the period of the Barracks Emperors. Legion fought legion to place its own commander on the throne, and as the frontiers were abandoned by their defenders, barbarians poured into the empire while rebel legionary generals seized large territories for themselves. There were times when the emperor in Rome ruled only over Italy and parts of North Africa. One emperor, Valerian, was captured by the Persians (260) and never heard from again. Another was killed fighting the Goths. Barbarians raided Athens. The economy of the empire collapsed as the coinage was devalued to almost nothing but worthless metal.

Surprisingly, Rome recovered under the forceful Emperor Diocletian (284–305). He managed to reconquer almost all the former territory of the empire and to restore the system of preclusive security.

Constantine the Great (d. 337) made a major modification to imperial grand strategy. Abandoning preclusive security, he turned instead to a system of defense in depth and created a large mobile army, strong in cavalry, stationed near the imperial residence, wherever it happened to be. To do this, he had to weaken the frontier forces, but his system worked well for a time, and the empire remained powerful. In the end, however, the results were catastrophic, as the frontier garrisons deteriorated in their now secondary strategic role. Infantry was generally neglected while cavalry became more important. Associated with this development was the increased use of barbarian mercenaries which led to a deterioration in training and discipline. While Constantine the Great lived, Rome remained dominant in the entire Mediterranean area, but under his successors in the fourth century, Roman armies began to suffer great defeats.

The Fall of the Roman Empire

The first major loss came in 363 when the Emperor Julian the Apostate led an invasion of Persia. The Sassanid Persians had replaced the Parthians in Mesopotamia in the third century, and the new Persian Empire became a formidable opponent. During Julian's invasion the Persians adopted a scorched earth strategy, and Julian, although he advanced to the Persian capital, Ctesiphon, in Lower Mesopotamia, withdrew. On the return he was killed in a skirmish with the Persians, and the new Roman Emperor, Jovian, was forced to negotiate a humiliating settlement.

Fifteen years later the Romans suffered an even greater defeat against the barbarian Visigoths at Adrianople (378 A.D.). The emperor of the Eastern Roman Empire, Valens, had agreed two years before to let the Visigoths cross the Danube into the empire. They had been driven in panic against the imperial frontier by the appearance of the Huns from the steppes of Asia into the region around the Black Sea. Because Roman authorities mistreated the

Visigoths when they made the crossing, the barbarians went to battle. Valens met them at Adrianople in 378, rushing there to get the glory before the Western Emperor Gratian, who was nearby, could arrive with reinforcements. On that Balkan battlefield the army of the Roman Empire, arriving little by little and engaging before it was fully deployed into line of battle, was badly beaten on a hot August afternoon. Valens was killed.

Theodosius the Great (379–95) took over in the East after Adrianople and by the time of his death had control of all the empire, East and West. Theodosius adopted a policy of appeasement and negotiation with the Persians and the barbarians, believing that he needed time to rebuild Roman military strength. He agreed to let the Visigoths stay in the empire as federated allies under their own kings and bearing their own arms. Never before had Rome made such a settlement with a Germanic tribe.

When Theodosius died, the Visigoths, under their new King Alaric, again attacked. The empire had been permanently divided between East and West on Theodosius's death; his son Honorius became emperor in the West and Arcadius in the East. Since Honorius was not yet ten years old, Theodosius appointed General Stilicho as regent in the West. At this period the West was weaker than the East. The East was richer, and the walls of Constantinople on the European side of the Bosphorus protected the capital and the rest of the Eastern Empire from invasion since the barbarians had no naval power for operations in the Eastern Mediterranean. So Alaric led the Visigoths first into the Balkans and then against Italy in the West. As long as Stilicho lived, he was able to keep Italy safe, but after his death in 408 Alaric put the city of Rome under siege. It fell to the Visigoths and was sacked for three days late in August, 410 A.D.

Earlier, in 407, Vandals, Suebi, and Alemanni had crossed the Rhine into Gaul and Spain. The entire western half of the empire was hard pressed, but the government of Honorius, now centered in the fortress of Ravenna on the northern Adriatic, held firm. Under a new military hero, Constantius, much of the West was retaken for a brief time, but Britain had been lost permanently in the crisis of 408–410, and the Visigoths had been allowed to settle in Aquitaine in southwestern Gaul.

Finally, in 429 Vandals moved from Spain into North Africa, and took Carthage in 439. The loss of North Africa, a major source of grain and money, was a strategic blow to the emperor in the West. In the meantime Burgundians and Alans had also settled in Gaul. The government of the Emperor Valentinian III (425–55) tried to keep things together, and with the help of the able General Aëtius did as much as possible under the circumstances. Militarily, the barbarian tribes relied heavily on infantry rather than cavalry, as is commonly believed, since only aristocratic tribesmen had horses. Generally, the Roman cavalry was better than the barbarian, but Roman infantry had declined drastically, and by the mid-fifth century it was not as good as the Germanic forces. In siege warfare and in naval warfare the barbarians were inferior to the Romans, but without good infantry Rome could not hold the western empire together. In the East this deterioration did not occur, mainly because the eastern army had not been so thoroughly barbarianized, and because discipline and training were much more rigorous.

The last great victory for Rome came in 451 at the Battle of Châlons when Aëtius organized an alliance of Romans, Visigoths, and Alans against Attila the Hun who had invaded Gaul. After this triumph, however, the alliance broke up, and on the deaths of Aëtius (454) and Valentinian III (455) the western empire nearly disappeared. For a generation it labored on under barbarian generals who ruled through puppets, but in 476 the last Roman emperor in the West, Romulus Augustulus, was deposed, and the western Roman Empire ceased to exist.

ARTHER FERRILL

SEE ALSO: Alexander the Great; Assyria, Military History of; Attila the Hun; Caesar, Julius; Graeco-Persian Wars; Hannibal Barca; Peloponnesian Wars; Persian Empire; Punic Wars; Roman Empire; Scipio Africanus; Tuthmosis III.

Bibliography

Campbell, J. B. 1984. *The emperor and the Roman army, 31 B.C.–A.D. 235.* Oxford: Clarendon Press.

Cheesman, G. L. 1914. *The auxilia of the Roman Imperial army.* Oxford: Clarendon Press.

Connolly, P. 1981. *Greece and Rome at war.* New York: Prentice-Hall.

Engels, D. W. 1978. *Alexander the Great and the logistics of the Macedonian army.* Berkeley, Calif.: Univ. of California Press.

Ferrill, A. 1985. *The origins of war: From the Stone Age to Alexander the Great.* New York: Thames and Hudson.

———. 1986. *The fall of the Roman Empire: The military explanation.* New York: Thames and Hudson.

Grant, M. 1974. *The army of the Caesars.* New York: Scribner.

Greenhalgh, P. A. L. 1973. *Early Greek warfare: Horsemen and chariots in the Homeric and Archaic Ages.* Cambridge, England: Cambridge Univ. Press.

Humble, R. 1980. *Warfare in the ancient world.* London: Cassell.

Keppie, L. J. F. 1984. *The making of the Roman army: From Republic to Empire.* Totowa, N.J.: Barnes & Noble Books.

Lazenby, J. F. 1985. *The Spartan army.* Warminster, England: Aris and Phillips.

Luttwak, E. N. 1976. *The grand strategy of the Roman Empire from the first century A.D. to the third.* Baltimore, Md.: Johns Hopkins Univ. Press.

Rodgers, W. L. 1964. *Greek and Roman naval warfare: A study of strategy, tactics, and ship design from Salamis (480 B.C.) to Actium (31 B.C.).* Annapolis, Md.: U.S. Naval Institute Press.

Schulman, A. R. 1964. *Military rank, title, and organization in the Egyptian New Kingdom.* Berlin: B. Hessling.

Speidel, M. 1984. *Roman army studies.* Amsterdam: J. C. Gieben.

Starr, C. G. 1960. *The Roman Imperial navy, 31 B.C.–A.D. 324.* New York: Barnes & Noble.

Turney-High, H. H. 1971. *Primitive war: Its practice and concepts.* Columbia, S.C.: Univ. of South Carolina Press.

Warry, J. G. 1980. *Warfare in the classical world.* London: Salamander Books.

Watson, G. R. 1969. *The Roman soldier.* Ithaca, N.Y.: Cornell Univ. Press.

Webster, G. 1969. *The Roman Imperial army of the first and second centuries* A.D. London: Black.

Yadin, Y. 1963. *The art of warfare in biblical lands in the light of archaeological study.* New York: McGraw-Hill.

HISTORY, EARLY MODERN MILITARY
[1453–1789]

In the mid-fifteenth century, while European princelings battled over a fragmented continent that was still trying to pull itself out of feudalism, an imperial era was reaching its crest throughout the rest of the world. Great empires were raised up and torn down by cavalry armies that swept through Asia. Magnificent pyramids and golden cities were built to mark the growing domains of the Aztecs and the Incas. Tribal chiefs were becoming kings in Africa. In this otherwise vital age, the fall of Constantinople, the last symbol of the great Roman Empire, to the Turkish sultan in 1453 appeared to mark the impotence and vulnerability of Europe.

From this nadir, however, the kings of Europe rose up, and in less than a century it was their empires that were on the advance. Their civilization, their religions, and their rule spread across the oceans, and the first true world empires were born. By 1789, Europeans dominated, ruled, or enslaved many of the other peoples of the globe. This imperial explosion was fueled by a complex military and technological revolution that began with these simple ingredients: 10 parts sulphur, 15 parts charcoal, and 75 parts saltpeter—the most popular formula for gunpowder.

Advent of Gunpowder Weapons

Gunpowder was not a European invention and was used against Europeans, rather than by them, for centuries. The stone walls of Constantinople, for example, which had shielded Europe from Islam for eight centuries, crumbled in 1453 when the sultan, Mohammed II, trained fourteen batteries of cannon on them. The largest of those five dozen guns was built, ironically, by a European, who cast the weapon in the European city of Adrianople. The gun, named Urban's Bombard after its creator, could hurl a 270-kilogram (600 lb.) stone ball over 1,600 meters (1 mi.). The huge bronze monster required about 60 kilograms (134 lbs.) of gunpowder for each such shot, and took so long to clean, load, and lay that it could only be fired seven times a day. The weapon, like many gunpowder engines of its day, frequently misfired. One such misfire burst the barrel and took the life of the gun's designer during the siege.

While Mohammed II's batteries pounded the imperial city, the Byzantine emperor, the eleventh Constantine to rule, had only a handful of small cannon mounted on his walls. The imperial artillery relied on catapults, ballistae, and dart throwers, which the first Constantine would have found familiar. The greatest city in Europe, moreover, could only muster 8,000 defenders for its population of 100,000. The sultan had more soldiers with him than the emperor had people in his capital.

The defense was desperate, brave, ingenious, and hopeless, as Mohammed's guns tore great gaps in the walls. Still, the defenders forced back the flood of feudal levies the Turks sent against them, and did not finally succumb until Mohammed sent in his elite corps of infantry, 12,000 Janissaries. After a day of looting by the Turkish horde, the Janissaries restored order, and Mohammed entered his city. With that procession, the last ancient empire fell.

Gunpowder was not a surprise to the Byzantine defenders. The explosive mixture had been in use in China since the start of the fourth century, about the same time that Constantinople was laid out by the engineers of Constantine the Great, the Roman emperor. Its reputation as a weapon in sieges in Asia was known in Europe by the ninth century, according to church manuscripts. By the twelfth century, Chinese inventors were building crude cannons, and Moorish invaders brought gunpowder weapons into Spain in 1118.

A century and a half later, small guns were being used in sieges throughout Europe, and by the time Urban cast his monster bombard for Mohammed, even larger bombards were in use by the rulers of Ghent, Scotland, and Muscovy. Cast-iron cannon balls and crude carriages were designed to replace the stone shot and immobile platforms of earlier guns, and within a century of the fall of Constantinople, a French inventor had built limbers that finally made guns mobile instruments of war that could be brought to the battlefield, rather than relegated to static siege work.

The proliferation of artillery swept aside the last remnants of feudalism in Europe. No castle, no matter how strongly built or stoutly defended, could withstand the thunder and lightning of artillery. The Europeans, once instructed in this new fact of life by the Turks, were quick to learn that lesson. Less than 40 years after Islamic power wiped out Europe's oldest empire, Spanish guns forced the surrender of Islam's oldest regime, Granada.

In 1481, Mulay Abdul Hassan, sultan of Moorish Spain, refused to pay tribute to Ferdinand and Isabella, the Christian rulers of Castile and Aragón. When asked for silver tribute, he replied, "Our mint at present coins nothing but blades of scimitars and heads of lances." Unfortunately for him and his subjects, the Spanish mints hired the best gunsmiths from France, England, Germany, and Italy, and one by one the Moorish castles and cities fell. On 2 January 1492, Mulay's successor, Boabdil, knelt before Ferdinand and Isabella, the walls of Granada breached by their guns. "These are the keys to the last relics of Arab empire in Spain," Boabdil told the Spanish rulers. "Thine, O sire, are our trophies, our kingdom and our person," Boabdil said as he gave up his crown. "Such is the will of Allah."

The "will of Allah" was heard in the blast of cannon both at Constantinople and at Granada, and at a hundred castles and cities from Scotland to Japan over the next 50 years. From one end of the Old World to the other, gunpowder crumbled principalities and built empires.

Into the Field

Cannon were expensive to cast and required miniature armies of specialists and laborers of their own just to move, use, support, and protect them. Feudal lords and minor nobles could neither remain safe behind ancient walls nor afford the expense of the new weapons. War became too costly for anyone but the wealthiest king, and his need for money to pay for war led the royal houses of Europe to demand taxes rather than military service from their vassals and subjects.

Some feudal armies, or at least feudal components of armies, would live on until the seventeenth century, especially in eastern Europe and the Ottoman Empire. In the 200 years after the fall of Constantinople, however, war would be decided as it had been during the age of Rome, in contests between increasingly larger and more professional armies that faced each other not from behind walls but across open fields.

While artillery forced armies out from behind castles and into the field, it was not mobile or powerful enough on its own to win, or even to be a decisive factor in, those field battles. The gunpowder revolution, however, did not stop. Although many artillery guildsmen worked to make bigger or more mobile guns, others put their talents to work making smaller, lighter weapons that individual soldiers could carry into battle. By the end of the fifteenth century, corps of handgunners could be found in most major armies. Although training men to use these short-range, slow-firing, cumbersome, inaccurate, and unreliable weapons was not difficult, their ineffectiveness led the more advanced armies of the age to retain their reliance on the proven weapons of antiquity: the bow, the pike, and the lance. That reliance, however, was about to change.

From the decline of the Roman Legion in the fourth century to the early fourteenth century, regular, reliable infantry had all but disappeared from the battlefield. Cavalry won the field battles for nearly a thousand years, and even at the time of the Siege of Constantinople, the horseman was still supreme from the shores of the China Sea to the Danube. The heirs of Tamerlane rode over the armies of the Delhi sultanate in India. Ming horsemen and the riders of the steppeland khanates ruled the Asian mainland. Turkish cavalry armies, for example, swept through the Balkans and North Africa in the years following the fall of Constantinople, and by 1477 the Ottoman horsemen were within sight of the defenses of Venice. Horsemen ruled the world, except in Europe.

The chivalry of Europe, the power of the feudal age, had fallen to the Welsh longbow and the Swiss and Flemish pikes, weapons wielded by common soldiers. The death knell of the knight was sounded by the Lombard citizen pikes at Legnano in 1176, and was heard again at Courtrai, Bannockburn, Morgarten, and a score of other battles throughout western Europe over the next 300 years.

The longbow, however, remained the weapon of a small handful of professionals, and except for limited use in Burgundy and Italy, was found exclusively in the small armies of the English kings. The pike, however, was the universal weapon that let the Swiss cantons and the Italian city-states and many cities and towns in between win their freedom from feudal lords. However, the masses of pikemen, the phalanxes of the fifteenth century, soon found themselves vulnerable to the long reach of gunpowder.

By the start of the Italian Wars (1494–1559), European generals had begun to experiment with lighter, long-range hand weapons called harquebuses. Select bodies of infantry armed with these weapons, the precursor of the musket, accompanied the pikemen into battle. Protected from cavalry by their own pikemen, they could shoot and kill the opposing pikes and hold off enemy crossbowmen or cavalry. Supported by artillery and their own cavalry, the combination of pike and shot dominated the battlefield in Europe and, shortly thereafter, the world. The use of gunpowder in weapons that a single man could wield gave rise to two very important and revolutionary factors that would forever change the face of war: the supremacy of infantry and the need for professional soldiers.

Infantry: The Queen of Battle

Despite the drubbing received from pikes, longbows, and harquebuses in the late sixteenth and early seventeenth centuries, the European nobility still preferred the saddle to shoe leather as a means of going into battle. The foot soldier, who had been looked upon as little more than an encumbrance or target for the last thousand years, now became the weapon of victory, and most nobles understood that. Even the aristocratic gendarmes of Catholic France, for example, were wise enough to bring Swiss pikemen with them into the fray against their Huguenot enemies during France's eight Wars of Religion (1562–98).

The foot soldier became the centerpiece around which a battle was planned. As feudal levies had proven worthless against the disciplined pikemen of Switzerland and the Italian cities, a new type of infantry was needed. In the 100 years following the fall of Constantinople, most major powers in Europe would form or hire units of full-time soldiers, the first regular infantry to march in western Europe since the fall of Rome.

In 1496, Ferdinand and Isabella raised the Spanish Infantry of the Ordinance, which by 1505 had been organized into *colunelas*, or regiments, that mixed pikemen and harquebusiers into battlefield units. Under able captains like Gonsalo de Córdoba, this infantry won battle after battle in Italy, defeating the pike masses of the Swiss at Cerignola (21 April 1503), annihilating the French on the Garigliano (30–31 December 1503), and winning other victories at La Motta (October 1513), La Bicocca (27 April 1522), and Pavia (24 February 1525).

Twenty of these regiments were formed initially, but by 1534 these had evolved into even larger units—brigades known as *tercios*. At first, the proportion of pikemen to harquebusiers was large, but the officers discovered that increasing the number of harquebusiers increased the effectiveness of the unit on the battlefield. Consequently, they gave more and more men harquebuses, until by 1550 just over one-half of the men carried firearms while the rest carried the long pike. By 1566, when the duke of Alva took his Spanish army into the Netherlands, the *tercios* included musketeers as well. The Spanish infantry (most of whom were from the Italian, German, and Walloon areas ruled by Spain) replaced the Swiss as the dominant force on the European battlefield, and they would retain that reputation for 150 years, until their defeat by the French at Rocroi on 19 May 1643.

France followed the Spanish model in 1531 when King Francis I created four "legions" of infantry, units that consisted of six "ensigns," each of 600 pikemen, 300 harquebusiers, and 100 halberdiers. The legion was bested by the *tercio* in several battles, notably at Ceresoles in 1544. In that fight, the French were saved at the last minute when their commander, Francis, prince of Enghien, turned the Spanish flank with his cavalry, showing that cavalry could still play an important battlefield role when properly combined with infantry and cannon.

Although not as successful as the Spanish *tercios*, the French infantry continued to grow, and two of the legions, named for the provinces of Picardy and Champagne, continued to exist in the French army without interruption until the revolution of 1789.

Other regular infantry forces also appeared in Europe. From the German states came mercenary pike units, with companies of harquebusiers and pikemen. Known as *landsknechts*, these units fought neither for king nor cause, but for cash. Similar mercenary infantry and cavalry units were raised by the condottiere captains of Italy. The Italian political philosopher Niccolò Machiavelli proposed a new type of Roman legion, which he called the *battaglione*, in 1525, which besides 9,000 men carrying pike, sword, and harquebus, would also have included detachments of cavalry and artillery, as well as its own supply corps. Machiavelli's ideas were never implemented by the Italian states, but some of his theories were adapted by the generals of a later age.

The Ottomans, of course, had their regular infantry, the Janissaries. By the time of the unsuccessful Ottoman siege of Malta in 1565, there were 40,000 Janissaries, armed with sword, bow, and harquebus. They carried the banners of the Turks from the shores of the Persian Gulf to the waters of the Red Sea, and from the deserts of Arabia to the Pillars of Hercules. Their march into Europe proper reached its crest at the walls of Vienna (1529 and 1683). For nearly 250 years after they had captured Constantinople, the Turks repeatedly tried to take Vienna, the capital of the Holy Roman Empire. The Janissaries' greatest defeat, however, was self-inflicted as the corps became embroiled in dynastic politics and was eventually purged. As a unit, however, it would remain part of the Turkish army until destroyed by other Turkish forces in 1826.

A similar fate befell the first professional infantry of eastern Europe, the Russian Streltsi. These regular infantry units of the czar were formed in the mid-1500s, about the time the Janissaries were trying to storm Malta and the Spanish had won the last battles of the Italian Wars. Armed with large axes and harquebuses, these professional soldiers became a class, with service in the unit hereditary. At first paid in saltpeter and lead, the Streltsi grew rich and influential and, like the Janissaries, had to be wiped out by the "new" regular infantry that came into being in the later years of the seventeenth century.

The rise of infantry was not confined to the world west of the Volga and the Caspian, however, but at least for a brief time the foot soldier built empires for eastern warlords. Babur, king of Kabul, conquered most of India with an army of harquebusiers supported by mobile artillery. Chinese, Korean, and other Asian armies also raised infantry units that relied on firepower.

In the mid- to late 1500s, Oda Nobunaga and his generals, Toyotomi Hideyoshi and Tokugawa Ieyasu, unified Japan with saltpeter as well as samurai. Nobunaga developed the concept of continuous infantry volley fire, in which an entire rank fired in a single blast, then stepped back while another rank came up and fired. Although the Spanish experimented with a march-countermarch fire system at about the same time, the volley tactic would not become common in Europe until John of Nassau used it in 1594, nearly 20 years after Nobunaga's use at Nagashino in 1575. Japanese firearms were lighter than those used in Europe and were just as important to victory. One of the most decisive battles in Japanese history, the battle of Sekigahara (the Barrier Field) on 21 October 1600, for example, was won by infantry firepower. The victor, Tokugawa Ieyasu, had learned his trade as a general under Nobunaga. The shogunate he established would last nearly a quarter of a millennia.

The military might of the shoguns, however, could not be effectively extended off their island. Despite invasions in 1592 and 1598, even nearby Korea proved too difficult for Hideyoshi's forces to conquer. Warlords, like Hideyoshi, learned that an invincible army needs an invincible navy if it is to conquer over water. That lesson was also being learned in Europe, as gunpowder, combined with sail power, brought a revolution at sea.

Wooden Ships and Iron Guns

Gunpowder went to sea in the early fourteenth century. The largest ships in the Genoese navy reportedly were armed with a few guns in the early 1300s, but the first time cannon were fired at sea was in 1340 at the naval battle of Sluys in the Hundred Years' War (1337–1453). The fight at Sluys, like most sea battles up to that date, resembled a land battle fought on water. The French fleet was chained together in three immobile lines in the estuary. Ahead of the line were floating traps made from small boats filled with timber, sharp sticks, and dirt. Five of the ships, however, had light cannon. Positioned ahead of and on the left of the first line so as to sweep the approaches, these five ships had an open field of fire on the advancing English. Their guns, however, were not very powerful, horribly inaccurate, and slow to load. Their effect on the battle could not have been very great, as four of the five cannon-armed vessels were taken and the French lost the battle. The battle at Sluys was won by hand-to-hand fighting as armored knights and foot soldiers boarded enemy vessels. There were no maneuvers, and the battle looked a lot like the storming of a castle. Still, the victory gave England command of the channel for 30 years.

Since antiquity, naval battles had been fought like land battles: masses of ships powered by oar closed with and tried to outflank one another while bowmen fired to kill enemy crewmen. For more than 2,000 years, from Salamis (480 B.C.) to Lepanto (1571), sea battles were decided by ramming and boarding.

By the mid-fifteenth century, however, ship design began to change. While the oar-powered galley and longboat still formed the mainstay of naval power, larger, taller sailing vessels were being built in the Atlantic and Baltic port cities of northern Europe and in the shipyards of China.

The Chinese were pioneers in seapower and in using navies to protect their might over long distances. A Muslim eunuch named Cheng Ho, for example, took his fleet of seagoing junks from Ming China to subjugate Sumatra, Ceylon, and much of the Indonesian archipelago in a series of great expeditions between 1405 and 1415. Over the next twenty years, Cheng Ho raided the coasts of the Indian Ocean, exacting tribute from Hormuz, on the Persian Gulf, and Mecca, on the Red Sea, in the early 1430s.

At about the same time, northern European shipyards were turning out relatively large merchantmen of up to 1,000 tons, while the merchant cities of Italy were building even larger vessels, called *uscieri*. Like Cheng Ho's junks, these ships depended solely on sail power and were designed for long-distance travel. The "great cogs" of the Baltic could carry up to 500 fighting men and, like the *uscieri*, were fitted with light cannon. By 1450, Venice and Genoa mounted scores of light cannon, called *petararae*, on their ships. The gun was not cast; instead, it was "built up," made of a tube that was reinforced with rings or strips of rope or, later, iron. A *petarara* fired a ball about the size of a man's fist and was designed to tear sails and kill men, not sink ships. One English vessel of the late fifteenth century, the *Regent*, mounted over 200 guns.

The effectiveness of these ships against oared galleys was demonstrated at the siege of Constantinople in 1453. In one battle, over 100 Turkish galleys tried to force their way into the harbor, but were blocked by ten Byzantine sailing ships. Although the galleys had a few small guns, they could not be raised to fire up at the larger ships, and the Turks were raked by plunging fire.

Later in the siege, three big Genoese ships, escorting a grain carrier, tried to reach the city. They were surrounded by 75 Turkish galleys, led by the sultan's most experienced admiral, Baltoghlu. In the short time between the defeat at the harbor and the battle with the convoy, Baltoghlu had made many changes in the Turkish fleet. Ships' guns had been elevated and remounted, walls of shields were erected along the sides of galleys, and a picked force of Janissaries was chosen to lead the boarding parties.

The Turks repeatedly swarmed around the Christian ships, which were becalmed when the light breeze changed direction. From morning until sunset, Baltoghlu's sailors tried to take the big ships, but each time they were repulsed by fire from above. The admiral even ordered his flagship to ram the grain carrier, but he, too, was repulsed. The four large Christian warships were lashed together and held the Turks at bay until a fresh night breeze carried them safely to Constantinople. Like the English admiral John Byng three centuries later, the luckless Baltoghlu was disgraced and stripped of command. The Turkish admiral, unlike Byng, who was executed for losing the Battle of

Minorca in 1756, was allowed to live, but only after he was given 100 lashes with a heavy golden rod.

Despite the proven power of the great sailing ships, the Turks, and most Mediterranean powers, continued to rely on galleys. Although some ships were powered by convicts or slaves, most rowers were paid professionals and were treated the same as any other member of the crew. These fast ships and their skilled soldiers did not disappear from naval history quietly, but went out with one last flourish of glory under two fifteenth-century admirals, Don John of Austria and the Muslim corsair Khair ed-Din.

Born a Greek Muslim, Khair ed-Din (also known as Barbarossa because of his red hair), was perhaps the greatest of the galley admirals. As dey of Algiers and vassal of the Ottoman sultan, Khair ed-Din scoured the Mediterranean, Aegean, and Adriatic seas throughout the early 1500s. He used his galleys for many different missions, including the conquest of North African states like Tunis and European seaports like Nice, which fell to him in 1543. His navy also harried Christian shipping and performed other complicated strategic missions, such as the evacuation of Spanish Moors (Moriscos) in 1533. Khair ed-Din died in 1546, 25 years before Don John led the last great galley fleet to victory at Lepanto.

Over 500 galleys of various sizes met off Lepanto in the Gulf of Corinth on 7 October 1571. Most of the ships, on both sides, had three to five light cannon mounted in their bows. The six largest ships, giant galleasses sent by Venice, also mounted guns along their sides. Many of the larger ships carried harquebusiers. Despite the guns, the battle was still one of ramming and melee. By the end of the day, nearly 200 Turkish ships had been sunk or captured, and nearly 20,000 rowers, soldiers, and sailors had been lost by the Ottomans. Although 15,000 Christians were killed or wounded, only thirteen of their ships were lost. The battle ended Turkish seapower forever, but despite the triumph of the Christian galley fleet, Lepanto was the last major naval action fought under oar.

The Armada

By the end of the fourteenth century, sails had long replaced oars in westernmost Europe, as they had in China. Christopher Columbus and Vasco da Gama had led sailing fleets across the Atlantic and down along the coast of Africa. Portugal's admirals reached China and Japan by the early 1500s, and Spanish explorers had penetrated the Pacific. None of these expeditions could have been made by galley fleets. In one of the rare galley versus sail battles of the era, a Turkish galley fleet sailing out of the Red Sea was forced back to port by a Portuguese sailing squadron. It was a defeat as important as Lepanto, as it forced the Ottomans away from Africa and opened up that continent, and the Asian sea routes, to the Europeans. Portuguese admirals like Francisco de Almeida and Afonso de Albuquerque fought off Muslim squadrons for 50 years throughout the first half of the sixteenth century, securing Indian Ocean sealanes for Portugal.

Portugal needed a navy to maintain an empire that reached from its Brazilian colonies to its Japanese trading posts. So did Spain, whose growing empire stretched to the Philippines. The Iberian ships were large two-, three-, and later four-masted sailing vessels capable of carrying cargo, crew, and the provisions for the crew great distances. The largest of these were the royal galleons of Portugal and the East India galleons of Spain. They also mounted a wide variety of cannon, ranging from small swivel guns to hull-rending culverins.

Other European powers also built navies, both for exploration and trade (Spain and Portugal) and for privateering (England). England had had a standing navy since Henry VII (1485–1509), who built five warships, among them the *Regent*, and who gave the navy a home base at Portsmouth.

Henry VIII established construction and repair yards along the Thames and enlarged both the navy and its ships. He also replaced the light weapons of his predecessor's reign with much larger, ship-killing guns. The heavier weight of these guns meant that they could no longer be mounted on the fore and stern castles or rails of the ships; for balance they had to be set on the upper or main deck of the vessel. The guns were mounted on carriages, or trucks, and portholes were cut in the sides so that the guns could be slid out and fired, then retracted. One of the first of this new type of broadside-gunned ship was Henry VIII's *Mary Rose*, built in 1509. It foundered and sank in 1545, but Henry and his shipwrights did not give up.

Although the fleet had decayed under Queen Mary (1553–58), Queen Elizabeth's admiral, John Hawkins, rebuilt and revitalized the fleet and its bases. Between 1577 and the year the Armada sailed (1588), Hawkins increased Britain's naval power to such an extent that he was able to put 197 armed ships in English waters that year. Only one of those, moreover, was oar powered.

The English also built flush-deck and race-built ships, which were much lower in the water than the great galleons. The lower English ships appeared small when seen next to the Spanish galleons, but many, like the *White Bear* and the *Triumph*, each of which was over 1,000 tons, were larger than many of the galleons, which averaged about 500 to 700 tons.

England waged a commercial war at sea against Spain and the Spanish treasure fleets. In April 1587, another of Elizabeth's admirals, Sir Francis Drake, sailed into Cádiz harbor. His squadron of seventeen ships fought off ten galleons, burned or captured 37 merchantmen, and then sailed off to seize the Azores. On the way home, he captured the Portuguese treasure ship *San Felipe*. Unable to protect the sea-lanes or his coasts from English raiders, King Philip II of Spain decided to strike the English in their den; he ordered his commanders to prepare an invasion of the British Isles.

Although Julius Caesar, Canute of Denmark, and William of Normandy had all crossed from the continent to England under oars, the Spanish fleet that was collected and built for that same goal in the years after Lepanto contained only eight ships propelled by oars. Four of those, moreover, were galleasses that depended on sails as their principal means of propulsion. Although Philip's chief planner, Alvaro de Bazan, Marquis de Santa Cruz, had commanded a squadron of galleys at Lepanto, he successfully argued for the creation of a sailing fleet for the invasion. He brought shipwrights and gunsmiths from all over Europe to Spain's Atlantic ports for the construction of a new fleet, the Armada. Santa Cruz recognized the value of the cannon used by Drake. Over 100 of the guns mounted on Armada ships were, in fact, made in England. A cannon foundry in the Forest of Dean made 100 guns for the warships of Spain, and merchants in Bristol shipped nine vessels loaded with long-range culverins to Spain for the Armada.

By the time it was ready to sail in May 1588, the Armada had over 130 warships, half of them classified as galleons or great ships. They mounted over 2,400 guns among them and were manned by 26,000 sailors and soldiers. The fleet even included 200 large boats that were carried aboard the big ships for the purpose of disembarking troops and guns. These were the sixteenth-century equivalent of modern landing craft.

Santa Cruz had died in February 1588, and Philip chose the richest, most powerful, and perhaps least-qualified man in Spain to succeed him, the duke of Medina Sidonia. Other experienced commanders were either passed over, relegated to subordinate positions, or detached to other theaters. When the fleet sailed in May 1588, moreover, its destination was not England, but the Netherlands, where it was to escort the duke of Parma's army across the channel.

Through a combination of Spanish luck and bickering among English commanders, Medina Sidonia sailed into the channel unopposed. On 30 July the entire Armada stood outside Plymouth, where two-thirds of the main English fleet lay at anchor, unprepared for battle. Rather than emulate Drake's Cádiz raid, Medina Sidonia remained on course. Over the next two weeks, the 130 ships of the Armada and the 118 warships sent after them by the English navy fought a series of running battles. Drake and Hawkins tried to stand off at long range with their guns, but during four battles in the channel sank only two galleons, one of which was lost because of fouled rigging. The Spanish, largely outranged, tried to close and board (at one point Medina Sidonia's flagship closed to within 100 meters [110 yds.] of the English line), but they too did little damage and reached Calais as planned on 6 August.

Although the Armada fight was the first time ships mounting broadside guns engaged in a large-scale fleet battle, the decisive moment came not at sea but in port, when English fireships were sent among the Armada. Although actual damage was minor, many Spanish captains cut their anchor cables to make way hurriedly, and Medina Sidonia's carefully ordered fleet degenerated into ad hoc squadrons and groups of stragglers.

Medina Sidonia managed to collect two dozen of the large galleons into a battle squadron, but after ten hours of combat on 8 August, both his fleet and the English had used up almost all of their powder and shot. The Armada sailed north, chased at a distance by the English, who after four days broke off the action and headed home. The Armada, in squadrons and by individual ship, tried to sail around England and Ireland. Half of the fleet was lost at sea. Of the 67 ships that made it back to Spain, nearly half were so badly damaged that they had to be broken up to repair the rest.

Spain built three more armadas, two of which were wrecked by storms. The fourth, sent to sea three years after Philip's death, landed a small army in Ireland in 1601, but to no avail. The two weary successors to Philip and Elizabeth made peace in 1604.

World Empires Made at Sea

Spanish seapower, although still great in terms of numbers of ships, never fully recovered. The English, who took credit for its demise, did not supplant the Spanish at sea, and were themselves nearly swept from the waves by the Dutch, whose navy was essentially a huge fleet of armed merchantmen. The Dutch, who gained their freedom from Spain in the 1630s, quickly built up a trading empire that brought spice from Asia and furs from the Americas. Colonies and trading posts from New Amsterdam (New York) to Nagasaki, Japan, served as bases for the trading navy, which in turn made Holland the warehouse of the world.

Civil wars in England (1642–51), unrest in France (1648–53), and a general malaise in the Iberian kingdoms gave the Dutch a head start toward building an empire and a fleet. When the rival navies finally began a twenty-year war for mastery of European waters and Atlantic trade routes, it was the Dutch, initially, who had the advantage, in terms of experience, numbers of ships, and money. By the middle of the century, Holland had over 10,000 sail and 168,000 seamen upon the water.

As the more maneuverable English had an advantage against the galleons, so Holland's lighter, flatbottomed ships often gave the Dutch an advantage over the English, French, and Spanish. Most of the battles between and among these forces in the seventeenth century were fought in coastal, tidal, or shoalfilled waters, where the Dutch were more maneuverable and less likely to run aground.

Naval battles of the period were contests of broadsides, but at first still resembled the melees of galley warfare. Fire ships were used to break up enemy formations in the same way that later navies would use torpedo boats. The Dutch, for example, took fire ships into the sea fight of Southwold Bay (Sole Bay) in 1672. By the end of the era, however, the tactical order of line abreast, used by galleys, was supplanted by the line ahead formation. This allowed the increasingly longer ranged guns to be best brought to bear in massive fleet broadsides.

England, France, and the Netherlands fought four naval wars in the second half of the seventeenth century, and although the Dutch fleet under De Ruyter once sailed up the Thames, it was the English who eventually triumphed.

Rather than armed merchantmen, the fleets of the late seventeenth century relied on ships designed solely for war. These vessels, known as ships of the line, mounted from 50 to as many as 130 guns of standard calibers. The bigger ships could even outgun coastal forts. The old iron trucks were replaced by wooden gun carriages, usually made of cedar or elm, and systems of ropes and pulleys allowed the guns to be fired, hauled in, reloaded, run out, and fired again in minutes. Unlike the Armada's guns, some of which had to be loaded by men leaning over the rails, these guns could be serviced from behind the protective sides of the warships.

The Dutch won most of the European naval actions, but the English kept coming back out to sea. They took the war to the colonies, moreover, and gained an empire. The commerce of England eventually surpassed that of Holland, and the Dutch, worried over the continental ambitions of France, made peace.

The French had an overseas empire, but they were not convinced of the advantages of maintaining a large blue-water navy. By the 1670s, the French decided to lay up their large warships and fight a war of privateers, preying on commercial vessels for profit and economic harm rather than contest the growing English mastery of the sea.

France produced its own class of courageous and innovative seamen, such as the privateer admiral Jean Bart and the fleet commander Tourville. Under Louis XIV, France made another, unsustained, bid for seapower, and built a new battle navy that by 1689 was nearly as large as the fleets of England and Holland combined. Unfortunately for France, England and Holland united. Despite inconclusive victories like Beachy Head (1690), the capture of an English treasure fleet from Jamaica, and the skillful retreat of La Hogue in 1692, the French decided again to break up their navy into commerce raiding. By the turn of the century, the French had all but disappeared from the sea, and the navies of England and its allies were able to sail anywhere at will.

This command of the sea allowed England to seize islands and raid ports, ravage coasts and capture strategic outposts such as Gibraltar, which fell to English forces in 1704. Spain, under the aggressive and talented royal minister Alberoni, tried to reestablish itself as a seapower, but the fleet was crushed at Cape Passaro in 1718, and the terms of peace imposed on it in 1719 forced Madrid to destroy the dockyards where the new navy was being built.

By 1740, the English fleet of nearly 100 ships of the line and an equal number of frigates (smaller and faster than ships of the line, mounting 20 to 40 guns), outnumbered that of its next largest rival, France, by two to one. That ratio grew as France and England went to war in the 1740s and 1750s. Although the English suffered a few defeats, such as Byng's failure at Minorca, the French were again forced to break up the navy and rely on a raiding strategy. At the end of the Seven Years' War (1756–63), the English navy outnumbered the French by three to one in ships of the line alone. Although French privateers captured or sank 2,500 English merchantmen during the war, over 8,000 remained to bring troops, supplies, and goods from one end of the growing British Empire to the other. Nearly 250 of the privateers had been captured by war's end, and by 1761 not a single French ship of the line was under sail. French commerce, moreover, was driven from the seas.

Command of the oceans allowed England to move armies at will, and not just in Europe. British forces captured the cities of rival European overseas empires. Quebec was taken from France in 1759, and Havana was wrested from Spain in 1762. Seapower also gave the British the opportunity to challenge the power of more distant kingdoms and to win an even larger empire in India.

While mastery of the sea gave the English, as it had the Spanish before them, the ability to reach across the ocean to build empires, those empires were won, and held, on the ground, and that was the job of the professional soldier.

Cannon, Cavalry, and Muskets

As the ship of the line became the main unit of mastery at sea, so the regiment became the instrument of victory on land. The regularity of warfare, both in Europe and overseas, and the increasing size of the armies needed to win those wars, led to the formation of standing armies of professional soldiers. Although all the powers of Europe relied on mercenaries or men who were forced or induced to join the colors to flesh out their armies, the central core of the Spanish, French, Swedish, and other important forces of the period were professional combat units of horse and foot.

The combination of pike and harquebus pioneered by the Spanish *tercios* became the model for all European armies by the turn of the seventeenth century. By 1618, at the start of Europe's last—and worst—great religious war, muskets had begun to replace the harquebus, giving infantry units a greater and more sustained reach across the battlefield. The 4–6-meter-long (4½–6½-yd.-long) spears carried by the pikemen, less an offensive weapon in an age when a musketeer could kill a man at 60 to 100 paces, were, however, still needed to protect the musketeer while he reloaded. Muskets easily became fouled by black powder, and a light drizzle could render the powder useless or put out the match that was used to ignite the powder in the musket pan. While the musket was put to use as a club in close fighting, particularly by the Irish regiments that fought for France and Spain, the pike was still needed to ward off cavalry and the opposition's own pike masses.

Throughout the Thirty Years' War (1618–48), European arms, tactics, and organizations went through a series of changes, most of them brought about by firepower. Artillery became more mobile, and light guns were used with great effect by Sweden's warrior king Gustavus Adolphus and his imitators. These light cannon, manned by a small crew, could keep pace with the advancing infantry, while the heavy guns remained comparatively immobile once in place. Gustavus at first used small guns made of copper tubes bound with iron hoops, cords, plaster, and leather, but he discarded these in favor of a cast-iron piece that fired a four-pound shot. It weighed only 200 kilograms (500 lbs.) and could be moved about by a two-horse team and a three-man crew.

The Swedish king attached a pair of these guns to each of his regiments and used them to plow great gaps in the massive squares of Imperial infantry that he faced at Breitenfeld, Lützen, and a dozen other battles of the Thirty Years' War. Accompanying light guns soon became standard equipment in the infantry regiments, a practice that continued throughout the musket era. As guns and muskets improved, the numbers of pikes dwindled in proportion, and generals and soldiers traded cold steel for hot powder.

For a time, even the cavalry of Europe came to rely on firepower. Pistol-armed horsemen had made their appearance in the French Wars of Religion half a century before, when Protestant cavalry combined sword and pistol in their duels with Catholic lancers. Large units of armored cavalry armed with pistols rode onto the battlefields of Germany in the early 1600s and performed a maneuver called the caracole, in which rank after rank of horsemen came forward, fired at their opponents, and wheeled to the side to let the rank behind come forward and fire.

This complete turnabout in tactics from shock to missile weapons by horsemen was short-lived, however, as Gustavus, England's Oliver Cromwell, and other generals raised new regiments of cavalry that were trained to charge at the gallop, wielding heavy steel swords. Lines of cavalry riding to the charge with swords remained the trademark of the heavy cavalry for 300 years, until the middle of the nineteenth century, when rifled muskets and quick-firing artillery were able to break up the horse regiments at ranges of several hundred meters.

The clumsy lance of the chivalric era was still carried by gendarmes and other heavy horse at the start of the seventeenth century, but by the end of the Thirty Years' War even they had discarded it in favor of the sword. Light horse units and eastern cavalry in general still carried a light lance, but even the Polish winged hussars stuck an axe, mace, or sword, and sometimes a brace of pistols, in their gear. The bow all but disappeared in the west, but remained an important tool of war from the Volga to the Yalu. The Manchu Banner cavalry, which overran Ming China in the 1600s, for example, fought with lance and bow, as did the Moghul cavalry in India. Japanese samurai also continued to use their bows.

Light cavalry also made a comeback on the European battlefield. The unarmored cavalry on their small ponies, such as the Hungarian hussars, performed the duties of scouting, patroling, and foraging for the army. On the battlefield, they usually kept to the far flanks, but were often used in harassing skirmishers, annoying flanks, and riding down already routed infantry units. European generals also experimented with units called *dragoons*, which moved and performed some of the duties of the light cavalry, but which usually fought on foot with muskets, firelocks, or carbines.

The use of such a variety of forces required the skill, timing, and discipline found only among well-led regular forces. The Stuarts were taught that lesson by Cromwell's New Model army, which, even when outnumbered, won impressive victories, like Naseby (14 June 1645). By the end of the Thirty Years' War, even the *tercio* had fallen to the more advanced combined arms tactics of men like the French general Louis duke of Enghien (later prince of Condé). The final day for the *tercio* came at the battle of Rocroi on 19 May 1643, when 18,000 Spanish infantry were broken by Enghien's army. The French cavalry defeated the Spanish horse, leaving the mighty *tercios* stranded. Still, the Spanish fought off a succession of French horse and foot attacks, until late in the day, when the duke brought his mobile guns up close and broke open the pike squares. Like the loss of the Armada, the destruction of the *tercios* was a defeat from which Spain could not recover, and Spanish dominance of land warfare was ended.

Spain was not the only empire whose sun had begun to set in the mid-1600s. By the end of the century, a new age had come about in Europe. With the last great gasp of Turkish power hurled back from the gates of Vienna by John Sobieski and his Polish cavalry in 1683, the Ottoman Empire began a rapid decline. By the end of that decade, the Turks had been forced out of Hungary, the Ukraine, and much of Greece and were in internal turmoil following a Janissary revolt and dynastic upheaval. Relieved of Ottoman pressure, another power in the east was also on the advance. Russia, whose cossacks had reached across Asia to Siberia and the borders of Manchu China by 1689, also turned westward, where it became embroiled in a series of wars with Poland and Sweden. By 1700, the last of the old empires had been beaten down, and those that rose to take their places engaged in a century-long world war.

The Rise of France

If any nation emerged victorious from the 30 years of destruction that left one-third of the population of central Europe dead or displaced, it was France. For the rest of the century following Enghien's victory at Rocroi, the French army was considered the best in Europe. Under Louis XIV it was certainly the largest and the best organized. By the 1660s, Louis had over 160 regiments of horse and foot in his army. Nearly a quarter of a million men marched under his royal banner.

Louis's generals also standardized and professionalized the French artillery. In the mid-seventeenth century, there was no standard artillery piece. The Spanish, for example, had over twenty different calibers of artillery, although they at least had them classified into four basic groups, which was far more ordered than most of their rivals. Louis's artillery regiment and his inspector of artillery, Claude du Metz, standardized the guns into six land and seven naval classes, categorized by weight of shot. Older guns were refounded, and new brass pieces were cast. Artillery would not become truly standardized until the French introduced their Système Vallière in 1732, the year that French gunners finally received military rank.

At the start of the 1700s, France was the leading power in Europe. Louis XIV had the largest army on the continent, and France itself was protected by a series of fortifications designed by the king's chief engineer, Vauban. The new style of fortress built by Vauban was designed to offset the power of artillery that had rendered stone castles obsolete. Combinations of stonework and dirt made the relatively low walls more resistant to the pounding of iron shot, while star-shaped gun positions, called bastions, were laid with an eye to establishing overlapping fields of long-range cannon fire.

As Vauban himself demonstrated, almost any fortress, even one modeled on his own designs, could be taken if the besieger had the time, manpower, will, and skill to do so. The Vauban fortress was not impregnable, nor was it intended to be. It was designed to slow an invasion and to allow small forces to buy time. While an invader was busy digging trenches and mines, foraging for food, and otherwise tied down in a siege, the opposing state could marshal an army of its own and march to the rescue. Such a rescue might involve a field battle, but more likely it could be accomplished by cutting off supply lines or threatening to lay siege to the invader's own bases. Tied to their depots, armies could not leave fortresses in their rear, unless they detailed large bodies of men to besiege or at least mask them. Such detachments would greatly weaken an invader, again helping the state under attack to even the odds.

Eighteenth-century warfare, however, was hardly the staid, bloodless chess match that the war of fortresses would suggest. In 1704, the English commander John Churchill, Duke of Marlborough, marched an Anglo-Dutch army from the Netherlands to Bavaria, knocked France's Bavarian ally out of the war and joined up with an Austrian Imperial army under Prince Eugene of Savoy, to win a bloody battle at Blenheim, near the banks of the Danube. At Blenheim, in August 1704, nearly 35,000 men, on both sides, were killed or wounded. Losses were even heavier at Malplaquet, another of Marlborough's victories, five years later.

The principal instrument of death in those battles, and in half a hundred other major engagements fought across Europe in that decade-long war, was the infantry musket. Unlike the clumsy matchlocks of the Thirty Years' War, the musket of 1700 was a flintlock weapon, a much more reliable and faster-to-load firearm than the matchlocks of the previous century. Louis XIV raised the first full regiment to be equipped with flintlocks in 1670, and they were the standard weapon throughout Europe by 1699. The last pikes disappeared in the West just about that time, although a few pike companies were still found in the Austrian, Russian, and Swedish armies in the first years of the century.

Infantry tactical formations went from men massed ten deep to more compact, linear formations three to six ranks deep. The troops fought in closely packed lines, with the purpose of bringing massive firepower to bear on other closely packed lines. Most firefights were fought at under 100 meters (110 yds.), and the slaughter was dreadful. When the mobile cannons were brought to the front by their regiments, the bloodletting was even worse.

Infantrymen were equipped with plug bayonets, which could be forced into the muzzle of a musket, and later with ring and socket bayonets (a Vauban invention), which could be fitted around the muzzle, thus permitting them to fire their muskets with bayonets fixed. However, cold steel was used more frequently by the cavalry, which continued to slash about at one another with heavy swords. The firepower of good, disciplined infantry gave them little to fear from cavalry approaching from the front, but the linear tactics dictated by the weapons made them more vulnerable on the flanks. While the infantry could still form a hollow square and hold off the horse with musket fire and a hedgehog of bayonets, an army whose cavalry was driven off the field could soon find itself in the position of the Spanish at Rocroi or the French at Blenheim.

The Great Wars for Empire

The eighteenth century saw the first true world wars in that great powers fought in several theaters of conflict. French, British, and Spanish fleets and armies, and the forces of their allies, fought each other in Europe, the Americas, India, and off the coasts of Africa and Asia. While most of the wars were initiated by dynastic squabbles in Europe, they mushroomed into world conflicts that decided or influenced the destiny of millions.

Some of these wars, however, were purely European in nature, such as the Great Northern War between Peter the Great of Russia and Charles XII of Sweden. Heir to Gustavus's tough little professional army, Charles triumphed over every army Peter sent against him for nearly a decade. The czar, however, learned from the Swedes, and when he met Charles on the battlefield of Poltava, in southern Russia in 1709, the weight of Russian numbers and artillery won the day. Russia replaced Sweden as the Baltic power, and for the next century would expand to the south and west at the expense of the Ottomans, the Poles, and the Swedes.

No longer threatened from the West, Russia also grew eastward, and became a great land empire and a power whose influence was felt from the privy council chamber in London to the Manchu court in Tientsin. Russia even launched its own bid for an overseas empire, with expeditions that sailed to Alaska and the Pacific coast of North America.

Unlike the Great Northern War, the wars initiated by Prussia's Frederick the Great involved coalitions that included nations with overseas empires. While his victories over Austrian, French, and Russian forces led to a battlefield legend for the Prussian disciplinarian and his army, battles fought outside of Europe by the allies and enemies of Frederick had at least as great an effect on world history.

In the two Frederickian wars of mid-eighteenth-century Europe (the War of Austrian Succession [1740–48] and the Seven Years' War [1756–63]), France and England sent fleets and armies to battle around the world. From the forests of New York to the plains of Delhi, small European regular forces, backed by colonial militia and local allies, fought and won huge empires that were out of all proportion in numbers of people and areas of land to the size of the armies engaged. The actions of a few thousand English troops on the Plains of Abraham (Quebec, 13 September 1759) and the mango grove at Plassey (23 June 1757) in India, ensured the ascendancy of Britain's world empire. Like Cortez's conquistadors, who conquered the Aztec Empire of Mexico 240 years before, those small numbers of professional, disciplined European firepower infantry proved more than a match for hordes of poorly trained feudal troops, even when, like the Nawab's army at Plassey, they also had gunpowder and courage to spare.

The World Turned Upside Down

The revolution in land and sea warfare that by 1763 had helped create the British Empire, the Prussian dominance of Central Europe, and the Russian colossus in the east did not end in the mid-eighteenth century (Fig. 1). The changes in warfare that had crumbled the last ancient empire at Constantinople in 1453 also contributed to the political and military revolution that came about in the closing decades of the eighteenth century.

Mark G. McLaughlin

See Also: American Revolutionary War; Charles XII, King of Sweden; Condé, Louis II de Bourbon, Prince de; Cromwell, Oliver; Eugene, Prince of Savoy-Carignan; France, Military Hegemony of; Frederick the Great; Gonzalo de Córdoba; Gustavus Adolphus; Italian Wars; Manchu Empire; Marlborough, John Churchill, Duke of; Moghul Empire; Musashi, Miyamoto; Ottoman Empire; Peter the Great; Prussia and Germany, Rise of; Saxe, Hermann Maurice, Comte de; Seapower, British; Seven Years' War; Spanish Empire; Suffren de St. Tropez, Pierre André de; Suvorov, Aleksandr Vasil'evich; Turenne, Henri

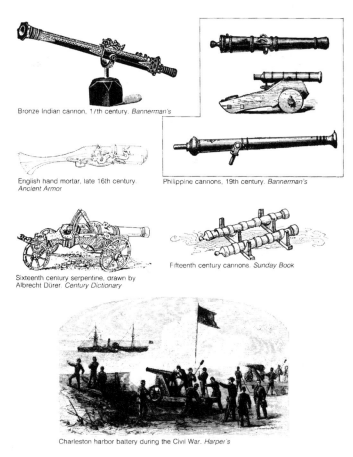

Bronze Indian cannon, 17th century. *Bannerman's*

English hand mortar, late 16th century. *Ancient Armor*

Philippine cannons, 19th century. *Bannerman's*

Sixteenth century serpentine, drawn by Albrecht Dürer. *Century Dictionary*

Fifteenth century cannons. *Sunday Book*

Charleston harbor battery during the Civil War. *Harper's*

Figure 1.Examples of fifteenth- through nineteenth-century cannon and a sixteenth-century mortar. (Source: Hart Picture Archives)

de La Tour d'Auvergne, Vicomte de; Vauban, Sébastien Le Prestre de; Washington, George.

Bibliography

Beeching, J. 1983. *The galleys at Lepanto.* New York: Scribner's.

Braudel, F. 1973. *The Mediterranean and the Mediterranean world in the age of Philip II.* 2 vols. Trans. S. Reynolds. New York: Harper and Row.

Chandler, D. G. 1974. *The art of warfare on land.* London: Hamlyn.

————. 1976. *The art of warfare in the age of Marlborough.* New York: Hippocrene.

Cipola, C. M. 1963. *Guns, sails, and empires.* New York: Minerva Press.

Corvisier, A. 1979. *Armies and societies in Europe 1494–1789.* Trans. A. T. Sidall. Bloomington, Ind: Indiana Univ. Press.

Duffy, C. J. 1975. *Fire and stone: The science of fortress warfare 1660–1860.* New York: Hippocrene.

————. 1988. *The military experience in the age of reason.* New York: Atheneum.

————. 1985. *Frederick the great: A military life.* New York: Atheneum.

Dupuy, R. E., and T. N. Dupuy. 1977. *The encyclopedia of military history.* New York: Harper and Row.

Fuller, J. F. C. 1967. *A military history of the western world.* New York: Minerva Press.

Guilmartin, J.F. 1974. *Gunpowder and galleys: Changing technology and Mediterranean warfare at sea in the sixteenth century.* Cambridge: Cambridge Univ. Press.

Hale, J. R. 1983. *Renaissance war studies.* London: Hambledon Press.

Hogg, I. V. 1975. *Fortress: A history of military defense.* New York: St. Martin's Press.

Koch, H. W. 1981. *The rise of modern warfare.* Greenwich, Conn.: Bison Books.

Lawford, J. 1976. *Cavalry.* New York: Bobbs-Merrill.

Leach, D. E. 1973. *Arms for Empire.* New York: Macmillan.

Machiavelli, N. 1965. *Chief works and others.* Trans. A. Gilbert. Durham, N.C.: Duke Univ. Press.

Mahan, A. T. 1918. *The influence of sea power upon history, 1660–1763.* Boston: Little, Brown.

Mallet, M. E. and J.R. Hale. 1984. *The military organization of a renaissance state: Venice, c. 1400–1617.* Cambridge: Cambridge Univ. Press.

Mattingly, G. 1959. *The armada.* Boston: Houghton Mifflin.

Oman, C. W. C. 1937. *A history of the art of war in the sixteenth century.* New York: E. P. Dutton.

Parker, G. 1972. *The army of Flanders and the Spanish road.* Cambridge: Cambridge Univ. Press.

————. 1988. *The military revolution: Military innovation and the rise of the West, 1500–1800.* Cambridge: Cambridge Univ. Press.

Roy, I. 1972. *The Hapsburg-Valois wars and the French wars of religion: Selections from the commentaries of Blaise de Monluc.* Hamden, Conn.: Archon Books.

Parkman, F. 1968. *The Seven Years' War.* New York: Harper-Torch.

Rogers, H. C. B. 1968. *Battles and generals of the civil wars.* London: Seeley.

Taylor, F. L. 1929. *The art of war in Italy, 1494–1529.* Cambridge: Cambridge Univ. Press.

Vale, M. G. A. 1982. *War and chivalry: Warfare and aristocratic culture in England, France, and Burgundy at the end of the Middle Ages.* Athens, Ga.: Univ. of Georgia Press.

Wedgewood, C. V. 1961. *The Thirty Years' War.* Garden City, N.Y.: Anchor Books.

HISTORY, MEDIEVAL MILITARY
[ca. A.D. 450–1450]

The medieval era (ca. A.D. 450–1450) is often regarded by military historians as devoid of significant developments, apart from the military system of the Mongols. This is unfortunate because numerous military developments occurred, many of them closely related to social changes that influenced the evolution of modern European military institutions. The decline and collapse of large empires in India, China, and the Mediterranean basin during the fourth century A.D. was followed by a prolonged period of political chaos. This situation endured longest and was most severe in Europe, but India remained politically fragmented for most of the ensuing ten centuries, and even China saw long periods of disorder and conflict between imperial regimes. By the mid-fifteenth century, though, Europe had achieved sufficient political organization and technological superiority to begin spreading its influence, marking the advent of the early modern era.

Dark Ages, A.D. 350–800

The collapse of the western Roman Empire in Europe had more profound results than the end of the Gupta Empire in India or the chaotic and sometimes anarchic period in China between the fall of the Later Han and the rise of the T'ang. Principal among these results was the change in the social fabric that followed the advent of the Germanic kingdoms in western Europe. The literate, urban society of the Roman Empire was replaced in less than a century by a collection of haphazardly organized successor-kingdoms ruled by kings who were little more than chiefs, and whose authority over their subjects was tenuous. Most cities in these kingdoms decayed, trade waned, and public order broke down as brigandage became common and quarrels among the new aristocracy became small wars. Perhaps most important, military service became linked to the ownership of land (the roots of manorialism); loyalty to the state or the emperor was replaced by personal, practical ties to a person's immediate overlord (the origins of feudalism). Some of these trends, like the decline of urban life and trade, and the beginnings of feudalism, were apparent as early as the mid-fourth century, but the collapse of the Roman Empire in the west in the fifth century hastened their development.

In terms of military organization and the conduct of warfare, these changes meant an end to the sophisticated warfare of Rome, and a return to days when campaigns were often expeditions for plunder, battles happened accidentally, and armies were usually poorly organized masses of armed men. Much the same could be said of the armies of the very late Roman Empire, however. The exception to this decline was in the Eastern Roman Empire where, with a more urban population, society did not regress even under the pressures of barbarian raids and crises of imperial succession nearly as badly as those in the west. The Eastern Empire's army, though at first staffed largely by *foederati* (allied barbarian soldiers serving for pay), retained most of the professionalism and technical expertise of the old Roman army.

A clear example of this is the Eastern Roman conquest of Italy, the so-called Gothic War of 534–54, undertaken by Justinian I's able generals Belisarius and Narses, less than 60 years after the fall of the Western Empire. Though handicapped by Justinian's notorious (and ultimately shortsighted) stinginess, Belisarius waged his campaigns with energy and speed, using his army's superior tactical skill to defeat much larger armies. At the Battle of Casilinum in 554, Narses's 18,000 men decisively defeated 30,000 Franks and Goths under the Frankish chieftains Buccelin and Lothair. Narses deployed his cavalry and archers on both flanks of his army, and when the Franks had committed themselves to the attack, he brought the wings of his army together, surrounding the Franks. After softening them up with arrows, Narses's cavalry charged and destroyed the Frankish army.

While the armies of the Germanic kingdom in western Europe were less organized than those of the Romans, they were not simply mobs. In theory all the adult male members of a tribe (around which each of the successor-kingdoms was originally created) were liable for military service, but in practice monarchs rarely summoned more than a small portion of the available manpower for service in a particular campaign. This self-imposed limitation occurred because a long campaign with an army based on universal compulsory service of adult males would wreak havoc on the subsistence agricultural economies of the barbarian kingdoms.

As military service was a significant economic burden (soldiers in the Germanic kingdoms were expected to show up with their own weapons, horses, and supplies when they were summoned), most of the kingdoms soon came to rely on their aristocracies, and those men who could be supported by them, to provide their armies. This practice kept armies relatively small, but it meant that the economic dislocation caused by raising troops was minimized, an important consideration in an economy just above the subsistence level. The tactics of these armies were simple: attack was an all-out charge, especially for the cavalry forces of the Goths and Lombards, and a defense was made by a dense mass of foot soldiers, all generally facing the enemy. Battles were usually confused and bloody, and commanders served less as tactical directors (battles in this period were nearly impossible to control once they began) and more as rallying points and champions. The strength of a soldier lay not in his tactical skill but in his personal prowess as a fighter.

This era lasted for approximately three centuries after the fall of the Roman Empire in the west and, although more primitive than the preceding or succeeding eras, it was not always lacking in sophistication, supplied by such monarchs as Theodoric the Great.

The Arab Conquests and the Rise of the Byzantine Empire, 630–800

The rise of Islam and the astoundingly rapid Arab conquest of North Africa, the Levant, and nearly all of Spain within a century of Muhammad's death in 632 had the most profound effect on military developments in Europe since the fall of the Roman Empire two and one-half centuries before. The Arab armies of the early Caliphate were primarily light troops, often poorly armed, but what they lacked in materiel they made up for in morale and esprit de corps. The Arab armies were also gifted with several brilliant generals, such as Khalid ibn al-Walid and Saad ibn ali-Waqqas, commanders who understood not only the strengths and weaknesses of their own troops but also those of their enemies. The best of the Arab generals also showed a clear grasp of strategy. Their campaigns employed the desert as a screen for their movements, a level of strategic sophistication almost entirely lacking in western Europe.

The most immediate result of the Arab conquests in Europe, other than the loss of Spain and destruction of the Visigothic kingdom, was the metamorphosis of the Latinized Eastern Roman Empire into the Greek-oriented Byzantine Empire, whose attentions were drawn to the east. The emperor who presided over this metamorphosis was Heraclius, a ruler and general of rare talent and ability. He became emperor (or "took the purple," as Byzantine chroniclers put it) as a result of a successful coup d'état against the notorious tyrant Phocas in 610. Heraclius came to the throne of an empire beset by Persian and Avar enemies, but his energy and ability enabled him to regain the initiative. Despite the loss of Egypt, the Levant, and most of Asia Minor he carried the war into the Persian homeland in a series of campaigns begun in 622.

The failure of the Persian siege of Constantinople, coupled with the effects of Heraclius's continued successes in Armenia, Anatolia, and Assyria, compelled the Persians to make peace in 628. Over the next few years, Heraclius busied himself restoring the Empire's prosperity after twenty years of war. Heraclius's restorations were interrupted by Arab attacks on the Levant, which began in the mid-630s. Despite valiant efforts, he was unable to halt the Arab advance, and when he died in 641, weary and despondent, the empire had lost Egypt and all of the Levant as far north as the Taurus mountains. The people in these areas were too tired of war to resist for long, and were further separated from the Imperial government by long-standing religious differences.

Heraclius's most important work, though, was his expansion of the ideas of Emperor Maurice (whom Phocas had murdered to seize the throne) on military administration, and his creation of the first *themes*, or military provinces, in Asia Minor in the 620s. The troops stationed in and recruited from each *theme* were to provide its defense, and were under the command of a *strategos* (general), who also acted as governor of the *theme*. The thematic system was patterned after the militarized administration of the exarchates of Ravenna and Africa, and represented a final break with the remnants of Diocletian's administrative system. The thematic system also provided the basis for Byzantine territorial defense and the army until the eleventh century, when the combination of the loss of Anatolia, the decreasing size of individual themes (and a corresponding increase in number), and the disappearance of the soldier-freeholder at last destroyed it.

Western Europe felt the Arab onslaught later than the East; Spain was not invaded until 711. Perhaps the most famous military incident of this period of

Arab conquests was the Battle of Tours in October 732. Charles Martel led an army of heavily armed and armored Franks against a large force of Arab raiders under their commander Abd er-Rahman, the governor of Muslim Spain. Despite repeated fanatical attacks, the light Arab cavalry was unable to make an impression on the well-armored Frankish troops, who had dismounted to fight. When the Arabs found that their commander had been killed in the fighting, they abandoned the field. The Battle of Tours showed that while the Arab armies were not invincible, they could be defeated only through careful and skillful generalship. Encounters with Arab and other Muslim armies in subsequent centuries showed that European commanders often lacked that quality.

Second Barbarian Assault: Vikings and Magyars, 800–1000

Western Europe, soon after stopping the Arab advance, was faced with two new threats: the Magyars from the east, and the Vikings from Scandinavia to the north. The Viking attacks began first, during the first decade of the ninth century. Although at first they only conducted raids for plunder, the warriors from the north began to settle along the coasts they raided, establishing networks of strongholds in the mid to late ninth century. Most of the Vikings who attacked England were Danes (the area they dominated was known later as the Danelaw), while the Norwegians (or Norse) operated primarily in Ireland and Scotland, and both Danes and Norse harassed the French coast. The Swedes took a different course and pressed deep into Russia, eventually arriving on the Black and Caspian seas, and even attacking Constantinople, albeit unsuccessfully.

Since the first Viking attacks were simply pirate raids, true armies of Vikings did not appear until the latter half of the ninth century. The physical prowess of the Vikings and their evident delight in violent activities did much to enhance their reputation as warriors, and the news that the Norsemen were coming was sometimes enough to empty a district of its population. Viking tactics, like those of their European opponents, were simple, but generally effective. These included the "shield wall," where defenders overlapped their shields for additional protection, and the use of *berserkers* (literally, "those without armor"), who worked themselves into a killing frenzy before a battle.

Viking generals also used ruses and stratagems, and their cunning and resourcefulness earned them many triumphs over more sophisticated opponents. Viking campaigns were at first constrained by the availability of water transport routes that their longships used to gain access to territories for pillage. When the Vikings later established local bases, they were able to mount some of their troops on horseback. While the Norsemen always fought dismounted, they used horses to increase their strategic mobility.

The strain of resisting the Viking depredations wrecked, or at least badly damaged, what little central government had developed in western Europe since the late fifth century. Authority naturally devolved onto those local leaders who could organize resistance or at least provide refuges for people fleeing Viking raids. In this fashion, especially in England and France, the Viking raids hastened the growth of feudalism. By the beginning of the tenth century, many of the Danes and Norse had settled in the lands they raided and often accepted the authority of the native rulers, if only in the same unruly fashion as other feudal magnates. The situation was different in England. By the end of the reign of Alfred the Great, the Danes and Anglo-Saxons had reached a happy accommodation. Alfred had also created a navy, which he and his successors used to guard their coast, to transport their troops, and to fend off enemy raiders.

While northern and western Europe endured the depredations of the Vikings, eastern Europe faced the onslaught of the Magyars, a nomadic people of Finno-Ugric ancestry. These people, defeated by an alliance of Patzinaks (Pechenegs) and Bulgars in southern Russia about 895, settled soon after in the Hungarian plain under their chieftain Arpad. There they allied with the remnants of Charlemagne's old enemies, the Avars. Even before settling in Hungary, the Magyars had raided eastern Germany, and they soon began again, raiding Germany and northern Italy, ranging as far afield as Rheims and Lyons. The highly mobile, bow-armed forces of the Magyars at first easily eluded the heavily armed and rather clumsy German cavalry.

The Germans responded, however, and worked better to protect their lands and to improve their armies. Henry the Fowler, then king of Germany, defeated a Magyar army at the Battle of Allstedt (near Erfurt) on 15 March 933. The Magyars, chastened by this reverse and frustrated by increasingly effective German frontier defenses, reduced their raiding activity during the next two decades. In 954, though, they assembled an army of at least 50,000 and swept through Bavaria into Franconia. German Emperor Otto I made a treaty with them and helped them move into Lorraine. The Magyars ravaged much of northeastern France, then crossed the Great St. Bernard Pass to conduct further pillage in Italy before crossing the Carnic Alps back into Hungary. In 955 the Magyars tried again, and advanced into Bavaria with another army of 50,000. They were besieging Augsburg when Otto I's army approached and compelled them to raise the siege on 9 August. The next day, the Magyars gained the advantage in the first clash, but Otto arrayed his heavy cavalry in line and delivered a charge that broke the more lightly armored Magyars and drove them from the field. Otto ordered a pursuit, and inflicted such losses on the Magyars that 75 years passed before another Magyar army invaded Germany.

The decentralization of power necessary to withstand these barbarian raids had effectively ended the last remnants of Carolingian state structure on the continent. Even under the well-organized Carolingians some decentralization was unavoidable given the state of communications at the time, and the strain of resisting raids nearly eliminated central government. Widespread raids could be resisted successfully only at a local level, and any local leader who defended his region against Viking or Magyar raiders was unlikely to surrender his authority to a distant monarch he had never seen and who had done little to help him. This strengthening of local authority, and the sporadic efforts of the kings to regain their paramount position, was the most important characteristic of medieval politics.

By 1000, feudal society was well established in most of western and central Europe. The situations in England and Italy were a little different. In England, the limited size of the realm and its well-defined boundaries made the task of the monarchy easier, and England was better administered and more tightly organized than other European kingdoms. In Italy, the high level of urbanization and the economic power of the cities (few had more than 10,000 people even in the late 1200s) limited the power of rural feudal magnates. Most feudal lords in northern and central Italy had become clients of neighboring towns by the mid-twelfth century, and many actually moved to the towns.

The Normans, the *Reconquista*, and the Crusades, 1000–1200

THE NORMANS

When the Norse chieftain Rollo, or Rolf the Granger (so-called because he was reputedly too tall to ride a horse), in 911 accepted the offer of King Charles the Fat of France to settle in the lands at the mouth of the Seine River in exchange for forgoing future raids on French lands, he founded a people who became famous for producing military adventurers. The region was soon called Normandy after its new inhabitants, who adopted many French customs, including their methods of making war. By 1050, following the same impetus that had driven their Norse forefathers to seek their fortunes outside Scandinavia, the Normans had gained considerable land and power in southern Italy.

Over the course of the next fifty years, the Normans achieved their three greatest military successes: the conquests of southern Italy, Sicily, and England. The conquest of England by William the Conqueror in 1066 is perhaps the best known of these, but is not necessarily the most spectacular. It is, however, illustrative of Norman capabilities. Harold Godwinson's Saxon army, which fought William's Normans at Hastings in October 1066, was a capable force built around a core of professional, heavily armed mounted infantry called *huskarls*. The bulk of the army was militia, though, and like many militia forces, the Anglo-Saxon army was not well-disciplined. The decisive point at Hastings came when the Normans feigned a retreat (a difficult maneuver, and indicative of notable tactical skill; it was also a favorite Byzantine tactic, and may have come to William's attention through Norman involvement in southern Italy) and enticed Harold's militia to make a hasty attack. As the Anglo-Saxons charged down off Senlac hill, the Normans rallied and launched a carefully timed counterattack, routing much of the militia and forcing the remnants of Harold's army back to the hilltop, where they were surrounded and destroyed by the Normans.

While William's Normans conquered England, other Normans under the adventurer turned state-builder Robert Guiscard were gaining control of southern Italy. The conquest of Sicily by Robert's brother Roger, begun in 1060, was not completed until 1091, delayed by the demands of Norman interests on mainland Italy, where Robert was involved in conflicts with the pope, the Byzantine Empire, and the quasi-independent feudal magnates of southern Italy. In 1071 Robert captured Bari, eliminating the last Byzantine foothold in

Italy. He then annexed the Duchy of Amalfi in 1073, and took Apulia in 1076. In 1081, he captured Corfu and prepared to invade the Byzantine Empire itself. He led his army into what is now Albania and besieged Durazzo, but he was opposed by the able and resourceful Byzantine Emperor Alexius II Comnenus. Robert eventually captured Durazzo (February 1082) despite the earlier loss of his fleet to a combined Venetian-Byzantine fleet. He left his son Bohemund to direct the advance overland against Thessalonica in the spring, while he responded to an urgent plea from Pope Gregory VII and returned to Italy. Bohemund had the worst of the Battle of Larissa against Alexius (1083), and a second naval encounter off Corfu was indecisive (1084). However, the death of Robert on Cephalonia (17 July 1085) compelled Bohemund to return to Italy to see to his father's dynastic interest.

Robert Guiscard's conquest of southern Italy and Sicily laid the foundations for a state that survived more than a century. During its existence it guarded the development of a remarkable culture, combining Norman, Byzantine, and Arab elements. This Sicilian Kingdom, as it is often called, also dominated the central Mediterranean, its fleets controlling the Ionian and Tyrrhenian Seas. It provided a powerful counterweight to the ambitions of the Holy Roman Empire in northern Italy, as it was also a strong ally of the papacy. The Sicilian Kingdom weakened in the latter half of the twelfth century, and in 1194 the throne was usurped by the Hohenstaufen Emperor Henry VI, who had a claim to the Sicilian throne through marriage.

THE RECONQUISTA

The Arab invasion of Spain, which destroyed the Visigothic Kingdom in the early eighth century, did not completely conquer Iberia. While most of Spain succumbed to the Arabs, the foothills of the Pyrenees, as well as Galicia and the northern coast along the Bay of Biscay, maintained a precarious independence. Charlemagne's conquest of the "Spanish March" along the modern French border in the northeast gave sorely needed help to the Christians in Spain. By 1000, five Christian states had arisen in Spain: (from west to east) the kingdoms of León, Castille, Navarre, Aragón, and the County of Barcelona. Barcelona was absorbed by Aragón soon after, and in 1034 the Christian cause gained an advantage by the dissolution of the Caliphate of Córdoba. Muslim-Arab Spain broke up into more than a dozen small states, which were (like their Christian rivals) as ready to fight each other as to fight their common enemy.

This situation was a great benefit to the Christian cause, which was further aided by the periodic arrival of knights from southern France, eager to fight the Muslims. The Christian reconquest of Spain, known in that country as the *Reconquista*, continued for over two centuries. The Christian progress southward was interrupted by the Almoravids, a tribal Islamic sect, who had conquered Morocco and responded to an appeal for help from the Muslim princes of Spain in 1085. Their general Ibn Tashfin defeated Alfonso VI of Castile at Zallaka, north of Badajoz, in 1086. Ibn Tashfin, though, was less successful in his campaigns against Rodrigo Díaz y Bivar, better known as El Cid, and his forces suffered heavily even though they had some successes against the Cid's armies. After Ibn Tashfin's death, Almoravid power waned and the Christians resumed their advance.

The Almoravids were overthrown by the Almohades, another tribal Islamic reform movement, in the mid-twelfth century. The Almohades also succeeded in blocking Christian conquests. By the time the Almohades conquered Morocco in 1147, the Christian states had taken both Toledo and Lisbon, and controlled the northern half of the Iberian peninsula. Over the next half-century, the Christian kingdoms made little progress in their struggle to drive out the Moors. However, on 6 July 1212, the Almohades suffered a crushing defeat at the Battle of Las Navas de Tolosa, and within forty years the kingdom of Castile (which had merged with León in 1230) ruled half of Spain. Castile blocked Navarre from contact with Muslim Spain, left Aragón in control of the northeast and east, and pushed southward to overrun the rest of Spain except for the Kingdom of Granada in the southeast. Farther west, the County of Portugal, which had become independent from León in 1140, forced the Muslims south of the Tagus River.

The warfare of the *Reconquista* was distinct from medieval warfare in northern Europe in several ways. First, the ruggedness of Iberian terrain limited the deployment of cavalry, and Spanish armies made wider and more effective use of foot soldiers than their French or German contemporaries. Second, the Spanish cavalry was notably more lightly equipped than its northern counterparts. In part, this was a result of climatic conditions, but it was also a response to the Muslim armies, whose horsemen were skirmishers and horse-archers. Most Spanish cavalrymen were *genitors*, men mounted on small, agile horses and armed with javelins, a sword, and often a shield. Many of the military lessons of the *Reconquista*, however, were ignored outside Spain.

The Christian states of Spain consolidated the gains won at Las Navas de Tolosa by the mid-thirteenth century, but because of civil strife and war among the Christian states, the kingdom of Granada remained independent for more than two centuries. King Ferdinand of Aragón and Queen Isabella of Castile brought the resources of their kingdom together, and between 1481 and 1492 conquered Granada. During this time, they undertook a major reform of their army (1483–87) and created a permanent national army. One of the leading commanders of the new army was Hernandez Gonzalo de Córdoba, later famous for his victories over the French in southern Italy. The conquest of Granada marked the entry of Spain into the ranks of major European powers.

THE CRUSADES

The Crusades, as a great manifestation of popular religious feeling, were more than a series of military expeditions. Yet even considered as merely military operations, the Crusades were interesting for several reasons. The idea of the "crusade" probably arose in Spain, as part of the warfare between Christian and Moor for control of the Iberian peninsula. The First Crusade was launched in 1096 and led by Norman and Flemish barons who had been inspired by the preaching of Pope Urban II. Over the ensuing 150 years, there were eight crusades, but only two, the First (1096–99) and the Third (1189–92), were successful. The First Crusade captured Jerusalem and brought most of what is now Lebanon, Israel, and coastal Syria under Christian rule. Some of the Crusader states thus created did not last long: the County of Edessa was destroyed in 1144, and frontier warfare against Muslim raiders was constant.

After the fall of Jerusalem to the Turkish-Egyptian monarch Saladin in 1187, the Crusader states (which the French called *Outremer*, "[the land] across the sea") waned, dwindling to a narrow coastal strip from Tripoli south to Jaffa and eventually to a few coastal enclaves. Despite military reversals, Europeans learned much of military value from the Crusades. The Crusaders gained from their Muslim adversaries an appreciation for light cavalry and its use in irregular warfare, the importance of scouting, ambushes, and surprise, and the importance of combining shock and missile action to gain success in battle. Most importantly, the Crusades introduced eastern, and especially Byzantine, fortification techniques to western Europe. These included concentric rings of walls and round towers, both previously unknown in the west.

Feudal Warfare and the Laws of War

The Middle Ages were an unusually violent period, marked not only by warfare between kings, but by warfare among a king's subjects, and between kings and their subjects. The frequency with which feudal lords resorted to war made warfare almost constant. The concept of war as a manifestation of private feud between two rival lords produced the concept of *dampnum*. Since it was usually impractical for one lord to strike at another directly, a lord instead injured his rival by destroying his crops, ruining his fields and villages, and killing or carrying off his serfs and livestock. This concept of striking at a lord through his subjects was called *dampnum*, and its widespread use was the main reason for the relative destructiveness of medieval warfare. It also tended to transform campaigns into semiorganized brigandage.

Some authorities, notably the church and royal governments, desired to limit the mayhem, and this desire, coupled with the medieval "laws of war" produced the idea of "just war." The medieval laws of war were not written statutes, but a compilation and distillation of traditions governing the exchange of envoys, the status of hostages, the treatment of prisoners, the granting of safe passage, the implementation of truces, and the like. A just war was characterized by three conditions: it was either a war against barbarians or infidels (in which case the laws of war among Christians did not generally apply), a war against rebels or outlaws undertaken by a legally constituted authority, or a defense against aggression. A war begun under any other conditions was unjust, and a war undertaken as part of a private quarrel was particularly unjust.

These conditions were applied most rigorously to lesser magnates, or to those who owed allegiance to a monarch. Matters were less clear-cut when dealing with disputes between monarchs, and the concept of just war at that level was honored more in the breach than the observance.

The Mongol Conquests and the Mongol System of Warfare, 1190–1280

The Mongols, who conquered most of Asia and half of Europe in less than 100 years, were the most efficient and ruthless war-makers of the Middle Ages. They were brought from obscurity to greatness by their chieftain Temujin, later called Genghis Khan. Genghis transformed the army of the nomadic Mongols from a simple force of horse-archers into a highly organized military force, adding armored lancers, an important shock element, to increase combat power. The Mongols were, by virtue of their harsh environment, hardy warriors, and under the command of a skilled general like Genghis, or his lieutenants Chepe Noyon and Subotai, an army of such men could achieve wonders.

Temujin unified the tribes of Mongolia over a sixteen-year period (1190–1206) and accepted the accolade-name of Genghis Khan ("Perfect War Emperor" or "Supreme Emperor") from the tribes. Over the next ten years, the Mongols overran most of northern central Asia, absorbing the empires of the Western Hsia, Chin, and Kara-Khitai. Genghis conquered the Khwarezmian Empire between 1218 and 1224, and by the time of his death in 1227 ruled an empire that stretched from the Urals to the Pacific and reached south into India and touched the Persian Gulf. Genghis's successors completed the conquest of the Chin (1231–34) and Sung empires in China (1234–79), and between 1237 and 1241 invaded eastern Europe, easily conquering Russia, Poland, and Hungary before the death of Khan Ogotai compelled them to withdraw. This was their high-water mark in Europe, but while they never again passed west of the Ukraine, they remained in Russia for three centuries.

Even the decline of the Mongol state, and its fragmentation into four major parts (the Khanate of the Golden Horde in Russia, the Il-Khan state in Persia, the Chagadia or Ili state in central Asia, and the Khanate of the Great Khan in Mongolia and China) did not end Mongol military power. The career of Tamerlane (Timur-e-lenk, or Timur the Lame), a Tatar who became chief of the Jagatai Mongols, is the greatest example. For over twenty years, from 1381 until his death in 1405, Tamerlane and his armies, operating from his capital at Samarkand, were the terror of the Middle East. Less an empire-builder than a plunderer, he conquered Persia and parts of central Asia, and invaded India (1398–99), Syria (1400), Iraq (1401), and Anatolia (1402). When in Iraq he sacked Baghdad, and in his invasion of Anatolia so mauled the Ottoman Turks at Angora (30 June 1402) that it took them years to recover.

The High Middle Ages and the Origins of Modern Warfare, 1150–1450

THE ENGLISH

By the middle of the twelfth century, feudalism and the manorial system had reached their greatest level of sophistication. In feudalism, an individual placed his services at the disposal of a more powerful person in exchange for that person's protection and access to his economic resources (the English word *lord* is derived from the Anglo-Saxon *hlaford*, or loaf-giver, meaning someone who provided food to his followers and supporters). The manorial system was a parallel to feudalism, and served to tie the holding of land (a fief) to obligations for military service (varying widely, but often fixed at a biblical 40 days). The gradual recentralization of political authority, which began to reach noticeable proportions in the twelfth century, made many rulers realize how little control they had over the military establishment. Their military vassals, in turn, became less eager to leave their homes and families for a campaign, even if for only six weeks.

The result of these two trends was the development of a money payment in lieu of service. Called shield money, or *scutage* in England, it allowed the knights and men-at-arms to remain happily at home, and it allowed the rulers to hire armies for as long as they wanted and as long as they could afford the expense. This practice began in England about 1176, where it was especially popular because of the difficulties of providing garrisons for the extensive Plantagenet holdings on the continent. The development of *scutage* indicates a revival of a money economy from one based on barter, which in turn shows renewed trade and a growth of urban centers. The institution of *scutage* proved so popular that by the time of King John's war against Philip II Augustus of France early in the first decade of the thirteenth century, more than half the troops in his army were mercenaries. The practice spread to France and the Low Countries, and eventually to Germany.

The widespread use of *scutage* in England led to another innovation in the late thirteenth century. King Edward I, exasperated by the continual political disarray in Wales, invaded and subjugated that country in a series of wars in the 1270s, 1280s, and 1290s. These campaigns were long-term operations, often lasting for several months, and they took place far enough from Edward's English bases that the traditional military institutions, even fortified by *scutage*, were inadequate to provide him with the necessary forces to conquer, and then garrison, his new domains.

Edward began two practices to give him the forces he needed. First, he instituted muster and review to raise foot soldiers: each county was to muster all its militia, essentially every free male in reasonable health from his late teens to his early sixties. The county officials (usually the sheriff) were then to review these men and select a number of them (specified by the king) to serve on a campaign. They were supposed to select the most eager and able men, arm them from the county armory, and send them to the army's concentration point. These men were paid regularly, usually three pence a day for foot soldiers (a rate comparable to what a skilled or semi-skilled worker would earn), and they were often provided with rations. Nonmilitary specialists like coopers, miners, carpenters, and blacksmiths were also raised in this fashion. Although the cost was high, England was able to manage the administrative burden imposed by this system, and the payoff in military efficiency was considerable.

Second, Edward I also began the practice of raising troops through indentures. An indenture was a written agreement between the king and one of his subjects (usually a man-at-arms or a knight) to provide the king with a specific number and type of soldiers, at a particular date and place, and for a specific period of time (at first three months, later raised to six, and then to a year). The indenture also specified how the men were to be equipped, how much they were to be paid, and so forth. The king agreed to pay a set sum of money to the subject, and the subject promised to get the specified troops to the right place at the right time.

These two methods of raising troops enabled Edward I and his successors to raise and maintain what amounted to standing armies, removing military service from the realm of traditional duties and obligations and placing it on an economic footing. Since all soldiers, including those holding indentures, were awarded a share of any plunder gained, or ransom received for captives, military service was popular, and raising troops was not a problem.

Edward and his grandson Edward III refined this system, so that when Edward III began the war with France in 1337 (the Hundred Years' War), the English possessed a military system superior to any in Western Europe. Edward III even began to issue indentures for supplies (mainly food), and began centralized, government-supervised manufacture of weapons, mainly at the Tower of London. These weapons were used to equip the troops raised by muster and review (a system that survived until 250 years later). This military system provided the English monarchy with armies that—while small (rarely more than 12,000 men, and often half that)—were cohesive, determined, and manned by a large proportion of experienced professionals, skilled not only in fighting, but also in the art of making war.

THE *CONDOTTIERI*

While the English were refining their systems of indenture, and muster and review, the Italians in the city-states of northern and central Italy were finding that warfare was costly and inefficient when waged by citizen levies. By the middle decades of the fourteenth century, most Italian city-states had begun making contracts (*condotta*) with independent soldier-entrepreneurs called *condottieri*. These contracts specified the number and types of troops, the duration of the contract, and the rates of pay. Many of the early *condottieri* were foreigners, including Germans, Frenchmen, and the notable English soldier Sir John Hawkwood, who went to Italy when he was left unemployed by the Peace of Brétigny in 1360.

The *condottieri*, like most mercenaries, were more interested in getting paid than in killing their fellow *condottieri*, who happened for the moment to be enemies. Consequently, Italian warfare during the last century of the Middle Ages was characterized more often by *ruses de guerre*, clever stratagems, and a great deal of maneuver than by actual fighting. However, Machiavelli's claim that the *condottieri* were militarily inept and commonly fought battles where armies numbering thousands suffered only a few fatal casualties is untrue.

The *condottieri* did professionalize the conduct of war. Mercenary bands, once assembled, tried to remain together, and soldiers who fought together for years developed considerable skill, unit cohesion, and efficiency. The officers in particular began to think and write seriously about the methods of waging war and fighting battles. These trends produced well-disciplined, well-organized forces, and increasingly sophisticated battle tactics. Further, the city-states that hired *condottieri* found it worthwhile to retain the same troops even in times of peace. This provided greater security for the states and, more important, created stronger ties between the mercenary and his employer. By the middle of the fifteenth century, the largest Italian states (Venice, Milan, Florence, and the Papal States) had all developed permanent standing armies of *condottieri*. These soldiers were not like their predecessors, who had been free agents; the *condottieri* of the mid-1400s were usually tied to a particular employer, and were *condottieri* only in the sense that they were hired through contractors, rather than directly by agents of the state. Those few *condottieri* who were still independent, like Federigo da Montefeltro or Sigismondo Malatesta, had their own principalities as power bases.

This institutional change in the status of the *condottieri* paralleled changes in warfare in Italy, especially in tactics and force structure. Early *condottieri* armies were dominated by the mounted man-at-arms, although some of the foreign *condottieri* like Sir John Hawkwood continued to rely heavily on infantry. The dominance of mounted troops became more widespread between 1390 and 1430 under Alberico da Barbiano and his protégés, Muzio Sforza and Braccio da Montone. Sforza, like his patron, favored the employment of troops in large bodies, unleashed at just the right moment in a mass attack. Braccio da Montone, in contrast, believed in operating in smaller units, which could maintain steady pressure on the enemy and be relieved by fresh troops when they became exhausted. Montone's system also allowed junior officers to exercise greater initiative. These rival "systems" and their followers, named "Sforzeschi" and "Bracceschi" after their patrons, dominated Italian military practice in the middle decades of the 1400s. Both systems had merit under different conditions.

By the later years of the 1400s, especially after the Peace of Lodi in 1454, the advent of infantry firearms began to change the face of battle. The campaigns of the late fifteenth century showed increased use of field entrenchments, and armies employed higher proportions of infantry, light cavalry, artillery, and engineers (Fig. 1). These changes, contemporary with the last stages of evolution from the old, entrepreneurial *condottieri* to the new, state-controlled mercenaries, foreshadowed the organization of French and Spanish armies in the early sixteenth century, an Italianization of European warfare that is often overlooked.

THE SWISS

The political history of the Swiss people began in the late thirteenth century, but their importance as a military force in central Europe was not immediately apparent. The Hapsburgs, feudal overlords of the Swiss cantons, were their first military opponents. In a series of conflicts lasting nearly 200 years, the Swiss Confederation (at first only the three cantons of Uri, Schwyz, and Unterwalden) freed themselves from Austrian domination.

The Swiss won their first victory at Morgarten on 15 November 1315 when their army of 1,500 spearmen and archers ambushed and routed an Austrian army of about 8,000 on a narrow battlefield between mountains and a lake.

Figure 1. The infantry carried long pikes to kill the horses, forcing the riders out of action. (SOURCE: Iconographic Encyclopaedia)

Seventy years later, an Austrian army 6,000 strong under Leopold III of Swabia was defeated at Sempach on 9 July 1386 by 1,600 Swiss. Although the Austrians fought dismounted and enjoyed initial success, they were soon exhausted by their exertions and fell victim to the more agile (and less heavily armored) Swiss halberdiers and pikemen. The Swiss warred again with Austria in 1415, 1460, and 1499. It was not until the Treaty of Basel on 22 September 1499 that the Swiss at last won independence.

During this period, the Swiss had also fought other neighbors; the French, Burgundians, and Milanese went to war with the Swiss between 1339 and 1450. Most of these clashes served to enhance the Swiss military reputation. A case in point was the Battle of St. Jakob, near Basel, fought on 24 August 1444. A French army of 30,000 men under Dauphin Louis (later King Louis XI) invaded Swiss territory as part of an alliance with Frederick III of Austria. This army was opposed by a Swiss force of 1,500 that fought to the last man, inflicted 3,000 casualties, and so disordered the French army that the French withdrew. The French were so impressed with the Swiss determination and ferocity that they changed sides and raided Frederick's domains in Alsace.

The Swiss armies, which performed so well in battle, differed in several ways from typical European armies of the day. First, since the troops were raised from a population of freeholders and town-dwellers of modest means, most of them were lightly armored infantrymen; Swiss armies contained few if any cavalrymen. The weapons of the infantry soldier changed over time. Initially, about one-third of the men used bows or crossbows, and the rest spears or halberds (a spear with an axe-blade at the end). As encounters with cavalry became more common, and as Swiss discipline and tactics improved, they adopted the pike in increasing numbers, eventually employing an 18- to 21-foot version. Swiss pikemen fought in large, dense columns and were trained to move at relatively high speed. Records of the period often refer to the speed with which Swiss troops moved to the attack, and the fearsome impact of their charge.

Fearsome as these pike phalanxes were, they were not invulnerable. They could be overwhelmed by superior numbers, as happened at St. Jakob, and they could be beaten by clever tactics and astute combat leadership. A Swiss army invaded the northern territories of Milan in 1422, as part of a sporadic border conflict that continued for years. About one-third of the Swiss army was pike-armed, while most of the rest had halberds, and only a small portion were armed with crossbows. At Arbedo, near Bellinzona, the invading Swiss met a Milanese army under the *condottiere* Francesco Bussone di Carmagnola on 30 June. Carmagnola's mounted attack was repulsed with heavy losses and, reverting to Hawkwood's tactics of 40 years before, he ordered his men-at-arms to dismount and fight on foot, covered by the fire of his crossbowmen. The dense blocks of Swiss troops suffered heavily from the Milanese crossbowmen, and hastily withdrew. So sobering was this defeat for the Swiss that they did not fight Milan again until 1478.

The strength of the Swiss lay in their effective combination of offensive power, from their halberds and pikes, with the ferocity and determination for which they were renowned. The latter characteristic was a product of strong traditions of community and local loyalty: no Swiss soldier would dare let his comrades down, and the *esprit de corps* that resulted gave Swiss armies remarkable cohesion. Swiss tactics, while aggressive and remarkably effective in many circumstances, did have limitations. Their pike columns could move rapidly, but were at a disadvantage on uneven ground, and were vulnerable to skirmishers. A lack of appreciation for troops equipped with crossbows or firearms also showed tactical narrow-mindedness. Still, the Swiss were formidable opponents; even after they abandoned an aggressive foreign policy in the 1520s, their mercenaries were in high demand, noted for their zeal and steadfastness.

The End of Medieval Warfare: The French Army of the *Compagnies d'Ordonnance*, 1445–90

The Hundred Years' War was dominated for the first 90 years (1337–1427) by the tactical superiority of the English. The French, despite numerous efforts to reorganize their armies and regularize their armament and quality, were unable to match the English in the field unless they were led by an unusually talented commander like Bertrand du Guesclin. After the defeat at Agincourt, where an English army of 6,000 under King Henry V defeated a French army of over 30,000 on 30 October 1415, French military fortunes declined steadily. By the time of Henry V's death in 1422, the English and their Burgundian allies held Paris and most of France north of the Loire River.

The advent of Jeanne d'Arc (Joan of Arc) and her leadership of the relief of Orléans from the Duke of Bedford's siege in 1429, provided the spark the French needed for revitalization. Within six years, the Burgundians had switched sides, the French had retaken Paris, and the English were on the defensive. This success, and the victories of the ensuing ten years, were accomplished by mercenary bands led by experienced professional soldiers. Many of the soldiers and their commanders were foreigners, and many of them were not far removed from brigands. In 1445, taking advantage of one of the periodic truces during the war, King Charles VII decided to place the army on a permanent footing.

On 26 May 1445, the King declared the *Grande Ordonnance*, which established a standing army. The new law granted official sanction to certain mercenary captains and made them royal officers. The soldiers of the *compagnies* were organized into lances, each of which contained a man-at-arms, a squire, two archers, and two pages (one for the archers and one for the man-at-arms and the squire). Each member of the lance had one horse, and the French authorities counted each lance as four combatants and six horses (although there were often extra horses, and some lances were understrength in manpower). The lances, which at first totalled about 1,800, were grouped into companies of 30 to 100 lances. The company commanders were paid on the basis of the number of lances fit and present, so royal inspection was frequent and precise.

Initially, the soldiers and officers of the *compagnies* were a surprisingly cosmopolitan group, only two-fifths being native Frenchmen. Further, many of the first group of leaders of the *compagnies* had unsavory careers, but transforming them into royal officials placed them under royal control, where their unruliness could be contained. To a large degree, the creation of the *compagnies d'ordonnance* paralleled the transformation of the *condottieri* from military entrepreneurs to state employees and, as a manifestation of the growing authority governments exercised over their territories and populace, serves to mark the end of the Middle Ages and the beginning of Early Modern Europe.

Meaning of Medieval Warfare

The military history of the medieval period is marked by two major characteristics. First, the control of military institutions was decentralized; it rested in the hands of local leaders rather than central or national governments. Second, these institutions were based on tradition and informal agreement, not on written law or formal decree. Similarly, command and organization were generally informal and irregular, based on groups of personal followers, or on fighters drawn from a particular region. Rank in the modern sense was virtually unknown, and a man who was commander of an army in one campaign could find himself, without having suffered disgrace, commanding a mere company in the next.

The regularization of these haphazard methods of making war, which began to spread through Europe in the last half of the fifteenth century, effectively ended medieval warfare. Regularly raised standing armies, firmly under the control of the central government, were a far cry from the feudal hosts of the eleventh or twelfth centuries. If nothing else, they could stay in the field for more than the traditional 40-day span of feudal obligations. Nevertheless, several crucial facets of medieval warfare had longlasting effects. The tradition of command by titled aristocrats lasted well into the modern era, and the traditions of chivalry and culture developed by the knightly class during the period had a long effect on European culture and military traditions.

David L. Bongard

SEE ALSO: Arab Conquests; Attila the Hun; Byzantine Empire; Charlemagne; Crusades; Edward I; Edward III; Feudalism; Genghis Khan; Gonzalo de Córdoba; Hundred Years' War; Khalid ibn al-Walid; Mongol Conquests; Normans; Persian Empire; Ruses and Stratagems; Tamerlane; Turkic Empire; Vikings.

Bibliography

Allmand, C. T., ed. 1973. *Society at war: The experience of England and France during the Hundred Years' War*. Edinburgh: Oliver and Boyd.

Beeler, J. H. 1971. *Warfare in feudal Europe*. Ithaca, N.Y.: Cornell Univ. Press.

Bloch, M. 1961. *Feudal society*. Trans. L. A. Manyon. Chicago: Univ. of Chicago Press.

Burne, A. H. 1956. *The Agincourt War: A military history of the latter part of the Hundred Years' War from 1369 to 1453*. London: Eyre and Spottiswoode.

―――. 1955. *The Crécy war: A military history of the Hundred Years' War from 1337 to the Peace of Bretigny*. London: Eyre and Spottiswoode.

Contamine, P. 1984. *War in the Middle Ages*. Trans. M. Jones. London: Basil Blackwell.

―――. 1972. *Guerre, état, et société à la fin du Moyen Age*. Paris: La Haye, Mouton.

Glubb, J. B. 1963. *The great Arab conquests*. London: Hodder and Staughton.

Hewitt, H. J. 1966. *The organization of war under Edward III, 1338–62*. Manchester: Univ. of Manchester Press.

Keegan, J. 1976. *The face of battle*. New York: Viking Press.

Keen, M. H. 1965. *The laws of war in the Late Middle Ages*. London: Routledge and Kegan Paul.

Kwantern, L. 1979. *Imperial nomads: A history of Central Asia, 500 to 1500*. Philadelphia: Univ. of Pennsylvania Press.

Mallet, M. E. 1974. *Mercenaries and their masters: Warfare in Renaissance Italy*. Totowa, N.J.: Rowman and Littlefield.

Norwich, J. J. C. 1967. *The Normans in the South, 1016–1130*. London: Longmans.

Oman, C. W. C. 1924. *The art of war in the Middle Ages*. 2 vols. London: Methuen.

Ostrogorsky, G. 1969. *History of the Byzantine State*. Trans. J. Hussey. New Brunswick, N.J.: Rutgers Univ. Press.

Runciman, S. 1964–67. *A history of the Crusades*. 3 vols. Cambridge and New York: Cambridge Univ. Press.

Smail, R. C. 1956. *Crusading warfare (1097–1193)*. Cambridge: Cambridge Univ. Press.

Trease, G. 1971. *The condottieri*. New York: Holt, Rinehart and Winston.

Turnbull, S. 1985. *The book of the medieval knight*. London: Arms and Armour Press.

Vale, M. G. A. 1981. *War and chivalry: Warfare and aristocratic culture in England, France, and Burgundy at the end of the Middle Ages*. Athens, Ga.: Univ. of Georgia Press.

HISTORY, MILITARY

At its core, military history is the analytic review of wars, campaigns, battles, and military institutions, including their economic, political, and social foundations and effects, and relationships between military and civil authorities.

A distinction may be made between professional, academic, and popular military histories.

At its most fundamental level, professional military history (or "operational history" as it is sometimes called) examines past conflicts in order to derive insights that might guide decision makers in preparing for contemporary or future warfare. In that capacity, it moves in the direction of military theory. To the extent that theoretical touchstones like the principles of war are subordinated to historical example, they belong in the realm of didactic military history rather than undiluted doctrine.

It is possible, while often not easy, to distinguish military history from general history. When the latter deals with armed conflict and military forces, these subjects have traditionally been treated as extraneous to the normal flow of events. As such, they are not discussed extensively.

Military history, as understood here, highlights such factors as the strategy, tactics, and logistics of a campaign; skill and knowledge of the commanders; characteristics or influence of weapons systems; and the composition and combat capabilities of the units engaged. Auxiliary, noncombatant services, such as advances in military medicine, the administration of field hospitals, and the prevention of tropical diseases, are also topics covered in military history studies, as are topics as diverse as arrangements for provisioning an army in the field, effects of various transport systems upon rates of advance, and techniques and devices for signals communications.

The military historian also analyzes the instruments that nations devise to ensure success in defending or advancing vital national interests. Such matters have long been considered by academic historians to be unworthy of attention, but this view has changed in the last thirty-five years.

In addition to critical accounts of wars, campaigns, and battles, military history includes institutional and administrative studies of armed forces that analyze their bureaucratic structure, managerial efficiency, and relationship to government and society. The social and economic background of enlisted personnel and officers and the cohesion of units also may be discussed in monographs, which do not necessarily include accounts of battlefield activities.

The academic variety of military history in particular includes assessments of the effects of war upon peoples and civilian institutions, participants and neutrals alike. The nature of modern "total war," harnessing all of the social and economic resources of the nation and endangering its very survival, has brought military history out from the constricted descriptive mode and into a broader context—what is now known as "war and society" studies. Academia has accepted the latter variety of military history. The concluding section of this article shows that some war and society scholars have strained so hard to avoid the "stench of cordite" that subscribers to military journals publishing their work may well wonder whether the editors have forgotten that combat is the *ultima ratio* of armies, navies, and air forces. On the other hand, the better operational historians are now borrowing from related disciplines to present a more rounded view of the relative military effectiveness of competing societies and economic systems.

On another level are unit histories. These are compiled from orders, dispatches, phone or radio message transcripts, logbooks, unit war diaries, citations, awards, and personal diaries of the fighting men. The least useful to military history are those composed simply to serve as souvenirs or memorials. As such, they may take the form of scrapbooks or captioned photo albums, patching together the bits and pieces of rosters, documents, and memorabilia with a cursory chronology of events, including sports and social festivities. The best of this type may be valuable as source material on daily routine and morale-building mechanisms. When the designated unit historian is also a practiced military historian, and affiliated with the unit, he may relate the unit's activities to events. British specialists like C. T. Atkinson, Sir Frederick Maurice, H. C. Wylly, and Dudley Ward have produced the best examples of this genre. Even then, the writer commissioned to memorialize the unit may hesitate to include incidents reflecting unfavorably upon the unit's performance. The British, French, and German models usually comprise valuable minihistories of the various wars, whereas American divisional, regimental, and battalion annals, with a few notable exceptions, tend toward the cut-and-paste commemorative approach.

Another variant, official history, has its own special credibility problems. The origin and development of this subgenre is discussed in the next section. Since the second quarter of the nineteenth century, defense establishments of major powers have commissioned official histories to distill lessons from past conflicts; to objectively record the role of the nation's armed forces, their triumphs, and errors; and to instill a sense of continuity and tradition among the troops. The last is an extension of the unit history's role to embrace the entire fighting force. Up until World War II, there was too often a built-in bias: to prove the correctness of prewar (or current) doctrine and to gloss over the mistakes of certain commanders or statesmen. The 1939–45 conflict produced official histories that employed the talents of trained historians who were asked to do their best to ascertain exactly what had transpired on the battlefield regardless of who won or lost.

Military memoirs and biographies highlight the military career of the subject. The subject's early life, training, emotional experiences, and so on, are presented only as background to his martial life. A few memoirs, such as those of Confederate artillerist Edward Porter Alexander and Wehrmacht Field Marshal Manstein, are depersonalized to the extent that they read like operational studies of the memoirist's campaigns rather than vivid personal recollections. A fascinating hybrid between the memoir and the troop orientation lecture can be found in Erwin Rommel's collection of World War I battle vignettes describing the exploits of his mountain infantry company on the Italian front. Finally, works such as G. F. R. Henderson's *Stonewall Jackson and the American Civil War* are really strategical studies of an epoch's prevailing doctrine as seen through the eyes of a preeminent practitioner and theorist.

A good deal of the "popular" military historical writing done for the enthusiast or "buff" is devised more to entertain than to inform. This ephemeral literature includes patriotic or macho tales of heroic deeds, a phenomenon of the nationalist ferment in the latter half of the nineteenth century that persists today in magazines appealing to would-be mercenaries, both armchair and active, and gun collectors. There is also the heavily illustrated coffee-table book or magazine article that is little more than extended captions for color pictures of uniforms, decorations, accouterments, weapons, and fanciful battle scenes.

However, one should not dismiss the output of hobbyists as irrelevant to the advancement of the form. The best of the semiamateur magazines written for (and often by) subscribers who are recreational war-gamers, modelers, collectors of militaria, and fanciers of military dress are thoroughly researched and documented. Dedicated and diligent buffs often add insights to their limited field that trained historians might utilize.

Origins of the Genre and Early Practitioners

From classical times through the seventeenth century, history was viewed as the doings of kings, nobles, ministers, and cabinet members. Because in ancient times warfare was endemic and preparation for it all-consuming, the written record is dominated by the martial exploits of rulers and lords. Scribes were not self-consciously writing military histories, but simply reflecting the dominant theme of societies organized for and preoccupied with war. Many of these works are didactic in that they set out to demonstrate the military genius of the subject ruler or the weakness resulting from the treacherous counsel of his or her internal enemies. Although one may learn of the nature of ancient armies and navies as well as their techniques and stratagems from these court histories, it was not until the advent of the "scientific" military historians at the end of the nineteenth century that students of military affairs had reliable guides to guide them through the "minefields" of the half-mythological tales of ancient and medieval chroniclers.

The histories of the wars of antiquity have come down to us through the writings of the Old Testament scribes and aristocratic intellectuals such as Herodotus, Thucydides, Xenophon, Polybius, and Arrian. Although their subject was warfare, they were writing for posterity rather than for the edification of future warriors.

Military biography and memoirs are among the earliest military histories. Ancient and early medieval historians wrote the "life and times" of great rulers who were, perforce, commanders as well. Although statesmanship was stressed, this often was seen as the diplomatic face of war, anticipating late nineteenth-century writers who looked beyond the battlefield to the cabinet chambers and ministries.

The Old Testament oral tradition, as written centuries after events, has left a sufficiently detailed record of bloody encounters among the great and small powers of the Fertile Crescent to enable modern military critics to reconstruct many of the pivotal battles among the Hebrews and their neighbors.

Herodotus, considered the father of history, wrote of the Persian wars in an epic-heroic vein. The history of Thucydides presents an analytic and critical treatment of the Peloponnesian Wars. Thucydides demonstrates a professional familiarity with strategy, tactics, and military organization and a scholar's concern with weighing conflicting sources in fixing relative numbers and positions as well as with explaining the reactions of the troops in human terms.

The campaign histories of Julius Caesar are replete with the dynamics of the various engagements but are obviously biased to present the most favorable picture of the author/protagonist/historian, and the student of the conquest of Gaul or the Roman civil wars must consult independent sources from archaeology and bardic sagas to obtain objective perspectives of Caesar's version of the events.

The medieval and Renaissance periods produced manuals on warfare, such as Maurice's *Strategicon*, Leo VI's *Tactica*, and Machiavelli's *The Art of War*, as well as renewed interest in Vegetius's *De Re Militari*. One must not overlook the ancient Chinese general Sun Tzu's treatise, *The Art of War*, which has served as a guide to Asian warlords for two millennia. But these were surveys of contemporary practice with an occasional snippet of relevant history rather than histories proper. To the extent that historical examples were included, they were often anachronistic, like those medieval miniatures depicting Joshua's Israelite warriors clad in suits of gothic armor. The authors viewed the ancient commanders as their contemporary colleagues in arms. Nonetheless, their historical examples help to illuminate both earlier and contemporary methods.

Although far from military history, the chronicles of the medieval and early Renaissance campaigns, such as the reminiscences of Joinville about St. Louis during the Seventh Crusade (1248–54) and Froissart's account of the first phase of the Hundred Years' War, are generally the only sources available. While conveying the authentic atmosphere of the times and presenting vivid portraits of the leading personalities, these chatty narratives are poor guides to details of battles or the size and composition of armies.

This is true not only of European writers but also of those in the Middle East, where the rise of Islam was writing a new and important chapter in military history that would be ignored in Europe until modern times due to a lack of militarily astute witnesses and the paucity of nineteenth-century scientific historians interested in sifting the dross from the early Arab commentators' accounts. The early Muslim historians, eager to record the great events of the Arab conquests of the seventh through ninth centuries, set out the various conflicting versions of the campaigns without evaluating their relative merits. They left this to their reader, with the admonishment, "And Allah knows best."

The Renaissance in the Mediterranean littoral of Europe witnessed a rediscovery of the texts of Vegetius and Maurice as well as the wars and campaigns that inspired them. Machiavelli's *Art of War* (1521) was more concerned with contemporary practice than the study of the military past. However, it did examine and embellish the arguments of the Roman historian Livy in support of a citizen army of native troops rather than mercenaries like the *condotierri*. Machiavelli's treatise also mines the works of Vegetius, Frontinus, and Polybius to lay out the precise organization, battle formations, logistical arrangements, campsites, chain of command, and so on of the Roman armies. His purpose was to hold up that ancient fighting machine as an ideal model for the forces of the

Florentine city-state. He dismissed the impact of modern artillery upon his Roman paradigm, since he estimated, erroneously, that the guns of his day were not much more mobile or effective than were the Roman siege engines.

Transition from War Histories to War Studies

It was not until the Enlightenment of the late seventeenth and eighteenth centuries that the "Great Captains" began to lay out their military maxims, based on concrete experience, so as to instruct the novice officer in the ways of war. The works of Marshal de Saxe, Chevalier de Folard, Guibert, Count Raimondo Montecuccoli, Henry Lloyd, and Frederick the Great—part military memoir and part distilled wisdom—are not so much military histories as rules and guidelines (practical hints for day-to-day troop management rather than principles of war) that assume that the reader is familiar with the political and technological context. Thus it was the immediate experience of contemporary wars rather than an idealized past that provided the ore for the metal of military wisdom.

Lloyd's *A History of the Late War in Germany* (1766) is widely regarded as the most influential elucidation of embryonic principles of war in a historical context. He admonished the reader that the best strategy was the slow and cautious advance along a short and well-protected line of communication of an undivided force that would, if possible, avoid battle. If a fight became necessary, Lloyd's intention was to lure a fragmented and ill-prepared enemy to attack well-prepared defensive positions. Lloyd was concerned more with preconceived notions of the character and qualities of physical force and the best methods of commanding troops than he was with recording accurately the progress of the Seven Years' War.

Perhaps the first truly modern military historian, as Peter Paret has pointed out, was Gerhard von Scharnhorst, who in 1797 published a history of the War of the First Coalition. Scharnhorst's avowed purpose was to identify and analyze crucial differences between the old monarchies and revolutionary France as demonstrated in their ways of war. Paret notes the distinction between Scharnhorst's treatment and that of other writers who found the key to French victory in such special techniques as the *levée en masse* or skirmishing. The pioneering German military educator noted instead that France enjoyed a more favorable strategic position, greater numbers, a unified political and military command, and stronger motivation. He also traced the origins and development of the French army's organization and methods and analyzed the strategy of the French revolutionary commanders as derived from the politico-military context. As an object lesson for his own Prussia of the early 1800s, Scharnhorst identified the psychological and social factors that generated superior moral force in a free political system that encouraged the participation of the common folk. Scharnhorst, who was the real founder of the Prussian German general staff system that dominated warfare for a century, was the first of a distinguished line of Prussian German military historian-theorist-generals. His major successors were Moltke and Schlieffen.

Emergence of Professional Military History in the Nineteenth Century

Scharnhorst's pupil, Karl von Clausewitz, who wrote from 1802 to 1832, is best known for his magisterial treatise *On War*. Besides distilling profound and widely applicable military truths (*not* readily memorized maxims) from the campaigns of Napoleon, he cautioned the would-be didactic military historian to examine his selected illustrative historical examples in depth to make certain that the circumstances do not invalidate the lesson derived. Book 7 of this work briefly surveyed the methods of making war employed by different European societies since ancient times. It concluded that one should not seek a single theory of war valid for all times, but that several different theories were necessary to account for the distinctive features of each epoch. The only immutable generalizations that could be sustained were those governing the psychological bases of human behavior under stress. His own study of the Thirty Years' War demonstrated how the men of the early seventeenth century behaved on the battlefield according to the dictates of economic and technological circumstances, as well as their political and religious motivations and mindsets.

Next, Clausewitz's contemporary and fellow veteran of the Napoleonic Wars, Antoine Jomini, drew upon a thorough survey of thirty campaigns of Frederick and Napoleon in order to deduce maxims and principles to guide apprentice military leaders. In that sense, Jomini's work was a logical extension of Lloyd's précis mentioned above. Much has been made of Jomini's deleterious effect upon British, Continental, and American commanders of the nineteenth century who slavishly followed his precepts without taking into account conditions of terrain, social background of the troops, and the character of the political and military leadership. However, Jomini qualified his published lectures (*Précis de l'art de la guerre*) by recognizing the importance of the personality of the general and the esprit of the men, as well as differences in the political impetus among wars. Since his works were clearly written and well organized, the newly established military educational institutions formed under the aegis of German-model general staff systems adopted the books of Jomini and his imitators as texts.

In Britain, a new precision was attained in the writing of military history with the publication of Sir William Napier's *History of the War in the Peninsula* (1828–1840). Based upon an exhaustive perusal of orders, dispatches, war diaries, and his own combat experiences in the campaign, Napier leavened his battle narrative with observations that fell between the precepts of Jomini and the intangibles of Clausewitz. So far as British military education was concerned, several prominent Staff College professors adapted Jomini's approach to their own uses, notably Maj. Gen. Patrick MacDougall, whose *Theory of War Illustrated by Numerous Examples from Military History* (1856) was a digest of Jomini, liberally sprinkled with examples from Napier, and represented the first in a line of British casebooks on military history. The most well known and durable of the didactic surveys was that done by Gen. Sir Edward Bruce Hamley, who provided the British Staff College (founded in 1858 after the exposure of British army shortcomings in the Crimean War) with its first "scientific" text consisting of heavily illustrated principles covering a wide range of problems confronting the apprentice field commander. His *The Operations of War Explained and Illustrated,* first published in 1866, went through seven editions (the last in 1922), taking Hamley's thematic campaign analyses through World War I. The book not only amplified Jominian precepts but also concurred with the Swiss theoretician's view of history as a treasurehouse to be plundered for proof of predetermined rules, rather than a body of knowledge to be studied for whatever insights it may happen to reveal. Hamley differed with MacDougall in questioning the relevance of combat predating the Seven Years' War to contemporary practice.

Late-nineteenth-century British military historian George F. R. Henderson, also a lead instructor at the Staff College, granted that *Operations* was an excellent teaching device but believed Hamley omitted crucial factors: the commander's leadership qualities and troop morale. While Henderson continued the emphasis upon tactical battle analysis, his work in this area is exemplary, bringing the student into the center of the action and to the seat of decision. This utilizing the vantage point of a single commander, with only that knowledge he possessed, was called the "applicatory" method of studying military history. Henderson emphasized the value of analyzing the neglected American Civil War at a time when most of European and America's service schools were digesting and regurgitating lessons from the great Prussian victories over Denmark (1864), Austria (1866), and France (1870). Henderson exploited fully his insights into human nature and the power of personality in war in his 1898 biography of Stonewall Jackson, which is in reality a personalized operational study of the first half of the Civil War in the eastern theater.

Part of the reason that Europeans were transfixed by the German Wars of Unification was the mystique of the German general staff under the direction of the great strategist, soldier's schoolmaster, and military historian Helmuth von Moltke. The latter's perfection of the general staff system included the creation of a historical section. This team of official researchers was entrusted with compiling the authorized, definitive histories of all of Germany's wars. These projects were the forerunners of all official history and, much as the German war directorate was copied by the leading nations of Europe, so was their history-writing function. Until the end of World War I, official history as written by the various armed forces was technically precise, highly detailed, and careful neither to stain national heroes nor to question the correctness of current military doctrine.

Since the study of warfare had been preempted by the military establishment, German academic scholars generally shied away from it. There were a few notable exceptions. German professional historians, led by Otto von Ranke, originated the modern methodical and scientific study of the past. In the mid-1800s, one of them, Friedrich Wilhelm Rüstow, dared to investigate the history of infantry (*Geshichte der Infanterie*) using the new critical techniques.

Inspired by Rüstow's independent analytical war studies and prompted by Clausewitz's dictum that war was but an extension of politics into a violent medium, Hans Delbrück's contribution to military history is arguably the most significant development in the field. Delbrück is generally considered the archetypical military historian. A highly trained and skilled professor of history, Delbrück was no mere armchair pedant. He had seen action in the Franco-Prussian War and was appointed as tutor to Waldemar, son of Crown Prince Frederick, where he was given wide access to army leaders and combat archives.

Appointed as Privatdozent to the University of Berlin in 1881, Delbrück began to concentrate upon the evolution of warfare as an extension of diplomatic intercourse. His authorized life of the great Prussian commander in the Napoleonic Wars, Field Marshal Graf August Neidhardt von Gneisenau, required an extensive grounding in Napoleonic strategy, for which he explored the works of Clausewitz and fused that great thinker's insights with the methods of Ranke and Rüstow. By the 1890s, Delbrück was making his mark as a master of military historical research. His contributions have been summed up by Richard Bauer as threefold:

1. Exposure and correction of many legends concerning the size of armies participating in ancient and medieval battles.
2. Division of all military strategy into the strategy of exhaustion (*Ermattungsstrategie*) and the strategy of annihilation (*Niederwerfungsstrategie*). The former was the preferred method in the eighteenth century, especially by Frederick the Great, and consisted of weakening the enemy gradually by a series of maneuvers without necessarily engaging his forces.
3. Explanation of the events of a war by going beyond mere descriptions of battlefield operations and considering the constraints imposed by technological and geographical limitations as well as the political intentions of the national leaders directing the war.

We can mark the beginning of the war and society trend with the advent of Delbrück, although Delbrück himself focused more on military organization, strategy, and tactics than upon social context as it has become known in the 1990s.

A contemporary of Delbrück, Otto Hintze, also placed warfare in its general context but found a new analytical touchstone in the relationship between military organization and political structure. In the process, he advanced the case for military history's relevance to the patterns of cultural and institutional development.

In England, Sir Charles Oman and Spenser Wilkinson, civilian scholars, advanced the study of military history by applying Delbrückian methods to, respectively, the wars of the Middle Ages and the military education of and influences upon the young Napoleon Bonaparte. The multivolume tour de force of John Fortescue, the preeminent historian of British land forces, is a masterpiece of traditional military history, but demonstrates the hold that battle narrative still exerted upon institutional studies.

Nineteenth-century French military history was principally the province of the officer-pedants attached to the general staff or instructors in the *Ecole de Guerre Supérieure*. Following the disaster at Sedan in 1870, the spirit and genius of Napoleon I was evoked to guide soldiers. A search for ways to revive the Napoleonic spirit permeated the prescriptive historical reviews churned out by the high command. "Drum and trumpet" histories, emphasizing élan, predominated. Several notable Napoleonic scholars rose above the hero worship of their fellow officers to produce fine critiques of the master's mind and method. The works of Palat, Bonnal, Camon, Vachée, Colin, and Pierron have enduring value.

American military historians covering land warfare worked under the shadow of Jomini. John Bigelow's 1895 primer on strategy was a Jominian survey of the Civil War, though his 1910 study of Chancellorsville represents, along with G. F. R. Henderson's tactical studies, the perfection of the campaign history. Matthew Forney Steele's 1909 West Point history text, *American Campaigns*, was the standard text for the institution's course in military art and engineering for almost fifty years. It also kept a "principles" scorecard for each major engagement from colonial times through the Spanish-American War.

It was only in the realm of naval history that American strategic thinkers broke new ground. Alfred Thayer Mahan's 1890 survey of seapower's influence upon world affairs in the age of sail also sought out eternal verities of naval warfare. But Mahan looked deeper for his principles of seapower than the landpower theoreticians' themes and found links between geographical configuration, demographic distribution and evolution, industrial infrastructure, political makeup, and the "control of the sea-lanes." His Darwinian racist credo and emphasis upon seeking decisive action between battle fleets on the high seas limited his influence to the first quarter of the twentieth century, yet his accent upon broader social and economic factors endures.

History Lessons for the Era of Total War

In the aftershock of World War I's slaughter, two British veterans of the trenches reexamined warfare to find formulas that might overcome the offense-defense deadlock.

J.F.C. Fuller searched the past to exhume its concealed "science of war," based upon immutable principles. His work in the 1920s is linked to the enumeration of discrete principles of war that found their way into the British field service regulations and the United States's field manual *Operations*, now designated *FM 100-5*. Fuller went beyond Jomini's list to evoke Darwin's evolutionary theories and devise a "law of military development," which held that armies must adapt to changes in their environment. Fuller turned to history to verify the natural laws of military science he had already divined. Much as Hamley did before him, Fuller plundered the historical data for insights without going into the primary sources. The result was lively and illuminating military history (especially his *Military History of the Western World*), albeit often wrong in the particulars.

Sir Basil Liddell Hart found his key to the puzzle of the World War I killing grounds in the "strategy of the indirect approach." In order to amass an inventory of examples proving that the indirect approach had been the determinant of success, Liddell Hart examined numerous battles throughout history, using the evidence selectively and, like Fuller, shunning primary sources or incidents that might contradict his hypothesis.

In short, both Fuller and Liddell Hart enriched the literature with provocative ideas and inspired much-needed investigation into contemporary doctrines. In their use of history they represent perhaps the last of the intellectual heirs of Jomini and Hamley.

While the British Committee of Imperial Defence supervised a meticulously detailed official operational history of the Great War, its editors were constrained to protect the reputations of much-decorated blunderers. The Americans did not hazard to analyze their brief participation. Rather than waste precious defense dollars on staff pedagogues, the U.S. War Department was content to assemble the various orders, corps, and division after-action reports and let the documents speak for themselves. The story of individual battles and campaigns was consigned to monographs that served as in-house teaching aids at the army's War College and at the Infantry School. In the mid-1930s, a new sophistication in prescriptive small-unit action studies was attained with the U.S. Army Command and General Staff College's *Infantry in Battle*.

The New Military History: 1945–2000

The Second World War inspired novel approaches in military history. At one level, official history had to shed its mask of self-exoneration and achieve greater depth and breadth than the up-the-hill, down-the-hill chronicle. The British version certainly bettered its World War I counterpart, especially in the "Grand Strategy" series, but did not match the ingenuity of the American method. The latter was developed by S. L. A. Marshall, a journalist-historian, who headed a talented academic team commissioned by the U.S. Army to write its combat history while it occurred. Marshall combined a survey of war diaries and orders and dispatches with group after-action debriefings to commence an innovative procedure in oral history. He extended this method to interrogations of captured German officers, who were assisted by access to captured documents.

A second level of analysis proceeds directly from Marshall's spotlight on small-unit interaction and cohesion under stress. As University of Chicago military historian Walter Kaegi has observed, it was sociologists and political scientists rather than historians who carried the study of men under fire to its next logical step: research on armies as social institutions, as bureaucracies, as political entities with internal rivalries and self-interests, and on their interactions with civilian agencies. Trailblazers of this aspect of war and society analysis include Samuel Huntington, Morris Janowitz, and S. E. Finer.

The sociological study of unit cohesion during World War II was embraced by erudite conflict historians in their investigations of the citizen at war in earlier periods. In France, Phillipe Contamine improved upon Oman's survey of medieval warfare by tracking religious, class, cultural, and ritual influences from village and manor to the field of battle. R. C. Smail did the same with crusading warfare for English-speaking readers.

In Britain and the United States, Michael Howard, John Shy, and Peter Paret brought new insights from the social sciences to bear upon multidimensional conflict studies, particularly the impact of the anticolonialist struggles in the Third World. Paul Kennedy has provided a holistic framework upon which to hang his explanation of the rise and fall of British naval mastery, which he later expanded to encompass the symbiosis between capital and military power since the Renaissance, updating Sombart and Nef to this effect.

Some practitioners of combat-oriented military history have been calling for a return to utilitarian considerations of military institutions as fighting instruments. Utilitarian military pedants believe that the scholarly approach toward military organizations and their impact on society has lost sight of the fact that their primary mission is combat or the threat of combat. Accordingly, since the mid-1980s there has been a fusion of the pristinely civilian outlook with the old emphasis upon battle. Exemplary American works are the U.S. Command and General Staff College's review of *America's First Battles* (meaning the American baptism of fire in each of its wars) and Ohio State University's three-volume project on military effectiveness, a concept that offers an excellent vehicle for combining the two approaches in a historical context.

Operations research (OR), or systems analysis, is another spin-off from World War II–stimulated progress in the social sciences that affected the writing of military history. This was an essentially algebraic procedure to solve special combat problems requiring a scientific approach. It was first devised to hunt submerged U-boats that evaded air and sonar search, and expanded to cover such questions as artillery fire plans, proper force mixture for different contingencies, bombing target priorities, and so forth. Its origins stretch back to William Lanchester's 1916 speculations upon the "force multiplier" effects of aircraft in combat. The British and American defense establishments adapted the method to solve postwar dilemmas. The harmful effects of OR upon American strategy in Vietnam somewhat discredited the technique as a planning tool and led to the revival of historical analogy in military education and planning.

Successful applications of OR concepts to professional war-gaming also have enriched the historian's craft. One example of this is American Col. Trevor Dupuy's quantified judgmental method. Applying statistically driven formulas covering such aspects as relative weapons lethality, effects of surprise, field fortifications, and troop density, Dupuy has isolated the factors explaining combat results over a wide range of historical battles. While critics have quibbled over the degree of precision one may expect, the method has enriched historical debate over what makes for success in battle.

Soviet historians have essentially utilized a variation of this method in their calculation of "norms" for artillery concentrations, armor dispersal, and the like for their World War II engagements.

Since the late 1960s, the vast expansion and refinement of the popular military hobby trade, including accurate scale models and diorama construction by gifted amateurs and the rise of recreational war-gaming, has created a demand for guides and authentic background information. Sometimes denigrated by academic military historians as mere buffs or enthusiasts, scale modelers, war-gamers, and reenactors often have made real contributions to military history.

A quick survey of the magazines catering to the hobbyists reveals a spectrum of professionalism ranging from fascination with uniform and equipment minutiae to erudite order-of-battle analysis. Necessarily, the modeling magazines are preoccupied with details of appearance, but this does not necessarily mean that the broader implications are ignored. Those directed to the more advanced creators of museum-quality reproductions often feature articles offering the historian hard-to-find information on matters pertaining to topics like unit insignia, weapons development and variants, equipment, camouflage techniques, and military costume.

There is considerable interaction between the hobby war-gaming industry and defense establishments, at least in the United States and Great Britain. The names of prominent Sandhurst and U.S. Army or Naval War College analysts appear regularly in the better historical simulations journals.

JAMES BLOOM

SEE ALSO: Ardant du Picq, Charles J. J. J.; Art of War; Caesar, Julius; Clausewitz, Karl von; Fuller, J. F. C.; Jomini, Antoine Henri; Mahan, Alfred Thayer; Moltke the Elder; Principles of War; Saxe, Hermann Maurice, Comte de; Scharnhorst, Gerhard Johann David von; Science of War; Sun Tzu.

Bibliography

Bauer, R. H. 1942. Hans Delbrück. In *Some historians of modern Europe*, ed. B. Schmitt. Chicago: Univ. of Chicago Press.

Best, G., B. Bond, D. Chandler, J. Childs, J. Gooch, M. Howard, J. C. A. Stagg, and J. Terraine. 1984. What is military history? *History Today* 34:5–15.

Dupuy, T. N. 1984. *The evolution of weapons and warfare*. Fairfax, Va.: Hero Books.

Earle, E. M., ed. 1943. *Makers of modern strategy from Machiavelli to Hitler*. Princeton, N.J.: Princeton Univ. Press.

Gooch, J. 1980. Clio and Mars: The use and abuse of military history. *Journal of Strategic Studies* 3:21–36.

Howard, M. 1962. The use and abuse of military history. *R.U.S.I. Journal* 117:4–10.

James, R. R. 1966. Thoughts on writing military history. *R.U.S.I. Journal*, May.

Jessup, J., and R. W. Coakley, eds. 1979. *A guide to the study and use of military history*. Washington, D.C.: U.S. Army Center of Military History.

Jones, C. 1982. New military history for old? War and society in early modern Europe. *European Studies Review* 12:97–108.

Luvaas, J. 1982. Military history: Is it still practicable? *Parameters* 12(1):2–14.

Millis, W. 1961. *Military history*. Washington, D.C.: Service Center for Teachers of History.

Millett, A. R. 1977. The study of American military history in the United States. *Military Affairs* 41:58.

Paret, P. 1971. The history of war. *Daedalus* 100:376–96.

———, ed. 1986. *Makers of modern strategy from Machiavelli to the nuclear age*. Princeton, N.J.: Princeton Univ. Press.

HISTORY, MODERN MILITARY
[ca. 1792–present]

Although the point at which modern warfare began is debatable, a good case can be made for the period of the French revolutionary wars. Dynastic conflicts for limited objectives faded, and the rise of nationalism dramatically changed the conduct of war. Organization at the national level and an approach toward total war marked the conflicts of the late eighteenth and early nineteenth centuries.

Naval warfare became highly organized and disciplined as wooden sailing ships reached their zenith. Battles were fought with heavier guns when large ships of the line appeared as precursors to the battleships of a later age.

Wars of the French Revolution

The revolution had a tremendous impact on the French army. Seventy percent of its officer corps and most of its trained men were lost in the chaos, leaving the French armed forces incapable of operating on the old model. In 1791, a new set of tactical concepts and reforms provided speed and flexibility in deployment for action.

European monarchs, alarmed at the spread of revolutionary ideals, reacted vigorously. By 1792, French volunteers and remnants of the Royal Army were in combat with the disciplined, professional armies of Prussia and Austria. The disorganized French forces were repeatedly defeated. Fortunately for the new government, the committed Prussian and Austrian forces were insufficient to subjugate France.

By 1793, France faced a coalition of Prussia, Austria, the Netherlands, Spain, and Great Britain and began drafting hundreds of thousands of men, many of whom were poorly trained and meagerly equipped. Nevertheless, the masses of men, revolutionary zeal, new tactics, and poor coordination of the coalition forces, along with the advantage of fighting from interior lines, enabled the French to hold their own.

In March 1796, 26-year-old Napoleon Bonaparte took command of a newly structured French army in Italy. His impact on military thought during this war-prone era was enormous. The old French officer corps was uprooted, the army rebuilt, and the obscure Corsican rose to leadership and later became emperor of France. Warfare was not greatly affected by new technology, though some innovations did appear, including Cugnot's invention of a steam-powered vehicle to haul cannon and the development of canned food to improve military diets.

Napoleon's initial campaigns in northern Italy were considered by some analysts to be his most brilliant. Even as he "learned his trade," he drove the competent but aging Austrian generals out of Italy in a series of short, sharp battles and maneuvers (April 1796–March 1797). Following an interlude in the Mideast, where he conquered Egypt but was checked in Acre, Palestine, he returned to France to face a revolt in the Vendée and the continuing war with

Great Britain and Austria, the latter having reconquered almost all of Italy by 1799.

Napoleon took over the government as first consul and prepared for more vigorous warfare. Since Great Britain could not be attacked directly, he targeted Austrian forces in Italy via Switzerland. Although nearly defeated at Marengo (14 June 1800), the French forced a temporary peace on Vienna.

Great Britain, along with Turkish troops, forced the French out of Egypt. Finally, in 1802, the Treaty of Amiens was signed and lasted fourteen months. Friction between France and England continued and, in May 1803, France declared war, seized Naples, occupied Hannover, and prepared for a channel crossing to invade Great Britain. British seapower proved too formidable and the invasion was never attempted.

Meanwhile Prime Minister William Pitt crafted another coalition, and by 1805, Russia, Austria, Naples, Great Britain, and Sweden had mobilized half a million men to fight the French. That autumn, Napoleon destroyed a major Austrian army at Ulm (17 October) before Russian forces arrived. Even in victory, however, a naval battle at Cape Trafalgar where a French-Spanish fleet was destroyed (21 October) ended any threat to Britain's sea supremacy.

Subsequently, at Austerlitz (2 December 1805), a Russian-Austrian army of 84,000 was shattered by Napoleon's army of 71,000. Vienna again sued for peace and the czar's army was sent reeling back into Poland.

On 7 August 1806, Napoleon secretly goaded the Prussians into a war declaration, and on 8 October, his columns crossed into Saxony. At the twin battles of Jena-Auerstädt (4 October 1806), the Prussian army was beaten and further shattered during its disordered retreat. Napoleon's month-long "lightning war" dragged on for six months, sustained by Prussia's iron-willed Queen Louise. Napoleon became master of most of Europe but there were still Russia and Great Britain to deal with. He tried an embargo to damage the British economy, but it failed.

Russian forces opened a winter offensive in northern Poland but were forced back after an indecisive battle at Eylau (8 February 1807). Napoleon won a notable victory at Friedland (14 June) and peace was finally achieved that month at a summit meeting between Czar Alexander and Emperor Napoleon. The French then faced a festering war on their southern flank as Portugal resisted invasion; however, shortly thereafter, Napoleon took over Spain, his nominal ally, and placed his brother on the throne.

The Spanish, with British backing, resisted, but were unable to repulse the French in the field. Widespread irregular warfare broke out; eventually, the Spanish, with the help of British forces under the Duke of Wellington, pushed the French out of Spain. In 1809, Austria reopened hostilities and Napoleon went on the offensive to win a costly victory at Wagram (5–6 July). A quarter of his men (32,000) were casualties, but the Austrians fared even worse. Napoleon's peace terms were accepted; however, this campaign was the last of his victories.

After two and a half years of relative peace, Napoleon again collided with the Russian Empire. In mid-1812, he assembled half a million men, many of whom were unwilling allies, and marched eastward. The Russians retreated until they reached Borodino, where they fought Napoleon almost to a draw in a bloody (about 80,000 casualties) twelve-hour battle (7 September). The Russians abandoned the field and the crippled French army marched on to Moscow.

Napoleon dallied in Moscow for several weeks and then began a disastrous retreat during which most of his invasion force was destroyed (October–December 1812). Following this fiasco, he created a new army to combat his persistent foes: Prussia, Austria, and Sweden. Campaigning began in Germany in April 1813, and his new French army fought well (although not up to 1809 standards), particularly when led by "the master." Napoleon's subordinates were less successful and more often targets of enemy attacks.

A major defeat at the Battle of Nations, at Leipzig on 16–19 October 1813, ended French hopes for a trans-Rhine empire. Napoleon refused a peace proposal that would have made the Rhine and the Alps France's frontier. The allies invaded France, captured Paris in March 1814, and forced the emperor's abdication.

Exiled to the island of Elba, he returned a year later, rallied his followers, drove out the French king, Louis XVIII, and began the "Hundred Days," in which he tried to reconstitute his empire. The allies relentlessly opposed these attempts. He was defeated at Waterloo by an allied Anglo-Prussian army (18 June 1815), which put an end to the great Napoleonic wars.

The Post-Napoleonic Era

Peace was not universal. In South America, revolutions led by Simón Bolívar, José de San Martín, Antonio José de Sucre, and others demolished the decrepit Spanish Empire between the years 1808 and 1828. Elsewhere, anti-Manchu uprisings in China, along with Great Britain's colonial wars in India, the French conquests in North Africa, local wars in the western Sudan, and a Greek revolt against the Turks kept warfare a means of solving ethnic, religious, and political conflicts. Strife in Italy led to the ousting of Austrians, and in 1848 there were widespread revolts of one kind or another in Europe.

During this period, weaponry was marginally improved while warfare characteristics remained generally unchanged. A Greek revolt, beginning in 1821 and threatened by an Egyptian army victory, brought European intervention (1827) as an allied fleet of British, French, and Russian ships, in the last major battle between wooden sailing vessels, annihilated Turkish and Egyptian fleets at Navarino (20 October 1827).

The Crimean War (1854–56) reflected the most changes in warfare since, perhaps, the advent of gunpowder. During this conflict, France, Great Britain, and later Sardinia came to the aid of the Ottoman Empire, which was on the verge of destruction by Russian attacks. On the naval side, steam overtook the fighting sail vessel. Armored floating batteries were used by the allies against the fortress of Kinburn (16 October 1855), presaging the widespread use of armor plate on naval vessels. Other innovations included use of a railroad to carry supplies from a landing area to the allied camps, the presence of war correspondents at the battlefields, and a reduction of mortality rates among the sick and wounded through the efforts of British nurse Florence Nightingale.

The siege of Sevastopol (8 October 1854–8 September 1855) was marked by hard-fought and confused battles with sustained bombardment of the city. The allies forced the Russians to withdraw and a peace settlement was concluded on 30 March 1856, thus preserving the Ottoman Empire.

The year 1859 was notable for several reasons. First, the French produced a steam-powered armored frigate, *Gloire*. It had a wooden hull, but its vitals were protected by armored plating. Second, during the Wars of Italian Independence, the battle of Solferino, fought by 120,000 Austrians and 118,000 French and Piedmontese (24 June 1859), forced the defeated Austrians to cede all of Lombardy to an emerging united Italy. Another major development that grew out of the carnage of Solferino was the formation of the International Red Cross. Swiss philanthropist Jean-Henri Dunant witnessed the battle and was horrified at the poor care the wounded received. His postbattle activism led to the founding of the organization, which has had a strong and continuing impact on the conduct of war, stimulating treaties governing the treatment of civilians in war zones, the treatment of prisoners, and the conduct of hostilities.

The War Between the States (1861–65)

Considerable new battlefield technology appeared during the American Civil War, including electrically fired land and naval mines, new forms of heavy artillery, a balloon observation corps, *Monitor*-type naval vessels (turreted armored warships), breech-loading and magazine rifles, and the Gatling gun (an early form of machine gun). The most important technology associated with this war was not really new at all: the railroad and the minié ball (previously used in combat by the Austrians).

The minié ball was a conoidal bullet with a hollowed-out base that was used in muzzle-loading rifles in standard infantry equipment. When the powder charge ignited, the hollow base expanded, making a gas-tight fit and forcing the soft lead to engage the rifling of the barrel. This spin-stabilized bullet maintained a relatively accurate trajectory over a long distance. In this way, every infantry musket (technically rifles, although still called muskets) became an accurate, long-range weapon infinitely superior to the inaccurate, smooth-bore muskets of the past. (Patch and ball rifles had long been used in warfare, but their slow rate of fire limited them on battlefields.)

Rifled muskets drastically changed battlefield tactics and campaign strategies. Field fortifications could no longer be charged with impunity unless attacks were made with overwhelming forces. Also, artillery could no longer unlimber at 270-meter (300-yd.) ranges and open fire on opposing infantry. The cannoneers would be wiped out by musketry.

Railroads had been around longer than the minié ball but, prior to 1861, had made only small contributions to warfare. Now their logistical importance became so great that battles and campaigns were planned around rail support. In addition to transport for men and supplies, the trains themselves could serve as semimobile artillery: gun tubes were sometimes mounted on rail trucks (e.g., the train-mounted mortars and guns used at the siege of Petersburg 1864–65).

Ultimately, the greater economic, demographic, and manufacturing base of the North provided the margin of victory in what was largely a war of attrition. Here, the United States Navy also played an important role, blockading the South and intercepting war materiel. Naval action included the first battle between ironclads—the *Monitor* and the *Virginia* (9 March 1862)—and later the widespread employment of this type of ship. The war ended with the surrender of Confederate general Robert E. Lee at the Appomattox Courthouse on 9 April 1865.

The Franco-Prussian War

After the Napoleonic wars, Prussia continued to improve its military staff system and reserve structure and began to move toward unifying Germany. Schleswig-Holstein was quickly wrested from Denmark in 1864. Austria was defeated in the Seven Weeks' War in which the two armies—some 170,000 on both sides—collided at Königgrätz (Sadowa) on 3 July 1866.

The next step toward unification was to defeat France. Both parties to the Franco-Prussian conflict wanted war: the Prussians to eliminate French influence and unify Germany, and Napoleon III, who hoped to regain the grandeur of the empire of Napoleon I.

On 19 July 1870, war was declared. The French had superior rifles and a "secret weapon," the *mitrailleuse*. Their mobilization, however, was chaotic and tactics obsolete. The mitrailleuse, a manually cranked precursor of the machine gun, had little impact because, to maintain secrecy, training was limited, and the guns were inappropriately used as artillery rather than as infantry weapons. The better organized and trained Prussian forces had superior artillery, better logistics support, and a better command structure. The French were beaten in every major engagement as the Prussians drove one French army into Metz to be captured later (27 October with 173,000 men) and then captured Napoleon with his entire army of 83,000 at Sedan on 2 September. France thereupon declared itself a republic, resolved to carry on the struggle, and ordered "war to the bitter end."

The Prussians surrounded Paris, initiating a famous siege that brought several innovations to warfare, including the use of balloons for communications and the use of microphotography to send messages attached to trained carrier pigeons. The Prussians also added a footnote to military intelligence history. They tapped an underwater telegraph line leading out of Paris and carried out what may have been the first signal intelligence intercept operation ever conducted in Europe (telegraph messages had been intercepted and decoded in the American Civil War). With besieged Parisians nearing starvation, the French government capitulated on 28 January 1871.

Colonial Wars, Rebellions, Spanish-American War, China, Boer War

Following the Franco-Prussian War, hostilities among major powers quieted as if bracing for the upcoming storm of World War I. There were, however, a host of revolutions, colonial wars, and minor conflicts throughout the world.

The Spanish-American War of 1898 was largely determined by two naval battles in which one Spanish fleet was destroyed at Manila in the Philippines (1 May) and another at Santiago, Cuba (3 July). Spanish soldiers ashore had superior personal weapons, including Mauser rifles and smokeless powder (developed by the French), but were quickly beaten. Spain capitulated and signed the Treaty of Paris (10 December 1898) and the United States emerged as a world power.

China was in almost continual warfare during the last half of the nineteenth century. As the Manchu dynasty weakened, the Sino-Japanese War, which ended in April 1895, provided victorious Japan with the island of Formosa, the Pescadores, a huge indemnity, and other considerations.

More widely publicized was the Boxer Rebellion of 1899, which was initiated by a xenophobic Chinese secret society and culminated in a siege of the foreign legation quarter in Peking (20 June–14 August 1900). Japanese, French, British, Italian, U.S., and Russian military forces (later joined by a German unit) relieved the legations, then fought with the Chinese for a year before peace was imposed (12 September 1901).

The Boer War (or South African War, 1899–1902) was a revolt of descendants of Dutch settlers in South Africa against British incursions. Early Boer successes were largely due to their accurate fire from magazine-fed rifles with smokeless powder. The British rapidly reinforced their troops, deploying 450,000 men against 90,000 Boers. Outnumbered, the Boers turned to guerrilla warfare, again with initial success; the British countered with effective, although harsh, antiguerrilla tactics. The war ended in May 1902 with the Boers accepting British sovereignty.

New, or relatively new, to warfare was the use of steam tractors to haul cannon and supplies, the use of armored and armed trains, and the large-scale employment of guerrilla and antiguerrilla warfare tactics such as concentration camps to segregate the civilian population from combatants. This tactic, pioneered by the Spanish in Cuba, presaged such later twentieth-century conflicts as Vietnam and Afghanistan.

Russo-Japanese War (1904–1905)

The Russo-Japanese War was, in many ways, a dress rehearsal for World War I. The naval battles included the use of breech-loading guns, mines, armor-piercing shells, wireless communications, and torpedoes at sea. On land were barbed wire, machine guns, and field artillery with recoil mechanisms. Naval actions and Japanese squadrons defeated Russian naval detachments; the Port Arthur squadron surrendered to besieging Japanese ground forces (2 January

1905), and a Russian squadron from the Baltic was destroyed at sea at Tsushima (31 May 1905). Although the Japanese were successful, they were hard- pressed to maintain the level of conflict as Russian ground reinforcements came east on the Trans-Siberian railroad.

A U.S. offer to act as mediator was accepted and the war ended with the Treaty of Portsmouth (5 September 1905). Japan's sphere of influence in Korea was recognized and both parties agreed to evacuate Manchuria.

World War I

The causes of World War I have been studied and argued for years. It is clear, however, that the great powers of Europe were, in the early 1900s, psychologically and militarily ready for combat, although few had any inkling of the tremendous bloodletting that lay ahead. Nationalism, Pan-Slavism, and desires for glory or revenge had turned Europe into a tinderbox that needed only a spark to set it ablaze. That spark came at Sarajevo, Bosnia, on 28 June 1914 when Archduke Francis Ferdinand, heir to the Austrian throne, was assassinated by Serbian radicals. In the aftermath, Europe began massive and complex mobilizations; war was inevitable.

Desperate, last-minute attempts to preserve peace failed, and war began with the Central Powers—Germany, Austria-Hungary, Turkey, and Bulgaria— opposed by the Entente headed by Russia, France, and the United Kingdom.

CHARACTERISTICS OF THE GROUND, NAVAL, AND AIR WAR

Ground warfare was markedly different from that of previous wars. Masses of manpower were employed on a scale never seen before. Europe's mass armies resulted from several factors, including long-term population growth; industrialization, which freed more manpower for combat; and nationalism, which sanctioned popular support for conscription. Most changes, however, involved technology. The large-scale, defensive use of machine guns, for example, led to development of vast field fortifications, miles in depth, that spread from the English Channel in the north to the Swiss-French frontier in the south. Combatants were supplied with magazine rifles, and artillery was equipped with recoil mechanisms and no longer bucked out of position with each discharge. Field telephones and to a lesser extent radios improved communications. Later in the conflict new ground force weapons, the tank and poison gas, appeared. One material-of-war on the western front was barbed wire, a relatively recent agricultural development now adapted to warfare. Thousands and thousands of miles of wire obstacles were strung before entrenchments, thus contributing to the static nature of combat on the western front.

Naval warfare was characterized by all-big-gun battleships (dreadnoughts), with ever larger guns, improved torpedoes and mines, better fire control systems, electrical shipboard communications, and wireless ship-to-shore and ship-to-ship communications. Oil-fired, turbine-driven ships became more common and, for the first time, submarines dominated the force at sea.

At the war's beginning, fixed-wing aircraft were few in number, balky, and limited to short-range reconnaissance missions. By war's end, thousands of aircraft from armies on both sides had taken to the skies. Range and speed improved many times over and new classes of aircraft were phased into combat so quickly that an aircraft design often had a useful life of only a few months. Machine guns appeared after a period in which planes were unarmed. Bombers emerged along with other specialized aircraft. Most aerial operations were tactical and aimed at supporting ground combat operations. Some longer range strikes on cities, however, were initiated by the Germans who used dirigibles and later long-range bombers. By the end of the war, the Allies were attacking distant communications centers and planning major strikes on German cities.

At the war's beginning, Germany had dirigible (zeppelin) capability and used airships extensively until incendiary machine-gun bullets exposed their vulnerability to fire. France and the United Kingdom also developed dirigibles, using them in various roles. Observation balloons were especially useful for artillery spotting on the western front.

Aerial warfare never impacted greatly on naval operations, but dirigibles and fixed-wing aircraft (both seaplanes and land-based) were important for reconnaissance.

WESTERN FRONT

Imperial Germany, knowing that the forces of the Central Powers would be greatly outnumbered by those of the Allies after all combatants were fully mobilized, determined to maximize its initial advantages: interior lines, better mobilization planning and execution, and better transportation. The strategy was to hold the slowly mobilizing Russians at bay while knocking France out of the war before the Russians could become a significant factor or before the British made large ground forces available in France. The concept was to sweep through Belgium, concentrate fast-moving German columns on the right wing of the advance, and envelop French forces with a vast turning movement. It was a strategy that demanded the German mobilization advantage not be squandered by drawn-out peace negotiations. On 3 August, Germany declared war and invaded Belgium.

The initial success failed partly because German generals did not rigorously adhere to the plan, partly because the small British Expeditionary Force (5 divisions, 70,000 men) became an unexpected obstacle. There was also the monumental calmness of the French commander, Gen. Joseph Joffre, who refused to panic or allow his forces to panic. Most important was a Russian offensive that forced the Germans to transfer badly needed troops to the east.

The Germans were halted at the First Battle of the Marne on 6–10 September, and shortly afterward both sides began to entrench along a 800-kilometer (500 mi.) front. At first the fortifications were simple breastworks, but these were steadily elaborated with extensive dugouts, barbed-wire obstacles, and defenses that defied attempts at breakthrough. The western front remained static until 1918.

In an attempt to break the stalemate, the Germans unleashed a chemical weapons attack at Ypres on 22 April 1915, killing 5,000 men, which opened a 6.4-kilometer (4- mi.) gap in Allied lines. The gap was soon sealed off by Allied reinforcements, but the precedent had been set for the use of gas for artillery preparation.

The British secretly developed armored tanks that protected crews from machine-gun fire when crushing barbed wire. Poor tactics and muddy battle-fields limited their effectiveness at Flers-Courcellette (15 September 1916), but they met with greater success in later battles, most notably the use of 350 of the tanks at the Second Battle of the Marne (15–17 July 1918).

EASTERN FRONT

In August, czarist armies, unready but responding to Allied pleas to relieve German pressure in the west, advanced into East Prussia. Germany was forced to shift troops to the east and recalled aging Gen. Paul von Hindenburg to duty to save the situation. Ably seconded by Erich Ludendorff, he soundly defeated the Russians at Tannenberg (26–31 August 1914).

Russian attacks against the heterogeneous armies of the Austro-Hungarian Empire were more successful, yet despite German reinforcements, by 1915 all fronts were in retreat.

OTHER FRONTS

The Japanese entered the war in 1914, attacking German colonies in the Far East; Turkey joined the Central Powers operating initially against Russia. Balkan, German, Austrian, and Bulgarian forces battled Serbia as the forces of the Central Powers overran much of that country. In October–November 1915, Romania joined the Allies but was defeated in December 1916. In Greece, King Constantine was deposed by pro-Allied forces, and war was declared on the Central Powers. The Allies sent an army to Salonika, where they defeated Bulgarian forces.

Britain occupied Egypt, and in Africa, British and French forces captured the German colonies of Togoland (1914), Kamerun (1916), and German Southwest Africa (1915). In German East Africa, Colonel (later general) von Lettow-Vorbeck fought vastly superior Allied forces, successfully operating in the field until after Germany itself surrendered.

In the Mideast, British troops carried the war to the Ottoman Empire, crossed into Palestine from Egypt, and attacked Mesopotamia to secure the Basra oil fields. Arabian allies, revolting against the Turks, were supplied with money, arms, and advisers. Among the latter was then-captain T. E. Lawrence, brought to fame by American journalist Lowell Thomas as "Lawrence of Arabia."

Allied naval and ground forces tried to open the Dardanelles in 1915 as a supply route to Russia, but they were stopped at Gallipoli by stubborn Turkish resistance on land and sea. A British army was forced to surrender at Kut in Mesopotamia (29 April 1916) after a five-month siege and the failure of relief efforts.

The Naval War

Germany was unable to directly challenge the strong British navy but did send several surface raiders to attack Allied shipping. After initial successes, the raiders were hunted down and destroyed. A German squadron destroyed a British one off Coronel, Chile, but was itself later destroyed off the Falkland Islands (Islas Malvinas). The most important naval battle was fought off Jutland on 31 May 1916 when the main British and German battle fleets engaged. The British incurred the most damage, including three battle cruisers. The German fleet, however, was driven back and never again challenged the British.

The Allies faced their greatest threat from German submarines. German U-boats did enormous damage to British merchant shipping until the institution of the convoy system and the development of such antisubmarine warfare (ASW) weapons as sonar, along with evasive tactics to reduce the damage from underwater warfare.

Final German Offensive

On 15 July 1918, Ludendorff launched an all-out offensive with three armies. By the evening of 17 July, massive Allied counterattacks had forced the Germans to retreat. On other fronts, the war was going badly for the Central Powers. Bulgarians asked for peace in September and the Austro-Hungarian Empire was fragmented beyond repair. Turkey, having lost Palestine, Mesopotamia, and Syria, asked for terms in November. Germany fought on until 11 November, when an armistice was signed.

World War I, the "War to End All Wars," was over. Eight million men had died, and the old order in Europe was destroyed forever.

Between the Wars

During the 1920s, there was prosperity in the United States until the 1929 stock market crash ushered in the Great Depression. With the election of Franklin Delano Roosevelt as president in 1933 came the devaluation of the dollar and a greater federal role in industry and farm production. New Deal programs were aimed at reducing unemployment.

America became isolationist as it saw that World War I had not brought peace, democracy, or disarmament, and European nations bickered as before. President Woodrow Wilson's Fourteen Points had been discarded and his concept of the League of Nations, adopted by many nations but refused in the United States, lacked authority to do more than issue verbal reprimands. Also, the United States believed that the two oceans would protect Americans from foreign belligerents.

In Russia, the November 1917 revolution, led by Vladimir Lenin, brought communism to power. After Lenin's death in 1924, Joseph Stalin became the dictator, later crushing all opposition by eliminating hundreds of thousands of intellectuals, army officers, and civil servants in the Great Purge of 1936–39. The fate of those purged was execution or labor camps in Siberia. Stalin's goal was to industrialize the USSR, nationalize steel and electrical plants, and seize private farms for use as collectives.

In the Far East, Japan and Korea (taken over by Japan in 1910) needed more territory to sustain the 65 million people, who increased by a million each year. The Japanese economy was hurt by the 1929 crash and it needed iron, coal, oil, and cereals in order to survive. Japanese forces overran nearby Manchuria in China in late 1931 and early 1932. When condemned by the League of Nations, Japan withdrew membership in 1933, signed an alliance with Germany and Italy in November 1936, and on 7 July 1937 declared war on China. Japanese armed forces attacked Peking, Nanking, Canton, and Shanghai. Entire village populations were slaughtered, and in the infamous Rape of Nanking, 20,000 were massacred in six weeks (13 December 1937–25 January 1938). Movietone News and graphic photography on the front pages of newspapers portrayed the horrors of war with the classic photograph of a Chinese child crying on the railroad tracks in Nanking.

In Europe, the civil war in Spain began as a rebellion by generals hostile to the Frente Popular and the Republican government (18 July 1936). The war ended in March 1939 with the victory of the rebels under dictator Gen. Francisco Franco. Adolf Hitler and Benito Mussolini backed the rebels, while the Soviet Union under Joseph Stalin and 45,000 volunteers from 53 countries under the banner of the International Brigade joined the Republican cause. Tens of thousands of civilians died, hundreds of thousands of soldiers were killed, and 350,000 people fled the country. Stalin bolstered the republic with arms and advisers and Hitler tested his weaponry.

In January 1933, Adolf Hitler became chancellor of the German Reich with the promise of righting the spiteful and selfish wrongs of the Versailles Treaty. At first he used ruses to avoid the clause that prohibited the manufacture of modern military equipment, such as tanks, planes, and submarines. Marshal Hermann Göring established a League of Air Sport, which actually trained future Luftwaffe pilots. Companies prepared prototypes of fighter planes and tanks for mass production.

In 1935, Hitler restored compulsory military service; France and Great Britain did nothing except express indignation. Meanwhile, Germany's arms industry flourished with steelworks, metallurgical and chemical factories, and the production of airplanes, tanks, and armored vehicles. Strategic roads and airfields were constructed and unemployment dropped. In March 1936, Hitler sent troops into the demilitarized zone of the Rhineland. Inaction by Britain and France emboldened Hitler, who supported Benito Mussolini's invasion and conquest of Ethiopia (October 1935–May 1936), and in March 1938, the Nazi dictator annexed Austria. In Czechoslovakia, which was carved out of the Austria-Hungary Empire in 1919, the Sudeten region, with its industries and large mineral resources and inhabited largely by Germans, was Hitler's next demand. In September 1938 at Nuremberg, annexation on threat of invasion was demanded. On 28 September 1938, in a conference with Hitler and French prime minister Edouard Daladier at Munich, British prime minister Neville Chamberlain refused to commit British troops "for this small nation," and promised "peace in our time." In March 1939, Nazis entered Prague, and Czechoslovakia was erased from the map.

Poland was next. Hitler demanded Danzig and free passage of the corridor that linked the port of Danzig with the rest of Poland. On 24 August 1939, Germany signed a secret nonaggression pact with Stalin's Russia and on 1 September, 2,000 Luftwaffe planes bombed Polish cities while troops and hundreds of tanks overwhelmed the country in a blitzkrieg ("lightning war"). France and Britain declared war but Poland fell in early October as Soviet forces occupied its eastern half.

World War II

WEHRMACHT OFFENSIVE IN WESTERN EUROPE

France had built the Maginot Line in 1932, a gigantic maze of underground works and barracks, all linked by tunnels and supplied with electric power, food, and ammunition. This great fortification was intended, in future war, to spare France the high casualties of World War I. Their guns, however, were short ranged, and only limited air defense was provided. Most important was the fact that it stopped at the Belgian border from which the Germans would invade France. Conversely, Germans had the Stuka dive-bomber that could make deadly attack dives, with the pilot-operated siren heightening the fear below.

In May 1940, using blitzkrieg tactics, German forces invaded the Netherlands, Belgium, and Luxembourg, smashing through defenses at Sedan in three days. British and French troops retreated to the Channel port of Dunkirk, and every available small boat from England sped to the rescue of 250,000 troops. The massive rescue saved 200,000, but the 50,000 left behind were either killed or became prisoners of war. The Germans crossed the Somme and Seine rivers, and on 10 June, Italy declared war on France. Italian advances were successfully repelled.

Meanwhile, the French army fell apart; hundreds of thousands of civilians filled roads with cars, carts, bicycles, and walking casualties, even as the government left Paris for Bordeaux. Paris was declared an open city and Marshal Henri Philippe Pétain told his people by radio to stop fighting. Although Pétain signed an armistice with Germany, Gen. Charles de Gaulle left for London on 17 June to organize a resistance movement.

BRITAIN ALONE

In July 1940, as the Nazi flag flew in France, Belgium, Denmark, and Norway, Prime Minister Winston Churchill in London gave his famous "Blood, toil, tears, and sweat" speech. Britain's ports were fortified and miles of trenches and shelters built to guard against invasion. But first, Hitler had to control the skies.

Battle of Britain. For 57 consecutive nights, 200 Luftwaffe bombers dropped explosives and incendiary and time bombs, leaving London in flames and many towns in the south almost completely destroyed. Still, the Germans failed to wreck British fighter bases, and the Royal Air Force and antiaircraft guns inflicted heavy damage on the German air force. (By 31 October 1940, the Luftwaffe had lost nearly 1,750 of the 2,200 planes initially employed.) Hitler saw that invading Britain was out of the question and canceled invasion plans on 12 October. Nevertheless, Air Marshal Göring persisted, sending 500 bombers carrying 600 tons of bombs to destroy the city of Coventry on 14 November.

The courageous Allied pilots were British, Norwegian, Dutch, Belgian, Polish, and French. Radar (radio detection and ranging) enabled the defenders to know when and where the Germans would strike. Britain girded for a long fight with the manpower and resources of its dominions (Australia, New Zealand, South Africa, and Canada), its colonies (in India, Kenya, and Nigeria), and its protectorates (such as Egypt) activated. Raw materials and arms were shipped from the United States.

Vichy France. Germany annexed Alsace and part of Lorraine and occupied the northeastern two-thirds of France. Southern France was declared a "free zone," headed by Marshal Pétain. He and Pierre Laval passed the Law on Jews and closely collaborated with Hitler. In November 1942, following Anglo-American landings in French-controlled North Africa, the Germans crossed into the "free zone," thus controlling the entire country.

BARBAROSSA

The Barbarossa plan (named for the 12th-century German emperor) ignored the nonaggression pact of 1939 in which Hitler and Stalin divided up Europe. Hitler had no fear of the Red Army after the fiasco in Finland, when the Soviets' mass attack on so small a nation during the Winter War (30 November 1939–13 March 1940) revealed poor leadership, coordination, and judgment. The 105-day war offered the go-ahead to invade Russia and reach Moscow, the Volga River, and the Caucasus Mountains before winter. Beginning on 22 June 1941, 3 million men, 3,000 tanks, and 3,000 planes crushed the surprised Soviet first line of defense. By 10 July, the Germans had advanced 400–800 kilometers (250–500 mi.) into Soviet territory. The Soviets lost hundreds of tanks; tens of thousands of men died and 300,000 were taken prisoner.

Stalin's defense during retreat was to destroy transportation, cattle, cereals, and oil and encourage guerrilla (partisan) attacks on the invaders. During these battles, the effectiveness of the Russian T-34 medium tank was an unwelcome surprise to the Germans. Hitler ordered some troops south to conquer Caucasia's oil fields and coal mines in the Donetz Basin. Others headed for Leningrad. On 30 August 1941, the Germans isolated Leningrad for a 900-day siege. The Soviets dug 480 kilometers (300 mi.) of trenches, put up 32 kilometers (20 mi.) of barricades, and built 15,000 blockhouses. Conditions during the siege were appalling, starvation was rampant, and many died of the cold. People ate crows, cats, and dogs and burned books and furniture for heat. Even so, half a million men, women, and children died before the siege was lifted in January 1944.

In October 1941, German forces totaling 1.5 million men, 1,800 tanks, and

1,500 planes pushed toward Moscow—320 kilometers (200 mi.) distant. The goal was to reach there before winter, but the "fifth element," weather, sided with the Soviets. Autumn rains and snowstorms stalled or halted the German advance, first with seas of mud, then with numbing cold. Reinforcements from the Far East, along with trenches, shelters, and antitank ditches hastily built by Muscovites, plus Marshal Georgi K. Zhukov's orders that "anybody leaving his post will be shot," helped even the odds. On 2 December, the Germans were within 24 kilometers (15 mi.) of Moscow, but they were exhausted, cold, and without sufficient food and fuel. On 6 December, the well-equipped and well-led Red Army launched a counteroffensive and pushed the Germans back. In retreat, they abandoned trucks, tanks, and other vehicles. The German losses in killed, wounded, or taken prisoner totaled 800,000.

PEARL HARBOR

At 7:50 A.M., Sunday, 7 December 1941, Japanese torpedo bomber and dive-bomber planes, backed by fighters, attacked Pearl Harbor, Hawaii, where most of the U.S. Pacific fleet was concentrated. The first bombs caught the Americans by surprise, and they were unable to respond. A second wave of 170 planes finished the job, and by 9:45 A.M. the attack was over. The damage: 2 battleships were sunk outright, 6 were damaged; 159 planes were destroyed; 2,334 Americans were killed and 1,341 wounded. The three U.S. aircraft carriers in the Pacific were at sea at the time and so were unhurt. The submarine base and shipyard, along with the vital underground oil storage tanks, also survived unscathed.

President Roosevelt addressed the nation by radio and referred to the attack as "a day which will live in infamy." Congress immediately voted funds, and four days later, Germany and Italy declared war on the United States. War was now on a truly global scale.

The Japanese captured the American possession of the Philippines in May after an unexpectedly difficult six-month campaign, and Gen. Douglas MacArthur, who had left for Australia in a submarine in March, vowed, "I shall return." In rapid succession, the Japanese captured the British colonies of Hong Kong in December 1941 and overwhelmed Dutch Indonesia in March 1942, Malaya and Singapore in April 1942, and Burma in May 1942.

The Americans soon struck back. On 18 April 1942, Gen. Jimmy Doolittle's "Tokyo Raiders" took off from the flight deck of the carrier *Hornet* and bombed Tokyo. A Japanese effort to seize strategic Port Moresby in southeastern New Guinea was foiled in the Battle of the Coral Sea (7–8 May 1942). The U.S. carrier *Lexington* was sunk, but the Japanese lost the light carrier *Shoho*. The fleet carrier *Shokoku* was damaged and the carrier *Zuikaku* lost so many aircraft that it, too, was out of action.

The decisive Japanese naval defeat came at Midway. On 5 May 1942, 6,000 soldiers and sailors, 40 large warships, 8 aircraft carriers with 500 planes, and 2 additional ships—all commanded by Adm. Isoroku Yamamoto—headed for Midway atoll, 1,440 kilometers (900 mi.) from Japan. The capture of Midway would give the Japanese protection against any surprise attack from the east while simultaneously threatening the U.S. west coast. American intelligence sources had broken the communications code used by the Japanese navy. This enabled Adm. Chester Nimitz to read Japan's plans.

On 3 June, Yamamoto's forces launched an air attack preparatory to troop landings. There was extensive damage, but the following day, waves of American dive bombers along with torpedo planes appeared, swooping down on the Japanese air and sea fleet. They destroyed rows of enemy planes readying for a strike on the flight decks, and set three of the four carriers aflame. Later, the fourth carrier was sunk by another U.S. air attack. Without air protection, Yamamoto ordered a retreat. His navy had lost a dozen ships, including a heavy cruiser and four of Japan's six fleet carriers; 250 planes were shot down. More than 3,500 men were killed, including 100 of Yamamoto's best airmen. The Americans lost one carrier, the U.S.S. *Yorktown*, which had been damaged at the Coral Sea battle. The Battle of Midway was mourned as a major defeat in Japan and showed that the aircraft carrier was the key to success in the Pacific.

BATTLE OF THE ATLANTIC (3 SEPTEMBER 1939–8 MAY 1945)

On 3 September, the day war was declared, German submarines sank the British liner *Athenian*. After the fall of France, the German U-boat blockade of Britain, under the command of Adm. Karl Dönitz and operating out of Brest, Lorient, Saint-Nazaire, and La Pallice, sank more ships than were built during that time. The British protected their shipping with convoys shepherded by escorts equipped with sonar; losses remained high in the Atlantic and elsewhere as 400 German submarines operated freely from Greenland to the Gulf of Mexico and roamed the east coastal waters of the United States and from the coast of Africa to South America. In five months, the United States lost 505 ships, of which 112 were oil tankers. The Germans increased their U-boat production from 60 in 1939 to 250 in 1942. They often operated at night in groups known as "wolf packs." They surfaced, fired torpedoes on convoys, then submerged. They hid in Norway's fjords to attack convoys heading for the USSR; in the Mediterranean, they attacked convoys sailing to the Middle East and Egypt. Allied convoys began sailing with warships and small aircraft carriers, employing improved detection procedures and depth charges, which finally reversed Allied losses. During 1943–44, U-boats suffered heavy losses; by the war's end, the Allies had sunk hundreds of German U-boats and 85 Italian submarines.

THE MEDITERRANEAN

Mussolini invaded Albania in 1939 and in September 1940 launched an attack on British-held Egypt from Italian-held Libya. Two months later, Italy attacked Greece. The Italians were poorly equipped and trained and their arms were often mediocre. The Greeks inflicted a humiliating rout on Italian forces there (December 1940) and the British mauled them in Libya, but Gen. (later field marshal) Erwin Rommel's Afrika Korps saved the Italians from total disaster. Provoked by an anti-Axis coup in Yugoslavia, the Germans invaded Greece and Yugoslavia in April 1942. Both countries surrendered within three weeks and

British Commonwealth forces sent to aid Greece were evacuated, some to Crete.

On 20 May, German paratroopers carried out the first large-scale airborne operation of the war as more than 20,000 paratroopers landed on Crete. By month's end the British had withdrawn and the island was in German hands.

In Libya, Rommel—nicknamed the Desert Fox—tangled with British, Canadian, New Zealand, Australian, Indian, and Free French forces in the desert. In the summer of 1942, Rommel overcame the British and occupied Tobruk, crossing the Egyptian border and opening the road to Alexandria and Cairo. At El Alamein, however, the British put up a solid defense and strengthened their position against the Afrika Korps (July–September). Rommel's forces were exhausted and their equipment worn out; in November, the British took the initiative. After a grueling battle (23 October–4 November 1942), Rommel retreated to Tunisia. North Africa was lost. By then, British and American troops had landed in Morocco and Algeria in Operation Torch (8–11 November 1942).

THE HOLOCAUST

In 1942, the Germans rounded up Jews by the thousands and deported them or packed them into ghettos. The Germans pillaged occupied countries for food and money and rationed everything. Food was a major problem as was manpower for factories. "Volunteers" from France, Belgium, and Holland were sent to Germany to work. In France, work service was mandatory. Special units (SS Einsatzkommando) were sent to Russia in 1941 to kill Jews. The "final solution," begun on 20 January 1942, involved shipping Jews to extermination camps where old people and children went directly to the gas chambers and able-bodied men were put on work details and given starvation rations until they died. Six million Jews perished in the genocide.

Although the Jews suffered the most, Gypsies and other ethnic minorities, homosexuals, and political and religious dissidents perished by the hundreds of thousands in death camps like Sobibor, Auschwitz, Treblinka, Bergen-Belsen, and Buchenwald.

STALINGRAD

The conquest of the USSR was critical, although the Wehrmacht was halted outside Moscow and Leningrad. Elsewhere, the industrial center and major port of Stalingrad spread over 40 kilometers (25 mi.) along the right bank of the Volga River. By the end of August, the German army of Gen. Friedrich Paulus was on the verge of success. The northern part of the city of 800,000 was aflame from bombings, and buildings had been reduced to rubble. Defenders formed groups and fought the enemy in bitter, costly street battles, often hand-to-hand, but by November, Paulus's forces controlled the city's center. Hitler ordered the offensive to continue even though Paulus reported his forces were weakened by the cold and snow.

Marshal Zhukov planned a large offensive, bringing together a million men, 6,000 tanks, and 3,000 planes. He organized them in pincers, and struck on 14

November 1942. Within five days he had surrounded 300,000 Germans; neither the Luftwaffe nor German armies from elsewhere could help Paulus's beleaguered Sixth Army. On 24 January 1943, Paulus informed Hitler of the desperate situation; 150,000 had already died. Hitler refused to allow surrender. On 31 January, Paulus and his staff were captured, German resistance stopped, and 99,000 were taken prisoner. Thousands of dead Germans were piled between railroad tracks and set afire. In Germany, there were two days of mourning.

During the Battle of Kursk (5–17 July) one of the largest tank battles in history was fought. The Wehrmacht deployed 3,200 tanks and 5,000 guns on a 256-kilometer (160-mi.) front. The Red Army's superior firepower resulted in a massacre, and after two days of fighting, hundreds of armored vehicles were destroyed and tens of thousands of men killed or wounded. The Germans were driven back hundreds of kilometers by partisans and guerrillas, obliterating any future offensives in Russia.

LOGISTICS

World War II was fought as much in factories as on the battlefield. Soldiers used highly sophisticated, costly equipment that was replaced when the old wore out or became outdated. Britain began the war with 185,000 soldiers and by mid-1940 had a million and a half. Those between the ages of 18 and 50 were mobilized and trained with broomsticks instead of guns. Women were recruited for passive defense or auxiliary forces.

In Germany, the Wehrmacht increased from 5.6 million in 1940 to 9.5 million in 1943. Albert Speer, Germany's minister of equipment and ammunition, was also responsible for armament and war production, increasing fighter plane production from 771 at the war's beginning to 12,740 during the last six months of conflict. In 1939–44, Britain had 70,000 planes and tripled its tonnage of ships. In the USSR, 1,300 factories were dismantled and transferred to the Ural region. Germans considered the Soviet T-34 tank the best of World War II. Until 1942, the Allies were the only ones who had radar, and by the end of 1944, the Luftwaffe became the first to use jet fighter planes. The Messerschmitt Me 262 was an effective fighter aircraft and the V-1 and V-2 rockets caused great damage in Britain during the last eleven months of war.

America's goal on 6 January 1942 was to produce 60,000 planes and 45,000 tanks that year, and 125,000 planes and 75,000 tanks the following year. Within four years, the United States built 65,000 landing craft, 320,000 pieces of artillery, 15 million small arms, and more than a million trucks, and produced 4 million tons of ammunition. The United States shipped aid to Stalin via Iran, building two ports linked to Teheran by a railway 1,100 kilometers (700 mi.) long. The United States supplied 35 percent of the arms used to fight Germany and 85 percent of the arms used against Japan.

At the war's beginning, there were 7 to 8 million Americans unemployed. All this changed as the young, elderly, and women moved from country to cities where defense industries provided jobs. Blacks left the south for California and the northern cities. Sweden designed a gun that required 450 hours of work in

Sweden but only 10 hours on American assembly lines. Shipbuilders put Liberty ships to sea in as little as twelve days and, at full capacity, Boeing built six B-29 bombers every day.

THE PACIFIC

The war in the Pacific was one against distances. The Americans crossed the longest distances ever imposed on vessels and merchant ships in a major war. For the Japanese forces, sea routes had to be protected from U.S. submarines, planes, and ships so that raw materials (metals, rubber, and copper) and fuel could reach factories in Japan. In the Pacific, economic strength counted as much or more than individual bravery, and Japan had only one-tenth of U.S. industrial and technical strength and power. Americans had sophisticated radar and antiaircraft guns on vessels and by mid-1942 were producing more and better aircraft than the Japanese. In the Solomon Islands during 1942–44, dependable supplies of modern planes and ships ensured U.S. victory.

Admiral Yamamoto was shot down during a flight over the Pacific on 7 August 1943, and a year later, the Americans launched an assault on the Mariana Islands. Japanese forces in their island garrisons often fought to the death, preferring suicide to surrender. During the reconquest of the Philippines from October 1944 to August 1945, the Japanese used bomb-loaded suicide planes—"kamikazes"—for the first time, and they were at first horribly effective. In the February 1945 Iwo Jima campaign, soldiers carrying explosives around their belts threw themselves against U.S. command posts or under planes on the ground. Improved tactics and warning gradually reduced the effect of aerial kamikazes, but the fanaticism disturbed U.S. strategists. The battle of Okinawa in the spring of 1945 was fanatical in the extreme. Only a few Japanese surrendered, preferring suicide to the dishonor of defeat. After three months of continual fighting, 100,000 Japanese were dead, including 7,000 kamikazes. U.S. losses were 12,000. The final step was to invade Japan itself, with 60 million people defending the homeland.

NORMANDY

On 5 June 1944, Allied convoys sailed across the English Channel toward the French coast. D-Day, code-named Operation Overlord, was planned by Gen. Dwight D. Eisenhower, with British Field Marshal Bernard L. Montgomery coordinating the movement of all Allied forces. Three million Allied soldiers and thousands of vessels were involved. British admiral Louis Mountbatten built artificial ports that were towed across the channel and assembled off the landing beaches, enabling 40,000 tons of equipment and 6,500 vehicles to be unloaded each week. Gas came by pipeline across the channel.

From midnight to dawn of that day, 10,500 British and American planes bombed the Normandy coast, and frogmen cut the barbed wire. At 2:00 A.M., 27,000 parachutists landed along the coast. On the so-called Longest Day, ten divisions with arms and supplies landed in Normandy. The British captured Bayeux on 8 June and linked with the Americans. The liberation of France had begun.

The Germans suffered a humiliating defeat. In the ensuing campaign, more than 500,000 of them were killed, wounded, or taken prisoner. Battlefields were littered with equipment and the rotting corpses of men and horses. On 15 August 1944, the Allies landed in the south of France and, with the help of Free French Forces, joined up in Burgundy a month later with the Normandy forces.

On 19 August, Paris revolted and was liberated with the help of the 2d Armored Division of Free French Forces under General Leclerc and American forces. An attempt by German officers to assassinate Hitler on 20 July failed, and 5,000 conspirators were executed. A counteroffensive in the Ardennes, beginning on 16 December 1944, resulted in the bitter and costly month-long Battle of the Bulge—a German defeat.

YALTA

Churchill, Roosevelt, and Stalin met at Yalta 2–10 February 1945 to plan the future. The USSR agreed to enter a war against Japan and the future occupation of Germany was settled, along with defining the role of the United Nations. As Germans retreated everywhere, Allied bombings had left their cities in ruins and 600,000 civilians dead. At the same time, 10 million refugees fled from the Soviets. Desperate for food, civilians found road and rail traffic at a standstill; trains had been bombed and no canals or rivers could be used.

THE END

Although V-2 rockets, Messerschmitt 262 jets, and sophisticated submarine equipment, including the snorkel, gave hope to the Germans, atomic scientists building nuclear weapons were the worst threat. Technology could not be perfected in time and countries fell one by one: Romania on 23 August 1944, Bulgaria on 28 October; Poland was liberated in January 1945 and Yugloslavia in April of that year.

On 7 March 1945, U.S. forces crossed the Rhine River, and in the east, the Russians approached the outskirts of Berlin. On 25 April, Russian and U.S. troops met on the banks of the Elbe. By the end of April, the Soviets had a million men and 15,000 guns encircling Berlin. Hitler entered his bunker with its fifteen-foot-thick walls and, on 30 April, committed suicide. On 8 May, in the French city of Rheims, Germany signed the unconditional surrender; on the following day, the ceremony was repeated in Berlin.

HIROSHIMA

After the fall of Okinawa, the U.S. blockaded Japan and during July 1945 bombed Tokyo every day. On 17–18 July, six waves of 1,500 bombers destroyed Osaka and Yokohama as the Japanese swore they would fight to the death to defend national soil. President Roosevelt died on 12 April 1945, and Harry S Truman became the U.S. president. Estimates were that it would cost a million U.S. casualties to conquer Japan proper, although these figures may have been too high. A secret weapon was needed to force Japan's surrender.

On 6 August 1945 at 8:15:17 A.M., the B-29 bomber *Enola Gay* opened its bomb-bay doors. Suspended from a parachute, a device descended on Hiroshima. Fifty-one seconds later, at almost 600 meters (2,000 ft.), it exploded. A gigantic mushroom cloud rose more than 14,900 meters (50,000 ft.) into the sky. Tens of thousands of people were buried in the rubble; many vanished and more were burned or mutilated. Fires were everywhere and the destruction was great. The atomic bomb killed 130,000, with survivors suffering irreversible changes in their bodies.

The USSR attacked Manchuria, and the United States dropped a second atomic bomb on Nagasaki, killing 35,000 and wounding 60,000. In a radio broadcast on 16 August, Emperor Hirohito announced to an astonished nation that Japan had surrendered. The six-year war was over.

Korea

Japan's defeat in World War II led to the partition of Korea along the 38th parallel. The cold war between the United States and the Soviet Union was the implied cause of the conflict in Korea in 1950–53.

It began on 25 June 1950 when the armies of North Korea, a protégé of the Soviet Union and Red China, invaded South Korea across the 38th parallel of latitude. The United Nations Security Council condemned the aggression, and on 27 June, President Truman ordered U.S. land, air, and sea forces to the defense of South Korea.

Eventually, fifteen UN members joined the U.S. "police action": Australia, Belgium, Canada, Colombia, Ethiopia, France, Great Britain, Greece, Holland, Luxembourg, New Zealand, the Philippines, South Africa, Thailand, and Turkey, with medical aid coming from Denmark, India, Italy, Norway, and Sweden.

At first, the Communists pushed back the UN forces nearly into the sea at Pusan. The United States was surprised and ill-prepared, while the People's Korean Army (PKA) had been well supplied by the Soviets with modern military equipment, including 150 T-34 tanks, 100 Yak fighters, and other heavy military equipment and artillery. There had been recruitment and training by Soviet advisers, and the PKA's 135,000 men were divided into seven infantry divisions with 122mm howitzers and self-propelled 76mm guns.

The Republic of Korea (ROK) forces were only an upgraded paramilitary constabulary of 95,000 men, with mortars and light artillery but no tanks. On 10 July, Gen. Douglas MacArthur was appointed commander in chief of the United Nations command and on 13 July Lt. Gen. Walton H. Walker (one of Patton's corps commanders in Europe during World War II) established his Eighth U.S. Army in Korea (EUSAK). On 23 December, General Walker was killed in a jeep accident and replaced by Lt. Gen. Matthew B. Ridgway. In the face of near defeat, Walker had ordered a defensive perimeter to protect the vital port of Pusan. There were 47,000 U.S. combat troops and 45,000 ROK troops holding the lines until reinforcements could be brought in. Names like "The Bowling Alley" appeared in news headlines to describe battles for the Naktong Bulge and the defense of Taegu. The ultimate success of the Pusan perimeter was due to the inability of the PKA to resupply its rapidly advancing troops. Conversely, U.S. forces were comparatively well supplied with men and materiel.

The Inchon landing had been carefully planned by MacArthur months in advance. A seaborne attack from the enemy's rear gained control of enemy communications in Seoul. Strategically, all north-south roads and rail links passed through the city, and to capture it proved politically significant to ROK forces. On 15 September 1950, the following forces participated in the massive Inchon operation: the 1st U.S. Marine Division from the U.S. mainland, the 7th U.S. Infantry Division stationed in Japan, 30 landing craft (LSTs) from Japan, the 5th Regiment of the 1st Marine Division from the Pusan perimeter, South Korean troops, the 7th Regiment U.S. Marines of the Sixth Fleet from the Mediterranean, and 230 ships from navies of the United States, Great Britain, Australia, Canada, New Zealand, South Korea, and France. On 25 September, aerial reconnaissance reported that PKA troopers were leaving Seoul, but some units remained behind to fight a desperate rearguard action. Three days later, UN forces had complete control of the city. Throughout the entire operation, fighting was furious and bloody, but the victory was decisive and took just thirteen days.

Of the 165,000 North Koreans who invaded the South, not more than 25,000 to 30,000 made it back to the North. Far East Air Forces (FEAF) under the command of Lt. Gen. George E. Stratemeyer provided essential air cover and close support.

Following the success of the Inchon operation, MacArthur ordered an invasion of North Korea and by late November UN troops occupied most of the country. But there were ominous signs of large-scale intervention by Chinese communist forces. Despite the lateness of the season and the Chinese communist threat, MacArthur launched an operation on 24 November to clear all of North Korea. Less than a day later, a massive Chinese offensive, employing 180,000 troops in eighteen divisions, outmaneuvered and nearly overran the UN troops. The 1st Marine Division was almost surrounded in the mountains around the Chosin Reservoir and had to fight its way out in the bitter cold through eight Chinese divisions over nearly impassable mountain terrain to reach the port of Hungnam for evacuation (27 November–9 December). The division's commander, Gen. Oliver Smith, was quoted as saying, "Retreat, hell! We're just attacking in a different direction!" General Ridgway eventually established a solid front line, running roughly along the 38th parallel.

UN forces had been driven from North Korea; over the next seven months, the front seesawed back and forth with vicious attacks and counterattacks (January–July 1951). The intent was to influence the intermittent peace talks at Panmunjom (November 1951–July 1953). On 27 July 1953, after a costly repulse of yet another Chinese communist offensive (10–30 June 1953), an armistice was signed. Neither the North nor South Korean regimes is reconciled to the permanent division of the nation, and the demilitarized zone (DMZ) remains heavily armed and patrolled. North and South Korea were admitted to the United Nations in 1991, along with the three Baltic nations and two South Pacific nations.

Vietnam (1961–75)

In July 1950, one month after the outbreak of the Korean War, the United States sent a Military Assistance and Advisory Group (MAAG), along with three DC-3 Dakotas, to bolster the French-supported puppet government of Emperor Bao Dai in Saigon. It was the beginning of the longest war in American history, but its roots went back to World War II, when President Roosevelt declared that Vietnam should not be returned to France as a colony. During the cold war, President Truman favored neutrality and withdrew American advisers of the OSS (later the CIA), who had been working with the guerrilla forces of Ho Chi Minh fighting the Japanese.

The French Indochina War of 1946–54 ended with the fall of the French fortress of Dien Bien Phu (7 May 1954). Indochina was divided into four parts: Laos, Cambodia, and two Vietnams divided along the 17th parallel. Ho Chi Minh's forces were in the north, and the Saigon government controlled the south. In 1956, a civil war broke out between the Communists in the north (Vietminh) and the "democratic" U.S.-backed nationalist forces in the south. Fighting was mainly guerrilla, the Viet Cong fighting the Army of the Republic of Vietnam (ARVN). In 1961, U.S. forces were authorized to fight alongside ARVN units, but they had virtually no authority over their ARVN counterparts, made no battlefield decisions, had no disciplinary role, and were unable to remove incompetent commanders. Americans advised ARVN forces on everything from battlefield tactics and logistics to communications and intelligence. They also worked with the CIA, AID, and USIA and helped with health matters, medicine, finance, and agriculture. The Green Berets (Special Forces) trained the South Vietnamese in commando tactics and worked with the ethnically different Montagnards, who disavowed loyalty to South Vietnam but nevertheless remained faithful to the Americans.

On 2 August 1964, North Vietnamese patrol boats reportedly attacked two U.S. destroyers in the Gulf of Tonkin. In hindsight, they probably did not actually attack the ships in international waters. At any rate, President Lyndon Johnson received congressional authority to repel armed attacks, and U.S. bombing raids began in earnest. American ground forces were sent to fight as allies alongside ARVN forces. North Vietnamese army units marched continually down the "spiderweb upon spiderweb," as the Ho Chi Minh Trail in Cambodia was called. Teaming up with the Viet Cong, their goal was to liquidate the enemy. By late 1967, there were half a million U.S. troops in Vietnam, and together with ARVN forces, they began "search and destroy" missions employing "free fire zones" coupled with a pacification policy to win the "hearts and minds" of the Vietnamese people. Meanwhile, there was continual bombing of Viet Cong targets and supply dumps in Cambodia.

In January 1968, the North Vietnamese Army (NVA) and the Communist-formed National Liberation Front (NLF) based on the Viet Cong launched the Tet Offensive against 36 cities. Intelligence had underestimated the strength of the Tet offensive—although the NLF and NVA forces were defeated and suffered heavy casualties, the U.S. and ARVN forces were also badly mauled. In the United States, antiwar demonstrations captured the headlines and by 1968–69 a policy of Vietnamization, in which the Vietnamese would do more of the fighting, gradually replaced the active participation of U.S. troops. Most of the 500,000 Americans were to be returned home, leaving behind the air force to continue air support.

On 30 March 1972, the NLF and NVA launched another major offensive, crossing the demilitarized zone (DMZ) at the 17th parallel and capturing a South Vietnamese province. After heavy combat, ARVN forces halted the offensive with the help of U.S. air support (May). At that point, the United States mined the Haiphong harbor and other North Vietnamese ports. Peace talks, which had been going on from time to time, broke down, and in December 1972, President Richard Nixon ordered eleven days of intensive bombing of North Vietnamese cities.

Eventually, peace talks were resumed and a cease-fire agreement was reached on 27 January 1973. Fighting continued, however, with each side accusing the other of violations. In 1974, the ARVN began withdrawing troops from distant outposts, and the NLF quickly took them over. In January 1975 the expected offensive began. The NLF gained the central highlands; when the South Vietnamese government evacuated the northern cities of Quang Tri and Hue, it was clear the struggle was nearing the end. Southern coastal towns and villages were abandoned; soldiers and civilians fled, and the remaining U.S. forces escaped by sea and air in ignominious defeat. On 30 April 1975, U.S. Marines serving as a rear guard were flown out of Saigon from the rooftop of the American embassy. Two hours later, Gen. Duong Van Minh, who had replaced President Thieu, announced Saigon's unconditional surrender in a radio and television broadcast. General Minh, who had led the coup that deposed Ngo Dinh Diem twelve years earlier (1–2 November 1963), appealed to all Saigon troops to lay down their arms and avoid further bloodshed. Fearing reprisals, ARVN troops hastily discarded uniforms and changed into civilian clothes.

Two hours later, North Vietnamese and Viet Cong troops rolled into the city on tanks, armored vehicles, and camouflaged Chinese-built trucks. The red, blue, and yellow-starred flag of the NLF was raised over the presidential palace; North and South Vietnam were formally reunited as the Socialist Republic of Vietnam on 2 July 1976.

Israel

The state of Israel was created in the aftermath of World War II to provide a homeland for survivors of the Holocaust. In 1947, the UN voted to replace the British mandate with a sovereign Jewish state in a part of Palestine. Arabs were opposed to this, and in May 1948 invaded Israel. In the end, after seven months of intermittent but bitter fighting, Israel occupied disputed areas in Palestine, and 400,000 Palestinian Arabs settled in refugee camps in neighboring Arab countries. In 1956, the nationalization of the Suez Canal by Egypt's president Gamal Abdel Nasser precipitated another crisis, leading to Israel's conquest of Sinai and the Gaza (29 October–6 November). In the end, Israel turned over the Gaza Strip, all of Sinai, and Sharm-el-Sheik to the United Nations forces.

The Six-Day War (5–10 June 1967), triggered by Nasser's militant nationalism, left Israel in possession of Sinai, the West Bank, Gaza, and the Golan Heights, but the basic causes of conflict were still unresolved. Egypt and Syria attacked Israel (6 October 1973), but at war's end (25 October), Israelis had gained the upper hand. Although Israel and Egypt signed a peace treaty after U.S.-moderated negotiations (26 March 1978), peace remained elusive. An Israeli invasion of southern Lebanon (June-August 1982) displaced the Palestine Liberation Organization (PLO) presence temporarily, but military action again failed to produce a lasting peaceful settlement.

Unrest continues in the Mideast as Israel swells the population of the West Bank and Gaza Strip with Jewish immigrants from the former USSR and elsewhere. Despite recent autonomy agreements, the Palestinians continue to be at odds with Israeli policies.

Gulf War, 1991

When his troops invaded Kuwait on 1 August 1991, Iraqi leader Saddam Hussein apparently expected neighboring Arab states to acquiesce to his aggression. Instead, the local wrath and concern that he provoked rapidly grew into worldwide condemnation. Only the PLO and a handful of countries—Jordan, Libya, Mauritania, the Sudan, and Yemen—gave Iraq any significant political support during the crisis. The opposing international coalition of 38 nations gathered under the UN aegis provided a textbook demonstration of the application of collective security.

After several months of threats and standoffs during Operation Desert Shield, the war began in earnest after Iraq ignored UN demands that it withdraw unconditionally by 15 January 1991. On 17 January the first phase of the air war began when U.S.-led air units launched a devastating series of attacks on targets in Iraq. The coalition quickly achieved air superiority and then proceeded to focus on targets of military significance within Iraq. These included command, control, and communications facilities; radar and surface-to-air missile sites; power-generating plants; transportation facilities (e.g., airfields, runways, bridges, and major roadways); and nuclear, biological, and chemical weapons development and production facilities. Toward the end of the air war (after about four weeks), coalition airpower began to concentrate on Iraqi forces in the field in preparation for the ground war. An intensive series of air strikes was launched, using precision-guided weapons against Iraqi armor and artillery, backed by B-52 and F-111 bombers and heavy attack fighters like the Tornado. Coalition airpower destroyed or incapacitated all of Iraq's nuclear reactor facilities, eleven chemical and biological weapons storage facilities and three production facilities, 50 percent of Iraq's major command centers, 70 percent of its military communications, 48 Iraqi naval vessels, and 75 percent of Iraq's electric power-generating capability. Iraq's only means of retaliation was to launch its long-range modified Scud missiles against Israel and Saudi Arabia and to set fire to about 600 Kuwaiti oil wells. The Scud attacks were largely ineffective, while the oil fires did nothing to affect allied air operations or slow the pace of the war.

With Iraq distracted by air bombardment (from both land and sea forces) and by the threat of an attack by amphibious forces stationed in the Gulf, coalition land forces moved secretly from the southeast Kuwait-Saudi border 320–480 kilometers (200–300 mi.) westward to the Iraq-Saudi border. The element of surprise played a key role when the ground war began on 24 February 1991. Within 48 hours, coalition troops from the south swept through Kuwait and established positions south and west of Kuwait City, while those forces that had secretly moved far to the west launched a deep strike northward into Iraq.

On 26 February, in the longest sustained armored advance in history, U.S. forces destroyed key Republican Guard divisions holding the area north of the Kuwaiti border, while other coalition forces began fighting for control of Kuwait City. A devastating series of engagements over the next two days virtually destroyed Iraq's remaining forces. British and U.S. Army forces liberated northern Kuwait, Saudi and other Arab forces liberated Kuwait City, and U.S. Marine forces secured the southern and western outskirts of Kuwait City.

The war was quick and decisive, due to the weakened and demoralized state of the Iraqi army and the superior technology and tactics wielded by the coalition's motivated, professional forces.

Summary

The 1991 Gulf War marked a major change in modern history and war. By the late twentieth century, many nations, both industrialized and developing, had acquired the modern equipment of war, including weapons of mass destruction. At the same time, with the dissolution of the Soviet Union, the long confrontation between the superpowers began to wind down. As of mid-1992, the threat of massive nuclear warfare has been significantly reduced, yet the threat of nuclear, chemical, and biological warfare at a lower level of intensity may be increasing dramatically. New states have been created and new power blocks and political/military alliances will continue to form; universal peace still lies in the future.

Relatively new features in conflict, primarily since World War II, are the increased use of peacekeeping forces to separate combatants and enforce truces and the use of multinational forces under UN or other aegis to restrain aggression (e.g., the Korean War, the 1991 Gulf War). The era of East-West polarity is apparently over, an era in which virtually every conflict of any magnitude involved and mirrored, in some way, the interests of the superpowers and the cold war. Although there may be more local conflict and tensions in the future, global conflict seems to be less of a danger.

During the past 200 years, military affairs have changed from relatively primitive strategy and weaponry to sophisticated computer-assisted long-range planning, "invisible" bombers, the Strategic Defense Initiative, and nuclear weaponry. Communications and airlift capabilities have brought conflicts into instant focus, but peace settlements and long-term resolution of ethnic, religious, economic, and political conflicts remain elusive. Environmental and social issues, migrations, and immigration are probable trouble areas of the future.

ELOISE H. PAANANEN

DWAYNE ANDERSON

SEE ALSO: Arab-Israeli Wars; Boer Wars; Civil War, American; Civil War, Russian; Civil War, Spanish; French Revolutionary–Napoleonic Wars; Gulf War, 1991; Korean War; Russo-Japanese War; Vietnam and Indochina Wars; World War I; World War II.

Bibliography

Allinson, A. R. 1926. *The war diary of Frederick III 1870–1891.* Westport, Conn.: Greenwood.

Bailer, S., ed. 1969. *Stalin and his generals.* New York: Pegasus.

Calvocoressi, P. , and G. Wint. 1972. *Total war: The story of World War II.* New York: Pantheon.

Catton, P. 1962. *The Army of the Potomac.* 3 vols. New York: Fairfax.

Chandler, D. G. 1966. *The campaigns of Napoleon.* New York: Macmillan.

Dupuy, R. E., and W. H. Baumer. 1968. *Little wars of the U.S.* New York: Hawthorne.

Engle, E., and A. Lott. *America's maritime heritage.* Annapolis: U.S. Naval Institute Press.

Engle, E., and L. Paananen. 1973 and 1992. *The winter war.* New York: Scribner's, and Harrisburg, Pa.: Stackpole.

Esper, G., and Assoc. Press. 1983. *The eyewitness history of the Vietnam War.* New York: Associated Press.

Fest, D. C. 1974. *Hitler* (Eng. transl.). New York: Harcourt Brace Jovanovich.

Harbottle, T. 1971. *Dictionary of battles.* New York: Stein and Day.

Humble, R. 1974. *Napoleon's peninsular marshals; a reassessment.* New York: Taplinger.

Moore, R. 1965. *The Green Berets.* New York: Crown.

Nevins, A. 1950. *The emergence of Lincoln,* vols. 1 and 2. New York: Scribner's.

Noyes, A. H. 1934. *Europe—Its history and its world relationships.* Boston: Heath.

Pierre, M., and A. Wieviorka. 1987. *The Second World War* (Eng. trans.). Morristown, N.J.: Silver Burdett Press.

Rees, D., ed. 1984. *The Korean War: History and tactics.* New York: Crescent.

Smith, S. E., ed. 1966. *The United States Navy in World War II.* New York: Morrow.

Warner, O. 1973. *Great battle fleets.* London: Hamlyn.

Welsh, D. 1982. *The USA in World War 2: The Pacific theater.* New York: Galahad.

HO CHI MINH [1890–1969]

In many senses Ho Chi Minh is the "father of his country"; he seems to have meant even more to Vietnam than Mao Tse-tung did to China or Joseph Stalin did to the Soviet Union. Ho Chi Minh ("He who Enlightens"), also known as

Nguyen Ai Quoc ("Nguyen the Patriot") as well as by a host of other aliases, led Vietnam for some 30 years. He was president from 1945 to 1969 and chairman of his party's Central Committee. More than just a Vietnamese patriot, Ho was one of Asia's foremost anticolonialists and one of the twentieth century's most influential leaders of communist movements.

The Early Years—The Wanderer

Ho was born Nguyen That Thanh (or Nguyen Sinh Cung) on 14 (or 19) May 1890 in Huong Tru hamlet, Nghe An Province, Central Vietnam—the French Protectorate of Annam, later to be North Vietnam. He was, like his colleague Vo Nguyen Giap, the son of a poor mandarin scholar. (His father, Nguyen Sinh Sae, left the family to become an itinerant teacher.) After a dreadful childhood, Ho managed to attend grammar school in Hue from age 14 to 18; later, as Van Bu, he taught school in various villages and also worked in Saigon. In 1911 (or 1912), Ho (now called Bu) became a cook on a French freighter and started his 30-year odyssey. Before he returned to Vietnam, he had visited such U.S. ports as Boston and New York. After sailing around the world for three years, he lived in Brooklyn for a year. Moving from the United States to London, he worked from 1915 to 1917 as a gardener, sweeper, waiter, photo retoucher, and stoker.

In the midst of World War I, Ho moved to France, where he remained until 1923. Then known as Nguyen Ai Quoc (Nguyen the Patriot), he organized a group of Vietnamese living in Paris. At Versailles, in 1919, Ho presented an eight-point petition to representatives of the Great Powers (Fig. 1). His demands centered on equal rights for Vietnam from the colonial French. There was little response from the great powers, but Ho became a hero to the Vietnamese.

Using his Nguyen Ai Quoc pseudonym, he was a founding member of the French Communist party on 30 December 1920. At that time, he was both speaking and writing on his primary ideological notion that anticolonial nationalism and socioeconomic revolution are inseparable. In 1922 (or 1924), impressed by Soviet victories—and tracked by French security—he went to Moscow to study Marxist doctrine at the School of Oriental Workers. He also met with the leaders of the Soviet Union. In 1925, he was assigned to Canton, China, as a Comintern agent. While in southern China, he formed the Vietnamese Revolutionary Youth League to campaign for Vietnamese independence. This led to the forming of the Indochinese Communist party (Lao Dong) in Hong Kong in 1930, with an amalgam of Vietnamese, Lao, and Khmer communist groups. The group received instructions from Moscow based on the Communist Internationale (Comintern). This activity led to Ho's imprisonment by the British in 1930. After his release in 1933, he traveled widely in China, Thailand, and elsewhere in Asia. In 1936, the French released his comrades, who fled to China. Ho returned to Moscow in 1938, remaining as one of the notably few Comintern agents to survive the Stalinist purges.

Figure 1. Ho Chi Minh as a member of the French Socialist party at the Versailles Peace Conference, 1919. (SOURCE: U.S. Library of Congress)

The Middle Years—Back in Vietnam

In 1940, the Japanese invaded Indochina. Ho aligned himself with the Allied powers, believing that Japanese domination was no better than French imperialism. Using the name Ho Chi Minh, he returned to Vietnam in May 1941 and organized the Vietminh (Vietnamese Doc Lap, Long Minh, or Dong Minh Hui—League for Vietnamese Independence). Initially, this was to be a coalition of all anti-French Vietnamese groups. Ho also chaired the eighth plenary session of the Indo-Chinese Communist party.

In 1942, Ho Chi Minh went to China again to ask the Chinese Nationalist government for help in operating against the Japanese, but he was arrested as a Communist agent and jailed until 1943, when the Chinese released him so he could organize an anti-Japanese resistance movement in Vietnam. Ostensibly copying Stalin, he proclaimed his movement "nationalist"—not Communist— anti-Japanese *and* anti-French.

During World War II, Ho cooperated with the Allies against the Japanese— and with the French, supposedly disbanding the Indo-Chinese Communist party in 1940. As Stalin was looked upon and called "Uncle Joe," so Ho Chi Minh became Vietnam's much loved "Uncle Ho." He cultivated a successful relationship with the United States through OSS agents who were acting against the Japanese in Indochina. In 1945, Bao Dai, the emperor of Vietnam who had cooperated with the Japanese, abdicated in Ho's favor.

By the end of the war, Ho was the most well known indigenous leader in Vietnam. On 2 September 1945, he declared Vietnamese independence, borrowing language from the U.S. Constitution as part of his declaration, and attained political power. In 1946, the French returned to Vietnam. Although at the May 1946 conference at Fontainebleau, Ho was prepared to compromise and work toward independence within a French union (to be something like the British Commonwealth), by September the plan broke down. By late 1946, the Vietminh were fighting the French forces using guerrilla tactics.

The Later Years—Independence

In 1950, Ho formed and proclaimed the Democratic Republic of Vietnam, which was rapidly recognized by China, the USSR, and many Soviet-bloc countries. True independence was won in battle when Vo Nguyen Giap and his Vietminh forces beat the French decisively at Dien Bien Phu. There had been peace talks in Geneva in April, and after Giap's 7 May victory, a truce was signed on 20 July 1954 that separated Vietnam into North and South; Laos and Cambodia were independent. The subsequent South Vietnamese Diem regime did not collapse as anticipated, and the United States supported it with both military and economic assistance. Ho, who had consolidated his power in the north between 1954 and 1960, organized, in 1960, the National Liberation Front and began supporting the (Laotian) Pathet Lao and (Cambodian) Khmer Rouge. He gave up his secretary-general post to lead more symbolically as the head of state. But Ho drove on to achieve his goal of Vietnamese unification and national independence together with domination of the French-created Indochina. Even though he used brutality to implement his plans, Ho Chi Minh was and is still recognized as the "father of his country."

Ho died 2 September 1969 and was accorded the dignity of a Leninist, Maoist-style mausoleum. In May 1975, when the North Vietnamese Army and Viet Cong forces captured Saigon and South Vietnam, Ho was further memorialized when the city of Saigon was renamed Ho Chi Minh City—an empty honor since Saigon remains the city's name to most of the world, including many of the city's own residents.

DONALD S. MARSHALL

SEE ALSO: Giap, Vo Nguyen; Vietnam and Indochina Wars.

Bibliography

Fall, B. 1968. *Ho Chi Minh on revolution.* New York: Signet.
Halberstam, D. 1971. *Ho.* New York: Random House.
Ho Chi Minh. 1966. *Prison diary.* Hanoi: Foreign Language Publishing House.
———. 1966–67. *Selected works.* 4 vols. Hanoi: Foreign Language Publishing House.
Lacoutre, J. 1968. *Ho Chi Minh: A political biography.* New York: Random House.

HUNDRED YEARS' WAR
[1337–1453]

This conflict, certainly the longest and possibly the most famous of medieval wars, dominated the history of both England and France from 1337 to 1453, a period of 116 years. Before it was over, it had involved Scotland, Castile, Aragon, Burgundy, and the Holy Roman Empire as well as France and England. Fighting was not continual over the entire period, as the frequent truces lasted as long as twelve years.

The Causes of War and the Combatants

The causes of the war lay in questions of suzerainty and dynastic precedence, exacerbated by economics. King Edward III, eager for military glory, cited all of these in his declaration of war. Although on paper a war between France and England looked very one-sided because England's population of perhaps 3.25 million was outnumbered by France's 16 million, the worth of armies is not determined by numbers alone. Although the French could field armies of 30,000 men, these forces were badly organized and poorly led. The individual quality of the mounted men-at-arms and sergeants was high, but these troops did not fight well in units and held their humble infantrymen-cum-followers, who were generally poorly trained and indifferently armed, in disdain. The French also used crossbowmen, many hired from Italy.

The English army, although rarely able to field forces larger than 6,000 men, was much better organized than the French. The need for standing forces during the Welsh and Scottish wars of Edward I had led the English to raise, equip, and maintain soldiers on a long-term basis. These troops had high morale, and their armament was superior as well. The infantry Edward I raised was at first equipped with pikes, but by the 1290s many of the troops were armed with the Welsh longbow. Made of yew and about 1.8 meters (6 ft.) long, the longbow fired 0.9-meter (3 ft.) steel-tipped arrows (the famous clothyard shaft) a distance of up to 228.6 meters (250 yd.) and at a rate (in trained hands) of six to twelve per minute. Longbowmen in units of twenty (*vintennis*) and 100 (*centennis*) were organized to deliver controlled, accurate, and rapid missile fire at the direction of the commander. The English armies could do things in battle utterly beyond French capabilities.

Edward III's War

The first three years of war, waged in Flanders, consisted largely of futile maneuver. No battles were fought, and the principal effect of hostilities was to drain Edward III's treasury. However, Edward's great victory at the naval Battle of Sluys on 24 June 1340 ensured his control of the English Channel. The onset of a succession crisis in Brittany in 1341 opened a new theater of war, and Edward dispatched troops there to support the ducal claim of John de Montfort. An English army of 3,000 men under the earls of Northampton, Derby, and Oxford won a notable victory over the French army of about 12,000 under Charles of Blois at Morlaix on 30 September 1342.

French efforts against English Gascony had been frustrated by Edward's able lieutenant there, Henry de Grosmont, earl of Derby, who defeated the French at Auberoche in October 1345 and beat them again at Aiguillon the next year. Edward invaded France directly by landing in Normandy near Cherbourg with an army of 12,000 men in July 1346. He captured Caen and, after feinting toward Paris and maneuvering in Picardy, gave battle near Crécy. Edward's leadership, superior English weapons and organization, and French tactical incompetence led to the virtual destruction of the French army and gave Edward a great victory, despite French numerical superiority of more than five to two.

Following the repulse of a Scottish invasion of England at the Battle of Neville's Cross on 17 October 1346 and the fall of Calais to Edward in September 1347, the outbreak of the Black Death produced a truce that was renewed for seven years. War again flared in 1354, partly because of the ruthless and devious Charles the Bad of Navarre. Edward III's eldest son Edward, often called "the Black Prince" from the color of the armor he supposedly wore at Crécy, led the English armies. He undertook great raids, called *chevauchées*, through central France, in order to wreak such damage that the French king would be forced to submit. Regardless of the oft-demonstrated English battlefield superiority, the French remained unsubdued, even after a disaster like the Black Prince's victory at Poitiers on 19 September 1356, where he captured King Jean II le Bel (the Good).

Despite this success and the associated negotiating advantage, the French continued to resist. Edward led another invasion at the head of a large army in October 1359. Marching through northern France against minimal opposition, he compelled the French to accept the Treaty of Brétigny on 8 May 1360 and so gained all of Guyenne, as well as Calais, Guines, and a ransom of three million gold ecus for Jean II. The terms were never fulfilled, and after the end of the Breton War the French began an earnest campaign. Poor English leadership, the discontent of local nobles, and the inspired leadership of the French constable, Bertrand du Guesclin, led to considerable French success. English *chevauchées* in 1369, 1370, and 1373 were fruitless, and an English fleet was smashed by France's Castilian allies off La Rochelle in 1372. The death of the Black Prince in 1376, of Edward III the following year, and of du Geusclin in 1380 caused hostilities to wind down.

Henry V's War

The next three decades saw only nominal combat but included a disastrous English expedition to Ypres and Dunkirk in 1383 and a planned but unexecuted French invasion of England in 1385–87. Truces and peace negotiations in the 1390s almost ended the war, but Henry IV's displacement of Richard II in 1399, coupled with the outbreak of the Burgundian-Armagnac civil war in France in 1407, led to renewed war after Henry V succeeded his father.

Henry, the ablest leader on either side since du Guesclin, landed with an army of perhaps 7,000 men in Normandy in August 1415. He besieged and captured Harfleur on 14 September and marched for Calais. He hoped to avoid the formidably large French army on the way but was compelled to give battle at Agincourt on 22 October, and his army, reduced to perhaps 5,000 archers and 800 men-at-arms, defeated the ill-led and ill-organized French army of at least 25,000, mostly dismounted men-at-arms.

Campaigning vigorously, Henry conquered Normandy between 1416 and 1420. He also secured the Treaty of Troyes, which made him heir to the French throne in preference to Charles VI's son the dauphin, later Charles VII, on 21 May 1420. Henry's death on campaign on 31 August 1422, however, left the English government in the hands of his able but unruly and less brilliant brothers. Without Henry's enterprise, the English conquest of France slowed, although an Anglo-Burgundian army under the earl of Salisbury won a victory over the French at Cravant (31 July 1423) and the English defeated a Franco-Scottish army at Verneuil (27 August 1424).

The French Recovery

The turning point in the war came when the duke of Bedford, one of Henry V's brothers, led a small army to besiege the city of Orléans in 1428 and begin the conquest of the Loire Valley. Invigorated by the example of Jeanne d'Arc (Joan of Arc), the French were able to break Bedford's siege. Although the comte de Clermont failed to capture Sir John Fastolf's supply convoy at the famous Battle of the Herrings (12 February 1429), Fastolf and John Talbot, earl of Shrewsbury, were defeated by Jeanne d'Arc's army at Patay on 18 June. Although Jeanne d'Arc was captured and executed soon after, the defection of Burgundy in 1435 doomed the English cause, and they were slowly driven from their holdings in France, outnumbered and, for the first time, outfought and "out-generaled."

In 1445, during a truce, French King Charles VII promulgated the *Grande Ordonnance* of 1445, which established a royal army composed of mounted men-at-arms, their pages and squires, and mounted archers, the first standing army in western Europe since the fall of Rome. This force, known as the *compagnies d'ordonnance* and backed by a large and efficient artillery train (largely the creation of the Bureau brothers), received its first test when the French invaded Normandy in 1449. An English army of 4,500 men under Sir Thomas Kyriell, sent to restore the situation, was destroyed at the Battle of Formigny on 15 April 1450 by two small French armies (a total of 5,500 men), under the count of Clermont and Artur de Bretagne, constable de Richemont. Turning their attention to Guyenne, the French conquered all of that area between 1451 and late 1452, except for the city of Bordeaux. The English dispatched an army under the earl of Shrewsbury to its relief, but Shrewsbury was killed and his army defeated when he launched a headlong and ill-considered attack on the fortified French camp at the Battle of Castillon on 17 July 1453. The fall of Bordeaux that October left the English holding only Calais and effectively ended the Hundred Years' War.

DAVID L. BONGARD

See Also: Edward I; Edward III; Feudalism; History, Medieval Military.

Bibliography

Allmand, C. I. ed. 1973. *Society at war: The experience of England and France during the Hundred Years' War*. Edinburgh: Oliver and Boyd.

———. 1976. *War, literature, and society in the late Middle Ages*. Liverpool: Univ. of Liverpool Press.

Burne, A. H. 1955. *The Crécy war*. London: Eyre and Spottiswoode.

———. 1956. *The Agincourt war*. London: Eyre and Spottiswoode.

Contamine, P. 1970. Les armées française et anglais à l'époque de Jeanne d'Arc. *Revue des Sociétés Savantes de la Haute Normandie: Lettres et Sciences Humaines*. 57:5–33.

———. 1972. *Guerre, état et société à la fin du Moyen Age*. Paris: La Haye, Mouton.

Cosneau, E. 1886. *Le Connétable de Richemont (Artur de Bretagne)*. Paris: A. Picard.

Curry, A. E. 1979. The first English standing army? Military organization in Lancastrian Normandy, 1420–1450. In *Patronage, pedigree and power in later medieval Europe*, ed. C. Ross. Gloucester and Totowa, N. J.: Rowman and Littlefield.

Fowler, K. A. 1969. *The king's lieutenant, Henry of Grosmont, First Duke of Lancaster, 1310–1367*. New York: Barnes and Noble.

———, ed. 1971. *The Hundred Years' War*. New York: St. Martin's Press.

Hewitt, H. J. 1966. *The organization of war under Edward III, 1337–1362*. Manchester: Univ. of Manchester Press.

Oman, C. W. C. 1924. *The art of war in the Middle Ages*. 2 vols. London: Methuen.

Seward, D. 1977. *The Hundred Years' War*. New York and London: Atheneum.

Solon, P. D. 1976. Valois military administration of the Norman frontier, 1445–1461: A study in medieval reform. *Speculum* 51:91–111.

Vale, M. G. A. 1982. *War and chivalry: Warfare and aristocratic culture in England, France and Burgundy at the end of the Middle Ages*. Athens, Ga.: Univ. of Georgia Press.

I

ITALIAN UNIFICATION WARS [1848–66]

During the Italian *Risorgimento*, or rebirth, which occurred between the years 1859 and 1861, Italy evolved from a fragmented and diverse group of kingdoms, duchies, and small states dominated by Austria, into a unified and respected member of the European community. Although complete unification did not occur until after World War I, the forging of a single Italian nation took place within this three-year period. Additions and annexations following this period are simply epilogues.

The freedoms granted by the Napoleonic Code, introduced by French occupiers in the early nineteenth century, awakened Italians to the possibilities of an enlightened government responsive to the basic needs of the people. Further, improvements in finance and communications implemented during the Napoleonic era by French-dominated governments had greatly benefited the Italians.

After the final defeat of Napoleon I in 1815, and the collapse of the Napoleonic organizational structure in the Italian states, there was a regression to fragmentation and autocracy. As provided by the Congress of Vienna of 1815, Austria maintained control over Venetia and Lombardy in northern Italy to prevent French influence from growing too strong there. The repressive Austrian presence in northern Italy, however, gave rise to a strong popular desire for independence and constitutional government.

Anti-Austrian sentiment grew beneath the surface for many years until it broke out in open revolt in Milan on 18 March 1848. The resulting "Five Day Revolt" (March 18–22) ended when Austrian Marshal Josef Radetzky withdrew his forces from the city. The rest of Lombardy and Venetia joined in the revolt and a coalition of Italian forces gathered in northern Italy to confront the Austrians. King Charles Albert of Piedmont (the Kingdom of Sardinia), the most competent and liberal leader in Italy, declared war on Austria on 22 March. The Italian coalition under Charles Albert, despite its numerical superiority, campaigned ineffectively against the Austrians, and suffered a severe defeat at the hands of Radetzky at the Battle of Custozza (24–25 July 1848).

Nevertheless, the Italian independence movement continued to grow.

Shortly after the Milan Revolt and the Piedmontese declaration of war, patriots under Daniele Manin declared an independent republic in Venice. In February the following year, Giuseppe Mazzini, with the support of soldier of fortune Giuseppe Garibaldi, declared the formation of a Roman Republic in the Papal States. Despite these events, Radetzky again decisively defeated Charles Albert at the Battle of Novara on 23 March 1849, and Charles Albert abdicated in favor of his son, Victor Emmanuel II.

A French expeditionary force landed at Civitavecchia on 24 April 1849 and moved on Rome, and after an initial repulse, finally forced Garibaldi and his "Legion" to surrender on 29 June. Following this setback, Garibaldi fled to America.

On 9 August Sardinia made peace with Austria, effectively ending the revolution. The Austrians regained firm control in northern Italy, and enacted harsh retaliatory measures, further antagonizing the Italians.

Despite the Austrian success, strong feelings for independence and unification continued to grow among the population. Piedmont, under the leadership of Count Camillo Benso di Cavour, again became the nucleus for the unification movement and for the removal of Austrian influence in Italy.

Although Cavour was trying to build a unified Italian state, he was concerned primarily with expanding the power and prestige of Piedmont. To accomplish this he entered the Crimean War on the side of Britain and France (1853–56), and concluded a secret alliance with Emperor Napoleon III of France at Plombières in 1858. The French promised aid to help drive the Austrians out of northern Italy, but only if this could be accomplished without France being charged with aggression. Following the expulsion of Austria from Italian territory, there would then emerge a federation of four states under the pope's presidency. For her part, France would receive Savoy and Nice from Piedmont.

After the assurance of French aid, Cavour provoked conflict with Austria by stirring up revolts in Lombardy and Venetia. An Austrian ultimatum to disarm was rejected by Cavour, and a brief but bloody war ensued, pitting Piedmont and France against Austria. The decisive Austrian defeat at Solferino (24 June 1859) by the combined French and Piedmontese forces effectively ended major fighting. The Austrian setback at Solferino was a signal for the small north Italian states of Tuscany, Parma, and Modena to overthrow their pro-Austrian leaders.

Napoleon III was alarmed by these revolutions in northern Italy. Hoping to prevent Prussia from entering the war on the side of Austria, he was anxious to end the war quickly and arranged a separate truce with Franz Josef of Austria. On 11 July 1859, at the peace conference held at Villafranca, it was agreed that most of Lombardy (except for the fortress cities of Mantua and Peschiera) would go to Piedmont. Venetia remained under Austrian control, the deposed leaders of Tuscany, Parma, and Modena were reinstated, and the pope was declared president of an Italian confederation.

Piedmont did not participate in the Villafranca meeting, but King Victor Emmanuel reluctantly accepted the terms because he was unwilling to face

Austria alone. Cavour then resigned as prime minister. The Treaty of Zürich, between Piedmont and Austria, ratified on 10 November 1859, essentially confirmed the Villafranca agreements.

The idea of an Italian Confederation under the pope was so distasteful to the northern Italian duchies of Parma, Modena, Tuscany, and Romagna that they agreed to be annexed by Piedmont. Napoleon III objected to this, but Cavour reemerged with a compromise solution. He suggested that the previously agreed cession of Nice and Savoy to France be carried out at once in return for Napoleon III's blessing. To this Napoleon agreed and he and Victor Emmanuel II signed the Treaty of Turin formalizing French annexation of Nice and Savoy.

In April 1860, King Francis II of the Kingdom of the Two Sicilies brutally suppressed revolts in Sicily and Naples, arousing indignation throughout Europe. With the covert support of Cavour and King Victor Emmanuel II, Garibaldi and his "Thousand Redshirts" sailed from Genoa and landed at Marsala, in Sicily, on 11 May. He quickly gained broad public support, and incited a revolt against Francis. Garibaldi defeated forces of the Kingdom of the Two Sicilies at Calatafimi on 15 May and took Palermo on 27 May. He again defeated royal forces at Milazzo on 20 July, and then, with British assistance, Garibaldi crossed the Straits of Messina to the mainland on 22 August. He marched northward, was greeted enthusiastically by the people, and occupied Naples on 7 September after meeting only light resistance.

While Garibaldi was engaged in the Kingdom of the Two Sicilies, unrest in the Papal States provided Cavour with the excuse to send in troops to restore order. Piedmontese forces crossed the border on 10 September and defeated Papal troops at Castelfidardo on 18 September. The Piedmontese then marched southward to link up with Garibaldi. This alarmed Napoleon III because of his desire to maintain the independence of Rome under the pope. French troops were landed and occupied Rome, while naval forces patrolled offshore.

Garibaldi, meanwhile, was able to achieve a victory over the Neapolitan forces at Volturno on 26 October, and then invested the stronghold of Gaeta in early November. The withdrawal of the French fleet in January allowed the Piedmontese navy to arrive and bombard the fortress, forcing its surrender on 13 February 1861.

An all-Italian parliament (with the exception of the papal territories around Rome) was convened on 17 March, and a united Kingdom of Italy was proclaimed with Victor Emmanuel as the first constitutional monarch. Continued French occupation of Rome prevented the inclusion of the Papal States in the new kingdom of Italy. Just three months after seeing his dream come to fruition, Cavour died, exhausted from years of carrying the burden of Italian independence and unification.

Garibaldi and his small army, again with the covert support of Victor Emmanuel, began planning to drive the French from Rome and unite all of Italy. In August 1862 Garibaldi marched northward through Naples toward Rome; however, Victor Emmanuel was not prepared to provoke a conflict with France and sent troops south to stop Garibaldi. The two forces met at Aspromonte on

29 August, where Garibaldi's army was defeated. Garibaldi was wounded and captured, but later released.

Italy now began to plan to recover Venetia from Austria. A treaty was concluded with Prussia in April 1866, and the outbreak of the Austro-Prussian War in June 1866 was followed by Italy's declaration of war against Austria on 20 June. Four days later an Italian army under Victor Emmanuel was defeated by a much smaller Austrian army under Archduke Albert at the Second Battle of Custozza.

Although the Austrians were decisively defeated by the Prussians at Königgrätz, or Sadowa (3 July 1866), and a treaty was concluded at Prague on 23 August, hostilities continued in Italy. Garibaldi won some minor battles in the Alps during July, but withdrew into Italy because Prussia would not agree to the Italian occupation of Trentine Tyrol.

On 20 July the Austrians defeated an Italian naval force at Lissa, in the Adriatic Sea, near Split. A treaty was concluded in Vienna on 12 October between Austria and Italy. Although the Austrians had generally been successful, they accepted the meditation of Napoleon III and ceded Venetia to Italy.

In December 1866 the French occupation force withdrew from Rome. This prompted Garibaldi to try again to force the Papal States into the Italian union. With covert Italian support, he led an invasion in January 1867, while the Italian government attempted to overthrow the papal government by covert and overt means. In October 1867, less than a year after they had been withdrawn, Napoleon again dispatched troops to occupy Rome.

Garibaldi met a French-Papal force at Mentana on 3 November, and was defeated with heavy losses, due primarily to superior French weapons. Garibaldi and his men fled to the Italian border and were arrested by Italian authorities.

The French remained in Rome until the outbreak of the Franco-Prussian War (1870), when they were withdrawn for the defense of France. An Italian army of 60,000 then marched across the border and besieged Rome. Following a brief bombardment, the city was assaulted and taken on 20 September after a short battle. Pope Pius IX, hoping to prevent further bloodshed, ordered his forces to lay down their arms. Rome was then annexed and, following a formal plebiscite, was declared the Italian capital.

Arnold C. Dupuy

See Also: Crimean War; Franco-Prussian War; History, Modern Military.

Bibliography

Delzell, C. F., ed. 1965. *The unification of Italy, 1859–1861: Cavour, Mazzini, or Garibaldi?* New York: Holt, Rinehart and Winston.
Dupuy, R. E., and T. N. Dupuy. 1986. *The encyclopedia of military history.* 2d rev. ed. New York: Harper and Row.
Leeds, A. C. 1974. *The unification of Italy.* New York: Putnam's.
Mack Smith, D. 1954. *Cavour and Garibaldi.* Cambridge, England: Cambridge Univ. Press.

———. 1956. *Garibaldi: A great life in brief.* New York: Knopf.
Trevelyan, G. M. 1911. *Garibaldi and the making of Italy.* New York: Longmans, Green.

ITALIAN WARS [1494–1559]

Italian wars is the collective name given to a series of wars between France and Spain that were fought primarily in Italy. These wars were characterized in part by the large-scale employment of mercenary soldiers by both sides, a growing use of artillery and other firearms, and the effects of the bastioned trace in fortifications. The end of the wars, brought about by the Treaty of Cateau-Cambrésis, created large numbers of unemployed soldiers in France, and so contributed to the unrest leading to the Huguenot Wars (1560–98).

Background

The collapse of the Hohenstaufen imperial regime in Italy in the early thirteenth century left Italy divided into numerous municipal republics, duchies, and counties that constantly quarreled and fought with each other. In such a chaotic political situation, foreign involvement was inevitable, and French, German, and Aragonese intervention played a significant role in Italian affairs.

France held the County of Asti from 1392, and briefly governed Genoa from 1458 to 1461. Further, the Kingdom of Naples was ruled by the House of Anjou from 1282 to 1442. Sicily, on the other hand, had fallen to Aragón in the aftermath of the Sicilian Vespers revolt against the Angevins in 1282. When King René of Naples died without heirs in 1442, he bequeathed his kingdom to the French throne. The French, deeply involved in the final stages of the Hundred Years' War, were unable to exploit their opportunity, and Aragón instead seized the Kingdom of Naples.

The Early Stages, 1494–1515

By the late fifteenth century, the major powers in Italy were Venice, Milan, Florence, the Papacy, and the Kingdom of Naples, and France, Aragón, and Austria all exerted considerable influence. King Charles VIII of France, who was only 24, determined to invade Italy, both to reassert French sovereignty in Naples and to secure a useful base for launching a crusade against the Turks (as he somewhat disingenuously asserted). He led his army across the Alps in September 1494, and this foreign invasion struck Italy like a thunderbolt. Not only was the ruthlessness and efficiency of French men-at-arms and Swiss pikemen an unwelcome surprise, but the relatively more mobile French artillery was also more effective than its Italian counterparts. The effect of these guns on fortifications was especially shocking, as the Florentine historian

Francesco Guicciardini wrote: "So violent was their battering that they could accomplish in a few hours what had previously required many days."

Charles's sudden success caused Ferdinand of Aragón to send a small army under Gonzalo de Córdoba to Italy in spring 1495, in part to succor Ferdinand's cousin King Ferrante of Naples, who had fled to Sicily as the French approached. In addition, Venice, Austria, Spain, Milan, and the Papacy joined in the League of Venice against France. Gonzalo's small army was brushed aside by a French army at Seminara in Calabria (28 June). In the meantime, with enemies gathering to his rear, Charles had realized his dangerous position and, leaving a large garrison in Naples, marched north with most of his army, some 4,100 horse and 7,500 foot. A league army of some 20,000 Italian mercenaries barred his way over the Apennines at Fornovo di Taro (southwest of Parma), but in a furious battle there on 6 July 1495, the French brushed them aside and moved calmly northward toward home.

The French withdrawal was only a pause in the conflict. War continued sporadically into 1496 and resumed in 1499 when France again invaded Naples. Despite some initial success, the French were unable to defeat Gonzalo, who destroyed one French army at Cerignola (21 April 1503) and another in a surprise winter attack at the Garigliano River south of Gaeta (30–31 December). These defeats ended French pretensions in southern Italy.

The League of Cambrai and Milan, 1508–1515

The French, turning their territorial ambitions toward Milan, returned in 1508 as part of the League of Cambrai against Venice. A French army smashed the Venetians at Agnadello (14 May 1509), but the league, led by Pope Julius II, turned on France the following year. A French army under the youthful and energetic Gaston de Foix won a bloody victory at Ravenna (11 April 1512), but Foix's death there spoiled the French success. The following year, a Swiss army routed a French army under Marshal Louis de la Tremoille at Novara (6 June 1513), but a Swiss invasion of France was averted when they accepted a French indemnity. Meanwhile, a Spanish army defeated a Venetian force (Venice had become France's ally) at La Motta (October), and French military prospects were bleak.

Francis I and Milan, 1515–25

Following the Swiss defection, France's other adversaries made peace. After King Francis I ascended the throne, he determined to invade Italy and seize Milan. In a bloody two-day battle at Marignano, Francis drove a Swiss army from the field (13–14 September 1515). This success gave him Milan, recognized by the Treaty of Noyon in 1516. Francis's fear and suspicion of Charles V, whose realm surrounded France on three sides, led to renewed war in 1521. An imperial army under the wily *condottieri* Prospero de Colonna captured Milan. Colonna's skillful use of field entrenchments, coupled with the difficulties French commander Odet de Foix, Marshal de Lautrec, had with his Swiss contingents (unpaid, they threatened to leave unless he launched an assault), gave Colonna a victory at the Battle of Bicocca (27 April 1522). Following the defeat, the battered remnants of Lautrec's Swiss troops left anyway, and Lautrec withdrew to France.

Francis sent a new army to Italy in 1523 under his favorite, Admiral Guillaume Bonnivet. Bonnivet, a soldier of small talent, was surprised and his army routed at La Sesia by Charles de Lannoy, the imperial viceroy of Naples (30 April 1524). Francis frustrated an imperial invasion of the French Riviera by crossing the Alps to the north and descending on Milan in October of that year. Hastening back to protect its Italian base, Lannoy's army waited while the French army besieging Pavia was weakened by disease and detachments.

Lannoy, joined by Charles, the renegade constable of Bourbon, attacked Francis's army on 24 February 1525, catching the besiegers by surprise. The French army reacted in a haphazard and uncoordinated fashion, and Francis led a locally successful cavalry charge into the imperial center. He realized his predicament only when he was surrounded by infantrymen screaming for his blood, and he was rescued only by the timely arrival of Lannoy himself. A captive of the Spanish, Francis was compelled to sign the ruinous Treaty of Madrid to secure his freedom in February 1526. As soon as he entered France, Francis repudiated the treaty and war resumed (May 1526).

The Hapsburg Valois Struggle, 1526–59

During indecisive campaigning in Italy, Lannoy sent the duke of Bourbon against the pope, who had become a French ally. Bourbon advanced on Rome, but after his death in the first assault his *landsknechts* (German mercenary infantry) went out of control and sacked the city (6 May 1527). The following year, the Marquis de St. Pol's French army was defeated at the Battle (or Rout) of the Landriano (19 June), and Genoa was lost to a revolt led by Andrea Doria. These French reverses led to yet another peace in 1529, but war returned from 1536 to 1538, and broke out again in 1542.

The French sent an army into northern Italy under the command of Francis of Bourbon, prince of Enghien. Enghien brought Marquis del Vasto's imperial army to battle at Ceresole, near Turin, on 14 April 1544. Through rare coordination between infantry and cavalry, the French drove the larger enemy army from the field, although an English-imperial invasion of northern France eclipsed Enghien's success. Peace returned in autumn 1544, but war was renewed in 1547.

In 1552, the French sent yet another army to Italy, this one under the Gascon general Blaise du Monluc. Operating in Tuscany in support of allies there, Monluc was defeated at Marciano by the marquis of Marignano (2 August 1553). Withdrawing into Siena, Monluc led an epic defense of that city against a siege until he was forced to surrender in 1554. Again, the focus of war shifted to northern France, where the last campaigns of the war were waged. French armies were defeated at St. Quentin (10 August 1557) and Gravelines

(13 July 1558) before the Treaty of Cateau-Cambrésis ended the conflict in April 1559.

Military Changes During the Wars

Armies had grown larger during the Italian wars, total strength rising from perhaps 12,000 for the French at Fornovo, and much less at Cerignola and the Garigliano, to twice that at Pavia. Alongside the increase in size, the proportion of cavalry had fallen from one-third at Fornovo to about one-eighth at Pavia and one-tenth at Ceresole; moreover, the ratio of heavy to light cavalry had dropped from at least 3:1 at Fornovo to about 1:2 at the later battles. French armies usually contained a larger proportion of cavalry—and a larger fraction of French cavalry was heavy—than did their opponents' armies, in part because the French recognized that one of their strengths was the superiority of their heavy horse, or *gendarmerie*.

Firearms became more common, and the use of artillery became more widespread. While handheld firearms were of minimal import at Fornovo, entrenched Spanish harquebusiers killed the duke of Nemours and broke his attack at Cerignola. A similar combination of entrenchments and firepower at Bicocca wrought fearful execution among the Swiss pike columns, and a Swiss attack at Pavia was handily repulsed by imperial harquebusiers in a wooded thicket on the French left.

Fortresses with bastioned walls proliferated. The ease with which Charles VIII's artillery had battered Italian citadels into submission accelerated the development of low-walled, bastioned fortresses. As sieges took longer (and were frequently no more than blockades, so strong were the new fortresses), the pace of warfare slowed. There were eight major battles in Italy during eleven years of war between 1494 and 1515, five in twelve years from 1515 to 1530, and only two in eighteen years from 1530 to 1559. Fortresses provided armies with safe havens in time of defeat, and as battles decided less and less, they declined in frequency. Warfare became a matter of sieges and "actions," the incessant skirmishes and ambuscades so familiar in the Dutch wars of the late sixteenth century.

MAX GEORGE KELLNER

SEE ALSO: Gonzalo de Córdoba; History, Early Modern Military; History, Medieval Military; Spanish Empire.

Bibliography

Benedetti, A. 1967. *History of the Caroline wars*. Ed. and trans. D. M. Schullian. New York: Frederick Ungar.

Commines, P. de. 1973. *Mémoires*. 2 vols. Ed. S. Kinser, Trans. I. Cazeaux. Columbia: Univ. of South Carolina Press.

Guicciardini, F. 1969. *The history of Italy*. Ed. and trans. S. Alexander. New York: Macmillan.

Machiavelli, N. 1965. *Chief works and others*. Trans. A. Gilbert. Durham, N.C.: Duke Univ. Press.

Mallet, M., and J. R. Hale. 1984. *The military organization of a renaissance state: Venice, 1400–1619*. Cambridge: Cambridge Univ. Press.

Monluc, B. de. 1964. *Commentaires.* Ed. P. Courteault. Paris: A. and J. Picard.

Oman, Sir C. W. C. 1937. *History of the art of war in the sixteenth century.* London: Methuen.

Taylor, F. L. 1921. *The art of war in Italy, 1494–1529.* Cambridge: Cambridge Univ. Press.

J

JACKSON, THOMAS JONATHAN
("Stonewall") [1824–63]

Thomas Jonathan ("Stonewall") Jackson (Fig. 1) was born in Clarksburg, Virginia (now West Virginia), on 21 January 1824, the third of four children and second son of Jonathan Jackson, a lawyer, and Julia Beckwith (Neale) Jackson. His parents died during his early childhood and he was raised by his uncle, Cummins E. Jackson. Thomas added the name Jonathan when almost grown.

Early Career

Jackson entered West Point in 1842 handicapped by inadequate prior education. However, he developed a demanding study regimen that enabled him to graduate seventeenth in a class of 59 when he graduated in 1846.

Upon graduation, Jackson was commissioned in the artillery. In the Mexican War he distinguished himself at Vera Cruz, Cerro Gordo, and Chapultepec, winning a succession of brevets to the rank of major. Afterward, he served at Fort Columbus, New York, in 1848–49; then at Fort Hamilton, New York, 1849–51; and finally in Florida. Jackson resigned from the army on 29 February 1852 to accept the professorship of artillery tactics and natural philosophy at the Virginia Military Institute (VMI), Lexington, Virginia.

Middle Years

Jackson was a poor teacher, and his stiff, formal manner and strict adherence to rules and regulations made him the butt of many cadet jokes. At VMI, he continued his strict personal study regimen and developed a strong Presbyterian religious conviction. His devoutness grew over the years.

On 4 August 1853, he married Elinor Junkin, the daughter of a Presbyterian minister, but she died suddenly on 22 October 1854, taking with her the child they were expecting. In 1856, Jackson spent five months in Europe. On 16 July 1857, he married his second wife, Mary Anna Morrison, also the daughter of a Presbyterian minister. This union produced two daughters, one of whom died in infancy.

Figure 1. Thomas "Stonewall" Jackson. (SOURCE: U.S. Library
of Congress)

Civil War Years

Jackson was in charge of the artillery detachment of VMI cadets at the hanging
of John Brown at Charles Town, Virginia, on 2 December 1859. Although he
did not support secession, Jackson believed that the South should fight for
states' rights. When Virginia seceded from the Union in April 1861, he cast his
lot with his state. He commanded the VMI corps of cadets, which left for war
service on 21 April.

Appointed a colonel in the Virginia forces on 27 April, he was sent to command Harpers Ferry but was soon superseded by Brig. Gen. Albert Sidney
Johnston. Jackson was promoted to brigadier general effective 17 June and
placed in command of a newly raised brigade.

Jackson earned the sobriquet "Stonewall" during the First Battle of Manassas

(First Bull Run), 21 July 1861. Brig. Gen. Barnard E. Bee, rallying his men, shouted: "There is Jackson standing like a stone wall. Let us determine to die here and we will conquer. Follow me." Bee was killed that day and Jackson was wounded in the middle finger of his left hand as he led his brigade of Virginia troops, famous that day forward as the Stonewall Brigade.

On 7 October 1861, Stonewall was promoted to major general of the Provisional Army of the Confederate States. On 4 November, he was given command of the Shenandoah Valley District. Between December 1861 and June 1862, he waged his famous Valley Campaign. His troops (rarely more than 15,000) were equally successful in maneuver and in battle. They tied down some 60,000 Federal troops, which were sorely needed for the campaign against Richmond, the capital of the Confederacy.

Recalled, with his command, to the main Army of Northern Virginia, then operating against the Army of the Potomac just east of Richmond, Jackson was slowed by his own physical exhaustion from the previous campaign and his unfamiliarity with the area. As a result, he failed to attack Federal positions at White Oak Swamp as expected on 30 June. This failure contributed to the disruption of Gen. Robert E. Lee's plan to envelop the Federal army's position. Nonetheless, in the ensuing Seven Days' Battle, the Union army was driven into its fortified base at Harrison's Landing, and Lee turned north to deal with Union general John Pope's Army of Virginia.

Jackson was again given a detached command. After defeating Pope's advanced corps (under Gen. Nathaniel P. Banks) at Cedar Mountain (9 August), he placed his command to the rear of Pope's army and initiated the Second Battle of Manassas, 29–30 August 1862. The arrival of Gen. James Longstreet's corps on Pope's left flank resulted in a crushing defeat of the Union army.

When Lee's army marched north into Maryland in September, Lee entrusted Jackson with five divisions to capture the Federal arsenal at Harpers Ferry. This he did on 15 September, then joined Lee at Sharpsburg. In the ensuing battle of Antietam, Stonewall steadfastly held the greatly outnumbered left wing of the Confederate army against almost overwhelming Union pressure (17 September).

Jackson was promoted to lieutenant general on 11 October 1862 and was given command of the Army of Northern Virginia's Second Corps. He distinguished himself at Fredericksburg on 13 December.

In late April 1863, the Union and Confederate armies were in Virginia's Wilderness region, south of the Rapidan River and west of Fredericksburg. On 1 May, Federal troops had taken up strong positions near Chancellorsville. On 2 May, Jackson led a great turning movement against the Union right flank and rear, wrecking one Union corps and driving the right wing into a constricted perimeter. Returning from reconnaissance forward of his main lines early that evening, General Jackson was mortally wounded when his own men fired into his party, believing them to be Federal troops. His left arm was amputated later that night and a musket ball was removed from his right hand. Moved to Guiney's Station, he died there, on 10 May 1863, of pneumonia. He was buried in Lexington, Virginia.

Assessment

In early life, Jackson suffered from a stomach ailment, causing him to adopt strict dietary and exercise habits the rest of his life. Jackson was five foot ten, slender and wiry, with large hands and feet, a high forehead, brown hair, blue eyes, and a Roman nose. Generally low-voiced and modest as a commander, and particularly in battle, Stonewall was aggressive, brave, determined, disciplined, and energetic. His command was dubbed Jackson's Foot Cavalry for its ability to march long distances in a short period of time. Yet while he asked much of his men, he also paid great attention to their needs and was popular with them. Lee could never replace this remarkable man, and the efficiency of the Army of Northern Virginia was irreparably damaged by his loss.

UZAL W. ENT

SEE ALSO: Civil War, American; Lee, Robert Edward.

Bibliography

Davis, B. 1954. *They called him Stonewall: A life of Lt. General T. J. Jackson, C.S.A.* New York: Rinehart.

Douglas, H. K. 1899. *I rode with Stonewall.* Chapel Hill, N.C.: Univ. of North Carolina Press (Douglas completed the manuscript in 1899, but it was not published until 1940).

Freeman, D. S. 1950. *Lee's lieutenants: A study in command,* vols. 1 and 2. New York: Scribner's.

Henderson, G. F. R. 1898. *Stonewall Jackson and the American Civil War.* 2 vols. London: Longmans, Green.

Vandiver, F. E. 1957. *Mighty Stonewall.* New York: McGraw-Hill.

JAPAN, MODERNIZATION AND EXPANSION OF

The 77 years between the Meiji Restoration and the end of World War II chronicle the emergence of Japan from self-imposed isolation, its transformation into an aggressive, militaristic state, and its near-catastrophic defeat. The evolution of Japan from a preindustrial, agrarian nation into an industrialized, Westernized power in such a short time still elicits admiration, and its aggressive expansionism still evokes bitter memories among the peoples of East and Southeast Asia.

The Meiji Restoration

On 2 November 1868, 265 years of military rule under the Tokugawa Shogunate came to an end. The Shogun Yoshinobu, faced with the continuing civil war launched by pro-imperial *daimyo* (high-ranking feudal lords)—Choshu, Satsuma, Tosa, and Hizen—formally resigned his post and surrendered all executive, legislative, and judicial power to the 14-year-old Meiji emperor (Mutsuhito).

The restoration of imperial power and the far-reaching political, economic, and social changes associated with the reign of the Meiji Emperor were the work of a small oligarchy drawn primarily from the proimperial feudal aristocracy. Spurred on by fears that Japan might suffer the fate of China at the hands of the Western powers, the emperor and his advisers decided to adopt certain elements of Western civilization. The primary objective of the Meiji Era statesmen was succinctly stated in the slogan "*fukoku kyohei*—a rich country, a strong army."

POLITICAL REFORMS

The imperial government's first political reform was the abolition of feudalism. In March 1869, the *daimyo* of Choshu, Satsuma, Tosa, and Hizen voluntarily returned their fiefs to the emperor. In return, the *daimyo* received the governorships of their former domains. Soon thereafter, the remaining *daimyo*, fearing possible government retaliation, also surrendered their fiefs to the emperor.

The emperor, on the advice of Ito Hirombi, decided to follow the Prussian model in the restructuring of the imperial government. According to the Meiji Constitution of 1889, the emperor held supreme power. Although a legislature, the Diet, was created, cabinet members were responsible only to the emperor. The ministers of the army and the navy also were responsible only to the emperor, and candidates for these posts could be nominated only by their respective service high commands.

ECONOMIC REFORMS

Japan's rapid industrialization during the Meiji Era was the result of centralized planning, financing, and control. The Japanese government obtained both foreign assistance and loans. Foreign loans were secured against imperial land revenues and land taxes. Between 1870 and 1900, the Japanese government built and operated steel mills, coal mines, railroads, and textile factories. Eventually the government sold these assets to private corporations.

Although Japan was able to go from a preindustrial to an industrialized society in a short time, industrial development was restricted to heavy industry (iron and steel), coal mining, and textiles. Little attention was paid to the development of light industry. The agricultural sector remained outside the scope of the Meiji reforms.

MILITARY MODERNIZATION

Because a primary reason for Japanese modernization was the threat of Western military power, the imperial government placed military modernization high on its priority list. Initially, the Japanese sought the assistance of the French in the creation of a modern army. In 1875, however, Yamagata Aritomo, the army minister, adopted the German general staff system rather than the French. Eventually the Japanese adopted the German system of military schools, including curricula, as well as the German divisional structure, with organic artillery support. Yamagata also reorganized the Army Ministry along German lines.

The Japanese sought the help of the dominant naval power of the day, Great Britain, in organizing and training the navy. In addition, British shipyards built the first Japanese warships.

Japanese Expansionism During the Meiji Era, 1868–1912

Although military modernization was initially a self-defense measure, the use of military force quickly became a tool of Japanese foreign policy. During the Meiji Era, the Imperial Japanese Army and Navy fought in two foreign wars: the First Sino-Japanese War and the Russo-Japanese War. The cause of both wars was the same: the status of Korea.

THE FIRST SINO-JAPANESE WAR, 1894–95

Disagreements between China and Japan over the status of Korea came to a head when Korean nationalists rebelled against the Korean government. Chinese troops, supporting the Korean government, clashed with Japanese troops. In the ensuing conflict, the numerically superior Chinese forces were soundly beaten by the modern Japanese army. At sea, the Japanese navy sank or captured elements of the Chinese North Seas Fleet, the most modern of China's naval forces.

The First Sino-Japanese War ended on 17 April 1895 with the signing of the Treaty of Shimonoseki. Both China and Japan recognized the independence of Korea. China agreed to pay Japan an indemnity of 200 million taels of silver, approximately US$66 million. Japan also received Taiwan (Formosa), the Pescadore Islands, and a lease to the Liaotung Peninsula. The Chinese also agreed to open the cities of Chungking, Soochow, and Hangchow to Japanese commercial enterprises.

THE RUSSO-JAPANESE WAR, 1904–1905

Having gained the Liaotung Peninsula, the Japanese were forced to return it to China due to pressure from France, Germany, and Russia. This Triple Intervention was shortly followed by German and Russian demands for economic enclaves—concessions—in China. Furthermore, Russia forced China to grant it a lease to the Liaotung Peninsula. The Japanese were outraged. Russia had replaced China as the main threat to Japanese interests. With its control of Liaotung and its penetration of Manchuria, Russia was in a position to dominate Korea and, therefore, threaten Japan.

Imperial Russia had many advantages: its size, population, rich natural resources, and a massive military establishment. Nevertheless, Japan decided to go to war. In order to offset the Russian advantages, the Japanese High Command ordered Adm. Togo Heihachiro to attack the Russian Asiatic Fleet at Port Arthur. The attack came without warning on 9 February 1904. The Russian fleet was bottled up in the harbor, and many ships were sunk or damaged at their moorings. The Japanese army landed and besieged Port Arthur, which finally surrendered on 1 January 1905. The Russian government, in an attempt to strike back, sent the Baltic Fleet halfway around the world. At the Battle of Tsushima Straits (27–28 May 1905), the outnumbered but more modern Japanese fleet outsailed, outmaneuvered, and outfought the Russians and inflicted on them one of the most decisive naval defeats in the history of sea warfare.

Meanwhile, the Japanese also had the best of the long, drawn-out fighting in Manchuria. The struggle took its toll of both governments. In Russia, the outcry against the war threatened revolution. In Japan, the war threatened bankruptcy. Therefore, when President Theodore Roosevelt offered to mediate, both governments accepted.

According to the terms of the Treaty of Portsmouth, signed 5 September 1905, Russia recognized Japan's paramount interests in Korea. Russia agreed to transfer to Japan, with Chinese approval, the lease to the Liaotung Peninsula, the southern section of the Chinese Eastern Railroad (in Manchuria), and the Russian-operated coal mines. Russia also ceded to Japan the southern half of Sakhalin Island. Both governments agreed to withdraw their forces from Manchuria.

THE ANNEXATION OF KOREA

On 22 August 1910, Japan solved the Korean problem by annexing the kingdom of Korea and placing it under the administration of the Imperial Japanese Army.

Japanese Expansion During the Taisho Era, 1912–26

The Taisho Era can be divided into two periods: the first ten years, 1912–22, during which Japanese expansionism followed the Meiji pattern; and the last four years, 1922–26, during which Japanese policy followed a less aggressive, more cooperative and conciliatory pattern.

THE FIRST WORLD WAR

World War I provided Japan with an opportunity to expand its economic foothold in China. Having declared war on Germany on 23 August 1914, the Japanese attacked German forces in Shantung, China. After securing Tsingtao on 7 November 1914, the Japanese occupied German possessions in the Pacific, the Marshall, Mariana, and Caroline islands. Japan's gains in China and the Pacific were formally recognized by the Treaty of Versailles.

THE LATE TAISHO ERA, 1922–26

The Washington Naval Conference of 1921–22 marked a change in the nature of Japanese foreign policy. In exchange for recognition as one of the five great naval powers and virtual naval control of the western Pacific, Japan agreed to return its concessions in Shantung to Chinese jurisdiction and pledged itself to defend Chinese sovereignty.

For the remainder of the Taisho Era and the first years of the Showa Era, Japan's policy toward China was one of conciliation and emphasis on the benefits of Sino-Japanese cooperation.

Japanese Expansion During the Showa Era, 1926–45

Japan's abrupt return to an aggressive policy of expansionism during the Showa Era can be traced to the economic distress caused by the Great Depression and the rise of militarism. The two were interrelated. The effects of the depression—rising food prices, falling silk prices, rapidly increasing rents, and the worsening condition of the peasants—convinced many members of the military high command that the party politicians who had succeeded the Meiji Era statesmen had sold out to the interests of big business and foreigners. All military factions—Black Dragon, Imperial Way, Control, Cherry Blossom, and the others—agreed that the politicians had abandoned the traditional values of the nation and betrayed the emperor. By 1929, the military had begun to formulate and follow its own foreign and domestic policies, policies often at odds with those of the government. By the late 1930s, the government had become, in effect, a tool of the military.

THE MANCHURIAN INCIDENT, 1931–32

The Kwantung Army—originally stationed in Manchuria to protect Japanese-owned railroads—took control of Manchuria without government approval. By 5 February 1932, the Kwantung Army had occupied all of Manchuria. Manchuria was detached from China and formed into the new state of Manchukuo with Henry Pu-yi, the last Manchu emperor of China, as emperor. Because the Japanese controlled all government functions, Manchukuo was, in reality, a Japanese puppet state.

JAPANESE AGGRESSION IN CHINA PROPER

The successful coup in Manchuria and the inability of the Japanese government to call the army to heel emboldened the militarists. From the creation of Manchukuo on 18 February 1932 to the Marco Polo Bridge Incident of 7 July 1937, the Japanese followed a policy of overt territorial expansionism. They hoped to detach the five northern provinces from China and form them into another puppet state. The Chinese Nationalist government, then embroiled in its anti-Communist extermination campaigns, tried negotiation and conciliation.

In December 1936, as a result of negotiations between Chou En-lai and Chiang Kai-shek, the Communist and Nationalist parties agreed to join forces in a united front against Japanese aggression. Faced with the possibility of a united China, the Japanese army fabricated the Marco Polo Bridge Incident. The Japanese expected the Chinese to request negotiations. Instead, the Chinese chose to fight.

THE SECOND SINO-JAPANESE WAR, 1937–45

The fighting in North China spread rapidly. The Japanese occupied Peking on 28 July and Tientsin the following day. In an attempt to outflank the Chinese defenses, 10,000 Japanese marines landed at Shanghai. Instead of a quick victory, Shanghai developed into a three-month-long battle that allowed the

Chinese government to fortify Nanking and make preparations for a withdrawal into the interior. Shanghai fell on 8 November, Nanking on 13 December. With the capture of Nanking, the Chinese capital, the Japanese hoped to end the China Incident. However, Chiang Kai-shek moved his capital to Chungking, and the Chinese fought on.

As the war dragged on, the Japanese government sought ways to end it. Both Britain and the United States condemned Japan's aggression and continued to supply China with war materiel through Burma.

The Greater East Asia War (World War II), 1941–45

American condemnation of Japanese policy in China took concrete form when, in 1940, the United States imposed a series of restrictions on the sale of oil, scrap iron, and other strategic materials to Japan. Faced with the specter of economic strangulation and continued Anglo-American support for China, the Japanese government, after long deliberation, decided to go to war. The plan was to neutralize the threat of American power by destroying the U.S. Pacific Fleet at Pearl Harbor and occupying the Philippines. The conquest of British-controlled Malaya and Burma would not only sever China's supply line but also secure for Japan the rubber and oil reserves of Southeast Asia.

What had begun as an attempt to gain economic control of the resources and markets of China and, therefore, economic security had led Japan into all-out war with China, Great Britain, and the United States. Although initially successful, Japan's limited industrial base and dependence on foreign raw materials severely hampered the war effort. By mid-1943, Japanese forces were in retreat in the Pacific and stalemated in Burma, while in China the fighting continued to drain the strength of the army. By the end of the war, Japan's military and civilian leaders, who had enthusiastically embraced the policy of expansionism, had, in effect, destroyed much of what their predecessors had achieved during the Meiji Era.

LAWRENCE D. HIGGINS

SEE ALSO: Chu-Teh; Giap, Vo Nguyen; Mao Tse-tung; Togo, Heihachiro; Wei Li-huang; Yamamoto, Isoroku; Yamashita, Tomoyuki.

Bibliography

Barnhart, M. A. 1941. *Japan prepares for total war: A search for economic security, 1919–1941.* Ithaca, N.Y.: Cornell Univ. Press.
Beasley, W. G. 1972. *The Meiji restoration.* Stanford, Calif.: Stanford Univ. Press.
Crowley, J. B. 1966. *Japan's quest for autonomy: National security and foreign policy.* Princeton, N.J.: Princeton Univ. Press.
Dower, J. W. 1988. *Empire and aftermath: Yoshida Shigeru and the Japanese experience, 1878–1954.* Cambridge: Harvard Univ. Press.
Francks, P. 1984. *Technology and agricultural development in pre-war Japan.* New Haven: Yale Univ. Press.
Hane, M. 1982. *Peasants, rebels, and outcasts: The underside of modern Japan.* New York: Pantheon Books.
Hattori, T. 1955. *Daitoa Senso Zenshi.* Tokyo: Hara Shobo.
Nobutaka, I. 1967. *Japan's decision for war: Records of the 1941 policy conferences.* Stanford, Calif.: Stanford Univ. Press.

Presseisen, E. L. 1965. *Before aggression: Europeans prepare the Japanese army.* Tucson: Univ. of Arizona Press.

Smith, T. C. 1988. *Native sources of Japanese industrialization, 1750–1920.* Berkeley: Univ. of California Press.

Totman, C. 1980. *The collapse of the Tokugawa Bakufu, 1862–1868.* Honolulu: Univ. of Hawaii Press.

JELLICOE, JOHN RUSHWORTH (1st Earl) [1859–1935]

Admiral of the Fleet Earl Jellicoe had a distinguished career in the Royal Navy from 1872 until 1924. A recognized expert at naval gunnery, Jellicoe was instrumental in modernizing the Royal Navy and superintending the Dreadnought construction program. His name has become enmeshed in the controversy surrounding the Battle of Jutland (31 May–1 June 1916) where Jellicoe commanded the Grand Fleet against the German High Seas Fleet. At this crucial engagement, which involved the two greatest fleets of dreadnoughts ever assembled, Jellicoe failed to defeat the Germans decisively. Afterwards his critics damned his caution as lacking the Nelson touch; his defenders echoed Churchill's comment that "Jellicoe was the only man on either side who could lose the war in an afternoon."

Early Life and Career

John Rushworth Jellicoe was born at Southampton, England, on 5 December 1859 to a family with a long tradition of maritime service. Jellicoe joined the training ship *Britannia* as a naval cadet in 1872, graduated at the top of his term in 1874, and received immediate promotion to midshipman.

Jellicoe's naval career began with service on the frigate *Newcastle* (1874–77) and the battleship *Agincourt* (1877–78) and then attendance at naval schools at Greenwich and Portsmouth. Subsequently Jellicoe served on the *Alexandra* in the Mediterranean and then returned to the *Agincourt* in time to combat the Arabi Pasha rebellion in Egypt in 1882.

Jellicoe next qualified as a gunnery officer, and in 1884 joined the staff of the *Excellent* gunnery school, commanded by Capt. (later Admiral of the Fleet Lord) J. A. Fisher. The following year Fisher became chief of staff of the *Minotaur*, and selected Jellicoe as his staff officer. Jellicoe's proficiency and abilities earned him a deserved place in the "Fishpond," a group of Fisher's proven protégés.

Service as gunnery officer on the *Monarch*, *Colossus*, and *Excellent* followed. In 1889 Fisher requested Jellicoe's transfer to the Admiralty, where he worked for two years before service on the *Sans Pareil*. Jellicoe then served as commander of the Mediterranean Fleet flagship *Victoria*. While Jellicoe was suffering from fever, Adm. Sir George Tryon, Fleet commander, made a tragic blunder in navigation that resulted in the *Victoria* ramming the *Camperdown*. The *Victoria* sank with the loss of nearly 400 men, including Tryon, but Jellicoe was able to swim free from the wreckage.

After recuperating, Jellicoe commanded the new flagship, *Ramillies*, from 1893 to 1896, at which time he returned to England to serve on the Ordnance Committee. He was promoted to captain in January 1897, and the next year became flag captain and chief of staff to Adm. Frederick Seymour in the Far East. Two years later, during the Boxer Rebellion, while Seymour commanded the international naval brigade, Jellicoe was shot in the left lung.

At the Admiralty

Jellicoe, after convalescing, served at the Admiralty where he was responsible for inspecting all ships under construction. A year later he took command of the armored cruiser *Drake*. This tour was interrupted by recall to the Admiralty, where he assisted in the development of the "all-big-gun" battleship *Dreadnought*, which made all earlier battleships obsolete.

In 1907 Jellicoe became second in command of the Atlantic Fleet and the next year returned to the Admiralty as controller and third sea lord. Three years later, Vice Admiral Jellicoe became commander of the Atlantic Fleet, after having supervised an increase in the Royal Navy of some 90 ships, including twelve battleships.

The Grand Fleet

Upon the outbreak of war in 1914, Jellicoe reluctantly assumed command of what was renamed the Grand Fleet. Most authorities and the public expected a major sea battle with the German High Seas Fleet soon after war broke out, but that opportunity never materialized. Jellicoe, however, needed to maintain his fleet in the highest state of readiness in the event the German fleet ventured into the North Sea.

The months of incessant training, drilling, and gunnery practice began to take their toll on Jellicoe's health, and he was increasingly pressured to take the offensive. The German fleet made a number of cautious sorties in an attempt to trap and destroy part of the Grand Fleet. On 30 May 1916 the Admiralty intercepted and decoded messages that warned that the German fleet would probably put to sea the following morning. Jellicoe led his fleet from the harbor that night.

At Jutland, the Grand Fleet's performance was marred from the beginning, primarily by signal errors. When Jellicoe sighted the German fleet, he instantly decided to deploy on his port column and subjected the enemy to withering fire as he crossed the German T on two occasions. As the Germans maneuvered away, Jellicoe, concerned about submarines and approaching nightfall, hesitated to follow. He positioned himself between the enemy and their ports and hoped to renew the action in the morning. The German fleet, however, escaped.

The Battle of Jutland is generally considered to have been inconclusive. The British fleet lost fourteen ships and 6,000 men, compared with the Germans' eleven ships and 2,500 men. Jellicoe's deployment is generally conceded to have been judicious and well executed, but his cautious decision to disengage—as if he had prized the Grand Fleet too highly to subject it to serious risk to win a decisive naval battle—prevented a sound British victory. The results of this battle, however, were due more to the rigidity of the tradition-bound Royal Navy, manifested in a centralization of authority and resultant lack of initiative shown by subordinates. Other factors included mediocre gunnery and defective projectiles. The onus of responsibility fell upon Jellicoe, although the controversy remains to this day.

Aftermath

In November 1916 Jellicoe became first sea lord, and his greatest concern became the German submarine menace and establishment of the convoy system. In the face of political pressure, he became increasingly fatigued and pessimistic. Due primarily to his reluctance to implement the convoy system, Jellicoe was relieved of his last wartime appointment on Christmas Eve 1917, after which he received a viscountcy.

Jellicoe served a successful tour as governor-general of New Zealand from 1920 to 1924 and then retired from the Royal Navy. In 1925 he received an earldom and, upon the death of Lord Douglas Haig in 1928, received the honor of being unanimously elected to fill the presidency of the British Legion. He held office until 1932, and died on 20 November 1935 from a cold caught while attending an Armistice Day ceremony.

Jutland was the apex of Jellicoe's career; the rest a "long, slow anti-climax" (Patterson 1969, p. 258). Jellicoe's renown will be based upon his command of the Grand Fleet against the German High Seas Fleet at Jutland, an action that marked the end of an epoch in naval warfare.

HAROLD E. RAUGH, JR.

SEE ALSO: Fisher, John Arbuthnot, 1st Baron of Kilverstone; Scheer, Reinhard; Schlieffen, Alfred, Count von; World War I.

Bibliography

Bennett, G. 1964. *The battle of Jutland*. London: Batsford.
Frost, H. H. 1936. *The battle of Jutland*. London: Stevens and Brown.
Gibson, L., and J. E. T. Harper. 1934. *The riddle of Jutland*. New York: Coward-McCann.
Jellicoe, J. 1920. *The crisis of the naval war*. London: Cassell.
MacIntyre, D. 1958. *Jutland*. New York: Norton.
Marder, A. J. 1961–70. *From the Dreadnought to Scapa Flow*. 5 vols. London: Oxford Univ. Press.
Patterson, A. T. 1969. *Jellicoe*. New York: Macmillan.

JOMINI, ANTOINE HENRI
[1779–1869]

Antoine Henri Jomini, a Swiss of French extraction, was a military historian and theorist who sought to define the principles of warfare systematically. Influenced by the Enlightenment and his observations of the Napoleonic wars, he endeavored to reduce battles, campaigns, and wars to theoretical systems that should govern their conduct. In the process he earned a place in the front rank of military theorists and coined words and concepts still in use.

Early Life and Military Career

Jomini was born into a bourgeois family at Payerne, Switzerland, where his father was syndic (municipal magistrate). Although he was expected to have a business career, he preferred military life. When the Swiss Revolution began, the 19-year-old Jomini left his post in a Paris bank to become first a member of the Swiss General Staff and then, at age 21, commander of a brigade. Subsequently he returned to Paris where he devoted himself chiefly to writing military history.

His first major work, *Traité des grandes opérations militaires*, was published in four volumes (1804–1805). Marshal Ney was so impressed by it that he had Jomini join his staff as volunteer aide-de-camp for the Austerlitz campaign. Napoleon appointed him a colonel in the French service in December 1805, and he became Ney's principal aide. Appreciative of Jomini's grasp of military strategy, Napoleon attached him to his general staff in 1806 for the impending campaign against Prussia. He was present at the battles of Jena and Eylau. For his service at Eylau, he was awarded the Legion of Honor. After Tilsit, he became Ney's chief of staff and was created a baron. Jomini gave Ney valuable advice in the Spanish campaign but vowed to leave French service following a quarrel with the marshal.

Napoleon refused to accept his resignation and compelled him to remain in the French army as a general of brigade, while allowing him to accept an appointment as general in the service of Alexander I of Russia. For a while Jomini held the rank of general in both the French and Russian armies, with the consent of both sovereigns. Because of this conflict of interest he was spared participation in Napoleon's Russian campaign. Jomini did take a command on the line of communication and was engaged there when the retreat from Moscow occurred.

War with Prussia ensued, and Jomini rejoined Ney for the battles of Lützen and Bautzen, where he served as chief of staff of Ney's group of corps. For Jomini's distinguished service at Bautzen, Ney recommended his promotion to general of division. This promotion was blocked by an old enemy, Alexandre Berthier, Napoleon's chief of staff, who erased Jomini's name from the promotion list and had him arrested and censured for failing to file a fortnightly report of strength on time. The charges were trivial and baseless; but the angry, frustrated Jomini joined the allied forces coalescing against France.

In August 1813 the czar appointed him a lieutenant general in the Russian army and a personal aide-de-camp. Jomini's old French comrades considered him treasonous, although in retrospect Napoleon forgave him because he was Swiss, not French. He withdrew from the Allied Army in 1814 when it violated Swiss neutrality by making a passage of the Rhine at Basel. Although Jomini took part in the Congress of Vienna, his influence had been undermined by his futile attempts after Waterloo to have Ney's life spared.

In 1823, after Jomini had spent several years in retirement, Alexander I appointed him full general in the Russian army and called him to Moscow. For the remainder of the decade, he spent his time principally in educating the czarevitch Nicholas and in organizing the Russian staff college, which opened in 1832. His last active service came in 1828 at the siege of Varna, where he was given the cordon of the Alexander order. After retiring from active service in 1829, Jomini spent the next 30 years in scholarly pursuits, chiefly in Brussels. He was called to St. Petersburg to serve as a military adviser to the czar during the Crimean War. Afterwards he settled at Passy near Paris where, until his death in 1869, he wrote treatises, pamphlets, and open letters on military subjects.

Literary Legacy

Jomini's reputation as a military commentator is based on a substantial literary legacy. Consisting of more than 30 volumes, his writings are both historical and theoretical in nature. The histories, issued originally in 27 volumes, discuss the wars of Frederick the Great and the wars of the French Revolution and Napoleon. The Seven Years' War and the revolutionary wars of the 1790s are treated in detail. Four additional volumes published in 1827 cover the political and military careers of Napoleon Bonaparte. But Jomini is best known for a single work entitled *Précis de l'art de la guerre*, published in Paris in 1838. Therein he developed his theories of war and contributed to the vocabulary of military science.

Military Thought

The *Précis* brought to fruition ideas Jomini had originally proposed three decades earlier in his study of the Seven Years' War (*Traité des grande opérations militaires*). In chapters 7 and 14 he speculated on the importance of lines of operation; in chapter 35 he advanced his belief that war was governed by immutable principles. Herein lies the corpus of Jomini's theory. Convinced that war was a rational activity, Jomini wrote the *Précis* in the belief that the central problem in military science was to comprehend and apply the natural laws of strategy. In the *Précis* he gave considerable attention to the definition of strategy, tactics, and logistics and explained their relationship. Noting that battles and campaigns must be meticulously planned, Jomini believed that victory would result from application of these eternal principles of strategy:

1. Massing the forces of an army successively on the decisive points of a theater of war, if possible upon the enemy's communications without endangering one's own;
2. Engaging this mass against fractions of the enemy's army by maneuver;
3. Directing by tactical maneuver one's massed forces to the decisive point of the battlefield, or to that portion of the enemy line which must be taken;
4. Contriving that these masses be brought into action with energy so as to produce a simultaneous effort.

To explain how these principles were to be applied, Jomini devised twelve model battle plans based on geographic formations. In each there was a theater of operations, a zone of operations, and a line of operations. The successful commander should choose a line of operations that would result in his domination of three sides of a rectangular zone of operations. The enemy would be forced either to surrender or to retreat. Because of his reliance on these geometric model battle plans, Jomini sometimes seems to be aloof from the reality of battle.

In summary, Jominian strategy consisted primarily of offensive action by massed forces that pursued vigorously after breaking the enemy's line.

Jomini's Influence

For two generations after Jomini published the *Précis*, it was considered the finest book on war. The *Précis* was studied wherever military leaders were trained or war plans developed. European staff officers held exercises based upon Jominian models and principles. Works by Dennis Hart Mahan, long an instructor at West Point, and Henry W. Halleck, his student, were derived principally from the *Précis*; thus a generation of professional officers entered the American Civil War schooled in Jominian strategy. Jomini's emphasis on the offensive may have affected such battles as Malvern Hill, Fredericksburg, Gettysburg, and Cold Harbor, where attacking armies were shattered by well-placed defenders armed with the rifle musket, a weapon unknown to Jomini. Alfred Thayer Mahan, son of Dennis Hart Mahan, acknowledged Jomini as the single most important influence in his thinking about naval strategy.

There were inherent weaknesses in Jomini's strategic thought (although some authorities have suggested that most of the criticism is debatable). Principal among these criticisms are the following:

• Jomini claimed war to be controlled violence fought according to unchanging principles; neither the validity nor the timelessness of these principles has been proven;
• He failed to understand the importance of strategic mobility, of the element of surprise, or of the role of chance in warfare;
• He urged concentration on one decisive point, with no important alternative objectives;
• He assumed that the enemy would act predictably;
• He tended to undervalue moral and psychological factors in war; and

• He had an inadequate appreciation of how science and technology change warfare.

It is possible, however, to refute each of these criticisms of Jomini by using selections from his own writings. He was neither as philosophical nor as profound as Clausewitz. Nevertheless, his conclusions and theories had much in common with those of Clausewitz.

MAX RAY WILLIAMS

SEE ALSO: Civil War, American; Clausewitz, Karl von; French Revolutionary–Napoleonic Wars; Napoleon I; Principles of War; Science of War; Seven Years' War.

Bibliography

Alger, J. I. 1975. *Antoine-Henri Jomini: A bibliographical survey.* West Point, N.Y.: U.S. Military Academy.

Brinton, C., G. A. Craig, and F. Gilbert. 1943. Jomini. In *Makers of modern strategy,* ed. E. M. Earle, pp. 77–92. Princeton, N.J.: Princeton Univ. Press.

Connelly, T. L., and A. Jones. 1973. *The politics of command: Factions and ideas in Confederate strategy.* Baton Rouge, La.: Louisiana State Univ. Press.

Hittle, J. D. 1975. *The military staff: Its history and development.* Westport, Conn.: Greenwood Press.

Jomini, Baron de. 1862. *The art of war.* Trans. G. H. Mendell and W. P. Craighill. Philadelphia, Pa.: Lippincott.

Shy, J. 1986. Jomini. In *Makers of modern strategy,* ed. P. Paret, pp. 143–85. Princeton, N.J.: Princeton Univ. Press.

Weigley, R. F. 1973. *The American way of war: A history of United States military strategy and policy.* New York: Macmillan.

Williams, T. H. 1981. *The history of American wars, from 1745 to 1918.* New York: Knopf.

KEMAL, MUSTAFA PASHA (Atatürk) [1881–1938]

At the conclusion of World War I, several empires—Russian, German, Austro-Hungarian, and Ottoman—collapsed. During the death throes of the latter, both a new leader (Mustafa Kemal) and a new nation (the Republic of Turkey) emerged in the place of the sultan and his empire. In recognition of Kemal's role in the evolution of the nation, the national assembly gave him the honorific Atatürk—Father of the Turks.

Mustafa Kemal lived through the breakdown of the once powerful Ottoman Empire—an empire by then derisively known as the "Sick Man of Europe." Born in Macedonia, the son of a customs officer, Kemal's home was in the port city of Salonika. Ottoman control over Macedonia faded rapidly as he became a young man. Through those years the "Eastern Question" kept the Ottoman Empire on the brink of crisis, yet for young Kemal good fortune radiated his way. He was selected to attend one of the few institutions—military school—that allowed a young man of humble origins to advance in the closed society of the Ottomans. Kemal graduated with honors as a second lieutenant. His education had been broad and considerably influenced by Western thought.

Reaction and Revolution

As a soldier Kemal quickly advanced in the ranks of the army. The sultan's corruption and autocracy led Kemal to question the status quo. Kemal, nurtured by his reading of Rousseau, Voltaire, Tolstoy, and others, soon advocated reform for the empire. He also resented foreign privilege that he had observed in Constantinople, especially the "Capitulations," which gave foreigners extraterritorial privileges that placed them above Turkish law. His newfound political awareness troubled the sultan's agents, but the Young Turk revolution of 1908 came from the army; Kemal was not in a position to play a key role.

War and Nationalism

The Italian attack on Tripoli in 1911 and the Balkan Wars of 1912 and 1913 foreshadowed the Great War of 1914. For Kemal it was a time of personal loss. As a soldier he experienced defeat in Tripoli, and as a Turk he lost his home to

Greece, although he took part in the recapture of Adrianople from Bulgarian troops in July 1913. Events moved into World War I following the assassination of Austrian Archduke Franz Ferdinand during the summer of 1914.

Kemal commanded the 19th Division at Gallipoli and so played a major role in halting the initial British attack there in April 1915. During the ensuing eight months of bitter fighting, Kemal was distinguished as the principal subordinate of German general Liman von Sanders. His performance in these battles won him renown and promotion, although he quarreled with War Minister Enver Pasha over growing German influence in the empire. He commanded the XVI Corps in eastern Anatolia from March to September 1916. Kemal's policy dispute with Enver Pasha continued, resulting in Kemal being placed on indefinite sick leave in late 1917. The deteriorating situation in Palestine led to his recall to command the Seventh Army there in summer 1918. Despite Kemal's best efforts, his meager forces were badly mauled by Allenby's offensive at Megiddo (19–22 September), but he was able to extricate much of his force. Although he reestablished a hasty line just north of Aleppo in late October, he was forced to withdraw as British troops approached; when the armistice was concluded in November, his force was in southeastern Anatolia.

The war had convinced Kemal that the future of his people rested with Turkish nationalism. He had witnessed before and during World War I the tide of nationalism within the empire. Kemal recognized that the multinational, multireligious empire led by the Ottomans would fail in the non-Turkish areas. He also concluded that a state based on a single, dominant faith (Islam) would also collapse for the same reason. Kemal had already observed the failure of the faithful to respond to the holy war (*jihad*) that the Ottomans had called during World War I. Last, he believed that a state that linked all Turks together would fail because Europeans dominated the region. Kemal realized that the Anatolian peninsula, peopled by Turks with a common heritage, represented the best opportunity of the Turks to survive a collapse of empire.

War of Independence

On 30 October 1918, the Turks had signed an armistice with the Allies. At the conclusion of the armistice, the Turks believed that an understanding had been reached with the Allies. Greece would not occupy Ismir (Smyrna), and the Allies would not occupy Constantinople. The war had been lost, but it seemed the territorial integrity of the Turkish heartland had been secured. The understanding was only an illusion.

In January 1919, the Allies assembled in Paris to determine the fate of Germany and its allies. The Paris Peace Conference focused on Europe and the competitive claims that the victorious Europeans had in their secret accords. Among them were plans for the dismemberment of the Ottoman Empire and cession of its territory to the prewar allies of Russia, Britain, and France. The Russian revolutions of 1917 caused Russia's claims to be discarded, but Britain and France had not been swayed by Woodrow Wilson's idealistic formula for peace. For the Ottomans, it meant the understandings of the previous October were to be betrayed. For Kemal, however, the betrayal provided an opportunity to ignite nationalism.

In February 1919, Allied troops entered Constantinople, and later that spring, Greece was granted the right to occupy Ismir. As a result, discontent and disorder emerged throughout Anatolia. Allied authorities and their puppet-sultan reacted by sending Kemal to quell the disturbances. The sultan named him inspector general with full power to combine civil and military authority to end the uprisings. Kemal's new position gave him what he had never possessed—legitimate authority. He then used this position to launch the struggle.

On 19 May 1919, Kemal ordered both military and civilian authorities to fight for Turkish dignity and honor. The sultan attempted to recall him, but it was too late. By September, Kemal had held several conferences that affirmed his aim of self-determination for the Turks. Early in 1920, the Allies moved against Constantinople and attempted to establish Armenia as an independent state. The Europeans played into Kemal's hands. Concurrently, the sultan assisted the nationalists when he signed the Treaty of Sèvres on 20 August 1920. In that treaty the sultan's government recognized the end of the Ottoman Empire, the return of the Capitulations, the acceptance of Allied economic controls, the demilitarization of the straits, and Allied intervention. The treaty gave new impetus to Kemal's movement.

Kemal, elected both president of the new national assembly in Ankara and head of the government in April, was faced with a desperate military situation. First, he seized the initiative and launched an offensive against the Armenians, subduing them in a brief campaign and concluding a peace at Alexandropol on 2 December. Meanwhile Kemal had appointed Ismet Pasha (later Ismet Inönü) commander in western Anatolia facing the Greeks. Ismet's success at First Inönü in January 1921 and Second Inönü in late March enabled Kemal's counteroffensive at Sakkaria (24 August–16 September) to be a resounding success.

Kemal spent some ten months reorganizing his forces and consolidating the new Turkish state. He launched his final drive against the Greeks in July 1922, capturing Afyon at the end of August and finally taking Smyrna in a bitter battle from 9 to 13 September. He then began an advance on Istanbul and negotiated the Convention of Mundania (3–11 October), by the terms of which the Allies agreed to withdraw their garrison from Istanbul. The last sultan departed Constantinople on 17 November 1922. The nationalists had won their War of Independence.

Kemal moved quickly to consolidate his triumph. By July 1923, he received international confirmation of his victory in the Treaty of Lausanne. In effect the Treaty of Sèvres was abrogated by the same powers that had imposed it on Turkey in 1920. The odious conditions of Sèvres were removed. On 29 October 1923, the Turkish national assembly created the Republic of Turkey, with Kemal as its president.

Kemalist Programs

The War of Independence had created a new nation. The victory had removed the chains of the Ottoman past and the shackles of imperialism, but Kemal recognized that more was needed to ensure his victory. Kemal's goal was to emulate success, and that meant westernization of the nation.

From the beginning of the republic to his death, the nation experienced radical changes as Kemalist reforms were enacted. Reforms included the abolition of the sultanate and caliphate, the introduction of the secular state, the westernization of the judicial system, the establishment of women's rights (including voting), the replacement of the Arabic alphabet with a Latin version, the acceptance of Western social and cultural lifestyles, and the adoption of Western economic and business standards.

To appreciate the enormity and rapidity of the Kemalist reforms, one not only would have to understand the empire's history, but also have some knowledge of Islam. In Islam there is no separation between secular and religious activities. Kemal's reforms challenged a way of life that had governed Turks for centuries, but he persevered and created a new way of life.

Kemal's program involved six guideposts: nationalism, republicanism, secularization, populism, statism, and reformism. The first three elements of his program had been seen in the war for independence (i.e., the subsequent establishment of the Republic and its secular reforms), but the last three require a brief explanation. Populism in its simplest form meant the abolition of privilege. Every Turk, no matter his station in life, was now equal before the law. Statism involved Kemal's effort to build the economic base of Turkey. In this program the state became a major player in economic development. The last element of his program was reformism. There he sought to continue the evolution of reform in the future. Kemal knew revolutions and their cycles. He warned that, historically, today's reformers become tomorrow's defenders of the status quo. Mustafa Kemal Atatürk tenaciously advocated reform until his death in 1938. His legacy is the modern Republic of Turkey.

J. E. WADE

SEE ALSO: Allenby, Edmund Henry Hynman; Balkan Wars; Ottoman Empire; Turkic Empire; World War I.

Bibliography

Berkes, N. 1964. *The development of secularism in Turkey*. Montreal: McGill Univ. Press.

Bodurgil, A. 1974. *Atatürk and Turkey: A bibliography, 1919–1938*. Washington, D.C.: Library of Congress.

Kinross, P. B. 1965. *Atatürk: A bibliography of Mustafa Kemal, father of modern Turkey*. New York: Morrow.

Lewis, B. 1961. *The emergence of modern Turkey*. London: Oxford Univ. Press.

Yalman, A. E. 1956. *Turkey in my time*. Norman, Okla.: Univ. of Oklahoma Press.

KESSELRING, ALBERT [1885–1960]

Field Marshal Albert Kesselring was a prominent German field commander of World War II. Although he was actually a Luftwaffe (air force) officer, Kesselring is noted for his superlative performance and conduct of the essentially ground operations of the Italian campaigns of 1943–45. As a result, Kesselring has been lauded as one of the most formidable technicians of war known to the twentieth century.

Early Life and Career

Albert Kesselring was born on 30 November 1885 in Bayreuth, Bavaria, where his father served on the town education committee. He studied at the local Classical Grammar School in 1904, but early in his youth decided on a career as a professional soldier. Kesselring later observed, "I wanted to be a soldier, indeed I was set on it, and looking back I can say that I was always a soldier heart and soul."

In 1904, Kesselring enlisted in the 2d Bavarian Foot Artillery as an officer candidate. Except for attendance at the Military Academy (1905–1906) and the Artillery School (1909–10), he served with his regiment in Munich until the outbreak of World War I.

Kesselring's service during the Great War was primarily as a staff officer. He served successively as adjutant in two Bavarian artillery units until the end of 1917, when he became a general staff officer and served on the eastern front. There, Kesselring conducted local armistice negotiations with a Russian counterpart. At the end of the war, Kesselring was serving on the Sixth Army staff at Lille, and in the immediate postwar years he served in the Bavarian army.

Kesselring was fortunate in being selected to serve in the 100,000-man Reichswehr (limited in size by the Treaty of Versailles), and after service as an artillery battery commander, returned to the staff. He was instrumental in designing the Luftwaffe and the panzer (armored) forces. In 1929, Kesselring was assigned to the Army Personnel Office in Berlin, and the following year he received two promotions, first to lieutenant colonel and then to colonel. In 1931, he returned to the troops as commander of the 4th Artillery Regiment in Dresden.

The advent of Adolf Hitler as chancellor of Germany in January 1933 provided the impetus for the clandestine establishment of the Luftwaffe. Kesselring, one of the first army officers to be transferred to the fledgling German air force, became an air commodore and learned to fly at age 48. The existence of the Luftwaffe was officially announced in March 1935, with Kesselring receiving promotion to major general in 1936 while continuing to urge the inauguration of a general staff for the air arm.

The Luftwaffe general staff was instituted on 1 August 1936, and Kesselring became chief of staff on 15 August 1936. Kesselring became embroiled in controversy over the issue of allocation of resources to strategic or tactical air forces and also over a power struggle with Gen. Erhard Milch, state secretary for aviation. Amid a Luftwaffe structural reorganization, Kesselring resigned as chief of staff only to receive an important command. Kesselring was only biding his time for more favorable political circumstances.

Kesselring's *Luftkreis* III was converted into 1st Group Command on 1 April 1939, which a year later became the First Air Fleet. His command then comprised a majority of the German air forces.

World War II

Kesselring energetically led his forces in support of Army Group North in the invasion of Poland in September 1939. He was largely responsible for eliminating resistance in Warsaw and received the Knight's Cross of the Iron Cross for his achievements during the first month of the war.

The relief of the commander of the Second Air Fleet early in 1940 was fortuitous for Kesselring, who succeeded to this command in the west. In the invasion of Holland in May 1940, Kesselring's command not only supported Army Group B in its blitzkrieg attack, but also conducted revolutionary airborne and glider-borne assaults. After the subjugation of France, the Battle of Britain began, and Kesselring's forces were initially so successful that, in recognition thereof, on 19 July 1940 he was promoted to field marshal.

Kesselring was informed in late 1940 of the plan to invade the Soviet Union, and he commanded the air fleet in support of Army Group Center's main attack when Operation Barbarossa commenced on 22 June 1941. Three months later it was determined that a stronger German presence was needed in the Mediterranean region, and Kesselring was reassigned to Italy in November 1941. He became commander in chief south, making him the superior of Gen. Erwin Rommel, commander of the German Afrika Korps.

With little guidance, Kesselring attempted to develop a strategy for his area of operations, although at this time he considered himself and his command as little more than a conduit for supplies for Rommel. This situation changed dramatically after the Allied invasion of North Africa on 8 November 1942. Stubborn delaying actions were fought in North Africa until the German evacuation on 12 May 1943.

The inevitable Allied invasion of Sicily (which occurred on 10 July 1943) was complicated for the Germans by the overthrow of Italian dictator Benito Mussolini two weeks later. On 1 September 1943 the Italians concluded an armistice with the Allies.

The Allies invaded the Italian mainland on 9 September 1943. On 21 November 1943, Kesselring was selected, over his now-rival Rommel, to be commander in chief of Army Group C and commander in chief southwest in Italy. By mid-January 1944, he had 21 divisions under his command. He tenaciously and skillfully defended the Italian peninsula against the Allied armies commanded by, first, Gen. (later Field Marshal Earl) Harold Alexander (until 12 December 1944), then by Lt. Gen. (later Gen.) Mark W. Clark.

On 8 March 1945, Kesselring succeeded Field Marshal Gerd von Rundstedt as commander in chief west. At this late stage the German surrender was only a matter of time.

Aftermath

Kesselring was imprisoned by the Allies after the German surrender. He was brought to trial in February 1947 for the murder of 355 civilians in the Ardeatine Caves in March 1944. Found guilty, Kesselring was condemned to death by shooting, but the sentence was later commuted to life imprisonment. He wrote his *Memoirs* (first published in 1953) while in prison. Kesselring was released from captivity in July 1952 when it was discovered he had throat cancer. He died on 20 July 1960.

Field Marshal Albert Kesselring, nicknamed "Smiling Albert" because of his omnipresent grin, had a rare blend of character and competence that permitted him to be the consummate staff officer as well as a dynamic, imaginative, and charismatic commander. At his funeral, Kesselring was fittingly eulogized by his former chief of staff as "a man of admirable strength of character whose care was for the soldiers of all ranks."

HAROLD E. RAUGH, JR.

SEE ALSO: Alexander, Harold Rupert Leofric George; Rommel, Erwin; World War II.

Bibliography

Blaxland, G. 1979. *Alexander's generals.* London: Kimber.
Clark, M. 1950. *Calculated risk.* New York: Harper and Row.
Irving, D. 1973. *The life of Erhard Milch.* London: Weidenfeld & Nicolson.
Jackson, W. G. F. 1967. *The battle for Italy.* London: Batsford.
————. 1972. *Alexander of Tunis as military commander.* New York: Dodd, Mead.
Kesselring, A. 1953. *Memoirs.* London: Kimber.
Linklater, E. 1977. *The campaign in Italy.* London: Her Majesty's Stationery Office.
Macksey, K. 1978. *Kesselring.* New York: David McKay.
Mason, H. M. 1973. *The rise and fall of the Luftwaffe.* London: Cassell.
Shepperd, G. A. 1968. *The Italian campaign, 1943–45.* New York: Praeger.

KHALID IBN AL-WALID [d. A.D. 642]

Known as "Chaledos" in the Byzantine chronicles, Khalid was an outstanding general, widely regarded as the preeminent war leader of the early Muslim conquests. His prowess in battle earned him the nickname *Sayf Allah* ("Sword of Allah"). He played a central role in the Muslim subjugation of Mesopotamia and Syria in the seventh century.

Background and Early Career

Of noble birth, Khalid was of the *banu-Quraysh*, the Prophet Muhammad's tribe, and a member of one of Mecca's wealthiest and most influential clans. His father, however, was sharply opposed to the nascent Islamic movement. In A.D. 625 the followers of the Prophet in Medina gained a victory over the nonbelieving Meccans at Badr. Seeking revenge the Meccans, including Khalid, who served as a subcommander, confronted the Muslims at Medina and taunted them by pasturing their horses and camels in the Medinans' field of unharvested grain near the hill of Uhud. When the Muslims attacked to drive the interlopers away from their crops, young Khalid led a successful local counterattack. Despite this success the Meccans lost the battle, but the Uhud fight established Khalid's reputation among his Muslim enemies as a tough, natural military genius.

About the time of the Muslim success at the Battle of the Trench (627), or shortly afterward, Khalid embraced Islam and joined the Muslim forces that conquered Mecca in 629. Although his conversion appears to have been opportunistic, Khalid soon demonstrated that he was an efficient, ruthless cavalry commander.

In the "War of Apostasy," or *riddah*, that followed Muhammad's death in 632, the Prophet's successor, Caliph Abu Bakr, dispatched eleven armies throughout Arabia to reestablish Muslim hegemony among tribes that were in revolt, led by "false prophets." In the military operations against the rebels (632–633) the most prominent commander was Khalid, leading the reconquest in the north and east. His ruthlessness shocked the caliph and Omar, who later succeeded Abu Bakr as caliph, but Khalid's success was such that he received only mild rebukes. His victory at Akraba (633) ended the Arab civil war and set the stage for the first expansion of Islam.

Operations in Syria and Palestine

When the traditional Arab border raids along the Arabian-Sassanid Persian (Iraqi) frontier became fused with the emerging Islamic *jihad*, Khalid led a raiding force into Iraq, conquering al-Hira (633). Tribute from al-Hira, along with that imposed on neighboring Sassanid districts, helped offset the loss of trade caused by the *riddah*. At the same time Khalid raided Iraq, another Arab army under Amr ibn al-As invaded Syria and Palestine, the eastern provinces of the Byzantine Empire.

In 634 several more Arab raiding columns entered Syria to reap supposedly easy pickings. The Arabs thrust into southern Palestine in search of booty, avoiding the still-formidable Byzantine *turmae* posted there. (A *turma* was the Byzantine equivalent of the old Roman legion.) However, Byzantine intelligence of the Arabs' operations was excellent, and the Byzantine *turmae* prepared to engage the interlopers. Discovering that the Syrian forces of Byzantine emperor Heraclius were seeking battle, the expeditionary leaders requested reinforcements from Abu Bakr. Having foresworn the military services of apostates, the caliph could find no forces at home to dispatch to Palestine and so sent for Khalid, still raiding in Iraq.

The urgency of Abu Bakr's message caused Khalid with 500 picked men to make a legendary forced march across 500 kilometers (300 mi.) of Syrian desert, reaching the Byzantine eastern frontier in the vicinity of Palmyra in eighteen days. Khalid's first military encounter in Syria was with a strong force of Byzantine auxiliaries, whom he defeated at their camp in Marj Rahit on the plain of Damascus (spring 634). He then joined forces with Amr ibn al-As, and the combined armies inflicted a crushing defeat on a Byzantine *thema* (two or three *turmae*) in July 634 at Ajnadayn on the Gaza-Jerusalem road. Following this victory, Khalid occupied Busra in the Hawran, south of Damascus. Another successful engagement at Fihl (January 635) gave the Arabs control of one of the most strategically important crossings of the Jordan River.

Khalid next moved his army toward Damascus, taking Marj al-Suffar en route. The six-month Muslim siege of Damascus that followed seems to have been brought to resolution by Khalid's conspiring with a disaffected monk within the city walls. Damascus surrendered to Khalid on 4 September 635. Following this, Khalid apparently led the columns that reduced Baalbek, Homs, and Hamah in rapid succession.

Alarmed, Heraclius ordered his general Theodore to marshal a major army—estimated at about 50,000—to deal a decisive blow to Khalid's force. Khalid fell back on a defensive position at the junction of the Yarmuk River within a defile known now as the Deraa Gap, near the southeastern shore of the Sea of Galilee. He positioned his cavalry with their backs to the desert.

When Theodore's Byzantine army attacked (20 August 636), a sandstorm blew up from the desert directly into the eyes of the oncoming Byzantine mass. Khalid's 25,000 men had the wind at their backs. Khalid also was aided by dissension between the Byzantine army's East Roman core and its disaffected Armenian and Arab auxiliaries. Khalid was nominally second in command at this battle—his impetuosity had always irked the new caliph, Omar, who appointed a more manageable commander in chief—but it is believed that Khalid actually directed the maneuvers that resulted in the destruction of the Byzantine army.

After Yarmuk

Khalid's great victory prepared the way for the expulsion of the East Romans from Syria and the consolidation of Arab power in the former Byzantine province (637–645). Khalid was rewarded with the governorship of a part of the new Arab Syrian province, holding this office until his death at Homs, where his tomb can still be viewed.

JAMES J. BLOOM

SEE ALSO: Arab Conquests; Byzantine Empire.

Bibliography

Akram, A. I. 1970. *The sword of Allah: Khalid ibn Al Waleed, his life and campaigns.* Karachi: National Publishing House.
Shaban, M. A. 1971. *Islamic history, A new interpretation* A.D. *600–750.* Vol. 1. London: Cambridge Univ. Press.

KING, ERNEST J. [1878–1956]

Ernest Joseph King, Fleet Admiral, U.S. Navy (Fig. 1), was supreme commander of all U.S. naval forces in World War II and principal naval adviser to President Franklin Roosevelt. As naval member of the Joint Chiefs of Staff and the Combined Chiefs of Staff, he participated in all interservice and international planning for the defeat of Germany and Japan.

Early Life and Career

King was born in Lorain, Ohio, on 23 November 1878. In August 1897 he entered the U.S. Naval Academy in Annapolis, Maryland. The following summer he served on the cruiser USS *San Francisco* and came under fire off Havana.

Figure 1. Adm. Ernest Joseph King. (SOURCE: U.S. Library of Congress)

Graduating in 1901 as a passed midshipman, King attended the Naval Torpedo School in Newport, Rhode Island, served as navigator on the geodetic survey ship *Eagle*, was aide to the admiral on the new battleship USS *Illinois*, and was in charge of a division of 40 enlisted men on the cruiser USS *Cincinnati* in 1903 when he was promoted to ensign. King went to the Far East on the *Cincinnati* and was there during the Russo-Japanese War. In October 1905 he married Martha Rankin Egerton. They had six daughters and one son.

While serving on the battleship USS *Alabama* in 1906, King was promoted to lieutenant. That fall he returned to the U.S. Naval Academy as instructor of ordnance, gunnery, and seamanship. In 1909 he went to sea again as flag secretary to Rear Admiral Osterhaus on the USS *Minnesota*. This duty was interrupted by a brief tour as engineer officer on the battleship USS *New Hampshire*. In 1912 King went back to Annapolis as executive officer of the Naval Engineering Equipment Station. In 1913 he was promoted to lieutenant commander.

World War I

King's first command, in April 1914, was the USS *Terry*, a reserve destroyer. He transferred to a new destroyer, the USS *Cassin*, in July. For a few months he was also aide to Capt. William S. Sims, commander of the Atlantic Fleet Destroyer Flotilla, and then commanded a destroyer division of four ships.

In December 1915 King reported as staff engineer to Vice Adm. Henry T. Mayo, Commander Battleship Force, Atlantic Fleet, and later Commander in Chief, Atlantic Fleet. Promoted to commander in July 1917, King twice traveled to Europe with Mayo during World War I to confer with British officials and inspect U.S. naval units. He received the Navy Cross and the temporary rank of captain.

King reopened the Naval Postgraduate School at Annapolis as commandant in the spring of 1919. His next command was a refrigerator supply ship, the USS *Bridge*. In 1922, with the permanent rank of captain, he took a four-month course at the submarine school in New London, Connecticut, and then was given command of a four-submarine division. He was commander of the submarine base in New London when he came to public attention as commander of the unprecedented operation that, under very difficult conditions, raised the submarine S-51, which had been rammed by a steamer and sunk off Block Island on 24 September 1925.

From submarines King went to naval aviation, as commander of the seaplane tender USS *Wright* from July 1926 to August 1928. He earned his wings at Pensacola, Florida, on 26 May 1927.

When the submarine S-4 was rammed and sunk off Provincetown, Massachusetts, in December 1927, King was abruptly summoned to command the effort to rescue the crew. The attempt had to be abandoned when a winter gale struck, and the rescue became another difficult salvage operation.

After serving briefly as temporary Commander, Aircraft Squadrons, Atlantic, King became assistant to the Chief of the Bureau of Aeronautics, Rear Adm.

William A. Moffett. In less than a year he became commander of the Norfolk Air Base in Virginia. In 1930 came a command he had eagerly sought, the aircraft carrier USS *Lexington*. From there he went to the senior course at the Naval War College in Newport. When Admiral Moffett died in the crash of the dirigible *Akron* in April 1933, King, now rear admiral, was made Chief of the Bureau of Aeronautics. Three years later he became Commander, Aircraft, Base Force, with responsibility for land- and sea-based patrol planes. In January 1938 he became Commander, Aircraft, Battle Force, with three aircraft carriers including the *Lexington*, all in the Pacific.

King's career-long hopes of the navy's top post, Chief of Naval Operations (CNO), were dashed in 1939, when Adm. Harold Stark was selected. King went to the Navy's General Board, one of ten admirals at the end of their careers who devoted full time to studying naval problems and advising the secretary of the navy, but his stay was brief.

World War II

In 1940 King accompanied outgoing Secretary Charles Edison and new Secretary Frank Knox on inspection trips. This led to a brief appointment as Commander, Patrol Force, U.S. Fleet. In January 1941, with the rank of vice admiral and soon admiral, King became commander of the new Atlantic Fleet, increasingly involved in assisting Great Britain with convoying and antisubmarine patrols. In August 1941 President Roosevelt traveled on King's flagship, the heavy cruiser USS *Augusta*, to Argentia, Newfoundland, and held meetings with British Prime Minister Winston Churchill.

After the Japanese attack on Pearl Harbor on 7 December 1941, King was called to Washington, D.C. On 30 December Roosevelt appointed him Commander in Chief, U.S. Fleet (CominCh), in supreme command of all naval operating forces. The division of tasks and responsibilities between CominCh and the CNO soon proved so uncertain that conflicts arose. In March 1942 Roosevelt sent Stark to England as Commander in Chief, U.S. Naval Forces, Europe, and made King both CominCh and CNO. As CominCh King was the principal naval adviser to the president on the conduct of the war and commander of all operating forces. As CNO he was responsible for the preparation, readiness, and logistic support of those forces. No U.S. naval officer had ever been given so much authority and responsibility. Few if any could have exercised it so well.

In 1943 King added another responsibility. To centralize all aspects of the antisubmarine war against German U-boats, he created the Tenth Fleet. Because no one else seemed to be available, he retained command of it himself.

Throughout his career King had been preparing for this wartime job, not only by personal experience in many areas but also by making a serious study of both sea and land warfare, in theory and in practice. As CominCh-CNO and as naval member of the U.S. Joint Chiefs of Staff and the U.S.-British Combined Chiefs of Staff, King contributed with professional expertise to strategic planning for the defeat of both Germany and Japan. He agreed with the decision that

Germany must be defeated first, but he insisted that pressure on Japan must be maintained and increased; he saw to it that as much materiel and men as possible went to the Pacific forces and that they advanced steadily north and west. Thus, when Germany surrendered, the defeat of Japan was only a few months behind.

On 13 December 1944, King was given the five-star rank of Fleet Admiral. Shortly after Japan's surrender in September 1945, on King's initiative, the post of Commander in Chief, U.S. Fleet, was abolished. King remained CNO until 15 December, when Fleet Adm. Chester W. Nimitz relieved him. King died in Portsmouth, New Hampshire, on 15 June 1956.

GRACE P. HAYES

SEE ALSO: Nimitz, Chester William; World War II.

Bibliography

Buell, T. B. 1980. *Master of sea power.* Boston: Little, Brown.
King, E. J., and W. M. Whitehill. 1976. *Fleet admiral King: A naval record.* New York: Norton.

KONEV, IVAN STEPANOVICH [1897–1973]

Marshal of the Soviet Union Konev—front commander in World War II, postwar deputy minister of defense, and commander of groups of Soviet forces in Eastern Europe—was one of the premier Soviet field commanders. Konev also served as a candidate member of the Central Committee (CC) of the Communist party of the Soviet Union (CPSU) from 1929 to 1952 and as a full member of the CC CPSU from 1952 to 1973. Konev was a delegate to the first through eighth sessions of the Supreme Soviet of the USSR.

Early Life

Konev was born on 16 (O.S.; 28 N.S.) December 1897, in the village of Lodeino (currently in the Podosinov raion of Kirov oblast) to Russian peasants. In 1916 he joined the Russian army and served as a junior NCO in an artillery battalion on the southwestern front. After demobilization in 1918, he joined the Communist party and served first as a member of the *Nikol'skii uezd* executive (*Volgodskii gubernia*), then as its military commissar following his induction into the Red Army in 1918. During the civil war Konev served as the military commissar of an armored train, infantry brigade, and infantry division, and then as a staff officer of the People's Revolutionary Army of the Far East Republic in Siberia opposite Kolchak, Semenov, and the Japanese intervention forces. While a delegate to the Tenth Congress of the Peasant and Workers Party (Bolshevik), Konev participated in crushing the Kronstadt revolt (1920). After the civil war Konev was political commissar of the XVII Maritime Rifle Corps.

He graduated from a command training course (1926), then commanded at the regimental (1926–30) and divisional (1930–32) levels. Konev graduated from the Frunze (command and staff) Academy in 1934, then commanded an infantry division (1934–37) and an infantry corps (1937–38). From 1938 to 1940 Konev commanded the Second Detached Red Banner Far East Army; in 1940 Lieutenant General Konev commanded first the Transbaikal, then the North Caucasus, Military Districts.

World War II

Konev's wartime exploits were marked by a bitter rivalry with Marshal Zhukov, which continued after the war. At the outbreak of World War II Konev was commanding the Nineteenth Army, which unsuccessfully defended Smolensk against the German invaders. In September 1941, Colonel General Konev assumed command of the Western Army Group (AG), which suffered serious reverses in the Battle for Moscow. He was relieved of command (10 October 1941) and replaced by Zhukov. A week later the Twenty-ninth, Thirtieth, and Twenty-second armies were combined to reconstitute the Kalinin AG (KAG), and Konev took command. The KAG launched the Soviet counteroffensive at Moscow on 5 December. From August 1942 to February 1943, Konev once again commanded the Western AG. During his command of the Steppe AG (July–October 1943) Konev's troops fought in the pivotal Battle of Kursk (21 July–23 August 1943) and the counteroffensive (Operation Rumiantsev) that liberated Belgorod and Kharkov (3–23 August). Konev commanded the 2d Ukrainian Army Group (2d UAG) (October 1943–May 1944) during the Korsun-Shchevchenkovskii operation (24 January–17 February 1944), which destroyed a large German force formed from Manstein's "South" group of armies and liberated the right bank of the Dnepr River. As commander of the 1st UAG (May 1944–May 1945), Konev was involved in the Lvov-Sandomir offensive (July 1944), the Vistula-Oder operation (12 January–7 February 1945), the Battle for Berlin (16 April–2 May 1945), and the liberation of Prague (one of his subsidiary tank forces occupied the city on 9 May). The Lvov-Sandomir offensive pitted Konev's 1st UAG against the German Northern UAG. Konev's force liberated the western Ukraine and southern Poland, captured Lvov, and established a beachhead across the Vistula River at Sandomir. The Vistula-Oder operation was the largest single Soviet operation in World War II. Fought by Zhukov's 1st Belorussian Army Group (BAG) and Konev's 2d UAG, the Soviets broke out of the Sandomir beachhead to destroy German forces between the Vistula and Oder rivers and created a similar beachhead across the Oder-Neisse River. The Berlin operation, which added a third force (Rokossovskii's 2d BAG to pin down German forces in the north on Zhukov's flank), performed a massive encirclement that surrounded, isolated, and destroyed the defending German Vistula AG and captured Berlin on 2 May. The Allies accepted a German unconditional surrender six days later. Stalin did not assign either commander the responsibility for actually capturing the city; instead he allowed the fierce rivalry between Konev and Zhukov to spur the attack along. Konev was the first to enter Berlin. He was promoted to marshal of the Soviet Union on 20 February 1944 (a rank he held until his death), was twice awarded Hero of the Soviet Union (29 July 1944 and 1 June 1945), and was one of only eleven commanders awarded the diamond-encrusted Order of Victory.

Postwar Career

Konev held a series of senior command positions in the Soviet Union and groups of Soviet forces in Eastern Europe following the war. From 1945–46 Konev was commander in chief (CINC) of occupation forces in Hungary and Austria; as such, he served as CINC of the Central Group of Forces (Hungary) and as supreme commissioner of Austria. In 1946 Konev became CINC, Ground Forces, Soviet Army and deputy minister of the armed forces (MAF). Four years later he was appointed chief inspector of the Soviet Army and deputy minister of defense (MAF was renamed Ministry of Defense in 1950). In 1951 Konev took command of the Carpathian Military District. Under Khrushchev he returned to Moscow in 1955 to become once again CINC, Ground Forces and deputy minister of defense (DMOD). The following year Konev was elevated to first DMOD and CINC, Warsaw Pact. Konev supported Khrushchev's ouster and exile of his rival, Marshal Zhukov, in 1957. In 1960 Konev became chief inspector of the General Inspectorate of the Ministry of Defense (GIMD), a semiretired position. During the Berlin crisis (1961), however, Konev was brought in to command the Group of Soviet Forces, Germany. He returned to the GIMD in April of 1962, where he served until his death on 21 May 1973; he was buried in the walls of the Kremlin. Konev was named Hero of the Czechoslovakian SSR (1970), the Ukrainian SSR (1970), and the Mongolian People's Republic (1971).

He was the author of *Sorok Piatyi* ['45] (published in 1970) and *Zapiski komanduiushchego frontom, 1943–44* [*Notes of a Senior Commander at the Front 1943–44*] (published in 1972). In an article entitled *Nachalo Moskovskoi bitvy* [*Beginning of the Battle of Moscow*] (*Voenno-istoricheskii zhurnal*, no. 10, 1966) Konev finally rebutted Zhukov's contention that he had been relieved of his command of the WAG in October 1941 when Zhukov replaced him.

DIANNE L. SMITH

SEE ALSO: Civil War, Russian; Manstein, Erich von; World War II; Zhukov, Georgi Konstantinovich.

Bibliography

Bialer, S., ed. 1969. *Stalin and his generals*. New York: Pegasus.
Erickson, J. 1975. *The road to Stalingrad*. London: George Weidenfeld and Nicolson.
———. 1985. *The road to Berlin*. London: George Weidenfeld and Nicolson.
Ziemke, E. 1968. *Stalingrad to Berlin: The German defeat in the East*. Washington, D.C.: U.S. Army Center of Military History.

KOREAN WAR (1950–53)

When Japan surrendered in World War II, a hurried Allied agreement (15 August 1945) established the 38th degree of latitude as an arbitrary dividing line, north of which the USSR would accept surrender of Japanese forces in Korea; Japanese south of the line would surrender to U.S. troops. Following the surrender, the USSR held the 38th parallel to be a political boundary, and dropped the Iron Curtain along it.

After two years of unsuccessful attempts to reach agreement on the unification of Korea, the United States referred the problem to the United Nations (UN). The UN proposed to establish an independent Korean government following free nationwide elections, but the USSR refused to cooperate. Consequently, the Republic of Korea was established in the southern zone (15 August 1947), with Seoul its capital. Declaring the action illegal, the USSR set up the Democratic People's Republic of Korea and organized a North Korean Army (NKA). Soviet troops allegedly evacuated the north in December 1948. U.S. troops completed evacuation of the south in June 1949; a small American military advisory group remained to reorganize a Republic of Korea (ROK) Army. In the following year, a barrage of Communist propaganda, raids, sabotage, terrorism, and guerrilla action was directed against the south, without breaking down the ROK government.

The Opposing Forces

Communist North Korea had a well-trained, Soviet-equipped army with a core composed of 25,000 veterans of the Chinese Communist campaign in Manchuria. The air force consisted of some 180 Soviet planes of World War II type. There were more than 100,000 trained reserves.

The ROK Army—little more than a national police force—consisted of about 100,000 men in eight divisions with little supporting artillery. It lacked medium and heavy artillery, tanks, combat aircraft, and reserves. Naval strength on both sides was negligible.

Operations

1950

On 25 June, North Korean forces crossed the border, driving on Seoul. Surprise was complete; the invaders broke through scattered resistance by elements of the ROK Army. Their objective was to seize the capital and occupy South Korea, thus presenting the free world with a fait accompli.

In reaction, the UN Security Council met in an emergency session (the USSR boycotted the Council) and called for an immediate end to hostilities and withdrawal of the NKA, asking member nations to assist. Meanwhile, President Truman (27 June) ordered Gen. Douglas MacArthur, commanding U.S. forces in the Far East, to support the ROK defense with air and sea forces. MacArthur effected a naval blockade of the North Korean coast and furnished air support. Reconnoitering the front in person (28 June), as Seoul fell, he reported the ROK Army to be incapable of stopping the invasion even with U.S. air support. Truman authorized the use of U.S. ground troops on 30 June.

Aside from the vessels of the U.S. Seventh Fleet and the Far East Air Force (8½ combat groups), U.S. ground forces in Japan consisted of four understrength divisions organized in two skeleton army corps. Infantry and artillery units were at two-thirds strength in personnel and cannon and short of antitank weapons. Corps troops, such as medium tanks, artillery, and other supporting arms, did not exist. On 30 June, the 24th Division (under Maj. Gen. William F. Dean) began movement piecemeal by sea and air into Korea.

One understrength battalion (two infantry companies) with one battery of artillery joined the ROK Army near Osan on 4 July. The next morning an NKA division with 30 tanks attacked. The ROK troops fled, but the battalion, completely surrounded, held out for seven hours. Then, ammunition exhausted, the survivors cut their way out, abandoning all materiel.

Between 6 and 21 July, the 24th Division partly snubbed the NKA advance down the peninsula, trading terrain for time while the 1st Cavalry and 25th Infantry divisions were being rushed from Japan. A five-day action at Taejon (16–20 July) ended when the NKA assaulted the 24th Division from three directions. Dean, personally commanding his rear guard while the remainder of his division withdrew, was captured. On 22 July his battered troops were relieved by the 1st Cavalry Division, while the 25th Division, on its right, together with reorganized ROK divisions slowed the NKA advance.

In response to a Security Council request to establish a unified command under a U.S. officer, President Truman named MacArthur commander in chief, UN Command, on 7 July. Lt. Gen. Walton H. Walker, commanding the U.S. Eighth Army, stabilized his defense on a thinly held line that ran north for 145 kilometers (90 mi.) along the Naktong River from Tsushima Strait to Taegu, and then east for 97 kilometers (60 mi.) to the Sea of Japan. The area embraced the southeast corner of the Korean peninsula, including Pusan, the one available port. In the north, five ROK divisions attempted to contain the invaders. The western flank, where the weight of the incessant NKA attacks fell, was held by U.S. troops, now including two additional infantry regiments and a Marine brigade. The Seventh Fleet protected both sea flanks and harassed NKA movements along the coast, while the Far East Air Force (augmented by an Australian group), together with carrier-based naval air, hammered at NKA lines of communication and furnished much-needed close support. Walker was able to shift a mobile reserve from point to point within the perimeter as the NKA attacks nibbled at his front. Several penetrations of the Naktong River line and a 132-kilometer (20-mi.) NKA advance in the north (August 26) were checked. NKA forces, estimated at fourteen infantry divisions supported by several tank regiments, continued a series of uncoordinated assaults all around the perimeter. A three-division attack in the north on 3 September necessitated committing the entire UN reserve (the 24th Infantry Division) north of Kyongju.

Arrival of the U.K. 27th Infantry Brigade (14 September) compensated for the withdrawal of the marine brigade, which was joining the 1st Marine Division for the Inchon landing.

MacArthur's plan for regaining the initiative in Korea and driving Communist forces from the south hinged on an amphibious landing at the port of Inchon, near Seoul. A successful assault there would cut Communist supply lines and compromise their entire military position in South Korea, at the same time avoiding a slow and costly overland advance from the Pusan perimeter.

At dawn on 15 September, the U.S. X Corps (Maj. Gen. Edward M. Almond commanding) began landing over the difficult and treacherous beaches at Inchon. The 1st Marine Division swept through slight opposition, securing Kimpo airport on 17 September. The 7th Infantry Division, following the Marines ashore, turned south, cutting the railroad and highway supplying the NKA in the south, and Seoul was surrounded.

Simultaneously, the Eighth Army broke out of the Pusan Perimeter, the 1st Cavalry Division leading. The NKA, its supplies cut off, and menaced from front and rear, disintegrated. The 1st Cavalry and 7th Infantry divisions met as Seoul was liberated on 26 September.

On 1 October, as directed by the United Nations and President Truman, MacArthur ordered ROK troops north across the 38th parallel. The Eighth Army followed on 9 October, leaving two divisions in the southern area to secure communication lines to Pusan and mop up remnants of the NKA. Pyongyang, the North Korean capital, was overrun (20 October) by a combined airborne landing and overland advance. But a serious military handicap was the injunction prohibiting UN aircraft from flying north of the Yalu River, in order not to provoke the Communist Chinese. The ROK 6th Division reached the Yalu River at Chosan and other ROK units fanned out behind it. By this time, other UN token forces had joined the Eighth Army and were integrated in existing U.S. divisional elements: a Turkish brigade and Canadian, Australian, Philippine, Dutch, and Thai battalions.

Reembarked at Inchon on 16 October, the X Corps was moved around to Wonsan on the east coast, which had already been captured by the ROK I Corps. A seven-day delay in landing was necessary to sweep the harbor clear of Soviet mines, which had been sown under the direction of Soviet experts with the NKA.

Peking had threatened intervention should UN troops cross the 38th parallel, and heavy concentrations of Chinese Communist troops were reported just north of the Yalu. MacArthur knew neither the full strength nor the dispositions of these troops, nor was he aware that Chinese in considerable numbers had already infiltrated south of the Yalu. On 1 November, the forward ROK divisions were ambushed by these Chinese divisions and a U.S. regiment at Unsan was severely mauled. Walker recalled his leading Eighth Army units and consolidated temporarily along the Chongchon River.

MacArthur's intention was still to advance up the entire front of the peninsula, the X Corps on the east coast, the Eighth Army on the west. The X Corps would turn west at the Yalu, making a sweeping envelopment, and drive all enemy forces south of the border against the Eighth Army. Since the rugged, desolate central massif precluded mutual support, the UN formations acted independently, their control and coordination directed by MacArthur in Tokyo. Almond's X Corps now consisted of the U.S. 1st Marine and 3d and 7th Army infantry divisions and the ROK I Corps (3d and Capital Divisions). The Eighth Army, nine divisions strong, was grouped in three army corps: from left to right the U.S. I and IX and the ROK II. The total combat strength of the entire command was about 200,000 men with perhaps 150,000 more in support functions in the rear. In addition to the ROK corps, some 21,000 more Korean troops were attached to or integrated in U.S. units.

MacArthur had believed that Communist China would not enter the conflict unless Manchuria itself were invaded. Truman, who had met with MacArthur at Wake Island on 15 October, knew this, and the U.S. Central Intelligence Agency held the same opinion. Yet now Chinese troops were in Korea. Since reconnaissance north of the Yalu was prohibited, MacArthur decided the only remaining course was to clarify the situation by a bold advance. Meanwhile, the X Corps had thrust north, widely distributed over an immense front. The ROK Capital Division had reached Chongjin on the coast and the U.S. 7th Division was on the Yalu at Hyesanjin.

MacArthur's "reconnaissance in force" with the Eighth Army began on 24 November. After advancing for 24 hours against practically no opposition, the Eighth Army was suddenly struck a massive blow on 25–26 November, the main effort being directed against its right flank. Some 180,000 Chinese troops, in 18 divisions, shattered and ripped through the ROK II Corps, hit the U.S. 2d Division on the right flank of the IX Corps, and threatened envelopment of the entire army. The 2d Division, attempting to reconstitute its right flank, fell into an ambush at Kunu-ri as the Chinese envelopment trapped its columns while passing through a defile in march order. Some 4,000 men and most of the divisional artillery were lost while trying to fight their way out. Walker threw in his reserves, the U.S. 1st Cavalry Division and the Turkish and 27th Commonwealth brigades. They staved off the envelopment, the Turks in particular taking heavy losses, and the Eighth Army managed to disengage. By 5 December, the Eighth Army, its right flank restored, had completely extricated itself, and the Chinese Communist drive was beginning to lose momentum (Fig. 1). The central and east-coast areas were wide open and a stronger defensive position was essential. Walker accordingly withdrew to the general line of the 38th parallel, slightly north of Seoul and some 130 miles below the 24 November situation. There, as the year ended, the Eighth Army awaited a new Communist offensive.

In the eastern zone, an additional 120,000 Chinese troops, advancing on both sides of the Chosin reservoir, isolated the 1st Marine Division and drove in elements of the 3d and 7th divisions, starting on 27 November. The ROK troops on the coastal flank were hurriedly withdrawn without much molestation. MacArthur then ordered evacuation of the entire force, since the Communist drive, directed on the ports of Hungnam and Wonsan, threatened its piecemeal destruction. The 1st Marine Division, under Maj. Gen. Oliver

Figure 1. Troops of the 24th Infantry Regiment leaving the Kunu-ri area in December 1950 for the Chongchon River bridge to confront the Chinese. (SOURCE: R. Dudley/77th ECC)

Smith, consolidated south of the Chosin reservoir. Surrounded by eight Chinese divisions, General Smith, announcing to his division that they were not retreating, but "attacking in another direction," moved southeast on Hungnam, supplied by the Far East Air Force. When the Communists destroyed the one bridge across a gorge otherwise impassable for the division's trucks and tanks, bridging material was flown in by air and the Marine southward "advance" continued. Thirteen days of running fight ended on 9 December when a relief column of 3d Division troops met the Marine vanguard outside the Hungnam perimeter.

Despite continued Communist attacks on both ports, evacuation by air and by sea went smoothly from 5 to 15 December. U.S. Air Force and Navy carrier-plane support, together with naval gunfire, facilitated the final embarkation.

Walker, killed in a jeep accident on 23 December, was replaced by Lt. Gen. Matthew B. Ridgway, who arrived on 26 December. MacArthur gave Ridgway command of all ground operations in Korea, retaining overall ground, air, and sea command.

EARLY 1951

The long-expected Communist assault crossed the 38th parallel at daybreak on 1 January 1951, its main effort in the western zone. Some 400,000 Chinese troops, with an additional 100,000 of the reconstituted NKA, pushed the 200,000-man Eighth Army back almost to Seoul. Then, on 3 January, a heavy penetration in the Chungpyong reservoir area overran the ROK divisions on both flanks of the U.S. 2d Division, which extricated itself only after serious fighting and the commitment of Ridgway's reserve—the 3d and 7th divisions.

Seoul was evacuated on 4 January, the third time the capital had changed hands. Stubborn resistance of ground troops, plus the Far East Air Force's close support and interdiction of the now-exposed Communist lines of communications, slowly checked the momentum of the drive. The UN position had stabilized by 15 January, some 80 kilometers (50 mi.) south of the 38th parallel, from Pyongtaek on the west coast to Samchok on the east.

Ridgway launched a series of limited-objective attacks, slowly driving north from 25 January to 10 February. A Communist counterattack near Chipyong and Wonju (11–18 February) checked the advance in the center, but on the west UN troops reached the outskirts of Seoul.

Operation Ripper, designed primarily to inflict casualties on the enemy, and secondarily to relieve Seoul and eliminate a large Communist supply base built up at Chunchon, opened on 7 March. The main effort, in the center, forced the Communists back. The Han River was crossed east of Seoul. Patrols of the I Corps found Seoul abandoned on 14 March. Chinese resistance then stiffened, but an airborne drop by a reinforced regiment at Munsan on 23 March forced a general Communist retirement. By 31 March, the Eighth Army was back roughly along the old 38th parallel front. MacArthur and Ridgway decided on further advance, toward the "Iron Triangle"—Chorwan-Kumhwa-Pyonggang, the major assembly and supply area and the communications center for the Chinese.

President Truman relieved General MacArthur of his dual command of UN and U.S. forces in the Far East on 11 April 1951. The president was exercising his prerogative as commander in chief. MacArthur was not in sympathy with the policy of limiting the war to the Korean peninsula and had not attempted to conceal his dissatisfaction with the restrictions placed on his operations. Ridgway was appointed in his place and Lt. Gen. James A. Van Fleet was hurried from the United States to command the Eighth Army.

April–December 1951

Aware of Communist preparations for a counteroffensive to blunt the threat to the Iron Triangle, General Van Fleet continued forward movement from 12 to 21 April, prepared to fall back, if necessary, to previously prepared defensive positions. There he planned to contain the enemy by heavy firepower and then counterattack.

The first phase of the expected Communist spring offensive began on 22 April; the first assault broke through the ROK 6th Division west of the Chung-pyong reservoir. The U.S. 24th Division on the left and the 1st Marine Division on the right promptly restored their respective flanks, but the penetration compromised Van Fleet's general position and he began withdrawal of his left—the I and IX Corps. The Chinese main effort developed against the I Corps, north of Seoul. Hasty withdrawal by the ROK 1st Division exposed the flank of the U.K. 27th Brigade on its right, and a battalion of the Gloucester-shire Regiment was cut off. Some 40 men escaped; the remainder were killed or captured. The Communist assault finally lost momentum and came to a pause by 30 April. The Chinese broke contact, retiring beyond UN artillery range. Communist losses in this phase were at least 70,000 men, while Eighth Army casualties were about 7,000.

The second phase of the Communist counteroffensive shifted the weight of their attack to the east. More than 20 Chinese divisions, with NKA divisions on their right and left, struck the right elements of X Corps—the ROK 5th and 7th Divisions. The U.S. 2d Division, next on the left, stood firm, but the ROK III Corps, farther east, went to pieces under heavy assault. The ROK I Corps, on the extreme right, restored its flank against the Communist surge through this wide corridor. The U.S. 2d Division (with French and Dutch battalions attached) and the 1st Marine Division, on the west side, promptly counterattacked. Van Fleet had expected the blow in this area and had already shifted his reserves. Their efforts snubbed the Communist offensive on 20 May. Attacks on the west flank, north of Seoul, and in the center, down the Pukhon River, had been repulsed.

The UN counteroffensive began on 22 May. It was preceded by limited attacks on the far left, anchoring the UN position on the Imjim River north of Munsan. The entire UN front moved north. The ROK Capital and 2d Divisions, on the extreme right, advanced up the east coast with little opposition, reaching Kansong. Advance was slower in the center, but was accelerating by month's end. But the U.S. government ordered Van Fleet to halt. Despite his plea for approval of "hot pursuit" against an enemy on the verge of collapse, the Joint Chiefs of Staff (JCS) refused either increased means or permission for another drive northward. The U.S. government, concerned by Soviet threats, had decided not to risk World War III.

With the advent of the rainy season in early June, Van Fleet decided to establish a defensive belt across Korea, from which he could keep the enemy off balance by a succession of JCS-approved limited-objective moves. Some gains were made at the base of the Iron Triangle and on the southern rim of the "Punchbowl," a fortified circle of hills northwest of Sohwa. Meanwhile, the Communists were organizing in depth to the north.

Soviet ambassador Malik made a cease-fire proposal in the UN on 23 June. It confirmed that the Chinese had been badly hurt in the previous six months' fighting. Estimated enemy losses totaled 200,000 men together with much materiel. UN air attacks also had foiled every attempt to install Communist air bases south of the Yalu. Delegations from both sides met at Kaesong. Negotiations opened in July, and the Communists took advantage of the location of Kaesong (just inside their lines), seizing every opportunity to delay progress while playing for time to recuperate from their mauling. Meanwhile, clashes between patrols and outposts continued all along the firing line as both sides sought to improve their positions. Negotiations broke down completely in late August.

UN forces resumed limited attacks. Van Fleet's troops cleared the Iron Triangle and the Punchbowl, driving the Chinese back from the Hwachon reservoir and the Chorwan-Seoul railway line. These successes brought prompt Communist requests for resumption of armistice discussions.

Discussions resumed on 12 November at Panmunjon, a village between the lines. General Ridgway ordered offensive operations stopped as talks began.

1952–53

While negotiations dragged out interminably at Panmunjon, minor actions flared continually all along the front. General Ridgway, ordered to replace General Eisenhower in command of NATO forces in Europe, was replaced by Gen. Mark W. Clark in May. The Communists continued building up their strength. By year's end an estimated 800,000 Communist ground troops, three-fourths of them Chinese, were in Korea, while heavy shipments of Soviet artillery were brought in.

Communist wranglings at the Panmunjon conferences centered on the disposition of prisoners of war. About 92,000 UN troops had fallen into Communist hands: 80,000 Koreans, 10,000 Americans, and 2,500 from other UN forces. Consensus of reports by returned POWs indicate that about two-thirds of U.S. prisoners died or were killed in the prison camps. No neutral or Red Cross inspections were ever allowed by the Communists. Some 171,000 Communist prisoners had fallen into UN hands—more than 20,000 of them Chinese. About 80,000 were assembled on the island of Koje, just off Pusan.

Meanwhile, along the front, a succession of attacks and counterattacks cost both sides great losses. In October, the negotiations at Panmunjon again broke off, while the war became a political football in the U.S. presidential election. The American people, tired of the struggle, elected Dwight D. Eisenhower, who had promised to bring about an honorable conclusion to the war.

Unexpectedly, but apparently in tune with internal unrest in the Communist world following Stalin's death (5 March), Premier Kim Il Sung of North Korea and Chinese general P'eng Teh-huai agreed to General Clark's previously ignored proposal for mutual exchange of sick and wounded POWs. They also urged resumption of the Panmunjon conferences. Extensive U.S. plans to renew offensive operations and possibly to extend the war were unquestionably major factors in the Communist change of heart. Operation Little Switch, an exchange of 5,800 Communists for 471 ROKs, 149 Americans, and 64 other UN personnel, took place in April.

In May South Korea's president Syngman Rhee flatly refused to become a party to any agreement that left Korea divided. Massive Communist attacks, mostly against ROK troops, began on 10 June to bring U.S. pressure on Syngman Rhee. On 18 June, Rhee demanded that the UN resume the military offensive. At the same time, he released from his own prison camps 27,000 North Korean POWs unwilling to be repatriated. When Rhee released the prisoners, the Communists, accusing the UN of bad faith, again broke off negotiations and on 25 June launched still another offensive against the ROK sector. Some slight gains were made, but quick shifts of U.S. reinforcements and the inability of the Chinese to exploit their penetrations brought the attack to a halt, with loss of some 70,000 Chinese troops.

Negotiations were resumed on 10 July, and a final armistice was hammered out on 27 July 1953.

The Costs

The Korean War cost the UN 118,515 men killed and 264,591 wounded; 92,987 were captured. (A great many of these died of mistreatment or starvation.) The Communist armies suffered at least 1.6 million battle casualties, 60 percent of them Chinese. An additional estimated 400,000 Communists were nonbattle casualties. U.S. casualties in addition to prisoners were 33,629 killed and 103,284 wounded. Of 10,218 Americans who fell into Communist hands, only 3,746 returned; the remainder (except 21 men who refused repatriation) either were murdered or died. In all, 357 UN soldiers (mainly Korean) refused repatriation. South Korea's toll—which can only be estimated—came to 70,000 killed, 150,000 wounded, and 80,000 captured. Approximately 3 million South Korean civilians died from causes directly attributable to the war.

Fourteen UN member nations besides the United States took part in this, the first war in which the UN had engaged. Britain and Turkey each contributed a brigade (each equivalent to half of a division). In addition, the United Kingdom furnished one aircraft carrier, two cruisers, and eight destroyers, with Royal Marine and supporting units. Canada sent one brigade of infantry, one artillery group, and one armored battalion; Australia, two infantry battalions, one air fighter squadron and one transport squadron, one aircraft carrier, two destroyers, and one frigate; Thailand, one regimental combat team; France, one infantry battalion and one gunboat; Greece, one infantry battalion and one air transport squadron; New Zealand, one artillery group and two frigates; Netherlands, one infantry battalion and one destroyer; Columbia, one infantry battalion and one frigate; Belgium and Ethiopia, one infantry battalion each; Luxembourg, one infantry company; and the Union of South Africa, one fighter squadron. All these elements bore themselves well and sustained substantial casualties. In addition, from Denmark, India, Italy, Norway, and Sweden came hospital or field-ambulance noncombat units.

The conflict reaffirmed the critical importance of airpower as an essential ingredient of successful combat; it was also a reminder that airpower alone can neither ensure adequate ground reconnaissance nor bring about the final decision in land warfare. The immediate superiority achieved by the UN in the air necessitated bringing in Soviet MiG-15s—then the latest USSR jet fighters, quite superior to America's F-84 and surpassing in some respects the F-86. MiGs, first seen in Korea in late 1950, and presumably all with Russian pilots, increased in number during 1951, but the training and competence of UN pilots—mostly American—compensated for any inferiority in materiel. While UN pilots were never permitted to pursue the MiGs across the Yalu, they were able to neutralize all Communist efforts to establish airbases south of the river. In air-to-air combat, 1,108 Communist planes were destroyed, including 838 MiG 15s; another 177 were probably destroyed, and an additional 1,027 were severely damaged, against a total UN loss of 114 aircraft. As the war drew to a close, U.S. F-86 jets were downing MiG-15s at the rate of 13 confirmed Communist losses to each F-86 shot down. UN plane losses to Communist antiaircraft fire, while giving magnificent close support to ground troops, were 1,213.

The potential of the helicopter as a new means of mobile transportation was clearly demonstrated. It was excellent for reconnaissance, evacuation of wounded, and rescue work.

American command of the sea was one of the principal handicaps to Communist success. The U.S. Seventh Fleet gave valuable gunfire support along the coast and carried out amphibious operations, while U.S. Navy and Marine air units participated in air force interdiction and close support to ground units. The navy's blockade of the peninsula prevented supply of Communist forces by water. Had it been possible to interdict ground-supply channels from Manchuria and Siberia in similar fashion, the war would have been over in short order.

This war was significant on several counts. It was the first major struggle of the nuclear age. While no nuclear weapons were employed, the threat of the atom bomb hung heavy over all concerned and throttled exploitation of success. It was a war between two differing ideologies, a war of stratagem and deceit in which roadbound superior firepower was canceled out by lighter-armed fluidity over desolate, trackless wastes.

TREVOR N. DUPUY

SEE ALSO: Cold War; History, Modern Military; MacArthur, Douglas A.

Bibliography

Appleman, R. 1961. *South to the Naktong, north to the Yalu*. Washington, D.C.: Government Printing Office.

Blair, C. 1987. *The forgotten war: America in Korea, 1950–1953*. New York: Times Books/Random House.

Cagle, M. W., and F. A. Manson. 1957. *The sea war in Korea*. Annapolis, Md.: U.S. Naval Institute Press.

Cumings, B. 1981. *The origins of the Korean War*. Princeton, N.J.: Princeton Univ. Press.

Futrell, J. A. 1961. *The United States Air Force in Korea 1950–1953*. New York: Duell, Sloan and Pearce.

Gugeler, R. A. 1954. *Combat actions in Korea*. Washington, D.C.: Combat Forces Press.

Hermes, W. G. 1966. *Truce tent and fighting front*. Washington, D.C.: Government Printing Office.

James, D. C. 1985. *The years of MacArthur*. Vol. 3 of *Triumph and disaster, 1945–1964*. Boston: Houghton-Mifflin.

Marshall, S. L. A. 1953. *The river and the gauntlet*. New York: Morrow.

Ridgway, M. B. 1967. *The Korean war*. New York: Doubleday.

L

LAND WARFARE

Land warfare is the organized use of military force by a nation-state to achieve political, economic, or social objectives. Military force is used directly to defeat the military forces of an adversary or indirectly—by threat—to cause an adversary to modify its political, economic, social, or military behavior. Trained and disciplined individuals are organized into military units that employ a variety of weapons in a coordinated fashion to subdue an enemy military force.

Land warfare is multidimensional. It involves the integration and maneuver of military formations (personnel, vehicles, weaponry, logistics, and communications) and the application of firepower (direct and indirect, air and naval) in a coordinated fashion to exploit an adversary's weaknesses and avoid his strengths, so that assigned objectives are accomplished with minimum expenditure of resources. Battles are orchestrated to accomplish campaign objectives that are aimed at winning wars to accomplish strategic objectives. To achieve those strategic objectives, landpower, seapower, and airpower must be fully interdependent.

Changes in technology have played a central role (and will continue to do so) in developing the doctrine and tactics of land warfare. The development of the bow allowed combatants to distance themselves from each other for the first time. That distance did not change again until the invention of gunpowder. The ability to fire a projectile further separated combatants, and that distance has continued to grow over the last 1,500 years. The 1991 war in the Persian Gulf served notice to land armies worldwide that targets to be engaged will be at even greater distances, and that the human face of the enemy increasingly will be replaced by a blip on an electronic device. Factors that are influencing the conduct of modern land warfare include the electronic battlefield; the increased use and coordination of joint and combined operations; the improved lethality and accuracy of weapons; an array of strategic, operational, and tactical sensors and detectors; the increased maneuverability of forces; the technological sophistication of lesser military powers; and growing requirements for rapid reaction capabilities at the strategic, operational, and tactical levels.

Historical Evolution

The tactics of land warfare emerged from the conflicts of the earliest civilizations. Opponents probably first engaged in personal, brutal, hand-to-hand combat using their bare hands. The first rudimentary handheld weapons were stones, clubs, and stone-head axes. Instruments that thrust objects at adversaries from afar—slings and bows, javelins and spears—further improved lethality while giving some protection by placing distance between combatants. Thus began the cycle of using advancing technology to improve the instruments of war. Improved weaponry meant a gain in advantage over an enemy force, which could lead to victory on the battlefield or, in modern parlance, deter the adversary from entering the fray.

The history and evolution of land warfare revolves around a number of factors: the tactical genius of a few great military leaders; the specific technological breakthroughs with potential military application; the overall modernization and industrialization of societies; and the developing art and science of land warfare as it has grown through analysis of battles, strategic principles, and proven or evolutionary doctrine.

Ancient Roots of Land Warfare

Although many early societies engaged in land warfare, the Assyrians left one of the earliest records of their weaponry, tactics, and battlefield engagements. As early as 1000 B.C., the Assyrians had made extensive use of military formations of soldiers armed with bows and arrows, spears and slings, on foot, on horseback, and in horse-drawn chariots. Formations of soldiers on foot and horseback would simultaneously launch a mass of projectiles—arrows, spears, and stones—against the enemy and then maneuver in a prescribed formation and direction to complete the task of subduing or destroying the remaining enemy forces.

Two elements of the Assyrians' military prowess continue to be fundamental to an effective military force today. The first factor is the combined use of massive firepower and maneuver of forces to overwhelm and demoralize the enemy. This psychological dimension of warfare at the level of the individual soldier's willingness to fight underlies such battlefield tactics as the employment of the sniper, shock action, blitzkrieg, carpet-bombing, and artillery raids. The second factor is related to the Assyrians' use of more readily available iron in lieu of bronze on the tips of arrows and spears and on body armor to improve personal protection from enemy projectiles and swords. The timely recognition and application of technology to land warfare can have a deterrent psychological effect on the enemy, as well as affecting the outcome of the battle.

While the Assyrians and Persians perfected the utility of massed firepower and maneuver, the Greeks countered with extensive use of large, advancing infantry formations of well-disciplined soldiers who were each protected by a large shield and armed with a particularly long, iron-pointed spear. They used this formation to overcome the shock effects of Persian massed fires, similar to those used by the Assyrians, at Marathon in 490 B.C. "With the spears of the first five or six rows of men protruding beyond the front rank to create a deadly hedge of iron points, the phalanx advanced to battle at a steady pace, protected from missiles by heavy shields, and ground [its] way through the enemy formation like a chopping machine" (Kendall 1957).

The Romans improved on the phalanx by making it a more flexible legion of smaller, spaced units and using spears that could be thrown by a soldier bearing a larger shield for greater protection. The legion was modified later to adapt to the need for better leadership and a more professional army in the far-reaching Roman empire. This professional army was recruited from the entire population, organized into 100-man cohorts, led by a professional soldier or centurion, and paid and equipped by the state. This last innovation would continue to come and go throughout the ages.

The ancient civilizations of the Mediterranean region and of China also contributed great strategists who have had lasting effects on the art and science of warfare. Their contributions to strategy, operational art, and tactics remain relevant to contemporary land warfare doctrine.

THE ANCIENT STRATEGISTS AND GREAT CAPTAINS

As ancient tribal behaviors coalesced into more complex societies, the emerging city-states were charged with securing the interests of their citizens. Individuals served in their respective armies through either conscription or civil obligation. To survive, these ancient societies had to conquer or be conquered. Consequently, they relied heavily on the skills of their military leaders, many of whom today remain central to our understanding of warfare, and land warfare in particular.

Among these ancient generals were Sun Tzu (ca. 500 B.C.), who enunciated well-defined fundamentals of war that underlie modern principles; Alexander the Great (ca. 300 B.C.), who conquered the civilized world from Persia to Egypt to India, adapting firepower, maneuver, and organization to surprise his enemies; Hannibal (ca. 200 B.C.), the Carthaginian, who made the strategic maneuver of crossing the Alps into Italy, thus avoiding the Romans' major force, and subsequently moving his force through foreboding terrain to surprise and defeat a force of Roman legions; and Julius Caesar (ca. 50 B.C.), who demonstrated a genius for adapting the tactics of the legion to the terrain and the enemy's formations and deployments, and engendering a discipline that ensured the commitment of forces to battle at the decisive time and place.

At the close of the last millennium B.C., the ancient great captains had secured their places of prominence in the study of military strategy, art, and tactics that underlie land warfare. The next great captains would not emerge until late into the second millennium A.D.: Gustavus Adolphus of Sweden (17th century); Marlborough of England (18th century); the Prussian, Frederick the Great (18th century); and Napoleon (19th century).

TRANSITION TO MODERN LAND WARFARE

In the first millennium A.D., emerging tactics included the use of horsemen (cavalry), light infantry, and heavy infantry, to be employed in various combinations and weightings. The extent of body armor covering head, chest, arms, and legs varied, as did the size and weight of shields and weaponry (javelin, spear, axe, dagger, sword, bow).

How armies fought also depended on the weaponry and tactics of adversaries. In the western Roman Empire at the start of the millennium, the response to continual barbarian raids on outposts was static defense; in the eastern Byzantine portion of the empire, cavalry prevailed by A.D. 500. The Byzantines codified their doctrine of warfare, focusing on defense in depth and conservation of resources (especially trained and expensive cavalry).

England and the western European tribes and enclaves of civilization were subject to Viking raids. To survive, they organized into protective fiefdoms and made extensive use of fortifications—at first, large earth and timber enclosures and later, walled castle keeps and cities. Siege warfare was common, and the techniques and equipment used to penetrate walls and engage distant targets became increasingly sophisticated.

Feudal armies were usually temporary, brought together for a particular purpose and then disbanded. They varied in size, on the average 5,000 to 10,000 men. Local vassals were eventually replaced by paid soldiers (mercenaries); as the strength of armies became more predictable, longer campaigns could be conducted. Through invasions and counterinvasions among France, England, and later Spain, and as a result of the Crusades and the Hundred Years' War, individuals built power bases and monarchies emerged. At first, the weapons of war and tactics of ancient periods were reinvented. However, with the advent of gunpowder, the relative lethality of infantry and cavalry changed forever; musket replaced bow, and cannon replaced catapult.

The Impact of Technology on Land Warfare

Before the invention of gunpowder, land warfare was fought in a destructive, personal manner, and at closer quarters. As crude weapons were gradually replaced by more effective devices, the nature of land warfare changed. Early man made only relatively simple advances in weaponry over several thousand years. But as man's ingenuity advanced through the first millennium A.D., significant advances in weaponry occurred more frequently.

The short bow, sling, and javelin brought about significant changes in how land wars were fought. Chariots gave archers and javelin throwers a mobile and stable platform from which to launch their projectiles. The use of helmet, breast plate, shin guards, and shield in combination with a spear, axe, or sword, and of lightly equipped soldiers on horseback (cavalry) continued well into the second millennium A.D. The effectiveness of this early weaponry was dependent on the mobility, maneuverability, and discipline of the military formation. Fortified defensive works of earth and stone were essential to the survival of entire city-states and date from earliest periods. These fortresses were besieged by armies using fighting towers, battering rams, catapults, and flame-tipped arrows and other flame devices.

During the first millennium A.D., the role of the soldier on horseback was enhanced by the use of saddle and stirrup, which provided a stable platform and leverage to use weapons while mounted. The cavalryman replaced the two-horsed chariot, which was an economical move in terms of the number of fighters per horse and the forage required for horses. Both the longbow (which required a well-trained archer to launch up to six arrows per minute to a range of 200 yd.) and the crossbow (which required less training and discipline, had a rate of fire of one to two arrows per minute to a range of 130 yd.) assumed prominent positions for organized use on the battlefield soon after the start of the second millennium A.D. (Macksey 1973). The use of gunpowder emerged soon thereafter.

GUNPOWDER AND THE INDUSTRIAL REVOLUTION

Over the centuries, weapons development focused on improving three elements: range, accuracy, and rate of fire. With the advent of gunpowder-propelled projectiles on the battlefield in the 1400s, science became a tool of the military in the search for ways to inflict more significant casualties on opponents. For the next 400 years, the sophistication and diversification of cannon, artillery, musket, pistol, and rifle revolutionized the conduct of land warfare. With each new invention—the cylindroconoidal bullet, improved explosives, smokeless powders, the fuse, shrapnel, rifling (to increase range and accuracy), breech-loading artillery, the repeating rifle, and the machine gun—rates of fire and the vulnerability of soldiers to long-range fire increased dramatically. The industrial revolution meant these weapons could be manufactured in mass quantities. The railroad, telegraph, and internal combustion engine brought military units a degree of mobility and responsiveness unimagined a century earlier (Garden 1989).

The leap in technology and invention in the nineteenth century continued the trend toward large land armies and greater casualties, as evident in the American Civil War and the Russo-Japanese War. World War I brought the artillery barrage, the machine gun, infantry attacks on entrenched enemy forces, and limited use of chemical weapons. World War I also saw the introduction of the airplane and the first armored vehicle (the tank) to be used in modern warfare to overcome the limitations of trench warfare (Macksey 1973). These two weapon systems have influenced land warfare in an unprecedented fashion. The pace and lethality of military operations was greatly accelerated by these weapon systems and by the application of electronics, including radar, high-speed communications, and encryption, in World War II.

The enhanced ability of opposing military forces to maneuver, employ firepower, and protect their resources brought about new operational methods involving the close coordination of airpower (strategic bombing and close air support) and landpower (rapid-moving armor units and artillery preparations) to engage an opposing force at its most vulnerable location and avoid its strengths. This form of warfare was used with great success by the Germans in World War II, to a lesser extent by the Allies.

MODERN TECHNOLOGY

The weapon systems of land warfare that emerged from World War II set the framework for weapons to follow. In spite of its power, the atomic bomb has proven unusable in a ground war. The potential for escalation, side effects of radiation, and political intervention have negated a direct role for nuclear weapons in land warfare. Instead, technology has focused on improvements to traditional applications of energy in weaponry and the vehicles that propel them.

The microminiaturization of equipment components, the microprocessor and computer, the development of sensors and detectors that respond to wide ranges of the electromagnetic spectrum (infrared and laser), electronic countermeasures, near-real-time dissemination of information, ground positioning systems, satellites, lasers, increased lethality of and accuracy of warheads, improved armor and munitions using depleted uranium, and countless related technological adaptations are having a profound effect on warfare. Targets can be detected, tracked, and engaged at ranges that far exceed those of World War II.

The high levels of reliability, protection, and lethality that have been attained can be illustrated by the modern battle tank. The performance of the U.S. Army M1A1 main battle tank in the 1991 war with Iraq reflects technological improvements applied to an established weapon system. After 100 hours of offensive operations, the tank's operational readiness exceeded 90 percent. In a night movement of 300 tanks across open desert, all of the tanks arrived at the destination. Several M1A1 tanks received direct hits from antitank rounds and sustained no damage, attesting to the effectiveness of special armor. The tank's thermal night sight allowed crews to see enemy tanks through smoke from oil well fires, use the laser range finder, maintain gun stabilization on the move, and destroy targets at ranges that exceeded 3,000 meters (9,900 ft.). The state-of-the-art antitank round fired by the 120mm gun of the M1A1 was able to fire through berms protecting enemy tanks and still destroy Soviet-origin T-72 tanks.

Modern land warfare uses technologically advanced systems at the level of the individual soldier to enhance fire support weapons. The individual soldier can be armed with night-vision equipment to allow him to "see daylight." He is also equipped with laser devices to designate targets for engagement by artillery and armed helicopters, and he is armed with individual antitank weapons that can launch smart rounds that stay on target until impact. He can engage enemy helicopters and aircraft using a shoulder-fired, heat-seeking antiaircraft missile and can locate his position within a few feet by using a hand-held global plotting device that receives satellite information.

Artillery weapons fire "smart rounds" that can seek out and destroy tanks from overhead and scatter antipersonnel and antitank mines. Radar systems can "backtrack" the path of enemy projectiles to the artillery location and automatically provide coordinates for counterartillery fires. Aircraft are used in traditional logistical and close air support roles. However, the armed helicopter is able to maneuver and engage enemy armor day or night using smart antitank missiles that respond to laser designation and infrared emissions.

Technology will continue to improve the overall capabilities of traditional land weapon systems. However, the limitations of technology and the man-machine interface will require continual attention. Success in warfare depends heavily on the ability of individuals to use weapons and information systems under battlefield conditions while maintaining the flexibility to adapt and take advantage of changing conditions. The advantages and economies of automation and robotics will have to be balanced with the human ability to process selective information to make good decisions—by a tank gunner's choice of target or a corps commander's timing of an attack.

Conceptual Foundation of Modern Land Warfare

The conduct of land warfare rests on three fundamental piers of analysis: strategy, operational art, and tactics. Successful military strategy achieves national and alliance political aims at the lowest possible cost in lives and national resources. Operational art translates those aims into effective military operations and campaigns. Sound tactics win battles and engagements that produce successful campaigns and operations (Department of the Army 1986).

In addition to these three components, modern land warfare doctrine reflects the precepts of ancient and modern theorists and strategists as reflected in principles of war and combat power (the ability to fight a war).

The classical principles of war were best articulated by British Major General J.F.C. Fuller during World War I. They remain valid today and are summarized below:

- Direct every military operation toward a clearly defined, decisive, and attainable objective.
- Seize, retain, and exploit the initiative.
- Concentrate combat power at the decisive place and time.
- Allocate minimum essential combat power to secondary efforts.
- Place the enemy in a position of disadvantage through the flexible application of combat power.
- For every objective, ensure unity of effort under one responsible commander.
- Never permit the enemy to acquire an unexpected advantage.
- Strike the enemy at a time or place, or in a manner, for which he is unprepared.
- Prepare clear, uncomplicated plans and clear, concise orders to ensure thorough understanding.

Combat power measures the effect of maneuver, firepower, protection, and leadership, which are defined as follows:

- *Maneuver* is the movement of forces in relation to the enemy to secure or retain positional advantage. It can involve concentrating forces at the critical point to achieve surprise and dominance over enemy forces; it also can be achieved by allowing the enemy to move into a disadvantageous position.

- Maneuver is linked to *firepower* to defeat the enemy's ability and will to fight; however, firepower can also be used independently of maneuver to destroy, delay, or disrupt uncommitted enemy forces.
- *Protection* involves the retention of fighting capabilities so they can be applied at the decisive time and place; this involves actions (such as camouflage, deception, dispersal, and air defense) to counter the enemy's ability to locate friendly forces and use firepower and maneuver against them.
- Competent and confident *leadership* provides purpose, direction, and motivation in land warfare.

Battlefield success is measured by the extent to which it accomplishes the operational goals of a campaign. In turn, the campaign is not successful unless the national security strategic objectives are met. Thus, clear statements of strategic purpose are essential. The effective application of combat power on the battlefield is defined in terms of doctrine.

MODERN BATTLEFIELD DOCTRINE

Battlefield doctrine addresses how to use combat power at the operational and tactical levels of warfare. Modern battlefield doctrine prescribes that friendly forces should gain and retain the initiative, act faster than the enemy, synchronize battlefield activities to produce maximum combat power, and operate in depth of space, time, and resources to win the battle.

The linear battlefield dominated the major land wars of the twentieth century. Trench warfare and the use of massive artillery fires in World War I resulted in mutual attrition and high casualties. World War II provided greater opportunities for coordination of mobile forces and firepower to gain the advantage over opposing forces; however, the linearity of the battlefield and heavy casualties still dominated, and rapid victory was elusive. However, the battlefield of the late twentieth century, as demonstrated in 1991 in the ejection of Iraqi forces from Kuwait (Operation Desert Storm), involves fast-paced, fluid operations. Depending on the assigned mission, units conduct close, deep, and rear operations.

Close operations involve units that are committed to battle, including support such as artillery, air defense, reconnaissance, and logistical units. At the operational level, close operations involve the activities of corps comprising divisions. At the tactical level, the subordinate units of the division, the brigades and battalions, fight battles (which can involve deep and rear operations as well). Close operations include maneuver, close combat (including close air support), indirect fire support (artillery or naval gunfire), combat support and combat service support of fighting units, and the necessary command and control (leadership and coordination) to ensure victory.

Modern battlefield doctrine incorporates deep operations to shape the operational situation in which later close operations will occur. Deep operations, which are not new to modern land warfare doctrine, include interdicting enemy supplies, reserves, and communications to minimize their impact on a current or future battle. With the increasing mobility and firepower available to modern tactical-level units, the ability of deep operations to influence the outcomes of battles and ensure early victory continues to grow. Deep operations are undertaken only against those enemy capabilities that can directly affect the conduct of friendly operations. They include deception operations, deep surveillance and target acquisition, interdiction by firepower and maneuver forces, and electronic warfare to disrupt enemy command, control, and communications.

Close and deep operations are closely coordinated with rear operations, which comprise activities to ensure freedom of maneuver and continuity of planned operations or opportunities to exploit success. Friendly reserve forces and fire support are positioned to successfully move and engage enemy formations while remaining secure from enemy observation or attack. Sufficient logistical support and services are conserved, without decreasing the support to currently engaged units, to ensure the sustainment of the reserves if committed.

These categories of operations reflect the fluid and nonlinear nature of the modern battlefield and provide a framework for the development of battle plans. Battle success depends ultimately on the ingenuity of the commanders, the readiness and training of individual soldiers and units, and their ability and flexibility to adapt to rapidly changing situations.

ORGANIZATION FOR LAND WARFARE

The doctrine of the modern battlefield is practiced by organizations within a designated operational area. Military operations are carried out in accordance with the strategic objectives established by national or international command authorities. A definite set of boundaries is established, rules of engagement are defined, and specific objectives are established. Land warfare operations are conducted in a theater of operations in coordination with air and sea forces (joint operations), to include the armed forces of allied countries (combined operations). A joint commander is designated who is responsible for coordinating all activities in the conduct of the campaign, to include all air, sea, and land forces operations. In a joint or combined command, a commander is designated for each of the air, sea, and land components. In a combined operation with forces from other countries, the joint commander may also be the combined commander, or a separate commander can be designated.

In the U.S. military, land forces at the operational level, where objectives are related to the accomplishment of specific strategic objectives, are organized into corps. One or more corps can operate under a theater army commander, who is responsible to the overall joint/combined commander. At the corps level, the operational objectives of the campaign are accomplished through the operations of subordinate tactical divisions: brigades and subordinate battalions and companies fight the battles and engagements.

The types of units assigned to each of these levels of organization—theater, corps, division, brigade—will depend on the overall purpose of the operation, the geographical location, the terrain and weather to be encountered, the sophistication of infrastructure in the theater of operation (i.e., ports, airfields, roadways), constraints of resources and time and, most important, the threat of enemy forces and their capabilities. Each level of organization is task organized to ensure the capabilities and functions necessary to achieve the objectives of the operation. Tactical-level combat units rarely operate as pure organizations; rather, they are augmented (task organized) with other types of units into a task force to take advantage of the combined effects of their capabilities.

Divisions are major ground combat units that have the command and control capabilities (commanders, staff, communications) to effectively plan for and implement operational plans at the tactical level. At this level, tactical missions are assigned, operational orders are developed and implemented, and the battle is fought by assigned units. Operational orders include clear statements of missions to be accomplished, a scheme of maneuver, a visualization of the operation, controls on the movement and firepower of units, assignment of different types of fire support (i.e., close air support, artillery support, naval gunfire support, air defense), priorities regarding transportation, allocation of fuel and ammunition, intelligence information, missions and actions of adjacent friendly units, and time lines for the start of the operation.

The number of personnel and units in a division will depend on the assigned mission, the operational environment, and the capabilities needed to defeat enemy forces. The number of personnel can range from 10,000 to 30,000. The units assigned to the division, like those assigned at the higher corps level and at subordinate brigade, battalion, and company levels, are categorized by their major functions: combat, combat support, and combat service support. Combat units include armor, mechanized, light infantry, air assault, and airborne. Each of these units has unique capabilities that makes it appropriate singularly or in combination with other types of units to conduct a ground operation. Combat support units include artillery, aviation, engineer, and air defense. Combat service support units include medical, transportation, supply, and construction.

Logistical Support

The combat service support units are often neglected in the study of land warfare. Their role is to support the deployment, movement, and sustainment of combat organizations. Functions involved include construction and transport; fuel, water, food, and ammunition resupply; and provision of spare parts and maintenance of equipment and weapon systems. The logistical situation and the support units involved will weigh heavily in decisions regarding the deployment of military forces.

Figure 1 portrays the Kuwait theater of operations that existed at the start of the Operation Desert Storm ground war in February 1991. To emphasize the important role of combat service support and logistical support, only the major combat service support units are displayed. Each of the divisions (displayed to the far right) has its own internal support command to meet short-term supply, maintenance, and medical needs. The corps-level logistical support structure

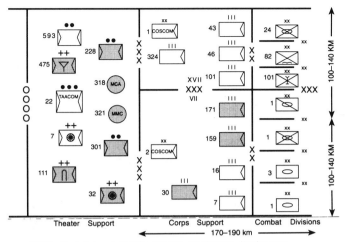

NOTE: Shaded boxes indicate Reserve Components Headquarters.

Figure 1. Operation Desert Storm: Kuwait theater of operations, 20 February 1991. (SOURCE: Association of the U.S. Army, 1991b.)

includes a corps support command (COSCOM) for each of the corps (XVIII and VII Corps), which provides a corps support group to support each division; in addition, a corps support group supports other units in the corps area. Each corps support group has a maintenance battalion, a supply and service battalion, and a transportation battalion. To the left are theater-level support units, including ammunition, fuel, spare parts, and transportation.

Land Warfare in the 1990s: Operation Desert Storm

States resort to warfare for many reasons: to promote and spread a political or religious ideology; to gain territory for resources and space for a growing population; to protect national interests in another region; and to conquer. In modern parlance, the reasons for going to war are usually expressed in terms of securing national, regional, or other international interests.

A case study can lend understanding to modern land warfare, and particularly to its complexity in light of the spread of technology and the availability of sophisticated weapons to adversaries. It can also provide some vision of how wars will be fought in the future. The 1990–91 war in the Persian Gulf, which involved Iraq, the United States, and a coalition of other countries, involved a definable threat to the national interests of several countries; international political, economic, and military cooperation and United Nations legitimacy; the use of strategic assets; definable operational campaigns; and the use of advanced weaponry and systems that had not been proven in combat.

THE STRATEGIC SETTING

Severely strapped for international exchange following an eight-year war with Iran, Iraq pressured Kuwait and other OPEC nations to raise oil prices and to reduce production. It accused the Kuwaitis of digging oil wells on Iraqi territory and extracting more than US$2 billion worth of oil, for which Iraq demanded compensation. Iraq also sought Kuwaiti oil fields near the Iraqi border and demanded a lease of Kuwait islands to gain a seaport on the Persian Gulf.

By late July 1990, Iraq had positioned a large force of troops along the Kuwaiti border. On 2 August, the Iraqi army invaded Kuwait and gained full control of the emirate within one day. That move was promptly condemned by the UN Security Council, which demanded the immediate withdrawal of Iraq's forces from Kuwait—a measure that Iraq chose to defy.

By 6 August, with Iraqi forces disposed along the Kuwaiti–Saudi Arabian border and postured for a possible attack on Saudi Arabia, the United Nations authorized worldwide economic sanctions against Iraq. Saudi Arabia, fearing imminent attack, requested assistance in defense of Saudi territory. Thereafter, support from the United States and many other countries moved at a rapid pace. The United States deployed land, air, and sea forces to the Persian Gulf region to deter or defend against an Iraqi invasion of Saudi Arabia. On 7 August, Operation Desert Shield officially began. A 2,300-man contingent of the U.S. Army's 82d Airborne Division immediately deployed by air. On 8 August, Iraq publicly annexed Kuwait and declared it a province of Iraq. The U.N. Security Council took positive and immediate action by approving a resolution that demanded unconditional and immediate withdrawal of Iraq's army.

OPERATION DESERT SHIELD

The national security objectives of Operation Desert Shield as outlined by the American president were:

- To protect the lives of American citizens
- To deter and, if necessary, repel further Iraqi aggression
- To effect the immediate, complete, and unconditional withdrawal of all Iraqi forces from Kuwait
- To restore the legitimate government of Kuwait

Rapid deployment of forces from all the services proceeded. The first requirement was to deter any further encroachment by Iraqi forces. U.S. naval forces in the region were reinforced and tactical air forces were moved to the theater of operations. Additional mobile light ground forces, including marine elements and the balance of the 82d Airborne Division, were also moved to the region. Troops of air assault and heavier armored and mechanized divisions, as well as air defense and corps support units, were airlifted to the Gulf, while combat equipment followed in the largest sealift of combat forces since World War II. To provide required combat and combat service support, units from the reserve components of all services were called to active duty. Also, equipment on pre-positioned ships deployed to the region.

Thirty-seven nations sent military forces or medical teams to the region. Ten nations pledged more than US$50 billion to defray the costs of the operation.

All U.S. forces deployed in Desert Shield came under the command of the commander in chief of U.S. Central Command (USCENTCOM).

USCENTCOM operated with the Saudi Joint Forces Commander through a Coordination and Communications Center. Initially, British forces were under U.S. operational control and French forces under Saudi control.

Arab and coalition forces were initially positioned behind the Saudi task forces arrayed along the Saudi-Kuwaiti border. The forces that were deployed by air were in place in the first weeks of August; the others arrived in increments through October. The major pacing factor for subsequent movements was the availability of airlift and sealift, with the equipment moving by sea and the troops flying to Saudi Arabia in time to marry up with their equipment. By early November, there was sufficient combat capability to provide an effective defense of Saudi Arabia.

Iraq continued to build its forces in the Kuwaiti theater to more than 400,000 troops, to include mass construction of hardened bunkers, tank traps, mine fields, and miles of earthen walls to reinforce positions along the frontier of Saudi Arabia. On 8 November, it was decided to develop an offensive capability with sufficient combat power to force the Iraqis out of Kuwait. At that point, the U.S. VII Corps from Europe and armored, mechanized, and support units from the United States were ordered to deploy, and the call-up of additional reserve units of all services was started. Toward the end of November, these units began to move, reaching full combat readiness in Saudi Arabia by early February.

In the first 80 days, more than 170,000 people and more than 160,000 tons of cargo were moved to Saudi Arabia by air from the United States. Over 7,500,000 square feet of cargo and equipment were moved by sea. By the time the coalition forces began the offensive on 17 January 1991, the United States had shipped some 460,000 tons of ammunition, 300,000 desert camouflage uniforms, 200,000 tires, and 150 million military meals to sustain the 540,000 soldiers, sailors, airmen, and marines deployed.

OPERATION DESERT STORM

The United Nations established a deadline of 15 January for Iraq to withdraw its forces from Kuwait, and authorized member nations to employ all necessary means to evict them if they did not withdraw. The Iraqis did not withdraw by the deadline. On 17 January 1991, Operation Desert Shield became Operation Desert Storm when the coalition initiated combat operations.

The initial phase, the air campaign, was intensive. The coalition forces employed its air resources—including armed helicopters, cruise missiles, and at least eighteen types of land- and sea-based aircraft—to maximum advantage. Electronic jammers, sophisticated sensors, night vision devices, and precision bombing technology destroyed Iraq's strategic capability.

Coalition air superiority was achieved early in the operation. The campaign was directed against Iraqi ground forces facing coalition units across the Kuwaiti–Saudi Arabian border. Thousands of sorties were flown each day attacking targets of military importance such as missile sites; command and control centers; telecommunications facilities; power generating plants; airfields and runways; aircraft storage shelters; bridges; Iraqi troop positions; and chemical, biological, and nuclear weapon development and production facilities. Air sorties against Iraqi military targets were conducted by U.S., Saudi, Kuwaiti, British, French, Canadian, Bahraini, Qatari, and Italian forces. The air and sea offensive continued for 38 days with a constant, around-the-clock bombardment that brought the war to Iraq.

Despite the high priority given to locating and destroying Iraqi SCUD ballistic missile launchers, missile attacks continued throughout the period, although in decreasing numbers. The SCUDs were intended as terror weapons against civilian targets and were never a serious military threat. U.S. Army Patriot missiles were used for the first time to defeat other missiles in a combat situation.

THE GROUND WAR

Two corps of more than 200,000 troops and thousands of tons of equipment started moving to the western part of Saudi Arabia on 17 January under the cover of air, sea, and artillery bombardments. Repositioning for a ground attack into Iraq and Kuwait was underway.

Sufficient fuel, ammunition, spare parts, water, and food were moved as much as 300 miles to establish a 60-day supply in preparation for the coming ground offensive. Special forces teams were inserted deep into Iraq to perform strategic reconnaissance and to report on troop movements. By 16 February, American and coalition forces were in positions spanning a distance of over 300 miles along the Saudi border.

Throughout this phase of the war, numerous feints, probes, and mock attacks were conducted by various elements of the coalition forces. On several occasions, the Navy and Marines rehearsed invasions from the sea and throughout maintained a large presence in Gulf waters off the shores of Kuwait. The American and coalition land forces executed reconnaissance missions all along the fortified borders of Kuwait and Iraq. By concentrating their forces along the southern Kuwaiti border and by fortifying the beaches east of Kuwait City, the Iraqis made it clear that they expected a headlong attack into their most heavily fortified areas.

By mid-February, the emphasis of the air campaign was clearly shifting to inflict maximum damage on Iraqi troop formations and defensive positions, softening them for the pending ground attack. By now, the U.S. Army had over 250,000 troops in the Persian Gulf area. Its combat elements were poised for the attack.

At 4:00 A.M. (Gulf time), 24 February 1991, the coalition forces launched the largest successful ground campaign since World War II. Along a 300-mile front, they rolled into Kuwait and Iraq to engage the world's fourth largest army. One hundred hours later, on 28 February, the coalition declared a temporary cease-fire.

Having maneuvered over 300 miles westward to reposition ground forces composed of two corps for the attack into Iraq and Kuwait, U.S. and coalition forces were positioned as portrayed in Figure 2. XVIII Corps included 82d

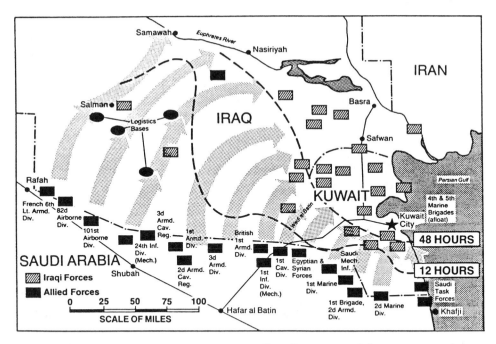

Figure 2. Operation Desert Storm: U.S. and coalition ground forces positioned for attack. (SOURCE: Association of the U.S. Army, 1991.)

Airborne, 101st Airborne Division, 3d Armored Cavalry Regiment, the 24th Infantry Division (Mechanized), and the French 6th Light Armored Division. Further east, VII Corps included the 1st and 3d Armored Divisions, the 2d Armored Cavalry Regiment, and the British 1st Armored Division. Near the confluence of the Saudi-Iraqi-Kuwaiti borders, were the 1st Infantry Division (Mechanized) and the 1st Cavalry Division. To their right was a pan-Arab force consisting of Saudi, Kuwaiti, Egyptian, and Syrian units at the western edge of the Saudi-Kuwaiti border. The 2d Marine Division and a brigade of the 2d Armored Division were positioned to the east of the pan-Arab force; the 1st Marine Division anchored the right flank. Two additional Saudi task forces were prepared to advance up the Persian Gulf coast, while Marines of the 4th and 5th Expeditionary Brigades were poised for amphibious operations off the Kuwaiti coast. Earlier, a number of Special Forces teams had been inserted deep in Iraq to track enemy movements and especially to locate SCUD missile sites.

The ground war started with two simultaneous attacks, one in the east, where pan-Arab forces and U.S. Marines breached the first line of Iraqi defenses and drove up the coast toward Kuwait City, and the other 300 miles west, consisting of the French 6th Light Armored Division and one brigade of the 82d Airborne Division attacking 90 miles into Iraq to seize the airfield at Salman and establish a security screen for the western flank. At the same time, the Marines in the Gulf, aided by intense naval gunfire, feinted an assault against Iraqi forces dug in along Kuwait's coast. Similarly, two brigades of the 1st Cavalry Division attacked about a dozen miles up the Wadi al Batin against sporadic resistance.

At 8:00 A.M., 23 February, the 101st Airborne Division launched the largest air assault operation in military history more than 70 miles into Iraq and then continued the attack to the Euphrates River. That afternoon, the 3d Armored Cavalry Regiment and the 24th Infantry Division (Mechanized) attacked north into Iraq.

In VII Corps' sector, the 1st Infantry Division breached Iraqi defensive positions and attacked north, followed by the British 1st Armored Division. The 2d Armored Cavalry Regiment and the 1st and 3d Armored Divisions attacked rapidly, bypassing hundreds of enemy positions. Along the coast, Saudi-led coalition forces breached defensive barriers and joined the marines in the attack on Kuwait City. By the end of 24 February, all major coalition forces were engaged.

On 26 February, elements of the XVIII Airborne Corps and VII Corps maneuvered to the east to trap and destroy what was left of the Iraqi forces. Having driven almost 100 miles into Iraq, the 24th Infantry Division and the 3d Armored Cavalry Regiment turned toward Basra to cut off retreating Iraqi forces. VII Corps units turned east to attack the Iraqi reserve. During the night, VII Corps, which now included the 1st Cavalry Division, conducted a coordinated attack and destroyed two Iraqi divisions. The 1st and 2d Marine Divisions also reached the outskirts of Kuwait City and fought for control of the international airport.

On 27 February, Kuwait was liberated. By the time a suspension of offensive combat operations was declared (at 8:00 A.M., 28 February 1991, Gulf time), U.S. and coalition forces had destroyed or rendered ineffective 43 Iraqi divisions, captured more than 80,000 prisoners, and destroyed or damaged 4,000 tanks, 2,100 artillery pieces, 1,800 armored personnel carriers, 7 helicopters, and 103 Iraqi aircraft.

The United Nations worked out the details of the formal cease-fire agreement, which was accepted by Iraq on 6 April and proclaimed on 10 April. Included in the U.N. action was the authorization of a 1,440-member observer team to oversee a newly created demilitarized zone (DMZ) between Kuwait and Iraq. Operation Desert Storm, preceded by Operation Desert Shield, became Operation Provide Comfort as some 13,000 coalition military personnel—including about 9,000 U.S. troops—turned their attention to giving food, shelter, and medical care to the refugees.

As U.S. and coalition forces redeployed, their troops in the DMZ were relieved by UN forces; the refugee support effort in the south was accepted by the Saudis. In the north, Operation Provide Comfort—support for the Kurdish refugees, much of which was rendered through Turkey—became the responsibility of the U.S. European Command.

Desert Shield and Desert Storm were the largest operational tests of modern military forces and doctrine since World War II.

The Future of Land Warfare

Land warfare, as the Desert Shield and Desert Storm operations indicate, involves the coordinated use of all military resources at a nation's disposal to achieve specific national objectives. The strategic, operational, and tactical settings of land warfare are shaped by airpower and seapower. Once strategically deployed and operationally positioned, the landpower component is charged with carrying the fight to the enemy land forces and dislodging them from the area of contention. Throughout, airpower and seapower continue to play a major role in maintaining supremacy in the skies and on the seas.

Ancient and medieval history and the technological impact of the industrial, atomic, and electronic ages have forged today's military doctrine. Operation Desert Storm reconfirmed many of the principles of war and provided some vision of land wars yet to be fought. Some of the parameters of future land warfare might be as follows:

- Early deployment of military forces, particularly land forces, to the area of contention is the clearest signal of national resolve in a crisis. An accompanying clear statement of the purpose and objectives of the military operation provides a framework for strategic and operational planning and judicious use of national resources.
- Developing nations have access to sophisticated, high-tech weaponry and, especially in the face of overwhelming opposing forces, are prepared to employ them to achieve national goals and resolve disputes with neighbors.
- Land forces are the major military resource of most countries. Therefore, nations will continue to use land warfare as the predominant instrument of military force, particularly at lower levels of conflict.
- A vast array of sensors is now available to detect, locate, and engage targets. Future land warfare may see most enemy capabilities engaged and rendered ineffective long before they can be maneuvered and employed.
- Operational doctrine will be broadened to more thoroughly encompass activities short of war, such as peacekeeping, refugee support and security, and environmental disaster relief.
- The interdependence of nations' interests and the number of nations with sophisticated armed forces point toward greater use of limited, multinational coalitions in future land wars. Temporary, opposing regional coalitions and more permanent international forces will probably be necessary to pool limited and complementary resources to mount a military operation.
- The accuracy and lethality of weapons available to opposing military forces will continue to improve. Successful and economical employment of these expensive and sophisticated weapons will depend on the skill of the individuals and crews that employ them. While modern technology will provide "smart weapons," simplicity of use will drive their success in battle engagements.

JAMES D. BLUNDELL

SEE ALSO: Alexander the Great; Art of War; Caesar, Julius; Clausewitz, Karl von; Fuller, J. F. C.; Napoleon I; Principles of War.

Bibliography

Association of the U.S. Army. 1991a. *The U.S. Army in Operation Desert Storm: An overview.* Arlington, Va.: AUSA Institute of Land Warfare.
————. 1991b. *Operations Desert Shield and Desert Storm: The logistics perspective.* Arlington, Va.: AUSA Institute of Land Warfare.
Bellamy, C. 1987. *The future of land warfare.* New York: St. Martins Press.
Gabriel, R. A. 1990. *The culture of war: Invention and early development.* Westport, Conn.: Greenwood Press.
Garden, T. 1989. *The technology trap: Science and the military.* London: Brassey's.
Jones, A. 1987. *The art of war in the western world.* Oxford: Oxford Univ. Press.
Kendall, P. 1957. *The story of land warfare.* Westport, Conn.: Greenwood Press.
Liddell Hart, B. H. 1991. *Strategy.* New York: Penguin Books.
Macksey, K. 1973. *The Guinness history of land warfare.* Enfield, England: Guinness Superlatives.
U.S. Department of the Army. 1986. *Field manual 100-5: Operations.* Washington, D.C.: Government Printing Office.

LATIN AMERICAN WARS OF INDEPENDENCE

The Latin American wars of independence were a series of early nineteenth-century conflicts in the areas of the Western Hemisphere governed by France, Spain, and Portugal. Although there were some linkages among them, it is helpful to analyze separately the independence wars of Haiti, of Mexico and Central America, of Spanish South America, and of Brazil. At the conclusion of these wars, only a few French Caribbean islands, Spanish Cuba, and Puerto Rico remained colonies of the Latin nations of Europe. From 1861 to 1865, Santo Domingo, for a time under Haitian rule and for a time independent, came briefly under Spanish rule again before peacefully regaining independence.

The military aspects of the wars can be described generally as struggles for independence fought between masses of Indian and mestizo (mixed Spanish-Indian) troops led on the one hand by small numbers of Spanish military professionals, and on the other by *criollos*, first- or second-generation Spaniards born in the colonies. The most noteworthy campaigns were those carried out by the Venezuelan Simón Bolívar and the Argentine José de San Martín, both of whom made epic crossings of the Andes Mountains to take the Spaniards by surprise.

The overall pattern of the Spanish American wars of independence was an initial period of political confusion stemming from Napoleon's occupation of the Iberian Peninsula in 1808, followed by declarations of independence first from Napoleon's puppet government in Madrid, and then from Spain as the mother country. These declarations were buttressed by a string of early patriot victories. But, after Spain threw off the Napoleonic yoke, it reconquered many of its American possessions, and this led to an extended period of conflict between Spaniards and rebels until the rebels gained final victory and independence in the early and mid-1820s (Fig. 1).

Figure 1. The Western Hemisphere at the end of the wars of independence (1826). (SOURCE: Jack Child, 1988)

Background of the Latin American Wars of Independence

GENERAL CAUSES

The general causes of the wars of independence lie in French, Spanish, and Portuguese neglect of their American colonies, their economic exploitation of them, and their feeling that the *criollos* in the colonies were politically, economically, and culturally inferior to their cousins on the Iberian Peninsula. Serious rebellions had been put down brutally in the late eighteenth century, and memories of these outbreaks were still fresh when winds of change began blowing in the Americas, fueled by the American and French revolutions, British-Spanish rivalry, and the ideas of the Enlightenment brought in by Freemasons and liberals.

THE INDEPENDENCE OF THE ISLAND OF HISPANIOLA

The first American colony to achieve independence after the United States was the black republic of Haiti on the island of Hispaniola, although the special circumstances of that event held little precedent for the other colonies in the hemisphere. The French Revolution had abolished slavery, and in Haiti, in the 1790s, this led to a civil war involving black former slaves (led by François Toussaint L'Ouverture), mulattoes, and French settlers. Napoleon's expeditionary force under General Leclerc managed to capture Toussaint, but it was eventually exhausted by disease and the firm resistance of the former slaves. It was only after a decade of bloodshed that Haiti's independence was achieved in 1804 on the western half of the island of Hispaniola. Santo Domingo, on the eastern half of the island, was to be under the intermittent control of Haiti, France, and Spain for another 40 years before achieving independence as the Dominican Republic in 1865.

THE IMPACT OF NAPOLEON'S INVASION OF IBERIA

The spark that set off the process of independence for the rest of Latin America was Napoleon's invasion of Spain and Portugal in 1808. In Portugal, the ruling Braganzas were able to escape the French armies and make their way to their colony of Brazil under the protection of British warships. From Brazil, they continued their rule and eventually returned to Portugal, thus avoiding the sharp splits that characterized the Spanish-American independence process. In Madrid, King Charles IV was forced to abdicate. His son Ferdinand was imprisoned by Napoleon, who placed his brother Joseph Bonaparte on the Spanish throne (1808–13). Spanish resistance to Napoleon was strong in the south of the peninsula, where a junta ruled in the name of Ferdinand. This political division provided Spain's American colonies with the opportunity to form their own local juntas and declare themselves independent from Napoleonic Spain. Many of the backers of this process expected that this would lead to full independence, which it eventually did after fifteen years of bitter struggle.

Mexico and Central America

The Viceroyalty of New Spain included what is today Mexico, Central America, and large portions of the southwestern United States. In 1808, the viceroy declared himself independent of Napoleon and established a government in the name of Ferdinand VII. This, however, was not good enough for the *criollos*, who had been conspiring for greater autonomy. On 16 September 1810, the priest Miguel Hidalgo launched the Mexican war of independence by ringing the bells of his parish church and uttering the "Cry of Dolores" against the Spaniards in the name of the Mexican Virgin of Guadalupe. Father Hidalgo organized a government in Guadalajara and led masses of Indians in battles against the Spanish authorities in Mexico City. Unfortunately, he proved to be a more effective spiritual and political leader than a military campaigner, and he was defeated by the viceroy's forces and captured early in 1811. He was condemned and excommunicated by the Inquisition. Shortly afterward he was tried and shot by the civil government. A fellow rebel priest, José Morelos, took up Hidalgo's banner and convened a congress that adopted a constitution and declared independence (November 1813). But Morelos, too, was defeated in battle and then executed by the Spaniards. It was left to the former Spanish professional soldier Augustín de Iturbide, who joined the patriot cause in 1820, to defeat the Spaniards, which he did in 1821, and consolidate the independence of a sovereign Mexican nation.

In Central America, there were several local independence movements in the period from 1811 to 1814, but these were crushed by the Spaniards. Central America finally achieved independence from Spain as a result of the victories of Iturbide, who invited the peoples of the old Capitancy-General of Guatemala (today's Central America) to join his Mexican Empire. But when Iturbide was overthrown in 1823, the Central Americans seceded from Mexico and established a federation of the "United Provinces of Central America," which lasted for a decade before splitting up into five of today's independent Central American nations.

Spanish South America

The military struggle for independence by Spanish South America was essentially a strategic pincer movement focusing ultimately on the Spanish stronghold of Peru and led from the north by the Venezuelan Simón Bolívar and from the River Plate area in the south by the Argentine José de San Martín. Both campaigns came after the 1810 declarations of rebellion against Napoleonic Spain and were characterized by initial victories that were followed by defeats as Spain temporarily regained her colonies, and then final independence in the mid-1820s.

SOUTHERN SOUTH AMERICA

The *criollos* of Buenos Aires had considerable confidence in their ability to make good their independence because they had defeated British invasions in 1806 and 1807, when the Spanish authorities abandoned the *criollos* to their fate. As a result, when news of Napoleon's invasion of Spain and of the incarceration of Ferdinand VII reached Buenos Aires, there was a firm determination to use the events in Madrid as the basis first to declare a break from Napoleonic Spain (25 May 1810) and then to effect a complete break from the mother country (9 July 1816). Gen. Manuel Belgrano was a key figure in this early period, but he suffered military reverses after Ferdinand VII was restored to the throne. This was also the period when Paraguay split off in its own independence movement, when the Uruguayan general José Gervasio Artigas was struggling against encroachments from both Argentina and Brazil, and when the Chilean patriot Gen. Bernardo O'Higgins was decisively defeated by the Spanish and had to retreat across the Andes Mountains into Argentina.

After 1812, military leadership of the southern South American independence movement passed into the able hands of José de San Martín. His strategic concept was to establish himself in western Argentina, then cross the Andes and strike the Spanish forces in Chile by surprise. From there he would head north to the center of Spanish authority in Peru, while Bolívar similarly headed south from his base in Venezuela. In early 1817, San Martín's forces, working with the Chilean patriots under General O'Higgins, crossed the Andes in an unprecedented feat and caught the Spaniards off guard, defeating them at Chacabuco (12 February 1817). A year later, at the Battle of Maipú (5 April 1818), he and O'Higgins consolidated the independence of Chile and began the campaign against the Spaniards in Peru. A fleet was organized with the help of Englishman Lord Thomas Cochrane. In July 1821, after victories on land and sea, San Martín entered Lima and proclaimed its independence. Important Spanish garrisons, however, remained in control of large sections of the region now encompassing Peru, Ecuador, and Bolivia. In July 1822, San Martín and Bolívar met privately for two days at Guayaquil, Ecuador, to plan the final campaign against the Spaniards. There is much mystery surrounding these meetings between the two liberators, but when the conversations ended San Martín withdrew from the scene and went into European exile, leaving to Bolívar the direction of the final stages of the wars of independence.

NORTHERN SOUTH AMERICA

The *criollos* of Caracas, like those of Buenos Aires, had declared their independence of Napoleonic Spain in 1810, and Simón Bolívar, the son of wealthy landowners, had led Venezuelan forces in a series of early victories against the Spanish. His War to the Death against the Spanish general José Boves was particularly bloody, and when the resurgent Spanish captured Caracas in 1814, Bolívar was forced to flee first to Bogotá (Colombia) and later to the island of Jamaica. Left behind to fight in the plains of the Orinoco Basin was Gen. José Antonio Páez, who led his irregular cavalry forces in a series of running battles against the Spanish.

Bolívar returned to Venezuela early in 1817 and began the second phase of the struggle against the Spanish. By late 1818, his forces, allied with those of

Páez, were in control of most of the Orinoco Valley. This permitted the patriots to declare independence formally at Angostura (20 November 1818) and to begin the campaign against the Spanish forces still holding Caracas. The final defeat of the Spanish in Venezuela was assisted by substantial numbers of foreign volunteers, mainly British. With Venezuela in his hands, Bolívar, like San Martín, planned a hazardous crossing of the Andes and a surprise attack on the Spanish garrison in what is today Colombia. He achieved this at the critical Battle of Boyacá (7 August 1819), finally expelling the last Spanish forces from northern South America at the Battle of Carabobo, on 25 June 1821. The following year, one of Bolívar's lieutenants, Gen. Antonio José de Sucre, obtained the independence of Ecuador at the Battle of Pichincha, 22 May 1822, fought on the slopes of a volcano just outside the capital city of Quito.

After the fateful meeting between San Martín and Bolívar in Guayaquil, Bolívar was left as supreme military commander of patriot armies in South America. Scattered Spanish forces held on, however, until decisively defeated by Bolívar and his generals first at the Battle of Junín (6 August 1824) and then at Ayacucho (9 December 1824).

Brazil

There were no wars of independence in Brazil, which separated from Portugal gradually and with little violence. The Portuguese Braganza dynasty had established itself in Brazil after Napoleon invaded the peninsula, and when Portuguese King John VI returned to Portugal, his son Pedro stayed behind. When Brazil obtained its independence from Portugal on 7 September 1822, it was as an empire, with the Braganzan Pedro I as its first sovereign.

JACK CHILD

SEE ALSO: Bolívar, Simón: San Martín, José de; Spanish Empire.

Bibliography

Anna, T. E. 1983. *Spain and the loss of America*. Lincoln: Univ. of Nebraska Press.
Bethell, L., ed. 1984. *The Cambridge history of Latin America*. Vol. 3: *From independence to 1870*. Cambridge: Cambridge Univ. Press.
Domínguez, J. I. 1980. *Insurrection or loyalty: The breakdown of the Spanish-American empire*. Cambridge: Harvard Univ. Press.
Herring, H. 1968. *A history of Latin America*. 3d ed. New York: Knopf.
Humphreys, R. A., and J. Lynch, eds. 1966. *The origins of the Latin American revolutions*. New York: Knopf.
Keen, B. 1986. *Latin American civilization: History and society, 1492 to the present*. 4th ed. Boulder, Colo.: Westview Press.
Lynch, J. 1973. *The Spanish American revolutions, 1808–1826*. New York: Norton.
Madariaga, S. de. 1947. *The fall of the Spanish American empire*. New York: Macmillan.
Prago, A. 1970. *The revolutions in Spanish America*. New York: Macmillan.

LEAHY, WILLIAM DANIEL [1875–1959]

Adm. William D. Leahy, U.S. Navy, served as a personal adviser to President Franklin D. Roosevelt during World War II (Fig. 1). In that capacity he had tremendous influence over America's wartime policies. He and Gen. George Marshall were so successful in the performance of their duties that many subsequent presidents came to rely on the U.S. military as a source of advisers.

Early Life and Career

Leahy was born on 6 May 1875 in Hampton, Iowa, and was graduated from the U.S. Naval Academy in Annapolis, Maryland, in 1897. As a midshipman during

Figure 1. William Daniel Leahy. (SOURCE: U.S. Library of Congress)

the Spanish-American War he was stationed aboard the battleship *Oregon* (BB-3), where he fought at the Battle of Santiago Bay in July 1898. He was then transferred to the second-class battleship *Texas* in October 1898. In 1899 he was sent to the Far East and saw action in the Philippine insurrection and the Boxer Rebellion, serving aboard the gunboat *Castine* and on the supply ship *Glacier* (AF-4), and as the commanding officer of the gunboat *Mariveles* in 1902. Leahy's duty assignments in the following years included: the new cruiser *Tacoma* (C-18); the protected cruiser *Boston* while it patrolled off the Panama Canal when that waterway was being built and later while *Boston* provided assistance to victims of the San Francisco earthquake of 1906; science instructor at the Naval Academy; navigator on the armored cruiser *California* (ACR-6) from 1909 to 1911; staff officer to fleet commander Adm. Chauncey Thomas on the same ship from 1911 to 1912; and chief of staff to Adm. W. H. H. Southerland on the flagship *West Virginia* (ACR-5) during the Nicaraguan intervention of 1912. He then served in various shore duty billets.

Prior to U.S. entry into World War I, Leahy at first continued his shore duty and then became commander of the dispatch gunboat *Dolphin* (PG-24) in the West Indies in 1915. While aboard, he participated in the occupation of Santo Domingo in 1916, in demonstrations off Mexico, and, following the U.S. declaration of war against Germany (6 April), in searches for German supply craft during the spring of 1917. He then became executive officer of the *Nevada* (BB-36), and served while it conducted wartime patrols out of Norfolk, Virginia. In April 1918, Leahy took command of the *Princess Matoika*, a troop transport that ferried elements of the American Expeditionary Force to Europe. It was during his command of this ship that he became friends with Franklin D. Roosevelt, who was then assistant secretary of the navy.

Senior Assignments in the U.S. Navy

Following the war, Leahy rose rapidly in the navy. He commanded the *St. Louis* (CA-18) while it was the flagship of U.S. naval forces off Turkey when that nation was torn with strife in 1921. He served as commander of the Atlantic Fleet's Mine Squadron One, and in 1922 as commander of the Control Force of submarines and smaller craft. From 1923 to 1926, he directed the officer personnel division of the Bureau of Navigation and then commanded the *New Mexico* (BB-40) before his promotion to rear admiral in 1927. While Leahy would have additional sea assignments, his administrative skills were his greatest strength, and it was in shore assignments that he had his greatest effect. From 1927 to 1931, he served as chief of the Bureau of Ordnance. Following a tour as chief of the Bureau of Navigation from 1933 to 1935, he was commander of Battleships Battle Force as a vice admiral, and commander of Battleships Force in the *California* (BB-44) as a rear admiral from 1936 to 1937. He served as chief of naval operations from 1937 to 1939 and virtually ran the navy in the absence of the secretary of the navy, Claude A. Swanson, who was ill during this period. Leahy was 64 (mandatory retirement age) when he retired as an admiral in July 1939.

Leahy as Statesman

Although Leahy never again served in the navy's chain of command, he served in several positions that had great effect on both naval and national policy. President Roosevelt made him governor of Puerto Rico in September 1939 and U.S. ambassador to the Vichy government of unoccupied France in November 1940—an assignment that required the greatest diplomatic skills, given German control over French foreign policy.

After America entered World War II, Leahy was recalled to active duty in July 1942 and was appointed to a newly created position, chief of staff to the president. He also served as chairman of the Joint Chiefs of Staff. He was promoted to fleet admiral in December 1944 and accompanied Roosevelt to all the strategic conferences of the Allies, including the Yalta conference in 1945.

After Roosevelt's death in April 1945, Truman retained Leahy as his chief of staff and he continued in his advisory role during the early years of the cold war. He retired at 73 in 1949 and wrote his memoirs, *I Was There: The Personal Story of the Chief of Staff to Presidents Roosevelt and Truman*, in 1950. He died on 20 July 1959.

Leahy's Significance

Admiral Leahy's historic significance lies in his diplomatic and administrative skills. During World War II he served as the senior military member of the small group of politicians and military men that dictated wartime military policy. His personal relationship with President Roosevelt gave him great influence in wartime decisionmaking. Additionally, because Leahy was considered so successful as a presidential adviser the practice of using high-ranking military officers in high-level government positions was continued. Such officers, regarded as competent and apolitical and offering no political threat, have served in many sensitive positions such as directors of the Central Intelligence Agency and the National Security Agency, and as national security advisers to presidents.

BRUCE W. WATSON

SEE ALSO: World War I; World War II.

Bibliography

Adams, H. H. 1985. *Witness to power: The life of fleet admiral William D. Leahy.* Annapolis, Md.: U.S. Naval Institute Press.

Leahy, W. D. 1977. *Diaries, 1939–1949.* Washington, D.C.: Library of Congress Photoduplication Service.

———. 1950. *I was there: The personal story of the chief of staff to Presidents Roosevelt and Truman.* New York: Whittlesey House.

Spiller, R. J. 1989. *American military leaders.* New York: Praeger.

Thomas, G. E. 1973. *William D. Leahy and America's imperial years, 1893–1917.* New Haven, Conn.: Gerald E. Thomas.

LEE, ROBERT EDWARD [1807–1870]

Born at Stratford, Westmoreland County, Virginia, on 19 January 1807, Robert E. Lee was the fifth child and third son of Henry ("Light Horse Harry") Lee, a distinguished cavalry officer of the American Revolutionary War, and his wife, Lucy Grymes Lee.

When his father died in 1818, Robert assumed the responsibility of caring for his partially disabled mother and an ailing sister. Scholastically, he excelled in mathematics.

Early Military Career

Lee graduated number two in the 1829 class of the United States Military Academy at West Point, New York, without a single demerit. He was breveted second lieutenant of engineers.

He subsequently served at Fort Pulaski, Georgia; as assistant engineer at Fort Monroe, Virginia (May 1831–November 1834); as assistant in the chief engineer's office in Washington, D.C. (November 1834–July 1837; helped survey the Ohio-Michigan border in 1835); as superintending engineer for St. Louis harbor and the Upper Mississippi and Missouri rivers (July 1837–October 1841); and at Fort Hamilton, New York (October 1841–August 1846).

On 30 June 1831 he married Mary Ann Randolph Custis, daughter of George Washington Parke Custis, grandson of Martha Washington. They were destined to have seven children.

Mexican War service provided Lee with lessons in the value of audacity and of a trained staff; of the relationship between careful reconnaissance and sound strategy; of the strategic possibilities of flanking movements; of the relationship of communications to strategy; and of the value of fortification. All of these lessons—acquired under the tutelage of Gen. Winfield Scott—proved of inestimable value to him in the forthcoming Civil War. He was cited by his superiors for bold reconnoitering, effectively emplacing artillery under heavy enemy fire, accurate reports, and well-thought-out recommendations. Slightly wounded at the battle of Chapultepec on 13 September 1847, he was sent home.

Lee had been promoted to first lieutenant in 1836 and captain in 1838. Brevet promotions during the Mexican War advanced him to colonel in 1848. From November 1848 to August 1852 he supervised construction at Fort Carroll, Baltimore, Maryland. Against his wishes, he was appointed superintendent of West Point. Lee did not feel experienced enough for this singular honor.

He was a diligent and efficient superintendent. He tightened academy discipline and academic standards, but also devoted personal attention to individual cadets.

In March 1855 Lee happily accepted appointment as lieutenant colonel of the 2d Cavalry, but was actually assigned to court martial duty most of the next two years.

When his father-in-law died in October 1857, Lee took leave from the army. Responsibilities as estate executor and caring for an ailing wife kept him from duty until 1859. That year he was sent to Harpers Ferry, Virginia (today, West Virginia), to quell an insurrection led by the abolitionist John Brown.

Civil War

Lee did not favor secession of the southern states from the Union, but he believed his principal allegiance was to his native state of Virginia.

Between February 1860 and February 1861, he commanded the Department of Texas. At the outbreak of civil war he was recalled to Washington and on 18 April was offered field command of the U.S. Army by General-in-Chief Scott. However, Virginia seceded, and Lee resigned his army commission.

Lee was then 54 years old. He stood 5 feet 11 inches tall and weighed just under 170 pounds. His physique was sound, his eyesight unimpaired, and he possessed great endurance (Fig. 1).

He was a disciplined professional soldier with good strategic sense, a master of reconnaissance, an excellent topographer, and had a superior knowledge of fortification. He had never, however, experienced defensive warfare, he had difficulty delegating work to others, and he lacked a good understanding of logistics.

Lee was nominated to command all Virginia troops on 23 April. In August he was appointed general in the Confederate States Army, to rank from 14 June, and appointed military adviser to President Jefferson Davis.

Between November 1861 and March 1862 he organized South Atlantic seaboard defenses. On 31 May 1862 he was appointed commander of the Confederate Army in Virginia, which he named "The Army of Northern Virginia."

In June, employing interior lines and brilliant maneuvering, Lee won a series of battles near Richmond, known as the Seven Days. In August he won the Second Battle of Manassas (Second Bull Run). However, when he moved north in September, he was checked by the Federals under Gen. George B. McClellan at Sharpsburg (Antietam) in Maryland. In December, Lee's well-positioned troops repulsed repeated Union assaults at Fredericksburg.

At Chancellorsville in May 1863, Lee defeated the Union army by dividing his army and enveloping the Union right wing. However, the price was high: Lt. Gen. Thomas Jonathan ("Stonewall") Jackson was lost, mortally wounded when shot by his own men. Lee moved north again in June but was decisively defeated at Gettysburg, Pennsylvania (1–3 July).

In 1864, Lee's army won tactical victories, but the persistent brilliance of Union general U.S. Grant, as well as the numerical, logistical, and transportation superiorities of the Union doomed Lee and the Confederacy to defeat. The end for the Army of Northern Virginia came on 9 April 1865 at Appomattox Court House, Virginia.

After the war, Lee became president of Washington College, Lexington, Virginia (today Washington and Lee University). He died 12 October 1870 and was buried in Lexington.

Figure 1. Robert E. Lee. (SOURCE: U.S. Library of Congress)

Conclusion

Lee successfully took chances with his army many times during the Civil War. A number of battles were won by the timely arrival of reinforcements at the critical point on the battlefield. However, he could never censure subordinates whose caution, independence, or disagreement with his ideas altered, or ruined, planned operations. He inspired confidence and was just and kind to all. The respect and admiration Robert E. Lee earned from friend and foe alike has grown with the passage of time.

UZAL W. ENT

SEE ALSO: Civil War, American; Grant, Ulysses Simpson; Jackson, Thomas Jonathan ("Stonewall"); Scott, Winfield.

Bibliography

Connelly, T. L. 1977. *The marble man: Robert E. Lee and his image in American society.* New York: Knopf.
Davis, B. 1956. *Gray fox: Robert E. Lee and the Civil War.* New York: Rinehart.
Dowdey, C. 1965. *Lee.* Boston and Toronto: Little, Brown.
Freeman, D. S. 1934–35. *R. E. Lee: A biography.* 4 vols. New York and London: Scribner's.
———. [1942] 1950. *Lee's lieutenants: A study in command.* 3 vols. New York: Scribner's.
Taylor, W. H. [1877] 1962. *Four years with General Lee.* Reprint. New York: Bonanza Books. Bloomington, Ind.: Indiana Univ. Press.

LIN-PIAO [1907–1971]

This article provides a brief glimpse into the life of Lin-Piao, a Chinese general and strategist, who played a major role in the military and political life of modern-day China.

Early Years: 1907–1934

Lin-Piao (Lin Biao) was born on 5 December 1907 to the family of a dye-house owner in Huanggang County, Hubei Province. He joined the Chinese Socialist Youth League in 1923, and in 1925, inspired by the 30 May Anti-Imperialist Movement, he threw himself into the student movement. He initiated the formation of the Gongjin Reading Society, and organized students to read progressive books and periodicals. He was elected by the Students' Union of Hubei Province as a delegate to the Congress of the Nationwide Students' Unions held in Shanghai. In winter of the same year (1925), the local Party organization recommended him to the Fourth Class of the Huangpu (Whampoa) Military Academy in Guangzhou (Canton). He subsequently joined the Chinese Communist Party (CCP) there. After his graduation in July 1926, he was assigned to Ye Ting's Independent Regiment, which belonged to the Fourth Army of the National Revolutionary Army, and took part in the Northern Expedition as a platoon leader. He participated in the Nanchang Uprising in August 1927 and after its failure followed Chu-Teh and Chen Yi to the borders of Fujian, Guangdong, and Jiangxi and was promoted to company commander. In January 1928, he took part in the South Hunan Uprising and then went to the Jinggang Mountains with the army. Serving in the Fourth Army of the Chinese Workers' and Peasants' Red Army, he became commander of the 1st Battalion of the 28th Regiment and later became the commander of the regiment itself. He took part in the struggle against the Kuomintang's (KMT) "encirclement and suppression" of the Red Army in the Jinggang Mountains Revolutionary Base. In the spring of 1929, he went to South Jiangxi and West Fujian with the main force of the Fourth Army as the commander of the First Column. He was promoted to commander of the

Fourth Army the following year, and later to commander of the First Army Corps. He led his troops in the campaigns of Changsha, Ganzhou, Zhangzhou, Naxiong Shuikou, and Yihuang of Le'an. He also took part in the defense against the KMT's five "encirclement and suppression" campaigns in the Central Revolutionary Base Areas (1930–34).

Military Exploits: 1934–49

Lin-Piao was subsequently elected a member of the First and Second Executive Committees of the provisional government of the Chinese Soviet Republic and member of the Central Revolutionary Military Committee. In October 1934, he led his troops in the retreat from the Central Revolutionary Base and joined in the Long March. En route he took part in the Xiangjiang Campaign and fought in the battles of Tucheng, in the forced crossing of the Dadu River, and in the taking of the Luding Bridge. In September 1935, he became the assistant commandant of the Shaanxi-Gansu Detachment, made up of the First and Second Red Armies, and commander of the First Column. When the Shaanxi-Gansu Detachment was renamed the First Front Army on arriving at the Shaanxi-Gansu Revolutionary Base, he was its commander in chief and then led his army in the Zhiluozhen and East Expedition campaigns. In 1936 he was made the president and political commissar of the Red Army Academy of Resistance against Japan and, later, the president of the Military and Political Academy.

After the outbreak of the War of Resistance against Japan (World War II) in July 1937, he became the commander of the 115th Division of the Eighth Route Army, and together with Nie Rongzhen, he led the troops on the North China front. In the first battle fought at Pingxing Pass, they badly mauled the Itagaki Division of the Japanese army and won the first important Chinese victory in the Anti-Japanese War. When marching past Xixian County, Shanxi Province, on 2 March 1938, he was accidentally wounded by KMT sentries of Yan Xishan's troops and returned to Yan'an for medical treatment. That same year he went to the Soviet Union for treatment and recuperation and acted as the representative of the Chinese Communist Party Central Committee's Delegation in Moscow. Returning to Yan'an in January 1942, he became the vice-president of the Central Party School of the CCP.

After the end of the victorious Anti-Japanese War in 1945, he was sent to North China and became commander in chief of the Northeastern People's Self-Governing Army, commander in chief and political commissar of the Northeastern Democratic United Army, commander and political commissar of the Northeast Military Area Command and Northeastern Field Army, and secretary of the Party's Northeast Bureau. He participated in planning and commanding the Linjiang Campaign; the summer, fall, and winter offensives in the Northeast in 1947; and the Liaoning-Shenyang Campaign, thereby playing a major role in the liberation of the northeast. He also led the reconstruction of the Liberated Areas in the northeast. In 1948 he led his troops down into the Shanhaiguan area and was appointed secretary of the Front Committee during the Beijing-Tianjin Campaign and, together with Luo Ronghuan and Nie Rong-zhen, exercised united command of the main forces of the Northeast Field Army and the troops of the North China Military Area Command. In April 1949 he led his troops to the mid-south of China in a strategic pursuit. He was made successively the commander of the Fourth Field Army (formerly the Northeast Field Army), commander of the Mid-China Military Area Command (later changed to Mid-South Military Area Command), and the first secretary of the Party's Mid-China Bureau (later changed to the Mid-South Bureau). He participated in commanding the campaigns of Hengbao, Guangdong, and Guangxi.

Political Advancement and the Cultural Revolution: 1949–71

With the founding of the People's Republic of China on 21 September 1949, Lin-Piao was appointed chairman of the Mid-South China Army and Government Committee and the Mid-South China Administrative Committee. Later he filled other positions such as vice-chairman of the People's Revolutionary Military Committee of the Central People's Government, vice-premier, and vice-chairman of the National Defense Council. In September 1955 he received the rank of field marshal of the People's Republic of China. In September 1959 he became the defense minister and then vice-chairman of the Central Military Committee, taking charge of its day-to-day work. From June 1945 on, he was a member of the Party Central Committee; from April 1955 on, a member of the Politburo of the CCP Central Committee; and from May 1958 on, a member and vice-chairman of the Standing Committee of the CCP Central Committee.

During the Cultural Revolution, Lin-Piao formed a counterrevolutionary clique with Chen Boda, Huang Yongsheng, Wu Faxian, Ye Qun, Li Zuopeng, Qiu Huizuo, and others. Hand in glove with Jiang Qing's counterrevolutionary clique, he schemed against and persecuted other party and state leaders, incited a movement for "overthrowing everybody and unleashing a comprehensive civil war," and plotted to usurp the supreme powers of the party and the state. On 8 September 1971, Lin-Piao issued an order for a coup, planning to assassinate Mao Tse-tung and set up another central authority. On 13 September 1971, when the conspiracy was uncovered, he tried to flee abroad, taking with him his wife, Ye Qun; his son, Lin Liguo; and other members of his clique. The plane carrying Lin-Piao's party crashed at Undurkhan in the People's Republic of Mongolia, killing all on board.

Final Comment

On 20 August 1973, the CCP Central Committee decided to expel Lin-Piao's name from the party. On 25 January 1981, he was condemned as the prime culprit of the counterrevolutionary clique by a Special Court of the Supreme People's Court of the People's Republic of China.

JIANG FENG-BO

SEE ALSO: Chu-Teh; Mao Tse-tung; World War II.

Bibliography

Institute of Military History of the Military Academy of the People's Liberation Army.
    1987. *Military history of the Chinese People's Liberation Army.* Vols. 1–3. Beijing:
    Military Science Press.
Research Office of the Party's History of the Party Central Committee. 1987. *Chronicles
    of the Chinese Communist Party.* Beijing: People's Publishing House.

LUDENDORFF, ERICH [1865–1937]

Erich Ludendorff is one of the most tragic figures in military history. A soldier
of great intellect and thorough competence, Ludendorff became the dominant
personality in the German war effort in World War I. Besides determining
national policy, Ludendorff also supervised and implemented changes in tactical doctrine that brought the German Army to a level of tactical excellence
that has seldom, if ever, been equaled. But, as one biographer has aptly stated,
Ludendorff was a "tormented warrior," a victim of his own terrible intensity.
Without others around him to help steady him, his behavior often exhibited
emotional instability, and his judgment would become distorted.

Career Prior to World War I

Erich Friedrich Wilhelm Ludendorff was born near Posen (Poznan), Prussia,
on 9 April 1865. His family was middle-class landowners; unlike many of his
Prussian military contemporaries, he was not an aristocrat. Tragedy touched
him early in his life when his father became bankrupt.

Ludendorff became a cadet at the age of 12 and quickly displayed a great
capacity for hard work, a characteristic that he retained all his life. Commissioned in the infantry, he was selected to attend the Kriegsakademie, the school
of the German General Staff, in 1893.

From 1904 to 1913 he served with the Great General Staff in Berlin. Ludendorff became deeply involved with the issue of army manpower, and he
pressed vigorously for increases. So doggedly did he pursue the issue that in
1913 he was posted to a regimental command out of Berlin, probably to get him
away from the capital and away from sensitive policy issues. During his posting
in Berlin, Ludendorff also met Margarethe Pernet, a divorced housewife with
four children, who, drawn to this intense army officer, married him. Vivacious
and beautiful, Margarethe helped Ludendorff display a warmer, more human
side. He was devoted to her children, who warmly returned his affection.

World War I

With the advent of the greatest war in Europe since Napoleon, Ludendorff was
a staff officer with the Second Army as it swept into Belgium, part of the great
turning movement of the so-called Schlieffen Plan. Taking over a brigade whose

commander had been killed, Ludendorff boldly directed the unit to take the critical Belgian fortress of Liège. With a combination of bluff and cool bravery, he persuaded the confused Belgian defenders to surrender the citadel. For this action, in which he demonstrated both great courage and great tactical skill (it was also his first experience under fire), he was awarded the nation's highest decoration.

Events on the eastern front now unexpectedly demanded Ludendorff's attention. As the bulk of German forces swept through Belgium in the attempt to defeat France quickly, the German Eighth Army in the east was to hold off the Russians until victorious forces from France could later be diverted to that theater. However, the commander of the Eighth Army began to panic as two Russian field armies massed on the borders of East Prussia. The German high command decided to appoint a new commander and a new chief of staff to that field army. General Paul von Hindenburg was called out of retirement to be the commander, and Ludendorff was named the chief of staff. The two men, who had never previously met, greeted each other at a railway station in Germany, and headed east on a special train. Thus began one of the most successful partnerships in military history. Hindenburg's calm, steady, and humane demeanor was the perfect complement to Ludendorff's brilliant but high-strung mind.

The Hindenburg-Ludendorff combination enjoyed immediate success. By concentrating first (near a town named Tannenberg) against one Russian field army, decisively defeating it, and then hitting the other army, the German Eighth Army drove the Russian forces out of East Prussia and inflicted severe casualties on them. By the end of 1914, as the war settled down to a long struggle, the Hindenburg-Ludendorff team (or H-L team, as Winston Churchill would call it) was placed in command of all German forces in the east. For the next two years these German forces hammered the Russians, driving them back deeper into Russia. In August 1916, frustration with German operations in the west caused the Kaiser to select the Hindenburg-Ludendorff team to direct the entire German war effort, with Hindenburg named as the chief of the general staff and Ludendorff as the first quartermaster general, a name he chose himself, not wishing to be a "deputy" or "second."

The Tactical Revolution

As Ludendorff now moved west to concentrate most of his efforts on the most crucial front, the western front, he must have been tempted to advocate "eastern" solutions. To his great credit, he set out to learn about the peculiar conditions of the western front, refraining from arrogantly imposing his own solutions from the experience in the east.

In adjusting to the tactical conditions of the western front and in directing changes in German tactics from 1916 to 1918, Ludendorff was at his most brilliant. By soliciting opinions and observations from the fighting units, Ludendorff's small operations staff developed new tactics; disseminated them to the units; refined them based on feedback; and then trained, organized, and equipped the army to apply them. Ludendorff was not the inventor; more important, he understood that tactical creativity existed *not* in a remote head-quarters, but in the fighting units, and he led the corporate effort to *discover* solutions to vexing tactical problems.

In 1917 the German forces in the west were on the defensive. Applying a new tactical concept, of the elastic defense-in-depth, the Germans absorbed the tremendous allied offensives and responded with mauling counterattacks. Many German observers remarked that Germany would not have survived the battles of 1917 had not Ludendorff managed the tactical changes so success-fully.

For offensive tactics (which the Germans applied in 1918), the Germans developed the concept of the sudden attack in depth, using carefully planned concentrations of artillery to disrupt the enemy, followed closely by infiltrating infantry units probing deeply, bypassing when necessary, constantly keeping the adversary off balance. Under the direction of Ludendorff, the German principles of offense and defense recognized that tactics had become decen-tralized in execution, that the small unit, even down to the squad, was a key element. The uniformly equipped rifleman was no longer the basic element of the tactical unit; soldiers with specialized weapons now had to be organized in the proper mix at the small-unit level. Special assault troops, called stormtroop-ers, were trained. The tactics also stressed the importance of combined arms, particularly the combination of infantry and artillery.

Strategic Errors

While Ludendorff was truly in his element directing the tactical innovation of the German Army, his influence in directing the entire German war effort led him into areas well beyond his expertise. The military talent that Germany possessed in abundance was not matched by political talent. Into this vacuum the dominant personality of Ludendorff penetrated, but the role exceeded even his capacity. The Hindenburg-Ludendorff team, dominated by Ludendorff, directed such diverse endeavors as the war economy and U-boat policy. In the latter case, their policy of unrestricted submarine warfare brought the United States into the war. When an opportunity for a negotiated peace emerged in 1917, Ludendorff ended it by making unrealistic territorial demands.

In order to destroy the Western powers before the full weight of the United States would tip the scales, Ludendorff decided to make one last offensive in the west in the spring of 1918. The great offensives that ensued were classic examples of German organizational ability. The new offensive tactics proved quite effective, as the Germans acquired more territory than had any army in the west since 1914. But the precarious position of Germany, with dwindling military resources and a suffering population at home, demanded a flawless strategic direction. This Ludendorff did not provide. He did not concentrate the German effort, nor did he reinforce success. Beginning in June 1918, the opposing allies, initially thrown into confusion, now rallied with counteroffen-sives of their own. Soon Ludendorff, completely exhausted, told Hindenburg that Germany should seek an armistice. Ludendorff found himself absorbing most of the blame for Germany's failure and resigned in October 1918. He eventually went to Sweden to write his memoirs, but before he left Germany he uttered the famous line that Germany had not been defeated, but had been "stabbed in the back" (referring to naval mutiny and political, revolutionary unrest that led a new German government to ask for an armistice).

Later Life

The strain upon Ludendorff during the war had been immense. In essence, he had directed the entire nation in 1917 and 1918; he had also suffered personal loss, for two of his stepsons had been killed in the war.

Returning to Germany in 1919, Ludendorff became involved in politics. (Figure 1 shows Ludendorff in 1921.) He seized upon extreme ideas of German ethnic "purity" and became an advocate of the newly formed National Socialist German Workers Party. In 1923 Ludendorff participated in the abortive Beer Hall Putsch with Adolf Hitler, was tried for treason, and was acquitted. Continuing in politics, he was elected to the Reichstag (parliament), but was disappointed by a dismal showing when he ran for president in 1925.

In his last years, Ludendorff retreated into his own world of disappointment and hatred. He divorced Margarethe in 1926 and married Dr. Mathilde von Kemnitz, whose bizarre ideas now appealed to him. He and his new wife

Figure 1. Gen. Erich Ludendorff is surrounded by high officers of the German Army at the funeral of ex-King Ludwig and the former queen of Bavaria, 1921. (SOURCE: U.S. Library of Congress)

indulged in pagan beliefs and racial hatred. Ludendorff became increasingly hostile to Hitler, who ironically continued to try to win the old general's approval. Estranged from his old commander, Hindenburg, Ludendorff nonetheless wrote to him when Hindenburg, as president of Germany, made Hitler chancellor. Ludendorff—with surprising prescience—warned that Hitler was a demagogue who would bring ruin to Germany. Just before his death in 1937, Ludendorff wrote *Total War*, in which he inverted Clausewitz's dictum subordinating war to politics, arguing that a military dictator should run the nation in war. (He appeared oblivious to the fact that his own experience disproved this thesis.)

Assessment

Ludendorff was an extremely able soldier, but he required the calming presence of others who were less intense. In politics, he was not in his element. While one can sympathize with his assuming great responsibility during the war because of an absence of competent political direction, his strange conduct after the war revealed a character that had lost its balance. In tactics, however, he was one of the most brilliant figures in military history. His conceptual tactical accomplishments in 1917 and 1918 have few parallels. Through his efforts, the theoretical foundations were laid for twentieth-century tactics. In the interwar years, his successors on the German General Staff added the benefits of mobility (mechanization and airpower) and radio communication to his tactical innovations of 1917 and 1918. The practitioners of blitzkrieg were the heirs of Ludendorff.

TIMOTHY T. LUPFER

SEE ALSO: Hindenburg, Paul von; Prussia and Germany, Rise of.

Bibliography

Barnett, C. 1963. *The swordbearers*. New York: Morrow.
Craig, G. A. 1964. *The politics of the Prussian army*. London and New York: Oxford Univ. Press.
Dupuy, T. N. 1970. *The military lives of Hindenburg and Ludendorff*. New York: Franklin Watts.
Goerlitz, W. 1953. *The German general staff*. New York: Praeger.
Goodspeed, D. 1966. *Ludendorff, genius of World War I*. Boston: Houghton Mifflin.
Ludendorff, E. 1934. *The general staff and its problems*. 2 vols. Trans. F. A. Holt. New York: Dutton.
———. 1919. *Meine Kriegserrinnerungen 1914–1918*. Berlin: Mittler.
Lupfer, T. T. 1981. *The dynamics of doctrine: The changes in German tactical doctrine during the First World War*. Fort Leavenworth, Kans.: Combat Studies Institute.
Middlebrook, M. 1978. *The Kaiser's battle*. London: Penguin.
Parkinson, R. 1978. *Tormented warrior*. New York: Stein & Day.
Tschuppik, K. 1932. *Ludendorff: The tragedy of a military mind*. Trans. W. H. Johnston. New York: Houghton Mifflin.
Wynne, G. [1940] 1976. *If Germany attacks*. Reprint. Westport, Conn.: Greenwood Press.

M

MACARTHUR, DOUGLAS [1880–1964]

Douglas MacArthur was born on 26 January 1880 in Little Rock, Arkansas, the son of Arthur MacArthur and Mary Pinkney Hardy. MacArthur's father was an army officer who had had a distinguished career as a commander during the Civil War, the Spanish-American War, and the Philippine Insurrection. Determined on an army career, MacArthur, with the help of his mother, won an appointment to the U.S. Military Academy at West Point. He graduated first in his class in 1903 and was commissioned a second lieutenant of engineers.

MacArthur's first assignment was as a junior construction engineer officer in the Philippines. Promoted to first lieutenant, he was then sent with an engineer party detailed to survey the Bataan Peninsula. In October 1904, MacArthur was transferred back to the United States. He was then assigned to the Golden Gate harbor defenses in San Francisco. In October 1904 he was sent to Tokyo as an aide to his father, now a major general assigned as an observer of the Russo-Japanese War. After the war he accompanied his father on an inspection tour of the Orient.

In late 1906, MacArthur returned to the United States to attend the Army Engineer School at Fort Belvoir, Virginia. During the winter while classes were not in session he served as a special aide to President Theodore Roosevelt. Graduating in August 1907, MacArthur was assigned to river and harbor duty in Wisconsin. In 1908 he was transferred to Fort Leavenworth, Kansas, and appointed a company commander in the 3d Battalion of Engineers. In 1909, MacArthur also became an instructor at the General Service, and later, the Cavalry School at Fort Riley, Kansas. On 27 February 1911 he was promoted to captain of engineers and appointed adjutant of the 3d Battalion.

From March to July 1911, MacArthur served in San Antonio, Texas, with the Maneuver Division, which had been raised in response to tension along the Mexican-American border. After the death of his father in September 1912, MacArthur requested a transfer in order to take care of his mother. In early 1913 he was sent to Washington, D.C., and assigned as a member of the Engineer Board. In May he was appointed superintendent of the State, War, and Navy Building. In September, MacArthur was named a member of the

General Staff. From May to November 1914 he took part in the Vera Cruz expedition and gathered intelligence on Mexico. In December he was promoted to major.

On 30 June 1916, MacArthur was assigned as military assistant to Secretary of War Newton D. Baker and appointed head of the Bureau of Information of the War Department. Secretary Baker and MacArthur developed a great respect for one another and worked closely together in developing the army. A champion of the new National Guard units, MacArthur was responsible for convincing the secretary that guard units could fight alongside regular army units in Europe if the United States became involved in World War I.

World War I

On 6 April 1917 the United States declared war on Germany. MacArthur was instrumental in organizing a multistate National Guard division, the 42d "Rainbow" Division, for service in France. On 5 August 1917 he was promoted to colonel of infantry in the National Army and was appointed the 42d's chief of staff. Sent to France with the division in October 1917, MacArthur fought in the Aisne-Marne operation from 25 July to 2 August 1918. With the brevet rank of brigadier general, he commanded the 84th Brigade at St. Mihiel on 12–17 September. During the Meuse-Argonne campaign (4 October–11 November), MacArthur became the youngest division commander of the war when he was appointed to lead the 42d in the "race to Sedan" (6–11 November). After the armistice, MacArthur remained in Germany as part of the occupation force until April 1919, when he was recalled to the United States.

Interwar Years

MacArthur was appointed superintendent of West Point in June 1919, and was promoted to brigadier general in the regular army in January 1920. He held the post of superintendent until late in 1922, when he was ordered to the Philippines. Before leaving on his new assignment, he married Louise Cromwell Brooks on 14 February.

MacArthur was promoted to major general on 17 January 1925. Shortly after, he returned to the United States and took command of the IV Corps Area in Atlanta. Later that year he was transferred to command the III Corps Area with headquarters in Baltimore. In October of that year, he was assigned the distasteful duty of sitting on the court-martial board of his childhood friend, Col. William "Billy" Mitchell. In September 1927, MacArthur accepted the post of president of the American Olympic Committee while still commanding the III Corps Area. In 1928 he returned to Manila as commander of the Department of the Philippines.

MacArthur was recalled to the United States in August 1930, and in November was appointed Chief of Staff of the Army with the temporary rank of general. Because the Great Depression imposed great fiscal constraints, MacArthur devoted his energies as chief of staff to preserving the meager strength of the army. He reorganized the tactical forces of the army by merging the corps areas into four armies, giving each a regional as well as a field responsibility. He backed the development of both a tank force and a modern air force, but the uncertainty of the national budget consistently thwarted his efforts.

In the summer of 1932, MacArthur was ordered by President Herbert Hoover to disperse some 11,000 unemployed protesters, nicknamed the "Bonus Army," who had camped in the Anacostia area of Washington. A large number of these men were World War I veterans who had been promised bonuses at the end of the war and had been given insurance policies instead. With the Depression in full swing, they had marched to Washington to demand cash for their policies, and threatened to wipe out a nearly empty treasury. Following orders, MacArthur led some 600 infantry and cavalry with six tanks against the hostile mobs and dispersed them in what the press cynically referred to as the "Battle of Anacostia Flats."

In late 1932, Franklin D. Roosevelt was elected president. When MacArthur's term as chief of staff expired in 1934, Roosevelt extended it for another year. In October 1935, MacArthur reverted to the permanent rank of major general and was sent to the Philippines to organize its defenses prior to its projected independence. In August 1936, MacArthur received a unique honor when he was appointed a field marshal in the Philippine Army by the Philippine government. Having divorced his first wife in 1929, MacArthur married Jean Marie Faircloth on 30 April 1937. This union produced a son, Arthur MacArthur IV. On 31 December, MacArthur retired from the U.S. Army and remained in the Philippines to help the government prepare for independence.

With the Japanese war of conquest in China threatening to break out into the rest of Asia, and the German conquests in Poland and France, U.S. strategists began to prepare for America's possible entry into the war. On 26 July 1941, MacArthur was recalled to active duty with the rank of lieutenant general and appointed commander of U.S. Army Forces in the Far East (USAFFE). He immediately set about trying to bolster the Philippine defenses against a possible Japanese invasion.

World War II

Following the Japanese attack at Pearl Harbor (7 December 1941), the United States entered World War II. Although informed of the attack on Pearl Harbor, MacArthur was still surprised when the Japanese launched air attacks against Clark and Iba airfields in the Philippines the following day. On 10 December the Japanese began their invasion of the Philippines, making small landings in northern Luzon. MacArthur realized these were only preliminary moves, and held back his forces for the main landings that he expected would come at Lingayen Gulf. When the Japanese landed in the gulf on 22 December, MacArthur's troops put up a desperate resistance. Since the Japanese possessed both sea and air superiority, however, MacArthur was soon forced to fall back. From 23 December 1941 until 1 January 1942, MacArthur surprised the Japanese by conducting a brilliant fighting withdrawal and sideslipping his army into partially prepared defensive positions on the Bataan peninsula. Forced from Bataan, MacArthur finally fell back to the fortified island of Corregidor in Manila Bay where, under heavy bombardment, he hoped to receive supplies and reinforcements. The situation was hopeless, however, and MacArthur was ordered by President Roosevelt in February 1942 to leave the Philippines. Against his will MacArthur, several members of his staff, and his family slipped out of the Philippines on 11 March and made their way to Australia. In a speech made on his arrival MacArthur gave his solemn pledge, "I came through and I shall return!"

On 28 March, MacArthur was awarded the Medal of Honor. In April he was appointed supreme commander, Allied Forces, Southwest Pacific Area, effectively splitting command in the Pacific with Adm. Chester W. Nimitz, commander in chief, Pacific Ocean Area. In command of one Australian and two U.S. divisions, MacArthur began planning a counteroffensive against the Japanese in New Guinea. From July to September 1942, his forces successfully repulsed a Japanese offensive against Port Moresby. MacArthur then launched his counteroffensive. From September 1942 to January 1943 his forces pushed across the Owen Stanley Range and captured the fortified Buna-Gona complex, driving the Japanese out of southeastern New Guinea.

During September and August 1943, MacArthur directed the U.S. Sixth Army in a series of amphibious leapfrog assaults, capturing the rest of New Guinea's strategic coastal points. In December he invaded New Britain to cut off and isolate the Japanese from their base at Rabaul. In February 1944, MacArthur personally led the attack that seized the Admiralties Islands. His brilliant victories at Hollandia and Aitape in April surrounded the Japanese Eighteenth Army and left it isolated and ineffective. MacArthur then resumed his leapfrog campaign west along the northern coast of New Guinea. On 30 July he captured Cape Sansapor, ending the campaign and effectively destroying Japanese power in New Guinea.

MacArthur then converged his offensive with that of Admiral Nimitz in the Central Pacific. In September, MacArthur took Molotai in the Molucca Islands while Nimitz took Pelelieu in the Palau Islands. When Nimitz encountered only light resistance along the Philippine coast, he recommended that proposed landings on Mindanao and Yap be canceled and an assault launched against Leyte in the central Philippines. MacArthur quickly agreed and, despite tremendous logistical difficulties, boldly moved up the scheduled invasion of the Philippines by two months. On 20 October, MacArthur landed with his troops on Leyte and spoke the words the Philippine people had waited two long years to hear, "I have returned."

Supported by Admiral Kincaid's Seventh Fleet, MacArthur expanded operations in the Philippines to Mindoro on 15 December. That month MacArthur was promoted to general of the Army (Fig. 1). On 9 January 1945 he invaded Luzon, retaking most of the island and completing the liberation of the Philippines in a bitter campaign that ended with the Japanese surrender on 15

Figure 1. Douglas MacArthur, General of the Army, in Manila.
(SOURCE: Robert F. Dorr Archives)

August. In April, MacArthur was appointed commanding general of U.S. Army Forces in the Pacific. In August he was also appointed supreme commander for the Allied Powers in Japan in order to take the Japanese surrender in Tokyo Bay (2 September 1945).

Postwar Years

After the Japanese surrender, MacArthur was appointed supreme commander of Allied Occupation Forces in Japan. For the next six years MacArthur—as virtual viceroy of Japan—directed the reorganization and reconstruction of the governmental, social, and economic systems of Japan. He saw to the elimination of Japan's ultranationalist, militarist, and feudal beliefs and traditions, replacing them with more liberal and democratic ideologies. He reformed Japan's political system, introducing a liberal constitution, and reformed the economy and improved rural life by introducing land reform. He changed outdated social norms by instituting women's rights. He modernized the health and welfare programs and the educational system and was responsible for improving relations between the United States and Japan. In January 1947, MacArthur was also appointed commander of the Far East Command, which comprised all U.S. forces in Japan, Korea, the Ryukyus, the Philippines, the Marianas, and the Bonin Islands.

Korean War

Shortly after the outbreak of the Korean War on 25 June 1950, MacArthur was ordered by President Harry S Truman to provide assistance to South Korea. The United Nations (UN) quickly passed a resolution calling for concerted military assistance to Korea, and on 8 July, MacArthur was appointed supreme commander of UN Forces in Korea.

The speed of the initial North Korean attack had overwhelmed the weaker South Korean Army and overrun most of the peninsula before U.S. forces could arrive. The UN forces—composed mostly of the U.S. Eighth Army, which had been on peacetime occupation duty in Japan—were virtually surrounded and reduced to holding a small perimeter around Pusan in southeast Korea. MacArthur managed to stop the North Korean offensive along the Naktong River and then directed the defense of the Pusan Perimeter. Over the objections of the Joint Chiefs of Staff, MacArthur created the X Corps and launched a daring amphibious landing at Inchon in the North Korean rear area on 15 September. This brilliant strategic envelopment resulted in the destruction of the North Korean forces in South Korea and led to the recapture of Seoul, the South Korean capital, on 26 September.

After receiving approval from the UN and the U.S. government, MacArthur invaded North Korea on 1 October. As his troops approached the Yalu River they were attacked by overwhelming Chinese forces on 25–26 November and forced to retreat south of the 38th Parallel. MacArthur conducted a skillful fighting withdrawal and managed to stabilize the front south of Seoul. Having received conflicting intelligence reports concerning Chinese intentions, MacArthur had chosen to discount the probability of Chinese troops engaging in the war and was taken by surprise. With China's entry into the conflict MacArthur was convinced that the UN was facing a "new war," and he advocated the use of airpower against targets in China. UN troops resumed the offensive in early 1951, taking Seoul on 14 March and again driving into North Korea.

MacArthur's public disagreement with U.S. policy and differences over civil-military relations and strategic direction of the war led to increasing tension with President Truman. Truman, without the consideration of forewarning MacArthur, publicly announced the general's dismissal on 11 April 1951. MacArthur learned of his dismissal from a friend who had heard the news on the radio and then reported it to the general. Shortly after, MacArthur received the official order.

Twilight Years

MacArthur had not been back to the United States since 1937; he returned to a hero's welcome, his parade resulting in the largest popular turnout in the history of New York City. On 19 April he delivered a farewell speech to Congress in which he uttered the unforgettable line, "Old soldiers never die, they just fade away." In 1952 he accepted the position of Chairman of the Board of the Remington Rand (later Sperry Rand) Corporation. MacArthur took up residence in the Waldorf Astoria Hotel in New York City and, with the exception of occasional speeches and his board duties, lived in relative seclusion. In 1961 he returned to the Philippines to help celebrate the fiftieth anniversary of that nation's independence. Invited to give the commencement address at West Point in 1962, he delivered the most memorable and moving of all his speeches. His memoirs, *Reminiscences*, were published in 1964. MacArthur died on 5 April 1964 at Walter Reed Army Medical Center in Washington, D.C.

MacArthur was one of America's greatest and, equally, most controversial generals. Reflecting a superb military mind, his amphibious campaigns in the Pacific and at Inchon were masterpieces of strategy, efficiency, and boldness. His knowledge and understanding of the culture and mentality of the Orient made possible the reconstruction of Japan as a modern democratic state. His love of the Philippine people was surpassed only by his devotion to his own country, and he is acclaimed as a Philippine hero even today. MacArthur's extraordinary life is best described by the three tenets he lived by—duty, honor, country.

                                                                                                        VINCENT B. HAWKINS

SEE ALSO: Korean War; Nimitz, Chester William; World War I; World War II; Yamashita, Tomoyuki.

Bibliography

Hunt, F. 1954. *The untold story of Douglas MacArthur*. New York: Devin-Adair.
MacArthur, D. 1964. *Reminiscences*. New York: McGraw-Hill.
Manchester, W. 1978. *American Caesar*. Boston: Little, Brown.
Mayer, S. 1971. *MacArthur*. New York: Ballantine Books.
———. 1971. *MacArthur in Japan*. New York: Ballantine Books.
Pfannes, C. E., and V. A. Salamone. 1981. *The great commanders of World War II*. Vol. 2: *The Americans*. New York: Kensington.

MAHAN, ALFRED THAYER [1840–1914]

Rear Adm. Alfred Thayer Mahan, U.S. Navy, stands as one of the world's most influential naval strategists (Fig. 1). Writing at a time of U.S. expansion westward and of an increasing U.S. role on the world scene, he had tremendous influence on naval thinking worldwide, on U.S. foreign policy, and on the naval development of many nations, including the United States, Great Britain, Germany, and Japan.

Early Life and Career

Alfred Mahan was born on 27 September 1840 at West Point, New York. His father, Dennis Hart Mahan, taught at the U.S. Military Academy and educated

Figure 1. Alfred Thayer Mahan, 1887. (SOURCE: U.S. Library of Congress)

an entire generation of American Civil War leaders in civil and military engineering. Mahan, however, pursued a different course. After attending Columbia College for two years, he entered the U.S. Naval Academy and graduated second in his class in 1859.

From 1859 until 1885, his career was unremarkable. During the Civil War he served on the screw steamer *Pocahontas* in the Port Royal, South Carolina, expedition of November 1861; on the screw sloop *Seminole* while it conducted blockade duty off Sabine Pass, Texas, in 1863 and 1864; in the South Atlantic Squadron aboard the *Alger* in 1864 and again in 1865; and on the *Philadelphia* as it operated off Charleston, South Carolina, in 1864. After the war, he had various sea and shore billets.

Teacher and Naval Theorist

Mahan's real talents were first revealed in 1883 when he published his first book, an account of U.S. naval operations during the Civil War. The book so impressed Capt. Stephen Luce that he adopted Mahan as his protégé. In 1885, Luce, then president of the newly established Naval War College at Newport, Rhode Island, invited Mahan to lecture on naval tactics and history at the college. Mahan taught there from 1886 to 1889 and also served as president of the college from 1886 to 1888. During this time he fought to ensure that the college was not absorbed into the navy's other training facilities and insisted that its curriculum stress the historical, theoretical, tactical, and strategic principles of naval warfare. His efforts were seminal in making the college the intellectual center of the new navy.

During his first tour at the college, Mahan wrote *The Influence of Sea Power upon History, 1600–1783*, which was based on his lectures at the college and published in 1890 (this book later brought him to the attention of Theodore Roosevelt). Mahan left the college in 1889 but returned in 1890 to write a sequel to *Influence* entitled *The Influence of Sea Power upon the French Revolution and Empire, 1793–1812*, published in 1892. He again served as president of the Naval War College in 1892 and 1893. After another tour of duty at sea, he returned to the college briefly before retiring in 1896 to devote full time to writing. His subsequent works included *The Interest of America in Sea Power, Present and Future* in 1897, *Sea Power in Its Relations to the War of 1812* in 1905, and *Naval Strategy* in 1911. He was recalled to active duty during the Spanish-American War, was an American delegate to the first Hague Peace Conference in 1899, and was promoted to rear admiral on the retired list in June 1906. Mahan, who raised the respectability of the field of naval history, was president of the American Historical Association in 1902 and foretold the defeat of the Central Powers and the German Navy in World War I. He died on 1 December 1914 at Quogue, New York.

Essence of Mahan's Theories

Concerning the United States, Mahan warned of the danger of neglecting seapower, a tendency he felt was inherent in democracies. Arguing that America's future lay in the seas, he cautioned against the nation's being distracted by the westward expansion that was then occurring across the continent.

Mahan made several other significant points. First, he placed great emphasis on the use of sea forces to project military power into areas controlled or threatened by enemy forces (sea power projection), arguing that U.S. coastal defense was a garrison function that most appropriately should be assigned to the army. Second, he stressed the great importance of a nation's sea lines of communication, those sea routes or lifelines across which its merchant ships and naval power pass. Third, he believed that while being first on the scene of a crisis was important for a navy, it was even more important to arrive with decisive naval superiority. Finally, in order to assure an adequate U.S. naval projection capability, Mahan said that it was necessary to have naval bases overseas. He recommended acquiring Hawaii and the Philippines in the Pacific and—placing great importance on the Panama Canal—he encouraged acquiring Cuba to assure control of the canal's eastern approaches.

Mahan's writings are more difficult to comprehend than those of Karl von Clausewitz and other military strategists, since they were based on his lectures at the Naval War College rather than being prepared as continuous narrative. For example, one must consult portions from several of his works to truly understand his views on the importance of the Panama Canal. Despite the difficulties, the U.S. Navy has followed Mahan's precepts concerning superior capability for power projection by sea and has also deemed it important to be on the scene of a crisis first with superior naval power. Using the resulting strategy, the navy has conducted its twentieth-century operations so effectively that, in terms of the frequency and success of its use of naval power, America may be viewed as history's preeminent sea power, challenged only by Great Britain's use of seapower in ages past. Additionally, by following Mahan faithfully the navy avoided suffering the great uncertainty and introspection that the U.S. Army endured after the American defeat in Vietnam. Often disparaged by some for the imperialistic aspects of his strategy, Mahan is responsible for the tremendous success of the U.S. Navy in the twentieth century.

Significance of Mahan's Theories

Written at a time of great and rapid technological advancement in navies, and immediately preceding emergence of the United States as a world power after the Spanish-American War (1898), Mahan's works profoundly affected both U.S. and worldwide naval developments before World War I. Because of a concord of interests and a personal relationship, Mahan regularly offered counsel to President Roosevelt and therefore had great influence on U.S. foreign policy and expansion overseas. His writings also considerably influenced battleship construction in the United States, Great Britain, Germany, Japan, and other nations.

BRUCE W. WATSON

SEE ALSO: Civil War, American; Naval Warfare.

Bibliography

Bowling, R. A. 1980. *The negative influence of Mahan on the protection of shipping in war.* Orono, Me.: Roland Alfred Bowling.
Hattendorf, J. B. 1986. *A bibliography of the works of Alfred Thayer Mahan.* Newport, R.I.: Naval War College Press.
Livezay, W. E. 1947. *Mahan on sea power.* Norman, Okla.: Univ. of Oklahoma Press.
Reynolds, C. G. 1978. *Famous American admirals.* New York: Van Nostrand Reinhold.
Spiller, R. J. 1989. *American military leaders.* New York: Praeger.
Taylor, C. C. 1920. *The life of Admiral Mahan, naval philosopher.* New York: George H. Doran.
Turk, R. W. 1987. *The ambitious relationship: Theodore Roosevelt and Alfred Thayer Mahan.* New York: Greenwood Press.

MANCHU EMPIRE (Qing, or Ch'ing Empire)

The Qing dynasty (1644–1911), the last in the 2,000-year-long feudal society in China, marked the transition of China from its early historical period to the modern period. Although some of the Qing dynasty rulers were able to provide periods of peace and prosperity to their nation, the corruption of officials, peasant rebellions, and wars eventually led to the overthrow of the Qing dynasty and the beginning of a new era in Chinese history.

Background

The Manchu, the dominant ruling class of the Qing dynasty, was an ancient nationality in China, previously living in the Heilongjiang River basin in the northeast. For 3,000 years, during the Shang (ca. 16th–11th centuries B.C.) and the Zhou (770–221 B.C.) dynasties, the ancestors of the Manchu were called the Sushen. Later they were called the Yilou (Han dynasty [206 B.C.–A.D. 220]), the Wuji (Southern and Northern dynasties [420–589]), and the Mojie (Sui dynasty [581–618]). When the Tang dynasty (618–907) set up a local authority in the Heilongjiang River valley in the eighth century, the area became Chinese territory.

In the early tenth century, the Mojie came to be called the Nuzhen, and they founded the kingdom of Jin (1115–1234) with Yanjing (present-day Beijing) as the capital. They ruled northern China, but in 1234 they were conquered by the Mongols and driven back to northeast China. In 1616, Nurhachi, chief of the Nuzhen branch in Jianzhou, unified the whole Nuzhen after 30 years of warfare and set up the state of Jin in 1616, making himself the khan. Nurhachi then declared war on the declining Ming dynasty. When he led his 60,000-man army in an attack on the strategic township of Ning Liao (present-day Xingcheng in Liaoning Province) on 2 March 1626, he was defeated by the 10,000-man Ming army, which defended the city with eleven Western cannon. Soon afterward, Nurhachi died of illness and was succeeded by his son, Abahai. In 1636, Abahai proclaimed himself emperor and changed Jin to Qing. He conquered Korea and Mongolia and removed the serious threats from the northeast. Qing troops then began to push south toward the Shanhaiguan Pass garrisoned by Ming soldiers. Abahai died suddenly in September 1643 and was succeeded by his six-year-old son, Fulin (Emperor Shun Di), with two princes (the late emperor's brothers) acting as regents. On 26 April 1644, a peasant army led by Li Zicheng seized Beijing and put an end to the Ming dynasty. The Manchus took advantage of the situation and marched southward. They defeated Li Zicheng's peasant army at the Shanhaiguan Pass and occupied Beijing on 6 July. Fulin made Beijing his capital in October. This marked the establishment of the central government of the Qing dynasty.

The Qing troops again marched southward to bring the whole country under their control, burning, killing, and looting indiscriminately. Further, the Qing government ordered the Han men to shave their heads or have them cut off, forcing them to shave off their hair on the front part of their crown and wear a pigtail at the back in accordance with the Manchu custom. This aroused great indignation in every stratum of the society. With the support of the masses, the peasant armies and the remnants of the Ming forces jointly waged wars of resistance against the Qing troops. The Qing court had to change its high-handed policy and learn to divide and be conciliatory to win over the rebels. It was only after several years of struggle that they gained control of the situation.

Unification and Expansion

The next emperor, Kangxi (1662–1722), learned from the mistakes of the Qing army in its southward march and formulated new policies in order to win the support of the local Han officials and intellectuals. To eliminate the strong barriers between the two nationalities, he respected the Han people's culture and adopted some of their customs and governmental traditions. He basically adopted the legal and official appointment systems of past dynasties in central China. To bring about economic recovery, he reduced taxes and encouraged land reclamation. He also had the Huanghe (Yellow) River harnessed to lessen the danger of floods. In addition, Kangxi strengthened the central government by removing dissidents from their posts. The peasants were able to enjoy a period of peace and prosperity, and the whole nation was rehabilitated. As a result, the Qing dynasty unified the country and expanded its territories. During the reigns of Emperor Kangxi, Emperor Yong Zheng (1723–35), and Emperor Qian Long (1736–95), Qing forces successively suppressed three revolts led by Han military governors in Yunnan, Guangdong, and Fujian; occupied Taiwan after overthrowing Zheng Chenggong's government; drove off the czarist Russian aggressors stationed in Yakesa on the north bank of the Heilongjiang River; and signed treaties that fixed the eastern portion of the boundary between China and Russia. They also subdued the Dzungars in Xinjiang Uygyr Autonomous Region, fought against Tibetan hereditary headmen in Dajinchuan and Xiaojinchuan in Sichuan Province, and posted high commissioners there to strengthen control over the minority regions in southwest China. Externally, the Manchu launched two expeditions against Burma, brought Annam into submission, and entered Nepal, forcing Kuorke to sue for peace.

By the mid- to late eighteenth century, the Qing territory stretched eastward to the sea, west to Lake Balkhash and the Pamirs, south to the islands in the South China Sea, and north to Gorno-Altay, Sayan Mountains. It reached the Outer Xingan Mountains and Okhotsk Sea in the northeast and Guangxi, Yunan, and Tibet in the southwest. With a population of about 300 million, China was the strongest country in Asia.

Military Strength

The pillar of strength of the Qing dynasty was its armed forces. In 1615 Nurhachi set up the Eight Banner system by which soldiers were also laborers during times of peace. Before the Manchus entered the Shanhaiguan Pass, the largest registered permanent units were the Gushans; each had a strength of

7,500 and a banner of a special color (called *qi*). In 1601, Manchuria had a small population and formed only four Gushans, which had yellow, white, red, and blue banners. Later, when another four Gushans were added, they hemmed the red banner with white edges and the other three banners with red edges. These were the eight original banners. By the time the Qing forces entered the Pass, there were already 24 banners, but the forces were still called the Eight Banner Troops.

Throughout the Qing dynasty, the main force of the Manchu army defended the capital. Those stationed in and outside Beijing city year-round amounted to over 100,000 men. Garrisons stationed at strategic points around the country and in northeast China and Inner Mongolia amounted to another 100,000 men. The overall strength of the Eight Banners never exceeded 300,000. In addition, there were the Green Battalions of Han origin, made up of Han recruits and some landlords' private armies. They were identified by their green banners. The name came from their unit battalion, which usually had a strength of about 600,000. The Eight Banners were better paid and better equipped than the Green Battalions. The two were the main military forces of the Qing dynasty before the Opium War (1840). Other military forces included some native armies (of minority nationality) and some local armies that were organized in times of emergency and disbanded or reorganized afterward.

A Declining Empire

In the early nineteenth century, because of huge financial expenditures required in protracted warfare and the embezzlement and corruption at all levels of government, social contradictions were sharpened and popular rebellions and uprisings took place in different parts of the country. The Qing dynasty had passed its heyday and was on the road to decline.

In the early 1840s, Britain unleashed a war of aggression against China, claiming that the Qing government had burned its opium; the British forced the Qing government to sign humiliating treaties. Other foreign governments followed suit and gradually turned China into a semicolonial and semifeudal country. Xianggang (Hong Kong), Aomen (Macao), and Taiwan and the Penghu Islands were occupied by Britain, Portugal, and Japan, respectively. The vast lands north of the Heilongjiang River, east of the Wusuli River, and that beyond the present boundary in Xinjiang were taken secretly by czarist Russia, and the Pamirs were divided up between czarist Russia and Britain.

The embryo of capitalism in China, which had germinated before the Opium War in trade and industries such as silk weaving, cotton dyeing, porcelain making, coal and iron mining, and cigarette and sugar production, was stifled. Production came to a standstill and the economy stagnated. The peasant revolution of the Taiping Heavenly Kingdom spread to eighteen provinces, and the Uprising of the Nian Forces in the north, operating in close cooperation with the Taipings, repeatedly defeated the Qing troops. The Qing court was shaken to its very foundations.

Beset with difficulties both at home and abroad, the Qing government staged a movement to make the country strong during the reigns of Emperors Tong Zhi and Guang Xu (1862–1908). Adjustments were made in the closed-door policy; observation groups and students were sent abroad to study or conduct investigations. With the financial aid of Britain, the United States, and France, officials such as Zeng Guofan and Li Hongzhang, who were of Han origin, initiated the Westernization Movement. They built modern munitions industries such as Jiangnan Machinery Manufacturing Bureau and Fuzhou Shipping Bureau, where the technical skills of the Western countries were adapted. They bought foreign warships and established the Northern Sea Fleet. And they set up a naval academy and defense academy to offer modern military education.

Troops of the Eight Banners and the Green Battalions were so corrupt after the Opium War that their combat capabilities had been greatly weakened. To suppress the strong Taipings and Nian Forces, Zeng Guofan and Li Hongzhang were sent to Hunan and Anhui to organize the new landlord army: the Hunan army and Huaihe River army. Marshals and commanders were granted military leadership with full powers by the central government, and foreign instructors and advisers were employed. Meanwhile, the National Guards, which recruited soldiers in the provinces, and the Lian Troops, which consisted of soldiers selected from the Green Battalions, were stationed at strategic points throughout the country. By the end of the nineteenth century, however, these troops also became corrupt and impotent. The government decided to organize a new army with Western military equipment and organization. But the plan was never carried out in full.

The Taiping Rebellion (1850–64), which spread to the greater part of China, and the Uprising of the Nian Forces, the Uprising of the Dagger Society in Shanghai, the Yunnan Hui People's Uprising, the Guizhou Miao People's Uprising, and the Hui People's Uprising in Shannxi and Gansu all dealt heavy blows to the ruling class despite the fact that these uprisings were suppressed by the government and ended in failure. The combined forces of the eight powers (Britain, the United States, Russia, France, Germany, Japan, Italy, and Austria) subsequently sacked Beijing and Tianjin, while czarist Russia also seized the opportunity to feather its own nest. This was the second time China had lost vast territories and her national sovereignty since the period of the Opium War. During the Sino-Japanese War of 1894–95, China's newly organized naval force was destroyed and its land forces suffered disastrous defeats.

The Hundred-Day Reform

The Qing rule was faced with a serious crisis. In 1898, with the support of the intellectuals and the masses, Kang Youwei, Liang Qichao, Tan Sitong, and other representatives of the national bourgeoisie and the enlightened gentry sent notice to the court demanding immediate constitutional reform. Emperor Guang Xu supported the reform and proclaimed new laws. The reform movement, however, was soon put down by the diehards led by Empress Dowager Ci Xi. Thus ended what is known in Chinese history as the "hundred-day reform." With its failure, the hope to save China through reform vanished. Filled with indignation at the danger of China being divided up among the imperialist powers, revolutionaries in Guangding and other places arose and eventually overthrew the Qing dynasty in 1911, putting an end to the feudal monarchy in China. The revolution of 1911 marked a new beginning in Chinese history.

ZHOU SHI-CHANG

SEE ALSO: Colonial Empires, European; Genghis Khan; Japan, Modernization and Expansion of; Mongol Conquests; Russia, Expansion of.

Bibliography

Cai Meibiao, et al. 1986. *A History of China.* Vol. 9. Ed. Kuo Muoruo. Shanghai: People's Publishing House.
Dai Yizhu, ed. 1980. *A concise history of the Qing dynasty.* Shanghai: People's Publishing House.
The great encyclopaedia of China military. 1988. Shanghai: China Great Encylopaedia Publishing House.
The Qing dynasty. 1980. In *Cihai Dictionary.* Shanghai: Shanghai Dictionary Publishing House.
Xiao Yishan. 1980. *The history of the Qing dynasty.* Rev. ed. Taipei: Taiwan Commercial Press.
Zheng Tianting, ed. 1981. *Documents on the history of the Ming and Qing dynasties.* Vol. 2. Tianjin: Tianjin People's Publishing House.

MANSTEIN, ERICH VON [1887–1973]

Fritz Erich von Manstein was born von Lewinsky on 24 November 1887 in Baden, Germany, the son of General of Artillery Eduard von Lewinsky. Upon the death of his parents Erich was adopted by Major General von Manstein, whose name he subsequently bore. Following in his father's footsteps, he was accepted into the Prussian Cadet Corps and upon graduation was commissioned an officer cadet in 1906.

World War I and Interwar Years

In 1914 Manstein attended the War Academy but it was closed after the outbreak of World War I. During the war he served on both the western and eastern fronts. In 1919 he was promoted to captain and upon the formation of the Reichswehr, Germany's postwar defensive force, was one of the few officers chosen to remain in service.

From 1919 to 1927, Manstein held a variety of troop and staff appointments before being transferred to the Reichswehr Ministry in 1927. Promoted to major, he remained with the ministry until Hitler's rise to the chancellorship of Germany in 1933. In that year Manstein was promoted to colonel and appointed a departmental chief on the General Staff. By 1935, he was appointed head of the Operational Section of the General Staff. In 1936 Manstein was promoted to *generalmajor* (brigadier general). In 1937 he served as 1st Deputy Chief of the General Staff under Gen. Ludwig Beck. After Beck's dismissal by Hitler in August 1938, Manstein was promoted to *generalleutnant* (major general) and given the command of a division in Silesia.

World War II

Prior to the outbreak of war in 1939, Manstein was appointed chief of the General Staff, Southern Army Group, under Gen. Gerd von Rundstedt. Manstein served well in this post during the Polish campaign, displaying a talent for planning operations.

In late 1939 the General Staff was considering plans for the invasion of France. Manstein submitted a plan that called for a rapid thrust of massed armored forces through the Ardennes Forest in Belgium to seize strategic crossing points on the Meuse River along the center of the French lines. This plan was first rejected, then adopted, by the chief of the General Staff, Franz Halder. Hitler became aware of Manstein's plan, was impressed by its daring nature, and approved it.

In January 1940 Manstein was given command of the XXXVIII Army Corps for the French campaign. On 10 May the operation began; Manstein's corps broke through the French lines and drove for the Meuse River. By 10 June his troops—the first German troops to cross the river—were pushing deep into the enemy's rear lines. Later that month Manstein was promoted to *general der infanterie* (lieutenant general) and in July was awarded the Knight's Cross.

Manstein was then appointed to command the landing forces for Operation Sea Lion, the planned cross-channel invasion of Great Britain. With the cancellation of Sea Lion, he was transferred to East Prussia and appointed commander of the LVI Panzer Corps in preparation for Operation Barbarossa, the invasion of Russia. The LVI Panzer Corps was one of the two corps that constituted the Fourth Panzer Group of Field Marshal Ritter von Leeb's Army Group North. For Manstein, command of a panzer corps was the culmination of a long-standing ambition.

Operation Barbarossa began on 22 June 1941. By 26 June, Manstein's forces had driven more than 320 kilometers (200 mi.) into enemy territory—80 kilometers (50 mi.) on the first day alone—reaching the Dvina River and establishing a bridgehead. The speed of his advance worked against him, however, since he was forced to halt due to the inability of the rest of the panzer group to protect his corps' exposed flanks.

The German advance recommenced on 2 July against stiffening Russian resistance. Manstein, ordered to advance his corps between Moscow and Leningrad, recommended that the Fourth Panzer Group be consolidated for a drive on Leningrad. In August, Hitler ordered the drive on Moscow halted and shifted the focus of his armies north to Leningrad and south to the Ukraine.

The Fourth Panzer Group was ordered to take Leningrad and Manstein's advance proceeded apace. Before he could link up with General Reinhardt's corps, however, Manstein's corps was pulled out of the line and sent toward Lake Ilmen to assist General Busch's Eighteenth Army, which was being severely pressed by Russian counterattacks. Manstein smashed into the flank of the Russian Thirty-fourth Army and rolled it up, relieving Busch's army.

For this victory Manstein was appointed commander of the Eleventh Army, Southern Army Group, on 12 September 1941. Manstein's primary objectives were to take Rostov and the Crimea but, realizing that his forces were not strong enough to do both, he concentrated his efforts on the Crimea. Manstein recognized that in taking the Crimea he could not only eliminate the Russian air threat to Romania's vital oil fields and secure the Eleventh Army's flank, but also provide an excellent staging area for a German offensive across the Kuban Isthmus into the Caucasus.

Realizing the threat, the Russians committed two armies to the Crimea in an offensive that resulted in heavy fighting in September and October. Manstein, hard-pressed and threatened with being cut off with his back to the Black Sea, was reinforced by Kleist's First Panzer Army, which drove down the Dneiper River into the Russian rear. By 5 October the Russians were stopped and Manstein immediately launched a counteroffensive. While Kleist moved against Rostov, Manstein pursued the Russians and cut off their escape from the peninsula by taking Kerch and Sevastopol. Kerch fell on 15 November and, after a long and arduous siege, Sevastopol fell on 4 July 1942. In roughly ten months the Eleventh Army, although greatly outnumbered, had taken the Crimea and captured more than 430,000 prisoners. Hitler, greatly impressed with the victory, awarded a special decoration to the soldiers of the campaign and promoted Manstein to field marshal (Fig. 1).

With the opening of the German summer offensive in June 1942, Manstein was given command of the Leningrad front with orders to take the city. With depleted forces and against his better judgment, Manstein attempted to obey Hitler's directives but failed to capture the city. He did, however, destroy a Russian army counterattacking in the Lake Ladoga sector.

By 20 November, the situation of Gen. Friedrich von Paulus's Sixth Army in Stalingrad had become disastrous. Manstein was given command of Army Group Don and sent to effect Paulus's relief. Realizing that the withdrawal of the Sixth Army would create a breach in the lines, Manstein at first attempted to reinforce Stalingrad. When this proved impossible because of Hitler's refusal to pull the needed forces from other areas of the front, Manstein tried to coordinate a breakout with Paulus. Despite the valiant efforts of Manstein's troops, the breakout was unsuccessful and the Sixth Army capitulated on 2 February 1943.

Due in large part to Manstein's persuasion, Hitler eventually allowed a withdrawal to the Mius River. On 14 February, with his army group redesignated Army Group South, Manstein launched an offensive to retake Kharkov. Setting a brilliant trap, Manstein lured the Russian Sixth Army to attack. Counterattacking against its flanks, he pushed the Russians back to the Donetz River, recapturing Kharkov. Although a great coup for Manstein, Kharkov was the last major German victory in the east.

Figure 1. Field Marshal Erich von Manstein (left) on an inspection tour in Russia. (SOURCE: U.S. Library of Congress)

Manstein had overall direction of the southern jaw of Operation Zitadelle, the German offensive against the heavily fortified Kursk salient, begun on 5 July. Although Manstein's forces breached the Russian defenses, they were too worn to deal with the Russian reserves and the ensuing counteroffensive.

After the disastrous defeat at Kursk on 11 July 1943, the initiative passed to the Russians, who began to push the Germans back step by step. Manstein argued persistently for a deliberate delaying strategy, with the German armies husbanding their strength instead of fighting costly defensive actions. Manstein believed that, if the Russians were allowed to penetrate deep into the German lines, he could strike the flanks of the penetrations with his panzers and destroy their spearheads, thus containing the threat and winning a war of attrition in the east. While Hitler sometimes allowed withdrawals to conserve forces, he vetoed Manstein's counteroffensive operations as too risky.

It was primarily due to Manstein's skill in maneuver that his army group was able to stave off disaster and withdraw to the Polish frontier. This success, however, did not save him from Hitler who, tired of constant retreats and arguments over strategy, relieved Manstein of command on 25 March 1944.

Manstein retired to his estates where he remained for the rest of the war. Eventually captured by the British, Manstein was taken to Hamburg to face war crimes charges. Although cleared of two counts of massacring Jews, Manstein was convicted on one count of failing to protect civilian lives and, on 19 December 1949, was sentenced to 18 years of imprisonment. This sentence was later commuted to 12 years, but in August 1952 Manstein was given a medical parole. Released in May 1953, Manstein served briefly as a military adviser to the Federal Republic of Germany. He died at his home in Irschenhausen on 12 June 1973.

Manstein was a brilliant, talented commander whose skill in operational planning was surpassed only by his leadership ability in the field. Manstein's talents contributed to many major German successes on the eastern front. Had Manstein been allowed to execute his concept of delay and counterstroke operations, the war in the east might have taken a different turn.

VINCENT B. HAWKINS

SEE ALSO: Guderian, Heinz; Konev, Ivan Stepanovich; Rokossovskii, Konstantin Konstantinovich; World War II; Zhukov, Georgi Konstantinovich.

Bibliography

Manstein, F. E. von. 1970. *Lost victories.* New York: Henry Regnery.
Pfannes, C. E., and V. A. Salamone. 1980. *The great commanders of World War II.* Vol. 1, *The Germans.* New York: Kensington.
Wistrich, R. 1982. *Who's who in Nazi Germany.* New York: Bonanza Books.

MAO TSE-TUNG [1893–1976]

No other twentieth-century figure has had as profound an effect on the strategy of modern politico-military conflict as Mao Tse-tung (Fig. 1). In a life that spanned 83 years, this revolutionary, common soldier, battlefield commander, commander in chief of armies, strategic thinker, and absolute ruler of the People's Republic of China left an indelible mark on his era. For good or ill, Mao guided the most populous nation, the largest Communist party, and the most sizable armed forces on earth at a critical time. This article focuses mainly on his influence in the military arena.

Early Education

Mao Tse-tung was born in 1893 in the Hunan Province village of Shaoshan. His father's relative prosperity, derived from ownership of some land and a small shop, afforded Mao the opportunity to study Chinese and Western classical literature. At a young age he had learned about Washington, Napoleon, Peter

Figure 1. Mao Tse-tung, chairman of the Central People's Government of the People's Republic of China. (SOURCE: U.S. Library of Congress)

the Great, and Sun Tzu and their contributions to both the military art and the national development of their countries. Mao's inclination in school toward philosophy, history, and geography rather than the sciences revealed an early interest in abstract theory and the sweep of events on a grand scale.

Mao combined this early instruction with practical experience when, in 1911, he became a soldier with the revolutionary forces that toppled the crumbling Ching dynasty. This brief exposure to conflict was followed by further study toward a teaching career in Hunan and at the University of Peking. During this time, he enthusiastically absorbed the radical ideas of Marx and Engels and the Russian writers Bakunin, Tolstoy, and Kropotkin.

Development of a Communist Revolutionary

After 1919, Mao was increasingly active in revolutionary politics. The 26-year-old teacher wrote, published, and distributed his writings and those of others espousing the radical Marxist approach to the revitalization of China.

On 1 July 1921, Mao Tse-tung joined eleven comrades in Shanghai to found the Chinese Communist party. During the next six years, Mao served the party in various capacities. He moved often between Shanghai, Canton, and Changsha in south-central China to avoid the police.

In this period, Mao was a strong proponent of Communist participation in a united front with the Kuomintang party, led by his later nemesis, Chiang Kai-shek. Mao became a firm believer in using such "marriages of convenience" to achieve ultimate victory.

The rising leader became identified with China's enormous peasant class, with whom he believed the nation's destiny resided. Mao's championing of the Chinese peasant catapulted him into a leading position in the Communist party when the urban workers—the preeminent revolutionaries in conventional Marxist theory—failed in their fight against Chiang in the wake of the united front's dissolution in 1927.

The Battlefield Classroom

Association with the Communist armed forces also fueled Mao's rise to the top. In 1927, with Chu-Teh, Chen-Yi, and Lin-Piao, who would thereafter be among his chief lieutenants, Mao formed the Red Army. Chu-Teh, schooled in traditional military thought, deserves much of the credit for refining Mao's early military ideas.

Mao's experiences in this period convinced him that any successful struggle against the entrenched power of the state would be protracted; victory would come only after a long, arduous politico-military effort to gain the allegiance of the Chinese peasants and through them control of the countryside. Only then could the Kuomintang-controlled urban centers be surrounded, isolated, and eliminated, one by one.

For this "revolutionary war" strategy to succeed, however, especially in the initial stages, the Red Army had to survive. In the early 1930s, Mao was unable to dissuade his comrades from engaging Chiang's stronger forces in open combat. The Communists were beaten at almost every turn. Finally, in October 1934, Chiang's armies closed in on the Communist forces at Juichin in Kiangsi Province for the coup de grace. As they would many times thereafter, the Communists wisely chose to retreat and save their army to fight another day. Strategic or tactical withdrawal in the face of unfavorable battlefield conditions became a primary principle of Mao's form of warfare.

Thus began the Long March. For the next year, the Red Army fought its way west to Siikiang Province and then north to a Communist base in remote Shensi Province—a distance of more than 9,600 kilometers (6,000 mi.). Although tens of thousands perished and the survivors suffered grievously on the rigorous trek, it forged a hardened, disciplined, and ideologically committed Red Army.

The Anti-Japanese War

The war against the Japanese, which broke out in earnest in 1937, provided Mao with another laboratory to test the politico-military concepts he had developed and to discover others for the eventual fight with the Chinese central government. Mao dispatched his forces from their stronghold at Yenan in Shensi Province against Japanese lodgments in northeastern China. Communist guerrilla forces, avoiding the well-defended cities and other strongholds, penetrated far into the Japanese rear. At the same time, Communist cadres worked among the peasants to develop paramilitary forces, establish local political control, and eliminate all opposition. This process was made easier by the hatred of the peasants for the brutal Japanese invaders. As a result of the struggle against the Japanese, Mao Tse-tung and his Communist Party became identified by many of the people as the embodiment of Chinese nationalism.

From a patchwork quilt of "liberated areas" behind enemy lines, the Communists implemented the mobile war phase of Mao's revolutionary war strategy. Main force units carried out lightning strikes on exposed Japanese positions and then withdrew to safety. Guerrillas raided supply depots, ambushed road and rail traffic, and sabotaged lines of communication. The Communists were never strong enough to destroy the Japanese army in northern China, but by September 1945 they had confined it to a few isolated bastions.

Civil War Victory

With the elimination of the Japanese threat in 1945, Mao prepared for the cataclysmic struggle with Chiang Kai-shek's government. The prize would be all of China. As during the Long March and the fight with the Japanese, however, the initial objective was to delay an all-out confrontation with Chiang's stronger Nationalist armies until a favorable balance of power developed.

By late 1946 and the breakdown of an American-arranged cease-fire, the Communist position was improving. In the Communist-controlled areas of China, the party had established a harsh, puritanical but efficient and relatively incorrupt administration. The battle-toughened Red Army was well supplied with Soviet and captured Nationalist arms. Of even greater importance was the fact that the Communists were convinced the national destiny of China was in their hands.

Conversely, the Nationalists were thoroughly disenchanted with Chiang's corrupt, politics-ridden, and paralyzed administration. Economic inflation was rampant; Nationalist forces had adequate materiel but lacked effective leaders, a sound strategy, and the will to win. Finally, the close association of Chiang's regime with the United States sullied its nationalist credentials in the eyes of many Chinese.

In the civil war that ensued on mainland China from 1946 to 1949, Mao put into practice all that he had learned in his long politico-military apprenticeship. In the last stage of revolutionary war, the general offensive, the Red Army's mobile columns outmarched, encircled, and routed one Nationalist unit in the field after another. Chiang's troops were compressed into urban enclaves, which were then reduced in turn. Operating from their heartland position in the north, the Communists overran Manchuria and central China where they destroyed Chiang's strongest armies. The Red Army, against diminishing opposition, then advanced across the Yangtze River and completed the conquest of mainland China. In large part, this victory was achieved by the Chinese Communist adherence to the strategy of revolutionary war developed by Mao Tse-tung.

Post–Civil War Years

In the following years, Mao's revolutionary war concept continued, with good and bad effect, to influence the employment of the Chinese armed forces. In the initial, fluid stages of the Korean War, Chinese units used their mobility and endurance to great advantage against United Nations' forces. In the conventional positional warfare along the 38th parallel, however, the relatively lightly armed Red Army suffered enormous casualties and failed to defeat its enemies.

Until his death in 1976, Mao remained an ardent proponent of maintaining large, ideologically inspired Chinese land armies, backed by regional militia, to defend the nation. He clashed with other Chinese leaders who called for greater emphasis on smaller, regular air, sea, and ground forces armed with sophisticated modern weapons. He prevailed more often than not.

The International Influence of Revolutionary War

During the post–civil war years, Mao had many disciples abroad. Cuba's Fidel Castro and Che Guevara, Cambodia's Pol Pot, and other revolutionaries throughout Asia, Africa, and Latin America followed his prescriptions for overthrowing governments defended by well-established armed forces and powerful allies. As adapted to the special conditions found in Southeast Asia, the strategy was successfully pursued by Vietnam's leaders in their long, bloody struggle against France, South Vietnam, and the United States. Clearly, the character of many of the modern world's conflicts reflects the revolutionary war concepts developed by China's Mao Tse-tung.

EDWARD J. MAROLDA

SEE ALSO: Chiang Kai-shek; Chu Teh; Korean War; Vietnam and Indochina Wars; World War II.

Bibliography

Archer, J. 1972. *Mao Tse-tung: A biography*. New York: Hawthorne Books.

Bartke, W. 1981. *Who's who in the People's Republic of China*. Armonk, N.Y.: M. E. Sharpe.

Boorman, S. A. 1969. *The protracted game: A Wei-Ch'i interpretation of Maoist revolutionary strategy*. New York: Oxford Univ. Press.

Chao, S. M., ed. 1961. *Chinese communist revolutionary strategy, 1945–1949*. Princeton, N.J.: Center of Public and International Studies, Woodrow Wilson School of Public and International Affairs, Princeton Univ.

Elliot-Bateman, M. 1967. *Defeat in the East: The mark of Mao Tse-Tung on war*. New York: Oxford Univ. Press.

Hook, B., ed. 1982. *The Cambridge encyclopedia of China*. Cambridge: Cambridge Univ. Press.

Mao Tse-tung. 1963. *Selected military writings of Mao Tse-tung*. Peking: Foreign Language Press.

O'Ballance, E. 1962. *The red army of China: A short history*. New York: Frederick A. Praeger.

MAPS, CHARTS, AND SYMBOLS, MILITARY

Maps and charts are graphic representations, normally on a plane (flat) surface, that depict natural or artificial features of part or all of the earth. They are prepared at an established scale and map features are positioned relative to a coordinate reference system. Man-made and natural features are represented by symbols, lines, colors, and forms.

To enhance the ability of map users to recognize features portrayed, such features are represented by conventional signs and symbols. Most symbols are exaggerated in size on maps beyond the point of what they actually represent. For example, on a 1:250,000-scale map, the symbol for any building occupies an area of some 500 square feet on the ground, while a road symbol, if in actual scale, would be over 500 feet wide.

Maps provide information on the existence of, location of, and distance between ground features (e.g., populated areas and routes of travel and communication). Maps also indicate variations in terrain; extent of vegetation; presence of streams, lakes, and oceans; and heights of natural terrain features. The proper use of maps by military personnel enables troops and materiel to be transported, stored, and placed into operation at prescribed places and times.

Classes of Maps by Type

Topographic maps portray terrain features as well as the horizontal positions of the features represented. Vertical positions, termed *relief*, usually are represented by contour lines.

Photomaps are first-instance or reproductions of aerial or satellite photographs on which grid lines, place names, route numbers, approximate scale, and other data have been superimposed.

Joint operations graphics are a series of 1:250,000-scale military maps designed for joint ground and air operations. These maps are published in air and ground versions with identical topographical data on each. Ground versions have elevations and contours in meters, air versions in feet. The air versions also have symbols that identify aids and obstructions to air navigation.

Photomosaics are assemblies of aerial photographs that are published when time does not permit compilation of a more accurate map. Accuracy of such maps depends on the methods employed in their preparation.

Military city maps are topographic maps, usually with a scale of 1:12,500 or 1:25,000, of cities that show important buildings, streets and their names, and other urban data of military significance.

Special maps are prepared for special purposes, such as trafficability, communications, or assaults. These maps usually are overprints of standard topographic maps with data not normally found on standard maps.

Classes of Maps by Use

Administrative maps are used to graphically record information pertaining to administrative matters, such as supply and evacuation installations, personnel and medical installations, straggler and prisoner-of-war collection points, service and maintenance areas, main supply routes, traffic circulation, and similar data.

Battle maps show ground features in sufficient detail for use by all combat forces, usually on a scale of 1:25,000 or 1:50,000.

Controlled maps have precise, or registered, horizontal and vertical ground control as their basis.

General maps have a small scale and are used for general planning purposes.

Line route maps, or map overlays, are used for signal communications operations and show actual routes and types of construction of wire circuits in the field. They also show the locations of telegraph stations and switchboards.

Map charts are representations of sea-land areas. They have the characteristics of a map to represent the land area and the characteristics of a chart to represent the sea area, with special characteristics added to make the map chart useful in military operations, usually amphibious operations.

Operation maps show locations and strengths of friendly forces involved in a given operation. They also may indicate predicted movements and locations of enemy forces.

Situation maps show the tactical, operational, or administrative situation at a given time.

Strategic maps have a medium or smaller scale, and are used for planning operations such as troop movements, concentrations, and logistics operations.

Tactical maps have a large scale and are used for tactical and administrative purposes.

Traffic circulation maps show traffic routes and measures for traffic regulation. They indicate the roads for specific classes of traffic, the locations of traffic control stations, and the directions in which traffic may move. They are also called *circulation maps.*

Weather maps show prevailing or predicted weather conditions over a large area. They are usually based on weather observations taken at the same time at a number of stations.

Classes of Maps by Scale

Map scale is expressed as the ratio of representational map distance to true ground distance (Fig. 1). Confusion can arise when the terms *small scale,* *medium scale,* and *large scale* are read in conjunction with the quantitative scale. Map scale classes and their general uses are:

Small-scale maps. These are maps of 1:600,000 and smaller scale which are used for general planning and for strategic studies. The standard small scale in the U.S. armed forces is 1:1,000,000.

Medium-scale maps. Maps at scales larger than 1:600,000, but smaller than 1:75,000, are used for planning operations such as troop movements and con-

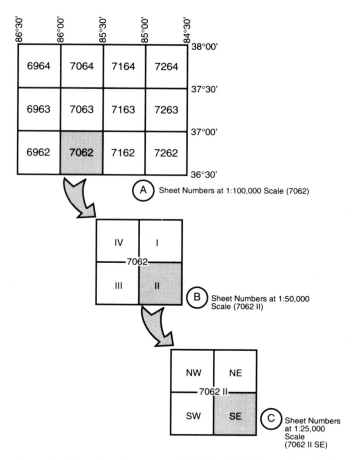

Figure 1. Map identification—1:100,000, 1:50,000, and 1:25,000 scales.

centrations and logistics operations. The standard U.S. medium scale is 1:250,000.

Large-scale maps. Such maps are used to meet the tactical, technical, and administrative requirements of field units. The standard U.S. large scale is 1:50,000.

Topographic Map Colors

Most military maps used in ground operations are topographic maps that differentiate among various types of terrain features through the use of different colors. This also may render the map a more nearly natural representation of the terrain. Colors usually found on North Atlantic Treaty Organization (NATO) maps are:

• Black—the majority of man-made or cultural features.
• Blue—water features such as lakes, rivers, and swamps.
• Green—vegetation such as woods, orchards, and vineyards.

- Brown—all relief features such as contours.
- Red—main roads, built-up areas, and special features.

Other colors are used to show special information on military maps. The meaning of these colors is, as a rule, indicated in the marginal information of the map. An example of such a color is purple, used in aeronautical symbols and related information on joint operations graphics.

Marginal Information

The marginal information found on almost all military maps can be considered a "user's guide" to the map in question. Within NATO most military maps are relatively standardized in their depictions of information, although there are exceptions. These exceptions are pronounced when maps from outside NATO are encountered. Nonetheless, almost all maps, regardless of their country of origin, have marginal information that informs the user of the map's peculiarities; therefore, marginal information on any map should be examined prior to map use. Most Western maps have similar types of marginal information. Some of the more important data elements to be found in marginal information are:

Sheet name. The name of the map sheet is usually found in two places on most military maps: the center of the upper right margin and in the lower right corner. Map sheets are usually named after their most prominent cultural or geographic feature. Usually the name of the largest city or town on the map is used.

Sheet number. The sheet number is usually found in the upper right corner and is used as a reference number for the map sheet. For small-scale maps (1:1,000,000 and larger) sheet numbers are based on an arbitrary system that facilitates the orientation of larger-scale maps.

Series name and scale. These data are normally found in the upper left margin of the map. A margin series usually comprises a group of similar maps with the same scale and format. The series name may also be a group of maps serving a common purpose, such as military city maps. The name of the series is that of the most prominent area.

Series number. This number normally appears in the upper right and lower left margins and is a comprehensive reference expressed either as a four-digit number (e.g., 1215) or as a letter followed by a three- or four-digit number (e.g., M221; R6221).

Edition number. The edition number, usually found in the upper margin and in the lower left margin, gives the age of the map relative to other editions of the same map and the agency responsible for its production. The highest number represents the most recent edition of the map. For example, EDITION 2-DMA indicates the second edition of a map prepared by the United States Defense Mapping Agency. The higher edition number usually supersedes previous editions of the same map.

Bar scales. These scales are usually found in the lower center margin and are used to convert map distance to ground distance. There are usually three or more bar scales, each with a different unit of measure.

Adjoining sheets diagram. Most military maps at standard scales contain a diagram that illustrates the adjoining sheets. On small-scale maps (1:100,000 and larger) the diagram is termed the *Index to Adjoining Sheets* and consists of as many rectangles as required to surround the sheet under consideration. All represented sheets are identified with numbers. Sheets of an adjoining series, which have the same scale, are represented by dashed lines whether they are published or merely planned. On maps of 1:50,000 scale, the sheet number and series number of the 1:250,000 scale map of the area are also shown below the Index to Adjoining Sheets.

Legend. The legend is located in the lower left margin of the map. It identifies and illustrates the topographic symbols used to depict the most common features on the map. Symbols are not always the same, hence the legend is critical to avoid errors in use.

Declination diagram. In large-scale maps, this diagram is located in the lower margin. It indicates the angular relationships of true north, magnetic north, and grid north. This diagram is crucial to using the map, as the map must always be aligned with the earth's surface prior to use by orienting it on the correct north-south ground alignment through the use of a compass. On maps of 1:250,000 scale this information is stated in a note in the lower margin.

Contour interval. This information appears in the center of the lower margin and states the vertical distance between adjacent contour lines on the map. It is an important datum, as it allows the user a ready means of computing his elevation.

The foregoing items of marginal information are only the most important ones; there are many data in the margins of military maps which the user must consider. A more detailed coverage of marginal information may be found in military map-reading manuals, such as the U.S. Army's *Field Manual 21–26*.

Map Grids

To use a map to determine one's position, a precise location system is required. Such a system should:

- require no knowledge of the geographic area in question.
- be applicable to large areas.
- require no landmarks.
- be applicable to all map scales.
- be simple to understand and use.

The traditional geographic coordinate system based on meridians of longitude and parallels of latitude has long been used for navigation at sea and in small-scale maps (Fig. 2). Both latitude and longitude represent a circle drawn

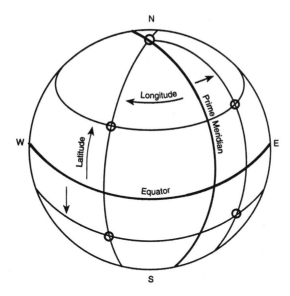

Figure 2. Longitude and latitude.

around the earth; geographic coordinates are expressed in angular measurement. Each circle is divided into 360 degrees, each degree into 60 minutes, and each minute into seconds. Longitude is measured east or west from the prime meridian at Greenwich, England; latitude is measured north or south from the earth's equator. It should be noted that many nations outside NATO do not use the Greenwich meridian as standard. While longitude and latitude are satisfactory for naval operations, there are two disadvantages to using this system for ground operations. First, latitude and longitude are curved lines, and second, the smallest subdivision of either is the second, which is accurate to only 24 meters (75 ft.). The curvature of the lines of longitude and latitude also cause quadrangles formed by the intersection of the parallels to be different sizes and shapes, which complicates measuring directions and locating points. Further, 24-meter (75-ft.) accuracy is not sufficiently precise for all military ground operations. Military grids overcome these problems, although longitude and latitude usually are also indicated on military maps.

Military grids are no more than a rectangular grid superimposed on the transverse Mercator projection normally used in military maps. The universal transverse Mercator (UTM) grid covers the earth between 84 degrees north and 80 degrees south latitude (Fig. 3). As its name implies, it is superimposed over the transverse Mercator projection. The earth has 60 UTM zones and the grid is identical in each. Base values in meters are assigned to the central meridian and to the equator, and the grid lines are fixed in parallel to these base lines. Each grid line is given a value indicating its distance from the origin. Each grid zone between 84 degrees north and 80 degrees south is 6 × 8 or 6 × 12 degrees of latitude and longitude in size, is given a designation (Fig. 4), and is further subdivided into 100,000-meter squares. Each 100,000-meter square is identified by a pair of letters that is unique within the area covered by the grid

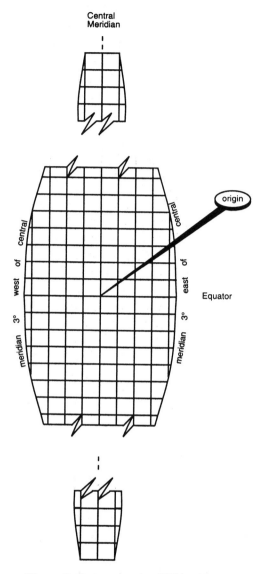

Figure 3. Representative UTM grid zone.

zone designation (Fig. 5). The identification of the 100,000-meter square identification letters usually is shown in the marginal information on most NATO military maps. This system ensures that no two locations can be located at the same point on the earth. Military maps are broken down from 100,000-meter squares through 1:50,000- and 1:25,000-scale sheets (see Fig. 1).

The regularly spaced grid lines that appear on all large-scale military maps are divisions of the 100,000-meter square and are spaced at 1,000- or 10,000-meter intervals. Each grid line has a specific designation that can be used to

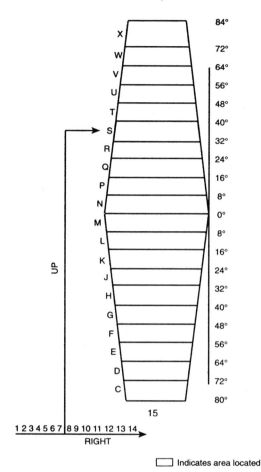

Figure 4. Grid zone designation.

pinpoint one's location. Most Western grid references are read from left to right, then up.

Military Symbols

Military symbols are graphic aids used on maps to identify items of operational interest. The keys to good military symbols are simplicity, uniformity, and clarity. Symbols are used to depict both friendly and enemy units, weapons, equipment, and activities. Within NATO, military symbols are governed by a standardization agreement (STANAG 2019) that generally defines the usage of symbols throughout the alliance, although there are variations.

Military symbols provide an easily recognizable means to express an operational plan, concept, or situation on a map. Under ideal conditions, colors are used to distinguish among friendly, enemy, and other symbols. The colors used within NATO are:

- Black or Blue—Friendly units, weapons, activities, and ground environment symbols not encompassed by other colors.
- Red—Enemy units, weapons, and activities.
- Yellow—Chemical, radiological, or biological areas, whether friendly or enemy.
- Green—Man-made obstacles, whether friendly or enemy.

Within NATO, fields around the basic symbol are used to display specific data regarding the symbol in question. The use of fields is necessary to clarify the status of the unit, weapon, or equipment depicted by the basic symbol.

Military symbols consist of a basic designator that indicates the type of organization represented, an interservice symbol, a size symbol, a unit role symbol, an equipment indicator, and various fields surrounding the basic symbol to further clarify and specify its identity. Representative NATO/U.S. military symbols are presented in Figures 6 through 10.

CHARLES Q. CUTSHAW

Bibliography

Pombrik, I. D., and A. N. Shevchenko. 1985. *Karta ofitsera* (The officer's map). Moscow: Military Publishing House.

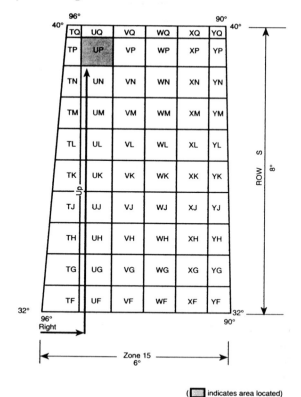

(▨ indicates area located)

Figure 5. 100,000-meter square representative designation.

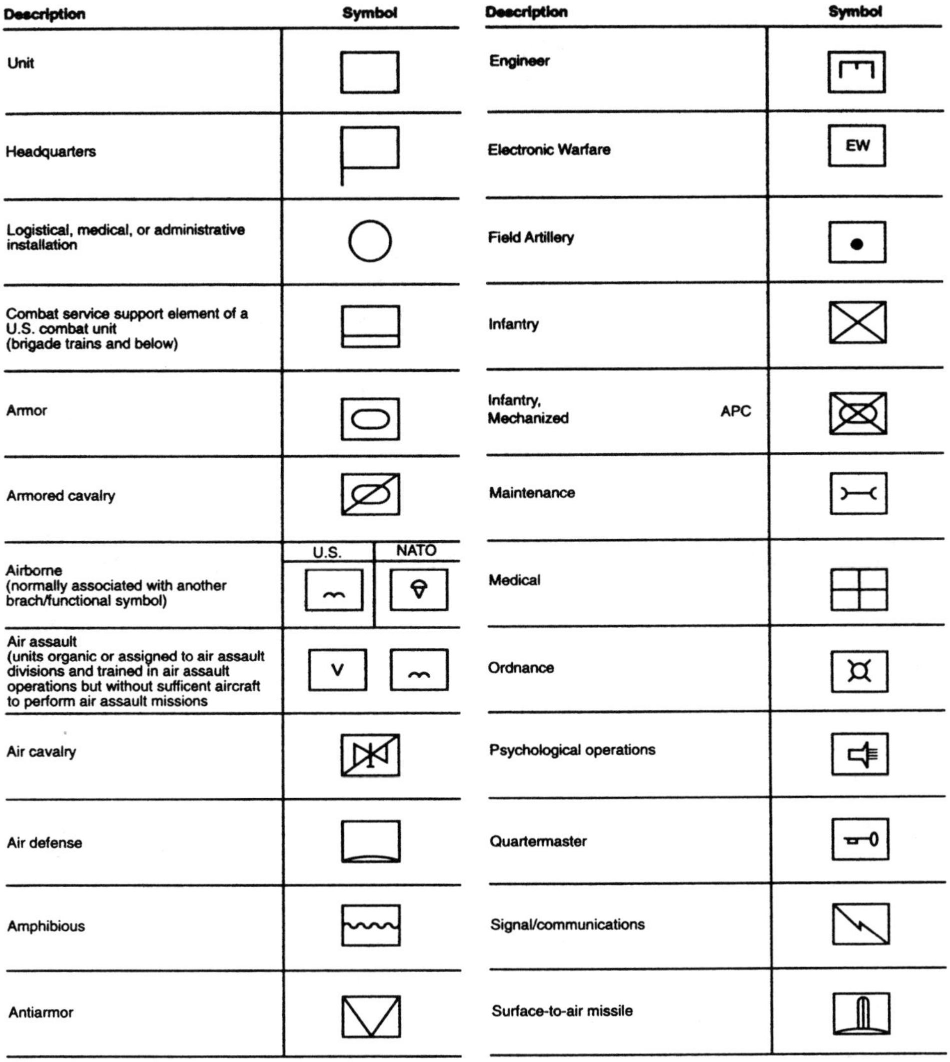

Description	Symbol	Description	Symbol
Unit		Engineer	
Headquarters		Electronic Warfare	EW
Logistical, medical, or administrative installation		Field Artillery	●
Combat service support element of a U.S. combat unit (brigade trains and below)		Infantry	
Armor		Infantry, Mechanized APC	
Armored cavalry		Maintenance	
Airborne (normally associated with another brach/functional symbol)	U.S. / NATO	Medical	
Air assault (units organic or assigned to air assault divisions and trained in air assault operations but without sufficent aircraft to perform air assault missions		Ordnance	
Air cavalry		Psychological operations	
Air defense		Quartermaster	
Amphibious		Signal/communications	
Antiarmor		Surface-to-air missile	

Figure 6. Basic military symbols.

U.S. Army. n.d. Field Manual 21–26. *Map reading.* Washington, D.C.: Headquarters, Department of the Army.

U.S. Defense Intelligence Agency (DIA). 1978. DDB-2680-41-78. *Handbook of Soviet armed forces military symbols.* Washington, D.C.: Defense Intelligence Agency.

Description	Symbol	Description	Symbol
Class I—Subsistence		Class VI—Personal demand	
Class II—Clothing, individual equipment, tentage, organizational tool sets		Class VII—Major end items	
Class III—POL Air Force		Class VIII—Medical materiel	
Class IV—Construction		Class IX—Repair parts	
Class V—Ammunition All types (less special)		Class X—Material to support nonmilitary programs	

Figure 7. Logistics role indicators.

Symbol	Description
xxxx / 8	Combat arms regimental system (CARS) Eighth Army
xxx / 3	III Corps
xx / 10 ... 3/8	10th Infantry Divsion, III Corps, Eighth Army
x / 1 ... 10/3	1st Brigade, 10th Infantry Divsion, III Corps
2-15 ... 1/10/3	2d Battalion, 15th Infantry, 1st Brigade, 10th Infantry Division, III Corps
A ... 2–15/1/10	A company, 2d Battalion, 15th Infantry, 1st Brigade, 10th Infantry Division
2 ... xx A/2-15/10	2d Platoon, A Company, 2d Battalion, 15th Infantry, 10th Infantry Division
1 ... 2/A/2-15	1st Squad, 2d Platoon, A Company, 2d Battalion, 15th Infantry

Figure 8. Representative fields for military symbols.

Weapons. Symbols are used to indicate the type and location of a weapon or group of weapons. When a weapon symbol appears on a map or overlay, the base of the shaft indicates the location of the weapon. To show the approximate size of a particular weapon, the procedure is as follows:

Select the appropriate weapon symbol.

↑ (light automatic weapon)	(gun)

Add horizontal bars (one for medium or two for heavy) to denote the size.

(medium machine gun)	(heavy gun)

If a weapon has a high trajectory, a O is placed at the base of the shaft. If the weapon has a flat trajectory, a ∧ is placed at the base of the shaft.

(medium mortar)	(light antitank gun)

If the weapon is primarily for air defense, a ⌒ is placed at the base of the shaft.

(air defense missile)	(air defense gun)

If the weapon is rocket launched, a ∧ is placed at the head of the shaft. If a weapon is also tracked, self-propelled vehicle, a ⌒ is placed below the weapon symbol.

(rocket launcher)	(a tracked, self-propelled medium howitzer)

Figure 9. Representative equipment symbols.

U.S. Description	STANAG 2019 Description	Symbol
Squad/crew	Smallest unit/UK section	
Section unit larger than a squad but smaller than a platoon	Unit larger than a U.S. squad/UK section but smaller than a platoon equivalent	
Platoon or detachment	Platoon/troop equivalent	
Company, battery, or troop	Company/battery/squadron equivalent	
Battalion or squadron	Battalion equivalent	
Group or regiment	Regiment/group equivalent	
Brigade	Brigade equivalent	
Division	Division	
Corps	Corps	
Army	Army	

Figure 10. Unit size designations.

MARLBOROUGH, JOHN CHURCHILL, DUKE OF
[1650–1722]

John Churchill, Duke of Marlborough (Fig. 1), was England's most successful military leader; he never lost a major battle, and he exhibited a brilliant grasp of tactics, strategy, and diplomacy. As commander of British forces fighting on the European continent during the War of the Spanish Succession, he was one of the two greatest soldiers of his day, the other being his ally and collaborator in his most famous victories, Prince Eugene of Savoy.

Early Years and Rise to Command

John Churchill was born 26 May 1650 into a family suffering from having been on the losing side in the English civil war. Even after the Restoration, the Churchill family possessed only modest means. At the age of 17, Churchill

Figure 1. John Churchill, Duke of Marlborough. (SOURCE: U.S. Library of Congress)

became a page to James, Duke of York, younger brother of King Charles II. Soon after, Churchill entered the Foot Guards as an ensign.

As a junior officer, Churchill first saw combat in 1668 with the English garrison of Tangier, where he took part in the mobile operations that were characteristic of skirmishes with the Moors. In 1670 he served with naval infantry in the Mediterranean. A brief interlude in England followed, during which he continued to develop close ties in the court. In 1672 Churchill served under the duke of Monmouth with English forces allied with France against the Dutch. During 1674 he distinguished himself in several battles and earned the praise of the great French marshal Turenne and King Louis XIV. In these years, Churchill served alongside several French officers against whom he would fight later in his career. He also learned much about the French army and acquired solid military experience.

Churchill became a close confidant of the duke of York and benefited considerably when the latter ascended the throne as James II (1685). Churchill also gained influence through his marriage to Sarah Jennings, a most influential lady-in-waiting to Princess Anne, daughter of James II and the future Queen

Anne. Churchill was given several diplomatic assignments. He received a colonelcy in 1677, and was made brigadier of foot in 1678. He defended James II against an attempted coup led by the duke of Monmouth (the illegitimate son of King Charles II), and fought against his old commander in the campaign of Sedgemoor (1685) in which Monmouth was defeated by the Royal Army. However, Churchill did not support James II when William of Orange (James's son-in-law) landed, at the invitation of English Protestants, at Torbay in 1688. Churchill deserted his longtime benefactor, James II, and the defection weighed heavily in the outcome and the accession of William and his wife, Mary (eldest daughter of James II), to the English throne.

Although Churchill was made the duke of Marlborough by the new monarch, his initial relationship with William III was not smooth. Marlborough assumed responsibility for the organization of the army and was promoted to lieutenant general even though William favored his own Dutch officers for senior positions and was not certain of Marlborough's loyalty. In 1690 Marlborough successfully commanded an expedition against Irish Jacobites. He was involved in court intrigues, which were always to plague his career, and was briefly imprisoned in the Tower of London (on accusations that later proved to be false), which kept him from serving in the latter part of the War of the League of Augsburg (1688–97) against the French.

War of the Spanish Succession

At the beginning of the War of the Spanish Succession (1701), Marlborough regained William's favor and was appointed captain-general of the English forces that were deployed to the continent and allied with Dutch forces against France. Marlborough's responsibilities included authority to negotiate the Second Grand Alliance against France. He was also designated allied commander but with considerable limitations on his authority, particularly with regard to his Dutch allies.

Marlborough's reputation was won in the ensuing war. His initial campaigns in the Netherlands and Rhineland (1702–1703) were hindered by the timidity of his Dutch allies, who were still in awe of the French army and unfamiliar with Marlborough's capabilities. From the beginning, Marlborough demonstrated a quick grasp of maneuver and a strong will to act.

Meanwhile, King William died and Queen Anne (to whom Marlborough's wife was still very close) assumed the English throne. From this point on, Marlborough's accomplishments can be summarized by four great battles.

Battle of Blenheim

In 1704 Marlborough executed his famous strategic march from the Spanish Netherlands (Belgium today) to the Danube to relieve his Austrian allies, who were threatened by a Franco-Bavarian army. The move was a masterpiece of logistical planning, deception, and drive. Once in southeastern Germany, Marlborough conducted a difficult assault of the Schellenberg (2 July 1704). Soon after, he joined forces with Eugene of Savoy, who commanded the Imperial army. Together they decisively defeated the French and Bavarians at the Battle of Blenheim (Blindheim, in Bavaria) on 13 August 1704. This victory exposed the relative deterioration of the French army since its preeminence in the earlier years of Louis XIV's reign.

The true significance of his victory was reinforced by the military achievements—often allied with Eugene on the battlefield—that followed.

BATTLES OF RAMILLIES AND OUDENARDE

In 1705 Marlborough, again commanding an allied force against the French, breached the fortified lines of Brabant along the eastern border of the Spanish Netherlands. In so doing, he demonstrated his mastery of strategic maneuver. His pattern, to be repeated in subsequent campaigns, consisted of a feint in one direction followed by a rapid movement and concentration of forces at another location to carry out his main thrust.

Marlborough's campaign in the Low Countries continued against Marshal Villeroi and the Elector of Bavaria. For the rest of 1705, Marlborough was on several occasions frustrated when, after successfully maneuvering the enemy into a potentially decisive battle, his Dutch allies refused to cooperate in a conclusive engagement. After a winter of travel to many capitals in Europe to gain support in the alliance, Marlborough returned to the Low Countries in the spring of 1706. He was surprised to find Villeroi ready to engage.

The resulting Battle of Ramillies (23 May 1706) evolved much like that of Blenheim. Following the failure of a major thrust on his right, Marlborough concentrated his cavalry on his left and personally led a series of charges that overwhelmed the French right so quickly that Villeroi was unable to use his reserves. In two hours the allies put the enemy to flight and followed up with a vigorous pursuit. Many cities fell, and all of Brabant and Flanders were won. Besides showing Marlborough's mastery of tactical command, the Battle of Ramillies demonstrated the superiority of the English line infantry of the time.

Marlborough was frustrated in his campaign of 1707 because he was unable to develop a major battle against a large French force under a new commander, Marshal Vendôme. Surprisingly, and for some unexplainable reason, Marlborough did not exhibit his usual dynamic, creative leadership. It was also a year of reverses for the allies on other fronts in Spain and Italy.

The inactivity of 1707 was compensated for when Marlborough confronted Vendôme at the Battle of Oudenarde, Spanish Netherlands (11 July 1708). Initially, Vendôme surprised Marlborough by rapidly placing the much larger French army in a position that threatened the English lines of communication to the North Sea. Prince Eugene, before his own forces could arrive, joined Marlborough and was there to assist in managing a desperate situation. He eventually took command of the allied right wing while Marlborough personally led the decisive flanking movement on the French right.

The allied victory was also helped when almost half of the French force was never committed. This was due to differences between Vendôme and the duke of Burgundy. The latter, as a "prince of the blood," had been given titular command but argued with Vendôme on almost every aspect of his plan. Still, the victorious outcome was another display of Marlborough's mastery of tactical command. His victory at Oudenarde freed the Spanish Netherlands from French control, although the French still held several fortresses. Marlborough undertook a series of successful sieges that further attested to his virtuosity. His aggressiveness and use of deception even made siege warfare appear more a war of maneuver.

MALPLAQUET AND RETIREMENT

In 1709 Marlborough confronted his most able French opponent, Marshal Villars, at the Battle of Malplaquet. Even with Eugene's able assistance and a considerable advantage in numbers going into battle, it was a most costly victory. Marlborough attempted his usual tactical scheme of throwing the opposing forces off balance and then exploiting a weakened sector of the enemy's defense. Villars, however, did not fall for any such ploy, and led his men inspirationally even though he had been seriously wounded. In some respects it was a Pyrrhic victory: the losses of the allies far exceeded those of the French and the disproportionate number of Dutch casualties did not sit well with the public. The battle did not help Marlborough with his political enemies back in England. These were gaining influence with Queen Anne as Marlborough's wife was losing favor with her former patron.

Marlborough had one more chance against Villars in the summer of 1711, in a campaign against the French *Non Plus Ultra* defense lines. At his best in deception and quick marches, Marlborough "out-generaled" his French adversary and successfully penetrated the line to besiege and take the town of Bouchain. Villars was unable to intervene. Unfortunately, Marlborough's political influence had disappeared in Queen Anne's court and he was relieved of command by the end of the year. With Marlborough absent, Marshal Villars prevailed on the battlefield; little of Marlborough's efforts were reflected in the Treaty of Utrecht in 1713.

Later Years

Marlborough retired to his estate in Woodstock, England, and continued supervising the construction of Blenheim Palace, richly decorated with paintings and memorabilia of his victories. For a time he traveled and received honors from many of the courts of Europe. Following the death of Queen Anne and the succession of the Elector of Hannover as George I to the English throne in 1714, Marlborough regained political influence. His health, however, had begun to deteriorate. In 1716, he suffered a stroke that left him partially paralyzed. He died in June 1722 after a second stroke.

Assessment

Marlborough's reputation as a great general is solidly established in military history. He was an excellent strategist, tactician, and battlefield leader. While he had problems in domestic politics, he demonstrated unusual aptitude as a commander. He was able to get the most from ineffective allies, and worked brilliantly with allied commanders.

ALBERT D. McJOYNT

SEE ALSO: Eugene, Prince of Savoy-Carignan; France, Military Hegemony of; History, Early Modern Military.

Bibliography

Barnett, C. 1974. *The first Churchill: Marlborough, soldier and statesman.* New York: Putnam.
Chandler, D. 1973. *Marlborough as military commander.* New York: Scribner.
———. 1976. *The art of warfare in the age of Marlborough.* New York: Hippocrene Books.
Churchill, W. S. 1968. *Marlborough, his life and times.* New York: Scribner.
Kemp, A. 1980. *Weapons & equipment of the Marlborough wars.* Poole, U.K.: Blandford Press.

MARSHALL, GEORGE CATLETT, JR. [1880–1959]

Gen. George C. Marshall was a principal architect of American military policy and strategy in World War II and went on to become one of the nation's most renowned statesmen. He did not achieve his military prominence as a field commander, but as the principal army adviser to two presidents of the United States. His civilian career led him to serve in the two most senior positions available to a nonelected American official.

Early Life and Career

George Catlett Marshall, Jr., was born in Pennsylvania on 31 December 1880. He graduated from the Virginia Military Institute (VMI) in the class of 1902, having been First Captain. He was commissioned into the United States Army. He endured the slow promotions of a peacetime army while serving in various assignments to midwestern posts, as well as two tours in the Philippines.

When the United States entered World War I in 1917, Marshall deployed to France with the 1st U.S. Division. General Pershing, commander of the American Expeditionary Forces, soon realized Marshall's staff skills and assigned him to the General Staff. Thus, Marshall did not realize his ambition of being a regimental commander. However, Pershing vested considerable trust and authority in Marshall's staff position.

Following the Armistice (November 1918) Colonel Marshall became Pershing's aide. Like most other Regular Army officers, he reverted to his peacetime rank (major). In 1921, Pershing became U.S. Army Chief of Staff. Marshall was promoted to lieutenant colonel and followed Pershing to Washington.

In 1924 Marshall received a regimental command, followed by a series of senior post assignments. As assistant commandant of the U.S. Army Infantry

School at Fort Benning, he started his famous "little black book," which listed young officers who had impressed him with their leadership abilities. Later, he served as commander of the Illinois National Guard division. In 1936 Marshall was promoted to brigadier general, and was in Washington as chief of Army War Plans in 1938. Shortly thereafter, he became deputy chief of staff.

World War II

Although Marshall's first meeting with President Roosevelt in 1933 went badly, Marshall's talents prevailed. In 1939 Roosevelt selected Marshall to be chief of staff over 32 senior officers. As Marshall put on his second star, war broke out in Europe with the German invasion of Poland.

The new army chief of staff faced and overcame difficult challenges. Marshall persuaded a reluctant Congress to provide funds for preparedness. He contended with various pressure groups: isolationists as well as zealous interventionists. In 1941 passage of the Lend-Lease Act interfered with the goal of readying U.S. forces, since much-needed equipment was diverted to the support of England and Russia. After the Japanese bombed Pearl Harbor in December 1941, America's priorities became clearer.

The American army was vastly enlarged with newly produced arms and with men who needed to be trained—a requirement that strained national mobilization plans. Worldwide operations were planned and directed through newly created allied and multiservice staffs. Senior officers were selected to command in the various theaters of operations. Crucial decisions had to be made in allocating the limited available resources to wage a global war.

Marshall participated in the high-level formulation of U.S. and Allied strategy and policy in the war. His vision was crucial in many fundamental force structure decisions. He recognized that U.S. armored and air forces had to be expanded far beyond envisioned programs. Marshall was daring in his support of a relatively "independent" U.S. Army Air Corps, with considerable leeway to pursue advanced airpower doctrines. He supported the "Europe first" strategy, much to the displeasure of General MacArthur and the U.S. Navy. But even here, he was at odds with the British allies—specifically Churchill. Marshall pushed for an early cross-channel operation as the most direct and quickest route to defeat Germany, rather than approach from the "soft underbelly" of south Europe. Most of Marshall's judgments proved correct. However, his advocacy of going immediately into Western Europe was premature, as events in North Africa proved. The American forces needed more combat experience.

As a "chief" and not a commander, Marshall's "battlefields" were usually conferences. A series of them marked the main decisions that shaped Allied strategy. The first two conferences (Arcadia in December 1941–January 1942 and Casablanca in January 1943) were tremendous tests for senior American military leaders. The British, who had considerable experience in combined and joint planning, dominated the initial conference. The concept of running a war through councils of military chiefs was new to the Americans, but Marshall learned fast. In the conferences that followed, Marshall generally was the dominant influence on matters of military policy and grand strategy.

By 1944 Marshall was directing action on six fronts. He and the other senior U.S. military chiefs were elevated to five-star rank to put them on a par with Allied field marshals. Unlike some other popular U.S. generals of the time, Marshall quickly stopped any pretensions to political ambitions.

Roosevelt died on 12 April 1945, and Marshall started to work with the new president, Harry Truman. He quickly won the highest respect from Truman, and the general's influence was at its peak.

Marshall reluctantly supported the use of the atomic bomb as the lesser of two evils when considering the alternative, the conquest of more Pacific islands and the invasion of Japan itself. Even then, he was not sure that the bomb would eliminate the need for an invasion of the mainland. After Japan surrendered in August 1945, Marshall immediately submitted his resignation and recommended Eisenhower for his job. Upon Truman's request Marshall delayed his retirement until November of that year.

The Statesman

President Truman asked Marshall to go to China ten days after his retirement. Marshall's assignment was to bring about reconciliation between the Nationalist government under Chiang Kai-shek and the Communist Party under Mao Tse-tung. It was a futile mission, an effort marked by American lack of understanding of the Chinese political situation.

In January 1947 Truman appointed Marshall Secretary of State. His first crisis was communist-inspired civil wars in Greece and Turkey. Three months later the "Truman Doctrine" was announced and the U.S. Congress voted to aid Greece in its fight against the communists. Marshall recognized that much of postwar Europe was destitute and vulnerable to communist subversion. On 5 June 1947 he announced a program whereby the United States would finance European economic recovery; this concept became known as the "Marshall Plan." Marshall's reputation contributed greatly to obtaining the necessary financial support for the project from the U.S. Congress. He oversaw the development of a massive foreign military assistance program to supply and train the military forces of democratic countries, so they would be prepared to defend both against communist subversion and possible communist aggression. His health forced him to resign in 1949.

In 1950 North Korea invaded South Korea and Truman appointed Marshall Secretary of Defense. This was a difficult period for the U.S. Army. Many contentious issues had to be faced, such as the racial integration of the military forces and the dismissal of MacArthur when he challenged the authority of the president. Political opportunists tried to rise to power on a tide of anticommunism. Even Marshall was accused of not being anticommunist enough. But his reputation was secure, and he resigned in September 1951 with a remarkable record of distinguished service to his country.

In 1953 Marshall was awarded the Nobel Peace Prize for the Marshall Plan.

After a lingering illness, he died on 16 October 1959 and was buried at Arlington Cemetery. A Marshall Foundation was formed in 1953. His papers are at VMI, where there is a museum in his honor. History remembers few military chiefs of staff, but Marshall will be an exception to that rule—not only because of his role as a soldier, but also his accomplishments as a civilian statesman.

ALBERT D. McJOYNT

SEE ALSO: Chiang Kai-shek; Eisenhower, Dwight David; Korean War; MacArthur, Douglas; Pershing, John Joseph; Mao Tse-tung.

Bibliography

Pogue, F. C. 1965–87. *George C. Marshall.* 4 vols. New York: Viking.
———. 1968. George C. Marshall: Global commander. In *Harmon Memorial Lectures in Military History 1968*, no. 10:1–20.
Bland, L. I., and S. R. Ritenour, eds. 1981–1986. *The papers of George Catlett Marshall.* Baltimore, Md.: Johns Hopkins Univ. Press.

MILITARY

The term *military* refers to those institutions of managed lethal violence that are legitimized by state control. The broad definition includes all the organized groups, regular and irregular, national and tribal, that use violence for political or social ends. A more narrow definition may distinguish among armies, navies, air forces, marines, and, in some cases, special forces, missile units, and other branches. Police, internal security forces, and intelligence agencies are usually excluded from the definition, although these may have attributes of military organization.

Military systems have existed at least since classical times, but the modern military is generally traced to the rise of west European nation-states in the sixteenth and seventeenth centuries. But from the beginning a distinction was made between officers, usually members of the nobility, and other ranks, typically drawn from the lower strata of the society. There also appeared early on a midlevel group of noncommissioned officers (NCOs) who directly supervised the lower ranks. This tripartite division of commissioned officers, NCOs, and enlisted personnel still characterizes almost all military organizations. Not only do uniforms separate military members from the civilian population, but insignia distinguish the ranks from each other within the military.

In the nineteenth century, the military became professionalized. Rank and authority derived from ascribed status gradually gave way to that based on competence and education. Military academies and schools arose, ranging from officer commissioning programs to colleges of advanced studies in warfare and strategy for senior officers. This era also saw the formalization of military law with a separate judicial, punishment, and incarceration system. A highly structured and disciplined organization continues to be a defining characteristic of the military.

Many of these military patterns of hierarchy, professionalization, and unique lifestyle spread from the west European heartland to the United States and other parts of Europe. These patterns were then adopted by the newly independent states in Latin America, by Japan and China, and, finally, by the successor states of defunct empires in Asia, Africa, and Oceania. By the mid-twentieth century, a military system was seen as a virtual prerequisite for national independence.

Military recruitment and formal organization vary in several ways. Recruitment depends on either volunteers or conscription. Military forces are usually composed of both active-duty units and reserve or militia components. Some military systems, however, consist solely of active-duty professional officers, NCOs, and lower-rank enlisted volunteers. Others consist of a small professional core with a large militia. Most military systems are mixed, with varying ratios of professional and nonprofessional members and varying components of active and reserve units. Despite these variations, a common imperative in all militaries is to maintain a corporate institutional sense of the membership while seeking to instill a moral commitment from the individual.

Although a long-standing institution, the military confronts special tensions in the contemporary world. For example, in less-developed countries, the tendency for the military to intervene in matters of civil order poses problems for democratic politics. In advanced democratic nations, the role of the military is subject to political influences as basic as budgetary control. In many nations, the very purpose of the military as defender of the homeland from external aggression is brought into question by pacifist groups, as well as by changes in the international strategic picture.

As the twentieth century closes, the military may assume new missions—for example, peacekeeping, multinational interventions, anti–drug trafficking, and environmental protection. In basic respects, however, the military in the foreseeable future will resemble the social organization that initially appeared with the rise of the nation-state.

CHARLES C. MOSKOS

Bibliography

Andrezejewski, S. 1954. *Military organization and society.* London: Routledge.

Edmonds, M. 1988. *Armed services and society.* Leicester, England: Leicester University Press.

Huntington, S. 1957. *The soldier and the state.* Cambridge, Mass.: Harvard University Press.

Janowitz, M., ed. 1964. *The new military.* New York: Russell Sage Foundation.

Moskos, C., and F. Wood, eds. 1988. *The military.* London: Pergamon-Brassey's.

MOGHUL EMPIRE

The Moghul Empire ruled northern India from 1526 to 1858. Founded by a descendant of both Genghis Khan and Tamerlane, the Moghuls were the last of the Turko-Mongolian dynasties that periodically dominated the urban civilizations of the Eurasian littoral.

Zahir-ad-Din Mohammad "Babur" (1483–1530)

Zahir-ad-Din Mohammad, better known in history as Babur, was born in 1483. His father, Omar Shaikh, the youngest son of Sultan Abu Sa'id, was king of Farghana. Through his father, Babur traced his ancestry back to Timur-i-lang (Tamerlane). Babur's mother was a daughter of Yunus Khan, king of the Chagatai Ulus. Through his mother, therefore, Babur traced his ancestry back to Genghis Khan.

The 78 years between the death of Tamerlane and the birth of Babur witnessed the decline of the Timurids. The cause of their decline was the internecine struggles for power among the Timurids themselves. Babur's own father, for example, faced an almost constant threat from his brothers and his cousins.

While the Timurids fought among themselves, the Uzbeks—an offshoot of the Golden (Kipchak) Horde—under Muhammed Shaibani (1451–1510), another descendant of Genghis Khan, encroached upon the Timurid patrimony. One by one, Babur's cousins and uncles fell before the Uzbeks. For a short time, Babur, king of Farghana since the age of 12, held Samarkand and sat on the throne of Tamerlane. By 1500, however, Muhammed Shaibani was master of both Bukhara and Samarkand and was poised to take Farghana and Tashkent. In June 1503, at the Battle of Akhsi, Babur lost Farghana forever. With a handful of followers, including his half-brothers Jahangir and Nasr—both of questionable loyalty—Babur sought refuge in the mountains of Afghanistan.

CONQUEST OF AFGHANISTAN

Ten years of warfare had taught Babur much. His defeats had resulted not only from his own inexperience but also from the machinations of allies and supporters to whom he had been no more than a pawn. The loss of Farghana freed Babur to follow his destiny.

Now a king without a kingdom, Babur had an army of less than 300 men. As he moved through the mountains, however, he attracted fighters from the local tribes, including the Mongol Hazaras. With this motley force, Babur conquered Badakhshan in 1503, and Ghazni and Kabul, which he made his capital, in 1504. Three years later, in 1507, he occupied Kandahar. Possession of Kabul gave Babur a route into northern India, but he was distracted from India by events in Central Asia. In 1505, and again in 1511–12, Babur attempted to regain his Timurid patrimony. After the Uzbek victory at Ghajdivan (1512), Babur confined his energies to strengthening his control of the kingdom of Kabul. By 1519 he was secure enough to begin raiding Hindustan (northern India).

CONQUEST OF THE SULTANATE OF DELHI

In 1524, Babur invaded the Punjab. As other Muslim conquerors had done before him, including Mahmud of Ghazni, Babur entered the Punjab by way of the Khyber Pass. After leaving a garrison to hold Lahore, Babur retired to Kabul. He returned to Hindustan in 1525. At Panipat, on 20 April 1526, Babur defeated Ibrahim Shah Lodi Afghan, Sultan of Delhi and Agra. Victories over the Rajputs at Khanua (1527) and Gogra (1529), completed Babur's conquest of the Sultanate of Delhi and placed the fledgling Moghul Empire on a firm foundation.

The Moghul Army

Babur conquered the Sultanate of Delhi with 12,000 troops. Cavalrymen, both armored and unarmored, predominated in the early Moghul army. Their armor ranged from the leather armor of the Kalmuks to Indo-Persian–style chainmail reinforced with iron plates. Weapons included the traditional weapons of the steppe: the sabre and bow.

Babur made an important addition to the traditional weapons of his people: firearms. He equipped a select number of infantrymen with matchlocks. Protected from enemy arrows by leather mantlets, these Moghul matchlockmen provided protective fire during siege operations; on the battlefield, they served as both a screen for the cavalry and a pivot for cavalry maneuvers.

Babur also used cannon. These weapons, manufactured and manned by Othmanli (Ottoman) Turkish gunners, along with the matchlockmen, gave Babur an important advantage over his Muslim and Hindu enemies in Hindustan.

MOGHUL ORGANIZATION

In general, the organization of the Moghul army followed that of the Mongol army of Genghis Khan, as had the army of Tamerlane. Some organizational flexibility was needed, however, given the mix of forces commanded by the Moghul emperor. Besides his own Turks, the emperor commanded contingents of Afghan tribesmen, Mongol freebooters, Persian mercenaries, and Indianized Turks from Delhi, as well as Rajput and other Hindu levees. There is evidence that the native contingents maintained their own battle order, while those from the Turkic and Mongol homelands adhered to the order mandated by the Yassa of Genghis Khan.

MOGHUL TACTICS

Moghul tactics were a mixture of the traditional and the modern. Babur used many of the same tactics successfully employed by both Genghis Khan and Tamerlane. These he wedded to the evolving tactics of the age of gunpowder. At the First Battle of Panipat (1526), Babur deployed his matchlockmen and gunners behind a defensive line formed by baggage wagons. The wagons, connected by lengths of rope and chain, left gaps in the line to allow cavalry sorties. After Moghul arrow and gunfire had driven the enemy wings in upon their own center, the Moghul cavalry—the right and left wings of Babur's own army—executed the famous and dreaded *tulughma*, the Banner Sweep.

At Khanua, 13 March 1527, Babur again deployed his infantry and artillery as he had at Panipat. At a critical point in the fighting, he abandoned the defensive and ordered the infantry and artillery to advance on the Rajput center. The Rajputs, re-forming to meet a frontal attack, broke off contact with the Moghul wings, which immediately executed the *tulughma*, and the slaughter of the Rajput army began. What his distant cousins, the Ottoman Turks, had done against the Persians at Chaldiran twelve years earlier, Babur did at Panipat and Khanua: combined the traditional tactics of the Turko-Mongolian steppe warrior with those of the dawning age of modern warfare.

Under Babur's successors, the Moghul Empire continued to expand despite occasional reverses of fortune. For a short time, the Moghul domain included virtually all of India.

Moghul Expansion Under Babur's Successors, 1530–1707

HUMAYUN (1530–56)

Humayun, Babur's son and successor, had a checkered career. Although he added Mandu and Champanir to the empire in 1535, Humayun was driven out of India by the Afghan, Sher Shah (1539–45), founder of the short-lived Sur Dynasty. Humayun spent sixteen years in exile, mostly in Persia, and was only able to return to Delhi in 1555, a year before his death.

AKBAR (1556–1605)

Akbar was the greatest of the Moghul emperors. Like his grandfather Babur, Akbar became king at an early age. Also like his grandfather, he learned to survive the court intrigues, jealousies, and conspiracies of relatives. With the help of Bairam Khan, his guardian, Akbar defeated both the court intriguers and, at the Second Battle of Panipat (1556), the Afghans. In 1561, he conquered Malwa and three years later, in 1564, the Chandels (Gonds) submitted. Chitor was occupied in 1568. The Kingdom of Gujarat submitted in 1573, Bengal in 1576, and Khandesh in 1577.

Akbar the conqueror was also Akbar the conciliator and administrative reformer. In 1562, the year he assumed full control of the government, he married a Hindu Rajput princess. The emperor wished to create a unified state in which both Muslim and Hindu could live together in safety and harmony. Akbar therefore abolished the *jizya*, the tax on nonbelievers. He also reformed the bureaucracy and recruited Hindus to staff its middle and lower echelons. By the end of Akbar's reign, Hindus made up 30 percent of the administrative staff.

Akbar also streamlined the administration by instituting the *mansabdari* system of civil service. *Mansabdars* (officials) were given military rank and were able to recruit and maintain troops appropriate to that rank. Therefore, although their primary duties were civil and fiscal, when occasion demanded, they could perform military duties.

To stimulate the economy and provide needed revenue, Akbar assumed control of all agricultural land in the realm. He abolished the traditional taxes and replaced them with a single tax: one-third of all agricultural and manufactured products.

JAHANGIR (1605–27)

During the reign of Jahangir, Moghul expansion stagnated. Jahangir, an indolent drunkard, was content to enjoy the wealth of the realm and the fermented juice of the grape.

SHAH JAHAN (1628–57)

Shah Jahan resumed Moghul expansion. Ahmadnagar was added to the empire in 1632, Golconda in 1635, and Bijapur in 1636.

Shah Jahan also initiated the last Moghul attempts to regain their Timurid legacy in Central Asia. Under the operational command of Aurangzib, the emperor's son, unsuccessful attempts were made to capture both Balkh and Badakhshan in 1647. From 1649 to 1653, the Moghuls tried to reconquer Kandahar, again without success. Shah Jahan was successful, however, in extending Moghul control over parts of the Deccan (central India).

The emperor's wars and the construction of the Taj Mahal nearly bankrupted the empire, and led to the revolt by Aurangzib. Deposed by his own son, Shah Jahan remained a prisoner until his death in 1666.

AURANGZIB (1658–1707)

Aurangzib expanded the Moghul Empire into central and southern India. In 1666, Chittagong was occupied. In 1679, the Moghuls won Marwar from the Rajputs. In 1685, Surat was seized. Between 1681 and 1692, Aurangzib personally led his army in the conquest of the Deccan and southern India. By 1692, he ruled virtually all of India. Shortly thereafter, however, rebellion broke out in the newly conquered territories, and Aurangzib spent the last fifteen years of his reign attempting to pacify the realm—in vain.

Aurangzib was also unsuccessful in his attempts to neutralize the growing power of the Marathas under their king, Sivaji. By 1674, the Marathas were the most dangerous rivals of the Moghuls.

The greatest danger to the Moghul Empire, however, proved to be Aurangzib's own domestic policy. Reversing the policy of Akbar, Aurangzib ended toleration of the Hindu religion, destroyed Hindu temples, and reimposed the *jizya*. The emperor expelled experienced Hindu bureaucrats from the administrative apparatus and replaced them with devout Muslims. By restoring Muslim purity, Aurangzib hoped to return the empire to the strict monotheism of Islam. The end result, however, was the rapid decline of the empire following his death.

Moghul Decline

During the reign of Bahadur Shah (1707–12), the Moghul Empire disintegrated. Territorial governors and local magnates became, in reality, independent rulers. The empire therefore repeated the pattern of dissolution followed by its Turkic and Mongol antecedents. Insubordinate governors, rebellious Hindu rajas, and British and French interlopers gradually reduced the Moghul realm to the Sultanate of Delhi. In the aftermath of the Indian mutiny, Bahadur Shah II (1837–57), the last of the Moghuls, was deposed, tried, and exiled to Rangoon, where he died in 1862.

LAWRENCE D. HIGGINS

SEE ALSO: Genghis Khan; Mongol Conquests; Ottoman Empire; Turkic Empire.

Bibliography

Beveridge, A. S., trans. 1922. *Babur, emperor of Hindustan: The Babur-nama.* 2 vols. London: Luzac.

Burn, R. 1937. *The Cambridge history of India.* Vol. 4, *The Mughal period.* Cambridge: Cambridge Univ. Press.

Gascoigne, B. 1971. *The great Moghuls.* New York: Harper and Row.

Habib, I. 1982. *An atlas of the Mughal empire.* New Delhi: Oxford Univ. Press.

Habibullah, A. B. M. 1945. *The foundation of Moslem rule in India.* Lahore: S. Muhammed Ashraf.

Lamb, H. 1964. *Babur the tiger: First of the great Moghuls.* New York: Bantam Books.

Lane-Poole, S. 1903. *Medieval India under Mohammedan rule, 712–1764.* New York: Putnam's Sons.

Moreland, W. H. 1920. *India at the death of Akbar.* London: Macmillan.

Sarkar, J. 1920. *Mughal administration.* Calcutta: Sarkar and Son.

Spear, T. G. P. 1951. *Twilight of the Mughals: Studies in late Mughal Delhi.* Cambridge: Cambridge Univ. Press.

MOLTKE THE ELDER
(Helmuth Karl Bernard, Graf Von) [1800–91]

Helmuth Karl von Moltke served as chief of the General Staff of the Prussian army from 1857 until 1888, playing a central role in Prussia's planning and preparation for its highly successful wars against Austria in 1866 and France in 1870–71. He is frequently referred to as Moltke the Elder to separate his identity from that of a nephew of the same name (Moltke the Younger) who was chief of the General Staff at the time Germany entered World War I. During the elder Moltke's tenure as chief of the General Staff, the Prussian army's General Staff acquired an unmatched reputation for excellence, and the Prussian army served as Prussian chancellor Otto von Bismarck's primary instrument for achieving Prussia's goal of a unified German state.

Early Years

Moltke was born in the northern German state of Mecklenburg on 26 October 1800. His family was part of the old Prussian nobility, but financially it was not well off. Moltke's father served as an officer in the Prussian army and later joined the Danish army. Moltke began his own military experience as a cadet in the Danish army. In 1821, Moltke transferred to the Prussian army to increase his prospects for advancement. He served briefly with troops before attending the Prussian army's war college, where he studied from 1823 to 1826. After two more years with a regiment, Moltke gained an assignment to the Prussian General Staff, where he stayed for the remainder of his career.

Moltke's early career was heavily influenced by the relative poverty of his family, and he turned to writing to supplement his meager income. Moltke's only direct experience with warfare began in 1835, when he received an assignment to Turkey as an observer and adviser to the Turkish army. In 1839, he accompanied the commander of a Turkish army that sought to drive an Egyptian army out of Syria. Here Moltke provided astute tactical and operational advice but saw his advice ignored. The Turkish army subsequently suffered a decisive defeat, and shortly thereafter Moltke returned to Prussia.

Moltke's Rise to Prominence

In 1842, Moltke married his sister's stepdaughter. This union, although a happy one, produced no children. Moltke continued to serve on a variety of staff assignments, while simultaneously publishing accounts of his experiences in Turkey.

At about this time, Moltke also began to receive assignments that brought him to the attention of the Prussian aristocracy. In 1845, he was appointed adjutant to Prussia's Prince Frederick. This brought him into frequent contact with both the current and future kings of Prussia. Moltke impressed both with his quiet diligence and brilliance as a staff officer and adviser. His unqualified support for the crown in its efforts to suppress the revolution of 1848 gained him favor as well.

In 1857, Moltke's loyalty and competence were rewarded with his appointment as chief of the General Staff of the Prussian army. Inheriting a position that had undergone a period of decline under his predecessors, Moltke played a major role in the restructuring of the Prussian approach to warfare.

Moltke as Chief of the General Staff

One of Moltke's most immediate and lasting achievements as chief of the Prussian General Staff was his success in implementing a military mobilization system within Prussia that capitalized on the tremendous strategic mobility potential of the newly invented railroads. Moltke demonstrated a clear understanding of how Prussia could use superior organization and speedy mobilization to help offset its vulnerable geographic location in central Europe and to gain strategic and operational advantages over its potential opponents.

Moltke also introduced into the Prussian army field telegraph units to speed the transmission of orders to subordinate unit staffs and commanders. Under Moltke, the German General Staff underwent a resurgence in the quality of its officer training and the efficiency of its organization that would produce stunning results in its subsequent wars against Austria and France.

War broke out first against Denmark in 1864. At this point, Moltke was still relatively unknown within Prussia; at the beginning of this war he was little more than an adviser to the Prussian war minister, who had the real responsibility for executing the king's directives and supervising the armies in the field. When the chief of staff of the army in the field was removed, however, Moltke temporarily assumed the post and helped direct the Prussian armies to victory.

Moltke intended to retire at this point, but he was persuaded by the war minister, Albrecht von Roon, to remain. Moltke was brought into the inner councils of policy making shortly afterward, a seemingly innocuous appointment at the time, but one that proved to be an important first step in the increasing importance of the chief of the General Staff's role in matters of state policy.

In 1866, war broke out with Austria. Here the fruits of Moltke's organizational and mobilization reforms were seen, as was his superb grasp of large-scale operations. Three Prussian armies rapidly mobilized, concentrated on the battlefield near Königgrätz under Moltke's direction on 3 July, and decisively defeated the main Austrian force in a great battle of encirclement. The Prussian victory permitted Bismarck to conclude a favorable peace with Austria (the Peace of Nikolsburg), which brought several smaller German states into a North German Confederation under Prussia's dominance.

Moltke remained chief of staff through the Franco-Prussian War of 1870–71. Again demonstrating a marked superiority in speed of mobilization, the Prussian armies struck into France. Despite a number of potentially serious mistakes by subordinate army commanders that undermined Moltke's concept for another battle of encirclement like that at Königgrätz, Prussian armies succeeded in surrounding one French army at Metz and, later, another at Sedan. Although the war continued for several months beyond the French defeat at Sedan, these two victories and the subsequent siege of Paris resulted in another set of favorable peace terms that brought about a final, successful chapter to Prussia's long-term efforts to establish a unified German state.

Final Years

Moltke's wife had died in 1868. With her death, he no longer had any desire to retire and so he continued to serve as chief of the General Staff until 1888, when a new kaiser, Wilhelm II, assumed the throne. In retirement, the officer who had done so much to create the Prussian army that crushed two rival powers in relatively short campaigns warned of the end of the era of short, decisive campaigns. He died peacefully on 24 April 1891, having seen the reputation of the Prussian army and its General Staff reach unparalleled heights during his long stewardship as chief. He remains today one of the great military figures of modern times.

DAVID A. NIEDRINGHAUS

SEE ALSO: Franco-Prussian War; Prussia and Germany, Rise of.

Bibliography

Addington, L. 1971. *The blitzkrieg era and the German general staff, 1865–1941.* New Brunswick, N.J.: Rutgers Univ. Press.
Craig, G. A. 1955. *The politics of the Prussian army, 1640–1945.* London: Oxford Univ. Press.
Dupuy, T. N. 1977. *A genius for war: The German army and general staff, 1807–1945.* Englewood Cliffs, N.J.: Prentice-Hall.
Gorlitz, W. 1953. *History of the German general staff, 1657–1945.* New York: Praeger.
Holborn, H. 1986. The Prusso-German school: Moltke and the rise of the general staff. In *Makers of Modern Strategy,* ed. P. Paret. Princeton, N.J.: Princeton Univ. Pres.
Kitchen, M. 1975. *A military history of Germany.* London: Weidenfeld and Nicholson.
Pflanze, O. 1973. *Bismarck and the development of Germany: The period of unification, 1815–1871.* Princeton, N.J.: Princeton Univ. Press.
Ritter, G. 1969. *The sword and the scepter: The problem of militarism in Germany,* vol. 1. Coral Gables, Fla.: Univ. of Miami.
Von Sybel, H. 1968. *The founding of the German empire.* New York: Greenwich.

MONGOL CONQUESTS

Under Genghis Khan and his successors the Mongols conquered the largest land empire in world history, an empire that extended over 90 degrees of longitude and included most of the Eurasian landmass. At its height (1206–94), the Mongol Empire encompassed many different nations and religions, all subject to the will of the Great Khan (Kha Khan) and to Mongol law (the Yassa). The Mongol army was the principal instrument used for the expansion and maintenance of the empire.

The Mongol Army

The Mongol army was one of the most efficient military machines in history. Well organized and well trained, the army was a professional fighting force, from its highest-ranking general to its lowest-ranking cavalryman.

COMPOSITION

The basic unit of the army was the *arban* (squad), composed of ten men. Ten *arban* formed a *jagun* (company), with a strength of 100 men. Ten *jagun* formed a *minghan* (regiment) of 1,000 men. Ten *minghan* formed a *tumen* (division), with a total strength of 10,000 men. Two or more *tumen* formed a field army, commanded by an *Or-Khan*.

The Mongol army was composed of light and heavy cavalry. Both the heavy cavalryman and his mount were armored. His weapons included a lance and a saber or mace. Some heavy cavalrymen also carried bows and arrows.

The light cavalrymen, the horse archers, were the core of the Mongol forces. They wore little or no armor, and carried a saber or two to three javelins, but their primary weapon was the bow and arrow. With their powerful, recurved bows, the light cavalry was able to deliver a devastating, almost continuous, suppressive fire at long range, and a deadly rain of armor-piercing arrows at short range.

With the subjugation of the northern portion of the Kin Empire, the Mongols drafted Chinese siege specialists into the army. These specialists played a significant role in the campaigns in China, the Middle East, and Eastern Europe.

BATTLEFIELD DEPLOYMENT

The army normally deployed in five ranks. The first two ranks were formed by the heavy cavalry; the remaining three ranks by the light cavalry. Units deployed so that the light cavalry *jagun* could advance and withdraw between the heavy cavalry formations.

The light cavalry initiated battle by delivering volleys of arrows. When the deluge of arrows had sufficiently disrupted the enemy ranks, the heavy cavalrymen charged. So devastating was the work of the horse-archers, that the enemy usually broke after one charge. The fleeing enemy was ruthlessly pursued and slain.

Discipline

Mongol discipline was harsh. The most common punishments were beatings and death. Death was the penalty for those who failed to obey orders in the field, broke ranks without orders, or looted without permission. To fail the commander of your *arban*, or your comrades, was the most serious offense.

The disciplinary code applied to officers as well as enlisted men. An officer was required to look after his men, ensure that they had the necessary equipment in good order, and that they received their share of the loot. Failure on the officer's part was punishable by flogging or death. Needlessly wasting the lives of his men was among the most serious offenses an officer could commit.

Size of the Mongol Army

Estimates of the size of the Mongol army vary. The Mongol core of the army may not have exceeded 130,000, but, as the empire expanded, the army added recruits from conquered territories. During his campaign against the Khwaresmian Empire, for example, Genghis Khan marshaled 150,000 troops, including contingents from allied and subject kingdoms. The Khwaresmian Army numbered at least 200,000. However, it was the Mongol organization, operational planning, firepower, mobility, and tactics that accounted for Mongol victories, not numbers.

Mongol Tactics

The Mongols used a number of tactics to gain victory, usually over much larger enemy forces. Their favorite tactic was wide envelopment of the enemy's force. This tactic, the *tulughma* or "Banner Sweep," had two variations: single envelopment and double envelopment. The Mongols also used the single envelopment and the double envelopment—the pincer movement—on the strategic level, as illustrated by the campaigns in North China, Transoxiana, and Eastern Europe.

Another tactic often employed was the feigned retreat, followed by counterattack. The Mongols would retreat before an enemy advance, often for days, and when the pursuing enemy had become sufficiently disorganized, the Mongols would turn and attack, usually from a prepared ambush.

The Mongols would sometimes leave an apparent avenue of escape open for a surrounded enemy. As the enemy troops fled through the gap in the Mongol lines, the horse-archers hunted them down.

Mongol Conquests

The Mongol Empire expanded during the reigns of Genghis Khan, Ogadai Khan, Mangu Khan, and Kublai Khan. The conquests followed a pattern of eastward—later southward—thrusts into China alternating with westward thrusts into Central Asia, Eastern Europe, and the Middle East. A brief chronology of the conquests follows:

Genghis Khan, 1206–27
1. Hsihsia, 1209; rebellion suppressed, 1227
2. Kara-Khitai, 1211
3. Inner Mongolia, western Manchuria, 1211–13
4. Peking, southern Manchuria, 1215
5. Khwaresmian Empire, 1219–22

Ogadai Khan, 1227–41
1. Conquest of the Kin Empire completed, 1234
2. Russia, Poland, Hungary, Wallachia, 1237–41

Mangu Khan, 1251–59
1. Yunnan Province (China), 1252
2. Tibet, 1252
3. Nan-chao, 1253
4. Persia, Iraq, Syria, 1252–58

Kublai Khan, 1260–94
1. Korea, 1259
2. Sung Dynasty (South China), 1267–79
3. Annam, 1288
4. Burma, 1297

Campaigns in North China and Eastern Europe

The manner in which the Mongols conquered their empire is best illustrated by the campaigns in North China and Eastern Europe.

INITIAL CAMPAIGNS AGAINST THE KIN EMPIRE, 1211–15

In 1211 Genghis Khan initiated a series of campaigns against the Kin that did not end until 1234, with the final defeat of these hereditary enemies of the Mongols. The campaign of 1211 was confined to western Manchuria and eastern Inner Mongolia, but in 1213, the Mongols attacked in force. Jebe, one of Genghis Khan's subordinates, feigned a retreat and lured the defenders of Nankou Pass into a prepared ambush, where they were annihilated by the main Mongol army under Genghis Khan.

The Mongol forces then divided into three columns. The left (eastern) column, under Genghis Khan and his youngest son, Tuli, moved south toward Shantung Province. The center column, under Jebe, moved through eastern Hopei Province. The right (western) column, under Juchi, Chagatai, and Ogadai, made a wide enveloping sweep around the Kin's left flank, and entered western Shansi Province from the southwest, behind the Kin defenses. Advancing along roughly parallel axes, the three columns moved south toward the Yellow River. Upon reaching the river, the columns reversed direction and converged on Peking, leaving devastation in their wake. Unable to take Peking, the Kin capital, after a long siege, Genghis Khan allowed the Kin emperor to ransom his city. The Mongols then returned to Mongolia with their loot.

In May 1215, the Mongols returned and captured Peking, but the Kin government had already moved to Kaifeng on the Yellow River. Mongol successes, especially in Peking and southern Manchuria, were aided by the revolt of the Khitans—distant cousins of the Mongols—whose own empire, the Liao, had been overthrown by the Kin a century earlier.

Realizing that the war against the Kin would be a protracted struggle, Genghis Khan named Mukhali viceroy, and charged him with the conquest of North China.

CAMPAIGNS IN EASTERN EUROPE, 1237–41

Ogadai Khan, in consultation with his generals, decided on the conquest of Eastern Europe during the grand council meeting in 1234. The emperor named his nephew Batu, son of Juchi, expedition commander, and the veteran general Subotai, deputy commander. In reality, Subotai was in operational command.

The Mongol attack on Russia was launched in the winter of 1237. The Khanate of Great Bulgary was smashed, and subsequently, the Turkic tribes along the Volga River submitted to the Mongols. The Russian city of Riazan was sacked in December 1237; Moscow, Suzdal, and Vladimir fell in February 1238; and Tver and Yaroslav were taken in March 1238. After regrouping, the Mongols moved into the Ukraine. On 6 December 1240, Mangu, eldest son of Tuli, captured and burned Kiev.

The Mongols paused after the sack of Kiev to rest and regroup. In the winter of 1241 they resumed their westward march. At Przemysl, the army was divided into three columns. Batu and Subotai, with the main army of 40,000, advanced toward Budapest, the Hungarian capital. The northern column, less than 30,000 strong, under the command of Ogadai's son Kaidu, swept into Poland and Silesia. At Liegnitz, 9 April 1241, Kaidu's army overwhelmed a joint German-Polish force of equal size, led by Prince Henry the Pious, Duke of Silesia. Turning southward, Kaidu rode through Moravia and on to Hungary. The southern column, under Kaidu's brother Kadan, about 20,000 strong, rode south through Galicia, then west through Moldavia, Wallachia, and Transylvania, before heading northwest toward Hungary.

King Bela IV of Hungary, with an army of Hungarians, Slovenes, Croatians, Germans, and French Templars (probably more than 80,000 men), set out to meet the Mongols. After a brief skirmish, the Mongols began to slowly withdraw, pursued by the allied army. At Mohi, on the Sajo River, the Mongols turned and attacked at dawn, 11 April 1241. Subotai, with a column of two or three *tumen*, crossed the river above the town, turned the enemy right flank, and attacked. The panic-stricken Europeans were allowed to escape through a gap in the Mongol lines, only to be hunted down and slain. At least 70,000 Europeans died at Mohi.

With Hungary secured, the Mongols began using it as a forward base. Columns raided Germany, Austria, and Dalmatia, and Europe stood open to a Mongol onslaught. Only the death of Ogadai, and the recall of the generals and princes of the empire, saved Europe from the Mongols.

End of the Conquests

The reign of Kublai Khan marked the zenith of Mongol expansion. Kublai's growing identification with China and Chinese civilization, however, was symptomatic of the growing divisions within the empire and the imperial family. In Persia, the Il-Khans (Vassal Kings) converted to Islam and adopted Persian customs. In Transoxiana (Russian Turkestan), the Chagatai Khans also converted to Islam and adopted Turkic customs. Only in the Mongolian Homeland and the Khanate of the Golden Horde did Mongols maintain their original customs. After the death of Kublai Khan, the empire split into five independent kingdoms, with only nominal allegiance to the Great Khan (Kha Khan).

LAWRENCE D. HIGGINS

SEE ALSO: Ghengis Khan.

Bibliography

Juvayni, A. 1958. *The history of the world-conqueror.* Tr. and ed. J. A. Boyle. 2 vols. Manchester: Manchester Univ. Press.

———. 1977. *The Mongol world empire.* London: Variorum.

Chambers, J. 1979. *The devil's horsemen: The Mongol invasion of Europe.* New York: Atheneum.

Grousset, R. 1952. *L'Empire des steppes.* Paris: Payot.

———. 1966. *Conqueror of the world.* New York: Orion Press.

Halperin, C. 1985. *Russia and the golden horde: The Mongol impact on medieval Russian history.* Bloomington, Ind.: Indiana Univ. Press.

Lamb, H. 1940. *The march of the barbarians.* New York: Literary Guild of America.

———. 1953. *Genghis Khan: Emperor of all men.* New York: Bantam Books.

Legg, S. 1970. *The heartland.* New York: Farrar, Straus and Giroux.

Liddell Hart, B. H. 1927. *Great captains unveiled.* London: Blackwood and Sons.

Martin, H. D. 1977. *The rise of Chingis Khan and his conquest of north China.* New York: Octagon Books.

McNeill, W. H. 1964. *Europe's steppe frontier, 1500–1800.* Chicago: Univ. of Chicago Press.

Prawdin, M. 1967. *The Mongol empire: Its rise and legacy.* New York: Free Press.

Saunders, J. J. 1972. *The history of the Mongol conquests.* New York: Harper and Row.

MONTGOMERY, BERNARD LAW [1887–1976]

British Field Marshal Viscount (Bernard Law) Montgomery was one of the most controversial and colorful senior Allied commanders of World War II (Fig. 1). His army career spanned half a century and culminated in service as Chief of the Imperial General Staff, but he is best known for his victory over the "Desert Fox," German Field Marshal Erwin Rommel, at the Second Battle of El Alamein, 23 October–3 November 1942.

Figure 1. Bernard Law Montgomery at a press conference in France, 1944. (SOURCE: U.S. Library of Congress)

Early Life and Career

Bernard Law Montgomery, the fourth of nine children of the Rev. Henry and Maude (Farrar) Montgomery, was born on 17 November 1887 in a London suburb. In 1889 the elder Montgomery was consecrated Bishop of Tasmania, and the entire family migrated to Hobart later that year.

Montgomery spent his early years in Tasmania, later noting, "Certainly I can say that my own childhood was unhappy," which he attributed to his tyrannical mother. The Montgomerys returned to England in October 1901. Bernard's elder brother Harold was granted a commission in the Imperial Yeomanry, and served in the final months of the Boer War. This perhaps influenced Bernard, who joined the army class at St. Paul's in 1902. During his four years at St. Paul's, Bernard excelled at cricket and rugby, but was considered "backward" academically, although he later felt ashamed of his "idleness."

After passing the competitive entrance examination in 1906, Montgomery entered Sandhurst in January 1907. Prior to his commissioning, however, he was involved in a "prank" which almost resulted in his expulsion. Apparently at the intervention of his mother, he was readmitted as a Gentleman Cadet, although his commissioning was delayed from January until the summer of 1908.

Montgomery was gazetted into the Royal Warwickshire Regiment on 19 September 1908 and served with its 1st Battalion in India (1908–12). In January 1913, shortly after the unit's return to England, he was appointed assistant adjutant.

World War I

England declared war on Germany on 4 August 1914. Montgomery's battalion arrived in France on 23 August 1914, and three days later he led his platoon into battle at Le Cateau. In the ensuing confusion Montgomery was listed as missing, and he never forgot the absence of proper planning which characterized the commitment of the British Expeditionary Force (BEF) in 1914.

On 13 October 1914, Montgomery was severely wounded while leading an assault during the first Battle of Ypres. For his conspicuous gallantry he was awarded the Distinguished Service Order and promoted to captain. After recuperating, Montgomery served as a brigade-major in England, and deployed with his unit (which later suffered severe losses on the Somme) to France in January 1916.

Montgomery's indefatigable diligence was recognized by his appointment as General Staff Officer 2 (GSO2), 33d Division, in January 1917, followed by selection as GSO2, IX Corps, six months later. He was promoted brevet major on 3 June 1918, and became, two weeks later, a temporary lieutenant-colonel and GSO1 (Chief of Staff) of the 47th Division. He ended the war in that position, having earned an outstanding reputation as an exceptional and ambitious staff officer.

Interwar Years

Montgomery attended the Staff College at Camberley in 1920, followed by service as a brigade-major in Ireland during the "troubles." He served with equal efficiency on the staff of a Territorial Army division (1922–25), as a company commander (1925–26), and as an instructor at the Staff College (1926–28). After a short stint on a War Office committee revising the *Infantry Training Manual*, Montgomery returned to his regiment in 1930 as second in command.

In 1931, he commanded the 1st Battalion, Royal Warwicks in Palestine. The battalion went to India in 1934, and Montgomery became chief instructor at the Staff College, Quetta, in June. He then commanded the 9th Infantry Brigade at Portsmouth (1937–38), and continued his quest for high command. As a major general, he briefly commanded the 8th Division in Palestine in 1938, but became quite ill and was sent home to England. After recuperating, he assumed command of the 3d Division on 28 August 1939, less than one week from the start of World War II.

World War II

Montgomery commanded his division as part of II Corps (commanded by Lt. Gen. Sir Alan Brooke, the future Chief of the Imperial General Staff) of the British Expeditionary Force, which landed in France on 30 September 1939. Montgomery incessantly trained his division during the interlude of the "phoney war." After the German onslaught of 10 May 1940, the 3d Division defended the city of Louvain, Belgium, and after the Allied forces disintegrated, his division participated in the retreat to Dunkirk. On 27 May 1940, the 3d Division conducted a night maneuver in the middle of a battle, which prevented the enemy from outflanking II Corps and the BEF. During the last few days of the Dunkirk evacuation, the imperturbable Montgomery commanded II Corps.

After his return to England, Montgomery resumed command of the 3d Division, was promoted to lieutenant general, and selected to command V Corps in July 1940. This was during the crucial period when a German invasion of England seemed imminent; nine months later Montgomery was transferred to command XII Corps. On 17 November 1940 Montgomery became general officer commander in chief South-Eastern Command.

Throughout 1942, the military situation in North Africa deteriorated, resulting in the relief, in August 1942, of Gen. Sir Claude Auchinleck and replacement by Gen. Sir Harold Alexander as commander in chief, Middle East. Montgomery, near the apex of his career, was selected to command the Eighth Army defending the approaches to Cairo. Montgomery restored cohesion and confidence throughout his command. Within a month, adopting Auchinleck's plan, Montgomery stopped Rommel's forces at the Battle of Alam Halfa (31 August–2 September 1942).

Montgomery then turned his attention to the logistical problems of operating in the desert, and planned the Second Battle of El Alamein. Starting on 23 October 1942, this rather unimaginative battle did not go as planned, but Montgomery responded to the changing situations and tenaciously continued the offensive. By 3 November, the Germans had literally run out of tanks.

Montgomery was very slow to exploit the victory at Alamein. He was outgeneraled by Rommel, but the tide of war had changed. Rommel's forces were eventually trapped by a giant pincer movement of the Eighth Army attacking from the east, and Allied forces (which had landed in North Africa in Operation "Torch" in November 1941) pushing from the west. Organized resistance in North Africa ceased on 12 May 1943.

Montgomery was involved in the planning for, and commanded the Eighth Army in, Operation Husky, the invasion of Sicily, 10 July 1943. He no longer had complete control, but had to work together with Americans, who were frequently annoyed and insulted by Montgomery's often condescending and boorish behavior.

After commanding the Eighth Army in Italy, Montgomery returned to England in December 1943 to command the 21st Army Group in the invasion of Europe. His Operation Goodwood (18–20 July 1944), an attempt to break out of the Normandy beachhead, was decisively repulsed. Subsequently, he was roundly criticized for the dilatory nature of his attempts to close the "Falaise gap"; however, the blame for the escape of thousands of retreating Germans must be shared by the American commander, Gen. Omar Bradley.

Montgomery's tenure as ground force commander came to an end in August 1944, when Supreme Commander Dwight D. Eisenhower took over direct control of ground force operations. Soon afterward Montgomery was promoted to field marshal.

Differing philosophies on how best to defeat Germany then divided the Allied High Command. Montgomery (like Bradley and Patton) favored a single, knife-like thrust—under his own command—to the Ruhr. (Bradley and Patton believed this should be an American offensive.) But Eisenhower's strategy was to attack Germany on a broad front. Despite the dismal failure of Operation Market Garden in September, the subsequent performance of 21st Army Group was typically efficient, but unimaginative. Montgomery responded well militarily to the German counteroffensive in the Ardennes, but his imprudent claims of having "saved" the Americans resulted in further alienation between himself and the senior American commanders. The Allied advance continued, and on 4 May 1945, Montgomery accepted the unconditional surrender of German forces in northern Europe, having reached the Baltic Sea, near Lübeck.

Aftermath

Montgomery was ennobled as Viscount Montgomery of Alamein on 1 January 1946, and served as chief of the Imperial General Staff from June 1946 to November 1948. He served as chairman of the Western Union Commanders-in-Chief Committee (1948–51), and then as deputy supreme allied commander Europe (1951–58), under Generals Eisenhower, Ridgway, and Gruenther. Montgomery retired in 1958 after a half-century as a serving officer.

The publication of Montgomery's *Memoirs* in 1958 caused a furor. He was accused of being grossly unfair to many people, especially Auchinleck. In retirement, Montgomery traveled extensively and wrote books and articles. While bearing the Sword of State at the 1968 opening of Parliament, Montgomery collapsed, and afterward faded from the public eye. After being bed-ridden for three years, Montgomery died at his home at Isington Mill, on 24 March 1976.

Field Marshal The Viscount Montgomery of Alamein, K.G., G.C.B., D.S.O., remains a controversial figure. Ruthlessly efficient, he was vain and at times a showman, and a rather unimaginative but highly charismatic commander. A German field marshal said that generals were like race horses. They were supposed to win and Montgomery won most of the time. That is how "Monty" will be remembered by many.

HAROLD E. RAUGH, JR.

SEE ALSO: Eisenhower, Dwight David; Rommel, Erwin; World War II.

Bibliography

Barnett, C. 1960. *The desert generals.* London: Kimber.

Carver, M. 1962. *El Alamein.* London: Batsford.

Chalfont, A. 1976. *Montgomery of Alamein.* New York: Atheneum.

Hamilton, N. 1981. *Monty: The making of a general, 1887–1942.* New York: McGraw-Hill.

————. 1987. *Monty: The final years of the field-marshal, 1944–1976.* New York: McGraw-Hill.

Lewin, R. 1971. *Montgomery as military commander.* New York: Stein and Day.

Montgomery, B. 1974. *A field-marshal in the family.* New York: Taplinger.

Montgomery, F-M. 1958. *Memoirs.* London: Collins.

————. 1968. *A history of warfare.* London: Collins.

Moorehead, A. 1946. *Montgomery.* London: Hamish.

MUSASHI, MIYAMOTO [1584–1645]

Miyamoto Musashi, formally Shinmen Musashi No Kami Fujiwara No Ginshin, more familiarly Niten (his artistic name) or Kensei, "Sword Saint," is Japan's equivalent in strategic thought to China's Sun Tzu or Germany's Clausewitz. His philosophy of military strategy lies midway between that of Sun Tzu and Clausewitz. Musashi's *A Book of Five Rings*, like Sun Tzu's *The Art of War*, has become a source for developing corporate business strategy—first by Japanese businessmen, now internationally. Musashi's book is not specifically *on* strategy, but is rather a guide for those who want to learn strategy. At first reading, the book may seem to be a manual on how to kill an opponent in a duel, but it incorporates ideas of potential military significance at several abstract levels of tactics and strategy.

Musashi the Individual

Exemplifying the *kendo* scholar's goal of "pen and sword in accord," Musashi was a Japanese martial equivalent of Europe's "Renaissance man"—although he was not unique in this (Lowry 1985, pp. 149–50). He devoted his life to the study of fighting and the development of a philosophy of fighting, killing every dueling opponent in the process (his first at age 13, more than 60 by age 29) and participating in six wars. But Musashi was also an accomplished painter, sculptor, poet, designer, and artisan. An orphaned but elite samurai of noble ancestry by inheritance and profession, he was in fact a *Rōnin* ("wave person"—an unemployed wandering warrior) for much of his life, as a result of the Battle of Sekigahara (15 September 1600).

Humble and serious when not actually mastering a foe in combat, in his lifetime Musashi became one of Japan's most renowned warriors. Today he is still a folk hero, more widely known to Japan's general populace than Sun Tzu to the Chinese or Clausewitz to the Germans. In World War II, Japan named a battleship *Musashi.* This vessel, and its sister ship, *Yamato,* were the largest battleships ever built.

Accomplishments

In combat, Musashi could only be termed invincible: he never lost. He became an expert with all manner of weapons, developing the two-sword way of fencing, *nitoryu*. Later in his career, however, he took to killing his opponents with wooden swords or even cruder weapons made on the spot, even when fighting against experienced and ambitious warriors armed with fine swords. Although his life was devoted to searching for and developing the "way of the sword," he is also noted for his artistic endeavors. His paintings are valued more highly than those of many artists in Japan, and his calligraphy, sculpture, and metalwork are treasured.

Musashi wrote down his final philosophic understanding of fighting while living in a cave in Kyushu, a few weeks before his death. Written as guidance for his pupil—and influenced by Zen, Shinto, and Confucianism— *A Book of Five Rings* is basic to any martial arts bibliography, as well as a guide for businessmen planning sales campaigns.

Musashi's first message, based upon his lifetime of combat experience and study, is that the warrior must recognize, accept, and be guided by the deadliness of his craft. He insists that strategy (in its broadest sense) is inherent in the individual duel. He stresses the overriding significance of understanding and benefiting from knowledge of what is involved in personal combat: Individual minds and movements can change and then be acted upon more swiftly than can those of an army or of any size unit of warriors. "Winning," with its attendant achievement of power and fame through the use of force (his clearly stated goal)—and possible subsequent employment by a lord—is achieved by overcoming other individuals or groups, using three elements of successful combat:

- resolute acceptance of the possibility of one's own death,
- intimate knowledge of the tools of one's trade, and
- a basic overall plan for the end result of one's work.

Musashi's translator uses the English term *strategy* as an equivalent to the anglicized Japanese *heiho*. Derived from the Chinese term for *military strategy*, the Japanese characters reveal a somewhat more complex set of concepts: *heiho*, translated as *hei* (soldier), and *ho* (method or form), should be considered relative to several field concepts of its written characters. These include strategy (the approach of a nation, corps, or division), tactics (small unit), and individual capabilities (in combat)—as well as mastery of such abilities as painting and poetry.

For Musashi, strategy encompasses all of the above. It must be employed by individual warriors and field commanders alike, whether in man-to-man or 10,000-on-a-side fights. Implicit in the above (made more explicit as Musashi treats—still metaphorically—his expanded views) is the significance of such items as

- considering *all* ("10,000") facts and factors involved;
- having intimate knowledge of *all* the weapons one may employ, and knowing just when and how to employ them;
- knowing other traditions and paths to knowledge;
- using, above all, rhythm and timing in execution.

Musashi's treatment of his "five books" (rings) stresses the significance of training and timing, as well as

- interrelating *all* the factors involved;
- using intuitive judgment;
- paying attention, even to trifles; and
- doing nothing that is of no use.

Future

Musashi's *Book of Five Rings* will become an increasingly significant text for military persons of East and West if users develop sufficient vision to sense the strategic and tactical implications of his empirically developed but philosophical metaphor.

DONALD S. MARSHALL

SEE ALSO: Art of War; Clausewitz, Karl von; Sun Tzu.

Bibliography

Kodansha. 1983. Musashi. In *Encyclopedia of Japan*. Tokyo: Kodansha.
Lowry, D. 1985. *Autumn lightning*. Boston: Shambala.
Musashi, M. 1982. *A book of five rings*. Trans. V. Harris. Woodstock, N.Y.: Overlook Press.
Yoshikawa, E. 1981. *Musashi*. Trans. C. S. Terry. Foreword by E. O. Reischauer. New York: Harper and Row/Kodansha.

N

NAPOLEON I [1769–1821]

Napoleon Bonaparte, one of history's greatest soldiers, was trained as an artillery officer under Louis XVI. Rising to prominence during the French Revolution, he overthrew the Directory government and seized power, becoming first consul and later emperor of the French. He capitalized on the military accomplishments of the Old Regime and the revolution, conquering most of Europe at the peak of his career (Fig. 1).

Education and Early Career

Napoleon was born 15 August 1769 at Ajaccio, Corsica. In 1778 he was sent to the *collège* at Autun and in 1779 to the academy at Brienne. In 1784 he matriculated at the Ecole Militaire in Paris and was commissioned an artillery sublieutenant in 1785. Early influences on Napoleon included the theoretical writings of Marshal Maurice de Saxe and the tactical ideas and innovations of Pierre de Bourcet, Joseph du Teil, and Jacques de Guibert. The army Napoleon entered had adopted the artillery reforms of Jean Baptiste Gribeauval, giving it the finest artillery in Europe, and it soon employed the combined-arms division and mixed order of lines, columns, and skirmishers. This force, enhanced by revolutionary changes such as conscription, was ultimately inherited by Napoleon and provided the basis for his conquests.

Napoleon first gained fame commanding the artillery at the siege of Toulon in 1793. The recapture of the city (19 December), due largely to Napoleon's guns, earned him promotion to brigadier general. But in 1794–95, his Jacobin connections and friendship with Augustin Robespierre led to disgrace and unemployment. He regained favor by his role in suppressing a royalist uprising in Paris (5 October 1795) with his famous "whiff of grapeshot." He was rewarded with the Army of Italy, his first independent field command.

Italian and Egyptian Campaigns

Napoleon led the Army of Italy to a series of victories, including Lodi (10 May 1796), Castiglione (5 August 1796), Arcola (15–17 November 1796), and Rivoli (14–15 January 1797). It also provided him with the opportunity to develop further his skills as a commander, and the peace he imposed on Austria in 1797

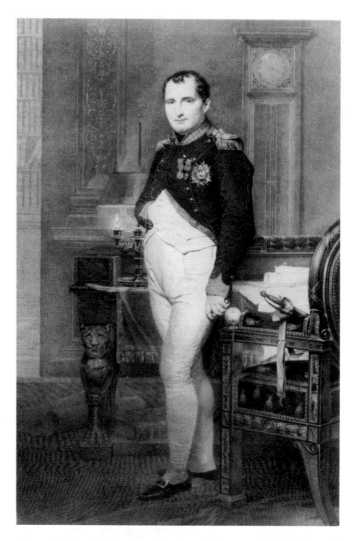

Figure 1. Napoleon, painted by David. SOURCE: (U.S. Library of Congress)

enhanced his fame in France. Returning to Paris, he discarded as impractical an invasion of England itself, instead embarking on an Egyptian campaign as a means of striking at Britain. After capturing Malta (12 June 1798), he landed in Egypt (1 July), but Lord Horatio Nelson's naval victory at Aboukir Bay (1–2 August) stranded him there. The easy conquest of Egypt led in 1799 to a campaign in Syria, possibly an effort to return overland to France. Stopped at Acre (March–May 1799), Napoleon returned to Egypt, where he learned things were going badly for the French armies in Europe. Napoleon abandoned his army in Egypt and returned to France (9 October) to assume the leading role in the overthrow of the Directory government and to make himself first consul (9–10 November 1799).

Campaigns and Reforms of the Consulate

Needing a victory to enhance his position, in 1800 Napoleon launched a second campaign in Italy, culminating in the victory—actually a near defeat salvaged by the arrival of Louis Desaix—at Marengo (14 June) and a peace with Austria (9 February 1801). Peace with Britain followed in March 1802, but it lasted only until the spring of 1803, although major hostilities did not resume in Europe until 1805.

In the meantime, Napoleon instituted several basic reforms. In 1801 he ordered a change in the artillery (the System of the Year IX). A six-pounder was to replace the four- and eight-pounders of the Gribeauval system, the twelve-pounder being retained. An army to invade England was established around Boulogne and carefully drilled until, as the Grand Army, it marched to victory at Ulm and Austerlitz. Napoleon had acquired enough popularity to be proclaimed emperor in May 1804; by this time his tactics and strategy had matured.

Tactics and Strategy

Napoleon capitalized on the idea of divisions operating independently of each other but capable of mutual support. In 1803 he adopted the army corps—typically, two to four infantry divisions, plus cavalry, artillery, and other services—as the largest field formation throughout the French army. Thus, the concept of mutual support, which he had previously applied to divisions, he now applied to army corps and even among various war theaters. Although Napoleon acknowledged no fixed principles of war, he gave great attention to such things as mobility, dispersal, concentration, and envelopment. Speed and mobility were critical, because they permitted Napoleon to keep his units dispersed and then concentrate them at the last moment to achieve local superiority over part of the enemy force. Interior lines of communication enhanced Napoleon's mobility, whether on the battlefield proper or throughout a theater. Mobility also permitted surprise and envelopment, both of which contributed to Napoleon's ability to maneuver the enemy out of position.

Napoleon always exercised direct tactical command in a battle, after laying careful plans in advance. He usually met with his major unit commanders very early on the morning of a battle, giving them last-minute instructions based on reconnaissance and then sending them out to implement his plans. He rarely interfered with their implementation, however, except in instances of failure or an unexpected change in the situation. Although his initial plans frequently went awry, he was quite adept at minimizing the effects of his own errors, seizing unforeseen opportunities, and capitalizing on enemy mistakes. With an army thus organized and led, well trained and rested, Napoleon embarked on perhaps his greatest campaign, the 1805 Ulm-Austerlitz campaign.

Campaigns of 1805–1807

When Austria and Russia attacked France in the fall of 1805, Napoleon moved the Grand Army into Central Europe, capturing one Austrian army at Ulm (20

October) and defeating the combined Austro-Russian armies at Austerlitz (2 December). This campaign serves as an excellent example of Napoleon's warmaking concepts. In 1806 Napoleon determinedly pressed for the political reorganization of Europe through military action, establishing the Confederation of the Rhine (12 July) and abolishing the Holy Roman Empire (1 August). This disruption of Germany angered Prussia, which, allied with Russia, declared war on France in 1806. This resulted in an overwhelming Prussian defeat at Jena and Auerstädt (14 October), the French occupation of Berlin, and the establishment of the Continental System (Napoleon's effort to break Britain by closing Europe's ports to British trade while stimulating French industry to fill the void). Prussia and Russia, however, continued the war, leading to a drawn-out winter battle at Eylau (8 February 1807) and another overwhelming French victory at Friedland (14 June). Napoleon's meeting with Czar Alexander I and the Treaties of Tilsit (7 and 9 July) ended this series of campaigns, temporarily brought Russia into the French system, and reestablished a Polish state: the satellite Grand Duchy of Warsaw.

Spanish and Portuguese Campaigns

The Iberian Peninsula, however, remained a breach in the Continental System. Therefore, Napoleon sent Marshal Andoche Junot into Portugal in late 1807. In 1808 Napoleon attempted to force the Spanish to accept Joseph Bonaparte as their king, but the people resorted to guerrilla warfare. Napoleon, having reassured himself of Central European loyalties at Erfurt (27 September–14 October 1808), then led an army into Spain. He defeated the Spanish army, restored Joseph to the throne of Spain, and achieved some success in driving the British out of the peninsula. In Paris, intrigues proliferated, and Austria grew restive. Napoleon returned to France in January 1809, never again setting foot in Spain, although the conflict there lasted until the French were finally driven out in late 1813.

1809 Campaign and the Austrian Marriage

While Napoleon was in Spain, Austria allied with England and in April 1809 invaded Bavaria, a French ally. Napoleon responded quickly, defeating Archduke Charles of Austria in a series of battles and occupying Vienna (13 May). However, during an attempted crossing of the Danube, Napoleon was defeated at Aspern and Essling (21–22 May). He then regrouped, defeated Archduke Charles at Wagram (5–6 July), and forced a peace on Austria.

In late 1809, Napoleon divorced his wife, Josephine Beauharnais, because she could not bear him an heir. He negotiated with both Austria and Russia for a new wife. He settled on Archduchess Marie Louise of Austria, rejecting Grand Duchess Catherine of Russia. Thus he contrived a marriage alliance with Austria, which France had defeated repeatedly, and angered Russia, which Napoleon had never been able to crush completely. Relations with Russia grew steadily worse.

The 1812 Russian Campaign

On 24 June 1812, Napoleon invaded Russia. The principal causes of the conflict were Russian humiliation over the marriage negotiations, Russian withdrawal from the Continental System, and disputes over Poland. The size of Napoleon's army, over 600,000 men, curtailed its speed and mobility. The Russians successfully withdrew (although one army was almost trapped at Smolensk), scorching the earth and making their first real stand at Borodino (7 September). This was a bloody, but indecisive, French success. Napoleon then marched to occupy Moscow, which the Russians had largely destroyed by fire. Napoleon, hoping to force the czar to make peace, waited in Moscow and disregarded warnings about the Russian winter. The French finally abandoned Moscow (19 October), but the weather grew extremely bitter, and the French retreat turned into disaster. Napoleon nonetheless outmaneuvered his Russian adversaries and fought his way out of an encirclement by forcing a costly crossing of the Beresina River (26–28 November). When he learned of a plot in Paris to overthrow him, the unsuccessful Malet Conspiracy (23 October), he abandoned his army at Smogorni (5 December) and returned to Paris. The pitiful remnants of the army continued the retreat to Germany.

Campaigns of 1813 and 1814

As the Russians advanced westward, Prussia allied with them, breaking its alliance with France. Napoleon built a new army of ill-equipped, half-trained recruits. He defeated the allies at Lützen (2 May 1813) and Bautzen (20–21 May). He then accepted an armistice (2 June–13 August) that worked to his disadvantage because, in the interim, Austria joined the allies. Napoleon defeated the Austrians at Dresden (26–27 August), but the numerically superior allies defeated him in a great battle at Leipzig (16–19 October), ending French power in Germany and resulting in French withdrawal west of the Rhine. The allies pursued.

For the 1814 campaign in France, Napoleon carried out a brilliantly conducted war of maneuvers, winning a series of minor victories, despite overwhelming allied strength. But the allies finally drove for Paris, which they entered on 31 March. With his army in disarray, his marshals disillusioned, and the people anxious for peace, Napoleon abdicated unconditionally (6 April). He was given the Mediterranean island of Elba to rule in exile.

The Hundred Days

Disgruntled over the failure of Marie Louise to join him, fearful of being deported elsewhere, and aware of widespread dissatisfaction with the reestablished Bourbon monarchy in France, especially among his former soldiers, Napoleon escaped from Elba and returned to France (1 March 1815). The allies quickly moved against Napoleon, who sought to defeat them before they could unite. He defeated the Prussians under Blücher at Ligny (16 June). The same day he defeated the British under the duke of Wellington at Quatre Bras. The main French force under Napoleon pursued Wellington's army toward Brussels. Wellington held Napoleon at Waterloo until the arrival of Blücher's Prussians, who had eluded the pursuit of Marshal Grouchy's detachment. The Anglo-Prussian allies then decisively defeated Napoleon (18 June). The French army disintegrated. Napoleon was exiled to the island of St. Helena, where, according to recent forensic discoveries, he likely died of arsenic poisoning on 5 May 1821.

Assessment

Napoleon's conquests, which had briefly given France dominion over most of Europe, had exhausted France. But the political and other changes that Napoleon had instituted did not vanish after Waterloo. The consolidation of German states remained, and the sense of German nationalism he had stimulated flourished anew a few decades later. Likewise, the nationalism his conquests had generated in Italy helped lead to that country's later unification. And while military technology soon changed, "Napoleonic" tactics and strategy and organizational innovations continued to affect warfare in many ways. Napoleon's military genius immediately earned him a permanent place among the great commanders of history.

JAMES K. KIESWETTER

SEE ALSO: Art of War; French Revolutionary–Napoleonic Wars; History, Modern Military; Jomini, Antoine Henri.

Bibliography

Chandler, D. G. 1966. *The campaigns of Napoleon.* New York: Macmillan.
Connelly, O. 1987. *Blundering to glory.* Wilmington, Del.: Scholarly Resources.
Dodge, T. A. 1904–1907. *Napoleon: A history of the art of war.* 4 vols. Boston: Houghton Mifflin.
Lachouque, H. 1961. *The anatomy of glory: Napoleon and his guard.* Providence, R.I.: Brown Univ. Press.
Quimby, R. S. 1957. *The background of Napoleonic warfare.* New York: Columbia Univ. Press.
Rothenberg, G. E. 1978. *The art of warfare in the age of Napoleon.* Bloomington, Ind.: Indiana Univ. Press.
Yorck van Wartenberg, M. 1902. *Napoleon as a general.* 2 vols. London: Wolsey Series.

NAVAL WARFARE

Naval warfare presupposes an organized state whose geography and national interests allow or impel the construction of organized sea-based forces to defend or advance the security, political position, and deterrent or compellent power of the state. Shaped by political purpose and organization, naval warfare is distinguished from piratical activities serving essentially private ends.

The Scope of Naval Warfare

The concept of naval warfare has traditionally referred to those military operations conducted in sea or ocean areas and in immediately adjacent land areas, control of which either contributes to or depends on the exercise of power on the seas. Naval warfare in modern times must necessarily be concerned with combat not only on the surface of the sea but also both under and over the sea, as well as in the air and on the ground in critical adjacent land areas. In a narrow sense, naval warfare concentrates on military instruments—such as surface vessels, submarines, naval aircraft, and amphibious troops—that are based in a navy and oriented toward specific naval missions (e.g., control or denial of the sea, projection and support of forces ashore, or land bombardment from the sea).

Although naval forces may act autonomously, most commentators agree that naval forces generally serve political purposes that can be achieved only by a combination of land, sea, and air forces. Writing in 1918, the British naval strategist Julian S. Corbett wrote:

> By maritime strategy we mean the principles which govern a war in which the sea is a substantial factor. Naval strategy is but that part of it which determines the movements of the fleet when maritime strategy has determined what part the fleet must play in relation to the action of the land forces; for it scarcely needs saying that it is almost impossible that a war can be decided by naval action alone.

Moreover, in contemporary times, the general range, accuracy, transparency, and destructiveness of weapons in all environments have further limited the autonomy of naval warfare. Although the special characteristics of weapons systems and missions that directly concern the sea can be distinguished, their contribution must be evaluated within a broader political, geographical, and technological context.

In general, three elements define the importance and meaning of naval warfare: geopolitics, political economy, and technology. On the specific end of the spectrum, one obvious factor—whose impact, however, is not self-evident—stands out: the sea—the medium that is transited, controlled, and contested and that gives rise in the first place to the specialized field of naval warfare.

Geopolitics and Naval Warfare

Crucial to the military posture of a state is the geographical position and location of its principal interests and potential allies and adversaries. The shape and strategy of a state's forces will differ depending on the society's degree of self-sufficiency, the security provided by geographical and topographical features, the existence of common borders with other states as well as the character of those states, and the requirements for moving forces to points distant from the state.

For example, a central continental state that is subject to direct invasion across its borders and that can secure its interests or extend its power by moving its forces across land will probably produce a different strategic perspective from that of an island state with no internal or external threats on the territory of the island and with interests across the sea, perhaps on the periphery of the continental state. The former state is likely to see naval warfare as an *adjunct* to land warfare—protecting the flanks from seaborne attacks and denying the secure use of the sea to any would-be enemy that might project power ashore or support land adversaries of the continental state. Conversely, the island state is apt to see naval warfare as the *foundation* of its territorial immunity and the *precondition* of its ability to protect its interests, secure its friends, and extend its power and influence.

A great continental state may ultimately seek to extend its control over the seas once it has secured itself on land, and an island state may establish and sustain a great land force on a distant continent. Statesmen from both countries, however, are likely to understand that the continental power's land force is central to the protection of the homeland and that the island state's naval force is equally crucial.

These examples represent ideal types, but they point to an important factor in the development of the concept of naval warfare: the meaning, dimensions, and centrality of naval warfare depend on the asymmetrical disposition of the states on the globe's surface. Most treatises on strategy and conflict have concerned land warfare. There is a scarcity of literature on seapower and naval warfare because few states have been dependent on or conceived their national identity in terms of control of the sea and the seaborne projection of major military force. At times, such concerns have animated many states, but consistent attention to these issues has engaged few historical powers—ancient Athens, the United Kingdom, Japan, and the United States among them.

Even in these states, the systematic examination of seapower and naval warfare came quite late despite the fact that commerce and war at sea occurred as far back as the ancient world and were crucial to the Athenians, the Phoenicians, a number of the Italian city-states, the Dutch, and the British. The late-nineteenth-century rise to prominence of studies of seapower and naval force may be attributed to two interrelated factors: the increasingly global basis of economic power, and changes in technology.

Political Economy and Naval Warfare

The eighteenth-century industrial revolution—essentially substituting machine power for human and animal power with all of the subsequent developments—not only generated an enormous increase in economic power but also led to a progressive interdependence of the national economies far beyond the international commerce of ancient times. The late twentieth century is heir to a revolution unleashed more than 200 years ago.

The expansion and diversification of production opened the possibility and desirability of expanded markets and the need for a whole range of mineral and fuel resources as well as raw materials generally. As the state in which the industrial revolution first took hold, Great Britain was impelled by the market-expansion dynamics unleashed by the industrial process to act on—and be dependent on—a broader global stage. Moreover, the preeminent power conferred by the wealth and technology produced catapulted Britain to a position of political preeminence. In some respects, the dynamics of Japanese developments in the late nineteenth and early twentieth centuries mirrored the British experience.

In addition to the broader global stage dictated by the economic developments following the industrial revolution, those same developments increased the complexity and costs associated with building and maintaining naval forces. Construction and outfitting of seagoing vessels have always been enormously expensive and required in the long term a thriving commercial base. If the sea were not central to a state's survival, vital interests, and political economy, then investment in naval forces could always be defined as a luxury that could be radically scaled back in times of economic stringency. That the ancient Athenians and the Dutch and British in early modern times did make such an investment is understandable, given the foundations of their wealth and security. If such forces have historically been costly, the period since the onset of the industrial revolution has seen an increase not only in the power and efficiency but also in the expense of naval forces, especially capital investments. Such costs are not limited to sea-related forces; land-based forces have also experienced cost increases. Nonetheless, so complex is the use and control of the sea—above, below, upon—as well as the projection of power ashore, that naval forces still require impressive geopolitical and economic arguments to justify the demands on the public purse. Ultimately such demands are related to technology.

Technology and Naval Warfare

Archer Jones, the eminent American military historian, has made the distinction between shock warfare and missile or artillery warfare. He states that naval warfare was fundamentally shock warfare until the sixteenth century, when advances in technology and mariners' skills gradually transformed such warfare into artillery warfare. *Shock* action or warfare refers to the direct contact of military platforms, personnel, and weapons—variations of hand-to-hand combat or ramming. *Missile* or *artillery* action involves the launching of projectiles at some distance and may precede, accompany, or substitute for shock action.

Naval warfare from ancient times until well into the age of sail was characterized either by hand combat of troops that had boarded another's ships or by ramming the ships themselves. As long as shock action dominated naval combat, warships were constructed to balance high speed, maneuverability, and a reinforced bow with a strong ram. This meant that vessels on attack were manned by many oarsmen to provide speed and independence from the wind, but the light weight of the ships (dictated by the desire for increased speed) meant that the sides of the ships were particularly vulnerable.

Clearly such narrow, long, light, oar-driven ships had an advantage over the broad, sturdy, sail-driven merchant ships, as the former could overtake and maneuver to ram the side of or board the merchant vessel. In combat with other warships, however, tactical and operational skills were crucial in maneuvering to ram the opposing ships' flanks or alternatively to bring the ships close enough together to lock on to each other and permit the embarked soldiers to engage in pitched battle.

Given the fragility, small carrying capacity, and large complement of oarsmen and soldiers, such naval combatants were tied much more closely to the shore than either the limited merchant ships of the day or, even more dramatically, later sailing or steam vessels. Logistic requirements made base support or shore raids critical to the maintenance of the warships, and the dangers of the open seas to the fragile vessels tethered them closely to the shoreline.

These ship characteristics ensured that sea control was always contested and that blockades could be only intermittent. Ships did not have the staying power to achieve complete dominance at sea or to prolong blockades. At the same time, these ships could convoy troop transports and attack merchant vessels. Command of the sea, blockade, power projection, convoying, commerce raiding—these naval roles were as evident in ancient as in modern times, but their conditions and effectiveness differed.

As the center of political gravity began to shift from the Mediterranean to northern Europe in the late Middle Ages, the large, turbulent Atlantic became more important. At the same time, improved ship design, enhanced mariners' skills in sailing their ships closer to the direction from which the wind blew, and the burdensome cost of supporting a fleet of galleys figured in the greater prominence of the sailing warship, which was not substantially different in design from the merchant ship. For a time, the oar-driven galley and the sailing ship coexisted, but in time the sailing ship supplanted the galley everywhere.

Sailing ships could no longer employ ramming as the dominant warfare tool but instead depended on independent ship action to close and grapple at close quarters with an opposing ship. Elaborate rope nets to forestall boarding and high structures called *castles,* from which the bowman could send his missiles, provided the basis for combat at sea. All this changed with the advent of the cannon, which transformed naval warfare from shock to artillery or missile combat and finally doomed the galley.

The larger size of the warship, increased maneuverability associated with improved ship design and sailing skills, and the "stand-off" attack allowed—and required—by cannon gave the warship in the late medieval and early modern period greater independence from the shore and increased range and staying power. In a fundamental sense, developments in the last 400 years have been but an extension of these capabilities.

Although the transition from sail to steam made reliance on coaling stations and later on oil depots—and therefore on increased base support—more pressing, the general trend has been toward less reliance on large numbers of bases, but critical dependence on the few far-flung bases that remain. This evolution is particularly evident with nuclear-powered craft. Ship repair, aircraft and weapons system maintenance, and personnel needs still tie ships to the shore. Nonetheless, the notion of a blue-water (i.e., open-ocean) fleet with tremendous reach and endurance is a product of the industrial revolution and the technological advances that flowed from it. At the same time, the ability to engage enemy vessels and to attack targets ashore from a very great distance confirms artillery or missile action flexibly deployed over wide areas as the hallmark of contemporary naval warfare. Modern technology also complicates and renders more expensive this expanded capability.

Five major technological developments have shaped the problems and prospects of contemporary naval warfare: (1) the advent of weapons of mass destruction, most particularly atomic, biological, and chemical weapons; (2) long-range, accurately guided aircraft and missiles; (3) powerful sensors that can locate and identify targets over a considerable range; (4) automation extending human control with great accuracy and speed over dispersed and varied forces; and (5) techniques of masking forces to escape the very detection inherent in the above-mentioned sensors. This cluster of advances adds up to an enormously extended battlefield over which contending forces can accurately deliver devastating destruction once the targets are located. Moreover, the line between the sea and the shore blurs under these conditions, and advantages accrue to the side that can bring to bear combined air, land, and sea forces. At the same time, the dimensions of the battlefield extend outside the earth's atmosphere.

If the contending parties to a conflict are equipped with comparable sea-based or other capabilities, the tendency is either toward preemption or, if both sides' forces are configured to be highly survivable, toward stalemate. Therefore, military doctrines generally have tended either toward concentration on the initiation and early stages of conflict or toward deterrence. Much of the literature on naval warfare has shared similar characteristics, although developments during the 1980s in U.S. maritime strategy gave more emphasis to protracted conflict and war termination.

U.S. maritime strategy was built on the premise that general nuclear war was not only not inevitable, but also increasingly unlikely; that is to say, even during conflict, given the strategic second-strike capability of the superpowers, the nuclear threshold would remain at a high level. If a relatively stable nuclear deterrence persists between superpowers and their alliances, some inhibition might also exist against the use of other weapons of mass destruction such as chemical and biological weapons. If comparable capabilities do not exist on these levels as well, however, this inhibition is far less certain. In any case, the possibility of protracted conventional conflict and the issue of finding ways to terminate conflict short of nuclear Armageddon become more salient. Moreover, in less than general war circumstances, conventional forces are likely to be dominant, if not exclusive. Nuclear arms agreements may only further the general trend toward increased development of conventional forces, strategies, and operational concepts. The nuclear umbrella remains as the foundation of the deterrence both of general war and of nuclear use itself, but many commentators now assume that, as long as the sides concerned maintain secure nuclear forces, the nuclear threshold will remain high and conventional action the typical form of armed conflict.

Two cautionary notes are in order. First, whether or not nuclear weapons are used in armed conflict, and leaving aside their deterrent function even during war, all sides to a violent contest must deal with the possibility that they might be used—with the consequent political, strategic, and operational implications. Therefore, a campaign plan that promises success through conventional operations must have mechanisms built into it for keeping the conflict conventional or, alternatively, for responding should the enemy decide to alter the course of battle through the use of nuclear—or chemical or biological—weapons. Second, even with exclusively conventional combat, the complexity and cost of operations are very high as a result of technological developments and of the dispersion of relatively sophisticated weapons among many potential combatants. This is readily apparent in naval warfare.

The irony of contemporary naval warfare is that technology has extended the range and power of naval forces but at the same time increased their vulnerability. The range and accuracy of sensors and of weapons, as well as the ability to control forces with speed and accuracy, give the contemporary naval force great power but also dictate that they be combined in order to defend against precisely the same kind of threats from an adversary. Moreover, as naval forces move in close to land, additional land-based air support is integral to fleet defense and offense. This dilemma holds true not only for armed conflict between major adversaries with comparable capabilities but even in actions where the contestants are unequal. So devastatingly accurate are many modern weapons and so widespread could be the political effects of a successful attack on the naval combatant of an adversary, especially if that enemy were a superior power, that a complex—and expensive—combination of sea, air, and land forces is required in order to both defend and threaten. Moreover, the cost of modern technology has driven all military establishments toward fewer, if more capable, military platforms, with their consequent heightened value. This trend is clearly visible in naval forces, where an enormous extension of power has been purchased at the cost of fewer vessels. This approach is reasonable, but it dictates strategies for joining forces to capitalize on strengths while reducing the vulnerabilities inherent in the spread of sophisticated weapons.

Advances in technology have both extended the capabilities and particularly complicated the problem of those states whose survival or interests depend on maintaining relative dominance at sea. If, for instance, the issue is sustaining by sea and the airspace over the sea interests or allies that lie directly on the periphery of a great land power, then sustained sea control is the absolute precondition. The issue facing the land power with internal land lines of communication is of a different order. It need but *deny* the effective use of the sea to the maritime adversary in order to prevail. A relatively small force of attack submarines might seriously complicate—if not make impossible in a timely fashion—the defense of the sea lines of communication. The notion from land warfare that a 2–3:1 force ratio is required to overwhelm a well-constructed defense might be misleading when applied to defense of the sea lines of communications (SLOCs). Given modern sensors, mining capabilities, submarine "quieting," stealth weapons, and precision-guided munitions, attacks on the SLOCs might be easier and their defense more demanding. For a sea-dependent state, however, mutual sea denial is not stalemate; it is victory for the land power.

Concepts of naval warfare developed by strategists of major maritime powers, therefore, tend to put heavy emphasis on early offensive action in the event of conflict in order to defeat or neutralize the potential threat to the SLOCs. At the same time, sea control, once achieved, can be used to project power ashore and threaten militarily significant targets deep inside the enemy state. Returning to an earlier point, therefore, a maritime power views naval warfare not simply as an adjunct to land combat but also as the foundation of its security and the precondition of its ability to sustain conflict across the seas.

The Sea and Naval Warfare

Discussions of naval warfare are often prefaced by a sharp distinction between land and naval warfare—a distinction that ultimately arises from the environment in which navies operate. The environment associated with the sea is distinct, but the differences can be overdrawn.

Both land and sea warfare may involve temporary intervention in hostile areas, and both may be relatively fixed in place in a restrictive maritime or land theater. Moreover, both land and sea warfare may engage in shock or artillery actions. Both can be aimed at the essentially logistical outcome of securing or denying lines of communication and of threatening or defending industrial and base infrastructure. Both can be used to achieve the neutralization or destruction of opposing forces. At the same time, although differences of scale exist between land and sea warfare, joint fleet action, as well as the combination of air, land, and sea forces, within maritime theaters of operation tends to narrow the differences. Finally, in practice, doctrines of land warfare have more flexibility and strategies of sea warfare have more rigidity than those who seek differences might allow. Nonetheless, important differences remain in the roles and missions of naval and land forces, and these differences are very much associated with the distinct environments.

Naval forces have the dominant role in sea control and power projection. The mission of sea control can connote either positive control of designated sea areas for specified times and purposes or generalized dominance on the world's oceans. It can also imply a negative role—denial of sea control to the other side in either a specific or general sense. The purposes to which naval force will be put depend on the geopolitical posture, resources, and strategic requirements of the states concerned, as well as their general foreign policy objectives.

The mission of power projection includes a broad spectrum of offensive naval operations aimed at carrying military power from the sea to the shore. It could include nuclear strikes from the fleet ballistic missile force, strikes from carrier-based aircraft, amphibious assault forces, and naval bombardment with guns or missiles. As with sea control, this mission can be defined negatively—that is, preventing the adversary from exercising power projection. Maintaining sea control includes securing the sea lines of communication and is an essential precondition of power projection. Both sea control and power projection include the task of sustaining overseas deployed forces.

Sometimes strategic nuclear deterrence is listed among naval missions, but in a real sense a deterrent posture is the outcome of both sea control and power projection capabilities—that is, the ability under a variety of conditions to target and destroy the enemy's forces; industrial and logistical bases; command, control, and communications; or populations. Although ballistic missile submarines are among the least vulnerable strategic nuclear forces and thus at present undergird a stable nuclear balance, the general point remains: to deter or to fight depends on the capabilities and general functions of one's forces.

The same argument holds true for other types of missions, including presence, diplomatic persuasion, and response to crisis: unless the action is purely symbolic, success in these areas depends on the degree to which a state's ability to control the sea and project power is perceived as *credible* and *decisive*. In effect, therefore, the naval warfare missions of sea control and power projection can without distortion generally encompass the many roles that might be undertaken.

If naval warfare concerns combat on the surface of the sea, under the sea, and in the air, then navies can reasonably be organized in three areas—surface, subsurface, and air—and basic warfare tasks—antiair, antisubmarine, antisurface ship, strikes ashore, amphibious assault, mining, and mine countermeasures—can be related to these areas. Surveillance, intelligence, command and control and communications, control of the electromagnetic spectrum, logistics, and nonconventional and clandestine special warfare may be designated as supportive of the warfare areas as well. However, the missions as divided into combat areas and tasks represent elements of naval warfare and not naval warfare itself.

Naval warfare strives to control the environment on, in, under, and around the sea, including critical adjacent land areas, in order to move forces and materiel, to sustain forces ashore, and to attack targets strategically significant to realizing objectives determined by political authority. The sea shapes the problems or the opportunities a nation faces. Naval warfare is a response to these problems and opportunities, but its ultimate significance depends both on the importance of the sea to the nation and the coordination of naval forces with the entire spectrum of military power.

ROBERT S. WOOD

Bibliography

Corbett, J. S. 1911. *Some principles of maritime strategy.* London: Longmans, Green.
Gorshkov, S. G. 1975. The development of the art of naval warfare. Trans. T. A. Neely, Jr. *U.S. Naval Institute Proceedings* 101 (6/868):54–63.
Hughes, W. P. 1986. *Fleet tactics: Theory and practice.* Annapolis, Md.: U.S. Naval Institute Press.

Jones, A. 1987. *The art of war in the western world.* Urbana and Chicago: Univ. of Illinois Press.

Landersman, S. 1982. *Principles of naval warfare.* Newport, R. I.: Naval War College Press.

Lautenschlager, K. 1984. *Technology and the evolution of naval warfare, 1851–2001.* Washington, D.C.: National Academy Press.

Levert, L. J. 1947. *Fundamentals of naval warfare.* New York: Macmillan.

Mahan, A. T. 1911. *Naval strategy: Compared and contrasted with the principles and practices of military operations on land.* London: Sampson, Low, Marston.

Moineville, H. 1983. *Naval warfare today and tomorrow.* Oxford, U.K.: Basil Blackwell.

Mordal, J. 1965. *Twenty-five centuries of sea warfare.* London: Souvenir Press.

Pemsel, H. 1975. *A history of war at sea: An atlas and chronology of conflict at sea from earlier times to the present.* Annapolis, Md.: U.S. Naval Institute Press.

Potter, E. B. 1981. *Sea power: A naval history.* 2d ed. Annapolis, Md.: U.S. Naval Institute Press.

Reynolds, C. G. 1974. *Command of the sea: The history and strategy of maritime empires.* New York: William Morrow.

Sanderson, M. 1975. *Sea battles: A reference guide.* Middletown, Conn.: Wesleyan Univ. Press.

Till, G. 1982. *Maritime strategy in the nuclear age.* London: Macmillan.

NELSON, HORATIO [1758–1805]

Horatio Nelson remains Great Britain's greatest naval officer. His expert seamanship, courage, intelligence, and his willingness to fight on in apparently hopeless situations enabled him to achieve a series of victories, culminating at Trafalgar in 1805, that provided Great Britain with undisputed mastery of the seas for over a century. Additionally, his standards of conduct and seamanship set a standard that is still emulated by officers in the Royal Navy.

Early Life and Career

Nelson was born 29 September 1758 at Burnham Thorpe, in Norfolk, England. The son of a clergyman, he went to sea as a midshipman at the age of 12. At the age of 18, he was promoted to lieutenant, and, because of his exceptional ability and devotion, he received an appointment as the captain of a sloop-of-war in 1779, and was then made captain of a frigate. Thus, at the age of 20, Nelson was the youngest captain in the history of the Royal Navy.

Nelson subsequently saw active service in the Americas, the Baltic, and the North Atlantic. From 1793 to 1796, he served three years of arduous service in the Mediterranean Sea. As captain of the 75-gun ship HMS *Agamemnon* in 1794, he was wounded during the occupation of Corsica and lost the sight of an eye. In 1797, as captain of the 75-gun ship HMS *Captain*, Nelson participated in the Battle of Cape St. Vincent on 14 February. During the battle, he engaged the largest ship in the world, the 130-gun Spanish flagship, *Santissima*

Trinidad, plus two 112-gun ships, and a 74-gun ship. His bravery and performance in this battle won him promotion to rear admiral and a knighthood. Later in the year, he was sent to capture Santa Cruz de Tenerife. He was repulsed and wounded in this engagement and his right arm was amputated.

Nelson returned to duty and commanded a squadron during the blockade of Cádiz. From there he was sent to seek out the French fleet in the Mediterranean. After several weeks of searching the central and eastern Mediterranean, he found the French fleet anchored at Aboukir Bay, near Alexandria, Egypt, on 1 August 1798. The speed and vigor of Nelson's attack and his tactics allowed him to bring greatly superior firepower to bear on selected portions of the French line, and victory in the ensuing night battle. The 120-gun *Orient*, the French flagship, was destroyed, and nine French ships were captured, while three ships and two frigates were able to escape. Although there were 900 British casualties, including another wound for Nelson, not a single British ship was damaged seriously. The French had lost ten of thirteen ships and had more than 5,000 casualties. This was one of the most overwhelming victories in naval history and sealed the fate of Bonaparte's army in Egypt.

Baron Nelson of the Nile spent the next year and a half involved in operations off the coast of Italy, in which he successfully eliminated the French influence from that portion of the peninsula. He returned to England in late 1800 and was promoted to vice admiral on 1 January 1801.

In February 1801 he became second in command, under Admiral Sir Hyde Parker, of a new fleet being prepared for operations in the Baltic. The objective of this fleet was to display a show of force or to use force, if necessary, to discourage an alliance of the neutral Baltic powers—Russia, Prussia, Denmark, and Sweden—from providing support to France in the ongoing war. The first major problem was that Denmark would not allow the British fleet to enter the Baltic. In late March, the British fleet approached Copenhagen, which was strongly defended by sixteen Danish ships and powerful shore batteries. On 1 April Nelson convinced Parker to allow him to take half of the fleet to attack the Danish fleet and coastal batteries. On 2 April Nelson took the twelve ships with the shallowest drafts and closed in, while Parker stood off to observe.

The resulting battle was one of the most bitterly contested in naval history. At one point, the situation looked so bad for Nelson that Parker signaled him by flag to discontinue the action. Knowing that the unfavorable winds would not allow him to withdraw without losing all of his ships, Nelson ignored the signal and ordered his captains to redouble their efforts. When his flag captain finally brought the signal to his attention, Nelson put his glass to his blind eye and responded, "You know, Foley, . . . I really do not see the signal." Nelson persevered, the Danes surrendered, and Denmark was forced to make peace and leave the alliance. Nelson, who expected to be court-martialed and possibly hung for disobeying orders, replaced Parker, who was relieved of his command.

In part because of Nelson's victory at Copenhagen, Great Britain and France signed a peace treaty in 1802. Hostilities were renewed in May 1803, however, and Nelson was sent to command again in the Mediterranean.

Prelude to the Battle of Trafalgar

For a year and a half the principal duty of the British Mediterranean fleet was to blockade the French fleet at Toulon. On 30 March 1805, however, French admiral Pierre Villeneuve was able to take advantage of bad weather to elude Nelson's blockade. Without being detected by the British, the French fleet sailed out of the Mediterranean and across the Atlantic to the West Indies.

After vainly searching throughout the Mediterranean for the French, Nelson also sailed for the West Indies. Upon learning that Nelson was approaching, Villeneuve set sail immediately for Europe. Nelson searched in vain for the French in the West Indies, and then he, too, sailed for Europe, about a month behind the French.

Villeneuve arrived at Cádiz on 20 August 1805, where he was joined by French and Spanish reinforcements, which brought his fleet strength to 39 ships of the line. He was promptly blockaded by a much smaller British squadron. Nelson joined the squadron on 28 September and took command of a combined force of 34 ships of the line.

Because of the initiation of intensive land campaigning in central Europe (the beginning of the Ulm and Austerlitz campaigns), Nelson expected that Villeneuve would be ordered by Napoleon to proceed into the Mediterranean. He also correctly believed that Villeneuve did not know that Nelson had arrived and that the blockading force was so strong. Thus, he expected the allied Franco-Spanish fleet to soon set sail for the Strait of Gibraltar.

Unable to talk at length personally with all of his captains, Nelson wrote them a lengthy memorandum explaining his concept of the battle that he expected to occur. He intended to concentrate part of his fleet under his second in command, Admiral Cuthbert Collingwood, against the enemy rear. Meanwhile, Nelson and the remainder of the fleet would threaten the leading ships of the enemy line, breaking through its center, and joining Collingwood in bringing overwhelming strength against the rear. "I look with confidence," he wrote, "to a victory before the van of the enemy could succour their rear." He concluded, "But in case signals can neither be seen or perfectly understood, no captain can do very wrong if he places his ship alongside that of the enemy."

The Battle of Trafalgar

On 19 October Villeneuve sailed from Cádiz with 33 ships of the line, heading for the Strait of Gibraltar. Nelson, with only 27 ships of the line, promptly moved to intercept him before he could reach the strait. As the British approached early on 21 October, Villeneuve changed course to the north in order to keep a line of escape to Cádiz open in case the coming battle did not go well. He formed his fleet in a line of battle.

During the morning, the British fleet converged on Villeneuve. The British were in two columns: Nelson was in the north and led eleven other ships from his flagship, HMS *Victory* (Fig. 1). Collingwood had fifteen ships in the southern column and approached the rear of the allied French-Spanish fleet. Just

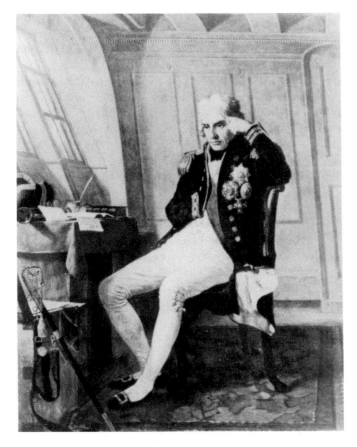

Figure 1. Nelson in the cabin of the Victory *(painting by Charles Lucy).* (SOURCE: U.S. Library of Congress)

before noon, as the fleets were almost within gunshot of each other, Nelson hoisted the flag signal: "England expects every man to do his duty." Collingwood opened the battle a few minutes later.

Although in his memorandum Nelson had written that "nothing is sure in a sea fight," the Battle of Trafalgar went exactly as he had planned. After threatening the lead allied ships, Nelson led his column to break the line between the thirteenth and fourteenth ships. Thus the British concentrated 27 ships against 20 enemy ships. The battle was over by 5:00 P.M., an overwhelming British victory. Nineteen French and Spanish ships were captured, without the loss of a single British ship.

The British had, however, suffered a loss far greater than one or more ships. Barely an hour after the battle had started, and as his *Victory* was alongside the French *Redoubtable*, Nelson was mortally wounded by a musket shot from a sniper positioned high on the mast of the French ship. He lived long enough to be told that his fleet had been victorious and replied, "Now I am satisfied. Thank God, I have done my duty."

Lord Nelson's Significance

Like Alexander the Great, Nelson died at the height of his career. Unlike Alexander, however, Nelson's crowning achievement endured for more than a century, as Great Britain exercised undisputed control of the oceans and seas of the world.

BRUCE W. WATSON

SEE ALSO: Seapower, British.

Bibliography

Mahan, A. T. [1887] 1984. *The life of Nelson: The embodiment of British sea power.* 4 vols. Reprint. New York: Found Class Reprints.

NIMITZ, CHESTER WILLIAM
[1885–1966]

Chester William Nimitz was born on 24 February 1885 in Fredericksburg, Texas. His father, Chester Bernard, died before Nimitz was born and his grandfather, Charles Henry, helped raise Nimitz until his mother remarried. The Nimitz family was of German descent and claimed ancestry from an order of Teutonic Knights. Charles Henry immigrated to Texas in 1840, where he built and ran a well-known inn.

Nimitz applied for admission to the U.S. Military Academy at West Point in 1900, but was informed by his congressman that all appointments had been filled for the next several years. Informed of an opening at the U.S. Naval Academy in Annapolis, he took and passed the entrance exams in April 1901 and was sworn in as a naval cadet on 7 September. Due to the rapid expansion of the navy and the need for junior officers, Nimitz was graduated a midshipman five months ahead of schedule on 30 January 1905.

Nimitz's first assignment was on the battleship *Ohio*, which was ordered to the Orient as flagship of the U.S. Asiatic Fleet. When the *Ohio* was ordered home Nimitz, opting to stay in the Far East, transferred to the cruiser *Baltimore*. He was commissioned an ensign on 31 January 1907, and shortly after was given command of the gunboat *Panay* in the Philippines. He later took command of the destroyer *Decatur*, which he ran aground on 7 July 1908. Court-martialed and charged with neglect of duty, he received only a public reprimand.

Transferred back to the United States in 1909, Nimitz was assigned to the First Submarine Flotilla and given command of the submarine *Plunger*. In early 1910 he was promoted to lieutenant, and in November of that year he took command of the submarine *Narwhal*. In October 1911 Nimitz was appointed commander of the Third Submarine Division, Atlantic Fleet, and in 1912 he was appointed Commander, Atlantic Submarine Flotilla. Nimitz married Catherine Freeman in April 1913, and the following month he was ordered to Europe to study diesel engines in Germany and Belgium.

On his return to the United States, Nimitz was assigned to the Brooklyn Navy Yard to supervise construction and installation of diesel engines on the oiler *Maumee*. After completion of the *Maumee* in 1916, he was assigned as its executive officer and chief engineer.

World War I

On the outbreak of war with Germany on 6 April 1917, the *Maumee* was ordered to the Atlantic to refuel destroyers. In August, Nimitz was promoted to lieutenant commander and assigned as an aide to Adm. Samuel S. Robison, the commander of Submarine Forces, Atlantic Fleet. Nimitz spent the remainder of the war accompanying Admiral Robison on inspection tours of British naval bases.

Interwar Years

In 1918, Nimitz served as senior member of the Board of Submarine Design at the Navy Department in Washington, D.C. In 1919 he was appointed executive officer on the battleship *South Carolina*. In June 1920, Nimitz was ordered to Pearl Harbor in Hawaii to construct a submarine base. He was promoted to commander in 1922, and from 1922 to 1923 he attended the Naval War College. After completing his tour at the war college, Nimitz was posted to San Pedro, California, and assigned to the battleship *California*, the flagship of the Pacific Fleet. Once again he was working under Admiral Robison, serving as aide, assistant chief of staff, and tactical officer. As Robison's assistant chief of staff, Nimitz was one of the six officers assigned to establish the Naval Reserve Officer's Training Corps (NROTC) in American universities. For three years Nimitz commanded the NROTC at the University of California, Berkeley. In September 1927 he was promoted to captain. In June 1929, Nimitz was appointed to command the Battle Fleet's Submarine Divisions; at the same time he also became Commander, Submarine Division 20, at San Diego. In 1931 he was appointed commander of destroyers at San Diego.

In 1933, Nimitz was appointed captain of the cruiser *Augusta*, which was later designated the flagship of the Asiatic Fleet and ordered to Shanghai. After serving two years in the Far East, Nimitz was transferred to Washington in 1935 as assistant to the chief of the Bureau of Navigation (later designated the Bureau of Personnel). Nimitz was promoted to rear admiral in July 1938. Appointed commander of Cruiser Division Two, San Diego, he was unable to take command due to a hernia operation. When he recovered, Nimitz was instead appointed commander of Battleship Division One, with the battleship *Arizona* as his flagship.

In January 1939, Nimitz was appointed commander of Task Force Seven, which consisted of the *Arizona*, a cruiser, a carrier, seven destroyers and auxiliaries, and one tanker. An enjoyable command for Nimitz, it was also a brief one, as he was transferred to Washington in June of that year and appointed chief of the Bureau of Navigation.

World War II

On 7 December 1941, the Japanese attacked Pearl Harbor and the United States entered World War II. Serving as Chief of Naval Personnel, Nimitz was faced with the enormous task of manning a wartime navy. On 31 December 1941, on the recommendation of Secretary of the Navy Frank Knox, President Franklin D. Roosevelt appointed Nimitz commander in chief, Pacific Fleet (CINCPAC), with the rank of full admiral. In April 1942, Nimitz was also appointed commander in chief, Pacific Ocean Areas (CINCPOA), effectively splitting the command of the Pacific with Gen. Douglas MacArthur, who was appointed supreme commander, Allied Forces Southwest Pacific Area.

Nimitz's first priority in the Pacific was to defend the Hawaiian Islands and Midway and to protect the lines of communication from the United States to Hawaii and Australia. His second priority was to launch offensive operations against the Japanese in the Central Pacific in an attempt to divert their attention from Singapore and the Dutch East Indies. Facing superior Japanese naval strength, Nimitz resolved to carry out a series of naval and air hit-and-run actions designed to deplete the enemy's strength. While these operations inflicted only minor losses, they did raise American morale.

Nimitz was greatly aided in his operations by Naval Intelligence which, due to U.S. code-breaking success, was able to give him accurate information of Japanese locations and movements. Using this information, Nimitz was able to anticipate and check Japanese naval operations against Port Moresby, New Guinea, at the Battle of the Coral Sea on 3–9 May 1942.

Nimitz was convinced that the Japanese target would be Midway Island. Again, his intelligence service proved invaluable. By way of a ruse, it discovered that Nimitz's hunch was correct and that the Japanese were planning to attack Midway and the Aleutian Islands. Nimitz knew he would face a superior force; he knew also that if he were defeated Hawaii and the United States' west coast would be left open to attack. Nevertheless, he decided to gamble on defeating the Japanese carrier force at Midway. The gamble paid off; on 3–6 June the smaller U.S. force mauled the Japanese, sinking four of their carriers and a heavy cruiser and downing 322 aircraft, against American losses of one carrier, one destroyer, and 132 aircraft. Midway was the turning point in the Pacific War. The Japanese offensive was stopped, and the initiative passed to the Allies.

Nimitz now turned to the offensive. Together with MacArthur he planned the overall strategy for the Pacific Theater as well as providing strategic direction for the major Allied offensive operations in the Central Pacific. Nimitz brilliantly directed the limited offensive against the Solomon Islands from August 1942 to February 1943. He followed this with successful campaigns in the Gilbert Islands on 20–23 November 1943, and in the Marshall Islands from 31 January to 23 February 1944. Nimitz then turned to the Marianas and directed the offensive against these islands from 14 June to 10 August. While directing operations in the Palau Islands from 15 September to 25 November, Nimitz also joined forces with General MacArthur in New Guinea to launch an invasion at Leyte Gulf in the Philippines on 20 October. On 15 December, Nimitz was promoted to the newly created rank of fleet admiral.

In January 1945, Nimitz moved his headquarters to Guam. From there he directed the operations on Iwo Jima from 19 February to 24 March, and then the invasion of Okinawa from 1 April to 21 June. Nimitz continued to direct naval operations against Japan until its capitulation on 14 August. On 29 August, Nimitz sailed into Tokyo Bay on board his flagship, the battleship *South Dakota*. On 2 September he boarded the battleship *Missouri* and, as the representative of the United States, signed the instrument of surrender.

In recognition of his wartime service, 5 October was designated Nimitz Day in Washington, and a grateful nation turned out to welcome its hero.

The Postwar Years

Nimitz's desire to succeed Adm. Ernest King as chief of Naval Operations (CNO) was granted, and on 15 December 1945 he was sworn in as the first postwar CNO. The job facing Nimitz was both difficult and trying, and he worked constantly and diligently at its success.

During his term as CNO, Nimitz was responsible for demobilizing the wartime navy and helping to determine the future status of America's armed forces. (The end result was the retention of the Joint Chiefs of Staff and the establishment of separate departments for the army, navy, and air force. Heading these departments would be a secretary of defense who would be a permanent member of the president's Cabinet.) Nimitz also played a role in the development of the first nuclear-powered submarine.

On 15 December 1947, Nimitz stepped down as CNO and retired to California with his wife and family. In 1948, he made himself available as a special assistant to the secretary of the navy. In March 1949 he was asked to come out of retirement to serve as good-will ambassador to the United Nations. Later that same year he became the UN commissioner for Kashmir, a post he held until 1951 when he returned to retirement.

Nimitz spent his remaining years in quiet, taking time to coauthor *Sea Power: A Naval History*, with E. B. Potter, which was published in 1960. In November 1965, Nimitz underwent surgery, and while in the hospital he contracted pneumonia. His health took a turn for the worse and late in January 1966, he went into a coma from which he never recovered. He died on Sunday, 20 February 1966; in accordance with his wishes, he was buried in Golden Gate National Cemetery.

Nimitz was one of America's greatest naval officers. An experienced commander of great foresight and ability, Nimitz performed arduous tasks skillfully and proficiently. Hardworking but with an easy manner, Nimitz was able to get the most from his subordinates and colleagues without antagonizing them. He was greatly admired and respected by both his sailors and his country. He provided the strategic direction and much of the impetus behind America's victory in the Central Pacific. Edwin Hoyt in his history of the Pacific War (1970) said of him, "The qualities of Nimitz's character were apparent in his face, in his career, and in his heritage; combined, these factors made him precisely the man he was and placed him in this particular situation at this moment in history."

VINCENT B. HAWKINS

SEE ALSO: King, Ernest J.; MacArthur, Douglas; World War II; Yamamoto, Isoroku.

Bibliography

Hoyt, E. F. 1970. *How they won the war in the Pacific.* New York: Weybright and Talley.

Morrison, S. E. 1947–62. *History of United States naval operations in World War II.* 15 vols. Boston: Little, Brown.

Nimitz, C. W., and E. B. Potter, 1960. *Sea power: A naval history.* Annapolis, Md.: U.S. Naval Institute Press.

Pfannes, C. E., and V. A. Salamone. 1983. *The great admirals of World War II.* Vol. 1, *The Americans.* New York: Kensington.

Potter, E. B. 1976. *Nimitz.* Annapolis, Md.: U.S. Naval Institute Press.

Reynolds, C. G. 1978. *Famous American admirals.* New York: Van Nostrand Reinhold.

NORMANS

The Normans were direct descendants of the Vikings, or Norsemen, fierce Scandinavian warriors who terrorized much of coastal and riverine continental Europe and the British Isles in the ninth and tenth centuries. In the early 900s, a Norse group seized and colonized Frankish territory at the mouth of the Seine River, a region known since as Normandy. Within a brief time, the Norse conquerors married local women, abandoned their pagan ways for Christianity, and many of them became civil administrators, church leaders, and crusaders in the Frankish kingdom. They had become Normans. A Norman force under William the Conqueror invaded and took England in 1066. This historic incursion marked the beginning of Norman rule in England and changed the course of Western history. Other Norman groups conquered southern Italy and Sicily, though their rule there did not last.

The Norman Conquest

Duke William of Normandy, a strong and respected leader, inherited his title at age eight. He soon became a noted warrior and put down a major revolt when he was twenty. He was related to the King of England, Edward the Confessor, who had granted him succession to the English crown. The Earl of Wessex, Harold Godwinsson, was the other principal contender. But Duke

William claimed that Harold, who had earlier been shipwrecked on the coast of Normandy, had sworn to support William's claim.

In 1066 Edward died. Harold was quickly named king by the Anglo-Saxon Grand Council (Witan). Duke William of Normandy also declared his right to the throne, obtained the pope's support, and began assembling an army. His forces made the channel crossing after a weather-induced wait of several weeks, landing without opposition at Pevensey Bay, near Hastings, on the Sussex coast. Harold was aware of William's preparations and was ready to oppose the invasion. However, an unexpected Norwegian invasion of northern England caused Harold to rush north to deal with that threat. Disposing of the Norwegians in a hard-fought battle, Harold backtracked south, after learning that William and his army had landed at Pevensey.

The Battle of Hastings

Harold and his army moved to Hastings by forced marches. He augmented his depleted force along the way from poorly armed and trained local militia. He and his Anglo-Saxon army met the Norman invaders on 14 October 1066 at the Battle of Hastings. The battle was joined at the hill of Senlac, near Hastings. Each side had approximately 7,000 men, though accounts differ on the exact numbers. Harold's forces, mostly dismounted, deployed on the hilltop as an infantry phalanx. The Norman army consisted of feudal cavalry supported by archers. Harold's forces were charged repeatedly by the Norman knights and showered by flights of arrows. Although the Norman charges failed to secure the heights, the Anglo-Saxons were gradually worn down. Harold was killed late in the afternoon by a Norman arrow. According to one account, the Normans defeated the defenders with another charge after Harold's death. Another account states that the Anglo-Saxons were tricked into rushing down the hill after a fake retreat by the Normans, who then turned and charged and overwhelmed the Anglo-Saxons. In any case, the Anglo-Saxon force was swept from the field that October day, leaving England open to invaders.

The Norman Subjugation of England

Hastings was really a battle between two would-be kings, both of whom had a claim to the throne. When William won he became, in fact, England's ruler and had to face no other major military confrontations. After their victory, the Normans moved quickly to London, where their leader was crowned William I on Christmas Day, 1066. Following his coronation, William spent several years trying to subdue the native Anglo-Saxons, but they resisted him stubbornly. William confiscated the land of most of the old English nobility and gave it to his loyal Norman followers. However, he let members of the old nobility keep their lands and titles if they swore allegiance to him. To consolidate his power through control of the feudal lords, William I ordered preparation of the Domesday Book in 1085. This was an inventory of the landholders in England and showed how their holdings were peopled. To accomplish this survey, the country was divided into districts, each surveyed by census takers familiar with the region. When the Domesday Book was completed in 1086, it became final and authoritative and formed the basis for the Norman administration of England.

The Normans as Warriors and Rulers

The Normans inherited their warlike tendencies and skills from their Norse ancestors. Their adoption of aggressive Frankish military tactics added to their prowess, and enabled them to overwhelm the basically defensive Anglo-Saxon posture.

But the real victory of the Normans in England lay in their ability as rulers and administrators. Their rule of England was capable and evenhanded. They installed an improved legal system and provided good government and security. Under their rule, England was largely free from internal strife and became a more cohesive nation.

Within a few centuries, a new England emerged, melded into one nation, with a common English tongue. The Norman conquest helped bring national unity to England and, eventually, status as a world power.

WALTER P. WHITE

SEE ALSO: Feudalism; History, Medieval Military.

Bibliography

Beeler, J. 1966. *Warfare in England, 1066–1189.* Ithaca, N.Y.: Cornell Univ. Press.
Douglas, D. C. 1977. *William the Conqueror: The Norman impact upon England.* London: Eyre Methuen.
Le Patourel, J. 1976. *The Norman empire.* Oxford: Clarendon Press.
———. 1971. *Normandy and England, 1066–1144.* Reading, England: Univ. of Reading.
Oman, Sir C. 1978. *A history of the art of war in the Middle Ages.* Vol. I: A.D. 378–1272. London: Methuen.
Sawyer, P. H. 1978. *From Roman Britain to Norman England.* New York: St. Martin's Press.

ORGANIZATION, AIR FORCE

Not unlike most large businesses, the military is organized to facilitate the flow of communication and control among all levels in the organization. Consequently, military organization charts often resemble a pyramid that rests at the working level and converges on top at the highest decision-making authority.

Because of the size of most military organizations, the critical process of planning, problem resolution, decision making, and policy implementation must be facilitated by levels or echelons of control that narrow toward the top of the organization through a formal chain of command at a number of subordinate headquarters. The structure of a military organization is important and, to a large extent, will ultimately determine the success or failure of assigned missions.

Characteristics of an Air Force

Within any military establishment, the organization of each component arm varies with the nature of its mission. Typically, air forces are charged with the responsibility to project military power quickly over long distances. Using aircraft equipped with complex weapon systems, air crews deliver lethal weapons and concentrate firepower in support of ground, sea, and other air forces. Consequently, air forces must be organized to accomplish such missions.

Due to the speed, range, and sophistication of modern aircraft and intercontinental missiles, the command and control of an air force is a critical factor in determining organizational structure. Most air forces are established as separate services that rely predominantly on a large officer corps to command and exercise control over forces provided to support the coordinated efforts of other services.

Most nations choose to staff their aircraft and missile launch facilities with skilled young officers who are physically fit and intellectually suited to the complexity of the task. As a result, air force officers rather than airmen or soldiers do the majority of fighting and training for combat. Enlisted personnel work mostly in jobs that support the aircraft, ballistic missiles, helicopters, and their crews. Air forces of major world powers are organized and trained to provide this support even when aircraft and units are deployed to distant locations.

Organization of an Air Force

Most armed forces are placed under the civilian control of the head of state of a nation and its governing political body. Typically, air force headquarters function in the chain of command alongside the other services under a ministry or department of defense headed by a minister or secretary who reports directly to the head of state on matters of defense policy and command authority. Politically, defense establishments should be subordinate to the policy of national legislatures on matters concerning their budget, funding, force structure, officer promotions, and procurement.

In the United States, the U.S. Air Force is a separate service organized as the Department of the Air Force under the secretary of the air force and a military chief of staff. The departments of the air force, army, and navy form the Department of Defense and report through the secretary of defense to the president and Congress of the United States. During a military emergency the three military service chiefs and the commandant of the Marine Corps can report directly through the chairman of the Joint Chiefs of Staff to the president as the commander in chief.

In the People's Republic of China the military is organized under the Ministry of National Defense, which reports politically to the Communist Central Committee and militarily to the Central Military Commission. The air force, artillery corps, navy, and People's Armed Police are separate service arms that make up the People's Liberation Army.

As a consequence of World War II, the Japanese military establishment was limited by treaty to provide for self-defense only. Although limited in its mission, Japan's Air Self-Defense Force is a formidable organization ranking as the fifth largest air force in the world with approximately 1,500 aircraft.

Similar to the U.S. Air Force, the Royal Air Force operates as a separate service within the British Ministry of Defence. Reporting to an Air Force Board, the Royal Air Force is split into three operating commands that are further broken down into air groups responsible for the operation of stations, units, and squadrons.

HEADQUARTERS FUNCTIONS

An air force headquarters is the top link in the chain of command between the civilian and political policymakers and the operating commands charged with accomplishing military missions. Headed by a military commander, chief of staff, or commander in chief, the headquarters staff formulates decisions regarding military policy and provides top-level policy guidance for operational planning, training, personnel, financial resources and budgeting, research and development, procurement, and logistic support for the operating commands and supporting elements.

MISSION AREA COMMANDS

To provide for increased span of control and to streamline the decision-making process, major commands are organized under the air force headquarters, usually by mission area. These commands should have the authority to make or delegate decisions in their specific mission areas so that commanders serving closest to operational problems can be effective and accountable for their actions.

Typical mission areas include aircraft and missile operations, personnel, training, communications, security, system development, procurement, and logistics support. Major commands that are assigned the responsibility for accomplishing these missions are as diverse in size and structure as the missions themselves.

The U.S. Air Force since its founding in 1947 had been organized along strategic and tactical lines. In 1992, after the end of the cold war, it restructured its operational forces into two global commands, the Air Mobility Command and the Air Combat Command. In addition, the Air Force Systems Command and Logistics Command were combined into one major command—the Air Material Command—responsible for research and development, procurement, and support of all air force systems and equipment. To accommodate the rapidly evolving air force mission in space, the U.S. Air Force has also formed a Space Command responsible for all air force space operations including missile launch, satellite control, reconnaissance, and space surveillance.

The Russian air forces are headed by a deputy minister of defense who reports to a general staff under the Ministry of Defense. The Russian air forces have three major components: frontal aviation, long-range aviation, and military transport aviation.

Equipped with fighter aircraft and armed helicopters, Russian frontal aviation is charged with the responsibility of maintaining battlefield air superiority and providing tactical support of ground operations.

Long-range aviation has about 900 long-range and medium-range bombers, which are capable of air-to-air refueling and can carry either nuclear or conventional weapons including air-to-air and air-to-surface missiles.

The responsibility for operation of Russian air defense fighter interceptors and long-range strategic missiles is not assigned to the air forces. Two other services, Troops of Air Defense and the Strategic Rocket Forces, are assigned these important mission areas.

OPERATING WINGS AND SQUADRONS

The organizational structure of an air force below the major command level is dependent upon its size, characteristics, and mission needs. Commands may be further broken down into air forces, divisions, and groups, but the ultimate operating unit is a wing comprising three or four squadrons of people and equipment.

In order to exercise full control of all units serving in the wing, the wing commander should have the authority to make decisions regarding the operation and support of the wing. He should also be accountable for all functions performed by the wing and its staff. Areas such as operations, training, standardization and evaluation, maintenance, supply, logistics support, security, transportation, and communications should also fall within the purview of the wing commander.

Because of its mission, a wing should be a homogeneous organization in its makeup and equipment. Furthermore, it should be a self-contained unit equipped with aircraft designed to perform assigned missions and manned with personnel specifically trained to operate and support those aircraft. The wing commander should have control of all of the resources needed to support the operation and deployment of the organization.

Within the structure of a wing, individual squadrons make up the basic fighting team of an air force. A squadron commander is assigned the personnel and equipment necessary to accomplish the squadron mission and ensure its support. The squadron chain of command usually flows through an operations officer to the flight commanders, typically four. The squadron commander and operations officer depend on the support of an executive officer, supply officer, chief of maintenance, and their staffs to conduct the duties of the squadron.

Squadrons vary in size depending on their mission, the number and type of aircraft assigned, and the extent to which the unit is supported integrally from within its own resources or is dependent on the combined support of outside organizations. Where practical, most flying squadrons perform best when they contain their own dedicated support personnel, mechanics, and technicians. With maintenance and support personnel assigned to a squadron under the direct, day-to-day control of the commander and maintenance officer, squadrons can best remain prepared and responsive to changing mission requirements. Unit deployments are greatly facilitated by the availability of squadron-dedicated maintenance.

Squadrons are the basic fighting teams of an air force; within fighter squadrons, flights form the basic combat elements. A formation of four modern fighters manned by highly skilled, well-trained, disciplined pilots can perform difficult missions with a high probability of success.

COMPOSITE ORGANIZATIONS

When rapid deployment and mission flexibility are essential to mission accomplishment, air force organizations can be structured as composite units. For example, a composite wing may operate more than one type of aircraft so that it can deploy rapidly and effectively accomplish a number of missions. A composite fighter wing may be equipped with several different types of fighters (such as air-to-air, air-to-ground, or night attack), tankers, airlift aircraft, and AWACS to form a fast-reaction combat team capable of deploying and operating on a worldwide basis.

SUPPORTING COMMANDS

Commands that play a supporting role in an air force generally conform to the organizational lines and structure of the flying units. In the U.S. Air Force, the organization of both the Materiel Command and the Training Command closely parallels the other major commands although their mission, day-to-day operations, titles, and unit designations may vary widely. In the supporting commands, emphasis is placed on management, technical expertise, and accountability for their specific contribution to the overall mission.

Interaction with an Army and Navy

Air forces seldom have or control all of the aircraft operated by a national defense force. Carrier-based naval aircraft and an assortment of army attack helicopters and support aircraft are important elements in most modern armed forces. These various air arms are charged with the responsibility to work together effectively and are often called upon to operate as an integrated team under a single commander. The conduct of Operation Desert Storm using the combined forces of several allied nations was a classic example of the success that can be achieved by an integrated task force.

Summary and Conclusion

Air forces vary in size, equipment, and mission but most share several unique characteristics—speed, complexity, and global reach. Organization may be tailored to individual capabilities and needs, but in every case the chain of command between the decision maker or commander and the air crews performing the mission must be streamlined and responsive. As air forces move into space, their responsiveness to command and control will be increasingly important.

As world tensions change, nations may be forced to reallocate their priorities, budgets, and missions. In the process, military organizations including the air forces will ultimately have to adapt to changing requirements. Furthermore, to maintain a credible force of air power within the constraints of shrinking resources, air forces will likely be forced to reduce the overhead of high-level headquarters by merging commands and staffs, particularly those of the supporting commands.

KENNETH H. BELL

SEE ALSO: Organization, Military; Organization, Naval.

Bibliography

Air Force Magazine. 1984. Soviet Air Force Almanac Issue, March.
———. 1991. 1991 Almanac, May.
Canan, J. W. 1991. No more SAC, TAC, and MAC. *Air Force Magazine*, October, pp. 13–15.
Central Intelligence Agency, Directorate of Intelligence. 1990. *Military organizations of the People's Republic of China.* Washington, D.C.: Library of Congress.
Katz, S. M. 1991. Israeli airpower on the rise. *Air Force Magazine*, November, pp. 46–51.
Mason, R. A. 1982. *The Royal Air Force: Today and tomorrow.* London: Ian Allan.
McMeiken, F. 1984. *Italian military aviation.* 1st ed. Midland Counties: Leicester.
North Atlantic Treaty Organization (NATO). 1978. *NATO facts and figures.* Brussels: NATO Information Service.

Sabin, P., ed. 1988. *The future of United Kingdom air power*. London and Washington: Brassey's.

Scott, H. F., and W. F. Scott. 1984. *The armed forces of the USSR*. Boulder, Colo., and London: Westview Press and Arms and Armour Press.

Smith, M. J. 1981. *The Soviet air and strategic rocket forces*. Santa Barbara, Calif.: ABC-Clio.

Tyushkevich, S. A. 1978. *The Soviet armed forces: A history of their organizational development, a Soviet view*. Washington, D.C.: U.S. Air Force.

Watanabe, A. 1985. *Japanese air arms*. Rev. ed. Japan: Saitama Komatsu.

Whiting, K. R. 1986. *Soviet air power*. Boulder, Colo.: Westview Press.

Wolk, H. S. 1984. *Planning and organizing the postwar air force 1943–1947*. Office of Air Force History. Washington, D.C.: U.S. Air Force.

ORGANIZATION, ARMY

All modern armies are organized similarly. All include the same basic functions necessary to conduct land combat with modern weapons. The proportions of these functions vary according to national preference and somewhat according to the weapons and equipment available, but all are present in the large combined arms organizations. Armies are designed to operate and fight on land, and are organized hierarchically in relatively fixed patterns from small units to large organizations. The functions of land combat are repeated at each level in the hierarchy, although smaller organizations may not include a separate unit for each function. Armies also tend to integrate their support units with their combat units at each level of the organizational hierarchy. When operating in the field, armies—unlike navies and air forces, which are tied to specific bases—bring their bases with them.

The evolution of army organization has been a process of creating and differentiating the functions of land combat. In early warfare, armies tended to have a single function—infantry combat. Over the course of history, new functions arose as technology evolved; the modern army is a complex and intricate organization requiring a high degree of management and leadership to do its work.

Basic Functions of Land Combat

The *command* function, sometimes called command and control, includes the decision, planning, direction, and feedback mechanisms that manage an army at each level in the hierarchy. At the lower levels, command is accomplished by an individual, sometimes with a deputy or assistant. At the battalion level and higher, commanders have staffs to help them accomplish the command function.

The *maneuver* function uses movement and firepower to seize or defend terrain features, destroy enemy forces, and weaken the will of the enemy to fight. Maneuver is accomplished by infantry or armored units, which alternately move and fire to accomplish military missions. Infantry usually fights on foot even though the troops may ride to the battlefield on horses, trucks, or armored personnel carriers. Mechanized infantry may fight while mounted in fighting vehicles. The infantry's role is to close with and destroy the enemy. Armor achieves shock power with its tanks and can penetrate enemy positions. Generally, the best results are achieved when infantry and armor work together in a combined arms team. The infantry protects the tanks from close-in fires, and the tanks protect the infantry from longer-range fires. Infantry units include considerable firepower capability at each level, and armor units have the firepower of their tanks as well as other fire support. A primary characteristic of modern armies is the integration of fire and maneuver, in which some elements provide a base of fire to facilitate the maneuver of other elements. Tactical missions are accomplished by a carefully concerted alternation of fire and maneuver by all elements in the hierarchy of army organization.

The *reconnaissance* or scouting function consists of finding the enemy, preventing surprise, and sometimes delaying or harassing enemy attackers. Reconnaissance elements are not intended for sustained combat, although they have the capability to fight. The reconnaissance function formerly was performed by foot skirmishers or light cavalry, but in modern armies it is accomplished by personnel in light tanks, high-speed vehicles, helicopters, or aircraft.

The *fire support* function is to destroy, damage, or deter the enemy by bringing fires to bear on his troops, support, or lines of communications. Fire support is performed by rifles, machine guns, mortars, howitzers, rockets, missiles, armed helicopters, and combat aircraft. It is provided by fire support elements in infantry and armor units, and by field artillery units, combat aviation units, naval guns and missiles, and air forces. Fire support provides protection for the maneuver elements by firing on enemy forces. One specialized part of the fire support function provides antiarmor weapons to destroy or damage opposing tanks and light armored vehicles.

The *air defense* function is to destroy, damage, or deter enemy helicopters, aircraft, and missiles. Air defense is performed by ground elements or aircraft armed with missiles and automatic guns designed specifically for this function. It is provided at each level of the hierarchy in armies, and is obtained also from naval and air forces.

The *combat engineer*, or pioneer, function is to assist the movement of the friendly forces and impede the movement of the enemy forces. The former is accomplished by building roads, airfields, bridges, and rafts and clearing obstacles; the latter is accomplished by damaging roads and airfields, destroying bridges, and constructing obstacles. Combat engineer elements may also build structures and utilities needed for military or related civil use, although engineer construction units are provided to do most of that kind of work.

The *communications*, or signal, function is to transmit messages among the elements of the army and other supporting services. It is accomplished by special sections within headquarters units and at the higher levels of the hierarchy by signal units.

Administration, or combat service support, includes several subfunctions pertaining to the operations of the army in all aspects other than combat itself.

Administration includes supply, maintenance, transportation, medical care, personnel management, and subsistence. There are administration elements at every level in the hierarchy starting with the company.

The *aviation* function includes operation of light aircraft and helicopters in support of the army. The aviation function is characterized by the use of aircraft to accomplish tasks of other functions: moving troops on the battlefield as part of the maneuver function; providing aerial reconnaissance; using armed helicopters for fire support; moving supplies, equipment, and wounded personnel; and allowing commanders to view the battlefield from above. Initially, the aviation function also included aerial combat, bombing, and close air support by high-performance aircraft, but most nations now perform these functions in air forces separate from their armies.

All of these functions except aviation are performed at each level in the hierarchy of army organization. As organizations become larger, these basic functions are accomplished by specifically designed and designated elements. The fundamental schema of army organization consists essentially of performing these same functions in an integrated and purposeful manner at each level in the hierarchy.

The historical evolution of army organization was achieved by adding new functional elements as compelled by the introduction of new technology. Initially, armies consisted entirely of two functions, command and maneuver; the maneuver elements were foot infantry, and the commanders led in person and even fought in battle. The introduction of horses and wheeled vehicles added heavy cavalry (armor) to the maneuver function and light cavalry to the reconnaissance function. The introduction of stand-off weapons, such as slings, bows, and finally guns, caused the fire support function to be differentiated in the form of a special corps—artillery. During the Middle Ages, the engineer function achieved independent status to build fortifications and manage the sieges to destroy them. The communications function was important from the earliest days but gained specific recognition with the introduction of heliographs, telegraphs, telephones, and radios. The essential function of feeding and paying the troops and providing weapons and munitions has always been a necessary part of an army, but as weapons grew more complicated and armies larger it became necessary to create specialized units to perform the administration function. The aviation function arrived with the introduction in World War I of workable aircraft and has evolved, despite the formation of separate air forces, into an important function for most modern armies. Similarly, the command function has evolved from a single general giving instructions by voice to an elaborate network of commanders at various levels, supported by staffs and numerous components, to achieve successful control of all of the other elements of the modern army.

The Hierarchy of Army Organization

Although the names, strengths, and specific roles vary somewhat, all modern armies include the same basic elements in the hierarchy of army organization.

Starting from smallest to largest, these are the squad, section, platoon, company, battalion, brigade, division, and army corps.

A *squad* consists of a squad leader (normally a sergeant) and seven to fourteen other soldiers. The squad is used in all branches of an army and is the smallest military organization. Originally, the size of a squad was determined by the ability of a single leader to command by voice, and it was employed as a single entity. However, the increased dispersion necessary to offset the increased lethality of modern weapons required the squad itself to be organized into teams.

The rifle squad is the basic element of infantry combat. There is great variety among rifle squads, but most modern rifle squads consist of a squad leader and two identical fire teams, each having a light machine gun as its principal weapon. Each fire team includes a leader, a machine gunner, and four to six riflemen, whose principal missions are to carry ammunition and protect the machine gunner. The fire teams alternate as maneuver or base of fire elements; that is, one fire team moves while the other team covers the movement with fire. Flexible interaction of fire and maneuver is the fundamental method of land combat at all levels.

A *section* is an organization larger than a squad and smaller than a platoon used within headquarters and in support organizations. It is led by a noncommissioned officer (NCO) and varies in strength from 10 to 40 personnel. In some armies, a section is also a combat element consisting of two or three squads.

A *platoon* consists of three or four squads and is led by a lieutenant or captain platoon leader assisted by a senior NCO—the platoon sergeant. The platoon is used in all branches of an army and has subelements for the maneuver, fire support, and command functions.

A generic rifle platoon includes three rifle squads as maneuver elements, a weapons squad as a fire support element, and a command section. Each rifle squad is a maneuver element for the platoon, although each contains both fire and maneuver capability internally. The weapons squad provides additional fire support with heavy machine guns to augment the fires of the light machine guns in the rifle squads. The command element consists of the platoon leader, the platoon sergeant, and a radio operator representing the communications function.

A generic tank platoon consists of four or five tanks with their crews and is commanded by a platoon leader in a tank. Each tank is a self-contained mobile fighting vehicle armed with a large flat-trajectory main gun, machine guns, and sometimes missiles. A tank platoon may fight in teams of two tanks, alternating fire and maneuver as directed by the platoon leader.

A *company* is a unit of 100–250 personnel consisting of several platoons and other elements. It is commanded by a captain, usually, although majors command companies in some armies. The functions of administration and air defense are introduced at the company level. Administration is performed by a first sergeant as senior NCO, a company clerk, a supply section, a maintenance section (depending on how much equipment the company has), and sometimes a mess section—all within a headquarters platoon. Command is accomplished by the company commander, the first sergeant, and several communications specialists.

A generic rifle company consists of three rifle platoons as maneuver elements, a weapons platoon to provide fire support, a headquarters platoon for administration, and a headquarters for command. A typical weapons platoon provides two new forms of fire support: high-angle fire using light (60mm or 81mm) mortars; and flat-trajectory light antitank fire with light antitank guns or missiles. The headquarters platoon contains small elements for personnel and supply. In the U.S. Army, the mess and maintenance functions for infantry units have been centralized at the battalion level.

A generic tank company consists of three tank platoons as maneuver elements and a company headquarters, which includes personnel and supply sections. Because of the heavy maintenance load for the tanks, company headquarters may also have a maintenance section.

A *battalion* is a unit of 400 to 1,200 personnel consisting of several companies and other elements. It is commanded by a lieutenant colonel and is the smallest organization with a staff to assist the commander. Most staffs are organized to provide principal staff officers for personnel, intelligence, operations, and logistics, although some nations combine intelligence and operations into a single operations staff element, and personnel and logistics into a single administrative staff element. The battalion is the basic unit for combat and combat support branches.

A generic infantry battalion is shown in Figure 1. It consists of three or four rifle companies as maneuver elements, a combat support company, a headquarters company, and a headquarters. The combat support company provides new weapons and equipment to augment those in the rifle companies, including a mortar platoon with medium mortars (107mm), tactical radar equipment, and an antiarmor platoon with heavy antitank missiles. The reconnaissance function is performed by a scout platoon in the combat support company. The air defense function may be introduced at this level by including in the combat support company a section armed with shoulder-fired air defense missiles. A separate engineer section or platoon is sometimes provided as well. The headquarters and combat support companies may be combined into a single unit. The headquarters company includes mess, maintenance, and signal sections,

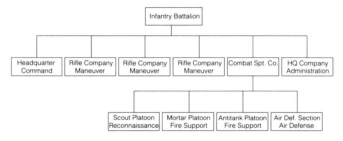

Figure 1. Organization of an infantry battalion.

and sometimes a transportation section as well. The headquarters includes the command, staff, and the personnel in the sections supporting the staff. An infantry battalion is a reasonably self-sufficient unit with explicit representation of six or seven of the nine functions of land combat.

A generic tank battalion is shown in Figure 2. It consists of four tank companies as maneuver elements, a headquarters, and a headquarters company. The headquarters company includes a medium mortar platoon for fire support and a scout platoon for the reconnaissance function, as well as a maintenance platoon and a support platoon to carry the battalion's basic load of ammunition and fuel. The combat engineer function is accomplished by an armored vehicle–launched bridge.

A *brigade* is an organization of units with an aggregate strength of from 2,000 to 8,000 personnel commanded by a brigadier general or colonel. A brigade is used to form combat, combat support, and combat service support units into functional or integrated combinations. Brigade headquarters are used to command engineer, transportation, signal, and artillery battalions in single-function organizations. They are also used to command combat service support battalions of different types—supply, maintenance, medical—in multifunction organizations. A group headquarters commanded by a colonel also may be used to command several battalions or companies and may be major subordinate elements of brigades. A regiment has about the same strength as a brigade but is a fixed organization with a definite internal composition, while a brigade is a flexible organization with an internal composition tailored to the specific combat environment. In the U.S. Army, the only regimental organization still in use is an armored cavalry regiment fulfilling the reconnaissance function for army corps. In some armies, the term *regiment* is used for smaller units comparable to battalions in the U.S. and (NATO) armies.

Combat brigades are combined arms organizations, in that they integrate infantry, armor, artillery, and cavalry units under a single commander for combat. A combat brigade may be organic to a combat division or may be a separate organization. An organic combat brigade is a tactical headquarters commanded by a colonel to which combat battalions and combat support units are attached or placed in direct support. Separate combat brigades are usually

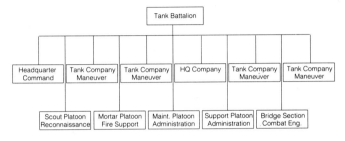

Figure 2. Organization of a tank battalion.

commanded by a brigadier general and are assigned its subordinate units on a permanent basis.

A generic separate combat brigade includes two to five infantry or tank battalions as maneuver elements, an artillery battalion for fire support, a cavalry troop (company) for reconnaissance, a combat engineer company, and a support battalion that includes the service support units. Brigades may be tailored for their intended missions, and an air defense battery or aviation company or battalion could be assigned as well. A separate brigade is a formidable combat force, and some nations use the separate brigade as their primary combat organization.

A *division* (Fig. 3) is a combined arms organization with 7,000–22,000 military personnel commanded by a major general. It includes three combat brigades as maneuver elements, an artillery brigade of three to five artillery battalions, a cavalry squadron with three or four cavalry troops (some of which may be air cavalry), a separate air defense battalion, a separate signal battalion, a support command with three or four service support battalions, and frequently an aviation battalion. The division artillery brigade commonly consists of a direct support battalion with light or medium (105mm, 152mm, or 155mm) howitzers for each brigade and one or two other battalions, including heavy (203mm or 240mm) howitzers or multiple-launch rocket launchers for general support of the division. Each of the nine basic functions of land combat is represented explicitly in a combat division.

In many armies, including the U.S. Army, the brigades organic to a division are tactical headquarters to which infantry and tank battalions are attached for a particular battle or campaign, while the rest of the brigade units—artillery battalion, engineer company, and combat service support elements—remain assigned to their own divisional units and placed in support of the brigade. This organizational concept allows a division commander to tailor his subordinate brigades to the combat situation and his mission. Other nations (Soviet Union, U.K.), treat the major subordinate elements of a division as regiments, or relatively fixed organizations. Whether a division is flexible or fixed in theory, division commanders tend to organize their divisions for combat as they perceive necessary to accomplish their missions.

There are many different types of combat divisions, depending on the nature and mix of the included infantry and tank maneuver battalions. Infantry divi-

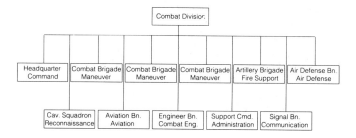

Figure 3. Organization of a combat division.

sions have from seven to ten foot-infantry battalions and one or two tank or mechanized infantry battalions. Light infantry divisions include nine or ten light infantry battalions designed for rapid strategic movement and trained for low-intensity conflict. Airborne infantry divisions are designed to conduct parachute assaults, so the nine infantry battalions and other division units (including sometimes a light tank battalion) are designed for this role, and all division personnel are qualified parachutists. The U.S. Army has an air assault division with nine light infantry battalions manned by soldiers specially trained in helicopter operations. Armored divisions and mechanized infantry divisions are composed of a mix of ten to twelve tank battalions and mechanized infantry battalions equipped with armored personnel carriers or infantry fighting vehicles. Tank battalions outnumber mechanized infantry battalions in armored divisions, while the converse is true in mechanized infantry divisions. In each of these divisions, the reconnaissance, artillery, engineer, and other units of the division base are equipped and trained to be compatible with the maneuver battalions. In an armored division, the artillery is all self-propelled on tracked vehicles, and the engineers ride in armored engineer vehicles. In a light infantry division, the artillery is light and towed by light vehicles, and the engineers have light trucks.

An *army corps* is the largest combined arms organization currently used as a standard army formation. It has a strength of 50,000 to 300,000 troops and is commanded by a lieutenant general. An army corps may consist of two to seven divisions and supporting units. A generic army corps is shown in Figure 4. It includes three divisions (two infantry and one armored), a separate combat brigade for augmenting a division or accomplishing a tactical mission, a corps artillery brigade with ten to fifteen artillery battalions organized into three or four artillery groups, an armored or air cavalry regiment with three or four cavalry squadrons, a corps support command with several area or functional commands, and brigades for the engineer, signal, air defense, and aviation functions.

The headquarters staffs for both division and corps are organized into more staff sections than are found at the division or brigade headquarters. In addition to staff sections for personnel, intelligence, operations, and logistics, there may be separate staff sections for planning, civil-military affairs, communications, and other special activities deemed important enough to warrant an additional principal staff officer.

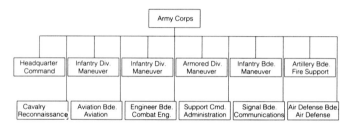

Figure 4. Organization of an army corps.

Army echelons above corps are organized for specific theaters and situations, but all include common elements for specific collateral functions of land combat. Field armies, consisting of two or more corps with an array of supporting organizations, and commanded by a full general, exist in the armies of the larger nations, but usually they are tailored for a specific mission. In the 1991 Gulf War, Third U.S. Army Headquarters commanded VII Corps and XVIII Airborne Corps as the army component of the unified theater command for the Persian Gulf. (The U.S. Army also maintains several "CONUS Armies," which are administrative headquarters responsible for specific regions of the United States and are not intended to serve as field armies.) The Soviet Union used the term *army* to mean a corps, and *front* to mean field army. In World War II the Allies, Germans, and Soviets formed army groups consisting of several field armies.

The collateral functions of land combat that are provided for in the echelons above corps include intelligence, military police, chemical, logistics, personnel replacement, and special operations. Intelligence units exist at battalion and higher levels in the form of staff sections. There are also intelligence units devoted to the collection and interpretation of intelligence. Some of these units exist at the division and corps level, but often they are organized into a single theater-wide intelligence command. The military police function also exists in the divisions and corps; there is a military police company in each U.S. division and one or more battalions in an army corps to provide law and order, area security, and battlefield circulation control. That part of the military police function involved with prisoners of war and criminal investigation often is organized into a single command under the army commander for a theater. Chemical units also are provided at every level, and there is a chemical company for each division, but the control of chemical assets, including smoke generator units, often is held at the theater or theater army level. The personnel replacement function normally is performed by a replacement command under the theater army commander.

Special operations forces include special forces, rangers, special operations aviation, civil affairs, and psychological operations units. These special operations forces usually are formed into a single command for theater-wide operations under the theater commander. In the war with Iraq, the United States assigned or attached civil affairs units to the corps and divisions, retained control of psychological operations at the theater level while placing units in support of the corps and divisions, and conducted special forces and ranger operations under a special operations command for the theater.

Finally, the echelons above corps include logistical commands to operate ports, railways, pipelines, highway transportation systems, supply depots, maintenance facilities, and other activities to support the operations of the corps. These logistical commands are organized either on an area basis with units of different functions or on a single-function basis for the entire theater. The exact variety and organization of the units operating at the echelons above corps depend on circumstances and national doctrine.

The organization of armies as national institutions tends to vary widely, but some common elements exist. The army headquarters is headed by a senior military officer who usually reports to a civilian minister of war or defense. The army is usually part of a unified military organization with the naval and air forces. The staffs at army headquarters are concerned with the normal staff functions for the army in the field, and in addition have to deal with budgeting, public relations, and political issues. Armies commonly have major commands for the following functions: centralized personnel management, development and procurement of weapons and equipment, wholesale logistics (supply and maintenance), training and education, doctrinal development, and health care. In addition, there may be organizations devoted to computers and electronics, munitions, industrial production, political affairs and propaganda, and testing of weapons and equipment. The exact organization and delineation of responsibilities varies widely according to national preference and the size of the army.

Armies are usually separated into two or more components according to readiness standards. The active component consists of units with equipment manned by full-time personnel. There are a wide variety of reserve component schemes, but they all involve only a few full-time personnel augmented in some cases by part-time reservists who train regularly and in other cases by reservists who will report to their units only upon mobilization. Most armies keep some of their units in a reserve component with the same organizational tables, tactical doctrine, and training standards as the active component, although with reduced readiness and cost.

It is likely that the historical trend toward greater complexity and specialization in army organization will continue. Once considered a low-tech organization compared with air forces and navies, armies are now using large amounts of sophisticated high-technology equipment and will use more in the future. Consequently, the proportion of the strength of an army that engages directly in combat will continue to shrink. Since the earliest days, when every member of an army fought on the battlefield, the evolution of army organization has increased the proportion of support troops to combat troops, until now only a few riflemen, machine gunners, and tank crews actually operate on the front lines.

This increase in support, however, has also resulted in a greater increase in the overall combat power of armies, so these fewer combat soldiers can deliver greater amounts of lethal munitions faster and more accurately than ever before. Because of the need to counter this increased lethality, armies will continue to move toward greater dispersion in tactical formations. Air power and longer-range weapons mean that armies must disperse in depth as well as laterally. The combat area is getting deeper and more difficult to distinguish from the rear areas, if indeed there are any rear areas remaining.

Finally, as armies are becoming more technical, more specialized internally, and more lethal, they are becoming smaller. During World War II, the U.S. Army had 8 million military personnel, the German army numbered 4.5 million, and the Red Army about 7 million. Even during the height of the cold war, the two major opposing coalitions were planning armies with at most 4 or 5 million on each side. Currently, armies of the NATO nations are being reduced in size as the threat of a major conventional war diminishes. The trend among industrialized nations is for smaller armies that are well trained and equipped with modern, sophisticated weapons. The United States is planning an army of slightly more than 500,000 active and 600,000 selected reserve personnel for the mid-1990s. However, China, Vietnam, North Korea, India, and perhaps the Commonwealth of Independent States and Iraq are likely to have active armies over 1 million strong for the foreseeable future. Despite reductions in size and the introduction of modern weapons, the fundamentals of army organization will tend to remain very much the same as they have been since Napoleon and Wellington collaborated unwittingly to combine respectively shock and firepower with linear tactics during the early years of the nineteenth century.

JOHN R. BRINKERHOFF

Bibliography

International Institute for Strategic Studies. 1990. *The military balance, 1990–1991.* London: Brassey's.
Isby, D. C., and C. Kamps. 1985. *Armies of NATO's central front.* London: Jane's.
Keegan, J. 1983. *World armies.* Detroit, Mich.: Gale Research.
Scott, H. F., and W. F. Scott. 1984. *The armed forces of the USSR.* London: Arms and Armour Press.
Thomer, E. 1984. *Die Bundeswehr Heute.* Herford und Bonn: E. S. Mittler und Sohn.
U.S. Department of the Army. 1987. *Staff officers field manual 101-10-1/1: Organizational, technical, and logistical data.* Vols. 1 and 2. Washington, D.C.: Government Printing Office.

ORGANIZATION, MILITARY

There are many definitions of *organization.* For the purpose of this article, organization is the process that provides a military activity with a methodical structure and then transforms that structure into full working order. To do this, life must be added to the activity's various functions in the shape and substance of individual persons, groups of people, and their interrelationships.

Organizational development entails identifying, specifying, and aligning the functions to be performed by each person or each group within an established system of formally regulated working relationships and procedures. It is the organization that binds these relationships and procedures together within the activity's structure, and links specific functions to the persons or groups charged with undertaking them. Organization is also the link between the activity's prescribed purpose and the method of executing or accomplishing that purpose.

Within the structure of military organization, the *unit* is the basic building block. Each unit has a specific combat or support role, and has an establishment (table of manpower and equipment) to enable it to carry out that role. The unit may be a battalion of infantry or a cavalry regiment, a formed column of horsedrawn wagons or a modern transport battalion, a supply depot or a maintenance workshop, a naval vessel or an aircraft wing, a joint headquarters or a communications center. Some units have a role only in war; they train in peacetime to remain operationally ready and fit for that role. Others have peacetime tasks that may change during transition to war. If a unit's organization changes in a crisis or in war, the amount of men and equipment it needs may change as well. There are also units that disband on the outbreak of war; their resources are transferred to other military purposes.

A *formation* is an operational grouping of combat and support units brought together permanently or temporarily for a specific mission. It may be a parachute brigade, an armored division, a logistic support group, or a joint task force comprising maritime, land, and air elements. It is, thus, an ordered arrangement or organization of army units composed of troops, vehicles, and equipments formed into a balanced and combined arms-services team; of ships in convoy or formed into a fleet; or of aircraft operating together. The term *formation* is also used to denote a tactical configuration of combat units, but this interpretation is outside the scope of this article.

Every unit and formation has a *commander* and a headquarters. On the one hand, a battalion commander has a small, mobile headquarters consisting of key officers and soldiers with well-defined operational or peacetime duties. The commander of a field formation, such as an armored division, has a larger, mobile headquarters comprising his general staff (operational planning staff), specialist support staff (artillery, supply, communications, intelligence, etc.), and a security and administrative element. The commander of an army, on the other hand, may well have a very large, static headquarters composed of his own personal and general staff, as well as others representing naval, air, or flanking forces.

The headquarters *staff* helps the commander to plan, direct, control, coordinate, supervise, monitor, and evaluate operations during an emergency or in war; the staff also assists with the regulation of peacetime training and domestic routine. Operational and administrative orders derive from the commander himself, although his staff may issue them on his behalf. The staff, collectively, and the chief of staff, individually, have no command authority over the units or formations in a military force; that is the sole preserve of the commander, who is the senior officer personally nominated and vested with that authority. A designated staff officer or another subordinate may be given powers, for example, to control the tactical movement of a unit or formation over an obstacle, or to control the release of operationally vital materiel in critical short supply. Nevertheless, these and other forms of control, which fall short of full delegated command, are always exercised directly on behalf of the commander.

A force structure that incorporates units and formations, commanders and staffs forms the foundations of military organization. The design, creation, and resources of that organization are its cornerstones and profoundly influence how well or how badly it functions, or whether or not it fulfills its mission. But it is people who actually make a chosen organization work and who principally determine its effectiveness.

History

A review of major organizational issues must start by outlining the evolutionary development of military structures during a long history of violent warfare, uneasy peace, and momentous change.

In prehistoric times, fighting men knew little, and needed to know little, about organization. Having found, made, or stolen their weapons, they roamed singly or in small groups, engaging or evading any threat that came their way. The most experienced and skillful—generally the elders of the group—made the decisions: where to go, when to leave and return to base, which route to use, and how to attack which prey. This required little organization.

This simplicity could not last. The groups of fighting men grew bigger and started to proliferate. Individuals had to be given additional duties: the young and fleet of foot reconnoitered and delivered messages, the less mobile and less aggressive pitched camp or found food for the combatants and others. Soon each fighting group needed several specialists to provide a variety of support, and the combatant troops themselves began to specialize as spearmen, bowmen, armed horsemen, and so forth.

ANCIENT AND MEDIEVAL MILITARY ORGANIZATIONS

Little detail is known of military organization before the rise of the Greek city-states in the early fifth century B.C. Earlier military structures, like those of Sumer, Akkad, Egypt, Assyria, and the Hittites, left little history, although some details of their equipment and tactics have come to light through archaeology.

Classical Greece and Macedon. The armies of the classical Greeks were built on a core of *hoplites*, armored spearmen who fought in close formation. Generally, the *hoplite* phalanx, usually eight men deep, and their supporting cavalry and light troops were organized in companies of 100 and "battalions" of 500 to 1,000. In the early fourth century B.C., for example, the Spartan army consisted of six or seven *morai*, each about 600 men strong. The organization of other Greek armies is less clear, but was probably broadly similar.

The Macedonian army of Philip II and his son Alexander III ("the Great") was organized differently. It was considerably larger than the Greek armies, and it relied to a greater degree on the offensive power of cavalry to achieve victory. The Macedonian *hoplites,* equipped with a pike (the *sarissa*) and a small shield, were called *pezetaeri* (foot companions) and were organized in *taxeis* (regiments) of about 1,500 men each, 16 men deep. The simple phalanx contained about 8,200 men. Alexander invaded Asia with four of these, leaving another three or four at home with the regent Antipater. The *pezetaeri* were supported by battalions, about 50 strong, of javelineers, archers, and *peltasts* (specially equipped light infantrymen). The final infantry force comprised the elite *hypaspists*, who were apparently trained to serve as either light troops or *pezetaeri*, as the occasion demanded; they wielded eight- to ten-foot spears and often served as the hinge between the phalanx and the cavalry.

The Macedonian cavalry was grouped in units about 500 strong. The horse *companions* (the royal bodyguard), Macedonians and Thessalians, were heavy shock troops equipped with armor, shield, sword, and lance. There were also lighter horsemen for scouting, skirmishing, and pursuit duties, often recruited from less-civilized peoples. Some 5,000 of the 35,000 men in Alexander's army when he crossed the Hellespont in 334 B.C. were cavalry, about evenly divided between light and heavy types.

In the 150 years after Alexander's death, the Hellenic successor-kingdoms in Greece and the Near East retained the basic structure of the Alexandrian army, although they added elephants and significant numbers of native troops. Without Alexander's genius, however, these armies were outmatched when they met the legions of Rome in the second century B.C.

The Roman Army. Under the Monarchy and the early Republic, the Roman army was no more than a Graeco-Etruscan phalanx supported by skirmishers and noble cavalry. Under Servius Tullius in the late fifth century B.C., Roman manpower was classified on an economic basis, with the wealthier sections of the population serving as either cavalry or *hoplites* and poorer citizens serving as light troops and servants. Each class was organized into *centuries* of 100 men each.

The reforms of Marcus Camillus in the early fourth century B.C. and modifications made after the Roman defeat by the Samnites at the Caudine Forks (321 B.C) produced a much more flexible force. Legionary infantry was divided into four groups, separated by age and equipment. The youngest men were employed as light infantry or *velites*. The *hastati*, *principes*, and the oldest troops, the *triarii*, were arrayed in successive lines on the field. A legion of about 3,500 men had ten cohorts (regiments), each one containing one *maniple* (battalion) of each troop type. Each maniple contained two centuries (companies) of 60 to 80 men, except for the maniple of *triarii*, which had only one century. The cohorts were deployed for battle in three lines in a kind of checkerboard or *quincunx* formation, with intervals between the cohorts in one line covered by those in the line behind. Each cohort also had a *turma* (troop) of 30 cavalry, but these fought separately from the cohort in consolidated cavalry units on the legion's flanks. Normally, each Roman legion was paired with a legion (or legion-sized force) raised from Rome's Latin and Italian allies. Two such legionary pairs formed a consular army of about 15,000 men. This tactical system was more flexible than the Graeco-Macedonian phalanx, and was both stronger and more resilient in action. This organization carried the Roman army through the Punic Wars, persisting for over 200 years until Gaius Marius undertook his military reforms about 105 B.C.

The "Marian" reforms simplified Roman organization considerably. The division of legionary infantry into four troops types was abandoned, and maniples were abolished. Under Marius, the legion contained ten cohorts, each of six 80-man centuries. The centuries of the first cohort were double-sized, so an ordinary legion's field strength totaled about 5,280 men. Each legionary was equipped as a heavy infantryman with *pilum* (a javelin also usable as a short spear), *gladius* (a broad, short sword about two feet in length), and shield. Cavalry and light infantry were provided by the *auxilia*, organized in 500- and 1,000-man cohorts, which were assigned to individual legions as required. This organization persisted almost unchanged until Diocletian's reforms in the late third century A.D.

The army of the late Roman Empire contained two separate forces. The frontier troops, or *limitanei*, were a quasi-militia force manning frontier fortifications. The mobile field army, consisting of the *comitatenses* and the *palatini* (imperial bodyguards), contained a large cavalry element, both for increased mobility and because the fighting quality of Roman infantry had declined as the standards of discipline had lapsed. Further, the late Roman army became increasingly made up of barbarians. By the start of the fifth century A.D., nearly all the *limitanei* and most of the field troops were barbarians; the senior commander in the Western Empire, Stilicho, was a Vandal, and many other senior commanders were barbarians.

From tribes to feudal armies, A.D. 476–1300. Although the barbarian tribes produced some cunning and capable warriors, their military sophistication came to them secondhand from the Romans. By the time the Western Empire collapsed in A.D. 476, most elements of Roman military organization had vanished from western Europe. In its place, the barbarian successor-kingdoms emplaced their own ruder military organization, based on clan, lineage, and personal loyalties rather than on formal units.

Germanic armies were led by chieftains, each of whom was accompanied into battle by a bank of warriors who had sworn to serve him. In exchange for their service and fealty, the chieftain undertook to provide sustenance for his followers. The economic aspects of this relationship were particularly important; the English word *lord* comes from the Anglo-Saxon *hlaford*, or loaf-giver, a person who provided sustenance to his followers. Chieftains in turn swore loyalty to higher-ranking chieftains, thereby providing a framework for controlling larger forces. This network of personal ties is the principal hallmark of feudalism, which dominated European social organization for nearly ten centuries after the fall of Rome.

As the social aspects of feudalism developed, many chieftains (or feudal lords) adopted the practice of providing for their followers by granting them land that could provide for their material needs. This practice, known as *manorialism,* is often linked with feudalism but is properly a separate development. For instance, the central governments of both the Byzantine Empire, with its *pronoia* military fiefs, and the Ottoman Empire, with its Timariot fiefs, made grants of land in exchange for military service by the fiefholder.

Outside the Byzantine Empire and the centrally organized Muslim states, military organization in medieval Europe was decentralized and irregular. Armies like those of the Vikings and Magyars consisted of war bands gathered around individual war chiefs, who sometimes banded together for particular operations. In the more "civilized" areas of western and southern Europe, armies consisted of feudal contingents provided to an overlord on demand. These contingents were limited in size and duration of service by tradition and mutual consent. A lord could extend the service of his followers (or vassals, the contemporary legal term) beyond the usual period if he paid them, as their usual service period was unpaid.

By the twelfth century, it became increasingly common in France, England, and the surrounding areas to replace individual service (always a nuisance for the vassal) with a cash payment. The lord could then hire mercenaries for as long as he liked (or could afford) with the money so received. After 1050 or so, most European armies contained a significant portion of mercenaries.

Typically, a feudal army fought in three parts, called *battles*. The vanguard, or forward battle, traditionally fought on the right wing; the main battle fought in the center of the line; and the rearguard or rear battle held the left. Each battle contained a variable number of separate contingents, most consisting of both infantry and cavalry. For purposes of combat, smaller groups of horse or foot soldiers were brigaded with other units of their type, but these groupings lasted only until the end of the battle. Mercenary forces often had a more permanent organization, and they were usually grouped in companies of 50 to 300 men. Larger organizations, as with the feudal troops, were strictly temporary.

Permanent armies: Muster and array, condottieri, and the Compagnies d'Ordonnance. By the beginning of the fourteenth century, most European states were making serious (if often unsuccessful) efforts to create permanent armies. The cost of such forces made the task difficult, but the English effort is especially noteworthy because it enabled a series of English monarchs to wage the Hundred Years' War against the vastly greater resources of France.

Under King Edward I, England undertook the conquest of Wales, a task that required not weeks but years. Feudal armies were unfit to perform such a task, and Edward introduced several reforms to enable him to keep an army in the field for months or years at a time. First, he issued "indentures" to individual lords, to provide specific numbers of troops with specified equipment, for a preset period of time. Second, he sent "commissioners of array" to the counties to muster the local militias and gather (or select) volunteers for service with the army. All these troops were paid and fed at royal expense, and were capable of serving abroad and for extended periods. This army, with foot soldiers armed with Welsh longbows, gave the English the military capacity to fight France (with five times' England's resources) for more than a century, twice nearly destroying the French kingdom.

Italy, because of the number of urban communities, had never developed the sort of feudalism present north of the Alps. Although Italian city-states at first depended on militia armies, they soon realized the costs and drawbacks associated with such forces. By the late thirteenth century, they began to employ mercenaries on a wide-scale basis, and by the mid-1300s the *condottieri* began to appear. These military entrepreneurs were a specific sort of mercenary; for a fee, a city could hire a general, who would in turn hire an army and conduct wars for the city-state. A written contract for such an agreement was called a *condotta*, whence the terms for the soldiers themselves. At first, the *condottieri* were free agents, switching their services from city to city as the situation dictated. By the 1420s and 1430s, however, they had lost much of their fiscal and political freedom and increasingly tended to spend their careers in the service of one state.

The armies of the *condottieri*, which often existed for long periods and indeed effectively became standing armies after 1440–50, were tightly organized. Troops were grouped in companies of several hundred men, generally armed and equipped similarly. Since most soldiers were long-term volunteer professionals, the sophistication of tactics and maneuver was considerable, and the ablest *condottieri*, like Francesco Sforze or John Hawkwood, were skillful generals indeed.

The effect of the *condottieri* was not limited to Italy alone. By the mid-fifteenth century, in the wake of the near-miraculous revival of French fortunes occasioned by the inspiration of Joan of Arc, the French undertook a major military reform. Until 1445, the French army consisted of numerous quasi-autonomous mercenary companies, many of them little more than bandits. In that year, King Charles VII (at the behest of his counselors) promulgated the *Grande Ordonnance*, which gave royal sanction and royal pay to some mercenary captains. Those mercenaries who did not gain official recognition were effectively outlawed. At one stroke, the French thereby created an army solely responsible to the crown, and at the same time cleared France of the bandit-mercenaries who had infested the country for decades.

Furthermore, this reform gave the French an army disciplined enough to drive the English from their shores, and effectively brought the Hundred Years' War to a close. This army consisted of a varying number of companies, each of between 30 and 100 "lances." Each lance contained a man-at-arms, his squire (counted as a soldier), two mounted archers, and two pages (both considered as noncombatants). The captain of the company was paid on the basis of the number of complete lances available in his unit, which was inspected regularly. As this army of the *Compagnies d'Ordonnance* (roughly translated as "legal companies") was also the first national standing army in Western Europe since the fall of the Roman Empire, it also served as a transition from the medieval to the modern.

THE BACKGROUND TO MODERN ORGANIZATION

Infantry on foot and cavalry on horseback received support from artillerymen, at first firing primitive cannon and later using weapons of ever-increasing sophistication and lethality. They were also supported by field engineers or pioneers who sapped at the walls of fortifications under siege and destroyed or built obstacles and bridges to make movement easier for their colleagues and more difficult for the enemy. As the means of mobility gradually improved, so the enhancement or obstruction of movement on and behind the battlefield became increasingly vital to operations.

Armed scouts were sent out to search for information and, when armed, found it easier to penetrate hostile areas, extricate themselves, and return to their leaders with the information gathered. Guides led mounted or dismounted troops through difficult terrain or to a special rendezvous. Signalers provided communications between groups and between leaders who shared a common cause; these were rudimentary systems initially, but as resourcefulness, ingenuity, and technology advanced, more reliable, secure communications became available and were used.

From earlier times, logisticians, accountants, paymasters, doctors, judges, police, and administrators of many types gave their services to those whose duty or vocation was to fight or provide direct support to the fighting. As fleets and armies grew in size, complexity, and power, the variety and amount of services needed to keep them at sea or on land in prime combat order multiplied.

Modern military organization comprising units, formations, and headquarters became discernible from the late sixteenth century onward in Europe. Armies had long consisted of cavalry, infantry (some armed with pikes, some with handguns), and artillery trains when, more than a century later, first Marlborough and then Frederick the Great took the field. However, the origin of the battalion or regiment as a basic military unit is a matter of some conjecture and dispute. There are those who claim the sixteenth-century Swiss and German mercenary *landsknechte* as the prototype, while others support the Italian *condottieri* as first.

Much of today's terminology was being developed at that time. The French word *bataillon* describes foot components of infantry or of artillery forming a subdivision of a regiment and itself comprising a number of companies. The French word *regiment* signifies a military component consisting of a number of battalions or cavalry squadrons commanded by a colonel. The term *formation*, also of French derivation, indicates a military organization composed of several diverse parts constituting a force, or a disposition of troops on the battlefield— for example, *formation dense* or *formation ouverte.*

The organization of European land forces was constructed from the bottom up: first the unit or battalion, then the regiment or brigade, later the division and larger formations. This continual, evolutionary process of development, experimentation, and refinement is well catalogued. As the scope of military strategies and commitments grew, as scientific discoveries and technological advances were made, so the structure and the capability of forces steadily expanded. In other parts of the world, forces were developed to match the prevailing local threat and conditions—terrorism, small wars, mountains, jungle, and desert. But it was mainly in Europe that most developments of modern force structure occurred and where the modern fighting formation became composed of a multiplicity of specialized, key units, many of them mutually supportive.

The organization of command and headquarters staff, on the other hand, was constructed from the top down: initially, a small group of senior officers and sometimes some civilians clustered around the commander, who was quite often the monarch. His force may have been relatively small, the number of his principal subordinates and levels of command within his force few, chains of command from top to bottom short, and the span of his command much narrower than in present-day forces. As the complexity of warfare and the size of forces grew, so the numbers on the staff of headquarters and their individual responsibilities grew. When a headquarters became too large to move frequently or to deploy far enough forward to observe and control the battle, the commander may have established a separate, small command group of himself and his principal tactical assistants. Then it became necessary to draw the distinction between the command group and the remainder of his staff. His headquarters and his staff there were instruments of command only when the commander was present with them or when he had formally delegated authority to another to act on his behalf.

During the late sixteenth and the seventeenth centuries, several important new senior staff appointments started to appear in the headquarters of European armies, among them a scoutmaster-general (reconnaissance), foragemaster-general (procurement), proviantmaster-general (supply), wagonmaster-general (transportation), provost, and camp and judge marshals. The German province of Brandenburg added adjutants-general, quartermasters-general, a commissary-general, supply master-general, auditor-general, and a staff quartermaster, field paymaster, chaplain, apothecary, and surgeon. After the Thirty Years' War, the French introduced the appointment of a *Maréchal Général des Logis* with responsibility for providing quarters and lodgings. Small functional organizations were formed around the holders of these early posts; these later became the supporting services of the armies.

Napoleon's *état-major* operated in two echelons: main and rear headquarters, in modern parlance. His *maison*, or group of immediate assistants, comprised a writing staff (intelligence, orders preparation), a fighting staff (operations), and a riding staff (aides, communications). Some distance back, Imperial Headquarters prepared the orders for nontactical movement, supervised artillery and engineer support, provided military police, and supplied maps. The logistics of Napoleon's armies was by no means neglected, for he was always personally involved with the planning and execution of logistic support, but the mainly civilian staff responsible for these functions was not part of the emperor's field headquarters.

Meanwhile, Napoleon's opponent, the Duke of Wellington, had an adjutant-general who dealt with reports, correspondence, orders preparation, and discipline; his quartermaster-general was concerned with supply, transportation, and quartering. In addition, the duke employed five chiefs of special corps for cavalry, artillery, engineers, provost, and guides, and five heads of civilian departments for the commissariat, purveyors, storekeepers, surgeons, and paymasters.

The Prussian quartermaster-general was also responsible for quartering and a widening range of logistic support. There was, however, an important difference between the status of this appointment and its equivalent in the British army. The Prussians incorporated their quartermaster-general firmly within their General Staff—the tightly knit, cohesively organized, and smoothly functioning branch of their headquarters comprehensively responsible, under a single chief of staff, for all operational intelligence and for strategic, tactical, logistical, and administrative planning of operations. The *Generalstabs Officier* had to respond to all calls and emergencies across the complete range of operational staff duties. In short, as it was said at the time: "The General Staff is intended to convert the ideas of the General commanding into orders, not only conveying [orders] . . . to the troops [general staff officers also needed to be bold riders], but also working out all matters of detail, thus relieving the General from a great amount of trouble" (Schellendorf 1905).

In the British army, the quartermaster-general has never been part of the General Staff, but has always headed a separate military staff department reporting directly to a government minister but under the general coordination of the chief of the General Staff. Efforts were made in the latter part of the nineteenth century to correct this deficiency and indeed to introduce a proper General Staff, but these failed. It is not surprising, therefore, that, at the higher levels of British defense organization, logistics has tended to be viewed as a separate matter. The recent, partial introduction of a General Staff organization at lower, formation headquarters level in the British Army has helped to rectify the shortcoming, though no single chief of staff appointment in these headquarters is yet vested with universal responsibility for the direction and coordination of all operational planning on behalf of each formation commander.

Still more men and still more support were required when the railroad, telegraph, and telephone were invented and when new weapons, new surface and aerial vehicles, and other new battle equipments came into military use. Procuring, supplying, maintaining, and accounting for the impressive array of military materiel required much manpower and expertise, over and above the troops who used it all in battle. The framework for harnessing this manpower and equipment and for bringing the expertise together and to bear in war was provided by military organization. As armed forces developed over the centuries, a structure of units evolved. When standing forces were introduced, the difference between peace and war organization became even more important.

Organizational developments were slow and unenterprising in the British and French armies during the second half of the nineteenth century; this was certainly not the case as far as the Prussians were concerned. They introduced a series of significant structural and procedural improvements. By 1870, when the Franco-Prussian War started, the Prussian General Staff had fully earned its admirable reputation for meticulous planning and the efficient execution of its wide-ranging operational duties. It became a model for emulation and for export beyond the continent of Europe.

Prussian headquarters were divided into four parts at army, army corps, and divisional levels: the General Staff (which did all the operational planning), the Routine Staff or *Adjutantur* (which dealt with mainly administrative matters and the domestic running of the formation and its headquarters), the Intendance, and the Legal Departments. The Intendance included supply, transportation, quartering, medical, veterinary, and religious affairs. In addition, there were advisers for artillery, engineers, military police, and communications, which incorporated railways, postal facilities, and the telegraph. A registrar, directly responsible to the chief of staff, supervised the clerks and orderlies; seven to thirteen clerks were allowed in each army corps with a special dispensation for more in times of exceptional stress. The ratio of one general staff officer per approximately 5,000 troops deployed in the field was stringently economical, particularly as, at that time, the introduction of new weapons and communications must have significantly increased the amount of staff work.

The German general von Moltke the Elder had devoted part of his immense energy and expertise to training the General Staff effectively and to supervising the planning and execution of the smooth, rapid mobilization, concentration, movement, and deployment of more than a million German officers and soldiers ready for operations against the French in 1870. In contrast, the *Corps d'Etat-Major* seemed a conservative outfit, isolated from the bulk of the French Army and lacking in efficiency.

Moltke had an advantage: he was chief of the General Staff and he was virtually commander in chief as well. However, at each formation level, there was also a chief of staff who supervised, coordinated, and generally ran the headquarters, freeing his own commander from overinvolvement with detailed planning, specialist support, and matters of routine. The concept and the practice of collegiality between commander and chief of staff had already begun, but was never present to the same extent in any other Western army. The issue of whether the general staff or any other staff department worked for the commander or the chief of staff was academic, for any difficulties were resolved by personalities and by thorough training, rather than by any contrived organizational adjustment.

FROM WORLD WAR II TO TODAY

The next major modification to staff organization happened during World War II, when General Eisenhower and others set up a unified command in the field for a campaign of indefinite length. The supreme Allied commander's naval, land, and air force subordinates had two roles: they helped Eisenhower develop plans, and they were then individually responsible to him for executing their respective parts of those plans, from the time of operations in the Mediterranean onward. Eisenhower consciously and conscientiously built up his Allied headquarters' organization from the bottom upward to avoid congestion at the top. He clearly appreciated and openly recognized the importance of integrated staffs through which the modern commander absorbs information and exercises his authority. He produced a fully interlocked, smoothly working mechanism and proceeded from the organizational and procedural assumption that all members of his staff belonged to a single nation, even though they were multinational.

In the latter stages of the campaign in northwest Europe, criticisms were raised that headquarters had become too large, unwieldy, and detached from the action, but the experience was of great value to the structure, functioning, and development of current, multinational, interservice staffs. The experience gained promoted similar initiatives within NATO that unfortunately have never been as successful, probably because what Eisenhower and his colleagues aimed to do was infinitely easier to achieve in wartime than in peacetime.

Issues in Modern Military Organization

The reader can find more specific details about modern military organizations in the separate articles on army, air force, and navy organization (keeping in mind that there are thousands of different military organizations contained within the armed services of the more than 150 countries that maintain modern military forces). There are, however, some central issues—some almost truisms—that are worth mentioning at the conclusion of this article.

MATCHING ORGANIZATION TO REQUIREMENT

Since World War II, some nations and their armed forces have tried to reconcile the different and often conflicting requirements of both general or total war and limited or small wars. The United States and the United Kingdom have found it necessary to develop separate forces for the North Atlantic Treaty Organization (NATO) and for their operations in other areas. The Soviet Union discovered that Afghanistan posed different requirements than those planned for its Warsaw Pact forces. On the other hand, in the case of the Federal Republic of Germany and the People's Republic of China, for example, armed forces have been tasked and organized for a single commitment, the defense of their own countries in a general war setting.

PEOPLE MAKE THE DIFFERENCE

Given that a particular civilian enterprise or military organization is founded on a sound structure, why does it not function at least as well as some closely comparable equivalents? The answer in most cases is people. People make organizations work; they achieve the objectives set with the resources allotted them. Even casual observers may be able quite quickly to detect the basic difference between a really professional outfit and a far less professional counterpart. The two may be organized identically, but differences may stem from the caliber of people employed.

To the qualified military observer or inspector, the difference between two identically organized units, formations, or headquarters may also highlight variable standards of training, equipment, leadership, decision making, military judgment, experience, expertise, commitment, discipline, motivation, teamwork, comradeship, and morale. Furthermore, the units, formations, commanders, and headquarter staffs of different nations may be identically organized, yet their military bearing, behavior, capacity, and performance may markedly vary. Organizing allied forces in the same way will not produce similar results. The crucial part people play in the functioning of any military organization has been amply demonstrated in major wars and has been illustrated again in recent operations such as the 1991 Gulf War. The standardization of structure within allied forces is nevertheless of vital operational importance, for it helps forces "to fit together to fight together," and it gives them a common, familiar working basis for cooperation and training in peacetime.

The Relevance of Organizational Theory

Organizational theory (with its charts, diagrams, matrices, functional titles, job descriptions, and lines of reporting) is like a computer system, a tool to be used rather than an idol to be set up and worshiped. It is helpful as an aid but has to be kept in perspective: "Organisations do not consist of tidy lines on charts, but of men working together; and in the long run it is the personalities, skills and capacity for cooperation of the people that will produce efficient administration; not intellectually satisfying models that look good on paper" (Howard 1970).

Nevertheless, organizations can be complicated, bewildering interrelationships of functions, persons, and groups. Some way must be found to record the structure so that it can be understood, rationalized, and improved. Lessons must be learned so that, when a similar activity has to be organized from first principles, former mistakes and pitfalls are avoided. Therefore, some knowledge and application of organizational theory is important. The difficulty is that developing a military organization often relies more on personal idiosyncrasies, preconceived ideas, and the protection of vested interests than on clear, logical thought and precise calculation. The objective is to select a structure that maintains continuity and stability yet also dynamically pursues change when change is needed, gives scope for improvement, and facilitates cooperation with others.

To the theorist, another difficulty is that military forces like to be different. They like to be differently organized and their regiments like to wear and display different uniforms. They take some pride in doing things differently as a mark of their distinctiveness and prestige. They eagerly protect long-established traditions while striving to keep pace with technological and other changes. This perhaps partially explains why the organizational structures of the national components of NATO's so-called integrated operational commands have tended to become more dissimilar, rather than more similar, over time. This is despite the fact that they have faced basically the same perceived threat, in the same geographical area. Witness the protracted, failed endeavor to introduce a standard division with NATO, or the several unilaterally inspired experiments with unit and formation structures almost designed to obstruct allied integration and cooperation. Compare this with the structural standardization achieved within the now-defunct Warsaw Pact forces and the potential, important operational benefits that could have accrued. There are many pertinent lessons to be learned when new, future military organization is designed and constructed.

Lessons for the Future

One lesson is that an individual, a unit, a formation, a commander, a head-quarters, or a national force may have to sacrifice what is considered the best organization for one that is commonly acceptable and attainable. Another lesson is that when change is necessary, the military inclination to remain the same must be overcome. Sometimes a fundamental reorganization is needed, yet the day is put off by tinkering with a comparatively small part of the structure. Expedient compromise and the selective application of this form of "spare-parts surgery" may do a great deal more damage to the organization and its collective purpose in the long run than if a fundamental, thorough reorganization had been courageously and effectively pursued from the outset.

Yet another lesson in designing efficient organizations is to eliminate the tendency in many nations to protect the military superstructures while cutting tactical forces. Often, those who wield the knife on these occasions are part of the monolithic, very expensive, overlarge defense ministries, departments, or higher military headquarters that form part of the superstructure. Headquarters staffs sometimes lose sight of the fact that once the purpose of an activity is decided, most of the execution or accomplishment of that purpose is in the hands of the working organization. In the military context, this means that when reductions are necessary, the cuts should most often be made in strict priority: superstructures first and forces last. If the carefully considered and calculated disarmament process now underway leads to a decision to reduce forces by a certain percentage, this reduction should be at least counterbalanced in the reduction of national and multinational superstructures.

Those who design future military organizations will face unique challenges that are emerging with the approach of the 21st century. Weapons systems are becoming ever more capable, with expanding ranges, lethality, destructive power, and precision. The future warrior will be highly and expensively trained; skill and quality will likely continue to replace brawn and quantity. Fewer warriors will pit their systems and machines against opposing systems at lengthening distances. The organizations supporting these war machines will grow even more complex. Defining the requirements for future military forces and organizations may become increasingly difficult, due to imprecision in identifying the enemy and the threat. Driving all of this will be a world that changes more rapidly each year, and that becomes more and more integrated and interdependent as the revolution in information availability spreads and multiplies. To meet these challenges, military planners in the industrialized world will find themselves with dramatically reduced budgets as the tensions of the cold war dissipate. Both East and West have been reorganizing their military forces, and this trend will persist as the pace of change in politics and technology continues to quicken.

J. H. SKINNER

SEE ALSO: Organization, Air Force; Organization, Army; Organization, Naval.

Bibliography

Barnett, C. 1970. *Britain and her army: 1509–1970*. London: Allen Lane.

Dupuy, T. N. 1977. *A genius for war: The German army and general staff: 1807–1945*. Englewood Cliffs, N.J.: Prentice-Hall.

Eisenhower, D. D. 1949. *Crusade in Europe*. London: Heineman.

Foster, H. 1913. *Organisation: How armies are formed in war*. London: Rees.

Hittle, J. D. 1944. *The military staff: Its history and development*. Harrisburg, Penn.: Military Service Publishing.

Howard, M. E. 1970. *The central organisation of defence*. London: Royal United Services Institute for Defense Studies.

Janowitz, M. 1964. *Changing patterns of organisation: The new military*. Los Angeles: Russell Sage Foundation.

Schellendorf, B. von. 1905. *The duties of the general staff*. London: Her Majesty's Stationery Office.

ORGANIZATION, NAVAL

Countries establish navy organizations in order to perform prescribed military missions, usually related to the oceans, lakes, and waterways of the world. Navy organization can refer to how the service fits into the defense organization of the government, how the service is organized to perform its mission, or how navy units are organized to carry out their assigned tasks. This article addresses the subject from each of those three points of view.

Each navy of the world has its own unique relationship to the other armed forces of the country, and each also maintains its own special organization within units. Because all the world's navies cannot be included in detail here, those of the United States and the former Soviet Union have been selected to provide examples of different organizational structures.

Organization of the U.S. Navy

The U.S. Navy Within the U.S. Government

Two command lines extend from the U.S. president down to the individual units of the navy (which includes the U.S. Marine Corps). The first is the operational chain of command, within which all operations of units are controlled. Within this operational command, the navy's mission is specified by law: to be prepared to conduct prompt and sustained combat operations at sea. The second is the administrative chain of command, which is responsible for administrative functions such as training, maintenance and upkeep, overhaul, protocol and ceremonies, and a variety of inspections.

The operational chain of command (Fig. 1) extends from the U.S. National Command Authority (the president and the secretary of defense) through the Joint Chiefs of Staff and the Unified and Specified Commanders, to the Naval

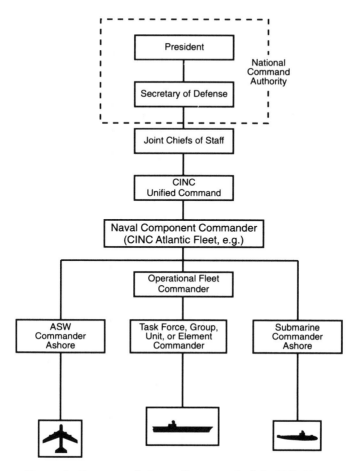

Figure 1. Operational chain of command of the U.S. Navy.

Component Commanders and the individual forces, groups, units, and elements.

Operationally, nearly all navy units fall under one of four geographically defined Unified Commanders in Chief (CINCs)—the commander in chief of the Atlantic, Pacific, European (while in the Mediterranean Sea), or Central (while in the Persian Gulf) command. Unified commands contain elements of all U.S. military services. Movement of a unit from one CINC's area to that of another requires a clearly defined change in operational control.

For administrative purposes a similar but separate chain of command is employed (Fig. 2). The unified commanders are not a part of this chain of command, but the secretary of the navy and the chief of naval operations (CNO) are in the chain of command that leads from the CNO through the fleet, type, group, squadron, and wing commander to the individual ships and aircraft.

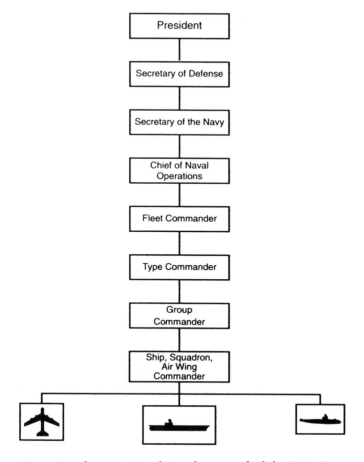

Figure 2. Administrative chain of command of the U.S. Navy.

The Internal Organization of the U.S. Navy

The U.S. Navy is also organized to carry out its three primary functions—sea control, power projection, and strategic sealift—along separate but interconnected operational and administrative lines. The U.S. Navy is divided, operationally and geographically, into four numbered fleets. In the Pacific Ocean area are the Third Fleet in the eastern Pacific and the Seventh Fleet in the western Pacific and the Indian Ocean. In the Atlantic Ocean area, the Second Fleet operates in the open Atlantic, and the Sixth Fleet in the Mediterranean Sea. The operational chain of command extends downward from the unified commander (CINCPAC for the Third and Seventh fleets, CINCLANT for the Second Fleet, and CINCEUR for the Sixth Fleet), then to task force, group, unit, or element commanders, and on to the ship, aircraft, or marine corps unit.

The administrative chain of command relies on type commanders to take care of training and administration for specific types of ships, aircraft, and other forces. Only CINCPAC and CINCLANT have type commanders assigned to them; the other area CINCs do not. Type commanders for the U.S. Pacific Fleet include: the Commanding General, Fleet Marine Force Pacific; Commander, Submarine Force, U.S. Pacific Fleet; Commander, Naval Logistics Command, Pacific Fleet; Commander, Naval Air Force, U.S. Pacific Fleet; Commander, Naval Surface Force, U.S. Pacific Fleet; and Commander, Training Command, U.S. Pacific Fleet.

INTERNAL ORGANIZATION OF U.S. NAVY UNITS

Depending on the kind of unit—air squadron or ship, for example—and the type—bomber or amphibious assault ship, for example—internal organization differs. In general, however, each unit has a commanding officer, executive officer, departments, and divisions. Exactly what departments and divisions are included in the organization depends on the kind and type of unit.

In some ways the internal organization mirrors the external organization—the commanding officer being responsible primarily for operational matters, and the executive officer bearing the brunt of the administrative duties. Ship and air organizations call for the execution of a variety of "bills" to regularize the activity of the crew. One example is the watch, quarter, and station bill, which details each man to a watch assignment and to battle and work stations.

Organization of the Soviet Navy

THE SOVIET NAVY WITHIN THE SOVIET GOVERNMENT

The Soviet organization was very different from that of the United States. Unlike the United States, which maintains the same organization in peace and war, the Soviet Union had separate organizations—or more accurately, evolving organizations—for wartime and peacetime. Figure 3 portrays the Soviet Navy high command organization.

This organization combined the operational and general administrative functions; with two exceptions—strategic aviation and airborne forces—operational and general administrative lines of control are identical. As a further indication of its pivotal position in the Soviet scheme, the general staff conducted the military planning for all the Soviet services, whereas in the United States that activity is performed at the level of the CINCs.

The Soviet Union maintained five military services: the strategic rocket forces, the national air defense troops, the ground forces, the air forces, and the navy. The Soviet equivalent of the U.S. Marine Corps, the Soviet Naval Infantry, was a small organization within the Soviet Navy.

The term *general administrative function* was employed above to distinguish it from *political administration*. The Soviet Navy was somewhat atypical in that it maintained yet another chain of command, that of political organization and administration. This chain of command had responsibility for political education, discipline and political reliability of the crew, and for agitation and propaganda activities. Soviet naval units had political officers, or *zampolits*, who had an independent chain of reporting for political matters. Despite Soviet efforts to maintain the principle of one-man command or sole command responsibility of the commanding officer, the very existence of the *zampolit*

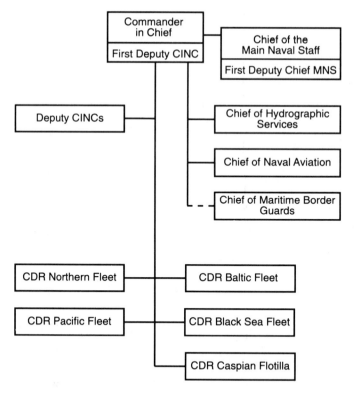

Figure 3. Soviet Navy high command organization. (SOURCE: U.S. Navy 1985)

brought into question the ability of the unit commander to execute the command requirements in an independent manner.

THE INTERNAL ORGANIZATION OF THE SOVIET NAVY

The Soviet Navy combined the operational and administrative functions in a high command with line organization under the commander in chief. The line organization included a main navy staff, five deputy commanders in chief, and separate chiefs for hydrographic services, naval aviation, and maritime border guards. The chief of the main naval staff was responsible for the day-to-day operational direction of the fleet. The deputy CINCs performed administrative, technical, logistic, and training functions. One of the deputies led the political directorate and provided the separate line of reporting for the political officers in the operational units. Beneath this "headquarters" level, the Soviet Navy was organized geographically into four fleets and one flotilla. The fleets, widely separated geographically, and thus disadvantaged by an inability to provide mutual support to one another, were the Red Banner Northern Fleet, the Twice-Honored Red Banner Baltic Fleet, the Red Banner Black Sea Fleet, and the Red Banner Pacific Ocean Fleet. Among the four fleets, the Pacific Fleet had the largest number of ships in its inventory. The single flotilla was the Red Banner Caspian Flotilla.

The various fleets were organized somewhat in a mirror image of the manner in which main headquarters was organized.

Under the commander of ship brigades, flotillas and *eskadras* (Soviet squadrons) were organized into *diviziya, brigada, divizions*, and *detachments*. Flotillas performed in-area functions, whereas *eskadras* were for operations out of area. Divisions constituted the main tactical formation of the same kind of ship of the second, third, or fourth rank.

Within the Soviet command structure were wartime commands called *theaters of military operations* (TVDs). Five of these TVDs were continental, four were intercontinental, and four were oceanic, coinciding with the four fleet areas: the Black, Baltic, Northern, and Pacific. In wartime the navy would conduct its operations within a TVD and under the operational command of a TVD commander. Direction for navy units, therefore, would emanate from the State Committee of Defense through the general staff, not from main navy headquarters.

INTERNAL ORGANIZATION OF SOVIET NAVY UNITS

The Soviet Navy classified its ships into four ranks. The first rank included the largest surface ships (air-capable ships and cruisers) and nuclear-powered submarines. The second rank comprised diesel submarines and large missile and antisubmarine warfare (ASW) ships and destroyers. In the third rank were minesweepers; small escort, patrol, and missile ships; and some amphibious warfare ships. The lowest rank contained boats such as torpedo boats, landing craft, and small minesweepers. The rank of the ship determined, inter alia, the seniority of the commanding officer and the level of logistic support the ship deserved.

Ships of the Soviet Navy were organized into seven primary departments: navigation, missile-gunnery, underwater weapons, surveillance-communications, engineering, aviation (where present), and command and control. There were also suborganizations for electronics, finance, supply-logistics, and chemical warfare. How the departments were organized depended, in part, on the ship's rank. Fourth-rank ships, for example, did not have departments, but the departmental functions were carried out by "teams."

The political officer, and subordinates if assigned, had a place in the organization outside the line departments and reported directly to the commander. The executive officer, the second in command, performed many of the same functions that the executive officer in the U.S. Navy carries out.

The organization of a Soviet ship to perform the various evolutions that might be required was established, like its U.S. counterpart, by the watch quarter and station bill. The *primary* control station was the location of the commanding officer during combat, from which weapons and sensors were controlled and damage-control operations were coordinated. Control stations were the locations of those who had responsibility to coordinate or direct actions of others.

Ships of the first, second, and third rank had primary control stations; fourth-rank ships had only control stations.

Concluding Observations

The ultimate test of a military organization is victory in battle. In peacetime the organization seeks to train forces so that they function most effectively should they be called upon to participate in combat. Historically, military organizations have demonstrated the complete range of effectiveness—from totally ineffective to highly effective. How armed forces are organized depends primarily on the political organization of the country and on its strategic culture. The purpose of this article has not been to evaluate the naval organizations of the United States and the Soviet Union; rather, it has been to describe those organizations from three points of view: how the service fits into the defense organization of the government, how the service is organized to perform its mission, and how units are organized to carry out their assigned tasks.

HIDEO SEKINO
SADAO SENO

Bibliography

U.S. Navy, Office of the Chief of Naval Operations. 1985. *Ship's organization and regulations manual.* OPNAV Instruction 3120.32 series. Philadelphia: Graceland Bros.

U.S. Navy, Office of the Chief of Naval Operations. 1985. *Understanding Soviet naval developments.* NAVSO P-3560. 5th ed. Washington, D.C.: Government Printing Office.

OTTOMAN EMPIRE

The Ottoman Empire existed for more than 600 years. At its greatest extent, the empire stretched from the Persian Gulf to Morocco, from Yemen to the outskirts of Vienna. As a European, as well as a Middle Eastern, power, the Ottoman Empire played a significant role in European military and diplomatic history from the midfourteenth century to the second decade of the twentieth century.

The Growth of the Ottoman Empire, 1290–1566

The Ottoman (Osmanli) Turks first appeared in historical records as a small, obscure Turkic clan. Fleeing from the Mongol conquest of Khwaresm, the Ottoman Turks found refuge in the emirate of Söğüt—in northwestern Anatolia—as vassals of the Seljuk Sultanate of Rum. At the Battle of Köse Dagh (1243), the Mongol Il-Khan of Persia defeated the Seljuks. Thereafter, the Seljuks and their vassals became tributaries of the Il-Khanate of Persia.

The Mongol victory at Köse Dagh precipitated the disintegration of the

Sultanate of Rum. Taking advantage of the breakdown of Seljuk authority, the emir of Sögüt, Osman (1290–1326)—in whose honor the Ottoman Turks named themselves—extended his authority northward over Brusa and Ephesus, at the expense of the Byzantine Empire.

Osman's successor, Orkhan (1326–62), added Pelekhanon, Nicaea, and Nicomedia to the Ottoman realm. The Ottomans first entered Europe in 1334, as allies of John Cantacuzene, a pretender to the Byzantine throne. The Turks entered Europe as Cantacuzene's ally again in 1352, against the Serbian king, Stephen Dushan. The Turks occupied Gallipoli in 1354 and began spreading out over Thrace.

EXPANSION INTO THE BALKANS

Ottoman expansionism followed a pattern of a westward thrust followed by an eastward thrust. Westward expansion took precedence over eastward expansion. As a result, the Turks were well entrenched in the Balkans long before they conquered eastern Anatolia, Syria, or Palestine.

The Turks took Adrianople in 1361, and the sultan, Murad I (1362–89), made it his capital in 1366. The primary objective of Murad's military expeditions was the conquest of Albania, Serbia, and Bosnia. Macedonia, Bulgaria, and the Byzantine emperor recognized Murad's overlordship in 1371, and Serbia submitted in 1386. However, in 1388, Bosnia, Serbia, and Bulgaria rebelled. After a series of rebel victories, Murad crushed a combined Bosnian and Serbian force at Kossovo (5 June 1389). Murad, however, was assassinated after the battle. In revenge, Bayazid, Murad's son and successor, executed Lazar of Serbia.

Bayazid I (1389–1402) continued his father's policy of expansion in the Balkans. In 1393, the Turks entered Bulgaria and, in April 1395, invaded Hungary. Bayazid crushed the Christian forces at Nicopolis on 25 September 1395.

Bayazid, having expanded Ottoman rule into Europe further than any of his predecessors, turned his attention to the conquest of eastern Anatolia. The sultan's actions in eastern Anatolia brought him into conflict with Tamerlane (Timur-i-lang), the most formidable conqueror since Genghis Khan. At the Battle of Ankara (28 July 1402), Tamerlane soundly defeated the Ottoman Turks and captured Bayazid. Confined in a cage, the once-proud sultan of the Ottoman Turks was put on display in town bazaars throughout Tamerlane's realm.

Bayazid's defeat and capture threw the Ottoman Empire into chaos, and ten years of civil war followed as his three sons fought each other for the throne. When Mohammed (Mehmed) I (1413–21) emerged victorious, the empire was on the verge of disintegration. Mohammed was able to reassert control over Anatolia by 1414 and, in 1417, was strong enough to commence military operations in Wallachia.

Sultan Murad II (1421–51) attempted to conquer Constantinople in 1424, without success. The sultan then renewed operations in the Balkans. He annexed Serbia in 1439 and besieged Belgrade in 1440. Turkish operations in Transylvania, however, were not successful. The Transylvanians and Hungarians, commanded by Janos Hunyadi, fought the Turks to a standstill. At Zlatica (1443), a Polish and Hungarian force defeated the Turks and retook Nish and Sofia. The Truce of Adrianople (2 June 1444) temporarily ended the fighting. The truce was soon broken by the "Varna Crusade" (mostly Hungarians and Wallachians), but on 10 November 1444, the Turks decisively defeated the crusaders. At the Second Battle of Kossovo (1448), the sultan defeated Hunyadi.

MOHAMMED (MEHMED) II, THE CONQUEROR, 1451–81

Mohammed II is best known in the West for the conquest of Constantinople. Mohammed, however, was more than a conqueror; he was an administrative reformer and a statesman.

Mohammed reorganized the political structure of the Ottoman Empire, rationalizing the slipshod, jury-rigged administration of his polyglot empire. To administer the empire, Mohammed selected the brightest youths from the *devshirme*—a tribute consisting of young boys from the sultan's Christian subjects imposed every five years—and trained them in the Palace School. Palace School graduates were appointed to civilian and military posts throughout the empire. Together with the *janissaries*, who were also recruited from the *devshirme*, these administrators formed the *askeri* (soldier) class, the civil and military elite of the Ottoman Empire.

The conquest of Constantinople. Shortly after he became sultan, Mohammed began planning the conquest of Constantinople. The city was nearly all that remained of the once mighty Eastern Roman (Byzantine) Empire. Anatolia, Thrace, and most of the Balkans were already under Turkish rule. Morea (southern Greece), the Dalmatian Coast, and the Greek Isles were controlled by Venice. Though politically insignificant, Constantinople remained of great symbolic value to both Christian and Turk.

After two years of preparation, Mohammed launched his attack on 6 April 1453. For 50 days, Turkish artillery battered the walls of Constantinople, while assault after assault failed. On 29 May the Turks successfully stormed the Romanos Gate, and the city fell. Constantinople secured, Mohammed rebuilt the city and made it the capital of the Ottoman Empire. A tolerant and farsighted statesman, Mohammed incorporated the leaders of the Latin Church, the Greek Church, and the Jewish community into the administrative apparatus of the state.

Operations in the Balkans. Between 1455 and 1459, Mohammed conducted operations against the Serbians. The Turks besieged Belgrade in 1456 but the intervention of Hunyadi prevented the capture of the Serbian capital. In the southern Balkans, the Turks were more successful, and by 1460, Morea was under Ottoman control.

The Turkish-Venetian War, 1463–79. The Turkish occupation of Morea directly challenged Venice, then the dominant seapower in the eastern Mediterranean. To meet the Venetian threat, the Turks developed their own naval capability. Although a Venetian-Papal fleet burned Smyrna in 1472 and threatened the Dardanelles, by the late 1470s, the Turks were winning the war at sea as well as on land. In 1477 the Turks raided the environs of Venice itself. In 1478 Kroia, Alessia, and Drivasto fell to the Turks. When the war ended in 1479, the Ottoman Empire was the dominant seapower in the eastern Mediterranean. The Second Turkish-Venetian War (1499–1503) resulted in the destruction of the Venetian fleet and the reduction of the Venetian trading empire to a few small islands.

THE CONQUEST OF EGYPT, 1516–17

When Mohammed II died, the Ottoman Empire was the strongest Muslim state in the Middle East. During the reigns of Bayazid II (1481–1512) and Selim I the Grim (1512–20), the Turks came into conflict with two neighboring Muslim states: Egypt under the Mamelukes and Persia under the Saffirid Dynasty. The First Turkish-Egyptian War, fought over control of the Kingdom of Cilicia, lasted seven years and was inconclusive. The Second Turkish-Egyptian War ended in the destruction of the Mameluke state and the incorporation of Egypt into the Ottoman Empire.

The Persian War, 1514–15. The Persians, under the fanatical Shiite, Shah Ismail—first of the Saffirid Dynasty—were a threat to the Orthodox Sunni Muslim states of Central Asia as well as to the Ottomans. Selim I declared war on Persia in 1514, on the grounds that the Persians had been fomenting rebellion among the Taurus Mountain tribes. On 23 August 1514, at Chaldiran, Turkish cannon and firearms prevailed over Persian cavalry. By 1515, eastern Anatolia had been pacified and Kurdistan had been annexed.

The Egyptian War, 1516–17. Turkish victory in the Persian War brought the Turks again into conflict with Persia's ally, Egypt. At the Battle of Marj Dabik (24 August 1516), the Turks defeated the Mamelukes and killed Kansu, the Mameluke sultan. Following their victory, the Turks received the submission of Aleppo and Damascus. When Tuman Bey, the new Mameluke sultan, refused to recognize Ottoman suzerainty, the war was renewed. On 22 January 1517, the Turks occupied Cairo. Tuman Bey was executed, and a Turkish governor-general was appointed to administer Egypt. Soon after his conquest of Egypt, Selim I received the submission of Medina, Mecca, and the Arab tribes.

SULEIMAN I (THE MAGNIFICENT), 1520–66

With Syria, Palestine, and Egypt under Ottoman rule, the sultan's attention once again turned northward, toward the Balkans and south-central Europe. In 1521, Suleiman I occupied Belgrade and prepared to invade Hungary.

Operations in Hungary. Suleiman invaded Hungary in 1526. At the First Battle of Mohacs, 29–30 August 1526, the Hungarians were routed and their king, Louis, slain. With Louis dead, two claimants to the Hungarian throne appeared: Ferdinand of Hapsburg, younger brother of Charles V, Holy Roman emperor (and king of Spain, under the designation Charles I); and John Zapolya, prince of Transylvania. Defeated by the Hapsburgs, Zapolya appealed to Suleiman for aid. In 1528, the Turks entered Hungary as allies of King John I Zapolya. From 26 September to 16 October 1526, the Turks besieged Vienna. Inclement weather, however, prevented them from properly deploying their artillery. Reluctantly, the sultan ordered their withdrawal, and in 1533, the Turks and Hapsburgs agreed to a truce. Hungary was divided unevenly between Zapolya and Ferdinand. For the small strip of Hungary awarded him, Ferdinand was required to pay annual tribute to Suleiman.

The Turkish-Venetian War, 1537–40. In March 1536 Francis I, king of France, and Sultan Suleiman I entered into a secret alliance against their common enemy, the Hapsburgs. In 1537, war again broke out between the Turks and the Venetians. The following year, the Papal States, Venice, and Charles V entered into an anti-Turkish alliance, the Holy League. Following the Turkish naval victory at Prevesa (1540), Venice sued for peace. The Turks received Nauplion and a large indemnity from Venice in exchange for peace.

Operations in Hungary. King John I Zapolya died in 1540, whereupon Ferdinand invaded Hungary. Suleiman supported the claim of Zapolya's son, John Sigismund, to the Hungarian throne. By 1541, Hungary was under effective Turkish control, and both sides agreed to another truce in 1547.

Sultan Suleiman spent 1548 fighting the Persians. In 1551, however, the sultan was again at war with Ferdinand of Hapsburg. This round ended with a truce and a return to the *status quo ante*.

The conquest of Mesopotamia. The Persian capture of Erzurum in 1552 precipitated another Turkish-Persian war. During the fighting, the Turks conquered Mesopotamia. After peace was negotiated in 1555, the Ottoman Empire retained possession of Mesopotamia.

The Ottoman Military Machine

The early Ottoman army, in common with most other Turco-Mongolian armies, was composed almost exclusively of cavalry. In exchange for a grant of land (*timar*), the landholder provided a fixed number of cavalrymen (*sipahi*) under his own command. When mobilized, the *sipahi* marshaled under the overall command of their provincial governor (*sanjak-bey*).

Infantry units were gradually incorporated into the Ottoman forces. At first, infantry was made up of provincial irregulars or vassal contingents. During the reign of Murad I, a regular, standing infantry corps was established, the *janissaries*.

THE JANISSARY CORPS

The *janissaries* were originally recruited from among Christian captives. By the reign of Mohammed I, recruits were drawn from the *devshirme*. *Janissary* recruits were trained in both the profession of arms and Islam. Though technically slave-soldiers, the *janissaries* enjoyed many privileges, but were not allowed to marry until after retirement.

The janissaries soon became the elite unit of the Ottoman army. The size of the corps grew from approximately 12,000 men during the reign of Mohammed the Conqueror to 40,000 men during the reign of Suleiman the Magnificent. Initially organized as foot archers, the janissaries were later armed with firearms.

ARTILLERY

The Ottoman Turks adopted both firearms and cannon from Western Europe. During the siege of Constantinople in 1453, the Turks used cannon cast by a Hungarian, Urban, and serviced, in part, by Italian mercenaries. The Turks used firearms and cannon to advantage against the Persians and the Mamelukes, as well as against European armies.

NAVAL FORCES

The Turkish navy was late to develop. Although the Turks had used flotillas of small craft as early as the reign of Murad I, it was not until the war with Venice (1463–79) that the Turks developed a navy strong enough to defeat the Venetian fleet. While Bayazid II and Selim I were involved in wars with Persia and Egypt, however, the Turkish navy languished. When Suleiman I intervened on the behalf of John Zapolya, the Turks faced not only the army of the Austrian Hapsburgs, but also the naval might of Hapsburg Spain.

The creation of Suleiman's new Ottoman navy was the work of Khair-ed-Din, "Barbarossa" (1478–1546). Born Khizr, the fourth son of a retired *janissary*, Khair-ed-Din joined his older brother, Aruj (the original Barbarossa), in the life of a corsair. Between 1504 and 1512, the Barbarossa brothers were based in Tunis. In 1516, Aruj became the *beylerbey* (ruler) of Algiers. When Aruj was killed in a battle with the Spaniards, Khair-ed-Din succeeded him as beylerbey.

From 1519 to 1533, Khair-ed-Din Barbarossa raided the lands of the Hapsburgs in Spain and Italy. So successful was the beylerbey of Algiers that, in August 1533, Suleiman I summoned him to Constantinople. The sultan charged Barbarossa with the reorganization of the Ottoman navy. Barbarossa's first task was to reorganize the Turkish shipyards and construct 61 new galleys.

In summer 1534 Barbarossa took part of his new fleet and raided the Kingdom of Naples. Italy was again subjected to massive Turkish raids between 1537 and 1540. During this period, Barbarossa and Andrea Doria, the celebrated admiral of Charles V, met at Prevesa. Barbarossa had 150 galleys under his command. Andrea Doria had 246 ships, including 50 galleons. Despite Doria's superiority in ships and firepower, Barbarossa outgeneraled and outsailed his adversary. Andrea Doria decided to withdraw rather than fight. Although the Christian forces had lost only seven galleys, the Venetians sued for peace.

In spring 1543 Barbarossa, the high admiral of the Ottoman navy, again raided southern Italy, with a fleet of 100 galleys. Barbarossa planned to inflict as much damage as possible on the Hapsburg lands in Italy. That summer, the Turkish fleet anchored in Toulon and, with the cooperation of his French allies, Barbarossa laid siege to Nice. After the surrender of Nice, the Turks returned to Toulon, while the French sacked and burned the city. Toward the end of summer, Barbarossa sent a flotilla to raid the coast of Catalonia.

The successes of Barbarossa and the Ottoman fleet in the central and western Mediterranean, and the success of the Ottoman army in Hungary, sent tremors of fear throughout Christian Europe.

The Decline of the Ottoman Empire

The reign of Suleiman the Magnificent was the golden age of the Ottoman Empire. The eastern Mediterranean was a Turkish lake, and, with the north African coast in Turkish hands, the Ottoman navy raided Hapsburg possessions at will. The Ottoman Empire was not only a great power, it was perhaps the greatest power of the sixteenth century. Yet, within 100 years of the death of Suleiman I, the empire was in decline.

The decline was gradual. Turkish forces, dominant in the midsixteenth century, suffered numerous reverses with only an occasional victory, from the midseventeenth century on.

MILITARY DECLINE

Under the first ten sultans, the Ottoman Turks had been an aggressive military power, open to technological innovation and improvement. The janissaries, the elite of the Ottoman army, dominated the battlefield. Turkish generals were the equal of the best Austrian, Spanish, and French field commanders. The sultan himself commanded his armies in the field.

By 1650 Turkish weapons were outmoded. Within the janissary corps, corruption and nepotism were rife. Instead of seeking battle, the janissaries sought comfort, wealth, and political influence. Not only did they occasionally make and unmake sultans, they also blocked all attempts to reform and modernize the army. At the very time that Austrian and Russian military strength increased, Turkish military strength declined.

MILITARY DEFEATS

The latter half of the seventeenth century was when the gradual Turkish retreat from the Balkans began. From 1682 to 1699, the Turks were at war with Austria and Poland. The failure of the Second Siege of Vienna (17 July–12 September 1683) was the first in a series of Ottoman defeats, broken only by the reoccupation of Belgrade in 1690. The Treaty of Karlowitz (26 January 1699) awarded Hungary, Transylvania, Croatia, and Slovenia to Austria; Podolia to Poland; Azov to Russia; and Morea and Dalmatia to Venice.

During the eighteenth century, the empire lost Little Wallachia, the Banat of Temesvar, Crimea, and northern Bosnia. The early nineteenth century was marked by increasing agitation for independence in Serbia, Wallachia, and Moldavia. Between 1821 and 1830, the Greeks of Morea fought for and won their independence. In 1832 Mohammed Ali Pasha, governor of Egypt, rebelled against the sultan. The success of the Egyptian forces further underscored the declining state of the Ottoman military.

MILITARY REFORMS

Faced with the constant threat of rebellion from within, and the constant threat of Austrian and Russian aggression, the Ottoman government attempted to reform and modernize its army. Previous attempts at military reform during the reign of Selim III (1789–1807) had been blocked by conservative factions within the government and by the janissaries. In 1826, Mahmud II (1808–39) disbanded both the janissary corps and the sipahi units and ordered the organization of a new army. In the 1830s, a Prussian military mission was active in Turkey, and, as a result, the new Turkish army had a definite Prussian look.

The Fall of the Ottoman Empire

The Ottoman Empire, on the verge of dissolution in 1833, enjoyed a brief period of renewed vigor. The outbreak of war with Russia in October 1853 found the Turks allied with the British and French in the Crimean War. At the Congress of Paris (25 February–30 March 1856) the Turks were accepted as members of the "Concert of Europe." On 15 April 1856, Great Britain, France, and Austria signed a treaty guaranteeing Turkish sovereignty. From 1856 to 1877, the empire enjoyed more than twenty years of relative tranquility.

THE YOUNG TURKS

In 1877 the Ottoman Empire was once again at war with Russia. The war ended with Serbia, Montenegro, and Romania independent. In 1881, France seized Tunis, and in 1882, Britain occupied Egypt. During the last decades of the nineteenth century, rebellions flared up in Crete and Armenia. In the Balkans, the various ethnic groups fought each other when not fighting the Turks.

In 1896, company- and field-grade officers stationed in Macedonia formed a secret political organization, the Young Turks. The majority of these officers had been trained in foreign military schools or the Turkish military schools established in the 1870s with Prussian help. In 1906, officers of the Third Army, including Enver Pasha, staged a coup, which failed. On 5 July 1908, the Young Turks mounted another coup, which was successful. The Young Turks restored the Constitution of 1876 and called parliament. The reactionary sultan, Abdul Hamid, was later deposed, and his brother Mohammed V enthroned (1910).

The establishment of parliamentary government, and the attempted reform of the empire, proved futile. In 1908, Bulgaria declared itself independent. Rebellion in Albania, and Serbian and Bulgarian victories during the First Balkan War (1912), removed the last Balkan province from Turkish control. Mounting fears of Russia, the pro-German attitude of Enver Pasha, and the need for a European ally drove the Young Turks closer to Germany. On 2 August 1914 Germany and the Ottoman Empire signed a secret military alliance. By 4 November 1914 the Turks were once again at war.

WORLD WAR I

During the First World War, the Turks again proved their fighting prowess. At Gallipoli, Turkish tenacity and bravery won the day. In 1916, Turkish arms also proved victorious against the British in Mesopotamia. Despite the bravery of the Turkish soldier, however, Turkish forces were everywhere in retreat by early 1917. By 4 October 1918, the Turkish army was finished.

The Treaty of Sèvres (20 August 1919) was a humiliation for the Turks. The British, in effect, controlled Constantinople and the government. A large portion of eastern Anatolia had been incorporated into the Armenian Republic, and Greek troops occupied Smyrna and threatened all of western Anatolia, with the blessings of the British government. General Mustafa Kemal, the hero of Gallipoli, broke with the Ottoman government and established a rival (Nationalist) government at Ankara. The Nationalists, led by Mustafa Kemal (Atatürk), eventually united the Turkish nation, drove out the Greek occupation forces, and won a revised peace treaty from the allies (Treaty of Lausanne, 1923). On 1 November 1922, the sultanate was abolished, and with it, the Ottoman Empire.

LAWRENCE D. HIGGINS

SEE ALSO: Byzantine Empire; Eugene, Prince of Savoy-Carignan; Genghis Khan; History, Early Modern Military; Kemal, Mustafa (Atatürk); Moghul Empire; Mongol Conquests; Peter the Great; Russia, Expansion of; Spanish Empire; Turkic Empire; World War I.

Bibliography

Barber, N. 1973. *The sultans.* New York: Simon and Schuster.

Bradford, E. 1968. *The sultan's admiral: The life of Barbarossa.* New York: Harcourt, Brace and World.

Coles, P. 1968. *The Ottoman impact on Europe.* London: Thames and Hudson.

Davison, R. H. 1968. *Turkey.* Englewood Cliffs, N.J.: Prentice-Hall.

Langer, W. L., and K. R. Blake. 1932. The rise of the Ottoman Turks and its historical background. *American Historical Review* 37:468–505.

Riggs, C. T., trans. 1954. *Kritovoulos: History of Mehmed the Conqueror.* Princeton, N.J.: Princeton Univ. Press.

Merriman, R. B. 1944. *Suleiman the Magnificent.* Cambridge, Mass.: Harvard Univ. Press.

Miller, B. 1941. *The Palace School of Mohammed the Conqueror.* Cambridge, Mass.: Harvard Univ. Press.

Rustow, D. A. 1959. The army and the founding of the Turkish Republic. *World Politics* 11:513–52.

Shaw, S. J. 1965. The origins of Ottoman military reform. *Journal of Modern History* 37:291–306.

Vucinich, W. S. 1965. *The Ottoman Empire.* Princeton, N.J.: Princeton Univ. Press.

Wittek, P. 1938. *The rise of the Ottoman Empire.* London: Royal Asiatic Society.

P

PANAMA, U.S. INVASION OF

On 20 December 1989, the United States launched Operation Just Cause and sent its military forces into combat in Panama against forces of Gen. Manuel Antonio Noriega Moreno. The use of American troops in Panama represented a failure of U.S. diplomacy and climaxed years of steadily deteriorating relations between Presidents Ronald Reagan and George Bush and General Noriega. In the two years preceding the U.S. invasion, Noriega had survived two coup attempts, a lost election, and U.S.-imposed economic sanctions.

In addressing the American public, President Bush said he had ordered Just Cause to protect the 35,000 Americans in Panama; to restore democracy in Panama; and to bring Noriega to trial in the United States on drug trafficking charges. It was explained that the operation was premised on rights afforded the United States under the terms of the Panama Canal treaties of 1977.

At the time it was conducted, Operation Just Cause was the largest American military operation since the Vietnam War (the U.S.-led coalition against Saddam Hussein, Operation Desert Storm in 1991, now has that distinction). It successfully removed Noriega from power (although he evaded capture, Noriega surrendered to U.S. forces on 3 January 1990), neutralized his military forces, drew overwhelming approval of the Panamanian and American people, and saw the installation of a new Panamanian government.

Background: Noriega Takes Control

The year 1968 is a watershed in Panamanian political history. In that year, the National Guard staged a coup and established an enduring pattern of direct and indirect military control of the government. Despite the subsequent construction of a democratic facade in the late 1970s, de facto control of the nation's policies in 1988 remained firmly in the hands of the commander of the National Guard's successor organization, the Panama Defense Forces (Fuerzas de Defensa da Panamá, FDP) which was created in 1983. (The terms *Panama Defense Forces* and *FDP* are used interchangeably throughout this article.)

The coup also represented a major turning point in Panamanian history because it brought to power Brig. Gen. Omar Torrijos Herrera, a charismatic leader who radically altered Panamanian politics. (It was during this time that the National Guard became the dominant political institution in the country.) In 1978, Torrijos stepped down as head of the government in favor of Aristides Royo who was chosen by the legislature to serve a six-year term as president. Torrijos remained, however, as commander of the National Guard and, as such, the holder of real power in Panama. His death in a July 1981 airplane crash gave rise to a power struggle in Panama that was filled by a succession of figurehead presidents controlled by a series of National Guard and FDP commanders who engaged in fierce internal maneuvering.

General Noriega, former head of military intelligence in Panama, assumed control of the National Guard in 1983 and launched a successful effort to consolidate his power. He oversaw the transformation of the National Guard from a small paramilitary organization into a much larger and more capable organization (the FDP), ostensibly capable of defending Panama's national territory and assisting the United States in defending the Panama Canal. Because of the strong U.S. vested interest in the security of the Panama canal, this transformation was accomplished with extensive U.S. training, equipment, and financial assistance.

It is ironic that the growing size and strength of the Panama Defense Forces, which were fostered in accordance with U.S. strategic interests, led to a situation that the United States increasingly regarded as inimical to its own interests, as well as those of the Panamanian people. The FDP, which had traditionally exhibited strong institutional cohesiveness and loyalty to its commander, increasingly became a formidable power base for enhancing and institutionalizing political control by the FDP commander.

The Crisis: A Chronology of Events

The crisis between the United States and Panama that culminated in Operation Just Cause began in June 1987. At that time, the former chief of staff of the FDP, Colonel Diaz-Herrera, who had been forced to retire, publicly charged that Noriega had personally ordered the execution of Dr. Hugo Spadafora, a vociferous Noriega critic. Spadafora was purported to have hard evidence of Noriega's involvement in drug trafficking and money laundering for the drug cartels. The allegation set off public protests in Panama against Noriega and the emergence of the National Civic Crusade (Cruzada Civilista Nacional, CCN), an organization in opposition to Noriega. Thousands of Panamanians participated in marches and street demonstrations to demand Noriega's resignation. Noriega and the FDP responded harshly, and there were credible reports of widespread police brutality.

These events led to direct U.S. involvement. On 26 June 1987, the U.S. Senate passed a resolution calling for a transition to genuine democracy in Panama. The Panamanian government responded by organizing a demonstration against the U.S. embassy and arresting U.S. diplomatic and military personnel. As a consequence, the United States suspended all military and economic assistance to Panama. By the end of 1987, the U.S. government apparently decided that Noriega was expendable and that serious efforts should be made to force him from power. U.S. Assistant Secretary of Defense Richard Armitage headed an end-of-the-year effort to draw up a plan for Noriega's departure from Panama. Noriega denounced the plan in January 1988.

The following month, Noriega, nominally the head of the FDP but in fact the actual leader of Panama, was indicted by a U.S. grand jury for narcotics trafficking and money laundering. This began a series of public statements and posturing both in the United States and Panama by President Reagan, U.S. Congressmen, and Noriega. On 25 February, Panamanian President Eric Arturo Delvalle Henríquez announced that he was replacing Noriega as the leader of the Panamanian Defense Force. Within hours of this announcement, the Panama General Assembly met and deposed Delvalle and installed a Noriega crony, Manuel Solís-Palma, as president. The United States announced that it did not recognize Solís-Palma; it supported Delvalle in his efforts to restore "democratic government and civilian constitutional order."

On 1 March, President Delvalle issued a proclamation that directed all payments to the government of Panama be made directly to the Delvalle government. In implementing this action, the Panamanian ambassador to the United States directed U.S. banks not to release Panamanian government funds and to freeze Panamanian accounts. In addition, Delvalle requested that payments under the Panama Canal Treaty be paid into an escrow account in the United States.

On 11 March, President Reagan announced suspension of trade preferences to Panama, the placing in escrow of those funds due to Panama that could be obligations to the government of Panama, and that certain payments due from the Panama Canal Commission would be placed in escrow. President Reagan also directed U.S. government agencies to increase their efforts against drug trafficking and money laundering in Panama.

Presidents Delvalle's and Reagan's actions resulted in economic paralysis and a series of strikes, supported by the CCN, and protests in Panama. In mid-March, a coup led by FDP officers was easily put down by Noriega. He also responded with violence to the strikes and, in reaction to the growing public and internal FDP opposition, declared a state of emergency and began to take over all economic sectors and government functions. In April, President Reagan declared a state of emergency, announced further restrictions of funds transfers to Panama, and instructed U.S. businesses to pay all funds due the government of Panama into escrow accounts.

These measures, according to Eliot Abrams, assistant secretary of state for inter-American affairs, had Noriega "hanging on by his fingertips." Noriega, however, countered them by "creative financing" which included the use of his own money, presumably drug money, to pay the FDP. He also took advantage of the situation by buying out or buying controlling interests in legitimate businesses that were in financial straits.

The U.S. economic sanctions prompted allies to help Noriega. Libya, for example, provided US$24 million to Noriega; 22 Latin American countries condemned the U.S. sanctions. Mexico offered oil to Panama under very favorable credit terms.

The United States began secret negotiations with Noriega in April 1988. The most important issue in these negotiations was the dropping of the drug indictments against Noriega. But when the negotiations became public, there was an outcry in the United States. The negotiations collapsed in May when Noriega refused to meet U.S. deadlines.

At this point, the situation in Panama threatened to become a factor in the 1988 U.S. presidential election because of the lack of agreement within the administration over the objective of U.S. policy and the ways and means to achieve it. Disagreements on the involvement of U.S. military forces in Panama between the Departments of State and Defense were the sharpest. Also, despite having knowledge of many of Noriega's illegal activities, the Central Intelligence Agency continued to support Noriega because of his intelligence work for the agency, as well as his support of the contras. The Drug Enforcement Agency also supported Noriega because of his antidrug work for them.

By mid-summer of 1988, the Reagan administration had made the Panama crisis a "nonissue"—it successfully removed Noriega and Panama from the public agenda by refusing to grant interviews to the media on the subject. The media quickly moved on to other issues. Without pressure from the United States, Noriega was able to resolve many of his short-term problems and assumed increased control over the country.

After the U.S. presidential election, it was determined that the May 1989 election in Panama was the best time to attack Noriega. U.S. officials expected the election to be fraudulent and that they would be able to expose it as such. Thus, Noriega would lose support of the poor and labor classes, the mainstay of the FDP's support. Once this support was gone, it was expected that Noriega would be removed from office.

As expected, the election went almost three to one against Noriega, but he annulled the election and appointed one of his cronies to serve as president. The election process involved violent attacks, witnessed by the world via television, on the opposition candidates. The United States recalled its ambassador to Panama and sent additional U.S. military forces to Panama.

In order to create international regional pressure on Noriega to step down from power, the United States turned to the Organization of American States (OAS). These negotiations, however, were a failure. Noriega had no intention of giving up power, and the OAS did not pursue the negotiations in a determined manner.

By the summer of 1989, the crisis in Panama was at a stalemate. U.S. economic sanctions and OAS negotiations continued but very little was expected of either. The United States hoped that internal opposition within the FDP would remove Noriega from office. Accordingly, U.S. officials continued to carefully distinguish between U.S. opposition to Noriega and support of the Panamanian Defense Forces as an institution.

In October 1989, the U.S. support of the FDP came to fruition in a coup led by a faction of the FDP. It was, however, a bungled attempt, and the violent reaction by Noriega created extreme criticism of President Bush. The United States then moved to a more covert plan of support for the opposition and a coup by FDP officers, but the plan became public and was terminated. By November 1989, it appeared that there were no options to effect the removal of Noriega from power except the use of U.S. military force.

U.S. Military Operations

On 20 December 1989, the United States, reacting to a declaration of war by Noriega, the killing of a U.S. serviceman, and the beating and harassment of another serviceman and his wife, invaded Panama in Operation Just Cause.

The Panamanian Defense Forces encompassed about 5,000 soldiers, with 8,000 paramilitary forces organized into "Dignity Battalions." However, once combat operations began, discipline of some of the Panamanian troops disintegrated and they offered little organized resistance to U.S. military forces.

Confronting the Panamanian forces were 13,000 U.S. forces, either permanently stationed in Panama or undergoing training at a jungle warfare school near Colón. These forces were reinforced by 9,500 soldiers that included a brigade from the 82d Airborne Division, three Ranger battalions, a battalion from the 7th Infantry Division (Light), and the 16th Military Police Brigade. U.S. special operations forces (SOF) participating in Just Cause consisted of Army Special Forces, aviators from Task Force 160, and Navy SEALS (Sea-Air-Landed forces).

In conducting their operations, U.S. military forces divided Panama into three areas of combat that were assigned to four task forces designated Red and Bayonet (which endured the heaviest fighting), Atlantic, and Semper Fidelis. The most severe action centered on Noriega's headquarters at the "Commandancia" in downtown Panama City. Additional heavy skirmishes occurred outside Fort Amador and at Rio Hato in western Panama (Fig. 1).

From the early morning hours of 20 to 24 December, the U.S. SOF conducted more than 40 operations across Panama aimed at capturing Noriega but failed in each attempt. At most target sites, the SOF found nothing. At others, they were told that Noriega had left minutes earlier. On 3 January 1990, Noriega surrendered to U.S. forces, thus bringing Operation Just Cause essentially to a close.

The operation was a military success that resulted in destruction of the FDP, establishment of a new democratic government, and overwhelming approval of the Panamanian and American people. In removing Noriega from power, U.S. military forces discovered more than 52,000 weapons including guns and ammunition of Russian, Chinese, Czechoslovak, Israeli, Belgian, and American manufacture, as well as armored personnel carriers, and rocket launchers.

Assessment

As a military operation, Just Cause was a success. It marked a watershed in modern warfare by demonstrating that the mixing of conventional forces with SOF was not only possible but enhanced the overall success of the operation. Furthermore, it showed that, with proper training and equipment, highly effective night operations are possible and even preferable in many cases to day

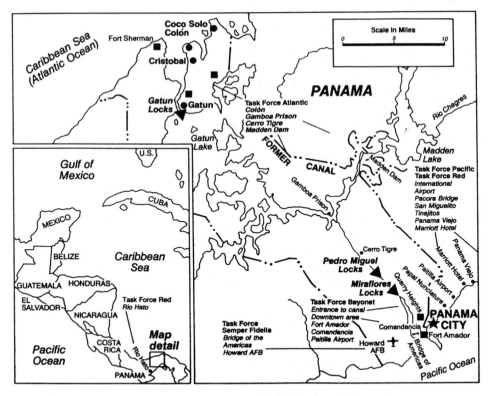

Figure 1. Operation Just Cause: U.S. military forces task force designation.

operations. Operation Just Cause proved that obedience to the often repeated but sometimes ignored principles of war—surprise, unity of command, and the offensive—pave the way for success in battle.

U.S. armed forces planned and executed a complex operation in pursuit of ambitious goals. Detailed planning, strict adherence to those plans, a short chain of command, and a long-term presence of in-country U.S. military forces with an intimate knowledge of most of the targeted assault sites were significant factors in the success of the operation.

Operation Just Cause was primarily an army show, but the U.S. Air Force made it possible for airborne, light infantry soldiers, and rangers to deploy from four U.S. bases and hit 27 targets simultaneously at H-hour, linking up with troops already in Panama. Although a military success, Operation Just Cause, as with any military operation, was not flawless. The most significant problems encountered were: the failure to capture Noriega as planned; a miscalculation of the tenacity of the Panamanian defenders (a similar shortcoming regarding Cuban defenders was experienced in the 1983 military action in Grenada); U.S. casualties from friendly fire; the failure to anticipate the widespread looting by Panamanian forces and the civilian population; the failure to drop a dozen planeloads of paratroopers at their designated drop zone; and the unsatisfactory results of the Stealth fighter's (F-117A) first combat mission (the mission was marred by pilot error resulting in a critical target being missed by hundreds of yards).

Overall casualties and equipment losses were small in comparison with the thousands of troops and hundreds of aircraft involved. Twenty-three U.S. soldiers and three American civilians died and another 324 were wounded. At least 314 Panamanians died defending Noriega and approximately 157 were wounded. It is estimated that the U.S. invasion also cost the lives of at least 202 Panamanian civilians and an uncounted number of wounded.

Incorporating lessons learned from Vietnam and Grenada, Operation Just Cause reflected the changing nature of U.S. military forces in a post–cold war world as they shift their focus from Central Europe to regional hot spots. The operation revealed capabilities that U.S. military forces will need in evolving world events, foreshadowed the equally impressive American victory in Operation Desert Storm, and demonstrated U.S. resolve to protect its citizens and its strategic interests. Noriega was placed in competent legal hands, and the Panama Defense Forces were shattered. With the FDP gone, Panama became a country in disarray. Pacification of the country strained military police and civil affairs units to their limits. Months after the ouster of Noriega and the establishment of a new government, Panama continued to experience severe economic problems and an uneasy security situation marked by crime, a floundering police force, and occasional violence against Americans. As of early 1992, indications are that the job is far from being completed, reflecting the need for increased emphasis within the U.S. military on training and doctrine for stability operations.

During Operation Just Cause, the battlefield was conquered rapidly by U.S. military forces. However, a combination of both tactical and operational advantages, from the training of the individual soldier and the ability to conduct extensive in-country rehearsals, to the acceptance and welcome by Panamanians of U.S. military forces as liberators, make the U.S. invasion of Panama an imperfect model for future U.S. military operations. In a historical perspective, the invasion may, in time, be viewed as an "example of a major power using disproportionate military power in the Third World to resolve a problem that better political and diplomatic management would have avoided in the first place" (Hoagland 1990).

JAMES B. MOTLEY

SEE ALSO: Dominican Republic: 1965 Crisis; Grenada, U.S. Intervention in; Gulf War, 1991; Principles of War.

Bibliography

Donnelly, T., M. Roth, and C. Baker. 1991. *Operation Just Cause: The storming of Panama*. New York: Lexington Books.
Hoagland, J. 1990. Sledge hammering an ant. *Washington Post*, 4 January, A-23.
Meditz, S. W., and D. M. Hanratty, eds. 1989. *Panama: A country study*. 4th ed. Federal Research Division. Washington, D.C.: Library of Congress.
Motley, J. B. 1991. *Beyond the Soviet threat: The U.S. Army in a post–cold war environment*. Lexington, Mass.: Lexington Books, D. C. Heath.

Ropelewski, R. R. 1990. Planning, precision, and surprise led to Panama successes. *Armed Forces Journal International*, February, pp. 26–32.

PATTON, GEORGE SMITH, JR. [1885–1945]

By May 1945, at the end of World War II in Europe, U.S. general George S. Patton, Jr. (Fig. 1) had emerged as one of the most visible and respected Allied military leaders of the war. Known as "Old Blood and Guts," he carried armored warfare to its highest level by aggressive and bold leadership, and was considered by both friend and foe as the most successful army commander in Europe. Frequently reprimanded for controversial actions, Patton nevertheless commanded U.S. forces in combat in North Africa, Sicily, France, Germany, and Czechoslovakia, and never experienced a serious setback.

Early Life and Education

Patton was born on 11 November 1885 in San Gabriel, California, into a wealthy family that was also rich in military tradition. After a year at the Virginia Military Institute, he gained an appointment to West Point in 1904. Because he suffered from dyslexia, which hampered his learning ability, he was "turned back" a year and graduated with the class of 1909. He received a commission in the cavalry, and at the 1912 Olympic Games became the first American to compete in the modern pentathalon. In 1913 he attended the French Cavalry School at Saumur and later attended and instructed at the U.S. Cavalry School at Fort Riley, Kansas.

World War I

Patton was assigned to the 8th Cavalry in Texas, but left in March 1916 to participate in the Mexican Punitive Expedition as an aide to Gen. John J. Pershing. In May of the following year he was promoted to captain and accompanied Pershing to France to organize and head the American tank training center at Langres.

Patton saw his first combat in a tank in August 1918. As temporary lieutenant-colonel, he organized and commanded the 304th Tank Brigade in the St. Mihiel and Meuse-Argonne offensives of 1918. He was wounded during the Meuse-Argonne offensive on 13 September and subsequently received the Distinguished Service Cross. When he left France in 1919, he was a colonel.

In the postwar demobilization, Patton reverted to the rank of captain, but was promoted to major in 1919 and assumed command of the 304th Tank Brigade at Fort Meade, Maryland. He was assigned to the Office of the Chief of Cavalry during the years 1928–31, graduated from the Cavalry School at Fort Riley, Kansas, in 1923, and from the General Staff School at Fort Leavenworth in 1924. Patton attended the Army War College in 1932 and was promoted to

Figure 1. Lt. Gen. George S. Patton viewing the troops in Tunisia, 1943. (SOURCE: U.S. Library of Congress)

lieutenant colonel in 1934. He was promoted to colonel in 1937, and commanded the 3d Cavalry during 1938–40.

World War II

As the army expanded prior to the United States's involvement in World War II, Patton saw rapid advancement. He was given command of the 2d Armored Division's 2d Armored Brigade in July 1940 at Fort Benning, Georgia, with the rank of temporary brigadier general. In April 1941 he received command of the division with the promotion to temporary major general. In January 1942 Patton assumed command of the I Armored Corps. Shortly thereafter, in March 1942, he established the Desert Training Center in California, but in July he was sent to Washington to assist in organizing the Allied invasion of North Africa (Operation "Torch").

CAMPAIGNS IN AFRICA AND SICILY

Patton commanded the Allied task force which landed on the west coast of North Africa on 8 November. Following the defeat of the Allies at Kasserine Pass, he took command of the demoralized U.S. II Corps (March 1943), which he quickly reorganized and led to victory against Axis forces in North Africa. He was promoted to lieutenant general in April and was given command of the U.S. Seventh Army prior to the invasion of Sicily.

The Seventh Army's role in Sicily was that of flank support for Gen. Bernard L. Montgomery's British Eighth Army drive along the east coast to Messina. However, shortly after landing, Montgomery's forces were slowed in the drive to Messina. Patton, unwilling to remain in a supporting role, asked for and received permission to take Palermo, which fell on 22 July. He then turned eastward and secured Messina, before the arrival of the Eighth Army.

While in Sicily, Patton slapped two hospitalized, but unwounded, soldiers whom he claimed were cowards and were shirking their responsibilities. As a result of this incident, Patton was left in Sicily on occupation duty and did not see further action in the Mediterranean.

CAMPAIGNS IN EUROPE

In January 1944 Patton was called to England to participate in the planning for the invasion of France. Shortly after arriving in England, Patton became the focus of an elaborate deception plan called "Fortitude." The plan had Patton commanding a fictitious army group with the purpose of convincing the Germans that the Allied invasion would occur in the Pas de Calais area. The results of "Fortitude" were positive: the Germans maintained large forces on the Pas de Calais to counter the expected invasion by Patton's Army Group.

In March he assumed command of the Third Army and prepared for operations on the continent. He arrived in France on 6 July, a month after the initial landing, and on 1 August the Third Army became operational against the Germans in Normandy.

The Allied breakout from the Normandy beachhead at Avranches on 1 August was exploited by the Third Army, which drove through the gap and swung west, south, and east, isolating Brittany. When Third Army troops reached Le Mans, they were redirected northward toward Argentan and subsequently trapped about 100,000 Germans in the Falaise-Argentan Gap on 13 August.

Following the victory at Falaise, Patton drove his army eastward across France until it ran out of fuel in late August at the Saar River. By September the Third Army began to move again, but was stopped at the fortifications on the German frontier. A lull in operations followed.

In December, while the replenished Third Army was conducting an offensive in the Metz area, the Germans launched the Ardennes offensive, known as the Battle of the Bulge. Patton halted his attack, shifted his army to the north, and drove into the southern flank of the German salient, which was eliminated by mid-January 1945. The Allies then returned to the offensive and drove through the defenses of the Siegfried Line and into Germany. Pushed aggressively by Patton, the Third Army raced through the Rhineland and crossed the Rhine River at Oppenheim on 22 March. As German resistance began to collapse, Third Army troops drove across Germany, taking thousands of demoralized prisoners. At the end of hostilities on 7 May 1945, Patton's army was inside Czechoslovakia.

Immediately after the war Patton was critical of the denazification program, due to his belief that the Soviet presence in central Europe was a serious threat to the region's stability. Because of his outspoken criticism in this matter, he was removed from command of the Third Army in October and placed in command of the Fifteenth Army, essentially a paper force.

On 9 December 1945 Patton was involved in a traffic accident and suffered a broken neck. He died in his sleep on 21 December 1945 in a hospital in Heidelberg, Germany.

ARNOLD C. DUPUY

SEE ALSO: Montgomery, Bernard Law; World War II.

Bibliography

Blumenson, M. 1974. *The Patton papers: 1940–1945.* Boston: Houghton Mifflin.
———. 1985. *Patton: The man behind the legend.* New York: William Morrow.
Farago, L. 1963. *Patton: Ordeal and triumph.* New York: Ivan Obolensky.
———. 1981. *The last days of Patton.* New York: McGraw-Hill.
Patton, G. S., Jr. 1947. *War as I knew it.* Boston: Houghton Mifflin.
Semmes, H. H. 1955. *Portrait of Patton.* New York: Appleton-Century-Crofts.

PELOPONNESIAN WARS [431–404 B.C.]

The Peloponnesian War took place in Ancient Greece, pitting Athens and its empire against its long-time rival, Sparta, and Sparta's allies including Thebes, Corinth, and Megara. Its final result was the end of Athens as a major power. Between 431 and 404 B.C., large-scale campaigns and heavy fighting took place from Sicily to the coast of Asia Minor and from the Hellespont and Thrace to Rhodes. It was the first war to be recorded by an eyewitness historian of the highest caliber. It has come down through history as the archetype of war between a commercial democracy and an agricultural aristocracy and of war between a maritime superpower and a continental military machine. Thucydides' history is itself a classic, and for generations was considered part of the foundation of a proper education.

The cities of the Boeotian Confederacy under Theban leadership were Sparta's allies from the first. Syracuse and other Sicilian cities gave active help in the last part of the war. Persia at first held aloof, waiting for an opportunity to regain her dominion over the Greek cities of the Asiatic seaboard, which Athens had liberated; it finally provided the crucial financial and logistic support Sparta needed to conduct a maritime offensive. Athens was unpopular with many members of its own empire, but held most under control by its maritime supremacy.

The war may be divided into three major periods or five phases:

- the Archidamian war: phase 1, 431–427; phase 2, 426–421
- the Sicilian war: 421–413
- the Ionian or Decelean War: phase 1, 412–408; phase 2, 407–404

The underlying cause of the war was Sparta's fear of the growing power of Athens under the leadership of Pericles. (This is Thucydides' own final judgment.) The immediate occasion of the start of the war was that Corinth, Sparta's chief naval ally, was concerned that Athens would block its commercial ties to the west, especially to Sicily. The Corinthians were supported by Megara, which had been nearly ruined by Pericles' economic boycott, and by Aegina, a reluctant member of the Athenian empire. But had Sparta not also been eager for war, then peace would have lasted.

The Archidamian War

PHASE 1, 431–427 B.C.

In a war between the main military and naval powers in Greece, a decisive result was unlikely to occur quickly. Sparta relied on the traditional strategy of Greek warfare. By invading Attica and destroying the crops, it hoped to force Athens either to sue for peace or to come out and fight the set-piece battle by which Greek wars typically were decided. In numbers as well as in discipline and combat effectiveness of troops, Athens was decidedly inferior to the Spartan-Theban forces. The defect in Sparta's strategy was that Athens, unlike other Greek cities, could not be starved into surrender nor be made to fight a pitched battle by occasional occupation of its individual citizens' farmlands. Athens's food supply came principally from Egypt and Crimea. Nevertheless, the Spartans were confident of a quick victory in pursuing their strategy of annihilation.

Pericles pursued an opposite strategy. He wanted only the status quo ante; conquest was well beyond Athens's means. Knowing his city walls were impregnable, that they connected Athens to the sea at Piraeus, and that his navy would be able to ensure the food supply, he opted for a defensive strategy of attrition. When the Spartans invaded, the rural population of Attica would move into the city. The Athenian fleet would secure the empire against revolt from within and attack from without, and would take the offensive to raid the Peloponnesian coast. Meanwhile, in spring and autumn the Athenian land army would devastate the lands of Sparta's allies (especially Megara) at the Corinthian isthmus, while the Spartans were home tending to their own crops. If Megara could be recovered, Sparta's land access to Attica would be blocked and her Theban allies would not dare come down from the north unaided.

Pericles' strategy also had weaknesses. He was fearful of the effect that high casualties would have on public sentiment in a democracy if he conducted more aggressive offensive military actions. He failed to see the opportunities for combined land and naval actions to intensify the war on Spartan territory with little risk and hasten the effect of attrition on Sparta. The Athenian people's morale proved unequal to the strain; after Pericles' death they undertook rash actions. Meanwhile, the Spartans were stoic and persistent in the face of failure until they found foreign resources sufficient to turn the tables on Athens.

Chance, too, entered the lists. In June 430, plague, brought with the vital grain from Egypt or Libya, devastated the city overcrowded with rural refugees. Pericles himself died in 429 and was succeeded by Cleon. Megara held out, although starving. The Athenian naval raids on Sparta's coastal allies were too feeble to bother Sparta. Therefore it was Athens that suffered the attrition intended for Sparta. Athens's vast financial resources were strained, and exacting ever more onerous taxation from the empire only engendered more unrest and rebellion.

Athens first offered peace in 430, but Sparta refused. In 430–429 Potidaea finally surrendered, and in the fall of 429 Athens won two great naval battles at Chalcis and Naupactus. In June 428 Mitylene on Lesbos revolted but was forced by Athens to surrender. But this was countered by the surrender in August of Athens's ally, Plataea, to a Theban army. In 426 Athens gained the upper hand in Corcyra. This brought the war to a near stalemate.

Phase 2, 426–421 B.C.

In 426 Athens began more active operations under direction of Cleon and Demosthenes. Despite the continued resistance of the upper classes led by Nicias, they initiated a vigorous offensive strategy. Athenian forces attempted to carry the war to Boeotia (Thebes), Sparta, and even Sicily but all offensives failed. A large Spartan army laid siege to Amphilochian Argos. Demosthenes won two great victories at Olpae and Idomene. This destroyed Spartan hegemony, pushed Arcania and Abracia out of the war, and opened the way for the Athenian navy to Sicily.

In 425 at the island of Sphacteria Athens won its greatest victory. An Athenian fleet under Demosthenes blocked the Spartan navy in Navarino Bay and cut off the Spartan force of 420 men on the island. Athens secured the surrender of the enemy fleet, leaving Sparta without a navy for many years. The Athenians captured the island and took 292 prisoners including 120 Spartans, who were taken to Athens. This was an unprecedented disgrace for Sparta. The "hostage" issue of these prisoners not only secured all Attica from Spartan attacks, but was played upon by Athens until Sparta sued for peace, which, foolishly, Cleon refused.

In 424 all Athenian offensive plans failed. The new Spartan commander, Brasidas, then marched full speed through Boeotia and Thessaly to Chalcidice, stirring up revolt and offering freedom. Amphipolis surrendered. Athenian reinforcements under Cleon arrived, and Brasidas sallied from Amphipolis. The Athenians were defeated, but both generals—the two most stubborn advocates and practitioners of offensive warfare—died in the battle. By April 421, Nicias concluded a peace treaty between Athens and Sparta that he hoped would end the war.

The Sicilian War, 421–413 B.C.

All the animosities and policy conflicts that divided the Greek cities remained unresolved during this period, as all strove to regain their strength. In 420 a new alliance of Athens, Argos, Mantinea, and Elis faced the Spartan-Boeotian alliance. Athens now had a new democratic leader in Alcibiades.

The remainder of the war was marked by the bitter internal political struggle between the democratic war party led by Alcibiades and the aristocratic (oligarchical) elements led by Nicias and others. This struggle led to outright treason, vicious internal partisan purges, and the final destruction of Athens's empire, authority, and very independence.

Athens's third offensive strategy was the most ambitious so far, but it was ultimately negated by the internal opposition of Alcibiades' political opponents. With its new allies in the Peloponnese, Athens forced Sparta into pitched battle on home territory. Sparta responded to the crisis by bringing forth another great military leader, King Agis, who brought up the full Spartan army and in August 418 won the largest land battle of the war at Mantinea. This not only restored Spartan self-confidence and prestige but also knocked out Athens's allies.

Athenian hopes now rested on an even bolder offensive to cut Spartan and Corinthian supplies from Sicily. In 416 B.C., Alcibiades promoted an ambitious strategic plan for conquering Syracuse, controlling all of Sicily, defeating Carthage, and then returning with greatly strengthened forces to the final defeat of a surrounded Peloponnese. The concept was brilliant, but it required the undivided support of the entire Athenian polity. The democrats embraced it with enthusiasm, but as usual Nicias opposed and recommended continued traditional operations in Chalcidice. The expedition to Syracuse was launched in June of 415, but with a fatally divided command of Alcibiades, Nicias, and the professional soldier, Lamachus. The campaign was barely begun when Alcibiades was recalled to stand trial on charges brought by his opponents, leaving the hopes of Athens in the hands of the chief opponent of the strategic plan. Rather than face certain execution, Alcibiades fled to Sparta.

Syracuse was duly invested by land and sea, but the half-hearted efforts of Nicias came to nothing. Lamachus died in battle; Demosthenes urged a general withdrawal to Athens, but Nicias would neither advance nor retire. The Athenian fleet was defeated. Nicias attempted to move the army inland, but it was massacred. Both generals were executed and the few Athenian survivors were enslaved.

The Ionian or Decelean War

PHASE 1, 412–408 B.C.

Sparta officially resumed the war in August 414 with a strong fleet and additional reinforcements from the west. Athens had lost its best sailors and nearly exhausted its treasury. In March 413, King Agis occupied Decelea to keep

Athens in a constant blockade. The Athenian empire began to fall apart, with one city revolt after another in 412 and 411. Finally Persia entered the contest by authorizing its satrap in Sardis, Tissaphernes, to support Sparta. Alcibiades fled from Sparta to Sardis where he persuaded Tissaphernes to withhold his support to Sparta. The Athenian navy recalled Alcibiades to command and resumed operations.

With the grain supply from Sicily in complete Spartan control and that from Egypt blocked by the same forces, Athens now was totally dependent on food brought from the Crimea through the Hellespont. There the Athenians defeated the Spartans at Cynossema in September of 411. In March 410, Alcibiades won a great victory over the opposing navy and supporting Persian army at Cyzicus on the Sea of Marmora, restoring Athens' maritime supremacy and a secure grain supply. Sparta again suggested peace, but the Athenians refused to listen.

PHASE 2, 407–404 B.C.

In autumn of 408 a new Spartan admiral, Lysander, arrived and began building a new fleet with the unlimited aid of the new Persian satrap, Cyrus. Finally Alcibiades was forced to divide his own fleet due to supply shortages. Leaving one force at Notium under Antiochus to observe but with strict orders to refuse battle, Alcibiades sailed north to reprovision. Lysander promptly sailed out and routed Antiochus. Alcibiades returned to renew the blockade but the damage was already done and he was dismissed.

For the next year Lysander was superseded by Callicratidas, who blockaded the Athenian fleet of Conon in Mitylene harbor. Another fleet sailed from Athens and in the battle of Arginusae in August 406 the largest fleets so far seen in the war entered battle. Callicratidas was drowned while losing and Sparta again offered peace. Again the Athenian democrats led by Cleophon refused. The new Athenian admirals now moved the entire fleet up to the open beach at Aegospotami on the Asiatic side of the Hellespont. Lysander lay opposite in a good harbor at Abydos. In vain Alcibiades warned his townsmen of their danger; his opponents would not listen. In September 405 Lysander captured practically the whole Athenian fleet without a blow and thus brought the entire war to an end in one stroke. With the grain supply now cut, Lysander could proceed to Athens itself to blockade it from the sea while the Spartan army under King Pausanius held the land side. After six months of starvation and with no prospect of relief, Athens surrendered on generous terms offered by Sparta. Corinth and Thebes protested, demanding total destruction, but Sparta did not want to create too great a power vacuum. The city walls and those connecting Athens to Piraeus were torn down and the empire of Athens dissolved.

JOHN F. SLOAN

SEE ALSO: Alexander the Great; Graeco-Persian Wars; History, Ancient Military.

Bibliography

Adcock, F. E. 1962. *The Greek and Macedonian art of war*. Berkeley, Calif.: Univ. of California Press.

Anderson, J. K. 1970. *Military theory and practice in the age of Xenophon*. Berkeley, Calif.: Univ. of California Press.

Connolly, P. 1977. *The Greek armies*. London: Macdonald Educational.

Green, P. 1970. *Armada from Athens*. London: Hodder and Stoughton.

Hanson, V. D. 1989. *The Western way of war*. New York: Alfred A. Knopf.

Nelson, R. B. 1973. *Warfleets of antiquity*. Sussex, England: Wargames Research Group.

Rogers, W. L. [1937] 1977. *Greek and Roman naval warfare*. Reprint. Annapolis, Md.: U.S. Naval Institute Press.

Sealey, R. 1976. *A history of the Greek city states 700–338 B.C.* Berkeley, Calif.: Univ. of California Press.

Ste. Croix, G. E. M. de. 1972. *The origins of the Peloponnesian War*. Ithaca, N.Y.: Cornell Univ. Press.

Thucydides. *The Peloponnesian War*. 1959. Trans. T. Hobbes. Ed. D. Grene. 2 vols. Ann Arbor, Mich.: Univ. of Michigan Press.

———. *The Peloponnesian War*. 1960. Trans. Crawley. Ed. R. Livingstone. New York: Oxford Univ. Press.

Xenophon. *Hellenica*. Vols. 1 and 2.

PERSHING, JOHN JOSEPH [1860–1948]

John Joseph Pershing, American army general, is chiefly noted for his command of the American Expeditionary Force (AEF) during World War I.

Early Career

The son of a small-town Missouri merchant, Pershing graduated from West Point in 1886, ranking in the middle third of his class academically but serving as first captain in his final year there in recognition of his outstanding soldierly qualities. Commissioned in the cavalry, he served at frontier posts in the west for five years and was involved in occasional minor hostilities with American Indians. He was a professor of military science from 1891 to 1895 at the University of Nebraska, where he also earned a law degree. Following additional frontier service, Pershing returned to West Point in 1897. There his rigidity in matters of discipline prompted cadets to dub him "Black Jack," a nickname meant to denigrate his service with the all-black 10th Cavalry Regiment; the nickname stuck and came to mean ramrod sternness. During the Spanish-American War, Pershing fought with the 10th Cavalry in Cuba, winning the praise of his superiors for coolness under fire.

Between 1899 and 1914 Pershing served three tours in the Philippines, mostly in Mindanao where fierce Moros resisted the imposition of American authority. Displaying tact in governing them and tenacity in fighting them, he brought the Moros under control with a minimum of bloodshed and instituted significant internal administrative improvements. Pershing's success in the

Philippines, the valuable reports he sent home while an observer during the Russo-Japanese War, and the political influence of his father-in-law (a prominent senator) all led President Theodore Roosevelt in 1906 to promote him from captain to brigadier general over 862 other officers superior in rank to him. Nine years later, while he was serving on the Mexican border, Pershing's wife and three daughters died in a fire at the Presidio in San Francisco. The tragedy destroyed much of his spirit and left him a stiff, taciturn man.

In 1916 Pershing was placed in command of the punitive expedition sent into Mexico in pursuit of Pancho Villa and his bandits after their raid on Columbus, New Mexico. Operating under tight restrictions, he never caught Villa. However, he broke Villa's power by forcing his bands to disperse. With some exceptions, he avoided confrontations with Mexican government troops that could have sparked war between the United States and Mexico. Equally important, the professional competence Pershing showed in carrying out his Mexican assignment and his unswerving loyalty to his political superiors, despite his own doubts about their Mexican policy, caused President Woodrow Wilson to entrust him with command of the AEF after American entry into World War I in April 1917.

World War I

Landing in France in June 1917, Pershing proceeded to build an army from scratch. Convinced that the stalemate on the western front could be broken only by an independent American army trained to fight in open-field operations, he rejected British and French arguments that Germany's manpower advantage demanded that he forgo the formation of his army and amalgamate his troops with the manpower-starved Allied armies, as the units arrived piecemeal from the United States. Only when the Allies were reeling under the weight of punishing German offensives in the spring of 1918 did he relent, and then only temporarily. As a result, contrary to Pershing's original design, American troops received their baptism of fire while integrated with Allied armies, acquitting themselves well in the summer of 1918 in battles at Cantigny, Château-Thierry, Belleau Wood, the Marne River crossings, Reims, and Soissons, which turned the tide in the war against Germany.

In September 1918, with more than 1 million American soldiers now available, an independent American army entered the fray. Its first test came in an assault against the St. Mihiel salient on 12 September. Using seven double-size divisions against eight battle-weary German divisions, Pershing reduced the salient in four days. Quickly shifting his forces in a spectacular logistical feat to join the giant Allied thrust all along the western front, Pershing then attacked the Hindenburg Line in the Meuse-Argonne sector on 26 September in a nine-division assault. For the next five weeks the Americans slugged it out with the Germans with minimal success, as the narrow confines and rugged terrain of the Meuse-Argonne severely limited Pershing's opportunity to demonstrate his tactical abilities. Casualties mounted at an alarming rate, and Pershing, unwilling to tolerate mediocre subordinates, ruthlessly relieved officers who did not measure up to his unceasing demands for progress. Finally, on 1 November the Americans cracked the German defenses, leading to the open warfare for which Pershing had planned. By the Armistice on 11 November, the earlier disappointments in the Meuse-Argonne were overshadowed by a surging American offensive.

The American performance in the Meuse-Argonne did not fully vindicate Pershing's commitment to open warfare, but he later argued with considerable justification that his offensive hastened the end of the war by compelling the Germans to deploy so many men to defend this sector and its vital rail communications that they had to withdraw all along the front or risk losing their forces facing the British and French to the northwest. By November, one-fourth of German forces in the west were facing the Americans on less than one-tenth of the front.

Postwar Career and Retirement

Raised to the rank of general of the armies, a rank previously held only by George Washington, Pershing served as Army chief of staff from 1921 until his retirement in 1924 (Fig. 1). The next year he headed the Tacna-Arica Plebiscitary Commission, which unsuccessfully attempted to settle a long-standing border dispute between Peru and Chile. Thereafter, Pershing devoted himself to his memoirs and his work as chairman of the American Battle Monuments Commission.

Figure 1. Gen. John J. Pershing in 1921. (SOURCE: U.S. Library of Congress)

Assessment

Although he had no opportunity to exercise strategic control of coalition armies, Pershing was a careful, determined commander who shaped and led the American army that tipped the balance against Germany in World War I. Moreover, Pershing both mirrored and helped bring about the transformation of the American army from an Indian-fighting constabulary into a decisive force in the international arena. Beginning his career when leadership was characterized by bold and dashing commanders, he became a manager of personnel, supply, and firepower on a massive scale. In this respect, he was America's first modern general and a model for the later generals who led the United States to victory in World War II.

JOHN KENNEDY OHL

SEE ALSO: Russo-Japanese War; World War I.

Bibliography

Coffman, E. 1968. *The war to end all wars: The American military experience in World War I*. New York: Oxford Univ. Press.

Pershing, J. J. 1931. *My experiences in the world war*. 2 vols. New York: Frederick A. Stokes.

Smythe, D. 1973. *Guerrilla warrior: The early life of John J. Pershing*. New York: Scribner's.

————. 1986. *Pershing: General of the armies*. Bloomington: Indiana Univ. Press.

Vandiver, F. E. 1977. *Black Jack: The life and times of John J. Pershing*. 2 vols. College Station: Texas A&M Univ. Press.

PERSIAN EMPIRE

The Persian Empire was the first "world" empire. At its height, the Persian Empire included three of the cradles of civilization—the river valleys of the Nile, the Indus, and the Tigris and Euphrates—as well as a large portion of the Greek-speaking world—Ionia, Thrace, Macedonia, and Thessaly. The empire fostered and safeguarded both the exchange of goods and the spread of ideas. Politically, the Persian Empire served as the model for the later empires of Macedonia and Rome.

Empire of the Medes

The immediate predecessor of the empire of the Persians was the empire of the Medes. The Medes were linguistic and cultural cousins of the Persians.

Cyaxares (625–585 B.C.) united the Medes into a single kingdom and extended his rule to include the Persian tribes. He then turned his attention to the destruction of the hereditary enemy of his people, the Assyrians. In 615 B.C., Cyaxares invaded Assyria and laid siege to Nineveh, the Assyrian capital. Unable to take Nineveh, Cyaxares occupied Assur. Nabopolassar, king of Babylon, entered into a secret alliance with Cyaxares, and in 612 B.C. the allies invaded Assyria, captured Nineveh, and razed it. The victors divided the Assyrian empire between them: the Medes took northern Assyria, Urartu, and the vassal states of Asia Minor; the Babylonians took the vassal states of Syria and Palestine.

Cyaxares was succeeded by his son Astyages (585–550 B.C.). During the latter's reign, relations worsened between the Medes and Babylonians. Nabonidus, king of Babylon, sought an ally against the powerful Median king. He found that ally in Cyrus II, king of Anshan.

Cyrus the Great, 550–530 B.C.

Cyrus the Great, creator of the Persian Empire, was the son of Cambyses I, king of Anshan, and Mandane, a daughter of Astyages. His kingdom was a confederacy of three tribes: the Pasargadai, Maraphioi, and Maspioi. Cyrus also was the acknowledged war leader of the other seven Persian tribes. As king of Anshan, Cyrus was a vassal of his maternal grandfather, Astyages.

The reasons for the rebellion of the Persians are unclear. In 550 B.C. Cyrus, supported by the princes of all ten Persian tribes and in collusion with certain officials of the Median empire, deposed Astyages and founded the kingdom of the Medes and Persians.

After receiving the submission of the Iranian tribes of Sogdiana (Transoxiana) and Bactria, Cyrus asserted his authority over the peoples of northern Mesopotamia and Asia Minor. In 547 B.C., Cilicia recognized Persian suzerainty. Lydia, which had withstood Cyaxares, fell to Cyrus in 546 B.C. The Greek city-states of Ionia were, in turn, reduced to tributary status.

Babylonia, Persia's former ally, had begun to decline in the latter years of King Nabonidus (555–539 B.C.). The king had become increasingly involved in a religious cult and had left the ruling of the country in the hands of his son, Belshazzar. Belshazzar's misrule resulted in growing disaffection among the Babylonians as well as among subject peoples. In 539 B.C., Cyrus advanced on Babylon. Instead of resisting, the Babylonians opened the city gates to the Persians. In eleven years, Cyrus the Great had created the first world empire, an empire that stretched from the Pamirs in the east to the Mediterranean Sea in the west, an empire that was both the heir to, and the culmination of, the ancient civilizations of the Middle East.

Cambyses II, 530–521 B.C.

During his final years, Cyrus the Great faced a persistent threat to the security of his northeastern frontier: nomadic raiders. While campaigning against the Massagetae, Cyrus was slain. He was succeeded by his eldest son, Cambyses.

The great achievement of Cambyses was the conquest of Egypt. By 522 B.C., Egypt had been secured and Cambyses was on his way back to Persia. Somewhere in southern Syria, the king learned of a revolt in Persia led by Gaumata, a Magian priest, who claimed to be the younger brother of Cambyses. Whether Cambyses became ill and died, killed himself, or was assassinated is unknown. His sudden death, however, emboldened the rebels and threatened the existence of the empire.

Darius, a cousin of Cambyses as well as commander of the king's bodyguard, assumed command of the army. With the army's support, Darius returned to the capital, Ecbatana, arrested Gaumata, and put him to death. The capital secured, Darius ascended the throne and began a two-year-long pacification campaign against the rebels. By 520 B.C., Darius had restored order throughout the empire.

The Persian Army

Under Cyrus the Great, the Persian army (*kara*) had consisted of the warriors of the Persian tribes. Darius transformed the *kara* into a professional standing army (*spada*). The *spada* consisted of the Immortals (imperial bodyguard), cavalry, infantry, and siege troops.

COMPOSITION

The strength of the imperial bodyguard always stood at 10,000 men. The elite of Immortals were the One Thousand, the royal bodyguard, under the command of the *hazarapat*. The *hazarapat* also commanded the Immortals, was operational commander of the Persian army, and in peacetime functioned as the Great King's chief minister. The Immortals were recruited from among the Medes, Persians, and Elamites. Their principal weapons were spears and bows and arrows.

The cavalry (*asabara*) was the traditional fighting force of both Medes and Persians. Cavalrymen were armed with bows and arrows. Additional weaponry included javelins and swords. Evidence suggests that by the reign of Artaxerxes III both rider and mount were armored.

The infantry (*pasti*) were armed with short spears, short swords, and bows and arrows. The cavalry and infantry were also composed of Medes, Persians, and Elamites.

ORGANIZATION

The Persian army was organized on a decimal basis, a system of organization inherited from the Medes and, ultimately, the Assyrians. A squad consisted of ten men; a company, 100 men. Ten companies formed a regiment of 1,000 men; ten regiments formed a division of 10,000 men. The divisions were organized into six field armies.

During wartime, the *spada* was augmented by satrapal (provincial) militias armed with the traditional weapons of the province. The mixture of professional and militia units and the different weapons produced vexing tactical problems for Persian commanders.

Persian Expansion Under Darius I, 521–486 B.C.

Darius I expanded the empire to both the east and the west. In the east, the Persians conquered Gandhara and the Indus Valley (521–519 B.C.). Darius also sent a naval force down the Indus into the Indian Ocean, with orders to sail west into the Red Sea. This expedition had both political and economic objectives: politically, it reinforced Persian control over the recalcitrant Egyptians; economically, it stimulated seaborne trade between India and Egypt.

Operations Against the Greeks

The existence of the independent, mainland Greek city-states posed a potential threat to Persian control over Ionia. Although the Ionian cities enjoyed virtual independence and the only obligation the Persians imposed upon them was an annual tax, the Ionians chafed against the Persian yoke. Both Athens and Sparta urged the Ionians to rebel.

Operations in Thrace, 492 B.C. Hoping to neutralize the Greek menace, Darius conducted operations against the Scythians in Thrace. Darius hoped to interdict the supply of timber from the Balkans to the Greek city-states and thereby pressure the Greeks to behave. Although the Scythians retreated before Darius, both Thrace and Macedonia submitted to the Great King.

The Greek reaction. Athens and Sparta were the leading Greek city-states. Sparta was solidly anti-Persian. In Athens, however, a faction favored recognition of Persian suzerainty. In 490 B.C., Darius attempted to win over the Greeks through diplomacy. This diplomatic offensive, however, was ruined when the Persian admiral, Datis, sacked Eretria and enslaved the population, contrary to the Persian policy of conciliation. The fate of Eretria convinced the Greeks that only slavery awaited them at the hands of Darius. When Datis landed his forces at Marathon (12 September 490 B.C.), the Athenians won a stunning victory.

Before Darius could mount another operation, his attention was diverted by a rebellion in Egypt. To Darius, Egypt was more important than Greece. Marathon had been a minor setback. A successful revolt in Egypt, however, could undermine the empire.

The Empire Under Xerxes I, 486–465 B.C.

Darius died in 486 B.C. His son Xerxes successfully suppressed the rebellion in Egypt as well as a revolt in Babylonia.

Xerxes Against the Greeks

Xerxes was initially unwilling to continue the struggle with the mainland Greeks. However, under pressure from his nobles and members of the royal family, Xerxes invaded Greece in 480 B.C. Once again the Macedonians recognized Persian suzerainty, as did the Thessalonians and the majority of the northern Greek city-states. Athens and the Peloponnesians—led by Sparta—resisted. The Persian advance on Athens was briefly delayed by Spartan and Thespian forces at Thermopylae. With Thermopylae neutralized, the advance resumed. The Persians occupied Athens, burned the citadel (Acropolis), and installed pro-Persian officials. Persian successes on land, however, were negated by the Athenian defeat of the Persian fleet at Salamis (479 B.C.). Although the Persian army was intact, Xerxes, in a rage, returned to Persia with a third of the army and left the army commander, the *hazarapat* Mardonius, to continue the campaign.

Mardonius first tried to open negotiations with the Greeks; his overtures were rebuffed. He then recommended military operations. At Plataea (479 B.C.) Mardonius was slain, and the Greeks won the day; however, the Persian army remained intact and formidable. When the supporting fleet was routed, the Persian commanders decided to withdraw from Greece. So ended the second and last Persian attempt to conquer the Greeks by force of arms. By 466 B.C., the Persians had been forced out of Europe.

Decline of the Persian Empire

The Great Kings who followed Xerxes added no new territory to the empire. Most of their efforts were directed toward maintaining the empire created by Cyrus and Darius, with varying success. Artaxerxes I (465–424 B.C.) lost the Greek city-states of Ionia. Darius II (424–404 B.C.) used Persian gold to help fuel the Peloponnesian War. Artaxerxes II (404–358 B.C.) survived an attempted assassination and the rebellion of his brother Cyrus to regain control over Ionia. Although he succeeded in playing the Greeks off against each other, Artaxerxes lost Egypt. In addition, central control over the satrapies weakened, and rebellions flared in Asia Minor and the Levant toward the end of his reign.

Artaxerxes III (358–338 B.C.) was able to restore central control throughout the empire by ruthlessly suppressing the rebels; in addition, he reconquered Egypt. To combat the growing strength of Macedonia, the Great King allied with the Athenians. In 338 B.C., Artaxerxes III, perhaps the ablest king since Darius I, died of poison. In the same year, the Macedonians defeated the Greeks at Chaeronea.

Darius III Codomannus (336–330 B.C.) was not up to the task facing him. He was outgeneraled and outfought by the young Macedonian king, Alexander III. Deserted by many of his nobles, his armies in disarray, Darius III fell victim to an assassin, and his empire fell to Alexander the Great.

LAWRENCE D. HIGGINS

SEE ALSO: Alexander the Great; Assyria, Military History of; Graeco-Persian Wars; History, Ancient Military; Peloponnesian Wars.

Bibliography

Cameron, G. C. 1936. *History of early Iran.* Chicago: Univ. of Chicago Press.
Culican, W. 1967. *The Medes and Persians.* New York: Praeger.
De Selincourt, A. 1951. *Herodotus: The histories.* Harmondsworth: Penguin.
Frye, R. N. 1963. *The heritage of Persia.* New York: New American Library (Mentor).
Ghirshman, R. 1961. *Iran: From the earliest times to the Islamic conquest.* Harmondsworth: Penguin.
Herzfeld, E. 1941. *Iran in the ancient East.* Oxford: Oxford Univ. Press.
Iliffe, J. H. 1953. *The legacy of Persia.* Oxford: Oxford Univ. Press.
Lamb, H. 1963. *Cyrus the Great.* New York: Bantam.
Olmstead, A. T. E. 1959. *History of the Persian Empire.* Chicago: Univ. of Chicago Press (Phoenix Books).
Warner, R. 1967. *Xenophon: The Persian expedition.* Harmondsworth: Penguin.

PETER THE GREAT (Peter I) [1672–1725]

In one generation, Peter the Great "Westernized" Russia and altered the balance of power in Eastern Europe. He founded the Russian Navy and, after capturing the Baltic coast, established a new capital at St. Petersburg. He completely revamped the Russian state through a series of reforms designed primarily to arm, man, finance, and feed his armed forces. Peter was not himself a revolutionary. He built upon the Westernizing heritage of his father, Alexei I, but this was not done without cost. His military adventures taxed the country to the limit, but his actual territorial gains were less in area and importance than those of Alexei had been. Serfdom increased, and the entire population was bound to lifelong state service. His transformation of Russia caused great social unrest. Peter won the Great Northern War, but he himself was not a "great captain." Rather, he had the knack of finding good people, and he valued talent over bloodlines. Peter was fascinated with technology and practical skills rather than ideas. Although known as a "Westernizer" and famous for his 1697 trip to the West, Peter favored absolutism rather than application of democratic limits to royal power as was advocated by thinkers in England and Holland. He wanted Western things but Russian ideas.

Youth

Two factors molded Peter's character: his status as a third son and his fascination with things and how they worked. During the reign of his older half-brother, Fedor I (1676–82), and the co-czar regency with his other half-brother, Ivan V (1682–89), Peter lived in the village of Preobrazhenskoe, where, free from the burden of the Muscovite court, he organized his "boyhood regiments" and staged mock battles. He studied mathematics and navigation, and socialized with foreigners in the city's German Quarter. In 1697 he visited the West. His studies of shipbuilding in Holland were cut short by news of an uprising of *strel'tsy* (musketeers), supposedly plotting to overthrow him (1698), which he cruelly suppressed.

Early Military Activities

Peter asserted his own rule following the death of his mother in 1694. The following year, he reopened Russia's struggle against the Turks to acquire a Black Sea port. His first attempt (1695) was unsuccessful for want of naval support. After building a fleet in Voronezh, Peter sailed down the Don River in 1696 to capture Azov. The 1700 Treaty of Constantinople ceded Azov (and Peter's newly built port at Taganrog) to Russia. Russia now had its first Black Sea ports.

Great Northern War (1700–21)

On the same day that Peter signed the treaty with the Turks, he declared war on Sweden, in collusion with Denmark and Saxony. Sweden, under the boy-king Charles XII, immediately took the offensive, drove Denmark out of the war, and destroyed a superior Russian force at Narva (1700), capturing all of Peter's artillery and routing his army. When Charles next turned his attention to Saxony, he gave Peter breathing space to rebuild his army, create a fleet, and build up an industrial base. In 1708 Charles invaded Russia but was pushed into the Ukraine, where the decisive battle of Poltava (27 June 1709–8 July, New Style) broke the back of the Swedish invaders. Peter's new navy defeated the Swedes at Hangö (1714) and Sweden sued for peace (Treaty of Nystadt) in 1721, ceding Estonia, Livonia, and the Baltic coast north to Vyborg to Russia.

Southern Campaigns

Success at Poltava was followed by disaster in the south against the Turks when Peter led an ill-advised, ill-planned invasion around the western shore of the Black Sea. After defeat on the River Pruth (1711), Peter was forced to abandon the southern fleet and return all of the 1700 gains. An expedition against Persia (1722–23) captured the southern coast of the Caspian Sea, but these gains were equally transitory (returned by Peter's successors in 1732).

Social Reforms

Peter's Westernization focused on the external forms, such as dress and manners. He founded the new capital at St. Petersburg (1703) to move court society from conservative Moscow. He adopted the Julian calendar (1699) and instituted an inheritance law (1714), which passed all property to one chosen son. His Table of Ranks (1722) established fourteen ranks through which all military, civil, and court servitors were promoted based on merit, but it involved only about 3,000 noble families (1 percent of the total population).

Religious Reforms

Upon the death of the Patriarch of the Russian Orthodox Church in 1700, Peter allowed the office to lapse. In 1721 he replaced it with a state office, the Holy Synod, headed by a lay official, the Oberprocurator. This subordinated the church to the state and made it a department of the government. The Holy Synod lasted until 1918.

Educational Reforms

Peter sought to develop technical schools to support his military reforms and to expand literacy. He founded the School of Mathematics and Navigation (1701) and the Naval Academy (1715). The Language Academy (1705–15) prepared students for study abroad. A simplified alphabet replaced Old Church Slavonic. Peter also laid the groundwork for the Academy of Sciences, but it was founded (1725) only after his death by his successor, Catherine I.

Administrative Reforms

Peter the Great's impetus to rationalize the running of the state was a desire to facilitate tax collection and army recruitment. More than half of the state revenues went to the military. Peter abolished the Boyar Duma (1711) and replaced it with a nine-man (later ten) Senate to supervise administration and justice in his absence. Peter abolished the haphazard, overlapping chancelleries and created nine governmental colleges (*collegia*) in 1717: foreign affairs, war, navy, finance (three), economic affairs (two), and justice. He conducted censuses in 1710, 1716, and 1718 and created a poll tax (1718). He reorganized provincial governments into 50 states, each headed by a governor responsible for law and order, financial affairs, tax collection, army recruitment, and health and education.

Military Reforms

Before Poltava, Peter sought to build a fleet and a permanent, standing army based on a Western model, replacing the outdated *strel'tsy* and the "new style" regiments of his father, which had relied heavily on foreign officers. He created engineering and artillery schools to lessen dependence upon foreign officers. He introduced linear tactics, learned from the Swedes. Peter developed the iron, woolen, and munitions industries to make his armed forces self-sufficient. After 1709 Peter rationalized and institutionalized the military by issuing a military manual, *Military Code of the Year 1716*, and creating a Military College (1718–20) to serve as a unified military command. His greatest achievement was the Russian navy, which by his death included nearly 50 warships and 700 smaller vessels. Peter continued the trend of his father by emphasizing infantry regiments, the most famous of which, the Preobrazhensky and Semenovsky Guards Regiments, were derived from his boyhood regiments. Peter was not an innovator, although Russia did develop the concept of the "flying corps" (an independent mobile formation), which was used successfully at Poltava. His writings, such as *Rules of Combat of 1708*, discussed practical examples from early Great Northern War battles and tried to integrate the theory of translated foreign theoretical texts with the realities of Russian battlefields.

DIANNE L. SMITH

SEE ALSO: Charles XII, King of Sweden; Ottoman Empire; Russia, Expansion of.

Bibliography

Anderson, M. S. 1978. *Peter the Great*. London: Thames and Hudson.

Duffy, C. 1981. *Russia's military way to the West: Origins and nature of Russian military power, 1700–1800*. London: Routledge and Keegan Paul.

Hellie, R. 1974. The Petrine army: Continuity, change, and impact. *Canadian-American Slavic Studies* 8:237–53.

Keep, J. 1985. *Soldiers of the Tsar: Army and society in Russia, 1462–1874*. London: Oxford Univ. Press.

Klyuchevsky, V. 1958. *Peter the Great*. New York: Random House.

Massie, R. 1980. *Peter the Great*. London: Penguin.

POWELL, COLIN L.
[1937–   ]

Colin L. Powell was appointed the twelfth chairman of the Joint Chiefs of Staff, Department of Defense, by President George Bush on 1 October 1989. He was reappointed for a second two-year term in October 1991 and served until his retirement on 30 September 1993. In this capacity, he served as the principal military adviser to the president, the secretary of defense, and the National Security Council. The position of chairman was strengthened significantly by the Goldwater-Nichols Act of 1986, which gave the chairman authority to express his personal views on military matters, not just the views of the Joint Chiefs of Staff. With a solid base of high-level experience from earlier assignments in the Office of the Secretary of Defense, Office of Management and Budget, and National Security Council, Powell carried out this expanded authority with dexterity and skill.

Figure 1. Colin L. Powell. (SOURCE: U.S. Army)

Powell was born in New York on 5 April 1937. He was raised in the South Bronx section of New York City by his parents, Maud and Luther, who were Jamaican immigrants. He graduated from the City College of New York in 1958 with a bachelor of science degree in geology. Because he was a distinguished military graduate of the Reserve Officer Training Corps (ROTC) program, he received a coveted regular army commission, rather than a reserve commission, as a second lieutenant of infantry. In addition to professional military schooling throughout his career, which included time at the U.S. Army Command and General Staff College and the National War College, Powell earned a master of business administration degree from George Washington University.

His military awards and decorations include the Defense Distinguished Service Medal with two oak-leaf clusters, Distinguished Service Medal (Army), Defense Superior Medal, Legion of Merit with oak-leaf cluster, Soldier's Medal, Bronze Star Medal, Purple Heart, Air Medal, Joint Service Commendation Medal, and Army Commendation Medal with two oak-leaf clusters. Powell also received the Presidential Medal of Freedom, President's Citizen's Medal, Secretary of State Distinguished Service Medal, and Secretary of Energy Distinguished Service Medal.

Powell is married to the former Alma Vivian Johnson, and they have three children: Michael, Linda, and Annemarie.

Military Career Highlights

After finishing the Infantry Officer Basic Course (IOBC) and Airborne and Ranger schools at Fort Benning, Georgia, Powell was assigned to the Federal Republic of Germany in October 1958. There, he served as a platoon leader, assistant adjutant, and company executive officer in the 3d Armored Division. He was reassigned to Fort Devens, Massachusetts, in December 1960, where he served as a company executive officer, rifle company commander, and battalion adjutant in the 5th Mechanized Division. As a captain, Powell went to Vietnam in late 1962, where he served briefly as an adviser at a Vietnamese self-defense corps training center and later as a senior adviser to a Vietnamese infantry battalion (where he earned the Purple Heart when he sustained a punji stake wound to his right foot) and as an operations adviser to the Vietnamese 1st Infantry Division.

From late 1963 to mid-1967, he served at the Infantry School at Fort Benning, Georgia, as a student attending the Infantry Officer Advanced Course (IOAC), weapons test officer, instructor, and writer. He was promoted early to major in May 1966 ahead of his contemporaries. Completing his tour at the Infantry School, he attended the U.S. Army Command and General Staff College at Fort Leavenworth, Kansas; he graduated second in his class of more than 1,200 students.

Powell returned to Vietnam in June 1968, serving in the U.S. 23d Infantry Division (American) as an infantry battalion executive officer, division operations (G3) officer, and later as deputy G3 (until a more senior officer slated for the G3 position arrived). Powell was awarded the Soldier's Medal for his role in rescuing other members of the division staff and the division commander when their helicopter crashed while landing to visit a deployed unit.

Returning to the United States in 1969, he undertook graduate studies and, in 1971, earned an MBA from George Washington University. (He was promoted to lieutenant colonel in July 1970.) After a year as an operations research analyst in the Office of the Assistant Vice Chief of Staff, Army, in 1972, Powell was selected to be a White House Fellow. He served his fellowship in the Office of Management and Budget. Initially, Caspar W. Weinberger and Frank C. Carlucci were the director and deputy director, respectively, of OMB in the Nixon White House. Powell would work for both of them later in his career as well.

In September 1973, Powell assumed command of the 1st Battalion, 32d Infantry, 2d Infantry Division in the Republic of Korea. He returned to the United States a year later, and after a brief stint as an operations research analyst in the Office of the Assistant Secretary of Defense for Manpower and Reserve Affairs, he attended the National War College, graduating in April 1976. By then promoted to the rank of colonel, he assumed command of the 2d Brigade, 101st Airborne Division (Air Assault) at Fort Campbell, Kentucky. The division commander was Maj. Gen. John A. Wickham, Jr., who would eventually become the Army chief of staff.

In 1977, Powell again returned to Washington to serve with the Office of the Secretary of Defense, then occupied by Carter administration appointees. Harold Brown was secretary of defense, and Charles Duncan was deputy secretary. Initially Powell served as executive to the special assistant to the secretary and deputy secretary of defense and then as senior military assistant to Deputy Secretary of Defense Duncan. Powell was promoted to brigadier general in 1979. For a brief period he served as executive assistant to Duncan when the latter became secretary of energy. Upon the defeat of President Carter in the November 1980 elections, the Reagan administration transition began. Already back at the Pentagon from his assignment at the Energy Department, Powell assisted the newly designated Secretary of Defense Caspar Weinberger and Deputy Secretary of Defense Frank Carlucci in the transition between administrations.

In June 1981, Powell became assistant division commander for operations and training, 4th Infantry Division (Mechanized), Fort Carson, Colorado. In August 1982, he became deputy commanding general of the U.S. Army Combined Arms Combat Development Center at Fort Leavenworth, Kansas. While in this assignment, Powell commanded a group of talented officers who were charged with advising the newly designated army chief of staff, Gen. John A. Wickham, Jr., in the development of his agenda for the army.

In July 1983, Powell returned to Washington to serve as senior military assistant to Secretary of Defense Weinberger. He was promoted to major general in August 1983. During this period the armed forces were undergoing modernization at a pace that would eventually build a force capable of easily overwhelming and defeating the Iraqis in Operation Desert Storm in February 1991. It was also the period of the Iran-Contra affair, which would eventually lead to the indictment—and later presidential pardon before a trial could get under way—of Weinberger.

In July 1986, Powell assumed command of V Corps in Frankfurt, Federal Republic of Germany, and was promoted to lieutenant general. His assignment to Germany, however, was to last only six months. Allegations in the Reagan White House of activities to circumvent laws prohibiting aid to Iran—the Iran-Contra affair—forced the resignation of Adm. John M. Poindexter as the national security adviser to President Reagan. Frank Carlucci was tapped to replace Poindexter; Carlucci in turn called on Powell to serve as his deputy. Powell officially assumed his duties in January 1987. When Carlucci eventually replaced Weinberger as secretary of defense in November 1987, Powell became the assistant to the president for national security affairs. He served in this capacity from December 1987 to January 1989.

Promoted to four-star general in April 1989, Powell became commander in chief, United States Forces Command, headquartered in Atlanta, Georgia. In October 1989, the presidency of George Bush now in place, he was appointed chairman of the Joint Chiefs of Staff and reappointed for a second two-year term in 1991.

Post–Cold War Military Leadership

While chairman of the Joint Chiefs of Staff, Powell oversaw two of the most successful military undertakings in the history of the U.S. armed forces: Operation Just Cause in 1989 and operations Desert Shield and Desert Storm in 1990 and 1991.

On 1 December 1989, Operation Just Cause was undertaken by a carefully planned and organized joint U.S. military force to eject Manuel Noriega from his dictatorial position in Panama and return him to the United States to face drug-trafficking charges. More than 25,000 U.S. troops conducted many carefully synchronized assaults to paralyze the Panamanian Defense Forces commanded by Noriega. The overall success of the precisely executed and thoroughly planned military operation demonstrated the capability of the U.S. armed forces to act decisively in international crises.

Iraq's invasion of Kuwait in August 1990 led to U.S. deployments (Operation Desert Shield) to deter expansion of Iraqi forces into Saudi Arabia. The continuing buildup of U.S. military forces and coalition forces reached a magnitude sufficient to eject the Iraqis from Kuwait (Operation Desert Storm) in February 1991; the ensuing ground campaign defeated Iraqi forces in 100 hours.

These successful operations established Powell as the country's newest military legend and hero. His ability to present information regarding military operations in an intelligible manner and his overall personable style reinforced his reputation as one of contemporary America's great soldiers.

The success enjoyed by the U.S. military in the Persian Gulf War was the high point of a process to rebuild the armed forces into a professional force in the years after the Vietnam War. Powell recognized that U.S. military modernization efforts in the 1980s had produced a professional force that could quickly defeat any adversary in the post–cold war era. Key elements were a revitalized operational doctrine, extensive force modernization, and realistic training, coupled with forward deployed and mobile forces. In combination, these elements gave the armed forces the capability to operate technologically advanced weaponry and rapidly defeat an opposing military force.

Political-Military Architect

As chairman of the Joint Chiefs of Staff, Powell was the principal military adviser to President Bush and Secretary of Defense Cheney. He was responsible for developing military options for their review and decision. In this regard, he had to ensure that the military objectives were clearly defined and in concert with the national objectives defined by the national command authorities. He had to recommend the magnitude and timing of U.S. military deployments to ensure success. The chief architectural responsibility for the most massive deployment of U.S. forces and material in U.S. history, Desert Shield and Desert Storm, therefore, fell on the shoulders of Colin Powell.

Powell's early military background, involving two tours in the Vietnam War and service at all levels of combat command, and his later experiences in the national security arena provided him with a blend of military savvy and an appreciation for things political.

At the conclusion of the Cold War, with the demise of the Soviet Union, Powell was charged with starting the process of partially dismantling the U.S. armed forces. At the same time, he had to advise a new administration on the use of military force in a number of regional crises, to include the Balkans and Somalia, where various U.S. peacekeeping elements are deployed. In this regard, his role was to advise his superiors on the importance of clearly defined national and related military objectives to ensure the success of a military operation.

Upon his formal retirement on 30 September 1993, Powell faced the prospect of new nonmilitary roles, possibly at the national level. His national popularity and stunning performance as a politico-military figure are characteristics that invite greater political involvement in the future.

JAMES D. BLUNDELL

SEE ALSO: Gulf War.

Bibliography

Adler, B. 1991. *The generals: The new American heroes.* New York: Avon Books.

Atkinson, R. 1993. *Crusade: The untold story of the Persian Gulf War.* New York: Houghton Mifflin.

Evertson, J. 1991. *Colin Powell.* New York: Bantam Books.

Haskins, J. 1992. *Colin Powell: A biography.* New York: Scholastic.

Means, H. 1992. *Colin Powell: soldier/statesman—statesman/soldier.* New York: Donald I. Fine.

Roth, D. 1993. *Sacred honor: A biography of Colin Powell.* Grand Rapids: Zondervan Publishing House.

PRINCIPLES OF WAR

Principles of war are a collection of basic experience parameters, rules, or maxims of conventional warfare for the successful conduct of military operations. They are the result of a comprehensive scientific analysis of campaigns and wars.

Purpose

The principles of war are used for the training and education of military commanders and for the conduct of military operations. For officers, knowledge of the principles of war promotes military expertise regarding developments and effects on the battlefield. The principles of war are also a suitable standard of comparison for the evaluation and assessment of completed operations, plans for operations, and new concepts.

In war, principles of war serve as a basis for command and control decisions. Their application enhances the ability to meet the challenges of complex and unforeseeable battlefield events with simple but effective responses.

Form and Applications

Generally, principles of war are expressed in one of three ways: as a list of key terms (e.g., offensive); in a form of sentence (e.g., adjust your ends to the means); or as text, where an aspect of decisive significance for the winning of military operations (e.g., mobility in defensive operations) is emphasized and explained.

The application of principles of war is not uniform and often is directly related to the form of presentation. The views range from rigid adherence to principles of war in all situations to flexible use, which is influenced by the conditions specific to each case. The more succinct the form of representation, the more dogmatic the application. In a mission-type order environment the application of the principles of war is dependent upon the evaluation of the given situation by the military commander.

The possibilities and limits of a meaningful application of principles of war vary with the level of command. Although principles of war are applicable at the strategic, operational, and tactical levels of command, the priorities and applications may vary due to different targets and situations at the different levels of command. For example, a principle such as "to mass forces at the decisive place and time" on the strategic level may call for dispersion of forces at the tactical level; or the application of the principle "offensive" in order to seize, retain, and exploit the initiative on an operational level may require a static defense by units on the tactical level.

Authors and Areas of Application

SUN TZU

The oldest statements on principles of war are ascribed to the military thinker and writer Sun Tzu (China, ca. 500 B.C.). He did not provide a list of principles of war; he proceeded from the assumption that the art of war does not have any fixed rules, that rules result only from the conditions of the concrete situation. Nonetheless, in *The Art of War*, he presented ten factors of decisive significance for victory or defeat in war, which are by their nature principles of war:

1. invincibility lies in the defense, the possibility of victory in the attack;
2. know the enemy and yourself;
3. strike only when the situation assures victory;
4. strike the enemy where he is least prepared;
5. weigh the situation before moving;
6. be flexible;
7. recognize the hazards and the weather;
8. deceive the enemy;
9. surprise the enemy;
10. separate the enemy from his allies.

KARL VON CLAUSEWITZ

Clausewitz recognized the usefulness of principles of war for the training and education of officers. But he also concluded that a capable and trained military leader must not adhere dogmatically to the principles of war; his military assessment should be determined by experience, intuition, and the conditions of the situation. An analysis of Clausewitz's *On War* reveals at least nine conclusions, which have the character of principles of war:

1. *Superiority of defense.* When Clausewitz had examined the arts of defense and offense and their relationship at the tactical and strategic levels, he concluded that defense is a stronger form of war than attack. Clausewitz placed a high value on defense, and felt that commanders should always consider the advantage of defensive actions to reach the military objective.

2. *Active defense.* Clausewitz visualized an active defense. Without this active element—more in tactics than in strategy—defense cannot exploit its advantages; to stay strictly defensive would mean to remain utterly passive. The defender must watch for opportunities to launch counterattacks to overcome and weaken the enemy whenever and wherever possible.

3. *Simplicity.* Simplicity as a requirement for planning and conducting actions on the battlefield is a matter of Clausewitz's own experience. In connection with friction he states, "Everything in war is very simple, but the simplest thing is difficult." Since war is the realm of uncertainty, and Clausewitz believed that three-quarters of the factors on which action in war is based are wrapped in a fog of greater or lesser uncertainty, all plans for operations must be very simple. Difficulties and complexity arise with and by the conduct itself.

4. *Offensive.* Although Clausewitz emphasized the relative strength of defensive combat more than that of offensive combat, he also emphasized that wars cannot be won by staying on the defensive. He pointed out that victory can be achieved only by taking the offensive.

5. *Concentration of forces.* Clausewitz frequently reminded his readers that numerical strength was an important ingredient for success in war. He stated that to assure numerical superiority, a commander must keep his forces con-

centrated, and avoid all temptations to detach elements from the main body except under the most urgent circumstances.

6. *Economy of force*. Clausewitz expressed this concept as the full employment of all elements of a command, with none allowed to remain idle. Although this is different from the meaning given to the concept by the U.S. Army (see below), there are some similarities, including Clausewitz's use of troops to occupy some of the enemy's forces and reduce his overall strength, and his view that economy of force is a corollary of concentration of force.

7. *Main effort*. Clausewitz mentioned the need for a main effort, or a strength, at the decisive place and time. When Clausewitz explained the advantage of the superiority of numbers of soldiers, he concluded that as many troops as possible should be brought into the engagement at the decisive point.

8. *Reserves*. Reserve forces and their use played a major role in Clausewitz's considerations. He taught that all the troops should not be brought into combat immediately; some should be held behind the front lines, far enough back to avoid envelopment of the total force by the enemy. Clausewitz felt that the commander should not give up the battle as long as he had sufficient reserves, and that their employment might determine the outcome of the battle.

9. *Surprise*. Clausewitz discussed the element of surprise as an independent principle both in tactics and strategy; he believed surprise to be a significant element in qualitative combat power. Surprising courses of action resulted in a disconcerted enemy. The best way to achieve surprise was with the rapid use of forces.

UNITED STATES ARMY

Principles of war have been presented by Clausewitz, Jomini, Douhet, and others. Modern versions of the principles of war, as understood by British and American forces, are based upon a formulation by the British theorist J. F. C. Fuller in 1920.

The tradition of the U.S. Army's principles of war can be traced back to December 1921, when nine principles were listed in *War Department Training Regulation no. 10-5:* (1) objective, (2) offensive, (3) mass, (4) economy of force, (5) movement, (6) surprise, (7) security, (8) simplicity, and (9) cooperation.

The 1986 edition of the U.S. Army's *Field Manual 100-5* also lists nine principles of war. They have withstood the test of analysis, experimentation, and practice; and they are applicable on the strategic, operational, and tactical levels.

The nine principles of war and their imperative definitions are:

1. *Objective*. Direct every military operation toward a clearly defined, decisive, and attainable objective.
2. *Offensive*. Seize, retain, and exploit the initiative.
3. *Mass*. Concentrate combat power at the decisive place and time.
4. *Economy of force*. Allocate minimum essential combat power to secondary efforts.

5. *Maneuver.* Place the enemy in a position of disadvantage through the flexible application of combat power.
6. *Unity of command.* For every objective, ensure unity of effort under one responsible commander.
7. *Security.* Never permit the enemy to acquire an unexpected advantage.
8. *Surprise.* Strike the enemy at a time or place and in a manner for which he is unprepared.
9. *Simplicity.* Prepare clear, uncomplicated plans and clear, concise orders to ensure thorough understanding.

The U.S. Army emphasizes the value of the principles of war in training and in the conduct of warfare. The principles of war serve U.S. Army officers as checklists for planning and operations. For the wargaming process they play a key role in the evaluation of each course of action and of the decision-making process.

ARMY OF THE FEDERAL REPUBLIC OF GERMANY

The German army's basic manual, *Heeresdienstvorschrift 100/100*, does not contain a list of principles of war. This is in accordance with traditional German doctrine since the era of Helmuth von Moltke in the nineteenth century. The command and control of forces is an art, a creative activity based on character, skill, and mental power.

The German army does not provide any rigid formulas or instructions on how individual operations should be conducted; but every commander must be guided by clear principles. Success is ensured only by giving commanders the freedom to judge and act within the scope of their missions, not by binding them strictly to principles of war. Only general principles are applied: active defense, fire and maneuver, building reserves, proper use of terrain, simplicity, surprise, and deception.

These general principles, which have the character of principles of war, provide the framework for training and peacetime exercises. They ensure a common understanding of tactical concepts and ideas for all officers, and form the basis for the application of mission-type orders.

GERTMANN SUDE

SEE ALSO: Clausewitz, Karl von; Douhet, Giulio; Fuller, J.F.C.; Jomini, Antoine Henri; Sun Tzu.

Bibliography

Alger, J. J. 1982. *The quest for victory: The history of the principles of war.* Westport, Conn.: Greenwood Press.
Clausewitz, C. von. 1976. *On war.* Ed. and trans. M. Howard and P. Paret. Princeton, N.J.: Princeton Univ. Press.
Sun Tzu. 1963. *The art of war.* Trans. S. B. Griffith. Cambridge: Oxford Univ. Press.
U.S. Department of the Army. 1986. *Field manual 100-5.* Washington, D.C.: Government Printing Office.

PRUSSIA AND GERMANY, RISE OF

Germany originated in one of the states created by the partition of Charle-magne's Frankish empire (A.D. 843). Among its numerous and semi-independent component states, Prussia eventually gained predominance and developed in the early nineteenth century what some regarded, until 1945, as the most efficient military system—others denounced it as an outgrowth of militarism. Also in the nineteenth century, Prussia united most of the German-speaking states, which already influential contemporaries (e.g., Benjamin Dis-raeli and William Gladstone) deplored as the overthrow of the balance of power in Europe; others contended that only a unified Germany could present a European balance to the visibly growing Russian potential. Finally, some argue that a Prussian mentality paved the way for Adolf Hitler, or at least was con-gruent with his ideology, while others hold the opposite view. After World War II, the Allies assigned large parts of Prussia and Germany to Poland and had the entire population expelled with huge loss of life. The Allies then dissolved the remainder of Prussia and divided what was left of Germany. This terminated the existence of Prussia and of Germany, two states whose role in history is still the object of considerable controversy. However, whereas a revival of Prussia seems impossible, the remnants of Germany were reunited in 1990.

The First German Reich (Empire)

In 843 and 870, Charlemagne's Frankish empire was partitioned first into three, then into two parts. Out of the eastern part grew the German Reich (state, empire). In 962, King Otto I assumed the title of kaiser (emperor), and his state became known officially as the Holy Roman Empire since it was considered the lawful continuation of the Imperium Romanum.

The emperors that followed Otto had no power base other than their own duchy—often insufficient to enforce their rule. Also, the king-emperors were elected by the most powerful nobles, who often wrested concessions from the candidate in return for their votes. Finally, the emperors who reigned from the eleventh to the thirteenth centuries became engaged in a bitter contest with the papacy over the proper relations between the spiritual and the secular powers. In 1250, imperial power collapsed and vanished completely for several decades.

Thereafter, the absence of a firm monarch and the consequent absence of an effective central power remained the salient features of German history. By the fifteenth century, the empire had become a patchwork of hundreds of secular territories, ecclesiastic territories, and free cities—all enjoying flourishing semi-independence. This permitted a beneficial, multicentered cultural diversity. It may also have assisted in the prevention of a degenerate absolutism. Finally, political freedom and civil liberties were less suppressed than in many other states, since most of the petty rulers and princes were too weak to abolish them. In many German states, diets continued to exist and a considerable number of them—for example, the "imperial free cities"—were organized as oligarchic republics.

On the other hand, the absence of a powerful center led to disintegration. In the thirteenth and fourteenth centuries, large areas (e.g., the Italian states, the cantons of Switzerland, the Netherlands, and Provence) established their independence. The Reformation exacerbated dissension within the Reich. Disaster struck with the Thirty Years' War (1618–48). It made the Reich the battlefield of Europe, leaving it utterly devastated, and further reduced the emperor's power. The Reich soon became the object of a two-pronged attack by France (1681 Strasbourg, capital of Alsace, occupied) and the Ottoman Empire (1683 Siege of Vienna). Alliances between the Reich's princes and foreign powers, especially France, became customary. In 1806, under French pressure, the last emperor abdicated the throne.

THE GERMAN CONFEDERATION (DEUTSCHER BUND)

After the Napoleonic Wars, the Congress of Vienna established the German Confederation, a loose association of 39 sovereign states. This left the door open for legal foreign interference, since three foreign monarchs were members through their possessions within the Confederation: the king of England as king of Hannover; the king of the Netherlands as grand duke of Luxembourg; and the king of Denmark as count of Holstein. The two most powerful members, Prussia and Austria, had large possessions outside the Confederation and were in constant rivalry. The Confederation thus proved unable to fill the power vacuum that had been advantageous primarily to neighboring nation-states.

The Rise of Prussia

What later became the kingdom of Prussia (Preussen) originated from two roots: the margraviate (frontier county) of Brandenburg and the state of the Teutonic Knights (Deutscher Ritterorden).

THE MARGRAVIATE OF BRANDENBURG

After about A.D. 300, Slavonic tribes (the Wends) resettled the area east of the lower course of the River Elbe, which Germanic tribes had vacated, migrating west and south. However, the vast lowlands remained sparsely populated and economically backward, which facilitated, after 900, conquest from the east by Poland and from the west by the Reich, and permitted penetration by German settlers. The very large number, if not preponderance of east German, especially Prussian, noble and common families with names of Slavonic origin, the preservation of Slavonic dialects in certain regions until the nineteenth and twentieth centuries, and the numerous villages with names prefixed, for example, by "Wendisch" (Slavonic) testify to the mix of old and new populations.

In 1140, the emperor created the margraviate of Brandenburg (region around Berlin) in the new territories. Since they ruled one of the more powerful principalities, by about 1250 the margraves were recognized as one of the seven electors (Kurfürsten) of the emperor.

The margraviate was ruled by various dynasties, until in 1415 the emperor appointed Friedrich I, a count from the south German family of Hohenzollern, as the new margrave. This dynasty ruled until 1918.

In 1506, the first university was founded. About 30 years later, Lutheranism peacefully replaced Catholicism. In 1614, the margraves inherited several principalities (Kleve, Mark, Ravensberg) far to the west on the lower Rhine. Four years later, they inherited the duchy of Preussen, which was located far in the east, outside the Reich, and legally under Polish suzerainty.

Thus, in the early seventeenth century, Brandenburg was spread out in bits and pieces over the whole north German lowlands. But little had happened that set it aside from other German states. With the family law of 1473, however, a first step toward primogeniture had been made. Also, when the margrave turned from Lutheranism to Calvinism in 1613, he refrained from the customary attempt to press his subjects into following suit. This initiated an almost uninterrupted history of religious tolerance, at the time almost unknown in Europe.

THE STATE OF THE TEUTONIC ORDER OF KNIGHTS

In the early thirteenth century, the Prussians, a Baltic people speaking a language akin to Lithuanian, lived east of the Vistula along the southeastern shores of the Baltic Sea. In 1226, Count Conrad of Masovia (the region around Warsaw in Poland) invited the Order of Knights of Christ and of the Hospital of St. Mary of the Teutons in Jerusalem, the Teutonic Knights, to convert the heathen Prussians, who frequently raided his territories. Emperor, pope, and Duke Conrad granted the order possession of the lands it would conquer.

The order soon moved its seat from the Holy Land to Venice and then to the Marienburg (St. Mary's castle, since 1945 Malbork) on the Vistula. About 1300, the order already ruled vast areas of what later became Estonia, Latvia, East Prussia, West Prussia, Posen (the "Polish Corridor"), and part of Pomerania. Numerous cities like Reval (Tallinn), Riga, Königsberg (since 1945 Kaliningrad), Danzig (since 1945 Gdansk), and Stettin (Szczecin) soon prospered.

However, the interests of the large commercial cities and of the landed gentry were at variance with government by a religious order. Several times cities or nobles allied themselves with foreign enemies of the order. Thus, in 1466, after several wars, Poland decisively defeated the order and annexed most of its possessions. The order retained only Prussia, albeit as a Polish fief.

The cultural level of the towns and bishoprics is illustrated by the career of the great astronomer Nicolas Copernicus (1473–1543), who first was adviser to his uncle, Bishop Lukas von Watzelrode, at Heilsberg (since 1945 Lidzbark Warminski), then chief administrator at Allenstein (now Olsztyn) and member of the Cathedral Chapter at Frauenburg (now Frombork).

In 1525, the grand master of the Teutonic Knights, Albrecht of Hohenzollern, embraced Lutheranism; the religious order's state became the secular duchy of Preussen (Prussia). When Albrecht's line died out in 1618, the duchy passed to Brandenburg.

From Electorate Through Kingdom to the Second Reich

In the Thirty Years' War (1618–48), Brandenburg tried vainly to stay neutral, but powerful neighbors made the weak state one of their preferred battlefields. The same threatened to happen in the ensuing wars between Sweden and Poland for supremacy in the Baltic region and between France and a coalition of various states for predominance on the continent. Obviously, for Brandenburg, consisting of several provinces scattered over northern Germany and devoid of natural borders, a powerful army and an effective administration were necessary for survival. Both were created by Friedrich Wilhelm, known as the Great Elector (1640–88). Brandenburg became the foremost German Protestant power, a position solidified by victory over the Swedes at Fehrbellin (1675). In addition, it established full sovereignty over Prussia.

In 1701, the ruling elector utilized the emperor's need for assistance in his bid for the vacant Spanish throne. In this way he gained recognition as "King in Prussia," taking the title from the province that lay outside the empire.

In 1740, the first king's grandson, Friedrich II (Frederick the Great), offered to support the daughter of the deceased emperor Charles VI in her candidacy for the imperial throne, normally open only to men. In return, he demanded the province of Silesia (now Slask), parts of which he claimed with dynastic arguments as complicated and contested as such arguments usually were. When the proposal was refused, Friedrich took by force what he then had to defend. Supported only by Britain, he survived the Seven Years' War (1756–63) against Austria, most states of the Reich, France, Sweden, Poland, and Russia. Prussia emerged from these wars with a treasury still well filled and as the fifth of the recognized major European powers.

By the late eighteenth century, Prussia had become exceptional in several respects: it possessed an army of unique size and great reputation, an administration so effective that it could support the army without imposing any unusual burden on the country, general primary education (introduced in 1717, cf. Britain 1872), no torture (banned in 1740), equality of nobles and commoners before the law, religious tolerance, no public debt, and a nobility accustomed and forced to satisfy its pride by service to the state.

Participation in the partitions of Poland and the wars against the French Revolution and Napoleon brought large ups and downs in the fate of Prussia, as well as the dissolution of most German ecclesiastic territories and their integration into the secular principalities. Finally, at the Congress of Vienna, the major European powers considerably enlarged Prussia: in the east it shared a common border with Russia, in the west with France. Rivalry with Austria was now inevitable. In the view of many, the power vacuum in central Europe and between France and Russia had to be filled. In addition, the nineteenth century demanded political rights for the masses. Finally, from Norway through Ireland and Italy to Greece, Romania, and Bulgaria, people considered a nation-state as indispensable.

In 1849, the Prussian king unilaterally imposed a constitution that, among other things, granted universal manhood suffrage. Critics pointed out that it was census-based; others emphasized that at the time it marked huge progress—in most states of the Americas, slavery was still legal, and even in Britain, less than 10 percent of the male population could vote at all.

Prussian-Austrian rivalry was settled by war in 1866 (Seven Weeks' War). Victorious Prussia demanded from the vanquished only their withdrawal from German affairs and the dissolution of the German Federation. Otto von Bismarck, Prussia's chancellor, however, knew that the First Reich had failed in part because the emperors never had a sufficient power base. Thus Prussia annexed most of those north German states that had been allied with Austria. Four years later, the troops from these states fought well under Prussian colors.

Possibly the war against France in 1870–71 was unavoidable. For more than two hundred years, France had dominated the continent of Europe, politically, militarily, and also culturally. A unified Germany inevitably would be a strong competitor because of its size, population, and potential. Few believed that France would voluntarily share its position of primacy with anyone or would even renounce it. The rivalry resulted in what incorrectly is called the Franco-Prussian War, since all German states participated voluntarily. In January 1871, during the Siege of Paris, the (Second) Reich was proclaimed at Versailles, with the Prussian king as hereditary emperor.

Barring Switzerland, the Second Reich was by far the most decentralized state of that time. The twenty-five component states (i.e., four kingdoms, six grand duchies, five duchies) retained important rights. Bavaria even retained the right to have it own army, its own general staff, and its own embassies abroad. Introduction of universal equal manhood suffrage was another unusual feature (Britain did not take this step until 1918), as was the secret ballot, unknown at the time even in Britain. Critics could point to deficiencies: Prussia was dominant, the Reich's chancellor required the kaiser's confidence only, and the Reichstag (parliament) could significantly influence the armed forces only through the budget. In defense, it could be stated that the Reich was one of the very few states that, because of the strength of the crown, passed from absolutism to constitutional monarchy without a transition through oligarchy, thereby sparing the lower classes much exploitation. The system of checks and balances was unique: the emperor retained in the Reich, and the princes retained in their states, important political rights; the upper class had the economic power but less political power than in most other countries of the time; the lower classes had little economic power, but through universal suffrage (equal suffrage in the Reich and in many of the component states), they had much political power and more than once they enjoyed additional support from the crown.

Visible decline of Prussia and Germany set in with World War I. Germany, often considered militaristic, had spent much less on its armed forces than its potential opponents—both in absolute terms and per capita. However, the finances were unquestionably used effectively to produce both an army and a navy of great efficiency. Nevertheless, the militaristic state entered a war in which time would clearly work in favor of its opponents with numerically inferior forces despite a large potential unused for military forces (Goodspeed

1977, pp. viii, 33, 51, 147; Wright 1942, App. XXII). The only hope lay in using the efficient army in a bid for rapid victory over one of its major opponents (Schlieffen Plan). When the general staff bungled it, ultimate defeat was almost inevitable. The peace of Versailles, in addition to heavy reparations and other onerous conditions, imposed important territorial changes. Some of these changes were in accordance with the wishes of the populations concerned (e.g., transfer of the province of Posen [Poznan] to Poland), but other changes were against the wishes of the population. The German portion of Austria-Hungary was forbidden to join Germany ("Anschluss"), despite a unanimous vote of its parliament.

The Third Reich and Collapse

World War II has been seen as a continuation of World War I. None of the German political parties endorsed the conditions imposed at Versailles—they only tolerated them. On the other hand, important politicians abroad continued to see Germany as a menace to the traditional balance of power in Europe, a balance that excluded Russia from consideration (Churchill 1949, vol. I, p. 208).

Hitler exacerbated the situation. Within a few years he broke what almost all Germans and many others considered "the chains of Versailles." This was popular in Germany but aroused concern and fear among other governments and peoples. He effected *anschluss* (joining) with Austria and absorption of the German Sudetens (from Czechoslovakia) and the Memel territory (from Lithuania), thereby strengthening his position with the population of Germany and of the territories gained. On the other hand, when what Hitler called the Third Reich occupied the rest of Czechoslovakia, it disrespected the right of self-determination of peoples at least as ruthlessly as the victors had done at Versailles. In addition, every territorial acquisition, even if justified by the desire of the population, exacerbated the problem of a Germany too large and too powerful for the comfort of many of its neighbors.

In 1939, Germany attacked Poland for the avowed purpose of solving the problems of Danzig (German in population but forced by Versailles to remain semi-independent under Poland's suzerainty) and of the Polish corridor (with mixed population and affecting Polish access to the Baltic and German access to East Prussia). When other states, outraged by this aggression, assisted Poland, the conflict expanded to World War II.

After the war, the victors gave the eastern provinces of Germany to Poland. The entire population was to be expelled, as well as all ethnic Germans from Czechoslovakia, Hungary, Yugoslavia, and Poland proper. The operation displaced more than 15 million people and was executed under conditions that took the lives of about 2.3 million, according to West German official statistics (Documents 1958; de Launay 1985; de Zayas 1977). Prussia (or rather the remainder of it) "which from early days has been a bearer of militarism and reaction in Germany [and which] has de facto ceased to exist . . . is abolished" (Decree no. 46 of the Allied Control Council, 25 February 1947). Critics could point out that "the bearer of militarism from early days" had been involved in significantly fewer wars than most of the nations who dissolved it, even according to an American study published during World War II (Wright 1942, pp. 641ff.). The rest of Germany was divided into four zones of occupation, with joint occupation of Berlin by the three victors and France. The future fate of the fragments was kept in abeyance because of disagreement among the victors.

Federal Republic, German Democratic Republic, and Berlin

Growing East-West tension motivated the Soviet Union and the Western occupying powers to completely reverse their occupation policy. Since they wanted a German military contribution, they had to integrate their fragments into their respective blocs and to restore a limited sovereignty. Thus, during most of the second half of the twentieth century, the Federal Republic was part of the Western system of alliances, the German Democratic Republic part of the eastern system, and Berlin was jointly occupied and under occupational jurisdiction of the victors. However, because of the largely peaceful revolution that swept through Eastern Europe in 1989–90, the three fragments of Germany were reunited in late 1990, and Berlin (the heart of historical Prussia) again became the capital of a united Germany.

FRANZ UHLE-WETTLER

SEE ALSO: Franco-Prussian War; Seven Years' War; Thirty Years' War; World War I; World War II.

Bibliography

Calleo, D. P. 1978. *The German problem reconsidered: Germany and the world order, 1970 to the present.* Cambridge: Cambridge Univ. Press.

Churchill, W. S. 1949. *The Second World War.* 6 vols. London: Cassell.

Documents on the Expulsion of the Germans from Eastern-Central Europe. 1958 seq. 15 vols. Bonn: Federal Ministry for Expellees, Refugees and War Victims.

Dupuy, T. N. 1984. *A genius for war: The German army and general staff 1807–1945.* Fairfax, VA: HERO Books.

Goodspeed, D. J. 1977. *The German wars 1914–1945.* New York: Bonanza Books.

De Launay, C. 1985. La grande débâcle. Paris.

Löwenstein, H. Prinz zu. 1962. *Deutsche Geschichte.* München and Berlin: Haude and Spenensche.

Ludwig, E. 1943. *How to treat the Germans.* New York: Willard.

Mann, G. 1958. *Deutsche Geschichte des 19. und 20. Jahrhunderts.* Frankfurt: S. Fisher Verlag.

Nizer, L. 1944. *What to do with Germany.* New York and Chicago: Ziff-Davis.

Taylor, A. J. P. 1962. *The origins of the Second World War.* New York: Atheneum Press.

Uhle-Wettler, F. 1984. *Höhe- und Wendepunkte deutscher Militärgeschichte.* Mainz: V. Hase und Koehler Verlag.

Wright, Q. 1942. *A study of war.* Chicago: Univ. of Chicago Press.

de Zayas, A. 1977. *Nemesis at Potsdam: The Anglo-Americans and the expulsion of the Germans.* London and Boston: Routledge and K. Paul.

ADDITIONAL SOURCES: *Preussen ohne Legende* (1979, Hamburg); *Germany Must Perish* (1941, Newark, N.J.).

PUNIC WARS

The Punic Wars were the three wars fought between Republican Rome and Carthage in the third and second centuries B.C. Originally an ancient Phoenician trading post on the northern coast of Africa, Carthage had become the dominant maritime and commercial power in the western Mediterranean by the third century B.C. Rome, which had consolidated control of the Italian peninsula by 265 B.C., could not ignore the imperialistic growth of Carthage, which had colonized Corsica, Sardinia, the Spanish coast, and western Sicily (the adjective *Punic* comes from *Poeni*, the Latin name for the Carthaginians).

First Punic War (264–241 B.C.)

The first war evolved from the growing political and economic rivalry between the two states over Sicily. The crisis that initiated the conflict was the seizure of the Sicilian city of Messana (Messina) by the Mamertini mercenaries of Campani. When the mercenaries were besieged by the armies of King Hiero II of Syracuse, they appealed to both Rome and Carthage for aid. The Carthaginians, who arrived first, occupied Messana and made peace with Syracuse. Rome, after some political vacillation, crossed the strait separating Sicily from Italy and in three campaigns drove the Carthaginians back into western Sicily, which they had occupied prior to the hostilities. The Romans could not expel the Carthaginians from western Sicily because of their excellent fortifications, which were easily supplied by their superior seapower.

Realizing their weakness, the Romans decided to challenge Carthage for control of the seas. Rome rapidly built its first great fleet while simultaneously training its oarsmen on the shore. Doubting their ability to outmaneuver the Carthaginians, the Romans equipped their ships with erect gangways with spiked ends. At close quarters, these gangways could be dropped onto the decks of enemy ships and serve as boarding bridges for the Roman soldiers, who excelled at hand-to-hand combat. In 260 B.C., the Roman admiral Gaius Duilius defeated a superior Carthaginian fleet at Mylae, off the northern Sicilian coast.

In 256 a large Roman fleet repelled the main Carthaginian fleet at Cape Ecnomus and went on to establish a Roman base at Clypea (Keliba in Tunisia). In 255, the Greek mercenary, Xanthippus, defeated the Romans commanded by Marcus Atillius Regulus near Tunis. A Roman fleet withdrawing the troops from Africa perished in a storm with a loss of nearly 100,000 men and 250 vessels. The remaining years of the war were fought in the area of Sicily as both sides began to feel the financial strain of the prolonged conflict. The only noteworthy feature of the land war was the emergence of Hamilcar Barca, who won several victories over Rome in Sicily. Rome rebuilt its navy and in 241 B.C. inflicted a disastrous defeat on the Carthaginian navy off the Aegates Islands near Sicily.

The Battle of Aegates gave Rome undisputed naval superiority and forced

Carthage to open negotiations that led to the Romans exacting an indemnity of 3,200 talents and the cession of Sicily and the Lipari Islands. Sicily was the first Roman overseas province and the initial step toward empire. During a mutiny in 238 B.C. by Carthaginian mercenaries in the "Truceless War," Rome seized Corsica and Sardinia from a politically divided Carthage.

Second Punic War (218–201 B.C.)

Carthage resented Rome's victory in the first Punic War and the subsequent seizures of Corsica and Sardinia. Under the leadership of the powerful Barca family, Carthage consolidated new sources of wealth and potential mercenaries in Spain. The Romans became concerned about the continued Carthaginian exploitation of Spain and negotiated a treaty in 255 B.C., establishing the Ebro River as a demarcation line between the rival nations. In 221 Rome supported an anti-Carthaginian party in the city of Saguntum, which was well within the Carthaginian sphere of influence. Carthage interpreted this as aggression and its military response opened the Second Punic War.

In 220 Hannibal, the 25-year-old son and successor of the deceased Hamilcar, attacked and took Saguntum. Rome officially declared war in 218. Anticipating Rome's response, Hannibal left his brother Hasdrubal as commander in Spain and marched a large army through Spain and Gaul, attacking the Romans in Italy before they could launch offensives into Carthage and Spain.

The boldness of Hannibal's strategy contributed to his success. After crossing the rugged Alps, he scored his initial victories on the banks of the Ticinus and the Trebbia in 218 B.C. In 217, with his 30,000 men reinforced by Gauls, he penetrated into Etruria and defeated a Roman force on the shores of Lake Trasimene. This disaster cost Rome over 15,000 men and opened the way for Hannibal to push deeper into Italy. Rome sent consuls Terentius Varro and Lucius Aemilius Paulus with 80,000 men to destroy Hannibal. This decision to depart from the successful delaying tactics of Quintus Fabius Maximus ("Cunctator") in 216 resulted in the bloodiest defeat in Roman history. On a level plain near the small fortress of Cannae in Apulia, Hannibal deployed his center, composed mainly of Spaniards and Gauls, in a convex formation. He posted his Carthaginian veterans behind the center. He permitted the superior Roman forces to push in his center until it was stabilized by his Carthaginians while his cavalry wheeled around to attack the Roman rear and flanks. The Romans, wedged into a tight pocket, could not use their weapons and were caught in a horrible massacre. Hannibal's classic victory at Cannae tactically depended on an unorthodox disposition of troops and careful timing and coordination. Seventy thousand Romans, including several senators, nobles, and the Consul Aemilius Paulus were killed at Cannae by Hannibal's double envelopment tactics.

Despite his military successes, Hannibal failed in his efforts and strategy to win over enough dissatisfied defectors from Rome. In addition, his requests for reinforcements and supplies were often ignored. Roman resumption of the Fabian strategy deprived Hannibal of additional victories. Hasdrubal valiantly crossed the Alps to reinforce his brother only to be defeated and killed at the Metaurus River in northern Italy in 207 B.C. Meanwhile, the Roman forces under Publius Cornelius Scipio, later named Scipio Africanus, had defeated the Carthaginians in Spain at Carthago Nova in 209. His victory at Ilipa, near Seville, in 206 resulted in the expulsion of Carthage from Spain. Having already defeated the Carthaginian forces in Sicily after several battles in 210, Rome had turned the war to its favor.

In 204 B.C., Scipio sailed a large force across to Africa. Initially pinned down on the coast, Scipio broke away to win several decisive battles over the Carthaginians and their ally, King Syphax of Numidia. Scipio restored King Masinissa to the throne of Numidia, from which Syphax had expelled him. Carthage was induced by these events in 203 to sue for peace, but before the negotiation could be concluded a reversal of opinion led to a resumption of the war.

Hannibal was recalled from Italy to defend Carthage. He had maintained his army and the military initiative in Italy for fifteen years. In Africa, he faced a formidable Roman army with a force of his veteran troops combined with mercenary and citizen levies. At the decisive Battle of Zama in 202, Scipio's infantry evaded an attack by the Carthaginian elephants and cut through the first two lines only to be stymied by Hannibal's veterans. The Romans, in a move recalling the tactics of Cannae, won the battle by attacking the Carthaginian rear with cavalry supplemented by Masinissa's troops.

The defeat at Zama forced Carthage to accept a Roman peace treaty in 201. Carthage surrendered its navy, ceded Spain and the Mediterranean islands, and paid an indemnity of 10,000 talents to Rome. Restricted in size, Carthage was no longer a great military or commercial power.

Third Punic War (149–146 B.C.)

During the second century B.C., Carthage again grew commercially powerful, which only served to irritate the Romans. The Roman censor Cato the Elder became obsessed with the belief that Carthage had to be eliminated. Again and again over the years, he voiced the phrase "Delenda est Carthago" ("Carthage must be destroyed"). During this time, Masinissa of Numidia took every opportunity available to encroach on Carthage, whose complaints to Rome resulted only in judgments in favor of Masinissa. The leadership of Carthage became exasperated by Numidian aggression. In 151 B.C., they exiled several of Masinissa's supporters and even attacked forces led by his sons when they tried to restore order. This led to war between Carthage and Numidia in 150. A more important result was that the Carthaginian war with Masinissa violated the terms of the Treaty of Zama and gave Rome a pretext for war.

Rome dispatched an army to Africa, where the desperate Carthaginians agreed to surrender their arms and make general reparations. They were goaded into war when the Romans added the further stipulation that they must renounce their commercial policies, abandon the coast, and immigrate to the African interior. The Roman siege of Carthage lasted three years. During the first two years the poorly disciplined Roman army was led by incompetent commanders. In 147 the command was given to Publius Cornelius Scipio Aemilianus, the adopted grandson of Scipio Africanus and a newly elected consul. The consul took Carthage in the spring of 146 in a six-day battle that raged from street to street and house to house until the city was razed. The surviving 50,000 people were sold into slavery and Carthage's ruins were included in the province of Africa Proconsularis. The story that Carthage was plowed under and the ruins covered with salt is based on exaggerated accounts by later writers. The impressive ruins remained for centuries, although they were constantly reduced for their quarried and dressed stones.

Conclusion

The issue between Rome and Carthage had been decided at the conclusion of the Second Punic War. The destruction of Carthage in the third war was simply primitive and brutal aggression by Rome. With the conclusion of the struggle with Carthage, Rome, the once small agricultural village of central Italy, became the master of a significant portion of the ancient world and the undisputed commercial power in the Mediterranean Sea.

PHILLIP E. KOERPER

SEE ALSO: Hannibal Barca; History, Ancient Military; Roman Empire; Scipio Africanus.

Bibliography

Caven, B. 1980. *The Punic wars.* New York: St. Martin's Press.
De Sélincourt, A. 1965. *Livy: The war with Hannibal.* Baltimore, Md.: Penguin Books.
Forde, N. 1975. *Cato the censor.* Boston: Twayne.
Harris, W. 1979. *War and imperialism in Republican Rome 327–70* B.C. Oxford: Clarendon Press.
Lazenby, J. 1978. *Hannibal's war: A military history of the second Punic war.* Warminster, Eng.: Aris and Phillips.
Liddell Hart, B. 1927. *Greater than Napoleon: Scipio Africanus.* Boston: Little, Brown.
Livy. 1981. *Rome and the Mediterranean.* New York: Penguin Books.
Lloyd, A. 1977. *Destroy Carthage.* London: Souvenir Press.
Scott-Kilvert, I., trans. 1979. *Polybius: The rise of the Roman Empire.* Harmondsworth, U. K.: Penguin Books.
Scullard, H. 1951. *A history of the Roman world from 753–146* B.C. London: Methuen.
———. 1970. *Scipio Africanus: Soldier and politician.* Ithaca, N. Y.: Cornell Univ. Press.
Thiel, J. 1946. *A history of Roman seapower.* Amsterdam: North Holland.
Toynbee, A. 1965. *Hannibal's legacy: The Hannibalic war's effects on Roman life.* 2 vols. Oxford: Clarendon Press.
Warmington, B. 1965. *Carthage.* London: Penguin Books.

R

ROKOSSOVSKII, KONSTANTIN KONSTANTINOVICH [1896–1968]

Marshal of the Soviet Union Rokossovskii—World War II front commander, Polish defense minister, postwar commander of groups of Soviet forces in Eastern Europe, and deputy minister of defense (DMD)—was one of the premier Soviet field commanders and specialists in mobile operations. Rokossovskii was one of the few Red Army purge victims to survive imprisonment and return to senior military command. He refused to support the Polish Home Army during its uprising in Warsaw in August 1944 (on Stalin's order) and was despised by the Poles when Stalin forced his appointment as Polish minister of national defense. Rokossovskii was a candidate member of the Central Committee (1956–58) and a delegate to the fifth through seventh sessions of the Supreme Soviet of the USSR.

Early Life

Rokossovskii was born on 9 (O.S.; 21 N.S.) December 1896 in Velikie Luki (Pskov oblast), the son of a Polish railroad machinist and a Russian mother. Orphaned in 1910, Rokossovskii became a construction worker. He was drafted into the czarist cavalry in 1914 and rose to the rank of sergeant with the 5th Dragoon Kargopol'skii Regiment. In October 1917 he joined the Red Guard; the following December he entered the Red Army. During the civil war Rokossovskii commanded a Red cavalry squadron of the 1st Urals Cavalry Regiment (CR) (October 1918); the 2d Urals Cavalry Division (CD) (June 1919); and the 30th CR (January 1920). In September 1920 he took command of the 35th CR. Rokossovskii joined the Communist party in 1919. Following the civil war he served in the Transbaikal where he commanded a cavalry regiment and the 5th Detached Kuban Cavalry Brigade. In 1925 he completed a training course for junior cavalry commanders; four years later he completed a course for senior cavalry commanders. In 1930 he took command of the 7th Samar CD, and in 1932–35 he commanded the 15th CD in the Transbaikal. In 1936 Rokossovskii commanded the V Cavalry Corps (CC) in Pskov. Arrested in August 1937, he was imprisoned until March 1940, when he was reinstated as commander of the V CC. In June he was promoted to major general and in December 1940 took command of the IX Mechanized Corps (MC) in the Kiev Special Military District (Ukraine).

World War II

At the outbreak of war, Rokossovskii still commanded the IX MC. On 19 July 1941 he was appointed commander of an operational-level army group near Smolensk, then commanded the Sixteenth Army during the Battle for Moscow (October 1941–March 1942), barring one of the German's main axes of advance. Rokossovskii was severely wounded on 8 March 1942 and not released from the hospital until the end of May. On 14 July 1942 he took command of the Briansk Army Group (AG) but remained only until September when he assumed command of the Don Front (1 October). The Don, Southwestern, and Stalingrad fronts encircled and destroyed 330,000 Axis troops during the Battle of Stalingrad (November 1942–February 1943). In February 1943 Rokossovskii took command of the Central AG (which absorbed the disbanded Briansk AG), then fought in the Battle of Kursk (July 1943), the largest tank battle in World War II. In October 1943 the Central AG split into the Belorussian AG (BAG) and the 1st Ukrainian AG; Rokossovskii took command of the BAG. By April 1944 the BAG liberated the Ukraine and Belorussia.

Rokossovskii's most controversial action took place in August 1944. Soviet forces in the Lvov-Sandomir offensive (July 1944) swept across the western Ukraine and southern Poland, liberating Lvov and establishing a bridgehead across the Vistula River. Expecting an immediate continuation of the drive toward Warsaw, the pro-Western Home Army rose up against the German garrison. But Soviet forces remained in place until mid-January 1945 as action shifted toward the Balkans; the Home Army was massacred while Rokossovskii's forces (on Stalin's orders) refused to come to their aid. Although Stalin claimed logistical shortcomings and refused to acknowledge the existence of the Home Army, it was probable that he hoped the Germans would rid him of potential postwar opponents and exhaust their men and supplies. Rokossovskii, however, bore the brunt of the blame in public opinion. In November 1944 Rokossovskii shifted to command of the 2d BAG (formed the previous February), where he remained until the end of the war. From January–March 1945 he led his armies in the East Prussian and East Pomeranian operations; in April–May 1945 he led one of the three army groups in the Berlin campaign. While his forces pinned down the Germans in the north, Zhukov's 1st BAG and Konev's 1st Ukrainian AG encircled Berlin (2 May). On 24 June 1945 Rokossovskii led the victory parade in Moscow. He was promoted to marshal of the Soviet Union on 29 July 1944 (a rank he held until his death). He was twice awarded Hero of the Soviet Union (29 July 1944 and 1 June 1945). Rokossovskii was one of eleven senior commanders awarded the diamond-encrusted Order of Victory.

Postwar Career

From 1945–49 Rokossovskii commanded the Soviet Northern Group of Forces in Poland. Exploiting the fact that Rokossovskii's father was Polish, Stalin forced the new satellite to appoint Rokossovskii Polish minister of national defense and deputy prime minister of the council of ministers of the Polish People's Republic. Rokossovskii was promoted to marshal of Poland and named a member of the Polish politburo and a delegate to the Polish parliament (*Sejm*). He held these positions until November 1956 when he returned to the Soviet Union and became a DMD and chief inspector of the Main Inspectorate. Rokossovskii was appointed commander of the Transcaucasus Military District in 1957, but returned to the Main Inspectorate in 1958, where he remained until he retired in 1962. After his retirement, Rokossovskii published his memoirs (*Soldatskii Dolg* [*A Soldier's Duty*]) in 1968 and an account of Stalingrad (*Velikaia Pobeda na Volge* [*Great Victory on the Volga*]) in 1965, and he participated in the Group of General Inspectors where he served until his death. He died on 3 August 1968 and was buried in the walls of the Kremlin.

DIANNE L. SMITH

SEE ALSO: Civil War, Russian; World War II; Zhukov, Georgi Konstantinovich.

Bibliography

Bialer, S., ed. 1969. *Stalin and his generals*. New York: Pegasus.
Erickson, J. 1975. *The road to Stalingrad*. London: George Weidenfeld and Nicolson.
————. 1985. *The road to Berlin*. London: George Weidenfeld and Nicolson.
Kardashov, V. 1980. *Rokossovskii* (in Russian). Moscow.
Svistunov, I. 1976. *Skazanie o Rokossovskom* (in Russian). Moscow.
Ziemke, E. 1968. *Stalingrad to Berlin: The German defeat in the East*. Washington, D.C.: U.S. Army Center of Military History.

ROMAN EMPIRE

The grand strategy and general military policy of the Roman Empire were responsible for Rome's success in providing centuries of military protection to the inhabitants of the Mediterranean area. Defending an imperial frontier that stretched nearly 9,700 kilometers (6,000 mi.) from Britain to Egypt and North Africa, the Roman army performed more cost-effectively than any military force in that large region before or since. Fifty million inhabitants were protected by an army 300,000 to 500,000 strong. Beneficiaries of rigorous and demanding military institutions, Romans were proud of their armed forces and looked with admiration on their empire. The army sometimes interfered in politics and did not always win its battles, but the army of ancient Rome ranks among the finest in the history of warfare.

The Late Republican Empire

The empire of the Late Republic (ca. 130–30 B.C.) set precedents for the Rome of the emperors. Much of the territory of the empire was taken in this period, including the great provinces of Gaul, Syria, and Egypt. Although many of the best armies of the Late Republic were levied on an ad hoc basis for specific campaigns, such as those of Marius, Sulla, Pompey the Great, and Julius Caesar, the Senate maintained a few standing armies for defense of some of the provinces. Marius abandoned the property qualification for service and accepted landless volunteers. The shift from a conscript army to a volunteer army gave the generals more power than ever because the commanders, not the government, usually delivered the bonuses and land grants to veterans. The inability of the Roman Senate to control the armies led to the failure of the Late Republic and to the rise of the emperors. They in turn depended on the loyalty of the legions to keep them in power.

Augustus and the Julio-Claudians

The Emperor Augustus (27 B.C.–A.D. 14) was the most important figure in the creation of the imperial army and in the development of Roman imperial grand strategy and defense planning. He transformed the semiprofessional Roman armies into regular, standing, fully professional forces. The pension system was standardized and so was length of service in the various branches of the armed forces. After the war with Antony and Cleopatra, the number of legions was reduced to 28, where it remained until the defeat of Varus in the Teutoberg Forest in A.D. 9, when three legions were lost. The Roman Empire was defended by only 25 legions from that time until the reigns of Caligula and Claudius.

Although Augustus is famous for introducing the period of the *Pax Romana*, the tranquility he so proudly proclaimed was only for the central core of the empire. On the frontiers the emperor waged relentless wars to extend the borders, particularly along the Rhine and Danube rivers. He dreamed of the conquest of Germany up to the Elbe, but the defeat of Varus forced the Romans to fall back to the Rhine. In the east Augustus dealt with the Parthians through diplomacy, and in North Africa the military threat was reduced by the vast Sahara Desert.

Augustus and his Julio-Claudian successors laid out the main lines of imperial defense for centuries. They often used client kings, especially in the east and in North Africa (e.g., Herod of Judaea) to serve as buffers and to relieve the pressure on the legions, but gradually, particularly under the Flavians and the Antonines, the Roman army took on full responsibility for defense of the frontier.

Flavians and Antonines (A.D. 69–180)

In this period the Roman frontier became more fixed and inflexible. Permanent stone fortresses were built along the Rhine and the Danube, and the emperors adopted a grand strategy of preclusive security that is best characterized by

Hadrian's Wall in England. Virtually all the legions, except for the two in Egypt, were stationed along the imperial frontier. The loyalty of Rome's subjects made it unnecessary to post troops in the interior to keep the population in subjection.

Some analysts have criticized Roman grand strategy because there was no central reserve. When an attack occurred at the frontier, it was necessary to move troops along well-maintained roads behind the frontiers to the critical point to achieve a reasonable mass of force against the enemy. This could be done easily when there was only one attack, but a war on two fronts strained Roman military resources considerably. However, that would have been true even if the Romans had maintained a central reserve. Roman grand strategy worked very well for two centuries, from the reign of Augustus to Marcus Aurelius; when it failed, it was mainly for internal political reasons.

The Third Century

Severe problems in the third century nearly led to the military collapse of the empire. Frontier defense broke down, barbarians made deep incursions, and civil war divided the empire into regional, nearly independent sectors. At the beginning of the century Septimius Severus strengthened the army. He increased its size from 30 to 33 legions and personally commanded the legions in campaigns in Parthia and in Britain. But his Severan successors were much weaker, and when the dynasty ended in a military mutiny in 235, a 50-year period of civil war and chaos produced more than twenty emperors, only two of whom died a natural death. Legion fought legion to place its own commander on the throne, and often the emperor in Rome controlled only a small portion of what had once been Roman territory. One of the emperors, Valerian, was captured by the Persians and never heard from again. Another, Decius, died fighting barbarians along the Danube. Regional rulers such as Postumus in Gaul, Britain, and Spain and Zenobia of Palmyra in the east took over large stretches of the Roman Empire. It was not until Diocletian came to the throne at the end of the century (A.D. 284–305) that the empire was reunited under central control. The legions returned to their frontier posts, and a strategy of preclusive security was restored.

Constantine the Great and Defense in Depth

In the fourth century Constantine the Great (d. A.D. 337) made a major modification to traditional Roman grand strategy. He created a central mobile reserve that was placed close to the emperor. To find the necessary troops he stripped the frontier defenses, and the new central army included a large cavalry contingent. The so-called *comitatus*, or army of the court, soon became an elite force distinctly superior to the *limitanei*, or border guards, which eventually became scarcely more than local militia. Some modern authorities praise the new grand strategy, although it was condemned in antiquity, and by Edward Gibbon in modern times. The army performed well under Constantine, who capably defended the frontiers. But under Julian the Apostate it suffered a humiliating defeat in Persia in 363 and fifteen years later was beaten badly by barbarian Visigoths at the Battle of Adrianople (378).

The Fall of Rome

In the 100 years from the Battle of Adrianople to the deposition of the last Roman emperor in the West in 476, the Roman army deteriorated drastically in fighting ability. Alaric and the Visigoths sacked Rome in 410, the Vandals took North Africa (429–439), Gaul and Spain were overrun, and Britain was permanently lost (ca. 410). Despite popular belief, Roman cavalry in this period was excellent. It was in the infantry, the traditional basis of Roman military power, that the decline of discipline and morale showed most markedly. The Roman analyst Vegetius advocated in the early fifth century a return to the old system of training but lamented that there was no one alive who was familiar with it and that it would have to be learned from books. Although Aëtius, "the last of the Romans," managed to rally an alliance of Romans and barbarians to repulse the invasion of Gaul by Attila and the Huns at the Battle of Châlons in 451, it was the last great Roman effort before their empire collapsed entirely in the West. By the time the empire disappeared, the once proud Roman army had ceased to exist.

The Roman Armed Forces

After the rule of Marius in the Late Republic, the Roman army and navy changed drastically. Marius organized the legions into cohorts, ten to a legion with six centuries of 80 men in each (except for the first cohort, which had only five). Each soldier carried two javelins and a short sword, wore a helmet and breastplate, and carried a shield and dagger. Caesar doubled the pay of the legionaries, but in the Late Republic it was the promise of booty and land grants at the end of the campaign that attracted men to the service. In addition to the legions, which were made up exclusively of Roman citizens, the Romans fielded noncitizen auxiliaries. Under the emperors, legionaries served for 20 years and auxiliaries for 25. The Pretorian Guards, created by Augustus, served for sixteen years and were better paid. The number of auxiliaries was normally equal to the number of legions. The Roman army, until the Late Empire, was traditionally weak in cavalry and often relied on allied and mercenary horsemen.

Infantry was the backbone of the Roman army of the Late Republic and Early Empire. The normal order of battle was three broad lines in a checkerboard pattern with the units of the second line in formation behind the gaps in the front line and the units of the third line behind the gaps in the second. But it was the constant peacetime training and drill that set the Romans apart from their opponents. Discipline and morale were the hallmarks of the Roman army. When on the march Romans stopped every afternoon and built a full camp for the night. They always took prudent precautions, and the feeling of security that resulted from this institutionalized behavior helped make the legions strong. The Romans had a strong system of logistical support. Their arsenals in the empire were extensive, and they had a network of military hospitals. Even on the far edges of the empire, for example at Hadrian's Wall in northern

England, latrines were flushed with running water. Their military engineers could build bridges, roads, catapults, and siege towers as needed. Although Roman special units were weak in archery and cavalry, the Roman army had its own slingers and hired mercenaries when necessary.

The imperial navy was based in two places in the Mediterranean—near Naples and in the upper Adriatic at Ravenna. Because Rome dominated the entire Mediterranean coastline, there were no major naval threats to its power until the Vandals took North Africa in the fifth century, but it was still necessary to police the seas. The Romans also maintained flotillas on the Rhine and Danube rivers.

ARTHER FERRILL

SEE ALSO: Attila the Hun; Caesar, Julius; Hannibal Barca; History, Ancient Military; Scipio Africanus.

Bibliography

Campbell, J. 1984. *The emperor and the Roman army*. Oxford: Clarendon Press.
Cheesman, G. 1914. *The auxilia of the Roman imperial army*. Oxford: Clarendon Press.
Ferrill, A. 1986. *The fall of the Roman empire: The military explanation*. New York: Thames and Hudson.
Grant, M. 1974. *The army of the Caesars*. New York: Scribner's.
Keppie, L. 1984. *The making of the Roman army*. Totowa, N.J.: Barnes and Noble.
Luttwak, E. 1976. *The grand strategy of the Roman Empire*. Baltimore, Md.: Johns Hopkins Univ. Press.
Speidel, M. 1984. *Roman army studies*. Amsterdam: J.C. Gieben.
Starr, C. 1960. *The Roman imperial navy*. New York: Barnes and Noble.
Watson, G. 1969. *The Roman soldier*. Ithaca, N.Y.: Cornell Univ. Press.
Webster, G. 1969. *The Roman imperial army*. London: Black.

ROMMEL, ERWIN [1891–1944]

Erwin Rommel (Fig. 1) was born on 15 November 1891 in Heidenheim, Germany, near Ulm, the son of Erwin and Helena Rommel. Erwin's father was a mathematician and schoolmaster; his mother was the eldest daughter of Karl von Lutz, president of the Duchy of Württemburg.

Rommel enlisted in the 124th Infantry Regiment as an officer cadet on 19 July 1910. Rising quickly, he was promoted to corporal in October and to sergeant in December. Rommel was then sent to the Infantry School at Danzig in March 1911 and, upon graduation, was commissioned a lieutenant in the 124th Regiment (January 1912).

World War I

At the outbreak of war Rommel's regiment was sent to France. His leadership qualities were quickly revealed, earning him the Iron Cross, First Class, on 29 January 1915 and a promotion to first lieutenant in September. After receiving

Figure 1. Erwin Rommel (SOURCE: U.S. Library of Congress)

mountain warfare training in Austria, Rommel's unit joined the Alpenkorps in Romania.

On 27 November 1916 Rommel married Lucie Marie Mollin; they had one child, Manfred.

At the Battle of Caporetto on 26 October 1917, Rommel demonstrated his talents for daring and bravery. At the head of two companies he overran and captured an Italian battery at bayonet point, then flanked and forced the surrender of an enemy battalion. Leading his men up a steep mountain face, he located the camp of the Salerno Brigade and, at the head of a few officers, demanded their surrender. In fewer than two days he had advanced more than 19 kilometers (12 mi.), climbed over 2,130 meters (7,000 ft.) up the mountainside, and—through maneuver and sheer audacity—captured 9,000 prisoners and 81 guns. For this incredible feat he was awarded the coveted Pour le

Mérite decoration and promoted to captain. He was then given leave and, to his chagrin, a staff appointment that he held until the end of the war.

Interwar Years

After the war Rommel was selected to join the Reichswehr, Germany's postwar defensive force, and on 21 December 1918 was reassigned to the 124th Regiment. After a short period in command of an internal security company in Friedrichshafen and Schwabisch-Gmünd, Rommel was appointed a company commander in the 13th Regiment on 1 January 1921.

Assigned as an instructor to the Infantry School in Dresden on 1 October 1929, Rommel spent the next four years lecturing on tactics. These lectures formed the basis for a book he began writing called *Infantry Attacks*.

Shortly after Hitler's election as chancellor on 31 January 1933, Rommel was promoted to major and on 10 October was appointed commander of the 3d Jaeger Battalion, 17th Infantry Regiment. In March 1935, under Hitler's orders, the German army began a rapid expansion program. Rommel was promoted to lieutenant colonel and on 15 October was assigned as an instructor at the Military Academy at Potsdam. While at the academy he was temporarily assigned to the Hitler Youth with orders to improve discipline.

In 1937 Rommel was promoted to colonel, and that same year his book was published. During the annexation of the Sudetenland in October 1938, Rommel was temporarily assigned as commander of Hitler's bodyguard, a post that was to have a dramatic effect on his career.

On 10 November, at the end of his tour in Potsdam, Rommel was appointed as commandant of the War Academy at Wiener Neustadt. He remained at the Academy until 23 August 1939, when he was promoted to *generalmajor* (brigadier general) and assigned to Hitler's headquarters, once again as commander of the bodyguard.

World War II

On 1 September, German forces invaded Poland; Rommel, from his position on the headquarters staff, was given a grand view of the operation. He was especially impressed with the tactical possibilities he saw offered by the combination of the panzers and close air support.

After the fall of Poland, Rommel continued to serve as bodyguard commander but was anxious for a field command. He approached Hitler on the subject, and on 15 February 1940 he was given command of the 7th Panzer Division at Godesberg.

On 10 May 1940 German troops invaded France and the Low Countries. Rommel's 7th Panzer Division was part of General Hoth's XV Panzer Corps, which was covering the right flank of General Kleist's Panzer Group. Kleist was to make the main thrust through the Ardennes Forest in Belgium. The role played by Rommel and his division in the drive to and beyond the Meuse River, however, was far from secondary. Keeping pace with Kleist's spearheads to the south, Rommel's 7th Panzer Division, nicknamed the "Ghost Division," was briefly halted by a British counterattack near Arras. Stopping and then throwing back the British, Rommel pushed ahead toward Dunkirk where, with the other pursuing panzer divisions, he was halted by Hitler's controversial order on 24 May.

In the subsequent Battle of France, Rommel's division led the drive of Hoth's Corps and the Fourth Army to Cherbourg. By the end of the campaign the 7th Panzer Division had captured 97,648 prisoners, 277 field guns, 64 antitank guns, 458 tanks and armored cars, 4,000 trucks, 1,500 cars, and more than 1,500 horse-drawn vehicles at a cost of 2,524 men and 42 tanks. The division was sent into winter quarters to refit, allowing Rommel time to work on his diary account of the campaign.

In January 1941 Rommel was promoted to *generalleutnant* (major general) and given command of the newly raised Deutsche Afrika Korps. The Afrika Korps, composed of one light and one panzer division, was formed to help the Italians hold North Africa against the British.

Rommel arrived in Libya in early February and by 11 March, with only a reconnaissance battalion and an armored regiment of his corps in hand, launched an advance toward El Agheila. Catching the British by surprise and overextended, he took El Agheila on 24 March. With his usual aggressiveness Rommel continued to advance, keeping the British off balance. With the arrival of the 15th Panzer Division, Rommel was able to continue his impromptu offensive until the middle of June, by which time he had captured Generals Philip Neame and Richard O'Connor, reconquered Cyrenaica, and invested Tobruk. Rommel had mastered the tactics of desert warfare as efficiently as he had panzer tactics and had earned for himself the nickname of the "Desert Fox."

On 15 June the British launched Operation Battleaxe, a hastily prepared offensive to retake Cyrenaica. The British attack was badly organized and understrength, and a counterattack by Rommel easily repulsed it.

During the remainder of the summer both sides took time to regroup and refit. As Hitler was completely occupied with the invasion of Russia, North Africa was deemed a secondary front, and reinforcements and supplies were few and long in coming. Rommel therefore reorganized his units into Panzer Kampfgruppen, self-supporting combined arms formations, which gave him a more balanced fighting force. He also devised new tactics to compensate for the enemy's growing superiority in armor.

On 18 November the British launched Operation Crusader, which drove Rommel back to Benghazi with severe losses. The British continued the offensive through December, and Rommel was forced to abandon Cyrenaica and fall back to defensive positions at El Agheila.

Reinforced on 5 January, Rommel launched a lightning counterattack against the overextended British on the 20th, catching them by surprise and forcing them back to Benghazi, which he recaptured on the 29th. Overwhelmed by the speed and tenacity of Rommel's advance, the British withdrew from Cyrenaica. On 30 January, Rommel was promoted to *generaloberst* (general).

In March 1942 Rommel flew to Berlin to request reinforcements from Hitler, but received only permission to launch a limited attack against Tobruk. On 26 May, Rommel began his Gazala offensive. Planned to last only four days, it took almost four weeks, culminating in the rout of the larger and better-equipped British Eighth Army and the capture of Tobruk on 21 June. The following day, in reward for this accomplishment, Rommel became one of Germany's youngest field marshals.

On 26 June, Rommel resumed his offensive, advancing into Egypt and taking Mersa Matruh on the 28th. He was halted on 30 June, however, by strong British defenses at El Alamein. Rommel's troops were exhausted and strung out more than 320 kilometers (200 mi.) from their supply base at Tobruk; the war settled into a stalemate and both sides regrouped.

The British Eighth Army, now commanded by Gen. Bernard Montgomery, began to build up strength behind the Alamein line. Unable to break the British defenses, Rommel was forced to concede the initiative to the British. Rommel was ill in Berlin with acute gastritis when Montgomery opened his offensive on 23 October. He hurriedly returned to the front. Faced with massive numerical superiority, Rommel's Panzergruppe Afrika was unable to stop the British attack, and by early November was in full retreat. Ignoring Hitler's orders to stand fast and fight to the last man, Rommel withdrew to Tunisia, fighting a series of skillful rearguard actions.

The Anglo-American landings in North Africa on 8 November resulted in Rommel's forces being attacked from two sides. Following a check at Kasserine Pass (14–23 February) and defeat at Médenine (6 March), Rommel was ordered by Hitler to leave North Africa (6 March), and his army (now known as the 5th Panzer Army) surrendered in May.

Although out of favor with Hitler for disobeying orders, Rommel was too popular and talented a commander to ignore. On 15 July 1943 he was appointed commander of Army Group B in Italy with the task of reorganizing the Axis defenses. Shortly afterward he was transferred to Greece to employ his organizational talents on that front. In November, Rommel was transferred to France and given command of Army Group B (Special Duties) under Hitler's personal direction with the task of strengthening the Atlantic Wall defenses against invasion by the Western Allies. Believing that the best way to defeat an invasion was to stop the landing forces on the beach, Rommel began improving the coastal defenses.

In January 1944, Army Group B was placed under the control of Field Marshal von Rundstedt as Commander in Chief West. At the same time, Rommel took over command of the Fifteenth Army and its area of responsibility from Ostend to the Loire River. While Rundstedt thought the Allies would land in the Pas de Calais, Rommel believed the Normandy coast the more likely site. He continued to improve and strengthen the defenses and by the end of May had doubled the number of mines—some 5,000,000 in all—and added more than 500,000 landing obstacles.

During the invasion preparations Rommel had been approached by an old friend, Dr. Karl Stroelin, mayor of Stuttgart and a member of the German resistance, and asked to lead a plot against Hitler. After some deliberation

Rommel consented to join the plot, believing that Germany's only chance of salvation lay in Hitler's death.

On 6 June the Allies landed at Normandy, and Rommel, on leave in Herrlingen to celebrate his wife's birthday, rushed to the front. Unable to prevent the invasion forces from establishing a beachhead, both Rommel and Rundstedt called on Hitler to release the panzer reserves to Army West control. Hitler, believing the Normandy landings were only a feint and that the real invasion would come at Calais, refused the request.

On 17 July, while making an inspection tour, Rommel was seriously wounded when his staff car crashed while being strafed by Allied fighter bombers. Three days later Hitler also escaped death from a bomb planted by the resistance. Hitler's investigators learned of Rommel's complicity in the plot. Rommel was at his home in Herrlingen, recovering from his injuries, when on 13 October he was visited by Generals Maisel and Burgdorf. They presented Hitler's terms: Rommel could stand trial for treason, would be found guilty and be executed with no provision for his family; or he could commit suicide by poison, his death would be attributed to his wounds, he would be given a state funeral, and his family would be left unharmed. Rommel chose the latter course. On 14 October he donned his Afrika Korps uniform, said goodbye to his wife and son, and rode away with Hitler's envoys. Within a short distance of his home he took the poison and was dead within seconds. Hitler kept his word and Germany mourned the loss of one of its greatest heroes.

Erwin Rommel was a brilliant, highly skilled commander who was respected and admired both by his soldiers and his enemies. Winston Churchill said of him, "We have a very skillful opponent against us, and, may I say across the havoc of war, a great general."

VINCENT B. HAWKINS

SEE ALSO: Cunningham, Sir Alan G.; Montgomery, Bernard Law; World War I; World War II.

Bibliography

Lewin, R. 1968. *Rommel as military commander*. New York: Ballantine Books.
Liddell Hart, B. H., ed. 1953. *The Rommel papers*. London: Collins Clear Type Press.
Pfannes, C. E., and V. A. Salamone. 1980. *The great commanders of World War II*. Vol. 1, *The Germans*. New York: Zebra Books.
Rommel, E. 1979. *Attacks*. Vienna, Va.: Athena Press.
Sibley, R., and M. Fry. 1974. *Rommel*. New York: Ballantine Books.
Wistrich, R. 1982. *Who's who in Nazi Germany*. New York: Bonanza Books.
Young, D. 1969. *Rommel, the Desert Fox*. New York: Berkeley.

RUSES AND STRATAGEMS

Stratagem signifies a commander's ingenious act and embraces the use of surprise, deception, trickery, and indirect means in war. Stratagems occur at all levels of military activity, whether strategy, operations, or tactics. *Ruse*, generally a synonym for *stratagem*, sometimes assumes a more specialized meaning in various modern theories of deception. Historically, stratagem can involve ambush, surprise attack, feigned retreat, disinformation, conditioning the enemy to expect a certain pattern of behavior, technological or tactical surprise (i.e., unexpected use of a new weapon, formation, or method), some commando/special forces operations, and various other tricks or deceptions. Stratagem may also denote inducement of betrayal or treason, bribery, assassination, some aspects of espionage, use of poison, and sophistic interpretation of terms of surrender, truce, or treaty. Designating any act a stratagem, however, as opposed to a routine or expected act, can be subjective and moot. The ingenuity of a stratagem may be called perfidy or illegal conduct, especially by its victim.

Stratagem is practically synonymous with warfare. Its prominence, particularly in the West, has varied throughout history in relation to the influence of chivalry and of advocates of the direct use of force. The Western military tradition typically emphasizes heroic action compatible with concepts of honor (e.g., direct confrontation, superior numbers, and firepower). Yet stratagem, often disdained as dishonorable and the expedient of the weak, can often provide a greater margin of victory by more economic means. The traditional contrast between Western force and Oriental trickery ignores both the Western tradition of stratagem found in practice and written theory since antiquity and Eastern (e.g., Chinese, Japanese) traditions of chivalry. Stratagems have characterized the generalship of numerous commanders known for creativity and unconventionality in many historical periods, but stratagem becomes especially prominent in ages of a balance of power or strong chivalrous impulses, and in situations where a numerically or technologically inferior party faces a superior foe. In current jargon, stratagem is a "force multiplier."

Besides its practical function, stratagem is a legal concept of the laws of war. Stratagem raises questions of legality by often straddling the line between honorable and dishonorable conduct. The distinction between stratagem and perfidy remains problematic even today. Current restrictions on specific types of ruse and the prohibition of perfidy represent only one point in the debate on the legal aspects of stratagem initiated by ancient philosophers and continued by medieval churchmen, early modern jurists, and statesmen of the last two centuries. Yet legal limits on stratagem present the paradox of restricting human ingenuity and circumscribing an idea whose essence derives from bending and breaking rules.

Vocabulary of Stratagem

English *stratagem* is derived from the Greek *stratēgēma*, first attested in the fourth century B.C. (Xenophon, *Memorabilia* 3.5.22) and initially meaning "principles or examples of generalship." By the end of that century it acquired the additional sense of "trick," which subsequently became the chief definition in both Greek and Latin. Cicero (*Letter to Atticus* 5.2.2.) attests its first appearance in Latin (51 B.C.). The word remained rare, as the ancients preferred to designate military ingenuity as trick, deceit, device, plan, skill, and wisdom.

Frontinus's collection of stratagems, *Strategemata* (composed in Latin 84–88), guaranteed survival of the word *stratēgēma* in later times. Frontinus became one source for late medieval handbooks of chivalry, such as Christine of Pisa's *Fayttes of Arms*. William Caxton's translation of this work (1490) introduced the word *stratagem* in English. The immense popularity of Frontinus from the fifteenth to the eighteenth century disseminated *stratagem* as the chief word for military trickery in European languages.

Ruse, a French word first attested in the thirteenth century, originally meant "deceit" or "lie." In late medieval treatises on hunting it acquired the technical sense of a deer backtracking to throw the dogs off its scent. By the eighteenth century *ruse* became the standard French equivalent for *stratagem*. The fetish among English speakers for eighteenth- and nineteenth-century French military thought popularized the term *ruse*.

In current military literature *stratagem* remains a relatively infrequent word, more often denoted by ruse, surprise, deception, feint, demonstration, or diversion.

History of Stratagem

PRIMITIVE WARFARE

Stratagem probably dominated the earliest warfare, if anthropological analysis of primitive (or pre-state) warfare offers a correct analogy to Neolithic practice. Intracultural conflicts, or wars between peoples of different cultures but in close proximity, could at times be governed by strict customary rules, often of a religious origin. Such rules, however, did not necessarily prohibit ambush or surprise attack on an enemy's village. No rules restricted conduct in intercultural conflicts, or wars with distant peoples. Treachery and trickery were the norm.

CHINA AND INDIA

The earliest Oriental tradition of stratagem in written form can be traced to the first Chinese military theory (fourth century B.C.), which reflected the abandonment of a strict code of chivalry among other military changes in the Warring States period (403–221 B.C.). *The Art of War* attributed to Sun Tzu became the classic work, although neither the earliest nor the only Chinese military treatise of its time. Sun Tzu's mystical, metaphysical views betray the close connection of military thought with the philosophical schools of Confucianism, Taoism, and Legalism. Sun Tzu's famous aphorism, "All warfare is based on deception," besides his emphasis on intelligent generalship, psychological factors, speed, and avoidance of battle, codified a Chinese doctrine of stratagem. The Chinese continued to study and write commentaries on Sun Tzu throughout their history. Japanese interest in Sun Tzu dates from the sixth century. Sun Tzu has also influenced the thought of Mao Tse-tung and modern guerrilla theorists.

India of the fourth century B.C., like China the victim of incessant warfare, produced its own military thought stressing stratagem. Kautilya's *Arthashastra*, probably written 321–296 B.C., espoused a Machiavellian approach to statecraft and contained military chapters emphasizing deception and trickery. Even the *Mahabharata* and the *Laws of Manu* (both reaching a final written form A.D. 330–445) do not consistently prohibit stratagem in the Hindu code of chivalry.

ANCIENT NEAR EAST (3000 B.C.–A.D. 641)

The earliest historical reference to stratagem occurs in the royal archives of Mari in Mesopotamia: by letter the Assyrian king Shamshi-Adad (1813–1781 B.C.) advised his son, the ruler of Mari, to beware of enemy stratagems and to devise stratagems against the enemy. In fact the second millennium B.C. was an age of stratagem, as seen in the extensive use of ambush, espionage, fifth columns, propaganda, provoking mutiny and rebellion, assassination, diversionary attacks, guerrilla tactics, and ruses of the Trojan-horse type. Traditions of pre-state warfare, religious concepts (e.g., holy war), invasions of new peoples, and a lack of international standards of conduct all contributed to the prevalence of stratagem in the earliest civilized warfare.

From the dawn of the Iron Age (ca. 1000 B.C.) to the Arab conquest, stratagems intermittently appeared in the wars of Assyrians, Achaemenid Persians, Parthians, and Sassanid Persians. No indigenous written military theory existed in the Near East before the Sassanids, and stratagem as a doctrine did not develop. Fragments of Sassanid treatises, preserved mainly by Muslim writers, attest to discussion of ambush and other stratagems, although Graeco-Roman influence on these works is likely.

CLASSICAL ANTIQUITY (750 B.C.–A.D. 565)

At the beginning of classical Greek civilization Homer's wily Odysseus and the Trojan-horse ruse provided a favorable precedent for stratagem. Yet Greek division into city-states, use of the phalanx, and the model of Achilles as the ideal warrior in aristocratic education favored, by the sixth century B.C., a chivalrous code of warfare shunning stratagem. Between the Persian Wars (490–478 B.C.) and the death of Alexander the Great (323 B.C.) revolutionary changes in the conduct of war modified or abolished aspects of this chivalrous code. Western military theory, a product of these changes and the new rationalization of war, began in the late fifth century. Homer's Odysseus and oral tradition had earlier been the medium of military theory and examples of stratagems. Thucydides' *History of the Peloponnesian War* attempted to turn history into military theory. His emphasis on shrewd generalship and psychological factors, when combined with his amoral attitude, led to the assertion that stratagems produce the greatest fame and success in war (Thucydides 5.9.4–5).

In the fourth century B.C. military theory became a distinct genre. Xenophon and Aeneas Tacticus, the earliest extant theorists, stressed the importance of stratagems. For Xenophon (*Agesilaus* 1.17, 6.5–8) deceit against the enemy was not only divinely approved and right but also a form of wisdom. Deceit brought the most profit in war and the greatest success (*Cavalry Commander* 5.9–11). Indeed every commander should be an inventor of stratagems (*Cyropaedia* 1.6.38). Aeneas Tacticus similarly emphasized stratagems. His *Strate-*

gika, a military encyclopedia, was read throughout antiquity and initiated the genre of treatises on siegecraft.

Alexander the Great returned Greek warfare to the standard of chivalry and pitched battle. The Hellenistic warfare of the dynasties of Alexander's successors displayed at times a penchant for chivalry, but by the second century B.C. Polybius (*Histories* 13.3) complained of living in an age of stratagem, in which observing the rules of conduct constituted poor generalship.

Rome's rise to empire in the fourth and third centuries B.C. rested on propagandistic claims of defensive just wars and scrupulous observance of good faith, which obscured Roman legal chicanery. The native Italian sagacity of Roman generals required no instruction from Hannibal or the Greeks about stratagems. Romans exemplified the principle that the most speciously honest are the best deceivers, and they delighted in vilifying opponents as perfidious tricksters (e.g., Hannibal).

When Roman military theory began in the second century B.C. with Cato's *De re militari*, the value of stratagem was already well known, but the bulk of Roman theory was produced under the empire. The *Strategemata* of Frontinus (d. 103) and the *Strategika* of Polyaenus (fl.160) constitute the only extant specimens of the literary genre of the collection of stratagems for military education and rhetorical use. The works of Frontinus, Polyaenus, and Vegetius (late fourth century) demonstrate, however, that stratagem had become not merely a major motif of ancient military thought but a doctrine. Classical theory taught that a general should have foresight to predict developments and should first await, then exploit, favorable opportunities. Battle should be avoided except when expedient. Stratagem could facilitate the proper occasion for battle, win the battle, or become an alternative to battle, since stratagems could bring victory without fighting, with fewer losses in battle, or win a war after defeat in battle. The ideal general of classical military thought worshiped at the shrine of Odysseus.

THE MIDDLE AGES (500–1500)

The Byzantines. The Byzantine Empire, the acknowledged continuation of the Roman Empire and of Graeco-Roman culture, made the classical doctrine of stratagem the basis of its strategy. Faced with numerically superior enemies on two, at times three, fronts the Byzantines maintained a defensive posture through avoidance of major battles, use of ambush and stratagems, and shrewd (occasionally treacherous) diplomacy. Byzantine military thought perpetuated the stratagem collection through numerous revisions and paraphrases of Polyaenus. The *Strategikon* of Ps.-Maurice (ca. 600) and the *Tactica* of Leo the Wise (ca. 900), largely borrowed from Classical Greek treatises, preached the virtues of stratagem, and added new material on how to fight contemporary enemies.

The Arabs. Traditions of pre-state, nomadic desert warfare promoted the use of stratagem in early Muslim conflicts. Moreover, Mohammed advocated trickery against enemies of Islam, a group against which restrictive rules would not apply. Yet stratagems could also be used against dissident Muslims as well as unbelievers. The Shiite cult, the Assassins (eleventh to thirteenth centuries), successfully pursued a strategy of terrorism derived from avoidance of battle and the principles of stratagem. By the ninth century a Muslim military theory in written form began, in part influenced by Greek, Byzantine, and Sassanid works. Arabs continued the Graeco-Roman genre of the stratagem collection, of which titles of the ninth century are known and a thirteenth-century work, *Coats of Fine Material in Clever Ruses* (R. Khawam, ed. and tr. 1976), survives. In the fourteenth century the significance of stratagem in Muslim military thought was further codified in Muhammed ibn 'Isā's *Complete Instruction in the Practices of the Military Art* and Iba Khalddun's *Introduction to History*.

The Medieval West. Although the works of Frontinus and Vegetius were read throughout the Middle Ages, early medieval stratagems were derived from expediency or from the traditions of pre-state warfare among Germanic and other peoples. Normans of the tenth and eleventh centuries became particularly famous for feigned retreat. As feudalism developed, warfare emphasized the siege of fortified strongholds. A trend to avoidance of battle contrasted with the impulse for feats of individual bravado in the chivalrous code of the knightly class, but chivalry remained an ideal rather than a reality in both battles and tournaments, where stratagems were never completely excluded. The dismal performance of Christian armies in the Crusades, nationalistic conflicts (e.g., the Hundred Years' War), and the increased use of mercenaries prompted, in the fourteenth and fifteenth centuries, written advocation of stratagems, *Realpolitik*, and credence to the writings of antiquity (e.g., Marinus Sanutus Torsellus, Christine of Pisa, Philippe de Commynes).

EARLY MODERN PERIOD (1500–1750)

The warfare of *condottieri* in Italy from the late fourteenth to the early sixteenth century (often not as bloodless as commonly believed) set the tone for early modern use of stratagems. As armies struggled to accommodate the new significance of infantry and the introduction of firearms, the waning influence of chivalry and the Catholic church (intensified by religious wars with the Protestants) left a void in standards of international and military conduct. Diplomatic duplicity, military ruse, and amorality characterized the age. Humanistic learning encouraged the study of classical texts now widely available in printed editions. Vegetius, Frontinus, Polyaenus, Leo the Wise, and others were zealously read to discover the secrets of the ancients' military success, in which stratagem played a prominent role. Contemporary military thought defined the ideal captain through citation of classical examples and imitated classical handbooks. Maurice de Saxe's *Mes rêveries* (1732) illustrates the continued importance of the classical doctrine of stratagem on early modern military thought.

1750–1914

The new age of mass armies, improved firearms, and worship of Napoleonic battle largely eliminated stratagem from Western military thought and practice. Although Napoleon had studied classical warfare and his emphasis on surprise, mobility, and deception incorporated principles of stratagem, his imitators and interpreters stressed numbers, firepower, and the frontal approach. Stratagem and ruse are scarcely mentioned in Jomini's *Précis de l'art de la guerre* (1838), which reflected in part the mathematical-mechanical school of Enlightenment military thought, seeking definite rules for the conduct of war. Clausewitz in *On War* (1831) largely relegated surprise and stratagem to tactics. Although, in his view, surprise underlies all military action, at the strategic level, time, space, and war's friction denied surprise a place among the key elements for military success. Effective surprise, he argued, most often depends on favorable circumstances, which cannot be readily created, or on one general's rare moral superiority over an opponent. Stratagem, which Clausewitz identified with disinformation and demonstration, likewise amounts to wasted effort.

Yet stratagems, never neglected at the tactical level, remained prominent in the new literature on small wars, colonial wars, and guerrilla warfare, which began in the second half of the eighteenth century. The surprises and ambushes of stratagem seemed to have a place in the use of small tactical units against irregulars and native tribes, as seen in C. E. Callwell's *Small Wars* (3d ed. 1906).

1914–1945

The absence of stratagem in nineteenth-century strategic thought contributed to the slaughter on World War I's western front. Before the war G. F. R. Henderson attempted to revive strategic interest in stratagem, speed, and deception through his biography of Stonewall Jackson and other writings. Henderson's students, Edmund Allenby and A. P. Wavell, would put some of his ideas into practice in the two world wars. In contrast, Alfred von Schlieffen's fascination with the battle of Cannae (216 B.C.), the model for the Schlieffen Plan, ignored Hannibal's stratagems. Schlieffen saw the battle only as proof of the effectiveness of flank attacks and as an example of a Clausewitzian battle of annihilation.

Strategic use of stratagem did occur on secondary fronts in World War I, such as Gallipoli (1915–16), East Africa (1916), and Allenby's campaign in Palestine (1917–18), where T. E. Lawrence exploited the principles of stratagem in his guerrilla warfare against the Turks. The war also produced new means for stratagem: the radio with its potential for gathering intelligence or spreading disinformation, and camouflage—the ancient practice of disguise now refined to counter aerial reconnaissance.

In the interwar period official doctrine again ignored stratagem and surprise. Nevertheless, B. H. Liddell Hart developed his theory of indirect approach in a series of military biographies, which led to his *Decisive Wars of History* (1929), subsequently revised as *Strategy* (1941, 1954, 1967). His emphasis on exploiting the line of least expectation, the enemy's psychological dislocation, deception/distraction, and the bloodless victory as the epitome of strategy incorporated various aspects of stratagem.

Similarly, the Germans turned to stratagem, as seen in Hitler's use of ruse.

They alleged to have learned stratagems from the Allies in World War I. Waldemar Erfurt's *Surprise* (1938; English tr. 1943), the first monograph on strategic surprise in over a century, added little new to previous thought, but stressed maneuver, deception, and creativity.

Hitler's surprise attack on Russia, the Japanese at Pearl Harbor, and Allied efforts to mask the timing and location of D-Day illustrate the tremendous increase of attention to stratagem in World War II. Winston Churchill, a proponent of stratagem since the early 1920s, first centralized and coordinated efforts at strategic deception in 1941–42 by emphasizing its importance for all strategic planning. The British chiefly promoted stratagem, from whom the Americans often reluctantly learned the advantages of deception. Less than 30 percent of land operations in World War II lacked the use of surprise and deception. Furthermore, the unparalleled vast scale of guerrilla warfare presented belligerents with innumerable problems in defining proper conduct.

1945–PRESENT

The "rediscovery" of stratagem in World War II led to its institutionalization as a major component of late twentieth-century warfare and military doctrine. The nuclear balance of power prompted theories of deterrence concerned with bluff and surprise. Limited conventional wars, such as the Six-Day War of 1967, have been hailed as stratagemic masterpieces. Trends toward guerrilla warfare and terrorism exploit the principles of stratagem in the interests of weak, small, or technologically inferior parties. With the unprecedented growth of national intelligence agencies, the issue is no longer use or nonuse of stratagem, but how to improve techniques and training in deception. Some would argue that the future of stratagem lies with computers and electronics specialists.

Stratagem as a Legal Concept

The legitimacy of stratagem in the Western tradition of laws of war involves two distinct issues: first, trickery in military operations, and second, perfidy (i.e., trickery concerning a pledge of good faith). Stratagems of the first type (excluding use of poison and assassination) have always been permitted, despite objections of illicit conduct resting more on concepts of fairness and chivalry than on any legal basis. The concept of just deceit, popularized by Greek sophists of the fifth century B.C and converted into the Stoic concept of *dolus bonus* (good trick), advocated stratagem for national defense or the public good. Roman law (*Justinian's Digest* 4.3.1.2–3) codified this Stoic concept and thus, with St. Augustine's biblical justification of stratagem (*On the Heptateuch* 6.10 concerning Joshua 8:2), the legitimacy of stratagem passed via Aquinas and Grotius into the modern tradition of international law.

Current prohibition of perfidy rests on the principles that violation of good faith aggravates the establishment of peace between belligerents and compromises protected persons (e.g., wounded, civilians, prisoners). Violations of oaths and good faith have always been condemned, but Cicero raised the issue of the validity of oaths only with equals in the international community. Hence in the Middle Ages and the Early Modern period the observance of pledged good faith with non-Christians, heretics, and peoples outside the European Christian community was debated. The United Nations Charter (1945), by including all sovereign states within the international community, has only partially resolved this issue, since national liberation movements now claim treatment as legitimate belligerents.

The Hague Regulations of 1907 (art. 22–24, 32–41) remain the basis of current law on stratagem and perfidy. Geneva Protocol I (1977) offers only some refinements to the Hague Regulations, although at this writing (1989) Geneva Protocol I has not been ratified by the major powers.

EVERETT L. WHEELER

SEE ALSO: Principles of War; Sun Tzu.

Bibliography

Bothe, M., K. Partsch, and W. Solf. 1982. *New rules for victims of armed conflicts.* The Hague: Martinus Nijhoff.

Fleck, D. 1974. Ruses of war and prohibition of perfidy. *Revue de droit penal militaire et de droit de la guerre* 13:269–314.

Greenspan, M. 1959. *The modern law of land warfare.* Berkeley: Univ. of California Press.

Whaley, B. 1969. *Stratagem: Deception and surprise in war.* Cambridge: M.I.T. Center of International Studies.

Wheeler, E. 1988. The modern legality of Frontinus' stratagems. *Militärgeschichtliche Mitteilungen* 44.1:7–29.

RUSSIA, EXPANSION OF

Through marriage, inheritance, a lack of natural borders, an aggressive military policy, and great rivers that traversed huge expanses of land, Russia expanded from the environs of Moscow to become the largest and longest-lasting multinational empire in the world. The bulk of expansion came through wars, but there was always a strong current of natural expansion away from the autocratic center by social outcasts, adventurers, and merchants. Russian expansion was always cyclical, moving into a void, being pushed back, then recovering lost territory.

Muscovy

The Grand Duchy of Muscovy was but one of several successor states of the Mongol Golden Horde claiming the right to dominate the steppes. Moscow conquered the Volga basin and the Baltic coast, and laid claim to Siberia in the sixteenth century. Russia's fortunes ebbed during the "Time of Troubles" as Sweden and Poland seized the western gains in the Baltic and Ukraine. The seventeenth century witnessed a constant struggle with Poland and Sweden to regain lost lands, and with the southern Cossack bands to capture the Ukraine and the mouth of the Don River at Azov.

In 1654, Russia supported the Ukrainian Bogdan Khmel'nitskii in his struggle with Poland; as a result, under the Truce of Andrussovo (1667), Moscow gained the left bank of the Dnieper as far as Moscow. Kiev and Smolensk were granted to Russia for limited time periods, but Moscow reneged and never gave them back. In its disputes with Sweden, Russia temporarily regained three Baltic ports in 1658, but they were returned to Sweden (Treaty of Kardis, 1661).

Muscovy was more successful expanding eastward into Siberia. Here there was no systematic policy, rather the gradual movement of settlers and fur traders. But exploration soon brought Russia into conflict with China. The resulting Treaty of Nerchinsk (1689), in which Moscow ceded the Amur Valley to China, stabilized the border with the Manchu dynasty for the next two centuries. In 1650 Semen Dezhnev reached the Kamchatka Peninsula, which projects from the Asian mainland between the Sea of Okhotsk and the Bering Sea and Pacific Ocean.

Peter the Great (1689–1725)

Under Peter the Great, Russia became the premier Baltic power and made gains against Turkey. The 1700 Treaty of Constantinople granted Moscow naval ports and the right to a fleet on the Black Sea. A second war with Turkey ending in 1711 forced Peter to abandon the fleet, but Russia retained Azov on the Don. The Great Northern War (1700–21) broke the back of Swedish power in the Baltic. Russia captured the Baltic coast and founded a new capital at St. Petersburg (1703). The peace treaty (Treaty of Nystadt, 1721) ceded Livonia, Estonia, part of Karelia, Vyborg, and the Baltic coast all the way to Riga to Russia in exchange for the return of Finland to Sweden. A war with Persia temporarily acquired Baku on the Caspian, but it was lost in 1732.

Post-Petrine

Peter's immediate successors focused their attention east and south. In 1728, Vitus Bering located the Northeast Passage; thirteen years later, Russian sailors discovered and claimed Alaska. Sailing farther south, Russia twice unsuccessfully (1739, 1809) sought to open Japan to foreign trade. Short wars with Turkey (Treaty of Belgrade, 1730) and Sweden (Treaty of Abo, 1743) brought minor territorial gains.

Catherine the Great (1762–96)

Catherine confronted the Ottoman Turks and Poland. The First Russo-Turkish War (Treaty of Kuchuk Kainarji, 1774) ceded to Russia strategic points in and near the Crimea and part of the Black Sea coast. Catherine's annexation of the Crimea in 1783 led to a Second Russo-Turkish War (Treaty of Jassy, 1793), gained additional fortresses and the Black Sea coast to the Dniester River, and opened the grain belt of the Ukraine to the sea. Catherine transformed Russia into a European power through its participation (with Prussia and Austria) in the partitioning of Poland. Under the First Partition (1772), Russia acquired

White Russia and all the territory to the Dvina and Dnieper rivers. The Second Partition (1793) added most of Lithuania and the western Ukraine. Following Kosciuszko's unsuccessful rebellion (1794), the three states absorbed the rest of Poland's lands. Catherine took the remainder of Lithuania and the Ukraine and the Duchy of Courland in the Baltic. Poland ceased to exist.

Wars of Revolution and Napoleon

Catherine's successors were involved in the wars against France to maintain the status quo in Central Europe and suppress revolutionary currents, while nibbling away at the borders of Russia's other neighbors. The Russian-American Trading Company, founded in 1799 to administer Alaska, was granted the right to make discoveries north of 50 degrees latitude and to claim lands for Russia. This led to the establishment of Fort Elizabeth, Hawaii, in 1804 and Fort Ross, California, in 1812. Both ventures ultimately failed because of foreign opposition and events in Europe that distracted Russian attention from them.

Alexander I, Catherine's grandson, joined the Third Coalition following the crowning of Napoleon as emperor in 1804. Although Alexander was defeated by Napoleon, under the Treaty of Tilsit (1807), the Russian and French empires emerged as the two continental powers: Russia received part of East Prussia while Napoleon carved out the new Duchy of Warsaw from lands taken by Prussia during the Partitions. After a short war, Sweden ceded Finland as an autonomous duchy ruled by Alexander as Grand Duke (Treaty of Frederickshavn, 1809). Russia annexed eastern Georgia in 1801; by the end of the decade Russia had annexed the rest. This action provoked a war with Persia (1804–13) that ended with Persia recognizing Russian rule in Georgia, while ceding Daghestan and Shemakha (Treaty of Gulistan, 1813). Turkey also fought a war over the Georgia gains (1806–12), which ended in a Russian success in 1812. Bessarabia and a strip on the eastern coast of the Black Sea (which put Russia at the mouth of the Danube) were granted to Moscow (Treaty of Bucharest, 1812). Under the Congress of Vienna (1815), Russia retained earlier gains in Finland, Poland, the Ukraine, and Bessarabia. The Duchy of Warsaw was reconfigured as a smaller Kingdom of Poland; with Alexander as king, he accepted a liberal constitution for his new kingdom.

A Century of Peace (1815–1914)

Nicholas I sought access to the Mediterranean by exploiting weaknesses within the Ottoman Empire (the "sick man of Europe") and gains in the Caucasus from Persia. The Russo-Persian War of 1826 gave Russia part of Armenia, including Erevan, and the right to a navy on the Caspian Sea (Treaty of Turkmanchai, 1828). War with Turkey in support of Greek rebels ended with the Russian conquest of the mouth of the Danube and Kars in the Caucasus (Treaty of Adrianople, 1829). In 1833 Russia "defended" the Ottomans against Egyptian rebels by landing troops in the Bosphorus; Russia and Turkey signed an eight-year mutual defense pact and Russia became the protector of Turkey (Treaty of Unkiar Skeliessi, 1833). When Russia, in 1853, suggested partitioning the Ottoman state, Great Britain and France supported Turkey. The 1856 Treaty of Paris forced Russia to cede to Turkey the mouth of the Danube, the Danubian provinces of Wallachia and Moldavia, and part of Bessarabia; the Black Sea was neutralized. The United States purchased Alaska in 1867.

During the last decades of the nineteenth century, Russia became increasingly involved in the Balkans, Central Asia, and the Far East. Russia retained territory acquired in Bessarabia and the Caucasus when the Treaty of Paris was rewritten at the Congress of Berlin (1878). Moscow moved into Central Asia with the conquest of Kokand, Bokhara, and Khiva (1865–76) and the annexation of the Transcaspian region in 1881. Russia also turned its attention to China and Japan. Russia exploited a period of civil war to force China to give over the left bank of the Amur River (Treaty of Aigun, 1858) and the Ussuri region (Treaty of Peking, 1860). In 1875 Russia exchanged with Japan the Kurile Islands for the southern half of Sakhalin Island. Russia's efforts to carve out its own sphere of influence in China through coercing the right to build the East China Railway, and a 25-year lease of the southern half of Liaotung Peninsula with Port Arthur in 1897–98, brought Russia into conflict with Japan, leading to a disastrous and humiliating war in 1904. Russia ceded to Japan the lease to Liaotung, part of the railway, and the southern half of Sakhalin Island (Treaty of Portsmouth, 1905).

Conclusion

Russia followed a consciously expansionist policy, but its land expansion only matched the voyages of exploration and creation of overseas colonies by Britain, France, Spain, Portugal, and Germany. Russian expansion was cyclical; territories were lost and regained according to the fortunes of war, but expansion was continual. Efforts to gain a readily accessible warm-water port were only successful on the distant Pacific shore; Baltic and Black Sea gains never produced free outlets to the open sea.

DIANNE L. SMITH

SEE ALSO: Charles XII; Civil War, Russian; Colonial Empires, European; French Revolutionary–Napoleonic Wars; Japan, Modernization and Expansion of; Manchu Empire; Mongol Conquests; Napoleon I; Ottoman Empire; Persian Empire; Peter the Great; Russo-Japanese War; Suvorov, Aleksandr Vasil'evich; Thirty Years' War; Togo, Heihachiro; World War I.

Bibliography

Eversley, G. J. S.-L. 1915. *The partitions of Poland.* London: T. F. Unwin.

Kaplan, H. H. 1962. *The first partition of Poland.* New York: Columbia Univ. Press.

Kerner, R. J. [1942] 1971. *The urge to the sea; the course of Russian history. The role of rivers, portages, ostrogs, monasteries, and furs.* Publication of the Northeastern Asia Seminar of the University of California. New York: Russell & Russell.

Lord, R. H. 1915. *The second partition of Poland: A study of diplomatic history.* Cambridge, Mass.: Harvard Univ. Press.

Pierce, R. A. 1965. *Russia's Hawaiian adventure, 1815–1817.* Berkeley: Univ. of California Press.

Sumner, B. H. 1951. *Peter the great and the emergence of Russia.* New York: Macmillan.

————. [1949] 1965. *Peter the great and the Ottoman empire.* Hamden, Conn.: Archon Books.

RUSSO-JAPANESE WAR
[1904–1905]

Between 1900 and 1903 Japan prepared for a limited war in Korea and Manchuria to crush Russia's growing power there, in revenge for Russian interference after the Sino-Japanese War, and to ensure Japan's hegemony over Korea. By 1904 Japan was ready to act.

Japanese deployment on the mainland was dependent upon command of the sea; hence an essential first step was to destroy the Russian Far East Fleet and capture its main base, Port Arthur, on the tip of Manchuria's Liaotung Peninsula. The second step was to destroy Russian land forces in Manchuria.

Russian naval strength in the Far East consisted of seven elderly battleships, nine armored cruisers, 25 destroyers, and some 30-odd smaller craft. The main fleet was based at Port Arthur; two cruisers lay at Chemulpo (Inchon), Korea, and four more at Vladivostok. Japanese naval strength consisted of six modern battleships, eight armored cruisers, 25 light cruisers, nineteen destroyers, 85 torpedo boats, and sixteen smaller craft. The Japanese army and navy were superior to Russia's in doctrine, training, and leadership.

Opening Moves

On 8 February 1904, without a previous declaration of war, Japanese torpedo boats launched a surprise attack on the Russian fleet at anchor in the harbor of Port Arthur, causing severe damage. At the same time, the main Japanese battle fleet of Vice Adm. Heihachiro Togo engaged the Russian shore batteries and fleet at long range and then blockaded the port. A Japanese armored-cruiser squadron destroyed the two Russian cruisers at Chemulpo.

On 20 February, Japan declared war. One week later Gen. Tamesada Kuroki's Japanese First Army debarked at Chemulpo and advanced northward through Korea to the Yalu River to cover operations at Port Arthur.

On 8 March the energetic and capable Russian admiral Stepan Makarov arrived to take command of the fleet. At once he began a series of sorties to harass the blockading Japanese cruisers, while avoiding Togo's battle fleet. On 13 April, Makarov's flagship struck a mine and sank with all on board. Thereafter the Russian ships remained passively in port. The loss of Makarov was a catastrophe for the Russians.

Gen. Alexei Kuropatkin assumed command of all field forces in the Far East. In April he began concentrating all available forces in three groups south of Mukden: General Stakelberg, with 35,000 men, directly north of Port Arthur; General Count Keller, with 30,000 troops, guarding the passes west of the Yalu River; and an advance guard of 7,000 under General Zasulich covering the Yalu crossings. Kuropatkin himself, with 40,000 men, lay in reserve at Liaoyang. An additional force under Gen. Anatoli M. Stesel garrisoned the powerful fortress of Port Arthur.

Recognizing the initial Japanese numerical advantage, Kuropatkin planned to permit them to besiege Port Arthur—which he felt sure could hold out—while he fell back, delaying the Japanese advance into Manchuria until reinforcements arrived from Russia. However, Adm. Evgeni Alekseev, appointed generalissimo by the czar, insisted upon an immediate offensive and ordered Kuropatkin to abandon his sound plan.

On 30 April Kuroki's First Army, arriving at the Yalu, was confronted by Zasulich, who gave battle against overwhelming odds. Zasulich was routed, and Kuroki advanced into Manchuria.

On 5 May the Japanese Second Army, under Gen. Yasukata Oku, landed northeast of Port Arthur. Moving south, the army was halted by a powerful Russian defensive position on Nanshan Hill at the narrowest part of the peninsula. Meanwhile, the Japanese Fourth Army disembarked at Takushan, west of the mouth of the Yalu River. As the Japanese net tightened around Port Arthur, Admiral Alekseev fled north to Kuropatkin's headquarters at Liaoyang.

The Siege of Port Arthur, 1904–1905

Nanshan Hill, outpost of the Port Arthur defenses, was attacked on 25 May by Oku's troops, and its defenders were forced to withdraw hastily. In ferocity the battle was a prototype of future Japanese assaults. The loss of Nanshan Hill uncovered the port of Dalny (Dairen), which became a Japanese base. Port Arthur was now ringed both on land and at sea. The Japanese Third Army, under Gen. Maresuke Nogi (captor of Port Arthur from the Chinese in 1894), began concentrating at Dalny.

The fortress complex at Port Arthur consisted of three main lines: an inner entrenchment surrounding the old town itself; the so-called Chinese Wall, some 3,700 meters (4,000 yd.) beyond, a ring of permanent concrete forts linked by strongpoints and entrenchments; and beyond that, outer works consisting of a series of fortified hills—some fully organized, others incomplete. The garrison of 40,000 men and 506 guns had a food supply sufficient for a moderate siege.

Nogi's strength increased, by the end of July, to more than 80,000 men with 474 field and siege guns. Even this imposing force, facing a skillful opponent, would have been insufficient for a successful assault against such a formidable fortified position. On 7–8 August, Nogi attacked the eastern hill masses of the outer defense and captured them after furious fighting. His objective was to get within artillery range of the harbor and the blockaded Russian ships.

The czar ordered Admiral Vilgelm Vitgeft (Makarov's successor) to break out and join the Vladivostok squadron, which was still at large. On 10 August, Vitgeft steamed out and Togo closed with him to begin the Battle of the Yellow Sea. Japanese gunnery was far superior to the Russian, and Togo's four modern battleships threw more metal than their six older Russian counterparts. Both fleets suffered severe damage. A shell struck Vitgeft's flagship, killing the admiral. Confusion followed, and the Russian ships fled in disorder; one was sunk, others ran for neutral ports, and most got back to Port Arthur.

On 14 August, four Japanese armored cruisers fell on the three remaining ships of the Vladivostok squadron in the Korea Strait; one was sunk, the others escaped. Japan now had complete command of the sea.

Nogi renewed his assault on Port Arthur on 19 August. In close-packed frontal attack, the Japanese struck from both the northeast and northwest. Russian machine-gun fire mowed the attackers down again and again; Nogi called off the attacks on 24 August. He had captured 174-Meter Hill and an outlying battery of the eastern defenses; otherwise the Russian position was unimpaired. Calling for heavy siege artillery, Nogi set himself to systematic sapping and mining of the fortifications. In another frontal assault on 29 September, most objectives were carried but 203-Meter Hill, the key point of the defense system, resisted all attacks.

Japanese siege artillery arrived, including nineteen 28cm howitzers throwing 500-pound projectiles 9,100 meters (10,000 yd.). Continuous bombardment hammered the Russian defenses. On 30 October, the Japanese struck the northern and eastern works simultaneously. Once more the Japanese infantry, in close columns, repeatedly attempted to claw through a rain of machine-gun, artillery, and hand-grenade fire and were repelled with tremendous losses. Within the fortress food was running short, and the sick list mounted. News that the Russian Baltic Fleet had left Libau cheered the defenders but spurred the besiegers.

On 26 November, Nogi launched his fifth general assault, which was repulsed at all points. He now concentrated on the 203-Meter Hill position—a huge redoubt, surrounded by barbed wire and flanked by smaller fortified hills, which looked down on the harbor only 3,700 meters (4,000 yd.) away. In Japanese hands, it would seal the fate of the Russian fleet. Bombardment of the crest continued. From 27 November until 4 December, the Japanese attacked in successive waves. Twice Russian counterattacks repelled detachments that had gained footholds in the redoubt. The last handful of the 2,200 defenders was overrun after about 11,000 Japanese had died. The next day Japanese artillery fire from the hill rained on the Russian fleet. Togo's fleet steamed home to refit.

Japanese assaults continued against the northern defenses of the fortress despite freezing weather and heavy snows. The last fort fell on New Year's Day 1905. On 2 January, Stesel surrendered about 10,000 able-bodied but starving survivors of his garrison. The Japanese captured a vast quantity of guns, small arms, and foodstuff (a reflection of Stesel's mismanagement).

Operations in Central Manchuria

On 14 June 1904, Stakelberg halted his advance toward Port Arthur and entrenched at Telissu, confronted by Oku's Second Army. Following a sharp encounter, Stakelberg retreated to avoid envelopment. Advancing, Oku attacked a Russian force at Tashichia, which successfully beat off the Japanese in a delaying action.

On 17 July, Keller's defensive group southeast of Liaoyang attacked Kuroki, who was advancing from the Yalu; Keller was repulsed. When Kuroki attacked in turn on 31 July, the battle ended in a stalemate.

Kuropatkin began pulling back his advance detachments on Liaoyang, toward which point the armies of Kuroki, Nodzu (coming from the coast), and Oku converged. In mid-August, Field Marshal Iwao Oyama assumed overall command of Japanese field forces.

Beginning on 25 August, Oyama gathered his armies against Kuropatkin's well-organized positions. Oyama's strength totaled 125,000 against 158,000 Russians, who had been reinforced by an army corps from Europe. Kuropatkin took the offensive but was checked by vigorous Japanese counterattacks. Another assault, against Kuroki's First Army on the Japanese left, was repulsed. Aggressive Japanese tactics overcame preponderance in numbers. The results of the Battle of Liaoyang were indecisive, but Kuropatkin believed himself defeated and began a systematic, well-managed withdrawal north toward Mukden. Oyama followed.

At the Sha-Ho River on 5 October, Kuropatkin turned on Oyama's forces. He concentrated his main effort against Kuroki's on the Japanese right. While Kuroki dug in to hold the Russian attack, Oyama counterattacked against the weakened Russian center. The severe Japanese assault eventually made Kuropatkin check his own assault to reestablish his center. Both sides renewed their efforts on 16 October without decisive results. Exhausted, both armies dug in.

With his reinforced troops organized in three armies, Kuropatkin again took the offensive at Sandepu (Heikoutai) on 26 January. He hoped to crush Oyama's armies before Nogi's troops arrived from Port Arthur. Attacking in a heavy snowstorm, the Russians came close to victory. After two days of bitter action, Oyama's counterattacks brought a temporary stalemate, and the Russians fell back.

Just south of Mukden the two entrenched armies, each about 310,000 strong, faced one another on a 64-kilometer (40 mi.) front. Beginning on 21 February, Oyama sought to envelop the Russians; attacks and counterattacks followed. Eventually, the Russian right flank was pushed back so far that Kuropatkin feared for his line of communications. On 8 March he disengaged in workmanlike manner and fell back on Tieling (Teihling) and Harbin, defeated but not routed. There was no further concerted action on land.

The Naval Campaign of Tsushima

Commanded by Adm. Zinovy P. Rozhdestvenski, on 15 October 1904 the Russian Baltic Fleet left its home ports of Revel (Tallin) and Libau (Liepaja). After endless problems and delays it reached Van Fong Bay in French Indochina, where the Russians prepared for battle. On 14 May, the fleet sailed for Vladivostok: eight battleships, eight cruisers, nine destroyers, and several smaller craft. Imposing in paper strength, the force was a conglomeration of obsolescent or obsolete vessels. Togo's waiting fleet comprised four battleships, eight cruisers, 21 destroyers, and 60 torpedo boats.

Rozhdestvenski entered Tsushima Strait early on 27 May in line-ahead formation, expecting battle. To the northwest, Togo was steaming northward in similar formation. The action opened in the early afternoon at a range of 5,900 meters (6,400 yd.). Togo, at fifteen-knot speed, overhauled the nine-knot Russians and quickly put two battleships and a cruiser out of action. Togo brilliantly maneuvered his faster force around the hapless Russians. By nightfall Rozhdestvenski had been wounded, three battleships (including his flagship) were sunk, and the surviving Russians, now under Admiral Nebogatov, were fleeing in confusion. Togo turned loose armored cruisers, destroyers, and torpedo boats to harry the exhausted Russians through the night.

Next day the destruction was completed. A cruiser and two destroyers reached Vladivostok; three destroyers got to Manila and internment. The remainder of the Russian fleet was sunk or captured, with 10,000 casualties. The Japanese lost only three torpedo boats and fewer than 1,000 men in all.

Treaty of Portsmouth

Both sides were ready to make peace. Japan's limited war objectives had been won; Russia, seething with internal discontent, had no stomach for continuing the fight. Through the efforts of U.S. president Theodore Roosevelt, peace negotiations at Portsmouth, New Hampshire, led to a treaty. Russia surrendered Port Arthur and one-half of Sakhalin Island and evacuated Manchuria. Korea was recognized as being within Japan's sphere of influence.

Conclusion

Tactically, the war on land made plain the enormous defensive value of the machine gun and the offensive value of indirect artillery fire. (Western observers failed to grasp fully the lesson of the machine gun.) The Russian soldier once more showed stoic courage in adversity. The Japanese displayed professional skill and fanatical devotion to duty. The Battle of Tsushima—the last great fleet action of the ironclad predreadnought era—was also the greatest naval battle of annihilation since Trafalgar. It emphasized that both seamanship and gunnery were still essential to victory at sea. Psychologically and politically, Japan's victory in the war marked a turning point in world history. Asia woke to the fact that the European was not always invincible; the concept of "white supremacy" was shown to be figurative rather than literal.

FRANKLIN D. MARGIOTTA

SEE ALSO: Japan, Modernization and Expansion of; Russia, Expansion of; Siege; Togo, Heihachiro.

Bibliography

Asakawa, K. 1972. *The Russo-Japanese conflict: Its causes and issues.* New York: Barnes and Noble Books.

Connaughton, R. M. 1988. *The war of the rising sun and tumbling bear: A military history of the Russo-Japanese War, 1904–5.* New York: Routledge.

Dupuy, R. E., and T. N. Dupuy. 1986. *Encyclopedia of military history.* New York: Harper & Row.

Fuller, J. F. C. 1956. *A military history of the western world.* New York: Funk and Wagnalls.

Hamilton, I. 1912. *A staff officer's scrap book.* London: Longmans, Green.

Martin, C. 1967. *The Russo-Japanese War.* London: Abelard-Schuman.

Novikoff-Priboy, A. 1937. *Tsushima.* New York: Knopf.

Warner, D. A., and P. Warner. 1974. *The tide at sunrise: A history of the Russo-Japanese War, 1904–1905.* New York: Charterhouse.

Westwood, J. N. 1986. *Russia against Japan, 1904–1905: A new look at the Russo-Japanese War.* Albany, N.Y.: State Univ. of New York Press.

S

SALADIN [1138–93]

Saladin was the most famous Muslim war leader of the twelfth century. He is best remembered for his victory over the Crusaders at the Battle of Hattin (1187), his recovery of Jerusalem for Islam, his founding of the Ayyubid dynasty in Egypt, and his defensive genius against the Third Crusade in the last decade of the twelfth century.

Early Career

Saladin (in Arabic, Salah al-Din Yusuf ibn Ayyub) was born of Kurdish parents in Tikrit, Mesopotamia, in 1138. His father (Ayyub) and other members of his family were prominent military and government leaders under the rule of the Syrian Zangid dynasty. Saladin joined the staff of his uncle Shirkuh in 1152 and by 1156 commanded the security forces of Damascus. He later served as a liaison officer between Sultan Nur al-Din and his commanders. Saladin served under Shirkuh in Egypt where he exhibited excellent organizational skills at the Battle of Bilbay (1164) and distinguished himself for his bravery at the Battle of al-Babayn (1167) and in the defense of Alexandria (1167). He was also instrumental in his uncle's conquest of the degenerate Egyptian Fatimid caliphate in 1169. When Shirkuh died suddenly, Saladin succeeded him as Fatimid vizier and commander of the Syrian forces in Egypt. Saladin strengthened his position and reputation as an aggressive military leader with successful campaigns against the Crusaders, Yemen, Nubia, and North Africa. In 1171 Saladin restored Egypt to the orthodox Sunnite form of Islam practiced by the Abbassid caliphate in Baghdad. He abolished the Fatimid dynasty in Egypt and replaced it with his own line, the Ayyubid dynasty.

Annexation of Syria and Palestine

When Nur al-Din, sultan of Damascus, died in 1174, Saladin exploited the political vacuum by capturing Damascus. Although his actions were resented by the Zangi and the heirs of Nur al-Din, Saladin continued to press his military and political aspirations in northern Syria, Mesopotamia, and eastern Anatolia. After twelve years of warfare, his efforts were rewarded with the submission of

Aleppo (1183) and Mosul (1186). The caliph at Baghdad quickly recognized and confirmed Saladin as sultan of Egypt and Syria. In thirteen years Saladin had consolidated his kingdom, encircled the Latin kingdom of Jerusalem, and united the Muslims against the Crusaders.

After reorganizing the political, administrative, and military structures of his extensive empire, Saladin proceeded to realize his lifetime ambition—defeating the hated Crusaders. In July 1187 his armies destroyed the forces of the king of Jerusalem and his allies at the Battle of Hattin. Most of the Crusaders were killed in the battle, and the majority of the others were taken captive. Saladin treated captured King Guy of Lusignan with the honor due his position, but the cruel Renaud of Chatillon and all the Hospitalers and Templars were executed for their cruelty to the Muslims. The Crusader states along the coast south of Tripoli, with the exception of Tyre and Ascalon, fell to Saladin within the next two months. Ascalon surrendered in September in exchange for King Guy's freedom. Saladin entered Jerusalem on 2 October 1187, and his humanitarian treatment of the Christian defenders stood in sharp contrast to the bloodbath staged by the Crusaders when they had captured the city in 1099. Only the great fortresses of Antioch, Tripoli, and Tyre on the Syrian littoral remained in the hands of the Crusaders. King Guy raised a new Crusader army and laid siege to Acre in August 1189. The long siege at Acre set the stage for the Third Crusade.

The Third Crusade (1189–91)

Saladin's conquest of Jerusalem, after nearly a century of Christian control, shocked Christian Europe and led to another Crusade. The three leading monarchs of Europe, Frederick Barbarossa of Germany, Philip Augustus of France, and Richard the Lionhearted of England, led this expedition against Saladin. Frederick was drowned while crossing a river en route to the Holy Land, and after a quarrel with Richard, Philip Augustus returned to France before the conclusion of hostilities. Most of the combat was between Saladin and Richard.

Saladin had been taken by surprise by the Christian attack on Acre. By the time he moved his army toward the city, the Crusaders besieging Acre had begun to receive reinforcements and supplies from the West. Although Saladin's field armies, his Egyptian fleet, and his elite forces in Acre were at the peak of military preparation, they were no match for the massive forces that Europe committed to the Battle of Acre. Although the Crusaders took Acre after a two-year siege, the heroic efforts of the besieged Muslim garrison and the rigorous military pressure by Saladin ruined the Christian plans to reconquer Jerusalem. They also hurt Saladin's prestige because his army lost its fanaticism against the Crusaders.

With his Egyptian supply base strained to the limit, his navy destroyed by the Italian fleets, and having suffered several setbacks from Richard the Lionhearted's armies, Saladin negotiated a three-year armistice on 2 September 1192. The provisions of the truce clearly underlined Saladin's successful policies. Except for a narrow coastal strip in Syria to be retained by the Christians, the rest of the contested territory, including Jerusalem, remained under Saladin's control. He did agree that Christian pilgrims could freely visit the holy shrines of Jerusalem and other holy places in Palestine. Saladin gained great respect from the Christians as well as Muslims for his generosity and chivalrous conduct. On 4 March 1193, Saladin died in Damascus after a short illness. His tomb was built next to the great mosque and has long been revered as a Muslim shrine.

Conclusion

Saladin brought unity to a divided Muslim region, vanquished the Crusaders in Palestine, and restored Egypt as a major power in the Middle East. His Ayyubid dynasty ruled Egypt and Syria until about 1250. In both history and legend Saladin's name has endured as the embodiment of Muslim chivalry and inspired such romantic literary works as Sir Walter Scott's novel *The Talisman*.

PHILLIP E. KOERPER

SEE ALSO: Arab Conquests; Crusades; History, Medieval Military.

Bibliography

Ehrenkreutz, A. 1972. *Saladin*. Albany, N.Y.: New York State Univ. Press.
Hindley, G. 1976. *Saladin*. London: Constable.
Lane-Poole, S. 1898. *Saladin and the fall of the Kingdom of Jerusalem*. London: G. P. Putnam's Sons.
Newby, P. 1983. *Saladin in his time*. London: Faber and Faber.
Slaughter, G. 1955. *Saladin, 1138–1193*. New York: Exposition Press.

SAN MARTÍN, JOSÉ DE [1778–1850]

The Argentine Gen. José de San Martín was one of two outstanding leaders of the independence movement in South America (the other being the Venezuelan Simón Bolívar). He conceived and directed the successful push from Argentina across the Andes and then north to the Spanish stronghold in Peru, and by his numerous victories he set the stage for the final expulsion of Spanish power from South America. He is also renowned for his sober and modest nature, for rejecting appeals to exercise dictatorial political power, and for declining many of the honors bestowed on him. On the eve of the independence movement's greatest military triumphs, he withdrew from command and went into exile in France. In Latin American politico-military history, he stands as symbol of a successful military figure who was singularly uninterested in the trappings of power or personal glory.

The Formative Years (1778–1816)

José de San Martín (Fig. 1) was born on 25 February 1778 in Yapeyú (northeastern Argentina), the son of a Spanish army captain assigned to the Viceroy-

Figure 1. Bust of José de San Martín (SOURCE: U.S. Library of Congress)

alty of the River Plate. The family returned to Spain when José was eight, and he soon began a military career in the service of the king. He served with distinction in campaigns against the Moors, as well as against Napoleon's forces in the Iberian Peninsula (1808–1811). During these years he became disillusioned with Spain's absolute monarchical system and was increasingly in touch with the *criollo* (first- or second-generation Spaniard born in the Americas) patriots of the Americas. In 1811 he resigned his commission and returned to Buenos Aires via London. Although he was viewed with some suspicion by the Buenos Aires revolutionary junta because of his long service to the king, his professional background was highly valued, and, beginning with an elite corps of mounted grenadiers, he played a significant role in forging the newly forming military forces of the United Provinces of the River Plate. He was also a founding member of the *Logia Lautaro*, a secret lodge society devoted to the cause of independence, with close links to Freemasonry. Whether or not San Martín himself was a Mason is controversial, but his contact with Freemasonry, a major channel bringing the liberal ideas of the Enlightenment and the French and U.S. revolutions to Spanish America, is not surprising.

San Martín's first military action in the service of the patriotic cause was at the Battle of San Lorenzo (3 February 1813). Here his career almost came to a premature end when his horse was killed and pinned him down in the midst of the action. He saw further service in northern Argentina in 1813 and 1814 until illness temporarily forced him to withdraw from military action. He then accepted the governorship of the western province of Cuyo. In this period he worked closely with the Chilean patriot Bernardo O'Higgins and developed his Continental Plan to free South America from Spanish control by crossing the Andes, liberating Chile, and finally taking the Spanish stronghold of Lima in the Viceroyalty of Peru.

The Years of Achievement and Triumph (1816–22)

A turning point in San Martín's life came with the 1816 Tucumán Congress, when he spoke out strongly in favor of a complete break with Spain and a formal declaration of independence, which the congress issued on 9 July. San Martín personally favored an enlightened limited monarchy, possibly enthroning a descendant of the pre-Columbian Inca royal family.

In early 1817 he made his epic crossing of the Andes by traversing passes as high as 5,000 meters (13,700 ft.), sharing his troops' severe hardships, and catching the Spanish forces by surprise at the battle of Chacabuco (12 February 1817). He declined the position of supreme director of Chile and suggested that O'Higgins assume the position instead. After suffering some reverses, the combined Argentine-Chilean forces consolidated their control of Chile following victory at the Battle of Maipú (5 April 1818).

The next phase of San Martín's plan involved a naval assault on Peru, and for this he enlisted the services of a former British naval officer, Lord Thomas Cochrane. When the Spaniards evacuated Lima, San Martín entered the city in July 1821 and proclaimed Peruvian independence. Shortly afterward, San Martín was named "Protector of the Freedom of Peru." That freedom was still in doubt, however, because the Spaniards maintained sizable forces in the Peruvian countryside and to the north in Ecuador.

After a brief period in Peru, San Martín traveled to Guayaquil (Ecuador) to meet with the liberator of northern South America, Simón Bolívar. The two generals met privately several times over a period of two days. Although no record exists of their talks, presumably they discussed plans for continuing the military campaign and the politics of governing the vast territories liberated from the Spanish. At the end of the second day of talks, San Martín withdrew mysteriously from Guayaquil, leaving to the Venezuelan the final military phase of the struggle for independence and the subsequent political spoils.

Renunciation and Withdrawal (1822–50)

San Martín's withdrawal was complete. After Guayaquil he paused briefly in Peru, then Chile, and finally Buenos Aires, shortly after the death of his wife. In early 1824 he sailed with his daughter to exile in France. In 1829 he returned briefly to the River Plate area. He refused an invitation from the Buenos Aires government to land and made only a brief stay in Montevideo before returning to Europe. Apparently he continued to be concerned that his presence and active participation in public life would contribute to the civil turmoil in his native country.

During his long period of expatriation in France, he continued to take an active interest in events in the Americas. He was particularly concerned over the joint British-French intervention in the River Plate against the Buenos Aires dictator Juan Manuel de Rosas; he offered his sword and moral support to Rosas as the defender of Argentine sovereignty against European aggression.

After a period of 28 years away from his native Argentina, Gen. José de San Martín died quietly in Boulonge-sur-Mer, France, on 17 August 1850.

JACK CHILD

SEE ALSO: Bolívar, Simón; Latin American Wars of Independence; Spanish Empire.

Bibliography

García-Godoy, C., ed. 1988. *The San Martín papers.* Washington, D.C.: San Martín Society.

Mitre, B. 1969. *The emancipation of South America.* Trans. W. Pillig. New York: Cooper Square.

Rojas R. 1945. *San Martín: Knight of the Andes.* Trans. H. Brickell. New York: Doubleday: Doran.

Schoellkopf, A. 1924. *Don José de San Martín, 1778–1850: A study of his career.* New York: Boni and Liveright.

SAXE, HERMANN MAURICE, COMTE DE
[1696–1750]

Hermann Maurice, comte de Saxe, commonly known as Maurice de Saxe, was one of the premier soldiers of the mid-eighteenth century. In addition to his talents as a general, he was a military theorist and strategist of unusual ability who wrote several notable books.

Early Life

Hermann Maurice was born in Saxony in 1696, the eldest of 364 acknowledged illegitimate children of Frederick Augustus I the Strong, elector of Saxony and king of Poland, and his then current mistress, the Swedish adventuress Aurora von Königsmarck. His father treated him well and enrolled the 12-year-old Saxe as an ensign in a Saxon infantry regiment. Saxe served under Marlborough and Prince Eugene in the campaign of 1709, and fought at Malplaquet on 11 September 1709. He was awarded the title count of Saxony by his father in 1711. In 1711–12 he fought in the Imperial armies against the Swedes in Pomerania. For his services at the siege of Stralsund in 1712, he was promoted to colonel of cavalry. He retired from active service in 1713 at the age of 17.

Military Apprenticeship

In 1713 Saxe married a very wealthy heiress three years his junior but swiftly squandered her fortune on his regiment and a stream of mistresses. Wearied by home life, he entered the Austrian service early in 1717 and accompanied Prince Eugene in his campaigns against the Turks. He fought at Eugene's successful siege of Belgrade (29 June–19 August 1717) and narrowly escaped death at the hands of Turkish cavalry while fighting in the Battle of Belgrade on 16 August, when Eugene repulsed a Turkish relief effort. Saxe returned to Dresden only after the Treaty of Passarowitz, ratified on 21 July 1718, restored peace between Austria and Turkey. His father purchased for him the colonelcy of a German regiment in French service in 1714, and Saxe began a long and fruitful career in France. His abilities soon earned him favor at the court of King Louis XV, as well as promotion to *maréchal de camp*, roughly analogous to the modern rank of brigadier general. Between 1720 and 1725, Saxe continued his pursuit of the ladies of the court and also began a serious study of the art of war based on his experiences under Eugene in Flanders and the Balkans.

This period ended when he became a candidate for the throne of the vacant duchy of Courland in 1725. He traveled there in 1726 and assumed the title against considerable opposition. Although he ruled wisely and well, he was unable to maintain his position, and returned to Paris in 1727. He resumed his previous peacetime pursuits and wrote his famous *Mes Rêveries* as he recovered from a fever in 1732, although the book was not published until after his death. The death of his father on 1 February 1733 triggered the War of the Polish Succession, and France entered the war against Saxony and Austria. Saxe served against both his erstwhile mentor, Prince Eugene, and his sole legitimate brother, Frederick Augustus II the Weak. Saxe won distinction several times, most notably when he commanded the covering force for the Duke of Berwick's siege of Philippsburg (25 May–27 July 1734) and stalled Prince Eugene's relief attempts. He was promoted to lieutenant general in 1736, and later, in part because of those achievements, he came to the attention of Louis XV's famous mistress, Mme. Pompadour. Saxe became her close friend, and she in turn furthered his career.

Saxe in Command

The outbreak of the War of the Austrian Succession in 1740 brought his return to active service. He accompanied Marshal François M. de Broglie's army of French "volunteers" in the invasion of Upper Austria from July to September 1741. He moved into Bohemia in October and won particular renown for his bloodless nighttime capture of Prague on 19 November. Saxe's capture of Prague was also unique for the order that he maintained among his army once the city had fallen.

The following spring, operating on his own, Saxe besieged and captured the fortress of Eger after a brief siege, lasting from 7 to 20 April 1742, but despite this success he was forced to withdraw by Austrian pressure. He obtained a leave of absence soon after to enable him to press his claims to the duchy of Courland, but he met with no more success than before and returned to France early in 1743. Promoted to marshal of France on 26 March 1743, he was soon deeply involved in plans to invade England and place Prince Charles Edward Stuart (Bonnie Prince Charlie) on the throne there. Poor weather and the wreck of the French fleet off Dunkirk in early 1744 halted these efforts, and after the French declaration of war against Austria in April that year he was given command of the main French army in Flanders.

Saxe outwitted the Austrians in a brief campaign of maneuver and gained control of the coastal areas of the Austrian Netherlands, but the illness of King Louis XV halted French operations in late August. Early the next spring, Saxe moved swiftly into Flanders and besieged Tournai, formally investing that fortress on 22 April 1745. The Duke of Cumberland's army hastened to Tournai's relief, but Saxe met them with his army at Fontenoy on 11 May 1745. To complicate Saxe's task, he was suffering terribly from dropsy and was compelled to command from a litter while a physician drained the fluid from his abdomen; he had also to contend with the presence of King Louis and the extensive royal retinue. Fortunately, Saxe was not bothered by these distractions, and he repeatedly repulsed Cumberland's infantry attacks. When Cumberland's massive infantry column of 15,000 men crashed through the French lines, Saxe hastily mounted a horse to direct the counterstroke personally and led a masterful counterattack employing infantry, guns, and cavalry in skillful combination to throw back the allies' effort. Tournai, despairing of relief, capitulated on 19 June, and the surrender of Ostend on 24 August left most of Flanders in French hands.

The following spring, he faced an Austrian army under the able and resourceful command of Charles of Lorraine. Saxe besieged and captured Brussels between 7 and 20 February 1746 and then marched on to capture Antwerp on 31 May. After further maneuver, he brought Charles to battle at Raucoux on 11 October, smashing the Austrian line with three parallel attacks by large columns. Only repeated charges by Lord Ligonier's cavalry prevented a decisive French victory. To capitalize on his achievements, Saxe invaded the Netherlands the following year. He was opposed by an allied army under the Prince of Orange and the Duke of Cumberland, who had returned from his campaign against Bonnie Prince Charlie in Scotland. Fortunately for the allies, they were assisted by the able Austrian commander Daun; with their army of 90,000, they trapped 30,000 French at Laufeldt. Saxe hurried to the relief of the trapped force by marching 80 kilometers (50 mi.) in two days at the head of 12,000 men. After a costly, seesaw battle for the village of Laufeldt itself, Saxe finally broke the center of the English line. So weary and bloodied was Saxe's army (his troops had suffered 14,000 casualties, his opponents more than 6,000) that the allies were able to withdraw almost unmolested. The next year, Saxe besieged and captured Maastricht between 15 April and 7 May 1748, thus earning promotion to marshal general, the first to hold that rank since Turenne 80 years before.

With the end of the War of the Austrian Succession, Saxe returned to Chateau de Chambord, a gift from an appreciative Louis XV. There he divided his time between experiments and drills with his private regiment and a series of remarkable debaucheries. He died there after "interviewing" a troupe of eight actresses on 30 November 1750. The official cause of his demise was noted on the death certificate as *une surfeit des femmes*.

Assessment

Saxe was a notable field commander who was aggressive, enterprising, and fortunate. His strategies were subtle and effective, his tactics carefully chosen to suit each occasion. His reputation is due as much to his writings, however, as to his considerable achievements in the field. In his *Mes Rêveries* he gave a great deal of advice on the art of war, some of it silly, such as the usefulness of plug bayonets and recommendations for the reintroduction of the pike. However, his thoughts on army reorganization were sound. He suggested the creation of 50,000-man armies of all arms, including 32,000 infantry and 17,000 cavalry as well as 20 twelve-pound and 160 half-pound cannon. His proposed military organization also emphasized the use of light infantry and combined-arms tactics, foreshadowing the corps of Napoleon. In sum, Saxe was the greatest soldier of the mid-eighteenth century.

DAVID L. BONGARD

SEE ALSO: Eugene, Prince of Savoy-Carignan; Organization, Army.

Bibliography

D'Auvergne, E. B. F. 1931. *The prodigal marshal.* New York: Dodd, Mead.
Blumenson, M., and J. L. Stokesbury. 1971. Maverick in warfare's formal age. *Army* 21(4):55–58.
Pichat, H. 1909. *La campagne du maréchal de Saxe dans les Flanders . . . suivis d'une correspondance inedité de Maurice de Saxe pendant cette campagne.* Paris.
Saint-René-Taillandier, R. G. E. 1865. *Maurice de Saxe: étude historique d'après les documents des archives de Dresde.* Paris: Michel Lévy frères.
Saxe, M. 1757. *Mes rêveries.* Paris: Desaint et Saillant.
White, J. E. M. 1962. *Marshal of France: The life and times of Maurice de Saxe.* Chicago: Rand McNally.

SCHARNHORST, GERHARD JOHANN DAVID VON [1755–1813]

Gerhard Johann David von Scharnhorst was a Prussian general during the Napoleonic Wars in Europe. As a child of the Enlightenment, Scharnhorst was one of the first to understand the transformation of war wrought by the armies of the French Revolution and Napoleon. When he moved to Prussia from his native Hannover in 1801, Scharnhorst had the opportunity to reform one of the great armies of Europe. He was blocked initially by the Prussian nobility until the defeat of the Prussian army at Jena and Auerstadt on 14 October 1806. That disaster opened the way for Scharnhorst, who converted his Age of Enlightenment notions of reform, education, and rationalism into a program that revolutionized the Prussian army. The dramatic success of that army during the Wars of German Liberation (1813–15) was a direct result of his reform program.

Scharnhorst's premature death in the 1813 campaign contributed to a resurgence of noble reaction after 1815, so that the full military-social-political implications of his program were never fully implemented. However, the purely military results became manifest in the Wars of German Unification and the Franco-Prussian War (1864–66 and 1870–71). After Prussia's spectacular victories in those wars, Scharnhorst's ideas, as carried out by Helmuth von Moltke, became the basis for the modernization of all the world's military powers.

Early Life

Scharnhorst was born of humble origins in Bordenau, a small village west of Hannover, on 12 November 1755. He grew up tenant farming with his father, a former sergeant in the Hannoverian cavalry. At 17 he entered the military academy of Count Friedrich Wilhelm Ernst zu Schaumburg-Lippe-Bückeburg (1724–77), one of the most enlightened and distinguished soldiers then living in Germany. Captivated by the spirit of the Enlightenment, Count Wilhelm introduced Scharnhorst to the profession of arms, emphasizing the integration of professional and technical knowledge with humanistic values. It was this concept of education that shaped Scharnhorst's entire military career.

Hannoverian Service

Scharnhorst was commissioned in the Hannoverian cavalry in 1778 and spent his first fifteen years of military service establishing a reputation as a military scholar and theorist. During this time he edited three journals and published two books. When Hannover joined the coalition against France in 1793, Scharnhorst left his faculty post and joined the Hannoverian army in Belgium. Throughout the campaign he demonstrated exceptional leadership under fire, but it was not until Menin, where he directed the successful sortie from that besieged fortress, that Scharnhorst secured his reputation as a fighting soldier. He was subsequently promoted and transferred to the commanding general's staff. Scharnhorst continued to serve with distinction, but received no further advancement. Frustrated by the lack of scope for his talents in Hannover, Scharnhorst accepted an appointment in the Prussian army in 1801.

Prussian Service

Scharnhorst's solid reputation as a soldier and scholar preceded him to Berlin. Once in Prussian service he agreed to direct the activities of the newly founded *Militärische Gesellschaft* (Military Society), whose purpose was to study the art of war. It was the first association of its kind and became the focal point of enlightenment in the Prussian army before 1806.

Realizing that the art of war had increased in scope and complexity, Scharnhorst and other members of the Military Society recommended the establishment of a permanent general staff system. Officers of the general staff would plan and coordinate the activities of war. Its chief would advise the monarch on all military matters. The primary source of general staff officers would be the reorganized Berlin Institute for Young Officers, which Scharnhorst had transformed into the army's central institution of higher military education. His goal was to replace the military aristocracy of birth with an aristocracy of education. When the first officers graduated from the Berlin Institute in 1804, the later famous philosopher of war, Karl von Clausewitz, stood at the head of the class.

Unfortunately, these measures came too late to prevent Prussia's catastrophic defeat by Napoleon in 1806 and 1807. Scharnhorst himself was chief of staff of one of the two armies Napoleon decisively defeated at Jena and Auerstadt. He was later taken prisoner with Blücher's forces near Lübeck, but was exchanged in time to play a critical role in checking Napoleon during the winter battle of Eylau in February 1807. Although many reputations were lost during Prussia's collapse, Scharnhorst demonstrated his superior strategic and tactical skills throughout the campaign.

After the Peace of Tilsit in 1807, Scharnhorst was charged with the reform of the Prussian military system. Learning from the American and French revolutions, and in close cooperation with civilian authorities, he abolished the mercenary character of the army and established a national army based on universal conscription. Corporal punishment was eliminated, military discipline was adjusted to meet the needs of a citizen army, and careers were opened to all men of talent and ability. With these reforms, Scharnhorst laid the foundation for a modern military organization.

Following Napoleon's defeat in Russia in 1812, Prussia once again took the field against the French. As chief of the newly established Prussian General Staff and minister of war, Scharnhorst planned the operations that eventually led to Napoleon's defeat in Germany. Unfortunately, he did not live to see his homeland freed. He was wounded in the first engagement at Grossgörschen (Lützen) in May 1813, and died on 28 June in Prague, where he had gone to negotiate Austria's entry into the war.

The Enlightened Soldier

Scharnhorst's great merit rests on his work as an educator and reformer, and on his unique ability to evoke the support of colleagues who, by nature and training, were unreceptive to new ideas. It is truly remarkable that Scharnhorst rose from humble origins to such high rank and influence in an army whose leaders came almost entirely from the hereditary nobility.

CHARLES E. WHITE

SEE ALSO: French Revolutionary–Napoleonic Wars; Prussia and Germany, Rise of.

Bibliography

Büschleb, H. 1979. *Scharnhorst in Westfalen: Politik, Administration, und Kommando im Schicksalsjahr 1795*. Herford: E.S. Mittler und Sohn.

Clausewitz, K. von. 1832. Ueber das Leben und den Charakter des Generals von Scharnhorst. *Historisch-politische Zeitschrift* 1:175–222.

Lehmann, M. 1886–87. *Scharnhorst*. Leipzig: S. Hirzel.

Paret, P. 1976. *Clausewitz and the state*. Oxford: Clarendon Press.

Stadelmann, R. 1952. *Scharnhorst: Schicksal und geistige Welt*. Wiesbaden: Limes Verlag.

White, C. 1989. *The enlightened soldier: Scharnhorst and the Militärische Gesellschaft in Berlin, 1801–1805*. New York: Praeger.

SCHEER, REINHARD [1863–1928]

Reinhard Scheer, commander of the German High Seas Fleet at the Battle of Jutland, was born in Oberkirchen near Bückeberge in 1863. He began a naval career of nearly 40 years by graduating second in his class from the Naval Training School in Kiel in 1880. As an ensign, Scheer entered a navy that soon became the prime instrument of Kaiser Wilhelm II's determination to make Germany preeminent among the great world powers. Scheer matured personally and professionally while Adm. Alfred von Tirpitz, Wilhelm's politically able state secretary of the Imperial Naval Office (*Reichsmarineamt*, or RMA), financed and fashioned a navy to satisfy his sovereign and extend Germany's political and economic influence around the world.

In a navy that placed a premium on experience at sea, Scheer experienced a fortunate balance between shore assignments and sea duty. He served most of his time ashore in Tirpitz's RMA, beginning his first tour in the Torpedo Section in 1897. By 1903, he had taken command of the RMA's Central Division, and his fitness reports described him as a selfless, technically competent officer with a high sense of duty.

Scheer's first assignments as a commissioned officer at sea took him to the East Africa Cruiser Squadron (1888–97), where his tour was interrupted only by two brief tours at the Naval Academy at Kiel (1894 and 1896) and a naval fact-finding trip to the Orient during the Sino-Japanese War of 1895–96. After various assignments as torpedo or navigation officer in the early 1900s, he left the RMA in 1907 to take command of the battleship SMS *Elsass*.

By age 44, Scheer had served in Africa as a newly commissioned ensign and in Asia as a lieutenant and had risen through the ranks as an expert in torpedo warfare and navigation both in the fleet and at the RMA. He reached the rank of lieutenant commander by 1900, commander four years later, and captain two years before he left the RMA to join the *Elsass*. In reviewing his performance with this vessel, Scheer's superiors extolled his competence as a commanding officer and his skill in gunnery and declared him suitable for a higher staff position.

With the elevation of his old friend Henning von Holtzendorff to command of the High Seas Fleet in 1909, Scheer left the SMS *Elsass* to serve as Fleet chief of staff. Less than six months later, he was selected for flag rank.

Character and Personality

According to officers who served with him, like Ernst von Weizsäcker and Erich Raeder, Scheer brought an openness, vitality, and delight in responsibility to command. When he left Holtzendorff's staff in 1911, he returned briefly to the RMA as the head of the General Naval Department before rejoining the High Seas Fleet as commander of the Second Squadron in 1913. He preferred assignments at sea, and there his staff and crew saw him as a cheerful, spirited, very adaptable man. His fitness report for 1 December 1915 described him as an energetic individual and an officer of accomplishment manifesting a high sense of duty and service, who "possessed the trust of his commanders and officers." As a commander Scheer trusted himself as much as his subordinates did, and this self-assurance gave his staff a vital sense of stability and confidence in his judgment.

Leadership and the First World War

Promoted to vice admiral in December of 1913, Scheer entered the war as a champion of an aggressive defense. Proponents of this strategic viewpoint suggested employing shore bombardments and other provocative tactics to draw elements of the British Grand Fleet into battle. If properly utilized, this strategy could provide the German High Seas Fleet with an opponent of manageable size and firepower. When the German battle cruiser force under Rear Adm. Franz Ritter von Hipper bombarded Scarborough and Hartlepool in January 1915, indeed Adm. David Beatty's battle cruisers were drawn into action. The commander in chief of the German High Seas Fleet, Adm. Friedrich von Ingenohl, refused to give battle, however; he was fearful that the Germans would encounter the entire Grand Fleet. When Ingenohl withdrew, Hipper, left to his own devices, crippled Beatty's flagship HMS *Lion* at the Dogger Bank while losing the SMS *Blücher* to British gunfire.

Ingenohl's behavior left an indelible impression on Scheer. Absolutely convinced of the strategy's validity, he felt deeply the irresponsibility of Ingenohl's action. The implication of cowardice aside, he felt very strongly that a commander's duty required taking the initiative and, in spite of the odds, seeking out and engaging the adversary.

When the results of the Dogger Bank encounter forced Ingenohl's resignation in February of 1915, he was replaced by the ailing Adm. Hugo von Pohl. Pohl's health forced his resignation after only a year at the helm, and Scheer took his place on 18 January 1916. In the face of the Royal Navy's numerical advantage, Scheer was determined to hold the initiative, take calculated risks, and rely on the proven expertise of his captains as his next most potent weapons after gunfire and torpedoes.

Confronted by the Grand Fleet at Jutland on 31 May 1916, Scheer displayed his willingness to take risks and employ the initiative to keep his foe guessing.

During the height of the battle, he twice employed the battle turn to starboard—a complete 180-degree change of course—to save his fleet. At 6:55 P.M. he actually used this tactic to assault the center of the Grand Fleet battle line in order to surprise Jellicoe and maintain the initiative. He felt that this tactic alone could preserve his command and satisfy the imperative to inflict maximum losses on his enemy.

Later Life

Hailed as a hero after Jutland, Scheer was promoted to admiral on 5 June 1916. He retained control of the High Seas Fleet until August 1918, when he assumed command of the newly created combined naval staff (*Seekriegsleitung;* Fig. 1). After the war ended in November, he retired from the navy and lived another decade to write his operational memoir of the High Seas Fleet (1919) and his autobiography (1925). Admiral Reinhard Scheer died in 1928 at Marktredwitz, at the age of 65.

GARY E. WEIR

SEE ALSO: Jellicoe, John Rushworth, 1st Earl; Tirpitz, Alfred von; World War I.

Bibliography

Campbell, N. J. M. 1986. *Jutland: An analysis of the fighting.* Annapolis, Md.: U.S. Naval Institute Press.

Figure 1. German Prince Henry (with glass) and Admiral Scheer on board the submarine tender Meteor, *2 October 1918 (captured German official photo).* (SOURCE: Naval Historical Center, official Navy Dept. photograph)

Forstmeier, F. 1961. Zum Bild der Personlichkeit des Admirals Reinhard Scheer (1863–1928). *Marine Rundschau* 58:73–93.
Herwig, H. 1987. *Luxury fleet*. Atlantic Highlands, N.J.: Ashfield Press.
Raeder, E. 1960. *My life*. Annapolis, Md.: U.S. Naval Institute Press.
Scheer, R. 1925. *Vom Segelschiff zum U-boot*. Leipzig: Verlag Quelle und Meyer.
———. 1934. *Germany's High Seas Fleet in the world war*. New York: Peter Smith.
von Weizsäcker, E. 1951. *Memoirs of Ernst von Weizsäcker*. London: Victor Gollancz.

SCHLIEFFEN, ALFRED, COUNT VON
[1833–1913]

Count Alfred von Schlieffen served as the chief of the General Staff of the German army from 1891 to 1906. He is primarily remembered as the architect of a German plan for waging a two-front war against France and Russia simultaneously. The German army implemented a modified version of the Schlieffen Plan when World War I broke out in 1914. The plan ultimately failed and was followed by four years of static trench warfare that characterized the fighting on the western front during World War I.

Early Years

Schlieffen, the son of a Prussian army major, was born in 1833. Educated in schools in Niesky and Berlin, in 1854 he joined the 2d Guards Uhlan Regiment as a second lieutenant. As a young officer, he lived a boisterous lifestyle—a sharp contrast to the dour, aloof character of his later years. Schlieffen was married for four years, the union ending with his wife's death. He never remarried.

In 1865 Schlieffen was assigned to the General Staff, where he spent most of the remainder of his career. He was a staff officer in the Prussian Cavalry Corps during Prussia's war with Austria in 1866. Here, Prussia's success in nearly encircling the Austrian army at Königgrätz seems to have made a great impression on the young officer. Schlieffen also served as a corps-level staff officer during the Franco-Prussian War of 1870–71.

Schlieffen subsequently served in a number of line and staff positions, including an eight-year stint as commander of the 1st Guards Uhlans, from 1876 to 1884. In 1889 he was selected as first deputy to the chief of the General Staff, Alfred von Waldersee. Two years later, Schlieffen himself became the chief of the General Staff when Waldersee was forced to resign.

Schlieffen as Chief of the General Staff

During his fifteen-year tenure as chief of the General Staff, Schlieffen oversaw several modernizing reforms within the Germany army. He introduced heavier, more mobile artillery, adopted new infantry regulations that emphasized *auftragstaktik* (mission tactics), and introduced greater numbers of machine guns, modern signal equipment, and even some motorized transport vehicles. His most significant efforts, however, concerned the development of the strategy that Germany would use at the outset of its next war.

In 1894, France and Russia joined in an alliance, thereby creating the sort of two-sided threat to Germany that Otto von Bismarck, the former chancellor, had taken such pains to avoid. This meant that the General Staff had to plan for a two-front war from a geographic position in central Europe that offered little in the way of defensible terrain. It was with this great problem that Schlieffen wrestled during the remainder of his service as chief of the General Staff.

Schlieffen's predecessors—Helmuth von Moltke (the Elder) and Waldersee—had also considered the problem of a two-front war before it became a virtual certainty. Their approach had been to defend in Lorraine against a French offensive and to seek a decision in the east. Schlieffen, assuming that the next war would likely be a short one because of the huge expense of maintaining the mass armies that all nations were now capable of fielding, concluded that an immediate decision against France was better. France could mobilize more quickly than Russia; therefore, to win a two-front war, that threat would have to be eliminated first. Then Germany could turn its attention toward the east. This concept formed the basis of the Schlieffen Plan.

The Schlieffen Plan

Schlieffen was fascinated by the concept of defeating an enemy through encirclement, along the pattern of Hannibal's famous victory over the Romans at Cannae in 216 B.C. He had seen this attempted in practice with Moltke's victory at Königgrätz, and he looked for ways that such a victory could be brought about on an even larger scale. Concluding that Germany's resources would not permit a Cannae-like double envelopment against France, with its substantial defensive fortifications on the Franco-German border, Schlieffen began to look at the idea of conducting a huge flanking movement—a single envelopment—that would bypass the French fortifications to the north and allow the German army to swing south and then east to encircle the French army and to strike it in the rear.

Schlieffen's plan called for placing a very small portion of Germany's army in the east, to delay any Russian advance into East Prussia or Silesia, while massing most of the German army in the west against France. He then planned to place the bulk of the projected German forces in the west on the right flank, and to leave a weak left flank that would withdraw in the face of the anticipated French offensive through Lorraine and Alsace. The huge right-flank force would need adequate room to maneuver if it were to skirt French defenses to the north; to do so would require German units to march through Belgium and the Netherlands, in both cases a breach of neutrality. Schlieffen also anticipated that, in order to protect its own flank, the flanking force would have to swing out wide enough to reach the English Channel. After swinging around Paris and crushing the French army against its own defenses, the units in the west would quickly be transported to the east to meet the slowly mobilizing Russians. In

1906 Schlieffen stepped down from the chief-of-staff post. By this time his plan formed the basis for virtually all German military and strategic planning for prospective conflicts.

Aftermath

During his retirement, Schlieffen continued to maintain great interest in the Schlieffen Plan. He offered suggestions to his successor as chief of staff, Helmuth von Moltke (the Younger), but his influence on German military policy had diminished considerably. He watched as the younger Moltke made a number of modifications to the Schlieffen Plan, to include a weakening of the right flank and a shortening of the great encircling wheel that Schlieffen had envisioned. Nineteen months before the outbreak of World War I, on 4 January 1913, Schlieffen died. Reputedly his dying words were: "Keep the right flank strong."

Supporters of Schlieffen and his plan were convinced that had it been executed properly and in its original form, Germany would probably have won World War I during the first few months. Detractors have pointed out that Germany's implementation of the plan helped to widen the war (to Germany's detriment), and that Schlieffen's plan was fundamentally flawed because it gave too much emphasis to military expediency while ignoring potential political consequences. The Schlieffen Plan's violation of Belgian neutrality is often cited as one of the major reasons for Great Britain's entry into the war on the side of the French and the Russians. (This is questionable, however, since Britain was firmly committed to its alliance with France and Russia.) One can still say with virtual certainty that Schlieffen's influence on both the outbreak and the outcome of World War I was of the highest order.

DAVID A. NIEDRINGHAUS

SEE ALSO: Moltke the Elder; Prussia and Germany, Rise of; World War I.

Bibliography

Addington, L. H. 1971. *The blitzkrieg era and the German general staff, 1865–1941.* New Brunswick, N.J.: Rutgers Univ. Press.
Craig, G. A. 1955. *The politics of the Prussian army, 1640–1945.* London: Oxford Univ. Press.
DeWeerd, H. A. 1941. *Great soldiers of the two world wars.* New York: Norton.
Dupuy, T. N. 1977. *A genius for war: The German army and general staff, 1807–1945.* Englewood Cliffs, N.J.: Prentice-Hall.
Gorlitz, W. 1953. *The German general staff: Its history and structure, 1657–1945.* London: Hollis and Carter.
Kitchen, M. 1975. *A military history of Germany.* London: Weidenfeld and Nicolson.
Nichols, J. A. 1968. *Germany after Bismarck.* New York: Norton.
Ritter, G. 1958. *The Schlieffen plan: Critique of a myth.* New York: Praeger.
———. 1970. *The sword and the scepter: The problem of militarism in Germany,* Vol. II. Coral Gables, Fla.: Univ. of Miami.
Rothenberg, G. 1986. Moltke, Schlieffen, and the doctrine of strategic envelopment. In *Makers of modern strategy,* ed. P. Paret. Princeton, N.J.: Princeton Univ. Press.

SCHWARZKOPF, H. NORMAN
[1934–   ]

General H. Norman Schwarzkopf assumed his duties as the commander in chief, United States Central Command, on 23 November 1988. His headquarters deployed to Riyadh, Saudi Arabia, in August 1990 to provide command and control for all U.S. forces deploying to the region for Operation Desert Shield. The invasion of Kuwait by the armed forces of Iraq prompted the United States to undertake the operation to deter further encroachment into Saudi Arabia. The overall mission of U.S. and coalition military forces in the region was changed to that of ejecting Iraqi forces from Kuwait and, on 17 January 1991, U.S. and coalition forces initiated combat operations. Schwarzkopf thus assumed command of Operation Desert Storm. The 42 days of intense air operations and 100 hours of lightning ground war ended when President Bush directed a cessation of hostilities against overwhelmed Iraqi armed forces on 28 February 1991. Desert Storm was a military success that proved the quality of the U.S. forces, their training, and the effectiveness of their weapon systems.

Schwarzkopf was born in Trenton, New Jersey, on 22 August 1934. After attending Valley Forge Military Academy, where he finished at the head of his class, he attended the U.S. Military Academy at West Point, New York. (His father, Herbert Norman Schwarzkopf, graduated from West Point in 1917.) Upon graduation in 1956, he was commissioned a second lieutenant in the infantry. In addition to professional military schooling throughout his career, to include the U.S. Army Command and General Staff College and the Army War College, Schwarzkopf earned a master's degree in guided missile engineering from the University of Southern California.

His military awards and decorations include the Distinguished Service Medal (Army) with two oak-leaf clusters, Silver Star with two oak-leaf clusters, Defense Superior Service Medal, Legion of Merit, Distinguished Flying Cross, Bronze Star Medal with Valor device and two oak-leaf clusters, Purple Heart with oak-leaf cluster, Meritorious Service Medal with two oak-leaf clusters, Air Medal, and Army Commendation Medal with Valor device and three oak-leaf clusters.

Schwarzkopf is married to the former Brenda Holsinger, and they have three children: Cynthia, Jessica, and Christian.

Military Career Highlights

After finishing the Infantry Officer Basic Course (IOBC) and Airborne School at Fort Benning, Georgia, Schwarzkopf was assigned to the 101st Airborne Division at Fort Campbell, Kentucky. There he served as a platoon leader, company executive officer, and assistant S-3 (air) or air operations officer. Reassigned in July 1959 to Berlin, he was a platoon leader, reconnaissance platoon leader, and liaison officer in the 2d Battle Group, 6th Infantry. Subsequently, he became the aide-de-camp to the commanding general, Berlin Command. Schwarzkopf thrived in this environment with a unit and troops

Figure 1. H. Norman Schwarzkopf. (SOURCE U.S. Army)

where there was a real-world military mission that contrasted with the spit-and-polish framework of his first assignment in the United States.

In September 1961, and by now a captain, Schwarzkopf attended the Infantry Officer Advanced Course (IOAC) at Fort Benning. He finished in the top third of his class, and his professional writing capabilities were recognized when he received the General George C. Marshall Award for Excellence in Military Writing. This professional military training was followed by two years of graduate studies at the University of Southern California, earning him a master's degree in guided missile engineering. In June 1964, he returned to West Point to serve on the faculty of the Department of Mechanics. His assignment there was interrupted after a year when he volunteered for duty in Vietnam. There he served as an adviser in the Vietnamese airborne brigade. Most of his tour was as an airborne task force adviser, and later on his tour of duty, exhausted from extensive military operations, he was the senior staff adviser for civil affairs to the Vietnamese airborne division. In his combat adviser role, he participated in seven major operations and received two Silver Stars for gallantry, three

Bronze Stars, and the Purple Heart. He was promoted early to major in 1965.

He returned to West Point in 1966 as an associate professor in the Department of Mechanics for two years. In August 1968, he was promoted early to lieutenant colonel and attended the U.S. Army Command and General Staff College, graduating in June 1969. Vietnam was his next assignment. He initially served as the executive officer to the chief of staff of U.S. Army, Vietnam. Schwarzkopf next assumed command of the 1st Battalion, 6th Infantry, 198th Infantry Brigade, 23d Infantry Division (Americal).

In July 1970, as a lieutenant colonel, Schwarzkopf returned to the United States and an assignment in Washington, D.C., in the army's infantry officer branch of the office of personnel operations. Serving in this position for two years, he was selected for attendance at the U.S. Army War College, Carlisle Barracks, Pennsylvania. In 1973, Schwarzkopf returned to Washington, D.C., to an assignment as military assistant in the office of the assistant secretary of defense for financial management, where he served for a little more than one year. An assignment to Alaska followed in December 1974, where he was the deputy commander, 172d Infantry Brigade at Fort Richardson. After two years—during which he was promoted to colonel—he moved on to Fort Lewis, Washington, in October 1976 to be a brigade commander in the 9th Infantry Division.

Embarking on a career in the general officers' ranks, he moved to a joint tour with a U.S. unified command, the U.S. Pacific Command, at Camp H. M. Smith, Hawaii, in 1978. This two-year tour was followed by a two-year assignment as the assistant division commander, 8th Infantry Division (Mechanized), in Germany. Promoted to major general, he returned to Washington, D.C., in 1982 and another assignment in the personnel arena, this time as director, military personnel management in the office of the deputy chief of staff for personnel, Department of the Army. He then became the commanding general, 24th Infantry Division (Mechanized) at Fort Stewart, Georgia, from June 1983 to June 1985. While in this assignment he acted as deputy director of Operation Urgent Fury, the Grenada invasion operation.

Schwarzkopf returned to the Department of the Army in Washington, D.C., as the assistant deputy chief of staff for operations for about a year and then was promoted to lieutenant general and assigned as the commanding general, I Corps, Fort Lewis, Washington. In less than a year, in 1987, he returned to Washington, D.C., to assume the prestigious position of deputy chief of staff for operations, Department of the Army. Later he was promoted to four-star general and assumed his position as the commander in chief, U.S. Central Command, MacDill Air Force Base, Florida, where he was responsible for contingency planning for possible U.S. and coalition operations in the Middle East.

"Stormin' Norman"

Schwarzkopf inspired his soldiers at the onset of the ground war in Desert Storm to be "the thunder and lightning of Desert Storm." In the Gulf War—

where the media were equipped with sophisticated equipment that enabled them to report the war's progress almost instantaneously—Schwarzkopf gave status reports of the war's progress in a briefing that, many pointed out, was indicative of the success to follow.

Schwarzkopf's leadership style is often compared with that of Gen. George S. Patton during World War II. Abrasive and confrontational, it is Schwarzkopf's approach to "getting the job done." Impatience has evidently been a personal characteristic throughout his career. His success can in part be attributed to extracting the most from his subordinates by focusing on the essential tasks to be performed and demanding superior results. In his autobiography, Schwarzkopf details a story about relieving a company commander who had failed to "take care of his troops" while he was a battalion commander in Vietnam. He goes on to point out that the officer was quite aware of his strengths and weaknesses and accepted his fate. They have subsequently come into contact on civil terms. The "Bear" has a bite, but also recognizes that soldiers have differing niches to fill to accomplish a mission.

Stormin' Norman notes in his autobiography that he came to appreciate the importance of leadership, the individual soldier, and his family during his early years of military service. Throughout his succeeding troop assignments he emphasized the role of subordinate commanders in leading their troops, receiving and integrating the newly assigned soldier into the unit, and addressing the needs of the soldier's family. Family programs and programs to generally improve the lot of the soldier became his trademarks. Finally, his experiences in Vietnam were not lost in the Gulf War. He played a major role in delaying any offensive action against Iraqi ground forces until there had been sufficient buildup of coalition and U.S. combat forces in the region. Though indeed a "can-do" soldier who demanded much from his staff and subordinate commanders, at the same time his military aggressiveness was kept in check until he could absolutely assure the U.S. political leadership of success in the Gulf War.

JAMES D. BLUNDELL

SEE ALSO: Gulf War.

Bibliography

Cohen, Roger, and Claudio Gatti. 1991. *In the eye of the storm: The life of H. Norman Schwarzkopf.* New York: Farrar, Straus and Giroux.
Scales, Robert H., Jr. 1993. *Certain victory: The U.S. Army in the Gulf War.* Washington, D.C.: Brassey's, Inc.
Schwarzkopf, H. Norman. 1992. *General H. Norman Schwarzkopf, The autobiography: It doesn't take a hero.* New York: Bantam Books.

SCIENCE OF WAR

In arriving at a definition of the *science of war*, one must acknowledge the differing viewpoints in the war-as-science versus war-as-art theories.

Science of War

According to one school of thought, the science of war is that part of the theory of war that attempts to establish a scientific basis for the decisions that affect the conduct of war. Those in this group believe that generalizations based on observations of past events are true for all future events as well as for past events that were unknown at the time the generalizations were made.

Art of War

Another school of thought sees war as group violence where the outcome is uncertain. Those holding this point of view believe that the outcome of war is not predictable through generalizations based on past wars, and hence, that there can be no true science of war. Those who maintain that war is too unpredictable to yield to science usually argue that war is an art. Favoring the term *art of war*, they contend that, while science can be learned from a book (like chemistry or physics), war can only be learned by practice. They argue further that, if war were a science, the "scientific" principles embraced by the war-is-a-science advocates would always be reproducible in all wars for all times.

Thus the "scientific" principle (repeated often in the paragraphs below)—namely, in order to win, one must gather superior forces at the decisive point—would have no exceptions. Yet there are historical deviations from this so-called principle because numerous human factors intrude on combat.

Science of War: A Definition

Despite difficulties of definition and the varied use of the term historically, the *science of war* can be useful in the study and understanding of war. In order to make use of it, a valid definition between the extremes is needed. The science of war, as examined in this article, is theory that is based on the systematic study of the past to make generalizations about the decision making in war that have been validated through application. The generalizations must affect decision making, and they must be prescriptive rather than descriptive. Some writers even maintain that the science of war implies that generalizations about war take the form of immutable principles.

From the Ancients to the Renaissance

The oldest military treatise known was written by the Chinese military philosopher Sun Tzu about 500 B.C. Although the work was entitled *The Art of War*, Sun Tzu undertook a systematic study by identifying components of war and by offering aphorisms based on his knowledge of war. "All warfare is based on deception" is among the most often quoted of his adages. He also wrote, "By discovering the enemy's dispositions and remaining invisible ourselves, we can keep our forces concentrated while the enemy must be divided." Such generalizations were clearly intended as guides to instruct future commanders in the conduct of war, and hence they mark Sun Tzu's work as the oldest known treatise on the *science* of war.

In ancient Greece and Rome, military theory was addressed by Thucydides and Xenophon in their histories of the Greek wars. Both descriptive and analytical, these histories were a part of both the art of war and the science of war.

Chief among the analysts of the ancient world was Flavius Vegetius Renatus, known generally as Vegetius. His book, *The Military Institutions of the Romans*, was written in the early fifth century, appeared in translations long before the printing press was invented, and, since the age of printing, has been available in translations throughout the world. Vegetius was not an experienced military leader, but through his study of ancient manuscripts, he imposed a new order on military theory and added new knowledge to the science of war. His generalizations were prescriptive and hence a part of the science of war: "Victory in war does not depend upon numbers or mere courage; only skill and discipline will ensure it. . . . It is better to have several bodies of reserves than to extend your front too much."

During the early Middle Ages, a step in the development of the concept of the science of war was taken by the Crusaders. No major treatise on war resulted from the expeditions of Christian soldiers to the Holy Land, but, by returning to western Europe with new ideas about fortifications and defensive works, the Crusaders brought an element that would link war with such accepted scientific studies as mathematics and geometry. This linkage also affected the way theorists thought about the conduct of war in general.

The renaissance in the study of war was manifested in the writings of Niccolò Machiavelli, whose principal military treatise was also entitled *The Art of War*. Like Sun Tzu, Machiavelli presented new ideas—especially regarding the need for new military institutions to deal more effectively with the political realities of renaissance Italy. Machiavelli also enumerated some "general rules" in his *Art of War;* among them, "to do of your own volition what your enemy endeavors to force you to do." Machiavelli's contribution to analysis and his evoking of rules thus qualifies him as a contributor to the evolution of the science of war.

During the seventeenth century, profound changes were made to the institutions of war by accomplished military leaders including Maurice of Nassau; Gustavus Adolphus; Henri de La Tour d'Auvergne, Vicomte de Turenne; the Great Condé; and the best-known soldier-intellect of the century, Raimondo Montecuccoli. It was Montecuccoli who wrote,

> I have attempted to encompass the vast areas of the only science vital for the monarch, and I have done my utmost to discover basic rules on which every science is based . . . and having considered the entire range of world history, I daresay I have not found a single notable military exploit which would not fit with these rules.

His treatise was an exhaustive study of all the components of war with which a general must concern himself, but it failed to identify a universal paradigm for the science of war. His ideas resulted in rigid dogmatism and, although he invoked the concept of science, his work, like the classics of Sun Tzu and Machiavelli, was entitled the *Art of War*.

The Age of Enlightenment

The close relationship between the *science* of war and the *art* of war became even closer in the contributions of Sébastien Le Prestre de Vauban. The military use of gunpowder and the role of fortifications in medieval Europe set the stage for Vauban to unite art and science, architecture and engineering, mathematics and mechanics. Vauban designed fortresses based on the range, accuracy, and trajectories of weapons. Each angle in his designs had its symmetry and purpose, and each measure its rationale—all derived from analysis, test, and conclusion. After designing fortresses that were close to impregnable, Vauban devised a system of siege warfare that was also based on scientifically determined distances and angles. Vauban brought the methods of science to the conduct of war, and he established a clear place for science in the study and theory of war.

In the eighteenth century, Marshal Herman Maurice, Comte de Saxe, reflected on the state of the theory dealing with the conduct of war. "War is a science," he wrote in his *Reveries, or Memoires upon the Art of War*, "so obscure and imperfect, that, in general, no rules of conduct can be given in it which are reducible to absolute certainties. . . . All other sciences are established upon fixed principles." He lamented that war has none and that books on war are generally difficult to understand. His book, however, despite the criticism in the preface, was organized much like the works of Montecuccoli and the others who had preceded him. It contained details on numerous topics, ranging from the raising of troops to organizations to the uses of colors and standards. His concluding chapter discussed the "qualifications necessary for the commander in chief of an Army." His was a book of analysis that covered the broad range of topics implicit in the profession of arms, but, like those before it, in the end it failed to present a scientific basis for the conduct of war.

At the time Saxe was writing his *Reveries*, the best-known eighteenth-century military leader, Frederick the Great of Prussia, was writing a set of instructions for his generals that seemed, at least from the title, to address Saxe's criticism regarding the state of military theory in the middle of the century. Frederick's terse handbook, written in 1747, appeared in 1748 under the title *General Principles of War*, but was known to posterity as *Instructions of Frederick the Great for His Generals*. Recipients of these books were ordered to take an oath that the book would not be taken on campaigns, and that when a recipient died, the book would be sealed and returned to Frederick. While the author of the book and the secrecy attached to it were clearly extraordinary, its contents were not. The book began with a section on "Prussian troops, their Deficiencies and their Advantages," and continued with a section on campaigns. The instructions were quite specific and were illustrated by examples, often taken from Frederick's recent campaigns: "The first rule is always to place magazines and fortified places behind the localities where you are assembling the army. In Silesia, our principal magazine has always been at Breslau." Such observations were sound and based on experience, but their universal application was subject to question. The work contributed to the science of war in its day, but it is now highly regarded more because of its author than because of its content.

In France in 1772, the young and brash Comte Jacques-Antoine de Guibert published his *General Essay on Tactics,* a book that angered Frederick because he believed it revealed too many of the concepts that he had worked to keep secret. Guibert, however, maintained that the book sought to raise tactics to the level of universal truth. Tactics, he claimed, was "the science of all times, all places, and all arms." The definition was broadly based and encompassed the wide range of topics covered in the works of both Frederick and Montecuccoli. Despite his objective of universality, Guibert's major theme was to call for a new army based on a broader recruiting base and on greater mobility; the universality of the book was reduced, however, when he repudiated many of its ideas in his second important book, *Defense of the Modern System of War.*

On the eve of the nineteenth century, Freiherr Heinrich von Bülow published his *Spirit of the Modern System of War,* a book that summarized many old concepts, was useful in defining key terms—like *strategy, tactics,* and *bases*—and finally, attempted to provide a geometric basis for the planning of campaigns. Bülow conceived of generalship as the combining of what he called the preparatory sciences: artillery, medicine, and logistics. He further called this combination the "true military science." He grasped many of the important changes in war that were taking place about him but left little legacy as a founder of the chief tenets of the science of war.

That science should hold a prominent place in the theory of war in the seventeenth and eighteenth centuries is not surprising when it is considered that science in general dominated the thinking of educated people in that period. Furthermore, the link between science and war was constantly in evidence at the distinguished schools of war established during this period. The British Royal Military Academy at Woolwich, for example, was founded to teach mathematics to military students who needed a greater knowledge of math for application in the artillery service. Near the turn of the century, engineering and math were the principal subjects taught at officer schools in Metz, Paris, and Sandhurst. At West Point, New York, in 1802, the U.S. Military Academy was founded to form "the basis in regard to science upon which the establishment rests." Scientific subjects dominated the curricula of these and other military schools, and the dominance of science is still evident today.

The Napoleonic Era

No individual has dominated the events of the era in which he lived more than Napoleon. He had a prolific mind and continually conceived new ideas, but he left no great treatise on war. He fought more battles than Alexander, Hannibal, Caesar, Gustavus Adolphus, and Frederick combined, but the fruits of his military experience had to be gleaned by others from his dictated memoirs and correspondence. It was typical of the age and indicative of Napoleon's military reputation that the military truths taken from his dictated letters and memoirs would be called "maxims." General Burnod, who compiled the first edition of Napoleon's maxims, claimed that the knowledge and genius of the commander are the same for all times, for all people, regardless of the arms employed. Burnod added that matters of detail are subject to change, but he provided no guide to distinguish the "knowledge and genius of the commander" from the "matters of detail." The distinction suggests, however, that the science of war exists not in matters of detail but in generalizations from the knowledge and genius of distinguished commanders.

The concept of principle exists in the maxims and thus sheds light on Napoleon's contribution to the science of war. Napoleon was quoted as saying, "It may be laid down as a principle . . . that by concentrating his forces, the commander cannot only prevent the junction of a divided enemy, but defeat them one by one." And he made the general statement that every war "should be conducted in conformity with principles and rules."

Although Napoleon's influence on the theory of war is limited to his example and to the aphorisms others gleaned from his writings, more complete treatises on war shaped by the Napoleonic experience were written by the most widely known of the military theorists of the nineteenth century: the Swiss Antoine Henri Jomini and the Prussian Karl von Clausewitz.

Jomini's first military volumes, *Treatise on Grand Tactics*, were inspired by the campaigns of Frederick the Great, not Napoleon. Jomini used the earlier writings of the Welshman Henry Lloyd on the campaigns of Frederick and through his own analysis sought to identify the underlying principles of war. Jomini acknowledged his debt to Lloyd when he stated that Lloyd convinced him that "the operations of war can be reduced to simple and incontestable principles." After studying Frederick's campaigns, Jomini sought to identify the principles demonstrated. One of his conclusions was that the choice of operational lines "forms the foundation of the science of war."

On occasion, Jomini combined his maxims into lists that would serve as guides for future commanders, and he identified the general principle on which all the operations of war rest. This principle was to put "a greater number of men than the enemy into action at the most important point." He continued, "All the rules of the art . . . are affiliated with this maxim." Jomini sometimes referred to maxims and principles as being part of the art of war and sometimes part of the science of war: it appears that differentiating between war as an art or a science was not important to him. However, it is a significant fact that he believed war was regulated by a small number of guiding principles.

Changes in Jomini's ideas occurred between 1805, when he published his *Treatise on Grand Tactics,* and 1837, when the *Summary of the Art of War,* the work that established him as the preeminent military writer of the nineteenth century, was published. In the *Summary,* Jomini claimed, "It is beyond question that war is a distinct science of itself." Yet the title spoke of the "art of war"; consistent with that view, Jomini wrote, "War is always to be conducted according to the great principles of the art." He also said, "Military science rests upon principles which can never be safely violated," and "a general's science consists in providing for his side all the chances possible." His interchangeable use of the terms *art* and *science* was indiscriminate, yet he was a key contributor to the development of the science of war wherein *science* is defined as the identification of generalizations that are based on analysis with the end result of being able to maximize the chances for success in military actions. Jomini's generalizations were sometimes stated as principles and sometimes as maxims, but he insisted that "war, far from being an exact science, is a terrible and impassioned drama, regulated by three or four general principles." Jomini's conclusion must have been that the conduct of war is *both* art and science, and that it is far from being an exact science.

Karl von Clausewitz, the spiritual father of the nineteenth- and twentieth-century German army, was a contemporary of Jomini and, like Jomini, he contributed to the development of the concepts of the art of war and the science of war. Unlike Jomini, whose writings analyzed past events and sought to provide generalizations on war and its conduct, Clausewitz's principal effort, *On War*, is a philosophical work that has a timeless quality.

Still, Clausewitz was concerned with teaching, and teachers tend toward analysis and generalization. In a didactic memorandum entitled "The Most Important Principles for the Conduct of War to Complete My Course of Instruction of His Royal Highness the Crown Prince," Clausewitz stated: "A fundamental principle is never to remain completely passive, but to attack the enemy frontally and from the flanks, even while he is attacking us." Entire sections of the memorandum contained "General Principles for Defense," "General Principles for Offense," "Principles Governing the Use of Troops," "Principles for the Use of Terrain," and "Principles for War in General." This exposition of principles, however, did not lead Clausewitz to conclude that war is a science, for he stated, "The most important thing in war will always be the art of defeating our opponent in combat."

In *On War*, Clausewitz devoted a chapter to the topic "Art of War or Science of War." He stated at the outset that the use of the terms is still unsettled, but that the facts of the matter are clear: "A book cannot really teach us anything, and therefore 'art' should have no place in its title." Clausewitz also concluded that the term *science* should be reserved for disciplines like math and astronomy, "whose object is pure knowledge." Ultimately, Clausewitz resolved the question of art or science by concluding, "War does not belong in the realm of arts and sciences; rather it is part of man's social existence."

Clausewitz further explained that because war is not an "exercise of the will directed at inanimate matter," but against an animate object that reacts, war cannot be codified using the same methods that concern the arts and sciences. He concluded, "It is clear that continual striving after laws analogous to those appropriate to the realm of inanimate matter is bound to lead to one mistake after another."

Such admonitions failed to clarify use of the terms *art of war* and *science of war*. An example of the confused use of the terms was aptly illustrated by a treatise on war written by Simon Gay de Vernon. His book was first published in France in 1805, and the literal translation of its title was "an elementary treatise on military art and fortification." In 1817, an English translation appeared in which the title read, *A Treatise on the Science of War and Fortification.* The confusion resulted in part from Gay de Vernon's own explanations. He maintained that the science of war was composed of three branches: (1) the art of choosing the best invasion route or the best defensive line; (2) the art of massing forces at the decisive point; and (3) the art of combat. He used the concepts of art and science, but the art, or skill, of war was subordinate to science.

Between the Napoleonic Era and World War I

Throughout the remainder of the nineteenth century, military theory was also strongly influenced by the positivist attitudes most clearly articulated in the writings of August Comte. Comte's positivist school maintained that the study of society was in its third and final phase—that is, the scientific phase. The study of man and his activities was thus a part of the "social sciences."

In the study of war, science also held a preeminent position. For example, at the U.S. Military Academy, reports filed during and after the American Civil War concluded that more instruction was needed in the science of war, and such was the case by the 1870s. A brief introduction to the course entitled "The Science of War" stated, "War is both an *art* and a *science*. When the rules for making campaigns, giving battle, conducting sieges, etc., are practically applied, war is an *art*. When the principles on which these rules are deduced and investigated and when analyses of military movements are made, war is a *science*." The notes concluded that war is an art when practical application is being made of the rules of war and that the term *science of war* applies when the "scientific principles upon which the art is founded are considered."

A similar explanation of the difference between the two occurred in the writings of Helmuth von Moltke, chief of the Prussian, and later German, general staff. In his *Questions on Applied Tactics*, Moltke wrote,

> One happily has recourse to principles and to doctrines, but principles and doctrines can only be furnished by science, and this science for us is strategy. However, strategy is not of the same essence as the abstract sciences. Those rest on immutable truths and good definitions that serve to build systems and lend themselves to all sorts of deduction.

Moltke and the German school of military theorists maintained that, while many principles regulate the conduct of war, these principles are not, as Jomini insisted, few in number, and their application is dependent on the specific conditions of any given situation.

Jomini had a large following in Europe and the United States. Henry W. Halleck, general in chief of the armies of the United States during the American Civil War, had earlier published a series of his lectures under the title *Elements of Military Art and Science*. Halleck made no claim to originality in the book;

instead, he sought to "embody, in a small compass, well-established military principles, and to illustrate these by reference to the events of past history, and the opinions and practice of the best generals." Halleck was a disciple of Jomini and presented terse principles, rules, and maxims throughout the book. A significant fact is that he used both *art* and *science* in the book's title—just as Jomini had used both terms in his writings.

Efforts to establish a scientific basis for the theory of war involved war on the sea as well as war on land. The most noted naval theorist of the nineteenth century was Alfred Thayer Mahan, and his lectures at the newly established U.S. Naval War College were inspired in part by Jomini and in part by the philosophy of the college's first president, Commodore Stephen B. Luce. Luce wrote in 1883 that the naval officer should "examine the great naval battles of the world with the cold eye of professional criticism and recognize where the principles of the science have been illustrated." In his opening address to students at the college, Luce elaborated: "Now naval history abounds in materials whereon to erect a science . . . there is no question that the naval battles of the past furnish a mass of facts amply sufficient for the formulation of laws or principles which, once established, would raise maritime war to the level of science." Mahan continued in the tradition of Luce, his mentor, and just months before Mahan gave his first lectures at the Naval War College, he determined that the few principles enunciated by Jomini were applicable by analogy to naval war. Following Jomini's lead, Mahan concluded that "concentration" was the "predominant principle" underlying the conduct of naval war. The Jominian tradition continued to bring the concept of science to the study and theory of war.

The role of science in social affairs was also evident in the writings of Karl Marx and Friedrich Engels. Their writings gained in significance after the success of the Bolshevik Revolution, but their reputation as ancestors of modern total war is based on ideas developed in the nineteenth century. Engels, in particular, wrote extensively on military topics, and his treatises on campaigns were marked by critical analysis and analogy. In a series of articles that appeared in the *New York Tribune* in 1851 and 1852, Marx and Engels claimed that insurrection is an art, but "subject to certain rules of procedure. . . . Firstly, never play with insurrection unless you are fully prepared to face the consequences. . . . Secondly, act with the greatest determination and on the offensive. . . . Surprise your antagonist. . . . Keep up the moral ascendancy."

The acceptance of principles as a basis for the science of war was widely debated among Russian military theorists. Maj. Gen. N. Medem, a professor of strategy and military history at the imperial military academy, stated, "Constant, absolute rules for actions themselves cannot exist." Gen. G. A. Leyer, professor and head of the staff academy for 40 years, however, presented a series of "basic principles": the principle of economy of forces, the principle of concentration of forces at the decisive point, the principle of surprise, the principle of security, and the principle of initiative and dominance over the enemy's will and mind. In spite of this identification of specific principles upon which a science of war might be established, the most widely known

Russian military writer of the nineteenth century, Gen. M. I. Dragomirov, concluded, "At the present time, it will enter no one's head to assert that there can be a military science; it is just as unthinkable as the sciences of poetry, painting, and music."

The role of principles and the belief in a science of war continued to be in evidence in France in the years following the Franco-Prussian War. Disciples of Charles Ardant du Picq (who was killed during that war) emphasized the role of moral factors as the primary cause of the French defeat, but the Jominian acceptance of a few immutable principles underlying the theory of war continued. Henri Bonnal, professor of military history, strategy, and general tactics at the French war college from 1887 to 1896, concluded, "There are a certain number of facts of experience, established by the most eminent men of war, which form the points of doctrine to which can be accorded the value of scientific truths." His points of doctrine were: (1) maintain your own liberty of action and limit that of the enemy; (2) impose your will on your adversary and do not submit to his; and (3) economize your forces in order to concentrate at a point suitably chosen and at the favorable time with a view toward producing a decisive result.

Bonnal's successor at the French war college was Ferdinand Foch. Like Bonnal and others of the French school, Foch adhered to Jomini's belief in the existence of a few immutable principles that form the foundation of the science of war. Foch differed from his predecessors, however, by enumerating four principles of war that make up the theory of war. These were: (1) the principle of economy of forces; (2) the principle of freedom of action; (3) the principle of free disposition of forces; and (4) the principle of security. Foch indicated there were other principles by concluding his list with the abbreviation, "etc." Like others of his day, he was a believer in the importance of moral factors in war, and he was a strong adherent of the primacy of offensive action.

Impact of the World Wars on Military Theory

After the initial months of World War I, offensive action on the part of all participants led not to victory but to death and self-destruction. Few practitioners of war took the time to reflect on the role principles play in war in light of the experiences of the battlefields, but a young British staff officer, J. F. C. Fuller, writing anonymously in the *Journal of the Royal United Service Institution*, soundly criticized official British doctrine for its omissions. He wrote that while the British *Field Service Regulations* mentioned that "the fundamental principles of war are neither very numerous nor in themselves very abstruse," the regulations failed to point out what the principles were. Fuller presented a list of eight, and he stated that he believed these to be "the leading ones in the science of war." He added, "The principles of war can be adhered to as are the principles in all the sciences by even the most indifferent of workers."

Fuller's identification of a definitive list of principles led to the adoption of a similar list in the British *Field Service Regulations*, which was revised after the war. In a subsequent journal article entitled "The Foundations of the Science of War," Fuller claimed that the principles were "eternal, universal, and fundamental." He said that they applied to every battle and to "every scientifically fought boxing match."

Fuller attempted to elaborate on the scientific basis for a theory of war in his book *The Foundations of the Science of War*, which was published in 1926. Here he hypothesized that war consisted of operations in three spheres—the mental, moral, and physical—and that each sphere was built around three principles of force. The book was not well received, and even Fuller later admitted that because it was the first of its kind, it was full of imperfections.

Despite the controversy over the existence of principles in war, the United States adopted a definitive list of principles in its *Training Regulations 10-5*, published in December 1921. No explanation of the principles was given; they simply appeared as a list of nine titles, taken from the lists of Fuller and the British regulations (which Fuller strongly influenced). The paragraph that followed the listing elaborated on their characteristics and meaning. It read:

> These principles are immutable. . . . Their proper application constitutes the true measure of military art, and it is the duty of all officers to acquire their true meaning by study, particularly the study of history, by reflection, and by practice, not only in purely military work, but in administration and business operation.

Opponents of the view that there are fixed principles called for the elimination of lists of titles of principles. The principles subsequently disappeared from the official publications of Great Britain for about a decade, but during World War II, Field Marshal Bernard Montgomery ordered their return. They continue to appear in doctrinal sources, but they are today more commonly referred to as "guides" or "tools" than as fixed and immutable laws upon which the science of war is based.

Among the proponents of this less rigorous view of principles was Mao Tse-tung, who wrote,

> In studying the laws for directing wars that occur at different historical stages, that differ in nature and that are waged in different places and by different nations, we must fix our attention on the characteristics and development of each, and must oppose a mechanical approach to the problem of war. . . . All the laws for directing war developed as history develops and as war develops; nothing is changeless.

Just as the navy, through the publications and speeches of Stephen B. Luce and Alfred Thayer Mahan, had accepted the principles and theory of land warfare espoused by Jomini, so the writers on airpower looked to land warfare for principles governing the conduct of air warfare. Giulio Douhet, whose treatise *Command of the Air* gave him just claim to the title Father of Airpower, accepted the applicability of "land and sea principles" to war in the air. He wrote that the first principle governing the operation of an independent air force is that it "should always operate in mass," and that the basic principle for war in the air is the same principle that governs warfare on land and sea: "Inflict the greatest damage in the shortest possible time." The principles of war adopted by the U.S. Air Force have closely followed the principles expressed in army doctrine. In 1951, an air force officer expressed a widely held belief in the efficacy of principles that govern the conduct of war on land, sea, and in the air. He wrote, "The principles of war are the result of the experience of mankind at war throughout the ages, irrespective of the type of weapons employed or the elements in which they are used."

Soviet views on the art and science of war originated during the German and Allied military interventions of 1918–20 and during the Russian Civil War. Soviet sources credit Lenin with many contributions in the development of Soviet military science, and M. V. Frunze, after whom the Soviet staff college is named, has been credited with generalizing the experience of past wars and developing the principles of military theory.

In the early 1940s, Soviet military doctrine emphasized a number of "permanently operating factors," which were said to "decide the course and outcome of wars." In 1942, Joseph Stalin codified these factors: (1) the stability of the rear; (2) the morale of the army; (3) the quantity and quality of divisions; (4) the armament of the army; and (5) the organizing ability of the command personnel. After Stalin's death, the "permanently operating factors" were replaced by similar concepts attributed to Lenin.

Col. Vasili Savkin, a member of the faculty at the Frunze Academy, published *The Principles of the Operational Art and Tactics* in 1972. Savkin observed that the principles of war as stated in Western doctrine were like the principles discussed in his book—except that the Soviet principles were properly derived from laws of war and armed conflict. He explained that bourgeois military theorists could not accept the existence of objective laws of social life.

New Methods in the Study of War

Since World War II, new analytic methods have been used in the study of war, and the debate over whether war is art or science has subsided. The general term for new methods of analysis is "operations research/strategic analysis" (ORSA). Mathematics, logic, and computers are the tools commonly used in ORSA. Attempts to predict the outcome of future battles, based on algorithms derived from the results of past battles, using in one case a quantified judgment method of analysis, have also sought to establish a scientific basis for the understanding of war and for predicting the outcome of future events and future war. Increased attention to long-range planning in the defense industry will likely guarantee a place for adherents of the science of war in the future.

JOHN I. ALGER

SEE ALSO: Ardant du Picq, Charles J. J. J.; Art of War; Clausewitz, Karl von; Condé, Louis II de Bourbon; Douhet, Giulio; Foch, Ferdinand; Frederick the Great; Fuller, J. F. C.; Jomini, Antoine Henri; Mahan, Alfred Thayer; Mao Tse-tung; Moltke the Elder; Napoleon I; Principles of War; Saxe, Hermann

Maurice; Sun Tzu; Turenne, Henri de La Tour d'Auvergne; Vauban, Sebastien Le Prestre de.

Bibliography

Alger, J. I. 1982. *Quest for victory*. Westport, Conn.: Greenwood Press.
Clausewitz, C. von. 1976. *On war*. Ed. and trans. M. Howard and P. Paret. Princeton, N.J.: Princeton Univ. Press.
Douhet, G. 1943. *Command of the air*. London: Faber.
Dupuy, T. N. 1979. *Numbers, predictions and war*. Indianapolis, Ind.: Bobbs-Merrill.
Fuller, J. F. C. 1926. *Foundations of the science of war*. London: Hutchison.
Halleck, H. W. 1846. *Elements of military art and science*. New York: Appleton.
Jomini, A.-H. 1862. *Art of war*. Philadelphia: Lippincott.
Mahan, A. T. 1911. *Naval strategy*. Boston: Little, Brown.
Paret, P., ed. 1986. *Makers of modern strategy*. Princeton, N.J.: Princeton Univ. Press.
Phillips, T. R., ed. 1940. *Roots of strategy*. Harrisburg, Pa.: Military Service.

SCIPIO AFRICANUS [237–183 B.C.]

Publius Cornelius Scipio Africanus was a noted Roman general who played an important role in the Second Punic War (219–202 B.C.), one of three wars fought between Rome and Carthage for control of the Mediterranean. The son of the Roman consul, Publius Cornelius Scipio, Scipio Africanus is most noted for his victories in Spain and his defeat of Hannibal at the battle of Zama (202 B.C.) in Africa, where his victory forced Carthage to sue for peace, thus ending the Second Punic War.

Scipio Africanus first encountered his great antagonist, Hannibal, in 218 B.C. while rescuing his father, who had been wounded and defeated during an engagement at the Ticinus (Ticino) River in northern Italy soon after Hannibal had emerged from the alpine passes.

A short time later the elder Scipio, consul and cocommander with the consul Sempronius, was again defeated by Hannibal on the Trebia River. While Scipio (Africanus) remained in Italy, his father joined his uncle, Cornelius Scipio Calvus, commanding general of Roman forces in Spain. In 216, young Scipio rallied the survivors of the Roman disaster at Cannae where his father-in-law, Lucius Aemilius Paullus, victor of the Second Illyrian War, died in battle.

Both Scipio's father and his uncle died in battle in Spain in 210 B.C. Despite his youth and political ineligibility, Scipio soon after was elected proconsul for Spain. He sailed for Spain with reinforcements, disembarking at Emporaiae to find all of Spain south of the Ebro River in Carthaginian hands. He quickly gained the loyalty of the veteran troops and then won over the Celtiberian hill tribes. In 209 he was at Tarraco with 28,000 infantry and 3,000 cavalry. He was opposed by three Carthaginian commanders—Hannibal Barca's brothers Hasdrubal and Mago, and Hasdrubal, son of Gisco. Each had about as many troops as Scipio, but the three were quarreling and so did not cooperate. Scipio made a rapid march south to surprise the Carthaginian main base and headquarters at New Carthage (modern Cartagena), and with the aid of his fleet, captured the city in a brilliant and bold operation.

Scipio trained his troops rigorously to improve their individual skills and their ability to operate in small units. In addition, he rearmed his troops with improved weapons.

In 208 he defeated Hasdrubal Barca at Baecula on the upper Guadalquivir River. Hasdrubal managed to pass around Scipio's force and march into Italy, attempting to join his brother, Hannibal. In Italy the following year, Hasdrubal was defeated and killed by the Roman general Claudius Nero at the Battle of the Metaurus River.

Hasdrubal's defeat changed the strategic situation dramatically. Hasdrubal Gisco now had to force the issue in Spain in order to help Hannibal. At the same time, Scipio could now afford to storm towns in southern Spain one at a time in order gradually to drive the Carthaginians out.

In 206 Hasdrubal marched from Gades (modern Cadiz) to Ilipa (near modern Cordoba) with 50,000 infantry, 4,000–5,000 cavalry, and elephants. Gaining help from Celtiberian chiefs, Scipio concentrated about 45,000 infantry and 3,000 cavalry and advanced on Ilipa. Not trusting his allies, Scipio executed an elaborate deception plan and eventually won a decisive victory that resulted in the virtual loss of Spain by the Carthaginians.

Scipio next visited the Numidian king, Syphax, in Africa in an unsuccessful attempt to win him to Rome's side. He then returned to Spain to quell a mutiny in his army. Having done this, he destroyed most Celtiberian resistance and also effectively eliminated the Carthaginian presence in Spain. He returned to Rome in time for the consular election of 205, in which he and P. Licinius Crassus were victorious.

Hannibal was blockaded in southern Italy by Crassus, and Scipio wanted to carry the war into Africa. He was strongly opposed by the Roman senate led by Q. Fabius Maximus. After a political struggle, Scipio prevailed and was given command of the two legions of survivors of Cannae in Sicily plus 7,000 volunteers he had raised himself. He was given unprecedented authority for the remainder of the war and sailed to Utica, northwest of Carthage, where he landed in spring 204.

Syphax, allied to Carthage in support of his new father-in-law, Hasdrubal Gisco, brought an army against Scipio, forcing the latter to raise the siege of Utica and fortify his own camp near Carthage (203). After inconclusive negotiations, Scipio launched a daring night attack and destroyed both the Numidian and Carthaginian armies. The Carthaginians raised two more armies, which Scipio destroyed in battle at Bacrades. Syphax was captured, deposed, and replaced by a Roman ally, Masinissa.

The Carthaginian government ordered Hannibal and Mago back to Africa. Mago, who had been seriously wounded in a battle in northern Italy, died en route, but much of his army joined near Carthage with Hannibal's remaining troops from Italy (fall 203). Scipio was in a difficult position on the coast awaiting his new Numidian allies, while Hannibal was training his new army. The approach of the Numidians forced Hannibal to attempt to block their junction with the Romans. In a brilliant strategic gamble Scipio began a campaign of destruction in the interior and moved southwest to join Masinissa, forcing Hannibal to give battle on the plain west of Zama before his army was fully ready.

Hannibal deployed his infantry in two echelons behind a strong skirmish line consisting of Ligurians, Celts, Balearic islanders, and Moorish mercenaries (mostly from Mago's army), with elephants in front. The weak cavalry contingent was deployed on both flanks, as usual. His plan was to hold off the Roman legions until the greatly superior Roman-Numidian cavalry could be lured away from the infantry combat by the weak Carthaginian cavalry posted on the flanks. Once the powerful Roman cavalry had been drawn off, he planned to fall on the flanks of the Roman infantry mass with the units of his second echelon, moving forward around both sides of the engaged first echelon.

Hannibal's first echelon consisted of 12,000 native Libyans and Carthaginians; the second echelon had 12,000 of Hannibal's Italian war veterans.

The Roman army, consisting of about 25,000 Roman and Italian legionaries and 10,000 Numidians, formed in its usual three lines of infantry; but instead of the usual *quincux* (checkerboard) deployment, Scipio formed his infantry in two echelons (like Hannibal), with the *hastati* (least experienced) in the first, and the *principes* and *triarii* (most experienced) in the second. Scipio placed his Italian cavalry on the left and Numidian cavalry on the right.

When the battle opened, Scipio's cavalry drove the Carthaginian cavalry off the field. At the same time the Carthaginian elephants and skirmishers engaged the Roman first echelon. Next, the Carthaginian first echelon engaged, and Hannibal began to execute the maneuver that had won Cannae, bringing his second echelon forward to extend the flanks of the first in an attempted double envelopment. Scipio, however, countered by also bringing forward and to the flanks the principes and triarii of his second echelon (who doubtless recalled their defeat at Cannae) to extend his line. The Romans had the better of the initial struggle, but were now opposed by Hannibal's veterans. The issue was still in doubt when the Carthaginians were attacked in the rear by the returning Roman cavalry. This resulted in the defeat of the Carthaginians, who lost about 15,000 killed and 15,000 captured to Roman losses of about 6,000 killed and wounded. Hannibal and a handful of survivors withdrew to Carthage.

The subsequent surrender of Carthage, ending the Second Punic War, was a turning point in the history of the ancient world.

Scipio lived in private life until 194 B.C., when he was elected consul to fight the Ligurian Gauls in northern Italy. In 190 he was legate to his brother Lucius, who was consul in command of the Roman army in the war against Antiochus III of Syria. They were credited with victory in the great battle of Magnesia in 190, although the real field commander was Domitius Ahenobarbus.

When they returned home, political enemies prosecuted the Scipio brothers in 187 on grounds of misappropriation of funds. Africanus tore up the account books, but Lucius was found guilty and fined. Scipio retired to Liternum where he died in 183 B.C.

Scipio was one of Rome's greatest generals, but for most of the Second Punic War he was overshadowed by three senior generals and consuls: Marcus Claudius Marcellus (conqueror of Syracuse), Quintus Fabius Maximus (dictator in 217, victor at Tarentum in 209), and C. Claudius Nero, victor at the Metaurus.

Skillful in both strategy and tactics, Scipio was a charismatic leader who inspired his soldiers with confidence, although his political enemies accused him of imposing discipline "like a king." F. E. Adcock (1960) comments that Scipio was "The first Roman commander . . . of whom it can be said with certainty that he added something to the art of war," and that as a strategist he was "far more daring than any other Roman general of the middle Republic." But Adcock also notes that Scipio owed much of his success in Spain to the incompetence of his enemies and the superior quality of his troops, and he has been criticized for allowing Hasdrubal to reach Italy.

Scipio was the political champion of the expansionist party that advocated a military strategy of annihilation, in contrast to the isolationist party led by Fabius Maximus that followed a military strategy of attrition. His appointment to military command was a precursor of the rise of professional generals, such as Marius, in the Roman army.

JOHN F. SLOAN

SEE ALSO: Hannibal Barca; History, Ancient Military; Punic Wars; Roman Empire.

Bibliography

Adcock, F. E. 1960. *The Roman art of war under the Republic.* New York: Barnes and Noble.

De Beer, G. 1969. *Hannibal.* New York: Viking Press.

Delbrück, H. 1990. *Warfare in antiquity.* Trans. W. J. Renfroe, Jr. Lincoln, Nebr.: Univ. of Nebraska Press.

Livy. 1960. *The war with Hannibal.* Trans. A. de Sélincourt. Harmondsworth, Middlesex: Penguin Books.

Polybius. 1979. *The rise of the Roman Empire.* Ed. F. W. Walbank, trans. I. Scott-Kilvert. Harmondsworth, Middlesex: Penguin Books.

Scullard, H. H. 1961. *A history of the Roman world.* London: Methuen.

SCOTT, WINFIELD [1786–1866]

Winfield Scott served on active duty as general officer longer than any other American officer. His military career spanned three major eighteenth-century American wars: the War of 1812, the Mexican-American War, and the American Civil War. Scott was appointed general in chief of the U.S. Army in 1841, in large measure because of the distinguished reputation he had earned in the War of 1812, and despite the animosity generated by his outspokenness and his sometimes abrasive personality. His command and leadership skills served him well in the 1847 Vera Cruz–Mexico City campaign, a series of bold operations and battles that culminated in the defeat of the Mexicans. Too old to serve actively in the American Civil War, he relinquished command of the army to Maj. Gen. George B. McClellan in November 1861. Scott lived until after the end of the Civil War, long enough to see the successful implementation by Gen. U. S. Grant of his proposed "Anaconda Plan," the combined sea blockade and land campaign that ultimately defeated the Confederacy.

Early Life and War of 1812

Scott was born at Laurel Branch, Virginia, near Petersburg, on 13 June 1786 to William and Ann Mason Scott. His father had served as a captain in the American Revolution. Scott briefly attended the College of William and Mary in 1805 but, dissatisfied with the college, left and began to study law in Petersburg. He subsequently enlisted in the cavalry (1807) and the following year was commissioned a captain of light artillery. While serving at New Orleans, Scott was relieved of his commission from 1809 to 1810 for labeling his controversial commander, Gen. James Wilkinson, "a traitor, liar, and scoundrel." (History has borne out Scott's judgment on all counts.) Both before and after that incident, Scott had grown so disaffected with military service that he twice contemplated a return to the legal profession.

Scott was promoted to lieutenant colonel in July 1812. During the War of 1812 he served in the northern theater. At the Battle of Queenston Heights (13 October 1812), he was captured while leading a small band of volunteers across the Niagara River to carry out an attack on the heights ordered by Gen. Stephen van Rensselaer. Exchanged in January 1813 and then promoted to colonel, he planned and led the amphibious operation that resulted in the capture of Fort George (27 May 1813), where he was wounded. After recovery from his wound, he commanded the fort's garrison and then served under his old adversary, Gen. James Wilkinson, in the ill-fated campaign to capture Montreal. In March 1814 Scott was promoted to brigadier general. He served under Gen. Jacob Brown in the Niagara River Campaign of 1814. At the Battle of Chippewa (5 July 1814), his brigade, which he had diligently trained, defeated a force of British regulars. On 25 July he was wounded at the hard-fought Battle of Lundy's Lane. Scott's brave and skillful performance in these battles earned him the brevet rank of major general and public acclaim.

Peacetime Military Service, 1815–46

Scott emerged from the War of 1812 as a national hero. For the next three decades he served in a number of prominent positions, eventually attaining the senior position in the army. During this period he devoted much of his energy to military studies, making two trips to Europe to study military developments there, assisting in formulating training manuals, and presiding over the army's Board of Tactics. Following the end of the War of 1812, he oversaw the reduction of the army and was instrumental in writing its first standard drillbook.

In 1815 Scott was made commander of the Northern Department, with headquarters in New York City. In 1828 he was passed over for promotion to commanding general of the army, in favor of a formerly junior officer. Indignant, he tendered his resignation, which was rejected, and in 1829 became head of the Eastern Division. In July 1832 he was in command of a force shipped by way of the Great Lakes to Wisconsin during the Black Hawk War. However, a cholera epidemic among his troops caused him to arrive too late to participate in the conflict.

In September 1832 Scott helped negotiate the Treaty of Fort Armstrong with the Sauk and Fox Indians. This treaty was the first of several diplomatic duties performed by Scott. In late 1832 his careful political maneuvering helped to defuse South Carolina's secessionist tendencies during the Nullification Crisis.

Scott's efforts to conduct operations in the Second Seminole War (1836) were handicapped by supply problems and poorly trained militia. He was removed from command and went before a court of inquiry in 1837. The court cleared him of all charges, however, and he soon returned to the duties of diplomat and negotiator.

Twice, in 1838 and 1839, Scott eased tension between the United States and Great Britain in border disputes along the New England–Canadian border. In 1838 he also supervised the forced removal of the Cherokee Indians from the southeastern United States to present-day Oklahoma. Promoted to major general and command of the army on 5 July 1841, he held this position for more than two decades until his retirement in November 1861.

Mexican-American War Service, 1846–48

War between Mexico and the United States broke out in 1846. Although the opening battles fought in northern Mexico were American victories, they were clearly not enough to have a decisive effect on the war. Disagreement between the administration of Pres. James K. Polk and Scott, and the president's wariness of the commanding general's popularity, delayed implementation of a proposal by Scott for an expedition to capture Mexico City in a decisive campaign. Polk eventually gave reluctant approval to the plan, and in March 1847 Scott put his troops ashore at Vera Cruz, Mexico, in the U.S. Army's first major amphibious landing. The port city capitulated on 27 March after a brief siege.

On 8 April Scott's army began its march inland from Vera Cruz. At Cerro Gordo (18 April) Scott defeated Mexican General Santa Anna's numerically superior army, using a flanking maneuver reconnoitered by the future Confederate leader Robert E. Lee to turn the Mexican left. After a three-month occupation of Puebla (May–August), during which he accumulated supplies and reinforcements, Scott boldly cut his lines of communications and advanced on Mexico City. South of Mexico City, at the battles of Contreras and Churubusco (19–20 August), Scott again outmaneuvered and defeated Santa Anna in victories that brought the Americans to the gates of the Mexican capital. Scott honored a Mexican request for an armistice to negotiate peace. When it became clear that Santa Anna was playing for time, Scott ended the truce. In bloody fighting his troops captured an arsenal at Molino del Rey (8 September) and stormed the fortress of Chapultepec (13 September). On the next day Mexico City capitulated.

Scott served as military governor in Mexico City until April 1848, when political machinations in the Polk administration and false accusations of misconduct caused him to return to the United States to face another court of inquiry. The court exonerated him of all charges, and the popularity he had achieved by his military successes soared.

Later Service, 1848–66

Scott lost the Whig Party presidential nomination in 1848. In 1852 he won the party's nomination but lost heavily in the presidential election to Franklin Pierce. Still in command of the army, he was promoted to the brevet rank of lieutenant general in February 1855. Scott's contentious personality led to frequent altercations with the men who served as secretary of war, his civilian superiors, in several administrations. His most serious disagreements of this sort were with Secretary of War Jefferson Davis. Paradoxically, he continued to show diplomatic skills, which served him well once again in September 1859, when he aided in settling a border dispute between the United States and Great Britain in the Puget Sound area.

With the approach of the Civil War, he urged in vain the strengthening of U.S. Army military installations in the South. Although a Virginian, his loyalty to the United States never wavered. His plan to defeat the Confederacy through naval blockade and control of the Mississippi River was maligned in the Northern press and derisively nicknamed the "Anaconda Plan." Its basic strategic concept eventually won the endorsement of Lincoln, and its implementation by Gen. Ulysses S. Grant ultimately spelled the end of the rebellion. On 1 November 1861 the aged Scott relinquished command of the army to Gen. George B. McClellan. Scott died at West Point on 29 May 1866, having lived long enough to see the vindication of his strategy for victory of the Federal forces.

Assessment

Nicknamed "Old Fuss and Feathers" for his insistence on drill and discipline, Scott served his country with distinction for more than half a century as a bold strategist and tactician and an accomplished organizer and theorist. His Valley of Mexico campaign ranks as one of the greatest in U.S. military history. His opinionated and outspoken character frequently estranged his civilian and army peers and superiors, but did not detract from his military capabilities and his faithful service to his country.

BRIAN R. BADER

SEE ALSO: Civil War, American; Grant, Ulysses Simpson; Lee, Robert Edward.

Bibliography

Dupuy, R. E., and T. N. Dupuy. 1959. *Brave men and great captains.* New York: Harper and Bros.
Elliot, C. W. 1937. *Winfield Scott: The soldier and the man.* New York: Macmillan.
Scott, W. 1864. *Memoirs of Lieut.-General Scott.* New York: Sheldon.

Smith, A. D. H. 1937. *Old Fuss and Feathers: The life and exploits of Winfield Scott.* New York: Greystone Press.

SEAPOWER, BRITISH

Great Britain, as an island nation, has a long and distinguished naval tradition stretching back to the time of Alfred the Great in the ninth century. Although the origins of the Royal Navy go back perhaps an additional 150 years, its advent as the premier European naval force lies in the mid-seventeenth century. At its height (ca. 1650–1918), the Royal Navy was the most powerful in the world and, together with British money, was frequently the great obstacle preventing domination of Europe by a single power.

Tudor Origins

The accession of King Henry VII and the resultant end of the Wars of the Roses in 1485 left England at peace both internally and externally for the first time in 70 years. Concern for English mercantile activities, coupled with the threat posed by a powerful and unified France, led Henry VII and his son Henry VIII to sponsor considerable naval activity. The elder Henry sent John Cabot of Genoa on several expeditions to the New World in the 1490s; although Henry VIII did not continue this policy, he took an interest in the royal fleet by adding several ships to it and encouraging the use of artillery as naval armament. Although neither Edward VI nor his elder sister Mary took much interest in naval affairs, Elizabeth, the fifth and last Tudor monarch, was an avid supporter of naval expansion. In its decades-long struggle with Spain, Elizabeth's small and relatively poor domain could not hope to compete with the Spanish on the European mainland, but its fleet gave it the ability to strike at the economic bloodlines of the Spanish Empire. Elizabeth's reign also demonstrated to the English, in the case of the Spanish Armada of 1588, that for them the possession of a strong naval force meant that they did not need a large army to protect them from invasion. Anyone who wished to invade England had to come by sea and would first have to deal with the English fleet. This fact was just as true for the Germans in the twentieth century as it was for the French in the eighteenth and nineteenth and the Spanish in the sixteenth.

Royal Navy in the Early 1600s

Elizabeth's navy, however, was not a real military force in the modern sense, as most of its ships spent the bulk of their useful lives laid up, and a majority of the English ships in the Armada battles were privately owned, as were nearly all those employed by commanders like Sir Francis Drake and Sir John Hawkins in their famous expeditions to the Caribbean in the 1580s and 1590s. This practice began to change in the 1600s under the Stuarts and even more rapidly under the Commonwealth. By the end of the English civil wars in 1651, the navy, which had generally sided with Parliament, was essentially a permanent force, although still relatively small. The Navigation Acts of 1651, 1661, and 1663 aimed at fostering English commerce by protecting English merchants and discriminating against foreign merchants who wished to trade with England. To enforce these measures, aimed largely at the extensive Dutch trade in bulk items (wood, grain, cloth, naval stores) to and from the Baltic, the English needed an effective and fairly large navy.

The First Anglo-Dutch War of 1652–54 marked the real beginning of English or British seapower. Not only did the English possess a sizable fleet and a clear goal but also two key technical advantages. The first of these was the technique of efficiently harnessing the recoil of fired guns to bring their muzzles inside the ship and so hasten reloading, thus greatly increasing their rate of fire. Coupled with this development, the "Generals at Sea" of Cromwell's navy created the famous *Fighting Instructions*, first issued in March 1653. This document made the line-ahead formation standard and so put to use the improvement in firepower to create an efficient and formidable battle array.

Components of English Seapower

This first war of the English navy thus clearly demonstrates two factors contributing to its naval superiority. First, the British had a clear goal for the navy. It was meant both to secure the flow of commerce to English ports, which already by the mid-seventeenth century was a vital part of the English economy, and to serve as the first bulwark against aggression upon England itself and thereby mitigate the need for a large army. This second portion of the navy goals also served a political purpose, for after the Restoration and the end of the Commonwealth in 1660, the English public showed great suspicion toward standing armies of any sort. Second, the navy maintained an interest in technical innovations, meaning not only new weapons and ship types but also new methods to command those ships more effectively, keep them at sea longer, and in general maintain as great a naval advantage over their mainland European naval rivals as possible.

As time went on, the British introduced or improved on several other naval innovations during the age of sail, including the use of copper sheathing on ship bottoms, thus greatly reducing fouling from barnacles and seaweed and so increasing speed. The British also steadily improved their methods of signaling during the 1700s; introduced items in the naval rations to prevent scurvy, the bane of long sea voyages in the early modern era; and invented the carronade, a short, iron cannon introduced in the 1770s. The carronade, although short of range, was lighter than a normal cannon of similar caliber and was ideal for short-range hammering of enemy ships, which dovetailed nicely with the British emphasis on close-range combat begun during the same period.

A final technical contribution to British seapower lay in ship design. Faced with limits of both finance and manpower, the Royal Navy designed ships that carried more guns per ton than anyone else's. Although British ships were often poor sailors, cramped, and relatively flimsy, they had more of them than any other navy, and they were armed just as well as the better-built but more expensive French and Spanish ships. Realizing their lack of endless manpower or endless money, the British built the best and largest fleet they could with what they had. They also made up whatever material weakness they may have possessed by fielding better-trained sailors and, above all, better officers than their opponents. Although by modern standards the methods of promotion and selection in the Royal Navy in the two centuries after 1651 were crude, status-ridden, and inefficient, they were notably superior to those of almost every other navy, and Royal Navy officers were in general well trained and well educated.

Employment of Seapower

This naval superiority gave to England (Great Britain existed only after the Act of Union of 1707) several important strengths. As already described, it made British trade secure from the depredations of their European opponents; indeed, the worst losses suffered by the British merchant fleet were inflicted by the tiny but superb American navy during the War of 1812. Naval superiority also lent the small British army great mobility and strategic superiority, partly compensating for its modest numbers. Their naval strength also allowed the British to support their colonies and to wage war against their enemies' overseas holdings as well. Largely due to their control of the sea, the British became the dominant power in both North America and India. These advantages did have their price, however. During the 130 years from 1685 to 1815, the British were at war with France no less than six times, for a total of 73 years. During that era the British were at war with virtually all the other European powers at one time or another; all these wars were undertaken to prevent the domination of the European mainland by any one continental power.

Even the decline of the masted sailing ship as the principal vessel of naval warfare did not end Great Britain's naval ascendancy. During the late nineteenth and early twentieth centuries, the Royal Navy pioneered iron warships (armored frigate HMS *Warrior* in 1860), torpedoes and submarines in the 1880s and 1890s, the dreadnought (all big gun) battleship in 1906, and both sonar (then called ASDIC by the British) and the aircraft carrier during World War I (see Fig. 1). The British maintained their naval policy goals, and Germany's race for naval parity in the early 1900s under the leadership of Admiral Tirpitz inevitably brought about a clash. The end of World War I left the Royal Navy in a commanding position, although less because of its technical achievements than because of the unenviable strategic position of the German High Seas Fleet. Nevertheless, the British development of sonar, however primitive by modern standards, played a major role in the ultimate frustration of Germany's submarine war against British shipping. In

Figure 1. A 1957 photo of the stern and flight deck of the HMS
Glorious, *a British cruiser converted into an aircraft carrier.*
(SOURCE: U.S. Library of Congress)

fact, only the growth of American and Japanese naval forces and the parallel
shift in naval attention from the northeast Atlantic to the Pacific spelled the
end of British naval supremacy, rather than any failure in either technical
achievement or strategic aim.

DAVID L. BONGARD

SEE ALSO: Colonial Empires, European; Fisher, John Arbuthnot; Jellicoe, John
Rushworth; Mahan, Alfred Thayer; Naval Warfare; Nelson, Horatio; Tirpitz,
Alfred von; Warships; World War I.

Bibliography

Corbett, J. S. 1912. *Drake and the Tudor navy.* London: Longmans.
———. 1918. *England in the Seven Years' War.* 2 vols. London: Longmans.
Corbett, J. S., and H. Newbolt. 1920–31. *Naval operations.* 5 vols. London: Longmans.
Ehrman, J. 1953. *The navy in the war of William III, 1689–1697.* Cambridge: Cambridge Univ. Press.
Kennedy, P. M. 1976. *The rise and fall of British naval mastery.* New York: Random House.
Lewis, M. A. 1948. *The navy of Britain: A historical portrait.* London: George Allen and Unwin.
———. 1960. *A social history of the navy, 1793–1815.* London: George Allen and Unwin.
Mahan, A. T. 1987. *The influence of seapower upon history, 1660–1783.* Mineola, N.Y.: Dover.
Marcus, G. L. 1971. *A naval history of England: The age of Nelson.* Boston: Little, Brown.
Mattingly, G. M. 1960. *The armada.* Boston: Houghton Mifflin.
Patterson, A. T. 1960. *The other armada: The Franco-Spanish attempt to invade Britain, 1779.* Manchester: Univ. of Manchester Press.

Richmond, H. W. 1946. *Statesmen and sea power.* London: Oxford Univ. Press.
Tedder, A. W. 1916. *The navy of the Restoration: From the death of Cromwell to the peace of Breda.* Cambridge: Cambridge Univ. Press.

SEVEN YEARS' WAR

The Seven Years' War foreshadowed the war of movement and maneuver later brought to perfection by Napoleon I. The war also set the stage for the rise of Prussia as one of the dominant military powers on the continent of Europe. It was during this time that Frederick II ("the Great"), King of Prussia, set the pattern for the development of the Prussian General Staff that later enabled Prussia to achieve most of its military objectives.

Prelude: War of the Austrian Succession (1740–48)

The Hapsburg Holy Roman Emperor Joseph I died in 1711, leaving no male heir. His only daughter, Maria Amelia, had married Charles of Wittelsbach, King of Bavaria. Joseph I was succeeded by his brother, who was crowned Emperor Charles VI. In turn, Charles VI, having no male heir, negotiated the Pragmatic Sanction with the Electors of the Empire (1713). Under this sanction Charles's eldest daughter, Maria Theresa, would ascend the throne as empress upon his death. While the majority of electors supported this agreement, Prussia did so with reservations that stemmed from its claims to Silesia. Bavaria refused to accept the sanction, since its king-elector had his own claims to the imperial throne.

When Charles VI died in October 1740, Maria Theresa did ascend the throne as empress. As expected, the king of Bavaria did not recognize her legitimacy. Frederick II of Prussia agreed to recognize her only if she ceded Silesia to him; he laid claim to it under a condition of Germanic law known as fraternal inheritance. Maria Theresa was not ready to accept this demand; however, she also was not ready for war.

At this time, Frederick possessed the best-trained and best-equipped army in Europe, numbering some 86,000 men, and was fully prepared to wage war. Allied with Saxony, France, and Bavaria, Frederick invaded Hapsburg territory. After defeats at Mollwitz (10 April 1741) and Chotusitz (17 May 1742), Maria Theresa ceded Lower Silesia to Frederick and Prussia withdrew from the war. As soon as Frederick's forces had withdrawn, Maria Theresa's Austrian troops quickly defeated the Bavarians and the French. Fearing an upset in the balance of power, Frederick reentered the war and, by his victories at Hohenfriedberg (4 June 1745), Soor (30 September 1745), and Katholisch Hennersdorf-Gorlitz (24–25 November 1745), forced Maria Theresa to come to terms with him and his allies. This resulted in the Treaty of Dresden on Christmas Day 1745.

Frederick II once more withdrew from the alliance, leaving France, Saxony, and Bavaria to deal with the Hapsburgs. Hostilities continued despite the treaty, and in the ensuing fighting Maria Theresa lost most of her possessions in the Netherlands to France. The war finally ended with the Treaty of Aix-la-Chapelle in 1748. Under this treaty, Frederick II received all of Silesia as a permanent possession, and Francis of Lorraine became Holy Roman Emperor alongside his wife, Maria Theresa, who remained the virtual ruler.

Following the war, Maria Theresa formed an alliance with France. She did this to counter the growing power of Prussia, now allied with and heavily funded by England, and as a means to end nearly two centuries of warfare between the French Bourbons and Austrian Hapsburgs.

The Global War

In many respects, the Seven Years' War was the first modern world war. It was not restricted to the power struggle between Maria Theresa and Frederick. In addition to the European theater, there was also significant fighting in India, in North America, and at sea. These overseas operations represented a continuation of long-standing commercial and colonial rivalries between France and Great Britain. Britain's alliance with Prussia and France's ties with Austria and Russia engaged the forces of those two powers in conflict worldwide.

THE SEVEN YEARS' WAR IN EUROPE

In 1756, the formation of a formidable anti-Prussian coalition of the empire (Austria), France, Russia, and Saxony prompted Frederick to strike without warning.

Frederick invaded Saxony (29 August 1756) and quickly overran the country. He led his army into northern Bohemia and won a narrow victory over Marshal M. U. von Browne's Austrian army at Lobositz (1 October). The following spring Frederick launched a major invasion of Bohemia (April 1757) and defeated Prince Charles of Lorraine's army outside Prague on 6 May. Frederick then besieged Prague, but could make little impression on that city's formidable defenses.

The approach of an Austrian relief army under Marshal Leopold J. von Daun compelled Frederick to respond. On 18 June 1757, near Kolin, he attacked the army of 60,000 men under Daun. This army now included several regiments of Hungarian hussars and light infantry (Maria Theresa was queen of Hungary). Most of the Hungarian troops were under the command of Count Ferenc Nadasdy. The furious counterattack of the Austrian and Hungarian cavalry left Frederick's army reeling. He lost 13,000 out of a force of 33,000 and was compelled to retreat to Prussian territory.

The coalition had concentrated nearly 390,000 troops against Frederick, who was closely allied with England. Events moved in quick succession. In June 1757, the French Marshal d'Estrées moved his forces into Hannover and on 26 July he defeated the English, under the Duke of Cumberland, at Hastenbeck. Simultaneously, a Russian army of 80,000 men moved into Prussia. Prussian Field Marshal Lehwaldt was dispatched by Frederick with an army of 25,000 to meet the Russians. Lehwaldt was defeated by the Russians at Gross-Jägersdorf. Fortunately for Frederick, the Russians were unable to capitalize on their victory because of a shortage of supplies.

Frederick's situation was desperate but not hopeless. He left a covering force of 41,000 men under the Duke of Bevern to block the 112,000-man army of Prince Charles of Lorraine and executed a forced march to Erfurt with the remainder of his forces. There he bribed the French commander, the Duke de Richelieu, with 100,000 gold thalers to keep his forces inactive. Frederick then followed the withdrawing French army under the Prince of Soubise and re-captured Gotha. At this point, Frederick had to break pursuit and make a forced march back to Berlin where a division of 4,500 Hungarian cavalry and light infantry, under Count András Hadik, had just occupied his capital.

The Hungarian forces had left Elsterwelde on 11 October 1757 and arrived at Berlin on 16 October. The following day they took the city by assault. Once Berlin was occupied, Hadik announced that he would burn the city to the ground unless he received 400,000 gold thalers from the Prussian treasury. The Prussians managed to pay him 280,000 thalers along with 4,000 white kidskin gloves. The Hungarians then quickly departed, careful to avoid any further contact with Prussian forces.

Frederick now joined forces with General Keith, bringing his army up to 22,000 men, and camped at Rossbach in Saxony. On 5 November 1757 he defeated a combined French and Imperial army commanded by the Prince of Soubise and the Duke of Saxe-Hildburghausen in a short, sharp battle that was a tactical masterpiece. The allies attempted to "turn" Frederick out of his position in the hills near Rossbach by marching in long, parallel columns around the left flank, toward the Prussian rear. Frederick shifted the bulk of his force under cover to a position confronting the left flank of the heads of the allied columns. He then attacked—before the allies had the opportunity to deploy for combat. The surprise was complete, and the allied columns were completely overthrown and driven pell-mell from the field. Prussian losses at Rossbach were 165 killed and 376 wounded. French losses were 3,000 killed and 5,000 taken prisoner, including eight generals and 300 officers. Frederick did not pursue, because of the continuing dangerous situation in Silesia.

The next day Frederick marched for Silesia. He arrived at Neumarkt on 3 December 1757, surprising Marshal Daun and Prince Charles of Lorraine, who thought Frederick would be too exhausted after Rossbach to resume campaign-ing. Daun and Charles departed Breslau (4 December 1757) with 51,000 in-fantry, 14,000 cavalry, and 230 guns, and took up a position near the town of Leuthen. Their right wing was under Lucchessi's command, the center was concentrated on the town of Leuthen, and the left wing, under Nadasdy, was at the town of Sagschutz. Frederick's forces numbered 24,000 infantry, 12,000 cavalry, and 167 cannon.

At 5:00 A.M. on 5 December 1757, in dense fog and cold, Frederick began his movement to contact. He sent a cavalry force toward the right flank of the Austrian line. Fighting in the dense fog, the Prussian cavalry probe was forced back. This action led Prince Charles to shift his cavalry reserve from the center of his position to his right. Frederick, meanwhile, took advantage of this diversion to lead his main force against the extreme left flank of the Imperial army. When the fog lifted, Frederick suddenly realized that the entire Austrian and Imperial army was deployed before him from Sagschutz to Nippern, a distance of 8 kilometers (5 mi.), and astride their left flank. He at once attacked with the full weight of his army. Nadasdy was forced back. By 1:30 P.M. Nadasdy's wing was routed by the Prussian cavalry. Prince Charles, having shifted his cavalry to Lucchessi, now made an effort to recall them to reinforce Nadasdy, but it was too late. The imperial army's resistance fell apart, and the defeat was complete. Breslau surrendered on 9 December 1757, Silesia was regained, and Prussia became the most powerful military entity in Western Europe. Prussian losses were 6,000 killed and wounded. Austrian and Imperial losses included some 10,000 dead and wounded and 21,000 taken prisoner. One hundred sixteen guns, 51 colors, and 4,000 wagons were also lost.

On 25 August 1758, Frederick defeated the Russians in a costly battle at Zorndorf, but by 14 October he was once again defeated by an Austrian army under Daun at Hochkirch. Nevertheless, Frederick managed to clear all Austrian forces from Saxony. On 12 August 1759 he suffered a terrible defeat at the hands of an Austro-Russian army at Kunersdorf. Within a year after this setback, on 15 August 1760, he defeated the Austrians at Liegnitz and overwhelmed their fortified camp in a costly attack at Torgau (3 November 1760).

By 1762, weary from six years of war and once again surrounded and outnumbered, Frederick and Prussia were in dire straits. Luck was on Frederick's side, however; in 1762 the czarina, Elizabeth, who intensely disliked him, died. This brought Peter III, an admirer of Frederick, to the throne of Imperial Russia. Without hesitation, Peter transferred his armies from the Hapsburg alliance to an alliance with Prussia and returned to Frederick all Prussian territory previously lost to Russia.

Without Russian help, Maria Theresa could not hope to recover Silesia from Frederick. The Treaty of Hubertusburg (16 February 1763) brought the Seven Years' War to a close with Maria Theresa's full recognition of Frederick II's right to Silesia.

THE SEVEN YEARS' WAR IN NORTH AMERICA

West of the Atlantic the Seven Years' War, known in North America as the French and Indian War, began in 1754, two years before Frederick II's invasion of Saxony. The basic causes of previous colonial conflicts between the French and the English in North America had not been settled. Both sides mounted expeditions to seize frontier posts. These attempts included George Washington's abortive expedition against Fort Duquesne (Pittsburgh) in the spring of 1754 and Gen. Edward Braddock's disastrous attack on Duquesne (April–July 1755).

On the oceans, British Admiral Boscawen tried and failed to halt a convoy of reinforcements and munitions for Quebec at Belle Isle (8 June 1755). The French seized the British base at Port Mahon on Minorca (20 May 1756), but otherwise their naval endeavors met with little success.

The British soon established a significant superiority at sea and moved considerable reinforcements to their important colonies in North America. Despite some minor successes in late summer 1755, however, the British achieved little in 1756 or 1757, and their expedition against Louisbourg failed completely (June–September 1757). New British generals, Jeffrey Amherst and James Abercrombie, provided the needed initiative, and 1758 saw a string of British victories: Louisbourg was captured on 27 July; Fort Frontenac (Kingston, Ontario) fell on 27 August; and Fort Duquesne was taken in November.

The following year, Amherst finally took Fort Ticonderoga (26 July 1759) after Abercrombie's costly defeat there in 1758. The great victory of 1759, however, was James Wolfe's capture of Quebec following his bold ascent of the cliffs overlooking the St. Lawrence River and his victory on the Plains of Abraham outside the city (13 September 1759). Both Wolfe and the French commander, Marquis Louis Joseph de Montcalm, were killed in the battle. Montcalm's death and the fall of Quebec sealed the fate of French North America. The next summer, following the failure of a desperate French attempt to retake Quebec (April 1760), the British captured Montreal and, with it, all of French Canada (8 September).

Part of the reason for the British success in North America was naval superiority. Despite some competent commanders and some sound plans, the French were unable to wrest control of the seas from the English, and their forces in Canada were usually outnumbered and undersupplied. Elsewhere in the Americas, the British captured Martinique (12 February 1762) and went on to besiege and capture Havana (20 June–10 August 1762), seizing twelve ships of the line and great wealth in booty and merchandise.

THE SEVEN YEARS' WAR IN INDIA

India had been the site of earlier Anglo-French clashes during the War of the Austrian Succession (1740–48), because of conflicting commercial interests. The British had established a base area in Bengal; the capital of French holdings was at Pondicherry, south of Madras (another British holding). Robert Clive's famous victory over Nawab Suraja Dowla of Bengal at Plassey (23 June 1757) was peripherally related to the war, but operations in India did not begin in earnest until the arrival of a French fleet under Count Anne Antoine d'Aché, carrying an expeditionary force led by Count Thomas Lally (March 1758).

D'Aché's fleet clashed several times with a British squadron under Adm. George Pocock (Bay of Bengal, 29 April 1758; Negapatam, 3 August 1758), but was unable to gain an advantage. After d'Aché's defeat at Pondicherry (10 September 1759), his fleet was so badly damaged that he departed for home waters, leaving the French in India to their fate. Meanwhile, on shore, Lally had besieged and captured British Fort St. David, south of Pondicherry (March–June 1758). His operations against Madras met with little success, partly due to a lack of naval support (December 1758–February 1759). A relief force under Francis Forde bested Lally at Masulipatam (25 January), and he lifted the siege soon after.

Dutch operations against the British were handily repulsed, and Forde captured the Dutch post at Chinsura (spring–summer 1759). The able British general Sir Eyre Coote gained an important victory over Lally at Wandiwash (22 January 1760) and drove the French into Pondicherry, where they were besieged. After resisting for nine months (April 1760–January 1761), Lally was compelled to surrender (15 January 1761), as there was no hope of reinforcement or relief. Although the French regained Pondicherry through the Treaty of Paris, their military influence in India was thereafter sharply limited.

Conclusion

The Seven Years' War solidified Prussia's position as a major power in central Europe, although Austria soon recovered from its losses. The war was more costly for the two colonial powers. France lost Canada, the centerpiece of its empire, and also suffered losses in India and the Caribbean. The British, although gaining much territory in America and a clear upper hand in India, were soon faced with additional problems. The cost of the war, including extensive subsidies to Prussia, was over £82 million. To ease the great burden on Britain, taxes were levied on the American colonies. Those measures (the Sugar, Stamp, Quartering, and Colonial Currency Acts) sparked fierce colonial resistance and contributed directly to the outbreak of the American Revolution twelve years later.

SZABOLCS M. DE GYÜRKY

SEE ALSO: Frederick the Great; History, Early Modern Military.

Bibliography

Duffy, C. J. 1985. *Frederick the Great: A military life.* New York: Atheneum.
———. 1988. *The military experience in the Age of Reason.* New York: Atheneum.
Fuller, J. F. C. 1955. *A military history of the western world.* 3 vols. New York: Funk and Wagnalls.
Mahan, A. T. 1918. *The influence of sea power upon history, 1660–1763.* Boston: Little, Brown.
Parkman, F. 1905. *Montcalm and Wolfe.* Boston: Little, Brown.
Peckham, H. H. 1964. *The colonial wars, 1689–1762.* Chicago: Univ. of Chicago Press.

SHERMAN, WILLIAM TECUMSEH [1820–91]

William Tecumseh Sherman is one of the most famous Union generals of the U.S. Civil War (Fig. 1). He is perhaps most remembered for his comment "war is hell" and for his ruthlessness. The latter was demonstrated when he burned Atlanta, Georgia (1864), and subsequently devastated the countryside during his march to the sea. Concerned that his capture of Atlanta might weaken the Union's resolve to resoundingly defeat the Confederacy, he wrote his wife that the only way to achieve peace was to annihilate what remained of Confederate

Figure 1. William Tecumseh Sherman. (SOURCE: U.S. Library of Congress)

resistance, including ravaging the enemy's land. To this end, Sherman favored a mobilization of all Northern men through a ruthless draft, sparing no one, ending only when the South was crushed.

Sherman was born in Lancaster, Ohio, on 8 February 1820. His father's premature death caused the family, particularly the younger children, to be apportioned among relatives and neighbors. The young Sherman was taken in by a close friend of his father's, Thomas Ewing, an influential Ohio lawyer who would serve in the U.S. Senate and in the cabinet of Pres. Zachary Taylor. Appointed to the Military Academy at West Point in 1836 by Ewing, Sherman graduated in June 1840 and was ordered to report to Florida, arriving in October of that year.

Early Military Career

As the U.S. government pursued its war against the Seminole Indians, Sherman found himself slogging through a trackless morass, pursuing small, elusive bands of Indians in small-unit actions. Promoted to first lieutenant in November 1841, Sherman remained in Florida until his regiment was rotated to Fort Moultrie, South Carolina. In 1844, he was assigned to Marietta, Georgia; while there, he explored the surrounding countryside and, in some cases, traveled the exact areas his armies would traverse twenty years later.

Much to his disgust, Sherman was given recruiting duty when war was declared against Mexico in 1846. Arriving in Monterey, California, in January 1847, he missed his chance for glory in Mexico, serving as an aide and adjutant under his commanding officers. His service, consisting of quartermaster duties, tempted Sherman to offer his resignation, the first of many times. Returning from California, Sherman married Ellen Boyle Ewing, the daughter of his sponsor and guardian, Thomas Ewing. In an often turbulent life, Sherman's marriage was to prove remarkably stable and often provided him with the emotional anchor he needed throughout his military career. After being promoted in the fall of 1850 to captain, Sherman became increasingly unhappy with what he considered to be a less-than-demanding position in the Commissary Department. Sherman tendered his resignation from the army three years later. After thirteen years of active service, Sherman returned to California to become a banker.

Transition

At first successful, Sherman was severely tested by the financial crisis of 1854–55, but he was able to guide his company through the panic with minimal loss. Sherman had encouraged his former West Point classmates to speculate in California securities, and when these defaulted, he felt honor-bound to cover any losses that his friends incurred, eventually compensating for all losses but almost bankrupting himself in the process. Moving to New York City, the ill-starred Sherman was to face a second financial crisis in October 1857, which led to the liquidation of his firm.

Leaving New York for Fort Leavenworth, Kansas, Sherman opened a real estate and law office, both unsuccessful. When the governor of Louisiana offered him the superintendency of a new military school in October 1859, Sherman accepted. Successful as superintendent, Sherman left his cadets in January 1861 because of the anticipated secession of Louisiana from the Union. Returning home, still searching for a career, Sherman became president of a street car company. Not surprisingly, when the Civil War erupted two months later, Sherman left his position and returned to active service.

Early Civil War Years

Commissioned colonel of the Regular 13th Infantry, Sherman reported to Washington. Due to the reorganization of the Union army, Sherman received command of a brigade that fought in Tyler's 1st Division at the First Battle of Bull Run, 21 July 1861. On 24 August 1861, Sherman was assigned to the Department of the Cumberland and received promotion to brigadier general of volunteers. Reporting to his new command, Sherman soon found himself in a tenuous position, assuming command in Kentucky in October 1861 when his superior resigned.

Overwhelmed by the demands of his new command, Sherman faced the prospect of poorly trained troops, an immediate invasion of Kentucky from Confederate-held Tennessee, and what appeared to be the indifference of Washington to his requests for assistance. At this time, Sherman was portrayed in the national press as an eccentric, rapidly losing control of his department as well as his head. In early November 1861, Sherman asked to be relieved of his command and to be returned to his old brigade, now in the Department of the Potomac. His request for relief was granted, but he was reassigned to the Department of the Missouri.

Sherman was able to regain his composure and his sense of direction in this department. Salvaging his reputation during the Battle of Shiloh, fought on 6–7 April 1862, Sherman's resistance in the face of an overwhelming Confederate attack enabled the Union command to reestablish its battle line. Although wounded, Sherman's leadership on the battlefield was a factor in the Union victory. His commanding officer, Gen. U. S. Grant, praised his subordinate's actions. Sherman, however, was incensed that Grant and he, indirectly, were criticized by several newspapers for their purported negligence on the battle-field. Shortly after the battle, Sherman wrote his wife that if he caught any newspaper reporters, he was going to hang them. Sherman was promoted to major general of volunteers on 1 May 1862.

After advancing into northern Mississippi from Shiloh, Sherman spent several months protecting the railroads in this area. Throughout the summer of 1862, as commanding officer of the District of West Tennessee, Sherman fought against Confederate guerrillas in a campaign notable for his development of the total war concept: war directed not only at the Confederacy and its armies but also at its civilians by the retaliatory destruction of small towns, farms, and plantations within the district.

American Warlord

Around this time, Sherman began his plans to desolate the Confederacy. In late November 1862, he was given the task of commanding the right wing of Grant's first drive on Vicksburg, Mississippi. Grant, commanding the center, was forced back, and the attack upon Vicksburg from the south was delayed because of the illness of the commanding officer. Consequently, Sherman's attack at Chicka-saw Bluffs on 27 December 1862 failed. Withdrawing after his defeat, but determined to crack the Confederate defenses on the Mississippi, Sherman planned the attack on Arkansas Post, a Confederate fort built to obstruct the navigation of the Mississippi River. At this he succeeded; Arkansas Post was captured on 11 January 1863.

Sherman's role in the capture of Arkansas Post, and his success at Memphis, marked him as one of the more capable Union generals. Unfortunately, he continued his poor relations with the press and attempted to arrest and execute one reporter as a spy. Counseled by his wife to cultivate the press, Sherman became increasingly frustrated by his inability to work with reporters. Concerned that his position was undermined by what he considered biased reporting, Sherman contemplated resigning, believing his removal from command was inevitable. However, he commanded the XV Corps with distinction during the Vicksburg campaign; and with Grant's capture of Vicksburg on 4 July 1863, a relieved Sherman wrote his wife that he could see the end of the Confederacy, and he celebrated the destruction of the enemy. Again for his services, Sherman received a promotion, this time to brigadier general in the regular army.

After the capitulation of Vicksburg, Sherman proceeded to ravage Mississippi, and he instructed his troops to destroy, remove, or eliminate everything that contributed to the Confederate war effort. He was so successful that his commanding officer, Grant, embarrassed by the actions of Sherman's troops, issued orders authorizing summary punishment for any troops caught in the act of pillaging. Fortunately for Mississippi, Sherman was ordered to Tennessee in October 1863 for the relief of Chattanooga, and the Confederate army was hurled back from that city. By February 1864 Sherman returned to central Mississippi during a month-long campaign. Returning to Nashville in March, Sherman began planning his Atlanta campaign.

On 12 March 1864, Sherman was assigned to command the Military District of the Mississippi. Grant, now the commanding general of all U.S. forces, ordered Sherman to break up the Confederate army. The Union army, poised above Dalton, Georgia, began its advance down the Western and Atlantic Railroad in May 1864. The Confederate army, commanded by Gen. Joseph E. Johnston, held a position considered impregnable by many, and stopped the initial Union attacks around Dalton.

Using these attacks as feints, Sherman, with his superior manpower, shattered Johnston's defenses when he pushed through Snake Creek Gap on 9 May, causing Johnston to begin his slow, fighting retreat to Atlanta. Sherman had completely baffled the Confederate high command, leaving Johnston no other option but to withdraw. In what was his finest performance as a general, Sherman pushed the Confederates back and across the Etowah River by a series of flanking movements.

Although pushed out of its defenses, Johnston's army was able to stop Sherman's army at New Hope Church on 25 May to 4 June 1864, and at Kennesaw Mountain on 27 June. Frustrated by Johnston's tactics, Sherman ordered a disastrous attack on Kennesaw Mountain, later writing to his wife that it was necessary for its effect on the enemy, who were impressed with the way Sherman's soldiers met their deaths on the slopes of Kennesaw.

The effort of forcing Johnston and his army from line after line of prepared defenses was beginning to have an effect on Sherman. Realizing that mounting casualties were beginning to hinder the performance of his army, Sherman resumed his flanking attacks, and again outmaneuvered and forced the Confederate army back to and across the Chattahoochee River to within sight of the city of Atlanta in early June 1864. Exasperated with Johnston's performance, the Confederate president, Jefferson Davis, replaced Johnston with Gen. John B. Hood on 17 July. Almost immediately, Hood attacked.

Hood's attacks on 20 and 22 July rocked Sherman but did not stop him. Later Confederate attacks on Sherman, as he circled to the south of Atlanta trying to cut the railroad lines, also failed. Hood's last attack—at Jonesboro, 31 August 1864—was crippled by tactical errors, and Sherman entered Atlanta on 2 September, proclaiming that Atlanta "is ours and fairly won." The Confederate army retreated to the north, closely followed by Sherman. Frustrated with his inability to catch Hood, Sherman called off the chase, detached part of his army to follow Hood, and returned to Atlanta, where he began his March to the Sea. Devastating large parts of Georgia, Sherman captured Savannah, Georgia, in late December.

Receiving the thanks of Congress for his march, Sherman veered northward into South Carolina, continuing to inflict as much destruction as possible to crush what remained of Confederate resistance. Unable to oppose the overwhelming Union army, the Confederate Army of the Tennessee, now under Johnston, surrendered to Sherman on 26 April 1865. Although acknowledged as one of the Union's heroes, Sherman was accused of offering Johnston overly generous peace terms, prompting newspapers to question his loyalty to his country. Compounding Sherman's problems, Grant's chief of staff, Henry Halleck, deeply embarrassed Sherman by openly questioning Sherman's motives. Furious at such treatment, Sherman came close to refusing to join the triumphal march through Washington during the grand review of the armies.

With Grant's election to the presidency in 1869, Sherman became the commanding general of the army, and supervised the contraction of the postwar army. Faced with an ever-growing problem with the various Indian tribes as the West was developed, Sherman typically advocated killing the Indians as being the most efficient way of handling the situation. Retiring from the army in 1883, Sherman was courted as a potential presidential candidate, but he declined the nomination. Dying on 14 February 1891, Sherman was eulogized as one of the great American patriots, and rightly belongs in the pantheon of American heroes.

GREG FORSTER

SEE ALSO: Civil War, American; Grant, Ulysses Simpson; History, Modern Military.

Bibliography

Clarke, D. L. 1969. *William Tecumseh Sherman: Gold rush banker.* San Francisco: California Historical Society.

Lewis, L. 1932. *Sherman fighting prophet.* New York: Harcourt, Brace and Co.

Marszalck, J. F. 1981. *Sherman's other war: The general and the civil war press.* Memphis, Tenn.: Memphis State Univ. Press.

Sherman, W. T. 1892. *Personal memoirs of Gen. W. T. Sherman.* 2 vols. New York: Charles Webster.

Sherman Family Papers. Univ. of Notre Dame Archives, South Bend, Ind.

Sherman, W. T. Papers. Henry E. Huntington Library, San Marino, Calif.

———. Papers. Manuscript Division, Library of Congress. Washington, D.C.

SLIM, WILLIAM JOSEPH (Viscount) [1891–1970]

One of the most charismatic and dynamic soldiers of the twentieth-century Indian army was William Joseph Slim, later Field Marshal the Viscount Slim. His adventure-filled military career started with his receipt of one of the first commissions in Lord Horatio Kitchener's New Army in 1914. Slim rose to the position of army commander in Southeast Asia in 1945, along the way commanding at every echelon from platoon to corps, all of them, with the exception of battalion, in combat. The culmination of Slim's military career was his appointment in 1948 as chief of the Imperial General Staff, the first Indian army officer ever to serve as the professional head of the British army.

Early Life and Civilian Career

Born on 6 August 1891 near Bristol, England, where his father owned a warehouse near the docks, Slim was raised without the wealth and social standing common to some of those who achieved high military command. Slim grew up during the Boer War, certainly an exciting event to an impressionable youth, and his martial ambitions were further awakened by his father, who regularly read selections from *British Battles by Land and Sea* to him and his brother.

Slim's father suffered a severe financial setback in 1903, which forced the family to relocate to Birmingham. There Slim attended a Catholic grammar school; in 1908, he transferred to King Edward's School where he later joined the Officer Training Corps (OTC). Although he wanted to attend Sandhurst, his father could not afford the tuition required at the time. To assist his family financially, Slim became a pupil-teacher, then an uncertified elementary teacher; but he found this mundane existence intolerable. Just prior to the outbreak of World War I, he joined the steel firm of Stewarts and Lloyds as a junior clerk.

Early Military Career

Lance Corporal Slim of the OTC became, on 22 August 1914, Second Lieutenant Slim of the 9th Service Battalion, Royal Warwickshire Regiment. His unit was sent to Gallipoli in July 1915. After spending a month in the trenches, Slim was seriously wounded: the bullet just missed his spine, collapsed his left lung, and passed through his shoulder. The doctor proclaimed Slim's military career over, but after recuperating, Slim proved the doctor wrong and proceeded to lead a draft of soldiers to Mesopotamia in late 1916. He won the

Military Cross in the attack on Baghdad and was wounded again shortly thereafter. Sent to recuperate in India, Slim was posted to Army Headquarters, India, in November 1917, and was transferred, with the rank of captain, to the Indian army in May 1919.

During the interwar years, Slim was able to put many of the lessons he had learned while on active service into practice, primarily at the regimental level. He served in the 1/6th Gurkhas from 1920 to 1925, then attended the Staff College at Quetta. This was followed by four more years at Army Headquarters, India, then a posting to the Staff College at Camberley, England, as the Indian army instructor (1934–36), where the commandant, Lord Gort, considered Slim an obvious commander.

After attending the Imperial Defense College (1937–38), Slim received a substantive lieutenant colonelcy and was selected for battalion command—a timely event because he was considering retirement at the time because of the slow promotions and advancement potential in the peacetime army. Slim returned to India. After attending the Senior Officers' School at Belgaum, he commanded the 2/7th Gurkhas, then returned to Belgaum as commandant with the local rank of brigadier—in time for World War II.

World War II

With the outbreak of World War II, Slim was selected to command the 10th Indian Infantry Brigade forming at Jhansi in northern India. He had almost a year to train his unit before it was shipped, as an element of the 5th Indian Division, to fight the Italians in Eritrea and the Sudan.

In November 1940, Slim's brigade was ordered to capture Gallabat. This objective was quickly seized, but the Italian air force inflicted heavy casualties and caused confusion in the attacking force. After consultation with his staff, Slim decided to evacuate Gallabat. His first battle of the war was, therefore, a tactical failure, for which he blamed himself: "When two courses of action were open to me, I had not chosen, as a good commander should, the bolder. I had taken counsel of my fears."

Despite this setback—and a minor wound received in Eritrea—Slim quickly achieved the rank of major general and in 1941 took command of the 10th Indian Division. He led this unit against the revolting Iraqis that year and later in the British occupation of Syria.

With the Japanese invasion of Burma on 16 January 1942, Slim was selected for the unenviable position of commander of the Burma Corps consisting of the 17th Indian Division and the 1st Burma Division. A month later, after defeat at the hands of numerically superior Japanese forces, he began the longest retreat the British army ever suffered, a thankless task that Slim accomplished quickly and skillfully.

In June 1942 Slim was appointed commander of the newly raised XV Corps and led it in the Arakan offensive, which was stalled in March 1943. Seven months later, he was confirmed in command of the Eastern Army, the name of which was soon changed to the Fourteenth Army. He began a limited offensive in February 1944 in Arakan, while part of his army was engaged in stopping a Japanese offensive into India through Imphal and Kohima. By June, Slim had decisively won the Imphal/Kohima battle. Thereafter, his "Forgotten Army" successfully advanced eastward and recaptured Burma. The glory of this campaign, however, was marred by a misunderstanding between Slim and his superior, Lt. Gen. Sir Oliver Leese, that resulted in Slim being advanced to Leese's former position.

The reconquest of Burma required an indefatigable, flexible, and courageous leader, and the names of Slim and the Fourteenth Army will remain inseparable in the annals of military history.

Aftermath

Slim served as commander in chief of the Allied Forces Southeast Asia for a year after the defeat of the Japanese; he then returned to England as commandant of the Imperial Defence College. He retired in 1947 but was recalled to active duty less than a year later to succeed Field Marshal Bernard Law Montgomery as chief of the Imperial General Staff, a post he held until 1952. From 1953 to 1960, Slim served as governor general of Australia, and was raised to the peerage in 1960.

The author of *Unofficial History* (1959) and *Defeat into Victory* (1961), Slim served as constable and governor of Windsor Castle from 1963 to 1969. He died peacefully the following year.

This courageous, self-effacing soldier was famous for the consideration with which he treated his subordinates, who affectionately nicknamed him "Uncle Bill." One cannot do better than that.

HAROLD E. RAUGH, JR.

SEE ALSO: Colonial Empires, European; World War I; World War II.

Bibliography

Allen, L. 1984. *Burma: The longest war 1941–45*. New York: St. Martin's Press.
Callahan, R. 1978. *Burma 1942–1945*. London: Davis-Poynter.
Evans, G. 1969. *Slim as military commander*. London: Batsford.
Lewin, R. 1976. *Slim the standardbearer*. London: Leo Cooper.
Slim, F. M. Viscount. 1961. *Defeat into victory*. New York: David McKay.
Slim, F. M. Sir W. 1959. *Unofficial history*. London: Cassell.
Smith, D. E. 1979. *The battle for Burma*. London: Batsford.
Thorne, C. 1978. *Allies of a kind*. New York: Oxford Univ. Press.

SPAATZ, CARL A. [1891–1974]

Carl A. Spaatz, along with airpower advocates Billy Mitchell and Hap Arnold, was one of the leading figures in the development of American strategic air doctrine between the First and Second World Wars. During World War II,

Spaatz (Fig. 1), as commander of U.S. Strategic Air Forces in Europe and later, the Far East, oversaw the implementation of that doctrine against both Germany and Japan. During the critical years 1944–45, Spaatz directed the bomber offensive against Germany and Japan that crippled their economies, making a significant contribution to the eventual Allied victory.

Early Years

Spaatz was born in Boyertown, Pennsylvania, into a Pennsylvania Dutch family, the son of a printer and a Democratic state senator. He entered the U.S. Military Academy at West Point in 1910 but nearly quit during his plebe year because of the hazing. It was at West Point that he received the nickname "Tooey" because of his resemblance to an upperclassman. The nickname remained with him for the rest of his life. Spaatz received a commission in the

Figure 1. Carl A. Spaatz, 1943. (SOURCE: U.S. Library of Congress)

infantry in 1914, and served with the 23d Infantry at Schofield Barracks, Hawaii.

After a year in Hawaii, Spaatz went to flying school at San Diego, and after learning to fly, transferred to the Air Service of the Signal Corps. He served in the 1st Aero Squadron during Gen. John J. Pershing's punitive expedition against Pancho Villa in Mexico (1916). He was promoted to captain in May 1917.

World War I and After

During World War I, Spaatz was assigned as a trainer at the Air Service School at Issoudun, France. His duties kept him away from the front, which conflicted with his aggressive nature. He took leave and flew combat missions with the 2d Pursuit Group, scoring two victories and earning a Distinguished Service Cross. He was promoted to major in August 1918.

In December 1925, Spaatz served as a defense witness in the Billy Mitchell court-martial. As a result of the trial and the subsequent setback to the concept of airpower, Spaatz became involved in publicity flights sponsored by the Air Service/Air Corps. During 1–7 January 1929, Spaatz, Ira C. Eaker, and Elwood Quesada—all of whom would become prominent air commanders in World War II—conducted an endurance refueling flight, staying in the air 151 hours. Major Spaatz won the Distinguished Flying Cross for the feat and was given command of the 7th Bomb Group, based at Rockwell Field, California.

Spaatz attended the U.S. Army Command and General Staff School at Fort Leavenworth, Kansas, during 1935–36 and was promoted to lieutenant colonel. After two and a half years at Langley Field, Virginia, he was assigned to Washington, D.C., as assistant executive officer to the chief of the air corps. While in Washington he was promoted to colonel (November 1939).

World War II

In 1940, during the Battle of Britain, Spaatz was sent to England as an observer. Later that year he was advanced to assistant to the chief of air corps and subsequently was promoted to brigadier general. As the United States prepared for war, Spaatz was assigned to head the War Department Plans Division and later became chief of the air staff. In January 1942, he became the chief of the combat command and was promoted to major general.

He returned to Britain in May 1942, this time as commander of the Eighth Air Force. On 7 July 1942, he was appointed commander of U.S. Army Air Forces in Europe. In accordance with the agreed Combined Bomber Offensive, the British bombers under Air Marshal Sir Arthur T. Harris would continue nighttime bombing missions, while the U.S. bombers would strike during the day. The first mission conducted by American bombers against a European target was on 17 August 1942 against the railroad marshaling yards at Rouen, France.

In autumn 1942, Spaatz commanded the Allied Air Forces under Gen. Dwight D. Eisenhower for the Operation Torch landings in North Africa. In

February 1943, he organized and commanded the Northwest African Air Force and was promoted to lieutenant general. He later became deputy commander of the Mediterranean Allied Air Forces but returned to England in early 1944. His new position was commander of U.S. Strategic Air Forces in Europe, which included the Eighth Air Force in England and the Fifteenth Air Force in Italy.

Shortly after taking command, Spaatz directed the effort against German aircraft manufacturing capabilities. The recent arrival of large numbers of P-51 Mustangs gave the bombers long-range fighter support, reducing their vulnerability to German fighter attacks. During 20–25 February 1944 ("Big Week"), bombers of the Eighth and Fifteenth air forces, supported by P-51 Mustangs, launched devastating attacks on German aircraft production facilities. The results of Big Week crippled the Luftwaffe, which was never able to fully recover, having also suffered crippling losses of trained pilots.

In the summer of 1944, the German transportation network and oil production facilities were targeted, paralyzing the German air and ground forces for lack of fuel and lubricant. Spaatz was promoted to general in March 1945. With Germany close to collapse in April 1945, Spaatz and Harris agreed to concentrate on German ground forces to hasten their surrender.

In June 1945, only a month after Germany's defeat, Spaatz was sent to Guam to command the U.S. Strategic Air Forces in the Far East. While in this position he oversaw the final months of American bombing raids over Japan, climaxed by the dropping of the atomic bombs on Hiroshima and Nagasaki.

Because of his position as the leading air figure in both the European and Pacific theaters, Spaatz was present at the signings of the unconditional surrenders of Nazi Germany and Imperial Japan. In February 1946, he was given command of the Army Air Force, succeeding Gen. Henry H. ("Hap") Arnold, who was in poor health. In September 1947, he was chosen by President Truman as the first chief of staff of the newly created United States Air Force, a fitting reward considering his strong support for an autonomous air force.

Final Years

Spaatz retired in 1948 but remained active in civilian life as national security affairs correspondent for *Newsweek* magazine. He was chairman of the Civil Air Patrol, the International Reserve Committee, and chairman of the board of the Air Force Association. He also served on the committee that chose Colorado Springs as the location for the U.S. Air Force Academy. Spaatz died in Washington, D.C., on 14 July 1974 and was buried at the Air Force Academy.

ARNOLD C. DUPUY

SEE ALSO: Arnold, H. H.; Douhet, Giulio; World War II.

Bibliography

Arnold, H. H. 1949. *Global mission*. New York: Harper and Brothers.
DuPre, F. O. 1965. *The air force biographical dictionary*. New York: Franklin Watts.

Eaker, I. C. 1974. Gen. Carl A. Spaatz, USAF: June 28 1891–July 14 1974. *Air Force Magazine* 57(9):43–52.
Mets, D. R. 1988. *Master of air power: General Carl A. Spaatz.* Novato, Calif.: Presidio Press.

SPACE WARFARE

A distinguishing characteristic of twentieth-century warfare has been the prosecution of military operations above the earth's surface. Since 1914, the airplane has offered unique possibilities for observation, bombardment, and transportation. In the 1950s, the development of long-range ballistic missiles and earth-orbiting satellites ushered in still another phase of warfare in which space systems gained an importance rivaling that of the airplane.

Characteristics of Space Warfare

For the purposes of this article, space warfare is characterized by the use of weapons and manned or unmanned vehicles that transit, or operate in, space to influence military operations conducted in space or on earth. In addition to weapons or space platforms—intercontinental ballistic missiles (ICBMs), antiballistic missile (ABM) weapons, launch rockets (boosters), satellites, antisatellite weapons (ASATs), manned spacecraft—an extensive network of surface-based radars and other space surveillance sensors, command and control centers, communications networks, and launch facilities support military operations in or through space.

The velocities required to attain earth orbit and the need to insulate space systems against the harsh space environment have led to the development of boosters, satellites, and manned spacecraft that are among the most technologically complex and expensive pieces of military equipment ever built. It is not surprising, then, that intercontinental ballistic missile and space operations have been dominated by the two superpowers, the United States and the Soviet Union. Still, the advantages offered by space operations are so great that other nations—France, Great Britain, China, and Israel, for example—have developed space programs with potential military applications. In the next century, the ability to conduct space operations may be as important an indicator of national power as is the ability to conduct air operations today.

Development of Space Warfare

Space warfare began with the German development of the V-2 medium-range ballistic missile (MRBM) in World War II. Successfully test-fired in October 1942, the missile, which carried a one-ton high-explosive warhead, was used to bombard Britain from launch sites along the North Sea coast in 1944–45. Unstoppable once launched, the missile presaged a new era in warfare.

After World War II the Soviet Union and the United States exploited captured German rockets and scientists and engineers in an effort to develop ballistic missiles. By 1957, the Soviets had produced a missile, the SS-6, capable of lofting a small satellite into low-earth orbit. The launch of *Sputnik I*, the first artificial satellite, on 4 October 1957 marked the beginning of the space age and the opening of a new arena for military competition.

Both Soviet and American booster development were characterized by the adaptation of ICBMs and MRBMs to space launch activities. Liquid-fuel ballistic missiles such as the SS-6, SS-4, Atlas, and Titan continue to serve as the basis for much of those countries' space launch programs. These missiles, coupled with subsequently developed systems such as the Soviet SL-16 booster and the U.S. space shuttle, have given the superpowers the access to space necessary to deploy and sustain the large variety of manned and unmanned space systems used in their military operations. The importance of maintaining access to space was underscored by the major problems posed to the American military space program by the explosion of the space shuttle *Challenger* in January 1986 and the subsequent grounding of the entire shuttle fleet.

Current Space Warfare Operations

As of the early 1990s, with the exception of strategic bombardment by ICBMs, military space activities primarily support the conduct of terrestrial military operations by enhancing communications, weather forecasting, navigation, surveillance, and mapping, charting, and geodesy. As the superpowers' ability to develop and use satellites to support these functions has increased, so too has their concern with being able to protect their own space assets and, if necessary in times of crisis or war, to destroy an enemy's space system.

In this regard, the development of military space operations has in some ways paralleled the development of aircraft operations in World War I. In the early days of that conflict the chief use of aircraft was observation, but weapons-carrying aircraft were rapidly developed in an attempt to deny the enemy the ability to conduct aerial reconnaissance.

Surveillance and Early Warning

The advent of ICBMs in the late 1950s, with their intercontinental flight times of less than 30 minutes, significantly increased the need for surveillance and early warning. Early-warning satellites detect the launch of a ballistic missile by using infrared sensors that detect the hot plume of plasma emitted by a rocket motor. They plot the source of infrared emissions over several scans by their sensors to see if it is moving or stationary, and then relay the information to ground sites where it is combined with data from ground-based radars to develop an assessment of the size of the attack and its targets.

In the United States, information from early-warning satellites provides launch notification and is combined with information from Ballistic Missile Early Warning (BMEWS) radars located in Britain, Greenland, and Alaska and from Pave Paws radars in the United States to provide national command authorities with information necessary to make reaction decisions. The importance of these early-warning satellites is that they double the approximately fifteen-minute warning American decision makers would have if only BMEWS were available to detect an ICBM attack. The satellites are critical in facilitating the launch of bombers and tankers in the event of an ICBM or a submarine-launched ballistic missile (SLBM) attack. A similar network of space-based infrared detection satellites and ground-based radars and command centers provides tactical warning and attack assessment information to the Soviet political and military leadership.

Space-based surveillance has also had an increasingly significant effect on tactical operations. An example is the Soviet use of radar ocean reconnaissance and electronic-intelligence ocean-reconnaissance satellites. The former satellites, first launched in 1967, detect and track naval surface units. The latter satellites collect electronic intelligence on enemy fleet dispositions. When combined at Soviet command centers, the data derived from these satellite systems provided the Soviets with a formidable capability to detect and track enemy naval surface units operating in the open sea or approaching the Soviet homeland. This information also gave the Soviets—and now Russia—a considerable ability to target enemy surface units, for the data are provided to naval and long-range aviation units, which are armed with long-range cruise missiles.

COMMUNICATIONS SATELLITES

The worldwide military operations of the superpowers have been greatly facilitated by the development and proliferation of communications satellites. The importance of these satellites may be seen in the direct conversations they allowed between the U.S. national command authorities in Washington, D.C., and the commando units at the Desert One landing zone in Iran during the failed American hostage rescue attempt in 1980. Approximately 70 percent of American overseas military and diplomatic communications are relayed by satellite, while some 95 percent of U.S. Navy communications rely on satellite transmissions. The first active repeater communications satellite, the U.S. Army's *Courier*, was launched in October 1960. The first launch of the current mainstay of the U.S. long-haul communications program, the Defense Satellite Communications System (DSCS), occurred in 1966. The capabilities provided by these satellites were rapidly exploited. Beginning in 1967 they linked South Vietnam, through Hawaii, to Washington, D.C., for the transmission of photoreconnaissance data used by the Pentagon and White House to quickly plan air strikes in Southeast Asia.

By the late 1980s, both the Soviet Union and the United States were operating extensive satellite communications systems. Because the demand for military satellite communications far exceeds the supply of available channels, both nations also use channels on civil and commercial communications satellites.

These space-based systems are central to the rapid dissemination of emergency action messages that control strategic nuclear forces. Without the information provided by early warning satellites and the ability to communicate rapidly with widely dispersed strategic forces, superpower fears of surprise attack would be significantly increased.

Communications satellites are also exploited by smaller military powers and alliances. For example, Britain has operated the Skynet system since 1969. British dependence on satellite communications to support Royal Navy operations was clearly demonstrated during the 1982 Falklands/Malvinas campaign, when a shortage of communications capability resulted in a British request to the United States to use circuits provided by the Defense Satellite Communications System. French military communications are relayed by the Syracuse package carried on Telecom satellites. Finally, NATO operates the NATO III satellite communications system, which is interoperable with the Defense Satellite Communications System and Skynet.

NAVIGATION AND POSITIONING SATELLITES

Space systems have also increased the accuracy of weapons delivery by serving as aids to navigation and providing data for mapping, charting, and geodesy. Both major space powers operate satellites that collect mapping and geodetic information. These data are especially important in programming the guidance systems of ICBMs, submarine-launched ballistic missiles, and cruise missiles, which require precise information on gravitational, magnetic, and terrain variations in their flight paths.

The first U.S. navigation satellite, *Transit*, was originally developed to enable Polaris submarines to determine their positions to within 150 meters (492 ft.). *Transit*, which became operational in 1964, continues to operate and will be replaced in the 1990s by the Global Positioning System (GPS). This multi-satellite network will transmit timing and ranging data which, when fully deployed, will allow military users to fix their position in three dimensions to within 16 meters (53 ft.) and determine their velocity to an accuracy of 0.03 meters (approx. 1.2 in.) per second. Signals will be continuously transmitted, allowing users to receive data passively, without having to interrogate the satellites. This is important, since the transmission of an interrogating signal would reveal the user's position. GPS data will also be available to U.S. and foreign civil and private users, although without the accuracy of data transmitted to U.S. and U.S.-allied military users. As of the late 1980s, the Soviets were developing a similar system, the Global Navigation Satellite System.

WEATHER SATELLITES

Because of their altitudes, space systems have an inherent capability to detect weather patterns over huge portions of the earth's surface. As a result, they have significantly improved the collection and dissemination of weather data. The chief U.S. military weather satellite system derives from the Defense Meteorological Satellite Program (DMSP), which dates to 1964. The satellites that make up this system use a variety of sensors to acquire daylight and infrared images that provide data on cloud cover, temperature, water vapor content, atmospheric density, and ionospheric conditions. These data are transmitted on demand directly to fixed ground sites for processing and dissemination to U.S. and allied military forces. U.S. aircraft carriers are also equipped to receive information from these satellites. Soviet Meteor satellites are comparable to DMSP.

Collectively, the development and application of these military space systems since 1957 have had far-reaching effects on the conduct of terrestrial military operations. Since the first powered aircraft flight in 1903, the focus of the ancient military maxim, "take the high ground," has shifted from the highest hill to military satellites now operating in geosynchronous orbit approximately 22,300 nautical miles above the surface of the earth.

Early warning, communications, weather, and navigation satellites, which in part evolved because of the need to conduct or defend against strategic missile operations, have come to exert a major influence on the execution of conventional military operations as well. As with the conduct of aerial operations in World War I, the increasing reliance on support activities in space has simultaneously stimulated efforts to deny those activities to an enemy and protect friendly space systems.

Space Control

Space control, in some ways analogous to sea control, involves integrated offensive and defensive military operations aimed fundamentally at ensuring one's own freedom to operate in space, while limiting or denying that freedom to an enemy. Most public and professional attention has centered on the development of antisatellite weapons to destroy threatening space systems, but space control involves far more than just these weapons.

SPACE CONTROL OPERATIONS

Negating enemy space systems may require direct attack with intent to destroy those systems using nuclear, directed energy, conventional fragmentation, or kinetic "hit to kill" weapons. Lasers can be used to "blind" sensors, while electronic attacks can jam communications channels or transmit false commands. Attacks can also be launched against the terrestrial facilities that support space operations by carrying out space surveillance and satellite tracking or providing telemetry and control support, all of which are involved in monitoring and directing satellite operations.

In an environment where attacks on friendly space assets are expected, techniques to improve survivability become important. These may involve interceptors aimed at attacking antisatellite weapons; hardening satellites against nuclear, directed energy, and jamming effects; deployment of spare satellites as replacements for battle losses; communications cross-links between satellites to reduce their dependence on ground stations; and improvements in the satellite's ability to operate autonomously for extended periods of time without ground control. In addition, mobile land- and sea-based control facilities can be used to reduce the vulnerability inherent in fixed control sites.

Antisatellite Weapons

Both superpowers have pursued the development of antisatellite (ASAT) weapons. From 1964 through 1975, the United States had a limited operational ASAT capability that involved using Thor intermediate-range ballistic missiles armed with nuclear weapons and based on Johnston Island in the Pacific. In the mid-1970s, the United States began development of a new system, in part spurred by Soviet ASAT development. The resulting weapon was an air-launched, two-stage missile carrying a miniature homing vehicle. The vehicle, guided to the target by an infrared sensor, did not carry an explosive warhead, but was designed to hit the target and destroy it by the force of impact. The weapon was successfully tested against an orbiting U.S. satellite in September 1985. Further testing was prohibited by a congressional ban, provided the Soviets refrained from ASAT testing. Although the program was subsequently cancelled, the U.S. Department of Defense has continued to investigate potential ASAT systems.

Soviet ASAT development began in the 1960s, with the first full operational test in 1968. The continuing Soviet development effort resulted in an operational capability in 1971. Testing continued until 1982, when the Soviets unilaterally declared a moratorium on the testing of ASAT systems. The Soviet ASAT, launched on a variant of an SS-9 booster, is guided to its target by either active radar or a passive infrared sensor. When close to the target, its warhead explodes into a cloud of fragments, much like a shotgun blast. The Soviet Galosh antiballistic missile interceptor, armed with a nuclear warhead, may also have a limited ASAT capability. Finally, two experimental ground-based lasers, constructed at the Sary Shagan research facility, may have some utility as ASATs.

Ballistic Missile Defense

Space operations, which in some ways began as a by-product of the ICBM, remain closely tied to the military challenge presented by that weapon. In the future, new developments in space systems may limit, or negate entirely, the strategic missile's effectiveness. The effort to develop ballistic missile defenses (BMD), now most closely identified with the U.S. Strategic Defense Initiative (SDI), offers the potential for reducing the ballistic missile threat.

Both superpowers began ballistic missile defense programs in the late 1950s. The U.S. Army developed a nuclear-armed ABM, the Nike-Zeus, intended for interception of incoming ballistic missile reentry vehicles (RVs) at a range of approximately 100 nautical miles. Although the system was never deployed, it figured in the development of two other nuclear-armed interceptor missiles, the Sprint and Spartan. The United States briefly deployed these in the 1970s as part of its Safeguard system, which was soon dismantled because of its high cost and limited effectiveness.

Strategic Defense Initiative

In March 1983 American BMD efforts received a significant boost when President Ronald Reagan announced his intention of conducting a vigorous research and technology development program aimed at eliminating the threat posed by ballistic missiles. The subsequent formation of the Strategic Defense Initiative Organization (SDIO) within the Department of Defense consolidated a number of existing BMD research and development programs under one organization and increased their funding and public visibility. SDI was not a program to produce and deploy specific weapons and supporting systems, but a research program designed to lead to what the administration called an "informed decision" in the early 1990s on which concepts and technologies to pursue.

BALLISTIC MISSILE DEFENSE CONCEPTS

By 1987, the preferred BMD concept, planned for initial deployment in the late 1990s, centered on three major groups of interrelated systems. The first group included sensors for space- and terrestrially based surveillance, target acquisition, target tracking, and assessment of BMD interception of enemy missiles and warheads. These sensors would provide targeting information to the second major group of systems, space, and terrestrially based kinetic-kill interceptors. Finally, command and control computers, software, and communications networks would tie together the targeting sensors, interceptors, and command centers from which the BMD battle would be directed. In addition, a new space booster, associated with the Advanced Launch System program, would be required to launch the large number of heavy, space-based sensors and weapons systems.

The forecasted BMD system faced a significant threat. In the event of a full-scale Soviet ICBM and SLBM attack against the United States, over 1,000 missiles could be launched in the first wave of the attack. Once the reentry vehicles (RVs) and their associated decoys and penetration aids separated into free flight, the defenses would have to identify and characterize over 100,000 objects, of which approximately 10,000 would be actual RVs. In addition, the space-based portion of the BMD network itself could be under attack from Soviet ASATs.

CONDUCTING THE BALLISTIC MISSILE DEFENSE BATTLE

The formidable technical considerations involved in defending against such an attack led the SDIO to plan the defense in two stages. In the first, or space-based portion, orbiting sensors would detect the launch of attacking Soviet missiles, determine their flight paths, and provide targeting data to kinetic-kill interceptors fired against those missiles in the boost and postboost phases of their flight, before the RVs separated into individual targets. The second phase of the battle would begin in the late midcourse phase of flight, when ground-based sensors and interceptors would conduct attacks against surviving RVs as they approached reentry into the earth's atmosphere.

The goal of the initial phase of the BMD system was not to defend the entire population, but to enhance deterrence by eliminating enough Soviet weapons to cause doubt in the minds of Soviet war planners that they could achieve their desired goals for destroying U.S. military targets, thereby reducing their incentive to attack. Only well into the next century, as new sensor and directed-energy technologies emerged, would the system approach the full protection of the population of the United States and its allies envisioned as its ultimate goal.

Improving relations between the two superpowers and the proliferaton of ballistic missile technology among regional powers led President George Bush in January 1991 to announce a major restructuring of the U.S. ballistic missile defense program. The goal was to develop, by the turn of the century, terrestrial- and space-based systems to protect the United States against accidental or unauthorized launches of ICBMs, and to defend U.S. forces overseas and allies against ballistic missile attack. While deployment decisions were deferred, the new system was to be significantly smaller than that envisioned in the original SDI concept. The new plan increased the emphasis given to the threat of short- and medium-range ballistic missile attacks in regional conflicts, such as those conducted by Iraq during the war over Kuwait in 1991.

SOVIET BALLISTIC MISSILE DEFENSES

The Soviets also pursued an active BMD program. Beginning with deployment of the Galosh interceptor missile in the mid-1960s, the Soviets upgraded both the number and the capabilities of their interceptors and supporting radars, and constructed 100 launchers for nuclear-armed interceptors that were capable of destroying RVs both in and outside the atmosphere. In addition, some of their surface-to-air antiaircraft missiles may have had a limited ABM capability. As of the late 1980s, the Soviets were also pursuing many of the target acquisition, tracking, and interception technologies being addressed in the United States as part of SDI.

Western military establishments have been especially concerned since the 1970s by Soviet construction of large, phased-array radars, especially at Krasnoyarsk, which provide an almost complete ring of ballistic missile detection coverage around the Soviet Union. While the Soviets argued that these radars were for warning and assessment of missile attack only, some Western analysts believed they could provide the Soviets with the tracking and targeting capability required to direct an active, nationwide ballistic missile defense. The Soviets eventually granted that the Krasnoyarsk radar was a violation of the ABM treaty and agreed to dismantle the facility there.

THE 1972 ANTIBALLISTIC MISSILE TREATY

For both superpowers, BMD development was caught up in complex political and technological disputes over restrictions contained in the 1972 Antiballistic Missile Treaty, which both signed. The treaty allows both to develop and deploy limited defenses. Deployment of space-based weapons, weapons based on new technologies such as directed energy, or space-based ABM radars remain contentious issues.

Military Applications of Manned Spaceflight

Yet another issue affecting space operations is the role of military personnel in space. From the earliest days of spaceflight, they have constituted the majority of astronauts and cosmonauts. In the 1960s the United States pursued several manned spaceflight initiatives—most important were Dynasoar and the Manned Orbiting Laboratory—designed to study and develop military capabilities. Much of this effort foundered on the lack of requirements and the high cost of manned space flight as compared with the cost of unmanned satellites. The United States has continued to explore, at a low level of effort, manned military spaceflight applications with the space shuttle and will perhaps expand this effort in the 1990s with the proposed space station.

In contrast, the Soviets pursued a vigorous manned spaceflight effort. They almost certainly, during *Soyuz* and *Salyut* missions, conducted extensive experiments designed to test the application of manned flight to military operations, especially surveillance, reconnaissance, and command and control.

Military Space Operations of Regional Powers

From the beginning of the space age, the superpowers have dominated military space operations, but other states are also developing space launch and satellite technologies that will significantly increase their terrestrial military capabilities. For Brazil, China, and India, the ability to control widely dispersed forces will be greatly increased by the deployment of weather and communications satellites. Although Japan's constitution restricts development of military capabilities, operations conducted by its self-defense forces will similarly be improved by satellite deployments. As indicated by Israel's launch of its first satellite in 1988, early warning of potentially hostile military deployments is a vital concern for the Israelis, as is the development of defenses against surface-to-surface missiles. For these regional powers, space systems will be increasingly integrated into terrestrial military operations in the twenty-first century.

Conclusion

Military space operations are both the latest fulfillment of the "take-the-high-ground" dictum and a departure point for new and potentially decisive applications of military power. As of the early 1990s, space systems largely support terrestrial operations. With success in space operations becoming a precondition for terrestrial victory, however, the development of ASAT and BMD weapons, although now clouded by technological, funding, and political uncertainties, may make space itself the decisive arena in some future international confrontation. Furthermore, the realm of space will become even more important if space-to-earth weapons are developed. At a minimum, space systems will grow in importance to national leaders as these systems continue their central role in the command and control networks that direct the employment of terrestrial forces.

GEORGE REED

Bibliography

Hobbs, D. 1986. *An illustrated guide to space warfare.* New York: Prentice Hall.
Johnson, N. L. 1987. *Soviet military strategy in space.* London: Jane's.
Karas, T. 1983. *The new high ground.* New York: Simon and Schuster.
McDougall, W. A. 1985. *. . . the heavens and the earth: A political history of the space age.* New York: Basic Books.

Stares, P. B. 1987. *Space and national security.* Washington, D.C.: Brookings.

Turnill, R., ed. 1986. *Jane's spaceflight directory, 1986.* London: Jane's.

U.S. Congress, Office of Technology Assessment. 1985. *Anti-satellite weapons, counter-measures, and arms control.* OTA-ISC-281. Washington, D.C.: Government Printing Office.

———. 1985. *Ballistic missile defense technologies.* OTA-ISC-254. Washington, D.C.: Government Printing Office.

U.S. Department of Defense. 1988. *Soviet military power: An assessment of the threat, 1988.* Washington, D.C.: Government Printing Office.

SPANISH EMPIRE

The Spanish Empire was the first global colonial empire. At its heart was Spain, modern Europe's first superpower. From the accession of Charles I (Holy Roman Emperor Charles V) in 1516 to the reign of Philip IV (1621–65), Spain dominated Europe politically and militarily. Spain continued to play a significant role in the political affairs of Europe and of the world long after it had lost its military preeminence.

The Origins of the Spanish Empire

The Spanish Empire developed from a combination of military conquests and fortunate marriages. The kingdom of Spain itself owed its existence to these same factors.

THE RECONQUISTA

In 711, the Muslims of northern Africa invaded the Iberian Peninsula. By 719, most of Iberia was in Moorish (Muslim) hands. The Visigothic kingdom had been pushed into the northern mountains and fragmented. From these fragments three kingdoms emerged: León, in the northwest; Navarre, in the Pyrenees; and Aragon, in the northeast.

The kings of León established a series of strongpoints along the border between León and the Moorish emirates. This border region became known as Castile because of its many castles. By 970 Castile was an independent kingdom, and in 1037 it absorbed León. Castile, Aragon, and Portugal gradually expanded their respective domains southward at the expense of the Moors. The last Moorish kingdom, Granada, capitulated to Isabella I (r. 1474–1504) of Castile and Ferdinand II (r. 1479–1516) of Aragon in 1492.

ARAGON AND THE WESTERN MEDITERRANEAN

The marriage of Isabella and Ferdinand in 1469 had united the two great kingdoms of Iberia in a personal union. Each kingdom, however, pursued its own interests. Aragon had ruled Sicily since 1409 and Naples since 1435. Ferdinand II had conducted operations against the Moorish emirates of Oran, Bougie, and Tripoli in 1509. By 1511 these North African states had accepted Aragonese overlordship.

CASTILE AND THE NEW WORLD

The kingdom of Castile was the vanguard of the *reconquista*. While Aragon developed a navy and merchant marine to exploit its interests in the western Mediterranean, Castile developed a professional army. The conquest of Granada and the seizure of Ceuta on the North African coast gave Castile control of the Straits of Gibraltar.

Although Aragon fought with the Muslims over control of the Mediterranean trade routes, Turkish control of the Middle East guaranteed the Muslim monopoly of overland trade with the Far East. The Portuguese controlled seaborne trade—via the Horn of Africa—with India and the Spice Islands. The expeditions of Christopher Columbus, commissioned by Isabella I to find a new trade route free from Portuguese control, found instead the New World. The conquests of Central and South America and the Philippine Islands provided Spain with not only hitherto undreamed of wealth but also a Spanish route to East and Southeast Asia.

THE HAPSBURG CONNECTION

The colonial empires of Aragon and Castile remained discrete entities during the reigns of Isabella and Ferdinand. Their eldest daughter and heir, Juana, married Philip of Hapsburg, son of Maximilian I, Holy Roman Emperor. After Philip died in 1506, Juana went mad. Ferdinand ruled Castile as regent on behalf of Juana's eldest son, Charles of Ghent. Upon Ferdinand's death in 1516 Charles became King Charles I, the first king of a united Spain, as well as ruler of the Aragonese and Castilian possessions in Italy, North Africa, and the New World. When Charles's Hapsburg grandfather, Emperor Maximilian, died, the Hapsburg lands of central and south-central Europe and the Burgundian lands (Duchy of Burgundy and the Netherlands) passed to Charles. His election as Holy Roman Emperor in 1519 made Emperor Charles V the secular head of western Christendom, a duty he vigorously discharged in his conflicts with "infidel" Turk and "heretical" Protestant.

Spain: Modern Europe's First Superpower, 1516–1643

The reigns of Charles V and Philip II are considered the Golden Age of Spain. During these years Spain dominated western Europe both politically and militarily. With the conquests of Mexico (New Spain), Peru, and the Philippines, Spain became the first global colonial power.

CHARLES V, R. 1516–56

While Cortes and Pizarro conquered Aztecs and Incas in his name, Charles V fought the French in the Netherlands, Italy, and the Rhineland; the Protestant princes, in Germany; and the Ottoman Turks, in the Mediterranean.

The French Wars. The Valois kings of France coveted the Rhineland, the Netherlands, and Italy. Linguistically the seventeen provinces of the Netherlands were unevenly divided into a French-speaking region (the modern Kingdom of Belgium and parts of northeastern France) inhabited by the Walloons, and a Dutch-speaking region (northern Belgium and the Kingdom of the Netherlands) inhabited by the Flemings and the Dutch. The Netherlands were the commercial crossroads of northern Europe and, therefore, a rich prize.

Charles V fought five wars against the French. The First French War (1521–26) was fought over the duchies of Burgundy and Milan. In February 1525, Charles V's army in Italy inflicted a crushing defeat on the French at Pavia and captured the French king, Francis I. Although Francis signed the Treaty of Madrid (1525), he later repudiated the treaty, claiming it had been signed under duress.

The results of the Second, Third, Fourth, and Fifth French Wars—the last concluded in the reign of Philip II—were the same: Spanish victories. France was forced to recognize Spanish sovereignty over the Netherlands, the duchies of Burgundy and Milan, and the Kingdom of Naples.

Wars of the Reformation. The Protestant Reformation produced both a religious and a political crisis for Charles V. The adherence of the North German princes to the teachings of Martin Luther threatened not only Christian unity but also the political unity and stability of the Holy Roman Empire.

As the guardian of the church, Charles V fought the Protestants with the same intensity he brought to bear against the French and the Turks. Unfortunately for Charles, he often had to fight more than one enemy at a time. As a result, while Charles was victorious over the French and held the Turks at bay, he had to settle for a compromise with the German Protestants. In 1555, the Religious Peace of Augsburg granted Lutherans freedom of worship.

Worn out by 39 years of rule, during which he was almost constantly at war, Charles V abdicated all his titles in 1556. Spain and her colonial empire, as well as the Burgundian lands, went to his son, Philip II. The Archduchy of Austria, the Kingdom of Bohemia, and the other Hapsburg holdings in Europe and the imperial crown went to Charles' brother, Ferdinand.

PHILIP II, R. 1556–98

The reign of Philip II witnessed the extension of Spanish power over Portugal and throughout Italy. In 1571 a combined Spanish-Papal-Venetian-Imperial fleet, commanded by Don Juan of Austria, defeated the Turks at Lepanto, thereby stemming the Turkish onslaught.

Philip II became king of Portugal following the death of Cardinal Henry in 1580. Although the Portuguese later rebelled and elected their own king (1640), for 60 years Iberia was united under the Spanish Hapsburgs. The acquisition of Portugal gave Philip not only the Portuguese commercial empire with its monopoly on seaborne trade with the Far East, but also a true, ocean-going navy.

The Spanish victories at St. Quentin (1557) and Gravelines (1558) brought the Fifth French War to an end. Philip's victories over the French and the Turks and his acquisition of Portugal were offset by the revolt of the Netherlands and the naval war with England.

The Revolt of the Netherlands, 1568–1648. The Netherlands served as the commercial center of the Spanish Empire and as an important source of tax revenue. Despite their importance, the Netherlands were ruled by a governor appointed by the Spanish king and responsible only to the Spanish king. Neither noble nor commoner, Walloon or Dutch, had any say in the governance of the provinces. Spanish absolutism conflicted with Calvinist demands for religious and political freedom, resulting in rebellion.

Philip II attempted to head off trouble by sending the duke of Alva to the Netherlands with 20,000 troops. The rebels, predominantly Dutch, could not meet the dominant European army of the day on an equal footing. Instead, the Dutch used their skills as seamen and conducted amphibious operations along the coast and the inland waterways, bypassing the Spanish garrisons. These "Sea Beggars"—a name adopted by the Dutch raiders—seized Brill in 1572. England, whose traditional alliance with Spain had withered after Henry VIII broke with Rome, secretly aided the "Sea Beggars" financially and allowed them the use of English ports.

Unable to defeat the rebels, Alva requested his recall in 1573. Alva's replacement, Luis de Requeséns y Zuñiga, defeated the Dutch rebels at the Battle of Mookerheide in 1574, and took and sacked Ghent and Maestricht. The string of Spanish victories, coupled with the sack of Antwerp by mutinous Spanish troops (October 1576), frightened not only the Calvinists but also the Catholics. Fearing the loss of their traditional privileges in the event of a complete Spanish victory, Catholic nobles joined forces with Calvinist nobles to oppose the Spaniards (Pacification of Ghent, November 1576).

Philip II appointed Alexander Farnese, later Duke of Parma, to command Spanish forces in the Netherlands in 1578. By combining military victories with diplomacy—he guaranteed the restoration and preservation of provincial privileges—Parma pacified the southern provinces (1579). The northern provinces, however, remained defiant and, in 1579, formed the Union of Utrecht. In 1581, the Union declared itself the independent United Provinces of the Netherlands, with William of Orange as its elected *stadtholder* (governor).

Parma's capture of Antwerp in 1584 convinced Elizabeth I of England that the Netherlands' revolt was in jeopardy. Accordingly, she ordered the earl of Leicester to the Netherlands with a force of 6,000 troops. England's intervention angered Philip. It was not until the execution of Mary, Queen of Scots (February 1587), however, that Philip decided to strike.

Philip asked his leading naval and military commanders, the marquis of Santa Cruz and the duke of Parma, to draw up preliminary operational plans. Philip hoped that by carrying war to England he could not only end English meddling in the Netherlands but also return the heretical English to the Roman Catholic fold.

Santa Cruz and the Armada. Philip's Captain-General of the Ocean, Don Álvaro de Bazán, marquis of Santa Cruz, was a veteran naval commander. In 1571 Santa Cruz had commanded the Christian reserves at Lepanto. His timely entry into the battle won the victory for the allies. In 1580 Santa Cruz secured the Portuguese capital of Lisbon and, with it, eleven ocean-going galleons. On 26 July 1582, Santa Cruz defeated a French fleet off Terceira in the Azores. The marquis of Santa Cruz was the obvious choice to command a seaborne attack on England.

Santa Cruz proposed to sail a large fleet, including troop transports, directly to England. The marquis wanted 510 ships, including 150 large ships—galleons and armed merchantmen. He listed his manpower requirements as 30,000 sailors and 64,000 soldiers (the invasion force).

The duke of Parma's proposal was more modest. Parma wanted the fleet to sail to the Netherlands. The fleet would then convoy the invasion force of 34,000 across the Channel to England. Parma requested sizable reinforcements to bring his army up to 34,000 troops.

After reviewing both proposals, Philip II decided to send limited reinforcements to Parma from Italy. The Armada, about one-half the strength of the force Santa Cruz had wanted, would sail first to the Netherlands and from there cover Parma's crossing to England. Once the invasion force was ashore, the Armada would maintain Parma's lines of communication. Only if necessary was the Armada to engage the English fleet.

Santa Cruz died on 9 February 1588, and Philip II appointed Don Alonzo Pérez de Guzmán, duke of Medina-Sidonia, the new commander of the Armada. Of the grand fleet Santa Cruz had requested, only 130 ships materialized. Instead of 50 galleons, only thirteen arrived. Medina-Sidonia was able to round up another seven galleons before the fleet set sail.

If the Armada was a secret, it was an open secret. Its passage through the English Channel was contested in a series of running battles. At the Battle of Gravelines (29 July 1588) the Armada was effectively neutralized. Battles with the English, however, accounted for perhaps 50 ships lost out of 130. Storms wrecked many ships along the coasts of Scotland and Ireland. Only 60 ships eventually returned to Spain.

The Twelve-Year Truce. The defeat of the Armada, although a blow to Spanish pride and a morale boost to the Dutch, did not end the conflict in the Netherlands. The war between the Spanish and the Dutch became stalemated. In 1609 both sides agreed to a twelve-year-long truce. When the truce expired, Spain renewed hostilities. The end result was again stalemate. It was not until the end of the Thirty Years' War that Spain grudgingly recognized the independence of the United Provinces of the Netherlands.

The Spanish Army

Spain's political preeminence during the sixteenth and early seventeenth centuries was, in large measure, the result of its military preeminence. The Spanish army was the first modern, professional national army in Europe. In its organization, training, weapons mix, and tactics, the Spanish army became the model for the armies of both friend and foe.

Spain in Decline, 1643–1714

The loss of the Netherlands cost Spain dearly. While it retained control of the Spanish Netherlands—the eight southern provinces—the 80-year-long struggle against the Dutch rebels had drained Spain financially. The financial distress caused by the war came at a time when Spain's domestic economy also was in decline.

Despite its troubles, Spain remained active in European political and military affairs. The Spanish Netherlands had to be protected from the Dutch and the French, especially the latter. As members of the House of Hapsburg, Spanish kings felt duty bound to aid their Austrian cousins whenever and wherever Hapsburg interests were threatened. The successors of Philip II also saw themselves as guardians of orthodox Catholicism.

THE THIRTY YEARS' WAR, 1618–48

During the early phases of the Thirty Years' War, Spain limited its active participation to General Spinola's operations in support of Count Tilly during the latter's invasion of Bohemia and the Palatinate (1620). Spinola was able to force the Protestant Union into neutrality (Treaty of Ulm) during Tilly's pacification campaign.

Following the pacification of the Palatinate, Spain's involvement took the form of financial assistance to the Austrian Hapsburgs, military advice, and finally direct military intervention. Its real enemy was France. Catholic France supported Protestant Sweden against the Hapsburgs, just as the French had supported Lutherans and Ottoman Turks during the sixteenth century. The French also renewed their attempts to acquire territory and influence at Spanish expense along the Rhine and in northern Italy.

The great conflict was pursued on land and sea with varying fortunes. An important turning point occurred on 19 May 1643 when the French, commanded by Louis de Bourbon, duke of Enghien, decisively defeated the Spanish at Rocroi. Not only had the Spanish lost a battle, the Spanish army had lost its aura of invincibility. New techniques of war, exemplified by the innovations of Gustavus Adolphus, triumphed over the weapons and tactics that had made the *tercio* the dominant military force for more than a century. The Franco-Spanish war ended in November 1659 (Treaty of the Pyrenees). Spain lost her border fortresses in Artois and Flanders as well as the province of Roussillon on the Franco-Spanish border.

THE WAR OF DEVOLUTION, 1667–68

The evident decline of Spanish power and the presence of a weak and sickly monarch, Charles II (r. 1665–1700), on the Spanish throne, emboldened Louis XIV of France. King Louis ordered Marshal Turenne to seize the provinces of Flanders and Hainault, while the Prince of Condé invaded Franche-Comté. The French king's gambit did not go unchallenged. On 23 January 1668 England, Sweden, and the United Provinces (Holland) formed a Triple Alliance against France. The war ended in May 1668 (Treaty of Aix-la-Chapelle) and, although Louis XIV returned Franche-Comté to Spain, he kept twelve fortresses in Flanders.

THE WAR OF THE GRAND ALLIANCE, 1672–78

Louis XIV invaded Holland in 1672. Spain allied with Holland and England to thwart Louis's aggression. By the Treaty of Nijmegen, Spain lost Franche-Comté to France as well as fourteen fortress towns in the Spanish Netherlands.

As compensation Spain received eight towns previously occupied by France, as well as Puycerda on the Catalonian coast. Spain joined the League of Augsburg against France in 1690, a move that cost it Haiti.

FROM HAPSBURG TO BOURBON

While France had been most active in acquiring territory at the expense of Spain, the other European powers also were interested in carving up the Spanish Empire. Charles II, without heirs, was the last of the Spanish Hapsburgs. Quite naturally, cadet branches of the Austrian Hapsburgs vied for the succession, as did Louis XIV of France (House of Bourbon). Louis's mother, Anne of Austria, was sister of Philip IV of Spain; Louis and Charles were first cousins.

On 11 October 1698 England, Holland, and France agreed to the dismemberment of the Spanish Empire upon the death of Charles II. Upon learning of this agreement, Charles was outraged. It was not until a year later, however, on 3 October 1700, that Charles II named as his successor his second cousin, Philip of Anjou, grandson of Louis XIV. Faced with the terrifying specter of a union of France and Spain under the House of Bourbon, England, Portugal, Holland, Austria, and Bavaria formed a new Grand Alliance and declared war on France.

THE WAR OF THE SPANISH SUCCESSION, 1701–1714

At first the war did not go well for the House of Bourbon. In the Netherlands allied armies commanded by John Churchill, duke of Marlborough, outfought the French. Archduke Charles of Hapsburg, second son of the Holy Roman Emperor, invaded Catalonia in 1703 and declared himself King Charles "III" of Spain. The English captured Gibraltar in 1704 and Archduke Charles occupied Madrid in 1706.

Faced with the worsening situation in Spain, Louis XIV sent French troops under the command of Marshal Vendôme and the duke of Berwick to help his Spanish allies. (James Fitzjames, duke of Berwick, was the illegitimate son of James II—the last Stuart king of England—and Arabella Churchill, sister of the Duke of Marlborough.) In October 1707 Berwick retook Madrid. At Almanza on 25 April 1708, Berwick's Franco-Spanish force defeated an Anglo-Dutch-Portuguese-Huguenot army. In 1710 Marshal Vendôme literally chased the allies across and out of Spain.

On 11 April 1713 Britain, Holland, Savoy, and Spain signed the Treaty of Utrecht. Philip of Anjou was recognized as King Philip V of Spain on the condition that the crowns of Spain and France would never be joined. Britain kept Gibraltar and obtained the island of Minorca, as well as permission to sell slaves in Latin America. The Duchy of Savoy received Sicily. By the Treaty of Rastatt and Baden (September 1714), Austria received the Spanish Netherlands, the Kingdom of Naples, and the Duchy of Milan. The Hapsburgs, however, refused to recognize the Bourbon succession in Spain.

SPAIN DURING THE EIGHTEENTH CENTURY

During the 34 years following the War of the Spanish Succession, Spanish military and diplomatic policy focused on attempts to regain Spain's lost Italian territories. The motivating force behind this policy was Elizabeth Farnese, second wife of Philip V. Elizabeth wanted to secure thrones for her children. Spain and its empire would, naturally, go to Philip's children by his first wife.

In 1717 Philip V secretly dispatched a military expedition to Sicily and Sardinia. When Philip's actions became known, Britain, France, Holland, and Austria formed a Quadruple Alliance (August 1718) to prevent Spain from upsetting the delicate balance of power in the Mediterranean. Philip ended his operations in Italy in exchange for an Austrian promise that Parma, Tuscany, and Piacenza would go to Charles, eldest son of Philip and Elizabeth Farnese (Treaty of the Hague, 1720). The Hapsburgs also renounced all claim to the Spanish throne. Savoy exchanged Sardinia for Sicily, while Austria received Sicily.

The Treaty of the Hague did not put an end to Spanish designs on Italy. To achieve its goals Spain allied with Britain and France in 1721 and with Austria against France in 1725. It then fought a two-year-long war against both Britain and France (1727–29). Surprisingly for a declining power, Spain actually profited from these maneuvers. In 1731 Prince Charles became duke of Parma in exchange for Spanish recognition of the Pragmatic Sanction. During the War of the Polish Succession, Spain invaded Lombardy, Naples, and Sicily. By the Treaty of Vienna (1738), Spain retained possession of Naples and Sicily, while Austria received Parma and Piacenza. Duke Charles became king of the Two Sicilies (Naples and Sicily). Spain allied with France during the War of the Austrian Succession, with the result that Philip, second son of Philip V and Elizabeth Farnese, became duke of Parma, Piacenza, and Guastalla (Treaty of Aix-la-Chapelle, 1748).

DEFENSE OF THE OVERSEAS EMPIRE

Charles, formerly king of the Two Sicilies, succeeded his half-brother, Ferdinand VI, on the throne. During the second half of the eighteenth century Spain, under Charles III (r. 1758–88), followed a policy of political centralization (absolutism) at home and alliance with France abroad.

Spain's alliance with France imperiled Spanish colonies overseas. During the Seven Years' War (1756–63), the British occupied Cuba and the Philippines (1762). Although Spain regained both, it lost Florida to Britain (Treaty of Paris, 1763). To compensate its ally, France ceded Louisiana to Spain.

In 1779 Spain once again joined France against Britain during the American Revolutionary War. Spain retook Florida and Minorca. On the high seas Spanish, French, and Dutch warships inflicted heavy casualties on the British merchant marine. Spain's possession of Florida was confirmed by the Treaty of Versailles (1783).

Spain and the French Revolutions

Initially Spain joined Britain and Austria against revolutionary France (War of the First Coalition). Spain invaded the French border provinces of Navarre and Roussillon, while the French invaded Catalonia and Guipuzcoa. The Treaty of Basel (1795) returned all occupied territory.

The Spanish king, Charles IV (1788–1808), unlike his father, was weak and irresolute; by 1796 he was completely under the influence of his queen's Francophile favorite, Manuel de Godoy. On 19 August 1796, Spain switched sides and allied with France (First Treaty of San Ildefonso). In the Second Treaty of San Ildefonso (1 October 1800), Spain ceded Louisiana to France in exchange for a French promise to enlarge the Duchy of Parma. Spain also agreed to try to wean Portugal away from its traditional alliance with Britain.

Spain's alliance with France during the War of the Second Coalition resulted in the recovery of Minorca (Treaty of Amiens, 1802). However, during the War of the Third Coalition, the Spanish fleet, along with the French, was defeated by the British at Trafalgar in 1805.

Unable to undermine Portugal's alliance with Britain, Spain and France agreed to invade and divide Portugal (Treaty of Fontainebleau, 1807). In two months, Portugal was overrun.

Godoy's Francophile policies and domestic misrule led to anti-Godoy demonstrations in Madrid (November 1807). Fearing revolution, Charles IV wanted to abdicate but was convinced by his family to remain on the throne. With Spain in turmoil and thus a security threat to the French southern flank, Napoleon invited both Charles IV and his son Ferdinand, Prince of the Asturias, to a conference in Bayonne. Napoleon first convinced Ferdinand to renounce the succession, then convinced Charles IV to abdicate in his, Napoleon's, favor. Napoleon then presented Spain to his brother, Joseph.

THE WAR OF RESISTANCE (PENINSULAR WAR), 1808–1814

French forces rapidly occupied the cities of Spain. King Joseph, however, did not long enjoy his new kingdom in tranquility. In May 1808 an uprising forced Joseph to flee Madrid. Although French troops retook Madrid on 20 July 1808, a Spanish force commanded by General Castaños defeated a force of 18,000 Frenchmen at Baylen (23 July 1808). The situation became so critical that Napoleon himself took the field. On 10 November, Napoleon defeated one Spanish army at Burgos and, the next day, a second Spanish army at Espinosa. Napoleon entered Madrid on 13 December 1808.

The British government sent an army to the Iberian Peninsula under the command of Sir John Moore, a leading advocate of the light infantry concept. On 16 January 1809 the French, commanded by Marshal Soult, defeated the British at Coruña. Moore was slain and the British troops evacuated by sea.

The French hold on Spain was insecure, despite French victories over both the Spanish and the British. The city of Cádiz, in the far southwest, remained defiant and free from French occupation. Throughout the countryside, local noblemen and peasants formed councils (*juntas*) to govern in the name of the Bourbon monarchy. Small bands of Spaniards, both professional soldiers and peasants without previous military training, raided French supply trains, intercepted French couriers, and executed *afrancesados* (pro-French collaborators). Unable to fight battles in the grand manner of regular armies, these small bands fought "little wars," or *guerrillas*. Under guerrilla leaders such as Don Julian Sancho, "El Empecinado" (Juan-Martin Diaz), and "El Marquisito," the "furor hispanicus" descended upon the heads of the hated French. Spain became for France what the Netherlands had been for Spain: an endless quagmire, the "Spanish Ulcer."

Arthur Wellesley, duke of Wellington, took command of British forces in Portugal in 1809. Working in cooperation with the Portuguese and especially with the Spanish guerrillas, Wellington set the stage for the liberation of Iberia. British officers gradually organized the guerrillas into battalions and regiments and trained them in the tactics of regular warfare. In 1811 the allies took the offensive and inflicted defeat after defeat upon the French: Fuentes de Oñoro (5 May 1811), Albuera (16 May 1811), Ciudad Rodrigo (19 January 1812), Badajoz (6 April 1812). At Salamanca (22 July), a Spanish division commanded by Charles of Spain took part in the battle. At Vitoria (21 June 1813), Colonel—later General—Pablo Morillo's Spanish brigade took the Puebla Heights, turning the French left flank; while General Longa's Spanish division turned the French right flank, thereby denying the enemy a line of retreat to Bayonne. During the enemy retreat to the border, guerrilla bands continually harassed the fleeing French.

With Spanish soil once again free of foreign occupiers Ferdinand, prince of the Asturias, was crowned King Ferdinand VII (March 1814).

REVOLUTIONS IN LATIN AMERICA

The French overthrow of the Spanish Bourbons precipitated uprisings in Spain's Central and South American colonies. At first these uprisings were pro-Bourbon. Gradually, however, the insurrectionists switched from fighting for Spain to fighting for independence from Spain. By 1825, the Central and South American colonies had declared their independence. Of its once great colonial empire, Spain retained only Cuba, Puerto Rico, and the Philippines.

Spain in the Nineteenth Century

FERDINAND VII, 1814–33

Ferdinand VII began his reign promising to rule Spain according to the Liberal Constitution of 1812. Ferdinand did the exact opposite. The king's mendacious behavior quickly lost him the popular support that had marked his accession.

In June 1833 Ferdinand set aside the Salic Law, which limited the succession to males only. Without sons, Ferdinand sought the succession for his infant daughter, Isabella. Following her father's death in September 1833, Isabella was named queen. Don Carlos, Ferdinand's brother and the heir presumptive, refused to recognize his niece.

Isabella II, 1833–68

Because Isabella was a child, her mother assumed the regency. Don Carlos and his supporters took to the hills and began the First Carlist War (1834–39). Britain, France, and Portugal supported the Spanish government and, with Spain, formed the Quadruple Alliance (April 1834) to prevent foreign intervention on behalf of the Carlists. Defeated, Don Carlos left Spain in August 1839, while his supporters went underground.

The Era of the Military Coup (pronunciamento). The end of the First Carlist War did not end the problems of the Spanish government. An uprising of Progressives, the more radical of the Liberals, had forced the government into issuing a new constitution. In October 1840 General Baldomero Espartero overthrew the government, forced the Queen Regent to flee the country, and assumed the regency himself. Espartero easily crushed uprisings of supporters of the Queen Regent (October 1841) and of the Catalans in Barcelona (November 1841).

Espartero's regency lasted until June 1843, when he was overthrown by General Ramon Narváez. In December 1852, the constitution was amended. The *cortes*—the Spanish legislature—lost all real power. Spain became a dictatorship ruled by military junta.

General Espartero and General Leopoldo O'Donnell overthrew Narváez in July 1854. Espartero once again became regent, while O'Donnell became prime minister.

Overseas Adventures, 1858–71. The Spanish government dispatched a military expedition to Morocco in 1859. Its objective was to secure the region between the Spanish enclaves of Ceuta and Melilla. This region eventually became the Protectorate of Spanish Morocco.

Spain joined British and French intervention in Mexico in 1861. Spain and Britain later withdrew in opposition to French colonial designs on Mexico.

Spain and Peru clashed over ownership of the Chincha Islands in 1864. The Spanish government sent a fleet to seize the islands. The Peruvian government sought to negotiate the matter after Spain had occupied the islands. A preliminary agreement had been reached that would have entailed Spanish recognition of Peruvian independence. However, a coup d'état replaced the government in Lima. On 14 January 1866, Peru declared war on Spain. Chile, Peru's ally, followed suit. The Spanish fleet blockaded Peru and shelled Valparaiso and Callao. The U.S. government eventually mediated an end to the war in 1871.

The First Spanish Republic

The deaths of O'Donnell in 1868 and Narváez in 1868 destabilized Spanish politics, while Queen Isabella's scandalous personal life weakened the popularity of the monarchy. On 18 September 1868, Admiral Juan Topete raised the flag of rebellion. He was soon joined by Liberal army officers. Ten days later Marshal Francisco Serrano defeated the royalists at Alcolea. The queen and her family fled the country. On 6 June 1869, a new constitution was proclaimed and Serrano assumed the regency. For the next two years the Spanish government searched for a new king. Amadeus of Savoy eventually accepted the crown. As Amadeo I, his reign was short and unhappy. In 1873 Amadeo abdicated and Spain was declared a republic.

The proclamation of the republic was met by a new Carlist uprising. In January 1874 Marshal Serrano overthrew the government. On 31 December 1874, Serrano himself was overthrown by generals favoring Isabella's son, Alfonso, Prince of the Asturias. Spain was once again a monarchy.

ALFONSO XII, 1875–85

Alfonso XII was an intelligent young man with a liberal philosophy of government. Unfortunately for Spain, he reigned for only ten years. His wife, Queen Maria Christina, ruled as regent for their son Alfonso. During her regency, control of the government alternated between the Progressives and the Liberals.

THE SPANISH-AMERICAN WAR, 1898

Cuba was swept by insurrectionary activity in 1895. The repressive measures of the Spanish colonial government outraged world, and especially American, public opinion. The U.S. government dispatched the battleship *Maine* to Cuban waters. On 15 February 1898, the *Maine* blew up in Havana Harbor. Holding the Spanish government responsible, the United States declared war on Spain on 25 April 1898.

The war was a disaster for Spain. Defeated, Spain was forced to grant Cuba independence and cede Puerto Rico, Guam, and the Philippines to the United States. The Spanish Empire had virtually ceased to exist.

LAWRENCE D. HIGGINS

SEE ALSO: Bolívar, Simón; Colonial Empires, European; Condé, Louis II de Bourbon, Prince de; France, Military Hegemony of; French Revolutionary–Napoleonic Wars; Gonzalo de Córdoba; History, Early Modern Military; History, Modern Military; Italian Wars (1494–1559); Napoleon I; Ottoman Empire; San Martín, José de.

Bibliography

Braudel, F. 1976. *The Mediterranean and the Mediterranean world in the age of Philip II*. 2 vols. New York: Harper and Row.

Elliot, J. H. 1964. *Imperial Spain, 1469–1716*. New York: Penguin.

Geyl, P. 1958. *The revolt of the Netherlands*. New York: Barnes and Noble.

Gibson, C. 1966. *Spain in America*. New York: Harper and Sons.

Graham, W. 1972. *The Spanish Armadas*. New York: Doubleday.

Mattingly, G. 1959. *The Armada*. Boston: Houghton Mifflin.

Merriman, R. B. 1962. *Philip the prudent*. Vol. 4, *The rise of the Spanish Empire in the Old World and in the New*. New York: Cooper Square.

Oman, C. W. C. 1937. *History of the art of war in the sixteenth century*. New York: Dutton.

Parker, G. 1972. *The army of Flanders and the Spanish road*. New York: Cambridge Univ. Press.

Parry, J. H. 1940. *The Spanish theory of empire in the sixteenth century.* Cambridge: Cambridge Univ. Press.

Pierson, P. 1975. *Philip II.* London: Thames and Hudson.

SPRUANCE, RAYMOND AMES [1886–1969]

Operational command of the main American naval force in the Pacific during World War II rested alternately with Admirals William F. "Bull" Halsey and Raymond A. Spruance. Spruance is best known as the victorious commander at the decisive Battle of Midway.

Early Career

Spruance was born in Baltimore, Maryland, on 3 July 1886, but grew up in New Jersey and Indiana. He entered the U.S. Naval Academy in Annapolis after high school, and after completing his academic studies in 1906, he served aboard the USS *Iowa* (BB-4) as a passed midshipman (September 1906–1907). He then transferred to the USS *Minnesota* (BB-22) to take part in the around-the-world cruise of the "Great White Fleet" from 16 December 1907 to 22 February 1909 and was commissioned an ensign in September 1908, while aboard the *Minnesota*. Spruance was promoted to lieutenant junior grade in 1913 and had as his first command the USS *Bainbridge* (DD-1) in the Asiatic Squadron during 1913 and 1914. For his next major assignment he helped outfit the new battleship USS *Pennsylvania* (BB-38), and later served aboard it as electrical officer from February 1916 to November 1917. By that time a lieutenant commander, Spruance worked at the New York Navy Yard as assistant engineer officer from late 1917 to late 1918, making frequent trips to Britain to study gunnery and fire control. Promoted to commander, he commissioned the USS *Aaron Ward* (DD-132) in April 1919 and commanded her as a station ship during the transatlantic flight of four Navy NC flying boats. Spruance moved to command of the USS *Perceval* from March 1920 until June 1921.

He then returned to shore duty as head of the electrical department of the Bureau of Naval Engineering between 1921 and 1924. After one year's service on the staff of U.S. Navy forces in Europe (1924–25), Spruance graduated from the Naval War College in 1927. Assigned to the Office of Naval Intelligence during 1927–29, he then returned to sea duty aboard the USS *Mississippi* (BB-41) between 1929 and 1931. Next, Spruance returned to the Naval War College as an instructor in 1931 and 1932 and was promoted to captain in June 1932. Assigned to the staff of the commander, Scouting Force, from 1933 to 1935, he returned to teach again at the Naval War College until 1938. He went back to sea duty as captain of the *Mississippi* from mid-1938 until he was promoted to rear admiral in December 1939.

Command and World War II

Spruance's first flag command was that of Naval District 10, headquartered at San Juan, Puerto Rico. He held that post from February 1940 to July 1941, when he moved on to serve as commander of the Caribbean Sea Frontier for a month, through August 1941. The following month, Spruance moved to Pearl Harbor as commander of Cruiser Division 5 in the Pacific Fleet, and in that capacity he escorted the USS *Hornet* (CV-8) during Col. James H. Doolittle's famous raid on Tokyo (April 1942). He took command of the heavily outnumbered American fleet during the Battle of Midway, replacing Adm. Frank J. Fletcher, whose flagship, the USS *Yorktown* (CV-5), was severely damaged by air attack on 4 June. Spruance, maintaining his habitual calm in moments of crisis, directed the limited American forces in exemplary fashion, helping to deal the Japanese a stunning defeat, turning back their attempt to land on Midway, and destroying four of their six fleet carriers.

Spruance was then named chief of staff to Adm. Chester W. Nimitz, and he subsequently became deputy commander of the Pacific Fleet and the Pacific Ocean Areas in September 1942. He was promoted to vice admiral in May 1943 and took command of the Central Pacific Area and Central Pacific Force, the latter soon renamed the Fifth Fleet. At the head of the Fifth Fleet, he directed operations against Tarawa and Makin in the Gilbert Islands 20–23 November 1943, against Eniwetok and Kwajalein 31 January–23 February 1944, and against Truk in the Marshall Islands during 17–18 February. Spruance was promoted to admiral in February. He directed his fleet west and north in the spring of 1944, striking at Japanese bases and shipping in the approaches to the Mariana Islands.

While directing the advance into the Marianas during June, July, and August, Spruance decisively defeated the fleet of Vice Adm. Jizaburo Ozawa at the Battle of the Philippine Sea on 19 and 20 August. In what was colloquially referred to as the "Marianas Turkey Shoot," Spruance's fighter pilots shot down 473 Japanese planes, virtually destroying Japanese carrier aviation. After this victory, Spruance returned to Pearl Harbor to plan the invasions of Iwo Jima and Okinawa. Halsey took command of the ships (renamed Third Fleet when he was in command) and directed naval operations during the liberation of the Philippines.

Spruance returned to command just before the invasion of Iwo Jima, and he directed the first carrier raids against Japan itself on 16 and 17 January 1945. He directed naval support for the marine assault and capture of Iwo Jima between 19 February and 24 March, and he went on to perform a similar role off Okinawa from 1 April to 22 June, where his forces were plagued by Japanese kamikaze attacks. He was subsequently involved in planning the invasion of Kyushu during the summer of 1945. After the war he served briefly as commander of the Pacific Fleet during November and December of 1945. He then became president of the Naval War College, where he served until his retirement in July 1948. After he left the navy, Spruance was U.S.

ambassador to the Philippines from 1952 to 1955. He died in Pebble Beach, California, on 13 September 1969.

Assessment

By nature quiet and unassuming, Spruance was a very effective fleet commander who maintained an unruffled calm even in moments of supreme crisis and urgency. Although often criticized for a tendency toward caution, this sprang from his desire to achieve his goals at minimum cost. While he is not as well known as his more flamboyant colleague, Admiral Halsey, he was almost certainly the better commander.

DAVID L. BONGARD

SEE ALSO: Halsey, William F.; Nimitz, Chester William; World War II; Yamamoto, Isoroku.

Bibliography

Buell, T. B. 1974. *The quiet warrior: A biography of Admiral Raymond A. Spruance.* Boston: Little, Brown.

Forrestel, E. F. 1966. *Raymond A. Spruance, USN: A study in command.* Washington, D.C.: Government Printing Office.

Morison, S. E. 1947–1962. *History of United States naval operations in World War II.* 15 vols. Boston: Atlantic, Little, Brown.

Reynolds, C. G. 1968. *The fast carriers: The forging of an air navy.* New York: McGraw-Hill.

STILWELL, JOSEPH WARREN [1883–1946]

Joseph Warren Stilwell, West Point graduate and veteran of both world wars, was a leading figure in Chinese-American military relations (Fig. 1). His understanding of Chinese culture and society, developed during three tours of duty in China between 1920 and 1939, led to his appointment as senior U.S. commander in Asia during World War II. He headed several Allied commands in the China-Burma-India (CBI) theater of operations, but his policies in the arena of coalition warfare were often opposed by China's President Generalissimo Chiang Kai-shek and the Nationalist Chinese government. Despite his outstanding military performance, his lack of tact caused such a deterioration in his relationship with Chiang Kai-shek that Stilwell was recalled to the United States in 1944. He served on Okinawa and at various other commands until his death in 1946.

Early Career and World War I

Stilwell was born on 19 March 1883 in Palatka, Florida, the first son of four children to Benjamin and Mary Stilwell. He spent his childhood in Massachusetts, and in Yonkers, New York. In 1900 his father, concerned about a recent

Figure 1. Gen. Joseph W. Stilwell, circa 1945. (SOURCE: U.S. Library of Congress)

blemish on his son's previously untarnished record of behavior, secured an appointment for Stilwell to the U.S. Military Academy. He proved an able student and in 1904 graduated 32d in a class of 124.

Upon graduation, Stilwell was commissioned a second lieutenant in the infantry and sent to the Philippines to serve with the 12th Infantry Regiment in antiguerrilla warfare. In 1906 he returned to West Point as an instructor in the Department of Modern Languages, and in 1910 he married Winifred A. Smith. In 1911 Stilwell returned to the Philippines, received his promotion to first lieutenant in March and, while on leave in November, made his first visit to China, then in the throes of revolution. Returning to the United States in January 1912, he spent a year at the Presidio of San Francisco and then four more years as a faculty member at West Point (1913–17). In 1916 he was promoted to captain. With the expansion of the U.S. Army in the following year, after the United States entered World War I, he received the temporary rank of major and was assigned as a brigade adjutant in the 80th Division.

Stilwell arrived in France in January 1918 to serve with Gen. John J. Pershing's American Expeditionary Force (AEF) as an intelligence officer, where his fluent French made him a valuable asset. Duty with the British 58th Division and the French XVII Corps, the latter unit at Verdun, familiarized Stilwell with conditions at the front. As chief intelligence officer of the U.S. IV Corps he helped plan the St. Mihiel offensive. This operation began in September 1918, the same month he was promoted to the temporary rank of lieutenant colonel. A wartime promotion to temporary colonel followed, and Stilwell held this rank throughout his service in the occupation army in Germany. He returned to the United States in 1919, and in the general reduction of the army in September 1919 he reverted to captain.

Interwar Service

Stilwell's interwar military career combined overseas service in China with study and command assignments in the United States. Prior to his departure in August 1920 for his first tour in China, Stilwell was promoted to major. He served in China from 1920 to 1923 as a language officer and as an assistant military attaché. Between 1923 and 1926 he attended the Infantry School at Fort Benning, Georgia, and the Command and General Staff School at Fort Leavenworth, Kansas. During his second tour in China (1926–29) he was first a battalion commander with the 15th Infantry Regiment stationed in Tientsin and then an acting chief of staff to the U.S. Army commanding general in China. While in the 15th Infantry, he served with Lt. Col. George C. Marshall, the regiment's executive officer and a man who helped to shape Stilwell's career in World War II. Stilwell was promoted to lieutenant colonel in 1928 and with the help of Marshall became head of the tactical section at the Infantry School in 1929. He held this position until May 1933 when he was assigned to reserve training in San Diego. In July 1935 Stilwell returned to China as military attaché and was promoted to full colonel. His position gave him the opportunity to travel extensively throughout the country. Prior to the outbreak of the Sino-Japanese War in 1937, he perceived the inherent dangers of Chiang Kai-shek's policy of focusing his efforts against the Chinese Communists without offering strenuous resistance to increasing Japanese aggression. In 1939 Stilwell returned to the United States where he was promoted to brigadier general and then major general while commanding several units, including the 3d Brigade, 2d Division; 7th Division; and III Corps.

World War II

In January 1942 U.S. Army Chief of Staff Gen. George Marshall appointed Stilwell commanding general of U.S. Army forces in the China-Burma-India (CBI) region and chief of staff to Chiang Kai-shek. Promoted to lieutenant general, Stilwell arrived in China in March 1942 during a major Japanese invasion of Burma. He subsequently took command of the Chinese Fifth and Sixth armies and, in cooperation with British forces, launched an unsuccessful counteroffensive to stop the Japanese drive. When the Allied operation collapsed, Stilwell led his headquarters group on a march through dense jungles and across high mountains to Imphal in India.

For the remainder of 1942, Stilwell supervised the training of the Chinese army in India and directed a supply airlift from India to China over the "Hump," the nickname given by U.S. Army Air Force pilots to the Himalayan barrier between India and China. In 1943 construction of an overland supply route to China from North India was begun under Stilwell's directions. In addition to his other duties, he was appointed deputy to British Vice Admiral Lord Louis Mountbatten, head of the newly operational Southeast Asia Command. This assignment further complicated Stilwell's command responsibilities, which included command of the China theater, the India-Burma theater, and the Northern Combat Area Command (NCAC). As commanding general of NCAC, he was subordinate to the commander of the British Fourteenth Army. His mission in command of NCAC was to reconquer northern Burma. The key operation in the campaign was the capture of Myitkyina in August 1944 during the height of the monsoon season. That same month Stilwell was promoted to full general. In October 1944 Chinese and U.S. forces under Stilwell renewed their attack in northern Burma. At the same time the Japanese were making large gains in an offensive in East China, intended to eliminate U.S. air bases in that region. Stilwell's relationship with Chiang Kai-shek had by this time severely deteriorated, and when President Franklin D. Roosevelt recommended that he be placed in charge of all Chinese forces, Chiang refused and insisted on Stilwell's removal. On 18 October 1944 Stilwell was recalled to the United States.

In January 1945 Stilwell became head of Army Ground Forces and in June, following the death of Gen. Simon Bolivar Buckner, took command of the U.S. Tenth Army on Okinawa. In January 1946 he was appointed commander of the U.S. Sixth Army and the head of the Western Defense Command, positions he held until his death of stomach and liver cancer on 12 October 1946.

Assessment

In World War I and in peacetime, Stilwell earned a considerable reputation among his colleagues for competent and sound leadership. Wartime service in the CBI, with its many responsibilities and equally numerous difficulties, put to the test all the skills he had developed between 1900 and 1941. Stilwell's irascibility, which earned him the nickname "Vinegar Joe," did not ideally suit the diplomatic requirements of coalition warfare, either with the British or the Chinese, as evidenced when his differences with Chiang Kai-shek led to his recall from the CBI. Stilwell was, however, respected and admired by the Chinese troops that served under his command. Whatever he lacked in tact he more than made up for in energetic and capable military leadership.

BRIAN RAYMOND BADER

SEE ALSO: Chiang Kai-shek; Marshall, George Catlett, Jr.; World War II.

Bibliography

Romanus, C., and R. Sunderland. 1953. *Stilwell's mission to China.* Washington, D.C.: Department of the Army, Historical Division.
Stilwell, J. W. 1948. *The Stilwell papers,* ed. T. White. New York: William Sloane.
Tuchman, B. W. 1970. *Stilwell and the American experience in China, 1911–1945.* New York: Macmillan.

SUFFREN DE ST. TROPEZ, PIERRE ANDRÉ DE [1729–88]

Suffren was the ablest and one of the most famous French admirals of the late eighteenth century. Renowned for his daring and aggressive battle tactics, he did not enjoy the successes his skills should have earned him during his campaign against the British in Indian waters because of the distrust, suspicion, and recalcitrance of his subordinates.

Early Life

Suffren was born on 17 July 1729 in the Château de Saint Canat in Aix, a younger son of the Marquis de St. Tropez. In September of 1743, having just turned 14, he entered the French navy as a *garde de la marine* (midshipman) aboard the ship of the line *Solide.* He served aboard the *Solide* in the Battle of Toulon on 11 February 1744 and then sailed to the West Indies the following year. He served in the Cape Breton expedition of 1746; when that effort ended in disaster, he returned to France. Suffren fought at the Second Battle of Cape Finisterre on 25 October 1747, where he was captured. The end of the war brought his release from British confinement, and he entered the service of the Knights of Malta in 1748. After eight years there, the outbreak of war with Britain led him to rejoin the French navy. Appointed a lieutenant in early 1756, he served under Adm. Augustin de La Galissonnière against Adm. John Byng at Minorca on 20 May. His further wartime efforts earned him promotion to captain, but he was captured at the Battle of Lagos on 18 August 1759.

Winning a Reputation

Released from imprisonment by the Treaty of Paris in 1763, Suffren again joined the navy of the Knights of Malta and commanded the xebec *Caméléon* against the Barbary pirates from 1763 to 1767. He performed the order's required "caravans," and thereby won promotion from knight to commander and gained eligibility for high and lucrative office. Soon after, however, Suffren reentered the French navy and secured command of a ship in the training and demonstration squadron formed to study tactics and maneuver. He eventually won commendation in 1778 for his skill and élan in handling his ship over the previous six years. He served under Adm. Charles Hector d'Estaing in North

American and Caribbean waters from July 1778 to November 1779 and won distinction in operations off Newport, Rhode Island, between 5 and 11 August 1778. He later led d'Estaing's battle line in command of *Fantasque* (64 guns) against British admiral John Byron off Grenada on 6 July 1779. His well-known dissatisfaction with d'Estaing's indecisive leadership did not prevent that admiral from recommending Suffren highly for independent command, perhaps in hopes of getting rid of a subordinate who was sometimes abrasive and acerbic.

Command in the Indies

Returning to France, Suffren was posted to command *Zèle* (74 guns) in the Atlantic during 1780, and he was then chosen to lead a squadron of five ships to the Cape of Good Hope to aid the Dutch and then go on to assist the French cause in India. He left Brest with Adm. François-Joseph-Paul de Grasse's fleet on 22 March 1781 but soon turned south. At Porto Praya in the Azores on 16 April, he surprised and badly mauled the British squadron of Comdr. George Johnstone, also bound for the Cape of Good Hope, although only two of his captains supported his attack. Suffren duly reached the Cape of Good Hope and reinforced the Dutch garrison there in June and then sailed on to Mauritius (called by the French Ile de France), where he joined forces with the six-ship squadron of Admiral d'Ovres on 25 October. The united force of eleven ships of the line and assorted supporting vessels sailed for the Bay of Bengal on 17 December; after d'Ovres died at sea on 9 February 1782, Suffren took command as a commodore.

The French fleet arrived off Madras on 15 February and won a narrow victory over the slightly smaller British squadron of Rear Adm. Edward Hughes two days later. Suffren went on to best Hughes a second time off Trincomalee, Ceylon, on 12 April but was himself surprised and roughly handled by Hughes and his squadron off Cuddalore on 6 July. Undeterred, Suffren descended on Trincomalee and captured that town on 31 August after a siege of just six days. When Hughes appeared offshore, Suffren attacked him with great vigor on 3 September but was yet again robbed of success by the recalcitrance of his subordinates. He waited out the monsoon and refitted at Achem on Sumatra from 2 November to 20 December and arrived back in Indian waters in early January 1783. Both he and Hughes received reinforcements, but despite material inferiority Suffren attacked Hughes off Cuddalore on 20 June 1783 in an effort to raise the British siege of that town. He forced the British to withdraw toward Madras, but the end of hostilities less than three weeks later, on 8 July, precluded further operations and left the victorious French squadron with little to do.

Last Years

Suffren soon sailed for France, and the warm and cordial receptions he received from British captains along the route pleased him greatly. During his absence, as word of his exploits reached France, he had been promoted to rear admiral, the Knights of Malta had named him *bailli* (bailiff), and Louis XVI created a special office of a fourth vice admiralty just for him on his return. Suffren died at Brest on 8 December 1788 on the eve of assuming command of a fleet gathering there. The official cause of death was listed as apoplexy, but his body servant later revealed that he had died of wounds from a duel with the Prince de Mirepoix, who was incensed at Suffren's brusque dismissal of the prince's plea to reinstate two of the prince's relatives whom Suffren had dismissed for misconduct.

Assessment

Suffren was the greatest French naval commander of the eighteenth century. In combat he was fiery, bold, and tenacious, and he always worked hard to seize and hold the initiative. He was further gifted with a fine strategic and tactical sense, but his efforts were hampered by uncooperative and unwilling or recalcitrant subordinates. However, he may have exacerbated the problem by his own impatience and vehemence, as demonstrated by the manner of his death.

DAVID L. BONGARD

SEE ALSO: American Revolutionary War; Colonial Empires, European; Seapower, British.

Bibliography

Cunat, C. 1852. *Histoire du bailli de Suffren.* Rennes: A. Manteville et Lefas.
Dupuy, R. E., G. Hammerman, and G. P. Hayes. 1977. *The American Revolution: A global war.* New York: David McKay.
Mahan, A. T. 1890. *The influence of seapower upon history, 1689–1783.* Boston: Houghton Mifflin.
Richmond, H. W. 1931. *The navy in India 1763–1783.* London: E. Benn.

SUN TZU

Chinese general Sun Tzu (ca. 400–320 B.C.) is now one of the most widely read writers on concepts of general as well as military strategy—and the art of war. Unlike the more familiar Clausewitz, the influence of Sun Tzu's philosophy of strategy reaches into the business world, being "taken into the boardrooms" of Western as well as Eastern corporations (Ramsey 1987). More specifically in the military arena, his ideas on the use of military forces and tactics to achieve larger strategic ends have influenced combat in recent wars, campaigns, and battles and the approach of successful national commanders and leaders such as China's Mao Tse-tung and Vietnam's Senior General Giap. Sun Tzu continues to influence the course of history. Paperback versions of his *Art of War*, edited by Wing (1988) and Clavell (1983), are selling as successfully as those of the Japanese strategist Musashi's *A Book of Five Rings*.

British military author and historian Liddell Hart, in a foreword to Griffith's

(1963) translation of Sun Tzu, wrote that Sun Tzu's essays "have never been surpassed in comprehensiveness and depth of understanding . . . concentrated essence of wisdom . . . only Clausewitz is comparable, and even he is more dated. . . . Sun Tzu has clearer vision, more profound insight, and eternal freshness."

Background

Little is known of Sun Tzu's birth, early circumstances, or appearance. Traditionally placed in the closing years of the sixth century B.C. (a chronology still maintained by some, including contemporary Chinese scholars), Griffith and others place his birth in the fourth century B.C. He was in the service of the king of Wu, credited with capturing Ying, capital of the Chu'u state, and defeating the northern states of Chi'i and Chin. There are stories of how Sun Tzu impressed his king in a demonstration drill with the system of disciplined soldiery he offered, immediately executing the king's foremost concubines when they did not follow his commands. But Sun Tzu's place in military history does not rest with personal military accomplishments or with examples of audacity for his king. His enduring value lies in his very brief, vivid treatise on the nature of war and how to win.

Only relatively recently has Sun Tzu become known to Western military scholars. The first known translation into a Western language was by a Jesuit missionary father J. J. M. Amiot in Paris in 1772. It was widely circulated and again published in a 1782 anthology. (Sun Tzu is only one of several significant Chinese authors of early military texts. Adm. Ko Tun-hwa [1972] notes several other well-written Chinese classic treatises that are appreciated by Asian soldiers, statesmen, politicians, diplomats, and businessmen—as well as by guerrilla fighters. Sun Tzu's 25,000-word treatise is much longer than those of Wu-Tzu [4,773 words] and Ssu-Ma [3,549 words]. There was also a Li-Tsin of the much later Tang dynasty. But these several brief treatises are not yet translated into Western languages, hence not yet generally available.)

Sun Tzu's Influence

Sun Tzu's work has influenced the course of history more through its impact on a few known—and many who are unknown—readers who have brought about that historical influence than from his own direct efforts. Some of that "hidden" influence is discussed by Stahel (1981) and Wass de Czege (1988). Other aspects are addressed in depth by Tashjean (1987). Sun Tzu's works had a significant influence on Mao Tse-tung and Vo Nguyen Giap, and on Sir Basil Liddell Hart and his "indirect strategy." Some say it also had an influence on Napoleon.

As to the nature of Sun Tzu's advice, according to Admiral Ko, his whole theory of winning is built on two foci: (1) make yourself impossible to be defeated, and (2) seek ways to defeat the enemy—preferably without fighting. While these may be too profound for most would-be users to apply to a practical situation, there are some straightforward observations that have become truisms, for example: "Know the enemy, know yourself—your victory will be inevitable"; "Know the ground, know the weather—your victory will be total." On the "indirect approach," Sun Tzu suggests: "Avoid strength, strike weakness." Another saying that is perhaps derived from Sun Tzu (if not from Clausewitz) is Mao's dictum: "Invincibility lies in the defense; the possibility of victory in the attack."

Perhaps the most controversial aspect of Sun Tzu is his more profound observation: "To triumph in battle is not the acme of skill; those skilled in war subdue the enemy without battle. They aim to take everything intact." Expressions of the art of offensive strategy include: "They defend when strength is inadequate; attack when strength is abundant."

But the above dicta—vaporous to some, profound to others—must be absorbed through considering the less quotable but seemingly more substantive supporting points obtained by careful reading and rereading of the several translations of works attributed to Sun Tzu. And even analyses made in wider context, like that of Ramsey (1987), are likely to come up with distilled lists that are suspiciously like the military professional's classic "principles of war"— Ramsey's reviewer Feinberg's citation of maneuver (flexibility), objective (clear goal), offense, surprise, economy of force, mass (concentration of strength), unity of command, simplicity, and security (secrecy).

Future Use of Sun Tzu's Works

Liddell Hart complained that national commanders failed to benefit from reading Sun Tzu—or, at least, failed to use his approach. This situation is likely to be negated by future generations of military and corporate business leaders who *will* read and benefit from Sun Tzu. This will depend upon the ability of Westerners to adapt their perceptions to the Eastern mode of presentation (see, e.g., Crossland 1983) and to translate the resultant ideas into operational terms for their staff and troops. Also it will have influence through wider reading, by both military professionals and business executives, in relevant, allied works, such as that by Musashi of the East and Fuller of the West. There are, however, fundamental ethical and cultural issues to be resolved in using the approaches of Sun Tzu, Musashi, and others, whose proposed deliberate use of bribery, treachery, and so forth, contradicts current (though often betrayed) Western ideals of ethics and morality.

It is probable that the strategic philosophy of Sun Tzu will become increasingly influential. It may remain stronger than that of Clausewitz because of the more concise ways in which Chinese Gen. Sun Tzu is now being presented by Wing and others.

DONALD S. MARSHALL

SEE ALSO: Art of War; Clausewitz, Karl von; Giap, Vo Nguyen; Mao Tse-tung; Musashi, Miyamoto.

Bibliography

Crossland, R. L. 1983. Review of *The art of war*. In *Naval Institute Proceedings*. November, pp. 105–6.

Liddell Hart, B. 1976. Sun Tzu—From The Art of War (from translation by S. B. Griffith). In *The sword and the pen—Selections from the world's greatest military writings*, ed. A. Liddell Hart. New York: Crowell.

Musashi, M. 1982. *A book of five rings*. Trans. V. Harris. Woodstock, N.Y.: Overlook Press.

Ramsey, D. K. 1987. *The corporate warriors*. Boston: Houghton Mifflin.

Stahel, A. A. 1981. Die Strategischen Konzeptionen von Clausewitz und von Sun Tzu: Gegensatze und Gemeinsamkeiten (The strategic conception of Clausewitz and Sun Tzu: Contrasts and mutualities). In *Schweizer Monatshefte*, November, 61 Jahr, Heft 11, pp. 860–70.

Sun Tzu. 1910. *Sun Tzu on the art of war, the oldest military treatise in the world.* Trans. and with an intro. and critical notes by L. Giles. London and Shanghai: Luzac.

———. 1963. *The art of war.* Trans. and with an intro. by S. B. Griffith. Foreword by B. H. Liddell Hart. New York and Oxford: Oxford Univ. Press.

———. 1983. *The art of war.* Ed. and with a foreword by J. Clavell. New York: Delacorte Press.

Tashjean, J. E. 1987. The classics of military thought: Appreciation and agenda. *Defense Analysis* 3(3): 245–65.

Tun-Hwa, K. 1972. An introduction to the Chinese military classics. *Military Review.* Fort Leavenworth, Kans.: U.S. Army Command and General Staff College.

Wass de Czege, H. 1988. Historical theories remain sound compass references; the catch is staying on course. *Army* (September), pp. 37–43.

Wing, R. L. 1988. *The art of strategy—A new translation of Sun Tzu's classic "The Art of War."* New York: Doubleday.

SUVOROV, ALEKSANDR VASIL'EVICH
[1729–1800]

Suvorov was the greatest tactical commander in Russian history. He never lost a battle—even his retreat through Switzerland enhanced his legend. In poor health and usually greatly outnumbered, Suvorov defeated Turks, Poles, French, guerrillas, and Russian rebels. His genius was hampered by jealous superiors and political intrigues at court. His suppression of Polish liberty and French revolution won condemnation in liberal circles, but he predated Napoleon in his adoption of mobile warfare, and he inspired the absolute devotion of his troops.

Suvorov's innovations must be viewed in light of contemporary military practice. Eighteenth-century armies were brutal and highly disciplined, relying on complex drills that were ponderous to execute. Warfare was limited. Political connections were more important for military rank than talent; boys were enrolled as officers at birth so that at maturity they could come on active duty as colonels or even generals.

Early Life

Suvorov's birthdate is unknown; sources list it as 1725, 1727, 1730, and (most likely) 1729. Suvorov was a sickly child and was enrolled in a regiment only at 13. He rose through the ranks of the Semenovskii Regiment and was commissioned in 1754 as a lieutenant in the Ingermanland Infantry Regiment. During the Seven Years' War as a lieutenant colonel and senior war commissioner, he saw his first action at Kunersdorf (1759). By 1762 he was colonel of the Astrakhanskii Regiment; later that year he commanded the Suzdal'skii Regiment, where he instituted his famous Suzdal' Regulations. In March of 1768, ill health forced a year's leave of absence, but he returned to fight the civil war in Poland and in March 1770 was promoted to major general.

First Russo-Turkish War (Rumiantsev's War)

In April of 1773 Suvorov was transferred to the Turkish front under Rumiantsev. For capturing the fortress of Turtukai, he was awarded the Order of St. George (second class). Ill health forced his return to Moscow. He returned in April 1774 as a lieutenant general but was junior in seniority to a younger general, Kamenskii, which caused friction when Rumiantsev failed to resolve the conflicting commands. However, Suvorov was victorious at Kozludzhi, where he was outnumbered five to one; the battle broke the will of the Turks, and they sued for peace (Kuchuk Kainarji, 10 July 1774).

Interwar Period

Suvorov missed the campaigns against Pugachev but commanded the detachment that brought the captured rebel to St. Petersburg. While restoring order in the region, his rule was marked by leniency and a regard for civil law. In 1776 Suvorov married Varvara Ivanovna Prozorovskaia, an ill-educated and extravagant woman with whom he had one daughter, Natalya; her infidelities brought about a lifelong estrangement. In November 1776 he commanded a division at Poltava under Rumiantsev's Ukrainian command. Two years later he commanded forces in the Kuban, where he established a cordon of military posts, the Kuban Line. He eventually was given command of the Crimea, Dnieper, and Kuban, where he put down an uprising after Russia's 1783 annexation of the Crimea. In 1787 he was appointed commander in chief of the Ekaterinoslav Army.

Second Russo-Turkish War

In 1787 the Ottomans renewed their war with Russia. Suvorov fought off an attack at Kinburn (1 October 1787), a psychological victory, if strategically unimportant. In the summer of 1788, Potemkin besieged the fortress of Ochakov rather than taking Suvorov's advice to storm the citadel. Suvorov argued that heavy battle casualties would still be less than those from disease and attrition. Potemkin's siege failed, but he put the blame on Suvorov, who returned to Kinburn in shame. Suvorov was then sent to Moldavia to bolster Russia's Austrian allies under Coburg. He beat a Turkish army at Fokshani (July 1789); then in September, outnumbered four to one, he routed an Ottoman army led by the grand vizier at the Battle of Rymnik. Suvorov was awarded the Cross of St. George (first class) and granted the title of Count Suvorov-Rymnikskii and a coat of arms depicting a streak of lightning aimed at a Turkish crescent. The Turkish fortress at Izmail remained the key to the Danube and the way to Constantinople. By a six-pronged land attack with a naval assault from the riverside, Suvorov captured Izmail in December 1790 and inflicted more than 26,000 Turkish casualties. This battle effectively ended the fighting, although the peace treaty (Jassy) was not signed until 1793.

Polish Wars

Suvorov was instrumental in suppressing the Kosciuszko revolt of 1794, although the overall commander, Potemkin, took the credit. On 24 October, Suvorov stormed the Praga fortress at Warsaw, destroyed the Polish army, and forced a peace. He was subsequently named proconsul of Warsaw (a Polish remnant state nullified by the final partition), where he carried out Catherine's revenge. At age 65 he was finally named field marshal (a title shared at that time only by Razumovskii and Rumiantsev), granted a huge estate, and given a new command at Tulchin in the south. In 1795 he published *The Art of Victory*, practical advice on tactics and the nature of combat.

War with France

Although Suvorov's star dimmed under Czar Paul I, who disdained anyone associated with Catherine and blindly admired anything Prussian, he was still held in high esteem by the Austrians, who in February 1799 requested his aid in defeating the French in northern Italy. The 69-year-old Suvorov left forced retirement, trained the Austro-Russian force in his style of fighting, and immediately defeated the French to open the way to Milan and Lombardy. His operations were hampered by the political ambitions of the Austrians, who wanted only to establish a *cordon sanitaire* rather than seek out and destroy French revolutionary forces, and the political guidance of Paul to crush the revolution and restore the old order in France. Unfortunately, Suvorov lacked sufficient forces to exploit his victories and drive into France. The Austrians did reward him with the title "Prince of Italy," but they also sent him next into Switzerland with too few troops and Austrian intelligence and logistics (both unreliable). Suvorov battled north into Austria via the St. Gotthard Pass (13 September 1799), Devil's Bridge at Andermatt (14 September), and Schwyz (19–20 September). Surrounded, having expended his artillery ammunition, without food, and with 50 percent casualties, Suvorov managed to escape north and save his army. Paul broke off the alliance with Austria in disgust and recalled Suvorov to Russia, where he granted Suvorov the title "Generalissimo."

Death

Developing a fever on his way home, Suvorov retired to his estate at Kobrin. Paul, learning that Suvorov had contravened his new petty regulations in Italy, called off the celebrations and told Suvorov he would not be welcome at court.

This rejection finally broke Suvorov's spirit; he died on 6 May 1800. His funeral was private, for Paul forbade any state arrangements or attendance by any guards regiments.

Suvorov's Art of War

Suvorov argued that destruction of the enemy army, not conquest of territory or capture of the enemy capital, was the key to victory. He emphasized realistic training, speed, the offensive, initiative, the shock value of the bayonet, independent actions by small formations, pursuit, the importance of morale and psychological factors, and coup d'oeil (the ability to size up a military situation quickly and devise an appropriate response). Fewer men were lost in an assault, he argued, than by disease and attrition during a prolonged siege. Mobility and surprise constantly allowed him to defeat much larger forces in encounter battles. He led by example and was often wounded. He trained and fought hard but looked after his troops' welfare instead of pocketing funds sent for their upkeep.

Conclusion

Suvorov's reputation has been hampered because he fought Turks and Poles, whereas Western historians focused on French, Prussian, and Austrian commanders. Also, his achievements were overshadowed by Napoleonic warfare and the great campaign of 1812, fought by men he trained (Kutuzov, Bagration, and Miloradovich). Nevertheless, his reputation survived into the Soviet period, including the creation of the Order of Suvorov in July 1942 and Soviet advocacy of his style of warfare.

DIANNE SMITH

SEE ALSO: French Revolutionary–Napoleonic Wars; Ottoman Empire; Russia, Expansion of.

Bibliography

Essame, M. G. H. 1961. The Suvorov legend. *Military Review*, January, p. 14.
Longworth, P. 1966. *The art of victory: The life and achievements of Field Marshal Suvorov, 1729–1800*. New York: Holt, Rinehart and Winston.
Maycock, F. W. U. 1910. Suvorov: Russia's greatest general. *United Service Magazine*, January, no. 974, pp. 407–14.

T

TAMERLANE [1336–1405]

Tamerlane, or more properly Timur, was the greatest Central Asian conqueror of the late Middle Ages. The common European form of his name, Tamerlane, comes from a derisive nickname common in Persian chronicles, Timur Lenk, or Timur the Lame.

Early Life and Career (to 1380)

Timur was born about 1336 at Kesh (modern Shahr-i-Sabz), near Samarkand, into the Turkic Barlas tribe, a Mongol group that had settled in Transoxania in the early thirteenth century after the campaigns of Genghis Khan's son Chagatai in the area. After the death of Transoxania's ruler Amir Kazgan in 1357, Timur swore allegiance to Tughluq Temur, khan of nearby Kashgar. When Tughluq made his son Ilyas Khoja governor of Transoxania in 1361, Timur became his vizier (prime minister). Soon after, however, Timur joined his brother-in-law Amir Husayn, a grandson of Amir Kazgan, and together they defeated Ilyas Khoja in 1364; within two years they had conquered Transoxania. About 1370, Timur turned against his brother-in-law and besieged him in Balkh. After Husayn was murdered, Timur declared himself ruler of the Chagatai line of khans and restorer of the Mongol empire.

Over the next decade, Timur waged war on the khans of Jatah and Khorezm (Kwarizm), finally capturing Kashgar, the seat of the Jatah khans, in 1380. He next lent armed support to Toktamish (Tokhtamysh), the Mongol khan of the Crimea, who had been driven from his throne by Mamai, khan of the Golden Horde, then ruler of much of modern Russia. Timur's troops defeated Mamai and replaced him as khan of the Golden Horde with Toktamish. Timur's army occupied Moscow in 1382 to punish its prince's defeat of Mamai in 1380; Timur's army also defeated a Lithuanian army near Poltava.

Conquests in the Middle East, Russia, and India (1381–99)

As the intervention in Russia ended, Timur began the conquest of Persia, a task made easier by the chaos in the country after the fall of the Il-khan dynasty in 1335. The rival successor-princes were unable to create a united front against

927

Timur. In 1381, he captured Herat, and by 1385 had overrun all of eastern Persia. Timur conquered western Persia, Azerbaijan, and Armenia in a series of campaigns in 1386–87.

His campaigns in Persia were interrupted by conflict with his erstwhile ally, Toktamish, who invaded Azerbaijan in 1385, defeating Timur's generals. Toktamish invaded Transoxania in 1388 but withdrew as Timur marched north from Persia. When Toktamish returned that winter, Timur decisively defeated him at the Battle of the Syr-Darya in early 1389. Timur then took the war to Toktamish's country, and in 1390–91 personally led an army into Russia, defeating Toktamish at the three-day Battle of Kandurcha (the Battle of the Steppes) in early 1391.

Timur returned to Persia to suppress a revolt by Shah Mansur, whom he defeated at the Battle of Shiraz in 1392. Timur then completed the conquest of western Persia, Armenia, and Azerbaijan in 1393–94. He also invaded Mesopotamia and captured Baghdad in 1393, and the next year subjugated Georgia. Meanwhile, Toktamish raised another army and again invaded the Caucasus, but Timur drove him out. Timur pursued him into Russia, sacking Astrakhan and Sarai (seat of the khans of the Golden Horde) and ruthlessly ravaging the countryside. His armies again occupied Moscow in 1395–96, but the outbreak of widespread revolts in Persia compelled him to return there. These revolts were suppressed with great cruelty: many cities were destroyed, and their populations massacred wholesale.

Having put down the Persian revolts, Timur mounted an invasion of India in 1398, on the pretext that the sultans of Delhi were showing too much tolerance to their Hindu subjects. He crossed the Indus River in late September and advanced on Delhi, carving a swathe of destruction along his route. He smashed Sultan Mahmud Tughluq's army at Panipat on 17 December, and afterward sacked Delhi, leaving it so ruined it did not recover for a century. By April 1399, he was back in his capital of Samarkand with huge quantities of plunder. To celebrate his triumph, he began the construction of a great mosque.

Final Campaigns: Mamelukes and Ottomans (1400–1405)

Angered by the seizure of border territories by the Mameluke sultan of Egypt and by the Ottoman sultan Bayazid I, Timur, now in his mid-sixties, prepared a great expedition against both of them. He recovered Azerbaijan and then invaded Syria. He defeated the Mameluke army near Aleppo on 30 October 1400 before storming and sacking both Aleppo and Damascus; he deported Damascus's artisans to beautify Samarkand. In 1401, he captured Baghdad, slaughtering 20,000 of its citizens and destroying its great buildings and monuments. He wintered in Georgia and then turned his efforts against Bayazid, the Ottoman monarch. Timur led his army into Anatolia, and at the Battle of Ankara on 20 July 1402 virtually destroyed the Ottoman army.

To further cement his success in the area, Timur captured Smyrna from the Knights of Rhodes, and received tribute from John VII (co-emperor of the

Byzantine Empire with Manuel II Palaeologus) and the sultan of Egypt early in 1403. He returned to Samarkand in 1404, where he began preparations for a great expedition against China. He set out in late December 1404, but fell ill at Otrar on the Syr-Darya, west of Chimkemt. He died there on 19 February 1405.

Timur's body was embalmed and taken to Samarkand in an ebony casket. He was interred in a magnificent tomb, the Gur-e-Amir. His will provided for his realm to be apportioned among his two surviving sons and his grandsons, but the settlement did not endure long. Around 1420, after years of bitter fighting, his younger son, Shahrukh (Shah Rokh), reestablished central control over much of his father's realm.

Assessment

Timur was the greatest Asian conqueror since Genghis Khan, but he was not a state builder. His conquests are notable not only for their military achievement but also for the apocalyptic ruin brought on the subjugated lands; stories of skulls heaped in great piles after a city was taken are common in the chronicles. Most of the vast riches he extracted from the conquered lands went to enrich and beautify Samarkand. Timur's historical legacy is significant, for among his numerous descendants is Babur, the founder of the Moghul dynasty of India.

DAVID L. BONGARD
TREVOR N. DUPUY

SEE ALSO: Genghis Khan; Moghul Empire; Mongol Conquests; Ottoman Empire.

Bibliography

Du Bec-Crespin, J. [1597] 1968. *The historie of the great Emperour Tamerlan.* Reprint. New York: Da Capo Press.
Gonzalez de Clavijo, R. [1859] 1970. *Narrative of the embassy of Ruy Gonzalez de Clavijo to the court of Timour at Samercand, A.D. 1403–6.* Trans. C. R. Markham. Reprint. New York: B. Franklin. Works issued by the Hakluyt Society, no. 26.
Ibn Arabshah, Ahmad ibn Muhammad. [1936] 1976. *Tamerlane: or, Timur, the great amir.* Trans. J. H. Sanders. Reprint. Lahore: Progressive Books.
Manz, B. F. 1989. *The rise and rule of Tamerlane.* New York: Cambridge Univ. Press.
Timur. [1783] 1972. *Political and military institutions of Tamerlane, recorded by Sharfuddin Ali Vezdi.* Reprint. Delhi: Idarah-i Adabiyat-i Delli.
Tovma Metsobetsi, V. 1987. *Tovma Metsobetsi's history of Tamerlane and his successors.* Trans. R. Bedrosian. New York: Sources of the Armenian Tradition.
Ure, J. 1980. *The trail of Tamerlane.* London: Constable.

TECHNOLOGY AND THE MILITARY

For all of history man has been exploring more effective ways to wage war. Much progress in science and technology has been inextricably linked to the needs of warfare. Science can offer more efficient ways to kill, better protection from an enemy, easier manufacturing processes for weapons, faster delivery systems, greater control of battles, and the myriad enhancements that make the difference between victory and defeat. Today technology is advancing so rapidly that the military implications are profound. As new capabilities are researched, countermeasures must also be developed. The costs of these innovations may become prohibitive, and new weapons may lead to less stability rather than more. The speed of progress is such that weapons are often obsolete by the time they are deployed.

Past Trends

Some technologies have led to fundamental changes in the conduct of war; others, despite their seeming promise, have not. At sea the development of steam power made sail obsolete for warships. When the attacker could ignore the vagaries of the wind, attack from any direction, and control his speed, he had a war-winning advantage. This was bought at the price of a new requirement for fuel, and hence for logistic support in the form of coaling stations. Similarly, on land, the advent of the steam railway and then of the internal combustion engine brought new and war-winning mobility to armies and their logistic supply lines. The advent of aircraft took this mobility into another dimension and again changed the nature of warfare. Technology gave military forces greater speed and range and the ability to exploit the sea—and under the sea—the land, the air, and eventually beyond the atmosphere into space.

While mobility has been a key factor in the changing nature of warfare, killing power has also been technology-dependent. From sword through longbow, musket, rifle, machine gun, howitzer, and bomber to the intercontinental nuclear ballistic missile, we can trace the increasing range and power of weapons. Technology has provided more effectiveness through chemical explosives and propellants, greater accuracy of delivery, munitions tailored to achieve specific effects, and the release of nuclear energy in both the atomic and the thermonuclear bomb.

If technology has been active in developing the sword and its many successors, it has also played a vital role in the development of the shield. As science has offered new offensive capabilities, it has also sought appropriate defensive countermeasures. The mobility and firepower of warships led to the development of heavier armor plate and bigger ships with more defenses, and then to the aircraft carrier. When the surface of the oceans was becoming inhospitable, the submarine used the cover of the seas to operate undetected. When the freedom of the air put land and sea forces at risk, radar provided the basis for an effective defense system.

With military technological development came an increase in the size of the battlefield. In the days of cavalry, control could be maintained by line-of-sight from a piece of high ground. While entire countries might be at war, the fighting took place in geographically limited areas. The use of airships and aircraft took war deep into rear areas and to the homelands of the protagonists. The advent of radio allowed control to be exercised over vast battles. The missile, the nuclear warhead, and satellite communications have made the entire world the potential battlefield.

Technology has also altered the classic "great powers" structure of international relations. While developments up to the end of World War II reinforced the power of the economic giants, technological innovations since have changed this. The power of nuclear weapons has made war between the major nations much less likely; at the same time, lesser nations have acquired the technological capability to wage more destructive war.

Finally, the economic aspects of technology must not be overlooked. The caveman's club was free and replacements were readily available. The new Stealth B2 aircraft was rolled out of the hangar in 1988 at a unit price of US$512 million. Between these extremes we have seen a complex relationship develop between capability and cost. While technology can offer improvements in military power, its costs may mean that fewer weapon systems can be bought and thus overall effectiveness may be reduced. Even when the net effectiveness is greater, dependence on a reduced number of systems may bring new vulnerabilities due to lack of redundancy and flexibility.

Military Technology

As we have seen from the historical overview, technology is the exploitation of science to improve military capability, be it offensive, defensive, or in support. The science of chemistry has been exploited in explosives, propellants, and chemical weapons. Physics has given more reliable and more accurate guns, nuclear weapons, jet engines, radar, and directed-energy weapons. Mathematics has provided ballistic tables, codes, and computer programs. Biology has provided both killing agents and life-saving drugs for battle casualties. Virtually every aspect of science has contributed in some way to military technology, and the pressure for new weapons has conversely contributed to the progress of science.

Looking to the future, we can anticipate similar patterns of activity. Each scientific discovery will be examined for a military implication. Does research into the spread and cure for the AIDS virus have biological-warfare applications? Does the development of parallel-processing three-dimensional computer chips have relevance to signal processors for electronic countermeasures? Does civil research into new and more efficient batteries have an application for submarine power sources? Scientific research is by its nature unpredictable and disparate. Pure research leads into unknown territory, and applications may be many years away. The theory of nuclear fission was well understood in the 1930s, but it took a monumental project to turn the theory into the first atomic bomb. Research is also conducted for specific commercial or domestic projects, and again the military applications may follow. The development of radio and television was spurred by civil applications but has had a profound effect on the conduct of war. The development of aircraft between the two world wars depended almost entirely on commercial concerns. The new materials being produced by new manufacturing processes today may have as great an influence on the conduct of war as the introduction of mass production had on the conduct of World War I.

Pure scientific research and commercial industrial research are inevitably a hit-or-miss method of military technology development. Defense research and development has become a major activity in the postwar era. The development of directed-energy weapons, chemical weapons, strategic defenses, fuel-air explosives, and many other military innovations must rely on specialized scientific work.

The key problem for technology and future military systems is the enormous choice available to nations and their potential enemies. No power can afford to follow every avenue for development, and once a new weapon system is produced, further decisions follow about numbers to be procured. When defense must operate within a finite budget, choices for investment must be made among research, development, procurement of new systems, training, force levels, and readiness. Every nation faces these choices, and the decisions will be based on political and economic factors as much as on military factors. Thus, while it is possible to speculate on the possibilities that science can offer the military in new technology, not all will come to fruition, and some that are developed may prove unaffordable as deployed weapon systems.

The technological search for longer range and greater power seems to have reached a plateau. The nuclear-tipped missile can deliver more firepower than any target requires to any point on earth, and there is no reliable defense in prospect. While nuclear deterrence has a unique place in military theory, the very power of nuclear weapons makes the search for a defense a continuing concern. The Strategic Defense Initiative was an indication of the resources one nation was prepared to allocate to counter nuclear vulnerability. The technologies involved are high risk and complex and cannot be tested convincingly before war. The costs are enormous and the countermeasures, it appears, relatively cheaper. The fear of nuclear weapons will ensure, however, that those nations that can afford to will seek ways to reduce vulnerability. In defense terms this is likely to mean research into terminal antiballistic missile systems, improved air defenses against cruise missiles and bombers, and research into directed-energy weapons. To counter such defenses, nuclear nations try to develop improved command and control systems for their nuclear assets, faster booster rockets, antisatellite weapons, and, if necessary, more warheads. Ensuring that each new measure is met by an effective countermeasure will require significant and continuing investment.

Nuclear Weapons Technology

Nuclear weapons can be developed to produce specific effects. Characteristics can be changed by exploding the weapon so that the fireball touches the ground, and some marginal enhancements are possible in the proportions of energy converted into heat, blast, and radiation. Third-generation nuclear weapons will offer a greater selection of effects. A weapon with a concentric cylinder blast effect might be more effective against missile silos. A weapon might be designed to produce the majority of its energy in the form of electromagnetic pulse designed to destroy the enemy's command and control systems. Such developments are possible but, given the political sensitivity to nuclear weapon design, little may be invested in this area of research.

In one area of the nuclear armory, however, there will be continuing interest. Deterrence rests ultimately on an assured retaliatory capability, which in turn has rested for twenty years on the invulnerability of the nuclear submarine. The continuance of this invulnerability plays a crucial role in assuring deterrence; research will therefore center on detection and destruction of strategic submarines and on the necessary countermeasures. A number of different technologies will be involved, such as using space-based laser systems to penetrate the ocean, developing biosensors to "sniff" the molecules released by a submarine, and seeking even more sensitive heat, magnetic, and gravitational detectors. All these will have roles to play in both offense and defense.

We must not ignore the potential of technology to provide easier methods of production for nuclear weapons. The relative success to date of the Non-Proliferation Treaty is at least to some extent due to the difficulties in processing and manufacturing these weapons. Laser fusion and separation techniques may make it much easier in the future to produce nuclear weapons, and the expanding civil use of satellites will make missile technology more available. Thus, technology may make the spread of nuclear capability, which has been forecast for many years, much more likely in the near future.

Nonnuclear Weapons Technology

Nonnuclear sciences also have much to offer the military. Wars will be fought on land, on and under the sea, in the air, and beyond the atmosphere. Commanders will need information about enemy dispositions and intentions, weapons to destroy enemy capabilities, and defenses to prevent the enemy from retaliating. A review of some of the main science research topics will give a feel for their potential military applications.

BIOTECHNOLOGY

In perceptions of weapon power, biological, toxin, and chemical warfare are often seen as only marginally less destructive than nuclear weapons. The use of such agents to date does not support the view of them as methods of mass destruction, but this may not be the case in the future. Civil research in biotechnology is progressing rapidly, and genetic engineering offers the prospect of tailoring agents to provide specific effects. While previous research centered on improving storage and handling characteristics of chemical agents, it will become possible to design substances that can penetrate protective clothing, fool detection systems, have accurately predictable persistence, and even be selective in target population. Civil biotechnology techniques will make these agents available to many more nations than other high-technology weapon systems. While arms-control negotiations may offer hope, the necessary level of verification seems at present impossible to achieve. It may be that this area of warfare is the one that holds the greatest potential danger. Research must continue into detection systems, protection, and antidotes. It seems likely that the advantage will be with the attacker in the future, and that the attacker could be a relatively unsophisticated enemy or terrorist group.

PHYSICS

Advances in physics will cause the most significant changes in the effectiveness of traditional war-fighting systems. Electronics has become the key to all aspects of future weapons. The delivery system—be it aircraft, ship, gun, missile, or tank—is positioned accurately, the warhead targeted precisely, the trajectory adjusted continually, and the attack coordinated, all though electronic command and control arrangements. Each warhead can carry its own "brain" to identify targets and ensure maximum effectiveness. The commander can survey the battlefield electronically and control his forces instantaneously.

The importance of this aspect of future wars has raised the science of developing countermeasures to a prime position. While nuclear weapons can destroy electronics through electromagnetic pulse (EMP), research will look for other nonnuclear methods to achieve the effect. While phased-array air defense radars become ever more discriminating, stealth, jammers, and countermeasures will make aircraft more difficult to detect by radar.

Identification of enemy targets remains a matter of great concern. Increases in computing power, new sensors, and better data fusion all offer the prospect for more reliable positive identification systems. The thermionic valve gave way to the transistor, which in turn has been replaced by ever more densely packed integrated circuits. The limits of component density have not yet been reached, and photonic computers offer the prospect for yet more powerful and smaller computers for weapon systems of the future. Electronics are also vital in communications, and the use of satellite relays, with aircraft backup, make the possibility of real-time exchange of information between a commander and his forces realizable.

If physics has had an influence on the development of existing weapon systems, it has also pointed the way toward new forms of weapons. The laser was originally an interesting demonstration of the discrete energy states in matter. Development of ever more powerful lasers has led to a number of current and potential technology applications. The use of directed energy from lasers, particle beams, and radio frequency sources has opened the prospect of a new class of weapons, directed energy weapons (DEW). While the death ray of science fiction seems initially exciting, these new weapons have limitations as well as advantages. A speed of delivery almost the speed of light simplifies aiming and gives more engagement time. The range of DEW is limited in the atmosphere by obscuration and field strength for lasers, and the earth's magnetic field for charged-particle beams. All such weapons suffer from dispersion problems, and countermeasures are available. While the projectile is virtually massless, such weapons still require fuel to power them. Directed energy weapons provide an excellent example of the problems of assessing the utility of particular technologies for future weapons. They offer novel capabilities, but at a high research and development cost, with the possibility that countermeasures may be cheaper to develop. The same money invested in more traditional weapons might produce more fighting power.

SPACE TECHNOLOGY

The dilemma of the allocation of assets is nowhere greater than in space technology. For the more than three decades that man has been able to place objects in orbit around the earth, the costs and risks have remained high. The rewards have also been significant. Worldwide communication, navigation, and reconnaissance have become possible through satellites. Some view space as the new high ground and believe that domination of space therefore is the key to security. Experience so far leaves this view arguable. Satellites, particularly in low orbit, are vulnerable to attack. Costs of raising heavy payloads into orbit make the basing of weapons in space an expensive activity. Despite the vast investment in research, the goal of a space-based defense system to counter a ballistic missile attack appears impossible if 100 percent success is required. The research has, however, produced technologies for other weapon systems: directed energy, hypervelocity guns, and antisatellite weapons (ASAT). It is this last class that offers perhaps the greatest threat to an advanced enemy who has become overdependent on the use of satellites.

MATERIALS SCIENCE

Materials technology has had much to offer in space and to weapon development on earth. New materials offer the prospect of lighter yet stronger platforms, materials that absorb rather than reflect incident radiation, easier and cheaper manufacturing techniques, or new and exciting properties (such as the recent production of high-temperature superconductors). Applications for these new materials may be in the field of electronic propulsion for vehicles, in the realm of superfast computers, or in new sensors.

Future Research and Development Strategy

Many areas of scientific research have great potential for military applications. Strategy for future research and development must weigh the balance of investment cost and true effectiveness. At sea, on land, and in the air and space, technology poses problems for the military: Will the submarine remain virtually undetectable? Will the helicopter replace the tank in future land battles? Can airfields be defended, or must future aircraft have vertical take-off and landing capability? Should increasing reliance be placed on satellites, or would ASAT weapons pay greater dividends? To what extent can artificial intelligence replace the human in the weapon system? Will the next generation of chemical weapons be potentially more devastating than nuclear weapons?

History provides many examples of the critical role that technology has played in military capability, but there are many other examples of technical breakthroughs that proved too expensive, ineffective, or impossible to develop. For example, the promise of atomic power did not lead to workable atomic aircraft. The development of modern jet aircraft was a story with many successes, but much money was spent on designs (such as the ill-fated British TSR2) that were never to provide any defense capability. The United States canceled a project for high-technology air defense guns late in development because of cost, lack of reliability, and inability to carry out the task.

Even when technology provides a new defense capability, it may be years before it is tested in combat, and it may then be found wanting. The shooting down of a civil airliner in the Persian Gulf by the U.S.S. *Vincennes* in 1988 caused many to question the adequacy of the most modern radar and command system in the world if it remained possible to mistake a nonmilitary aircraft for a hostile fighter. The revelations in the aftermath of the U.S. space shuttle disaster showed the dependence of high technology on the reliability of a multitude of subsystems.

What, then, should be our strategy for research and development? Nations must prepare for the developing capabilities of their potential enemies, but the research that they undertake on new weapon systems may not increase security. A new weapon system may be technically flawed; it may work perfectly, but be flawed in concept; in either case, the resources spent could have produced more effective defense if invested elsewhere. An increasing dependence on a highly capable technical device makes for greater vulnerability to effective countermeasures. Nations need a way to decide which technologies can best improve future security. Each nation has different security concerns, resource constraints, scientific bases, and industrial capabilities. Nevertheless, some generalizations from the past indicate possible approaches for the future.

ACADEMIC SCIENTIFIC RESEARCH

Pure scientific research is a key to both commercial and military technology. In many cases, interesting scientific discoveries are turned into commercial products, which in turn lead to military capabilities. (The laser is a recent example.) Without pure, nonapplied research, radical innovation is unlikely. A breakthrough in pure research areas in general requires free interchange of information between academic institutions, and academic research thrives on debate and criticism. Such open discussion and publication often, however, seem to work against their use in military applications.

DEFENSE-RELATED RESEARCH

Whatever the source of funds, the potential military applications of new discoveries must be a key interest of the defense establishment. It is necessary to have expert opinion available that can spot potential applications at an early stage. Such groups exist in military research establishments, but may have a narrow view of future military requirements. It is desirable to harness the imagination of the scientist-engineer in the service of national defense needs. Ideally, defense policymakers should have a good scientific background; in practice few, whether political, military, or government officials, are likely to be so qualified. While scientific specialists can be engaged, they will be likely to respond to the direction given by the nonspecialist leaders. Defense industries and the government should seek to fund university departments where research may have benefit for weapon technology, yet where researchers would be given freedom to choose their own avenues of research.

RESEARCH AND DEVELOPMENT COSTS

A different approach to the problem of increasing costs for new technologies is to accept second place in the race for innovation. This option will not appeal to defense industries or the military, but it has a number of advantages for both. The key concern for the future is the increasing costs of weapon systems, given the finite resources available. In some cases, the advantages of reliable mature technologies at lower cost may outweigh the promise of new, expensive, and unproven systems.

If all nations adopted such a wait and see approach, then new weapons would not be developed. Unlikely as this may seem now, it may become increasingly the pattern in the future as cost and resource constraints affect even the superpowers. It may be that the current flurry of activity in arms control is the first indication of such a new approach. If the current optimism on arms reductions is carried through to significant decreases in levels of armament, then there may be much less enthusiasm for new weapon technologies. (Alternatively, the focus may merely shift to noncontrolled types of armaments.) While such moves could improve stability between the superpowers, they would not affect the risks presented by modern weapons in the hands of less stable regimes. Indeed it is already clear that technology is offering considerable capabilities to those involved in low-intensity conflict around the world. It may be that the high-technology nations will need to direct more effort to prevention of the spread of the more damaging developments. Biotechnology is but one area where proliferation of production techniques for chemical, toxin, and biological agents could be very dangerous.

Technology and Education

A key to the effective application of science to the military is as broad an education as possible for all those involved in developing weapons. The scientist needs to be aware of what he is doing in the strategic context if he is to spot the innovations that are worth developing. The policymaker must be able to make intelligent judgments on the relative merits of different technologies, and for this needs both basic scientific and strategic grounding. The organization must be sufficiently responsive to correct its procurement strategy when circumstances change. Judging the balance of risk will never be easy, but the options must be continually reexamined.

The military man must remain responsive to new ideas, yet skeptical of "magic" forecasts. The decision maker must weigh costs against benefits and be prepared to review decisions in the light of developments. The effect of the introduction of new weapons on stability and opportunities for arms control must not be ignored. The changing nature of the threat will mean that high-cost weapons should be flexible in application as insurance against an uncertain future. Science and the military will continue to be necessary partners until conflict is no longer possible. Technology is, as it has always been, a two-edged sword.

TIMOTHY GARDEN

SEE ALSO: Technology and Warfare.

Bibliography

Barnaby, F. 1984. *Future war*. London: Joseph.
Bertram, C., ed. 1979. *New conventional weapons and East-West security*. London: Macmillan.
Brodie, B., and F. M. Brodie. 1973. *From crossbow to H-bomb*. Bloomington, Ind.: Indiana Univ. Press.
Dunnigan, J. F. 1982. *How to make war*. London: Arms and Armour.
ESECS. 1983. *Strengthening conventional deterrence*. London: Macmillan.
Garden, T. 1989. *The technology trap*. London: Brassey's.
Geissler, E., ed. 1986. *Biological and toxin weapons today*. Stockholm: SIPRI.
Graham, D. O. 1983. *The non-nuclear defense of cities*. Cambridge, Mass.: Abt.
Holley, I. B. 1953. *Ideas and weapons*. New Haven, Conn.: Yale Univ. Press.
Kirby, S., and G. Robson. 1987. *The militarisation of space*. Brighton: Wheatsheaf.
Mason, R. A., ed. 1986. *War in the third dimension*. London: Brassey's.
O'Neill, R., ed. 1985. *New technology and Western security policy*. IISS. Hamden, Conn.: Shoe String Press.
Prentis, S. 1985. *Biotechnology*. London: Orbis.
Wright, D. M., and L. J. Paszek. 1969. *Science, technology and warfare*. Colorado Springs, Colo.: U.S. Air Force Academy.

TECHNOLOGY AND WARFARE

Technology has played a major role in war since ancient times, changing the nature of warfare many times throughout history. Almost all technologies are used in war: weapons and other specific military equipment technologies, civilian technologies, and system technologies. These technologies have had a major impact on the way wars are fought, on force structure, and on doctrine and tactics. Beyond that, superiority in military technology has quite often led to political supremacy and domination, as in the case of European colonization.

On the other hand, war and the preparation for war in peacetime have had a pronounced impact on the advance of technology, in particular its rapid implementation under crisis conditions. There is thus a complex web of interactions between technology and the conduct of war.

Those interactions have become more intensive and rapid in the last 150 years, and even more so in the twentieth century, during which weapons innovation has become an organized and directed process. The process is based on many research and development (R&D) establishments all over the world, heavily supported by governments and industry. The purposeful, organized, and rapid military-technological innovative process of this century is quite different from that of previous periods in organization, methods, and the very close relations between the military and the scientific-industrial establishment.

Technological innovation is the prime engine of the technological arms race. This qualitative race, which may lead to radical changes in strategy, force structure, doctrine, and tactics, is now perhaps more important than the mere quantitative arms races of the past (and present). The potential of the military-technological innovative process to cause upheavals in existing military postures requires an understanding of the dynamics of this process and the roles of the various players.

Undoubtedly the future will bring more radical changes, such as the capacity for space war, an increasing threat to mobility arising from the diffusion of precision firepower, and others yet unknown.

Historical Perspective

Examples of the effect of technology on warfare include the use of stone weapons in prehistoric times; the invention of the wheel and war chariots; bronze and iron weapons; the longbow defeating armored, mounted medieval knights; artillery destroying feudal castles and extending war to rear areas; and the farther extension to the rear by aerial bombing and missiles in the twentieth century.

The character of the interaction between the evolution of technology and the evolution of society (including the evolution of warfare) has changed markedly through history. This changing interaction may be divided roughly into the following periods according to the pace and process of technological change:
1. until A.D. 1500, very slow random pace based mostly on accidental discoveries without any theoretical background
2. between 1500 and 1800, increasing pace, still based mostly on trial and error—very limited theoretical background
3. in the nineteenth century, rapid pace of change based more and more on increasing scientific and technological theory and infrastructure
4. in the twentieth century, worldwide organized and directed innovative processes based on formal R&D establishments using the most advanced knowledge base, its rapid pace due to heavy support by governments and industry.

The purposeful, organized, and rapid weapon innovation process of the twentieth century is quite different from that of previous periods. This article will therefore concentrate on the interactions between technology and warfare in our era, including future trends.

Overall Relations Between Technology and War

There are three types of technologies used in war:
1. military technologies connected specifically with military artifacts
2. civilian technologies (e.g., transportation, communications, and medical) that are important in war
3. system technologies applied to the preparation for and conduct of war.

All influence and are influenced by war.

INFLUENCE OF WAR ON THE EVOLUTION OF TECHNOLOGY

The influence of war on the evolution of technology has been important in long wars that last for years and involve many campaigns (e.g., World War I and World War II). During a long war the development of military equipment is accelerated, although it may take years for development to be completed and for the resultant equipment to arrive on the battlefield in meaningful quantities. Also, such development is nearly always derived from basic scientific and technological work, often done many years before the war. The case of radar, which played a major role in the battle of Britain in 1940, is typical. The first observations of radio reflection from aircraft were made at His Majesty's Signal School in 1923. Similar observations were made by the British Post Office in 1931. The British decision to proceed with full-scale development and construction of a net of radar stations to protect southeast England was made in 1935, only after the danger from a rearming Germany became clear.

New weapons that entered service in World War II, such as radar, proximity fuzes, jet aircraft, and missiles were based on technologies developed in the 1920s and 1930s. Some, like radar, had a major impact. Others, such as the German jet fighters, which entered service in small quantity in 1944, had a negligible influence in that war. Note that in the case of the German jet fighters, the decision to mount a large-scale effort was not made until after the beginning of the war. Thus even a long war is, in most cases, not long enough for a completely new technological development to achieve a considerable impact on the battlefield.

One famous exception was the atomic bomb. A large number of technologies were developed from scratch in the course of the project. The success of this exception was made possible by the expenditure of tremendous resources, by using many parallel approaches to ensure success, and by the extremely low number of weapons required to produce a decisive impact on the outcome of the war.

INFLUENCE OF MILITARY DEVELOPMENT IN PEACETIME ON THE EVOLUTION OF TECHNOLOGY

Arms races have been commonplace in human experience for a long time. Since the industrial revolution, the qualitative, technological component of these races has increased steadily. Following World War II, the official doctrine of the West was to counter Soviet quantitative superiority with qualitative, technological superiority. The East, while not forsaking quantity, also joined this intensive technological arms race, which became a prominent feature of international relations in the late 1900s. This competition has been a prominent factor in the rapid evolution of many post–World War II technologies such as solid state electronics, jet transports, nuclear power stations, and satellites.

Is military development necessary for the evolution of technology and economic growth? Definitely not, as can be observed from the highly successful post–World War II economic development of the Federal Republic of Germany and Japan. Those countries, which were not allowed to build military equipment after that war, channeled all their resources, as well as very substantial resources provided by their recent conquerors, toward the achievement of their remarkable economic success. Thus, economic growth and the advance of technology may be facilitated in various ways.

INFLUENCE OF SHORT RECURRENT WARS ON THE EVOLUTION OF TECHNOLOGY

The Arab-Israeli conflict provides a good example of the impact of short recurrent wars. Israel, faced with a huge numerical disadvantage, had to choose quality and build a large scientific and industrial defense establishment to achieve a qualitative technological edge on the battlefield. That was made possible by the high quality of its manpower, both in the laboratories and on the battlefield, along with massive financial and technological assistance from governmental and private sources in Western countries. Recurrent wars every decade led to the rapid evolution of new, sometimes innovative, weapon systems and their first use in combat. The 1982 Lebanon War furnished quite a few examples, including surveillance by remotely piloted vehicles (RPVs) and reactive armor for tanks. Note, however, that almost no basic advances in military technology were made by Israel. The outcome of the pressures of short recurrent wars is in this respect quite similar to the case of a long war. Building on basic scientific and technological advances made before the war (in the case of World War II and the Vietnam War) or elsewhere (in the Israeli case), the pressing need leads to accelerated development and fielding of military equipment.

INFLUENCE OF TECHNOLOGICAL SURPRISE ON WAR

The influence of technology on the nature of warfare and on history was discussed briefly in the beginning of this article. Here the issue is: Can a technological advantage, cloaked in secrecy and applied by surprise, decide the results of a war? Again, it is necessary to differentiate between long wars and short wars. In a long war, with many campaigns over a large territory or even worldwide (e.g., World War II), one campaign is usually not decisive. Thus, the highly successful Japanese surprise at Pearl Harbor could not decide the outcome of World War II in the Pacific. On the other hand, in a geographically limited war, where a single campaign can be decisive, surprise by technological or other means (e.g., strategic or tactical) may determine the outcome. The almost total destruction of Arab air forces on the ground by the Israeli air force surprise attack at the very beginning of the 1967 war, for example, sealed the outcome of that war.

In order to achieve not just surprise but decisive advantage, by means of a secret technological advantage, it must be combined in sufficient quantity with other necessary equipment, force structure, doctrine, tactics, and meticulous, flexible mission planning, as was the case in the destruction of the Syrian ground-to-air missile array in the Bekaa Valley during the 1982 Lebanon War. Otherwise, the results will be disappointing, as in the case of the surprise appearance of 49 tanks on the Somme battlefield in 1916. The tanks were mechanically unreliable, and only nine returned from the battle under their own power. There was also practically no comprehension of suitable doctrine and tactics for their use in battle. As a result, their impact on that battle was negligible.

Technological-Military Innovation Process

Technological-military innovation involves two types of players acting in a two-sided environment, the military establishment and the relevant industrial-scientific establishment. The environment in which they operate includes the political and economic climate of a country and those of its adversaries. This discussion will first concentrate on the process itself and the role of the two players; and then on the influence of the environment on the process.

WEAPON SYSTEMS DEVELOPMENT AND BATTLEFIELD SYSTEMS EVOLUTION

It is important to stress that the introduction of a weapon or weapon system embodying a new technology is not an end in itself. It must become a part of and contribute to the success of a larger battlefield system (BFS) that is composed of personnel and weapons of various types integrated by suitable structure, doctrine, and tactics (e.g., a combined arms team or an air defense system). In many cases, an improved weapon can be accommodated within an existing, unchanged battlefield system (as when a larger diameter tank gun is retrofitted). In many cases, however, a substantial change in fighting capabilities requires substantial battlefield system innovation, not just weapon innovation.

Weapon innovation differs from BFS innovation in the process of its evolution and in the locus of innovation. The evolution of a weapon or a weapon system occurs through successive generations. A weapon system has a finite life, during which it may be improved by various modifications. At some point, however, it inevitably becomes obsolete and is replaced in toto by a new-generation system. A BFS, on the other hand, is not built in one piece. It evolves gradually, mostly through incremental changes in equipment, personnel, structure, doctrine, and tactics.

As for the locus of innovation, radical weapon innovation is usually driven by technology push, led by the scientific-industrial establishment, often without an understanding of battlefield realities. Improvements in existing weapons, by contrast, are triggered most often by military need and usually follow the path of normal evolution.

BFS innovation, stimulated by new technology or other factors, is properly in the province of the military. But since such innovation is often disruptive and threatening to established military institutions, military personnel often have no incentive to advance it.

Successful technologically based military innovation requires the proper meshing of weapon and weapon system development with BFS evolution, a meshing of two different processes with two very different players.

BFS Evolution

Problem of feedback. Evolution requires feedback on systems operations in the real world. Without such feedback, natural selection, the survival of the systems best suited for real-world conditions, cannot function properly. For most military systems, real feedback is not available in peacetime, despite all the simulations, field exercises, and other substitutes for combat used by military organizations. Hence, equipment selection in peacetime is often shaped by other forces. Political, bureaucratic, industrial, and scientific pressures, which often determine the selection of weapons in peacetime, by no means lead to survival of the weapons best suited for wartime. A case in point was the resistance of most air forces and some industries to the widespread application of unmanned aerial vehicles (UAVs).

Normal and radical evolution. Complex systems evolve in various ways, ranging from normal to radical. Normal evolution proceeds within the existing framework and results in incremental change. Radical evolution involves, in the long run, far-reaching changes resulting in a basically different system. In both cases the process of change is slow and gradual, but the outcomes are very different.

Normal evolution leads to improved performance of an existing BFS within the currently perceived battlefield scenario. Such a course may result in defeat when the battlefield scenario undergoes substantial changes. Radical evolution may lead, if successful, to large and qualitative expansion of present capabilities, including completely new capabilities within a new environment (an example is SDI, the Strategic Defense Initiative).

The opportunity for radical change is often opened by a new technology, as night vision technology opened up the possibility of 24-hour-a-day battles. Obviously, the realization of such a possibility requires a great deal more than technology alone.

BFS evolution paths. The evolution of BFS may proceed via several paths:
1. improving present system performance, which is the fastest process
2. introducing new operating methods without change in equipment
3. introduction of new equipment without structural change, a hardware change, a common path for the introduction of new technology
4. system restructuring, including further changes in equipment—a very slow process
5. radical structural change without change in equipment, usually a response to crisis conditions
6. combined radical change, involving radical hardware and software changes (this path is rare).

Normal evolution follows paths 1–4. Radical evolution proceeds via paths 5 and 6. New technology is involved in paths 3, 4, and 6.

Succeeding generations of a new technology may enter into weapon systems and BFS along different paths. First of all, the new technology is usually introduced in an independent item of equipment (e.g., night vision goggles). Later generations will find their way into complex battlefield systems, at first within the existing structure (following the path of least resistance and of higher incentives to both producers and users). Only much later will the "new" (by now old) technology be combined with system restructuring. This multistage process, wherein force structure and tactics are adapted to make full use of the new technology, is slow and expensive, and involves a long delay in the application of new technology to the battlefield. Also, without real feedback in peacetime, it does not always result in an effective new system.

Combined radical change is risky and rare. It involves larger technological and tactical uncertainties than those present in normal evolution. More important, it faces organizational resistance embodied in the present force structure and sometimes in the political system. Nevertheless, there have been some very successful changes of this type.

The introduction of the tank offers an excellent example of the different evolution paths that may be followed for the same weapon system by different countries during the same time period. Before World War II, Guderian in Germany combined the emerged technologies of his time—tanks, radio communication, and dive bombers—into a new force structure and tactics to create the blitzkrieg innovation. The British and the French, on the other hand, although they had more tanks than the Germans, dispersed them as supporting weapons in their infantry divisions. This doctrinal choice was a major factor in their defeat in 1940.

Guderian did not invent the concept of the armored force. It had already been advocated by the British general Fuller in 1919. Small armored unit tactics were developed by the British in the 1920s. Guderian's success in the transition to the large-scale blitzkrieg concept was due to many factors, including: (1) the destruction of the old German army as a result of the Versailles peace treaty, and (2) an active search for a solution to the 1914–18 stalemate so that the offensive doctrine of Nazi Germany could be implemented.

Another example of successful radical evolution is the Israeli navy's missile boat system. This novel system was created in one direct leap. The vessel, the Gabriel sea-to-sea missile, and other equipment, doctrine, and tactics were all developed in parallel. The decision to implement this risky approach was sealed by the destruction of the old destroyer system (the sinking of the *Eilat* in 1967). This demonstrated how a high-risk situation can force radical combined change under difficult conditions.

THE INNOVATION PROCESS: PROPERTIES AND PROSPECTS

The present state of technological-military innovation in most advanced countries may be summarized as follows:

1. A large worldwide R&D establishment is advancing the scientific and technological base on a broad front, creating a large menu of opportunities for new weapons and weapon systems.
2. Normal evolution produces, through a slow and lengthy process, new and improved weapon systems every year. These systems enhance performance

within the present framework. Some are overtaken by the changing battle-field scenario and are never completed. This happened to the U.S. DIVAD (division air defense gun), which could not cope with an increasing helicopter threat.

3. The introduction and acceptance of radical innovations are rare and very slow. RPV technologies, for example, have been available for many years. Still, even after the successful application of RPVs by Israel in the 1982 Lebanon War, progress in adopting them in other countries has been slow.

Basic improvements in this process will probably require broadening and combining the weapon development process within the larger BFS evolution process. A great deal depends on the environment, which will be discussed later. Some possible changes in the process itself will be addressed now.

The proper meshing of equipment and BFS development depends on the opportunity or need for radical change. Where a new technology apparently offers such an opportunity, the new system concept should be explored in tactical experiments, even before the new equipment is built. Such experiments, leading to a decision to develop or reject a new tactical system concept, may often be performed with surrogate equipment. Using a manned aircraft as a surrogate for an RPV in a tactical experiment, for example, can yield valuable information on the preferred characteristics of the RPV system itself, as well as its relationship with other systems on the battlefield. Such experiments have been useful in the past, as when Guderian developed the blitzkrieg doctrine in field experiments using dummy tanks made of sheet iron set up on cars and trucks.

The first generation of a radically new system is almost never a dominant design, technically or operationally. It usually serves as an experimental generation, pointing the way to further evolution.

The split responsibility in most armies for training, combat development, requirements generation, and technical program management is not conducive to an overall system view or overall responsibility and accountability. It actually promotes normal, incremental, disjointed evolution. This problem is more serious in ground forces because of their complexity and diffused decision mechanisms.

The radical evolution of strategic forces after World War II, involving the development of completely new weapons, doctrine, and force structure, was accomplished by specific organizations designed to accomplish radical system change. Similar approaches may be necessary in the future to utilize technological opportunities for radical change.

Influence of the Environment

INTERNAL POLITICAL ENVIRONMENT

The political and economic environments of a country and its adversaries play a major role in the application of technology to military objectives. Political decision making is concerned not only with grand strategy, overall missions, and budget allocations, but also with such other considerations as general technological advance, economic growth, and employment. Investment in military technology is sometimes justified by projected spin-offs to the general economy. As mentioned before, direct investment in civilian R&D is probably a better way to promote economic growth not dependent on large military exports.

Policy makers, notably in the United States, are involved in detailed line-by-line management of the defense budget, often motivated by local considerations. Such scrutiny is not well suited to maintaining an overall system view. Economic considerations often push politicians to call for premature and even dangerous equipment standardization. In a world full of operational and technological risks, variety is often a very necessary insurance policy.

TECHNOLOGICAL ARMS RACE

The pace of military development and procurement is to a large extent determined by relationships with adversary countries. The technological arms race of the twentieth century has become more expensive every decade. Attempts to arrest the increasing cost of new weapon systems have been only marginally successful. The hopes for cheap, smart weapons in the future are also quite exaggerated, because military requirements are performance-oriented, not cost-oriented like many civilian products. Each generation of a specific military product is considerably different from the previous one. Therefore, unit cost increases as a result of increased product complexity and production diseconomies.

The technological arms race between the United States and the former Soviet Union has become, by and large, an economic contest. Many development and procurement decisions are heavily influenced by the relative economic costs of actions and counteractions. Forcing the adversary to spend much more than one's own nation is a valid and important objective and is sometimes unconnected with preparations for a real war.

The evermore expensive race cannot be arrested at the technical level and cannot be sustained economically at higher and higher levels, even by superpowers. It can be arrested only by reduction in political conflict and by arms control. In recent years, the economic imperative imposed by the rising costs of the race was one of the main factors that led to the end of the cold war and wholesale reductions in military forces.

Future Trends

SHORT AND LONG CYCLES IN THE LIFE OF WEAPON SYSTEMS

Before discussing possible future trends, it is useful to discuss a few characteristics of weapon systems' life cycles. Perhaps the best-known phenomenon is that of the continual contest between systems, countersystems (or countermeasures), counter-countermeasures, and so on. Over a certain period, a system is preponderant; later a countersystem is invented or improved, and the balance tilts in its favor for a while. In the meantime, the original system is improved, and the balance tilts back. This pendulum of dampened oscillations creates a balance zone between system and countersystem, with neither becoming absolutely dominant (Fig. 1a). The contest between tanks and antitank weapons, which has continued for more than half a century, is a good illustration of this oscillating balance. From time to time the lethality of antitank weapons is improved, giving them an advantage for a while, only to be countered by improved armor a few years later.

This common wisdom must be qualified by two important points. First, the contest between sophisticated weapon systems is often characterized by large oscillations and temporary absolute dominance of one side or the other. The contest for superiority between aircraft and air defense is illustrative. In the 1967 Arab-Israeli War, Israeli aircraft enjoyed almost absolute superiority. By 1973 the Arabs had deployed a massive air defense complex, enabling them to inflict heavy losses on the Israeli air force and reduce its effectiveness drastically. In the 1982 Lebanon War, the Israeli air force destroyed almost all Syrian air defense batteries in the Bekaa Valley without sustaining any losses (Fig. 1b). This trend in favor of the air arm was demonstrated vividly again, albeit under very special conditions, in the 1991 Gulf War. In the future, air defense may again gain the upper hand.

Second, these oscillations, with a period of five to ten years, describe only the short-term picture. Over a much longer period, half a century or more, we observe the decline of previously dominant systems and their replacement by completely different systems, which then play the major role. Battleships be-

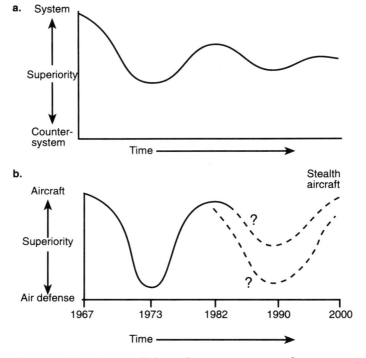

Figure 1. The changing balance between systems and counter-systems.

came dominant by the end of the nineteenth century, ruling the seas during World War I. By 1939, with the ascendance of aircraft and the deployment of aircraft carriers, battleships were already obsolete. For a time, this was hardly noticed. The truth was perceived suddenly in December 1941 when carrier-launched Japanese aircraft sank and damaged many American ships in Pearl Harbor and, shortly afterward, two major British ships off the coast of Malaya. Now, perhaps the day of aircraft carriers and other large ships is over. There have already been several ominous signs of the capabilities of antiship missiles: the sinking of the *Eilat* in 1967 by a Russian Styx sea-to-sea missile, the Falklands/Malvinas War, and the Persian Gulf confrontations between Iran and Iraq.

The long life-cycle waves are often obscured by short-period oscillations. While discussing future trends, it is difficult to discriminate between a down wave in a short-period oscillation and a permanent long-term decline. It is nevertheless necessary to try to point out cases where a long-wave decline may be approaching.

TRENDS IN COMBAT COMPONENTS

The first guided missiles were invented in Germany during World War II. Within a few years Germany had developed a wide variety, from small antitank guided missiles to large V-2 ballistic missiles. Since then the accuracy and lethality of precision firepower have improved steadily. Missiles are already dominant in naval and air warfare. On land, their progress has been much slower because of the inherent difficulties of the ground medium. Improving guidance methods, including automatic target acquisition, will solve problems of detection, discrimination, and target acquisition against the difficult land background. High-energy weapons may contribute to the direct-fire battle. But the greatest impact of precision firepower on land warfare may be in the extension of the current battle forward beyond the hill. Indirect precision fire can kill tanks out of sight, before they reach direct fire positions.

Successful, even if partial, bypassing of terrain line-of-sight restrictions can lead to radical change in land warfare. Such a change is dependent on timely, highly responsive surveillance and target acquisition. The combination of behind-the-hill surveillance, target acquisition, and lethal indirect fire, both day and night, is going to increase the scope of the current land battle in both space and time.

In general, the ascendancy of precision firepower calls into question the viability of the major mobile platforms: ships, aircraft, and tanks. The problem of large ships has already been discussed. Indeed, it is not necessary to sink a ship; simply causing enough damage to take it out of action for a long time (as happened with the USS *Stark* in the Persian Gulf) will suffice. Hence, the future may belong to small, fast boats and submarines.

As for aircraft, their survivability problem may be solved by stand-off weapons and, in the future, by massive and expensive transition to stealth aircraft (but the present estimated cost for one stealth bomber is US$450 million). Whether such solutions will be cost-effective and permit full air participation in the air-land battle remains to be seen.

The problem of mobility on the land battlefield is even more serious. In the future, the vulnerability of tanks is going to increase considerably. The advent of top attack weapons creates a very difficult problem. Weight limitations make it practically impossible to protect completely against such weapons by covering all the soft top of the tank with heavy armor. Thus, tanks will perhaps become almost as vulnerable as light armored vehicles. Mobility will be threatened also by attack on the soft belly of the tank by new, smart, rapidly dispersed mines. Some observers contend that we are approaching the final decline of the heavy battle tank as the major mobile platform on land. Many welcome this prospect, seeing it as leading to superiority of the defense. Others fear a return to the bloody stalemate of World War I.

Electronic and electro-optical countermeasures will blunt to some extent the impact of missiles and combat intelligence. Because of the variety of communication, guidance, and sensor types, methods, and wavelengths, however, their overall effect will be limited. They thus do not offer a panacea for the mobility problem. Communication jamming, when successful, will complicate the problems of mobile warfare even further, making coordination among moving troops more difficult.

After the turn of the century, mobile survivability on land will probably depend more on mobility and agility than on heavy armor. Those are much easier to achieve with light armor or helicopters. The helicopter's freedom from terrain constraints enables it to employ fast-moving concealment tactics better than any land vehicle. Such properties have moved some observers to claim that the helicopter is going to become the next major fighting platform in land warfare, but these ideas are immature and do not yet form a coherent, accepted concept anywhere. The point is that, in order to prevent a World War I–type stalemate, it is necessary to seek actively new, radical solutions to the land warfare survivable mobility problem. Such an active search is not evident in present land forces programs.

Another long-term solution to the land warfare mobility problem might be the use of robots or unmanned vehicles (UVs). Unmanned aerial vehicles (UAVs) already exist as stand-off weapons and RPVs. In all cases such vehicles must be survivable enough to perform their missions. Land UVs face the additional difficult problem of traveling over rough terrain and man-made barriers. Future land UVs might therefore be UAVs.

The application of computers improves the efficiency of many military tasks. Can they improve command and control effectiveness? It all depends on the way they are applied. One approach is to collect centrally more and more data from more and more sources about enemy and friendly dispositions. The data are fused, analyzed, and presented to the high-level decision makers. Orders and processed intelligence are then disseminated to the fighting units. Such tightly coupled, critical nodes, however, dependent on a supersystem, could easily collapse under the stress of war.

Effective command and control in the current battle requires that units be capable of dealing autonomously with most immediate contingencies affecting them. This calls for local self-contained BFSs loosely connected to higher levels. In computer language, it is the personal computer against the mainframe. The technology is already available to build almost any system desired. Specifications should evolve from the perceived logic of the battlefield, verified by early tactical experiments, and not from notions taken from the way banks control their branches.

TECHNOLOGY AND HUMAN PERFORMANCE

The increasing complexity of military equipment has often raised the question of whether it can be used effectively by regular troops. It is necessary to differentiate between single-purpose weapons and multipurpose weapon systems. The first, even if complex internally, can be used very effectively by technically untrained fighters, as was the Stinger portable surface-to-air missile in the hands of the Afghan guerrillas.

On the other hand, multipurpose systems possess high external complexity in that they may be used in many different battlefield scenarios and situations. The effective application of such systems requires much more sophistication. Understanding how the system works, how its parts interact, and what its real capabilities are under various conditions is necessary for achieving the full performance spectrum of the system. In these systems, such as aircraft, high-caliber personnel and long training are essential.

As external complexity increases, however (for example, when the amount of information from various sources that must be processed rapidly by the operator or pilot increases), even highly skilled personnel may be overwhelmed. Computerized decision aids and synthetic displays are used to alleviate this problem. Heads-up displays in high-performance aircraft and other complex situation displays are examples. In the future, better displays and computerized expert systems that mimic the human expert, such as the so-called pilot's associate, may be of further help.

A note of caution is necessary. Such aids to the human operator are based on complex computer programs that cannot be tested completely and always retain some hidden errors. Moreover, preprogrammed decision laws and synthetic displays, by their very nature, ignore and suppress some information. In certain unanticipated and undesigned-for situations, the lack of this very information or the sudden appearance of a hidden error could cause catastrophic results. The shooting down of an Iranian civil airliner by a U.S. warship over the Persian Gulf is a vivid example of this danger.

Such caveats are even more relevant in the case of very complex systems that must operate very rapidly under extreme conditions, perhaps in a fully automatic mode (such as antiballistic missile defense systems).

TRENDS IN COMBAT DIMENSIONS

The scope, intensity, and pace of combat will increase with improved operational capabilities in the following dimensions:

1. The deep three-dimensional battlefield. Long-range surveillance and precision firepower, and airborne VTOL (vertical takeoff and landing) mobility result in a far deeper battlefield. Missiles will also be used against civilian populations in rear areas, as was done in the war of the cities in the Iran-Iraq War.

2. The 24-hour battle. The availability of continually improving night vision sensors suggests the possibility of a round-the-clock battle. It is quite difficult to implement, but if successful would confer considerable advantage on the battlefield.

The optimal use of space and time is not achieved by spreading resources evenly over all ranges and hours. The debate within the North Atlantic Treaty Organization (NATO) about the meaning and preferred ranges for follow-on forces attack illustrates the necessity of choice.

SPACE WAR

The discussion to this point has dealt mostly with conventional warfare. A few comments will now be made about other types of war. The use of space for peaceful and military applications began in 1958 with the Soviet Sputnik, the first satellite. Since then the use of space for communications and intelligence gathering has become widespread and highly important. In the last few years the proposed SDI has focused attention on other major military missions that can perhaps be implemented in space.

Space is the only major new niche introduced since the invention of aircraft at the beginning of the century. Meaningful utilization of such a new niche would require a tremendous initial investment, dwarfing the Manhattan and Apollo projects. Also, no defense establishment can abandon old niches simply because a new one appears. Thus the growth of the space niche will mean a considerable increase in defense budgets, unless limited by arms control agreements.

From a technological evolution point of view, the idea of building a tightly coupled, strategic defense super system in one piece is not realistic, all the less so considering the multitude of large operational and technological uncertainties involved and the impossibility of real testing in peacetime. Some observers therefore claim that strategic defense is infeasible. In any case, evolution of strategic defense requires a slow and gradual approach aimed at achieving a collection of loosely coupled systems, each one capable by itself of performing effectively a worthwhile mission.

Large, tightly coupled systems, whether in C^3I (communications, command, control, and intelligence) or strategic defense, are sensitive to various disturbances and especially to wartime actions that often cause their rapid collapse.

NUCLEAR WAR

Future developments will emphasize technologies connected with arms control agreements: verification and violation detection. Still, the belief that technology can ensure 100 percent compliance is somewhat optimistic. As in electronic warfare, for every measure there is a countermeasure, not necessarily technological.

SUBCONVENTIONAL WAR

Terrorism and guerrilla warfare have been very common since World War II. It may be argued that they have become the leading form of real warfare in our era. Technology has been widely applied to covert operations and terrorism. Many special types of miniature equipment, both lethal and nonlethal, have been developed for these activities.

As for guerrilla warfare, the common wisdom has been that only simple and light weapons from the arsenal of large-scale conventional war are suitable (such as the RPG-7, a Soviet short-range, man-portable antitank rocket). Obviously, guerrilla fighters need weapons that are simple to operate, but not necessarily simple inside. To counter Soviet helicopters in Afghanistan, the complex but easy to use Stinger missile was required. Guerrillas fighting a modern army often need and obtain sophisticated weapons to counter their opponent. The development of special light equipment for light infantry in the advanced countries will increase the available menu for guerrilla operations.

Concluding Remarks

Technology will continue to affect pervasively all types and aspects of warfare, offering solutions and creating problems. Some important future issues are mobility in land warfare, the increasing use of space in warfare, the dangerous attraction to complex super systems, the role of technology in arms control, and the deficient process of military-technological innovation.

ZEEV BONEN

SEE ALSO: Technology and the Military.

Bibliography

Bonen, Z. 1981. Evolutionary behavior of complex sociotechnical systems. *Research Policy* 10:26–44.
———. 1984. The technological arms race—An economic dead end? In *Israeli security planning in the eighties*, ed. Z. Lanir, pp. 108–30. New York: Praeger.
Deitchman, S. J. 1983. *Military power and the advance of technology*. Boulder, Colo.: Westview Press.
Handel, M. I. 1986. Clausewitz in the age of technology. In *Clausewitz and modern strategy*, ed. M. I. Handel, pp. 51–94. London: Frank Cass.
Handel, M. I. 1987. Technological surprise in war. *Intelligence and National Security* 2:5–53.
Isenson, R. S. 1969. Project Hindsight: An empirical study of the sources of ideas utilized in operational weapon systems. In *Factors in the transfer of technology*, ed. W. H. Gruber and D. G. Marquis. Cambridge, Mass.: MIT Press.
Simpkin, R. E. 1985. *Race to the swift*. London: Brassey's.
Van Creveld, M. 1991. *Technology and war: From 2000 B.C. to present*. London: Brassey's.

TERRORISM

Modern terrorism burst on the scene over twenty years ago with three shocking incidents: at Dawson Field, Jordan, where the PFLP blew up two planes in full view of the preassembled media; at Lod Airport, where the Japanese United Red Army and the PFLP massacred 26 people; and at Munich, where the Black September Palestinian group seized and murdered Israeli athletes within the Olympic Village. The West was stunned and largely unprepared; no one knew quite how to respond.

Today, victim nations have slowly and painfully learned how to defend themselves against some forms of terror. There is near universal screening of tens of millions of airline passengers to prevent a handful of terrorists from boarding planes with guns or bombs. Concrete barricades, ill-disguised as planters, surround many U.S. government buildings to deter suicide bombers. The critical question is whether the nations of the world are able to deal with future mutations of threat.

For some nations, terrorism is ranked high on the list of pressing security concerns, equated at least rhetorically with the prevention of nuclear war and major policy objectives. It is not readily apparent why terrorism should loom so large on any nation's security agenda. More citizens are killed crossing the street each year than in terrorist attacks. No gang of terrorist thugs, religious fanatics, or political nihilists is a match for even a major metropolitan police force. Yet the problem continues to grow—the terrorists skillfully seeding shock, panic, and horror around the globe.

One of the basic problems is definitional. Terrorism has been defined by the U.S. Department of Defense as a "premeditated, politically motivated violence perpetrated against non-combatant targets by subnational groups or clandestine state agents usually to influence an audience." In practice, this violence ranges from plane hijackings by frustrated Cubans to kneecappings by Italian Red Brigades to assassinations planned by drug cartel kingpins to embassy bombings by Shiite fanatics.

Some incidents appear to be inspired, supported, and actively abetted by state sponsors. Some terrorists, like the Peruvian Shining Path, confine their attacks within their nation's borders. Armenian separatists and Palestinian Liberation Organization (PLO) members conduct their operations across the world stage. Some terrorist attacks are a form of warfare directed against the West, others are acts of rage by frustrated intellectuals or idealists. Some have a political motivation. Others, such as attacks by the drug cartels, appear to be economically inspired.

Indeed, terrorism is so broadly defined that it encompasses almost every form of violent action short of large-scale conventional warfare. By describing the terrorism phenomena as a single entity, it becomes an insurmountable policy problem. The reality is that there is no single terrorism, only separate and distinctive terrorisms.

In addition, despite strong rhetoric, it is not clear that the United States or its allies are equally concerned with all forms of terrorist violence. For example,

Great Britain complained for years that the United States refused to take vigorous action to stem the flow of U.S. financial support and arms to the Irish Republican Army (IRA); the Basque separatists are a concern only to the Spanish government, the Shining Path only to the Peruvians.

Terrorist groups receive international attention basically for three reasons:

- their attacks capture the attention of the world's media;
- they are often acting at the behest of a state sponsor or, in the case of the drug kingpins, a quasi-state sponsor; and
- they are potentially able to employ sophisticated means of mass disruption or mass destruction.

A more detailed discussion of these reasons follows.

Media Involvement

The media plays a major role in terrorist incidents. It molds public perceptions about the success or failure of a terrorist operation, about official competence in the face of the threat, and about the prowess of the terrorist organization. Examples include: Israel's high-risk rescue at Entebbe, Uganda, which was cast as a major triumph; and the German rescue of a Lufthansa jet in Mogadishu, Somalia, which basked in the same affirmative limelight. By contrast, the U.S. experience in the Iranian desert was depicted not simply as a difficult attempt that failed but as a debacle, a symbol of U.S. military impotence and presidential bungling.

Terrorists rely on a free and unfettered media, particularly the visual media, to provide a springboard onto the world stage. Media coverage makes larger than life an act that, on its own, might simply be viewed as barbaric.

Terrorists understand the leverage that media coverage provides and make certain that the TV cameras have access to themselves and their hostages. Televised captives, whose faces are broadcast not once but over and over again, become familiar friends whose fates concern us directly. Television coverage can be orchestrated to make the terrorists look sympathetic, even statesmen-like. Pictures of Yasir Arafat hugging babies or making pleas for moderation in the Mideast peace negotiations alter the perception that he sits atop the largest and most brutal terrorist organization in the world.

Television, by capturing only one slice of reality, changes that reality. Perhaps the most egregious case of a misleading media occurred during the TWA hijacking in 1985. Nabih Berri, justice minister for the essentially nonexistent government of Lebanon, was asked by one network anchor if he had any final words for President Ronald Reagan. By being asked this question, Berri, inextricably linked to the terrorist group that staged the incident, was put on a political par with the president of the United States.

This is precisely what terrorists hope for. They do not expect that a bombing incident, hijacking, or embassy seizure will bring a great power to its knees. Instead, by using the media as an unwitting but not unwilling partner, they seek to create panic and doubt about the competence of elected governments.

The government that is the object of an attack that receives extensive media coverage cannot ignore the situation, but it is not always prepared or able to respond. The terrorist's goal, often realized, is that the attack will force a target government into paralyzing impotence (the Iranian embassy seizure) or blind overreaction (the Iran-Contra affair), thereby discrediting itself.

State Sponsorship

One of the fundamental changes that occurred in terrorism during the 1980s was not so much in the attacks themselves but in the willingness of states to train, equip, and sponsor the terrorists. As international power has grown increasingly diffuse—with arsenals of modern weapons widely scattered—the ability of small nations to threaten large ones, using the tactics of terror, has become painfully obvious. As a strategic tool, terrorism works. It works so well that it appears to be emerging as the political instrument of choice for adversarial states who cannot compete on a more conventional battlefield. For such states as Libya, Iran, and Syria, terrorism has become warfare on the cheap.

As a result, many terrorist activities have less to do with frustrated idealism than with the realpolitik of international conflict. Terrorists can no longer be viewed as the disaffected children of Europe, the displaced refugees of the Middle East, or the disillusioned peasants of the developing world. With increasing frequency, state-sponsored terrorists tend to be trained professionals, well financed, well equipped, and potentially able to exploit a range of modern technologies from satellite communications to possibly the dispersal of chemical, biological, or radiological materials.

In the foreseeable future, it would not be surprising to see an increase in both the absolute number of violent acts and in their qualitative importance. The possibility of high-tech terrorism has historically been discounted for a number of reasons. First, there was doubt that terrorist groups had the technological infrastructure or the know-how to achieve mass disruption. Even if the technological hurdles were surmountable, it was assumed that such groups would be refused safe haven if they went too far. No country could afford to be associated with madmen or risk retaliation for harboring them. Second, it was assumed that as long as terrorists maintained an aura of social revolution, any action that threatened the lives of hundreds of innocent people would be difficult to defend.

Events like the bombing of the U.S. Marine Corps barracks in Lebanon in 1983, the Labelle disco bombing in 1986, and the downing of Pan-Am Flight 103 over Scotland in 1988 have shattered many of the myths about what terrorists will or will not do. Since nations have begun to sponsor these events, there can be no question about technological capability or lack of safe haven. Also, the pretext of social justice appears threadbare when Japanese Red Army faction terrorists are caught carrying bombs on the New Jersey Turnpike or drug dealers sponsor hit teams to eliminate U.S. federal prosecutors.

What is becoming clear is that it is no longer possible to guess where the line of destruction will be drawn—or, indeed, if a line will be drawn at all. Recent attacks worldwide demonstrate a growing level of technological competence. The hijacking of a Kuwaiti airliner in 1988 by Shiite terrorists offers an illustrative case. In that episode, the terrorist team included at least one veteran of a hijacking as well as a pilot qualified to fly the plane. The hijackers reportedly blocked entry points on the plane and wired it with explosives, rendering the plane impervious to rescue. Similarly, the bombing of Pan-Am Flight 103 later that year, using a multiphased trigger that sensed barometric pressure, takeoff and landing cycles, as well as time, demonstrated genuine technical expertise.

For the 1990s, the worry is that state sponsors will provide the wherewithal for even more devastating attacks—technoterrorism. These kinds of attacks will significantly increase the importance of terrorism.

Potential for Superviolence

The proliferation of chemical, biological, and nuclear arsenals among the state sponsors of terrorism may be the trigger for massively destructive attacks. In the area of chemical warfare, Western intelligence services estimate that 15 to 30 countries have or are actively working to possess chemical munitions. In this case it is not so much a matter of technological prowess as it is sheer availability. The internationalization of the chemical industry—petrochemicals, fertilizers, and insecticides—has put chemical warfare technology within reach of developing countries and their terrorist protégés and virtually out of reach of any meaningful control.

Terrorists have long had more than a passing interest in the extortion potential of chemical warfare. In recent years, Israeli security agents and police found canisters of a potent poison, presumed to have been brought in by terrorists, in Tel Aviv. Between 1978 and 1979, approximately 400 kilograms (880 lb.) of intermediate compounds, used for manufacturing nerve agents, were discovered at a safe house in West Germany. In 1975, German entrepreneurs were apprehended in Vienna attempting to sell nerve agents to Palestinian terrorists. In 1991, a plot by neo-Nazi "skinheads" to pump hydrogen cyanide gas into a synagogue was thwarted.

Far more lethal alternatives are in the toxin family, the poisonous by-products of microorganisms, plants, or animals. Toxins actually fall somewhere between chemical and biological weapons; they are synthesized from living material but are not living themselves.

Probably the best-known toxin causes botulism, which is found virtually everywhere. When compared with the most dangerous nerve agents, botulinal toxins are a thousand times more effective. The average lethal dose is probably as low as a few tenths of a microgram. One group of terrorists apparently thought it could find a use for botulinal toxin. In a raid on a Red Army Faction safe house in 1980, French police found flasks of the unpurified toxin stored in the bathtub. A decade later in Paris, another Red Army Faction safe house (equipped with a primitive lab) was raided and found to have quantities of botulinal toxin.

More ominous still is the untapped potential for biological warfare: tiny microorganisms such as fungi, bacteria, or viruses that are cultured in concentration. Among the most serious viral agents are those that produce smallpox, yellow fever, and influenza. Bacterial agents include anthrax, plague, or typhoid fever.

Although biological weapons are more dangerous for the handler because they are designed to be infectious, their effects are also far greater. Only a small quantity is sufficient to devastate a crowded urban area, killing hundreds of thousands, even millions of people.

Today, stunning advances in the field of biotechnology have made biological weapons a more attractive option. It is now possible to synthesize agents tailored to specification. New weapons can be produced in hours while antidotes may take years. New technology can also yield agents against which an attacker could immunize himself in advance. This would tend to enhance the utility of biological over chemical weapons, against which neither side is immune.

The apparent ease by which a person can order biological organisms was demonstrated in 1984 when two Canadians, posing as microbiologists from the Canadian firm ICM Science, ordered pathogens over the telephone from a laboratory in Maryland that routinely stocks biological cultures for research and clinical purposes. When the laboratory routinely sent a copy of the sales invoice to ICM Science, the large quantity of tetanus ordered caught their attention. ICM Science recognized that it had not ordered the cultures and had no employees of the names given.

In 1990, Saddam Hussein, the leader of Iraq, demonstrated the growing threat of biological terrorism with his possession of massive quantities of botulinal toxin and the biological agent anthrax. A considerable portion of his lethal feedstock was ready to use as weapons.

Ironically, it was the U.S. Army that first tested the way in which biological agents could be used in a terrorist attack. In the late 1950s and early 1960s, government personnel conducted experiments to gauge the effects of biological attacks in the United States. Using a nonlethal substitute for dry anthrax, they dropped light bulbs full of the powder in the subway system of New York City. The enormous winds in the tunnels distributed the powder throughout the system, creating the probability of hundreds of thousands of deaths in a real attack. Other tests involved the dispersal of pseudotoxins, located in cleverly designed attaché cases at bus and airport terminals and on boats, equipped with aerosol sprays, in inland waterways. In all, the army found that such a series of attacks might yield tens of millions of casualties.

What makes the prospect of biological weapons so nightmarish is the catastrophic power of even modest attacks. With a small nuclear device, the fatalities, even in a major urban center, would be on the order of several hundred thousand. A chemical attack with the best agents available would probably not exceed a few thousand fatalities. But for biological weapons, the number of fatalities could theoretically run into the millions.

And there is no guarantee that the victim government would be able to trace the origin of attack or even be certain the epidemic was deliberately rather than naturally induced. With new self-cleaning production techniques, biologicals can be truly anonymous weapons of attack.

Vulnerable Infrastructure

Terrorists need not use massively destructive weapons to bring about utter devastation. They are becoming more adept not only in the weapons available to them but also in their ability to analyze and target the more complex infrastructure targets that modern civilizations rely on for basic survival—electric power, oil and natural gas networks, telecommunication and computer networks, potable water systems, and transportation networks—all of which are inextricably linked. The possibility of successful attacks on infrastructure is a crisis manager's nightmare because massive failure in any one system can mean a cascading disruption in many others.

In the United States, the vulnerability of infrastructure is acute. Thousands of miles of electric power lines and petroleum pipelines represent exposed targets; publicly available maps show where they may be severed to isolate entire regions of the country. A handful of people could turn off three-quarters of the oil and gas supply to the East Coast without ever leaving the state of Louisiana. Just one pipeline system, dependent on a single control center, carries half the barrel miles of refined products shipped in the United States.

Electric power facilities pose a special threat. As was demonstrated in the 1977 New York blackout, the loss of power brought the sanitation, food, mass transportation, and water systems to a halt. Indeed, even routine law enforcement procedures were stymied because the electric typewriters in the New York Police Department did not function. Hundreds of looting cases were thrown out of court for lack of adequate arrest records.

As a result, electric power facilities, precisely because they are an embracing system upon which almost all other services depend, have become a target of choice for terrorists worldwide. There are few damage control options once an electric facility has been taken off line.

In the United States, the New World Liberation Front—a consumer protest group in the Pacific Northwest—targeted the Pacific Gas and Electric Company more than ten times during the 1970s. In 1978, in the Philippines, the Moro National Liberation Front blacked out almost half of the island of Mindoro. In Chile, in November 1980, members of the Movement of the Revolutionary Left (MIR) cut off power to Santiago, Valparaiso, and Vina del Mar. In Italy, the Red Brigades have targeted the electric power grid for two decades with varying degrees of success. The Shining Path in Peru blacked out Lima on several occasions during the late 1970s and 1980s.

One group in Japan, the Chukaku-Ha or Middle Core, has made attacks on the transportation infrastructure a particular specialty. In 1978, the group cut the cables leading to the control tower at Tokyo International Airport, shutting down air traffic. A much more sophisticated attack was launched in 1985. Acting with military precision, the terrorists simultaneously attacked 34 nodes on the national railway system, idling 18 million commuters. According to press reports, they then tried to increase the panic by jamming police communications with a special radio transmitter.

For the future, there is concern that new technologies are opening up far more disruptive avenues of attack. In particular, the data processing and communications linkages that underpin the global economy are vulnerable to attack. It is estimated, for example, that computer outages can cost anywhere from $10,000 to $1 million per company per minute in real dollars. State and local governments in the United States estimate the cost of computer outages at $65,000 per day. Only about 20 percent of U.S. companies have a data recovery plan in the event of disaster.

Even more worrying is the potential for disruption of computer software through the so-called computer virus. In biological terms, a computer virus is a disease that is 100 percent infectious, spreads instantaneously at the moment of contact, and has no detectable symptoms until the moment it strikes.

Computer viruses are actually lines of code hidden within normal programming instructions. They have the capability to clone themselves and then to bury that copy inside other software programs. A single strategically placed computer with an infected memory—for example, a central banking computer—could rapidly infect thousands of smaller computers.

Viruses have been discovered worldwide in recent years at such corporations as IBM, Hewlett-Packard, and Apple; at major university centers; and in Israel, West Germany, Switzerland, Britain, Italy, and the United States. For example, in 1988, a Cornell computer whiz created a virus program that disrupted operations in an estimated 6,000 computers in the United States for over a 24-hour period. Fortunately, the virus was not instructed to damage operating systems or destroy information, only to consume unused memory banks in the network by reproducing data files. But what began as a prank led to the most intensive interagency scrutiny of U.S. vulnerability to computer sabotage.

A more insidious terrorist attack by computer virus was accidentally discovered in Israel in 1988. The virus code contained a "time bomb" that would have caused all infected programs to erase their files on May 13, the fortieth anniversary of the creation of the state of Israel. The virus was discovered because of an error in its program that did not allow it to distinguish between already infected and uninfected programs. Because it continued to add copies of itself to infected software, in some cases hundreds of times, the extra lines in the software began to flood the disk memories. Although one or two lines of virus code would have been almost impossible to detect, the anomaly of so many lines of repetitive programming proved to be easier to spot.

The damage potential of computer viruses is so enormous that it may be impossible to calculate. Suppose, for example, someone managed to hide a computer virus among the millions of lines of programming instructions in the strategic defense control systems. Experts claim that it is difficult enough to identify random bugs in the system; it would be virtually impossible to spot any Trojan horse lines of code. But quite conceivably, a weapons system could be presabotaged to fail at a moment of crisis. Ultimately, international security—not to mention economic stability—hinges on the ability to prevent insertion of such a virus into computers that communicate with other computers. In practice, however, no reliable way has been identified to insulate computers from such attacks.

Coping with Terror

Although U.S. policymakers have spent a great deal of time over the past twenty years trying to forge credible antiterrorism policies, the record can only be described as dismal. Various approaches have been tested by successive U.S. administrations. None has proven truly effective in meeting the terror challenge.

Under Richard Nixon's collective security approach, it became apparent that not all U.S. allies were prepared to follow the U.S. policy lead. Under Jimmy Carter, it was discovered that humanitarian aid is not a complete solution, since redress of grievances is not always the raison d'être for terrorist attacks. Ronald Reagan promised swift retribution to terrorists (who might run but could not hide) only to find that in many cases, notably Lebanon, the terrorists enjoyed relative immunity from U.S. reprisals.

These policy problems have their roots, at least in the United States, in the "can-do" attitude of U.S. leaders. Each administration has foolishly promised counterterrorism miracles, deluding itself and the public that the terrorism problem is amenable to a U.S.-imposed solution.

The reality is that neither the United States nor any other government can solve the terrorism problem. Regardless of actions taken, terrorism or loss of life cannot always be prevented. Nor will governments always be able to identify or apprehend the criminals or punish their state sponsors, or resolve every incident on favorable terms.

Accordingly, policies are needed that reflect the limitations inherent in dealing with terrorism. Terrorists retain all the advantages of the clandestine offense; they control the targets, timing, and often the tempo of the event. Although governments possess counterterrorism options, the perception that a government must be able to protect its citizens and assets everywhere against every kind of attack lays the groundwork for eventual humiliation. Combating terrorism requires resources and encompasses a wide range of organizational and operational talents, including flexible diplomatic and economic options, upgraded law enforcement intelligence capabilities, military force (both overt and covert), expanded use of high technologies in the counterterrorism arena, and a wide crisis management apparatus.

LAW ENFORCEMENT

Effective law enforcement is an indispensable tool in the counterterrorism arsenal of free societies. When it works, it reflects the democratic system at its best. The problem is that law enforcement doesn't always work against all types of terrorism. For example, regarding domestic terrorism, the issues are relatively straightforward. In the United States and elsewhere, law enforcement authorities have achieved notable successes against both left- and right-wing groups. Groups like the Weathermen, the Symbionese Liberation Army, Posse Comitatus, FALN, Aryan Nation, and the United Freedom Front have faded in turn from the front pages, due in large measure to high-quality police work.

Terrorist attacks that occur abroad, however, pose an entirely different set of law enforcement dilemmas. Questions of access, jurisdiction, and national sovereignty invariably complicate a response. While there have been efforts to foster an international regime of legal cooperation, it is difficult to force an unwilling foreign government, which may fear retaliation, to extradite or prosecute terrorists and equally difficult to conduct unilateral operations on foreign soil without the approval of the host government.

In fact, even friendly governments have resisted U.S. extradition requests. For example, after the series of kidnappings began in Lebanon in the early 1980s, the United States asked informally for custody of Imam Mugniyah, one of the most powerful of the terrorist leaders. French authorities, however, alerted Mugniyah, who was then able to slip away. In the 1986 *Achille Lauro* case, the Italian and Yugoslav governments spirited the mastermind of the operation, Muhammed Abul al-Abas (disguised as a flight attendant), out of their territories even as the United States was issuing an extradition request. In 1987, the German government was extorted into refusing extradition to the United States of Mohammed Hamadei, a terrorist accused of participating in the hijacking of TWA Flight 847. To pressure the German government, Hamadei's Hizbollah "family" in Beirut arranged the kidnapping of two West German businessmen.

Because the diplomatic channels are often blocked, U.S. law now sanctions the extradition of terrorists to the United States by legal or other means (generally taken to imply forcible abduction). The court is supposed to turn a blind eye to the issue of how a defendant came before it, judging the criminal case only on its merits. This authority was used in the abduction of Fawaz Younis— one of the terrorists who stormed a Royal Jordanian airliner in 1985 and blew it up on the tarmac.

Although satisfying when it succeeds, this approach has several limitations. As a practical matter, it takes months, perhaps years, of concerted effort to capture a single terrorist. Then, terrorists tend to take sanctuary with their state sponsors, making covert operations a risky business. Efforts to lure high-ranking terrorists out of hiding may be substantially more difficult. Younis was not one of the most notorious international targets, merely one of the most accessible ones since he was living openly in Beirut and running short of money.

There has, however, been some progress internationally in bringing terrorists to justice. Despite political pressures for appeasement, increasing numbers of terrorists are being tried worldwide. In London, Nezar Hindawi received a life sentence for his attempt to use his unwilling pregnant girlfriend to blow up an Israeli jumbo jet. In Paris, George Ibrahim Abdullah received a life sentence for his role in the murder of a U.S. Army attaché. In Madrid, a Palestinian terrorist was sentenced to 47 years for directing a 1986 bombing attempt against an El Al plane.

Because terrorism cuts across national boundaries, efforts to combat it will require a great deal of cooperation among the law enforcement authorities of victim governments. Although multinational conventions and national legislation now exist to provide legal authority to prosecute terrorists, much more needs to be done to lay the practical groundwork for regular communication and ongoing cooperation between law enforcement agencies.

IMPROVED INTELLIGENCE

Intelligence efforts designed to thwart terrorist attacks are obviously another critical component of counterterrorism.

In the United States, there is clearly substantial room for improvement. During the 1970s, intelligence capabilities were virtually decimated by legislative fiat. By 1980, the intelligence community had lost a quarter of its people; three-quarters of the overseas station chiefs were eligible for retirement. Less than half of the CIA's intelligence analysts spoke the language of the country they were assigned to cover. An even smaller proportion had even visited the countries in which they were supposed to have expertise. Information transmitted by satellite rather than human intelligence on the ground came to dominate (and restrict) America's intelligence-gathering capabilities.

These events contributed to some spectacular failures. After the shah was permitted entry to the United States, perhaps the U.S. government should have anticipated the seizure of the embassy in Teheran by Iranian radicals. Indeed, Israel passed on warnings that such an event might occur. Yet the obvious step—to reduce the number of embassy personnel down to a skeleton staff—was not taken; thus Iran's Revolutionary Guard was able to capture and hold hostage 66 Americans. In 1983, the U.S. Marine compound in Lebanon was virtually a sitting duck for attack. But the intelligence expertise that might have predicted the event had been wiped out in the Beirut embassy bombing a few months before.

In the late 1980s, efforts were made to upgrade domestic analytic capabilities as well as international intelligence sharing. Within the FBI, analytical capabilities were vastly upgraded, including the Bomb Data Center, the Terrorist Research and Analytical Center (TRAC), and the Special Operations and Research Unit (SOAR). For many years, Interpol—the international police organization—refused to become involved with terrorism, treating it as a political crime and therefore out of its jurisdiction. But in 1986, Interpol created a specialized unit to compile information on terrorist groups and transmit this data to its worldwide network.

Data collection and analysis alone will not be sufficient to predict all terrorist operations. Rather, good intelligence plays a critical role in the deft handling of terrorist crises: gauging the technical credibility of the terrorist threat (whether the group is willing and able to carry it out) and providing behavioral assessments of the group (willingness to negotiate, leadership structures, command and control structures, and motivation).

How well a government responds to terrorist acts depends a great deal on how much is known about the terrorists. Issues of culture, demography, and individual psychology create a unique internal dynamic in each incident. Despite the ongoing efforts of psychologists, diplomats, and police, there is still a great deal to be learned about analyzing and integrating these intelligence factors into the response calculus.

USE OF FORCE

The 1980s trend in the United States toward a more forceful response to terrorism stemmed in part from President Reagan's belief that the United States had been too passive in dealing with terrorists. According to his secretary of state George Shultz, the issue was no longer whether the United States would retaliate, but when and how and under what circumstances.

Bold rhetoric aside, deciding when and how to deploy military force is itself difficult. The use of force is clearly not applicable in every terrorist incident and generally requires a fair amount of luck, as was demonstrated in the *Achille Lauro* affair. Had the hijackers thought to bring along a few hostages for insurance, the U.S. response may have been quite different.

Moreover, military force in the *Achille Lauro* affair proved to be an insufficient tool. Although the midair interception of the Air Egypt flight carrying the hijackers out of Egypt was flawlessly executed, the mission rapidly unraveled once it was on the ground. U.S. special operations forces—deployed to take the hijackers into custody—were pinned between armed terrorists in the jet and armed Italian troops on their rear with orders to block the American action. The U.S. forces withdrew to let the diplomats work out an extradition arrangement. By the following day, however, the Italian government had already spirited al-Abas, the terrorist leader, out of Italy.

Similarly, the aircraft raid on Libya, designed to topple Muammar Qadhafi's government, also experienced problems from the outset. The F-111 bombers, based in England, were denied overflight rights by France and forced to fly an exhausting 6½ hours in formation over international waters. Subsequently, most of the attack jets and bombers missed their designated targets, with nearly five tons of explosives landing on residential neighborhoods, killing or wounding 130 people.

Questions of distance and sovereignty complicate military responses to terrorist acts. Projecting power quickly over thousands of miles is an arduous logistical and operational task. With a few exceptions, countries are generally forced either to wait for an invitation to intervene, hope for a weak central government (such as the Germans enjoyed in Somalia and the Israelis in Uganda), or rely on the good offices and counterterrorism capabilities—competent or not—of the government in power.

The use of military force cannot always be a counterterrorism solution. However, the resolve to use force lends credibility to a host of other options. First, a military option keeps the terrorists off-balance, forcing them to devote more attention and resources to protecting themselves than to planning new attacks. Second, it can enhance the perceived prowess of the victim governments to respond to terrorists' attacks. Finally, it can galvanize other countries into a firmer stand against terrorism. For example, after the U.S. raid on Libya,

Europe, which had been reluctant to impose any joint sanctions against Libya for its support of terrorism, moved quickly at the prospect of nonmilitary cooperation. Within a few days, the ministers of the European Economic Community (EEC) had agreed to expand intelligence sharing with the United States, to reduce the size of Libya's diplomatic missions in Europe (which served as command posts for its terrorist operations), and to ensure that Libyans expelled from one EEC country could not seek haven in another.

Covert Operations

One counterterrorism tool that usually receives less attention is covert operations. This term is generally taken to mean those operations, for example, subversion, assassination, or psychological warfare, that are planned and executed so as to conceal the identity of, or permit plausible denial by, the sponsor.

Democratic societies tend to resist this alternative, viewing covert operations as ethically repugnant and a misuse of power. Response to terrorists, it is argued, must be fashioned within the tradition of due process. Although it is popularly believed that Soviet negotiations for the release of four kidnapped Soviet diplomats involved kidnapping the family members of the terrorists and dismembering one of them, success at any price is not a concept with which many in the West feel comfortable.

If the principle is accepted that covert force may occasionally be a necessary and legitimate tool in the counterterrorism arsenal, then governments must begin to define with considerable rigor and in open debate the parameters for its conduct. If there is to be secrecy, then there must be diligent oversight. When covert responses are mandated, then they must be conducted by agencies that fall under legislative or parliamentary purview. Otherwise, far more may be lost than is gained in the struggle against terrorism.

Use of Technology

If terrorists are becoming more technologically sophisticated, so, too, are the potential counterterrorism applications. Technology can provide new capabilities to help prevent terrorists from achieving their goals, new physical safeguards against attack, and a more effective real-time response. From remote sensing devices to rapid-entry techniques, technology offers the potential for new offensive and defensive approaches to countering terrorists.

The range of counterterrorism technologies on the shelf or on the horizon is staggering. Solid-state television cameras, smaller than a quarter, can be invisibly hidden in advance to monitor a hijacking in progress. Long-range infrared devices, which detect motion or placement of individuals inside a hostage barricade, are also available. Fiber optics, tiny hairlike strands of glass with a lens cover, can generate television pictures of events taking place inside an area occupied by terrorists.

Laser technologies offer a host of previously inconceivable capabilities. By aiming lasers through the windows of an aircraft or the glass panes of a building onto such items as a piece of paper, one can actually listen in on conversations inside a hostage area. Similarly, lasers can be used as a means of communication to individual hostages by modulating the tiniest concentrations of organic vapors to convey sound. Such techniques can also be used offensively to envelop a target in sound.

Techniques have been developed to wall off communications around a particular target such as a commercial airliner sitting on the ground. Other devices, including specialized explosives, high-powered sound, or lasers can be used to disintegrate brick and mortar to allow for rapid entry. Related techniques have been used for antipersonnel objectives—for example, to create temporary mental confusion and loss of bodily controls.

Although the emerging technological arsenal offers some extraordinary possibilities, there is no room for complacency. Without a well-directed and adequately funded U.S. program of research and development, counterterrorism technological potential cannot be further explored.

There is also a pressing need for threat anticipation in order to predict some of the countermeasures that may be needed in the future. For example, it is known that terrorists have downlink satellite receivers to monitor cable and network reports of their operation and that they have experimented with uplink satellite transmitters to broadcast internationally. Thus, governments should prepare the capability to selectively block transmissions in or out of a hostage site or hijacked plane. Without innovative research and development applied to the terrorism problem, governments will remain perpetually in a reactive mode—always one step behind the terrorists.

Crisis Management

Of all the potential tools in the counterterrorism arsenal, the ability to manage the aftermath of a major incident has received the least attention. The last defense against terrorists is probably the most critical: to prevent them from achieving the depth of political, economic, or social disruption they seek.

Ironically, the United States' greatest protection comes not through preemption or retaliation but through imaginative planning and a well-oiled crisis management apparatus. If deterrence fails, victim governments must be able to limit the consequences of attack. As the potential for terrorist incidents of mass disruption increases, containment and restoration must become integral elements of the counterterrorism arsenal.

What is clear, particularly in the United States, is that it is no longer possible to rely on blind faith that such attacks cannot occur in the United States or on sheer luck that things will work out somehow. Effective crisis management should prepare for the next set of crises, not the last.

The reality is that governments are rarely prepared to respond to most kinds of emergencies except on an interim and ad hoc basis. There are few contingency plans that would stand up to even casual scrutiny. Responsible reactions to terror require an emergency apparatus that can respond quickly and decisively and is the result of coordinated efforts at the highest levels of government.

If coping with terror were easy, the problem would have been solved long ago. Thus, the governments of the world must be prepared for the fact that terrorists and their sponsors will always exist.

Robert H. Kupperman

Debra van Opstal

Bibliography

Douglass, J. D., Jr., and N. C. Livingstone. 1987. *America the vulnerable: The threat of chemical and biological warfare.* Lexington, Mass.: Lexington Books.

Kupperman, R. H. 1983. *Technological advances and consequent dangers: Growing threats to civilization.* Washington, D.C.: Center for Strategic and International Studies.

Leventhal, P., and Y. Alexander, eds. 1987. *Preventing nuclear terrorism.* Lexington, Mass.: Lexington Books.

Levitt, G. M. 1988. *Democracies against terror.* New York: Praeger.

Livingstone, N. C., and A. E. Terrell, eds. 1988. *Beyond the Iran-Contra crisis.* Lexington, Mass.: Lexington Books.

Marks, E., and D. Van Opstal. 1986. *Combatting terrorism: A matter of leverage.* Washington, D.C.: Center for Strategic and International Studies.

Martin, D. C., and J. Walcott. 1988. *Best laid plans: The inside story of America's war against terrorism.* New York: Harper and Row.

Revell, O. 1988. *Terrorism: A law enforcement perspective.* Washington, D.C.: U.S. Department of Justice, Federal Bureau of Investigation.

Wilcox, R. H., and P. J. Garrity, eds. 1984. *America's hidden vulnerabilities: Crisis management in a society of networks.* Washington, D.C.: Center for Strategic and International Studies.

THEORY OF COMBAT

A theory of combat is the embodiment of a set of fundamental principles governing or explaining military combat, whose purpose is to provide a basis for the formulation of doctrine, and to assist military commanders and planners to engage successfully in combat at any level. Such a theory includes the following elements:

1. identifying the major elements of combat and the combat processes through which they operate and patterns in the interactions and relationships among them,
2. describing combat structures and patterns of interactions and relationships of variable factors that constantly shape or determine the outcome of combat, and
3. expressing in quantitative terms the patterns so identified and described.

Elements of a Theory of Combat

Military combat can be defined as a violent, planned form of physical interaction (fighting) between two hostile opponents where at least one party is an organized force (recognized by governmental or *de facto* authority) and one or both opposing parties hold one or more of the following objectives: to seize control of territory or people; to prevent the opponent from seizing and controlling territory or people; to protect one's own territory or people; to dominate, destroy, or incapacitate the opponent.

The above definition refers to interactions and levels of combat. This is a recognition of the fact that fighting between armed forces—while always having the characteristics noted above, such as fear and planned violence—manifests itself in different fashions from different perspectives. In commonly accepted military terminology, there is a *hierarchy of combat*, with war as its highest level, followed by campaign, battle, engagement, action, and duel.

Search for a Theory of Combat

Since the early days of civilization men have sought general rules about the nature of war that could help them prevail in future conflicts.

The oldest surviving military treatise is *The Art of War*, written by Sun Tzu in China about 500 B.C. Over the next 2,300 years, others tried to formulate a theoretical approach to warfare. Sextus Julius Frontinus wrote *On Military Affairs* and *Strategems* in the first century. Two centuries later, another Roman, Flavius Vegetius Renatus, wrote a book also entitled *On Military Affairs* (more generally known as *Military Institutions of the Romans*), which was often used as a reference by the military scholars of Medieval Europe. There were several theoretical works on war by Byzantines: Mauricius's *Strategikon*, *The Tactica* of Leo the Wise, and others. In the century before Napoleon, there were such writings as *Reveries on the Art of War* by Count Maurice of Saxe and *Instructions to His Generals* by Frederick the Great of Prussia.

THE GREAT THEORISTS

Napoleon. Napoleon Bonaparte, more than any other, was responsible for stimulating the search for a theory, science, or collection of laws on war. Although he never committed his ideas on military theory to paper in a coherent, unified form, he did leave an extensive collection of empirical—as opposed to conceptual or theoretical—maxims. From these maxims, and from analyses of his performance on the battlefield, others have distilled the principal elements of his theoretical ideas. In his correspondence and recorded statements, as in his *Maxims*, Napoleon made it clear that his concepts and thinking on war had been derived basically from the study of the campaigns of earlier generals.

As noted, Napoleon never articulated his theory or theories of war, except for occasional passages in his letters—for instance the letter of 27 August 1808, written to try to teach his brother Joseph how to rule Spain, in which he implied that "the moral is to the physical as three is to one"—and the uneven litany of concepts to be found in his *Maxims*. It was necessary for his younger contemporaries, Antoine Henri Jomini and Karl von Clausewitz, to attempt to give these concepts the theoretical substance they deserved.

Jomini and Clausewitz. It is doubtful that Jomini and Clausewitz met during the short period when they were both in the service of the czar or later. During the 1820s each was very familiar with the writings of the other and, as somewhat jealous rivals, each was critical of the other's work.

Jomini tried to explain Napoleon's ideas on theory. But in his many writings, Jomini was never able to capture the philosophical aspects of Napoleon's thinking on war satisfactorily or to distill the essence of his theory. The result was a somewhat mixed bag of discussion, rules, aphorisms, and maxims.

Clausewitz was able to capture Napoleon's philosophy and to add to it some ideas of his own, but he also found himself baffled by the problems of distilling a theory out of this philosophy. Like the bible in theology, Clausewitz can be quoted to support both sides of almost any argument in military affairs, or as a source for almost any sound or unsound concept that one might desire to document. Such quotations are usually out of context, or else the seeming contradictions result from the fact that he never had a chance to edit a final version of his master work.

Clausewitz is often quoted erroneously as ridiculing the idea that there could or should be any fixed set of principles of war. Although some of his words out of context could be so interpreted, he devotes several chapters of *On War* to a discussion of a theory of war, and affirmed that there *are* principles. He lists, though not in sequential fashion, eight of the nine principles usually accepted by modern military scholars, but he admitted implicitly that the formulation of the theory would require an effort beyond that of *On War*, or possibly beyond the limits of what could be accomplished in terms of the scientific method of his time. He did decry attempts to produce precise and mathematical rules for combat to be followed by generals on the battlefield. Yet Clausewitz did think mathematically and quantitatively, and from that thinking he provided the rudiments of the most substantial theory of combat so far produced.

Much has been made of the differences between Jomini and Clausewitz, but these differences were not great and were essentially philosophical rather than interpretive or practical. Both were stimulated to prolific writing on war by the example of Napoleon, and both drew essentially the same conclusions from their respective studies of that example. Both were convinced that Napoleon demonstrated that there is—or should be—a theory of war, and that such a theory was based upon fundamental principles. They generally agreed on what those principles were: such things we now call mass, maneuver, objective, and surprise.

There were two principal differences. The first was in their approaches; Jomini was more doctrinaire, Clausewitz more philosophical. Jomini tried to derive a framework of rules for battlefield success in war from his identification of principles used by Napoleon. Clausewitz, equally impressed by the principles, did not consider it possible for those principles to provide more than general guidance for a subsequent commander, who should adapt his understanding of the principles to his own "genius." There are many indications in the text of *On War* that Clausewitz believed that it might some day be possible to formulate a more comprehensive, more scientific body of theory in the form of laws and principles than he believed was possible in the 1820s. In his time, however, he was convinced that such a formulation was impossible, and thus he was very critical of Jomini's efforts to draw up rules for generalship.

The second difference was intellectual. Jomini was unquestionably a man of great analytical ability, highly intelligent, even brilliant. Clausewitz was an intellectual giant worthy of comparison not only with a Napoleon and a Scharnhorst, but also with the contemporary philosophers Kant and Hegel. Jomini studied, and understood very well, the warfare of his time. Clausewitz recognized the relationship of the warfare of his time with the behavioral, social, and political natures of man. Jomini identified the trees of war. Clausewitz not only knew the trees; he saw the forest.

Other theorists since Napoleon. Ten other theorists since Napoleon have influenced the course of the search for military theory. There is not likely to be complete agreement among military scholars as to which names should be included in such a list. It would, however, be difficult to ignore the contributions made by any of the following men.

Denis Hart Mahan was essentially a follower of Napoleon through Jomini. He was the first great American military theorist. He compiled maxims and rules that he thought were relevant to military theory in America, but he never tried (so far as is evident from available writings) to produce a theory.

Helmuth von Moltke was both an eminent historian and an eminent military thinker. He was also a superb organizer and director of combat. He did little, however, to advance military theory per se, other than in unrelated, although perceptive, comments such as that addressing the need to combine the tactical defensive with the strategic offensive. He was essentially a manifestation of the capabilities of an institution of genius; any number of his Prussian contemporaries could have done as well had they been in his place.

Charles J. J. J. Ardant du Picq was perhaps the most perceptive writer on the subject of moral forces (behavioral considerations) in war. His book *Battle Studies* (1921) is one of the best of a handful of truly great military classics. He was killed in battle in the Franco-Prussian War before his work could be incorporated into any kind of theoretical context, which was unfortunate for France.

Alfred Thayer Mahan was an American military theorist in the style of Jomini, of his own father (Denis Hart Mahan), and of Moltke. His focus was on naval warfare and theory. A profound and gifted thinker on military and naval affairs, he well understood the relevance of military history to the contemporary military problems of his time. He dominates the roster of naval theorists much as Clausewitz stands out over other theorists of land warfare. He recognized principles and analytically employed them but never attempted a scientific, analytical approach to military theory.

Count Alfred von Schlieffen served after Moltke's successor as chief of the German General Staff. He was another studious, profound thinker on war who never attempted to distill a theory of combat from his knowledge of military history and the warfare of his own time. The so-called Schlieffen Plan has become a matter of controversy that has inhibited serious study of his military genius by writers or readers of the English language. Perhaps the best-known work in German was by a worthy successor, Groener (1927). As a soldier and a general, Schlieffen was probably superior to Moltke, but he never had an opportunity to command in battle or war.

Baron Colmar von der Goltz was one of a number of German military thinkers who emerged from that institution of genius, the German General Staff, during its heyday under Moltke and Schlieffen. In his two best-known works, *The Nation in Arms* (1887) and *The Conduct of War* (1908), he refers frequently, if somewhat vaguely, to the theory of war and to its principles. He may not deserve to be included in the intellectual company on this list, other than as a representative of an extremely prolific and thoughtful group of German writers from the General Staff. His work had great influence in Germany, in France, and particularly in Britain.

Ferdinand Foch was a disciple of both Clausewitz and Ardant du Picq. He probably understood Clausewitz as well as anyone ever has—certainly better than most Germans. Paradoxically, he misread his countryman, Ardant du Picq. He did try to think and write in scientific, theoretical terms, and there was much that was sound in his approach to analyzing military history. However, his influence and his devotion to the moral significance of *l'offensive à outrance* nearly ruined the French Army at the outset of World War I. But his leadership in the recovery from that near disaster was brilliant.

Giulio Douhet was the first and most important theorist of air warfare. Like many other early adherents of airpower, he greatly exaggerated the potential of the military aircraft of his time. What distinguished him from others was his development (in his book *Command of the Air*, published in 1921) of a coherent, consistent theory of air warfare that correctly anticipated (even if it overestimated) the dominant role of airpower in all subsequent wars. Douhet's name is often linked with the contemporary air warfare apostles of Britain and the United States: Marshal of the Royal Air Force Sir Hugh Trenchard and U.S. Maj. Gen. William Mitchell. Neither of these men, however, had the influence, even in their own countries, that Douhet exercised upon airpower development and trends through the twentieth century.

John F. C. Fuller was perhaps the greatest military thinker of this century, and probably the most important since Clausewitz (Trythall 1977). In his earlier writings he tended to downgrade Clausewitz, but in later years he began to recognize that his own approach to military theory was essentially Clausewitzian. He was immodest enough to compare himself (and Clausewitz) with Copernicus, Newton, and Darwin. Fuller was the first important armored warfare tactician and theoretician as a combat staff officer in World War I. He was the first to codify the "principles of war" as they have been known for most of this century. Underlying this seminal production was a conviction that there must be laws of combat, or a science of war. Fuller knew that there should be more content and more scientific rigor to a theory of combat than just the principles of war, but he never quite succeeded in formulating such a theory.

Fuller wrote extensively on armored warfare, military theory, the science and philosophy of war, and military history in general. Despite his brilliance,

Fuller was never fully understood or liked by the majority of his fellow officers in the British army. He continued to write and to criticize with acid pen and tongue after he was retired as a relatively youthful major general.

A fellow countryman and contemporary of Fuller, Frederick William Lanchester, was also concerned with the application of the "principle of mass" on the battlefield. An early aeronautical engineer, Lanchester wrote an article entitled "The Principle of Concentration," which was published in October 1914 in the British journal, *Engineering*. That article has had profound impact on the evolution of a theory of combat. Like Fuller, Lanchester's ideas (expressed in the form of two differential equations) about the "principle of concentration" (or mass) were based upon his analytical reading of military history. This is somewhat ironic in view of the fact that many who have exploited Lanchester's ideas have rejected the relevance of history to modern warfare.

In essence, the Lanchester equations show the effects of force concentration upon the loss rates of two opposing sides in a simple, uncomplicated combat situation under each of two general conditions of combat: (1) when one or both of the sides have only a general knowledge of the location of the other (as in a meeting engagement, or as in the case of an attacker against defenders concealed behind prepared or fortified defenses); and (2) when one or both sides have accurate information of the location of the other (as, for instance, a defender in most prepared and fortified defense situations, or two forces opposing each other on a broad, flat desert). Whether these equations represent combat realistically and accurately is debatable. What is not debatable is that Lanchester profoundly influenced military theory in the late twentieth century.

SOVIET SEARCH FOR A THEORY OF COMBAT

Soviet military structure tends toward greater rigidity and conservatism than its counterparts in the West. The magnitude of the Soviet effort in pursuit of a theory of combat is impressive. Officers are schooled in the scientific method far more thoroughly than their Western counterparts. Quantitative analytical techniques are taught throughout the Soviet military educational system, not just as a specialty to a few officers. The Soviets have dozens of officers with doctoral degrees in military science conducting research and publishing treatises on all aspects of war.

Soviet planners apply the data derived from historical research to their operational plans. They press hard to avoid leaving anything to chance. They do not see themselves as practitioners of an art, but rather as scientists and engineers applying the scientific process.

The ultimate expression of the Soviet application of military history to contemporary military science is in what they call the *correlation of forces and means*. This is both a mathematical model of combat and a theory of combat. The official statement of this concept, in greatly abridged form (Belyakov 1979), is:

The Correlation of Forces and Means is an objective indicator of the fighting power of opposing sides, showing the degree of superiority of one over the other. It is determined by comparison of existing quantitative and qualitative data of opposing forces.

An analysis of the correlation of forces permits a deeper investigation into the essence of past battles and engagements.

It is usually calculated during preparation for battle. An estimate is made of the quantity of forces and means necessary for accomplishing missions.

A correlation of forces was estimated during the great patriotic war based on the combat and numerical strength of our own forces and the enemy's. This method of calculating the correlation of forces is also useful today.

Where combat capabilities differ significantly, estimated coefficients of comparability of combat potentials are used. The following are also taken into account: opposing organizations, training, nationality, moral and fighting qualities, armament and equipment, leadership, terrain, etc. Factors are compared with the aid of coefficients.

Those factors which lend themselves to a mathematical expression are compared with the aid of one or another of the coefficients, while the rest are expressed in terms of "superior" or "inferior." Modern computer equipment is used for speeding up the computation of the correlation of forces and means. Possible changes in the correlation of forces and means during combat operations can be determined with the aid of modeling.

It would appear that Soviet theory skillfully integrates the past, the present, and the future.

American Search for a Theory of Combat

In general, and with only a few significant exceptions, American military theorists have shown little interest in the concept of a comprehensive theory or science of combat. While most Americans who think about such things are strong believers in the application of science to war, they seem not to believe, paradoxically, that waging war can be scientific, but instead consider it an art rather than a science. Even scientists involved in military affairs, who perhaps overemphasize the role of science in war, also tend to believe that war is a random process conducted by unpredictable human beings, and thus not capable of being fitted into a scientific theoretical structure.

That aspect of the paradox relating the application of science to war became increasingly pronounced during and since World War II. This has been manifested in two principal activities: the application of technology to the design and development of improvements of weapons, and the study of a wide variety of combat phenomena through military operations research.

American scientists have been generally successful in the first of these activities, but this success has not produced the results that might have been anticipated. Despite the unquestioned lead of the United States and its allies in technology, the Soviet Union, with its relatively inferior technology, has been able to produce comparable weapons just as rapidly.

The experience of American scientists in military operations research has been, if anything, even more frustrating. Despite brilliant success solving individual problems, operations research has not been able to verify its accomplishments or to distill them into a coherent theory. In fact, the opposite may be true, because the results of operations research tend to be confusing without an overall theory to place them into context.

The situation is particularly disappointing in the field of combat modeling. Elegant mathematical formulas abound, purporting to describe the battlefield operations and interactions of weapons and forces in detail, from duels between individual combat soldiers through engagements between small units to battles involving larger aggregations of units. Thousands of computers are used by the American defense research community to operate combat models and simulations, producing results designed to provide useful insights to planners and commanders on how to achieve success in battle. Unfortunately there is a major problem: no two sets of results agree. The combat models are not validated, and there is a general lack of confidence in them.

In 1978 an informal group (first called a Committee to Develop a Theory of Combat, later The Military Conflict Institute) was formed to foster a scientific understanding of the nature of military conflict. Its first goal was to produce a theory of combat, a draft of which was completed in early 1989. Concurrently, one group member found that, since the fundamental problem in any effort to generalize and formulate theories of combat was the influence of presumably unpredictable human behavior on outcomes of battle, the key to developing theories of combat was a systematic study of military history. A method for determining these human behavioral patterns evolved after a long and difficult review of the specifics of a large number of conflicts (Dupuy 1987).

Conceptual Components of Combat

Just as there are different levels in the waging of combat, and largely because of those different levels, there are also different levels in conceptualizing combat. Traditionally there have been two principal conceptual components or levels of combat: strategy and tactics.

About 1830 Clausewitz defined *strategy* as "the use of engagements to attain the object of the war." *Tactics*, he wrote, is "the use of the armed forces in engagements" (Clausewitz 1984). About the same time Jomini defined *strategy* as "the art of getting the armed forces onto the field of battle," and as comprising "all the operations embraced in the theater of war in general." Jomini went on to define *tactics* as "the maneuvers of an army on the day of battle; its contents, its concentrations, and the diverse formations used to lead the troops to the attack" (Jomini 1830, pp. 58–60). In theory the distinction between strategy and tactics was clear; in practice the line was slightly fuzzy.

As war became more complex and as its scope expanded early in the twentieth century, it became evident to military theoreticians, particularly those on the German General Staff, that strategy's scope was correspondingly expanded, dealing often with more than one theater of war, and even embracing such nonmilitary considerations as economics and politics. This expansion, of course, was at the "upper end" of strategy. It also meant that the nature of the authority and responsibility for those concerned with the upper level of strategy at the national capital and in the headquarters of a commander in chief was very different from those of the theater and army commanders at the lower end.

The Germans began to refer to the lower level of strategy as *operations*, a term that—according to Gen. Hermann Foertsch in the late 1930s—was "frequently employed to indicate a sub-concept of strategy. Strictly speaking, operations are the movements of armed forces preparatory to battle, but the fighting itself is usually also included in the concept. There is no definite line of demarcation between the two in ordinary usage" (Foertsch 1940). Foertsch then provided a diagram to help clarify the distinctions among tactics, operations, and strategy as seen by the Germans at that time. For the Germans, warfare comprised three conceptual levels, divided by theoretically clear but practically fuzzy lines.

At the same time other theorists, particularly in Britain, had adapted a term used by Jomini—*grand tactics*—to deal with the area of warfare the Germans called operations, and coined the term *grand strategy* to distinguish that form of strategic thinking applicable to the conduct of war at the highest levels of government. There were, however, no generally accepted definitions of *grand tactics* or *grand strategy*. Furthermore, it was clear that the concept of grand tactics was really part of the realm of strategy as originally visualized by both Jomini and Clausewitz.

In the United States after World War II a clearer understanding of the relationships of the upper levels of strategy emerged, through the development of concepts of "national strategy" and "military strategy." This has led to a new set of definitions for strategy in general and for its upper levels, as follows:

Strategy is the art and science of planning for the use of, and managing, all available resources in the waging of war by those in high levels of national and military authority.

National strategy is the art and science of developing and using political, economic, psychological, social, and military resources as necessary during war and peace to afford the maximum support to national policies and—in the event of war—to increase the probabilities and favorable consequences of victory and to lessen the chances of defeat. Art predominates over science in national strategy.

Military strategy is the art and science of developing and employing in war military resources and forces for the purpose of providing maximum support to national policy in order to increase the probabilities and favorable consequences of victory and to lessen the chances of defeat. Science predominates over art in military strategy. The difference between military competence and military genius at the strategic level is greater artistry by genius. This definition covers a very broad range of the activities of warfare, from the global deployments of armed forces to the theater-level activities the Germans called operations.

Soviet military theorists have also devoted their attention to the relationship between the lower and intermediate levels of strategy by characterizing the lower level as the conceptual area of the operational art. To end fuzziness of distinctions, they arbitrarily define *tactics* as that aspect of the art of war that is the responsibility of division commanders and lower; operational art is the responsibility of army and front (army group) commanders; strategy is the domain of higher commanders. This arbitrary distinction may have ended the practical fuzziness, but it tends to blur the concepts, since it is not possible to make a firm distinction between the concepts of strategy, operations, and tactics simply on the basis of command levels.

Despite the theoretical problems clouding the concept of the operational art, the United States early in the 1980s adopted the concept, following the Soviet example perhaps more closely than would be desirable for conceptual clarity. A definition of *operations*, or *operational art*, generally consistent with that recently adopted by the U.S. Army, is as follows:

Operations involves the control and direction of large forces (usually armies or army groups) in combat activities within a single, discrete theater of combat. Operations can be considered a separate conceptual level of combat lying between strategy and tactics.

Thus, the classic duality of the conceptual components of combat as visualized by Clausewitz and Jomini has become in the twentieth century a trilogy in the current military doctrines of many major military powers. The classic definitions of tactics by Clausewitz and Jomini require some adjustment to fit into this trilogy:

Tactics is the technique of deploying and directing military forces (troops, ships, or aircraft, or combinations of these, and their immediate supporting elements) in coordinated combat activities against the enemy in order to attain the objectives designated by strategy or operations.

Another word often used in relation to the conceptual components of combat is *doctrine*. Interestingly, the Germans have no such term in their military lexicon, apparently because of its imprecision. However, it is a useful word and concept, and the following definition attempts to limit its inherent imprecision.

Military doctrine is the combination of principles, policies, and concepts into an integrated system for the purpose of governing all components of a military force in combat, and assuring consistent, coordinated employment of these components. The origin of doctrine can be experience, theory, or both. Doctrine represents the available thought on the employment of forces that has been adopted by an armed force. Doctrine is methodology, and if it is to work, all military elements must know, understand, and respect it. Doctrine is implemented by tactics.

APPLICABILITY TO AIR AND NAVAL WARFARE

Discussed earlier were twelve military theorists since the time of Napoleon whose writings have contributed to the inchoate effort to produce a theory of combat. Only one of the twelve was a naval combat theorist, although mankind has been fighting on, in, and over the water almost as long as it has on land; and only one was an air combat theorist.

If the list were expanded to include all possible contributors to significant military theory, the proportion of naval theorists would not rise much above 10 percent. The proportion of air theorists would probably be even smaller, in part because manned flight and air combat has been possible for less than a century. In any event, there is reason to believe that a general theory of combat for land warfare is likely to be applicable—probably with some modifications—to both naval and air warfare.

Clausewitz's Theory of Combat

To provide background for a discussion of Clausewitz's basic theory of combat, it is useful to survey what he wrote in *On War* about his philosophy of war.

CLAUSEWITZ'S PHILOSOPHY OF WAR

One of the three most profound theoretical statements that Clausewitz made about war had to do with his philosophy of war; that is, his statement of the relationships of war to politics.

War as a continuation of politics. This is perhaps the most fundamental element of Clausewitz's philosophy of war. War is, and must always be, subservient to politics.

"Absolute" war in theory and war in practice. In theory, Clausewitz points out, war is an act of violence to be carried out to the utmost limits of the lethal capabilities of the opponents. In practice, however, war will be carried out only to the degree of violence consistent with the politics motivating the opponents. This is mainly because war is an instrument of policy, but it is also because of the realities that led him to develop his concept of friction. From this duality of theory and practice emerge two more significant characteristics of war.

Total war or limited war. War can be conducted with as much force as is possible—thus approaching the theoretical absolute war—in order to overthrow an opponent, if that is the aim of policy. Or else it can be carried out in more limited fashion for the purpose of achieving lesser policy goals.

Ends and means in war. When the ends of war are total (i.e., the overthrow of the opponent, or survival against such an effort), the means will be violent to the utmost capability of the contestants. If the ends of war are less than overthrow of the enemy, then the means will be less violent.

The activities of war. Clausewitz divides the activities of war into two principal categories: fighting, or combat; and preparation for fighting, or administration.

In sum, Clausewitz thought in theoretical terms and saw war as having both quantitative and qualitative aspects. He also made it very clear that the general philosophy of war—dealing primarily with strategy—was essentially qualitative, and probably not amenable to quantitative analysis. On the other hand, when he was writing about tactics—in other words, dealing with actual fighting or combat—he saw much in terms of scale, degree, or quantity.

Next to be examined is the concept that was the essence of Clausewitz's quantitative approach to combat theory.

THE "LAW OF NUMBERS"

It has been obvious to most soldiers and scholars who have studied *On War* that it is the most profound book on military theory ever written. Although it is an unfinished work, it is thought that if Clausewitz had been able to complete it in the fashion that he planned, he might have been able to integrate its many brilliant thoughts and concepts into a single, comprehensive theory.

One of the most important passages in *On War* was Clausewitz's discussion of numbers, the essence of which is a passage called the "Law of Numbers."

> If we . . . strip the engagement of all the variables arising from its purposes and circumstances, and disregard the fighting value of the troops involved (which is a given quantity), we are left with the bare concept of the engagement, a shapeless battle in which the only distinguishing factor is the number of troops on either side.
>
> These numbers, therefore, will determine victory. It is, of course, evident from the mass of abstractions I have made to reach this point that superiority of numbers in a given engagement is only one of the factors that determines victory. Superior numbers, far from contributing everything, or even a substantial part, to victory, may actually be contributing very little, depending on the circumstances.
>
> But superiority varies in degree. It can be two to one, or three or four to one, and so on, it can obviously reach the point where it is overwhelming.
>
> In this sense superiority of numbers admittedly is the most important factor in the outcome of an engagement so long as it is great enough to counterbalance all other contributing circumstances. It thus follows that as many troops as possible should be brought into the engagement at the decisive point.
>
> Whether these forces prove adequate or not, we will at least have done everything in our power. This is the first principle of strategy. In the general terms in which it is expressed here it would hold true for Greeks and Persians, for Englishmen and Mahrattas, for Frenchmen and Germans. (Clausewitz 1984, pp. 194–95)

Just as important as the actual numbers—or perhaps more important—are the variable factors describing the engagement, which must be "stripped out" for analysis. Clausewitz also states specifically that the fighting value, or effectiveness, of a military force is a given quantity (i.e., quite measurable), and he implies clearly that the quality of forces will vary from nation to nation and among units within national forces. Finally, he tells us that his formulation of the relationship of numbers to victory is historically timeless and applicable in any geographic setting. The "law of numbers" is a clear, unambiguous statement of a mathematical theory of combat, which Clausewitz asserts is valid throughout the course of history.

It is necessary to reconcile this interpretation of the law of numbers with the passages in Book Two of *On War*, where Clausewitz argues with himself the twin questions of whether war is a science or an art, and whether or not war is amenable to theory. It is necessary also to reconcile this deterministic statement with the many references throughout *On War* to the role of chance in war, which has led many of his readers to assume that Clausewitz saw war as a random process with unpredictable results, rather than the mathematical process implied so clearly in the above quotation.

Despite some passages in *On War* that could be interpreted that way, Clausewitz did *not* think of chance as a roll of the dice determining victory or defeat. As is clear, for instance, in his famous quotation on "friction," he looked upon chance much as he did upon friction: one of many factors contributing to the confusion and chaos of battle. Indeed, the two concepts of chance and friction seem to have overlapped in his mind.

To Clausewitz the word *chance* meant that there will always be problems in battle that a commander cannot possibly foresee, problems that arise either because of the "innate perversity" of inanimate objects, or of nature, or of man himself. Even though not individually foreseeable, these problems of chance are things that a commander can—if he is ready—deal with and control by means of his "genius" in the same way in which his genius will enable him to overcome the even less predictable actions and reactions of his opponent.

What Clausewitz wrote about chance is fully reconcilable with his law of numbers. The outcome of the battle will be determined by the genius of the commander in bringing to the critical point on the battlefield a force superior in numerical combat power; by his genius in being adaptable, and taking advantage of the "circumstances of the combat," including most of the variables of combat (not excepting friction and chance); and by his genius in assuring the highest value (quality) of his troops.

Even though Clausewitz did not specifically say so, and even though he might not even have recognized the fact at the time of writing, his law of numbers is, indeed, a synthesis of a comprehensive theory of combat. Although Clausewitz never expressed that law as a formula, it is stated so clearly, and in such mathematical terms, that such a formula was unquestionably in his mind.

First we see Clausewitz's concept of battle outcome as a ratio:

$$\text{Outcome} = \frac{N_r \times V_r \times Q_r}{N_b \times V_b \times Q_b}$$

where:

N = numbers of troops
V = variable circumstances affecting a force in battle
Q = quality of force
r = red force identifier
b = blue force identifier

If that is a valid relationship—as Clausewitz asserts—then the following equation can be written for the combat power, P, of each of the opposing sides:

$$P = N \times V \times Q$$

Just as Newton's physics can be summarized by the simple equation $F = MA$, so, too, can Clausewitz's theory of combat be summarized in an equally simple equation: $P = NVQ$.

Future of a Theory of Combat

Although Clausewitz's Law of Numbers was published a century and a half ago, it has only recently been seriously proposed as the basis for a comprehensive theory of combat. This is probably because Clausewitz expressed his essentially mathematical concept in words rather than in equations. Therefore it has been ignored by theorists seeking a theory expressed mathematically, because they have been looking for a mathematical form. It may be some time before the profundity and universality of Clausewitz's theory is accepted by those who have hitherto overlooked it in their search for *the* theory.

It may be safely predicted, however, that any alternative approach will have to take Clausewitz's theory into consideration and will have to come to terms with it, either consciously or unconsciously. Any alternative inconsistent with Clausewitz's theory, as presented above, will almost certainly be demonstrably invalid. Any alternative that is consistent with it cannot be fundamentally different.

TREVOR N. DUPUY

SEE ALSO: Clausewitz, Karl von; Friction; Jomini, Antoine Henri; War.

Bibliography

Ardant du Picq, C. J. J. J. 1921. *Battle studies.* New York: Macmillan.

Belyakov, V. I. 1979. Correlation of Forces and Means. *Sovetskakila voennakila entsiklopedkila.* (Soviet military encyclopedia). Moscow: Voyenizdat.

Clausewitz, C. von. 1976 [1832]. *On war.* Reprint. Ed. and trans. M. Howard and P. Paret. Princeton, N.J.: Princeton Univ. Press.

Dodge, T. A. 1889–1907. *Great captains.* 6 vols. Boston: Houghton Mifflin.

Douhet, G. 1942. *The command of the air.* Trans. D. Ferrari. New York: Coward-McCann.

Dupuy, T. N. 1987. *Understanding war.* New York: Paragon House.

———, C. Johnson, and G. P. Hayes. 1986. *Dictionary of military terms.* New York: Wilson.

Earle, E. M., ed. 1971. *Makers of modern strategy.* Princeton, N.J.: Princeton Univ. Press.

Foch, F. 1970. *The principles of war.* Trans. J. de Morinni. New York: AMS Press.

Foertsch, H. 1940. *The art of modern warfare.* Trans. T. W. Knauth. New York: Veritas.

Fuller, J. F. C. 1961. *The conduct of war, 1789–1961.* London: Eyre and Spottiswoode.

Groener, W. 1927. *Das Testament des Grafen Schlieffen.* Berlin: E. S. Mittler & Sohn.

Jomini, A. H. 1830. *Tableau analytique des principales combinaisons de la guerre, et de leurs rapports avec la politique des états, pour servir d'introduction au Traité des grandes opérations militaires.* Paris: Anselin.

———. 1851. *Traité des qrandes opérations militaries, ou Histoire critique des guerres de Fréderic le Grand comparées au système moderne.* Paris: J. Dumaine.

Lanchester, F. W. 1914. The principle of concentration. *Engineering,* 2 October.

Mahan, A. T. 1884. *The influence of sea power on history, 1660–1783.* Boston: Little, Brown.

Paret, P., ed. 1986. *Makers of modern strategy.* Princeton, N.J.: Princeton Univ. Press.

Schlieffen, A. G. von. 1931. *Cannae.* Fort Leavenworth, Kans.: Command and General Staff School Press.

Sun Tzu. 1963. *The art of war.* Trans. S. B. Griffith. Oxford: Oxford Univ. Press.

Trythall, A. J. 1977. *"Boney" Fuller: The intellectual general.* London: Cassell.

U.S. Military Academy, Dept. Of Military Art and Engineering. 1944. *Jomini, Clausewitz, and Schlieffen.* West Point, N.Y.: Dept. of Military Art and Engineering, U.S. Military Academy.

Wright, Q. 1942. *A study of war.* Chicago: Univ. of Chicago Press.

Yorck von Wartenburg, M. Graf. 1902. *Napoleon as a general.* 2 vols. London: K. Paul, Trench, Trubner.

THIRTY YEARS' WAR

The Thirty Years' War was a major European conflict that took place from 1618 to 1648 and, at one time or another, involved every European state either directly or indirectly. The war, which was in fact a series of closely related wars, was Europe's most destructive conflict, in terms of both human life and property, until surpassed by the wars of the Napoleonic era.

It is traditional to view the events of the Thirty Years' War within a chronological framework of four "periods," each named for the leader of a series of anti-Hapsburg coalitions. The periods are: Bohemian (1618–23); Danish (1625–29); Swedish (1630–35); and French (1635–48). Within that framework occurred no fewer than "13 distinct but overlapping wars, involving over 50 bilateral wars" (Wright, Vol. I, Table 33, facing p. 642).

Background

The conventional interpretation of the war—as a religious-political conflict pitting the militant Protestant states of North Europe against Hapsburg Austria and Spain, the champions of the Catholic Reformation—is attractive in its simplicity but ignores some basic facts of seventeenth-century European political life. Chief among these is the fact that the religious issue was not the principal dynamic (although it was a convenient motivational instrument, and an important theme in the plentiful propaganda of the time). In the first great armed confrontation of the war the Protestant powers of North Europe maintained a studied neutrality while their co-religionists in Bohemia were crushed, Lutheran Saxony joined the emperor against the Bohemians, and Catholic Savoy provided an army to the Protestant rebels. Indeed, the final defeat of the Catholic powers was ensured by the intervention of Catholic France, first by subsidy to Sweden, the "Protestant Champion," then by military force. And the architects of French policy were both cardinals of the Catholic church.

In fact, the war had a multiplicity of causes, some of which were religious issues. The rise of Calvinism, unanticipated at the time of the Catholic-Lutheran settlement of the Peace of Augsburg (1555), complicated matters. The Lutheran-Calvinist schism (1561) was the first important division among the Protestants, and the Calvinists were often rebellious proselytes who threatened the status quo of *cuius regio, eius religio* ("he who holds the region determines the religion") established by the Peace of Augsburg. The possibility that the Holy Roman Empire might fall into the hands of a Calvinist (and the status of Calvinism within the empire) was the proximate cause of the war.

In general, however, the war was the working out of the future status of the great House of Hapsburg. The Hapsburgs controlled central Europe by virtue of the fact that one branch of the family usually supplied the Holy Roman (i.e., German) Emperor; they also aspired to world empire, since the other branch provided the hereditary monarchs of Spain. Although in 1618 the House of Hapsburg was in decline, the disorganization, timidity, and selfishness of its myriad enemies prevented the fact from becoming apparent.

Bohemian Period, 1618–23

Decades of tension and threatening conflict in the Holy Roman Empire culminated in open rebellion in Bohemia (Czechoslovakia). There, the Bohemian Diet had recognized as king Ferdinand of Styria, the Catholic cousin (and designated successor) of the aged, ailing emperor Matthias. It then reversed itself and elected the Calvinist Frederick, Elector Palatine, as king in defiance of the emperor.

The new "king of Bohemia" was an ambitious but politically naive youth who aspired to the imperial throne and was chief of the Protestant Union, a league of German Calvinist states that had the nominal support of England and Holland—Spain's archenemies. With an imperial election imminent, Ferdinand could not permit Bohemia and its "swing vote" to fall into the hands of his enemies.

Despite the rebellion, Ferdinand was elected emperor (28 August 1619) and, with his allies Spain and the Catholic League, moved to restore imperial authority in Bohemia. Frederick garnered remarkably little support. He and his allies were decisively defeated at the White Mountain, near Prague (8 November 1620), by an Imperial League army commanded by Charles Bonaventure de Longueval, Count of Bucquoi, and Johan Tserclaes, Count of Tilly.

Frederick fled, and his followers were delivered up to a fearful retribution. Bohemia would not again enjoy independence until 1918.

The suppression of the rebellion in Bohemia allowed the emperor to transfer military operations into the Rhine Valley, the seat of power of the Protestant Union. In a series of battles in 1622, Tilly, aided by the Spanish under Gonzalo de Córdoba, defeated the generals and confederates of Frederick: Ernst, Count Mansfeld; George Frederick, Margrave of Baden-Durlach; and Christian of Brunswick. The principal battles in this phase were fought at Wimpfen (6 May), where Tilly and Gonzalo defeated Baden-Durlach; at Höchst (20 June), where

Tilly defeated Christian; and at Fleurus (29 August), where Gonzalo, though hard-pressed, defeated and pursued Mansfeld and Christian. The results at Wimpfen and Höchst caused the Palatine to withdraw from the conflict; Mansfeld and Christian became freebooters, without allegiance to any state or cause, save the black flag of pillage and rapine.

Danish Period, 1625–29

Christian IV, Protestant king of Denmark, alarmed by Tilly's success and desirous of extending Danish influence over the rich ports of the North Sea and Pomerania, advanced himself as Protestant champion. While the Imperial generalissimo Albrecht, Count Wallenstein, a Czech, administered the coup de grace to Mansfeld at the Battle of Dessau Bridge (25 April 1625), Tilly defeated Christian and his allies in a series of battles, the most important of which was Lutter (27 August 1626).

The defeat of the Danish king and the defeat and death (from natural causes) of both Mansfeld and Christian of Brunswick created the possibility of peace in the empire. Emperor Ferdinand, however, missed the opportunity for reconciliation by issuing the Edict of Restitution (1629), a revolutionary document that proposed to restore to the Church all property seized and secularized in the three-quarters of a century since the Peace of Augsburg. The measure was patently illegal and had little support, even among Catholics, but despite profound resentment there was no resistance, since all Germany was cowed by the emperor's military success.

Swedish Period, 1630–35

On 4 July 1630 the 36-year-old king of Sweden, Gustavus Adolphus, already an accomplished warrior, landed with his army in northern Germany. He was the latest Protestant champion, "the Lion of the North," and it mattered little that behind the hagiography Gustavus was little interested in the more mundane aspects of the outcome of his invasion—his primary aim was to add Germany's Baltic littoral to the Swedish empire.

Augmented by the Saxon army, the Swedes defeated Tilly at Breitenfeld I (17 September 1631) and at the Lech (15–16 April 1632), where Tilly was killed. Gustavus's progress was checked at the Alte Veste near Nürnberg (3–4 September 1632) by Wallenstein, but at Lützen (16 November 1632) the Swedes defeated Wallenstein in a sanguineous fight made dearer by the loss of the king. The mantle of leadership passed to Gustavus's gifted lieutenant, Bernhard of Saxe-Weimar.

In the aftermath of this battle, Wallenstein was basely murdered by some of his officers at the emperor's behest. It seems that he had grown too powerful and, indeed, had entered into negotiations with high officers of the other side.

At Nördlingen (6 September 1634) Archduke Ferdinand, King of Hungary and the emperor's son, and Ferdinand, Cardinal-Infante of Spain, decisively defeated Saxe-Weimar and the Swedish marshal Gustav Horn in a great battle that had far-reaching implications. The battle showed that Sweden and Bernhard's "Weimarians," however game, were no match for the combined power of the empire, Spain, and Bavaria. France's Cardinal Richelieu, implacable enemy of the Hapsburgs, decided to intervene in the war to redress the balance.

French Period, 1635–48

France brought immense resources and military power potential into the arena and assumed leadership of the anti-Hapsburg coalition. Sweden, subsidized by France, was now led by the able chancellor Axel Oxenstierna.

Capitalizing on Nördlingen, the empire countered by concluding the Peace of Prague with Saxony (1635). The terms of the peace were accepted eventually by all the important German states. With Germany united behind him, the emperor was able to move strongly against the foreign powers. In the thirteen remaining years of war, however, the Imperial armies enjoyed little success. Mainly, this was due to poor leadership. With the sole exception of the brilliant Franz, Baron von Mercy, Imperial commanders in the war's last phases were mediocre and even incompetent. One of these heirs of Tilly and Wallenstein, Matthias, Count Gallas—who had profited immensely by Wallenstein's downfall—was so palpably inept that he was nicknamed "the destroyer of armies" (i.e., his own). By contrast, the leaders of the armies of the Franco-Swedish alliance were generally able and occasionally gifted or truly great.

The first test of the new alignment came at Wittstock in Brandenburg, where the Swedish marshal Johan Baner routed a combined Saxon-Imperial army under Melchior, Count von Hatzfeld, and John George, Elector of Saxony (4 October 1636). The victory restored the reputation of the Swedish army and ensured the continuation of the war in central Germany.

Despite his talents, Baner eventually evidenced ambition almost as colossal and dangerous as Wallenstein's. His death in 1641 precluded any attempt to usurp the Swedish crown.

Baner was succeeded by Lennart Torstensson, a thorough, no-nonsense soldier who set about the task of finally dismantling the empire. Torstensson destroyed an Imperial army commanded by the archduke Leopold William at Breitenfeld II (2 November 1642) and followed up by ravaging Bohemia and Moravia.

In 1643 at Rocroi, in the Ardennes region on France's northeastern frontier, a Spanish invasion army under Francisco Melo de Braganza was destroyed by a French army led by Louis, duc d'Enghien (the future "Great Condé"). Enghien's victory ended 150 years of Spanish military preeminence and heralded the military ascendancy of France. Also, by eliminating the Spanish threat to France in that quarter, it permitted Enghien to transfer his army to the Rhine region; this he did effectively in 1644 and 1645, checking and defeating Mercy in both instances.

Enghien's triumph at Rocroi was almost negated by the French disaster at Tuttlingen; there on 24 November 1643 Mercy surprised and smashed the French Army of Germany, which was led by the Danish soldier of fortune,

Josias von Rantzau. The rout of Tuttlingen diminished French prestige and seriously compromised the efforts of French diplomats at the preliminary peace negotiations of the Congress of Munster (1644).

Henri, vicomte de Turenne, one of history's great captains, took command of the demoralized remnants of Rantzau's army, which he reorganized in Lorraine. Mercy, meantime, descended on the key Black Forest city of Freiburg im Breisgau and besieged it (July 1644).

Turenne called for help, and Condé led his army to Breisach, where it joined Turenne's. As a prince of the blood, Condé commanded the united armies, which marched immediately against Mercy. In a furious three-day battle (3, 5, 9 August 1644) Mercy was driven from Freiburg and into Würtemberg.

On 6 March 1645, Torstensson defeated Hatzfeld at Jankau in Bohemia, destroying the emperor's last field army. Joined by George I Rakoczy, Prince of Transylvania, he marched on Vienna. The fickle Rakoczy's unexpected defection ended this threat to the empire, and Torstensson fell back into Bohemia.

Turenne, meanwhile, invaded Bavaria. He was surprised by Mercy at Mergentheim and defeated (2 May 1645). Retreating into Hesse, he rallied his men and prevented a greater disaster by his skillful handling of a potentially disastrous situation. Once again, Condé came to Turenne's aid. His army joined Turenne's remnants, and the united force advanced into Bavaria. Mercy fell back before the French.

At Allerheim (Nördlingen II) on 3 August 1645, Mercy gave battle. In a desperate, bloody battle, Mercy came close to winning but was killed by a musket shot. His successor, Johann von Werth, withdrew the Bavarian army. The French were too shattered to pursue.

The war's final campaigns resembled in some respects the "broken-back war" predicted for the aftermath of nuclear holocaust. The relatively efficient French armies of Condé and Turenne continued to win victories, but the Swedes failed in Bohemia. Turenne finally forced Bavaria to submit, and Condé's great victory over the Spanish and Lorrainers at Lens (10 August 1648) induced the emperor Ferdinand III (r. 1637–57) to sign the Peace of Westphalia, which ended the war. (The war between France and Spain continued until 1659.)

The Peace of Westphalia

The various treaties that made up the Peace of Westphalia greatly diminished the emperor's power. France and Sweden gained territories within the empire (Sweden on the Baltic littoral, France along the Rhine). The triumph of particularism in Germany was fatal; it created a political weakness that was practically an invitation to aggression, as had been the case in Italy in the previous century. The chief aggressors in the next half-century were the guarantors of the Peace: France and Sweden.

The Peace resulted in the breakup of the powerful but often strained Spanish-Austrian alliance, in effect achieving Richelieu's objective in entering the war. France, though mired in civil war (the *Fronde*), was now Europe's greatest power. It is ironic that the nation that would later administer the first rude checks to French ambition was born in the negotiations ending the Thirty Years' War. On 30 January 1648 Spain officially ended its 80-year-long war with the rebellious provinces of the Netherlands and recognized Holland as a sovereign power.

Military Aspects of the War

The war was remarkable chiefly for the introduction and triumph of the linear tactical system of Gustavus Adolphus. This system marked the final transition from the ponderous, deep formations of the sixteenth century to the more modern, shallow tactical formations emphasizing firepower that characterized combat in the Age of Marlborough and Frederick the Great. Gustavus emphasized combined arms combat, firepower, and maneuver in a rationalized system made possible by discipline and drill. His armies were recognizably "modern" in most respects. The inheritors of his legacy were Turenne on the Continent (and through him the armies of Louis XIV) and Cromwell and Montrose in the British Isles (and through them the army of Marlborough).

Cost of the War

The human and economic toll of the war can never be known with certainty. The most reliable statements of the human cost estimate 180,000–325,000 battle deaths and a total population decline in the empire of "considerably less than one-third"—that is, less than ten million (Urlanis 1971, p. 149; Ergang 1956, pp. 24, 27). Since the principal war theaters encompassed parts of central and eastern Europe outside the empire as well as border regions of Spain and France, there were undoubtedly significant civilian casualties not included in the above enumeration.

The war supposedly devastated the once-thriving economy of Germany and crippled its socioeconomic life. In fact, although certain districts suffered terribly from the war, the economic eclipse of the region began as early as 1550 and continued unabated until revived by industrialization and unification in the nineteenth century. The war certainly accelerated the decline, but the fragmentation of the empire and the intensified economic particularism that were debilitating consequences of the peace treaties were, in the long term, far more serious.

CURT JOHNSON

SEE ALSO: Condé, Louis II de Bourbon, Prince de; France, Military Hegemony of; Gustavus Adolphus; Prussia and Germany, Rise of; Spanish Empire; Turenne, Henri de La Tour d'Auvergne, Vicomte de.

Bibliography

Chapman, B. 1856. *The history of Gustavus Adolphus and of the Thirty Years' War.* London: Longman, Brown.

Charvériat, E. 1878. *Histoire de la guerre de Trente Ans.* Vol. 1: *Période palatine et période danoise (1618–1630)*; vol. 2: *Période suédoise et période française (1630–1648)*. Paris: Plon.

Chudoba, B. 1952. *Spain and the Empire, 1519–1643.* Chicago, Ill.: Univ. of Chicago Press.

Ergang, R. 1956. *The myth of the all-destructive fury of the Thirty Years' War.* Pocono Pines, Pa.: The Craftsmen.

Maland, D. 1980. *Europe at war, 1600–1650.* Totowa, N.J.: Rowman and Littlefield.

Malleson, G. B. [1884] 1971. *The battlefields of Germany.* Reprint. Westport, Conn.: Greenwood.

Pagès, G. 1939. *La Guerre de Trente Ans, 1618–1648.* Paris: Payot.

Polisensky, J. V. 1971. *The Thirty Years' War.* Trans. R. Evans. London: Batsford.

———. 1978. *War and Society in Europe, 1618–1648.* New York: Cambridge Univ. Press.

Steinberg, S. H. 1975. *The Thirty Years' War and the conflict for European hegemony.* London: Edward Arnold.

Urlanis, B. 1971. *Wars and population.* Moscow: Progress.

Wedgwood, C. V. 1938. *The Thirty Years' War.* London: J. Cape.

Wright, Quincy. 1942. *A study of war.* 2 vols. Chicago: Univ. of Chicago Press.

TIRPITZ, ALFRED VON [1849–1930]

Alfred von Tirpitz was among the most able naval administrators of modern history and the architect of the Imperial German Navy that fought World War I.

Tirpitz, a commoner, enlisted in the German navy in 1865 and became an officer four years later. In 1888 he was promoted to captain and, in 1895, to rear admiral. In March 1897 Kaiser Wilhelm II appointed him state secretary of the Navy Office (Reichs-Marine-Amt) to build up the German navy, a task to which he devoted the next nineteen years.

Wilhelm II, who became kaiser in 1888, reversed Bismarck's sound policy of keeping the German navy small. He saw the navy as an important element in his aggressive foreign policy (*Weltpolitik*). It would provide diplomatic leverage, protect Germany's growing colonial empire and overseas trade, and, in the event of war, prevent the nation from being cut off from vital imports. In 1895, while ranking second in world trade, Germany was only fifth in naval strength.

Before Tirpitz became state secretary of the Navy Office, great strides had been made in such areas as ordnance, armor, and shipbuilding. Tirpitz insisted on full control over naval construction, rejected the cruiser fleet concept that the kaiser advocated, and agreed with Mahan's idea that the emphasis must be on battleships. Although Tirpitz did not acknowledge it publicly, his battleship fleet was obviously directed against Britain, and the decision to build a powerful German fleet ushered in one of history's greatest arms races. Tirpitz succeeded by virtue of his force of personality, his ability as a publicist, and growing support in influential circles within Germany for a large navy.

The first naval construction bill passed the Reichstag in April 1898. It called for the construction of nineteen battleships, eight armored cruisers, twelve large cruisers, and 30 light cruisers by April 1904.

In 1900 Tirpitz took advantage of the troubled international situation (the recently concluded Spanish-American War and the ongoing Boer War and Boxer Rebellion) to secure passage of a second Navy Bill. This doubled the size of the projected navy within twenty years to a total of 38 battleships, 20 armored cruisers, and 38 light cruisers (by comparison, the British Home Fleet had at the time about 32 battleships). Supplemental naval authorizations came with international crises over Morocco in 1906 and 1912. The rapid construction of newer vessels reduced the average age of ships in service. The Kiel Canal was also widened to allow the passage of the larger new vessels from the Baltic to the North Sea. In 1912 the fleet, to be maintained at full readiness, was projected at 41 battleships (in five squadrons) and twenty large and 40 light cruisers.

Tirpitz kept pace with British innovations, responding to both the new dreadnought and battle cruiser classes. Although less heavily gunned than their English counterparts, German dreadnoughts and battle cruisers were better protected, and hence less vulnerable.

Tirpitz was absolutely opposed to any reductions in naval construction and was prominent in scuttling British War Minister Haldane's 1912 mission to Germany in which he attempted to reduce the naval race.

Tirpitz was a late convert to the potential of submarines. The first German *Unterseeboot* (i.e., submarine), U1, was completed only at the end of 1906, and it was several years before the submarine's potential was realized. There were to be 72 such boats, but there was no plan to use them for warfare against commercial shipping. By 1913 Tirpitz had also been won over to the value of naval airships.

The Tirpitz program was supposedly based on the "risk theory." Tirpitz felt that the German fleet should be sufficiently powerful to deter a potential enemy from risking an all-out encounter that might result in losses sufficient to make that power prey to other navies. He also maintained, contrary to the views of Bismarck, that a powerful fleet would make Germany a valuable potential ally.

By 1920 the Imperial Navy was to have 60 capital ships in full readiness, but these were by no means all Tirpitz wanted. He saw the navy as the key to Germany's future existence (*existenzfrage*). His chief concern was that the British might try to "Copenhagen" the fleet before it was ready to compete against them on equal terms (this refers to the 1801 Battle of Copenhagen in which the British navy destroyed the Danish fleet, through a surprise attack and without a declaration of war). Privately Tirpitz spoke of a great future sea battle (*entscheidungsschlacht*) with the British, possibly joined by the Americans, to decide world mastery.

The risk theory makes sense only if it is seen as cover for a plan to build the world's most powerful navy. Tirpitz viewed the German army as second in importance to the navy, which he considered the future chief instrument of *Weltpolitik*; by 1914 the German navy was the second largest in the world. Although the army had again been given priority for spending in 1908, the naval buildup prior to that had already consumed precious and limited resources.

The British had a "two-power" naval policy; they maintained a navy equal in strength to the next two naval powers combined. Britain was better able to bear the financial burden of the naval race than Germany and, as an island nation dependent upon imports of food and raw materials for survival, the navy was indeed the key to Britain's *existenzfrage*. The naval race had also driven Britain into an alliance with France. A 1912 agreement between the two countries enabled the British to withdraw naval units from the Mediterranean and deploy them in the North Sea, giving Britain naval superiority over the Germans there.

Tirpitz gave his attention to the development of the fleet rather than to its employment, and he was not consulted on important decisions over its use during the First World War. He believed that Britain would remain neutral, and when that did not occur, he favored risking a decisive battle early in the war. However, with the exception of the submarines, the German High Seas Fleet remained in port most of the war. The chief exception was the Battle of Jutland in 1916, which was tactically indecisive, but which strategically confirmed Britain's mastery of the seas.

In the winter of 1915–16 Tirpitz pushed for a resumption of unrestricted submarine warfare. When his advice went unheeded, he submitted a letter of resignation, which Wilhelm II accepted on 10 March 1916.

Tirpitz later entered politics, helping to found the Fatherland Party. From 1924 to 1928 he was a Nationalist member of the Reichstag. He died on 6 March 1930.

SPENCER C. TUCKER

SEE ALSO: Scheer, Reinhard.

Bibliography

Herwig, H. 1980. *"Luxury" fleet. The imperial German navy, 1888–1918.* London: George Allen and Unwin.

Tirpitz, Grand Admiral Alfred von. 1919. *My memoirs.* New York: Dodd, Mead.

TOGO, HEIHACHIRO [1848–1934]

Admiral Heihachiro Togo (Fig. 1) was Japan's naval leader whose fleet utterly defeated numerically superior forces during the Russo-Japanese War. As the capstone of a military career that paralleled Japan's rise from a feudal state to a world power, his victory at the battle of Tsushima in 1905 is considered by many the most sweeping naval success in all of history.

Background and Early Career

Togo was born into a samurai family on 27 January 1848 at Kajiya, Satsuma. At age 15, wearing two swords at his waist, he helped serve the muzzle-loading

Figure 1. Togo Heihachiro. (SOURCE: U.S. Library of Congress)

cannon defending Kagoshima against a British punitive squadron. In 1866 Togo entered the new Imperial Navy. A most promising junior officer, Togo spent a seven-year apprenticeship with the Royal Navy at Portsmouth and studied math at Cambridge. Upon his return to Japan in 1878, he advanced rapidly. By 1888, he was a full captain and in 1893 took the cruiser *Naniwa* to Hawaii during the unrest coincident with the coup against Queen Liliuoikalani.

Sino-Japanese War of 1894 and Afterward

On 25 July 1894, Togo's cruiser probably fired the first shots of the Sino-Japanese War against Chinese warships off Korea and, later the same day, created an international incident by sinking with a torpedo the British-flagged transport *Kowshing*, which was loaded with Chinese troops. Although Togo rescued the British personnel of the vessel, he refused to pick up drowning Chinese and sank two of their lifeboats.

Playing a conspicuous part in the major sea actions of the war, Togo also led the naval forces assigned to the seizure of Formosa. After his promotion to rear admiral, plum assignments followed: president of the Naval Technical Council (1895) and of the Higher Naval College (1896), leader of the squadron dispatched against the Boxers (1900), and finally in October 1903, commander of the Standing and Combined Squadrons—virtually the entire Japanese navy. He chose the English-built battleship *Mikasa* as his flagship.

Russo-Japanese War, 1904–1905

In planning for war against an increasingly hostile Russia, Togo faced a serious numerical disadvantage in major warships. Excluding the Black Sea Fleet, the Russians listed sixteen battleships in commission or close to completion and four armored cruisers. Seven of the Russian battleships were in the Far East. Togo in January 1904 could muster six battleships and eight armored cruisers with no reinforcements in the offing.

EARLY ENGAGEMENTS

His force did possess certain advantages: better-trained personnel, a higher fleet speed, and an enemy navy divided between European and Asian waters. Togo intended to capitalize on these advantages by defeating the Russian fleet in detail. On 7 February 1904, Togo launched, prior to his country's declaration of war, a night torpedo attack against the czarist Far Eastern fleet at its principal base, Port Arthur. Although only partially successful, Togo's destroyers did cripple the best Russian battleships.

For the next year, Togo kept the Russians off balance with a variety of offensive operations despite the loss of two battleships in May to Russian mines. On 6 June, he was promoted to full admiral. On 23 June and again on 10 August at the Battle of the Yellow Sea, he repulsed sorties by the larger Russian Port Arthur squadron. Togo remained on blockade duty until the surrender of the Russian base to Japanese land forces at the end of 1904.

TSUSHIMA STRAITS

Togo then turned to deal with the Russian Baltic Fleet, which was approaching by way of the Indian Ocean. Although the opposing forces were closely matched in size, the Japanese held the upper hand in training, morale, and the physical condition of their ships. Togo intended to fight a battle of annihilation, beginning with a gunnery duel in the Tsushima Straits, between Korea and Japan, followed by night torpedo attacks.

Early in the action of 28 May 1905, Togo made a risky "in-succession" turn to achieve a decisive position ahead of the Russian force. With his advantage in speed, Togo then chose the range that best suited his fleet's superior main battery gunnery. Despite deteriorating weather conditions and smoke, the well-trained Japanese sailors quickly scored crippling hits. By the next day, the Russians had lost all twelve of their major ships; one Japanese cruiser suffered damage. Personnel casualties were similarly disproportionate: 4,830 Russians dead to 110 Japanese. The Russian admiral, Zinovy Rozhdestvensky, was captured.

Tsushima was Togo's masterpiece. Never in history had a naval battle between apparently closely matched forces ended with a victory so complete or so one-sided. The famed American naval theorist Alfred Thayer Mahan praised Togo's "personal skill and sound judgment." The official British history summarized: "While his conduct of the whole campaign claims admiration and the completeness of his final triumph compels something akin to wonder, it is easy to underrate the less obtrusive side of his action—the strategical insight, the determination and the restraint which gave him strength to wait."

Later Career

A grateful nation showered Togo with honors. He became chief of the Naval General Staff and was made a count. He represented Japan at the coronation of King George V. In 1913 the Imperial Palace elevated him to the rank of admiral of the fleet, and the next year it entrusted him with overseeing the studies of Crown Prince Hirohito. With the completion of that task in 1921, Togo retired from active duty.

He did retain his seat as the only naval representative on the Board of Field Marshals and Fleet Admirals, and in 1930 the octogenarian hero became a rallying point for the big navy advocates resisting the London Naval Treaty. Afflicted with throat cancer, he died on 30 May 1934, the day after he was named marquis. He received a state funeral; his flagship *Mikasa* has been preserved as a memorial.

Summary

Although unassuming in disposition, Togo won the admiration of his men by his remarkable endurance and his surehanded command of the fleet. Respecting international law only when it served Japan's interests, Togo was ruthless in action. He reminded some British observers of Lord Horatio Nelson in many of his personal qualities, in his devotion to his profession, in his close relationship with his principal subordinates, and in the veneration he inspired from his nation. And Togo's crowning achievement, Tsushima, ranks with Trafalgar in its military and political significance.

MALCOLM MUIR, JR.

SEE ALSO: Japan, Modernization and Expansion of; Russo-Japanese War.

Bibliography

Ballard, G. A. 1921. *The influence of the sea on the political history of Japan*. London: John Murray.
Lloyd, A. 1905. *Admiral Togo*. Tokyo: Kinkodo.
Ogasawara, N. 1934. *Life of Admiral Togo*. Trans. I. Jukichi and I. Tozo. Tokyo: Seito Shorin Press.
Warner, D., and P. Warner. 1974. *The tide at sunrise: A history of the Russo-Japanese War, 1904–1905*. New York: Charterhouse.
Westwood, J. N. 1970. *Witnesses of Tsushima*. Tokyo: Sophia Univ., with Diplomatic Press of Tallahassee.

TRENCHARD, SIR HUGH MONTAGUE
[1873–1956]

During the early days of World War II, when the fate of Great Britain rested on the Royal Air Force (RAF), came Prime Minister Winston Churchill's now famous remark: "Never in the course of human conflict was so much owed by so many to so few." Knowing the history of British airpower, Churchill certainly included Lord Trenchard in that praise in view of the vital role he played in developing the Royal Air Force.

Early Years

Hugh Montague "Boom" Trenchard was born on 3 February 1873 in Taunton. His father was a lawyer who went bankrupt about the time that Trenchard was ready for advanced education. Not a particularly gifted student, Trenchard failed to qualify for training as a naval cadet, but on his third try, and with extensive cramming, he won a commission in the army and was assigned to the Royal Scots Fusiliers.

Joining his unit in India in 1893, Trenchard quickly developed a strong interest in polo and horses, which proved highly useful during his service in the Boer War. He began his service in that war as an infantry captain but was soon asked to form a mounted unit that he led with vigor until he suffered a severe lung wound in October 1900. At first given up for dead, he recovered and returned to England for recuperation. By May 1901 he was able to return to South Africa and at the end of the war was a major in command of a newly formed mounted infantry regiment.

After the Boer War, Trenchard thought of leaving the service but decided to remain when he was offered the position of second in command of the South Nigerian Regiment. While in Africa he won several commendations for his leadership during campaigns, but alienated many fellow officers because of his strict regulations about gambling and drinking. He returned to England twice due to illness during this period, once with black-water fever and once with an abscess on the liver.

While in England, Trenchard became excited about the future of airpower and, at age 39, entered the Central Flying School. While not a distinguished pilot, he did complete the course and became one of the army's first dozen pilots. He was assigned to the permanent staff of the school even before he completed the course and in August 1913 was made its commandant.

World War I

At the outbreak of war in August 1914 the school expanded and the Royal Flying Corps, as it was called then, prepared to expand from its 105 officers and 755 men. This involved a continuing struggle to balance resources for training new air personnel with the need to send every available pilot and mechanic to the front.

In November 1914, Trenchard was assigned to command the first of three air wings in the British Expeditionary Force (BEF). His planes fought German aircraft, strafed ground troops, began rudimentary bombing, and experimented with aerial photography.

By 1915, Trenchard had been promoted to brigadier general and was assigned to command all air groups in the BEF, working closely with its commander, General Haig. Trenchard would seldom turn down an air mission requested of his command and was criticized for his willingness to accept high casualties in order to complete key missions. He was also criticized because he was more interested in supporting the hard-pressed British ground troops than in diverting planes to help protect Britain when the Germans attacked London by air. He was quoted as saying he did not favor British pilots wearing parachutes because he wanted them to stick with their planes if they went down.

A separate Air Ministry was created in 1917 and while Trenchard did not like its first head, Lord Rothermere, he agreed to serve as its first chief of air staff, hoping to serve the interests of the Royal Flying Corps and the Naval Air Service. He discovered, however, that Lord Rothermere was more interested in discrediting General Haig than in supporting him with airpower, and, as a result, Trenchard resigned as air chief in April 1918, only a few days before Lord Rothermere also left office. The new air minister offered Trenchard a variety of positions and he chose to raise a bomber group in France, but the war ended before the group became fully operational.

The Royal Air Force (RAF) was officially created 1 April 1918 and by the end of the war it had 25,000 officers and 140,000 men.

The Battle for the RAF

When Winston Churchill became minister of war and air in 1919, one of his first moves was to persuade Trenchard to serve again as chief of air staff. He had hardly begun when he learned that Prime Minister Lloyd George assumed that the air force would be dissolved and its resources divided between the army and navy. To make matters worse, many of its best officers were seeking discharges.

As commander of the RAF, Trenchard was appointed marshal of the Royal Air Force in 1919 but found that the heads of the army and navy were determined to abolish the separate air force. Finally, in December 1919, the First Sea Lord, Admiral Beatty, agreed to give Trenchard a year to develop the Royal Air Force.

Trenchard developed plans for training institutes for flight officers and technical personnel, technical centers to conduct research, and a system of regular and reserve pilots. Despite these plans, his colleagues in the "sister services" maintained that the air force should be divided between them. In the face of this disagreement, the prime minister asked Lord Balfour to arbitrate the dispute. Balfour spent two months studying the problem and finally recommended that the Royal Air Force be maintained as a separate service.

The role of the air force was supported by its success in helping to maintain peace in the empire. It replaced expensive ground troops in many areas and proved useful in surveying vast areas in Asia and the Middle East.

In December 1929 Trenchard retired from active military service, not knowing that he was soon to begin a new career.

Police Commissioner

In 1919 Trenchard had won recognition for his role in quelling a mutiny by 20,000 British troops in Southampton who refused to accept further orders.

This earlier success in handling dissident troops may have been the reason Prime Minister Ramsey MacDonald asked Trenchard in 1931 to become commissioner of London's Metropolitan Police. After investigating the situation, Trenchard agreed, as he felt that efficiency and discipline were the chief needs. Not surprisingly, Trenchard proved a stern leader, quick to investigate charges of corruption and anxious to add more science to police work. He was not popular with many on the force, however, and had the bad fortune to have to defend wage cuts, which were typical of that period. He retired from the police position in 1935.

World War II

Trenchard was 66 years old when the Second World War broke out, and was not forgotten as Britain prepared for war. In 1940, he received a number of offers to return to active duty, and when he rejected all of them, no further overtures were made. He declined the chance to organize the training of RAF pilots in Canada, the job of "camouflaging the whole of England," and organizing the defense of aircraft factories. In May 1940, Churchill offered him one of Britain's highest posts: commander in chief of the Home Forces. When Trenchard asked for too much independent authority, Churchill became angry and withdrew the offer. Trenchard did, however, visit many air bases during the war to provide moral support.

Personal

Trenchard was a tall, vigorous, self-confident man who thought and moved quickly. A determined leader, he was popular with pilots who respected his view of airpower, although some disagreed with him on the role of fighters. Trenchard felt that while "the airplane was the best offensive weapon that has ever been invented, it is a shockingly bad weapon of defense."

His major weakness as a leader was his inarticulateness. His mind always worked faster than his tongue. He was not intellectual but had a flair for getting to the core of a problem and for establishing steps to achieve a general goal.

At age 47 Trenchard married Katharine Boyle, the widow of a friend who had been killed early in the war. Unfortunately, one of his two sons and two of his three stepsons were killed during World War II.

After leaving the London Police, Trenchard served as director of several companies and was chairman of the United Africa Company.

Knighted in 1918, Trenchard was created a baronet in 1919, a baron in 1930, and a viscount in 1936. He died in London on 10 February 1956 at the age of 83.

ROBERT CALVERT, JR.

SEE ALSO: Airpower, History of; Boer Wars; World War I.

Bibliography

Baring, M. 1930. *Flying corps headquarters, 1914–1918*. London: Heinemann.
Boyle, A. 1962. *Trenchard*. London: Collins.
Richards, D. 1953. *The Royal Air Force*. Vol. 1. London: Her Majesty's Stationery Office.
Townsend, P. 1970. *Duel of eagles*. New York: Simon and Schuster.

TROTSKY, LEON [1879–1940]

Leon Trotsky, Russian revolutionary and Communist, was a key figure in the Bolshevik seizure of power in Russia in 1917 and the subsequent Communist victory in the Russian Civil War. As commissar for war in the young Soviet Government, Trotsky organized the newly formed Red Army and played a major role in the consolidation of power by Lenin. His achievements in organizing and leading the Red Army were instrumental in the Communist success in the civil war. However, Trotsky's failure to act decisively in the power struggle following Lenin's death precluded his effective participation in the political development of the Soviet Union during the 1920s, and led to his banishment by Joseph Stalin.

Prerevolutionary Life

Trotsky was born Lev Davidovich Bronstein in the Ukrainian town of Yanovka on 7 November 1879 to Jewish *kulak* (well-to-do farmers) parents. Following schooling at the St. Paul *Realschule* in Odessa, he nurtured his political development under the repressive governmental policies of Imperial Russia by first espousing Populism and then becoming a Marxist. In 1898 he was arrested for his activities with the revolutionary South Russian Workers' Union and was eventually convicted and sentenced to exile in eastern Siberia. In 1900, prior to his journey to Siberia, he married his first wife, Alexandra Sokolovskaya, while in a holding prison in Moscow.

Trotsky remained in Siberia for two years. In 1902 he escaped and traveled across Russia to Austria using a forged passport identifying him as Trotsky, a name taken from a former prison guard in Odessa. From Austria he went to Paris and then to London where he met Lenin. For the next three years he lived in various European cities and participated in the activities of Russian political emigres and exiles. He helped to publish *Iskra* (*Spark*), a popular organ of the exiled Russian Marxists and for a while joined the Menshevik faction of the Russian Social Democratic Party. In Paris he met Natali Sedova, who later became his second wife and who remained with him until his death.

Upon learning of the Russian workers' massacre in St. Petersburg in January 1905, Trotsky left Geneva for the Russian capital. Trotsky's oratorical skills became evident during the revolutionary upheavals of 1905. In December, however, the revolutionary movement suffered a fatal reverse when czarist authorities arrested the entire St. Petersburg Soviet of Workers' Deputies. Trotsky, chairman of the soviet, was convicted of insurrection and in 1906 was sentenced to exile for life in Siberia.

He escaped during the journey through Siberia and traveled to Finland. In the decade between his escape and the Russian Revolution, he worked for the Russian Marxist cause but did not commit to either the Bolshevik or Menshevik factions of the movement. His political ambivalence and flexibility earned him both the disfavor and the respect of his revolutionary colleagues. From 1908 to 1914 he lived in Vienna and served as a war correspondent in the Balkan Wars. In 1916 he was expelled from France for his antiwar writings and in January 1917 traveled to New York City. He stayed in the United States briefly before returning to Russia in the spring of 1917 at the outbreak of the Russian Revolution.

Revolution and Civil War

From his arrival in Petrograd (as St. Petersburg had been renamed in 1914) until the overthrow of the Russian Provisional Government, Trotsky played a major part in the Communist accession to power. He did not immediately join the Bolsheviks upon his return to Russia, but headed a small party of independent social democrats. In August 1917 he formally joined the Bolshevik party and was named to the party's Central Committee. With Lenin in seclusion in the autumn of 1917, Trotsky almost single-handedly engineered the overthrow of the Provisional Government. Using the Red Guard, sailors from the Kronstadt Naval Base, and units of the Petrograd garrison to occupy strategic buildings and installations of the Russian capital, the Bolsheviks conducted a successful and almost bloodless revolt against the government on 6–7 November. On 12 November he participated in repulsing a loyal government force of Cossacks advancing against Petrograd.

Trotsky was appointed commissar for foreign affairs soon after the Bolshevik seizure of power. His unsuccessful efforts to ameliorate German territorial demands during the Brest-Litovsk Peace Conference (December 1917–February 1918) resulted in the imposition of even harsher terms on the Soviet government and the loss of large parts of Russian territory when the peace treaty was finally signed on 3 March. He thereupon resigned his position and became commissar of war.

As commissar of war Trotsky helped lead the defense against internal and external military threats to the Communist regime. The methods he used to organize the Red Army into an efficient and victorious fighting force, particularly the employment of ex–Imperial Army officers as "military specialists," were effective but often alienated other Soviet leaders. In August–September 1918 the Red Army defeated a White Army and Czech Legion force at Kazan on the Upper Volga River. The Red Army achieved another military victory at Tsaritsyn in the autumn of 1918, but, during this campaign, a disagreement arose between Stalin and Trotsky over the use of former czarist officers. In March 1919 the Red Army defeated a force commanded by Adm. Alexander Kolchak advancing from Siberia, and in November Trotsky concluded a successful defense of Petrograd against an army under Nikolai Yudenich. During 1920 and 1921, he oversaw the elimination of the remnants of the White Army. In the Soviet war with Poland, he opposed the Soviet drive against Warsaw, arguing that the Red Army was incapable of offensive action. Also in 1921, Trotsky played a minor role in the suppression of the sailors' revolt at Kronstadt.

Death of Lenin and Exile

Stalin's appointment as general secretary of the Communist Party and Lenin's decline in health marked the beginning of Trotsky's decline in power. His belated union with the Bolsheviks and Stalin's campaign to discredit him eroded his power after Lenin's death in 1924. In January 1925, Trotsky lost his position as commissar of war. In 1926 his efforts to forge an alliance with other opponents of Stalin failed, and in the following year he was ousted from the Communist Party. In January 1928 he was deported to Soviet Central Asia for alleged counterrevolutinary activities. Stalin banished him from the Soviet Union in 1929. He spent the next decade in Turkey, France, Norway, and Mexico, writing his autobiography, *My Life,* and other political and anti-Stalinist works. On 20 August 1940 a Stalinist agent assaulted him with an ice pick in his home in Mexico City. On the following day he died from injuries sustained in the attack.

Trotsky's organization and leadership of the Red Army during the formative revolutionary years of the Soviet Union were largely responsible for the Bolshevik seizure and consolidation of power. During much of the revolution Trotsky traveled in the specially equipped armored train to different sectors of the front, and his frequent appearance in threatened regions often bolstered Red Army morale. However, he lacked the political leadership qualities needed to stand up to his determined rival, Stalin, and so suffered the fate of most of the political opponents of the ruthless Soviet dictator.

BRIAN R. BADER

Bibliography

Deutscher, I. 1954. *The prophet armed, Trotsky: 1879–1921.* London: Oxford Univ. Press.
———. 1959. *The prophet unarmed, Trotsky: 1921–1929.* London: Oxford Univ. Press.
———. 1963. *The prophet outcast, Trotsky: 1929–1940.* London: Oxford Univ. Press.
Liddell Hart, B. H., ed. 1956. *The Red Army: The Red Army—1918 to 1945, the Soviet Army—1946 to the present.* New York: Harcourt, Brace.
Payne, R. 1977. *The life and death of Trotsky.* New York: McGraw-Hill.
Trotsky, L. 1960. *My life.* New York: Grosset and Dunlap.

Von Laue, T. H. 1966. *Why Lenin? Why Stalin?* London: Weidenfeld and Nicholson.
Worth, R. D. 1977. *Leon Trotsky.* Boston: G. K. Hall.

TUKHACHEVSKY, MIKHAIL NIKOLAEVICH
[1893–1937]

Mikhail Nikolaevich Tukhachevsky (16 February 1893–11 June 1937) was a marshal of the Soviet Union, hero of the Russian civil war, member of the Communist party from 1918, leader of the Red Army, military theorist, and victim of Joseph Stalin. He was a youthful, charismatic, brilliant, and audacious soldier-revolutionary.

Early Life and Career

Born to a modest gentry family in Smolensk Guberniia in 1893, Tukhachevsky graduated from the First Moscow Catherinian Cadet Corps in 1911 and from the Aleksandrovsky Military School in 1914. Posted to the Semenovsky Guards Regiment as a young lieutenant, he fought on the Galician front in World War I and was awarded the Order of St. Vladimir. Captured by the Germans in February 1915, his repeated escape attempts brought his transfer to stricter prisoner of war camps. (At Ingolstadt, one of his fellow inmates was Capt. Charles de Gaulle.) In 1917, Tukhachevsky's escape attempt proved successful, and he made his way back to Russia.

Russian Civil War

With the October Revolution, Tukhachevsky, in spite of his noble status and Guards connections, sided with the Bolsheviks. In 1918, he became one of the first commissars of the newly established Red Army of Workers and Peasants (RKKA). In April of that year, he joined the Communist Party. Tukhachevsky quickly rose in the RKKA, serving first as commissar of Defense of the Moscow Region. In July 1918, he took command of a group of detachments which he transformed into the First Revolutionary Army fighting on the eastern (Volga and Urals) front. Tukhachevsky's First Army played a decisive role in the defeat of Komuch (Committee of the Constituent Assembly) forces in the fall of 1918, and in the spring of 1919 he commanded the Fifth Army during the final campaign against Adm. Alexsandr Kolchak in Siberia. Because of the tactical limitations of his forces, Tukhachevsky had to use concentric attacks in this battle to exploit open flanks and threaten the enemy with envelopment. Given the low density of forces, such attacks often led to wholesale routs and the enemy's destruction during sustained pursuit. Appointed commander of the Caucasian front in January 1920, he conducted the final operations against Gen. Anton Ivanovich Denikin's Volunteer Army. In February, he launched an offensive into the Kuban, using S. M. Budennyi's First Cavalry Army as a mobile group to disrupt the enemy's rear. In the ensuing retreat, Denikin's force disintegrated; the operation culminated in the Whites' frantic evacuation of Novorossiisk.

In March 1920, Tukhachevsky took command of the western front and planned the Soviet counteroffensive against Marshal Jozef Pilsudski's Polish army in Belorussia. Tukhachevsky's offensive, "the campaign beyond the Vistula" of July–August, was conceived and executed as an attempt to bring about "the revolution from without," using conventional warfare and class struggle to bring Soviet power to Central Europe. Ineffective command and control of Soviet forces (the refusal of Budennyi, Kliment Voroshilov, and Joseph Stalin to attack with the First Cavalry Army toward Lublin), insufficient mass, chaotic logistics, poor intelligence, and the political stability of the Polish rear combined to undo initial success. Pilsudski counterattacked before Warsaw and drove the Red Army back toward Belorussia and the Ukraine. The "campaign beyond the Vistula" became one of the most studied topics in Soviet military science in the 1920s. Tukhachevsky himself wrote a remarkably candid essay on the operation.

In the final stage of the civil war, Tukhachevsky commanded the Seventh Army during the suppression of the sailors' revolt at Kronstadt in March 1921 and ran the antipartisan war against the Antonovshchina (a peasant revolt in Tambov Province) in 1921–22.

Post–Civil War Era

Following the civil war, Tukhachevsky headed the Military Academy of the RKKA, where he played a leading role in the Military-Scientific Society; commanded the western front, 1922–24; and then served as deputy chief and later chief of staff of the RKKA, 1925–28. From 1928 to 1931, he commanded the Leningrad Military District, where he conducted tactical-operational tests with mechanized and airborne forces. Beginning in 1931, he served as deputy peoples commissar for military and naval affairs, chairman of the Revolutionary Military Council of the USSR, and director for armaments. In 1936, he was named first deputy commissar for military-naval affairs and director of the Department for Combat Training.

Tukhachevsky played a prominent role in developing Soviet military science. One theme of his early writings was the relationship between regular (i.e., national) warfare and class (i.e., partisan) warfare. His contributions to the development of the concept of successive operations, deep battle, and deep operations were significant. In a major polemic with A. A. Svechin over strategy, Tukhachevsky championed a strategy of "crushing" (*sokrushenie*), using operations during the initial period of war to disrupt enemy mobilization and defeat his forces in detail. His concept of future war was one of mass, where mechanized armies of tank, tactical aviation, and airborne forces played a decisive role. He played a leading role in introducing these concepts and capabilities into the Red Army of the early 1930s and played a major role in the drafting of the RKKA Field Regulations of 1929 and 1936. With Mikhail Frunze,

Tukhachevsky recognized the linkage between modern war and total mobilization of the national economy and, in the 1920s, was one of the most prominent military supporters of "militarization" of the national economy. His concept of the war economy anticipated the Stalinist program of superindustrialization and provided a national security rationale for the brutal force applied during industrialization and collectivization. In 1934, he was made a candidate member of the Central Committee of the Communist Party. By 1936, Tukhachevsky considered Nazi Germany the most serious challenge to Soviet security and foresaw the blitzkrieg capabilities that German rearmament was making possible.

Once Stalin's purge of the old Bolsheviks took on universal scope, Tukhachevsky and like-minded Red commanders emerged as a potential threat to Stalin's power. Political denouncements by lesser colleagues at show trials were the first indications of Stalin's assault on Tukhachevsky in the spring of 1937. A provocation staged by Reinhard Heydrich, head of the S.S. Security Service, planted "evidence" of Tukhachevsky's involvement in a conspiracy with conservative German generals. This "information" was passed on to Stalin as legitimate intelligence by the Czechoslovak government and provided Stalin with the pretext to arrest Tukhachevsky and extend the mass terror to the military. In mid-May 1937, just prior to his arrest, Tukhachevsky was reassigned to command the Volga Military District. He and his closest comrades were arrested shortly thereafter. The Military Collegium of the Supreme Court tried them in camera and found them guilty of treason. They were secretly executed. Over the next several years, Stalin extended the terror throughout the Soviet high command, decapitating it. During Khrushchev's de-Stalinization, Tukhachevsky was posthumously rehabilitated.

JACOB W. KIPP

SEE ALSO: Civil War, Russian.

Bibliography

Butson, T. G. 1984. *The tsar's lieutenant, the Soviet marshal.* New York: Praeger.
Ivanov, V. M. 1985. *Marshal M. N. Tukhachevskii.* Moscow: Voenizdat.
Nikulin, L. 1964. *Tukhachevskii, biograficheskii ocherk.* Moscow: Voenizdat.
Nord, L. 1978. *Marshal M. N. Tukhachevsky.* Paris: Lev.
Simpkin, R. 1987. *Deep battle: The brainchild of Marshal Tukhachevskii.* In association with J. Erickson. London: Brassey's.
Tukhachevsky, M. N. 1964. *Izbrannye proizvedeniia.* 2 vols. Moscow: Voenizdat.

TURENNE, HENRI DE LA TOUR d'AUVERGNE, VICOMTE DE [1611–1675]

A splendid soldier, Turenne (Fig. 1) was gifted both as a tactician and a strategist. With Prince Louis II of Condé (the Great Condé), and the marshal-duke of Luxembourg, he was one of the three great commanders who led the armies

Figure 1. Vicomte de Turenne, 1643. (SOURCE: U.S. Library of Congress)

of the French King Louis XIV to a succession of startling victories during the mid to late seventeenth century.

Early Life

Turenne was born in Sedan on 11 September 1611, the son of Henri, duke of Bouillon and Elizabeth I of Nassau, and the nephew of the famous Dutch general Maurice of Nassau (1567–1625). He showed an early interest in military affairs and in the deeds of Julius Caesar and Alexander the Great, and entered his uncle's army as a private soldier in 1625.

Military Career

He entered French service in 1630 and was given the colonelcy of an infantry regiment. He served against the Spanish between 1630 and 1634, and led the successful assault on the fortress of La Motte. In recognition of his achievements, he was promoted to *maréchal de camp*, and served under Cardinal La Valette in the Rhineland in 1635.

Turenne saw further action in August 1638 when he accompanied Marshal Guébriant's reinforcement of the army of Bernhard of Saxe-Weimar, then besieging Breisach. Turenne served with the covering force until Breisach surrendered to Bernhard on 17 December. He next served in Italy under the duke of Harcourt (1639–41), and fought at the Battle of Casale (29 April 1640) and the siege of Turin (14 May–24 September 1640). His elder brother's involvement in the Cinq Mars conspiracy cost Turenne his lands in 1642, but despite this, Cardinal Mazarin had him made a marshal of France on 16 November 1643. Baton in hand, Turenne was sent to command and rebuild the French army in Germany after its defeat at Tuttlingen (24 November 1643). He led his troops across the Rhine into the Black Forest, but withdrew from Bavarian Gen. Franz von Mercy's superior forces in June 1644. He joined Condé and the Army of Champagne at Breisach, and together they took the offensive and defeated Mercy at the bloody Battle of Freiburg (3–9 August). The next year Turenne led the Army of Germany into Franconia, but Mercy surprised and defeated him at Mergentheim (5 May 1645) and forced him to withdraw into Hesse. Rebuilding his force, he absorbed the small Hessian army and once again sent to Condé for assistance.

After Condé arrived, the combined Franco-Hessian force invaded Bavaria and defeated Mercy at the hard-fought Battle of Allerheim on 3 August 1645, where Mercy was killed. Despite this success, the Austrian Archduke Leopold and his army forced them back to Phillipsburg, and Condé then returned to France. On 10 August 1646 Turenne joined forces with Wrangel's Swedish army near Geissen and together they invaded and ravaged Bavaria, forcing Bavaria to accept the Truce of Ulm on 14 March 1647. Still in Germany, Turenne suppressed a mutiny among the long-serving Weimarian troops and repulsed a Spanish attack in Luxembourg (May 1647). Bavarian intransigence led to a second invasion of that country, again in company with Wrangel, and together the allies defeated Gen. Peter Melander at Zusmarshausen on 17 May 1648, where Melander was killed.

Turenne returned to France, which was in the grip of the Fronde rebellion, and he supported the rebel Parlément of Paris in January and February of 1649, but he was forced to flee to the Netherlands. Following the imprisonment of Condé and the other princes, Turenne returned and assumed military leadership of the second Fronde in early 1650. He joined with the Spanish and led an army to the relief of Rethel, but his army was nearly destroyed by Marshal Choiseul at Champ Blanc on 15 October. When the princes were released the following February, he returned to Paris; despite divided loyalties, he remained faithful to Louis XIV and Mazarin during

Condé's revolt and the outbreak of the Third (or Spanish) Fronde (September 1651). He led a vigorous campaign against Condé in the Loire Valley and defeated his former comrade at Gien on 7 April 1652 and at Porte St. Antoine on 5 July. When King Louis XIV returned to Paris (21 October 1652), followed by the return of Mazarin in early February 1653, the Third Fronde was over. Condé, however, remained in the field in command of Spanish forces, and the Franco-Spanish War continued. The next year Turenne again waged a successful campaign, checking Condé's invasion, and in 1654 he captured Stenay and defeated the Spanish at Arras on 25 August. He captured three more towns in 1655, and although he besieged Valenciennes with Marshal La Ferté, he was defeated by Condé's relief effort on 16 July 1656. Turenne's efforts against Cambrai were frustrated by Condé the following summer, but he took Venant and Mardyck anyway, assisted in the latter instance by English aid.

In May 1658 Turenne besieged Dunkirk, and resoundingly defeated the relieving army of Don John of Austria and Condé at the Dunes on 14 June, ensuring by this victory both the fall of Dunkirk and the successful conclusion of the war, ended by the Treaty of the Pyrenees on 7 November 1659. For his services he was created Marshal-General by Louis XIV on 4 April 1660 giving him authority over all the other marshals. He was the de facto commander of the French invasion of Flanders during the brief War of Devolution in the spring of 1667, although King Louis was in titular command.

At the outbreak of the War of the Triple Alliance in 1672, he led the French army on the left bank of the Rhine. He crossed the Rhine, outmaneuvering the combined armies of Raimondo Montecuccoli and Frederick William of Brandenburg, and forcing the latter out of an anti-French alliance by the Treaty of Vassem (6 June 1673). Refused reinforcements by French Minister of War Louvois, he was driven back across the Rhine into Alsace that fall. Ordered to defend Alsace, he recrossed the Rhine in a preemptive attack and defeated Charles of Lorraine and Caprara at Sinzheim (16 June 1674). Following further maneuvers along the Rhine, Turenne seized Strasbourg on 24 September, and subsequently won a victory over Bournonville's army at Enzheim on 4 October. Turenne then regrouped his forces and launched a surprise winter campaign against the reinforced allied forces in December, employing the Vosges Mountains to screen his movements. He defeated Bournonville a second time at Mulhouse on 29 December. Following this success, he attacked Bournonville at Turckheim on 5 January 1675 and shattered the enemy army, thus freeing Alsace and completing a brilliant campaign. During the spring campaign, he kept Montecuccoli out of Strasbourg, and caught the Austrian army at a disadvantage at Sasbach on 27 July, but he was killed by a cannonball during a reconnaissance mission.

Summary

In the course of a 50-year career, Turenne showed himself a master strategist and tactician, and he often achieved near-miracles because of the respect and love he had earned from his troops. He was a bold and energetic commander and a capable administrator, who twice reorganized armies broken in battle and led them to victory within months of their defeat. Compared with his comrade and sometime opponent Condé, who usually won his successes through sheer grit and determination, Turenne was a more farsighted and intellectual soldier, though no less formidable on the battlefield. Of their campaigns, it is said that while Condé was as bold at the end of his career as he was at the beginning, Turenne grew more daring and resourceful as his career progressed.

DAVID L. BONGARD

SEE ALSO: Condé, Louis II de Bourbon, Prince de; France, Military Hegemony of; Thirty Years' War.

Bibliography

Longueville, T. 1907. *Marshal Turenne*. London: Longmans, Green.
Picavet, C. G. 1919. *Les dernières années de Turenne (1660–1675)*. Paris: Calman-Levy.
Roy, J. 1896. *Turenne: Sa vie, les institutions militaires de son temps*. Paris: A. Le Vasseur.

TURKIC EMPIRE

The Turks played a significant role in the history of Central Asia, the Middle East, and Eastern Europe during the period A.D. 600–1194. Under the leadership of the Ghaznavids, Seljuks, and Osmanlis, the Turks became the dominant force within, and the cutting edge of, Islam.

First Turkic Empire

Turkic origins are obscure. The Turks first appeared in Chinese records as the *t'u-chueh*, and along with their Liang overlords were identified as descendants of the Hsiung-nu (Huns). After the Northern Wei (*Toba*) destroyed the Northern Liang kingdom in A.D. 439, the *t'u-chueh* placed themselves under the protection of the khan of the Juan-Juan (Avars).

In 546, a revolt broke out within the Juan-Juan Empire. The Turks, under their chief Tumin, remained loyal to the Juan-Juan khan and aided in the suppression of the rebels. As a reward for his services, Tumin sought the hand of the khan's daughter. The khan refused. Tumin then conspired with the king of the Northern Wei. When the latter attacked the Juan-Juan, the Turks rose in rebellion. Caught between the Turks and the Wei, the Juan-Juan Empire disintegrated.

Tumin established the First Turkic Empire in 552. He did not, however, live to enjoy his new role as khan. Within a year of his victory over the Juan-Juan, Tumin died.

KHANATES OF EAST AND WEST

After Tumin's death, the empire was divided into two khanates. Muhan, Tumin's son, succeeded his father as khan and ruled the eastern khanate as his personal domain. Istemi, Tumin's brother, ruled the western khanate as *jabghu* (prince). The eastern khanate included Outer and Inner Mongolia as well as parts of the modern Chinese provinces of Kansu and Hsinchiang. The western khanate included the Ili, Chu, Talas, and Yulduz river valleys.

Expansion of the Western Khanate. Istemi sought to expand the western khanate into Transoxiana (Sogdiana). Therefore, he entered into an alliance with the Persian (Sassanid) king, Khosrau I Anoshirvan, against the Hephthalites (White Huns). In 567, the allies defeated the Hephthalites and divided the spoils. Persia recovered Bactria while the Turks occupied Transoxiana.

When Istemi died in 575, he was succeeded by his son, Tardu. Taking advantage of the confusion following the death of Muhan Khan, Tardu proclaimed himself khan and attempted to seize control of the eastern khanate. Tardu's imperial ambitions, and his mendacious rule, provoked a rebellion in 603, which resulted in his death and the breakup of the western khanate.

The eastern khanate fared little better. Weakened by the struggles that followed Muhan's death and Tardu's attempted usurpation, the eastern Turks bowed before a resurgent China and in 630 recognized Chinese suzerainty. The western Turks followed suit in 639.

KHANATE OF THE BLUE TURKS

Chinese control over Mongolia began to weaken after the Tibetans invaded the Tarim Basin in 670. In 682, Kutluk Khan reestablished the eastern khanate as the Khanate of the Blue Turks. Khapghan, Kutluk's brother, extended control over the Togesh, the Kirghiz, and the Turks of Transoxiana. The western Turks formally recognized Khapghan as khan in 694. The empire founded by Tumin was once again united.

Despite his achievements, Khapghan Khan could not solve the perennial problems of the Turks. Clan feuds, as well as inter- and intratribal vendettas, continued to threaten the stability, unity, and existence of the empire of the Blue Turks. Khapghan Khan was ambushed and slain in 716. His successors, Kul-tegin and Bilge, faced sporadic rebellions. Kul-tegin died in 731, Bilge in 734. With Bilge's death, the empire of the Blue Turks fell apart, prey to the Karluks, Basmil, and Uighers, as well as the Arabs and the Chinese.

In the west, the Turgesh had emerged as the dominant tribe, but a serious threat confronted them. In 642, Arabs completed the conquest of Persia. Although Arab armies had crossed the Syr Darya (Oxus River), internal political conflicts had halted their advance. In 705, Kutuyba ibn Muslim resumed the Arab advance, and by 715, had conquered Transoxiana and Farghana. The Arab victory over a Chinese expeditionary force on the Talas River (751) ended Chinese attempts to reassert control over the western Turks.

Impact of Islam

The 246 years between the Arab conquest of Transoxiana and the emergence of the first Turkic emirate witnessed the conversion of the Turk and the transformation of the erstwhile pagan Turk into the foremost promoter and protector of Islam.

Turkic ascendancy within the political and military life of Islam was the result of the Arab practice of using slave-soldiers as bodyguards. Given the rampant political and clan feuds that plagued the Arabs—a common problem in both Europe and Asia at that time—loyalty was at a premium. By using slaves, Muslim notables hoped to ensure their safety against the machinations of peers and subordinates.

The Turkic slave-soldiers were initially drawn from prisoners of war. Later, pagan Turks found a lucrative trade in selling other pagan Turks to the Arabs. Eventually, pagan Turks were attracted to service in the slave-armies by the promise of fighting and loot. Individually and by clans, pagan Turks entered the service of Islam.

In addition to his love of battle, the Turk brought to the service of Islam his skill as a mounted archer. Traditionally, Arab cavalry had relied on sword and lance. The addition of the Turkic horse-archer gave an Arab commander a highly mobile, rapid-fire, long-range projectile weapon.

First Turkic Emirates

Arab control over Iran (Persia) and Central Asia weakened in the early ninth century. By 850, native Persian dynasties had arisen. The Saffarids ruled Khorasan, Fars, and Sistan; the Samanids, Transoxiana.

GHAZNAVID EMIRATE

The Samanids continued the Arab practice of recruiting Turkic slave-soldiers, many of whom rose to command rank. In 962, Alp-tegin, the Turkic commander of the royal bodyguard, fled to Ghazni after his role in a plot against the Samanid ruler was uncovered. At Ghazni, Alp-tegin founded the first Turkic emirate. The Samanids eventually recognized Alp's son, Ishakh, as emir (governor) of Ghazni and guardian of the southern frontier.

In 977, Sebuk-tegin ascended the throne of Ghazni. He invaded northern India in 977 and came to the aid of his Samanid overlord in 993 during a rebellion in Khorasan. As a reward for his aid, the Samanid shah invested Sebuk with the governorships of Ghur, Bamiyan, and Balkh, and appointed Sebuk's son, Mahmud, military commander of Khorasan. Mahmud of Ghazni (998–1030) continued his father's policy of Ghaznavid expansion in northern India.

KARA-KHANIDS

Samanid control of Transoxiana was seriously threatened by a new tribe of pagan Turks, the Kara-Khanids, a branch of the Karluks. Although the Kara-

Khanids converted to Islam about 950, they continued raiding Samanid territory and occupied Bukhara in 999. To combat the Kara-Khanid threat, the Samanids called upon their vassal, Mahmud of Ghazni. Instead of aiding his suzerain, Mahmud allied with the Kara-Khanid king and attacked the Samanids. With the destruction of the Samanid kingdom, the Kara-Khanids took Transoxiana and Mahmud took Khorasan. Soon thereafter, the erstwhile allies quarreled over Khorasan.

Rise of the Seljuks

The Seljuks, a branch of the Oghuz (Ghuzz) Turks, had settled along the lower Syr Darya in the vicinity of Jand and had converted to Islam. Israil ibn Seljuk had aided the Samanids against the Kara-Khanids in 992. With the defeat of the Samanids, the Seljuk chief, Toghrul Beg, and his brother, Chaghri Beg, had occupied Bukhara and Samarkhand. After the brothers had recognized Mahmud of Ghazni as suzerain, Mahmud had invested Toghrul with the governorship of Nishapur and Chaghri with Marv (1037).

The Seljuks remained loyal to Mahmud. After his death, however, neither Toghrul nor Chaghri felt the same loyalty to Mahmud's successor. In 1040, the Seljuks roundly defeated the Ghaznavids at Dandarkhan and extended their control over Khorasan and Afghanistan. Thereafter, the Ghaznavids were restricted to northern India.

SELJUK WESTWARD EXPANSION: TOGHRUL BEG (1055–63)

Following his victory over the Ghaznavids, Toghrul Beg assumed the title of king. With Transoxiana, Khorasan, and Afghanistan in Seljuk hands, Toghrul turned his armies westward. Chaghri Beg conquered Khwarezm in 1042, thereby bringing the Seljuks into conflict with the Bouids, the Persian rulers of western Iran and Iraq.

Toghrul exploited the Sunni-Shiite split in his struggle with the Bouids. The Bouids were Shiite, while both the caliph (the spiritual ruler of Islam) and Toghrul were Sunni. In a symbolic act, Toghrul placed the caliph under his personal protection, even though the Seljuks were not yet strong enough to directly challenge the Bouids.

Toghrul's objective was Baghdad, at the time the religious capital of Islam. A westward advance, however, would expose the Seljuk right (northern) flank to possible Byzantine attack. To forestall such an attack, Toghrul sent his cousin, Ibrahim Inal, into Armenia with orders to probe the Byzantine defenses. Ibrahim's raiding parties roamed as far north as Trebizond on the Black Sea (1045). In 1049, Toghrul invaded the kingdom of Georgia and in 1054 conquered Azerbaijan. Seljuk victories, and Toghrul's support of the caliph, won over many Persian nobles. In 1055, Al Ka'im, the caliph, declared the Bouid sultan deposed and recognized Toghrul as the new sultan—that is, the temporal ruler of Islam.

Seljuk Westward Expansion: Alp Arslan (1063–72)

Toghrul was succeeded by his nephew, Alp Arslan. Two powers now threatened the Seljuks: the Byzantines and the Egyptians. The Byzantines were the strongest Christian power. The Egyptians, under the Shiite Fatimid dynasty, were both a political and a religious threat to the orthodox Seljuks. Alp Arslan feared an alliance between the Byzantine Empire and Egypt. To prevent such an alliance, the Seljuk sultan initiated a series of limited, spoiler raids against the Byzantines.

In 1064, the Seljuks conquered Armenia and seized the Byzantine fortress-towns of Melitene and Sebastea. The Seljuks attacked Caesarea in 1067 and raided the environs of Konya in 1069. By 1070, Seljuk raiding parties were active on the Aegean coast. Confident that he had secured his right flank, Alp Arslan commenced operations in Syria as a prelude to an invasion of Egypt.

The Seljuk sultan, however, had miscalculated. Romanus Diogenes, the Byzantine emperor, fearing the Seljuk raids were the first phase of an all-out invasion, assembled 60,000 troops and marched eastward. His objective was to reconquer Armenia.

Romanus first secured Sebastea, then advanced toward the source of the Euphrates River. The Byzantines recaptured the fortress of Erzurum, on the north branch of the river, then advanced on Manzikert, on the south branch. On reaching Manzikert, Romanus divided his forces. While Romanus laid seige to Manzikert, Roussel de Bailleul, with a force composed mostly of west European mercenaries (Franks), marched on Akhlat. After Manzikert surrendered, Romanus sent half his heavy infantry to aid Roussel.

Romanus believed that Alp Arslan, with the bulk of the Seljuk forces, was still in western Iran. Actually, the sultan was marching through Syria when word reached him of the Byzantine attack. Alp Arslan quickly countermarched his troops northward and sent word to his emirs in Iran and Transoxiana to assemble their troops at Khoi, approximately 480 kilometers (300 mi.) east of Lake Van.

With his assembled forces, approximately 40,000 men, Alp Arslan marched west, then southwest. Neither Romanus nor Roussel knew of the rapidly approaching Turks. Skirting the southern shore of Lake Van, the sultan surprised Roussel, who, along with his troops, fled westward.

Romanus, upon learning of the approach of the Turks, evacuated Manzikert and marched southward to reinforce Roussel, unaware that the latter had fled. On 19 August 1071, the Seljuk and Byzantine armies met. Deserted by Andronicus Ducas, the general commanding the reserves—and a political as well as a personal enemy of the emperor—Romanus and his command were beaten.

The Seljuk victory at Manzikert was followed by others. Jerusalem fell in late 1071. Under Malik Shah (1072–92), most of Asia Minor as well as Antioch were added to the Seljuk realm. Sulaiman, a cousin of Malik Shah, formed the Seljuk territories in Asia Minor into the Sultanate of Rum (Rome), while the sultan himself reduced the Kara-Khanids to vassalage.

When Malik Shah died, the Seljuk Empire was at its height. After Malik Shah, however, rivalries within the ruling clan effectively divided the empire into a number of separate states with only nominal allegiance to the sultan. Sanjar the Great (1117–57) directly ruled only Khorasan and exercised an often loose suzerainty over Khwarezm, Transoxiana, and Ghuri. Transoxiana was lost to the Buddhist Kara-Khitans in 1141.

Sanjar also had problems with his vassal Astiz (d. 1156), the emir of Khwarezm, who on occasion acted too independently. Following Sanjar's death, Arslan (1156–72), the son of Astiz, assumed the Iranian title shah. Threatened by the Karluks to the north and the Ghurids to the south, Arslan recognized the emperor of the Kara-Khitai—the Gur-khan—as his overlord. Tekish Shah (1172–1200) defeated and killed the last Seljuk sultan at Rayy in 1194. Tekish, a Shiite, also challenged the Sunni caliph's right to rule. Tekish's son, Al-din Mohammed Shah (1200–22), destroyed the Ghurids at the Battle of Balkh (1204) with the help of the Gur-khan. Mohammed occupied Herat in 1206 and Ghazni in 1215. When the Gur-khan was deposed by his son-in-law, Mohammed seized control of Transoxiana (1210).

Mohammed Shah had secured control of Muslim Central Asia by 1215. In 1217, he declared the Sunni caliph deposed and named a Shiite to replace him. Mohammed seemed destined to repeat the career of Toghrul Beg when, in 1218, he ordered the execution of a foreign ambassador on a charge of espionage. Perhaps unwittingly, by this action Mohammed had signed his own death warrant and that of many thousands of his subjects. The slain ambassador had been the personal representative of Genghis Khan, and the Mongol khan's vengeance was swift and terrible.

LAWRENCE D. HIGGINS

SEE ALSO: Arab Conquests; Byzantine Empire; Genghis Khan; History, Medieval Military; Mongol Conquests; Persian Empire.

Bibliography

Barthold, V. V. 1958. *Turkestan down to the Mongol invasion*. 2d ed. Oxford: Oxford Univ. Press.
Frye, R. N., and A. M. Sayili. 1943. Turks in the Middle East before the Saljugs. *Journal of the American Oriental Society* 63:194–207.
Grousset, R. 1952. *L'Empire des Steppes*. Paris: Payot.
Hambly, G., ed. 1969. *Central Asia*. New York: Delacorte.
Jahn, K. 1967. Zu Rasid Al-Din's "Geschichte der Oguzen und Türken." *Journal of Asian History* 1:45–63.
Legg, S. 1970. *The heartland*. New York: Farrar, Straus, and Giroux.
Rice, T. T. 1961. *The Seljuks*. London: Thames and Hudson.
Samolin, W. 1964. *East Turkestan to the 12th century*. The Hague: Mouton.
Saunders, J. J. 1972. *The history of the Mongol conquests*. New York: Harper and Row.
Sinor, D. 1953. The historical role of the Turk empire. *Journal of World History* 1:23–55.

TUTHMOSIS III [ca. 1485–1425 B.C.]

Sometime around 1485 B.C., Eset, a concubine in the harem of Tuthmosis II, the fourth king of the Eighteenth Dynasty of ancient Egypt (1550–1307 B.C.), bore a male child. Also named Tuthmosis (a Grecized form of the Egyptian *Djehutimose*), he was saved from the obscurity common for harem children by the premature death of his royal father without a direct heir and his subsequent elevation to the throne by the oracle of the national and dynastic cult god Amun-Re.

Tuthmosis' reign extended from 1479 to 1425 B.C. During the early years, his stepmother Hatshepsut, the widowed chief wife of Tuthmosis II, acted as regent. Soon after, however, she entered into a coregency with the young king, assuming the role of senior partner and the full pharaonic titulary normally reserved for the male monarch, a state of affairs in which the young Tuthmosis apparently acquiesced.

Tuthmosis attained sole rule on the death of Hatshepsut circa 1458 B.C., the 22d year of his reign. Thereafter he initiated a series of aggressive military campaigns in the Levant, pursuing the expansionist policies of his dynastic forebears. Achieving great success in these enterprises, particularly the crucial battle of Megiddo circa 1457 B.C. (the first decisive military encounter for which there are contemporary records), Tuthmosis made Egypt the foremost power in the Bronze Age Middle East and established his family on the throne for nearly 200 years.

Politico-Military Antecedents

On Tuthmosis' accession circa 1458 B.C., only 92 years had passed since Ahmosis, the founder of the dynasty, had driven the Semitic Hyksos (Egyptian *heq-khasut*, "foreigner rulers") out of the Delta, reestablishing Egyptian suzerainty over the whole Nile valley for the first time in a century. Ahmosis' three successors, Tuthmosis I, Amenophis I, and Tuthmosis II, had in varying degrees used a similar "national security" rationale for creating an imperium over the Levant that would secure Egypt from foreign invasion. It was natural, therefore, for Tuthmosis to do the same.

Changes in the status of kingship had accompanied these developments. The cult of a warrior king "smiting the Asiatics" as the earthly representative and son of an increasingly imperial universal god, Amun-Re, while not unique to this dynasty, certainly underwent growth and sophistication. Unlike earlier times, such as the reign of Senwosret III in the Twelfth Dynasty (1878–1841? B.C.), when similar propaganda was current on royal monuments, Egypt now had a large standing army with vested interests in its continued existence and in the political power and economic benefits to be gained from aggressive, expansionist imperialism. In addition to these factors, the young Tuthmosis, aged between 25 and 30 at the time of Hatshepsut's death, probably felt strong personal and political reasons for taking his nation to war. He was not secure in his claim to the throne, and success in "extending the frontiers" could only strengthen his position, demonstrating through "trial by combat" that the god Amun-Re supported his "son" Tuthmosis as king.

World Politics (ca. 1450 B.C.)

Empire is a misleading term in the context of the Bronze Age Middle East; it conjures up nineteenth-century notions of close, centralized rule by an occupying power. The Tuthmosid empire, like those of its neighbors, was more a loose feudal "sphere of influence" maintained primarily by fear of the nearest great power and its propensity to conduct punitive raids if tribute was not regularly forthcoming from the local vassal chieftains. Frequent military campaigns by a great power were therefore an important part of maintaining this form of imperium even if expansion was not intended.

Earlier in the dynasty, Tuthmosis I (1504–1492 B.C.) had expanded the boundaries as far as the banks of the Euphrates in northern Syria, primarily because no other great power existed to challenge him. Although these "possessions" had soon fallen from Egypt's control, a large part of the southern Levant remained under its suzerainty.

At the time of Tuthmosis III, three other great powers existed to contend for dominance over the petty states in this region, which corresponded roughly to present-day Syria, Lebanon, Israel, and Jordan. These were the Khatti (the Hittites), based in central Turkey to the north; the Naharin (the Mittani), based in Syria; and Babylon in Mesopotamia to the east. During Hatshepsut's rule, Egypt had largely abandoned military expeditions, and the loyalty of the Levantine vassals had evaporated. At the same time the power of the Mittani had grown, extending their influence to the south and west. A conflict was inevitable.

Megiddo and After

Matters came to a head in 1457 B.C., the 23d year of Tuthmosis' reign. A coalition of petty states led by the king of Kadesh and supported by the Mittani threatened Egyptian influence from Lebanon southward. Swift action was required, and Tuthmosis responded handsomely, leading his army out of Egypt in two forced marches of ten days that brought them to the Carmel range, 32 kilometers (20 mi.) south of modern Haifa.

What followed was recorded many years later in florid and often incomprehensible prose on the walls of the temple to Amun-Re in Luxor and has been translated by Pritchard (1969), with a good commentary by Gardiner (1964). Although some of the narrative may be dismissed as mere rhetoric and hyperbole to please a royal master, the overall description tallies with the topography of the region and may be regarded as reliable (see Nelson 1913).

Learning that the "vile man of Kadesh" had encamped at Megiddo, Tuthmosis decided to surprise his enemy by making a bold march over a narrow mountain defile, the route least expected. The gamble paid off, and at 7:00 in the evening the battle was joined. Tuthmosis fought valiantly, and the Egyptians routed their foes, who escaped to the town of Megiddo itself while the

Egyptian army began looting. Subsequently besieged, Megiddo held out for eight months with most of the hostile princes of the Levant cooped up inside. Tuthmosis' archivists recorded that "the capture of Megiddo is the capture of a thousand towns," and so it proved, this decisive victory assuring Egyptian dominance in the region.

Over the remaining 31 years of his reign Tuthmosis conducted fifteen more campaigns in Syria, the Levant, and Nubia. Victorious in his exploits, he made Egypt an undisputed great power for the rest of his lifetime and beyond, and truly deserves the epithet "Egypt's Napoleon."

MICHAEL A. MABE

SEE ALSO: History, Ancient Military.

Bibliography

Baines, J. S., and J. Malek. 1980. *An atlas of ancient Egypt.* Oxford: Phaidon.

Drower, M. S. 1973. Syria ca. 1550–1400 B.C. In *The Cambridge ancient history*, vol. 2, part 1, chap 10. Cambridge: Cambridge Univ. Press.

Gardiner, A. H. 1961. *Egypt of the pharaohs.* London: Oxford Univ. Press.

James, T. G. H. 1973. Egypt from the expulsion of the Hyksos to Amenophis I. In *The Cambridge ancient history*, vol. 2, part 1, chap. 8. Cambridge: Cambridge Univ. Press.

Kemp, B. J. 1978. Imperialism and empire in New Kingdom Egypt (ca. 1575–1087 B.C.). In *Imperialism in the ancient world*, ed. P. D. Garnsey and C. R. Whitaker, pp. 7–57, 284–97, 368–73. Cambridge: Cambridge Univ. Press.

Nelson, H. H. 1913. *The battle of Megiddo.* Chicago: Univ. of Chicago Press.

Pritchard, J. B., ed. 1969. *Ancient Near Eastern texts relating to the Old Testament.* 3d ed. Princeton, N. J.: Princeton Univ. Press.

U

UNIFORMS AND ACCOUTERMENTS

Uniforms, with their accounterments, are the distinctive dress worn by members of the armed forces to distinguish them from civilians. Uniforms also help identify friends from foes; provide protection from the weather and hazards of campaign and combat; identify the wearer's rank, branch of service, unit, and nationality; and foster morale and esprit de corps.

Uniforms

For centuries, soldiers have been wearing clothing that might be called uniforms. Roman soldiers dressed alike in that most wore the same kinds of body armor over simple tunics, although the color might have been varied to differentiate units. They also wore similar styles of helmets and used fairly standard weapons and shields. The clothing of their leaders, the centurions and tribunes, however, varied considerably according to the individual's wealth and taste—and his commander's wishes.

During the Middle Ages, feudal lords were required to provide kings or overlords with fighting men. In many cases, these men simply wore whatever they had, but some lords did provide clothing and armor. In those cases, the clothing would often be of one color—usually a color from the lord's heraldic device—and might include the lord's emblem. The cross was a popular device used on the surcoats or shields of crusaders and other European knights. Colored scarves or sprigs of leaves might be used as recognition devices ("field signs"). Some cities had forces of fighting men or watchmen who wore similar surcoats with emblems.

Groups of mercenary soldiers often wore clothes of the same color and style because their captain furnished or specified what the members of his company would wear. Since these were businessmen concerned with the bottom line, it made sense to them to buy a large amount of one type of cloth and have it cut the same for everyone. They usually followed the current civilian styles, so the results were groups dressed alike who were differentiated from civilians by the armor some wore and the weapons and other combat gear they carried. They also might have had shields, helmets, and banners.

The two oldest uniforms still in use are that of the Swiss Guard of the Vatican, said to have been designed by Michelangelo, and that of the English Yeomen of the Guard. The Yeomen's dress of red coats, breeches, and caps might have originated with King Henry VIII before 1520 and been modified later. The Swiss Guard wear Swiss pikemen's garb in the blue, gold, and red colors of the Medici family of Florence, Italy. Their uniform dates to about 1506, when the guard was first raised.

Uniforms as we understand them today did not come into general use until the beginning of standing national or royal armies in the seventeenth century. Among the first armies to wear "real" uniforms were those of King Gustavus Adolphus of Sweden, who dressed three elite regiments in green, blue, and yellow; Oliver Cromwell's New Model Army, which wore the famous British red coat; and Louis XIV's soldiers in light gray with colored facings. National colors appeared around the end of the seventeenth century as a result of either royal whim or the availability of various cheap dyes. The British used russet followed by red and then scarlet. The French started with gray and went to white until 1789 when the revolutionaries changed the predominant uniform coat color to blue—white was associated with the old regime and the royal house of Bourbon.

Other nations dressed their soldiers in a variety of colors and styles, but there were some basic similarities. During much of the seventeenth century, the main garment was a coat that, for the cavalry, featured long skirts. The headdress was often a steel cap or cloth hat. Soldiers usually wore their hair long. In the latter part of the seventeenth century, the long-skirted coat became the main garment along with a broad-brimmed hat. The cavalry still wore some armor. Officers were recognized by their sashes, long wigs, and better-quality clothes. The exact form and ornamentation of the officers' dress was usually left to the individual.

During the eighteenth century, uniforms began to differ from civilian fashions. The coat became double-breasted and turned back at the chest to form lapels. The skirts were also turned back and became narrower. Collars got bigger. Turned-back cuffs became smaller and sleeves narrower. The felt hat began to be turned up on two or three sides and decorated with tape. Canvas leggings appeared to help contend with the mud of the Low Countries. The hair was worn in a queue, and beards gave way to clean-shaven faces. Officers showed their status with gorgets, sashes, sword knots, and embroidery.

The first half of the nineteenth century saw soldiers wearing single- or double-breasted coatees with long or short skirts. Hats gave way to shakos, although cavalry used leather helmets with combs and crests. Hair queues became rare, with preference given to short hair. Around the middle of the nineteenth century, single- or double-breasted tunics of medium length became common, along with spiked helmets. The shako remained popular in the Latin countries but gradually became smaller. Officers showed rank with lace, epaulettes, shoulder straps, and badges. Uniforms became loose and simple for combat but tight and ornate for parades and other noncombat times. Armies copied the styles of successful foreign or allied forces. During the 1860s, many armies adopted the French kepi, frock coat, and Zouave dress. In the 1870s, the German spiked helmet became popular with just about every army except the French.

Drab- or camouflage-colored field uniforms came into general use during the early twentieth century along with steel helmets, especially during World War I, when automatic weapons forced the infantry to stay close to or under the ground. After the war, many nations copied the British service dress, which featured patch pockets on the coat's breast and skirts. Colors might be brown, khaki, olive drab, light blue, or gray-green. Steel helmets and fore-and-aft-shaped caps were usually worn during field duty and peaked caps after duty. Officers reduced the conspicuousness of their rank badges during the wars but afterward usually adopted bright markings.

After 1940, uniforms were often designed for specific tasks or environments. These included the paratrooper outfit, jungle uniforms of lightweight cotton or synthetic materials in green or camouflage patterns, mountain and arctic uniforms, and steel or fiber helmets and body armor colored to match the uniform. Parade and semidress uniforms are more ornate and colorful, while the full dress is very colorful and similar to the uniforms of the nineteenth century.

Uniforms have often been anything but uniform. Today, they are fairly standard within national armies and strictly controlled within the individual units, but many units strive to include something to differentiate them from other units. Such differences might include metal badges, cloth patches, various colored braids, unique belt buckles, and hat cockades. But historically there were often considerable differences within an army. Cavalry might wear a uniform very different from the infantry in color, cut, and style, as would the support units. Bandsmen often wore uniforms whose colors contrasted sharply with those of the other members of their armies. Artillerymen, who were originally civilian specialists, belonged to a kind of international guild and wore similar uniforms of dark blue coats with red linings and gold buttons and braid. Sometimes, native items of dress were worn, or adapted, such as the Scottish kilt or American hunting shirt. Each regiment of an army might have its own brightly colored uniform, perhaps decorated with braid, fur, or metal trimmings. When an army assembled, it might present a rainbow of colors, and glitter with the many bits of brass, silver, and gold trimmings.

Navy uniforms for officers came about in the mid-eighteenth century and have usually been dark blue, cut according to current civilian styles with gold buttons, braid, and shoulder marks. Many navies have used the uniforms of the British Royal Navy as models. Khaki and white uniforms for warm weather wear are also used.

Enlisted sailors generally wear blue or white jumpers with bell-bottom trousers for service uniforms. The uniforms were based on the need for freedom of movement when working aloft on sails or on muzzle-loading guns on a heaving deck. There was no need for the individual to blend into the background as on land. These conditions led to the bell-bottom trousers that could be rolled up easily; a shirtlike upper garment, with an open neck, instead of a coat; a short jacket for cold weather instead of an overcoat with skirts; and a cap that would stay on the head in a wind. Naval uniforms, little changed despite the disappearance of sails and muzzle-loading guns, came from the clothes worn by merchant seamen. Until the early part of the nineteenth century, sailors usually provided their own clothes or bought garments from the ship's slop chest. After the Napoleonic Wars, the British began regulating the dress of their sailors, and other navies soon did the same.

The air forces favor sky-blue uniforms in styles similar to their national armies. Marines also wear uniforms similar to that of the army, but they make certain to include enough differences to maintain a clear identity. Both British and American marines use a blue dress uniform and a drab or camouflage service uniform.

Accouterments

The basic uniform of tunic or jacket, shirt, trousers, and boots or shoes usually includes such accouterments as buttons, belts, buckles, badges, rank insignia, headgear, and a whole range of pouches.

Buttons have been on uniforms for as long as they have been used on civilian clothes. The first uniforms, after all, were simply civilian clothes of the same color and cut to help make a group of soldiers look alike. Buttons for officers were often elaborate and decorative, frequently made of gold or silver, while buttons for enlisted personnel were of cheaper metals, bone, or plastic. Metal buttons made especially for use on uniforms are often stamped or embossed with national emblems, unit numbers, or other military designs.

Buttons are also sometimes used simply for decoration. Among the more common uses of decorative buttons are the rows of brass or other shiny metal buttons on some dress uniforms and the buttons on sleeves that seem to serve no purpose. In fact, the early sleeve cuffs were intended to be lowered to protect hands in cold weather. This was not done with any concern for the soldiers' comfort in mind but in recognition that frozen fingers interfered with the loading and firing of weapons. When the cuffs were folded back, the buttons kept them in place. Since the buttons were often of a hard substance—such as cheap metal—and uniforms were of low-quality cloth, the buttonholes tore or quickly became worn. This led to strengthening the buttonholes with loops of cloth or braid. Later, as the buttons became ornamental rather than functional, the loops also remained as forms of decoration. These, in turn, became more and more elaborate, sometimes covering large portions of the sleeve, tunic, and trousers.

Belts originated as strips of leather, cloth, or rope on which the soldiers carried weapons and other items. The belts were worn around the waist or as straps across the shoulders. The width and thickness of the belts depended on the size and weight of the items attached to them; for instance, as swords became smaller or lighter, the belts used to carry them became thinner.

Many belts worn by members of today's military services are of webbing. While that material may not be as elegant as polished leather, it is more durable, easier to clean and maintain, and certainly better suited to today's combat conditions.

One of the more recognizable belts of recent military history is the Sam Browne, a broad leather belt with a double-claw brass buckle and one or two cross straps across the shoulders. It was named for British general Sir Sam Browne, who lost an arm fighting in the Indian Mutiny. Not a man to let the mere loss of an arm slow him down, Browne found he needed a better way to carry his sword than by the long frog attached to the belt, the popular method at the time. Accordingly, he adopted the belt with two cross straps so he could attach his sword on one side and his pistol on the other. The belt became very popular not only because it was practical but also because it looked elegant, especially when polished. When the pistol was not worn, just one cross strap was needed. During the first decades of the twentieth century, the Sam Browne belt with one cross strap, often without sword or pistol, became a required part of an officer's uniform in many armies and police forces. Its popularity declined in the 1940s and 1950s as did the routine wearing of swords; the belt now appears most frequently during formal occasions when swords are worn. Some cadet and police units, however, still wear the belt.

Buckles hold belts together by means of hooks, claws, clasps, and loops or by the sliding pin or rod in a brass case that was adopted by the United States Army in the 1940s and now used by many other military services. Since a buckle can be designed to include a generous flat, curved, or rounded face, it is also frequently used as a place for an insignia, unit number, or other decoration. Sometimes the decorations are elaborate to the point of being done with gold or silver and precious stones. The buckles now worn mostly at the waist are descended from the decorative and highly polished plates worn on the crossbelts of earlier times, which can still be seen on some dress and guards uniforms. The crossbelts, often white, with shiny plates fell from favor as soldiers began to spend more and more time close to or under the ground as weapons and artillery became more effective.

Rank insignia varies about as much as other items of military wear. Early badges included the cudgel or rod (which might have been made of twisted grape vines and used by Roman centurions as aids to "instructing" their troops), staffs with various decorations, batons, spontoons, special weapons, gorgets, epaulettes, rows of buttons, lace in all sorts of patterns, sashes, cut and quality of clothing, and even cockades on hats. Today's armed forces use fairly standard rank insignia of metal, plastic, cloth, or embroidery attached to the hat or some portion of the top half of the uniform. The insignia might be stars, bars, crowns, eagles, chevrons, stripes, or any designs that are standard at least within each nation's armed forces and usually easy to understand with a bit of study or instruction.

The variety of insignia can cause confusion when members of several nations' military serve together. For example, some nations use stars (either gold or silver) to designate all their officer ranks, so that a young captain might wear three silver stars. This could surprise forces from another nation (where only generals wear stars) when they see such a young soldier wearing what they think are general's stars.

Shoulder patches, unit emblems, cap badges, ribbons, and special skill badges are often rich in history and tradition.

Pouches, bags, and holsters of many shapes and sizes are clipped, strapped, snapped, and otherwise attached to the soldier's uniform. The attachments are usually designed for specific items, such as ammunition, gas masks, first-aid kits, weapons, and other tools needed in combat.

One popular attachment is the canteen or water bottle, which often has its own specially designed pouch of cloth or plastic. The word *canteen* comes from the Italian *cantina*, or wine cellar, and once meant the place on a military reservation where soldiers could get refreshments. *Canteen* was still used in this sense as late as World War II, when a squad leader, when asked to account for three absentees, is supposed to have responded: "One's in the canteen, one's in the latrine, and one I ain't never seen." Later, canteen became the name for the water bottle carried by each soldier.

The sabretache is an attachment seen today mostly in pictures of old cavalry uniforms. It started out as a haversack worn by Hungarian Hussars and was widely adopted by cavalrymen as a map and writing case. It hung by a long strap or frog from the cavalryman's waist. Often it was near the sword and served to help keep the sword from flying about when galloping. Being a flat and visible surface, the sabretaches soon became heavily embroidered and decorated, making them almost useless except as weights.

Headgear has the obvious function of protecting the head but has been used at various times to make the wearers look more intimidating, as was the case with the tall shakos, mitrecaps, bearskins, and spike helmets of the nineteenth and early twentieth centuries. Huge feathers or tall plumes also enhanced the effect. These have given way to the helmet of steel or composition plastic for combat wear. The word *helmet* comes from the Anglo-Saxon word *helm*, which means to cover. Helms used by knights during the medieval period covered the entire head with only slits or small holes for seeing and breathing; they became smaller as armor went out of fashion because of the increasing effectiveness of firearms. By the sixteenth century, the helmet or "little helm" served mostly to protect the top of the head as it does today, but there were extra pieces of metal attached to help protect the eyes, nose, ears, and neck. Even those helmets were generally out of use by the end of the seventeenth century, only to be replaced by hats of felt, fur, leather, or brass. The most popular hat among the European and American armies was probably the tricorner or cocked hat that in the nineteenth century gave way to the kepi and the shako. However, helmets were retained in the dress uniforms of the cavalry units of several nations.

World War I brought the steel helmet back in an effort to cope with the dramatically increased effectiveness of firepower. As usual, each nation's helmet had a different shape, although initially this was more by happenstance than design. This situation helped identify friend from foe because the helmet might often be the only thing visible through the smoke or above the trenches.

The colors of the helmets are also important because unpainted steel "pots" would make easy targets. Combat helmets during World War I were painted various shades of gray, brown, green, or blue. In later wars, camouflage patterns appeared. Fabric covers of various patterns are also used as well as nets in which the wearers can place leaves, grass, twigs, and other materials as camouflage.

For noncombat wear, many military services use the "flying saucer"—a round cap with visor—or the fore-and-aft garrison cap. For fatigue wear, there are caps with bills and often soft crowns, which soldiers can stiffen with plastic or cardboard inserts if they want to appear more formal.

Summary

All items of military uniforms and accouterments originated as practical solutions to problems of combat. Even the bright colors of the early uniforms and the bright metal of some badges and buckles served a purpose—that of permitting recognition by friendly troops or of frightening enemy troops. As combat came to be dominated by modern rifles, automatic weapons, cannon, and aircraft, uniforms changed to adopt the colors of the earth to provide concealment. Accouterments changed from bright objects to subdued ones. The plumes and brilliant coat facings of the earlier era still exist, but only for pomp and ceremony. The dress uniforms today's military forces wear at social events and on parade reflect in many cases the combat uniforms of earlier times. The combat uniforms of today are drab and utilitarian, but they still serve to unify the fighting force and to provide an element of morale.

RAYMOND OLIVER

SEE ALSO: Decorations, Honorary Orders, and Awards.

Bibliography

Allen, K. 1972. *Fighting men and their uniforms.* New York: Hamlyn Publishing Group.
Boatner, M. M. 1976. *Military customs and traditions.* Westport, Conn.: Greenwood Press.
Castano, J. B. 1975. *The naval officer's uniform guide.* Annapolis, Md.: U. S. Naval Institute Press.
The Company of Military Historians. 1977. *Military uniforms in America.* Vol 2: *Years of growth, 1796–1851.* Novato, Calif.: Presidio Press.
Crocker, L. P. 1988. *The army officer's guide.* Harrisburg, Pa.: Stackpole Books.
Elting, J. R. 1974. *Military uniforms in America, the era of the American revolution 1755–1795.* Novato, Calif.: Presidio Press.
Fitzsimons, B. 1973. *Heraldry and regalia of war.* New York: Beekman House.
Funcken F., and L. Funcken. 1972. *Arms and uniforms 2, 18th century to the present day.* London: Ward Lock.
———. 1974. *Arms and uniforms, the first world war.* London: Ward Lock.
Gordon, L. L. 1971. *Military origins.* New York: A. S. Barnes.
Humble, R., and R. Scollins. 1986. *The soldier.* New York: Crescent Books.
Kerrigan, E. E. 1967. *American badges and insignia.* New York: Viking Press.
Knotel, H., and H. S. Knotel. 1980. *Uniforms of the world.* New York: Scribner's.
Lovette, L. P. 1959. *Naval customs, traditions and usage.* Annapolis, Md.: U.S. Naval Institute Press.
Mack, W.P., and R. W. Connell. 1980. *Naval ceremonies, customs, and traditions.* Annapolis, Md.: U.S. Naval Institute Press.
Martin, P. 1967. *European military uniforms, a short history.* London: Spring Books.

Military Collector & Historian, journal of the Company of Military Historians, West-brook, Conn.

Mollo, J. 1972. *Military fashion.* New York: Putnam's.

Mollo, J, and M. McGregor. 1975. *Uniforms of the American revolution.* New York: Macmillan.

Rankin, R. H. 1962. *Uniforms of the sea services.* Annapolis, Md.: U.S. Naval Institute Press.

――――. 1967. *Uniforms of the army.* New York: Putnam's.

Rosignoli, G. 1986. *The illustrated encyclopedia of military insignia of the 20th century.* Secaucus, N.J.: Chartwell Books.

Schick, I. T. 1978. *Battledress, the uniforms of the world's great armies 1700 to the present.* Boston: Little, Brown.

Steffen, R. 1977. *The horse soldier 1776–1943.* 4 vol. Norman, Okla.: Univ. of Oklahoma Press.

Tily, J. C. 1964. *The uniforms of the United States Navy.* New York: Thomas Yoseloff.

Todd, F. P. 1980. *American military equipage 1851–1872.* New York: Scribner's.

Wilkinson, F. 1970. *Battle dress.* Garden City, N.Y.: Doubleday.

Wilkinson-Latham, R. J. 1975. *Collecting militaria.* London: John Gifford.

Windrow, M., and G. Embleton. 1973. *Military dress of North America 1665–1970.* New York: Scribner's.

VASILEVSKII, ALEKSANDR MIKHAILOVICH
[1895–1977]

Marshal of the Soviet Union Vasilevskii—first Soviet commander of a High Command of Forces (HCF) in a Theater of Strategic Military Operations (TSMO), chief of the Soviet General Staff, and minister of war—was one of the foremost operational planners and commanders of World War II. Vasilevskii was also a delegate to the 19th and 20th Communist party of the Soviet Union (CPSU) party congresses and a member of the Central Committee of the CPSU (1952–61). He served as a delegate to the second through fourth sessions of the Supreme Soviet of the USSR.

Early Life

Vasilevskii was born on 18 (O.S.; 30 N.S.) September 1895 in Novaia Gol'chika (previously in the Keneshevskii *raion* of Ivanov oblast), the son of a Russian Orthodox priest. Vasilevskii initially attended a theological seminary, but joined the czarist army in 1915. After completing the Alekseev Military School (1915), he served as a junior officer in the Novokhpoersk Regiment of the 103d Infantry Division (ID) of the Ninth Army. He commanded a company, then a battalion (as a captain). During the civil war, Vasilevskii joined the Red Army (1919) and began service as an assistant platoon commander in a reserve battalion in Efremov, then commanded a company and detachment. By October 1919 Vasilevskii was a battalion commander; he next took command of the 5th Infantry Regiment of the 2d Tula ID (later renamed the 48th ID). While assistant commander of a regiment of the 11th Petrograd Division, Vasilevskii fought in the Russo-Polish War (1920). During the first two decades of the Red Army, Vasilevskii excelled as a staff officer, planner, and educator. From May 1920 to 1931, Vasilevskii served as assistant regimental commander, commander of divisional schools, and regimental commander (for eight years) within the 48th ID. In 1931 he was transferred to the Department of Combat Training of the General Staff where he helped develop the "Instructions on Service of Staffs" and "Instructions Concerning the Conduct of Deep Battle." That same year he joined the CPSU. Vasilevskii directed military training in the Volga Military

District (1934–36) before attending the newly formed General Staff Academy (1936–38). A protégé of Marshal Shaposhnikov, Major General Vasilevskii remained with the General Staff after graduation as assistant chief of the Operations Directorate (1940).

World War II

Soon after the outbreak of war, Colonel General Vasilevskii became the chief of the Operations Directorate and assistant chief of the General Staff (August 1941). In May 1942 Vasilevskii (now Army General) replaced the ailing Marshal Shaposhnikov as chief of the General Staff. From October 1942 he simultaneously served as deputy minister of the Armed Forces (MAF, renamed Ministry of Defense in 1950). He left the actual operation of the General Staff to his deputy, General Antonov, while he went to the front to coordinate the planning and execution of multifront operations and where he also served as Supreme Headquarters (STAVKA) representative. He coordinated operations at Stalingrad (November 1942–February 1943); the 1943 Ostorozhsko-Rossoshanskii operation on the Voronezh front; the Voronezh and Steppe Army Groups (AGs) during the Battle of Kursk (July 1943); the southern and southwestern fronts for the liberation of the Don Basin (Donbas); the 3d and 4th Ukrainian AGs at Krivoi Rog and Nikopol (January–February 1944); the liberation of the Crimea (April 1944) where he was wounded; the 3d Belorussian, 1st Baltic, and 2d Baltic AGs in Belorussia (June 1944); and the East Prussian operation (February 1945). During the last campaign (17 February 1945) Vasilevskii was replaced by Antonov as chief of the General Staff and appointed field commander of the 3d Belorussian AG, which destroyed a major German group in East Prussia and captured Koenigsberg (present-day Kaliningrad). At the Tehran Conference Stalin agreed to declare war against Japan three months after Germany's surrender (Japan and the USSR had signed a non-aggression pact in 1940). In the autumn of 1944 Vasilevskii was assigned the task of preparing covertly for operations in the Far East in Manchuria (both in the planning of the campaign and the secret buildup of supplies and equipment to execute it). In June 1945 he was appointed supreme commander of the HCF of the Far Eastern TSMO, the first such command in Soviet history. Initiated after the United States dropped two atomic bombs, the lightning campaign of maneuver and operational surprise (9 August–2 September 1945) pitted Vasilevskii's three fronts (Transbaikal, 1st Far East, and 2d Far East) against the Japanese Kwantung Army of one million men. Vasilevskii quickly overwhelmed the Japanese forces in Manchuria, forced a Japanese unconditional surrender, and occupied Manchuria and Korea. In 1943 Vasilevskii was promoted to marshal of the Soviet Union (a rank he held until his death). He was twice awarded Hero of the Soviet Union (29 July 1944 and 8 September 1945). Only eleven Soviet commanders were awarded the diamond-encrusted Order of Victory; Vasilevskii (and Zhukov) were awarded the order twice.

Postwar Career

Marshal Vasilevskii remained as Far Eastern commander until 1946 when the theater was abolished. He once again became chief of the General Staff and deputy MAF in 1946, overseeing the demobilization and reorganization of the Soviet army (Antonov reverted to his deputy). In November 1948 he became minister of the armed forces, and following Stalin's death in March 1953, Vasilevskii reverted to deputy minister of defense (DMD). From 1956–1957 he became DMD for Military Science, but retired due to ill health from 1957 to 1959. He returned to service in the General Inspectorate in January 1959, where he remained in semiretirement until his death. Vasilevskii published his memoirs, *Delo Vsei Zhizhni* (*A Complete Life*), in 1973, and died on 5 December 1977.

DIANNE L. SMITH

SEE ALSO: Civil War, Russian; World War II.

Bibliography

Bialer, S., ed. 1969. *Stalin and his generals.* New York: Pegasus.
Erickson, J. 1975. *The road to Stalingrad.* London: George Weidenfeld and Nicolson.
———. 1985. *The road to Berlin.* London: George Weidenfeld and Nicolson.
Glantz, D. 1983. *August storm: The Soviet 1945 strategic offensive in Manchuria.* Fort Leavenworth, Kans.: Combat Studies Institute.
Ziemke, E. 1968. *Stalingrad to Berlin: The German defeat in the East.* Washington, D.C.: U.S. Army Center of Military History.

VAUBAN, SEBASTIEN LE PRESTRE DE [1633–1707]

Vauban (Fig. 1) is perhaps the most famous fortification engineer of all time and certainly one of the most accomplished. He raised the craft of fortification design to a science, and to counter his improvements in defense he designed a system of siegecraft to capture any fortress. He possessed a clear sense of strategy and intended his frontier fortresses to serve as bases of operation as well as strategic refuges.

Early Career

Vauban was born at St. Leger Vauban in Burgundy in 1633, but the exact date is unknown. He received some education during his youth in nearby towns and, when he was eighteen years old, enlisted as a cadet in the army of Prince Louis II de Condé (the Great Condé), at the start of the third Fronde, in September 1651. Young Vauban took advantage of the pardon offered by King Louis XIV in 1653 and entered the French service. He soon won distinction under the Chevalier de Clerville, the leading French military engineer of his

Figure 1. Sébastien Le Prestre de Vauban. (SOURCE: U.S. Library of Congress)

time and was made an *ingénieur ordinaire du roi* (royal engineer) in 1655. From 1659 to 1667, he worked under Clerville's direction to improve and rebuild frontier fortresses and won further note for his performance during the War of Devolution in 1667 and 1668. He was rewarded with an appointment from minister of war Louvois as *commissaire général* (director) of all engineering work in his department.

Builder and Breaker of Fortresses

During the Dutch War of 1672–78, Vauban directed several sieges, notably those of Maastricht (5–30 July 1673), Valenciennes (28 February–17 March 1677), and Ypres (13–26 March 1678). Building on his wartime experience, he instituted his "second system" of fortification when he improved the fortresses Belfort and Bensançon by utilizing corner towers and semidetached bastions to create defense in depth, although the changes from the standard pattern based on a curtain wall were forced on him by the problems of terrain at Belfort. This style replaced his former bastion and curtain wall "first system," which he had used in earlier fortresses. Vauban again took the field during the War of the League of Augsburg, and conducted the sieges of Mons (15 March–10 April

1691), Namur (25 May–1 July 1692), and Ath (15 May–5 June 1697), the last notable for Vauban's use of ricochet fire to breach the walls.

Following the Peace of Ryswick in September 1697, he continued to work at improving and rebuilding fortresses. He developed a "third system" of fortification that utilized an extension of his ideas on defense in depth, although he used this method only in the construction of the great fortress of Neuf-Breisach. He was rewarded further with promotion to marshal of France on 14 January 1703. This honor marked the close of his active military career, but he continued to write until his death on 20 March 1707.

Evaluation

Vauban was a first-class military engineer; his efforts to systematize French frontier defenses, although ultimately frustrated by political factors beyond his control, reveal his perception of strategic problems and opportunities. He wrote widely on a variety of subjects, including *Traité des mines*, *Traité de l'attaque des places*, and *Projet d'une dix royale*, a proposal for fiscal reform that was suppressed by Louis XV.

DAVID L. BONGARD

SEE ALSO: France, Military Hegemony of; History, Early Modern Military.

Bibliography

Blomfield, R. T. 1938. *Sebastien le Prestre de Vauban, 1638–1707*. London: Methuen.
Duffy, C. 1979. *Siege warfare: The fortress in the early modern world*. London: Routledge and Kegan Paul.
Guerlac, H. 1986. Vauban and the impact of science on war. In *Makers of modern strategy*, ed. P. Paret. Princeton, N.J.: Princeton Univ. Press.
Parent, M. 1982. *Vauban, un encyclopédiste avant la lettre*. Paris: Berger-Levrault.
Vauban, S. le P. 1968. *A manual on siegecraft and fortification*. Trans. and ed. G. Rothrock. Ann Arbor, Mich.: Univ. of Michigan Press.

VIETNAM AND INDOCHINA WARS

Four Vietnamese conflicts in Indochina since World War II (1946–1989) have continued the millennia of turbulence within and among the evolving nation-states of peninsular Southeast Asia. Pressures from larger outside powers— China, Japan, France, etc.—seeking to impose their will on smaller states frequently have worsened the continuing conflicts within Indochina. The turbulence also has been related to continual Vietnamese expansion down the peninsular coast on the South China Sea and inland over Indochina. Quarrels between island, peninsular, and mainland participants over ownership of the several island clusters in the South China Sea reflect a continuing dynamic factor of the Indochina Wars: the Vietnamese protagonist, almost always divided within itself, fending off (or, for a while, expediently submitting to) suzerainty of powerful external states, while itself absorbing territories of lesser states.

During the last two millennia, Indochina has been a mingling ground for indigenous traits and for intrusive Indian and Chinese religious, linguistic, and other cultural patterns. The resulting mixture was made increasingly complex by the sequential arrival of various eighteenth- and nineteenth-century forces of Western colonization—first religious, then economic, then military. The early twentieth century brought further disruptive influences through the spread of Soviet communist ideology and of Western economic development, complicated by the surge of Japanese imperialism in the 1930s and 1940s. Post–World War II French recolonization attempts were actively opposed by armed Vietnamese resistance made stronger by the leadership of such unique personalities as Ho Chi Minh and General Giap. The resultant complex internal and external quarrels characterize the four post–World War II Indochina-Vietnam Wars (see Table 1).

The Indochina Arena

The artificial domain of Indochina was first created politically in 1887 as the Indochinese Union, to satisfy nineteenth-century French colonial ambitions. It was reaffirmed by the post–Vietnam War Vietnamese political-military activity and goals. Indochina includes the present-day Vietnam, Laos, and Cambodia. Diffuse political borders link Indochina to surrounding Burma, Thailand (and the Malaysian extension of peninsular Southeast Asia), and mainland China. The lengthy Mekong River provides an important route for commerce within Indochina and among other parts of peninsular Southeast Asia, as it winds from Burma through the Laos/Thailand border, Cambodia, and Vietnam.

Increased French influence from 1850 to 1893 enabled these colonial rulers to establish an Indochinese Union that helped govern the area. Royal families of Cambodia, Laos, and Vietnam periodically seemed to cooperate in enabling a central federal government to be run by a French governor, responsible to the French minister of trade. This central administration handled defense, foreign relations, finance, customs, and public works.

The term *Indochina* continues to have meaning in Southeast Asia and elsewhere. During the Vietnam War the Chinese recognized, assisted, and applauded an "Indochinese revolutionary coalition." Not only was *Indochina* related to the historic development of Indochinese Communism and to the four Indochina wars described below, but *Indochinese* is still a means of collective reference to those refugees who fled the area by land, sea, and air. These departures occurred following expulsion of the Japanese in 1945, the French in 1954, the United States and its allies in 1975, and the internal Cambodian turbulence of 1975–1989.

The First Indochina War (1946–54)

Often identified as the Viet Minh War, this conflict joined Vietnamese nationalists and communist anticolonialists in fighting against various French regular and colonial forces from 1946 to 1954. Significant U.S. logistic support was

TABLE 1. *The Indochina-Vietnam Wars (1946–89)*

FIRST:	VIET MINH WAR (1946–54)
Start:	23 November 1946—French cruiser shells Haiphong/Hanoi; 19 December —Viet Minh respond by attacking French forces.
End:	22 July 1954—French and Viet Minh high commands sign truce at Geneva (Dien Bien Phu fell 8 May 1954, after U.S. refused to intervene militarily).

SECOND:	VIETNAM WAR (1959–75)
	Democratic Republic of (North) Vietnam (DRV) supported by China, the USSR, and other socialist states in its invasion of the South *vs.* Republic of (South) Vietnam (RVN) supported by the U.S., some Asian-Pacific nations, and other Free World allies. Significant revolutionary elements of the South Vietnamese were organized as a National Liberation Front (NLF), its fighters popularly known as Vietcong (VC, "Vietnamese Communists").
Start:	January 1959—DRV Executive Committee changes its strategy toward RVN from "political struggle" to "armed struggle."
End:	30 April 1975—DRV forces capture Saigon.

THIRD:	VIETNAMESE INVASION & OCCUPATION OF KAMPUCHEA/CAMBODIAN-VIETNAMESE CONFLICT (1978–89)
Start:	25 December 1978—PAVN (People's Army of Vietnam) crosses border into Cambodia.
End:	September 1989—Vietnam reportedly withdraws all combat troops from Cambodia.

FOURTH:	CHINA-VIETNAM BORDER WAR/SINO-VIETNAMESE CONFLICT (1979)
Start:	17 February 1979—Chinese forces cross Vietnam border.
End:	16 March 1979—Chinese return across border with Vietnam.

Note: There have been many other Indochina/Vietnam Wars: French Indochina Wars of 1858–63, 1873–74, 1882–83; Vietnamese-Cambodian war of 1738–50; Vietnamese-Cham Wars of 1000–1044, 1068–74, 1103, 1312–26, 1446–71; Vietnamese-Chinese Wars of 1405–1407, 1418–28; Vietnamese civil wars of 1400–1407, 1772–1802; 1955–65; Vietnamese Khmer War of 1123–36; Vietnamese-Mongol War of 1257–88; Vietnamese uprisings of 1930–31.

provided to the French for Vietnamese colonial troops to use during that period. Other than the reality that Vietnamese "rebels" eventually won, this was a classic colonial war.

Before World War II, the French had maintained their hold over Indochina through some 70,000 poorly equipped members of the French Expeditionary Corps (FEC), first formed in the 1880s. In August 1945, the Viet Minh seized control of Hanoi and forced the abdication of Emperor Bao Dai, who had made no real effort to govern under the late–World War II control of the Japanese. Great Britain rearmed the French troops. Ho Chi Minh permitted some 15,000 of them to enter North Vietnam, to help get the Chinese Allied Forces out faster. Despite the proclamation of the French military commander of Indochina that "we have come to reclaim our inheritance," and the U.S. announcement that it would respect French sovereignty over Indochina, Ho proclaimed an independent Democratic Republic of Vietnam (DRV) on 2 September 1945. On 26 September, for unknown reasons, Ho Chi Minh's troops killed Maj. Peter Dewey, head of the American OSS unit in Saigon—the first of many American military casualties in Vietnam.

France had hoped to regain control over Vietnam as a colony, but soon realized that at least some kind of a "free association" with former colonies would be needed. They agreed to recognize Vietnam as a free state within the French Union. French and Vietnamese representatives signed an accord on 6 March 1946. A subsequent conference at Fontainbleu began on 1 June, but on 6 December 1946, the French Navy shelled Haiphong, killing some 6,000 civilians. On 19 December, the Viet Minh retaliated by attacking French forces in Tonkin. After the French occupied Haiphong, Ho declared the Viet Minh at war with the French. At that time fewer than 20,000 French troops opposed over 50,000 Viet Minh insurgents, a number that increased in 1947 to 115,000. On 5 June 1948, France named Emperor Bao Dai as head of state in Vietnam.

By 1950, the French had 150,000 troops in Vietnam. On 14 January, Ho reproclaimed the Democratic Republic of Vietnam ("Hanoi"), stating that it was the only legal government of Vietnam; the Soviet Union and the People's Republic of China promptly recognized the DRV. In February, the United States recognized Emperor Bao Dai as head of state of Vietnam ("Saigon"), and Pres. Harry S Truman authorized US$10 million in military aid for French forces in Indochina. In August, the United States opened a 35-person Military Assistance and Advisory Group in Saigon, and in December signed a mutual defense agreement with France, Vietnam, Cambodia, and Laos. By this time, the Viet Minh had rejected any element of French authority.

During this period, guerrilla activity in the countryside had increased. French outposts along the border of China were attacked, and the Viet Minh received significant military equipment and other aid from China. In 1951, the Vietnamese created a common front with Communist groups in Laos and Cambodia. The United States increased its aid to France and its Vietnamese colonial troops, concerned over potential "Soviet Russian imperialism." By 1954, the United States was supplying up to 80 percent of the French military cost of the war. Continuing military activity enabled the Viet Minh to increase their control of the countryside. The internal political situation in France was increasingly unsettled, with seventeen successive governments in the period 1945–54.

The decisive battle of the war unexpectedly took place at the upland valley town of Dien Bien Phu. The French commander had occupied the area late in 1953, attempting to cut enemy supply lines into Laos and to establish a base of mobile operations against communist forces. Mobility was not to be achieved on the rugged terrain. The French then established a net of eight strongholds, with substations and varied weapons and numbers of tanks.

The Viet Minh soon cut all ground routes to Dien Bien Phu. Still confident of superiority, the French were supplied by air. But Gen. Vo Nguyen Giap had not only surrounded the French force with some 40,000 troops, but brought in heavy artillery (some of it U.S.-made, captured by the Chinese in Korea) over seemingly impossible terrain. The Viet Minh opened their artillery fire on 13 March 1954. The battle lasted 56 days. (On 17 March, U.S. president Dwight D. Eisenhower first spoke of "dominoes" in connection with Indochina.) The French troops and their colonial forces fought valiantly, while their leaders sought active U.S. military assistance. They not only proposed that the U.S. Air Force intervene, but suggested the use of nuclear weapons. Although Washington continued to provide supplies and equipment, the United States decided not to intervene actively.

The Viet Minh steadily overcame the French and Vietnamese colonial troops' resistance. The French forces ran low on ammunition, and most of their heavy guns were destroyed. The French commander surrendered on 7 May 1954. In the battle of Dien Bien Phu, 2,080 French were killed in action and 5,613 wounded; 7,900 Viet Minh were killed and 15,000 wounded. The war cost the French forces 75,867 dead and 60,175 wounded; their Indochinese troops lost 18,714 killed and 13,002 wounded. Current estimates state that a total of 600,000 lives (including civilians) were lost.

For all practical purposes, the battle of Dien Bien Phu signaled the French loss of the war. The 1954 conference at Geneva, originally convened to discuss settlement of the Korean War and the restoration of peace in Indochina, began on 8 May 1954—the day after the fall of Dien Bien Phu. By 21 July it was agreed that a cease-fire line along the seventeenth parallel in Vietnam would be created and 300 days allowed for each side to withdraw troops to each side of the line. For all practical purposes this line created North and South Vietnam, separated by a demilitarized zone (DMZ). All-Vietnamese elections were to be held before 20 July 1956, to reunite the country. Communist troops and guerrillas were to leave Laos and Cambodia, where free elections would be held in 1955. The particular cease-fire line "should not in any way be interpreted as constituting a political or territorial boundary." The agreement was signed by French, Vietnamese, Laotian, and Cambodian representatives. Although eight of the nine countries that participated agreed to the provisions, the United States made clear that it was not bound by them.

Interim

In 1954, Emperor Bao Dai had asked Ngo Dinh Diem to act as premier. On 23 October 1954, President Eisenhower pledged U.S. aid and support to South Vietnam, in a letter to Prime Minister Diem. The United States also helped form the Southeast Asian Treaty Organization (SEATO) to assist in combating communist aggression in Vietnam, Cambodia, and Laos. SEATO came into being on 1 January 1955, and the U.S. Senate ratified the treaty on 1 February by a vote of 82 to 1.

After proclamation of the independent Republic of (South) Vietnam (RVN) in 1955, Diem became president, and took control of the newly formed army. He used it to defeat three rebel groups: the Binh Xuyen, Cao Dai, and Hoa Hao. But when he did not hold the agreed-upon election in 1956, the North Vietnamese had communist South Vietnamese rebels (who had formed a front in

1955) begin guerrilla warfare and terrorist activity to attempt the overthrow of the Diem regime. These forces included from 5,000 to 10,000 former Viet Minh, plus a fifth column of internal dissidents. They were particularly strong in the southern Mekong Delta and along the Laos and Cambodian border. In 1956, the United States began training RVN troops in Vietnam, the Philippines, and the continental United States. By 1957, the rebels in the south had formed 37 armed guerrilla companies in the western Mekong Delta. Thirteen U.S. advisers were wounded by rebel actions. A campaign of guerrilla action and terrorism to overthrow South Vietnam had begun.

The Vietnam War (1959–75)

The Vietnam War pitted communist Vietcong (VC) guerrillas within South Vietnam, and North Vietnam Army (NVA) forces and their supporters within South Vietnam, Cambodia, and Laos (as well as external supporters from China, the Soviet Union, North Korea, and Eastern Europe)—against anticommunist South Vietnamese. South Vietnam was directly assisted by the United States and its armed forces, together with sundry forces from Australia, New Zealand, South Korea, and the Pacific islands.

This second Indochina War is variously listed by different historians as beginning in 1945 (hence overlapping the first, anti-French colonial war), 1954, or 1959, and extending through the decisive North Vietnamese victory in April 1975. This article takes as a starting point the North Vietnamese Communist Party decision in January 1959 to change from covert political-military activity in South Vietnam to overt military actions: the "armed struggle" phase of their efforts to unify Vietnam as a communist nation. The decision, Resolution 15, was endorsed in May, but it took up to six months to notify all the Vietcong cadres in South Vietnam.

On 4 April 1959 at Gettysburg, Pennsylvania, President Eisenhower declared that "our own national interest demands [that] the U.S. support South Vietnam." This was the first of many subsequent official U.S. statements committing the United States to maintain South Vietnam as an independent nation. On 8 July 1959, the Vietcong killed two U.S. soldiers at Binh Hoa. By the end of 1959, 760 U.S. military personnel were in Vietnam. The United States soon sent a Special Forces White Star training team into Laos to help train the Laotian Army. Meanwhile, the North Vietnamese People's Army of Vietnam (PAVN) established Group 559, to construct and maintain the Ho Chi Minh trail, and Group 259, to commence sea infiltration of the south. The trail through Laos and Cambodia, attributed to the strategic genius of General Giap, became a mainstay of DRV operations and a major component of their victory over South Vietnam and its allies.

PHASE I: 1960–65

The first phase of the Vietnam War was the revolutionary guerrilla war period, and lasted from 1960 to 1965 (see Pike 1988). The DRV imposed universal military conscription in April 1960 and began infiltrating cadres into South Vietnam. In South Vietnam, Diem was busy suppressing an internal military revolt against his rule. In September, the DRV leaders called for an intensified struggle in South Vietnam, and on 20 December 1960, the National Front for the Liberation of South Vietnam (NLF) was formed. At the end of the year, there were still only 900 U.S. military in Vietnam. In 1961, a U.S. counterinsurgency plan for Vietnam was approved. U.S. Vice President Lyndon B. Johnson visited Vietnam in May and recommended a strong U.S. commitment to the gathering conflict; later, Gen. Maxwell Taylor urged that the United States send 8,000 combat troops to Vietnam. Diem soon asked for troop training by U.S. advisers and subsequently requested a bilateral defense treaty. In December 1961, the United States had 3,205 troops in South Vietnam, and Pres. John F. Kennedy again committed the United States to helping achieve an independent South Vietnam.

By February 1962, Gen. Paul Harkins had established the U.S. Military Assistance Command, Vietnam (MACV) Headquarters. U.S. advisers were authorized to "return fire," and the buildup of U.S. forces began in earnest. The United States and South Vietnam began a strategic hamlet campaign to resettle peasants in defended towns and protect them from the Vietcong; the U.S. Air Force deployed its 2d Air Division to Vietnam. In early 1963, the Vietcong achieved a decisive, widely publicized defeat of U.S.-advised South Vietnamese Army forces at Ap Bac.

President Diem's opposition to Buddhist protests had already led to riots and self-immolations in South Vietnam, which brought him unfavorable international publicity. Moreover, South Vietnamese Army attacks on Buddhist pagodas received widespread attention. The U.S. State Department asked Ambassador Henry Cabot Lodge to reduce the influence of Diem's relatives, the Nhus, on South Vietnam affairs. However, on 2 March, both Ngo Dinh Diem and Ngo Dinh Nhu were assassinated in a military coup. The government of South Vietnam was in disarray. By the end of 1963, the United States had 16,300 military in Vietnam.

On 7 February 1964, the United States removed the dependents of military and other U.S. government personnel from South Vietnam. By April, North Vietnam began infiltrating regular People's Liberation Army forces into South Vietnam. In June, Gen. William Westmoreland took over as commander of U.S. forces in Vietnam, and General Taylor replaced Ambassador Lodge as U.S. Ambassador to the RVN.

On 2 August 1964, North Vietnamese patrol boats attacked the USS *Maddox* in the Tonkin Gulf, leading to the Gulf of Tonkin Resolution by the U.S. Congress—a resolution later considered to have been used to give the president wide powers for war making. In October, the arrival of the Fifth U.S. Special Forces in Vietnam was overshadowed by news of China having exploded a nuclear weapon. By December, the South Vietnam armed forces had increased their personnel allocation to 514,000, and there were 23,300 U.S. military in Vietnam.

Phase II: 1965–69

The regular force strategy period (1965–1969; see Pike 1988) opened on 7 February 1965 with a Vietcong attack on U.S. installations. On 2 March, the U.S. air war Operation Rolling Thunder began. The 3d U.S. Marine Corps Regiment arrived on 8 March, followed in April by the U.S. Army's First Logistic Command and subsequent major troop units. The first U.S. "teach-in" protesting the war was held in Michigan on 24 March, but President Johnson's peace proposal was rejected by the DRV on 7 April. By June, the U.S. Arclight bombing operation began, and Australian troops were deployed to Vietnam. New Zealand troops arrived in July, Korean troops in October. The 1963 coup had brought a disastrous succession of leaders. Now an Armed Forces Council headed by Generals Ky and Thieu was managing the government of South Vietnam.

The first major U.S. armed forces battle of the Vietnam War took place in the Ia Drang Valley, from 14 to 18 November 1965. This was a test of U.S. airmobile tactics and equipment, as well as U.S. armed forces' combat capability against North Vietnamese regular armed forces. Although the U.S. forces "won" when the PAVN troops withdrew, General Giap was deliberately using the battle to study U.S. combat tactics and equipment, in order to develop means to resist and defeat them in future actions. By the end of the year, President Johnson suspended the bombing of North Vietnam and invited negotiations. There were now 184,300 U.S. troops in-country.

In May 1966, the United States bombed the Vietcong in Cambodia and in June bombed the oil facilities in Haiphong and Hanoi. President Johnson visited U.S. troops in Vietnam on 26 October. By 31 December there were 385,300 U.S. troops in Vietnam, and 6,664 U.S. troops had been killed in action. In May of 1967, the United States bombed the Hanoi power plant. Ambassador Ellsworth Bunker replaced Lodge, and Robert Komer was appointed deputy to commander, U.S. Military Assistance Command, Vietnam (COMUSMACV) with the rank of ambassador. Komer's appointment reflected acknowledgment by U.S. leaders that the war in Vietnam was more than a "war of the big battalions," and that there was indeed a need to deal with the (often mocked) "hearts and minds" of the Vietnamese people themselves. Gen. Nguyen Van Thieu was elected president of South Vietnam in September. On 21 October in the United States, 50,000 antiwar protestors demonstrated at the Pentagon against the war.

The most significant year of the sixteen-year conflict was 1968. On 21 January, the PAVN laid siege to the U.S. base at Khe Sanh, and on 30 January the Vietcong and PAVN Tet Offensive began. By 24 February, South Vietnam and its allies had defeated that offensive and decimated the Vietcong within South Vietnam. Nonetheless, the U.S. public lost confidence in the ability of U.S. forces to help the South Vietnamese resist the PAVN forces. Despite U.S. troop success in resisting the PAVN siege of Khe Sanh, General Westmoreland's request for 206,000 more troops, combined with news of the massacre of women and children by U.S. troops at My Lai, brought increased doubts as to the purpose and capabilities of having U.S. forces in Vietnam.

In April 1968, U.S. troops in Vietnam reached their peak figure of 543,378. The United States now declared the need to "Vietnamize" the war and on 3 May President Johnson announced that formal peace talks with the DRV would begin. On 3 July 1968, Gen. Creighton W. Abrams replaced Westmoreland as commander of U.S. forces in Vietnam; on 31 October, President Johnson announced the end of bombing North Vietnam. By 31 December, U.S. military personnel in Vietnam had dropped to 536,000.

PHASE III: 1969–72

The neo-revolutionary war period (1969–72; see Pike 1988) began with the election of Richard M. Nixon as president of the United States. Nixon brought an agenda and a strategy for "honorably" ending the Vietnam War. The Battle of Hamburger Hill (May 1969) in the A Shau Valley, near the Cambodian border by elements of the 101st Airborne Division, again had raised serious questions as to the purpose and value of U.S. military operations in Vietnam: soldiers had fought to gain the top of a hill at great cost of lives, only to have the hill abandoned shortly thereafter. Nixon's accelerated Vietnamization plan pulled the U.S. 9th Division out of Vietnam on 27 August and the U.S. 3d Division on 30 November. By the end of 1969, there were 475,200 U.S. troops in Vietnam, with 40,024 U.S. troops now having been killed in action. Ho Chi Minh's death during this time (3 September 1969) had little effect on the course of the war, other than to deprive General Giap of his patronage.

During 1970, U.S. forces kept up their accelerated departure from Vietnam: the U.S. 1st Division on 15 April, followed by the 4th Division on 7 December

Figure 1. North Vietnamese troops man an antiaircraft gun in 1972. (SOURCE: U.S. Air Force photo; Robert F. Dorr Archives)

and the 25th on 8 December. The U.S. invasion of Cambodia (29 April–30 June 1970) raised a crescendo of objections in the United States and was followed by the unsuccessful U.S. raid on Son Tay Prison in North Vietnam (21 November) in the vain hope of liberating U.S. prisoners of war. American citizens' confidence in their government and its conduct of the Vietnam War was further shaken by a series of events. Perhaps most significantly, both in emotional cost to U.S. citizens and in lessened congressional support to the war, was the Kent State University tragedy, in which four student protestors were killed by nervous National Guardsmen. The unsuccessful operation Lam Son 719, an effort to have the Vietnamese troops enter Laos between 8 February and 6 April, was followed by the *New York Times'* publication of the "Pentagon Papers," obtained from Daniel Ellsberg and subsequently the subject of futile legal actions and bumbling government efforts to bring retribution. Troops continued to flow back to the United States: the Fifth Special Forces and the 11th Armed Cavalry Regiment in March, the Third Marine Amphibious force in April. By the end of December 1971, only 156,800 U.S. troops were in Vietnam. However, Congress had placed no restrictions on airpower. Therefore, to persuade the DRV to negotiate an end to the conflict, President Nixon ordered a resumption of the bombing of North Vietnam.

PHASE IV: 1972–74

Nixon's visit to China (February 1972) brought about a decline thereafter in the strength of Chinese support of North Vietnam and marked the beginning of the negotiated settlement strategy period (see Pike 1988). Although the 101st Airborne Division left Vietnam on 10 March, President Nixon suspended the Paris Peace Talks, and on 30 March, the PAVN began its Eastertide Offensive. On 15 April, the United States began bombing Hanoi. The Paris Peace Talks resumed on 27 April, but by 1 May, PAVN forces captured Quang Tri Province. On 4 May, the United States again suspended the Paris Peace Talks, and on 8 May, the U.S. Navy mined the North Vietnamese ports. By 15 September, South Vietnam had recaptured Quang Tri, and peace negotiations were again underway in Paris. But the United States believed North Vietnam required further incentive to negotiate, and ordered the "Christmas Bombing" of the north. On 15 January 1973, Nixon ordered an end to all U.S. offensive operations, and on 27 January 1973, the Peace Pact was signed by the United States, South Vietnam (RVN), North Vietnam (DRV), and by the National Liberation Front (NLF) of South Vietnam. The North Vietnamese released the first of the U.S. prisoners of war on 12 February, and on 29 March, MACV headquarters was closed. By 31 December 1973, only 50 U.S. military personnel were left in Vietnam and no other Free World forces remained. The United States lost 46,163 service persons in the war.

On 20 August 1974, the U.S. Congress reduced American aid to South Vietnam, and the South Vietnamese forces found themselves short of weapons, munitions, and spare parts. The hard-won peace terms had not been observed, and fighting now resumed. In late December, the PAVN began their Phuoc Thanh Offensive, and on 8 January, they began a massive invasion of South

Vietnam. They had not expected to finish the war so soon, but a demoralized RVNAF collapsed sooner than the PAVN expected; they rapidly followed up their advantage. President Thieu resigned on 12 April, and on 30 April 1975, the last Americans left Vietnam by helicopter from the roof of the American Embassy. North Vietnamese forces entered Saigon, and the Vietnam War was over—not just in Vietnam, but in all of Indochina.

The United States had slipped into the Vietnam/Indochina quagmire, lacking an agreed purpose and realistic, agreed-upon objectives. Valiant fighting by U.S., South Vietnamese, and Free World armed forces had won many battles, but the war was decisively lost.

The Cambodian-Vietnamese Conflict (1978–89)

North Vietnamese troops and People's Liberation Front fighters passed through, took supplies from, and sought sanctuary in Cambodia during the Indochina War, and the Cambodian people suffered retaliatory blows from U.S. and RVN military forces. Dissident faction leader Lon Nol deposed Prince Norodom Sihanouk on 18 March 1970 and declared Cambodia the Khmer Republic. Sihanouk went to China (in 1966, Sihanouk had made a deal with China for delivery through Cambodia of supplies for the VC) and from Peking headed up both the government-in-exile and the internal National Front of Cambodia, which was determined to overthrow the U.S.-supported Lon Nol regime. The Lon Nol regime was also actively opposed by other revolutionary forces, including North Vietnam, the Vietcong, and the Khmer Rouge rebels. In January 1975, the rebels cut Phnom Penh off from the Mekong River, and in April Lon Nol fled the city. Sihanouk returned to Cambodia as head of state for three months. Then chaos reigned: Cambodia was taken over by the Khmer Rouge, and Pol Pot became premier. His Chinese-supported government was directly responsible for the deaths of between 2 and 4 million people. The Soviet-supplied Vietnamese communist government, motivated not only by world horror at the situation in Cambodia, but also drawing upon traditional Khmer-Vietnamese mutual hatred and the Vietnamese tradition of conquest, then inflicted its own military forces on fragmented Cambodia.

Following the fall of Saigon and Phnom Penh to the communists in 1975, Vietnamese and Cambodian forces had clashed near offshore islands in the Gulf of Thailand. In April 1977, Vietnamese and Cambodian military forces fought along the border between the two nations, leading to a break in relations between the two governments. Cambodia protested Vietnamese efforts to form a Saigon-dominated "Indochina Federation." Vietnam responded with charges of Cambodian attacks on Vietnamese territory.

On 25 December 1978, some 200,000 Vietnamese troops invaded Cambodia, against the advice of Vietnam's own General Giap. By 9 January 1979, Phnom Penh was taken by the Vietnamese forces. Dissident Khmer Rouge official Heng Samrin became president of a Vietnamese-supported Khmer government. Yet despite Vietnamese occupation forces, dissident Khmer Rouge forces survived in the jungle and in rural areas, avoiding major battles and attacking government forces and Vietnamese supply lines. Despite past atrocities of his regime, Pol Pot's Khmer Rouge continued to be recognized by the United States and China, who would not accept the results of Soviet-backed Vietnamese aggression. U.S. and ASEAN unwillingness to normalize relations with Vietnam until PAVN troops were fully removed from Cambodia became a significant factor in resolving that conflict.

By 1986 there were three major competing anti-Vietnamese forces in the Cambodian countryside, including the Khmer Rouge. They had formed an uneasy coalition to attempt to get rid of the Vietnamese occupiers and unseat the regime then in power. The United Nations then recognized Prince Sihanouk as president of a Khmer government-in-exile. Despite continued internal bickering and fighting between military forces of the three parties, with the help of the ASEAN nations (particularly Indonesia) and in light of Vietnam's disastrous economic situation, the last Vietnamese military forces departed Cambodia in December 1989. An agreement between the three internal parties was then tortuously hammered out. By early 1992, there appeared to be greater hope for a less bloody internal Cambodian political relationship and better international relations than the past twenty years had allowed.

The Sino-Vietnamese Conflict (17 February–16 March 1979)

Considered by some scholars to be only a part of the "third" Indochina War/ Vietnamese incursion into Cambodia, this fourth war involved a 29-day punitive incursion into Vietnam in early 1979 by substantial People's Republic of China military forces. The People's Republic of China had declared itself as close as "lips and teeth" to Vietnam during the Vietnam War, serving as a conduit for Soviet aid and itself providing war materials and labor forces to Vietnamese and Laotian communist forces. However, after the Vietnam War, China and Vietnam, traditional enemies, soon reverted to quarreling. A tense relationship with China increased when the Vietnamese strengthened their relations with the Soviets, more so when Vietnam invaded Laos and Cambodia in 1978. China became seriously upset when the Vietnamese expelled more than 200,000 Chinese, some of whose families had carried on much of the business activity in Vietnam for generations.

The China-Vietnam Border War followed China's international posturing and threats to "teach a lesson" to Vietnam. China invaded northern Vietnamese territory on 17 February 1979, calling it a "counterattack in self-defense." Before dawn, up to 125,000 Chinese troops with approximately 1,200 tanks poured over the border at several points. Several towns were taken as the Chinese penetrated up to 25 miles into Vietnamese territory. Assisted by terrain favorable to the defenders and for which the Chinese were inadequately equipped, the Vietnamese put up stiff resistance. Bringing troop divisions from Cambodia, they mounted an unsuccessful counterattack in an area opposite the Chinese Province of Yunan.

The Chinese soon captured the cities of Lao Cai and Cao Bang, then Lang Son, the central city of the Northern Provinces, on 3 March. After strong resistance from Vietnamese troops, other Chinese troops took the coastal town of Quang Yen, some 100 miles from Hanoi. Despite purported gains, however, the Chinese invasion was then stopped. After some fifteen days of fighting, the Chinese declared they had accomplished their mission and started withdrawing. On 15 March, the Chinese troops were back behind their border, and the government claimed "success."

Recently published casualty figures indicate that the Chinese lost 26,000 killed; 37,000 wounded; 260 prisoners of war; 420 tanks and armored vehicles; 66 heavy mortars and guns; no missile stations. The Vietnamese suffered 30,000 dead; 32,000 wounded; 1,638 prisoners of war; 185 tanks; 200 heavy mortars and guns; six missile stations. Despite the heavy losses, neither side used significant air forces or naval forces.

Many subsequent exchanges of fire and various troop engagements have continued along the border. Although an accord was reached after many discussions, no settlement was achieved nor treaty signed. Analysts have suggested that Chinese government officials were surprised and disappointed at the modest results of the conflict, and that this led to subsequent efforts to modernize the Chinese military forces. However, adverse morale problems and inexperience were also major factors. The Vietnamese also were concerned with the inconclusive results. After public calls for improvement, their military forces were increased from 600,000 to well over a million within a year. Military equipment also was increased in number and improved in quality.

Future Vietnam-Indochina Wars

As of 1992, the Vietnamese have made a political rapprochement with China, brought their armed forces back from Cambodia, and effectively been influenced by ASEAN to reduce their aggressive behavior and efforts to control and colonize other Indochinese countries. Their national economic situation, while slowly improving, still borders on the desperate. Their armed forces suffer from economic constraints, but remain proportionally one of the largest military organizations in the world. Their communist party and government continue to rule.

A more hopeful indicator of reduced future conflict in Southeast Asia is the 1991 political accord in Cambodia, reached after years of effort on the part of the United Nations, ASEAN, and specific Southeast Asian nations such as Indonesia. Similarly, the changed political climate of what once was the Soviet Union and its reduced support to Vietnam may assist in moving the country toward a more peaceful environment. Nevertheless, the plethora of arms, munitions, would-be leaders, and splintered political parties, along with the continuation of ancient enmities, indicate the need for caution in any forecast for continuing peace in Indochina.

Recurring political-economic–based military clashes, with some shots fired and (presumed) casualties, have occurred over the Spratly and Paracel island clusters in the South China Sea. These islands are variously claimed by (some islands are occupied with military forces of) the People's Republic of China,

Taiwan (Republic of China), the Philippines, Malaysia, and Vietnam. Although the conflicts have not yet intensified to the level of "wars," the potential for such a situation exists.

Despite the 1975–90 Vietnamese internal political problems and economic failures, the threat of revolt (whether or not externally supported) appears improbable. In the political climate of the late twentieth century, it seems unlikely that any external major power would give significant support to militarily subversive actions in Vietnam or Indochina. However, if such actions did occur in the future, they might stem from the following scenarios (in decreasing degree of likelihood):

- Military clashes in the contested Spratly or Paracel Islands of the South China Seas
- Renewed military activity in Cambodia, particularly should there be significant border incursions into Vietnam
- Increased military clashes on the Vietnam-China border
- Internal conflict generated by either externally introduced former South Vietnamese paramilitary forces, externally led internal resistance forces, or (least likely) revolt by schismatic elements of the Socialist Republic of Vietnam.

DONALD S. MARSHALL

SEE ALSO: Giap, Vo Nguyen; Ho Chi Minh.

Bibliography

Boston Publishing Company. 1981–1989. *The Vietnam experience* (series). Boston, Mass., and Alexandria, Va.: Time-Life Books.

Buttinger, J. 1958. *The smaller dragon: A political history of Vietnam.* New York: Praeger.

———. 1967. *Viet-Nam: A dragon embattled.* 2 vols. New York: Praeger.

Chang, P. M. 1986. *The Sino-Vietnamese territorial disputes* (Foreword by D. Pike). New York: Praeger.

Chen, K. C. 1987. *China's war with Vietnam, 1979—Issues, decisions, and implications.* Stanford, Calif.: Hoover Institution Press.

Dunn, P. M. 1985. *The first Vietnam war.* New York: St. Martin's Press.

Fall, B. B. 1967. *Hell in a very small place—The siege of Dien Bien Phu.* Philadelphia: J.B. Lippincott.

———. 1966. *Vietnam witness, 1953–1966.* New York: Praeger.

———. 1964. *Street without joy: Insurgency in Indochina.* Harrisburg, Pa.: Stackpole.

———. 1963. *The two Vietnams: A political and military analysis.* New York: Praeger.

Gardner, L. C. 1988. *Approaching Vietnam: From World War II through Dien Bien Phu, 1941–1954.* New York: W. W. Norton.

Ginnekin, J. van. 1983. *The third Indochina War: The conflicts between China, Vietnam and Cambodia.* Netherlands: Univ. of Leiden.

Herrington, S. 1982. *Silence was a weapon.* Novato, Calif.: Presidio Press.

———. 1983. *Peace with honor.* Novato, Calif.: Presidio Press.

Karnow, S. 1991. Rev. ed. *Vietnam.* New York: Viking Press.

McGregor, C. 1988. *The Sino-Vietnamese relationship and the Soviet Union.* Adelphi Papers #232. London: International Institute for Strategic Studies.

Olson, J. S. 1988. *Dictionary of the Vietnam War.* Westport, Conn.: Greenwood Press.

Pike, D. 1966. *Viet-Cong—The organization and techniques of the National Liberation Front of South Vietnam.* Cambridge, Mass.: M.I.T. Press.

————. 1986. *PAVN: People's Army of Vietnam.* Novato, Calif.: Presidio Press.
————. 1988. *The history of the Vietnam War.* Microfiche from the Indochina Archive.
    Ann Arbor, Mich.: University Microfilms International.
Shaplen, R. 1965. *The lost revolution.* Rev. ed. New York: Harper and Row.
————. 1969. *Time out of hand: Revolution and reaction in Southeast Asia.* New York:
    Harper and Row.
Summers, H. G., Jr. 1985. *Vietnam War almanac.* New York: Facts on File.
————, ed. Var. issues. *Vietnam* Magazine. Leesburg, Va.: Empire Press.

VIKINGS

"From the fury of the Northmen deliver us, O Lord." Such was the oft-repeated prayer of the inhabitants of those regions of the medieval world that were visited by the Scandinavian raiders. These fierce warriors held Europe under their spell for almost 300 years starting with the infamous raid in 793 on the English monastery of Lindisfarne and ending roughly with the Battle of Hastings in 1066.

Who Were the Vikings?

Reading some of the hair-raising accounts of contemporary chroniclers, one can easily get the impression that the Vikings were nothing but marauders who looted and plundered wherever they went. However, looking at the Viking age from the distance of centuries, one can see that they were not solely raiders. They were also traders and explorers and settlers; sometimes one man was all of these—a different Viking for different seasons.

Why the Vikings emerged from their northern homelands and swarmed over much of the civilized world is not clear—and many reasons have been advanced, from climatic changes to overpopulation and internal power struggles. But there is general agreement that, whatever the reason, their endeavors could not have been so successful and their impact so strong if they had not achieved extraordinary advances in boatbuilding (as well as in navigational skills). Their famous "long ships" were of unparalleled beauty and incredibly light and flexible. Even the flat-bottomed cargo ships were marvels of technology.

The Vikings' raiding/trading and settlement routes stretched from the British Isles, Iceland, and Greenland to America in the west and to the Caspian Sea, the land of Khazars, and the city of Baghdad in the east. They settled in Italy, Spain, Morocco, Egypt, and Jerusalem and served in the emperor's bodyguard in Byzantium—the legendary Varangian Guards. When the famous Battle of Hastings was fought in 1066, toward the end of the Viking era, it was a clash between two military leaders with varying degrees of Viking ancestry: Duke William of Norman's ancestor was the great Viking Rolf, or Rollo, of Normandy; Harold, earl of Wessex, was a descendant of Danes.

The location of a particular country largely determined the direction of expansion during the Viking age (a distinction not made by the victims of the Viking raids, who simply referred to their tormentors as *Northmen* and their language as the *Danish tongue*).

The Swedes are associated with the movement east. The Rus (as in Russia), as the Swedes were often called, traveled regularly along the eastern part of the Baltic, where the island of Gotland was an important center (and a rich source of archaeological finds in later times), and also along the Dnieper and Volga rivers, from which they entered the Arab markets and the Byzantine Empire. These rivers were extremely hazardous routes of cataracts and rapids, and no doubt many a Viking never carried home the luscious silks and beautiful objects he had coveted in the East. But many who made it to *Miklagard* (the *great city* in Norse), Constantinople, gained fame and money as merchants or soldiers and lived to tell those who had stayed at home faithfully tilling the soil.

Westward Viking is an appropriate term for the Norwegians and the Danes. The Norwegians settled Iceland in 870. In 930, they established an independent republic that flourished until 1262, when it was forced to submit to the Norwegian king. From there, Norsemen moved to Greenland. Although their lives were full of toil and trouble, they succeeded in triumphing over their inhospitable surroundings. The colony, however, disappeared in the early 1300s—although several theories offer an explanation, to this day no one knows why.

The lure of the west did not stop with Greenland. The first sighting of America was recorded in 985, and the first Norseman to step onto the shores of the New World bore the fitting nickname of "Leif the Lucky"—Leif Eriksson. It is still not known exactly where the Vikings settled in North America, but the settlement on Newfoundland at L'Anse aux Meadows is no doubt associated with Norse expeditions.

The history of the British Isles is intimately connected with the Vikings. After the famous first raid of Lindisfarne in 793, Danish and Norwegian men and women put down roots and gave names in their native tongue to settlements, from Jarlshof in the Shetland Islands to Wexford in Ireland; and at the end of the ninth century, the *Danelaw*, which included the kingdoms of York and East Anglia, was established, with Danish rule and Danish laws. In Ireland, the Vikings developed a Norse kingdom with Dublin as its capital, and many important archaeological finds from the Viking age come from the Islandbridge cemetery outside Dublin. The Irish still commemorate the famous Battle of Clontarf (23 April 1014), in which the legendary Irish king Brian Boru died a heroic death in victory over the Nordic troops. In the waning years of the tenth century up to roughly A.D. 1050, Vikings looted England under the rule of different Norse kings, who, in many cases, established themselves as rulers not only over the Danelaw but at times over almost all of England. Those threats forced the inhabitants of those areas to pay *Danegeld* (protection money) to be left in peace (in some years amounting to almost US$100,000).

Viking Weaponry

The Viking warriors who approached the coasts of England in the eleventh century, or those who invaded the Frankish Empire, where they plundered Paris in 845 and the Moorish kingdom in Spain at about the same time, must have been fearsome indeed. Not only were they fearsome in battle, where they sometimes slipped into the famous *berserk fury*, the rage of the *bear skins* or the *bare skins*, but the Vikings had also streamlined the use of their weaponry and equipment in ways that were unique in the Middle Ages. Drawing on their own native traditions, ruthlessly discarding what seemed outmoded and/or inefficient, and, drawing on ideas and techniques picked up from their southern neighbors, the Vikings were able to develop military equipment best suited to their needs and time.

A Viking's weapons were more than utilitarian tools. From ancient times in Scandinavia, a man's weapons were looked upon as an extension of himself. These weapons were often imbued with magical powers. Icelandic sagas abound with stories of cursed swords, halberds that bled in anticipation of battle, and other supernatural events involving weapons. Viking warriors also gave their weapons names—for example, the sword of the mythical hero Sigurd (Wagner's Siegfried) was named Gram and it imbued its owner with unusual prowess. And the powers continued after the owner's death. Viking warriors were often buried with their weapons and one sometimes hears of graves in foreign lands being denuded of their weapons in an effort to transfer "Viking power" to a new owner.

A Viking warrior's equipment consisted of sword, axe, club, spear, and bow and arrows. Although the protective gear varied, it normally included a shield, helmet, and, for those who could afford it, a coat of mail.

In literature and lore, the most cherished of weapons, the royal weapon, was the sword. The Viking sword was often of Frankish origin, or at least the blade was. The area around contemporary Cologne was famous for its swordsmiths, and many archaeological finds and contemporary witnesses attest to the quality of the damascened sword (i.e., the wire was inlaid into the blade in wavy patterns) of the Franks. The typical sword was double-edged, made of iron with elaborately gilded hilts (in the case of a wealthier owner), and a triangular or semicircular pommel, most often of Scandinavian origin in typical Scandinavian "beast" ornamentation or in contrasting material (some were made of elk antlers).

The most common weapon after the sword was the spear. The thinner, lighter ones were the javelins, the heavier of the lance type. Like swords, they varied in appearance depending on the owner's wealth. The conical socket, which fits into the shaft, is often decorated in silver and other metals. On the Bayeux tapestry, embroidered in memory of the battle of Hastings and a veritable encyclopedia of knowledge about Viking weapons, charging cavalry is shown thrusting lances and throwing javelins at their enemy.

The most dreaded weapon of the Vikings, and the one that is most often mentioned by the terrified chroniclers of their times, is the battle axe. While it was characteristic of the Vikings at that time, it was largely out of use in the rest of Europe. The axe has a long tradition in Scandinavia connected with rites and rituals; axe-carrying celebrants are found in Bronze Age rock carvings. Stone slabs from that time depict curved axes, and there is little doubt that the axe is associated with the worship of the sun god.

Although the axe of the Viking age could be the most utilitarian of tools or the most deadly of weapons, some highly decorated axes, which were clearly of neither type, have been found in graves. They could have been ritual weapons associated with Thor, the god of thunder and lightning and the guarantor of stability and order. The proverbial Viking warrior is often depicted brandishing a sword and/or an axe. Normally, this axe had to be carried by two hands, but there are accounts of smaller and lighter ones being used in battle. Two principal types existed: the beard axe, where the blade is extended at the bottom like a beard; the other is the so-called broad axe, which came into use around A.D. 1000, where the blade is often decorated with animal motifs or inlays of precious stones.

The bow and arrow played a role in references to the Vikings; unfortunately only the points of the arrows have survived to our times.

As mentioned, the protective gear was a shield, which was most often a round wooden board with a central boss, a helmet, and a mail coat. Few helmets have survived to modern times, but it can never be stressed often enough, in light of Hollywood's depictions of the Vikings, that the Vikings did not wear horned helmets. Such helmets went out of style after the Bronze Age (1500–500 B.C.). The Viking's headgear was a conical leather cap with a nose-guard of a type shown on the Bayeux tapestry. All in all, it was an unglamorous appearance to the inhabitants of the threatened lands, but nevertheless one to strike terror in their hearts.

Remnants of the Past

How are we able to conjure up the image of the Vikings and their daily life so well after so many centuries? Our sources are many and varied, among them Icelandic prose and poetry from the Middle Ages, memorial stones raised by the survivors of the raiders and traders of these unruly times, pictorial stones on which warriors and heathen gods and their rites and rituals are depicted, Arab merchants describing their encounters with the Vikings in the East, and the names on the map of England where "Denby" is a modern version of "Dana by"—the Danish village/town. But the earth itself is the most generous provider of knowledge, always yielding new finds to archaeologists. Thousands of household tools and weapons have come to light from all over the Viking territory. The aforementioned cemetery of Islandbridge alone supplied 40 swords, 35 spearheads, 26 shield bosses, and two axe heads.

New excavations furnish new clues and new knowledge. The Viking age may have ended by A.D. 1100, but modern archaeology continues to stimulate our interest in one of the most intriguing and dramatic periods in world history.

ROSE-MARIE G. OSTER

SEE ALSO: History, Medieval Military; Normans.

Bibliography

Brondsted, J. 1965. *The Vikings.* London and Baltimore: Penguin.
Foote, P. G., and D. M. Wilson. 1970. *The Viking achievement.* New York: Praeger.
Graham-Campbell, J. 1980. *The Viking world.* New Haven, Conn.: Ticknor and Fields.
———, and D. Kidd. 1980. *The Vikings.* London: British Museum.
Jones, G. A. 1968. *A history of the Vikings.* London and New York: Oxford Univ. Press.
Magnusson, M. 1980. *Vikings.* New York: E. P. Dutton.

W

WAR

Throughout recorded history, man's outlook upon war has changed many times. Different civilizations in different times have evaluated war in different ways and have fought their wars according to different rules. War has not only been the object of man's interpretation, it has also actively and deeply influenced the religious, philosophical, and material fundamentals of man's life. The history of man's outlook upon war, therefore, is a major part of the history of human civilization.

War (from late Anglo-Saxon *werre*, related to French *guerre*, German *wirr* = confusion [i.e., confusion of the normal and peaceful order], hence also dissension, strife) denotes a conflict between major groups such as clans, tribes, religious or social congregations, states, and alliances. Usually, the term refers to armed conflicts, but Bernard Baruch coined the term *cold war* after World War II to denote a relation of bitter hostility and competition but short of open use of arms.

Traditionally, the term *war* has been used only when the quarreling parties were sufficiently equal in power to feed hostilities of considerable duration and magnitude. Wars against peoples considered "primitive" have often been called *military expeditions* or *pacification*; wars against much smaller states have been called *surgical strikes* or *reprisals*; in civil wars terms like *revolt* or *uprising* have been preferred. Such terminology has sometimes been adopted in all sincerity, without hypocrisy, and with some justification. At times the driving motive has been the desire to avoid embarrassing questions and constitutional, legal, or political problems.

Causes of War

Since early times, philosophers and religious men have tried to identify and then analyze the causes of war. Some merely wanted to know and to explain; others hoped to reduce the number of wars and their horrors. Human nature, economic causes, man's depravity, the conditions of man's existence in this imperfect world, and other causes have been invoked. None of these theories came anywhere near universal acclaim.

Recently the search for the causes of war has gained a new impetus due to the terrific destructive power of modern weapons and the consequential fear with which war is regarded. Peace research has tried to become a recognized academic activity. Certainly it is justified by its claim, its purpose, and its aspirations, although in the view of some it is not yet justified by its results. The powerful and prestigious disciplines of psychology and sociology have intervened in force.

However, all the research has brought little to light that explains much more than the age-old justification for colonialism: gold, gospel, and glory.

Gold, in this context, is but a short term for riches (i.e., for gold in the narrow meaning of the word and for a host of other basically economic motives, such as overpopulation, change of climate, competition for mineral resources, for pasture, water, energy), in short, competition for *lebensraum* (space for existence). Many wars trace their origin to one or more of these causes. At least one, the Opium War (1840–42), took its name from the cause.

Gospel, of course, stands for idealistic, ideologic, and crusading reasons, for the desire to spread a religious creed such as Islam or Christianity, or a secular creed (form of living) such as Marxism-Leninism or democracy. Many wars originated from one of these causes, for example, the Crusades, which were intended to spread Christianity. In modern times, wars were to spread what was proclaimed to be *liberté*, *égalité*, and *fraternité*. One country entered World War I in order "to make the world safe for democracy." During World War II, one country decorated its soldiers with a "Crusade" medal, and one of the more prominent military leaders titled his memoirs *Crusade* (in Europe).

Glory stands for such reasons as preservation of status, preservation of power or of the balance of power, nationalism, and, indeed, plain love of hero worship. Therefore, one could mention in this context man's aggressive nature and man's depravity.

In addition, it has been noted that some states, not all of them small and located in remote corners, have been involved in remarkably few wars (e.g., Switzerland, Sweden, Denmark, Prussia, and Japan), whereas others (e.g., France, Great Britain, and Russia) have participated much more frequently (Wright 1942, p. 641ff.), not always as victims of aggression. Thus, there is strong evidence for a polyphyletic explanation of war. It is primarily, and understandably, only the Marxists that do not accept this view. "All history of man is a history of class struggles" reads the opening sentence of the *Communist Manifesto's* first chapter. But otherwise there seems to be widespread recognition that there are many causes for war and that most wars have more than one cause.

Obviously, the two theories have consequences that differ in important aspects. If the Marxist theory explains the causes of war correctly, then war will cease by itself once exploitation and class struggle have been abolished through transition of mankind into a socialist and, thereafter, communist world. On the other hand, if there are multiple causes for war, and if the wars that do occur have interacting causes, then abolition of war will be much more difficult. Removal of all causes would then require the reconstruction of man, the reconstruction of human society, and a most fundamental change in the political and economic order of the world. This would be a herculean task, and therefore, abolition of the causes for war appears to be impossible.

Under such circumstances, wars could probably more easily be reduced or abolished through enhancement of the fear of war. In this process, sooner or later a level will be reached where even the victor can gain nothing by his sacrifices. War could then justifiably be regarded as a means unsuited to improve anyone's condition and as unable to fulfill any rational purpose.

Since 1945–46, the world has seen the bitter confrontation of two mighty blocs, both armed with all the horrific modern means of destruction. Many events have occurred during this time that formerly might have initiated an armed conflict, in comparison to which the murder at Sarajevo that started World War I was a mere trifle. None of the causes which have brought about innumerable wars has been eliminated. The causes were all there, but peace has been preserved because both sides feared the consequences of the first shot. This has been interpreted as indicating that the causes of war can indeed be controlled, and that they can best be controlled through widespread fear of war (the concept of deterrence).

Levels of War

The forms of peace may vary from sincere friendship between factions or states to bitter confrontation. The only and minimum requirement for peace is the absence of open use of arms. Conversely, war requires use of arms, although the forms of war may also vary widely. There is no universally accepted terminology for the various forms of war, but the following usage is fairly widespread:

Total war means the complete utilization of all resources available to a belligerent. The totality will normally be solicited by the war aims pursued. Nations threatened by the demand for unconditional surrender or a Carthaginian peace will mobilize all economic, political, and social resources and thereby force their opponents to similar efforts.

General war is closely related to total war, but the term emphasizes the total use of military means. It often denotes a war in which nuclear, biological, and/or chemical weapons are used. But the term is also used to denote an unrestricted conventional war.

In a *limited war* the aims of the belligerents are restricted. This permits the warring parties to limit utilization of their political, economic, and social means (no total war) and also to limit use of their military means (no general war).

A *conventional war* is fought without the use of nuclear, biological, or chemical weapons, although their availability may have a noticeable influence on the war aims, strategy, and tactics of the opponents.

The term *low-intensity conflict* has been introduced in recent years, but it has not yet been generally accepted. The term covers military action in the gray area between peace and open warfare, such as gunboat diplomacy, military assistance to insurgents or to countries fighting insurgents, reprisals by military means, and so forth. The forces and methods used are strictly limited. Often, but not always, the duration is limited to a few hours or days. There is no declaration of war; often diplomatic relations continue to exist. Normally, the political aim is clearly limited and clearly defined, which may lead to tight political control. At the high end of the spectrum are punitive actions such as those carried out by China against India in 1962 and Vietnam in 1979, and Cuban military involvement in several African countries. A medium position is illustrated by the raids carried out by armed forces of the Republic of South Africa into various neighboring states. At the lower and lowest end are the use of various nations' ships to protect international shipping in the Persian Gulf in the late 1980s, or the employment of very high-altitude reconnaissance aircraft (U-2) over various countries by the United States. In all cases, the aims pursued by the parties involved in low-intensity conflicts determine the intensity of the confrontation and thereby the level at which it is fought below the level of what generally is being called "war."

Man's Concept of War

THE AGE OF HUNT

In prehistoric times, war probably resembled hunting, and among cannibal tribes or those who needed prisoners for religious sacrifice, the purpose of war and the purpose of hunting may have been quite similar. Even a writer as late as Aristotle (394–322 B.C.) argued that hunting, which he considered as one of the acquiring professions, had two different modes: the hunt of animals and the hunt of human beings (i.e., war). After all, for him there were human beings whose destinies were to serve, but who would not do it voluntarily, so they were forced to do so (*Pol.* I, 8, 1256b; VII, 2, 1324b).

THE AGE OF FEUD

The close relationship between war in its modern meaning and the feud of individuals is still apparent in the fact that the Latin words for feud (*duellum*) and for war (*bellum*) have the same root, whereas the word for hunt (*venatio*) has a different origin. Apparently hunt and armed conflicts separated very early and in conjunction with the growing sophistication of human thought, behavior, and social structure. The new and larger social bodies, such as tribes, city-states, and kingdoms pursued objectives in their wars much different from the hunt for human beings. This forced them to organize conflicts for their special purpose, and soon resulted in forms and rituals wholly incompatible with the way the hunt for animals had to be conducted.

Many early epics and records reflect this stage in the development of man's attitude toward war. Homer and the Vedas already knew about the immunity of heralds and about certain rituals at the opening of wars and battles. Many early civilizations established locations, time periods, or specific events (e.g., the Olympic games or the celebrations of the Latin League) during which all hostilities were interrupted. The early Romans had a special college of priests, the Fetiales, which was responsible for specific aspects of relations with other states (e.g., for the safety of heralds and the rites obligatory upon initiation and cessation of hostilities). The Indian epics established an elaborate code of chivalry, demanding, for example, that foot infantry fight only foot infantry; chariots, only chariots; cavalry, only cavalry; and elephants, only elephants. The stage of ritualization was reached when rules were developed that, when observed, were detrimental to straightforward effectiveness (e.g., the soldiers had to call and warn an enemy before attacking him, and if the enemy was exhausted an attack was considered unfair).

Among the epics originating from tribal societies, there is one, however, that pays little attention to ideas of chivalry that are so important for many other epics. The Kitab-i-Dede Korkut tells of many battles fought after about A.D. 1200 by Turkish tribes against unbelievers, often Christians, in the steppes north and south of the Caucasus. Obviously, rules of chivalry applied only in battles against members of the same supergroup. The rules could be disregarded in conflicts against peoples of widely different ideals, culture, or religion. The strictly limited applicability of ethical rules, tribal mores, and religious ordinances is a feature not uncommon up to our time, especially in wars with racial or crusading undertones. Since oldest times religious or ideological leaders were permitted to order the annihilation of entire peoples, overriding even the decisions of military commanders (e.g., Num. 31, V, 7–18).

During European antiquity, some attempts were made to restrict the destructiveness of war. Plato (427–347 B.C.) taught that wars should be fought in a manner that does not exclude later reconciliation. Aristotle condemned enslavement of the vanquished. But again such limitations were demanded only for wars between members of the same supergroup, in this case Hellenes. Further on, these exhortations did not bear much fruit even in wars between Hellenes (e.g., Thucydides, III, 82) and a theoretical justification for outlawing even members of the same supergroup was often readily at hand (Thucydides, V, 84–116).

Since religion dominated many of the early societies, it also deeply influenced their interpretation and conduct of war. Many early peoples saw wars and battles as a divine trial. The outcome was seen as preordained by the gods, who often intervened in person to assure the desired result. This is true for monotheistic and polytheistic religions alike, as is evidenced by the Old Testament (notably Exod. 14), by almost every battle Homer describes (e.g., Iliad XVI, 775–810), and the Bhagavadgita, which tells at length how the god Krishna participated in the decisive battle of Kurukshetra as King Arjuna's charioteer.

Those who believed that battles reflect divine decision could well consider ruses of war as an unethical attempt to frustrate divine writ. Tribes professing such faith often prearranged time and location of battles, marched straight into it, waited until the enemy had prepared for battle, and then fought it out. Without much tactics and maneuver, they simply fought as hard and as courageously as they could, since this was the only way to win the good will of the gods and thereby victory. Such prearranged battles were even possible between peoples and armies from different supergroups (e.g., Herodotus, I, 205ff.). Naturally, such armies were at a serious disadvantage when they fought a more sophisticated, wilier enemy.

However, throughout European antiquity, and despite the growing sophistication and secularization of human thought, no one challenged the view that war was a principle of the universe; as Heraclitus of Ephesus (ca. 550–475 B.C.) had put it at the dawn of Greek philosophy. Neither custom nor religion, philosophy nor law, questioned the basic propriety of war. Even the individual's right (under certain conditions) to take up arms and to start a private war or a feud in order to further his own purposes was challenged only in a few highly organized states. This attitude toward war and this seeming neglect of the suffering war causes corresponds to an interpretation of human dignity, human rights, and the value of human life quite different from the individualistic view developed later and preponderant in the late twentieth century. This is illustrated by the widespread use of corporal punishment, by slavery, by the gladitorial games, and by the custom of sacrificing humans, which prevailed even in Rome well into the time of the Punic Wars (Livius, VII, 57). Life was considered less precious and suffering less important than other values. "For the honourable man disgrace is worse than death" (Bhagavadgita II, 35) was a view dominating all early societies and remaining influential almost to the present day. But honor was not an individualistic principle. The individual's honor was derived from the prestige and the honor of the family and the clan, as illustrated by the fact that in many early societies a stain on the honor of a family, for example, the murder of a family member, could be avenged by killing any member of the murderer's clan (e.g., Edda, Hrafnkell saga, death of Eyvind), not necessarily the individual who had caused the stain. Where the individual counted so little, his death and suffering could hardly be important enough to question the righteousness of war.

In a similar societal structure, although later in time, Islam developed concepts not much different from the early European ones, although the influence of a revealed religion naturally proved to be very strong and very direct (*Koran* II, 190ff.; IX, 5, 29, 36, 41ff). Farther east, however, remarkable views evolved that the European western civilization did not develop even at later stages. In India under the influence of Buddhism, Emperor Ashoka (ca. 272–231 B.C.), one of the greatest rulers of the subcontinent, erected inscriptions in many conspicuous places across his large empire, confessing his shame for having initiated wars of aggression and thereby having caused untold suffering (Edict no. 13). In China, on one hand Sun Tzu (ca. 350 B.C.) wrote a masterly *Art of War* without even paying lip-service to divine law, holy writ, chivalry, or any other code of comportment in war and interstate relations. On the other hand, in China great captains and conquerors never gained the respect and esteem that their peers received in Western civilization, from Alexander the Great to Napoleon I, and later personalities. It is significant that none of the mythological first emperors, Yao, Shun, and Yue, gained preeminence through martial activities.

called for state prosecution of those who preferred to trust the old gods. Soon there was widespread agreement among Catholic Christian writers that the just cause required for a just war was always available when Catholic Christians met heretics or unbelievers. This presaged trouble, especially when the so-called heretics subscribed to the same dangerous and troublesome view.

The dangerous consequences of the doctrine of just wars can be illustrated by the decrees of the Lateran Councils. The decrees of 1139 and 1179 banned enslavement and execution of prisoners as well as the use of the crossbow. The councils argued that these were hateful, sin, and loath unto the Lord. However, these restrictions did apply only in wars against members of the same supergroup (i.e., Catholic Christians). In wars against infidels (nonbelievers), the restrictions did not apply. Apparently the councils held that in such cases the usages did not displease the Lord.

Thus Catholic Christianity often continued the ancient practice of considering outsiders as beyond ethical ordinances. Those who refused the "right" faith refused what the Lord had offered them. This made heretics, heathen, and witches liable for *iustitia vindicativa*, for punishment. Often crusades, just wars, inquisitions, and savage cruelty have been brethren, not only in their ultimate aim (conversion to the "right" faith), but also in their disregard for *caritas* (i.e., in the means they used). Few wars in antiquity were conducted with such cruelty as the wars against heretics, such as the Cathari, Albigenses, and Waldenses, or with the cruelty displayed in many pogroms against the Jews and in the campaigns against the Islamic communities in Southern Italy and Spain, none of which survived.

The danger posed by the doctrine of just wars was exacerbated by a peculiar feature: Antiquity had outlawed other supergroups because they were unknown (i.e., by a principle which could easily be corrected), whereas Christianity often excluded other supergroups on the basis of religion, which could only be corrected by conversion. Thus, in antiquity a group could incorporate others into its own supergroup and could make ethical considerations applicable to them once enough contact had been established; seldom has a vanquished age-old foe been treated more chivalrously than the Persians by Alexander the Great, who himself married a princess from southern Siberia, the heart of Asia. Such chivalry has seldom been possible and hardly ever been practiced in the crusades of old and of the present time.

But the doctrine of just wars was dangerous not only in wars against infidels and heretics. Its effect in wars between members of the same supergroup, Catholic Christianity, could be equally negative. From the belief to fight a just war it was only a short step to the view that the other side fought an unjust one. This ominous view was supported by the fact that medieval writers never developed a theory which permitted neutrality; there were only just and unjust wars, but no wars in which both sides had justified causes. From there, it was very close to the conclusion that those who stuck to a seemingly unjust cause were morally inferior. Thus they were liable to punishment. The minimum treatment necessary was (or is) quarantine and re-education, the official program of many a crusade including those of the twentieth century.

Thus, the consequences of the doctrine of *bellum iustum* are Janus-faced. It ennobled war and the military profession by providing them with a noble cause, thereby raising them far above bludgeonry and selfish purposes. On the other hand, it converted war from a duel into a *bellum punitivum* and more often than not into a *bellum internecinum*. In consequence, this doctrine also excluded other supergroups, as had been done by almost all early societies. But the exclusion was effected on the basis of religion (i.e., a semipermanent mark). Thus the doctrine opened the door to many crusades in which remarkable deeds could be done with the very good conscience of a Christian soldier marching onwards to smite, punish, and re-educate the wicked.

Quite different was the interpretation of war in the Christian communities outside of Catholicism, especially in the Holy Orthodox Catholic Apostolic Eastern Church. Here, for historic reasons, neither the four original Patriarchates nor those that arose later gained the supremacy that the Patriarch of Rome gained in western and central Europe. Thus, a normative summary of the obligatory creed could not be produced. In addition, the eastern churches were less influenced by Roman law than the western ones, whereas the influence of Greek, and often of Platonic or neo-Platonic, thought was much stronger. Eastern theology was much more concerned with theology in its narrower meaning, with the nature of the godhead and its relation with manhood in the incarnation. Thus a normative theory of war, binding all parishes and all believers, has never been evolved. Faith continued to be seen primarily as adoration and confession. In conjunction with the absence of a centralized spiritual authority, this saved the eastern churches from the dangerous, and from the positive, consequences of the doctrine of *bellum iustum*.

TOWARD MODERNITY: WAR AS THE CONTINUATION OF POLICY

The essence of the doctrine of *bellum iustum* is the close link between religion and the interpretation of war. Obviously, this doctrine was to lose credibility in surroundings less dominated by religion than the European Middle Ages.

The door to a new age was opened in the country that gave birth to the Renaissance (i.e., to a movement that deliberately reverted to a pre-Christian era). The stage for a fundamental change in man's outlook upon war was set by Niccolò Machiavelli (1469–1527), significantly a man who was everything but a devout Christian.

Typical for the time to come, Machiavelli considered this world only when he analyzed war. Indeed, he denied any writ superior to the aspirations of the warring parties. The idea of a *bellum iustum*, of war as an act rendering justice, appeared meaningless to him. Since there were neither just nor unjust wars, a *ius ad bellum*, a right and a justification for initiating war, was no longer required. Thus Machiavelli emancipated war from religion, theology, and ideology and he even went far toward emancipating war from morals. As he saw it, "that cannot be called war where men do not kill each other, cities are not sacked nor territories laid waste" (*Istorie Fiorentine* V, 1).

It is illustrative that Machiavelli explicitly applauded Cato for having expelled all philosophers from ancient Rome. His supreme authority was not the teaching of religion or philosophy, but reason of state. He interpreted the life of states as a constant struggle for survival among the aspirations of neighboring states. Therefore, the primary duty of governments was to care for survival through preservation and, if possible, enlargement of the state's power base. Literally everything was subordinate to the requirements resulting from such reason of state: "Where the very safety of a country depends upon the resolution to be taken, no considerations of justice or injustice, humanity or cruelty, nor glory or shame should be allowed to prevail" (*Discorsi* III, 41).

In our time, such statements give a shrill sound indeed, not only because of their unusual frankness. However, when Machiavelli excluded religion and even morals from war, he also excluded all crusading attitudes, pretexts, and hypocrisies. Thereby, he also excluded the crusader's fanaticism and the belief that their noble ends justify many means. Closing the door to crusades, Machiavelli opened the door for a more dispassionate, more rational, and often more humane conduct of war. This positive feature was strongly reinforced by the fact that the new doctrine did not exclude or outlaw certain groups or even supergroups. The unrestricted applicability of the theory of war was an important new feature in European political thought.

Moreover, while Machiavelli disallowed religion, ideology, and even ethics to dominate war, he did not at all deny them. When he insisted that reason of state necessity may force a prince to commit wicked deeds, he never denied that they were wicked by all moral standards. "Religion, laws and armed forces" for him are the fundamentals of a state (*Disc.* II, Intro.). Finally, and most important, Machiavelli's new supreme authority, reason of state, often called for strict limitation of violence, and a later writer, Karl von Clausewitz (1780–1831) even considered policy the most powerful moderating factor in war.

Machiavelli's detached, wholly secular, and almost pagan consideration of war did not, however, have much effect upon the world. Reformation and Counterreformation caused a noticeable revival of religious influence on political philosophy and the interpretation of war.

Protestantism, rising shortly before Machiavelli's death, naturally disclaimed the view that wars against heretics were always justified. Otherwise, the deeply religious Protestant theologians, offspring of the same root as Catholic Christianity, had little difficulty with the theory of *bellum iustum*.

Writing amidst the horrors of the religiously motivated Thirty Years' War, Hugo Grotius (1583–1645) also retained much of the doctrine of just war. But he had studied history extensively and had wide experience as a high-ranking and influential diplomat. Thus he knew that there could well be wars in which both sides sincerely believed themselves to be defending a valid cause and possibly even did have such justification. If that happened, other states did not have any moral reason to intervene. Instead, they were well advised if they observed impartiality in thought as well as in action (*De iure belli ac pacis* III, 17, sec. 3). This led to a theory of neutrality which had been largely neglected in the age of just wars. It prevailed until the twentieth century when the climate dominating the two world wars made neutrality again a dubious attitude.

The Enlightenment eroded the doctrine of *bellum iustum* even further. Emeric de Vattel, a Swiss lawyer, raised the important question as to who was entitled to judge whose cause was just and whose was unjust. As he saw it, those who attempted to judge this issue thereby superimposed their authority over the authority of states and princes, who by definition were sovereign. This theory struck at the root of any just war theory. However, the issue Vattel had raised lost importance with the waning of the influence of the *bellum iustum* doctrine. When the theory was revived in the twentieth century, the League of Nations and the United Nations (UN) had to decide again as to who was entitled to determine whose cause was just and whose cause was unjust.

When Machiavelli and later writers justified war for reasons of state only, they did not straightaway designate the objects of military actions. The opposing state consisted of armed force, fortresses, civilians, villages, fields, forests, and so forth. Who and which of these should be the object of war? During the Age of Enlightenment, the continental European states developed a theory which differentiated clearly between combatants and noncombatants. As an ideal, King Frederick the Great of Prussia endeavored to fight wars so that noncombatants were aware of a war only when they read about it in the gazettes. Of course, reality often fell short of the ideal. But how far governments were ready to go was shown by Frederick again. When two Prussian provinces were occupied by French and Russian troops, the inhabitants initiated a resistance movement. But their own king threatened them with severe punishment, lest the difference between armed forces and civilians be obliterated. The attitude prevailing on the continent can best be illustrated by a quotation from J. J. Rousseau (1712–78; *Contr. Soc. Ouevres*, Paris 1964, III, p. 357): "War is not a relation from man to man, but a relation from state to state. Therein, the individuals are enemies by accident only, not as human beings, and not as civilians but as military men."

Differentiation between combatants and noncombatants was more difficult for countries with strong seagoing interests. Thomas Hobbes (1588–1679; *Lev.* XIII) considered, and later John Locke (1632–1704; *Two Treatises* II, 2, sec. 13)) followed him in many respects: Hobbes considered the original state of mankind as a war of everyone against everyone. When states came into being, they suppressed this universal enmity, but only between their own citizenry and between their citizens and befriended states. In war, the original hostility is revived, and all citizens of the enemy state are again the enemies of the state's own citizens. This doctrine facilitated sea warfare, since most merchantmen were armed. But it also facilitated blockade and sea warfare against entire peoples through its denial of an essential difference between combatants and noncombatants, which the continental European theory had evolved.

The doctrine of war justified by reason of state found its most acclaimed and most influential proponent in Karl von Clausewitz (1780–1831) and his major work *Vom Kriege* (*On War*). Clausewitz believed in the tradition of those who were not concerned with the moral justification for war. For Clausewitz, war was one of the means by which states pursue their interests and implement their political aims. Therefore, it seemed meaningless to ask for a justification of war—a view perhaps understandable for someone who first saw war as an officer cadet at the age of twelve and thereafter lived and fought through the wars of the French Revolution and of the Napoleonic age.

In the nature of pure war, Clausewitz saw nothing that moderated the innate violence. Thus he argued in a way reminiscent of Machiavelli: "We do not want to hear of captains who are victorious without shedding blood. When bloody butchery is a dreadful spectacle that should merely be the reason to analyze war more, but not to allow our swords to grow blunt by and by through humanitarianism" (Clausewitz 1976, chap. 4). War by itself and without the influence of other factors (i.e., "absolute" or "perfect" war) "is an act of violence pushed to the extremes."

In real life, however, Clausewitz pointed out that there is no absolute, no perfect war. There are always powerful factors which limit the exertions of both parties and thereby the violence of war. One of these factors is friction, which results from faulty information, chance, physical exhaustion, danger, fear, and many other factors. Friction ensures that "in war everything is very simple but the simplest thing is difficult" (Clausewitz 1976, chap. 1).

In all wars, however, the most powerful moderating factor is politics. Clausewitz emphasized that "war is nothing else than a continuation of political transactions." The political purpose of wars determines what methods the belligerents activate to achieve their aims. To be sure, in all centuries there have been wars with almost unlimited aims, wars which sought Carthaginian victories that delivered the vanquished helplessly to the victor's dictated decisions. In such wars, both parties activated all means at their disposal, so that real war approached what Clausewitz called perfect or absolute war. But in most European wars of the eighteenth and nineteenth centuries, the political aims were much more restrained. Thus the political domination of war exerted a powerful moderating influence. In these wars, the difference between real and perfect war has been very pronounced. Often the treaties that concluded the war were not sources of new hatred, but were acceptable to both sides and succeeded in installing a more peaceful order.

It is important, however, that in Clausewitz's view, although it dominates war, "the political purpose is not a despotic legislator" (Clausewitz 1976, chap. 1). The relation between the politician and the military, between policy and war, is not a one-way street. They interact. The political purpose must constantly be adjusted to the military means available. Therefore, it undergoes frequent change. It is also important that the politicians know their military instrument lest they ask it to do what it cannot possibly achieve. Therefore, if the politician and the *generalissimus* are not the same person, the *generalissimus* should be made a member of the cabinet to ensure "that war completely follows policy and policy is completely in line with its military means" (Clausewitz 1976, chap. 8).

It is regrettable that Clausewitz never wrote a treatise *On Policy* as a corollary to his *On War*. Possibly, as a serving Prussian officer, he wanted to avoid trespassing into the political sphere, which he himself had so emphatically placed above the military one. Thus we do not know in detail which requirements he considered imperative for policy and politicians.

But Clausewitz allows us to catch a glimpse of what he had in mind. In the first book of *On War*, the only one he considered finished, he describes the "strange trinity" that war consists of (chap. 1). First, there is the "original enmity" (i.e., the hatred and the violence). They are like a "blind instinct" and are the part the peoples play. The second element of the trinity is the interaction of probabilities and chance, of courage and talents; this is where the armed forces and their leadership play their role. Third, war has the subordinate character of a tool for policy "and thereby it becomes subject to pure reason" (*"wodurch er dem blossen Verstande anheimfällt"*).

Policy, for Clausewitz, was far removed from the marketplace, from political rallies, and from the madding crowd. It is not exempt from error, but it is shielded from emotions, from rabblerousing, from the hatred and the "blind instincts" of the masses. The policy that guides the military is the result of dispassionate reflection: a matter of "pure reason."

This indicates the high degree to which Clausewitz's teachings are the result of the age he lived in. He did not foresee that soon technology would create destructive capabilities that called war as a means of policy into question. Also, his interpretation of war and policy reflects attitudes of the eighteenth and nineteenth centuries, when wars were fought for limited aims that were established not by the "blind instincts" of the masses, but by rational reflection. Thus Clausewitz's doctrine reflects a time when victor and vanquished could jointly establish a new order which was advantageous for the victor but also tolerable for the vanquished.

Clausewitz interprets war convincingly from the perspective of Metternich, Talleyrand, and Castlereagh, of Washington and Bismarck. It is interesting that his contemporary, de Tocqueville, also did not foresee the gigantic problems that technology and the participation of the masses would create for war and peace (*La démocracie en Amérique*, vol. 2, III, chap. 26).

MODERNITY: *BELLUM IUSTUM* WITH MODERN WEAPONRY

The transition to modernity can be illustrated by a historical reminiscence: At the outbreak of World War I, the president of the United States called upon his people to be "impartial in thought as well as in action." He stated the doctrine of neutrality as it had evolved since man had realized that seldom did the justified causes belong only to one of the warring parties. The president had quoted the famous farewell address that George Washington had presented to his country should war break out elsewhere.

But the tide of the new age was already rising; the president's statement was widely criticized. Less than three years later, 1917, the president declared war. He was not satisfied with a definable political aim, but he set the purpose "to make the world safe for democracy." It was to be "a war to end wars," and the masses were satisfied with this reversion to a crusading spirit.

Thus a new age of just wars began, of good wars fought by the righteous and peaceloving against Huns, Boches, and Krauts. The latter, however, equally satisfied with their righteousness, considered themselves victims of crafty machinations and encirclement by perfidious and revengeful peoples. One side sang "Onward Christian Soldiers," the other side cried "Gott strafe England" ("may He punish Britain"), an attitude revived in even more venomous form during World War II and several of the lesser wars of the twentieth century.

The most important factor that drove the transition to a new age of just wars (crusades) was probably the growing influence of the masses. Modern war requires active participation by the entire nation as well as the readiness to bear the burden and sufferings connected with it. Active participation of the masses could most easily be achieved if the loftiest war aims were proclaimed and the enemy were depicted in the darkest colors. What the age requires is the "demonization" of the enemy, comparable to the exclusion of foreign supergroups, which man had practiced since time immemorial until the age of Machiavelli and Clausewitz. Demonization was accomplished by both sides in both great wars. Either the enemy's race was denounced or it was shown that the enemy's civilization suffered an age-old propensity toward evil.

Clausewitz had wanted to exclude the "blind instincts" of the masses when policy was formulated, and Bismarck had been able contemptuously to refuse German and British proposals to try Napoleon III for crimes against peace. But soon the masses tightened their grip on governments; less than half a century after Bismarck one of the warring prime ministers conducted his reelection campaign and won under the slogan "Hang the Kaiser."

Thus the restrictions on violence developed over two centuries of noncrusading wars, were nullified within a few years. Chivalry was still upheld by many individuals on both sides, but it was seldom supported by those in government and often denounced by those who felt responsible for kindling the fighting spirit of the nation.

In a marked change from the previous century, formal declarations of war have become unusual. This tendency is supported by the high prize which modern technology offers for a successful first strike. It is further reinforced by the desire to negate participation in, and especially initiations of, war: when one nation invaded northern China in 1931, it called it a reprisal, and when three nations invaded Egypt in 1956, two of them posed as honest brokers and harbingers of peace.

The civilian population is no longer exempt. For centuries it had been part of the soldier's honor not to use his arms against the unarmed. But in the twentieth century the entire civilian population of the enemy's country can easily become not only the target of naval blockades but also of large-scale air bombardment and of reprisals. At the end of hostilities, the civilians see their private property expropriated at a scale unknown since antiquity. In addition, many millions are expelled from their ancestral homelands and no crusader's conscience is moved when hundreds of thousands of them lose their lives. Thus war has intruded into the civilian sphere on an unprecedented scale in modern times. On the other hand, the civilians also enter into the military sphere. What in previous times were considered *franctireurs*, guerrillas of doubtful standing, have now become the heroes of many nations, although their very existence and often their way of fighting is incompatible with all traditional standards.

War termination also takes a new form. The *bellum iustum* age's custom is revived to deny the defeated the status of a lawful belligerent; the First World War was terminated by dictated, not negotiated, instruments. Prisoners of war are again retained by all victorious powers for many years after the end of hostilities, reviving a very ancient custom.

Thus methods of waging war, which had fallen into disuse since the Middle Ages and the Thirty Years' War, have been revived. Two features stand out. The first is the clear conscience of those who promote it. Due to the widespread violation of the traditional rules, both sides can claim that the enemy has little right to invoke those rules. Both sides are able to justify their methods as reprisal, retribution, and well-deserved punishment of those who are guilty of horrible deeds. An unsurpassable climax was reached when the World War II leaders of Germany invoked such rationale to justify genocide.

The second feature, and perhaps more important for analyzing the second age of *bellum iustum*, is that the enemy is again considered a supergroup beyond the applicability of traditional and professed rules of warfare and ethical standards, a revival of ancient and medieval customs. This makes a Carthaginian war termination possible or even imperative. Such a development is abetted by the strong passions that were whipped up during the war and could not be switched off when the enemy was defeated. The sacrifices and the suffering of the people call for revenge and the damage calls for reparations. Revenge, hatred, and fear inflate all war aims. Although Clausewitz is quoted more often than ever, in fact the Clausewitzian purpose and justification of war, realization of a rational political aim, is more and more in jeopardy. Thus war becomes unable to accomplish any aim beyond the destruction of the hated and feared enemy, and loses the only justification it can offer for the suffering and destruction it causes.

This process is reinforced by the simultaneous dramatic development of technology. Even before the advent of nuclear weapons, the destructive power of war had been multiplied. On one hand, this reinforced the crusading attitudes: modern war cannot be justified by small war aims, but only by the claim, hypocritical or not, to defend pseudo-religious and more lofty aims. On the other hand, World War I showed that in modern war even the victor can hardly gain anything worth his sacrifices. This grim reality was reinforced by World War II, and nuclear weapons removed any doubts concerning the validity of the reality.

Thus, toward the second half of the twentieth century, the destructive power of modern war and the difficulties to conclude a rational peace under the tremendous pressure of the agitated masses, called war itself into question.

OUTLAWING WAR?

For the first time in history, war as such is in doubt. It is no longer generally accepted as one of the unavoidable universal principles, as antiquity had seen it. It is no longer seen as a means to implement or protect a divine order, as the *bellum iustum* theory had held. It can no longer continue policy by more powerful means, since its destructive power is almost beyond control and war aims are too often established by what Clausewitz had called the "blind instincts" of the masses.

The transition to a new interpretation of war was not made simultaneously everywhere. Minor wars, which fulfill the victor's war aims at an acceptable price, still occur. However, in a world getting smaller and smaller, there is the danger that a local conflagration will spill over and that distant states will use such wars for their own purposes of war by proxy. Those small wars can then become very destructive and war termination can become very complicated. Thus even the wars fought below the level of the two World Wars are more and more in danger of losing their capability to fulfill a rational purpose at a price worth the victor's sacrifices.

The consequences of the new development were drawn relatively early. After World War I, the Covenant of the League of Nations went far toward limiting the *ius ad bellum*, the right to initiate a war, which before had been a jealously guarded component of a nation's sovereignty. Articles 11 and 12 obliged all member states to undergo a complicated procedure of mediation and "cooling off." In articles 13–15, sanctions were foreseen if members did not comply. Participation in sanctions was made obligatory by articles 16 and 17, which made neutrality legally impossible. In addition, between 1928 and 1939, 63 states signed the Kellogg-Briand Pact, thereby formally renouncing war as a means of their policy, as stated in article 1.

Church leaders were not slow to draw conclusions from World War II. In his 1944 Christmas message, the pope stated that the theory that regarded war as a means of policy was no longer applicable, a view reiterated before the World Medical Congress on 30 September 1954. This paved the way for an important shift of emphasis: Not only should wars be just, but man's primary duty is preservation of peace. This interpretation of peace and war was formalized in the encyclical *Pacem in Terris* (1963). The World Council of (non-Catholic) Churches stated at its Amsterdam meeting in 1948 that the tremendous destructive power of modern war challenges the traditional doctrine of *bellum iustum*. In February 1986, the Holy Synod of the Russian Orthodox Church published a "Message concerning the Problem of War and Peace in the Nuclear Age." It confirmed the theory of just wars, but stated explicitly that the advent of nuclear weapons and their destructive power forces a change in "all our traditional concepts of war, peace and justice" (paras. 1.7, 1.8, 2.11 and 2.16). Finally, the Charter of the United Nations forbids the use and even the threat of force (Art. 2, para. 4). Only self-defense is allowed and such sanctions as are imposed by the United Nations (Art. 41, 42, 51).

However, this raises the problems that man has had to deal with since he first tried to restrict war: Is aggression the first shot fired or is it the creation of conditions intolerable for the opponent? Who has the right to designate an aggressor? Who has the right to determine sanctions?

The Charter of the United Nations entrusts all these important responsibilities to the Security Council (Art. 24 and 39). The council's five permanent members have a veto right. If they agree among themselves, they need but three more votes from the ten nonpermanent members to see their wishes prevail. This gives them extensive rights and considerable power without any controlling authority. Unfortunately, the composition of the Security Council raises credibility problems that could affect its functioning. The elevated status of one or two of the members reflects a Eurocentric view, which was already dated in 1945. Several of the five nations who entrusted peacekeeping to themselves have a record of extensive participation in wars.

The new rules for neutrality also are remarkable. The Charter obliges all members to participate in sanctions (Art. 2, para. 5; Art. 25; Art. 43, para. 1). It is the Security Council, with its powerful influence of the five permanent members, that decides sanctions. All UN members are represented in the General Assembly, which can influence the Security Council only by the weight of would-be public opinion.

This arrangement has not prevented numerous wars and armed conflicts in many areas of the world. Therefore, states and alliances still must seek security in a world devoid of a supreme, credible, and powerful law enforcement agency. Interpreting war, man is still where St. Augustine stood: man is forced to take up arms when threatened by evil. The dilemma thereby created is still indicated by Vitoria's view that war cannot be just when it causes more destruction that it should prevent.

The present discussion of war still very much revolves around the problems long ago indicated by St. Augustine and Vitoria, thus illustrating the difficulty of finding a satisfactory solution. Most of the democratically elected governments, and therefore most of the peoples of the world, hold that the only solution to the problem lies in a strategy of deterrence: the sword is kept sharp and ready so that its use may never be forced upon its bearer.

Theoretical considerations provide support for such a strategy. The fear of war has grown in proportion to its destructive power. Thus there is reason to believe that nobody will voluntarily start a conflict as long as he is threatened in retaliation by modern war's full destructive power. As Winston Churchill said, "Peace may become the sturdy child of terror."

There is also practical experience to support a strategy of deterrence. Most of the wars fought after World War II originated when one or more national leaders believed that little of the most modern weaponry would be used and that nuclear escalation was impossible. Fear of war and deterrence of war had not yet reached its peak.

It is possible to argue that a strategy of deterrence can succeed in preserving peace and in avoiding the intolerable alternative of either fighting a disastrous war or surrendering to every threat of aggression. Thus would Immanuel Kant's (1724–1804) prediction of two hundred years ago be realized (*Idee zu einer allgemeinen Geschichte in weltbürgerlicher Absicht, 7.Satz*). As the Prussian philosopher saw it, there can be no doubt that one day war will end. Not through rebuilding human society, through reconstruction of man, or through realization of other dreams. War will simply end because man will realize through war's destructive power what pure reason could have taught him long before: that war does no longer pay, not even for the victor, and that therefore other ways must be found to protect the rights and the security of states.

CHALLENGES TO THE STATE'S MONOPOLY ON VIOLENCE

In the past, man's concept of war developed gradually; major parts of the old and superseded concept were retained. For instance, even in this second age of *bellum iustum*, the traditional rules of warfare, although often artfully circumvented, were seldom openly denied. To the contrary, they were loudly reconfirmed to support the claim of fighting a just war against evil opponents.

In the twentieth century, however, theories have evolved that aim at more profound changes in man's concept of war than previous changes. They have several roots, the most important of which is probably Marxism. The first chapter of the *Communist Manifesto* interpreted all government as a means of class struggle designed to facilitate exploitation of the vast majority by a small minority. Engels expanded this theory (i.a. *Anti-Dühring* II, 2; III, 5), Mao Tse-tung confirmed it, and the Soviet official textbooks reconfirmed it as one of the cornerstones of the Marxist creed (*Osnowy marksistskoi filosofii*, Moscow 1959 II, XV 2–4; *Osnowy marksisma-leninisma, utschebnoe posobie*, 2d ed., Moscow, 1962, V, 2). This theory grants the exploited, the vast majority, and possibly every individual, the right to resist the presocialist state. Also, the theory goes far toward denying that a nonsocialist state is a lawful repository of violence.

The second root of the new theories dates back to colonialism. The nationalism of European nations spilled over into their colonies, some of which soon asked why they were denied the right of self-determination, which their masters so loudly professed but so seldom applied to their colonies or to those whom they had vanquished in war. In addition, many colonials had been forced to participate in the European wars of their masters, so that they lost whatever feeling of military inferiority they may have had. Of those who became famous, Mahatma Gandhi was the first to openly proclaim that even legal colonial government could be unethical and that the individual's resistance was legitimate. (It is interesting that similar ideas had been presented nearly two centuries earlier in the British colonies in America by the likes of Samuel Adams and Thomas Paine.)

Much may be argued in support of the new theories of war and progressive violence. But it is difficult to see how the complicated fabric of modern industry, trade, society, and international relations can function without a rule-enforcing authority that protects the weak, checks the strong, and acts as a safeguard and mediator. It could well be argued that the new creed overestimates the individual's capability to judge his own cause impartially.

In short, it is possible that a new kind of violence springs into life—not in the international arena and between states, but within the states themselves. Numerous countries have already experienced large uprisings. Almost all countries have seen how a few can challenge the laws of the state, often with the applause of many. In many countries the low end of progressive violence— blockades, sit-ins, and so forth—have become a normal feature. Thus there is indeed a theory that powerfully proclaims a new age of progressive wars and of progressive violence and there are many examples.

On the other hand, there is less and less justification for colonial wars of liberation. Many believe that those theories that interpret the state only as a means of structural violence are losing credibility. Therefore, it is possible that future generations will see such theories as strange aberrations. If that happens, it should be evaluated together with the fact that large international wars become more and more improbable. Therefore, there is a chance that more and more generations of man in wider and wider regions of the world can hope to live without exposure to the grandeur and horror of war.

FRANZ UHLE-WETTLER

Bibliography

Aquinas, St. Thomas. 1912–25. *The "Summa Theologica" of St. Thomas Aquinas*. 21 vols. New York: Benziger Bros.

Aron, R. 1986. *Clausewitz, Philosopher of war*. C. Booker and N. Stone, trans. New York: Simon & Schuster.

Ballis, W. B. 1973. *The legal position of war: Changes in its practice and theory from Plato to Vattel*. New York: Garland.

Beaufre, A. 1972. *La guerre revolutionnaire*. Paris: Gallimard.

Clausewitz, C. von. 1976 [1832]. *On war*. Ed. and trans. M. Howard and P. Paret. Princeton, N.J.: Princeton Univ. Press.

De Tocqueville, A. 1944. *Democracy in America*. P. Bradley, ed. 2 vols. New York: Knopf.

Douhet, G. 1942. *The command of the air*. D. Ferrari, trans. New York: Coward-McCann.

Dupuy, T. N. 1987. *Understanding war*. New York: Paragon House.

Ferrill, A. 1985. *The origins of war: From the stone age to Alexander the Great*. New York: Thames and Hudson.

Fuller, J. F. C. 1961. *The conduct of war, 1789–1961*. London: Eyre and Spottiswood.

Howard, M. E. 1976. *War in European history*. New York: Oxford Univ. Press.

Kondylis, P. 1988. *Theorie des Krieges—Clausewitz, Marx, Engels, Lenin*. Stuttgart: Klett-Cotta.

Mahan, A. T. 1987. *The influence of sea power upon history 1660–1783*. Boston: Little, Brown.

Morisi, A. 1936. *La guerra nel pensiero Christiano dalle origini alle crociate*. Firenze: Feltrinelli.

Otterbein, K. 1970. *The evolution of war*. New Haven, Conn.: HRAFP.

Paret, P., ed. 1986. *Makers of modern strategy*. Princeton, N.J.: Princeton Univ. Press.

Schlieffen, A. G. von. 1913. *Gesammelte Schriften*. Berlin: E. S. Mittler.

Walzer, M. 1977. *Just and unjust wars*. New York: Basic.

Wright, O. 1942. *A study of war*. Chicago: Univ. Of Chicago Press.

ADDITIONAL SOURCES: A. Jomini, *Précis de l'art de la guerre (Paris, 1938)*.

WARSHIPS

Warship is a generic term for a seagoing naval vessel whose primary purpose is to use weapons against an enemy. Other types of naval ships carry weapons for their own defense but their principal missions are different—such as mine-sweeping, landing amphibious forces, or resupply and fueling of task forces.

Early Warships

The earliest warships were not specifically built for fighting but were modified, as needed, for war service. Their weapons consisted of the small arms of their crews, and the craft were primarily used to land raiding parties rather than to fight actions at sea. Specially configured fighting ships appear in dynastic Egypt as galleys with platforms for soldiers; a ram and a masthead fighting top for archers were added later. The earliest recorded naval action was fought by galleys of Ramses III off the Sinai coast against attackers identified as the Sea People; ramming and archery decided the day for the Egyptians.

Crete had an organized navy that cooperated with Egypt in clearing the eastern Mediterranean of pirates. While Egyptian warships were originally modifications of the existing merchant galley design, the Cretans are believed to have been the first to design specialized fighting ships. At about this time a distinction begins to appear between the beamy merchant sailing ship and the narrow "long ship" that cruised under sail and went into action under oars. Cretan, and later Phoenician, warships were slim, single-masted galleys with a heavy ram as their principal weapon.

The early Greeks used galleys and "round ships" alike for exploration and

Figure 1. Warship (three views of a French ship of the line, ca. 1850). (SOURCE: Iconographic Encyclopaedia)

trading. Their ships were used to carry landing forces rather than to fight at sea; in the *Iliad*'s account of the war with Troy, nothing is said about sea fighting. Eventually, war galleys appeared, and became gradually larger and more powerful. Because the effectiveness of a galley's ram depended on the ship's propulsion, efforts were made to improve the arrangement of oars and rowers. The exact nature of these arrangements is still disputed; in recent years the *Mariner's Mirror* (England) has published a number of studies based on archaeological and empirical evidence. Greek and Roman war galleys carried marines, who boarded after ramming. They also used archers and slingers for short-range combat. One of Alexander the Great's successors, Demetrius Poliorcetes, is thought to have introduced heavy catapults to his warships, providing them with longer-range capability. The Roman navy was organized around heavy war galleys and lighter *liburnians*. Julius Caesar described his troops' landing in Britain, supported by missile fire from their ships. During the Punic Wars, the Romans fitted their galleys with the *corvus*, a hinged bow ramp with a grappling spike at its forward end. On ramming, the *corvus* was dropped and the Roman ship's large force of marines swarmed across it. In later years the *corvus* was discarded; by Caesar's time a Roman warship was a ram-galley with one or two elevated platforms for archers, slingers, and catapults.

With the fall of the western Roman Empire, naval forces fell into decay, although for a while fragmentary attempts were made by some of the surviving remnants of Roman rule to keep control of the seas. In what became the Byzantine Empire, the navy was maintained and developed. Byzantine warships continued to be galleys, called by the Greek word *dromon* (runner). As with the Roman galleys, *dromons* evolved into larger battle force ships and smaller cruising warships. The Byzantines produced large catapults, some throwing missiles weighing as much as 450 kilograms (1,000 lb.) up to 700 meters (750 yd.). In the seventh century or before, "Greek fire" was invented. Consisting of various combinations of resin, crude petroleum, and nitrates, "Greek fire" was considered Byzantium's most formidable weapon and was long kept a closely guarded secret. Devastating to wooden ships, it was thrown in containers from catapults or projected from bow tubes and could not be extinguished with water.

NORTHERN EUROPE

Roman Gaul and Britain used warships of the existing Roman pattern. By about A.D. 800, however, the Viking ship, a single-masted galley with a square sail, had evolved in Scandinavia. Viking ships were large open boats, used at first in war and peace alike. By the eleventh century, three general sizes had evolved. The largest were powerful, but costly and not too maneuverable. The medium galley became the principal warship for the Vikings, as would the midsize ship of the line for eighteenth-century Europe.

The first English warships were similar to their Viking contemporaries and were merchant vessels mobilized in time of need. Alfred, King of Wessex (r. 871–899), built large war galleys to counter the Danish invasions. During the thirteenth and fourteenth centuries, such technical changes as the invention of the stern rudder to replace the steering oar; the bowsprit; additional masts and sails; and deep-draft seagoing hulls combined to produce true sailing ships that could tack into the wind as well as run or reach before it. These square-rigged ships were owned by monarchs, nobles, or merchant traders and used as merchantmen in peacetime. In an emergency, the ports were closed, and king's officials commandeered or hired suitable ships for their purposes. Wooden fore- and aftercastles were added for archers and catapults, and a force of soldiers was embarked. Tactics were still a matter of short-range missile fire followed by grappling and boarding, as in such engagements as the English victory over the French at Sluys (1340) and the Genoese victory over Pisa at Meloria (1284).

MEDITERRANEAN AREA

The war galley continued to serve in the Mediterranean long after passing out of use elsewhere. It was the principal Mediterranean warship into the seventeenth century and remained in limited use until the early 1800s. The best-known galley actions of this period were fought by allied European fleets against the Ottoman Turks at Prevesa (1538) and Lepanto (1571). The first was a draw, although a large Venetian sailing ship demonstrated the value of the broadside-armed ship. At Lepanto four galleasses (broadside ships with oars) did considerable damage. Although both actions involved the traditional ramming and boarding by galleys, the broadside ships had an impact out of proportion to their numbers and gave evidence of things to come.

GUNPOWDER

Small antipersonnel guns are believed to have been used at sea in the fourteenth century, mounted in the castles of ships to supplement other missile weapons. They had no effect on the configuration of ships. Early guns were relatively light, wrought iron breechloaders with detachable powder chambers. They were erratic and incapable of more than low power and were soon relegated to a secondary role by larger, cast muzzleloaders of bronze or iron. The new guns became larger; during the second half of the sixteenth century 50- and 60-pounders (smoothbore artillery was identified by the weight of the solid shot it threw) came into naval use. Bronze was preferred over iron from the late 1500s to the 1700s, but as gun makers gradually learned to process iron reliably and to produce iron cannon that were lighter and cheaper than their bronze equivalents, iron guns became preferable for use at sea, where weight was critical.

Sailing Warships

Ships of Henry VIII's time carried large arrays of guns, most of which were still relatively light. At this time the gunport, cut into a ship's side, was introduced. It permitted a ship's battery to be carried low enough to allow numbers of heavy pieces to be mounted and made the warship a more effective weapon system. Through the seventeenth century, guncasting and powder were improved, and gun sizes and calibers tended toward standardization. By the late

1600s a typical European warship was a wooden square-rigger with one or more broadside decks of heavy—for their time—smoothbore guns mounted on simple wooden carriages controlled by the muscle of their gun crews with the help of levers and heavy tackle. The smoothbore was hardly a weapon of precision; its crudely cast iron round shot rapidly lost accuracy—such as it was—beyond point-blank range, about 300 or so yards, and practical naval shooting was done at close quarters. Because sailing ships depended on their topside forest of sails, spars, and rigging for propulsion, and because practical shipboard artillery was relatively light by modern standards (the heaviest eighteenth-century ship guns were 32- to 42-pounders), all-around fire was not a practical option. Ship guns were mounted behind hull ports along the broadside, and the column or "line ahead" soon became the preferred battle formation. Ships in column had an unimpeded field of fire for their broadside batteries and could support one another's vulnerable flanks—their bows and sterns, which for structural reasons could not be armed. The combination of satisfactory sailing ships and effective ordnance made worldwide European expansion possible during and after the Renaissance.

DEVELOPMENT OF SAILING FLEETS

The sailing warship continued to evolve from the sixteenth into the nineteenth centuries. The high-castled carrack (or great ship)—exemplified by Henry VIII's *Henri Grace A Dieu* (Great Harry) and the recently salvaged *Mary Rose*—was essentially an adaptation of the merchant ship of its time. It was supplanted in the late 1500s by the galleon. The popular image of the galleon is really that of the earlier carrack; the actual galleon was a trimmer and more streamlined vessel with three or four masts and a projecting beakhead in place of the high forecastle of the carrack. Its broadside battery was increased, with one or two gun decks running the length of the ship. During the Armada action of 1588, it demonstrated both its speed and agility.

The galleon, armed with relatively heavy broadside guns and built with a pronounced tumble-home (its sides sloping inward from the lower deck up to the weather deck, concentrating upper deck weight closer to the centerline and improving stability), continued to develop during the seventeenth century. The Armada demonstrated the ability of heavy guns to cripple and even sink ships, although recent research has shown that the accepted concept of the Armada fight as a fight between long-range English guns and short-range Spanish guns has been exaggerated.

As warships increased in size, so did the weight of guns they could carry. Larger ships could carry more guns of heavier caliber than could smaller ones. In 1618 James I of England categorized his ships by size and firepower. This process continued through the age of sail because wooden warships did not, with a few exceptions, differ in fundamental concept; from large to small, all were essentially "sisters under the skin." By the second half of the seventeenth century, English warships were identified by "rates." First-rates, the biggest, carried up to 100 heavy guns; sixth-rates, the smallest, mounted as few as two light carriage pieces. This general system prevailed in other navies as well. As warships gradually became larger, the rates themselves escalated. By the turn of the nineteenth century, a first-rate might have 120 to 130 guns, arranged on three gun decks.

Refinements of design included capital ship hulls able to carry large numbers of heavy guns and smaller ships capable of higher speeds; staysails and jibs, permitting more varied canvas to be carried; and the helm, or steering wheel, in place of the old whipstaff, or tiller. The large fleet actions of the Anglo-Dutch Wars of the mid-1600s showed that battle fleets required standardization. Earlier actions were fought by fleets of ships differing considerably in strength, and the smaller ones simply could not hold their own. Only the bigger and more formidable vessels were capable of "lying in the line of battle"; they came to be called *line-of-battle ships*, the term evolving into *battleship* during the late 1800s. As the Vikings had discovered centuries before, the medium-sized ship of the line became the most generally useful version of its type, big enough to give and take punishment but not so large as to be cumbersome or uneconomical of seamen. Most of the sailing battleships of the highly developed sail navies of the late 1700s and into the 1800s were 74-gun third-rates; smaller numbers of bigger ships served primarily as flagships.

CRUISING WARSHIPS

The frigate, ancestor of the modern cruiser, developed during the eighteenth century as a fast fleet scout, convoy escort, and commerce raider. Where the ship of the line carried its guns on two or three covered gun decks, the frigate had one gun deck with additional guns on the quarterdeck. As frigates grew in size, guns were added to the forecastle. Quarterdeck and forecastle evolved into a single weather deck, or spar deck, in the big frigates of the 1800s.

Smaller ships supplemented frigates. Single-masted cutters and two-masted brigs and schooners performed many subsidiary tasks. Two-masted sloops-of-war evolved by the late 1700s into three-masted ship-sloops, some of which became as powerful as early frigates had been. These sloops carried their guns on a single spar deck. Former merchantmen, armed for naval service, saw auxiliary wartime duty. Supply ships were armed for their own protection; mortar vessels, usually ketch-rigged with an open foredeck armed with one or two heavy mortars, were used to attack land targets.

Steam

Steam engines were tried in the late eighteenth century but did not see naval service until the 1820s. Side-wheel steamers were first used as tugs to manipulate sailing warships in harbors; the British-manned Greek steamer *Karteria* (1820s) was the first steamer to see war service (against Turkey) and the first ship to use shell-firing naval guns in combat. Other small steamers were used in such peripheral roles as operations against pirates. During the years that followed, steam engines were gradually tested in seagoing warships. Early steam plants, cantankerous and uneconomical, were used as auxiliaries to sail. Steam warships normally cruised under sail, using their engines only in restricted waters or in action.

The conspicuous paddleboxes of side-wheel steamships made natural targets for gunfire and reduced the broadside space available for guns. Invention of the screw propeller did away with paddles and allowed machinery to be placed lower in the hull, where it was better protected from damage. As steam systems became prevalent, nations developed an interest in coaling stations in distant parts of the world and acquired or leased places, often of little or no intrinsic value, that could be used as fueling points for coal-burning ships. Boilers and engines gradually improved in efficiency to a point where, during the second half of the nineteenth century, navies could begin to discard sails.

Heavy Ordnance

By the early 1800s some small warships were being armed with one or two heavy guns on centerline pivot carriages, which allowed use of larger ordnance than could be handled on conventional broadside carriages. Pivot carriages continued in service through the rest of the era of sail. Although they did not permit all-around fire—which was not possible in a sailing ship, with its masts and rigging—they allowed heavy guns to be trained to the side where needed and represented more economical use of ship weight. Ship guns increased in size as designers experimented with new materials and techniques. In the 1820s the French general Henri-Joseph Paixhans convinced his navy that explosive shells could safely be used at sea, and large-caliber "shell guns" were tested to good effect. The French navy adopted shell guns, and other fleets were not slow in following. As mentioned, shell guns were first used in the Greek war of independence in the 1820s; a French squadron bombarded Vera Cruz, Mexico, with them in 1838; the fleets of Mexico and independent Texas dueled with them in 1843; and a Russian fleet destroyed a weaker Turkish squadron with them at Sinope in 1853. Sinope attracted the attention of naval powers and confirmed the value of the new artillery.

Larger guns that could fire heavier shells with larger charges of black powder became possible when cast iron guns could be replaced by wrought iron guns and, eventually, steel guns. Gun tubes were reinforced by outer cylinders of iron and could accommodate the higher chamber pressures generated, although mistakes were inevitably made.

Armor

To protect against heavy explosive shells, designers turned to armor. This was hardly new; the Korean admiral Yi Sun-sin had used oar-propelled "turtle ships" armed with cannon and protected by a carapace of wood plated with iron against Hideyoshi's Japanese fleets in the 1590s. Sail-powered, protected Spanish *barcazas espines*—floating batteries—had been used in an unsuccessful siege of Gibraltar in 1782.

Floating steam batteries—slow, shallow-draft craft carrying heavy guns and protected by iron plating with massive wooden backing—were built for use in the Black Sea during the Crimean War. French and British ironclad batteries were soon followed by seagoing ironclads. In 1859 France launched *Gloire,* a wooden-hulled ship protected by a wrought iron belt. England replied with the iron-hulled *Warrior*. Both ships were soon followed by various types of broadside ironclads and armored rams. When steam made propulsion independent of the wind, the ram returned to the naval arsenal, and great things were expected of it. Although it was used to effect by an Austrian squadron in its defeat of an Italian force at Lissa in 1866, the ram eventually demonstrated that it was more dangerous to friend than foe, and it was discarded as improving artillery made it tactically useless.

Ironclad river and coastal ships saw extensive service during the American Civil War. These included types of broadside ships, with guns in side and end ports, and the shallow-draft, low-freeboard turret ironclads given their generic name by John Ericsson's *Monitor* of 1862. Although not suited to sea service, these ships did valuable work in the shallow waters where most of the Civil War was fought. Armed with 11-inch (27.9-cm) and 15-inch (38-cm) smoothbore shell guns in two-gun revolving turrets, they foreshadowed the gun warships that would follow.

Toward the Modern Warship

The second half of the nineteenth century was a period of transition and upheaval. Steam machinery continued to develop; triple- and quadruple-expansion piston engines and more efficient boilers lessened the need for sail and eventually displaced it entirely. When sail rig was finally dispensed with, designers could combine the hull and machinery of the seagoing warship with big guns in positions that allowed good fields of fire for the heaviest ordnance ships could carry. For a while some uncertainty existed as to the best arrangement for a ship's main batteries. Guns were mounted in "box batteries" amidships, with wide ports on the broadside and angled toward bow and stern. All-around fire was considered vital because naval actions were thought of in terms of short-range melees involving ramming; some ships had their big guns in two echeloned mounts arranged as far to port and starboard as possible so that both mounts could—theoretically—fire close to the centerline. The British battleship *Devastation*, commissioned in 1873, pioneered what would become a standard gun-warship configuration. Its four 12-inch guns were mounted in twin turrets forward and aft, and it had heavy armor arranged in a citadel around machinery and magazines.

Steel-hulled warships, armed with new steel breech-loading rifles, were introduced toward the end of the nineteenth century and continued this trend. Where the capital ships of the age of sail had carried large numbers of iron muzzle-loading smoothbores, their descendants mounted a small number of much more powerful weapons. Rifling gave the new guns increased range but only a fraction of this range was usable at first because weapon control was primitive and early turret guns were still individually controlled by their crews. Adjustable gun sights, telescopic sights, electrical transmission of gun orders, and optical range finders made centralized control of ship gunfire possible. The poor performance of naval gunners around the turn of the century spurred reform-minded officers, conspicuous among whom were Percy Scott in England and William Sims in the United States, to stress the need for careful training and continuing practice. Improved material, such as smokeless powder and faster-acting breech mechanisms for light and heavy guns, contributed to solutions. Mechanical and later electromechanical analog computers were coupled with gunfire spotting (adjustment of observed fire onto a target) to give gunners a reasonable chance to hit a moving target from a moving ship at an unknown range. Intensive practice and competitive shooting helped to make the naval gun a more effective weapon.

UNDERSEA WEAPONS

During the American Revolution David Bushnell's experiments demonstrated that the force of an underwater explosion, concentrated by the surrounding water—rather than dispersed, as was thought—could damage a ship. Bushnell and, later, Robert Fulton tried various devices that were not accepted. During the Crimean War, Russia used moored underwater charges that came to be called torpedoes. Fighting for the most part on the defensive, Confederate forces made and used similar devices during the American Civil War. The Union navy was required, perforce, to organize the first minesweeping operations to counter them. In 1866 an Austrian, Giovanni Luppis, and the Englishman Robert Whitehead devised an underwater weapon driven by a compressed-air motor. Early "automobile torpedoes" were slow, inaccurate, and short-ranged, but the value of the weapon was clear. Through the late 1800s and into the 1900s, improvements followed. Heated-air, then air-steam, engines increased speed and range. Control mechanisms kept torpedoes at their proper course and depth; later devices let torpedoes be fired on one bearing and then turn to another. The first warheads were filled with guncotton; later ones used dynamite and then high explosives. The increasing range of the torpedo was one of the factors contributing to the rapidly increasing gunnery ranges of the years before World War I. Electric drive and acoustic homing appeared during World War II; some postwar torpedoes have been wire-guided.

TORPEDO BOATS AND DESTROYERS

With the torpedo came a new generation of torpedo boats, small steam-driven craft armed with one or more torpedo tubes and small-caliber guns and intended to operate in poor visibility. The torpedo boat was seen as a great equalizer and a serious threat to large warships. All navies built or acquired them; some, notably France and Germany, thought that they might counter conventional battle fleets. Like other ultimate weapons, the torpedo failed to do away with its opposition, although it did prove powerful and valuable in service. Its descendants are still a prominent part of the naval arsenal.

The torpedo boat stimulated development of smaller-caliber, rapid-firing guns, numbers of which were mounted in big ships and used in coordination with searchlights. The need to defend heavy warships from torpedo attack led to a new type of ship, somewhat larger and more seaworthy than the torpedo boat but small enough to be produced in quantity. Its original function was defense of battleship and cruiser forces against torpedo attack, hence its original name of *torpedo-boat destroyer,* later shortened to *destroyer.* Although its functions have repeatedly changed, the type is still essential to many navies.

SUBMARINES

During the nineteenth century, inventors in a number of countries began serious experiments with undersea craft, although sporadic efforts in this direction had occurred as far back as the time of Alexander the Great. Advances in materials and weapons—originally the spar torpedo, a powder charge on the end of a boom projecting from the bow—made it possible to think seriously about what was first called the *submarine torpedo boat,* eventually shortened to *submarine.* The torpedo was a natural weapon for submersible craft and, by the turn of this century, navies were acquiring numbers of small submarines armed with one or more torpedo tubes.

Invention of the periscope and the diesel-electric power plant, with high-capacity storage batteries powering electric motors for underwater navigation, enabled submarines to operate completely beneath the surface. Torpedo-firing diesel-electric submarines saw their first combat in World War I. German submarines in that conflict, as well as German and American submarines in World War II, inflicted damage on their opponents' navies but scored most heavily on their supply lines. Antisubmarine warfare (ASW) became a major priority for their opponents; well-escorted convoys, sonar and depth charges, radar, high-frequency radio direction finders, and—in the Atlantic during World War II—cryptographic intelligence and seaborne aviation all helped to counter the submarine. Through World War II the submarine was still essentially a surface ship capable of operating at slow submerged speeds for relatively short periods of time; when batteries ran down and air gave out, it had to surface. Postwar development of high-performance submarines made ASW more difficult; nuclear propulsion, with techniques for purifying and oxygenating breathing air, created the true submarine, able to operate at high speeds at depth for long periods of time.

Twentieth Century

From the late 1800s through World War II, warships tended to fall into fairly well-defined categories, although the particular characteristics of these categories grew and developed. The core of a major navy was the battleship, heavily armored and armed with the heaviest guns. Into the early 1900s, battleships were armed with a small number of big guns—usually four—backed up by an intermediate battery of cruiser-weight guns, all of which formed the ship's offensive armament. As heavy-gun performance improved and torpedo ranges increased, battle ranges were extended to a point where the lighter guns lost their value and were supplanted by "all-big-gun" armaments. The first ship to mount such a battery, the British battleship *Dreadnought,* gave its name to the new category of battleship, which would continue to be built through World War II.

Earlier battleships were powerful but relatively slow. They were supplemented by armored cruisers, big ships with medium-caliber guns and armor and massive power plants for speed. With the coming of the dreadnought, the armored cruiser gave way to the battle cruiser, similarly big, fast, and more lightly protected but armed with battleship-caliber guns. During World War I the battle cruiser proved too lightly protected for gunnery duels with capital ships—a task for which they were really never intended—but some of them survived through World War II.

A moratorium on capital ship construction was negotiated through arms limitation treaties after World War I, and no new capital ships were built until the naval limitation system began to break down in the 1930s. By then naval architects had learned a great deal about improved performance. The new battleships built in the decade before and during World War II combined protection and firepower with the speed of the battle cruiser. They served throughout the war; Britain, Italy, and France each operated a battleship or two for some years afterward. The USSR used the former Italian *Giulio Cesare* for some years. The newest American battleships, the Iowa class, performed bombardment and gunfire support work during the Korean conflict (1950–53). During the 1980s they were armed with cruise missiles and new electronics and returned to service as modern surface warships.

CRUISERS

Cruisers were the workhorses of most navies, including those that did not feel a need for a large battleship force. During the earlier years of this century, *cruiser* identified a wide spectrum of types, from the big armored cruiser to protected cruisers—their vitals shielded by an armored deck—and light cruisers, fast fleet reconnaissance ships. It also included small unprotected ships that would later be classed as gunboats.

The armored cruiser, as noted above, had developed into the battle cruiser by World War I. The relatively slow, protected cruiser had become obsolescent by that time. Light cruisers were used in large numbers, not only as fleet scouts but also as destroyer flotilla flagships, their gunfire supporting the smaller ships in attack or in defense of the battle line.

After World War I the cruiser became a fast, powerful element of the surface fleet. Ironically, cruiser design benefited from the naval limitation treaties signed in Washington and London because they were limited in numbers and in overall size, and designers were stimulated to search for ways to pack more power into a hull. Machinery had evolved into geared turbines and became more efficient, and hull materials were used more effectively to save weight. The Washington Treaty (1922) limited cruiser displacement; the London Treaty (1930) limited their numbers and categorized them as light or heavy based on gun caliber. This terminology remained in use until guns were replaced by missiles.

During World War II, cruisers fought surface actions, took part in task force operations with carriers and battleships, and performed bombardment and gunfire support duty. They operated as surface raiders or protected shipping against attack. Japanese cruisers had catapult floatplanes for fleet reconnaissance mission, a mission that was performed in the American service by carrier scouting planes. Cruiser antiaircraft (AA) batteries were progressively strengthened, both for their own protection and to enable them to take their part in task force AA screens. Postwar gun cruisers, embodying wartime experience, had rapid-firing guns with radar-equipped directors.

In the 1950s guided missiles were first added to cruiser batteries. Early missile cruisers were modified gunships with some tube artillery replaced by guided weapons; by the 1960s all-missile types, such as the Soviet *Kynda* and *Kresta* and the American *Leahy* and *Belknap*, were being built in numbers. Modern missile cruisers are large ships, capable of independent operation as well as service with task forces. A fairly typical ship of this type has a mix of short- and long-range antiair and antiship missiles, with antisubmarine weapons and short-range automatic guns for self-defense. Newer cruisers, such as the American Ticonderoga class, with the long-range Aegis fire control system, are intended to coordinate the weapons of an entire task force. Some Soviet and American cruisers, such as the Soviet Kirov class, are nuclear-propelled for high-speed strategic mobility.

DESTROYERS

Like other warships, destroyers steadily increased in size, from 1,000- or 1,500-ton ships armed with torpedo tubes and light guns, to large, sophisticated gas-turbine ships armed with guns, missiles, and antisubmarine ordnance controlled by digital computers. From World War II to the present, the destroyer category has included full-size fleet destroyers and smaller destroyer escorts (frigates). Destroyers are often thought of as convoy escorts. Although they did perform this task, their primary mission was offensive action with surface or carrier task forces. They fought in large numbers in every theater during World War II. As that conflict went on, they acquired such new missions as search-and-rescue and task force radar picket duty. Antisubmarine armaments were updated in the postwar years to cope with high-performance submarines; stand-off weapons, capable of carrying a depth charge or torpedo a distance from the firing ship, were introduced. As with cruisers, guided missiles began to be added during the 1950s. Current destroyers and frigates resemble cruisers in their general capabilities; they normally have antisubmarine, gun, and self-defense missile systems, and many have long-range missiles as well.

MODERN WARSHIPS

Contemporary warships include a variety of types, limited only by the needs and resources of their users. Some larger fleets use aircraft or helicopter carriers of varying sizes; virtually every other type except small attack craft can accommodate, or at least operate, helicopters or V/STOL airplanes. Some argue that the big American-type carrier is a vulnerable, expensive target and that ships more along the line of Britain's Invincible-class light carriers would be more cost-effective and survivable. Advocates of the large carrier, however, emphasize its power, versatility, and ability to protect itself while extending its striking power over wide areas of land and sea.

Surface warships have taken a new lease on life from new missile systems and computerized electronics. Long- and short-range antiaircraft missiles, backed up by quick-reaction, high-performance, smaller caliber guns, give them an ability to defend themselves against aircraft and antiship missiles. Surface-to-surface missiles, such as the new generation of cruise missiles, let them attack ships and land targets formerly out of reach. The Soviet fleet was the first to operate surface warships with surface-missile capability, but such weapons are now widely distributed. Such missiles as Exocet, Tomahawk, and the Soviet SS-N-12 permit standoff engagement at ranges measured in hundreds of miles. Nuclear propulsion lets ships steam long distances at high speeds, gives them true strategic mobility, and saves considerable internal weight and space for other uses. Gas turbines also save weight and space, provide high performance, and are much easier to maintain than steam systems.

Missiles, automatic guns, and high-performance hull forms and power plants have combined to produce effective new fast attack craft. These give considerable hitting power for their size and are useful to large and small fleets. Since the 1960s, these craft, both conventional-hull and hydrofoil, have become a significant element of naval power. Rapid-firing shell guns controlled by radar-equipped systems—the newer ones using digital computers—make them effective against smaller warships; long-range missiles make them a threat to large ships.

The modern nuclear-powered submarine is fast and difficult to detect and counter. Armed with conventional torpedoes, it has added cruise missiles and, in some ships, ballistic missiles, as well as stand-off weapons for use against other submarines. Its nuclear reactor lets it cruise at depth for long periods; hull forms are designed for optimum submerged performance because a contemporary submarine needs to surface only when entering or leaving port. Submarine design emphasizes noise reduction and submerged speed and agility. Weapon development is concerned with the ability to detect and counter faster, deeper-diving opponents.

Warships have inevitably grown. A modern destroyer is close to a World War II cruiser in size, and frigates are now larger than wartime destroyers. As missiles and their control systems have developed, increasing amounts of space are required to accommodate them. Although a modern missile can do many things beyond the capacity of one round of gun ammunition, it is considerably bigger and heavier, and its shipboard control system is much bulkier than the fire control systems and radars of World War II.

Future Developments

The history of the second half of the twentieth century makes it clear that predictions are risky. Aircraft carriers, however, appear to have reached their limit; any future ships of this type will, in general, probably resemble their immediate predecessors. Smaller aircraft ships, particularly as V/STOL and "convertiplane" technology improves, will take naval aviation to sea in coordination with the aircraft complements of other types of warships. The surface warship will continue to develop, possibly along "stealth lines"—omitting large topside structures for minimum radar reflection. Missiles and control systems will continue to develop, incorporating countermeasures and counter-countermeasures as the old contest between attack and defense is played out on this new field. These will improve the effectiveness of surface ships but will also give submarines enhanced ability to attack surface and shore targets. Satellites play important navigation, communications, and reconnaissance roles, and will continue to be vital to modern naval operations. Antiair and antisubmarine systems and tactics will continue to receive high priority. Guns, which have made a remarkable comeback, will continue to develop with their control systems; emphasis will be placed on accuracy, volume of fire, and rapid reaction. New hull forms, such as hydrofoils and the promising small-waterplane-area-twin-hull (SWATH) concept, will extend their uses; they appear particularly promising for use in submarine-infested waters. Gas turbines will continue to extend their usefulness in surface warships. Increasing automation will permit sophisticated systems to be used by smaller crews, although experience has shown that too much cannot be left to automation, particularly in combat situations. The human element is, and will continue to be, as indispensable as ever.

JOHN C. REILLY, JR.

SEE ALSO: Naval Warfare.

Bibliography

Brodie, B. 1941. *Sea power in the machine age.* Princeton, N.J.: Princeton Univ. Press.
Cipolla, C. M. 1965. *Guns, sails and empires.* New York: Minerva.
Cowburn, P. 1965. *The warship in history.* New York: Macmillan.
Friedman, N. 1979. *Modern warship design & development.* New York: Mayflower.
Hovgaard, W. 1920. *Modern history of warships.* London: Spon.
Howard, F. 1979. *Sailing ships of war, 1400–1860.* Greenwich, U.K.: Conway Maritime.
Jane's fighting ships. Annual. 1898– . London: Jane's.

WASHINGTON, GEORGE [1732–99]

George Washington (Fig. 1) is the most famous American hero, remembered as the "father of his country" for his distinguished service as commanding general of the revolutionary army that won independence, and for his exemplary performance as the first president of the United States. His military accomplishments are not popularly appreciated for two reasons: his distinction as first president of the new nation was unique and his enduring achievement; and his military operations, as important as they were, were not based upon a series of conquests or large-scale battles. Nevertheless, Washington's military career

Figure 1. Painting of George Washington by Gilbert Stuart.
(SOURCE: U.S. Library of Congress)

provides a model of leadership and strategic and tactical expertise, surprising for one not specially trained for, or engaged in, a full life of military campaigning.

Early Life and Military Experience

Washington was born on 22 February 1732 in Virginia. His early years as a surveyor provided him with an understanding of terrain and broadened his knowledge of territories outside of Virginia. When his half brother died in 1752, George inherited Mount Vernon, a sizable estate near Alexandria, Virginia. He now had the wealth and prestige of a large landowner. Mount Vernon plantation was the focus of his life, from which he was frequently separated by military duties and political responsibilities.

Washington's military experience began in the French and English struggles for domination of the upper Ohio Valley. Washington's surveying experience made him a logical choice to lead Virginian expeditions into the western territories, where he had a series of encounters with the French. In one encounter, in May 1754 near French Fort Duquesne (modern Pittsburgh), Washington's force ambushed a French detachment. Soon afterward, Washington was forced to surrender his outnumbered force to the French and returned disarmed to Williamsburg.

The British sent General Braddock to Virginia to lead an expedition against the French. As an aide-de-camp, Washington marched with Braddock's army to the Monongahela River, south of Fort Duquesne. The French and their Indian allies surprised the British with an attack in which Braddock was killed. Washington led the remnants of the force in an orderly withdrawal. The Virginia governor rewarded Washington with the rank of colonel and placed him in command of the colony's troops, with the main mission of guarding the western frontier.

During the French and Indian War, Washington developed a resentment against British rule and military administration. He observed that British professionals were ignorant of the conditions of colonial warfare and arrogant toward colonial leaders. Washington was particularly disappointed when he was refused acceptance in the British regular military service. At the end of the war, Washington resigned his militia commission and returned to Mount Vernon.

Interim Military Period as a Farmer and Virginia Politician

Disenchantment with British rule followed Washington into civilian life. He resented commercial restrictions and was especially upset when the British canceled colonists' claims to settlements in the Ohio Valley, where he had considerable holdings.

When elected to the Virginia House of Burgesses, Washington actively opposed the Townshend Revenue Act of 1767. With other colonial leaders he found British tax policies tyrannical and recommended a "continental congress" to watch over the interests of the colonies. He was elected as one of Virginia's seven delegates to the First Continental Congress, which voted to forbid the importation of goods subject to British taxes. It authorized towns and counties to set up committees of safety to enforce its provisions. Washington spent most of 1774–75 in Virginia organizing independent military companies to aid the local committees in enforcing the Continental Association.

The American War for Independence

After the battles of Lexington and Concord, and while the New England colonial militia invested British forces in Boston, the Second Continental Congress met on 10 May 1775 in Philadelphia. Washington's appearance in military uniform at the Congress expressed support for the militia and his readiness to fight. In June, Congress authorized the creation of the Continental Army and unanimously elected Washington commander in chief.

Washington's appointment was motivated largely to gain the support of the powerful Virginia colony. His selection was resented by several men with equal, or more, professional military experience. This caused some dissension which continued during more than half of the war. In hindsight, Washington's selection was fortuitous for the rebel cause. Few of the potential contenders evidenced the special character and military leadership traits which allowed Washington to prevail in his unique mission. Not only did he have to adapt to irregular and varied military situations, but he had to pioneer in commanding an army placed specifically under civilian rule. That civilian rule was the newly created Congress—an unproven political institution which had not fully defined its goals and policies. No less a challenge, Washington had to lead the fight against one of the world's finest professional armies.

Taking command of the forces besieging the British in Boston in July 1775, Washington exhibited a remarkable strategic awareness for one who had only militia command experience. He initiated a campaign to gain allies, a policy to deal with Loyalists, and a directive to establish a navy. His first tactical maneuver, carried out in the winter, was the occupation of Dorchester Heights, where he positioned artillery brought from Fort Ticonderoga. This forced the British to evacuate Boston in March 1776.

Anticipating the British, Washington proceeded to New York and fortified Brooklyn Heights to defend the approaches to New York City. The British commander, Gen. Sir William Howe, made a flanking move which drove Washington from Long Island and forced him to retreat to Harlem Heights. Using naval transport, Howe again outflanked the Americans, forcing Washington to withdraw to White Plains. With the capture of a significant portion of the American army at Fort Washington, the British acquired an undisputed hold on New York City. Washington's army was compelled to retreat through New Jersey and to cross the Delaware River into Pennsylvania in December 1776. American spirits were low, as approximately 34,000 British regulars confronted Washington's army of 3,000.

At this point, Washington made a daring, and probably his most famous, tactical move. On the cold and stormy night of 25–26 December, he recrossed the Delaware in a surprise attack against the Hessian garrison of Trenton, New Jersey, and captured nearly 900 prisoners. Washington avoided entrapment by a large British force deployed to Trenton under Earl Charles Cornwallis's command. In withdrawing to Princeton, Washington was able to defeat another small British force under Lt. Col. Charles Mawhood on 2 January 1777. These successes compelled the British to withdraw to eastern New Jersey, and revived American hopes. Washington had not only avoided a serious defeat and held his army together in the face of overwhelming odds, he had won two battlefield victories and achieved a strategic success.

In July 1777 General Howe departed New York by sea with a large force, intending to capture the Revolutionaries' capital of Philadelphia. Washington met Howe's force and was defeated at Brandywine Creek in September, and, after the British occupied Philadelphia, at Germantown, in October. But Howe failed to follow up his victories vigorously. The American Congress relocated to York, Pennsylvania.

These tactical setbacks do not reflect favorably on Washington's military abilities unless put into a broader context. Washington was forced to fight long before his army was prepared to engage well-trained regulars. He not only had to attempt to defend Philadelphia, he had decided to send his best troops north to stop the dangerous threat of an invasion from Canada by a British army under General Burgoyne. The broader strategic implications of Washington's actions must be recognized. By his endeavors in the fall of 1777, Washington prevented General Howe from going to the aid of Burgoyne, who was forced to surrender 5,000 British soldiers at Saratoga on 17 October 1777. Although Washington was not present at Saratoga, he was instrumental in that victory because of the troops he had sent there. As he took his army into winter quarters at Valley Forge in the winter of 1777–78, Washington realized that he had to train a more professional force before spring.

Gen. Sir Henry Clinton, who relieved Howe, evacuated Philadelphia in June 1778. Washington intercepted Clinton's withdrawal at Monmouth, New Jersey, before the British reached New York. American Gen. Charles Lee initially bungled the attack, and only Washington's personal intervention prevented a serious mistake. Importantly, the battle proved that the American army could stand against British regulars following the winter of training at Valley Forge.

Nevertheless, 1778 was a disappointing year for Washington. Savannah fell to the British, and the first combined operation with French forces, under the Comte d'Estaing, failed at Newport. The next year proved also to be frustrating. Washington remained stalemated against the British at New York. D'Estaing failed in another allied operation at Savannah in September and October. Washington wintered with his army at Morristown, New Jersey.

In 1780, unable to defeat Washington in the north, the British shifted their main effort to the south. They invaded North Carolina and Virginia, and took Charleston, South Carolina. Morale was waning in the Continental Army from lack of pay, and Washington was confronted with the first of several mutinies. In July a large French expeditionary force under Rochambeau arrived at Newport and placed itself under Washington's supreme command. Unfortunately, the allied force was too small to challenge the British concentration around New York.

The main focus for the year remained in the south. In August, the Americans suffered a serious defeat at Camden, South Carolina, which discredited General Gates, who had continually sought to replace Washington as overall commander. This provided Washington with the opportunity to appoint more capable leaders in the south.

In 1781, the effect of the French military support, in conjunction with some minor American tactical victories in the south, became apparent. Washington's command of the superbly executed French-American combined and joint operations in the Yorktown campaign proved decisive. It created a military situation which was untenable to the British national leaders. The surrender of General Cornwallis was a crushing setback for the British efforts to subdue the rebellion. British leaders could no longer maintain support for the war and were forced to negotiate the peace which recognized American independence.

Post-Revolution

Washington continued to play a dominant role in the postwar development of the United States. He was instrumental in leading the young nation through a series of challenges and crises. As a hero, Washington was elected unanimously as the first U.S. president. His pathfinding role as the first executive leader of the new nation was as great an accomplishment as was his generalship of the revolutionary army. Again, he proved his leadership skills. His special talent was an ability to obtain cooperation from strong-minded subordinates and to project a reasonable and fair bearing. His calm, authoritative manner prevailed in postrevolutionary politics as it had in war councils. In 1796, he returned to his beloved Mount Vernon and a very public "private life." He died at Mount Vernon on 14 December 1799.

Assessment

George Washington's military skills were largely derived from practical experience. He lacked familiarity with formal large-scale military operations and direct knowledge of preparing forces for many of the tactical maneuvers required in open combat. His weaknesses, however, were compensated for by his innate understanding of strategy and tactics, and his willingness to seek and accept professional advice. He was also favored by an imposing stature and, more importantly, by a combination of wisdom and skill, the talent to inspire a complex array of his fellow citizens—soldiers and politicians alike.

ALBERT D. MCJOYNT

SEE ALSO: American Revolutionary War; Seven Years' War.

Bibliography

Carrington, H. B. 1899. *Washington the soldier.* New York: Scribner.
Flexner, J. T. 1965–72. *George Washington.* 4 vols. Boston: Little, Brown.
Freeman, D. S. 1948–57. *George Washington: A biography.* 7 vols. New York: Scribner.
Irving, W. n.d. *The life of Washington.* 4 vols. New York: John Wanamaker.

WAVELL, ARCHIBALD PERCIVAL (1st Earl) [1883–1950]

Rated one of Britain's top generals at the outbreak of World War II, Wavell had the misfortune to be overall commander in the Middle East when early defeats were suffered in the Western Desert and in Greece and Crete. By mid-1943, despite some remarkable local successes, he had lost the confidence of Prime Minister Winston Churchill and was relieved and assigned to command Imperial forces in India.

Early Years

Archibald Percival Wavell was born on 5 May 1883 in Colchester into a military family. His father, grandfather, and great-grandfather all had been major generals. He attended Winchester College and graduated from the Royal Military College at Sandhurst in time to serve with the 42d Royal Highland (Black Watch) Regiment in the final months of the South African (2d Boer) War.

Like most junior officers in this period, he served a tour of duty in India and saw action in 1908 fighting the Zakka Khel tribesmen on the northwest frontier. However, his next career move was quite unorthodox as he asked for a year's leave of absence to live in Moscow and study Russian. Later, as captain, he was sent back to Russia to observe the 1911 army maneuvers.

World War I and Afterward

With the outbreak of war, he was assigned to the staff of the general headquarters but was not content to remain far behind the lines. During a 1916 visit to the front line he was badly wounded and lost an eye. After recovering, he was sent as liaison officer to the Russian Army of the Caucasus. He returned from Russia in April 1917 and was posted as liaison officer between the War Office and the Egyptian Expeditionary Force. Later, he was chief staff officer for the XX Corps during Gen. Sir Edmund Allenby's successful 1917–18 campaign in Palestine.

Wavell's career between the wars was varied and marked him as one destined for high command should combat recur. He served on Allenby's staff in Egypt and later wrote two books based on this experience. He also had a tour with the Black Watch in the Rhineland, duty with the War Office, and was an aide to King George V.

Beginning in 1930, with command of the Sixth Brigade, he received a series of progressively more responsible troop commands. In 1933 he was promoted to major general and shortly afterward took command of the Second Division. After six months' service in Palestine and Trans-Jordan in 1937–38, he returned home with promotion to lieutenant general and was given the key Southern Command.

World War II

At the outbreak of war, Wavell was commander in chief, Middle East Forces, with the rank of general.

In June 1940, Italy entered the war and poured half a million men into Africa in an attempt to expand its empire. Facing this force was a small British army of fewer than 100,000 men, scattered in seven different countries. Wavell adopted aggressive tactics to disguise his real strength and, fortunately, the Italians proved cautious. On 9 December 1940 the Western Desert Force (only

31,000 men) attacked 80,000 Italians and in three days took 38,300 prisoners, losing only 624 men. By the time this campaign was over, Wavell's forces had captured 130,000 Italians and had given Britain its first major triumph of the war.

Wavell then moved against Italian forces led by the Duke of Aosta in East Africa. While the Italian army far outnumbered the British, many of its soldiers were native troops whose loyalty was suspect. Aosta managed to hold the British at Keren for eight weeks but was forced back to a pass at Amba Alagi between Asmara and Addis Ababa and finally surrendered on 17 May 1941.

Despite these successes, Churchill was not satisfied with Wavell. Because he feared his plans might leak out, Wavell often failed to keep London posted on forthcoming operations. Churchill also became angry when Wavell, criticized for abandoning British Somaliland early in the war, replied that "a big butcher's bill is not necessarily evidence of good tactics."

Early in 1941, German troops began to support the Italian invasion of Greece and in February Churchill ordered Wavell to reinforce the Greek army with British troops. However, overwhelming German power and poor Greek tactics led to a debacle and on 27 April the Nazi Swastika was hoisted atop the Acropolis. Of some 58,000 British troops committed in Greece, all but 11,000 were evacuated in late April and early May, but most of the equipment was abandoned.

Many of these troops were evacuated to Crete, expected to be the scene of the next German attack. This proved correct: on 20 May the Germans launched an invasion with 6,000 paratroopers. Despite heavy casualties, the paratroopers managed to establish a bridgehead and took the key Maleme airfield on the second day. This permitted airborne reinforcements to arrive at the rate of twenty planes per hour and sealed the fate of Crete. Once again, evacuation of British forces began and 15,000 were rescued, but 13,000 British plus 5,000 Greek soldiers were left behind.

While the evacuation of Crete was underway, the German Afrika Korps in the Western Desert, under General Erwin Rommel, was being strengthened and took the offensive (31 March). In two months Rommel captured most of the territory taken in Wavell's first campaigns.

With access to the German's secret code, Churchill knew Rommel's strength and problems and was upset at how British forces were being mauled. He blamed Wavell. On 21 June 1941 Wavell was removed from his Middle East command and appointed commander in chief of British forces in India.

In India, Wavell's initial task was to continue the expansion of the Indian army, which grew from 189,000 in 1939 to 2,500,000 in 1945, and to send trained units to combat theaters. When Japan entered the war and its forces moved against British possessions in the Far East, Wavell was appointed supreme commander of Allied Forces in the Southwest Pacific. In this role, he had the unhappy task of presiding over the loss of Malaya, Singapore, and Burma to the Japanese. In the spring of 1942, his Southwest Pacific command was abolished and Wavell returned to the Indian command.

Anticipating a Japanese invasion of India, Wavell worked hard on the defense of the subcontinent. This involved coordination with the hard to get along with Generalissimo Chiang Kai-shek of China and American Gen. Joseph W. Stilwell. The first Arakan campaign to retake Burma ended in failure, but fortunately Gen. William Slim arrived to revitalize the field army and Brigadier Orde Wingate conducted a well-publicized and apparently successful campaign behind Japanese lines with his Chindits.

In January 1943, Wavell was appointed field marshal by Churchill.

Viceroy of India

In June 1943 Wavell was appointed viceroy of India, and, despite the widespread perception that this was a demotion engineered by Churchill, entered into his new post with vigor. His two major problems were food for the thousands who were starving in Bengal and India's desire for independence. Wavell wanted to assemble nationalist leaders and ask their support of the war effort while promising steps toward independence later. This was vetoed by Churchill who, at the time, was committed to keeping India under British rule. However, a key meeting was held at Simla in June 1945 which did not provide a solution, but began the process of formal discussions.

Following the British elections of 1945, Clement Atlee succeeded Churchill as Prime Minister. He was no more partial to Wavell than Churchill had been. He decided that Wavell should be made an earl and retired from India in 1947.

Wavell felt that India needed about fifteen years after the war to prepare for independence. If that was not possible, his inclination was that freedom should be given slowly, province by province. What actually happened, however, was that Lord Louis Mountbatten replaced him as viceroy in 1947 and an accelerated timetable was adopted for British withdrawal. In the resulting civil strife, hundreds of thousands of civilians were killed.

Personal

Much of Wavell's problem with Churchill was due to his personality. He was reserved in public, some felt remote and aloof. As a commander he often kept his plans to himself and was faulted for not insisting on higher standards of performance by subordinates. He was extremely frank and honest when he spoke, and with troops was more concerned with winning their confidence than with being popular. Friends, however, reported him warm, outgoing, witty, and very human. His closest staff always referred to him as "The Chief."

An unabashed intellectual, he was a scholar of Latin and Greek and often began a talk with a quotation from Socrates. In contrast to many World War II generals who used ghost writers to prepare their memoirs, Wavell was a widely published author whose works included *Allenby: A Study in Greatness* (1940), *Generals and Generalship* (1941), *Allenby in Egypt* (1943), *Generally Speaking* (1946), and *The Good Soldier* (1948), as well as a book of poems, *Other Men's Flowers* (1944).

In 1915, he married Eugenie Marie Quirk. They had three daughters and one son. The son, Archie John Wavell, served in his father's Black Watch regiment in World War II and survived the war, only to be killed by the Mau Mau in Kenya in 1953.

Wavell lived for only a short time after leaving India, dying in London on 24 May 1950 at age 68.

ROBERT CALVERT, JR.

SEE ALSO: Allenby, Edmund Henry Hynman; Chiang Kai-shek; Rommel, Erwin; Stilwell, Joseph Warren; World War II.

Bibliography

Connell, J. 1969. *Wavell: Supreme commander*. London: Collins.
Fergusson, B. 1961. *Wavell: Portrait of a soldier*. London: Collins.
Lewin, R. 1980. *The Chief: Field Marshal Lord Wavell*. New York: Farrar, Strauss, Giroux.
Wavell, Field Marshal Earl. 1971. *The viceroy's journal*. London: Oxford Univ. Press.
Woollcombe, R. 1959. *The campaigns of Wavell 1939–1943*. London: Cassell.

WEI LI-HUANG [1897–1960]

Wei Li-huang (1897–17 January 1960) was a general officer in the Nationalist Army of China during the 1930s and 1940s. Although he lost his most important campaign by losing Manchuria to the Communists, Wei was generally respected as a tough, competent military leader.

Early Life and Career

Wei Li-huang was born in 1897 in Hefei, the capital of Anhui Province, China. His military career began when he joined the forces of Wu Chung-hsin, a local warlord. Wu was sufficiently impressed with Wei's talents to make him a member of his bodyguard in 1920. Wei left Wu a short time later and rose from squad leader to division commander in one of the military forces that were later combined into the National Revolutionary Army. In 1926 he assumed command of the 3d Division of the First Army. This brought Wei into contact with the inner circle of Chiang Kai-shek's associates in the Kuomintang (KMT) because the First Army was created from the student body and cadre of the Whampoa Military Academy. After participating in the first stage of the Northern Expedition against China's warlords, Wei was appointed commander of the Third Column of the Northern Anhwei garrison forces in 1927. In the following years he served as deputy commander of the Ninth Army of the 1st Army Group, commander of the 45th Division (later the 10th Division) and bandit suppression commander for Northern Anhwei Province.

In the early 1930s, Wei served in various positions during Chiang's "Encirclement Campaigns" against the Chinese Communists. He achieved national prominence in 1932 when his troops captured the Chinese Communist base at

Chinchia-chai in the rugged Taipieh Mountains along the Anhwei-Hunan border. This victory earned Wei the accolades of Chiang Kai-shek who ordered the town renamed Lihuang to honor Wei. By 1933 Wei's successes against the Communists had earned him the nickname "Ever Victorious General" (Ch'ang-sheng Chiang-chun) and a large financial reward.

Wei attended the Central Military Academy in 1933–34 and returned to field duty as commander of the eastern sector of the Bandit Suppression Force for Kiangsi, Kwangtung, Fukien, Hunan, and Hupeh. In 1935 Wei was promoted to general and elected to the Central Executive Committee of the KMT. He participated in the operations to mop up the Communist bases in Hunan-Hupeh-Anhwei-Kiangsi after the Communist forces left on the "Long March." In 1936 Wei was appointed commander in chief of the KMT forces in this area.

World War II and the Chinese Civil War

After the war with Japan began in July 1937, Wei served as Deputy Commander of the Second War Zone in Shansi. The Japanese objective in this area was the provincial capital of Taiyuan. Wei Li-huang assumed command of the troops facing the Japanese 5th Division along the Peiping-Suiyuan railroad. Wei's force outnumbered the Japanese but were not as well equipped. The battle was joined at Hsin-kou on 13 October. By 9 November the Japanese had seized Taiyuan by approaching from the east. The Japanese lost 20,000 men at Hsin-kuo, but Chinese casualties were probably substantially greater. The battle for Taiyuan is noteworthy for one other reason: it was one of the high points of KMT–Chinese Communist Party (CCP) cooperation against the Japanese. Wei Li-huang's forces were supported by elements of the CCP's Eighth Route Army, which conducted guerrilla attacks on the Japanese forces.

As the war moved south, Wei became commander of the First War Zone (Honan and southern Shensi). Concurrently, he commanded the Third Group Army and, in 1939, became governor of Honan. In 1940 Wei became commander of the Hopei-Chahar War Zone and Chief of the Hopei-Chahar Party-Government Committee. He was relieved of these posts late in 1941, possibly because he failed to take forceful action against the Communists in his region.

The break in Wei Li-huang's service was short. In 1942 he was appointed to the Military Affairs Commission of the KMT and was made commander of the Chinese Expeditionary Force in southwest China which was established to invade Burma in 1942. After an extensive period of training and reorganization, elements of Wei's command, commonly known as "Y Force," crossed the Salween River on 11 May 1944 to open a new axis of attack against the Japanese in northern Burma. After desultory fighting through the monsoon season, Wei's force linked up with the Chinese "X Force" (based in Burma and India) on 21 January 1945, thereby opening the Burma Road.

After the defeat of Japan, Wei toured Europe and the United States. He returned to China at a time when the civil war between the Communists and Nationalists was going badly for the Nationalists. He was named commander of the Northeast Bandit Suppression Headquarters in Manchuria in January 1948.

His troops were demoralized and his logistical support was plagued by corruption. In September 1948, Lin Piao led a Communist army of 700,000 men against Wei's force of 450,000 isolated Nationalists. Lin surrounded Chinchow while feinting toward Changchun. Chiang Kai-shek ordered Wei to relieve Chinchow. Wei refused the order because he believed a sortie from his main base in Shenyang would lead to an ambush by Lin's forces, who were hoping for such an opportunity. Finally, on 1 October Wei carried out Chiang's orders and directed the dispatch of a relief force. The Communists captured Chinchow on 15 October, then encircled the relief force on 26 October. Wei was forced to withdraw from Shenyang on 2 November 1948. After the failure of the Manchurian Campaign, Wei was relieved and imprisoned in Nanking. In April 1949 he went to Hong Kong.

Last Years

Wei returned to China on 15 March 1955 and served as a delegate and national committeeman at the Second Chinese People's Political Consultative Conference in January 1956. In 1958 he represented Anhwei Province at the National People's Congress, and from 1959 until his death he served as a standing committee member of the Kuomintang Revolutionary Party, one of the few minor parties authorized by the Chinese Communist Party. He was appointed a vice-chairman of the National Defense Council in April 1959, and at the same time was elected to the Standing Committee of the Third Chinese Political Consultative Conference. Wei died in Peking on 17 January 1960.

Wei Li-huang was probably the most competent of the KMT generals during the civil war and World War II. He was never completely trusted by Chiang Kai-shek, and he never got along well with Gen. Joseph W. Stilwell, the nominal commander of the Chinese effort against the Japanese in Burma.

EDWARD C. O'DOWD

SEE ALSO: Chiang Kai-shek; Civil War; Stilwell, Joseph Warren; World War II.

Bibliography

Boorman, H. L. 1967. Wei Li-huang. In *Biographical dictionary of republican China.* Vol. 2. New York: Columbia Univ. Press.
Levine, S. I. 1987. *Anvil of Victory: The communist revolution in Manchuria 1945–1948.* New York: Columbia Univ. Press.
Wilson, D. 1982. *When tigers fight: The story of the Sino-Japanese war, 1937–1945.* New York: Viking Press.
Whitson, W. W. 1973. *The Chinese high command: A history of communist military politics, 1927–1971.* New York: Praeger.

WORLD WAR I

World War I is the most common name given to the great international conflict of 1914–18, which began in Europe with the alliance of Germany and Austria-Hungary against the alliance of Britain, France, Russia, and Serbia, and eventually involved over 30 nations in theaters around the globe. The war ended in the defeat of Germany and its allies, but the rivalries were renewed a mere twenty years later. The cost of World War I was enormous, with battle deaths approaching the 10 million mark. The war had profound impact on the political and economic structure of the world and is generally considered to be the pivotal event in the decline of European influence in the world.

Origins of the War

Despite the accusations and hatred generated during the war, no single nation desired or planned the conflagration. Europe blundered into a war that proved to be far different from what most experts had anticipated.

ALLIANCES

From the end of the Franco-Prussian War (1870–71) until the outbreak of World War I, European nations aligned themselves in increasingly rigid military alliances. While such brilliant politicians as Bismarck (German chancellor, 1871–90) could keep national commitments amazingly fluid, the politicians of the turn of the century were less enlightened. The major nations of Europe gradually coalesced into two military alliances: the Central Powers (Germany, Austria-Hungary, and Italy) and the Entente Powers, or Allies (Britain, France, and Russia). Many of the agreements between nations were secret (in some cases even the governments were unaware of the full extent of their countries' military commitment), and the flexibility of governments to operate in an international crisis became increasingly restricted.

NATIONAL RIVALRIES AND POPULAR EMOTIONS

The general air of animosity was reinforced by a strong sense of nationalism throughout Europe. National identities and sensitivities became a powerful element of the mass culture. The opportunity for expression of national pride was extensive, from colonial competition to military spending.

LEGACY OF THE FRANCO-PRUSSIAN WAR

The most recent major war in Europe had been the conflict between France and a uniting Germany in 1870–71. Although restricted to these two powers, the apparent lessons of that war were widely digested by European powers during the long period of peace to 1914. One of the most compelling lessons from the war had been the importance of rapid mobilization of a nation's forces in accordance with a comprehensive strategic plan.

Immediate Cause of the War

The war could well have been started over any number of incidents, but the immediate cause was a terrorist (or patriotic, depending on one's point of view) incident in a restless part of Austria-Hungary.

THE ASSASSINATION

The heir to the Hapsburg throne, Archduke Franz Ferdinand, was shot and killed (as was his wife) by a Serbian nationalist at Sarajevo on 28 June 1914. The small nation of Serbia was implicated in the assassination, and Austria-Hungary was intent on punishing it. Once Austria-Hungary began to mobilize, an irreversible process began wherein most members of the alliances (Italy was the exception) began to mobilize. National leaders were faced with the terrible realization that so heavily did military success depend on rapid mobilization and execution of movement plans that no one would risk putting a stop to the process.

NATIONS GO TO WAR

The continental powers, with the lesson of the Franco-Prussian War in mind, hurried to assemble their mass armies. British politicians agonized over the prospects of war and decided to alert the fleet and send the small British professional army to France. Germany, facing belligerents on two fronts, began to execute a bold and intricate plan, the Schlieffen Plan, in which a relatively small force would hold the Russians in the east while a huge concentration of forces swept through Belgium and Luxembourg into the heart of France. (This was a classic case of the German tendency to hazard everything on one throw, for the German armies violated Belgian neutrality, assuring British entry into the war.) Thirsting for revenge from the Franco-Prussian War, France, with a much-improved mobilization system, hurled its armies directly against the German border. Russia appeared to be able to muster her ponderous resources faster than expected, while Austria-Hungary had an embarrassingly difficult time crushing tiny Serbia.

1914

WESTERN FRONT

The first major battles occurred in August 1914 as the German forces swept through Belgium and Luxembourg. The German forces were enormous (and larger than the Allies had expected) because the Germans had integrated their well-trained reserves into the standing army. Seven field armies were arrayed against France, and the German chief of the general staff (Helmuth von Moltke, nephew of Field Marshal von Moltke) had great difficulty in directing these large formations. While the French vainly hurled their forces against the Germans in Alsace-Lorraine, the bulk of the German forces wheeled through Belgium into northern France. By late August, it appeared as if the German plan would work and Paris would be encircled. But German confusion about the movement of their field armies in France, and the incredible steadiness of the French commander, Gen. Joseph J. C. Joffre, combined to produce the Battle of the Marne (5–10 September 1914), in which the German wheel was stopped before Paris. The armies in northern France, including the small British Expeditionary Force, began to consolidate their positions and extend their lines toward the channel, each side vainly attempting to outflank its opponents.

As positions were established, the power of the machine gun and, more importantly, artillery required extensive defensive fieldworks.

EASTERN FRONT

As the Austrian forces attacked Serbia, and found the task extremely costly, the Russians mobilized with a speed that alarmed the Central Powers. The Austrians deployed forces in Galicia, where the Russians inflicted such severe casualties on them that Austria never fully recovered. Two Russian field armies crossed the border into northeast Germany. After some confusion on the German side, a newly appointed command team of Paul von Hindenburg and Erich Ludendorff inflicted a crushing defeat on one of the Russian armies at Tannenberg (26–31 August).

OTHER ACTIONS

The German navy was effectively swept from the high seas by Britain's Royal Navy, with the bulk of the German fleet being bottled up in the North Sea. German cruisers, especially the SMS *Emden*, enjoyed some success as commerce raiders, but in the end all were sunk or captured. Likewise, Admiral von Spee's Asiatic Squadron smashed a British force at Coronel (1 November 1914), but in the end fell victim to Admiral Sturdee's battlecruisers at the Falklands (8 December 1914). The Germans began to explore the uses of the submarine as a means to break the British naval blockade that was strangling German access to the seas. The Japanese, siding with the Allies, seized German outposts in the Pacific and China by early November 1914. The Ottoman Empire (Turkey) joined the war on the side of the Central Powers, and in response, the British occupied oil facilities in Mesopotamia.

1915

WESTERN FRONT

The belligerents began to recognize that the course of the war was taking turns that no one had anticipated. In the west, it was solidifying into a war of position characterized by trench warfare where the defense had most of the advantages. Germany decided to remain on the defensive in the west. The French and the British (whose armies increased in size) threw their forces against the German positions and suffered heavy casualties. The year 1915 was the most costly of the war for the French in terms of casualties. Artillery continued its dominance and a severe munitions shortage developed. The Germans employed poison gas at Ypres (Fig. 1).

EASTERN FRONT

As the Austrian forces were depleted, the Germans came to dominate operations in the east, but cooperation between the two powers was often strained. In contrast to the stalemated situation in the west, the battles in the east included bold maneuvers and great movements. By the end of 1915, the Russians had been driven deeper into Russia and had suffered enormous casualties, perhaps as many as 2 million in 1915 alone.

Figure 1. British soldiers in the trenches prepared for poison gas attack. (SOURCE: Imperial War Museum)

OTHER FRONTS

Serbia was finally crushed by the combined efforts of Austria-Hungary, Germany, and Bulgaria (which had joined the Central Powers). Italy entered the war on the side of the Allies but could do very little against the Austrian defensive positions along the common border.

Great Britain (with the reluctant acquiescence of France) decided upon an "eastern" strategy designed to: (1) knock Turkey out of the war, (2) bring succor to the hard-pressed Russian armies, and (3) provide the western Allies with access to the rich granary of the Russian Ukraine. This was to be accomplished by a powerful Allied naval thrust from the Mediterranean to the Bosphorus. The plan was based on a bold and brilliant strategic concept formulated by Britain's First Lord of the Admiralty, Winston Churchill.

However, the Allied naval effort was repulsed (barely) by Turkish coastal defenses in the Dardanelles. Thereupon the Allies decided to implement this eastern strategy by an amphibious assault to seize the land shores of the Dardanelles strait. The main effort was made by forces of the British Empire, including an Australian and New Zealand army corps (ANZAC) landing on the Gallipoli Peninsula, north of the strait. Bad naval-ground forces, inept field leadership, and the quick reactions of the Turks and Germans (notably the actions of Mustafa Kemal, later known as Ataturk) confined the British troops to shallow beachheads, where they languished. The forces of the British Empire were eventually evacuated (8–9 January 1916).

In Mesopotamia, a British expedition pushing to Baghdad was surrounded by the Turks at Kut (December) after the failure of an offensive against Baghdad in November.

At the urging of their German allies, the Turks launched an attack across the Sinai against the vital Suez Canal. The assault was repulsed by British troops in a series of engagements (14 January–3 February), although at one point Turkish advance forces crossed the canal in assault boats provided by the Germans. The Turks withdrew and made no further attacks that year, and the British began a gradual buildup of their forces in Egypt for a counteroffensive.

In Africa, British and South African forces conquered German Southwest Africa (now Namibia), capturing the town of Windhoek in May and securing the surrender of all German forces in July. Operations in the Cameroons were hampered by terrain, climate, and stubborn German resistance. Although French and British forces overran the coastal areas by autumn, the capital at Yaoundé did not fall until New Year's Day, 1916, after a bitter eight-week campaign. German forces in German East Africa (now Tanzania) were led by the able and resourceful Gen. Paul von Lettow-Vorbeck. Although his forces were outnumbered and outgunned, he employed what resources he had to frustrate a British invasion at Tanga in November 1914. East Africa was not high on Britain's list of strategic priorities, and there was no major offensive action there until 1916.

1916

WESTERN FRONT

Under the direction of the chief of the general staff, Gen. Erich von Falkenhayn (who had succeeded Moltke in 1914), the Germans attacked French positions around Verdun (February 1916). While trying to draw the French into a battle of attrition and wear them down, Falkenhayn's German forces also suffered heavy casualties as the campaign dragged on for many months. Verdun came to symbolize the relentless and grinding nature of combat on the western front. Perhaps more soldiers were killed in combat in the area of Verdun than on any other battlefield in history.

To relieve the French forces (which were now beginning to suffer considerably from the losses of the war), the British army, now a large mass army fed by conscription and commanded by Gen. Sir Douglas Haig, launched an offensive on the Somme (July). This massive effort, particularly the tremendous use of artillery, inflicted severe casualties on the Germans and diverted German efforts at Verdun. The British, however, never achieved the breakthrough for which they had hoped, and suffered over 400,000 casualties in the process. The British also introduced a new weapon, a tracked armored vehicle known by its deceptive name, the tank. Like other technological innovations introduced during the war (such as poison gas), the tank was committed to battle before an effective method of employment, in conjunction with surprise and reinforcement, had been developed.

EASTERN FRONT

The summer of 1916 saw the last great Russian offensive of the war. General Brusilov, in a well-planned attack, crushed the Austrian forces opposite him. German forces (including some originally destined for Verdun) were rushed in to stop the collapse, and Brusilov's offensive was finally contained. The Austrian army was ruined, and the Russian forces were exhausted.

OTHER ACTIONS

In May, the German High Seas Fleet made its one attempt to break into the open sea. The British Grand Fleet made contact with the German fleet and, after a tactical draw near Jutland, the Germans withdrew. The frustration of the British blockade and the German surface fleet's inability to break it made the use of submarine warfare (which the Germans were increasingly employing) even more appealing to the German High Command. In Mesopotamia, the British force at Kut surrendered to the Turks in April after relief efforts failed.

On the Sinai front, the British gradually constructed a combined water pipeline and railway across the desert to support projected operations in Palestine. A Turkish attack against the British railhead at Rumani, again made at German urging, was repulsed handily on 3 August. The British were also involved in sending support to the anti-Turkish Arab revolt in the Hejaz and in suppressing the anti-Allied Senussi revolt in Libya.

By the start of 1916, Lettow-Vorbeck's forces in East Africa totaled nearly 15,000. Operations began in earnest when South African general Jan Smuts took command in February. Mounting an offensive in daunting conditions of terrain and climate, his forces had driven the Germans from the northern half of East Africa by early autumn, but Allied casualties had been heavy and Lettow-Vorbeck's forces remained intact. Smuts's troops continued to push south, joined by Belgian troops from the Congo and British forces from Nyasaland (now Zambia). Lettow-Vorbeck evaded them and inflicted several sharp defeats on individual columns, but superior Allied numbers compelled him to retreat farther.

HOME FRONTS

By the end of 1916, the frustration with the war was immense among the population of all the participants. Germany and Austria-Hungary were suffering from the effects of the Allied blockade. Russia was exhausted and politically restless. In France and Britain, however, the governments would eventually be dominated by politicians—Georges Clemenceau and David Lloyd George—who had the ruthless energy to continue the war. While political leadership in

Germany was weaker, it was dominated by the successful military team of Hindenburg and Ludendorff, and thus Germany was equally determined to fight through to victory. The societies of all combatants were harnessed for the prodigious war effort by industrial organization imposed on the nations at large. Britain was probably the most successful in this regard.

1917

WESTERN FRONT

The Germans opted to remain on the defensive in the west. The German High Command was now directed by the team of Hindenburg and Ludendorff, recently having arrived in France from the eastern front. Ludendorff, the more brilliant (but also erratic) of the two, carefully examined the tactical experiences of the western front in order to redirect tactical efforts in France. The test of German skill came in two major Allied offensives in 1917—a French offensive in April and a British offensive (Third Ypres) in the summer and autumn.

After the failure of the French offensive, French units began to mutiny out of frustration and resentment. Henri Pétain, the hero of Verdun, became commander of French forces and skillfully defused the desperate situation. By the end of 1917, the German forces still maintained a coherent defense in northern France and had inflicted considerable casualties on the Allies.

The Allies, however, now had a new partner. The United States had entered the war against Germany, principally because of the German policy of unrestricted submarine warfare. This was a significant turning point in the history of the United States, which had previously avoided political entanglements in Europe.

One of the most important Allied developments of this time was the convoy system, which proved successful in mitigating the effects of the German submarines. The manpower of America was thus able to reach France.

EASTERN FRONT

In March, moderate Russian politicians forced Czar Nicholas II to abdicate. In the confusion that followed, a party of Marxists known as Bolsheviks (led by Vladimir Lenin) asserted themselves and by November had taken over the government in the capital (Petrograd, later renamed Leningrad). The German army continued to press against the Russians, so the Bolsheviks concluded an armistice with the Germans at Brest-Litovsk in December. Russia was now out of the war. (A peace treaty was signed on 3 March 1918.)

OTHER ACTIONS

The Italian front broke wide open as the Austrians and Germans inflicted a serious defeat on the Italians at Caporetto in October. With French and British help, the Italians stabilized the front along the Piave River. While 1917 was frustrating for the Allies on the western front and disastrous for them on the eastern and Italian fronts, in other theaters they enjoyed considerable success.

Following the disaster at Kut, the British had revamped their military efforts in Mesopotamia, bringing in reinforcements from India and placing Gen. Frederick Maude in command. Maude captured Baghdad in March, and by autumn was driving on the Mosul oil fields when he died of cholera (18 November); he was replaced by Gen. William R. Marshall. On the Sinai front, British forces under Gen. Archibald Murray opened offensive operations, but British efforts against Gaza were repulsed twice (26 March and 17–19 April) because of supply problems and cautious generalship on the part of Murray and Gen. Charles M. Dobell. Concerned about another stalemate, the British sent Gen. Sir Edmund Allenby, one of their ablest field commanders, to replace Murray. Allenby captured Gaza and Beersheba on 31 October, outflanking Turkish defenses from the southwest and then driving northward. Allenby's forces entered Jerusalem on 9 December, giving the Allies a valuable victory.

British–South African operations continued against Lettow-Vorbeck's forces in East Africa. Under heavy British pressure, Lettow-Vorbeck's forces were gradually hemmed into the southeast corner of the country, but the Germans continued to maul British columns. In October, Lettow-Vorbeck invaded the Portuguese colony of Mozambique, largely to secure supplies of food, medicine, and munitions for his troops, which now numbered barely 2,000. By year's end, he and his increasingly ragged troops were still unbeaten.

1918—Year of Decision

WESTERN FRONT

The question before the Germans was how to end the war before the full potential weight of the United States (which was pitifully unprepared for war) could be brought to bear against Germany. After harsh peace terms were imposed on the Russians, the Germans transferred units from the east to the western front and gained temporary advantage before the bulk of U.S. forces reached Europe. Ludendorff, who had assumed responsibility for the direction of the German war effort, decided to make one last attempt to defeat the French and British forces in France. The German offensives of the spring of 1918 were a masterpiece of tactical planning. New techniques of attacking in depth, coordinating various arms (particularly artillery and infantry), and directing fluid battle were derived from the experiences of the western front. The initial results were spectacular, but the strategic direction of the effort was flawed. The efforts of German field armies were not complementary. The Germans simply could not afford any wasted effort.

The Allies had developed a Supreme Command under Gen. Ferdinand Foch that gave coherence and unity to Allied actions. The forces of the British Empire had developed tactics employing tanks and surprise. The Americans were beginning to arrive in France in force, and they plugged critical gaps in the Allied line when the issue was in doubt during the German assaults. By the summer of 1918, the German forces were exhausted and the home front was demoralized. The Allies displayed new determination and began to drive the German forces back decisively. With revolution brewing at home and their army clearly outmatched, the German High Command asked for an armistice. On 11 November 1918, the war in Europe ended.

Africa and Asia

As 1918 began, Turkish armies in Palestine and Mesopotamia, despite expanded German assistance, were growing less capable of resistance. In Mesopotamia, British attention was diverted by events in southern Russia following the Bolshevik Revolution. The British launched a final offensive in late October and eventually captured Mosul, although not until after the armistice (14 November). Operations in Palestine were more extensive. Determined to liberate Palestine and Syria, General Allenby launched a major offensive near Megiddo on 19 September, and within a week had completely ruptured the Turkish front in a spectacularly successful attack. Allenby's forces, acting in cooperation with Arab irregulars, captured Damascus on 1 October and Aleppo in northern Syria on 25 October.

In the winter of 1917–18, nearly 70,000 Allied troops were arrayed against Lettow-Vorbeck's 2,000 troops in Mozambique. But the canny German commander continued to elude Allied forces, overwhelming isolated garrisons and chewing up outlying columns. In late September, Lettow-Vorbeck's forces reentered German East Africa; at the time of the armistice, his forces, still unbeaten, were operating in Northern Rhodesia (now Zambia). When Lettow-Vorbeck heard of the armistice (14 November), he opened negotiations and surrendered to the British at Abercorn on 25 November, the last German force to surrender.

Legacy

The hatred that had characterized the war affected the peace. Despite the counsel of the U.S. president Woodrow Wilson (who is still either condemned for being naive or praised for being farsighted), a harsh settlement was imposed on Germany. The resentment of the Germans, in combination with the economic disruption caused by the Great Depression in the 1930s, led to the emergence of National Socialism in Germany and World War II. In military matters, World War I had a profound impact. New weapons—tanks, airplanes, submarines, chemical munitions, assault guns, and machine guns—all became part of the world's arsenals. More important was the fact that the full weight of mobilized national industry was dedicated to war. This is what gave the war its terrible scope. In many respects, World War II was simply a continuation of World War I.

Timothy T. Lupfer

See Also: Allenby, Edmund Henry Hynman; Balkan Wars; Civil War, Russian; Colonial Empires, European; Fisher, John Arbuthnot; Foch, Ferdinand; Franco-Prussian War; Hindenburg, Paul von; History, Modern Military; Jellicoe, John Rushworth; Kemal, Mustafa Pasha; Ludendorff, Erich; Moltke the Elder; Pershing, John Joseph; Scheer, Reinhard; Schlieffen, Alfred; Tirpitz, Alfred von.

Bibliography

There are several works that cover this epic war. The official histories are mammoth, and official points of view are still controversial (as are the casualty figures). Particularly recommended are the British official histories and the German official histories. The following are the best general works available in English.

Agnew, J. B., W. R. Griffiths, and C. Franks. 1977. *The great war.* West Point, N.Y.: Department of History, United States Military Academy (now available through Avery Press, N.Y.).

Balck, W. 1922. *Development of tactics—world war.* Trans. H. Bell. Fort Leavenworth, Kans.: General Service Schools Press.

Barnett, C. 1963. *The swordbearers.* New York: William Morrow.

Cruttwell, C. R. M. F. 1934. *A history of the great war, 1914–1918.* Oxford, U.K.: Clarendon Press.

Esposito, V., ed. 1959. *The West Point atlas of American wars.* Vol. 2. New York: Praeger.

Falls, C. 1959. *The great war.* New York: Capricorn Books.

Fussell, P. 1975. *The great war and modern memory.* New York: Oxford Univ. Press.

Horne, A. 1962. *The price of glory.* New York: St. Martin's Press.

Liddell Hart, B. H. 1930. *The real war 1914–1918.* Boston: Little, Brown.

Ludendorff, E. 1919. *Ludendorff's own story.* 2 vols. (English trans.). New York: Harpers.

Middlebrook, M. 1972. *The first day on the Somme.* New York: Norton.

———. 1978. *The Kaiser's battle.* London: Penguin.

Pitt, B. 1963. *1918: The last act.* New York: Norton.

Spears, E. L. 1939. *Prelude to victory.* London: Jonathan Cape.

Stone, N. 1975. *The eastern front 1914–1917.* New York: Scribner's.

Tuchman, B. 1962. *The guns of August.* New York: Macmillan.

Watt, R. 1963. *Dare call it treason.* New York: Simon and Schuster.

Wolff, L. 1958. *In Flanders fields.* London: Longmans Green.

Wynne, G. C. [1940] 1976. *If Germany attacks.* Reprint. Westport, Conn.: Greenwood Press.

WORLD WAR II

World War II (1939–45), along with several years of preliminaries and after-shocks, was the most costly and violent war in human history. Nearly 50 million people were killed; over 70 million troops participated. Most of the planet's population was involved and operations took place in every time zone and on nearly every continent. As with most large wars, the conflict was actually a series of smaller wars fought concurrently. The two main wars were those involving the aggressions of Germany and Japan. These two nations were also the focus of numerous other disputes in their respective regions.

Participants

The participants of World War II, their populations, and the number of mo-bilized soldiers and casualties are shown in Table 1.

The Soviet-German war accounted for most of the deaths, a fact that is

TABLE 1. *Participants of World War II*

	POPULATION (MILLIONS)	MOBILIZED SOLDIERS (THOUSANDS)	CASUALTIES (THOUSANDS)
Axis powers			
Bulgaria	7	60	50
Finland	4	80	42
Germany	85	14,000	7,000
Hungary	9.2	100	40
Italy	43.6	4,500	250
Japan	71	7,400	3,000
Romania	20	260	300
Thailand	16	150	20
Allied powers			
Albania	2	50	25
Australia	9	50	30
Belgium	8	60	10
Brazil	3	200	1
Britain	48	4,200	300
Canada	11	100	40
China	700	8,000	3,000
Denmark	4	50	10
Ethiopia	30	100	5
France	41	6,000	500
Greece	7	140	10
Iran	26	300	45
Iraq	4.5	100	25
Netherlands	8.7	100	6.2
New Zealand	1.8	60	17.3
Norway	2.9	50	5
Poland	33	300	6,000
South Africa	10	50	8.7
Soviet Union	170	20,000	25,000
United States	130	16,000	408
Yugoslavia	15.4	500	1,500

often overlooked in the West. Russia mobilized over 20 million troops for the war and more than half were casualties. Of Russian civilians, 10 to 15 million died as a result of the war, making total Russian deaths nearly 25 million people. Germany mobilized 14 million troops of which 4 million died, plus 3 million civilians dead. In addition, German authorities killed 6 million Poles and several million other civilians of various nationalities. Of the 50 million World War II deaths, over 75 percent were a result of military operations or occupation and extermination policies involving Germany. The fiscal cost, in 1990 dollars, was over US$10 trillion.

Campaigns

The war followed several well-defined phases. First there were the German actions against Poland in 1939 and France (and adjacent countries) in 1940. In mid-1941 the principal event was the German invasion of Russia. The Soviet-German war continued unabated until early 1945. The fighting in North Africa and the Mediterranean grew from skirmishes in 1940 to a bloody campaign in Italy in 1943–44. The Japanese began their portion of the war in December 1941 with a series of attacks in the Pacific. It took the United States more than three years to recapture everything Japan seized. Through all this, submarine campaigns against shipping went on in the North Atlantic and Pacific.

The German invasion of Poland in September 1939, after previous aggressions against Austria and Czechoslovakia, caused France and Britain to declare war on Germany and its ally Italy. Various other minor powers made declarations, while the United States and Russia remained neutral for the moment. Most Americans did not want to get involved. Russia was waiting for a better opportunity to jump in. For six months nothing more happened, except for Russia's invasion of Finland and the fighting between Italy and Britain in Africa.

In the spring of 1940, Germany overran Denmark, Norway, the Netherlands, Belgium, and France. Britain went to the aid of France and was promptly ejected from the continent. Throughout the rest of 1940 and into early 1941, Germany and Britain fought an air war that both sides thought, for a while, would be a prelude to a German invasion of Britain. But the Germans lost 1,400 aircraft, the British only 800, and the Germans turned their attention eastward.

In the spring of 1941, Germany invaded the Balkans, swiftly conquering Yugoslavia and Greece. The British forces aiding Greece were driven out, and the Germans crossed the sea into North Africa to assist their faltering Italian allies. The Balkan invasion was but a prelude to the June 1941 invasion of Russia. This caught the Russians completely unaware and led to a devastating string of German victories that did not end until early 1942, when the exhausted German forces stalled before Moscow and Leningrad.

At the same time, Germany continued a largely ineffective bombing campaign against British cities and a more successful submarine offensive against British shipping. The commerce battle had been going on since late 1939, and Germany's submarine building program was beginning to make itself felt. Until 1943, Britain's major danger was German submarines, not German ground forces or aircraft. At the end of 1939, Britain had access to less than 20 million tons of merchant shipping. The battle against the German submarines was inconclusive for three years, until the United States entered the war and was able to contribute antisubmarine forces and an enormous shipbuilding capability. By the end of 1942 the German subs had been put on the defensive, and the pool of available shipping had grown to over 100 million tons. Nineteen million tons had been destroyed by Germany and its allies ("the Axis"), 75 percent by submarines.

German military success in World War II peaked in December 1941. In that month, Japan attacked the United States—bringing it into the war and initiating the process that led to Germany's decline and eventual defeat.

The Pacific war had its origins in previous conflicts. Japan had taken Korea and parts of Manchuria from Russia during the 1904–1905 war. In the early 1930s, Japan began invading the rest of China, a piece at a time. Continued tensions with Russia led to some fighting on the Russo-Manchurian border in 1939, ending badly for the Japanese. Russia and Japan then entered into a non-aggression pact. Japan also made an alliance with Germany, so when France fell in 1940, Japan was able to take over French possessions in Indochina. Dutch possessions in Indonesia received British support and remained free of Japan's control. Most of Japan's oil came from Dutch-controlled oil fields in Indonesia. Moreover, Britain and the United States constantly pressured Japan to cease its aggression in China. In late 1941, Britain, the United States, and the Netherlands threatened to cut off oil shipments to Japan if aggression in China did not cease. Japan responded in December 1941 by attacking Dutch, U.S., and British possessions in the Pacific. A major contributing factor to this decision was Germany's success against Russia, Britain, France, and the Netherlands.

Like their German allies, Japanese forces initially swept all before them. But six months later they suffered a serious defeat off Midway Island. Four carriers were lost and their naval superiority in the Pacific quickly disappeared. Even without the disaster at Midway, the Japanese were in big trouble. In 1940 the United States had begun a major ship-building program. By late 1942 the first light carriers began to appear, along with destroyers and cruisers. By 1945, America would possess over 100 aircraft carriers plus numerous destroyers, cruisers, submarines, battleships, amphibious craft, and merchant shipping. The U.S. industrial capacity was ten times that of Japan. In the long run there was no contest. After Midway, there was no real chance for a Japanese victory.

While the Japanese prepared for a long siege, Germany made another attempt to revive its prospects. Stalled before Moscow and Leningrad, it made a major effort in the south against Stalingrad, the Volga River, and the Caucasus. All three of these objectives were part of Russia's link to the military and economic aid coming in from Britain and the United States. By late 1942, German troops were fighting inside Stalingrad and advancing into the Caucasus toward Russia's oil fields on the Caspian Sea. The German forces in Stalingrad were besieged, while those in the Caucasus quickly withdrew lest they, too, be cut off. Attempts to relieve the German forces in Stalingrad failed, and the surrounded Sixth Army was lost. German forces fell back before a Russian spring offensive but regrouped and rebuilt in anticipation of one more lunge eastward.

The resulting Battle of Kursk in July 1943 was the largest armor battle to date. The Germans lost the battle. Germany then began its twenty-month retreat from Russia, toward Berlin and ultimate defeat. Russia battled with most of Germany's ground forces throughout the war, but this was not the only scene of German defeat.

A North African campaign, begun as a minor operation in 1941 to bail out its Italian ally, was turning into a substantial drain on dwindling German resources. In late 1942, victorious British forces were driving the Germans away from the Egyptian border when U.S. forces landed in Algeria, putting German forces between the two Allied armies. The Germans retreated to Sicily, which the Allies promptly invaded. The German and Italian forces then fell back to the Italian mainland in 1943.

The Allies then invaded Italy, and the Italians surrendered in mid-1943. Italian combat troops in Italy and the Balkans had to be replaced with German forces taken largely from the garrisons in France and the already weakened armies in Russia. The German troops moving into the Balkans found that the numerous and well-organized partisans had not only seized much of the Italian weapons but had recruited many of the surrendering Italians as well. The tempo of fighting picked up immediately and eventually went against the Germans as Yugoslavia became the only occupied country to liberate itself.

The Japanese also had a bad year in 1943. U.S. naval, air, and ground forces continued the island-hopping strategy begun in August 1942 at Guadalcanal. The inadequacies of the Japanese military and industry began to show as an unbroken string of defeats spread from 1943 into 1944 and 1945. U.S. forces advanced from island to island, bypassing many Japanese after sinking their warships and destroying their aircraft, leaving many of them to starve to death before the war was over. Few Japanese surrendered. Those islands that the U.S. forces did take were large enough to hold airfields for heavy bombers. By late 1944, bombers began flying missions against Japan itself from bases in the Marianas. Japanese industry was brought to a standstill by the U.S. submarine campaign against Japanese shipping (90% destroyed by 1945). In 1945 the Japanese population faced the potential for millions of starvation deaths should the war extend into 1946.

The only area where Japanese aggression was successful was in China. From the late 1930s to early 1943, Japanese forces had been largely confined to Manchuria, parts of northern China, and the major coastal cities. In 1943, U.S. engineers began building air bases in central China for use by heavy bombers. In 1944, Japan made several major efforts to overrun these bases and was partially successful. However, Japanese ground forces were stretched too thin against the more numerous but less efficient and politically divided Chinese forces. Also, many of the best Japanese units had been shipped off to the Pacific in 1943 and 1944. By late 1944 the war in China was settled, for neither side had the strength to do anything to their opponent.

In June 1944, Allied forces invaded France at Normandy (Fig. 1). A month later, a smaller invasion was launched through the southern French port of Marseilles. In September, German forces were able to halt the invaders along the German border. In December, Germany mustered its last reserves for a final offensive in the Ardennes area of south Belgium. This failed. In January the Allies renewed their advance, and in March they crossed the Rhine. In early May, Allied and Russian forces met in central Germany and the war in Europe was almost over. Back in western Russia, nationalist and anti-Communist partisans fought on until the early 1950s.

In the Pacific, British and Indian forces finally pushed Japanese forces out of Burma by summer 1945. In August 1945 the United States dropped two atomic bombs on Japan. This caused the Japanese to lose all hope and hastened their surrender. A week before the bombing, Russia entered the war against Japan with an enormous armored invasion of Manchuria. Japanese forces in that area had never been very powerful to begin with. Calls for reinforcements from

Figure 1. American soldiers land on the beach at Normandy.
(SOURCE: U.S. Coast Guard)

southern China and the Pacific had taken away some of the best units. The result was one of the most spectacularly successful mechanized operations of the war. Russian military academies still use this operation as an example of what a mechanized offensive should be.

Outcomes

Outcomes varied greatly from nation to nation. The only "winner" in World War II was the United States, which suffered insignificant damage to its homeland. American industrial facilities were greatly expanded to support the war effort. When the shooting stopped, the other major industrial nations found themselves largely devastated and dependent on the United States for manufactured goods and capital for reconstruction. America held onto this dominant position for over 25 years.

Political borders were radically redrawn in central and eastern Europe. Germany lost East Prussia to Russia, Silesia to Poland, and Alsace-Lorraine to France. The remainder of Germany was partitioned. Poland lost part of its eastern territory to Russia in return for parts of Germany. More than 12 million Germans fled in response to these changed borders. More than 10 million other people became refugees because of the fighting and redrawn borders. Various other East European nations traded bits and pieces of territory. World War II also loosened Europe's grip on its colonies, most of which became independent within the next twenty years. Russia refused postwar aid from the United States and prevented East European nations it controlled from accepting any, which slowed the rebuilding of these nations. By the 1980s, Russia and its East European "allies" were significantly behind Western nations in economic development.

In Asia, Japan lost all its colonies and some of its northern islands. One former colony, Korea, was partitioned, which led to a bitter and costly civil war. Japan accepted U.S. economic aid and soon grew into an economic superpower. China fell to the Communists, an event that finally resolved 40 years of revolution and civil war. The Nationalists, defeated in the Chinese civil war, "set up shop" on the island of Taiwan and, with the help of U.S. aid, developed a strong economy. This highlights another legacy of World War II. After the war, many nations came under the domination of Communist governments. After 30 years of trying to make this form of socialism work, the cold war between communism and capitalism came to an end in the late 1980s.

Innovations

World War II was notable for a number of military innovations. Some of these follow:

Air-to-air missiles: German R4M missiles were unguided but caused great damage against tightly packed formations of Allied heavy bombers.

Aircraft ground support: The Germans were the first to perfect the techniques of using aircraft to support ground operations. First came their Stuka dive bombers and later heavily armed antitank aircraft. Allied forces used large numbers of heavily armed fighter-bombers and highly effective use of ground-to-air radio links with the ground combat forces.

APCs and MBTs: Only rudimentary armored vehicles were used in World War I. At the start of World War II, most tanks were armed with only machine guns or light cannon. By 1942 the heavily armored Main Battle Tank (MBT) with a large-caliber gun was the norm. It was quickly demonstrated that these MBTs could not long survive on the battlefield without their infantry escorts riding in armored personnel carriers (APCs).

Beyond visual range (BVR) combat: BVR combat came of age during World War II. Radar and sonar allowed weapons to be used effectively against unseen targets.

Command, Control, Communications, and Intelligence (C^3I): The modern concept of C^3I came of age during World War II. The proliferation of radios, and an organizational structure that could make the best use of them, made rapid, wide-ranging mobile warfare possible.

Carrier warfare: The basic techniques of carrier warfare were perfected during World War II and are still in use.

Guided missiles: The German V-1 was the prototype of the cruise missile. Indeed, Russia still uses numerous improved versions of the original German "buzz-bomb." The V-2 ballistic missile was the source of most post–World War II missile research and development. The Germans also pioneered the use of guided air-to-surface missiles, using them to sink two Italian warships.

Jet aircraft: During the 1930s, Germany, Britain, and the United States were working on jets, but Germany got its into action first. Bureaucratic and political fumbling prevented earlier and more extensive deployment.

Mechanized warfare: British theorists took the lead during the 1920s and 1930s in developing the concepts, but the Germans perfected the ideas for battle-field use. After World War II, Russia revised its mechanized warfare organization and doctrine to absorb many German ideas. To this day, most mechanized doctrine and tactics can be traced to what the Germans developed between 1935 and 1945.

Nuclear weapons: The atomic bomb may be the most significant product of World War II. Its use against Japan could be considered decisive, although it was not really needed to ensure Allied victory. Only the Allied nations had the resources and the will to bring this enormous research and development project to fruition in less than four years. Had the fighting with conventional weapons gone against the Allies, their nuclear weapons could have saved them from defeat.

Self-propelled artillery: First seen in crude form during the last year of World War I, armored, self-propelled artillery became the third critical weapon for the new armored divisions that matured during World War II.

Stategic bombing: This concept was developed during the 1920s and 1930s, but it was never really perfected in practice. Extensive studies after the war show that most of the Allied strategic bombing had little effect on the war's outcome. What impact there was resulted more from chance than from design. This was largely because of faulty analysis of the target economies. The key German target system was electrical power. The next most critical target system was the transportation net, which was hit toward the end of the war. The damage done proved invaluable in crippling the German war effort. Nevertheless, German weapons production peaked only six months before the war ended. Experience during the war did much to advance the technology of heavy, long-range bombers.

World War II also represented significant advances in the lethality and scope of warfare:

Genocide: Many previous wars were notable for attempts to exterminate ethnic or religious groups, yet this was a particularly ugly aspect of World War II. The Germans mounted a systematic campaign against Jews, Gypsies, Slavs, and other minority groups. Over 12 million people died because of these extermination programs.

Industrial mobilization: For 200 years before World War II, major wars had seen greater and greater mobilization of national economies to support the military effort. In World War II, many nations devoted more than half their productive capacity to directly supporting the war. This was one reason the war was so destructive and lasted so long.

Global warfare: The intensity and universality of the fighting in World War II were unprecedented. Those areas that were not fought over were drawn into the economic mobilization. No significant population on the planet was unaffected by the war effort.

JAMES F. DUNNIGAN

SEE ALSO: Arnold, H. H.; Brooke, Alan Francis, 1st Viscount Alanbrooke; Chiang Kai-shek; Cunningham, Sir Alan G.; Doenitz, Karl; Douhet, Giulio;

Fuller, J. F. C.; Guderian, Heinz; History, Modern Military; Japan, Modernization and Expansion of; King, Ernest J.; MacArthur, Douglas; Manstein, Erich von; Marshall, George Catlett, Jr.; Nimitz, Chester William; Patton, George Smith, Jr.; Prussia and Germany, Rise of; Rommel, Erwin; Slim, William Joseph; Spaatz, Carl A.; Stilwell, Joseph Warren; Trenchard, Sir Hugh Montague; Tukhachevsky, Mikhail Nikolaevich; Wavell, Archibald Percival; Yamamoto, Isoroku; Yamashita, Tomoyuki; Zhukov, Georgi Konstantinovich.

Bibliography

Arnold-Forster, M. 1973. *The world at war*. New York: Stein and Day.

Bayliss, G. M. *Bibliographic guide to the two world wars: An annotated survey of English-language reference materials*. New York: Bowker.

Campbell, C. 1986. *The World War Two fact book, 1939–1945*. New York: Harper and Row, Salem House.

Detwiler, D. S., ed. 1979. *World War Two German military studies*. 23 vols. New York: Garland.

Dupuy, E. R. 1969. *World War II: A compact history*. New York: Hawthorne.

Goralski, R. 1981. *World War II almanac*. New York: Putnam.

Keegan, J., ed. 1977. *The Rand-McNally encyclopedia of World War II*. Chicago: Rand-McNally.

Morison, S. E. 1963. *The two-ocean war: A short history of the United States Navy in the Second World War*. Boston: Little, Brown.

Stokesbury, J. L. 1980. *A short history of World War II*. New York: Morrow.

Vatter, H. G. 1988. *The U.S. economy in World War Two*. New York: Columbia Univ. Press.

Y

YAMAMOTO ISOROKU [1884–1943]

Yamamoto Isoroku, admiral in the Imperial Japanese Navy and commander of the Japanese Combined Fleet at the decisive World War II Battle of Midway (June 1942), was born at Nagaoka, Niigata Prefecture, Japan, as Takano Isoroku, the sixth son of Takano Sadayoshi, a disgraced, penniless Samurai. He was later adopted by Yamamoto Tatewaki, whose surname he adopted in 1916.

Early Career

After graduation from the Japanese Naval Academy in 1904, Yamamoto served as an ensign on board the armored cruiser *Nisshin* with Admiral Togo's fleet at the Battle of Tsushima (27 May 1905), in which he was severely wounded, losing two fingers of his left hand. He subsequently held a number of shipboard assignments and continued his professional education, graduating from torpedo school in 1908 and naval gunnery school in 1911.

From 1914 to 1916 he was a student at the Navy Staff College; promoted to lieutenant commander in 1915, he was graduated in 1916. In 1915, just five years after U.S. Navy pilot Eugene B. Ely made the first successful takeoff of an airplane from a makeshift "flight deck" fitted on the cruiser USS *Birmingham*, Yamamoto predicted that ships carrying aircraft would be the most important warships of the future.

In 1918 Yamamoto married. From 1919 to 1921 he was a student at Harvard University in Cambridge, Massachusetts, during which time he was promoted to commander. Returning to Japan, he was posted to the Naval Staff College as an instructor for two years. Following an observation tour of Europe and the United States (1923–24) he served as second in command of the Kasumigaura Naval Air Station (1924–25). From 1925 to 1928 he was the Japanese naval attaché in Washington. In 1929, after a brief period as captain of the aircraft carrier *Akagi*, he was promoted to rear admiral.

With the exception of two military-diplomatic assignments (delegate to the London Naval Conference, 1929–30, and chief of the Japanese delegation to the London Naval Conference, 1936), Yamamoto's career in the 1930s was bound intimately with the progress of naval aviation in Japan. As chief, Technological Division, Technical Department (1930–33); commander, 1st Naval Air Division (1933–34); chief, Naval Aviation Headquarters (1935–36); and Navy vice minister (1936–39), he enthusiastically advocated a strong naval air arm and the use of the aircraft carrier as the main naval offensive weapon. He was promoted to vice admiral in 1934. The early and unparalleled successes of the Japanese navy in World War II, due entirely to the strength and mobility of the Combined Fleet's aircraft carrier force, were the fruition of Yamamoto's efforts during this period.

Commander, Combined Fleet

In 1939, with extremists in the Japanese government and armed forces pushing increasingly for armed confrontation with the West, Yamamoto, a moderate, found himself virtually isolated in the Cabinet. Because of his opposition to the belligerent views of his colleagues he was removed from the Cabinet and appointed commander, Combined Fleet (August 1939). In this position he formulated a plan for a surprise attack against Pearl Harbor, Hawaii, to destroy the U.S. Pacific Fleet at its base in one blow using aircraft launched from the Combined Fleet's carrier force. A realist, Yamamoto predicted that Japan would enjoy a brief period of success in a naval war against the West, but would eventually be overwhelmed by the West's mobilized industrial and military capacity. His view is said to have been influenced by his reading of the British journalist Hector Bywater's remarkably prescient novel, *The Great Pacific War* (1925).

The Pearl Harbor operation was a striking success for Yamamoto and the Combined Fleet and was followed in rapid succession by other victories in the East Indies and the Indian Ocean. However, the U.S. Pacific Fleet's aircraft carrier task forces, which were not at Pearl Harbor at the time of Yamamoto's attack, remained to be dealt with; augmented, they eventually became the decisive force in the naval war in the Pacific and the chief agent of Japan's defeat.

After Pearl Harbor

Yamamoto's reputation as a naval strategist rests primarily on the string of victories achieved by the Combined Fleet in the six months between Pearl Harbor and the great air-sea battle of Midway (4 June 1942). But Japan's loss at Midway, the first Japanese naval defeat in 350 years, was due as much to Yamamoto's errors of judgment as to the U.S. success in decoding Japanese naval communications. The failure at Midway ended Japan's superiority in carriers and prevented Yamamoto from thereafter contending against the U.S. Pacific Fleet on anything like terms of equality. Ironically, the Admiral's death resulted from the American ability to decipher a coded Japanese wireless transmission that described the itinerary of a flight Yamamoto was to make to inspect Japanese facilities at Bougainville. Acting on this intelligence, an American fighter shot down his aircraft in the South Pacific on 18 April 1943.

Yamamoto was succeeded by Adm. Mineichi Koga, who said, "There was only one Yamamoto, and no one can replace him."

CURT JOHNSON

SEE ALSO: Japan, Modernization and Expansion of; Nimitz, Chester William; World War II.

Bibliography

Agawa, H. 1979. *The reluctant admiral: Yamamoto and the Imperial Navy.* Trans. J. Bester. New York: Kodansha International.

Davis, B. 1969. *Get Yamamoto.* New York: Random House.

Dull, P. S. 1978. *A battle history of the Imperial Japanese Navy (1941–1945).* Annapolis, Md.: U.S. Naval Institute Press.

Glines, C. V. 1990. *The attack on Yamamoto.* New York: Orion Books.

Hoyt, E. P. 1990. *Yamamoto: The man who planned Pearl Harbor.* New York: McGraw-Hill.

Oide, H. 1983. *Bonsho Yamamoto Isoroku.* Tokyo: Gendaishi Shuppankai; Hatsubai Tokuma Shoten.

Potter, J. D. 1965. *Yamamoto: Admiral of the Pacific.* New York: Viking.

Toyama, S. 1978. Years of transition: Japan's naval strategy from 1894 to 1945. *Revue Internationale d'Histoire Militaire* 38:162–82.

Tsumoda, J., and K. Uchida. 1978. The Pearl Harbor attack: Admiral Yamamoto's concept with reference to Paul S. Dull's "A battle history of the Imperial Japanese Navy (1941–1945)." *Naval War College Review* 31(2):83–88.

Wible, J. T. 1988. *The Yamamoto mission: Sunday, April 18, 1943.* Fredericksburg, Tex.: Admiral Nimitz Foundation.

YAMASHITA, TOMOYUKI [1885–1946]

Known to many Allied soldiers as the Tiger of Malaya, Imperial Japanese Army general Tomoyuki Yamashita was one of the most gifted military leaders of World War II. Born a commoner on 8 November 1885 in Kochi Prefecture on Shikoku Island, the son of a country medical doctor, Yamashita was fifteen years old at the beginning of the new century when the Japanese nation was caught in political-economic turbulence that was to end in World War II. On the side of the vanquished in 1945, Yamashita surrendered to American forces in the Philippines. Charged with being a war criminal, he was tried and found guilty by an American military commission of five U.S. Army generals appointed by Gen. Douglas MacArthur. Yamashita was sentenced to death by hanging and executed on the scaffold at Luzon Prisoner of War Camp at 3:02 A.M., 23 February 1946.

Early Career and World War I

By the summer of 1899, the young Yamashita wanted desperately to become an army officer. His ambition was realized through hard work and an excellent academic record, first at the Hiroshima District Military Preparatory School and later at the Military Academy in Tokyo. Commissioned a second lieutenant of infantry in June 1906, Yamashita was industrious and popular with both superiors and subordinates. Promoted to first lieutenant in December 1908, by 1911 he was appointed to the staff of the infantry school. During much of World

War I, Yamashita was a very successful student at the prestigious Army Staff College, essential for junior officers who sought successful careers and promotion to high rank. Graduating near the top of his class in November 1915, he spent the next two years attached to the army general staff in Tokyo.

The decade of the 1920s was a formative period for Yamashita. Significantly, his professional career was enhanced by foreign travel as well as study in Tokyo of the peacetime requirements of the Japanese army. Yamashita enjoyed a mixture of European attaché assignments (in Switzerland, 1919–22, and in Austria and Hungary, 1927–29) where he and fellow officer Hideki Tojo, the future prime minister (1941–44), toured the battlefields of the western front and studied various European armies. In February 1922 he was promoted to major. Between the end of his first attaché assignment in Europe and the beginning of his second, 1922 and 1927, Yamashita, a lieutenant colonel by August 1925, was staff officer, Military Policy Bureau in the War Ministry. As such, he diligently carried out War Minister Kazushige Ugaki's orders by helping to demobilize four divisions. Thus, the 13th Division at Takata, 15th Division at Toyohashi, 17th Division at Okayama, and 18th Division at Kurume were stricken from the Imperial Japanese Army in April 1925. Yamashita's association with the Ugaki scheme to reduce the size of the army was heavily criticized by many fellow army officers, one of whom was Tojo.

Although Yamashita and Tojo knew each other from their time together in Switzerland, their rivalry became serious during the 1930s when they both became lieutenant generals. It is likely that Tojo was envious of Yamashita. More significantly, however, the two belonged to rival factions, each faction seeking to become the stronger influence in the army. Yamashita was a member of the *kodo* faction, which sought reconstruction at home and an aggressive military policy against Russia. In 1936, members of the *kodo* faction—especially the younger, mostly field-grade officers—were responsible for the army revolt against the *tosei* faction, which controlled most Japanese army affairs. Tojo belonged to the *tosei* faction and supported its China expansion policy. The 1936 revolt failed, and subsequently the *tosei* faction became more powerful and the dominant influence, which culminated in Tojo's premiership in October 1941.

World War II

Nevertheless, Yamashita's important duty assignments and promotions were a reflection of his ability. He was promoted to colonel in August 1929 and to major general in August 1934. As a member of the *kodo* faction, he acted as a successful mediator in the young officers' revolt in 1936, and later became commander of an infantry brigade in Korea. He was promoted to lieutenant general in November 1937. Despite the pervasive influence of the *tosei* faction, Yamashita's abilities were so outstanding that success could not be denied, although he realized that his career remained perilous. In late 1940, he traveled across the Soviet Union to Berlin at the head of a Japanese military mission to Germany and Italy. Yamashita was surprised by the apparent failure of the

Maginot line in France and impressed by the way the Germans maneuvered their tanks in the 1940 campaign. Returning to Japan, Yamashita reported in June and July 1941 that the Japanese army lagged behind European armies and that the service was especially deficient in heavy bomber aircraft and medium tanks. Tojo, soon to be prime minister, and other high-ranking army officers downplayed Yamashita's reports and soon had him transferred out of the limelight to command the Kwantung army in Manchukuo. On the eve of the Pacific war, however, Yamashita was recalled to Tokyo and in November 1941 was given command of the Twenty-fifth Army. Known as an able strategist, he was assigned the task of capturing Singapore, the citadel of British power in East Asia.

The Twenty-fifth Army comprised a combined arms force of three infantry divisions and their supporting regiments of heavy field artillery, a tank brigade, and army and navy air groups that totaled nearly 600 aircraft; total strength was 60,000 men. Yamashita's staff had been hastily assembled from commands throughout the Japanese army, but the new commander's strong personality and leadership produced much loyalty among his officers while they all worked to achieve one of Japan's greatest military triumphs. From 8 December 1941, the Japanese pushed larger British and empire forces hundreds of miles through the jungle and down the Malay Peninsula until their full withdrawal to Singapore Island was completed by the end of January 1942. On 15 February, after a successful landing on Singapore, General Yamashita demanded and received the unconditional surrender of the British commander, Lt. Gen. Arthur Ernest Percival.

Even during his moment of triumph, Yamashita had to contend with old foes of the *tosei* faction. He was recalled from Singapore soon after his victory, for Tojo was insistent that the popular hero be reassigned as quickly as possible and kept away from Tokyo and the seat of power. As prime minister, Tojo made certain that Yamashita was not permitted to have an audience and report to Emperor Hirohito; this was exceptional and was outrageous treatment of such a successful field commander. In July, Yamashita was transferred back to Manchukuo to command the First Area Army, a remote assignment in view of an earlier headquarters decision not to attack the Soviet Union.

Yamashita, however, remained popular in some circles and widely respected. Promoted to full general in February 1943, he was briefly considered as a candidate for war minister when Tojo's cabinet fell in July 1944, but elements of factional struggle in the 1930s still had influence among several high-ranking generals. Instead of a cabinet appointment, he was made commander of the Fourteenth Area Army in the Philippines in September 1944 (Fig. 1). Sadly, this appointment proved to be his nemesis. Defense of the Philippines was considered a dangerous assignment, and many Japanese placed much hope in Yamashita's leadership in the coming decisive battle.

American landings on Leyte occurred the month after Yamashita arrived in the Philippines. Ten months of heavy fighting remained in the Pacific war, during which time Yamashita was increasingly hampered by poor communications with both superiors and subordinates, dwindling and limited ground re-

*Figure 1. Gen. Tomoyuki Yamashita (photo taken between Feb-
ruary 1943 and the end of World War II).* (SOURCE: Carl Boyd)

inforcements, and dissipating air strength. Yet he executed a masterful delaying
campaign, finally withdrawing into the mountainous areas of Luzon where
formidable defensive works had been prepared. He surrendered on 2 September 1945, several weeks after the Tokyo government offered to surrender and
after, indeed, the Allied occupation of the home islands had begun.

The victors' justice was swift and ominous. In October, Yamashita was indicted as a war criminal, particularly in connection with atrocities committed by
some Japanese troops during the defense of Manila. The prosecution maintained that Yamashita, as the commanding general in the Philippines, was
responsible for everything his troops did during the time he commanded.
MacArthur urged conviction of Yamashita as soon as possible. Seemingly in a
final touch of retribution, the U.S. military commission hearing Yamashita's

case restricted its deliberations and hurried to announce its findings and sentence on the fourth anniversary of the Japanese attack on Pearl Harbor, 7 December 1945, although, from their side of the International Date Line, the Japanese recognized 8 December as the date of the attack. Gen. Tomoyuki Yamashita, dressed in an American khaki shirt and trousers, without insignia of rank or military medals, was executed in an austere and sober setting. Calm and brave, as an admiring U.S. Army eyewitness recorded, the Tiger of Malaya bowed reverently toward the Imperial palace in Tokyo and then stepped into place on the execution platform to await the hangman's noose.

CARL BOYD

SEE ALSO: World War II.

Bibliography

Kenworthy, A. S. 1953. *The tiger of Malaya: The story of General Tomoyuki Yamashita and "Death March" General Masaharu Homma.* New York: Exposition Press.
Kojima, Y. 1969. *Shisetsu Yamashita Tomoyuki.* Tokyo: Bungei Shunju-sha.
Oki, S. 1959. *Ningen Yamashita Tomoyuki, higeki no shogun.* Tokyo: Nihon Shuho-sha.
Redford, L. H. 1975. The trial of General Tomoyuki Yamashita: A case study in command responsibility. Master's thesis, Old Dominion University, Norfolk, Va.
Reel, A. F. 1949. *The case of General Yamashita.* Chicago: Univ. of Chicago Press.

Z

ZHUKOV, GEORGII KONSTANTINOVICH
[1896–1974]

Georgii Konstantinovich Zhukov is considered the first among what Soviet military historians have called the "pleiad of great captains" who led the Soviet forces to victory on the German-Soviet front during World War II. Zhukov stands out not only for the number and scale of his victories, but also for his great operational and strategic talent. He had a strong influence on the development of postwar Soviet operational art. Zhukov's inordinate pride in his accomplishments and the fear, envy, and spite his fame and popularity engendered among the chronically insecure Soviet political leadership caused him to suffer through two separate periods of persecution and exile totaling almost one-third of his life.

Career Prior to World War I

Georgii Konstantinovich Zhukov was born on 1 December 1896 in the village of Strelkovka in what is now Kaluga Oblast. His father was an impoverished shoemaker-peasant; his mother was a physically powerful woman who could easily lift 180-pound sacks of grain to supplement the family income. At the age of ten, he completed the local three-year parochial school with praise. The next year he was apprenticed to a successful Moscow furrier. At age fifteen, by taking courses at night, he successfully passed the city equivalency examinations and that same year became a "submaster furrier."

World War I and the Russian Civil War

In 1915, Zhukov was conscripted into the cavalry and selected for noncommissioned officer training, arriving at the front in August 1916. By October, when he was wounded and evacuated, he had been awarded two Crosses of St. George. After the February Revolution of 1917, Zhukov became a Bolshevik sympathizer. He joined the 4th Cavalry Regiment of the 1st Moscow Cavalry Division in August 1918 and was accepted as a member of the Communist Party in March 1919. In the spring of 1919, Zhukov saw action in the Russian Civil War in the Southern Urals, but he was wounded in the fall of that year and sent home to recover. He served as a squadron commander in the mopping-up actions that marked the end of the Civil War in 1920.

Peacetime Service, the Purges, and Khalkin Gol

Zhukov advanced to regimental command in the Red Army in 1923. He was ordered to Moscow in 1931 as assistant to the inspector of cavalry of the Red Army, S. M. Budenniy, the famed commander of the First Cavalry Army in the Civil War. Budenniy personally selected Zhukov to revive a cavalry division in the Belorussian Military District in 1933. There, Zhukov served as a division and corps commander under I. P. Uborevich, one of the first military victims of the purges of 1937–38. His association with Uborevich almost drew him into the maelstrom, but he was saved by an assignment to Mongolia, where he organized and commanded the Soviet and Mongolian troops defending against the Japanese incursion at Khalkin Gol. In August 1939, his troops inflicted some 61,000 casualties on the invaders, and drove them back over the Mongolian-Manchurian border. Zhukov was promoted to general of the army, given command of the Kiev Military District, and made a hero of the Soviet Union—and he met Josef Stalin for the first time.

World War II: Glory and Disgrace

When Hitler launched his attack on the Soviet Union on 22 June 1941, Zhukov had been chief of the Soviet General Staff for less than five months. His efforts to prepare the Soviet forces for the attack had been frustrated by Stalin's conviction that Hitler was occupied in the West and would not attack that year. Stalin either disregarded intelligence to the contrary or considered it a provocation designed to draw the Soviet Union into the war. Once the war started, Stalin used Zhukov as a troubleshooter and a coordinator as the invaders drove toward Moscow. Zhukov initially was sent to Kiev; Stalin believed that the Ukraine would be Hitler's first objective. Next, Zhukov organized the defense of Leningrad, and, in October 1941, he assumed command of the collapsing western front.

Zhukov's success in halting the Wehrmacht before Moscow, the first serious setback to Hitler's grandiose plans, attracted world attention. Even before Moscow, he had demonstrated the leadership style and skills that he applied throughout the war. Iron will and determination, the uncanny ability to anticipate the enemy's future course of action and to skillfully apply all available assets, and the courage to withstand the dictator's ire when making contrary recommendations made him a tower of strength in a crisis. But in combination with his own vanity, these qualities would also earn him numerous enemies, not only among Stalin's supporters and sycophants but also within the senior military leadership.

In January 1942, Zhukov opposed Stalin's plan to turn the defensive success at Moscow into a general offensive on the grounds that there were insufficient resources; he was overruled. The result was a series of failed operations that set the stage for the German advance to Stalingrad that summer. Zhukov was dispatched to that city along with the man who eventually succeeded him as chief of staff, Aleksandr Mikhailovich Vasilevskii. Together, they organized its defense and the counteroffensive of November 1942–February 1943, which resulted in the destruction of the German Sixth Army.

Stalin accepted Zhukov's recommendation in 1943 that the Soviets await the German onslaught on the Kursk salient and then counterattack. The result was a German defeat and a Soviet counteroffensive that drove the enemy to the Dnieper. Zhukov coordinated the operations of Rokossovskii and Konev that drove the Germans out of Belorussia in 1944. Stalin then placed Zhukov in command of the First Belorussian Front in November 1944. In April 1945, that front entered Berlin and on 9 May it accepted the surrender of the German forces.

These victories and the attendant honors and applause (Fig. 1) strained the relations between Stalin and Zhukov. Stalin, urged on by his close political and security operatives Beria, Molotov, and Malenkov, became jealous of Zhukov's fame and popularity and irritated by his independence. As Soviet high commissioner for occupied Germany, Zhukov was exposed to Western press conferences for the first time, and he was not modest in his appraisal of his role in the Soviet victories. Zhukov also challenged Beria's secret police emissaries in Germany. In 1946, he was recalled to Moscow, accused of attempting to arrogate all credit for Soviet military success to himself and, more ominously, of plotting against the regime. His military colleagues agreed with most of the accusations against his personal conduct but did not accept that he had plotted

Figure 1. Georgii Konstantinovich Zhukov, Deputy Supreme Soviet Commander (on the left), dining with U.S. General Dwight D. Eisenhower (center) and British Marshal Bernard L. Montgomery (on the right), SHAEF Headquarters in Frankfurt, Germany. (SOURCE: U.S. Library of Congress)

against Stalin. He was sentenced to exile from Moscow to command a secondary military district.

Return to Moscow and Second Disgrace

After Stalin's death in March 1953, Zhukov was named deputy minister of defense by the successor leadership. He immediately began to study the effect of nuclear weapons on modern war. He also became directly involved in the contest among Stalin's heirs for political power, which ended with Nikita Khrushchev's victory over the "anti-Party group" in 1957. He personally organized the arrest of secret police chief Beria in 1953. The "resignation" of Malenkov in 1955 was accomplished with military support, and Zhukov subsequently became minister of defense in that year. Khrushchev's emergence as party and government leader in June 1957 was due, in part, to Zhukov's strong support in the contest with the anti-Party group. As a reward, Zhukov was co-opted by the Communist Party Presidium (the successor to the Politburo)—the first professional military man ever to be selected.

While Zhukov was on an official visit to Yugoslavia and Albania in October 1957, Khrushchev organized and coordinated a case against him similar to that used by Stalin. The charge of "Bonapartism" was included to suggest that Zhukov was plotting to seize control of the government. It was revealed that Zhukov had approved the formation of a 2,000-man special-forces-type unit without informing the political leadership. This, coupled with his statement during the anti-Party group confrontation that he would use the army to enforce any decision of the Party Central Committee, caused the political leadership, always concerned about its legitimacy, to fear a military seizure of power. Zhukov was removed from all of his party and government posts, but was allowed to live in the Moscow area in virtual exile from his military comrades.

Isolation

The removal of Khrushchev from power in 1964 permitted some relaxation of the conditions of Zhukov's "exile." His recollections of his career up to 1946 were published in 1969 in a heavily censored edition. But he was not allowed to appear at officers' clubs or at major party functions. In his later years, he was concerned that his version of the great events in which he participated become available to historians; he succeeded only partially in this by the time of his death in 1974.

Assessment

Zhukov as a military commander was a prime example of the Stalinist style of leadership. He demanded and got obedience. He was ruthless toward those who in his opinion could not or would not execute his orders. For him, achieving the objective was paramount; anything less was unsatisfactory. In retrospect, he admitted that he had little tolerance for those around him who were not doing their share. Working directly for an exacting taskmaster, he sometimes seemed to exceed Stalin in his disregard for human frailty. In his defense, it should be noted that the times, the circumstances of the German attack, and the relatively low level of Soviet military culture in the early months of the war demanded extraordinary measures to survive.

As a soldier, Zhukov was an extraordinary tactician. He understood the importance of terrain; before major operations, he reconnoitered the front lines and verified the plans and assessments of his subordinates. He also believed in exhaustive efforts to obtain and use intelligence, and depended on his specialists for aviation, artillery, engineer, and signal support. He would calculate carefully the correlation of forces and avoid attacking when they were unfavorable. He never hesitated to request reinforcement, and he understood that to continue a successful attack, even when taking heavy losses, is less costly than to halt and reorganize. In sum, Zhukov was the outstanding field commander of World War II.

WILLIAM J. SPAHR

SEE ALSO: Civil War, Russian; World War I; World War II.

Bibliography

Zhukov, G. K. 1990. *Vospominaniia i razmyshleniia* [Reminiscences and reflections]. 10th ed. Moscow: Novosti.

Pavlenko, N. G. 1988. Razmyshleniia o sud'be polkovodtsa [Reflections on the fate of a great captain]. *Voennoistoricheskii zhurnal*, nos. 10, 11, 12.

Simonov, K. M. 1987. Zametki k biografii G. K. Zhukova [Notes to a biography of G. K. Zhukov]. *Voennoistoricheskii zhurnal*, nos. 6, 7, 9, 10, 12.

INDEX

Main encyclopedia entries are in boldface; references to illustrations are italicized.